Rick Steves®

GREAT BRITAIN

CONTENTS

To Marylebone → Station

LEGEND

- - - - Rail Line
Pedestrian-Friendly Area
Popular Shopping Area
- - - - Pedestrian Path
⊖ Underground/Tube Station
⇌ Train Station
■ Point of Interest
ℹ Tourist Information

0 km   0.5 km
0 mi   0.25 mi

SIGHTS

1 #10 Downing Street
2 Apsley House (Wellington Museum)
3 Banqueting House
4 British Museum
5 Buckingham Palace & Queen's Gallery
6 Changing of the Guard
7 Churchill War Roo[m]
8 Covent Garden
9 Horse Guards
10 Houses of Parliame[nt] & Big Ben
11 Leicester Square
12 National Gallery

To Wallace ► Collection & Madame Tussauds

HARROW RD.

N. WHARF RD.

PADDINGTON STATION (TRAINS TO HEATHROW)

Paddington

BAYSWATER

CRAVEN RD.   PRAED SUSSEX GDNS. SPRING SUSSEX TERR. LANCASTER PLACE

Lancaster Gate

BAYSWATER RD.

N. CARRIAGE DR.

EDGWARE RD.

WIGMORE ST.

Marble Arch

MARBLE ARCH

OXFORD ST.

SELFRIDGES

SPEAKERS' CORNER ■ 18

CUMBERLAND GATE

UPPER BROOK ST.

US EMBASSY

UPPER GROSVENOR

MOUNT ST.

PARK ST.   N. AUDLEY

Grosve[nor] Squa[re]

S. AUDL[EY]

Hyde Park

PARK LN.   PARK LN.

To Kensington Palace ←

Kensington Gardens

The Serpentine

SERPENTINE GALLERY ■

DIANA FOUNTAIN

ROTTEN ROW

BANDSTAND

ROSE GARDEN

APSLEY HOUSE

W. CARRIAGE DR.

ALBERT MEMORIAL ■

S. CARRIAGE DR.

KENSINGTON RD.

KNIGHTSBRIDGE

HARVEY NICHOLS

WELLING[TON] A[RCH]

Hyde Park Corner

GROSVENOR CRESCENT

16 ROYAL ALBERT HALL

PRINCE CONSORT RD.

Knightsbridge ⊖

THE CAPITAL HOTEL ■

LOWNDES SQ.

Belgrave Square

CRESCENT WILTON CHAPE[L]

PRINCE'S GDNS.

ENNISMORE GDNS.

RUTLAND GATE

HARRODS

BASIL ST.

IMPERIAL COLLEGE RD.

EXHIBITION RD.

BROMPTON RD.

BEAUCHAMP PL.

PONT. ST.

SLOANE ST.

CADOGAN LN.

EATON PL.

BELGRAVE

SCIENCE MUSEUM

NATURAL HISTORY MUSEUM 14

VICTORIA & ALBERT MUSEUM 22

BROMPTON

PAVILION RD.

BELGRAVIA

CROMWELL ROAD

Thurloe Square

WALTON ST.

HASKER ST.

MOORE ST.

EATON PL.   KING'S RD.   LYALL ST.

THURLOE PL.

PELHAM ST.

DRAYCOTT AVE.

CADOGAN PL.

Sloane Square

CHESTER   EATON [T]ER.

OLD BROMPTON

SUMNER PL.

South Kensington ⊖

Onslow Square

ONSLOW GDNS.

PELHAM ST.

FULHAM RD.

DRAYCOTT AVE.

SLOANE AVE.

IXWORTH PL.

ELYSTAN ST.

DRAYCOTT PL.

Sloane Square ⊖

KING'S RD.

LOWER SLOANE

HOLBEIN PL.

BOURNE ST.   EBURY

SOUTH KENSINGTON

CALE ST.

CHELSEA

To National Army Museum ↓

PIMLICO RD.

West London

To British Library & St. Pancras, Euston & King's Cross Stations

- 13 National Portrait Gallery
- 14 Natural History & Science Museums
- 15 Piccadilly Circus
- 16 Royal Albert Hall
- 17 Royal Mews
- 18 Speakers' Corner
- 19 St. Martin-in-the-Fields
- 20 Tate Britain
- 21 Trafalgar Square
- 22 Victoria & Albert Museum
- 23 Westminster Abbey

BLOOMSBURY

BRITISH MUSEUM

CARTOON MUSEUM

SOHO

CHINATOWN

COVENT GARDEN

Leicester Square

MAYFAIR

NATIONAL GALLERY

Trafalgar Square

ADMIRALTY ARCH

Green Park

St. James's Park

HORSE GUARDS PARADE

DOWNING ST.

CENOTAPH

BUCKINGHAM PALACE

QUEEN VICTORIA MEMORIAL

Parliament Square

BIG BEN

HOUSES OF PARLIAMENT

ROYAL MEWS

WESTMINSTER ABBEY

WESTMINSTER

JEWEL TOWER

VICTORIA STATION (TRAINS TO GATWICK)

WESTMINSTER CATHEDRAL

Smith Square

ST. JOHN'S

Westminster School Playing Fields

TATE BRITAIN

PIMLICO

Thames River

MILLBANK PIER

East London

SIGHTS

1. Borough Market
2. BFI Southbank (Cinema)
3. City Hall
4. The Clink Prison Museum
5. Courtauld Gallery
6. Covent Garden
7. To Geffrye Museum
8. Golden Hinde Replica
9. HMS Belfast
10. Houses of Parliament & Big Ben
11. Imperial War Museum
12. The Inns of Court
13. Jubilee Walkway
14. Leadenhall Market
15. London Duck Tours
16. London Eye
17. London Transport Museum

18. Millennium Bridge
19. The Monument
20. Museum of London
21. Old Bailey
22. Old Operating Theatre Museum & Herb Garret
23. Royal Courts of Justice
24. Shakespeare's Globe
25. Sir John Soane's Museum
26. Southwark Cathedral
27. St. Bride's Church
28. St. Paul's Cathedral
29. The Shard (Observation Decks)
30. Tate Modern
31. Temple Church
32. Tower Bridge
33. Tower of London
34. Vinopolis

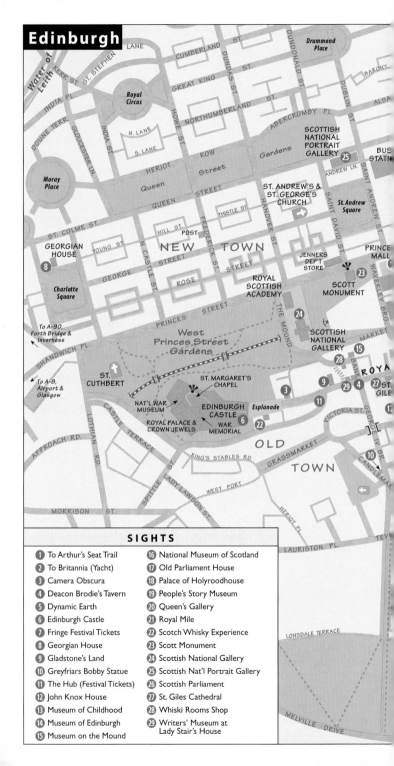

Edinburgh

NEW TOWN

OLD TOWN

SIGHTS

1. To Arthur's Seat Trail
2. To Britannia (Yacht)
3. Camera Obscura
4. Deacon Brodie's Tavern
5. Dynamic Earth
6. Edinburgh Castle
7. Fringe Festival Tickets
8. Georgian House
9. Gladstone's Land
10. Greyfriars Bobby Statue
11. The Hub (Festival Tickets)
12. John Knox House
13. Museum of Childhood
14. Museum of Edinburgh
15. Museum on the Mound
16. National Museum of Scotland
17. Old Parliament House
18. Palace of Holyroodhouse
19. People's Story Museum
20. Queen's Gallery
21. Royal Mile
22. Scotch Whisky Experience
23. Scott Monument
24. Scottish National Gallery
25. Scottish Nat'l Portrait Gallery
26. Scottish Parliament
27. St. Giles Cathedral
28. Whiski Rooms Shop
29. Writers' Museum at Lady Stair's House

Great Britain

What's so great about Britain?
Plenty. You can watch a world-class
Shakespeare play, do the Beatles blitz in
Liverpool, and walk along a windswept
hill in the footsteps of Wordsworth.
Climb cobblestone streets as you wander
Edinburgh's Royal Mile, or take a ferry
to a windswept isle. Ponder a moody
glen, wild-ponied moor, lonesome stone
circle, or ruined abbey. Try getting your
tongue around a few Welsh words, relax
in a bath in Bath, and enjoy evensong
at Westminster Abbey. Stroll through a
cute-as-can-be Cotswold town, try to
spot an underwater monster in a loch,
and sail along the Thames past Big Ben.
Great Britain has it all.

Regardless of the revolution we had 230-some years ago, many American travelers feel that they "go home" to Britain. This most popular tourist destination has a strange influence and power over us. The more you know of Britain's roots, the better you'll get in touch with your own.

The Isle of Britain is small (about the size of Idaho)—600 miles long and 300 miles at its widest point. Britain's highest mountain (Scotland's Ben Nevis) is 4,409 feet, a foothill by our standards. The population is a fifth that of the United States. At its peak in the mid-1800s, Britain owned one-fifth of the world and accounted for more than half the planet's industrial output. Today, the empire is down to the Isle of Britain itself and a few token scraps, such as Northern Ireland, Gibraltar, and the Falklands.

And yet, culturally, Britain remains a world leader. Her heritage, culture, and people cannot be measured in traditional units of power. London is a major exporter of actors, movies, and theater; of rock and classical music; and of writers, painters, and sculptors.

On the other hand, when it comes to cuisine, Britain has given the world...fish-and-chips and haggis. Bad, bland British food is almost a universal joke, headed by dishes with funny names like "bubble and squeak" and "toad in the hole." Traditionally, Britain was known for heavy, no-nonsense meals. The day started with a hearty breakfast of eggs and bacon, followed by meat pies and beer for lunch, and finished with a filling dinner of red meat and thick sauces.

But the cuisine has improved. The British have added fresh fruits and vegetables to their diet, and many regions pride themselves on using locally grown foods to make lighter, more creative variations of old favorites. Foreign influences—

especially Indian and Chinese imports—are especially popular, having been adapted to local tastes.

Thankfully, one distinctive British tradition remains popular: afternoon tea served with biscuits, cookies, or little sandwiches. This four o'clock break is part pick-me-up and part social ritual.

Ethnically, the British Isles are a mix of the descendants of the early Celtic natives (in Scotland, Ireland, Wales, and Cornwall), the invading Anglo-Saxons who took southeast England in the Dark Ages, and the conquering Normans of the 11th century...not to mention more recent immigrants from around the world. Cynics call the United Kingdom an English Empire ruled by London, whose dominant Anglo-Saxon English (50 million) far outnumber their Celtic brothers and sisters (10 million).

It's easy to think that "Britain" and "England" are one and the same. But actually, three very different countries make up Great Britain: England, Wales, and Scotland. (Add Northern Ireland and you've got the United Kingdom—but you'll need a different guidebook.) Let's take a quick cultural tour through Great Britain's three nations.

England

Even today, England remains a cultural and linguistic touchstone for the almost one billion humans who speak English. It's the center of the United Kingdom in every way: home to four out of five UK citizens, the seat of government, the economic powerhouse, the center of higher learning, and

Britain Almanac

Official Name: The United Kingdom of Great Britain and Northern Ireland (locals say "the UK" or "Britain").

Population: Britain's 62 million people include a sizable and growing minority of immigrants, largely from India, Pakistan, and Eastern Europe. Seven in ten British call themselves Christian (half of those are Anglican), but in any given week, more Brits visit a mosque than an Anglican church.

Latitude and Longitude: 54°N and 2°W. The latitude is similar to Alberta, Canada.

Area: From "Britannia's" 19th-century peak of power, when it dominated much of the globe, the British Empire shrunk to a quarter of its former size. Today, this nation is 95,000 square miles (about the size of Michigan). It's composed of one large island and a chunk of another large island.

Geography: Most of the British Isles consists of low hills and rolling plains, with a generally moderate climate. The country's highest point is 4,409-foot Ben Nevis in western Scotland. Britain's longest river, the Severn, loops 220 miles from the mountains of Wales east into England, then south to the Bristol Channel. The Thames River runs 215 miles east–west through the heart of southern England (including London).

Biggest Cities: London is the capital, with 7.8 million people. Industrial Birmingham has about 1 million, Glasgow 600,000, Edinburgh 500,000, and the port of Liverpool 450,000.

Economy: The Gross Domestic Product is $2.25 trillion and the GDP per capita is $36,000. Moneymakers include banking, insurance and business services, energy production, agriculture, shipping, and trade with the US and Germany. Heavy industry—which once drove the Industrial Revolution—is now in decline.

Government: Queen Elizabeth II officially heads the country, but in practice it's the prime minister, who leads the majority party in Parliament. Since 2010, the British House of Commons has had 650 members. (The House of Lords is now a mere advisory body.) Britain's traditional two-party system—Labour and Conservatives ("Tories")—now has a smaller third player, the Liberal Democrats ("Lib Dems"). The current prime minister, Conservative leader David Cameron, came to power in May 2010, unseating Labour Party rival Gordon Brown. Britain is a member of the European Union (but not the euro system) and is one of five permanent members (with veto power) of the UN Security Council. In 1999, Scotland, Wales, and Northern Ireland were each granted their own Parliament—and, with that, more autonomy in their domestic affairs. However, independence movements still run strong, particularly in Scotland; a referendum on Scottish independence will take place in September of 2014.

Flag: The "Union Jack" has two red crosses on a field of blue: the English cross of St. George and the Scottish cross of St. Andrew.

The Average Brit: Eats 35 pounds of pizza and 35 pounds of chocolate a year, and weighs 12 stone (170 pounds). He or she is 40 years old, has 1.66 children, and will live to age 80. He/she drinks 2.5 cups of tea a day and 2.5 glasses of wine a week (Americans drink less than half that). He/she has free health care, and gets 28 vacation days a year (versus 13 in the US). He/she sleeps 7.5 hours a night, speaks one language, and loves soccer.

the cultural heart. And, although it lacks some of the Celtic color of other parts of Britain, you'll find plenty of variety even in "plain vanilla" England.

North England tends to be hilly with poor soil, so the traditional economy was based on livestock (grazing cows and sheep). Today it has

some of England's most beautiful landscapes, but in the 19th century it was dotted with belching smokestacks as its major cities and its heartland became centers of coal and iron mining and manufacturing. Now its working-class cities and ports (such as Liverpool) are experiencing a comeback, buoyed by higher employment, tourism, and vibrant arts scenes.

South England, including London, has always had more people and more money than the north. Blessed with rolling hills, wide plains, and the Thames River, in the past this area was rich with farms, its rivers flowed with trade, and high culture flourished around the epicenter in London. And today, even though London is a thriving metropolis of nearly eight million people, much the same can still be said.

The English people have a worldwide reputation (or stereotype) for being cheerful, courteous, and well-mannered. Cutting in line is very gauche. On the other hand, English soccer fans can be notorious "hooligans." The English are not known for being touchy-feely or physically demonstrative (hugging and kissing), but they sure do love to talk. When times get tough, they persevere with a stiff upper lip. The understated English wit is legendary—when someone dies, it's "a bit of a drag" (but if the tea is cold, it's "ghastly"!).

For the tourist, England offers a little of everything we associate with Britain: castles, cathedrals, and ruined abbeys; chatty locals nursing beers in village pubs; mysterious prehistoric stone circles and Roman ruins; tea, scones, and clotted cream; hikes across unspoiled, sheep-speckled hillsides; and drivers who cheerfully wave from the "wrong" side of the road. And then there's London, a world in itself, with monuments (Big Ben), museums (the British Museum), royalty (Buckingham Palace), theater, and nightlife, throbbing with the pulse of the global community.

You can trace England's illustrious history by roaming the countryside. Prehistoric peoples built the mysterious stone circles of Stonehenge and Avebury. Then came the Romans, who built Hadrian's Wall and baths at Bath. Viking invaders left their mark in York, and the Normans built the Tower of London. As England Christianized and unified, the grand cathedrals of Salisbury, Wells, and Durham arose. Next came the castles and palaces of the English monarchs (Windsor and Warwick) and the Shakespeare sights from the era of Elizabeth I (Stratford-upon-Avon). In following centuries, tiny England became a maritime empire (the *Cutty Sark* at Greenwich) and the world's first industrial power (Ironbridge Gorge). England's Romantic poets were inspired by the unspoiled nature and time-passed villages of the Lake District and the Cotswolds. In the 20th century, the gritty urban world of 1960s Liverpool gave the world the Beatles. Finally, end your journey through English history in London—on the cutting edge of 21st-century trends.

For a thousand years, England has been a major cultural center. Parliamentary democracy, science (Isaac Newton), technology (Michael Faraday), and education (Oxford and Cambridge) were nurtured here. In literature, England has few peers in any language, producing some of the greatest legends (King Arthur, *Beowulf*, and *The Lord of the Rings*), poems (by Chaucer, Wordsworth, and Byron), novels (by Dickens, Austen, and J. K. Rowling), and plays (by William Shakespeare, England's greatest writer). London rivals New York as the best scene for live theater. England is a major exporter of movies and movie actors— Laurence Olivier, Alec Guinness, Ian McKellen, Helen

Mirren, Judi Dench, Kate Winslet, Keira Knightley, Ralph Fiennes, Hugh Grant, Ricky Gervais, and on and on.

In popular music, England remains neck and neck with America. It started in the 1960s with the "British invasion" of bands that reinfused rock and blues into America—the Beatles, the Rolling Stones, and the Who. Then came successive waves in the 1970s (Elton John, Led Zeppelin, David Bowie, Pink Floyd, Queen, Black Sabbath, the Clash, the Sex Pistols); the '80s (Dire Straits, Phil Collins and Genesis, Elvis Costello, the Cure, the Smiths, the Police, Depeche Mode, Duran Duran, Wham!); the Britpop '90s (Oasis, Blur, PJ Harvey, Spice Girls, the rave scene); and into the 21st century (Coldplay, Adele, M.I.A., Radiohead, the late Amy Winehouse).

Wales

Humble, charming little Wales is traditional and beautiful—it sometimes feels trapped in a time warp. When you first enter Wales, it may seem like you're still in England. But soon you'll awaken to the uniqueness and crusty yet poetic vitality of this small country and realize...you're not in Oxford anymore. And don't ask for an "English breakfast" at your Welsh B&B—they'll smile politely and remind you that it's a "Welsh breakfast," made with Welsh ingredients.

For the tourist, Wales is a land of stout castles (the best are at Conwy and Caernarfon), salty harbors, chummy community choirs, slate-roofed villages, and a landscape of mountains, moors, and lush green fields dotted with sheep. Snowdonia National Park is a hiker's paradise, with steep but manageable mountain trails, cute-as-a-hobbit villages (Beddgelert and Betws-y-Coed), and scenery more striking than most anything in England. Fascinating slate-mine museums (such as at Blaenau Ffestiniog), handy home-base

towns (Conwy and Ruthin), and enticing, offbeat attractions round out Wales' appeal.

Perhaps Wales' best attraction is hearing the locals speak Welsh (or Cymraeg, pronounced kum-RAH-ig). The Welsh people often use this tongue-twisting and fun-to-listen-to Celtic language when speaking with one another, smoothly switching to English when a visitor asks a question. With its sometimes harsh, sometimes melodic tones, Welsh transports listeners to another time and place.

Culturally, Wales is "a land of poets and singers"—or so says the national anthem. From the myths of Merlin and King Arthur to the poetry of Dylan Thomas (1914-1953), Wales has a long literary tradition. In music, the country nourishes its traditional Celtic folk music (especially the harp) and has exported popular singers such as Tom Jones, Charlotte Church, and Jem. Popular actors born in Wales include Richard Burton and Catherine Zeta-Jones.

Scotland

Rugged, feisty, colorful Scotland is the yin to England's yang. Whether it's the looser, less-organized nature of the people, the stone and sandstone architecture, the unmanicured landscape, or simply the haggis, go-its-own-way Scotland still stands apart. The home of kilts, bagpipes, whisky, golf, lochs, and shortbread lives up to its clichéd image—and then some.

While the Scots are known for their telltale burr—and more than a few unique words (aye, just listen for a wee blether)—they're also trying to keep alive their own Celtic tongue: Gaelic (pronounced "gallic"). While few Scots speak Gaelic in everyday life, legislation protects it, and it's beginning to be used on road signs.

That's just one small sign of the famously independent Scottish spirit. Since the days of William "Braveheart" Wallace, the Scots have chafed under English rule. Thanks to the relatively recent trend of "devolution," Scotland has become increasingly autonomous (even opening its own Parliament in 1999). On September 18, 2014, Scottish citizens will vote on whether Scotland should be an independent country, with full control over all taxes and laws.

Visitors divide their time between the two Scotlands: the Lowlands (the flatter, southern area around Edinburgh and Glasgow, populated by yuppies) and the Highlands (the remote, rugged northern area, where proudly traditional Scots eke out a living).

In the Lowlands, don't miss the impressive Scottish capital of Edinburgh, with its attraction-lined Royal Mile and stirring hilltop castle. Nearby, the rival city of Glasgow offers a grittier (but quickly gentrifying) urban ambience. And golfers can't miss the seaside town of St. Andrews, with its world-famous links, vast sandy beaches, colorful university life, and evocative ruined cathedral.

To commune with the traditional Scottish soul, head for the Highlands. Here you'll find hills, lochs (lakes), "sea lochs" (inlets), castles, and a feeling of remoteness. The "Weeping Glen" of Glencoe offers grand views and a sad tale of Scottish history. The provincial city of Inverness is a handy home base for venturing to uniquely Scottish sights (including the historic site of "Bonnie" Prince Charlie's disastrous Battle of Culloden). Ever-present whisky distilleries offer the chance to sample another uniquely Scottish "spirit," and viewing the engineering feat of the Caledonian Canal—not to mention

famous Loch Ness—inspires awe (say hi to Nessie). Hardy souls can set sail for some of Scotland's islands: Iona and Mull (from Oban), or the super-scenic Isle of Skye.

Whether going to England, Wales, Scotland, or (my choice) all three, you'll have a grand adventure—and a great experience—in Great Britain. Cheerio!

INTRODUCTION

This book breaks Great Britain into its top big-city, small-town, and rural destinations. It gives you all the information and opinions necessary to wring the maximum value out of your limited time and money in each of these locations. If you plan a month or less for Britain and have a normal appetite for information, this book is all you need. If you're a travel-info fiend, this book sorts through all the superlatives and provides a handy rack upon which to hang your supplemental information.

Experiencing British culture, people, and natural wonders economically and hassle-free has been my goal for more than three decades of traveling, tour guiding, and travel writing. With this new edition, I pass on to you the lessons I've learned, updated for your trip. (Note that Northern Ireland—which is part of the UK, but not Great Britain—is covered in my book *Rick Steves' Ireland*.)

While including the predictable biggies (such as Big Ben, Edinburgh, Stratford-upon-Avon, and Stonehenge), this book also mixes in a healthy dose of Back Door intimacy (windswept Roman lookouts, angelic boys' choirs, and nearly edible Cotswold villages). It is selective. For example, while Hadrian's Wall is more than 70 miles long, I recommend visiting just the best six-mile stretch.

The best is, of course, only my opinion. But after spending half my adult life researching Europe, I've developed a sixth sense for what travelers enjoy. The places featured in this book will knock your spots off.

About This Book

Rick Steves' Great Britain is a personal tour guide in your pocket. The book is organized by destinations. Each is a mini-vacation

Map Legend

⚬ Viewpoint	✈ Airport	)▬▬(Tunnel
↟ Entrance	Ⓣ Taxi Stand	▦▦▦ Pedestrian Zone
⊕ Tourist Info	Ⓣ Tram Stop	--·-- Railway
WC Restroom	Ⓑ Bus Stop	·········· Ferry/Boat Route
⬗ Castle	Ⓟ Parking	⊢—⊢ Tram
⌂ Church	⊖ Tube	▮▮▮▮ Stairs
▪ Statue/Point of Interest	)(Mtn. Pass	· · · · Walk/Tour Route
⬯ Pub	▢ Park	- - - - Trail

Use this legend to help you navigate some of the maps in this book.

on its own, filled with exciting sights, strollable neighborhoods, homey and affordable places to stay, and memorable places to eat. In the following chapters, you'll find these sections:

Planning Your Time suggests a schedule for how to best use your limited time.

Orientation includes specifics on public transportation, helpful hints, local tour options, easy-to-read maps, and tourist information.

Sights describes the top attractions and includes their cost and hours.

Self-Guided Walks take you through interesting neighborhoods, with a personal tour guide in hand.

Sleeping describes my favorite hotels, from good-value deals to cushy splurges.

Eating serves up a range of options, from inexpensive pubs to fancy restaurants.

Connections outlines your options for traveling to destinations by train, bus, and plane, plus route tips for drivers.

The **Britain: Past and Present** chapter is a quick overview of British history and culture.

The **appendix** is a traveler's tool kit, with telephone tips, useful phone numbers and websites, transportation basics (on trains, buses, car rentals, driving, and flights), recommended books and films, a festival list, a climate chart, a handy packing checklist, and a fun British-Yankee dictionary.

Browse through this book, choose your favorite destinations, and link them up. Then have a brilliant trip! Traveling like a temporary local, you'll get the absolute most out of every mile, minute, and dollar. I'm happy that you'll be visiting places I know and love, and meeting my favorite British people.

Key to This Book

Updates
This book is updated every year, but things change. For the latest, visit www.ricksteves.com/update.

Abbreviations and Times
I use the following symbols and abbreviations in this book:
Sights are rated:

▲▲▲	**Don't miss**
▲▲	**Try hard to see**
▲	**Worthwhile if you can make it**
No rating	**Worth knowing about**

Tourist information offices are abbreviated as **TI,** and bathrooms are **WC**s. To categorize accommodations, I use a **Sleep Code** (described on page 23).

Like Europe, this book uses the **24-hour clock** for schedules. It's the same through 12:00 noon, then keeps going: 13:00, 14:00, and so on. For anything over 12, subtract 12 and add p.m. (14:00 is 2:00 p.m.).

When giving **opening times,** I include both peak season and off-season hours if they differ. So, if a museum is listed as "May-Oct daily 9:00-16:00," it should be open from 9 a.m. until 4 p.m. from the first day of May until the last day of October (but expect exceptions).

For **transit** or **tour departures,** I first list the frequency, then the duration. So, a train connection listed as "2/hour, 1.5 hours" departs twice each hour, and the journey lasts an hour and a half.

Planning

This section will help you get started on planning your trip—with advice on trip costs, when to go, and what you should know before you take off.

Travel Smart

Your trip to Great Britain is like a complex play—it's easier to follow and really appreciate on a second viewing. While no one does the same trip twice to gain that advantage, reading this book in its entirety before your travels accomplishes much the same thing.

Design an itinerary that enables you to visit sights at the best possible times. Note festivals, holidays, specifics on sights, and days when sights are closed. To get between destinations smoothly, read the tips in this book's appendix on taking trains and buses, or renting a car and driving. A smart trip is a puzzle—a fun, doable, and worthwhile challenge.

INTRODUCTION

Top Destinations in Great Britain

ISLE OF SKYE

OBAN & SOUTHERN HIGHLANDS

INVERNESS & NORTHERN HIGHLANDS

BETWEEN INVER. & EDIN.

ST. ANDREWS

GLASGOW

EDINBURGH

LAKE DISTRICT

DURHAM & N.E. ENGLAND

LIVERPOOL

YORK

NORTH WALES

IRONBRIDGE GORGE

WARWICK & COVENTRY

STRATFORD

THE COTSWOLDS

GREENWICH WINDSOR & CAMBRIDGE

LONDON

NEAR BATH

BATH

DCH

When you're plotting your itinerary, strive for a mix of intense and relaxed stretches. To maximize rootedness, minimize one-night stands. It's worth a long drive after dinner to be settled into a town for two nights. Hotels and B&Bs are more likely to give a better price to someone staying more than one night. Every trip (and every traveler) needs slack time (laundry, picnics, people-watching, and so on). Pace yourself. Assume you will return.

Reread this book as you travel, and visit local TIs. Upon arrival in a new town, lay the groundwork for a smooth departure; get the schedule for the train or bus that you'll take when you depart. Drivers can study the best route to their next destination.

Get online at Internet cafés or at your hotel, and carry a

mobile phone (or use a phone card) to make travel plans: You can find tourist information, learn the latest on sights (special events, tour schedules, etc.), book tickets and tours, make reservations, reconfirm hotels, research transportation connections, check weather, and keep in touch with your loved ones.

Enjoy the friendliness of the British people. Connect with the culture. Set up your own quest for the best pub, cathedral, or chocolate bar. Slow down and be open to unexpected experiences. You speak the language—use it! Ask questions—most locals are eager to point you in their idea of the right direction. Keep a notepad in your pocket for noting directions, organizing your thoughts, and confirming prices. Wear your money belt, learn the currency, and figure out how to estimate prices in dollars. Those who expect to travel smart, do.

Trip Costs

Five components make up your trip costs: airfare, surface transportation, room and board, sightseeing and entertainment, and shopping and miscellany.

Airfare: A basic round-trip US-to-London flight can cost, on average, about $1,000-1,800, depending on where you fly from and when (cheaper in winter). Smaller budget airlines may provide bargain service from several European capitals to many cities in Great Britain. If your trip extends beyond Britain, consider saving time and money by flying into one city and out of another—for instance, into London and out of Amsterdam.

Surface Transportation: For a three-week whirlwind trip of all my recommended British destinations, allow $550 per person for public transportation (train pass, key buses, and Tube fare in London). For a three-week trip by car, allow $300-450 per person (based on two people sharing; not including gas, insurance, or taxes)—or look into leasing, which can save you money on insurance and taxes for trips of this length. Car rentals and leases are cheapest when arranged from the US. Train passes are normally available only outside Europe. You may save money by simply buying tickets as you go. Don't hesitate to consider flying, as budget airlines can be cheaper than taking the train (check Skyscanner.com for intra-European flights). For more on public transportation and car rental, see "Transportation" in the appendix.

Room and Board: Outside of London, you can thrive in Britain on $120 per day per person for room and board. This allows $15 for lunch, $35 for dinner, and $70 for lodging (based on two people splitting the cost of a $140 double room that includes breakfast). Allow about 15 percent more for your days in London or other big cities. Students and tightwads can enjoy Britain for as little as $60 ($30 for a bed, $30 for meals and snacks).

Great Britain at a Glance

England

▲▲▲**London** Thriving metropolis packed with world-class museums, monuments, churches, parks, palaces, theaters, pubs, Beefeaters, telephone boxes, double-decker buses, and all things British.

▲▲**Greenwich, Windsor, and Cambridge** Easy side-trips from London: famous observatory at the maritime center of Greenwich, the Queen's palace at Windsor, and England's best university town, Cambridge.

▲▲▲**Bath** Genteel Georgian showcase city, built around the remains of an ancient Roman bath.

▲▲**Near Bath** England's mysterious heart, including the prehistoric-meets-New Age hill at Glastonbury, spine-tingling stone circles at Stonehenge and Avebury, enjoyable cathedral towns of Wells and Salisbury, and rugged sights of South Wales.

▲▲**The Cotswolds** Remarkably quaint villages—including the cozy market town Chipping Campden, popular hamlet Stow-on-the-Wold, and handy transit hub Moreton-in-Marsh—scattered over a hilly countryside and near one of England's top palaces, Blenheim.

▲**Stratford-upon-Avon** Shakespeare's hometown and top venue for seeing his plays performed.

Warwick and Coventry England's best medieval castle, in pleasant Warwick, and the stirring bombed-out husk of an ancient cathedral, in Coventry.

▲**Ironbridge Gorge** Birthplace of the Industrial Revolution, with sights and museums that tell the earth-changing story.

▲**Liverpool** Rejuvenated port city and the Beatles' hometown.

▲▲**The Lake District** Idyllic lakes-and-hills landscape, with enjoyable hikes and joyrides, time-passed valleys, William Wordsworth and Beatrix Potter sights, and the charming home-base town of Keswick.

▲▲▲**York** Walled medieval town with grand Gothic cathedral, excellent museums (Viking, Victorian, Railway), and atmospheric old center, with the windswept North York Moors at its doorstep.

▲**Durham and Northeast England** Youthful working-class town with magnificent cathedral, plus (nearby) an open-air museum, the Roman remains of Hadrian's Wall, Holy Island, and Bamburgh Castle.

Wales
▲▲▲**North Wales** Scenically rugged land with the castle towns of Conwy, Caernarfon, and Beaumaris; natural beauty of Snowdonia National Park; tourable slate mines at Blaenau Ffestiniog; colorful Welsh villages like Beddgelert and Ruthin; and charming locals who speak a tongue-twisting old language.

Scotland
▲▲▲**Edinburgh** Proud and endlessly entertaining Scottish capital, with an imposing castle, attractions-studded Royal Mile, excellent museums, and atmospheric neighborhoods.

▲**St. Andrews** Sandy beach town that gave birth to golf and hosts Scotland's top university.

Glasgow Scotland's gritty but gentrifying, cultural "second city," a hotbed of 20th-century architecture.

▲**Oban and the Southern Highlands** Handy home-base town of Oban—with boat trips to the isles of Mull and Iona—and the stirring "Weeping Glen" of Glencoe.

▲**Isle of Skye** Remote, dramatically scenic island with craggy mountainscapes, jagged Trotternish Peninsula, castles, and distilleries.

▲**Inverness and the Northern Highlands** Regional capital with easy access to more Highlands sights, including Culloden Battlefield (Scotland's Alamo) and monster-spotting at the famous Loch Ness.

Between Inverness and Edinburgh Whisky mecca of Pitlochry and stately castle and battlefield at Stirling.

INTRODUCTION

Britain's Best Three-Week Trip by Car

Day	Plan	Sleep in
1	Arrive in London, train/bus combo or direct bus to Bath	Bath
2	Bath	Bath
3	Pick up car, Avebury, Wells, Glastonbury	Bath
4	South Wales, St. Fagans, Tintern	Chipping Campden
5	Explore the Cotswolds, Blenheim	Chipping Campden
6	Stratford, Warwick, Coventry	Ironbridge Gorge
7	Ironbridge Gorge, to North Wales	Conwy
8	Highlights of North Wales	Conwy
9	Liverpool	Liverpool
10	South Lake District	Keswick area
11	North Lake District	Keswick area
12	Drive up west coast of Scotland	Oban
13	Highlands, Loch Ness, Scenic Highlands Drive	Edinburgh
14	Edinburgh	Edinburgh
15	Edinburgh	Edinburgh
16	Hadrian's Wall, Beamish, Durham's Cathedral and evensong	Durham
17	North York Moors, York, turn in car	York
18	York	York
19	Early train to London	London
20	London	London
21	London	London
22	Whew!	

While this three-week itinerary is designed to be done by car, it can be done by train and bus or, better yet, with a BritRail & Drive Pass (best car days: Cotswolds, North Wales, Lake District, Scottish Highlands, Hadrian's Wall); for more on the pass, see page 1012. For three weeks without a car, I'd cut back on the recommended sights with the most frustrating public transportation (South and North Wales, Ironbridge Gorge, and the Scottish Highlands). Lacing together the cities by train is very slick, and buses get you where the trains don't go. With more time, everything is workable without a car.

...g and Entertainment: Figure about $15-35 ... (Stonehenge-$13, Shakespeare's Birthplace in ..., Westminster Abbey-$29, Tower of London-$35, ... astle-$25), $7 for minor ones (climbing church towers), and ...-40 for splurge experiences (e.g., bus tours, concerts, discounted tickets for plays). For information on various sightseeing passes, see page 21.

Fortunately, many of the best sights in London are free, including the British Museum, National Gallery, National Portrait Gallery, Tate Britain, Tate Modern, British Library, and the Victoria & Albert Museum (though most request donations). An overall average of $30 a day works in most cities (allow $50 for London). Don't skimp here. After all, this category is the driving force behind your trip—you came to sightsee, enjoy, and experience Britain.

Shopping and Miscellany: Figure roughly $2 per postcard, $3 for tea or an ice-cream cone, and $5 per pint of beer. Shopping can vary in cost from nearly nothing to a small fortune. Good budget travelers find that this category has little to do with assembling a trip full of lifelong and wonderful memories.

Sightseeing Priorities

Depending on the length of your trip, and taking geographic proximity into account, here are my recommended priorities:

3 days:	London
5 days, add:	Bath and the Cotswolds
7 days, add:	York
9 days, add:	Edinburgh
11 days, add:	Stratford, Warwick, Blenheim
14 days, add:	North Wales, Wells/Glastonbury/Avebury
17 days, add:	Lake District, Hadrian's Wall, Durham
21 days, add:	Scottish Highlands, Liverpool, Ironbridge Gorge
24 days, add:	Choose two of the following—St. Andrews, Glasgow, Cambridge, South Wales, Isle of Skye

This list includes virtually everything on my "Britain's Best Three-Week Trip by Car" itinerary and map (see page 81).

Note: Instead of spending the first few days of your trip in busy London, consider a gentler small-town start in Bath (the ideal jet-lag pillow), and let London be the finale of your trip. You'll be more rested and ready to tackle Britain's greatest city. Heathrow Airport has direct bus connections to Bath and other cities. (Bristol Airport is also near Bath.)

Your itinerary will depend on your interests. Nature lovers will likely put the lovely Lake District, the Scottish Highlands, and North Wales nearer the top of their list, while engineers are drawn like a magnet to Ironbridge Gorge. Beatlemaniacs make a pilgrimage to Liverpool. Literary fans like Cambridge, Stratford, Bath, and the South Lake District.

When to Go

In most of Britain, July and August are peak season—my favorite time—with very long days, the best weather, and the busiest schedule of tourist fun. For Scotland, the weather is best in May and June.

Prices and crowds don't go up during peak times as dramatically in Britain as they do in much of Europe, except for holidays and festivals (see "Holidays and Festivals" in the appendix). Still, travel during "shoulder season" (May, early June, Sept, and early Oct) is easier and can be a bit less expensive. Shoulder-season travelers usually enjoy smaller crowds, decent weather, the full range of sights and tourist fun spots, and the ability to grab a room almost whenever and wherever they like—often at a flexible price. Winter travelers find absolutely no crowds and soft room prices, but shorter sightseeing hours and reliably bad weather. Some attractions are open only on weekends or are closed entirely in the winter (Nov-Feb). The weather can be cold and dreary, and nightfall draws the shades on sightseeing well before dinnertime. While rural charm falls with the leaves, city sightseeing is fine in the winter.

Plan for rain no matter when you go. Just keep traveling and take full advantage of bright spells. The weather can change several times in a day, but rarely is it extreme. As the locals say, "There is no bad weather, only inappropriate clothing." Bring a jacket and dress in layers. Temperatures below 32°F cause headlines, and days that break 80°F—while more frequent in recent years—are still rare in Britain. Weather-wise, July and August are not much better than shoulder months. May and June can be lovely anywhere in Britain. (For more information, see the climate chart in the appendix.) While sunshine may be rare, summer days are very long. The midsummer sun is up from 6:30 until 22:30. It's not uncommon to have a gray day, eat dinner, and enjoy hours of sunshine afterward.

Know Before You Go

Your trip is more likely to go smoothly if you plan ahead. Check this list of things to arrange while you're still at home.

You need a **passport**—but no visa or shots—to travel in Great Britain. You may be denied entry into certain European countries if your passport is due to expire within three to six months of your ticketed date of return. Get it renewed if you'll be cutting it close. It can take up to six weeks to get or renew a passport (for more on passports, see www.travel.state.gov). Pack a photocopy of your passport in your luggage in case the original is lost or stolen.

Book rooms well in advance if you'll be traveling during peak season and any major **holidays** (see list on page 1033).

Call your **debit- and credit-card companies** to let them know the countries you'll be visiting, to ask about fees, to request your PIN code (it will be mailed to you), and more. See page 16 for details.

Do your homework if you want to buy **travel insurance.** Compare the cost of the insurance to the likelihood of your using it and your potential loss if something goes wrong. Also, check whether your existing insurance (health, homeowners, or renters) covers you and your possessions overseas. For more tips, see www.ricksteves.com/insurance.

Consider buying a **railpass** after researching your options (see page 1014 and www.ricksteves.com/rail for all the specifics). If traveling to continental Europe on the **Eurostar** train, you can order a ticket in advance or buy it in Britain; for details, see page 224.

If you're planning on **renting a car** in Great Britain, arrange it ahead of time.

If you'll be in London or Stratford and want to **see a play,** check theater schedules ahead of time. For simplicity, I book plays while in Britain, but if there's something you just have to see, consider buying tickets before you go (for tips, see page 159, and for a current schedule of London plays and musicals, visit www.officiallondontheatre.co.uk). Tickets to performances at Stratford's Royal Shakespeare Theatre are likely to sell out (see www.rsc.org.uk), but if it's just Shakespeare you're after—with or without Stratford—you can see his plays in London, too.

To attend the **Edinburgh Festival** (Aug 8-31 in 2014 and Aug 14–Sept 6 in 2015), you can book tickets in advance (for details, see page 802).

If you want to **golf at St. Andrews' famous Old Course,** reserve a year ahead, or for other courses, reserve two weeks ahead (see page 838).

At **Stonehenge,** anyone can see the stones from behind the rope line (and for most people, this is sufficient), but if you want to go inside the stone circle, you'll need reservations (see page 346); book it when you know the date you'll be there. You can also reserve a tour of the Lennon and McCartney homes in Liverpool (figure on two weeks ahead in peak season, otherwise just a few days; see page 525).

If you plan to hire a **local guide,** reserve ahead by email. Popular guides can get booked up.

If you're bringing a **mobile device,** download any apps you might want to use on the road, such as maps and transit schedules. Check out **Rick Steves Audio Europe,** featuring audio tours of major sights in London, hours of travel interviews on Great

Britain, and more (via www.ricksteves.com/audioeurope, iTunes, Google Play, or the Rick Steves Audio Europe smartphone app; for details, see page 54).

Check the **Rick Steves guidebook updates** page for any recent changes to this book (www.ricksteves.com/update).

Because **airline carry-on restrictions** are always changing, visit the Transportation Security Administration's website (www .tsa.gov) for an up-to-date list of what you can bring on the plane with you and what you must check. Some airlines may restrict you to only one carry-on (no extras like a purse or daypack); check with your airline or at Britain's transportation website for the latest (www.dft.gov.uk).

Practicalities

Emergency and Medical Help: In Great Britain, dial 999 for police help or a medical emergency. If you get sick, do as the Brits do and go to a pharmacist for advice. Or ask at your B&B or hotel for help—they'll know the nearest medical and emergency services.

Theft or Loss: To replace a passport, you'll need to go in person to an embassy or consulate (see page 1006). If your credit and debit cards disappear, cancel and replace them (see "Damage Control for Lost Cards" on page 17). File a police report, either on the spot or within a day or two; you'll need it to submit an insurance claim for lost or stolen railpasses or travel gear, and it can help with replacing your passport or credit and debit cards. For more information, see www.ricksteves.com/help. Precautionary measures can minimize the effects of loss—back up photos and other files frequently.

Time Zones: Britain, which is one hour earlier than most of continental Europe, is five/eight hours ahead of the East/West coasts of the US. The exceptions are the beginning and end of Daylight Saving Time: Europe "springs forward" the last Sunday in March (two weeks after most of North America), and "falls back" the last Sunday in October (one week before North America). For a handy online time converter, try www.timeand date.com/worldclock.

Business Hours: In Britain, most stores are open Monday through Saturday from roughly 10:00 to 17:00. In London, stores stay open later on Wednesday or Thursday (until 19:00 or 20:00), depending on the neighborhood. Saturdays are virtually weekdays, with earlier closing hours. Sundays have the same pros and cons as they do for travelers in the US: Sightseeing attractions are generally open; banks and many shops are closed; public transportation options are fewer (for example, no bus service to or from smaller towns); there's no rush hour. Rowdy evenings are rare on Sundays.

Watt's Up? Europe's electrical system is 220 volts, instead of North America's 110 volts. Most newer electronics (such as laptops, battery chargers, and hair dryers) convert automatically, so you won't need a converter, but you will need an adapter plug with three square prongs, sold inexpensively at travel stores in the US, and in British airports and drugstores. Avoid bringing older appliances that don't automatically convert voltage; instead, buy a cheap replacement in Europe. Low-cost hairdryers and other small appliances are sold at Superdrug, Boots, and Argos stores (ask your hotelier for the closest branch).

Discounts: Discounts (called "concessions" or "concs" in Britain) are not listed in this book. However, many sights offer discounts for youths (up to age 18), students (with proper identification cards, www.isic.org), families, seniors (loosely defined as retirees or those willing to call themselves a senior), and groups of 10 or more. Always ask. Some discounts are available only for EU citizens.

Money

This section offers advice on how to pay for purchases on your trip (including getting cash from ATMs and paying with plastic), dealing with lost or stolen cards, VAT (sales tax) refunds, and tipping.

What to Bring

Bring both a credit card and a debit card. You'll use the debit card at cash machines (ATMs) to withdraw pounds for most purchases, and the credit card to pay for larger items. Some travelers carry a third card, in case one gets demagnetized or eaten by a temperamental machine.

For an emergency reserve, bring several hundred dollars in hard cash in $20 bills. If you have to exchange the bills, go to a bank; avoid using currency-exchange booths because of their lousy rates and/or outrageous fees.

Cash

Cash is just as desirable in Britain as it is at home. Small businesses (hotels, restaurants, and shops) prefer that you pay your bills with cash. Some vendors will charge you extra for using a credit card, and some won't take credit cards at all. Cash is the best—and sometimes only—way to pay for bus fare, taxis, and local guides.

Exchange Rate

I list prices in pounds (£) throughout this book.

1 British pound (£1) = about $1.60

While the euro (€) is now the currency of most of Europe, Britain is sticking with its pound sterling. The British pound (£), also called a "quid," is broken into 100 pence (p). Pence means "cents." You'll find coins ranging from 1p to £2, and bills from £5 to £50. Counterfeit pound coins are easy to spot (real coins have an inscription on their outside rims; the rims on the fakes look like tree bark).

London is so expensive that some travelers try to kid themselves that pounds are dollars. But when they get home, that £1,000 Visa bill isn't asking for $1,000...it wants $1,600. (Check www.oanda.com for the latest exchange rates.)

Scotland and Northern Ireland issue their own currency in pounds, worth the same as an English pound. English, Scottish, and Northern Ireland's Ulster pound notes are technically interchangeable in each region, although Scottish and Ulster pounds are considered "undesirable" and sometimes not accepted in England. Banks in any of the three regions will convert your Scottish or Ulster pounds into English pounds for no charge. Don't worry about the coins, which are the same throughout the UK.

Throughout Europe, ATMs are the standard way for travelers to get cash. Most ATMs in Britain are located outside a bank. Stay away from "independent" ATMs such as Travelex, Euronet, and Forex, which charge huge commissions and have terrible exchange rates.

To withdraw money from an ATM (which locals call "cashpoints"), you'll need a debit card (ideally with a Visa or MasterCard logo for maximum usability), plus a PIN code. Know your PIN code in numbers; there are no letters on European keypads. Although you can use a credit card for an ATM transaction, it only makes sense in an emergency, because it's considered a cash advance (borrowed at a high interest rate) rather than a withdrawal. Try to withdraw large sums of money to reduce the number of per-transaction bank fees you'll pay.

For increased security, shield the keypad when entering your PIN code, and don't use an ATM if anything on the front of the machine looks loose or damaged (a sign that someone may have attached a "skimming" device to capture account information). Some travelers make a point of monitoring their accounts while traveling to detect any unauthorized transactions.

Pickpockets target tourists. Even in jolly olde England, you'll need to keep your cash safe. Wear a money belt—a pouch with a strap that you buckle around your waist like a belt and tuck under your clothes. Keep your cash, credit cards, and passport secure in your money belt, and carry only a day's spending money in your front pocket.

Credit and Debit Cards

For purchases, Visa and MasterCard are more commonly accepted than American Express. Just like at home, credit and debit cards work easily at larger hotels, restaurants, and shops. I typically use my debit card to withdraw cash to pay for most purchases. I use my credit card only in a few specific situations: to book hotel reservations by phone, to cover major expenses (such as car rentals, plane tickets, and long hotel stays), and to pay for things near the end of my trip (to avoid another visit to the ATM). While you could use a debit card to make most large purchases, using a credit card offers a greater degree of fraud protection (because debit cards draw funds directly from your account).

Ask Your Credit- or Debit-Card Company: Before your trip, contact the company that issued your debit or credit cards.

• Confirm your card will work overseas, and alert them that you'll be using it in Europe; otherwise, they may deny transactions if they perceive unusual spending patterns.

• Ask for the specifics on transaction **fees.** When you use your credit or debit card—either for purchases or ATM withdrawals—you'll typically be charged additional "international transaction" fees of up to 3 percent (1 percent is normal) plus $5 per transaction. If your card's fees seem high, consider getting a different card just for your trip: Capital One (www.capitalone.com) and most credit unions have low-to-no international fees.

• If you plan to withdraw cash from ATMs, confirm your daily **withdrawal limit**, and if necessary, ask your bank to adjust it. Some travelers prefer a high limit that allows them to take out more cash at each ATM stop (saving on bank fees), while others prefer to set a lower limit in case their card is stolen. Note that foreign banks also set maximum withdrawal amounts for their ATMs.

• Get your bank's emergency phone number in the US (but not its 800 number, which isn't accessible from overseas) to call collect if you have a problem.

• Ask for your credit card's **PIN** in case you need to make an emergency cash withdrawal or encounter Europe's "chip-and-PIN" system; the bank won't tell you your PIN over the phone, so allow time for it to be mailed to you.

Chip and PIN: Europeans are increasingly using chip-and-

PIN cards, which are embedded with an electronic security chip (in addition to the magnetic stripe found on American-style cards). With this system, the purchaser punches in a PIN rather than signing a receipt. Your American-style card might not work at automated payment machines, such as those at train and subway stations, toll roads, parking garages, luggage lockers, and self-serve gas pumps.

If you have problems using your American card in a chip-and-PIN machine, here are some suggestions: For either a debit card or credit card, try entering that card's PIN when prompted. (Note that your credit-card PIN may not be the same as your debit-card PIN; you'll need to ask your bank for your credit-card PIN.) If your cards still don't work, look for a machine that takes cash, seek out a clerk who might be able to process the transaction manually, or ask a local if you can pay them cash to run the transaction on their card.

And don't panic. Many travelers who use only magnetic-stripe cards never have a problem. Still, it pays to carry plenty of cash (you can always use an ATM to withdraw cash with your magnetic-stripe debit card).

If you're still concerned, you can apply for a chip card in the US (though I think it's overkill). One option is the no-annual-fee GlobeTrek Visa, offered by Andrews Federal Credit Union in Maryland (open to all US residents; see www.andrewsfcu.org).

Dynamic Currency Conversion: If merchants offer to convert your purchase price into dollars (called dynamic currency conversion, or DCC), refuse this "service." You'll pay even more in fees for the expensive convenience of seeing your charge in dollars.

Damage Control for Lost Cards

If you lose your credit, debit, or ATM card, you can stop people from using your card by reporting the loss immediately to the respective global customer-assistance centers. Call these 24-hour US numbers collect: Visa (tel. 303/967-1096), MasterCard (tel. 636/722-7111), or American Express (tel. 336/393-1111). European toll-free numbers (listed by country) can be found at the websites for Visa and MasterCard.

Providing the following information will allow for a quicker cancellation of your missing card: full card number, whether you are the primary or secondary cardholder, the cardholder's name exactly as printed on the card, billing address, home phone number, circumstances of the loss or theft, and identification verification (your birth date, your mother's maiden name, or your Social Security number—memorize this, don't carry a copy). If you are the secondary cardholder, you'll also need to provide the primary cardholder's identification-verification details. You can generally receive a temporary card within two or three business days in Europe (see www.ricksteves.com/help for more).

If you report your loss within two days, you typically won't be responsible for any unauthorized transactions on your account, although many banks charge a liability fee of $50.

Tipping

Tipping in Britain isn't as automatic and generous as it is in the US, but for special service, tips are appreciated, if not expected. As in the US, the proper amount depends on your resources, tipping philosophy, and the circumstances, but some general guidelines apply.

Restaurants: At pubs where you order at the counter, you don't have to tip. (Regular customers ordering a round sometimes say, "Add one for yourself" as a tip for drinks ordered at the bar—but this isn't expected.) At a pub or restaurant with waitstaff, check the menu or your bill to see if the service is included; if not, tip about 10 percent. Many restaurants in London now add a 12.5 percent "optional" tip onto the bill—read your bill carefully, and tip only what you think the service warrants.

Taxis: To tip the cabbie, round up. For a typical ride, round up your fare a bit (for instance, if the fare is £4.50, give £5; for a £28 fare, give £30). If the cabbie hauls your bags and zips you to the airport to help you catch your flight, you might want to toss in a little more. But if you feel like you're being driven in circles or otherwise ripped off, skip the tip.

Services: In general, if someone in the service industry does a super job for you, a small tip of a pound or two is appropriate, but not required. If you're not sure whether (or how much) to tip for a service, ask your hotelier or the TI.

Getting a VAT Refund

Wrapped into the purchase price of your British souvenirs is a Value-Added Tax (VAT) of 20 percent. You're entitled to get most of that tax back if you spend a significant amount, set by the retailer (Harrods, for example, won't process a refund unless you spend at least £50). Typically, you must ring up the minimum at a single retailer—you can't add up your purchases from various shops to reach the required amount.

Getting your refund is usually straightforward and, if you buy a substantial amount of souvenirs, well worth the hassle. If you're lucky, the merchant will subtract the tax when you make your purchase. (This is more likely to occur if the store ships the goods to your home.) Otherwise, you'll need to:

Get the paperwork. Have the merchant completely fill out the necessary refund document (either an official VAT customs form, or the shop or refund company's own version of it). You'll have to present your passport at the store. Get the paperwork done before you leave the shop to ensure you'll have everything you need (including your original sales receipt).

Get your stamp at the border or airport. Process your VAT document at your last stop in the European Union (such as at the airport) with the customs agent who deals with VAT refunds. Arrive an additional hour early before you need to check in for your flight, to allow time to find the local customs office—and to stand in line. Keep your purchases readily available for viewing by the customs agent (ideally in your carry-on bag—don't make the mistake of checking the bag with your purchases before you've seen the agent). You're not supposed to use your purchased goods before you leave. If you show up at customs wearing your new Wellingtons, officials might look the other way—or deny you a refund.

Collect your refund. You'll need to return your stamped document to the retailer or its representative. Many merchants work with a service, such as Global Blue or Premier Tax Free, which have offices at major airports, ports, or border crossings (either before or after security, probably strategically located near a duty-free shop). These services, which extract a 4 percent fee, can refund your money immediately in cash or credit your card (within two billing cycles). If the retailer handles VAT refunds directly, it's up to you to contact the merchant for your refund. You can mail the documents from home, or more quickly, from your point of departure (using an envelope you've prepared in advance or one that's been provided by the merchant). You'll then have to wait—it can take months.

Customs for American Shoppers

You are allowed to take home $800 worth of items per person duty-free, once every 30 days. You can also bring in duty-free a liter of alcohol. As for food, you can take home many processed and packaged foods: vacuum-packed cheeses, dried herbs, jams, baked goods, candy, chocolate, oil, vinegar, mustard, and honey. Fresh fruits and vegetables and most meats are not allowed. Any liquid-containing foods must be packed in checked luggage, a potential recipe for disaster. To check customs rules and duty rates, visit http://help.cbp.gov.

Sightseeing

Sightseeing can be hard work. Use these tips to make your visits to Britain's finest sights meaningful, fun, efficient, and painless.

Plan Ahead

Set up an itinerary that allows you to fit in all your must-see sights. For a one-stop look at opening hours in the bigger cities, see the "At a Glance" sidebars throughout this book. Most sights keep stable hours, but you can easily confirm the latest by checking with the TI or visiting museum websites.

Don't put off visiting a must-see sight—you never know when a place will close unexpectedly for a holiday, strike, or restoration. Many museums are closed or have reduced hours at least a few days a year, especially on holidays such as Christmas, New Year's, and Bank Holidays in May and August. A list of holidays is on page 1033; check museum websites for possible closures during your trip. Off-season, many museums have shorter hours.

Going at the right time helps avoid crowds. This book offers tips on specific sights. Try visiting popular sights very early, at lunch, or very late. Evening visits are usually peaceful, with fewer crowds. For specifics on London at night, see the sidebar on page 105.

Study up. To get the most out of the self-guided walks and sight descriptions in this book, read them before you visit.

At Sights

Here's what you can typically expect:

Entering: Be warned that you may not be allowed to enter if you arrive 30 to 60 minutes before closing time. And guards start ushering people out well before the actual closing time, so don't save the best for last.

Some important sights require you to check daypacks and coats. To avoid checking a small backpack, carry it tucked under your arm like a purse as you enter.

At ticket desks, you'll constantly see references to "Gift Aid"—a complicated tax-deduction scheme that benefits both museums (which are often classified as charities) and their patrons who are British taxpayers. Unless you pay taxes in Britain, you can ignore this.

Photography: If the museum's photo policy isn't clearly posted, ask a guard. Generally, taking photos without a flash or tripod is allowed. Some sights ban sights ban photos altogether.

Temporary Exhibits: Museums may show special exhibits in addition to their permanent collection. Some exhibits are included in the entry price, while others come at an extra cost (which you may have to pay even if you don't want to see the exhibit).

Expect Changes: Artwork can be on tour, on loan, out sick, or shifted at the whim of the curator. To adapt, pick up a floor plan as you enter, and ask museum staff if you can't find a particular item.

Audioguides: Many museums rent audioguides, which generally offer excellent recorded descriptions (about £3.50; sometimes included with admission). If you bring your own earbuds, you can enjoy better sound and avoid holding the device to your ear. To save money, bring a Y-jack and share one audioguide with your travel partner. Increasingly, museums are offering apps (often free) that you can download to your mobile device. I've produced free, downloadable audio tours of the major sights in London; see page 54.

Services: Important sights and cathedrals may have an on-site café or cafeteria (usually a good place to rejuvenate during a long visit). The WCs are usually free and nearly always clean.

Before Leaving: At the gift shop, scan the postcard rack or thumb through a guidebook to be sure you haven't overlooked something that you'd like to see.

Every sight or museum offers more than what is covered in this book. Use the information in this book as an introduction—not the final word.

Sightseeing Memberships and Passes

Many sights in Britain are managed by English Heritage, the National Trust, Cadw (Welsh organization), or Historic Scotland; but the sights don't overlap. Both the English Heritage and National Trust sell annual memberships that allow free or discounted entry to the sights they supervise; you can join either organization online or at just about any of their sights. English Heritage, Cadw, and Historic Scotland also sell passes.

Membership in **English Heritage** includes free entry to more than 400 sights in England and half-price admission to about 100 more sights in Scotland and Wales. For most travelers, their **Overseas Visitor Pass** is a better choice than the pricier one-year membership (Visitor Pass: £24/9 days, £28/16 days, discounts for couples and families; Membership: £48 for one person, £84 for two, discounts for seniors and students, children under 19 free; toll tel. 0870-333-1182, www.english-heritage.org.uk).

Membership in the **National Trust** is best suited for garden-and-estate enthusiasts, ideally those traveling by car. It covers more than 350 historic houses, manors, and gardens throughout Great Britain. From the US, it's easy to join online through the Royal Oak Foundation, the National Trust's American affiliate (one-year membership: $65 for one person, $95 for two, family and student memberships, www.royal-oak.org). Children under age five are always admitted free to National Trust properties (www.nationaltrust.org.uk).

Cadw and **Historic Scotland** offer Explorer Passes that cover many sights. For Scotland, see page 740 (www.historic-scotland .gov.uk/explorer); for Wales, see page 689 (www.cadw.wales .gov.uk).

Factors to Consider: If you have children over the age of five and you're all avid sightseers, consider the National Trust family membership—but remember that your kids get in free or cheaply at most sights. Similarly, people over 60 get "concessions" (discounted prices) at many British sights (and can get a senior discount on an English Heritage membership). If you're traveling by car and can get to the more remote sights, you're more likely to get your money's worth out of a pass or membership, especially during peak season (Easter-Oct). If you're traveling off-season (Nov-Easter) when many of the sights are closed, the deals are a lesser value.

The Bottom Line: These various deals can save a busy sightseer money, but only if you choose carefully. Make a list of the sights you plan to see, check which ones are covered (visit the websites for each pass), and then add up the total if you were to pay individual admissions to the covered sights. Compare the total to the cost of the pass or membership. Keep in mind that an advantage to any of these deals is that you'll feel free to dip into lesser sights that normally aren't worth the cost of their admission.

Sleeping

I favor hotels and restaurants that are handy to your sightseeing activities. In Britain, small bed-and-breakfast places (B&Bs) generally provide the best value, though I also include some bigger hotels. Rather than list lodgings scattered throughout a city, I describe two or three favorite neighborhoods and recommend the best accommodations values in each, from dorm beds to fancy doubles with all the comforts. Outside of pricey London, you can expect to find good doubles for £50-100 ($80-160), including cooked breakfasts and tax. (For specifics on London, see page 170.)

A major feature of this book is its extensive and opinionated listing of good-value rooms. I like places that are clean, central, relatively quiet at night, reasonably priced, friendly, small enough to have a hands-on owner and stable staff, run with a respect for British traditions, and not listed in other guidebooks. (In Britain, for me, six of these eight criteria means it's a keeper.) I'm more

Sleep Code

(£1 = about $1.60, country code: 44)

Price Rankings

To help you easily sort through my listings, I've divided the accommodations into three categories based on the price for a double room with bath during high season:

$$$ **Higher Priced**
$$ **Moderately Priced**
$ **Lower Priced**

I always rate hostels as $, whether or not they have double rooms, because they have the cheapest beds in town. Prices can change without notice; verify the hotel's current rates online or by email.

Abbreviations

To pack maximum information into minimum space, I use the following code to describe accommodations in this book. Prices listed are per room, not per person. When a price range is given for a type of room (such as double rooms listing for £80-120), it means the price fluctuates with the season, size of room, or length of stay; expect to pay the upper end for peak-season stays.

S = Single room (or price for one person in a double).

D = Double or twin room. "Double beds" can be two twins sheeted together and are usually big enough for non-romantic couples.

T = Triple (generally a double bed with a single).

Q = Quad (usually two double beds; adding an extra child's bed to a T is usually cheaper).

b = Private bathroom with toilet and shower or tub.

s = Private shower or tub only. (The toilet is down the hall.)

According to this code, a couple staying at a "Db-£80" B&B would pay a total of £80 (about $130) for a double room with a private bathroom. Unless otherwise noted, breakfast is included and credit cards are accepted. For most places, the rates I list include the 20 percent VAT tax—but it's smart to ask when you book your room.

There's almost always Wi-Fi and/or a guest computer available, either free or for a fee.

impressed by a convenient location and a fun-loving philosophy than flat-screen TVs and a pricey laundry service.

Book your accommodations well in advance if you'll be traveling during busy times. Mark these dates in red on your travel calendar: New Year's Day, Good Friday through Easter Monday, the Bank Holidays that occur on the first and last Mondays in May and on the last Monday in August, Christmas, and December 26 (Boxing Day). See page 1033 for a list of major holidays and festivals in Britain; for tips on making reservations, see page 28.

Britain has a rating system for hotels and B&Bs. Its diamonds and stars are supposed to imply quality, but I find that they mean only that the place sporting these symbols is paying dues to the tourist board. Rating systems often have little to do with value.

Rates and Deals

I've described my recommended accommodations using a Sleep Code (see sidebar). Prices listed are for one-night stays in peak season, usually include a hearty breakfast, and assume you're booking directly (not through an online hotel-booking engine or TI). Booking services extract a commission from the hotel, which logically closes the door on special deals. Book direct.

Many hotels use "dynamic pricing," which means room rates change from day to day depending on demand. This makes it extremely difficult to predict what you will pay. When possible, I've tried to list just one price, which is what you'll most likely pay for a standard room during the busy season (but ignoring the dramatically inflated rates hotels charge for special events a few days each year). This rate is intended as a rough guideline, and may vary significantly based on demand—check the hotel's website, or email them, to find out specifics for the date of your visit. For other hotels, I list a range of prices. If the rate you're offered is at or near the bottom of my printed range, it's likely a good deal.

Given the economic downturn, hoteliers and B&B operators are often willing and eager to make a deal. I'd suggest emailing several hotels or B&Bs to ask for their best price. Comparison-shop and make your choice.

As you look over the listings, you'll notice that some accommodations promise special prices to Rick Steves readers who book directly with the hotel. To get these rates, you must book direct (that is, *not* through a booking site like TripAdvisor or Booking. com), mention this book when you reserve, and then show the book upon arrival. Rick Steves discounts apply to readers with ebooks as well as printed books. Because we trust hotels to honor this, please let me know if you don't receive a listed discount. Note, though, that discounts understandably may not be applied to promotional rates.

In general, prices can soften if you do any of the following: offer to pay cash, stay at least three nights, or mention this book. You can also try asking for a cheaper room or a discount, or offer to skip breakfast. When establishing prices, confirm if the charge is per person or per room (if a price is too good to be true, it's probably per person). Because many places in Britain charge per person, small groups often pay the same for a single and a double as they would for a triple. In this book, however, room prices are listed per room, not per person.

Types of Accommodations

Hotels

Many of my recommended hotels have three floors of rooms and steep stairs; expect good exercise and be happy you packed light. You'll generally find an elevator (called a "lift" here) only at larger hotels. If you're concerned about stairs, call and ask about ground-floor rooms or pay for a hotel with a lift. Air-conditioning is rare (I've noted which of my listings have it), but most places have fans. On hot summer nights, you'll want your window open—though in big cities, you may have to put up with street noise.

"Twin" means two single beds, and "double" means one double bed (but in my listings, I list all two-person rooms as "doubles," regardless of bed type). If you will take either bed configuration, let the hotel know, or you might be needlessly turned away. Most hotels offer family deals, which means that parents with young children can easily get a room with an extra child's bed or a discount for larger rooms. Call to negotiate the price. Teenage kids are generally charged as adults. Kids under five almost always sleep free.

Understand the terminology: "En suite" (pronounced "on sweet") means the room has a bathroom (toilet and either a tub or shower). Hotels sometimes call a basic en-suite room a "standard" room to differentiate it from a fancier "superior" or "deluxe" room—if you're not sure, ask for clarification.

Note that to be called a "hotel," a place technically must have certain amenities, including a 24-hour reception (though this rule is loosely applied). TVs are standard in rooms, but may come with only the traditional five British channels (no cable). All of Britain's accommodations are now non-smoking.

If you're arriving early in the morning, your room probably won't be ready. You should be able to safely check your bag at the hotel and dive right into sightseeing.

Hoteliers (and B&B hosts) can be a great help and source of advice. Most know their city well and can assist you with everything from public transit and airport connections to finding a good restaurant, the nearest Internet café, or a self-service launderette.

Even at the best places, mechanical breakdowns occur: Air-conditioning malfunctions, sinks leak, hot water turns cold, and toilets gurgle and smell. Report your concerns clearly and calmly at the front desk. For more complicated problems, don't expect instant results.

If you suspect night noise will be a problem (if, for instance, your room is over a pub), ask for a quiet room in the back or on an upper floor. To guard against theft in your room, keep valuables out of sight. Some rooms come with a safe, and other hotels have safes at the front desk. I've never bothered using one.

Checkout can pose problems if surprise charges pop up on your bill. If you settle up your bill the afternoon before you leave, you'll have time to discuss and address any points of contention (before 19:00, when the night shift usually arrives).

Above all, keep a positive attitude. Remember, you're on vacation. If your hotel is a disappointment, spend more time out enjoying the city you came to see.

Modern Hotel Chains: While most travelers prefer the classic British hotel or B&B experience, chain hotels—which are popping up in bigger cities all over Britain—can be a great value. They offer simple, clean, and modern rooms for up to four people (two adults/two children) for £60-100, depending on the location (more expensive in London). Rooms come with a private shower, WC, and TV. Some hotels are located near the train station, on major highways, or outside the city center. What you lose in charm, you gain in savings.

These hotels are as cozy as a Motel 6, but they are especially worth considering for families, as kids sometimes stay for free. There's usually an attached restaurant, good security, an elevator, and a 24-hour staffed reception desk. Breakfast is always extra.

Book through the hotel's website, as it is often the easiest way to make reservations, and will generally net you a discount. To find the going rate, punch in your dates on the hotel's online reservation form. Like airline tickets, pricing changes from day to day or week to week according to demand. Expect higher rates on weekdays in business-travel destinations, and pricier weekends in tourist-oriented places. Either way, Sunday nights can be shockingly cheap. The best deals typically require a prepaid, nonrefundable, three-week advance purchase.

The biggest chains are **Premier Inn** (www.premierinn.com, reservations tel. 0870-242-8000) and **Travelodge** (www.travelodge .co.uk, reservations tel. 0870-085-0950). Both have attractive deals for prepaid or advance bookings. Other chains operating in Britain include the Irish **Jurys Inn** (www.jurysinns.com) and the French-owned **Ibis** (www.ibishotel.com). Couples can consider **Holiday Inn Express,** which is spreading throughout Britain. Like a Holiday Inn lite, with cheaper prices and no restaurant, many of these hotels allow only two people per room, although some take up to four (make sure Express is part of the name or you'll be paying more for a regular Holiday Inn, www.hiexpress.co.uk).

EasyHotel is a different animal—an extremely basic, pay-as-you-go bargain chain with several branches in London (see page 187 for details).

For recommendations for online hotel deals in London, as well as using auction-type sites, see page 170.

Hotels Beyond This Book: If you're traveling beyond my recommended destinations, you'll find accommodations where you need them. Any town with tourists has a TI that books rooms or can give you a list and point you in the right direction—but remember to book direct for the best prices. In the absence of a TI, ask people on the street or in pubs or restaurants for help. Online, visit www.smoothhound.co.uk, which offers a range of accommodations for towns throughout the UK (searchable by town, airport, hotel name, or price range).

Small Hotels and B&Bs

Places with "townhouse" or "house" (such as "London House") are like big B&Bs or small family-run hotels—with fewer amenities but more character than a hotel. B&Bs range from large guesthouses with 15-20 rooms to small homes renting out a spare bedroom, but they typically have six rooms or fewer. The philosophy of the management determines the character of a place more than its size and facilities offered. I avoid places run as a business by absentee owners. My top listings are run by people who enjoy welcoming the world to their breakfast table.

Compared to hotels, B&Bs give you double the cultural intimacy for half the price. While you may lose some of the conveniences of a hotel—such as fancy lobbies, in-room phones, and frequent bedsheet changes—I happily make the trade-off for the lower rates and personal touches. If you have a reasonable but limited budget, skip hotels and go the B&B way. Many B&Bs now take credit cards, but may add the card service fee to your bill (about 3 percent).

You'll generally pay £30-50 (about $45-80 per person) for a double room in a B&B in Britain. When considering the price of a B&B or small hotel, remember you're getting two breakfasts (up to a £25 value) for each double room.

Remember, "en suite" means a room with an attached bathroom. A room with a "private bathroom" can mean that the bathroom is all yours, but it's across the hall. Some B&Bs have rooms with access to a bathroom that's down the hall and shared with other guests. Figuring there's little difference between en

Making Hotel Reservations

Reserve your rooms several weeks in advance—or as soon as you've pinned down your travel dates—particularly if you'll be traveling during peak times. Note that some national holidays jam things up and merit your making reservations far in advance (see "Holidays and Festivals" on page 1033).

Requesting a Reservation: It's usually easiest to book your room through the hotel's website. Many have a reservation-request form built right in. (For the best rates, be sure to use the hotel's official site and not a booking agency's site.) Simpler websites will generate an email to the hotelier with your request. If there's no reservation form, or for complicated requests, send an email (see below for a sample request). The hotelier wants to know:

- the number and type of rooms you need
- the number of nights you'll stay
- your date of arrival
- your date of departure
- any special needs (such as bathroom in the room or down the hall, cheapest room, twin beds vs. double bed, crib, air-conditioning, quiet, view, ground floor or no stairs, and so on)

If you request a room by email, use the European style for writing dates: day/month/year. For example, for a two-night stay in July 2015, ask for "1 double room for 2 nights, arrive 16/07/15, depart 18/07/15." Make sure you mention any discounts—for Rick Steves readers or otherwise—when you make the reservation.

Confirming a Reservation: When the hotel replies with its room availability and rates, just email back to confirm your reservation. Most places will request a credit-card number to hold your room. While you can email it (I do), it's safer to share that confidential info via a phone call, two emails (splitting your number between them), or the hotel's secure online reservation form. On the small chance that a hotel loses track of your reservation, bring along a hard copy of their confirmation.

Canceling a Reservation: If you must cancel your reservation, it's courteous—and smart—to do so with as much notice as possible, especially for smaller family-run places. Simply make a quick phone call or send an email. Request confirmation of your cancellation in case you are accidentally billed.

Be warned that cancellation policies can be strict; read the fine print or ask about these before you book. For example, if

suite and private rooms, some places charge the same for both. If you want your own bathroom inside the room, request en suite.

B&Bs are not hotels. Think of your host as a friendly acquaintance who's invited you to stay in her home, rather than someone you're paying to wait on you.

B&B proprietors are selective as to whom they invite in for

From:	rick@ricksteves.com
Sent:	Today
To:	info@hotelcentral.com
Subject:	Reservation request for 19-22 July

Dear Hotel Central,

I would like to reserve a room for 2 people for 3 nights, arriving 19 July and departing 22 July. If possible, I would like a quiet room with a double bed and a bathroom inside the room.

Please let me know if you have a room available and the price.

Thank you!
Rick Steves

you cancel on short notice, you could lose your deposit, or be billed for one night or even your entire stay. Internet deals may require prepayment, with no refunds for cancellations.

Reconfirming a Reservation: Call to reconfirm your room reservation a few days in advance. Smaller hotels and B&Bs appreciate knowing your estimated time of arrival. If you'll be arriving late (after 17:00), let them know.

Reserving Rooms as You Travel: You can make reservations as you travel, calling hotels and B&Bs a few days to a week before your arrival. If you'd rather travel without any reservations at all, you'll have greater success snaring rooms if you arrive at your destination early in the day. When you anticipate crowds (weekends are worst), call hotels at about 9:00 or 10:00 on the day you plan to arrive, when the receptionist knows who'll be checking out and which rooms will be available.

Although most TIs in Britain can book you a room in their town, and also often in nearby towns, they generally charge a booking fee, and you'll pay a small deposit. While this can be useful in a pinch, it's a better deal for everyone (except the TIs) to book direct, using the listings in this book.

Phoning: For tips on how to call hotels overseas, see page 998.

the night. At many B&Bs, children are not welcome. If you'll be staying for more than one night, you are a "desirable." In popular weekend-getaway spots, you're unlikely to find a place to take you for Saturday night only. If my listings are full, ask for guidance. Mentioning this book can help. Owners usually work together and can call up an ally to land you a bed.

Small places usually serve a hearty fried breakfast of eggs and much more (for details on breakfast, see page 36). Because your B&B owner is also the cook, the time span when breakfast is served is usually limited (typically about an hour—confirm before you turn in for the night). It's an unwritten rule that guests shouldn't show up at the very end of the breakfast period and expect a full cooked breakfast (try to arrive at least 15 minutes before the ending time). If you do arrive late (or need to leave before breakfast is served), most hosts are happy to let you help yourself to cereal, fruit, juice, and coffee; ask if it's possible.

Most B&Bs stock rooms with an electric kettle, along with cups, tea bags, and coffee packets.

Americans sometimes assume they'll get new towels each day. The British don't, and neither should you. Hang towels up to dry and reuse.

Be aware of luggage etiquette. A large bag in a compact older building can easily turn even the most graceful of us into a bull in an English china shop. If you've got a backpack, don't wear it indoors. If your host offers to carry your bag upstairs, accept—they're adept at maneuvering luggage up tiny staircases without damaging the walls and banisters. Finally, use your room's luggage racks—putting bags on empty beds can dirty and scuff nice comforters. Treat these lovingly maintained homes as you would a friend's house.

Electrical outlets sometimes have switches that turn the current on or off; if your electrical appliance isn't working, flip the switch at the outlet. When you unplug your appliance, don't forget your adapter—most B&Bs have boxes of various adapters left behind by guests (which is handy if you left yours at the last place).

You're likely to encounter unusual bathroom fixtures. The "pump toilet" has a flushing handle that doesn't kick in unless you push it just right: too hard or too soft, and it won't go. (Be decisive but not ruthless.) There's also the "dial-a-shower," an electronic box under the shower head where you'll turn a dial to select the heat of the water and (sometimes with a separate dial or button) turn on or shut off the flow of water. If you can't find the switch to turn on the shower, it may be just outside the bathroom.

Many B&Bs and small hotels are in older buildings, with thin walls and doors, and sometimes creaky floorboards. This can make for a noisy night, especially with people walking down the hall to use the bathroom. If you're a light sleeper, bring earplugs. And please be quiet in the halls and in your rooms (talk softly, and keep the TV volume low). Those of us getting up early will thank you for it.

Your B&B bedroom probably won't include a phone. In this

mobile-phone age, street phone booths can be few and far between. Some B&B owners will allow you to use their phone, but many are disinclined to let you ring up charges. That's because most British people pay for each local call, and rates are expensive. Therefore, to be polite, ask to use their phone only in an emergency—and offer to use an international calling card or to pay for the call. If you plan to be staying in B&Bs and making frequent calls, consider buying a British mobile phone (see page 999).

With so many people traveling these days with a laptop or mobile device, nearly every B&B comes equipped with free Wi-Fi (as noted in my accommodations listings); however, the signal frequently won't reach up many stairs, so you may have to sit in the lounge to access it.

Many B&B owners are also pet owners. And, while pets are rarely allowed into guest rooms, and B&B proprietors are typically very tidy, visitors with pet allergies might be bothered. I've tried to list which B&Bs have pets, but if you're allergic, ask about pets when you reserve.

Remember that you may need to pay cash for your room. Plan ahead so you have enough cash to pay up when you check out.

Hostels

Britain has hundreds of hostels of all shapes and sizes. Choose your hostel selectively. Hostels can be historic castles or depressing tenements, serene and comfy or overrun by noisy school groups. You'll pay about £20-25 ($32-40) for a bed. Travelers of any age are welcome if they don't mind dorm-style accommodations and meeting other travelers. Most hostels offer kitchen facilities, guest computers, Wi-Fi, and a self-service laundry. Nowadays, concerned about bedbugs, hostels are likely to provide all bedding, including sheets. Family and private rooms may be available on request.

Independent hostels tend to be easygoing, colorful, and informal (no membership required); Hostelworld.com is the standard way backpackers search and book hostels these days, but also try www.hostelz.com, www.hostels.com, and www.hostelbookers.com.

Official hostels are part of Hostelling International (HI) and share an online booking site (www.hihostels.com). HI hostels typically require that you either have a membership card or pay extra per night. For more English and Welsh hostel listings, check www.yha.org.uk; for Scotland, consult www.hostel-scotland.co.uk.

Other Options

Whether you're in a city or the countryside, renting an apartment, house, or villa can be a fun and cost-effective way to delve into Europe. Websites such as HomeAway.com and its sister site VRBO.com let you correspond directly with European property owners or managers.

Airbnb.com makes it reasonably easy to find a place to sleep in someone's home. Beds range from air-mattress-in-living-room basic to plush-B&B-suite posh. If you want a place to sleep that's free, Couchsurfing.com is a vagabond's alternative to Airbnb. It lists millions of outgoing members, who host fellow "surfers" in their homes.

Eating

Great Britain's reputation for miserable food, while once well-deserved, is now sorely dated. A few names familiar stateside—Jamie Oliver, Gordon Ramsay, Nigella Lawson—are just the tip of the culinary iceberg of British celebrity chefs prodding their national cuisine forward. Over the last generation, British cooking has embraced international influences and good-quality ingredients, making "modern British" food something to be truly proud of. While some dreary pub food still exists, you'll generally find the cuisine scene here lively, trendy, and pleasantly surprising. (Unfortunately, it's also expensive.) Even the basic, traditional pub grub has gone upmarket—more and more "gastropubs" are serving locally sourced meats and fresh vegetables. Even basic pubs are more likely to dish up homemade, creative dishes rather than microwaved pies, soggy fries, and mushy peas.

All indoor British eateries are now smoke-free. Establishments keep their smokers contented by allowing them to light up in doorways and on outdoor patios.

When restaurant-hunting, choose a spot filled with locals, not tourists. Venturing even a block or two off the main drag leads to higher-quality food for less. Locals know they can eat better at lower-rent locales.

Budget Eating Tips

You have plenty of inexpensive choices: pub grub, daily lunch and early-bird specials, ethnic restaurants, cafeterias, fast food, picnics, fish-and-chips, greasy-spoon cafés, pizza, and more.

I've found that portions are huge and, with locals feeling the economic pinch, **sharing plates** is generally just fine. Ordering two drinks, a soup or side salad, and splitting a £10 meat pie can make a good, filling meal. If you are on a limited budget, share a main course in a more expensive place for a nicer eating experience.

Pub grub is the most atmospheric budget option. You'll usually get hearty lunches and dinners priced reasonably at £6-10 under ancient timbers (see "Pubs," later). Gastropubs, with better

---

Sounds Bad, Tastes Good

The Brits have a knack for making food sound funny. Here are a few examples:

Toad in the Hole: Sausage dipped in batter and fried

Bubble and Squeak: Leftovers, usually potatoes, veggies, and meat, all fried up together

Bap: Small roll

Treacle: Golden syrup, similar to light molasses

---

food, are more expensive.

Classier restaurants have some affordable deals. Lunch is usually cheaper than dinner; a top-end, £25-for-dinner-type restaurant often serves the same quality two-course lunch deals for £10-12. Look for early-bird dinner specials, allowing you to eat well and affordably (usually last order by 18:30 or 19:00).

Ethnic restaurants from all over the world add spice to Britain's cuisine scene. Eating Indian, Bangladeshi, Chinese, or Thai is cheap (even cheaper if you do takeout). Middle Eastern stands sell gyro sandwiches, falafel, and *shawarmas* (lamb in pita bread). An Indian samosa (greasy, flaky meat-and-vegetable pie) costs £2, can be microwaved, and makes a very cheap, if small, meal. (For more, see "Indian Food," later.) You'll find all-you-can-eat Chinese and Thai places serving £5-7 meals and offering even cheaper take-away boxes. While you can't "split" a buffet, you can split a take-away box. Stuff the box full, and you'll have Britain's cheapest hot meal.

Fish-and-chips are a heavy, greasy, but tasty English classic. Every town has at least one "chippy" selling a take-away box of fish-and-chips in a cardboard box or (more traditionally) wrapped in paper for about £4-7. You can dip your fries in ketchup, American-style, or "go British" and drizzle the whole thing with vinegar.

Most large **museums** (and some historic **churches**) have handy, moderately priced cafeterias.

Fast food places, both American and British, are everywhere.

Inexpensive chain restaurants serve middle-of-the-road food in family-friendly settings (£7-12 meals). For specific chains to keep an eye out for, see "Good Chain Restaurants," later.

Bakeries sell yogurt, cartons of "semi-skimmed" milk, pastries, meat pies, and pasties (PASS-teez). Pasties are heavy, savory meat pies that originated in the Cornish mining country; they had big crust handles so miners with filthy hands could eat them and toss the crust. The most traditional filling is beef stew, but you'll also find them with chicken, vegetable, lamb and mint, and even Indian flavors inside.

Picnicking saves time and money. You can easily get prepared food to go. Munch a relaxed "meal on wheels" picnic during your open-top bus tour or river cruise to save 30 precious minutes for sightseeing.

Stop at a good **sandwich shop** or corner **grocery store** for boxes of orange juice (pure, by the liter), fresh bread, tasty British cheese, meat, a tube of Colman's English mustard, local eatin' apples, bananas, small tomatoes, a small tub of yogurt (drinkable), trail mix, nuts, plain or chocolate-covered digestive biscuits, and any local specialties. At **open-air markets** and **supermarkets,** you can get produce in small quantities. Supermarkets often have good deli sections, even offering Indian dishes, and sometimes salad bars. Decent packaged sandwiches (£3-4) are sold everywhere (for a few options, see "Carryout Chains," later).

Good Chain Restaurants

I know—you're going to Britain to enjoy characteristic little hole-in-the-wall pubs, so mass-produced food is the farthest thing from your mind. But several excellent chains with branches across the UK can be a nice break from pub grub.

Sit-Down Chains

Most branches of the chains listed here open daily no later than noon (several at 8:00 or 9:00), and close sometime between 22:00 and midnight. Occasionally a place may close on Sundays or in the afternoon between lunch and dinner, but these are rare exceptions.

Wagamama Noodle Bar, serving up pan-Asian cuisine (udon noodles, fried rice, and curry dishes), is a noisy, organic slur-pathon. Portions are huge and splittable. There's one in almost every midsize city in the UK, usually located in sprawling halls filled with long shared tables and busy servers who scrawl your order on the placemat. While the quality has gone downhill a bit as they've expanded, this remains a reliable choice with reasonable prices (£8-12 main dishes big enough for light eaters to share, good veggie options, www.wagamama.com).

Côte Brasserie is a contemporary French chain serving good-value French cuisine in reliably pleasant settings, and at the right prices (£9-14 main dishes, early dinner specials, www.cote-restaurants.co.uk).

Byron, an upscale-hamburger chain with hip interiors, is worth seeking out if you need a burger fix. While British burgers aren't exactly like American ones—they tend to be a bit overcooked by our standards—Byron's burgers are your best bet (£7-10 burgers, www.byronhamburgers.com). **Gourmet Burger Kitchen (GBK)** provides a cheaper alternative, serving burgers that are, if not quite gourmet, very good. Choices range from a simple cheeseburger to more elaborate options, such as Jamaican. Choose a table and order at the counter—they'll bring the food to you (£7-11 burgers).

Loch Fyne Fish Restaurant is part of a Scottish chain that raises its own oysters and mussels. Its branches offer an inviting, lively atmosphere with a fine fishy energy and no pretense (£10-18 main dishes, two- and three-course specials often available before 19:00, www.lochfyne-restaurants.com).

Nando's is understandably popular as a casual, affordable place to get flame-broiled chicken with a range of Portuguese and South African flavors (£10 meals, www.nandos.co.uk).

At **Yo! Sushi,** sushi dishes trundle past on a conveyor belt. Color-coded plates tell you how much each dish costs (£1.90-5), and a picture-filled menu explains what you're eating. For £1.50, you get unlimited green tea (water for £1.05). Snag a bar stool and grab dishes as they rattle by (www.yosushi.com).

Ask and **Pizza Express** serve quality pasta and pizza in a pleasant, sit-down atmosphere that's family-friendly. **Jamie's Italian** (from celebrity chef Jamie Oliver) is hipper and pricier, and feels more upmarket.

Carry-Out Chains

While the following places might have some seating, they're best as an easy place to grab some prepackaged food on the run.

Major supermarket chains have smaller, offshoot branches that specialize in sandwiches, salads, and other prepared foods to go. These can be a picnicker's dream come true. Some shops are stand-alone, while others are located inside a larger store. The most prevalent—and best—is **M&S Simply Food** (an offshoot of the Marks & Spencer department-store chain; there's one in every major train station). **Sainsbury's Local** grocery stores also offer some decent prepared food; **Tesco Express** and **Tesco Metro** run a distant third.

Some "cheap and cheery" chains, such as **Pret à Manger, Eat, Apostrophe,** and **Pod** provide office workers with good, healthful sandwiches, salads, and pastries to go. Among these, Eat has a reputation for slightly higher quality...and higher prices.

West Cornwall Pasty Company and **Cornish Bakehouse** sell a variety of these traditional savory pies for around £3—as do many smaller, independent bakeries.

The Great British Breakfast

The traditional "fry," or "full English/Scottish/Welsh breakfast"—generally included in the cost of your room—is famous as a hearty

way to start the day. Also known as a "heart attack on a plate," the breakfast is especially feast-like if you've just come from the land of the skimpy continental breakfast across the Channel.

The standard fry gets off to a healthy start with juice and cereal or porridge. (Try Weetabix, a soggy cousin of shredded wheat

and perhaps the most absorbent material known to human-kind.) Next, with tea or coffee, you get a heated plate with eggs (cooked to order—poached is the only style not floating in grease), Canadian-style bacon or sausage, a grilled tomato, sautéed mush-rooms, baked beans, and sometimes hash browns, kippers (her-ring), or fried bread (sizzled in a greasy skillet). Toast comes in a rack (to cool quickly and crisply) with butter and marmalade. This protein-stuffed meal is great for stamina and tides many travelers over until dinner.

You'll figure out quickly which parts of the fry you like and don't like. Your host will likely ask you this up front, rather than serve you the whole shebang and risk having to throw out uneaten food. There's nothing wrong with skipping some or all of the fry—few Brits actually start their day with this heavy breakfast. Many progressive B&B owners offer vegetarian, organic, or other cre-ative variations on the traditional breakfast.

These days, the best coffee is served in a *cafetière* (a French press). When your coffee has steeped as long as you like, plunge down the filter and pour.

Afternoon Tea

People of leisure punctuate their day with an afternoon tea at a tearoom. You'll get a pot of tea, small finger foods (like sand-wiches with the crusts cut off), homemade scones, jam, and thick clotted cream. A lighter "cream tea" gets you tea and a scone or two. Tearooms, which often serve appealing light meals, are usu-ally open for lunch and close at about 17:00, just before dinner. For more on this most British of traditions, see page 211.

Pubs

Pubs are a basic part of the British social scene, and, whether you're a teetotaler or a beer guzzler, they should be a part of your travel here. "Pub" is short for "public house." It's an extended living room where, if you don't mind the stickiness, you can feel the pulse of Britain.

People go to a public house to be social. They want to talk. Get vocal with a local. This is easiest at the bar, where people assume you're in the mood to talk (rather than at a table, where you're allowed a bit of privacy). The pub is the next best thing to having relatives in town. A cup of darts is free for the asking.

Smart travelers use the pubs to eat, drink, get out of the rain, watch sporting events, and make new friends. Unfortunately, many city pubs have been afflicted with an excess of brass, ferns, and video slot machines. The most traditional, atmospheric pubs are in the countryside and in smaller towns.

Pub hours vary. Pubs generally serve beer (and food for shorter hours; see below) Monday to Saturday 11:00-23:00 and Sunday 12:00-22:30, though many are open later, particularly on Friday and Saturday. As it nears closing time, you'll hear shouts of "Last orders." Then comes the 10-minute warning bell. Finally, they'll call "Time!" to pick up your glass, finished or not, when the pub closes.

Pub Grub

Pub grub gets better each year. In London, it offers the best indoor eating value. For £6-10, you'll get a basic budget hot lunch or dinner in friendly surroundings. The *Good Pub Guide* is excellent (www.thegoodpubguide.co.uk). Pubs that are attached to restaurants, advertise their food, and are crowded with locals are more likely to have fresh food and a chef—and less likely to be the kind of pub that sells only lousy microwaved snacks.

Pubs generally serve traditional dishes, such as fish-and-chips, vegetables, "bangers and mash" (sausages and mashed potatoes), roast beef with Yorkshire pudding (batter-baked in the oven), gammon (ham steak), and assorted meat pies, such as steak-and-kidney pie or shepherd's pie (stewed lamb topped with mashed potatoes). Side dishes include salads (sometimes even a nice self-serve salad bar), vegetables, and—invariably—"chips" (French fries). "Crisps" are potato chips. A "jacket potato" (baked potato stuffed with fillings of your choice) can almost be a meal in itself. A "ploughman's lunch" is a traditional British meal of bread, cheese, and sweet pickles that nearly every tourist tries...once. These days, you'll likely find more Italian pasta, curried dishes, and quiche on the menu than traditional fare.

Meals are usually served from 11:00 or 12:00 until 21:00 or later, although some pubs close the kitchen between lunch and dinner. There's often no table service. Order at the bar, then take a seat and they'll bring the food when it's ready (or sometimes you pick it up at the bar). Pay at the bar (sometimes when you order, sometimes after you eat). Don't tip unless it's a place with full table service. Servings are hearty, service is quick, and you'll often eat for £10 or less per person. (If you're on a tight budget, consider sharing a meal—note the size of portions around you before ordering.) A beer or cider adds another couple of pounds. (Free tap water is always available.)

If you want food that's a notch above, seek out a **gastropub.** Although similar to a regular pub, a gastropub pays more attention to the quality of its menu—with accordingly higher prices (£10-15 meals). You'll find a few gastropubs in the towns and cities, but some of the best are in countryside villages.

Beer and Other Beverages

The British take great pride in their beer. Many Brits think that drinking beer cold and carbonated, as Americans do, ruins the taste. Most pubs will have **lagers** (cold, refreshing, American-style beer), **ales** (amber-colored, cellar-temperature beer), **bitters** (hop-flavored ale, perhaps the most typical British beer), and **stouts** (dark and somewhat bitter, like Guinness).

Order your beer at the bar and pay as you go, with no need to tip. An average beer costs £3. Part of the experience is standing before a line of "hand pulls," or taps, and wondering which beer to choose. Long-handled pulls are used to draw traditional, rich-flavored "real ales" up from the cellar. Short-handle pulls at the bar mean colder, fizzier, mass-produced, and less interesting keg beers. Mild beers are sweeter, with a creamy malt flavoring. Irish cream ale is a smooth, sweet experience. Try the draft cider (sweet or dry)...carefully.

Even if you enjoy fizzy beer, you should at least sample a **real ale** while in Britain. These are the connoisseur's favorites and often come with fun names. Served straight from the brewer's cask at cellar temperature, real ales finish fermenting naturally and are not pasteurized or filtered, so they must be consumed within two or three days after the cask is tapped. Naturally carbonated, real ales have less gassiness and head; they vary from sweet to bitter, often with a hoppy or nutty flavor.

As dictated by British law, draft beer and cider are served by the pint (20-ounce imperial size) or the half-pint (9.6 ounces). (It's considered almost feminine for a man to order just a half; I order mine with quiche.) The government recently sanctioned an in-between serving size—the two-thirds pint—hoping that more choice will woo more beer drinkers (a steady decline in beer consumption, which is taxed, has had a negative effect on tax revenues). Proper British ladies like a **shandy** (half beer and half 7-Up).

Besides beer, many pubs actually have a good selection of wines by the glass, a fully stocked bar for the gentleman's "G and T" (gin and tonic), and the increasingly popular bottles of alcohol-plus-sugar (such as Bacardi Breezers) for the younger, working-class set. **Pimm's** is a refreshing and fruity summer liqueur, traditionally popular during Wimbledon. It's an upper-class drink—a rough bloke might insult a pub by claiming it sells more Pimm's than beer.

Teetotalers can order from a wide variety of soft drinks—both the predictable American sodas and other more interesting bottled drinks, such as ginger beer (similar to ginger ale but with more bite), root beers, or other flavors (Fentimans brews some unusual options that are stocked in many pubs). Note that in Britain, "lemonade" is lemon-lime soda (like 7-Up). Children are served food and soft drinks in pubs, but you must be 18 to order a beer.

Indian Food

Eating Indian food is "going local" in cosmopolitan, multiethnic Britain. You'll find recommended Indian restaurants in most cities, and even in small towns. Take the opportunity to sample food from Britain's former colony. Indian cuisine is as varied as the country itself. In general, they use more exotic spices than British or American cuisine—some hot, some sweet. (But if you like your food very hot, you'll find that Indian restaurants dull the spice for timid British palates—you'll have to be insistent if you want four-star heat.) Indian food is very vegetarian-friendly, offering many meatless dishes to choose from on any given menu.

For a simple meal that costs about £12-14, order one dish with rice and *naan* (Indian flatbread that can be served plain, with garlic, or other ways—usually one order is plenty for two people to share). You'll generally pay £2-3 extra for an order of rice (it's not included in the price of the main dish). Many restaurants have a fixed-price combination meal that offers more variety, and is simpler and cheaper than ordering à la carte. For about £20, you can make a mix-and-match platter out of several sharable dishes, including *dal* (simmered lentils) as a starter; one or two meat or vegetable dishes with sauce (for example, chicken curry, chicken *tikka masala* in a creamy tomato sauce, grilled fish tandoori, chickpea *chana masala*, or a spicy *vindaloo* dish); *raita* (a cooling yogurt that's added to spicy dishes); rice; *naan;* and an Indian beer (wine and Indian food don't really mix) or chai (a cardamom- and

INTRODUCTION

British Chocolate

My chocoholic readers are enthusiastic about British chocolates. As with other dairy products, chocolate seems richer and creamier here than it does in the US, so even the basics like Kit Kat (which was actually invented in York—see page 600) and Twix have a different taste. Some favorites include Cadbury Gold bars (filled with liquid caramel), Cadbury Crunchie bars, Nestlé's Lion bars (layered wafers covered in caramel and chocolate), Cadbury's Boost bars (a shortcake biscuit with caramel in milk chocolate), Cadbury Flake (crumbly folds of melt-in-your-mouth chocolate), Galaxy chocolate bars (especially the ones with hazelnuts), and Aero (a light-as-air chocolate bar filled with little bubbles). Thornton shops (in larger train stations) sell a box of sweets called the Continental Assortment, which comes with a tasting guide. The highlight is the mocha white-chocolate truffle. British M&Ms, called Smarties, are better than American ones. At ice-cream vans, look for the beloved traditional "99p"—a vanilla soft-serve cone with a small Flake bar stuck right into the middle. For a break from chocolate, buy a roll of wine gums—similar to Jujubes, but tangier and less sweet (Maynards is the biggest brand).

cinnamon-spiced tea, usually served with milk). An easy way to taste a variety of dishes (especially for a single diner) is to order a *thali*—a sort of sampler plate, generally served on a metal tray, with small servings of various specialties.

Desserts

To the British, the traditional word for dessert is "pudding," although it's also referred to as "sweets" these days. Sponge cake, cream, fruitcake, and meringue are key players.

Trifle is the best-known British concoction, consisting of sponge cake soaked in brandy or sherry (or orange juice for children), then covered with jam and/or fruit and custard cream. Whipped cream can sometimes put the final touch on this "light" treat.

Castle puddings are sponge puddings cooked in small molds and topped with Golden Syrup (a popular brand and a cross between honey and maple syrup). Bread-and-butter pudding consists of slices of French bread baked with milk, cream, eggs, and raisins (similar to the American preparation), served warm with cold cream. Hasty pudding, supposedly the invention of people in a hurry to avoid the bailiff, is made from stale bread with dried fruit and milk. Queen of puddings is a breadcrumb pudding

How Was Your Trip?

Were your travels fun, smooth, and meaningful? If you'd like to share your tips, concerns, and discoveries, please fill out the survey at www.ricksteves.com/feedback. I value your feedback. Thanks in advance—it helps a lot.

topped with warm jam, meringue, and cream. Treacle pudding is a popular steamed pudding whose "sponge" mixture combines flour, suet (animal fat), butter, sugar, and milk. Christmas pudding (also called plum pudding) is a dense mixture with dried and candied fruit served with brandy butter or hard sauce. Sticky toffee pudding is a moist cake made with dates, heated and drizzled with toffee sauce, and served with ice cream or cream. Banoffee pie is the delicious British answer to banana cream pie.

The British version of custard is a smooth, yellow liquid. Cream tops most everything custard does not. There's single cream for coffee. Double cream is really thick. Whipped cream is familiar, and clotted cream is the consistency of whipped butter.

Fool is a dessert with sweetened pureed fruit (such as rhubarb, gooseberries, or black currants) mixed with cream or custard and chilled. Elderflower is a popular flavoring for sorbet.

Scones are tops, and many inns and restaurants have their secret recipes. Whether made with fruit or topped with clotted cream, scones take the cake.

Traveling as a Temporary Local

We travel all the way to Britain to enjoy differences—to become temporary locals. You'll experience frustrations. Certain truths that we find "God-given" or "self-evident," such as cold beer, ice in drinks, bottomless cups of coffee, and bigger being better, are suddenly not so true. One of the benefits of travel is the eye-opening realization that there are logical, civil, and even better alternatives. A willingness to go local ensures that you'll enjoy a full dose of British hospitality.

Europeans generally like Americans. But if there is a negative aspect to the British image of us, it's that we are loud, wasteful, ethnocentric, too informal (which can seem disrespectful), and a bit naive.

The British (and Europeans in general) place a high value on speaking quietly in restaurants and on trains. Listen while on the bus or in a restaurant—the place can be packed, but the decibel level is low. Try to adjust your volume accordingly to show respect for their culture.

While the British look bemusedly at some of our Yankee excesses—and worriedly at others—they nearly always afford us individual travelers all the warmth we deserve.

Judging from all the happy feedback I receive from travelers who have used this book, it's safe to assume you'll enjoy a great, affordable vacation—with the finesse of an independent, experienced traveler.

Thanks, and have a brilliant holiday!

Back Door Travel Philosophy
From *Rick Steves' Europe Through the Back Door*

Travel is intensified living—maximum thrills per minute and one of the last great sources of legal adventure. Travel is freedom. It's recess, and we need it.

Experiencing the real Europe requires catching it by surprise, going casual..."through the Back Door."

Affording travel is a matter of priorities. (Make do with the old car.) You can eat and sleep—simply, safely, and enjoyably—anywhere in Europe for $120 a day plus transportation costs. In many ways, spending more money only builds a thicker wall between you and what you traveled so far to see. Europe is a cultural carnival, and time after time, you'll find that its best acts are free and the best seats are the cheap ones.

A tight budget forces you to travel close to the ground, meeting and communicating with the people. Never sacrifice sleep, nutrition, safety, or cleanliness to save money. Simply enjoy the local-style alternatives to expensive hotels and restaurants.

Connecting with people carbonates your experience. Extroverts have more fun. If your trip is low on magic moments, kick yourself and make things happen. If you don't enjoy a place, maybe you don't know enough about it. Seek the truth. Recognize tourist traps. Give a culture the benefit of your open mind. See things as different, but not better or worse. Any culture has plenty to share.

Of course, travel, like the world, is a series of hills and valleys. Be fanatically positive and militantly optimistic. If something's not to your liking, change your liking.

Travel can make you a happier American, as well as a citizen of the world. Our Earth is home to seven billion equally precious people. It's humbling to travel and find that other people don't have the "American Dream"—they have their own dreams. Europeans like us, but with all due respect, they wouldn't trade passports.

Thoughtful travel engages us with the world. In tough economic times, it reminds us what is truly important. By broadening perspectives, travel teaches new ways to measure quality of life.

Globetrotting destroys ethnocentricity, helping us understand and appreciate other cultures. Rather than fear the diversity on this planet, celebrate it. Among your most prized souvenirs will be the strands of different cultures you choose to knit into your own character. The world is a cultural yarn shop, and Back Door travelers are weaving the ultimate tapestry. Join in!

ENGLAND

ENGLAND

England (pop. 53 million) is a hilly country the size of Louisiana (50,346 square miles) that's located in the lower two-thirds of the isle of Britain. Scotland is to the north and the English Channel to the south, with the North Sea to the east and Wales (and the Irish Sea) to the west. Fed by ocean air from the southwest, the climate is mild, with a chance of cloudy, rainy weather almost any day of the year.

England has an economy that can stand alongside many much larger nations. It boasts high-tech industries (software, chemicals, aviation), international banking, and textile manufacturing, and is a major exporter of beef. While farms and villages remain, England is now an urban, industrial, and post-industrial colossus.

England traditionally has been very class-conscious, with the wealthy landed aristocracy, the middle-class tradesmen, and the lower-class farmers and factory workers. While social stratification is fading with the new global economy, regional differences remain strong. Locals can often identify where someone is from by their dialect or local accent—Geordie, Cockney, or Queen's English.

One thing that sets England apart from its fellow UK countries (Scotland, Wales, and Northern Ireland) is its ethnic makeup. Traditionally, those countries had Celtic roots, while the English mixed in Saxon and Norman blood. In the 20th century, England welcomed many Scots, Welsh, and Irish as low-wage workers. More recently, it's become home to immigrants from former colonies of its worldwide empire—

England

particularly from India/Pakistan/Bangladesh, the Caribbean, and Africa—and to many workers from poorer Eastern European countries. These days it's not a given that every "English" person speaks English. Nearly one in three citizens does not profess the Christian faith. As the world becomes interconnected by communications technology, it's possible for many immigrants to physically inhabit the country while remaining closely linked to their home culture—rather than truly assimilating into England.

This is the current English paradox. England—the birthplace and center of the extended worldwide family of English-speakers—is losing its traditional Englishness. Where Scotland, Wales, and Northern Ireland have cultural movements to preserve their local languages and customs, England does not. Politically, there is no "English" party in the UK Parliament. While Scotland, Wales, and Northern Ireland have their own parliaments to decide local issues, England must depend on the decisions of the UK government at large. Except for the occasional display of an English flag at a soccer match (the red St. George's cross on a white background), many English people don't really think of themselves as "English"—more as "Brits," a part of the wider UK.

Today, England tries to preserve its rich past as it races forward as a leading global player. There are still hints of its legacy of farms, villages, Victorian lamplighters, and upper-crust dandies. But it's also a jostling world of unemployed factory workers, investment bankers, soccer matches, rowdy "stag parties," and faux-Tudor suburbs. Modern England is a culturally diverse land in transition. Catch it while you can.

LONDON

London is more than 600 square miles of urban jungle—a world in itself and a barrage on all the senses. On my first visit, I felt extremely small.

London is more than its museums and landmarks. It's the L.A., D.C., and N.Y.C. of Britain—a living, breathing, thriving organism...a coral reef of humanity. The city has changed dramatically in recent years, and many visitors are surprised to find how "un-English" it is. ESL (English as a second language) seems like the city's first language, as white people are now a minority in major parts of the city that once symbolized white imperialism. Arabs have nearly bought out the area north of Hyde Park. Chinese takeouts outnumber fish-and-chips shops. Eastern Europeans pull pints in British pubs. Many hotels are run by people with foreign accents (who hire English chambermaids), while outlying suburbs are home to huge communities of Indians and Pakistanis. London is a city of eight million separate dreams, inhabiting a place that tolerates and encourages them. With the English Channel Tunnel and discount airlines making travel between Britain and the Continent easier than ever, London is learning—sometimes fitfully—to live as a microcosm of its formerly vast empire.

The city, which has long attracted tourists, seems perpetually at your service, with an impressive slate of sights, entertainment, and eateries, all linked by a great transit system. With just a few days here, you'll get no more than a quick splash in this teeming human tidal pool. But with a good orientation, you'll find London manageable and fun. You'll get a sampling of the city's top sights, history, and cultural entertainment, and a good look at its ever-changing human face.

Blow through the city on the open deck of a double-decker orientation tour bus, and take a pinch-me-I'm-in-London walk through the West End. Ogle the crown jewels at the Tower of London, hear the chimes of Big Ben, and see the Houses of Parliament in action. Cruise the Thames River, and take a spin on the London Eye. Hobnob with poets' tombstones in Westminster Abbey, and visit with Leonardo, Botticelli, and Rembrandt in the National Gallery. Enjoy Shakespeare in a replica of the Globe theater and marvel at a glitzy, fun musical at a modern-day theater. Whisper across the dome of St. Paul's Cathedral, then rummage through our civilization's attic at the British Museum. And sip your tea with pinky raised and clotted cream dribbling down your scone.

Planning Your Time

The sights of London alone could easily fill a trip to Great Britain. It's a great one-week getaway. But on a three-week tour of Britain, I'd give London three busy days. You won't be able to see everything, so don't try. You'll keep coming back to London. After dozens of visits myself, I still enjoy a healthy list of excuses to return. If you're flying in to one of London's airports, consider starting your trip in Bath and making London your finale. Especially if you hope to enjoy a play or concert, a night or two of jet lag is bad news.

Here's a suggested three-day schedule:

Day 1

9:00	Tower of London (crown jewels first, then Beefeater tour and White Tower; note that on Sun-Mon, the Tower opens at 10:00).
13:00	Grab a picnic, catch a boat at Tower Pier, and relax with lunch on the Thames while cruising to Westminster Pier.
14:30	Tour Westminster Abbey, and consider their evensong service (usually at 17:00, at 15:00 on Sun and off-season Sat, never on Wed).
17:00 (or after evensong)	Follow my self-guided Westminster Walk. When you're finished, if it's a Monday or Tuesday, you could return to the Houses of Parliament and possibly pop in to see the House of Commons in action.

Day 2

8:30	Take a double-decker hop-on, hop-off London sightseeing bus tour (from Green Park or Victoria Station), and hop off for the Changing of the Guard.
11:00	Buckingham Palace (guards change most days May-July at 11:30, alternate days Aug-April—confirm online).
12:00	Walk through St. James's Park to enjoy London's delightful park scene.
13:00	After lunch, tour the Churchill War Rooms.
16:00	Tour the National Gallery.
Evening	Have a pub dinner before a play, concert, or evening walking tour.

Day 3 (or More)

Choose among these remaining London highlights: National Gallery, British Library, Churchill War Rooms, Imperial War Museum, the two Tates (Tate Modern on the South Bank for modern art, Tate Britain on the North Bank for British art), St. Paul's Cathedral, Victoria and Albert Museum, National Portrait Gallery, Natural History Museum, Courtauld Gallery, or the Museum of London; take a spin on the London Eye or a cruise to Kew Gardens or Greenwich; enjoy a play at Shakespeare's Globe;

do some serious shopping at one of London's elegant department stores or open-air markets; or take another historic walking tour.

Orientation to London

To grasp London more comfortably, see it as the old town in the city center without the modern, congested sprawl. (Even from that perspective, it's still huge.)

The Thames River (pronounced "tems") runs roughly west to east through the city, with most of the visitor's sights on the North Bank. Mentally, maybe even physically, trim down your map to include only the area between the Tower of London (to the east), Hyde Park (west), Regent's Park (north), and the South Bank (south). This is roughly the area bordered by the Tube's Circle Line. This four-mile stretch between the Tower and Hyde Park (about a 1.5-hour walk) looks like a milk bottle on its side (see map on next page), and holds 80 percent of the sights mentioned in this chapter.

With a core focus and a good orientation, you'll get a sampling of London's top sights, history, and cultural entertainment, and a good look at its ever-changing human face.

The sprawling city becomes much more manageable if you think of it as a collection of neighborhoods.

Central London: This area contains Westminster and what Londoners call the West End. The Westminster district includes Big Ben, Parliament, Westminster Abbey, and Buckingham Palace—the grand government buildings from which Britain is ruled. Trafalgar Square, London's gathering place, has many major museums. The West End is the center of London's cultural life, with bustling squares: Piccadilly Circus and Leicester Square host cinemas, tourist traps, and nighttime glitz. Soho and Covent Garden are thriving people zones with theaters, restaurants, pubs, and boutiques. And Regent and Oxford streets are the city's main shopping zones.

North London: Neighborhoods in this part of town—including Bloomsbury, Fitzrovia, and Marylebone—contain such major sights as the British Museum and the overhyped Madame Tussauds Waxworks. Nearby, along busy Euston Road, is the British Library, plus a trio of train stations (one of them, St. Pancras International, is linked to Paris by the Eurostar "Chunnel" train).

The City: Today's modern financial district, called simply "The City," was a walled town in Roman times. Gleaming skyscrapers are interspersed with historical landmarks such as St. Paul's Cathedral, legal sights (Old Bailey), and the Museum of London. The Tower of London and Tower Bridge lie at The City's eastern border.

London's Neighborhoods

The Tube's Circle Line

Regent's Park

NORTH LONDON

BRITISH MUSEUM

BAYSWATER

BLOOMSBURY

NOTTING HILL

Hyde Park

SOHO

MAYFAIR

WEST END

TRAFALGAR SQ.

EAST END

WEST LONDON

BELGRAVIA

PIMLICO

CENTRAL LONDON

THE CITY

TOWER OF LONDON

ST. PAUL'S

SOUTH KENSINGTON

WEST-MINSTER

Thames River

BIG BEN

CHELSEA

LONDON EYE

SOUTH BANK

To the Docklands

Not to Scale

LONDON

East London: Just east of The City is the East End—the increasingly gentrified former stomping ground of Cockney ragamuffins and Jack the Ripper.

The South Bank: The South Bank of the Thames River offers major sights (Tate Modern, Shakespeare's Globe, London Eye) linked by a riverside walkway. Within this area, Southwark (SUTH-uck) stretches from the Tate Modern to London Bridge. Pedestrian bridges connect the South Bank with The City and Trafalgar Square.

West London: This huge area contains neighborhoods such as Mayfair, Belgravia, Pimlico, Chelsea, South Kensington, and Notting Hill. It's home to London's wealthy and has many trendy shops and enticing restaurants. Here you'll find a range of museums (Victoria and Albert Museum, Tate Britain, and more), my top hotel recommendations, lively Victoria Station, and the vast green expanses of Hyde Park and Kensington Gardens.

Outside the Center: The Docklands, London's version of Manhattan, is farther east than the East End; Queen Elizabeth Olympic Park is just north of the Docklands. Historic Greenwich is southeast of London and across the Thames. Kew Gardens and Hampton Court Palace are southwest of London.

Tourist Information

For such a big and important city, it's amazing how hard it can be to find unbiased sightseeing information and advice in London. You'll see "Tourist Information" offices advertised everywhere, but most of them are private agencies that make a big profit selling tours and advance sightseeing and/or theater tickets; others are

LONDON

Rick Steves Audio Europe

If you're bringing a mobile device, be sure to check out **Rick Steves Audio Europe,** where you can download free audio tours and hours of travel interviews (via the Rick Steves Audio Europe smartphone app, www.ricksteves.com/audioeurope, iTunes, or Google Play).

My self-guided **audio tours** are user-friendly, easy to follow, fun, and informative, covering the major sights and neighborhoods in London: the British Museum, British Library, St. Paul's Cathedral, The City, and my Westminster Walk. Compared with live tours, my audio tours are hard to beat: Nobody will stand you up, the quality is reliable, you can take the tour exactly when you like, and they're free.

Rick Steves Audio Europe also offers a far-reaching library of intriguing **travel interviews** with experts from around the globe.

run by Transport for London (TFL) and are primarily focused on providing public-transit advice.

The only publicly funded (and therefore impartial) "real" TI is the **City of London Information Centre** (Mon-Sat 9:30-17:30, Sun 10:00-16:00; across the busy street from St. Paul's Cathedral—around the right side as you face the main staircase, in the modern, angular building just toward the Millennium Bridge; Tube: St. Paul's, tel. 020/7332-1456, www.visitthecity.co.uk). While officially a service of The City (London's financial district), this office also provides information about the rest of London. It sells Oyster cards, London Passes, and advance "Fast Track" sightseeing tickets (all described later), and stocks various free publications: *London Planner* (a free monthly that lists all the sights, events, and hours), some walking-tour brochures, the *Official London Theatre Guide*, a free Tube and bus map, the *Guide to River Thames Boat Services*, and brochures describing self-guided walks in The City (various themes, including Dickens, modern architecture, and film locations). They give out a free map of The City, and sell several city-wide maps; ask if they have yet another, free map with a coupon good for 20 percent off admission to St. Paul's. I'd skip their room-booking service (charges a commission) and theater box office (may charge a commission).

Visit London, which serves the greater London area, doesn't have an office you can visit in person—but does operate a call center and website (tel. 0870-156-6366, www.visitlondon.com).

Fast Track Tickets: To skip the ticket-buying queues at certain London sights, you can buy Fast Track tickets in advance—and they can be cheaper than tickets sold right at the sight. They're particularly smart for the Tower of London, the London Eye, and Madame Tussauds Waxworks, all of which get very busy in high season. They're available through various sales outlets around London (including the City of London TI, souvenir stands, and faux-TIs scattered throughout touristy areas).

London Pass: This pass, which covers many big sights and lets you skip some lines, is expensive but potentially worth the investment for extremely busy sightseers (£47/1 day, £64/2 days, £77/3 days, £102/6 days; days are calendar days rather than 24-hour periods; comes with 160-page guidebook, also sold at major train stations and airports, tel. 0870-242-9988, www.londonpass.com). Among the many sights it includes are the Tower of London, Westminster Abbey, St. Paul's Cathedral, and Windsor Castle, as well as many temporary exhibits and audioguides at otherwise "free" biggies. Think through your sightseeing plans, study their website to see what's covered, and do the math before you buy.

Arrival in London

For more information on getting to or from London by train, bus, plane, and cruise ship, see "London Connections," near the end of this chapter.

By Train: London has nine major train stations, all connected by the Tube (subway). All have ATMs, and many of the larger stations also have shops, fast food, exchange offices, and luggage storage. From any station, you can ride the Tube or taxi to your hotel. For more info on train travel, see www.nationalrail.co.uk.

By Bus: The main intercity bus station is Victoria Coach Station, one block southwest of Victoria train/Tube station. For more on bus travel, see www.nationalexpress.com.

By Plane: London has six airports. Most tourists arrive at Heathrow or Gatwick airport, although flights from elsewhere in Europe may land at Stansted, Luton, Southend, or London City airport. For specifics on getting from London's airports to downtown, see "London Connections" near the end of this chapter; for hotels near Heathrow and Gatwick, see page 188.

Helpful Hints

Theft Alert: Wear your money belt. The Artful Dodger is alive and well in London. Be on guard, particularly on public transportation and in places crowded with tourists, who, considered naive and rich, are targeted. The Changing of the Guard scene is a favorite for thieves. And more than 7,500 purses are stolen annually at Covent Garden alone.

Pedestrian Safety: Cars drive on the left side of the road—which can be as confusing for foreign pedestrians as for foreign drivers. Before crossing a street, I always look right, look left,

Affording London's Sights

London is one of Europe's most expensive cities, with the dubious distinction of having some of the world's steepest admission prices. Fortunately, many sights are free.

Free Museums: Many of the city's biggest and best museums won't charge you a dime. Free sights include the British Museum, British Library, National Gallery, National Portrait Gallery, Tate Britain, Tate Modern, Wallace Collection, Imperial War Museum, Victoria and Albert Museum, Natural History Museum, Science Museum, Sir John Soane's Museum, the Museum of London, and the Geffrye Museum.

About half of these museums request a donation of a few pounds, but whether you contribute or not is up to you. If I spend money for an audioguide, I feel fine about not otherwise donating. If you can afford it, donate.

Free Churches: Smaller churches let worshippers (and tourists) in free, although they may ask for a donation. The big sightseeing churches—Westminster Abbey and St. Paul's—charge higher admission fees, but offer free evensong services nearly daily (though you can't stick around afterward to sightsee). Westminster Abbey also offers free organ recitals most Sundays at 17:45.

Other Freebies: London has plenty of free performances, such as lunch concerts at St. Martin-in-the-Fields (see page 104) and summertime movies at The Scoop amphitheater near City Hall (see page 170). For other freebies, check out www.free londonlistings.co.uk. There's no charge to enjoy the pageantry of the Changing of the Guard, rants at Speakers' Corner in Hyde Park (on Sun afternoon), displays at Harrods, the people-watching scene at Covent Garden, and the colorful streets of the East End. It's free to view the legal action at the Old Bailey and the legislature at work in the Houses of Parliament. And you can get into a bit of the Tower of London and Windsor Castle by attending Sunday services in each place's chapel (chapel access only).

Greenwich makes for an inexpensive day trip (see next chapter). Many of its sights are free, and the journey there is covered by a cheap Zones 1-2 Tube ticket or pass.

Sightseeing Deals: If you buy a paper One-Day Travelcard at a National Rail station (such as Paddington or Victoria), you may be eligible for two-for-one discounts at many popular sights, such as the Churchill War Rooms, London Eye, Tower of London, and Madame Tussauds. (This also works with paper train tickets bought in person at the station—if you'll be riding into London and visiting one of these sights later in the day.) See page 62 for details.

Good-Value Tours: The city walking tours with professional guides (£6-9) are one of the best deals going. (Note that the guides for the "free" walking tours are unpaid by their companies, and they expect tips—I'd pay up front for an expertly guided tour instead.) Hop-on, hop-off big-bus tours, while expensive (£24-30), provide a great overview and include free boat tours as well as city walks. (Or, for the price of a transit ticket, you could get similar views from the top of a double-decker public bus.) A one-hour Thames ride to Greenwich costs £12 one-way, but most boats come with entertaining commentary. A three-hour bicycle tour is about £20.

Pricey...but Worth It? Big-ticket sights worth their hefty admission fees (£13.50-17.50) are Kew Gardens, Shakespeare's Globe, the Churchill War Rooms, and Kensington Palace.

The London Eye has become a London must-see—though if you're on a tight budget, it's difficult to justify its very high cost (£19). While Hampton Court Palace (£18) is expensive, it is well presented and a reasonable value if you have an interest in royal history. The Queen charges royally for a peek inside Buckingham Palace (£19, open Aug-Sept only), and her art gallery and carriage museum (adjacent to the palace, about £9 each) are expensive but interesting. Madame Tussauds Waxworks is pricey but still hard for many to resist (£30, see page 120 for info on discounts). Harry Potter fans gladly pay the Hagrid-sized £29 fee to see the sets and props at the Warner Bros. Studio Tour (but those who wouldn't know a wizard from a Muggle shouldn't waste the time or money).

Many smaller museums charge relatively low admission. My favorites include the Courtauld Gallery (£6, £3 on Mon) and the Wellington Museum at Apsley House (£6.70).

Totally Pants (Brit-speak for Not Worth It): The London Dungeon, at £24.60, is gimmicky, overpriced, and a terrible value...despite the long line at the door. It doesn't make sense to spend your pounds on Winston Churchill's Britain at War Experience (£14.50) when the Churchill War Rooms (£17.50) and the Imperial War Museum (free) cover the same themes much better.

Theater: Compared with Broadway's prices, London's theater is a bargain. Seek out the freestanding tkts booth at Leicester Square to get discounts from 25 to 50 percent on good seats (and full-price tickets to the hottest shows with no service charges; see page 163). Buying direct at the theater box office can score you a great deal on same-day tickets, and even the most popular shows generally have some seats under £20 (possibly with obstructed views)—ask. A £5 "groundling" ticket for a play at Shakespeare's Globe is the best theater deal in town (see page 142). Tickets to the Open Air Theatre at north London's Regent's Park start at £15 (see page 168).

London doesn't come cheap. But with its many free museums and affordable plays, this cosmopolitan, cultured city offers days of sightseeing thrills without requiring you to pinch your pennies (or your pounds).

then look right again just to be sure. Most crosswalks are even painted with instructions, reminding foreign guests to "Look right" or "Look left." While locals are champion jaywalkers, you shouldn't try it; jaywalking is treacherous when you're disoriented about which direction traffic is coming from.

Medical Problems: Local hospitals have good-quality 24-hour-a-day emergency care centers, where any tourist who needs help can drop in and, after a wait, be seen by a doctor. Your hotel has details. St. Thomas' Hospital, immediately across the river from Big Ben, has a fine reputation.

Getting Your Bearings: London is well-signed for visitors. Through an initiative called Legible London, the city is erecting thoughtfully designed, pedestrian-focused maps around town. In this sprawling city—where predictable grid-planned streets are relatively rare—it's also smart to buy and use a good map. *Benson's London Street Map*, sold at many newsstands and bookstores, is my favorite for efficient sightseeing.

Festivals: For one week in February and another in September, fashionistas descend on the city for **London Fashion Week** (www.londonfashionweek.co.uk). The famous **Chelsea Flower Show** blossoms in late May (book ahead for this popular event at www.rhs.org.uk/chelsea). During the annual **Trooping the Colour** in June, there are military bands and pageantry, and the Queen's birthday parade (www.trooping-the-colour.co.uk). Tennis fans pack the stands at the **Wimbledon Tennis Championship** in late June to early July (www.wimbledon.org), and partygoers head for the **Notting Hill Carnival** in late August.

Traveling in Winter: London dazzles year-round, so consider visiting in winter, when airfares and hotel rates are generally cheaper and there are fewer tourists. For ideas on what to do, see the "Winter Activities in London" article at www.ricksteves.com/winteracts.

Getting Online with a Mobile Device: In addition to the Wi-Fi that's likely available at your hotel, it's smart to get a free account with **The Cloud,** a free Wi-Fi service found in many convenient spots around London, including most train stations and many museums, coffee shops, cafés, and shopping centers. Sign up at www.thecloud.net/free-wifi, where you'll have to enter a street address and postal code; it doesn't matter which one (use your hotel's, or the Queen's: Buckingham Palace, SW1A 1AA). Your Wi-Fi may be limited to 15 or 30 minutes at a time; if you max out, simply log in again.

Most **Tube stations** and trains have Wi-Fi, but it's free only to those with a British cellular account. However, the

Tube's Wi-Fi always lets you access Transport for London's Journey Planner (www.tfl.gov.uk), making it easy to look up your city transit options—and get real-time updates on delays—once you're in a station. To access the rest of the Web using the Tube's Wi-Fi, you can pay £2 for a one-day pass, or £5 for a one-week pass (easy sign-up and credit-card payment at http://my.virginmedia.com/wifi). The Wi-Fi can falter inside Tube tunnels, but generally comes right back as you approach the next station.

Useful Apps: While the Transport for London's Journey Planner works great for people with access to the Internet, the **MX Apps free Tube map** works even when you're not online, showing the easiest way to connect station A to station B. When you are online, the app provides live updates about Tube delays and closures. (It doesn't, however, look up bus connections, and MX Apps' "Bus London" map isn't very useful offline.) **City Maps 2Go** ($2) lets you download searchable offline maps; their London version is quite good. **Time Out London's** free app has reviews and listings for theater, museums, movies, and more (download the "Things to Do" version, which is updated weekly, rather than the boilerplate "Travel Guide" version).

Travel Bookstores: Located between Covent Garden and Leicester Square, the very good **Stanfords Travel Bookstore** stocks current editions of many of my books (Mon and Wed-Fri 9:00-20:00, Tue 9:30-20:00, Sat 10:00-20:00, Sun 12:00-18:00, 12-14 Long Acre, second entrance on Floral Street, Tube: Leicester Square, tel. 020/7836-1321, www.stanfords.co.uk).

Two impressive **Waterstones** bookstores have the biggest collection of travel guides in town: on Piccadilly (Mon-Sat 9:00-22:00, Sun 11:30-18:00, Costa Café, great views from top-floor bar—see sidebar on page 128, 203 Piccadilly, tel. 0843-290-8549) and on Trafalgar Square (Mon-Sat 9:30-21:00, Sun 12:00-18:00, Costa Café on second floor, tel. 0843-290-8651).

Baggage Storage: Train stations have replaced lockers with more secure left-luggage counters. Each bag must go through a scanner (just like at the airport), so lines can be slow. Expect long waits in the morning to check in (up to 45 minutes) and in the afternoon to pick up (each item-£8.50/24 hours, most stations daily 7:00-23:00). You can also store bags at the airports (similar rates and hours, www.excess-baggage.com). If leaving London and returning later, you may be able to store a box or bag at your hotel for free—assuming you'll be staying there again.

"Voluntary Donations": About a half-dozen sights automatically add a "voluntary donation" of about 10 percent to their admission fees (these are noted in the listings). The price posted and quoted includes the donation, though it's perfectly fine to say you want to pay a cheaper price without the donation.

Updates to This Book: Check www.ricksteves.com/update for any significant changes that have occurred since this book was published.

Getting Around London

To travel smart in a city this size, you must get comfortable with public transportation. London's excellent taxis, buses, and subway (Tube) system make a car unnecessary (see page 71 for details on driving in London—and why it's a bad idea).

The helpful *Welcome to London* brochure, produced by the mayor's office and Transport for London (TFL), includes both a Tube map and a handy schematic map of the best bus routes (available free at TFL offices—such as the one in Victoria Station, the City of London TI, and at museums and hotels all over town). For specific directions on how to get from point A to point B on London's transit, call TFL's automated info line at 0843-222-1234.

Public-Transit Passes

London has the most expensive public transit in the world—save money on your Tube and bus rides by using a multiride pass. You have three options: Pay double by buying individual tickets as you go; buy a £5 Oyster card and top it up as needed to travel like a local for about £1-2 per ride; or get a Travelcard for unlimited travel on either one or seven days.

The transit system has six zones. Since almost all of my recommended accommodations, restaurants, and sights are within Zones 1 and 2, those are the prices I've listed here; you'll pay more to go farther afield. Specific fares and other details change constantly; for a complete and updated list of prices, check www.tfl.gov.uk.

Individual Transit Tickets

These days in London, individual paper tickets are obsolete; there's no point buying one unless you're literally taking just one ride your entire time in the city. Because individual fares (£4.50 per Tube ride, £2.40 per bus ride) are about double the cost of using a pay-as-you-go Oyster card, in just two or three rides you'll recoup the £5 added deposit for the Oyster. If you do buy a single ticket, avoid ticket-window lines in Tube stations by using the coin-op machines; practice on the punchboard to see how the system works (hit "Adult Single" and your destination). These tickets are valid only on the day of purchase.

Oyster Cards

A pay-as-you-go Oyster card (a plastic card embedded with a computer chip) is the standard, smart way to economically ride the Tube,

buses, Docklands Light Railway (DLR), and Overground. (Note that the Oyster card may begin to be phased out in 2014 and replaced with direct payments using bank debit cards.) On each type of transport, you simply lay the card flat against (or sufficiently near) the yellow card reader at the turnstile or entrance, it flashes green, and the fare is automatically deducted. (You'll also tap your card again to "touch out" as you exit the Tube and DLR turnstiles, but not to exit buses.)

With an Oyster card, rides cost about half the price of individual paper tickets (£2.10 or £2.80 per Tube ride—depending on time of day, £1.40 per bus ride). You buy the card itself at any Tube station ticket window for a refundable £5 deposit, then load it up with as much credit as you want. (For extra peace of mind, ask about registering your card against theft or loss.) When your balance gets low, simply add credit—or "top up"—at a ticket window or machine. A price cap on the pay-as-you-go Oyster card guarantees you'll never pay more than the One-Day Travelcard price within a 24-hour period.

You can see how much credit remains on your card by touching it to the pad at any ticket machine. Oyster card balances never expire (though they need reactivating at a ticket window every two years), so you can use the card whenever you're in London, or lend it to someone else.

When you're finished with the card (and if you don't mind a short wait), you should be able to reclaim your £5 deposit at any ticket window. However, to make it as easy as possible to recoup your deposit, you should always use the same mode of payment: For example, if you pay the deposit in cash, you need to top up with cash. If you pay the deposit in cash and top up with a credit card, or vice versa, it can be more difficult (or impossible) to get your deposit back.

Transfers: You can change from one Tube line to another on the same Oyster journey (as long as you don't leave the station); however, if you change between buses, or change between bus and Tube, you'll pay a new fare.

Travelcards

Like the Oyster card, Travelcards are valid on the Tube, buses, Docklands Light Railway (DLR), and Overground. The difference is that Travelcards let you ride as many times as you want within a one- or a seven-day period, for one fixed price.

Before you buy a card, estimate where you'll be going; there's a card for Zones 1 and 2, and another for Zones 1-6 (which includes Heathrow Airport). If Heathrow is the only ride you're taking outside Zones 1-2 (which is likely), you can pay a small supplement to make the Zones 1-2 Travelcard stretch to cover that one ride.

The **One-Day Travelcard** gives you unlimited travel for a day (Zones 1-2: £8.80, off-peak version £7.30; Zones 1-6: £16.40, off-peak version £8.90; off-peak cards are good for travel after 9:30 on weekdays and anytime on weekends). This Travelcard works like a traditional paper ticket: Buy it at any Tube station ticket window or machine, then feed it into a turnstile (and retrieve it) to enter and exit the Tube. On a bus, just show it to the driver when you get on.

The **Seven-Day Travelcard** is a great option if you're staying four or more days and plan to use buses and the Tube a lot. It's issued as credit on your plastic Oyster card, and gives you unlimited travel anytime, anywhere in Zones 1 and 2 for a week (£30.40 plus the refundable £5 deposit for the Oyster card). As with a standard Oyster card, you'll touch it to the yellow card reader when entering or exiting a Tube turnstile, or when boarding a bus. It's smart to keep an extra £5-6 worth of credit on your Oyster card on top of the Travelcard to cover travel outside zones 1-2 or after your Travelcard runs out.

Discounts

Groups: A gang of 10 or more adults can travel all day on the Tube for £4.50 each (but not on buses). Kids ages 11-17 pay £1.70 when part of a group of 10.

Families: A paying adult can take up to four kids (ages 10 and under) for free on the Tube, Docklands Light Railway (DLR), and Overground all day, every day (kids 10 and under are always free on buses). At the Tube station, use the manual gate, rather than the turnstiles, to be waved in. Other child and student discounts are explained at www.tfl.gov.uk/tickets. Or simply show up at a Tube ticket window with your family; the clerk will tell you which deal is best.

River Cruises: A Travelcard gives you a 33 percent discount on most Thames cruises (see "Cruises," later). If you pay for Thames Clippers (including the Tate Boat museum ferry) with your pay-as-you go Oyster card, you'll get a 10 percent discount.

Sightseeing Deal: By buying a paper One-Day Travelcard at a train station, you can qualify for two-for-one discounts at many popular sights. If two of you will be visiting a pricey sight (such as the Tower of London, Churchill War Rooms, London Eye, or Madame Tussauds) and getting a One-Day Travelcard anyway, this is a smart move. But it only works if your paper Travelcard is issued through a National Rail train-station machine or ticket counter, and the sight discount must be used on the day the ticket is valid. It doesn't work if your Travelcard is loaded onto an Oyster card, or if you get your Travelcard in a Tube station. Look for brochures with coupons at major train stations, or print vouchers at www.daysoutguide.co.uk.

The Bottom Line

Struggling to choose which pass works best for your trip? First of all, skip the individual tickets. On a short visit (three days or fewer), get an Oyster card and pay as you go (remember, even if you'll be zipping around a lot, using an Oyster card means you'll never pay more per day than the cost of a One-Day Travelcard). If you're in London four days or longer, the Seven-Day Travelcard will likely pay for itself.

By Tube

London's subway system is called the Tube or Underground (but never "subway," which, in Britain, refers to a pedestrian under-

pass). The Tube is one of this planet's great people-movers and usually the fastest long-distance transport in town (runs Mon-Sat about 5:00-24:00, Sun about 7:00-23:00). Two other commuter rail lines, while technically not part of the Tube, are tied into the network and use the same tickets: the Docklands Light Railway (called DLR, runs to the Docklands, Greenwich, and Olympic Park) and the Overground.

Get your bearings by studying a map of the system (free at any station).

Each line has a name (such as Circle, Northern, or Bakerloo) and two directions (indicated by the end-of-the-line stops). Find the line that will take you to your destination, and figure out roughly which direction (north, south, east, or west) you'll need to go to get there.

You can use an Oyster card, Travelcard, or individual tickets (all explained earlier) to pay for your journey. At the Tube station, touch your Oyster card flat against the turnstile's yellow card reader, both when you enter and exit the station. If you have a regular paper ticket or a One-Day Travelcard, feed it into the turnstile, reclaim it, and hang on to it—you'll need it later.

Find your train by following signs to your line and the (general) direction it's headed (such as Central Line: east). Since some tracks are shared by several lines, double-check before boarding a train: First, make sure your destination is one of the stops listed on the sign at the platform. Also, check the electronic signboards that announce which train is next, and make sure the destination (the end-of-the-line stop) is the direction you want. Some trains,

particularly on the Circle and District lines, split off for other directions, but each train has its final destination marked above its windshield.

Trains run about every 3-10 minutes. For a rough idea of how long it takes to get from point A to point B by Tube, estimate five minutes per stop (which includes time to walk into and out of stations, and to change trains). So a destination six stops away will take you about 30 minutes.

If one train is absolutely packed and another to the same destination is coming in three minutes, wait to avoid the sardine routine. Rush hours (8:00-10:00 and 16:00-19:00) can be packed and sweaty. Bring something to do to make your waiting time productive. If you get confused, ask for advice from a local, a blue-vested staff person, or at the information window located before the turnstile entry.

At most stations, you can't leave the system without touching your Oyster card to an electronic reader, or feeding your ticket or One-Day Travelcard into the turnstile. (If you have a single-trip paper ticket, the turnstile will eat your now-expired ticket; if it's a One-Day Travelcard, it will spit out your still-valid card.) Some stations, such as Hampton Court, do not have a turnstile, so you'll have to locate a reader to "touch out" your Oyster card. If you skip this step and leave the station, the system assumes you've ridden to the most remote station, and highest fare will be deducted from your card. When leaving a station, save walking time by choosing the best street exit—check the maps on the walls or ask any station personnel.

The system can be fraught with construction delays and breakdowns (the Circle Line is notorious for problems). Most construction is scheduled for weekends. Closures are publicized in advance (online at www.tfl.gov.uk and with posters in the Tube; Google Maps also has real-time service alerts for the Tube, and

TFL does a fine job of tweeting updates). Pay attention to signs and announcements explaining necessary detours. Closed Tube lines are often replaced by temporary bus service, but it can be faster to figure out alternate routes on the Tube; since the lines cross each other constantly, there are several ways to make any journey. For help, check out the "Journey Planner" at www.tfl.gov .uk, which is accessible (for free) on any mobile device within most Tube stations.

Tube Etiquette

- When your train arrives, stand off to the side and let riders exit before you try to board.
- Avoid using the hinged seats near the doors of some trains when the car is jammed; they take up valuable standing space.
- If you're blocking the door when the train stops, step out of the car and off to the side, let others off, then get back on.
- Talk softly in the cars. Listen to how quietly Londoners communicate and follow their lead.
- On escalators, stand on the right and pass on the left. But note that in some passageways or stairways, you might be directed to walk on the left (the direction Brits go when behind the wheel).
- When leaving a station, it's polite to hold the door for the person behind you.
- Discreet eating and drinking are fine (nothing smelly); drinking alcohol and smoking are not.

By Bus

If you figure out the bus system, you'll swing like Tarzan through the urban jungle of London (see sidebar for a list of handy routes).

Pick up a free bus map; the most user-friendly is in the *Welcome to London* brochure (mentioned earlier). You can also find thicker, more in-depth maps of various sectors of the city (most useful is the Central London Bus Guide). Bus maps are available at Transport for London offices, the City of London TI, and other tourist spots around town. With a mobile phone, you can find out the arrival time of the next bus by texting your bus stop's five-digit code (posted at the stop, above the timetable) to 87287 (if you're using your US phone's SIM card, text the code to 011-44-7797-800-287).

Buses are covered by Travelcards and Oyster cards. You can also buy individual tickets from a machine at bus stops (no change

Handy Bus Routes

Ever since London instituted a congestion charge for cars, the bus system has gotten faster, easier, and cheaper. Tube-oriented travelers need to get over their tunnel vision, learn the bus system, and get around fast and easy. The best views are upstairs on a double-decker.

Here are some of the most useful routes:

Route #9: High Street Kensington to Knightsbridge (Harrods) to Hyde Park Corner to Piccadilly Circus to Trafalgar Square. This is one of two "Heritage Routes," using some old-style double-decker buses.

Route #11: Victoria Station to Westminster Abbey to Trafalgar Square to St. Paul's and Liverpool Street Station and the East End.

Route #15: Regent Street to Piccadilly Circus to Trafalgar Square to St. Paul's to Tower of London. This is the other "Heritage Route," also with old-style double-decker buses.

Routes #23 and #159: Paddington Station to Oxford Circus to Piccadilly Circus to Trafalgar Square; from there, #23 heads east to St. Paul's and Liverpool Street Station, while #159 heads to Westminster and the Imperial War Museum. In addition, several buses (including #6, #13, and #139) also make the corridor run between Marble Arch, Oxford Circus, Piccadilly Circus, and Trafalgar Square.

Route #24: Pimlico (near Tate Britain) to Victoria Station to Westminster Abbey to Trafalgar Square to Euston Square, then all the way north to Camden Town (Camden Lock Market) and Hampstead Heath.

Route #38: Victoria Station to Hyde Park Corner to Piccadilly Circus to British Museum.

Route #RV1 (a scenic South Bank joyride): Tower of London to Tower Bridge to Southwark Street (five-minute walk behind Tate Modern/Shakespeare's Globe) to London Eye/Waterloo Station, then over Waterloo Bridge to Aldwych and Covent Garden.

Route #148: Westminster Abbey to Victoria Station to Notting Hill and Bayswater (by way of the east end of Hyde Park and Marble Arch).

Check the bus stop closest to your hotel—it might be convenient to your sightseeing plans.

given), but you can't buy tickets on board. Any bus ride in downtown London costs £2.40 for those paying cash, or £1.40 if using an Oyster card (with a cap of £4.40 per day).

The first step in mastering London's bus system is learning how to decipher the bus stop signs (see photo). In the first column, find your destination on the list—e.g., Paddington. In the next column, find a bus that goes there—the #23. The final column has a letter within a circle (e.g., "H") that tells you exactly which bus stop you need to stand at to catch your bus. (You'll find the same letter marked on a neighborhood map nearby.) Make your way to that stop—you'll know it's yours because it will have the same letter on its pole—and wait for the bus with your number on it to arrive. Hop on, and you're good to go.

O		
Oakwood ⊖	N91	ⓣ ⓧ
Old Coulsdon	N68	Aldwych
Old Ford	N8	Oxford Circus
Old Kent Road Canal Bridge	53, N381	ⓣ
	453	ⓐ ⓞ
	N21	ⓖ
Old Street ⊖ ≋	243	Aldwych
Orpington ≋	N47	ⓖ
Oxford Circus ⊖	Any bus	ⓣ
	N18	ⓖ

P		
Paddington ⊖ ≋	23, N15	ⓗ ⓙ ⓣ
Palmers Green ≋	N29	ⓖ
Park Langley	N3	ⓐ ⓜ
Peckham	12	ⓐ ⓟ
	N89, N343	ⓖ
	N136	ⓐ ⓝ
	N381	ⓟ
Penge Pawleyne Arms	176	ⓖ
	N3	ⓐ ⓞ
Petts Wood ≋	N47	ⓖ
Pimlico Grosvenor Road	24	ⓞ ⓝ
Plaistow Greengate	N15	ⓞ ⓟ
Plumstead ≋	53	ⓟ
Plumstead Common	53	ⓟ

As you board, touch your Oyster card to the card reader, or, if you have a paper ticket or a One-Day Travelcard, show it to the driver. On "Heritage Routes" #9 and #15 (some of which use older double-decker buses), you may still pay a conductor; take a seat, and he or she will come around to collect your fare or verify your pass. There's no need to tap your card or show your ticket when you hop off.

If you have an Oyster card or Travelcard, save your feet and get in the habit of hopping buses for quick little straight shots, even just to get to a Tube stop. During bump-and-grind rush hours (8:00-10:00 and 16:00-19:00), you'll usually go faster by Tube.

By Taxi

London is the best taxi town in Europe. Big, black, carefully regulated cabs are everywhere. (While historically known as "black cabs," some of London's official taxis are covered with wildly colored ads.) Some cabs now run on biofuels—a good way to dispose of all that oil used to fry fish-and-chips.

I've never met a crabby cabbie in London. They love to talk, and they know every nook and cranny in town. I ride in a taxi each day just to get my London questions answered (drivers must pass a rigorous test on "The Knowledge" of London geography to earn their license).

If a cab's top light is on, just wave it down. Drivers flash lights when they see you wave. They have a tight turning radius (on new cabs, the back tires actually pivot), so you can hail cabs going in either direction. If waving doesn't work, ask someone where you can find a taxi stand. Telephoning a cab will get you one in a few minutes, but costs a little more (tel. 0871-871-8710; £2 surcharge, plus extra fee to book ahead by credit card).

Rides start at £2.40. The regular tariff #1 covers most of the day (Mon-Fri 6:00-20:00), tariff #2 is during "unsociable hours" (Mon-Fri 20:00-22:00 and Sat-Sun 6:00-22:00), and tariff #3 is for nighttime (22:00-6:00) and holidays. Rates go up about 15-20 percent with each higher tariff. All extra charges are explained in writing on the cab wall. Tip a cabbie by rounding up (maximum 10 percent).

Connecting downtown sights is quick and easy, and will cost you about £6-10 (for example, St. Paul's to the Tower of London, or between the two Tate museums). For a short ride, three adults in a cab generally travel at close to Tube prices—and groups of four or five adults should taxi everywhere. All cabs can carry five passengers, and some take six, for the same cost as a single traveler.

Don't worry about meter cheating. Licensed British cab meters come with a sealed computer chip and clock that ensures you'll get the correct tariff. The only way a cabbie can cheat you is by taking a needlessly long route. One serious pitfall, however, is taking a cab when traffic is bad to a destination efficiently served by the Tube. On one trip to London, I hopped in a taxi at South Kensington for Waterloo Station and hit bad traffic. Rather than spending 20 minutes and £2 on the Tube, I spent 40 minutes and £16 in a taxi.

If you overdrink and ride in a taxi, be warned: Taxis charge £40 for "soiling" (a.k.a., pub puke).

If you forget this book in a taxi, call the Lost Property office and hope for the best (tel. 0845-330-9882).

By Bike

London is keeping up its push to become more bike-friendly. Since 2010, it's operated a citywide bike-rental program similar to ones in other major European cities, and new bike lanes are still cropping up around town. Still, London isn't (yet) ideal for biking. Although the streets are relatively uncongested, the network of designated bike lanes is far from complete, and the city's many one-way streets (not to mention the need to bike on the "wrong" side) can make biking here a bit more challenging than it sounds. If you're accustomed to urban biking, it can be a good option for connecting your sightseeing stops, but if you're just up for a joyride, stick to London's large parks.

Barclays Cycle Hire bikes, intended for quick point-to-point trips, are fairly easy to rent and a giddy joy to use, even for the most jaded London tourist. These "Boris Bikes" (as they are affectionately called by locals, after cycle enthusiast and mayor Boris Johnson) are cruisers with big, cushy seats, a bag rack with elastic straps, and three gears.

Approximately 600 bike-rental stations are scattered throughout the city, each equipped with a computer kiosk. To rent a bike, you need to pay an access fee (£2/day or £10/week). The first 30 minutes are free; if you hang on to the bike for longer, you'll be charged (£1 for 1 hour, £4 for 1.5 hours, £6 for 2 hours, and much steeper beyond that).

When you're ready to ride, press "Hire a Cycle" and insert your credit card when prompted. You'll then get a ticket with a five-digit code (using a combination of 1s, 2s, and 3s). Take the ticket to any bike, then wake up the machine by pressing any button on the panel near the front tire. When the light comes on, punch in the number. After the yellow light blinks, a green light will appear: Now you can (firmly) pull the bike out of the slot.

When your ride is over, find a station with an empty slot, then push your bike in until it locks and the green light flashes.

You can hire bikes as often as you like (which will start your free 30-minute period over again), as long as you wait five minutes between each use. There can be problems, of course—stations at popular locations (such as entrances to parks) can temporarily run out of bikes, and you may have trouble finding a place to return a bike—but for the most part, this system works great. To make things easier, get a map of the docking stations—pick one up at any major Underground station. It's also available online at www.tfl.gov.uk (click on "Barclays Cycle Hire") and as a free smartphone app (http://cyclehireapp.com).

Helmets are not provided, so ride carefully. Stay to the far-left side of the road and watch closely at intersections for *left*-turning cars. If riding on crowded streets feels intimidating, stick to parks and quiet back lanes. Be aware that in most parks (including Hyde Park/Kensington Gardens) only certain paths are designated for bike use—you can't ride just anywhere. Maps posted at park entrances identify bike paths, and non-bike paths are generally clearly marked.

Some bike tour companies also rent bikes—for details, see page 77.

By Car

If you have a car, stow it—you don't want to drive in London. If you need convincing, here's one more reason: A £10 **congestion charge** is levied on any private car entering the city center during peak hours (Mon-Fri 7:00-18:00, no charge Sat-Sun and holidays, fee payable at gas stations, convenience stores, and self-service machines at public parking lots, or online at www.cclondon.com). Traffic cameras photograph and identify every vehicle that enters the fee zone; if you get spotted and don't pay up by midnight that day (or pay £12 before midnight of the following day), you'll get socked with a penalty of at least £60. The system has been effective in cutting down traffic jam delays and bolstering London's public transit. The revenue that's raised subsidizes the buses, which ARE now cheaper, more frequent, and even more user-friendly than before. Today, the vast majority of vehicles in the city center are buses, taxis, and service trucks.

Tours in London

To sightsee on your own, download my series of free audio tours that illuminate some of London's top sights and neighborhoods (see sidebar on page 54 for details).

▲▲▲Hop-On, Hop-Off Double-Decker Bus Tours

Two competitive companies (Original and Big Bus) offer essentially the same two tours of the city's sightseeing highlights, with nearly 30 stops on each route. Big Bus tours are a little more expensive (£30), while Original tours are cheaper (£24 with this book) and nearly as good.

These two-to-three hour, once-over-lightly bus tours drive by all the famous sights, providing a stress-free way to get your bearings and see the biggies. They stop at the same core group of sights regardless of which overview tour you're on: Piccadilly Circus, Trafalgar Square, Big Ben, St. Paul's, the Tower of London, Marble Arch, Victoria Station, and elsewhere. With a good guide and nice weather, I'd sit back and enjoy the entire tour. (If you don't like your guide, you can hop off and try your luck with the next departure.)

Each company offers at least one route with live (English-only) guides, and a second (sometimes slightly different route)

Combining a London Bus Tour and the Changing of the Guard

For a grand and efficient intro to London, consider catching either of the bus companies' overview tours at 8:30, riding 90 percent of the loop (which takes just over two hours, depending on traffic), and hopping off at Buckingham Palace in time to catch the Changing of the Guard ceremony. Choose between the Big Bus Tour (catch it at the Green Park Tube station) or the Original Bus Tour (catch it at Grosvenor Gardens, a block from Victoria Station). If you miss the 8:30 bus, you could catch the next one (generally about 20 minutes later), though it may get you to the ceremony a bit late (check with the driver).

comes with recorded, dial-a-language narration. In addition to the overview tours, both Original and Big Bus include the Thames River boat trip by City Cruises (between Westminster and the Tower of London) and three 1.5-hour walking tours.

Pick up a map from any flier rack or from one of the countless salespeople, and study the complex system. Sunday morning—when the traffic is light and many museums are closed—is a fine time for a tour. Unless you're using the bus tour mainly for hop-on, hop-off transportation, consider saving time and money by taking a night tour (described later).

Buses run about every 10-15 minutes in summer, every 10-20 minutes in winter, and operate daily. They start at about 8:30 and run until early evening in summer or late afternoon in winter. The last full loop usually leaves Victoria Station at about 19:00 in summer, and at about 17:00 in winter (confirm by checking the schedule or asking the driver).

You can buy tickets from drivers or from staff at street kiosks (credit cards accepted at kiosks at major stops such as Victoria Station, ticket good for 24 hours).

Original London Sightseeing Bus Tour

They offer two versions of their basic highlights loop: **The Original Tour** (live guide, marked with a yellow triangle on the front of the bus) and the **City Sightseeing Tour** (essentially the same route but with recorded narration, a kids' soundtrack option, and a stop at Madame Tussauds; bus marked with a red triangle). Other routes include the blue-triangle **Museum Tour** (connecting far-flung museums and major shopping stops), and green, black, and purple triangle routes (linking major train stations to the central route). All routes are covered by the same ticket. Keep it simple and just take one of the city highlights tours (£28, £4 less with this book, limit four discounts per book, they'll rip off the corner of this page—raise bloody hell if the staff or driver won't honor this discount; also online deals, info center at 17 Cockspur Street, tel. 020/8877-1722, www.theoriginaltour.com).

Big Bus London Tours

For £30 (up to 30 percent discount online—requires printer), you get the same basic overview tours: Red buses come with a live guide, while the blue route has a recorded narration and a one-hour longer path that goes around Hyde Park. These pricier Big Bus tours tend to have better, more dynamic guides than the Original tours, and more departures—meaning shorter waits for those hopping on and off (daily 8:30-18:00, winter until 16:30, info center at 48 Buckingham Palace Road, tel. 020/7233-9533, www.bigbustours.com).

London by Night Sightseeing Tour

This tour offers a 1.5-hour circuit, but after hours, with no extras (e.g., walks, river cruises), and at a lower price. While the narration can be pretty lame, the views at twilight are grand—though note that it stays light until late on summer nights, and London just doesn't do floodlighting as well as, say, Paris (£19, £15 online). From June through late September, open-top buses depart at 19:00, 20:00, 20:45, 21:30, 22:10, and 22:55 from Victoria Station (Jan-May and late Sept-late Dec departs at 19:00, 20:45, and 22:10 only with closed-top bus, no tours between Christmas and New Year). Buses leave from near Victoria Station (in front of Grosvenor Hotel on Buckingham Palace Road; or you can board at any stop, such as Marble Arch, Trafalgar Square, London Eye, or Tower of London; tel. 020/8545-6110, www.london-by-night.net). For a memorable and economical evening, munch a scenic picnic dinner on the top deck. (There are plenty of take-away options within the train stations and near the various stops.)

▲▲Walking Tours

Several times a day, top-notch local guides lead (sometimes big) groups through specific slices of London's past. Look for brochures at TIs or ask at hotels, although the latter usually push higher-priced bus tours. *Time Out*, the weekly entertainment guide, lists some, but not all, scheduled walks. Check with the various tour companies by phone or online to get their full picture.

To take a walking tour, simply show up at the announced location and pay the guide. Then enjoy two chatty hours of Dickens, Harry Potter, the Plague, Shakespeare, Legal London, the Beatles, Jack the Ripper, or whatever is on the agenda.

London Walks

This leading company lists its extensive and creative daily schedule on their amusing website, as well as in a beefy, plain *London*

Daily Reminder

Sunday: The Tower of London and British Museum are both especially crowded today. Speakers' Corner in Hyde Park rants from early afternoon until early evening. These places are closed: Sir John Soane's Museum, and legal sights (Houses of Parliament, City Hall, and Old Bailey; the neighborhood called The City is dead). Westminster Abbey and St. Paul's are open during the day for worship but closed to sightseers. With all these closures, this morning is a good time to take a bus tour. Most big stores open late (around 11:30) and close early (18:00). Street markets are flourishing at Camden Lock, Spitalfields (at its best today), Petticoat Lane, Brick Lane, and Greenwich, but Portobello Road and Brixton markets are closed (though the Brixton farmers market is open 10:00-14:00). Theaters are quiet, as most actors take today off. (There are a few exceptions, such as Shakespeare's Globe, which offers Sunday performances in summer, and family-oriented fare, including *The Lion King,* offered year-round.)

Monday: Virtually all sights are open, except Apsley House, Sir John Soane's Museum, Vinopolis, and a few others. The Houses of Parliament may be open as late as 22:00.

Tuesday: Virtually all sights are open, except Vinopolis and Apsley House. The British Library is open until 20:00, and the Houses of Parliament may be open as late as 22:00. On the first Tuesday of the month, Sir John Soane's Museum is also open 18:00-21:00.

Wednesday: Virtually all sights are open. Vinopolis is open until 21:30 and the Houses of Parliament may be open as late as 22:00.

Thursday: All sights are open, plus evening hours at the National Portrait Gallery (until 21:00) and Vinopolis (until 21:30).

Walks brochure (available at St. Martin-in-the-Fields' Café in the Crypt on Trafalgar Square and at the City of London TI). Just perusing their fascinating lineup of tours inspires me to stay longer in London. Their two-hour walks, led by top-quality professional guides (ranging from archaeologists to actors), cost £9 (cash only, walks offered year-round, private tours for groups-£130, tel. 020/7624-3978 for a live person, tel. 020/7624-9255 for a recording of today's or tomorrow's walks and the Tube station they depart from, www.walks.com).

London Walks also offers day trips into the countryside, a good option for those with limited time and transportation (£12-16 plus £10-50 for transportation and any admission costs, cash only: Stonehenge/Salisbury, Oxford/Cotswolds, Cambridge, Bath, and so on). These are economical in part because everyone gets group

Friday: All sights are open, except the Houses of Parliament. Sights open late include the British Museum (selected galleries until 20:30), National Gallery (until 21:00), National Portrait Gallery (until 21:00), Vinopolis (until 21:30), Victoria and Albert Museum (selected galleries until 22:00), and Tate Modern (until 22:00). The Tate Britain is open until 22:00 on select Fridays.

Saturday: Most sights are open, except legal ones (Old Bailey, City Hall; skip The City). The Houses of Parliament are open only with a tour. Vinopolis is open until 21:30 and the Tate Modern until 22:00. The Tower of London is especially crowded today. Today's the day to hit the Portobello Road street market; the Camden Lock and Greenwich markets are also good.

Notes: St. Martin-in-the-Fields church offers concerts at lunchtime (Mon, Tue, and Fri at 13:00) and in the evening (several nights a week at 19:30, jazz Wed at 20:00).

Evensong occurs nearly daily at St. Paul's (Sun at 15:15 and Tue-Sat at 17:00), Westminster Abbey (Sun at 15:00, Mon-Tue and Thu-Sat at 17:00 except Sat at 15:00 Sept-April), and Southwark Cathedral (Sun at 15:00, Tue-Fri 17:30, Sat at 16:00). For a description of evensong services, see page 169.

London by Night Sightseeing Tour buses leave from Victoria Station each evening (six departures 19:00-22:55; at 19:00, 20:45, and 22:10 in winter).

The London Eye spins nightly (last departure between 20:30 and 21:30, depending on the season).

In winter, Apsley House is open only on weekends (closed Mon-Fri).

LONDON

discounts for transportation and admissions.

Sandemans New London "Free Royal London Tour"

This company employs students (rather than licensed guides) who recite three-hour spiels covering the basic London sights. While the fast-moving, youthful tours are light and irreverent, and can be both entertaining and fun, it's misleading to call the tours "free," as tips are expected (the guides actually pay the company for the privilege of asking for tips). Given that London Walks offers daily tours at a reasonable price, taking this "free" tour makes no sense to me (daily at 11:00 and 13:00, meet at Wellington Arch, Tube: Hyde Park Corner, Exit 2). Sandemans also has other guided tours for a charge, including a Pub Crawl (£20, nightly at 19:30, meet at Verve Bar at 1 Upper St. Martin's Lane, Tube: Leicester Square, www.newlondon-tours.com).

Beatles Walks

Fans of the still-Fab Four can take one of three Beatles walks (London Walks has two that run 5 days/week; Big Bus includes a daily walk with their bus tour; both listed earlier). For more on Beatles sights, see page 121.

Jack the Ripper Walks

Each walking tour company seems to make most of its money with "haunted" and Jack the Ripper tours. Many guides are historians and would rather not lead these lightweight tours—but, in tourism as in journalism, "if it bleeds, it leads" (which is why the juvenile London Dungeon is one of the city's busiest sights).

Two reliably good two-hour tours start every night at the Tower Hill Tube station exit. **London Walks'** leave nightly at 19:30 (£9, pay at the start, tel. 020/7624-3978, recorded info tel. 020/7624-9255, www.jacktheripperwalk.com). **Ripping Yarns,** which leaves earlier, is guided by off-duty Yeoman Warders—the Tower of London "Beefeaters" (£7, pay at end, nightly at 18:45, no tours between Christmas and New Year, mobile 07813-559-301, www.jack-the-ripper-tours.com). After taking both, I found the London Walks tour more entertaining, informative, and with a better route (along quieter, once-hooker-friendly lanes, with less traffic), starting at Tower Hill and ending at Liverpool Street Station rather than returning to Tower Hill. Groups can be huge for both, but there's always room—just show up.

Private Walks with Local Guides

Standard rates for London's registered Blue Badge guides are about £150-165 for four hours and £250 or more for nine hours (tel. 020/7611-2545, www.guidelondon.org.uk or www.britainsbest guides.org). I know and like four fine local guides: **Sean Kelleher** (tel. 020/8673-1624, mobile 07764-612-770, seankelleher@bt internet.com), **Britt Lonsdale** (£230/half-day, £330/day, great with families, generous with pre-trip advice, tel. 020/7386-9907, mobile 07813-278-077, brittl@btinternet.com), and two others who work in London when they're not on the road leading my Britain tours, **Tom Hooper** (mobile 07986-048-047, tomh@ricksteves .net) and **Gillian Chadwick** (mobile 07889-976-598, gillychad @hotmail.co.uk).

Driver-Guides

These two guides have cars or a minibus (particularly helpful for travelers with limited mobility): **Robina Brown** (£330/half-day, £475/day, £660 outside London, £40 more for groups of 4-6 people, also does overnight tours farther afield, tel. 020/7228-2238, www.driverguidetours.com, robina@driverguidetours.com) and **Janine Barton** (£350/half-day, £470/day within London, £550 outside London, tel. 020/7402-4600, http://seeitinstyle.synthasite .com, jbsiis@aol.com).

London Duck Tours

A bright-yellow amphibious WWII-vintage vehicle (the model that landed troops on Normandy's beaches on D-Day) takes a gang of 30 tourists past some famous sights on land Big Ben, Trafalgar Square, Piccadilly Circus—then splashes into the Thames for a cruise. All in all, it's good fun at a rather steep price. The live guide works hard, and it's kid-friendly to the point of goofiness. Beware: These book up in advance (£21, April-Sept daily, first tour 9:30 or 10:00, last tour usually 18:00, shorter hours Oct-March, 1-4/hour, 1.25 hours—45 minutes on land and 30 minutes in the river, £3 booking fee by phone or online, departs from Chicheley Street—you'll see the big, ugly vehicle parked 100 yards behind the London Eye, Tube: Waterloo or Westminster, tel. 020/7928-3132, www.londonducktours.co.uk).

LONDON

Bike Tours

London, like Paris, is committed to creating more bike paths, and many of its best sights can be laced together with a pleasant pedal through its parks. A bike tour is a fun way to see the sights and enjoy the city on two wheels.

London Bicycle Tour Company

Three tours covering London are offered daily from their base at Gabriel's Wharf on the South Bank of the Thames. Sunday is the best, as there is less car traffic (**Central Tour**—£19, daily at 10:30, 6 miles, 2.5 hours, includes Westminster, Covent Garden, and St. Paul's; **West End Tour**—£19, April-Oct daily at 14:30, Nov-March daily at 12:00 as long as at least 4 people show up, 7 miles, 2.5 hours, includes Westminster, Buckingham Palace, Hyde Park, Soho, and Covent Garden; **East Tour**—£22, April-Oct Sat-Sun at 14:00, Nov-March only on Sat at 12:00, 9 miles, 3.5 hours, includes south side of the river to Tower Bridge, then The City to the East End; book ahead for off-season tours). They also rent bikes (£3.50/ hour, £20/day; office open daily April-Oct 9:30-18:00, Nov-March 10:00-16:00, west of Blackfriars Bridge on the South Bank, 1a Gabriel's Wharf, tel. 020/3318-3088, www.londonbicycle.com).

Fat Tire Bike Tours

Daily bike tours cover the highlights of downtown London, on two different itineraries (£2 discount with this book): **Royal London** (£20, daily March-Nov at 11:00, mid-May-mid-Sept also at 15:30, 7 miles, 4 hours, meet at Queensway Tube station; includes Parliament, Buckingham Palace, Hyde Park, and Trafalgar Square) and **River Thames** (£28, March-Nov Thu-Sat at 10:30, nearly daily in summer, 5 hours, meet at Waterloo Tube station—exit 2; includes London Eye, St. Paul's, Tower of London, Trafalgar Square, Covent Garden, and boat trip on the Thames). The spiel is light and irreverent rather than scholarly, but the price is right. Reservations are easy online, and required for River Thames tours and kids' bikes (off-season tours can be arranged, mobile 078-8233-8779, www.fattirebiketourslondon .com). Confirm the schedule online or by phone.

Weekend Tour Packages for Students

Andy Steves (Rick's son) runs **Weekend Student Adventures,** offering experiential and active three-day weekend tours from €199 designed for American students studying abroad (see www .wsaeurope.com for details on tours of London and other great European cities).

▲▲Cruises

London offers many made-for-tourist cruises, most on slow-moving, open-top boats accompanied by entertaining commentary about passing sights. Several com-panies offer essentially the same trip. Generally speaking, you can either do a **short city-center cruise** by riding a boat 30 minutes from Westminster Pier to Tower Pier (particularly handy if you're interested in visiting the Tower of London anyway), or take a **longer cruise** that includes a peek at the

East End, riding from Westminster all the way to Greenwich (save time by taking the Tube back).

Each company runs cruises daily, about twice hourly, from morning until dark; many reduce frequency off-season. Boats come and go from various docks in the city center (see sidebar). The most popular places to embark are Westminster Pier (at the base of Westminster Bridge across the street from Big Ben) and Waterloo Pier (at the London Eye, across the river).

A one-way trip within the city center costs about £10; going all the way to Greenwich costs about £2 more. Most companies charge around £3 more for a round-trip ticket, and others sell hop-on, hop-off day tickets (around £19). But I'd rather just savor one cruise, then zip home by Tube—making these return tickets not usually worthwhile.

You can buy tickets at kiosks on the docks. A Travelcard can snare you a 33 percent discount on most cruises (just show the card when you pay for the cruise); the pay-as-you-go Oyster card only nets you a discount on Thames Clippers. Because companies vary in the discounts they offer, always ask. Children and seniors gen-erally get discounts. You can purchase drinks and scant, overpriced snacks on board. Clever budget travelers pack a picnic and munch

Thames Boat Piers

While Westminster Pier is the most popular, it's not the only dock in town. Consider all the options (listed from west to east, as the Thames flows—see the color maps in the front of this book):

Millbank Pier (North Bank), at the Tate Britain Museum, is used primarily by the Tate Boat service (express connection to Tate Modern at Bankside Pier).

Westminster Pier (North Bank), near the base of Big Ben, offers round-trip sightseeing cruises and lots of departures in both directions (though the Thames Clippers boats don't stop here). Nearby sights include Parliament and Westminster Abbey.

Waterloo Pier (a.k.a. **London Eye Pier,** South Bank), right at the base of the London Eye, is a good, less-crowded alternative to Westminster, with many of the same cruise options (Waterloo Station is nearby).

Embankment Pier (North Bank) is near Covent Garden, Trafalgar Square, and Cleopatra's Needle (the obelisk on the Thames). This pier is used mostly for special boat trips (such as some RIB—rigid inflatable boat—trips, and lunch and dinner cruises).

Festival Pier (South Bank) is next to the Royal Festival Hall, just downstream from the London Eye.

Blackfriars Pier (North Bank) is in The City, not far from St. Paul's.

Bankside Pier (South Bank) is directly in front of the Tate Modern and Shakespeare's Globe.

London Bridge Pier (a.k.a. **London Bridge City Pier,** South Bank) is near the HMS *Belfast*.

Tower Pier (North Bank) is at the Tower of London, at the east edge of The City and near the East End.

St. Katharine's Pier (North Bank) is just downstream from the Tower of London.

Canary Wharf Pier (North Bank) is at the Docklands, London's new "downtown."

In outer London, you might also use the piers at **Greenwich, Kew Gardens,** and **Hampton Court.**

while they cruise.

The three dominant companies are **City Cruises** (handy 30-minute cruise from Westminster Pier to Tower Pier; www.city cruises.com), **Thames River Services** (fewer stops, classic boats, friendlier and more old-fashioned feel; www.thamesriverservices .co.uk), and **Circular Cruise** (full cruise takes about an hour, operated by Crown River Services, www.crownriver.com). I'd skip the **London Eye**'s River Cruise from Waterloo Pier—it's about the same price as Circular Cruise, but 20 minutes shorter. The speedy

Thames Clippers (described later) are designed more for no-non-sense transport than lazy sightseeing.

For details—including prices, schedules, and exactly which piers each company uses—check their websites or look for ticket kiosks at the docks. If you'd like to compare all of your options in one spot, head to Westminster Pier, which has a row of kiosks for all of the big outfits.

Cruising Downstream, to Greenwich: Both **City Cruises** and **Thames River Services** head from Westminster Pier to Greenwich. The cruises are usually narrated by the captain, with most commentary given on the way to Greenwich. The companies' prices are the same, though their itineraries are slightly different (Thames River Services makes only one stop en route and takes just an hour, while City Cruises makes two stops and adds about 10 minutes). The **Thames Clippers** boats, described later, are cheaper and faster (about 45 minutes to Greenwich), but have no commentary and no seating up top. To maximize both efficiency and sightseeing, I'd take a narrated cruise to Greenwich one way, and go the other way on the DLR (Docklands Light Railway), with a stop in the Docklands (Canary Wharf station).

Cruising Upstream, to Kew Gardens and Hampton Court Palace: Boats operated by the **Westminster Passenger Services Association** leave for Kew Gardens from Westminster Pier (£12 one-way, £18 round-trip, cash only, 2-4/day, 1.5 hours, about half the trip is narrated, www.wpsa.co.uk). Most boats continue on to Hampton Court Palace for an additional £3 (and another 1.5 hours). Because of the river current, you can save 30 minutes cruising from Hampton Court back into town (depends on the tide—ask before you commit to the boat). Romantic as these rides sound, it can be a long trip...especially upstream.

Commuting by Clipper

Thames Clippers, which uses fast, sleek, 220-seat catamarans, is designed for commuters rather than sightseers. Think of the boats as express buses on the river—they zip through London every 20-30 minutes, stopping at most of the major docks en route (including Canary Wharf/Docklands and Greenwich). They're fast: roughly 20 minutes from Embankment to Tower, 10 more minutes to Docklands, and 10 more minutes to Greenwich. However, the boats are less pleasant for joyriding than the cruises described earlier, with no commentary and no open deck up top (the only outside access is on a crowded deck at the exhaust-choked back of the boat, where you're jostling for space to take photos). Any one-way ride costs £6.50, and a River Roamer all-day ticket costs £15 (discounts with Travelcard and Oyster card, www.thamesclippers.com).

Thames Clippers also offers two express trips. The **Tate Boat** ferry service, which directly connects the Tate Britain (Millbank Pier) and the Tate Modern (Bankside Pier), is made for art lovers (£5.50 one-way, covered by River Roamer day ticket; buy ticket at gallery desk or on board; for frequency and times, see the Tate Britain and Tate Modern listings, later, or www.tate.org.uk/visit /tate-boat). The **O2 Express** runs only on nights when there are events at the O2 arena (departs from Waterloo Pier).

Self-Guided Walk

Westminster Walk

Just about every visitor to London strolls along historic Whitehall from Big Ben to Trafalgar Square. This walk gives meaning to that touristy ramble (most of the sights you'll see are described in more detail later). Under London's modern traffic and big-city bustle lie 2,000 fascinating years of history. You'll get a whirlwind tour as well as a practical orientation to London. (You can download a free, extended audio version of this walk to your mobile device; see page 54.)

Start halfway across ❶ **Westminster Bridge** for that "Wow, I'm really in London!" feeling. Get a close-up view of the **Houses of Parliament** and **Big Ben** (floodlit at night). Downstream you'll see the **London Eye.** Down the stairs to Westminster Pier are boats to the Tower of London and Greenwich (downstream) or Kew Gardens (upstream).

En route to Parliament Square, you'll pass a ❷ **statue of Boadicea**, the Celtic queen defeated by Roman invaders in A.D. 60.

For fun, call home from near Big Ben at about three minutes before the hour to let your loved one hear the bell ring. You'll find four red phone booths lining the north side of ❸ **Parliament Square** along Great George Street—also great for a phone-box-and-Big-Ben photo op.

Wave hello to Winston Churchill and Nelson Mandela in Parliament Square. To Churchill's right is **Westminster Abbey**, with its two stubby, elegant towers. The white building (flying the Union Jack) at the far end of the square houses Britain's **Supreme Court**.

Head north up Parliament Street, which turns into ❹ **Whitehall**, and walk toward Trafalgar Square. You'll see the thought-provoking ❺ **Cenotaph** in the middle of the boulevard, reminding passersby of the many Brits who died in the last century's world wars. To visit the **Churchill War Rooms**, take a left before the Cenotaph, on King Charles Street.

Continuing on Whitehall, stop at the barricaded and guarded

Westminster Walk

LONDON

❶ Westminster Bridge
❷ Statue of Boadicea
❸ Parliament Square
❹ Start of Whitehall
❺ Cenotaph
❻ #10 Downing Street & Ministry of Defence
❼ Banqueting House
❽ Horse Guards
❾ Trafalgar Square

❻ **#10 Downing Street** to see the British "White House," home of the prime minister. Break the bobby's boredom and ask him a question. The huge building across Whitehall from Downing Street is the **Ministry of Defence** (MOD), the "British Pentagon."

Nearing Trafalgar Square, look for the 17th-century ❼ **Banqueting House** across the street and the ❽ **Horse Guards** behind the gated fence.

The column topped by Lord Nelson marks ❾ **Trafalgar Square**. The stately domed building on the far side of the square is the **National Gallery**, which has a classy café in the Sainsbury wing. To the right of the National Gallery is **St. Martin-in-the-Fields Church** and its Café in the Crypt.

To get to Piccadilly from Trafalgar Square, walk up Cockspur Street to Haymarket, then take a short left on Coventry Street to colorful **Piccadilly Circus** (see map on page 106).

Near Piccadilly, you'll find a number of theaters. **Leicester Square** (with its half-price "tkts" booth for plays—see page 163) thrives just a few blocks away. Walk through seedy **Soho** (north of Shaftesbury Avenue) for its fun pubs. From Piccadilly or Oxford Circus, you can take a taxi, bus, or the Tube home.

Sights in Central London

Westminster

These sights are listed roughly in geographical order from Westminster Abbey to Trafalgar Square, and are linked in my self-guided Westminster Walk, above.

▲▲▲Westminster Abbey

The greatest church in the English-speaking world, Westminster Abbey is where the nation's royalty has been wedded, crowned, and buried since 1066. Indeed, the histories of Westminster Abbey and England are almost the same. A thousand years of English history—3,000 tombs, the remains of 29 kings and queens, and hundreds of memorials to poets, politicians, scientists, and warriors—lie within its stained-glass splendor and under its stone slabs.

Cost and Hours: £18, £36 family ticket (covers 2 adults and 1 child), cash or credit cards accepted (line up in the correct queue to pay), ticket includes audioguide and entry to cloisters and Abbey Museum; abbey—Mon-Fri 9:30-16:30, Wed until 19:00 (main

LONDON

church only), Sat 9:30-14:30, last entry one hour before closing, closed Sun to sightseers but open for services; museum—daily 10:30-16:00; cloisters—daily 8:00-18:00; no photos, café in cellar, Tube: Westminster or St. James's Park, tel. 020/7222-5152, www.westminster-abbey.org. It's free to enter just the cloisters and Abbey Museum (through Dean's Yard, around the right side as you face the main entrance), but if it's too crowded inside, the marshal at the cloister entrance may not let you in.

When to Go: The place is most crowded every day at mid-morning and all day Saturdays and Mondays. Visit early, during lunch, or late to avoid tourist hordes. Weekdays after 14:30 are less congested; come after that time and stay for the 17:00 evensong. The main entrance, on the Parliament Square side, often has a sizable line. Of the two queues (cash or credit) at the admissions desk, the cash line is probably moving faster.

Music and Services: Mon-Fri at 7:30 (prayer), 8:00 (communion), 12:30 (communion), 17:00 evensong (except on Wed, when the evening service is generally spoken—not sung); Sat at 8:00 (communion), 9:00 (prayer), 15:00 (evensong; May-Aug it's at 17:00); Sun services generally come with more music: at 8:00 (communion), 10:00 (sung Matins), 11:15 (sung Eucharist), 15:00 (evensong), 18:30 (evening service). For more on evensong, see page 169. Services are free to anyone, though visitors who haven't paid church admission aren't allowed to linger afterward. Free organ recitals are usually held Sun at 17:45 (30 minutes). For a schedule of services or recitals on a particular day, look for posted signs with schedules or check the Abbey's website.

Tours: Entertaining guided tours of the Abbey (£3, 1.5 hours, schedule posted outside and inside entry) are offered up to 5/day in summer, 4/day in winter.

❷ Self-Guided Tour: You'll have no choice but to follow the steady flow of tourists through the church, following the route laid out for the audioguide. My tour covers the Abbey's top stops.

• *Walk straight in through the north transept. Follow the crowd flow to the right and enter the spacious...*

Nave: Look down the long and narrow center aisle of the church. Lined with the praying hands of the Gothic arches, glowing with light from the stained glass, it's clear that this is more than a museum. With saints in stained glass, heroes in carved stone, and the bodies of England's greatest citizens under the floor stones, Westminster Abbey is the religious heart of England.

The king who built the Abbey was Edward the Confessor. Find him in the stained glass windows on the left side of the nave (as you face the altar). He's in the third bay from the end (marked *S: Edwardus rex...*), with his crown, scepter, and ring. The Abbey's 10-story nave is the tallest in England.

Westminster Abbey Tour

1. Nave
2. Choir
3. Coronation Spot
4. Shrine of Edward the Confessor
5. Tomb of Elizabeth I & Mary I
6. Chapel of King Henry VII
7. Royal Air Force Chapel
8. Tomb of Mary, Queen of Scots
9. Poets' Corner
10. Cloisters & Abbey Museum
11. Coronation Chair

On the floor near the west entrance of the Abbey is the flower-lined Tomb of the Unknown Warrior, one ordinary WWI soldier buried in soil from France with lettering made from melted-down weapons from that war. Contemplate the million-man army from the British Empire, and all those who gave their lives. Their memory is so revered that, when Kate Middleton walked up the aisle on her wedding day, by tradition she had to step around the tomb (and her wedding bouquet was later placed atop this tomb, also in accordance with tradition).

• *Walk up the nave toward the altar. This is the same route every future monarch walks on the way to being crowned. Midway up the nave, you pass through the colorful screen of an enclosure known as...*

The Choir: These elaborately carved-wood and gilded seats are where monks once chanted their services in the "quire"—as it's known in British church-speak. Today, it's where the Abbey boys' choir sings the evensong. The "high" (main) altar, which usually has a cross and candlesticks atop it, sits on the platform up the five stairs in front of you.

• *It's on this platform—up the five steps—that the monarch is crowned.*

The Coronation Spot: The area immediately before the high altar is where every English coronation since 1066 has taken place. Royalty are also given funerals here. Princess Diana's coffin was carried to this spot for her funeral service in 1997. The "Queen Mum" (mother of Elizabeth II) had her funeral here in 2002. This is also where most of the last century's royal weddings have taken place, including the unions of Queen Elizabeth II and Prince Philip (1947), Prince Andrew and Sarah Ferguson (1986), and Prince William and Kate Middleton (2011).

• *Veer left and follow the crowd. Pause at the wooden staircase on your right.*

Shrine of Edward the Confessor: Step back and peek over the dark coffin of Edward I to see the tippy-top of the green-and-gold wedding-cake tomb of King Edward the Confessor—the man who built Westminster Abbey. God had told pious Edward to visit St. Peter's Basilica in Rome. But with the Normans thinking conquest, it was too dangerous for him to leave England. Instead, he built this grand church and dedicated it to St. Peter. It was finished just in time to bury Edward and to crown his foreign successor, William the Conqueror, in 1066. After Edward's death, people prayed at his tomb, and, after getting good results, Pope Alexander III canonized him. This elevated, central tomb—which lost some of its luster when Henry VIII melted down the gold coffin-case—is surrounded by the tombs of eight kings and queens.

• *At the top of the stone staircase, veer left into the private burial chapel of Queen Elizabeth I.*

Tomb of Queens Elizabeth I and Mary I: Although there's only one effigy on the tomb (Elizabeth's), there are actually two queens buried beneath it, both daughters of Henry VIII (by different mothers). Bloody Mary—meek, pious, sickly, and Catholic—enforced Catholicism during her short reign (1553-1558) by burning "heretics" at the stake.

Elizabeth—strong, clever, and Protestant—steered England on an Anglican course. She holds a royal orb symbolizing that she's queen of the whole globe. When 26-year-old Elizabeth was crowned in the Abbey, her right to rule was questioned (especially by her Catholic subjects) because she was considered the bastard seed of Henry VIII's unsanctioned marriage to Anne Boleyn. But Elizabeth's long reign (1559-1603) was one of the greatest in English history, a time when England ruled the seas and Shakespeare explored human emotions. When she died, thousands turned out for her funeral in the Abbey. Elizabeth's face on the tomb, modeled after her death mask, is considered a very accurate take on this hook-nosed, imperious "Virgin Queen."

• *Continue into the ornate, flag-draped room up a few more stairs, directly behind the main altar.*

Chapel of King Henry VII (a.k.a. the Lady Chapel): The light from the stained-glass windows; the colorful banners overhead; and the elaborate tracery in stone, wood, and glass give this room the festive air of a medieval tournament. The prestigious Knights of the Bath meet here, under the magnificent ceiling studded with gold pendants. The ceiling—of carved stone, not plaster (1519)—is the finest English Perpendicular Gothic and fan vaulting you'll see (unless you're going to King's College Chapel in Cambridge). The ceiling was sculpted on the floor in pieces, then jigsaw-puzzled into place. It capped the Gothic period and signaled the vitality of the coming Renaissance.

• *Go to the far end of the chapel and stand at the banister in front of the modern set of stained-glass windows.*

Royal Air Force Chapel: Saints in robes and halos mingle with pilots in parachutes and bomber jackets. This tribute to WWII flyers is for those who earned their angel wings in the Battle of Britain (July-Oct 1940). A bit of bomb damage has been preserved—look for the little glassed-over hole in the wall below the windows in the lower left-hand corner.

• *Exit the Chapel of Henry VII. Turn left into a side chapel with the tomb (the central one of three in the chapel).*

Tomb of Mary, Queen of Scots: The beautiful, French-educated queen (1542-1587) was held under house arrest for 19 years by Queen Elizabeth I, who considered her a threat to her sovereignty. Elizabeth got wind of an assassination plot, suspected Mary was behind it, and had her first cousin (once removed) beheaded. When Elizabeth—who was called the "Virgin Queen"—died heirless, Mary's son, James VI, King of Scots, also became King James I of England and Ireland. James buried his mum here (with her head sewn back on) in the Abbey's most sumptuous tomb.

• *Exit Mary's chapel. Continue on, until you emerge in the south transept. You're in...*

Poets' Corner: England's greatest artistic contributions are in the written word. Here the masters of arguably the world's most complex and expressive language are remembered: Geoffrey Chaucer *(Canterbury Tales)*, Lord Byron, Dylan Thomas, W. H. Auden, Lewis Carroll *(Alice's Adventures in Wonderland)*, T. S. Eliot *(The Waste Land)*, Alfred, Lord Tennyson, Robert Browning, and Charles

LONDON

Dickens. Many writers are honored with plaques and monuments; relatively few are actually buried here. Shakespeare is commemorated by a fine statue that stands near the end of the transept, overlooking the others.

• *Exit the church (temporarily) at the south door, which leads to the...*

Cloisters and Abbey Museum: The buildings that adjoin the church housed the monks. Cloistered courtyards gave them a place to meditate on God's creations.

The small Abbey Museum, formerly the monks' lounge, is worth a peek for its fascinating and well-described exhibits. Look into the impressively realistic eyes of Elizabeth I, Charles II, Admiral Nelson, and a dozen others, part of a compelling series of wax-and-wood statues that, for three centuries, graced coffins during funeral processions. The once-exquisite, now-fragmented Westminster Retable, which decorated the high altar in 1270, is the oldest surviving altarpiece in England.

• *Go back into the church for the last stop.*

Coronation Chair: A gold-painted oak chair waits here under a regal canopy for the next coronation. For every English coronation since 1308 (except two), it's been moved to its spot before the high altar to receive the royal buttocks. The chair's legs rest on lions, England's symbol.

▲▲Houses of Parliament (Palace of Westminster)

This Neo-Gothic icon of London, the royal residence from 1042 to 1547, is now the meeting place of the legislative branch of government. Like the US Capitol in Washington, DC, the complex is open to visitors. You can view parliamentary sessions in either the bickering House of Commons or the sleepy House of Lords. Or you can simply wander on your own (through a few closely monitored rooms) to appreciate the historic building itself.

The Palace of Westminster has been the center of political power in England for nearly a thousand years. In 1834, a horrendous fire gutted the Palace. It was rebuilt in a retro style that recalled England's medieval Christian roots—pointed arches, stained-glass windows, spires, and saint-like statues. At the same time, Britain was also retooling its government. Democracy was on the rise, the queen became a constitutional monarch, and Parliament emerged as the nation's ruling body. The Palace of Westminster became a symbol—a kind of cathedral—of democracy. A visit here gives both UK residents and foreign tourists alike a chance to tour a piece of living history and see the British government inaction.

Cost and Hours: Free, open to visitors whenever Parliament is in session—generally Oct-July, Mon-Thu. If you see a light on above Big Ben's clock and a flag atop Victoria Tower (at the south end of the building), then Parliament is in session.

The House of Commons is usually in session Oct-July Mon 14:30-22:00, Tue-Wed 11:30-19:00, Thu 9:30-17:30; House of Lords is typically in session Oct-July Mon-Tue 14:30-22:00, Wed 15:00-22:00, Thu 11:00-19:00; last entry usually around 20:00, both houses closed Fri-Sun except for Sat tours. During the Aug-Sept recess, the only way to visit is on a guided tour (see below). Tube: Westminster, tel. 020/7219-4272 or 020/7219-3107, see www.parliament.uk for schedule, or visit www.parliamentlive.tv for a preview.

Dealing with Lines: Expect lines—it may take a while to get through security, plus another 20-60 minutes once inside to be admitted to the house chambers. Lines are longest at the start of each day's session (when the most fiery debate often occurs), and especially bad on Wednesdays, when the prime minister normally attends. The later in the day you enter, the less crowded (and less exciting) it is. Visiting after 18:00 is risky, as sessions tend to end well before their official closing time, and visitors aren't allowed in after the politicians call it a day.

If you only visit one of the bicameral legislative bodies, I'd choose the House of Lords. Though less important politically, the lords meet in a more ornate room, and the waiting time is shorter (likely less than 30 minutes). The House of Commons is where major policy is made, but the room itself is sparse, and waiting times are longer (30-60 minutes or more). If you just want to see the grand halls of this majestic building (without visiting either of the legislative chambers), you won't have any waiting once you're through security.

Tours: When Parliament is in recess during much of August and September, you can get a behind-the-scenes peek at the royal chambers of both houses by taking a tour (£15, 1.25 hours, generally Mon-Sat, times vary, so confirm in advance; book ahead by calling 0844-847-1672 or through www.ticketmaster.co.uk). The same tours are offered Saturdays year-round 9:15-16:30.

◑ Self-Guided Tour: Enter midway along the west side of the building (across the street from Westminster Abbey), where

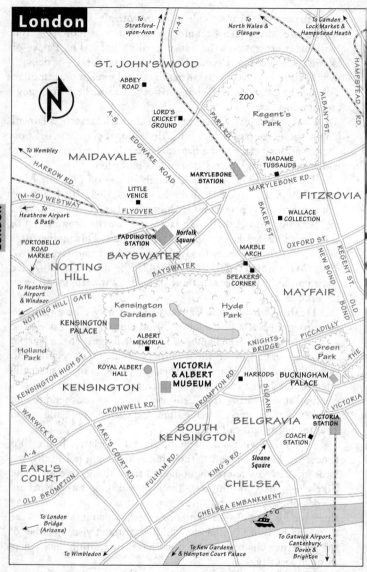

London

To Stratford-upon-Avon

To North Wales & Glasgow

To Camden Lock Market & Hampstead Heath

ST. JOHN'S WOOD

ABBEY ROAD

ZOO

Regent's Park

LORD'S CRICKET GROUND

To Wembley

MAIDAVALE

MADAME TUSSAUDS

MARYLEBONE STATION

MARYLEBONE RD.

FITZROVIA

LITTLE VENICE

(M-40) WESTWAY

To Heathrow Airport & Bath

FLYOVER

WALLACE COLLECTION

PORTOBELLO ROAD MARKET

PADDINGTON STATION

Norfolk Square

OXFORD ST.

MARBLE ARCH

BAYSWATER

NOTTING HILL

BAYSWATER

SPEAKERS CORNER

To Heathrow Airport & Windsor

NOTTING HILL GATE

Kensington Gardens

Hyde Park

MAYFAIR

KENSINGTON PALACE

ALBERT MEMORIAL

KNIGHTS-BRIDGE

PICCADILLY

Green Park

Holland Park

ROYAL ALBERT HALL

VICTORIA & ALBERT MUSEUM

HARRODS

BUCKINGHAM PALACE

KENSINGTON

CROMWELL RD.

BROMPTON RD.

VICTORIA

WARWICK RD.

SOUTH KENSINGTON

BELGRAVIA

VICTORIA STATION

EARL'S COURT

FULHAM RD.

KING'S RD.

COACH STATION

Sloane Square

To London Bridge (Arizona)

CHELSEA

OLD BROMPTON

CHELSEA EMBANKMENT

To Wimbledon

To Kew Gardens & Hampton Court Palace

To Gatwick Airport, Canterbury, Dover & Brighton

LONDON

there's a tourist ramp leading to the visitor entrance. As you enter, you'll be asked if you want to visit the House of Commons or the House of Lords. I choose "Lords" (because the line is shorter), but it really doesn't matter. Once inside, you'll be able to do whatever you please: switch houses, see them both, or see neither and just browse through the other public spaces. If you have questions, the attendants are extremely helpful.

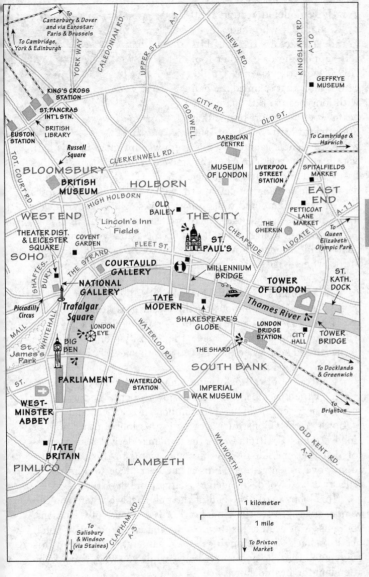

At the airport-style security, you're photographed and given a (Lords or Commons) badge. Continue past the Jubilee Café (which has live video feeds of Parliament in session), pick up helpful brochures at the information desk, and take in the cavernous...

Westminster Hall: This vast hall—covering 16,000 square feet—survived the 1834 fire, and is one of the oldest and most important buildings in England. Begun in 1097, the hall was greatly remodeled around 1380 by Richard II, who made it the grandest space in Europe. His self-supporting oak-timber roof (1397) wowed everyone. Unlike earlier roofs that spanned the hall with long beams, this "hammer-beam" roof uses short beams that jut horizontally out from the

walls. England's vaunted legal system was invented in this hall, as this was the major court of the land for 700 years. King Charles I was tried and sentenced to death here. Guy Fawkes was condemned for plotting to blow up the Halls of Parliament in 1605. (He's best remembered today for the sly-smiling "Guy Fawkes mask" that has become the symbol of 21st-century anarchists.)

Walking through the hall and up the stairs, you'll enter the busy world of today's government. You soon reach St. Stephen's Hall, where visitors wait to enter the House of Commons Chamber.

St. Stephen's Hall: This long, beautifully lit room was the original House of Commons for three centuries (from 1550 until the fire of 1834). MPs sat in church pews on either side of the hall—the ruling party on one side, the opposition on the other—a format they'd keep when they moved into the new chambers.

Next, you reach the...

Central Lobby: This ornate, octagonal, high-vaulted room is often called the "heart of British government," because it sits midway between the House of Commons (to the left) and House of Lords (right). Constituents come to this lobby to petition, or "lobby," their MPs (from which the term may derive). Video monitors list the schedule of meetings and events in this vast 1,100-room governmental hive. This is the best place to admire the Palace's carved wood, chandeliers, statues, and floor tiles.

This lobby marks the end of the public space where you can wander freely. To see the House of Lords or House of Commons, you must wait in line. Just before entering either chamber, you'll need to check your belongings—bag, camera, phone, even this guidebook. Read up on the info below while you wait, and ask the attendant for any brochures.

When you're done visiting the chambers, you'll backtrack through the same halls, where you can sightsee leisurely on your way back out into a well-governed London.

House of Lords: When you're called, you'll walk to the Lords Chamber by way of the long Peers' Corridor. Paintings on the corridor walls depict the anti-authoritarian spirit brewing under the reign of Charles I. When you reach the House of Lords Chamber, you watch the proceedings from an upper-level gallery.

The House of Lords consists of 750 members, called "Peers." They are not elected by popular vote. Some are nobles who've inherited the position, others are appointed by the Queen. These days, their role is largely advisory. They can propose, revise, and filibuster laws, but they have no real power to pass laws on their own. On any typical day, only a handful of the 750 lords actually show up to debate.

The Lords Chamber is church-like and impressive, with stained glass and intricately carved walls. Once you're seated in the galleries, your gaze will likely go to the Queen's gilded throne at the far end of the room. She's the only one who may sit there, and only once a year, when she gives a speech to open Parliament.

The benches where the lords sit are always upholstered red. (The House of Commons is green.) The ruling party sits on one side, the opposition on the other, and unaffiliated "crossbenchers" in between. In the center of the room sits the "Woolsack"—a cushion stuffed with wool. Here the Lord Speaker presides, with his/her ceremonial mace placed behind the backrest.

House of Commons: On the way to the House of Commons Chamber, you first pass through the long Commons Corridor, which spills into the Members' Lobby. In the lobby, MPs check their message box with its state-of-the-art 1960s technology; they enter the chamber through a stone archway that still bears bomb damage from the Nazi Blitz; and as they enter, many rub the Churchill statue's golden toe for good luck.

The Commons Chamber may be much less grandiose than the Lords Chamber, but this is where the sausage gets made. The House of Commons is as powerful as the lords, prime minister, and Queen combined. It was destroyed in the Blitz, and Churchill rebuilt the surprisingly small chamber with the same cube-shaped floor plan. Of today's 650-plus MPs, only 450 can sit—the rest have to stand at the ends.

As in the House of Lords, the ruling party sits on the left, opposition on the right. Keep an eye out for two red lines on the floor, which cannot be crossed when debating the other side. (They're supposedly two sword-lengths apart, to prevent a literal clashing of swords.) Between the benches is the canopied Speaker's Chair, for the chairman who keeps order and chooses who can speak next. The clerks sit at a central table that holds the ceremonial mace, a symbol of the power given Parliament by the monarch. Also on the table are the two "dispatch boxes"—old wooden chests that serve as lecterns, one for each side.

The Queen is not allowed in the Commons Chamber. When the prime minister visits, he speaks from one of the boxes. His ministers (or cabinet) join him on the front bench, while lesser

London at a Glance

▲▲▲**Westminster Abbey** Britain's finest church and the site of royal coronations and burials since 1066. **Hours:** Mon-Fri 9:30-16:30, Wed until 19:00, Sat 9:30-14:30, closed Sun to sightseers except for worship. See page 83 .

▲▲▲**Churchill War Rooms** Underground WWII headquarters of Churchill's war effort. **Hours:** Daily 9:30-18:00. See page 96 .

▲▲▲**National Gallery** Remarkable collection of European paintings (1250-1900), including Leonardo, Botticelli, Velázquez, Rembrandt, Turner, Van Gogh, and the Impressionists. **Hours:** Daily 10:00-18:00, Fri until 21:00. See page 99 .

▲▲▲**British Museum** The world's greatest collection of artifacts of Western civilization, including the Rosetta Stone and the Parthenon's Elgin Marbles. **Hours:** Daily 10:00-17:30, Fri until 20:30 (selected galleries only). See page 114.

▲▲▲**British Library** Impressive collection of the most important literary treasures of the Western world. **Hours:** Mon-Fri 9:30-18:00, Tue until 20:00, Sat 9:30-17:00, Sun 11:00-17:00. See page 118.

▲▲▲**St. Paul's Cathedral** The main cathedral of the Anglican Church, designed by Christopher Wren, with a climbable dome and daily evensong services. **Hours:** Mon-Sat 8:30-16:30, closed Sun except for worship. See page 123 .

▲▲▲**Tower of London** Historic castle, palace, and prison housing the crown jewels and a witty band of Beefeaters. **Hours:** March-Oct Tue-Sat 9:00-17:30, Sun-Mon 10:00-17:30; Nov-Feb Tue-Sat 9:00-16:30, Sun-Mon 10:00-16:30. See page 129 .

▲▲▲**Victoria and Albert Museum** The best collection of decorative arts anywhere. **Hours:** Daily 10:00-17:45, Fri until 22:00 (selected galleries only). See page 150 .

▲▲**Houses of Parliament** London's Neo-Gothic landmark, famous for Big Ben and occupied by the Houses of Lords and Commons. **Hours:** Generally Mon-Tue 14:30-22:00, Wed 11:30-22:00, Thu 9:30-19:00, closed Fri-Sun and most of Aug-Sept. Can visit on Sat via guided tour only. See page 88 .

▲▲**Trafalgar Square** London's heart, where Westminster, The City, and the West End meet. **Hours:** Always open. See page 98 .

▲▲**National Portrait Gallery** A *Who's Who* of British history, featuring portraits of this nation's most important historical fig-

LONDON

ures. **Hours:** Daily 10:00-18:00, Thu-Fri until 21:00, first and second floors open Mon at 11:00. See page 103 .

▲▲**Covent Garden** Vibrant people-watching zone with shops, cafés, street musicians, and an iron-and-glass arcade that once hosted a produce market. **Hours:** Always open. See page 108.

▲▲**Changing of the Guard at Buckingham Palace** Hour-long spectacle at Britain's royal residence. **Hours:** Generally May-July daily at 11:30, Aug-April every other day. See page 111.

▲▲**London Eye** Enormous observation wheel, dominating—and offering commanding views over—London's skyline. **Hours:** Daily July-Aug 10:00-21:30, April-June 10:00-21:00, Sept-March 10:00-20:30. See page 136.

▲▲**Imperial War Museum** Exhibits examining the military history of the bloody 20th century. **Hours:** Daily 10:00-18:00. See page 138.

▲▲**Tate Modern** Works by Monet, Matisse, Dalí, Picasso, and Warhol displayed in a converted powerhouse. **Hours:** Daily 10:00-18:00, Fri-Sat until 22:00. See page 141.

▲▲**Shakespeare's Globe** Timbered, thatched-roofed reconstruction of the Bard's original "wooden O." **Hours:** Theater complex, museum, and actor-led tours generally daily 9:00-17:00; in summer, morning theater tours only. Plays are also staged here. See page 142.

▲▲**Tate Britain** Collection of British painting from the 16th century through modern times, including works by William Blake, the Pre-Raphaelites, and J. M. W. Turner. **Hours:** Daily 10:00-18:00, select Fridays until 22:00. See page 147.

▲▲**Kensington Palace** Recently restored former home of British monarchs, with appealing exhibits on Queen Victoria, as well as William and Mary. **Hours:** Daily 10:00-18:00, until 17:00 Nov-Feb. See page 149.

▲▲**Natural History Museum** A Darwinian's delights, packed with stuffed creatures, engaging exhibits, and enthralled kids. **Hours:** Daily 10:00-17:50. See page 151.

▲**Courtauld Gallery** Fine collection of paintings filling one wing of the Somerset House, a grand 18th-century palace. **Hours:** Daily 10:00-18:00. See page 109.

MPs (the "backbenchers") sit behind. It's often a fiery spectacle, as the prime minister defends his policies, while the opposition grumbles and harrumphs in displeasure. It's not unheard-of for MPs to get out of line and be escorted out by the Serjeant at Arms. One furious MP even grabbed the Serjeant's hallowed mace and threw it to the ground. His career was over.

Nearby: Across the street from the Parliament building's St. Stephen's Gate, the **Jewel Tower** is a rare remnant of the old Palace of Westminster, used by kings until Henry VIII. The crude stone tower (1365-1366) was a guard tower in the palace wall, overlooking a moat. It contains a fine little exhibit on Parliament and the tower (£4, April-Oct daily 10:00-17:00; Nov-March Sat-Sun 10:00-16:00, closed Mon-Fri; tel. 020/7222-2219). Next to the tower (and free) is a quiet courtyard with picnic-friendly benches.

Big Ben, the 315-foot-high clock tower at the north end of the Palace of Westminster is named for its 13-ton bell, Ben. The light above the clock is lit when Parliament is in session. The face of the clock is huge—you can actually see the minute hand moving. For a good view of it, walk halfway over Westminster Bridge.

Other Sights in Westminster
▲▲▲Churchill War Rooms

This excellent sight offers a fascinating walk through the underground headquarters of the British government's fight against the Nazis in the darkest days of the Battle for Britain. It has two parts: the war rooms themselves, and a top-notch museum dedicated to the man who steered the war from here, Winston Churchill. For details on all the blood, sweat, toil, and tears, pick up the excellent, essential, and included audioguide at the entry, and dive in. Allow yourself 1-2 hours for this sight.

Cost and Hours: £17.50 (includes 10 percent optional donation), £5 guidebook, daily 9:30-18:00, last entry one hour before closing; on King Charles Street, 200 yards off Whitehall, follow the signs, Tube: Westminster, tel. 020/7930-6961, www.iwm.org .uk/churchill. The museum's gift shop is great for anyone nostalgic for the 1940s.

Cabinet War Rooms: The 27-room, heavily fortified nerve center of the British war effort was used from 1939 to 1945. Churchill's room, the map room, and other rooms are just as they were in 1945. As you follow the one-way route, be sure to take advantage of the audioguide, which explains each room and offers first-person accounts of wartime happenings here (it takes about 45 minutes, not counting the Churchill Museum). Be patient—it's well worth it. While the rooms are spartan, you'll see how British gentility survived even as the city was bombarded—posted signs informed those working underground what the weather was like outside, and a cheery notice reminded them to turn off the light switch to conserve electricity.

Churchill Museum: Don't bypass this museum, which occupies a large hall amid the war rooms. It dissects every aspect of the man behind the famous cigar, bowler hat, and V-for-victory sign. It's extremely well-presented and engaging, using artifacts, quotes, political cartoons, clear explanations, and high-tech interactive exhibits to bring the colorful statesman to life; this museum alone deserves an hour. You'll get a taste of Winston's wit, irascibility, work ethic, passion for painting, American ties, writing talents, and drinking habits. The exhibit shows Winston's warts as well: It questions whether his party-switching was just political opportunism, examines the basis for his opposition to Indian self-rule, and reveals him to be an intense taskmaster who worked 18-hour days and was brutal to his staffers (who deeply respected him nevertheless).

A long touch-the-screen timeline lets you zero in on events in his life from birth (November 30, 1874) to his first appointment as prime minister in 1940. Many of the items on display—such as a European map divvied up in permanent marker, which Churchill brought to England from the postwar Potsdam Conference—drive home the remarkable span of history this man lived through. Imagine: Churchill began his military career riding horses in the cavalry and ended it speaking out against the proliferation of nuclear armaments. It's all the more amazing considering that, in the 1930s, the man who would become my vote for greatest statesman of the 20th century was considered a washed-up loony ranting about the growing threat of fascism.

Eating: Get your rations at the Switch Room café (in the museum), or for a nearby pub lunch, try Westminster Arms (food served downstairs, on Storey's Gate, a couple of blocks south of the museum).

Horse Guards
The Horse Guards change daily at 11:00 (10:00 on Sun), and a colorful dismounting ceremony takes place daily at 16:00. The rest of the day, they just stand there—terrible for video cameras (on Whitehall, between Trafalgar Square

and #10 Downing Street, Tube: Westminster, www.changing-the-guard.com). Buckingham Palace pageantry is canceled when it rains, but the Horse Guards change regardless of the weather.

▲Banqueting House

England's first Renaissance building (1619-1622) is still standing. Designed by Inigo Jones, built by King James I, and decorated by his son Charles I, the Banqueting House came to symbolize the Stuart kings' "divine right" management style—the belief that God himself had anointed them to rule. The house is one of the few London landmarks spared by the 1698 fire and the only surviving part of the original Palace of Whitehall. Today it opens its doors to visitors, who enjoy a restful 20-minute audiovisual history, a 30-minute audioguide, and a look at the exquisite banqueting hall itself. As a tourist attraction, it's basically one big room, with sumptuous ceiling paintings by Peter Paul Rubens. At Charles I's request, these paintings drove home the doctrine of the legitimacy of the divine right of kings. Ironically, in 1649— divine right ignored—King Charles I was famously executed right here.

Cost and Hours: £5 (includes 10 percent optional donation), includes audioguide, daily 10:00-17:00, last entry at 16:30, may close for government functions—though it promises to stay open at least until 13:00 (call ahead for recorded information about closures), aristocratic WC, immediately across Whitehall from the Horse Guards, Tube: Westminster, tel. 020/3166-6154, www.hrp.org.uk.

▲▲Trafalgar Square

London's central square—at the intersection of Westminster, The City, and the West End—is the climax of most marches and demonstrations, and a thrilling place to simply hang out. A recent remodeling of the square has rerouted car traffic, helping reclaim the area for London's citizens. At the top of Trafalgar Square (north) sits the domed National Gallery with its grand staircase, and to the right, the steeple of St. Martin-in-the-

Fields, built in 1722, inspiring the steeple-over-the-entrance style of many town churches in New England. In the center of the square, Lord Horatio Nelson stands atop his 185-foot-tall fluted granite column, gazing out toward Trafalgar, where he lost his life but defeated the French fleet. Part of this 1842 memorial is made from his victims' melted-down cannons. He's surrounded

Trafalgar Square Area

COVENT GARDEN

LISLE ST.

GARRICK

KING ST.

CRANBOURN

NEW ROW

BEDFORD

Leicester Square

CHARING CROSS ROAD

ST. MARTINS LANE

Leicester Square

CHANDOS PL.

To Courtauld Gallery & The City

■ TKTS

IRVING

PANTON

WHITCOMB STREET

ORANGE ST.

THE CHANDOS PUB

THE HARP PUB

NATIONAL PORTRAIT GALLERY

WILLIAM IV ST.

CRYPT, CAFÉ & SHOP ENTRANCE

THE STRAND

To Piccadilly

NATIONAL GALLERY

ST. MARTIN-IN-THE-FIELDS

✚

DUNCANNON

To Embankment

SAINSBURY WING

GEORGE WASH.

SOUTH AFRICA HOUSE

Charing Cross

VILLIERS

HAYMARKET

FOURTH PLINTH

Trafalgar ⚓ Square

⊖ Charing Cross

CHARING CROSS STATION

PALL MALL

COCKSPUR ST.

NELSON'S COLUMN

CANADA HOUSE

CHARLES I

⊖ Charing Cross

To St. James's Palace

Charing Cross

SHERLOCK HOLMES PUB

NORTHUMBERLAND

ADMIRALTY ARCH

SITE OF OLD SCOTLAND YARD

WHITEHALL

To Buckingham Palace

THE MALL

OLD ADMIRALTY

GREAT SCOTLAND YARD

WHITEHALL PL.

Green Park

To Big Ben & Westminster

200 Meters

200 Yards

by spraying fountains, giant lions, hordes of people, and—until recently—even more pigeons. A former London mayor decided that London's "flying rats" were a public nuisance and evicted Trafalgar Square's venerable seed salesmen (Tube: Charing Cross).

▲▲▲National Gallery

Displaying Britain's top collection of European paintings from 1250 to 1900—including works by Leonardo, Botticelli, Velázquez, Rembrandt, Turner, Van Gogh, and the Impressionists. This is one of Europe's great galleries. You'll peruse 700 years of art—from gold-backed Madonnas to Cubist bathers.

Cost and Hours: Free, but suggested donation of £4, temporary (optional) exhibits extra, daily

MEDIEVAL & EARLY RENAISSANCE
❶ ANONYMOUS – The Wilton Diptych
❷ UCCELLO – Battle of San Romano
❸ VAN EYCK – The Arnolfini Portrait

ITALIAN RENAISSANCE
❹ LEONARDO – The Virgin of the Rocks
❺ BOTTICELLI – Venus and Mars
❻ CRIVELLI – The Annunciation, with Saint Emidius
❼ LEONARDO – Virgin and Child with St. Anne and St. John the Baptist

VENETIAN RENAISSANCE
❽ TITIAN – Bacchus and Ariadne
❾ TINTORETTO – The Origin of the Milky Way

HIGH RENAISSANCE
❿ MICHELANGELO – The Entombment
⓫ RAPHAEL – Pope Julius II
⓬ BRONZINO – An Allegory with Venus and Cupid
⓭ HOLBEIN – The Ambassadors

NORTHERN PROTESTANT ART
⓮ VERMEER – A Young Woman Standing at a Virginal
⓯ VAN HOOGSTRATEN – A Peepshow with Views of the Interior of a Dutch House
⓰ REMBRANDT – Belshazzar's Feast
⓱ REMBRANDT – Self-Portrait at the Age of 63

BAROQUE & FRENCH ROCOCO
⓲ RUBENS – The Judgment of Paris
⓳ VELÁZQUEZ – The Rokeby Venus
⓴ VAN DYCK – Equestrian Portrait of Charles I
㉑ CARAVAGGIO – The Supper at Emmaus
㉒ BOUCHER – Pan and Syrinx

BRITISH
㉓ CONSTABLE – The Hay Wain
㉔ TURNER – The Fighting Téméraire
㉕ DELAROCHE – The Execution of Lady Jane Grey

To Leicester Square (5 min. walk)

SAINSBURY WING

ENTRANCE ON LEVEL 0

SELF-GUIDED TOUR STARTS ON LEVEL 2

TOUR BEGINS

SAINSBURY ENTRANCE

10:00-18:00, Fri until 21:00, last entry to special exhibits 45 minutes before closing, no photos, on Trafalgar Square, Tube: Charing Cross or Leicester Square.

Information: Helpful £1 floor plan available from information desk; free one-hour overview tours leave from Sainsbury Wing info desk daily at 11:30 and 14:30, plus Fri at 19:00; excellent £3.50 audioguides—choose from one-hour highlights tour, several theme tours, or tour option that lets you dial up info on any painting in the

National Gallery

⊠ Elevator/Lift

30 Meters

30 Yards

ORANGE ST. ENTRANCE

21 22
20 18 23 17 14
19 16 24 25 15
26 27 28
17 15 29 30 31 20
16 18 19 21 32 33 22
14 SUNLEY ROOM 37 24
WOHL ROOM 10 11 13 CENTRAL HALL 39 38 36 35 34
LINK 9 12 23
8 9 5 SHOP 40
12 11 6 4 2 32 44 43 27 41
10 8 45 25
13 31 30 28 29 42
46 26

PORTICO ENTRANCE

GETTY ENTRANCE (LEVEL 0)

STAIRS DOWN TO NAT'L CAFÉ & **WC**

LONDON

Trafalgar Square ⚓ NELSON'S COLUMN

To Charing Cross ⊖ (2 min. walk) →

IMPRESSIONISM & BEYOND

㉖ MONET – Gare St. Lazare
㉗ MONET – The Water-Lily Pond
㉘ MANET – Corner of a Café-Concert
㉙ RENOIR – The Skiff

㉚ SEURAT – Bathers at Asnières
㉛ VAN GOGH – Sunflowers
㉜ CÉZANNE – Bathers

museum; ArtStart computer terminals help you study any artist, style, or topic in the museum, and print out a tailor-made tour map (located in the comfy Espresso Bar on the ground floor of the main building; a few more non-printing terminals are inside the entrance to the Sainsbury Wing); info tel. 020/7747-2885, switchboard tel. 020/7839-3321, www.nationalgallery.org.uk.

Eating: Consider splitting afternoon tea at the excellent-but-pricey National Dining Rooms, on the first floor of the Sainsbury

Wing. The National Café, located near the Getty Entrance, also has afternoon tea (see page 212 for more info on both).

○ **Self-Guided Tour:** Go in through the Sainsbury Entrance (in the smaller building to the left of the main entrance), and approach the collection chronologically.

Medieval and Early Renaissance: In the first rooms, you see shiny paintings of saints, angels, Madonnas, and crucifixions floating in an ethereal gold never-never land.

After leaving this gold-leaf peace, you'll stumble into Uccello's *Battle of San Romano* and Van Eyck's *The Arnolfini Portrait,* called by some "The Shotgun Wedding." This painting—a masterpiece of down-to-earth details—was once thought to depict a wedding ceremony forced by the lady's swelling belly. Today it's understood as a portrait of a solemn, well-dressed, well-heeled couple, the Arnolfinis of Bruges, Belgium (she likely was not pregnant—the fashion of the day was to gather up the folds of one's extremely full-skirted dress).

Renaissance: In painting, the Renaissance meant realism. Artists rediscovered the beauty of nature and the human body, expressing the optimism and confidence of this new age. Look for Botticelli's *Venus and Mars*, Michelangelo's *The Entombment*, Raphael's *Pope Julius II,* and Leonardo's *The Virgin of the Rocks.*

Hans Holbein the Younger's *The Ambassadors* depicts two well-dressed, suave men flanking a shelf full of books, globes, navigational tools, and musical instruments—objects that symbolize the secular knowledge of the Renaissance. So what's with the gray, slanting blob at the bottom? If you view the blob from the right-hand edge of the painting (get real close, right up to the frame), the blob suddenly becomes...a skull, a reminder that—despite the fine clothes, proud poses, and worldly knowledge—we will all die.

In *The Origin of the Milky Way* by Venetian Renaissance painter

Tintoretto, the god Jupiter places his illegitimate son, baby Hercules, at his wife's breast. Juno says, "Wait a minute. That's not my baby!" Her milk spurts upward, becoming the Milky Way.

Northern Protestant: Greek gods and Virgin Marys are out, and hometown folks and hometown places are in. Highlights include Vermeer's *A Young Woman Standing at a Virginal*

and Rembrandt's *Belshazzar's Feast.*

Rembrandt painted his *Self-Portrait at the Age of 63* in the year he would die. He was bankrupt, his mistress had just passed away, and he had also buried several of his children. We see a disillusioned, well-worn, but proud old genius.

Baroque: The museum's outstanding Baroque collection includes Van Dyck's *Equestrian Portrait of Charles I* and Caravaggio's *The Supper at Emmaus.* In Velázquez's *The Rokeby Venus,* Venus lounges diagonally across the canvas, admiring herself, with flaring red, white, and gray fabrics to highlight her rosy white skin and inflame our passion. This work by the king's personal court painter is a rare Spanish nude from that ultra-Catholic country.

British: The reserved British were more comfortable cavorting with nature than with the lofty gods, as seen in Constable's *The Hay Wain* and Turner's *The Fighting Téméraire.* Turner's messy, colorful style influenced the Impressionists and gives us our first glimpse into the modern art world.

Impressionism: At the end of the 19th century, a new breed of artists burst out of the stuffy confines of the studio. They donned scarves and berets and set up their canvases in farmers' fields or carried their notebooks into crowded cafés, dashing off quick sketches in order to catch a momentary...impression. Check out Impressionist and Post-Impressionist masterpieces such as Monet's *Gare St. Lazare* and *The Water-Lily Pond,* Renoir's *The Skiff,* Seurat's *Bathers at Asnières,* and Van Gogh's *Sunflowers.*

Cézanne's *Bathers* are arranged in strict triangles. Cézanne uses the Impressionist technique of building a figure with dabs of paint (though his "dabs" are often larger-sized "cube" shapes) to make solid, 3-D geometrical figures in the style of the Renaissance. In the process, his cube shapes helped inspire a radical new style—Cubism—bringing art into the 20th century.

Other Sights on Trafalgar Square
▲▲National Portrait Gallery

Put off by halls of 19th-century characters who meant nothing to me, I used to call this "as interesting as someone else's yearbook." But a selective walk through this 500-year-long *Who's Who* of British history is quick and free, and puts faces on the story of England.

Some highlights: Henry VIII and wives; portraits of the "Virgin Queen" Elizabeth I, Sir Francis Drake, and Sir Walter Raleigh; the only real-life portrait of William Shakespeare; Oliver Cromwell and Charles I with his head on; portraits by Gainsborough and Reynolds; the Romantics (William Blake, Lord Byron, William Wordsworth, and company); Queen Victoria and her era; and the present royal family, including the late Princess Diana.

The collection is well-described, not huge, and in historical sequence, from the 16th century on the second floor to today's royal family on the ground floor.

Cost and Hours: Free, but suggested donation of £5, temporary (optional) exhibits extra, floor plan-£1; daily 10:00-18:00, Thu-Fri until 21:00, first and second floors open Mon at 11:00, last entry to special exhibits one hour before closing; audioguide-£3, no photos, basement café and top-floor view restaurant, entry 100 yards off Trafalgar Square (around the corner from National Gallery, opposite Church of St. Martin-in-the-Fields), Tube: Charing Cross or Leicester Square, tel. 020/7306-0055, recorded info tel. 020/7312-2463, www.npg.org.uk.

LONDON

▲St. Martin-in-the-Fields

The church, built in the 1720s with a Gothic spire atop a Greek-type temple, is an oasis of peace on wild and noisy Trafalgar Square. St. Martin cared for the poor. "In the fields" was where the first church stood on this spot (in the 13th century), between Westminster and The City. Stepping inside, you still feel a compassion for the needs of the people in this neighborhood—the church serves the homeless and houses a Chinese community center. The modern east window—with grillwork bent into the shape of a warped cross—was installed in 2008 to replace one damaged in World War II.

A freestanding glass pavilion to the left of the church serves as the entrance to the church's underground areas. There you'll find the concert ticket office, a gift shop, brass-rubbing center, and the recommended support-the-church Café in the Crypt.

Cost and Hours: Free, but donations welcome; hours vary but generally Mon-Fri 8:30-13:00 & 14:00-18:00, Sat 9:30-13:00 & 14:00-18:00, Sun 15:30-17:00; £3.50 audioguide at shop downstairs, Tube: Charing Cross, tel. 020/7766-1100, www.smitf.org.

Music: The church is famous for its concerts. Consider a free lunchtime concert (suggested £3 donation; Mon, Tue, and Fri at 13:00), an evening concert (£8-28, several nights a week at 19:30), or Wednesday night jazz at the Café in the Crypt (£5.50 or £9, at 20:00). See the church's website for the concert schedule.

The West End and Nearby

To explore this area during dinnertime, see my recommended restaurants on pages 199-204.

London for Early Birds and Night Owls

Most sightseeing in London is restricted to the hours between 10:00 and 18:00. Here are a few exceptions:

Sights Open Early

Every day, several sights open at 9:30 or earlier.

St. Paul's Cathedral: Mon-Sat at 8:30.

Shakespeare's Globe: Daily at 9:00.

Madame Tussauds Waxworks: Daily mid-July-Aug at 9:00, Sept-mid-July Mon-Fri at 9:30, Sat-Sun at 9:00.

Tower of London: Tue-Sat at 9:00.

Churchill War Rooms: Daily at 9:30.

Kew Gardens: Daily at 9:30.

Westminster Abbey: Mon-Sat at 9:30.

British Library: Mon-Sat at 9:30.

Buckingham Palace: Aug-Sept daily at 9:30.

LONDON

Sights Open Late

Every night in London, at least one sight is open late (in addition to the London Eye and Madame Tussauds). Keep in mind, however, that many of these stop admitting visitors well before their posted closing times.

London Eye: Last ascent July-Aug daily at 21:30, April-June at 21:00, Sept-March at 20:30.

Madame Tussauds: Mid-July-Aug daily until 19:00.

Clink Prison Museum: July-Sept daily until 21:00, Oct-June Sat-Sun until 19:30.

British Library: Tue until 20:00.

Sir John Soane's Museum: First Tue of month until 21:00.

British Museum (some galleries): Fri until 20:30.

National Portrait Gallery: Thu-Fri until 21:00.

Vinopolis: Thu-Sat until 21:30.

National Gallery: Fri until 21:00.

Victoria and Albert Museum: Fri until 22:00 (selected galleries).

Tate Modern: Fri-Sat until 22:00.

Tate Britain: Select Fridays until 22:00 (check online or call to confirm).

West End & Nearby

FITZROVIA

Cavendish Square

MARGARET ST.

OXFORD STREET

Oxford Circus

SOHO

Hanover Square

LIBERTY DEP'T STORE

HAMLEYS

SOTHEBY'S AUCTION HOUSE

REGENT STREET

Golden Square

MAYFAIR

Berkeley Square

Piccadilly Circus

EROS STATUE

BURLINGTON ARCADE

ROYAL ACADEMY OF ARTS

ST. JAMES

FORTNUM & MASON

St. James's Square

Green Park

RITZ HOTEL

ST. JAMES'S

CHRISTIE'S AUCTION HOUSE

PALL MALL

PICCADILLY

Green Park

THE MALL

ST. JAMES'S PALACE

200 Meters
200 Yards

Piccadilly and Soho
▲Piccadilly Circus

Although this square is slathered with neon billboards and tacky attractions (think of it as the Times Square of London), the surrounding streets are packed with great shopping opportunities and swimming with youth on the rampage.

Nearby Shaftesbury Avenue and Leicester Square teem with fun-seekers, theaters, Chinese restaurants, and street singers. To the northeast is London's Chinatown and, beyond that, the funky Soho neighborhood (described next). And curling to the northwest from Piccadilly Circus is genteel Regent Street, lined with the city's most exclusive shops.

▲Soho

North of Piccadilly, seedy Soho has become trendy—with many recommended restaurants—and is well worth a gawk. It's the epicenter of London's thriving, colorful youth scene, a fun and funky

Sesame Street of urban diversity.

Soho is also London's red light district (especially near Brewer and Berwick Streets), where "friendly models" wait in tiny rooms up dreary stairways, voluptuous con artists sell strip shows, and eager male tourists are frequently ripped off. But it's easy to avoid trouble if you're not looking for it. In fact, the sleazy joints share the block with respectable pubs and restaurants, and elderly couples stroll past neon signs that flash *Licensed Sex Shop in Basement*.

Covent Garden and Nearby
▲▲Covent Garden

This large square teems with people and street performers—jugglers, sword swallowers, and guitar players. London's buskers

(including those in the Tube) are auditioned, licensed, and assigned times and places where they are allowed to perform.

The square's centerpiece is a covered marketplace. A market has been here since medieval times, when it was the "convent" garden owned by Westminster Abbey. In the 1600s, it became a housing development with this courtyard as its center, done in the Palladian style by Inigo Jones. Today's fine iron-and-glass structure was built in 1830 (when such buildings were all the Industrial Age rage) to house the stalls of what became London's chief produce market. Covent Garden remained a produce market until 1973, when its venerable arcades were converted to boutiques, cafés, and antique shops. A market still thrives here today (for details, see page 159).

The "Actors' Church" of St. Paul, the Royal Opera House, and the London Transport Museum (described next) all border the square, and theaters are nearby. The area is a people-watcher's delight, with cigarette eaters, Punch-and-Judy acts, food that's good for you (but not your wallet), trendy crafts, and row after row of boutique shops and market stalls. For better Covent Garden lunch deals, walk a block or two away from the eye of this touristic hurricane (check out the places north of the Tube station, along Endell and Neal Streets).

▲London Transport Museum

This modern, well-presented museum, located right at Covent Garden, is fun for kids and thought-provoking for adults (if a bit overpriced). Whether you're cursing or marveling at the buses and Tube, the growth of Europe's third-biggest city (after Moscow and Istanbul) has been made possible by its public transit system.

After you enter, take the elevator up to the top floor...and the year 1800, when horse-drawn vehicles ruled the road. Next, you descend to the first floor and the world's first underground Metro system, which used steam-powered locomotives (the Circle Line, c. 1865). On the ground floor, horses and trains are replaced by motorized vehicles (cars, taxis, double-decker buses, streetcars), resulting in 20th-century congestion. How to deal with it? In 2003, car drivers in London were slapped with a congestion charge, and today, a half-billion people ride the Tube every year.

Cost and Hours: £15, ticket good for one year, kids under 16 free, Sat-Thu 10:00-18:00, Fri 11:00-18:00, last entry 45 minutes before closing, pleasant upstairs café with Covent Garden view, in southeast corner of Covent Garden courtyard, Tube: Covent Garden, switchboard tel. 020/7379-6344, recorded info tel. 020/7565-7299, www.ltmuseum.co.uk.

LONDON

▲Courtauld Gallery

While less impressive than the National Gallery, this wonderful and compact collection of paintings is still a joy. The gallery is part of the Courtauld Institute of Art, and the thoughtful description of each piece of art reminds visitors that the gallery is still used for teaching. You'll see medieval European paintings and works by Rubens, the Impressionists (Manet, Monet, and Degas), Post-Impressionists (such as Cézanne and an intense Van Gogh self-portrait), and more. Besides the permanent collection, a quality selection of loaners and temporary exhibits are often included in the entry fee. The gallery is located within the grand Somerset House; enjoy the riverside eateries and the courtyard featuring a playful fountain.

Cost and Hours: £6 (£3 on Mon); open daily 10:00-18:00, last entry 30 minutes before closing, occasionally open Thu until 21:00—check website, café, at Somerset House along the Strand, Tube: Temple or Covent Garden, recorded info tel. 020/7848-2526, shop tel. 020/7848-2579, www.courtauld.ac.uk.

Buckingham Palace

Three palace sights require admission: the State Rooms (Aug-Sept only), Queen's Gallery, and Royal Mews. You can pay for each separately, or buy a combo-ticket.

A combo-ticket for £32 admits you to all three sights; a cheaper version for £16 covers the Queen's Gallery and Royal Mews. Many tourists are more interested in the Changing of the Guard, which costs nothing at all to view.

▲State Rooms at Buckingham Palace

This lavish home has been Britain's royal residence since 1837. When the Queen's at home, the royal standard flies (a red, yellow, and blue flag); otherwise, the Union Jack flaps in the wind. The Queen opens her palace to the public—but only in August and September, when she's out of town.

Cost and Hours: £19 for lavish State Rooms and throne room, includes audioguide; Aug-Sept only, daily 9:30-18:30, until 19:00 in Aug, last admission 16:45 in Aug, 15:45 in Sept; limited to 8,000 visitors a day by timed entry; come early to the palace's Visitor Entrance (opens 9:15), or book ahead in person, by phone, or online (£2.50 extra); Tube: Victoria, tel. 020/7766-7300, www .royalcollection.org.uk.

Queen's Gallery at Buckingham Palace

A small sampling of Queen Elizabeth's personal collection of art is on display in five rooms in a wing adjoining the palace. Her 7,000 paintings, one of the largest private art collections in the world, are actually a series of collections, which have been built upon by each successive monarch since the 16th century. The Queen rotates the paintings, enjoying some privately in her many palatial residences while sharing others with her subjects in public galleries in Edinburgh and London. The exhibits change two or three times a year and are lovingly described by the included audioguide.

Because the gallery is small and security is tight (involving lines), I'd suggest visiting this gallery only if you're a patient art lover interested in the current exhibit.

Cost and Hours: £9.25 but can change depending on exhibit, combo-ticket with Royal Mews saves about £2, daily 10:00-17:30, opens at 9:30 Aug-Sept, last entry one hour before closing, Tube: Victoria, tel. 020/7766-7301—but Her Majesty rarely answers. Men shouldn't miss the mahogany-trimmed urinals.

Royal Mews

Located to the left of Buckingham Palace, the Queen's working stables are open to visitors. The visit is likely to be disappointing unless you follow the included audioguide or the hourly guided tour (April-Oct only, 45 minutes), in which case it's fairly entertaining—especially if you're interested in horses and/or royalty. You'll see a few of the Queen's 30 horses, a fancy car, and a bunch of old carriages, finishing with the Gold State Coach (c. 1760, 4 tons, 4 mph). Queen Victoria said absolutely no cars. When she died, in 1901, the mews got its first Daimler. Today, along with the hay-eating transport, the stable is home to five Bentleys and Rolls-Royce Phantoms, with one on display.

Cost and Hours: £8.50, combo-ticket with Queen's Gallery saves about £2, April-Oct daily 10:00-17:00, Nov-March Mon-Sat 10:00-16:00, closed Sun, last entry 45 minutes before closing,

Buckingham Palace Area

St. James's Park

LONDON

1 Changing of the Guard
2 Victoria Memorial (Best Views)
3 Wellington Barracks
4 St. James's Palace
5 Spur Road

guided tours on the hour in summer, Buckingham Palace Road, Tube: Victoria, tel. 020/7766-7302.

▲▲Changing of the Guard at Buckingham Palace

This is the spectacle every visitor to London has to see at least once: stone-faced, red-coated, bearskin-hatted guards changing posts with much fanfare, in an hour-long ceremony accompanied by a brass band.

It's 11:00 at Buckingham Palace, and the on-duty guards (the "Queen's Guard") are ready to finish their shift. Nearby at St. James's Palace (a half-mile northeast), a second set of guards is also ready for a break. Meanwhile, fresh replacement guards (the "New Guard") gather for a review

LONDON

Changing of the Guard Timeline

When	What	Where
10:30	Tourists begin to gather (arrive now for a spot by the fence)	Fence outside the palace
11:00	Victoria Monument gets crowded	Middle of traffic circle in front of palace
11:00-11:15	"New Guard" gathers for inspection	Wellington Barracks
11:00 (10:00 Sun)	Horse Guard changing of the guard	Horse Guards Parade (opposite end of St. James's Park)
11:15-11:30	Tired St. James's Palace guards and Horse Guard both head for the palace	Down the Mall
11:15-11:30	Fresh replacement troops head from Wellington Barracks to Buckingham Palace	Down Spur Road
11:30-11:45	All guards gradually converge	Around Victoria Monument in front of the palace
11:45-12:00	The Changing of the Guard ceremony	Inside fenced court-yard of Buckingham Palace
12:00-12:10	Tired guards head for Wellington Barracks	Up the Mall
12:00-12:10	Fresh guards head for St. James's Palace	Up Spur Road
12:15	Smaller changing of the guard ceremony	In front of St. James's Palace

and inspection at Wellington Barracks, 500 yards east of the palace (on Birdcage Walk).

At 11:15, the tired St. James's guards head out to the Mall, and then take a right turn for Buckingham Palace. At 11:30, the replacement troops, led by the band, also head for Buckingham Palace. Meanwhile, a fourth group—the Horse Guard—passes by along the Mall on its way back to Hyde Park Corner from its own changing-of-the-guard ceremony on Whitehall (which just took place at Horse Guards Parade at 11:00, or 10:00 on Sun).

At 11:45, the tired and fresh guards converge on Buckingham

Palace in a perfect storm of Red Coat pageantry. Everyone parades around, the guard changes (passing the regimental flag, or "colour") with much shouting, the band plays a happy little concert, and then they march out. At noon, two bands escort two detachments of guards away: the tired guards to Wellington Barracks and the fresh guards to St. James's Palace. As the fresh guards set up at St. James's Palace and the tired ones dress down at the barracks, the tourists disperse.

Cost and Hours: Free, daily May-July at 11:30, every other day Aug-April, no ceremony in very wet weather; exact schedule subject to change—call 020/7766-7300 for the day's plan, or check www.royalcollection.org.uk; Buckingham Palace, Tube: Victoria, St. James's Park, or Green Park. Or hop into a big black taxi and say, "Buck House, please."

Sightseeing Strategies: Most tourists just show up and get lost in the crowds, but those who know the drill will enjoy the event more. The action takes place in stages over the course of an hour, at several different locations. The main event is in the forecourt right in front of Buckingham Palace (between Buckingham Palace and the fence) from 11:30 to 12:00. To see it close up, you'll need to get here no later than 10:30 to get a place right next to the fence.

But there's plenty of pageantry elsewhere. Get out your map and strategize. You could see the guards mobilizing at Wellington Barracks or St. James's Palace (11:00-11:15). Or watch them parade with bands down The Mall and Spur Road (11:15-11:30). After the ceremony at Buckingham Palace is over (and many tourists have gotten bored and gone home), the parades march back along those same streets (12:10).

Pick one event and find a good, unobstructed place from which to view it. The key is to get either right up front along the road or fence, or find some raised elevation to stand or sit on—a balustrade or a curb—so you can see over people's heads.

If you get there too late to score a premium spot right along the fence, head for the high ground on the circular Victoria Memorial, which provides the best overall view (come before 11:00 to get a place). From the memorial, you have good (if more distant) views of the palace as well as the arriving and departing parades along The Mall and Spur Road. The actual Changing of the Guard in front of the palace is a nonevent. It is interesting, however, to see nearly every tourist in London gathered in one place at the same time.

If you arrive too late to get any good spot at all, or you just don't feel like jostling for a view, stroll down to St. James's Palace and wait near the corner for a great photo-op. At about 12:15, the parade marches up The Mall to the palace and performs a smaller changing ceremony—with almost no crowds. Afterward, stroll through nearby St. James's Park.

Sights in North London

▲▲▲British Museum

Simply put, this is the greatest chronicle of civilization...anywhere. A visit here is like taking a long hike through *Encyclopedia Britannica* National Park. While the vast British Museum wraps around its Great Court (the huge entrance hall), the most popular sections of the museum fill the ground floor: Egyptian, Assyrian, and ancient Greek, with the famous frieze sculptures from the Parthenon in Athens. The

museum's stately Reading Room—famous as the place where Karl Marx hung out while formulating his ideas on communism and writing *Das Kapital*—sometimes hosts special exhibits.

Cost and Hours: Free but a £5 donation requested, temporary exhibits usually extra (and with timed ticket); daily 10:00-17:30, Fri until 20:30 (selected galleries only), least crowded weekday late afternoons; multimedia guide—£5, free Rick Steves audio tour available—see page 54, Great Russell Street, Tube: Tottenham Court Road, general info tel. 020/7323-8000, ticket desk tel. 020/7323-8181, collection questions tel. 020/7323-8838, www.britishmuseum.org.

Information: Information desks offer a £1 basic map or £2 version highlighting important pieces, but neither is essential; the *Visitor's Guide* (£3.50) offers 15 different tours and skimpy text. Free 30-minute **eyeOpener tours** are led by volunteers, who focus on select rooms (daily 11:00-15:45, generally every 15 minutes). Free 45-minute **gallery talks** on specific subjects are offered Tue-Sat at 13:15; a free 20-minute highlights tour is available on Friday evening. The £5 **multimedia guide** offers dial-up audio commentary and video on 200 objects, as well as several theme tours (must leave photo ID). There's also a fun children's audioguide (£3.50). General info tel. 020/7323-8000, ticket desk tel. 020/7323-8181, collection questions tel. 020/7323-8838, www.britishmuseum.org.

◆ Self-Guided Tour: From the Great Court, doorways lead to all wings. To the left are the exhibits on Egypt, Assyria, and Greece—the highlights of your visit.

Egypt: Start with the Egyptian section. Egypt was one of the world's first "civilizations"—a group of people with a government, religion, art, free time, and a written language. The Egypt

British Museum Overview

MONTAGUE PLACE

MONTAGUE PLACE ENTRANCE

To Fitzrovia & Charlotte Place Eateries

Russell Square

UP TO MUMMIES

CAFÉ

EGYPT

ASSYRIA

ROSETTA ■STONE

READING ROOM & SHOP

PARTHENON GALLERIES

GREECE

THE KING'S GALLERY

MONTAGUE ST.

WINGED LIONS

THE GREAT COURT

INFO ■

INFO ■

BLOOMSBURY ST.

BOUTIQUE

CAFÉ

CLOAK- ROOM

BOOK- SHOP

COLUMNS

Not to Scale

MAIN ENTRANCE

GREAT RUSSELL STREET

To Tottenham Court Road ⊖ (10 min. walk)

To Holborn ⊖ (10 min. walk)

LONDON

we think of—pyramids, mummies, pharaohs, and guys who walk funny—lasted from 3000 to 1000 B.C. with hardly any change in the government, religion, or arts. Imagine two millennia of Nixon.

The first thing you'll see in the Egypt section is the **Rosetta Stone.** When this rock was unearthed in the Egyptian desert in 1799, it was a sensation in Europe. This black slab, dating from 196 B.C., caused a quantum leap in the study of ancient history. Finally, Egyptian writing could be decoded.

It contains a single inscription repeated in three languages. The bottom third is plain old Greek, while the middle is medieval Egyptian. By comparing the two known languages with the one they didn't know, translators figured out the hieroglyphics.

Next, wander past the many **statues,** including a seven-ton Ramesses, with the traditional features of a pharaoh (goatee, cloth headdress, and cobra diadem on his forehead). When Moses told the king of Egypt, "Let my people go!" this was the stony-faced look he got. You'll also see the Egyptian gods as animals—these include Amun, king of the gods, as a ram, and Horus, the god of the living, as a falcon.

At the end of the hall, climb the stairs to **mummy** land (use the elevator if it's running). To mummify a body, you first disembowel it (but leave the heart inside), then pack the cavities with pitch, and dry it with natron, a natural form of sodium carbonate (and, I believe, the active ingredient in Twinkies). Then carefully bandage it head to toe with hundreds of yards of linen strips. Let it sit 2,000 years, and...*voilà!* The mummy was placed in a wooden coffin, which was put in a stone coffin, which was placed in a tomb. The result is that we now have Egyptian bodies that are as well preserved as Joan Rivers. Many of the mummies here are from the time of the Roman occupation, when fine memorial portraits painted in wax became popular. X-ray photos in the display cases tell us more about these people. Don't miss the animal mummies. Cats were popular pets. They were also considered incarnations of the cat-headed goddess Bastet. Worshipped in life as the sun god's allies, preserved in death, and memorialized with statues, cats were given the adulation they've come to expect ever since.

Assyria: Long before Saddam Hussein, Iraq was home to other palace-building, iron-fisted rulers—the Assyrians, who conquered their southern neighbors and dominated the Middle East for 300 years (c. 900-600 B.C.). Their strength came from a superb army (chariots, mounted cavalry, and siege engines), a policy of terrorism against enemies ("I tied their heads to tree trunks all around the city," reads a royal inscription), ethnic cleansing and mass deportations of the vanquished, and efficient administration (roads and express postal service). They have been called the "Romans of the East."

Standing guard over the Assyrian exhibit halls are two human-headed **winged lions**. These stone lions guarded an Assyrian palace (11th-8th century B.C.). With the strength of a lion, the wings of an eagle, the brain of a man, and the beard of ZZ Top, they protected the king from evil spirits and scared the heck out of foreign ambassadors and left-wing newspaper reporters. (What has five legs and flies? Take a close look. These quintupeds, which appear complete from both the front and the side, could guard both directions at once.)

Carved into the stone between the bearded lions' loins, you can see one of civilization's most impressive achievements—writing. This wedge-shaped **(cuneiform)** script is the world's first written language, invented 5,000 years ago by the Sumerians (of southern Iraq) and passed down to their less-civilized descendants, the Assyrians.

The **Nimrud Gallery** is a mini version of the throne room and royal apartments of King Ashurnasirpal II's Northwest Palace at Nimrud (9th century B.C.). It's filled with royal propaganda reliefs, 30-ton marble bulls, and panels depicting wounded lions (lion-hunting was Assyria's sport of kings).

Greece: During their civilization's Golden Age (500-430 B.C.), the ancient Greeks set the tone for all of Western civilization to follow. Democracy, theater, literature, mathematics, philosophy, science, gyros, art, and architecture, as we know them, were virtually all invented by a single generation of Greeks in a small town of maybe 80,000 citizens.

Your walk through Greek art history starts with **pottery**, usually painted red and black and a popular export product for the sea-trading Greeks. The earliest featured geometric patterns (eighth century B.C.), then a painted black silhouette on the natural orange clay, then a red figure on a black background. Later, painted vases show a culture really into partying.

The highlight is the **Parthenon Sculptures**, taken from the temple dedicated to Athena, goddess of wisdom and the patroness of Athens—the crowning glory of an enormous urban-renewal plan during Greece's Golden Age. The sculptures are also called the Elgin Marbles, for the shrewd British ambassador who had his men hammer, chisel, and saw them off the Parthenon in the early 1800s. Though the Greek government complains about losing its marbles, the Brits feel they rescued and preserved the sculptures. These much-wrangled-over bits of the Parthenon (from about 450 B.C.) are indeed impressive. The marble panels you see lining the walls of this large hall are part of the frieze that originally ran around the exterior of the Parthenon, under the eaves. The statues at either end of the hall once filled the Parthenon's triangular-shaped pediments and showed the birth of Athena. The relief panels known as metopes tell the story of the struggle between the forces of human civilization and animal-like barbarism.

The Rest of the Museum: Be sure to venture upstairs to see artifacts from Roman Britain that surpass anything you'll see at Hadrian's Wall or elsewhere in the country. Also look for the Sutton Hoo Ship Burial artifacts from a seventh-century royal burial on the east coast of England (Room 41). A rare Michelangelo cartoon (preliminary sketch) is in Room 90 (level 4).

North London

400 Meters
400 Yards

To Zoo

Regent's Park

To Abbey Road

Queen Mary's Gardens

SHERLOCK HOLMES MUSEUM & BEATLES STORE

Baker Street

MADAME TUSSAUDS WAXWORKS

Regent's Park

MARYLEBONE ROAD

MARYLEBONE

WALLACE COLLECTION

POLLOCK'S TOY MUSEUM

Great Portland St.

Warren Street

Euston Square

ST. PANCRAS INTERNATIONAL STATION

KING'S CROSS STATION

EUSTON STATION

EUSTON ROAD

BRITISH LIBRARY

FITZROVIA

Goodge Street

Russell Square

BLOOMSBURY

GUILFORD STREET

THEOBALD'S RD.

BRITISH MUSEUM

Bedford Square

SIR JOHN SOANE'S MUSEUM

CARTOON MUSEUM

Holborn

Lincoln's Inn Fields

CHARLOTTE PLACE EATERIES

WIGMORE ST.

SEYMOUR

OXFORD STREET

Marble Arch

Bond St.

OXFORD STREET

NEW OXFORD ST.

Tottenham Court Rd.

Oxford Circus

Soho Square

SOHO

MARBLE ARCH

Hyde Park

To Trafalgar Square

SHAFTESBURY

To Trafalgar Square

THE STRAND

To The City

Other Sights in North London
▲▲▲British Library

The British Empire built its greatest monuments out of paper; it's through literature that England has made her lasting contribution to history and the arts. Here, in just two rooms, are the literary treasures of Western civilization, from early Bibles, to the Magna Carta, to Shakespeare's *Hamlet,* to Lewis Carroll's *Alice's Adventures in Wonderland.* You'll see the Lindisfarne Gospels transcribed on an illuminated manuscript, as well as Beatles lyrics scrawled on the back of a greeting card. Pages from Leonardo da Vinci's notebook show his powerful curiosity, his genius for invention, and his famous backward and inside-out handwriting, which makes sense only if you know Italian and have a mirror. A *Beowulf* manuscript from A.D. 1000, *The Canterbury Tales,* and Shakespeare's First Folio also reside here. (If the First Folio is not out, the library should have other Shakespeare items on display.)

Exhibits change often, and many of the museum's old, fragile manuscripts need to "rest" periodically in order to stay well-preserved. If your heart's set on seeing that one particular rare Dickens book or letter penned by Gandhi, call ahead to make sure it's on display.

Cost and Hours: Free, but £5 suggested donation, admission charged for some (optional) temporary exhibits; Mon-Fri 9:30-18:00, Tue until 20:00, Sat 9:30-17:00, Sun 11:00-17:00; 96 Euston Road, Tube: King's Cross St. Pancras or Euston, tel. 019/3754-

British Library Highlights

MAGNA CARTA

SACRED TEXTS

PRINTING

PRINTED PRAYER SHEET

GUTENBERG BIBLE

To Café

CODEX SINAITICUS

ILLUMINATED MANUSCRIPTS

SCIENCE

FIRST FOLIO

ENTRANCE

BEOWULF

CHAUCER

TEMPORARY EXHIBITS

SHAKE-SPEARE

HISTORICAL DOCUMENTS

LITERATURE

MAPS

SIR JOHN RITBLAT GALLERY

MUSIC

ELEV. BEATLES HANDEL

MAIN STAIRS UP

STAIRS UP TO RITBLAT GALLERY

INFO DESK

PACCAR GALLERY (TEMPORARY EXHIBITS)

STAIRS DOWN

SHOP

MAIN ENTRANCE

NEWTON STATUE

Piazza

To Euston Road Entrance

LONDON

6060 or 020/7412-7676, www.bl.uk.

Tours: While the British Library doesn't offer an audioguide or guided tours of the permanent collection, you can download a free Rick Steves **audio tour** that describes its highlights (see page 54). Guided tours are offered of the building itself—the archives and reading rooms.

▲Wallace Collection

Sir Richard Wallace's fine collection of 17th-century Dutch Masters, 18th-century French Rococo, medieval armor, and assorted aristocratic fancies fills the sumptuously furnished Hertford House on Manchester Square. From the rough and intimate Dutch lifescapes of Jan Steen to the pink-cheeked Rococo fantasies of François Boucher, a wander through this little-visited mansion makes you nostalgic for the days of the empire. While this collection would be a big deal in a mid-sized city, it's small potatoes here in London...but enjoyable nevertheless.

Cost and Hours: Free, daily 10:00-17:00, audioguide-£3, free guided tours or lectures almost daily—call to confirm times, just north of Oxford Street on Manchester Square, Tube: Bond Street. Tel. 020/7563-9500, www.wallacecollection.org.

▲Madame Tussauds Waxworks

This waxtravaganza is gimmicky, crass, and crazily expensive, but dang fun...a hit with the kind of tourists who skip the

British Museum. The original Madame Tussaud did wax casts of heads lopped off during the French Revolution (such as Marie-Antoinette's). She took her show on the road and ended up in London in 1835. Now it's all about squeezing Tom Cruise's bum, gambling with George Clooney, and partying with Beyoncé and Brangelina. In addition to posing with all the eerily realistic wax dummies—from Johnny Depp to Barack Obama to the Beatles—you'll have the chance to tour a hokey haunted-house exhibit; learn how they created this waxy army; hop on a people-mover and cruise through a kid-pleasing "Spirit of London" time trip; and visit with Spider-Man, the Hulk, and other Marvel superheroes. A nine-minute "4-D" show features a 3-D movie heightened by wind, "back ticklers," and other special effects.

Cost: £30, 10 percent discount and no waiting in line if you buy tickets on their website (also consider combo-deal with London Eye, sold cheaper online), £25.50 Fast Track ticket (see page 54), often even bigger discount—up to 50 percent—if you get "Late Saver" ticket online for visits later in the day, 2-for-1 rail vouchers accepted (see page 63). Kids also get a discount of about £4, and those under 5 are free.

Hours: Mid-July-Aug and school holidays daily 9:00-19:00, Sept-mid-July Mon-Fri 9:30-17:30, Sat-Sun 9:00-18:00, these are last entry times—place stays open roughly two hours later; Marylebone Road, Tube: Baker Street, tel. 0871-894-3000, www .madametussauds.com.

Crowd-Beating Tips: This popular attraction can be swamped with people. To avoid the ticket line, buy a Fast Track ticket or reserve online. If you wait to buy tickets at the attraction, you'll discover that the ticket-buying line twists endlessly once inside the door (believe the posted signs warning you how long the wait will be—an hour or more is not unusual at busy times). If you buy your tickets at the door, try to arrive after 15:00—a smart move even with advance tickets, as the crowds inside thin out later in the day.

▲Sir John Soane's Museum

Architects love this quirky place, as do fans of interior decor, eclectic knickknacks, and Back Door sights. Tour this furnished home on a bird-chirping square and see 19th-century chairs, lamps, and carpets, wood-paneled nooks and crannies, and stained-glass skylights. (While some sections may be closed for restoration through 2014, the main part of the house will be open.) The townhouse is cluttered with Soane's (and his wife's) collection of ancient relics, curios, and famous paintings, including Hogarth's series on *The Rake's Progress* (read the fun plot) and several excellent Canalettos. In 1833, just before his death, Soane established his house as a museum, stipulating that it be kept as nearly as possible in the state he left it. If he visited today, he'd be entirely satisfied. You'll leave wishing you'd known the man.

Cost and Hours: Free, but donations much appreciated, Tue-Sat 10:00-17:00, open and candlelit the first Tue of the month 18:00-21:00, closed Sun-Mon, last entry 30 minutes before closing, long entry lines on Sat and first Tue, good £1 brochure, £10 guided tour Sat at 11:00, free downloadable audio tours on their website, 13 Lincoln's Inn Fields, quarter-mile southeast of British Museum, Tube: Holborn, tel. 020/7405-2107, www.soane.org.

Beatles Sights

London's city center is surprisingly devoid of sights associated with the famous '60s rock band. To see much of anything, consider taking a guided walk (see page 76).

For a photo op, go to **Abbey Road** and walk the famous crosswalk pictured on the *Abbey Road* album cover (Tube: St. John's Wood, get information and buy Beatles memorabilia at the small kiosk in the station). From the Tube station, it's a five-minute walk west down Grove End Road to the intersection with Abbey

Road. The Abbey Road recording studio is the low-key, white building to the right of Abbey House (it's still a working studio, so you can't go inside). Ponder the graffiti on the low wall outside, and...imagine. To re-create the famous cover photo, shoot the crosswalk from the roundabout as you face north up Abbey Road. Shoes are optional.

Nearby is **Paul McCartney's current home** (7 Cavendish Avenue): Continue down Grove End Road, turn left on Circus Road, and then right on Cavendish. Please be discreet.

The **Beatles Store** is at 231 Baker Street (Tube: Baker Street). It's small—some Beatles-logo T-shirts, mugs, pins, and old vinyl like you might have in your closet—and has nothing of historic value (open eight days a week, 10:00-18:30, tel. 020/7935-4464, www.beatlesstorelondon.co.uk; another rock memorabilia store is across the street).

Sherlock Holmes Museum

A few doors down from the Beatles Store, this meticulous re-creation of the (fictional) apartment of the (fictional) detective sits

at the (real) address of 221b Baker Street. The first-floor replica (so to speak) of Sherlock's study delights fans with the opportunity to play Holmes and Watson while sitting in authentic 18th-century chairs. The second and third floors offer fine exhibits on daily Victorian life, showing off furniture, clothes, pipes, paintings, and chamber pots; in other rooms, models are posed to enact key scenes from Sir Arthur Conan Doyle's famous books.

Cost and Hours: £8, daily 9:30-18:00, last entry at least 30 minutes before closing, expect to wait 15 minutes or more, large gift shop for Holmes connoisseurs, Tube: Baker Street, tel. 020/7935-8866, www.sherlock-holmes.co.uk.

Sights in The City

When Londoners say "The City," they mean the one-square-mile business center in East London that 2,000 years ago was Roman Londinium. The outline of the Roman city walls can still be seen in the arc of roads from Blackfriars Bridge to Tower Bridge.

Within The City are 23 churches designed by Sir Christopher Wren, mostly just ornamentation around St. Paul's Cathedral. Today, while home to only 7,000 residents, The City thrives with nearly 300,000 office workers coming and going daily. It's a fascinating district to wander on weekdays, but since almost nobody actually lives there, it's dull in the evenings and on Saturday and Sunday.

You can download a free Rick Steves **audio tour** of The City, which peels back the many layers of history in this oldest part of London (see page 54).

▲▲▲St. Paul's Cathedral

Sir Christopher Wren's most famous church is the great St. Paul's,

its elaborate interior capped by a 365-foot dome. There's been a church on this spot since 604. After the Great Fire of 1666 destroyed the old cathedral, Wren created this Baroque masterpiece. And since World War II, St. Paul's has been Britain's symbol of resilience. Despite 57 nights of bombing, the Nazis failed to destroy the cathedral, thanks to the St. Paul's volunteer fire watchmen, who stayed on the dome.

Cost and Hours: £16, includes church entry, dome climb, crypt, tour, and audioguide; Mon-Sat 8:30-16:30, last entry for sightseeing 16:00 (dome opens at 9:30, last entry at 16:15), closed Sun except for worship, sometimes closed for special events, no photos, café and restaurant in crypt, Tube: St. Paul's. If interested, check the website for worship times the day of your visit. Communion is generally Mon-Sat at 8:00 and 12:30. On Sunday, services are held at 8:00, 10:15 (Matins), 11:30 (sung Eucharist), 15:15 (evensong), and 18:00. The rest of the week, evensong is at 17:00 Tue-Sat (not Mon). For more on evensong, see page 169. If you come 20 minutes early for evensong worship (under the dome), you may be able to grab a big wooden stall in the choir, next to the singers. On some Sundays, there's a free organ recital at 16:45.

Information: Admission includes an **audioguide** as well as a 1.5-hour guided tour (Mon-Sat at 10:00, 11:00, 13:00, and 14:00; confirm schedule at church or call 020/7246-8357). Free 15-minute talks are offered throughout the day, and a stand-up, wrap-around **film** program titled *Oculus: An Eye into St. Paul's* gives some historical background and shows the view from atop the dome (find it near Nelson's tomb). You can also download a free Rick Steves **audio tour** of St. Paul's (see page 54). Recorded info tel.

The City, The Tower & East London

020/7236-4128, reception tel. 020/7246-8350, www.stpauls.co.uk.

○ **Self-Guided Tour:** Even now, as skyscrapers encroach, the 365-foot-high dome of St. Paul's rises majestically above the rooftops of the neighborhood. The tall dome is set on classical columns, capped with a lantern, topped by a six-foot ball, and iced with a cross. As the first Anglican cathedral built in London after the Reformation, it is Baroque: St. Peter's in Rome filtered through clear-eyed English reason. Often the site of historic funerals (Queen Victoria and Winston Churchill), St. Paul's most famous ceremony was a wedding—when Prince Charles married Lady Diana Spencer in 1981.

Inside, this big church feels big. At 515 feet long and 250 feet wide, it's Europe's fourth largest, after Rome (St. Peter's), Sevilla, and Milan. The spaciousness is accentuated by the relative lack of decoration. The simple, cream-colored ceiling and the clear glass in the windows light everything evenly. Wren wanted this: a simple, open church with nothing to hide. Unfortunately, only this entrance area keeps his original vision—the rest was encrusted with 19th-century Victorian ornamentation.

The **dome** you see from here, painted with scenes from the life of St. Paul, is only the innermost of three. From the painted interior of the first dome, look up through the opening to see the light-filled lantern of the second dome. Finally, the whole thing is covered on the outside by the third and final dome, the shell of lead-covered wood that you see from the street. Wren's ingenious three-in-one design was psychological as well as functional—he

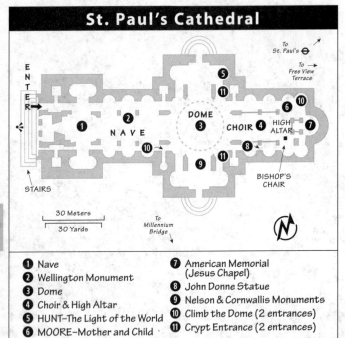

St. Paul's Cathedral

To St. Paul's ⊖

To → Free View Terrace

ENTER →

❺

⓫

❻ ❿

DOME ❸

CHOIR ❹ HIGH ALTAR ❼

❶ NAVE ❷

❿ →

❽ →

❾ ⓫

BISHOP'S CHAIR

STAIRS

30 Meters
30 Yards

To Millennium Bridge

Ⓝ

❶ Nave
❷ Wellington Monument
❸ Dome
❹ Choir & High Altar
❺ HUNT–The Light of the World
❻ MOORE–Mother and Child

❼ American Memorial (Jesus Chapel)
❽ John Donne Statue
❾ Nelson & Cornwallis Monuments
❿ Climb the Dome (2 entrances)
⓫ Crypt Entrance (2 entrances)

wanted a low, shallow inner dome so worshippers wouldn't feel diminished.

Do a quick clockwise spin around the church. In the north transept (to your left as you face the altar), find the big painting *The Light of the World* (1904), by the Pre-Raphaelite William Holman Hunt. Inspired by Hunt's own experience of finding Christ during a moment of spiritual crisis, the crowd-pleasing work was criticized by art highbrows for being "syrupy" and "simple"—even as it became the most famous painting in Victorian England.

Along the left side of the choir is the modern statue *Mother and Child,* by the great modern sculptor Henry Moore. Typical of Moore's work, this Mary and Baby Jesus—inspired by the sight of British moms nursing babies in WWII bomb shelters—renders a traditional subject in an abstract, minimalist way.

The area behind the altar, with three bright and modern stained-glass windows, is the **American Memorial Chapel**—honoring the Americans who sacrificed their lives to save Britain in World War II. In colored panes that arch around the big windows, spot the American eagle (center window, to the left of Christ), George Washington (right window, upper-right corner), and symbols of all 50 states (find your state seal). In the carved wood beneath the windows, you'll see birds and foliage native to the US. The Roll of Honor (a 500-page book under glass, immediately behind the altar) lists the names of 28,000 US servicemen and women based in Britain who gave their lives during the war.

Around the other side of the choir is a shrouded statue honoring **John Donne** (1621–1631), a passionate preacher in old St. Paul's, as well as a great poet ("never wonder for whom the bell tolls—it tolls for thee").

In the south transept are monuments to military greats **Horatio Nelson**, who fought Napoleon, and **Charles Cornwallis**, who was finished off by George Washington at Yorktown.

Climbing the Dome: During your visit, you can climb 528 steps to reach the dome and great city views. Along the way, have some fun in the Whispering Gallery (257 steps up). Whisper sweet nothings into the wall, and your partner (and anyone else) standing far away can hear you. For best effects, try whispering (not talking) with your mouth close to the wall, while your partner stands a few dozen yards away with his or her ear to the wall.

Visiting the Crypt: The crypt is a world of historic bones and interesting cathedral models. Many legends are buried here—Horatio Nelson, who wore down Napoleon; the Duke of Wellington, who finished Napoleon off; and even Wren himself. Wren's actual tomb is marked by a simple black slab with no statue, though he considered this church to be his legacy. Back up in the nave, on the floor directly under the dome, is Christopher Wren's name and epitaph (written in Latin): "Reader, if you seek his monument, look around you."

Near St. Paul's Cathedral
▲Old Bailey

To view the British legal system in action—lawyers in little blond wigs speaking legalese with an upper-crust accent—spend a few minutes in the visitors' gallery at the Old Bailey, called the "Central Criminal Court." Don't enter under the dome; continue down the block about halfway to the modern part of the building—the entry is at Warwick Passage.

Cost and Hours: Free, generally Mon-Fri 9:45-13:00 & 14:00-16:00 depending on caseload, last entry at 15:40 but often closes an hour or so earlier, closed Sat-Sun, fewer cases in Aug; no kids under 14; no bags, mobile phones, cameras, iPods, or food, but small purses OK; you can check bags at the Capable Travel agency just down the street at Old Bailey 4—£5/bag, £1 per phone or camera; 2 blocks northwest of St. Paul's on Old Bailey Street, follow signs to public entrance, Tube: St. Paul's, tel. 020/7248-3277.

▲Museum of London

This museum tells the fascinating story of London, taking you on a walk from its pre-Roman beginnings to the present. It

London's Best Views

Though London is a height-challenged city, you can get lofty perspectives on it from several high-flying places. For some viewpoints, you need to pay admission (cheapest at The Monument), and at the bars or restaurants, you'll need to buy a drink; the only truly free spots are Primrose Hill, the rooftop terrace of a shopping mall next to St. Paul's Cathedral, and the viewpoint in front of Greenwich's Royal Observatory.

London Eye: Ride the giant Ferris wheel for stunning London views. See page 136.

St. Paul's Dome: You'll earn a striking, unobstructed view by climbing hundreds of steps to the cramped balcony of the church's cupola. See page 127.

Rooftop Terrace: Get fine, free views of St. Paul's Cathedral and surroundings—nearly as good as those from St. Paul's Dome—from the rooftop terrace of the shopping mall just behind and east of the church.

Tate Modern: Take in a classic vista across the Thames from the museum's level-6 restaurant and bar. See page 141.

The Monument: Though surrounded by modern buildings in the financial district, this 202-foot column memorializing the Great Fire of 1666 affords a nice view of The City. See page 129.

National Portrait Gallery: A mod top-floor restaurant peers over Trafalgar Square and the Westminster neighborhood. See page 103.

Waterstones Bookstore: Its hip, low-key, top-floor café/bar has reasonable prices and sweeping views of the London Eye,

features London's distinguished citizens through history—from Neanderthals, to Romans, to Elizabethans, to Victorians, to Mods, to today. The museum's displays are chronological, spacious, and informative without being overwhelming. Scale models and costumes help you visualize everyday life in the city at different periods. In the last room, you'll see the museum's prized possession: the Lord Mayor's Coach, a golden carriage pulled by six white horses, looking as if it had pranced right out of the pages of *Cinderella*. There are enough whiz-bang multimedia displays (including the Plague and the Great Fire) to spice up otherwise humdrum artifacts. This regular stop for the local school kids gives the best overview of London history in town.

Cost and Hours: Free, daily 10:00-18:00, galleries shut down 30 minutes before closing, see the day's events board for special talks and tours, café, £1 lockers, on London Wall at Aldersgate Street, Tube: Barbican or St. Paul's plus a five-minute walk, tel. 020/7001-9844, www.museumoflondon.org.uk.

Big Ben, and the Houses of Parliament (see page 59, on Sun bar closes one hour before bookstore, www.5thview.co.uk).

OXO Tower: Perched high over the Thames River, the building's upscale restaurant/bar boasts views over London and St. Paul's, with al fresco dining in good weather (Barge House Street, Tube: Blackfriars, tel. 020/7803-3888, www.harvey nichols.com/restaurants/oxo-tower-london).

London Hilton, Park Lane: You'll spot Buckingham Palace, Hyde Park, and the London Eye from Galvin at Windows, a 28th-floor restaurant/bar in an otherwise nondescript hotel (22 Park Lane, Tube: Hyde Park Corner, tel. 020/7208-4021, www.galvina twindows.com).

The Shard: The observation decks that cap this 1,020-foot-tall skyscraper offer London's most commanding views, but at an outrageously high price. See page 145.

Primrose Hill: For dramatic 360-degree city views, head to the huge grassy expanse at the summit of Primrose Hill, just north of Regent's Park (off Prince Albert Road, Tube: Chalk Farm or Camden Town, www.royalparks.gov.uk/The-Regents-Park).

The Thames River: Various companies run boat trips on the Thames, offering a unique vantage point and unobstructed, ever-changing views of great landmarks (see page 78).

Royal Observatory Greenwich: Enjoy sweeping views of Greenwich's grand buildings in the foreground, the Docklands' skyscrapers in the middle ground, and The City and central London in the distance.

The Monument

Wren's 202-foot-tall tribute to London's Great Fire was restored a few years ago. Climb the 331 steps inside the column for a view of The City that is still monumental.

Cost and Hours: £3, daily 9:30-18:00, until 17:30 Oct-March, last entry 30 minutes before closing, junction of Monument Street and Fish Street Hill, Tube: Monument, tel. 020/7626-2717, www .themonument.info.

▲▲▲Tower of London

The Tower has served as a castle in wartime, a king's residence in peacetime, and, most notoriously, as the prison and execution site of rebels. You can see the crown jewels, take a witty Beefeater tour, and ponder the executioner's block that dispensed with Anne Boleyn, Sir Thomas More, and troublesome heirs to the throne.

Cost and Hours: £22, family-£57 (both prices include a 10 percent optional donation), entry fee includes Beefeater tour (described later); March-Oct Tue-Sat 9:00-17:30, Sun-Mon 10:00-17:30; Nov-Feb Tue-Sat 9:00-16:30, Sun-Mon 10:00-16:30; last entry 30 minutes before closing; skippable audioguide-£4, Tube: Tower Hill, switchboard tel. 0844-482-7777, www.hrp.org.uk.

Advance Tickets: To avoid the long ticket-buying lines at the Tower, buy your ticket at the Trader's Gate gift shop, located down the steps from the Tower Hill Tube stop (tickets here are generally slightly cheaper than at the gate; similar, discounted Fast Track tickets are sold at various locations, such as travel agencies, throughout London). You can also buy tickets, with credit card only, at the Tower Welcome Centre to the left of the normal ticket lines—though on busy days, it can be crowded here as well. It's easy to book online (www.hrp.org.uk, £1 discount, no fee) or by phone (tel. 0844-482-7799 within UK or tel. 011-44-20-3166-6000 from the US; £2 fee), then pick up your tickets at the Tower.

More Crowd-Beating Tips: It's most crowded in summer, on weekends (especially Sundays), and during school holidays. Any time of year, the line for the crown jewels—the best on earth—can be just as long as the line for tickets. For fewer crowds, arrive before 10:00 and go straight for the jewels. Alternatively, arrive in the afternoon, tour the rest of the Tower first, and see the jewels an hour before closing time, when crowds die down.

Yeoman Warder (Beefeater) Tours: Today, while the Tower's military purpose is history, it's still home to the Beefeaters—the 35 Yeoman Warders and their families. (The original duty of the Yeoman Warders was to guard the Tower, its prisoners, and the jewels.) The free, worthwhile, one-hour Beefeater tours leave every 30 minutes from inside the gate (first tour at 10:00, last one at 15:30—or 14:30 in Nov-Feb). The boisterous Beefeaters are great entertainers, and their historical talks include lots of bloody anecdotes and corny jokes.

Sunday Worship: For a refreshingly different Tower experience, come on Sunday morning, when visitors are welcome on the grounds for free to worship in the Chapel Royal of St. Peter ad Vincula. You get in without the lines, but you can only see the chapel—no sightseeing (9:15 Communion or 11:00 service with fine choral music, meet at west gate 30 minutes early, dress for church, may be closed for ceremonies—call ahead).

Visiting the Tower: William I, still getting used to his new title of "the Conqueror," built the stone "White Tower" (1077-

Tower of London

LONDON

- ❶ Entrance Gate
- ❷ Traitor's Gate
- ❸ White Tower Museum
- ❹ Execution Site
- ❺ Crown Jewels
- ❻ Wall Access
- ❼ Chapel Royal of St. Peter ad Vincula
- ❽ Cafeteria
- ❾ Trader's Gate Gift Shop (Tower Tickets)

1097) to keep the Londoners in line. Standing high above the rest of old London, the White Tower provided a gleaming reminder of the monarch's absolute power over subjects. If you made the wrong move here, you could be feasting on roast boar in the banqueting hall one night and chained to the walls of the prison the next. The Tower also served as an effective lookout for seeing invaders coming up the Thames.

Henry VIII
(1491-1547)

The notorious king who single-handedly transformed England was a true Renaissance Man—six feet tall, handsome, charismatic, well-educated, and brilliant. He spoke English, Latin, French, and Spanish. A legendary athlete, he hunted, played tennis, and jousted with knights and kings. He played the lute and wrote folk songs; his "Pastime with Good Company" is still being performed. When 17-year-old Henry, the second monarch of the House of Tudor, was crowned king in Westminster Abbey, all of England rejoiced.

Henry left affairs of state in the hands of others, and filled his days with sports, war, dice, women, and the arts. But in 1529, Henry's personal life became a political atom bomb, and it changed the course of history. Henry wanted a divorce, partly because his wife had become too old to bear him a son, and partly because he'd fallen in love with Anne Boleyn, a younger woman who stubbornly refused to be just the king's mistress. Henry begged the pope for an annulment, but—for political reasons, not moral ones—the pope refused. Henry went ahead and divorced his wife anyway, and he was excommunicated.

The event sparked the English Reformation. With his defiance, Henry rejected papal authority in England. He forced monasteries to close, sold off some church land, and confiscated everything else for himself and the Crown. Within a decade, monastic institutions that had operated for centuries were left empty and gutted (many ruined sites, including the abbeys of Glastonbury, St. Mary's at York, Rievaulx, and Lindisfarne, can be visited today). Meanwhile, the Catholic Church was reorganized into the (Anglican) Church of England, with Henry as its head. Though Henry himself basically adhered to Catholic doctrine, he discouraged the veneration of saints and relics, and commissioned an English translation of the Bible. Hard-core Catholics had to assume a low profile. Many English welcomed this break from Italian religious influence, but others rebelled. For the next few generations, England would suffer through bitter Catholic-Protestant differences.

Henry famously had six wives. The issue was not his love life (which could have been satisfied by his numerous mistresses), but the politics of royal succession. To guarantee the Tudor family's dominance, he needed a male heir born by a recognized queen.

Henry's first marriage, to Catherine of Aragon, had been arranged to cement an alliance with her parents, Ferdinand and

Isabel of Spain. Catherine bore Henry a daughter, but no sons. Next came Anne Boleyn, who also gave birth to a daughter. After a turbulent few years with Anne and several miscarriages, a frustrated Henry had her beheaded at the Tower of London. His next wife, Jane Seymour, finally had a son (but Jane died soon after giving birth). A blind-marriage with Anne of Cleves ended quickly when she proved to be both politically useless and ugly— the "Flanders Mare." Next, teen bride Catherine Howard ended up cheating on Henry, so she was executed. Henry finally found comfort—but no children—in his later years with his final wife, Catherine Parr.

In 1536, Henry suffered a serious accident while jousting. His health would never be the same. Increasingly, he suffered from festering boils and violent mood swings, and he became morbidly obese, tipping the scales at 400 pounds with a 54-inch waist.

Henry's last years were marked by paranoia, sudden rages, and despotism. He gave his perceived enemies the pink slip in his signature way—charged with treason and beheaded. (Ironically, Henry's own heraldic motto was "Coeur Loyal"—true heart.) Once-wealthy England was becoming depleted, thanks to Henry's expensive habits, which included making war on France, building and acquiring palaces (he had 50), and collecting fine tapestries and archery bows.

Henry forged a large legacy. He expanded the power of the monarchy, making himself the focus of a rising, modern nation-state. Simultaneously, he strengthened Parliament—largely because it agreed with his policies. He annexed Wales, and imposed English rule on Ireland (provoking centuries of resent-ment). He expanded the navy, paving the way for Britannia to soon rule the waves. And—thanks to Henry's marital woes— England would forever be a Protestant nation.

When Henry died at age 55, he was succeeded by his nine-year-old son by Jane Seymour, Edward VI. Weak and sickly, Edward died six years later. Next to rule was Mary, Henry's daughter from his first marriage. A staunch Catholic, she tried to brutally reverse England's Protestant Reformation, earning the nickname "Bloody Mary." Finally came Henry's daughter with Anne Boleyn—Queen Elizabeth I, who ruled a prosperous, expanding England, seeing her father's seeds blossom into the English Renaissance.

London abounds with "Henry" sights. He was born in Greenwich (at today's Old Royal Naval College) and was crowned in Westminster Abbey. He built a palace along Whitehall and enjoyed another at Hampton Court. At the National Portrait Gallery, you can see portraits of some of Henry's wives, and at the Tower you can see where he executed them. Henry is buried alongside his final wife at Windsor Castle.

This square, 90-foot-tall tower was the original structure that gave this castle complex of 20 towers its name. William's successors enlarged the complex to its present 18-acre size. Because of the security it provided, the Tower of London served over the centuries as a royal residence, the Royal Mint, the Royal Jewel House, and, most famously, as the prison and execution site of those who dared oppose the Crown.

You'll find more bloody history per square inch in this original tower of power than anywhere else in Britain. Inside the White Tower is a **museum** with exhibits re-creating medieval life and chronicling the torture and executions that took place here. In the Royal Armory, you'll see some suits of armor of Henry VIII—slender in his youth (c. 1515), heavyset by 1540—with his bigger-is-better codpiece. On the top floor, see the Tower's actual execution ax and chopping block.

The **execution site,** however, in the middle of Tower Green, looks just like a lawn. It was here that enemies of the crown would kneel before the king for the final time. With their hands tied behind their backs, they would say a final prayer, then lay their heads on a block, and—*slit*—the blade would slice through their necks, their heads tumbling to the ground. Tower Green was the most prestigious execution site at the Tower. Henry VIII axed a couple of his ex-wives here (divorced readers can insert their own joke), including Anne Boleyn and his fifth wife, teenage Catherine Howard (for more on Henry, see the sidebar on page 132).

The Tower's hard stone and glittering **crown jewels** represent the ultimate power of the monarch. The Sovereign's Scepter is encrusted with the world's largest cut diamond—the 530-carat Star of Africa, beefy as a quarter-pounder. The Crown of the Queen Mother (Elizabeth II's famous mum, who died in 2002) has the 106-carat Koh-I-Noor diamond glittering on the front (considered unlucky for male rulers, it only adorns the crown of the king's wife). The Imperial State Crown is what the Queen wears for official functions such as the State Opening of Parliament. Among its 3,733 jewels are Queen Elizabeth I's former earrings (the hanging pearls, top center), a stunning 13th-century ruby look-alike in the center, and Edward the Confessor's ring (the blue sapphire on top, in the center of the Maltese cross of diamonds).

The Tower was defended by state-of-the-art **walls** and fortifications in the 13th century. Walking along them offers a good look at the walls, along with a fine view of the famous Tower Bridge, with its twin towers and blue spans (described next).

After your visit, consider taking the boat to Greenwich from here (see cruise info on page 80).

Near the Tower of London
Tower Bridge

The iconic Tower Bridge (often mistakenly called London Bridge) has been recently painted and restored. The hydraulically powered drawbridge was built in 1894 to accommodate the growing East End. While fully modern, its design was a retro Neo-Gothic look.

You can tour the bridge at the **Tower Bridge Exhibition,** with a history display and a peek at the Victorian engine room that lifts the span. It's overpriced at £8, though the city views from the walkways are spectacular (daily 10:00-18:00 in summer, 9:30-17:30 in winter, last entry 30 minutes before closing, enter at the northwest tower, Tube: Tower Hill, tel. 020/7403-3761, www.tower bridge.org.uk).

The bridge is most interesting when the drawbridge lifts to let ships pass, as it does a thousand times a year, but it's best viewed from outside the museum. For the bridge-lifting schedule, check the website or call (see above for contact info).

Nearby: The best remaining bit of London's **Roman Wall** is just north of the Tower (at the Tower Hill Tube station). The chic **St. Katharine Dock,** just east of Tower Bridge, has private yachts, mod shops, the recommended medieval banquet, and the classic Dickens Inn, fun for a drink or pub lunch. Across the bridge, on the South Bank, is the upscale Butlers Wharf area, as well as City Hall, museums, the Jubilee Walkway, and, towering overhead, The Shard. Or you can head north to Liverpool Street Station, and stroll London's East End (described next).

Sights in East London

▲East End

The East End has a long history as London's poorer side of town—even in medieval times. These days, it still lacks the posh refinement of the West End—but the area just beyond Liverpool Street Station is now one of London's hippest, most fun spots. It boasts a colorful mix of bustling markets, late-night dance clubs, the Bangladeshi ghetto (called "Banglatown"), and tenements of Jack the Ripper's London, all in the shadow of glittering new skyscrapers. Head up Brick Lane for a meal in "the curry capital of Europe," or check out the former Truman Brewery, which now houses a Sunday market, cool shops, and Café 1001 (good coffee). This neighborhood is best on Sunday afternoons, when the Spitalfields, Petticoat Lane, and Backyard markets thrive (for more on these markets, see page 156).

▲Geffrye Museum

This low-key but well-organized museum—housed in an 18th-century almshouse—is located north of Liverpool Street Station in the hip Shoreditch area. Its displays give a historical overview of the "middling sort" (middle class), as seen through the prism of home decor. Walk past 11 English living rooms, furnished and decorated in styles from 1600 to 2000, then descend the circular stairs to see changing exhibits. In summer, explore the fragrant herb garden.

Cost and Hours: Free, fees for (optional) special exhibits, Tue-Sat 10:00-17:00, Sun 12:00-17:00, closed Mon, garden open April-Oct, 136 Kingsland Road, tel. 020/7739-9893, www.geffrye-museum.org.uk.

Getting There: Take the Tube to Liverpool Street, then ride the bus 10 minutes north (bus #149 or #242—leave station through Bishopsgate exit and head left a few steps to find stop; hop off at the Hoxton Station stop, just after passing the brick museum on the right). Or take the East London line on the Overground to the Hoxton stop, which is right next to the museum (Tube tickets and Oyster cards also valid on Overground).

Sights on the South Bank

The South Bank of the Thames is a thriving arts and cultural center, tied together by the riverfront Jubilee Walkway.

▲Jubilee Walkway

This riverside path is a popular, pub-crawling pedestrian promenade that stretches all along the South Bank, offering grand views of the Houses of Parliament and St. Paul's. On a sunny day, this is the place to see Londoners out strolling. The Walkway hugs the river except just east of London Bridge, where it cuts inland for a couple of blocks. It was recently expanded into a 60-mile "Greenway" circling the city, including the 2012 Olympics site.

▲▲London Eye

This giant Ferris wheel, towering above London opposite Big Ben, is one of the world's highest observational wheels and London's answer to the Eiffel Tower. Riding it is a memorable experience, even though London doesn't have much of a skyline, and the price is borderline outrageous. Whether you ride or not, the wheel is a sight to behold.

The experience starts with a brief (four-minute) and engaging show combining a 3-D movie with wind and water effects. Then it's time to spin around the Eye. Designed like a giant bicycle wheel, it's a pan-European undertaking: British steel and Dutch engineering, with Czech, German, French, and Italian mechanical parts. It's also very "green," running extremely efficiently and virtually silently. Twenty-five people ride in each of its 32 air-conditioned capsules for the 30-minute rotation (you go around only once). Each capsule has a bench, but most people stand. From the top of this 443-foot-high wheel—the second-highest public viewpoint in the city—even Big Ben looks small.

Cost: £19, family ticket available, about 10 percent cheaper if bought online. Buy tickets in advance at www.londoneye.com, by calling 0870-500-0600, or in person at the box office (in the corner of the County Hall building nearest the Eye). Combo-tickets that also cover Madame Tussauds Waxworks cost roughly twice as much (also cheaper online).

Hours: Daily July-Aug 10:00-21:30, April-June 10:00-21:00, Sept-March 10:00-20:30, these are last-ascent times, closed Dec 25 and a few days in Jan for annual maintenance, Tube: Waterloo or Westminster. Thames boats come and go from Waterloo Pier at the foot of the wheel.

Crowd-Beating Tips: The London Eye is busiest between 11:00 and 17:00, especially on weekends year-round and every day in July and August. When it's crowded, you might have to wait up to 30 minutes to buy your ticket, then another 30-45 minutes to board your capsule. If you plan to visit during a busy time, call ahead or go online to pre-book your ticket. Once at the sight, you punch your confirmation code into the automated machine in the ticket office (otherwise, you can pick up your ticket in the short "Groups and Ticket Collection" line at desk #5). Even if you pre-reserve, you still have to wait a bit to board the wheel. You can pay an extra £7-10 for a Fast Track ticket that lets you jump the queue, but the time you save is probably not worth the expense.

By the Eye: The area next to the London Eye has developed a cotton-candy ambience of kitschy, kid-friendly attractions. There's

The South Bank

an aquarium, game arcade, and London Film Museum dedicated to movies filmed in London, from *Harry Potter* to *Star Wars* (not to be confused with the far-superior British Film Institute, a.k.a. the BFI Southbank, just to the east).

▲▲Imperial War Museum

This impressive museum covers the wars of the last century—from World War I biplanes, to the rise of fascism, to Montgomery's Africa campaign tank, to the Cold War, the Cuban Missile Crisis,

the Troubles in Northern Ireland, the wars in Iraq and Afghanistan, and terrorism. Rather than glorify war, the museum does its best to shine a light on the 100 million deaths of the 20th century. It shows everyday life for people back home and never neglects the human side of one of civilization's more uncivilized, persistent traits.

Allow plenty of time, as this powerful museum—with lots of

artifacts and video clips—can be engrossing. The highlights are the new WWI galleries and the WWII area, the "Secret War" section, and the Holocaust exhibit. (Some sections may be closed for renovation in early 2014.) War wonks love the place, as do general history buffs who enjoy patiently reading displays. For the rest, there are enough interactive experiences and multimedia exhibits and submarines for the kids to climb in to keep it interesting.

Cost and Hours: Free, daily 10:00-18:00, last entry 17:45, temporary exhibits extra, audioguide-£3.50, guided tours usually Sat-Sun at 11:30 and 13:30—confirm at info desk, Tube: Lambeth North or Elephant and Castle; buses #3, #12, and #159 come here from Westminster area; tel. 020/7416-5000, www.iwm.org.uk.

Visiting the Museum: Start with the museum's latest pride and joy: the **WWI galleries,** newly souped up for the centennial anniversary of the start of the "Great War." Exhibits cover the various theaters and the war at sea, as well as the home front, and the Treaty of Versailles and interwar years. The Trench Experience lets you walk through a dark, chaotic, smelly WWI trench. Then head into the **WWII section** that explains the Blitzkrieg and its effects (see an actual Nazi parachute bomb like the ones that devastated

London). The Blitz Experience is a walk-through simulator that assaults the senses with the noise and intensity of a WWII air raid on London (begins every 10 minutes). End with a visit to a special exhibit celebrating Field Marshal Bernard Montgomery, and the displays about conflicts since 1945.

The **cinema** on the ground floor shows a rotating selection of films. Up on the first floor, you'll get the best view of the entry hall's **large exhibits**—including Monty's tank, several field guns, and, dangling overhead, vintage planes. Imagine the awesome power of the 50-foot V-2 rocket (towering up from the ground floor)—the kind the Nazis rained down on London, which could arrive silently and destroy a city block.

Near the first-floor stairwell is the **"Secret War"** exhibit, which peeks into the intrigues of espionage and poses challenging questions about the role of secrecy in government.

The second floor has temporary exhibits and the **John Singer Sargent room,** an art gallery of military-themed works; hiding behind the entryway is Sargent's *Gassed* (1919) and other giant canvases. Across the hall is a provocative 30-minute **film** about genocide, *Crimes Against Humanity.* The third-floor section on the **Holocaust,** one of the best on the subject anywhere, tells the story with powerful videos, artifacts, and fine explanations.

The museum (which sits in an inviting park equipped with an equally inviting café) is housed in what had been the Royal Bethlam Hospital. Also known as "the Bedlam asylum," the place was so wild that it gave the world a new word for chaos. Back in Victorian times, Londoners—without reality shows and YouTube—paid admission to visit the asylum on weekends for entertainment.

From Tate Modern to City Hall

These sights are in Southwark (SUTH-uck), the core of the tourist's South Bank. Southwark was for centuries the place Londoners would go to escape the rules and decency of the city and let their hair down. Bearbaiting, brothels, rollicking pubs, and theater—you name the dream, and it could be fulfilled just across the Thames. A run-down warehouse district through the 20th century, it's been gentrified with classy restaurants, office parks, pedestrian promenades, major sights (such as the Tate Modern and Shakespeare's Globe), and a colorful collection of lesser sights. The area is easy on foot and a scenic—though circuitous—way to connect the Tower of London with St. Paul's.

▲▲Tate Modern

Dedicated in the spring of 2000, the striking museum across the river from St. Paul's opened the new century with art from the pre-

vious one. Its powerhouse collection of Monet, Matisse, Dalí, Picasso, Warhol, and much more is displayed in a converted powerhouse.

The permanent collection is on levels 2 through 4. Paintings are arranged according to theme, not chronologically or by artist. Paintings by Picasso, for example, are scattered all over the building. Don't just come to see the Old Masters of modernism. Push your mental envelope with more recent works by Pollock, Miró, Bacon, Picabia, Beuys, Twombly, and others.

Of equal interest are the many temporary exhibits featuring cutting-edge art. Each year, the main hall features a different monumental installation by a prominent artist—always one of the highlights of the art world. The Tate is constructing a new wing to the south, which will double the museum's exhibition space. The new wing is opening bit by bit and, once it's finished, the permanent exhibits will likely be rearranged, with some pieces moving to the new section.

Cost and Hours: Free, but £4 donation appreciated, fee for special exhibitions, open daily 10:00-18:00, Fri-Sat until 22:00, last entry to temporary exhibits 45 minutes before closing, especially crowded on weekend days (crowds thin out on Fri and Sat evenings), audioguide-£4, free 45-minute guided tours are offered about four times daily (ask for schedule at info desk), no photos beyond entrance hall, coffee shops and restaurant, tel. 020/7887-8888, www.tate.org.uk.

Getting There: Cross the Millennium Bridge from St. Paul's; take the Tube to Southwark, London Bridge, or Mansion House and walk 10-15 minutes; or catch Thames Clippers' Tate Boat ferry service from the Tate Britain (£5.50 one-way or £15 for day ticket, discounts with Travelcard or Oyster card, buy ticket at gallery desk or on board, departs every 40 minutes from 9:55 to 17:00, about 15 minutes, check schedule at www.tate.org.uk/visit/tate-boat).

▲Millennium Bridge

The pedestrian bridge links St. Paul's Cathedral and the Tate Modern across the Thames. This is London's first new bridge in a century. When it first opened, the $25 million bridge wiggled when people walked on it, so it promptly closed for repairs; 20 months and $8 million later, it reopened. Nicknamed the "blade of light" for its sleek minimalist design (370 yards long, four yards wide, stainless steel with teak planks), its clever aerodynamic handrails deflect wind over the heads of pedestrians.

▲▲Shakespeare's Globe

This replica of the original Globe Theatre was built, half-timbered and thatched, as it was in Shakespeare's time. (This is the first thatched roof constructed in London since they were outlawed after the Great Fire of 1666.) The Globe originally accommodated 2,200 seated and another 1,000 standing. Today, slightly smaller and leaving space for reasonable aisles, the theater holds 800 seated and 600 groundlings. Its promot-

ers brag that the theater melds "the three A's"—actors, audience, and architecture—with each contributing to the play. The working theater hosts authentic performances of Shakespeare's plays with actors in period costumes, modern interpretations of his works, and some works by other playwrights. For details on attending a play, see page 166.

Cost: £13.50, includes Exhibition, audioguide, and 40-minute tour of the Globe; tickets good all day; when the Globe theater is closed, you can tour the Exhibition only for £10, or take a guided tour of the nearby Rose Theatre (also £10, only available some afternoons).

Hours: The complex is open daily 9:00-17:00. Exhibition and tours: May-Sept—Globe tours offered mornings only with Rose Theatre tours some afternoons; Oct-April—Globe tours run all day, tours start every 15-30 minutes. Located on the South Bank directly across Thames over Southwark Bridge from St. Paul's, Tube: Mansion House or London Bridge plus a 10-minute walk; tel. 020/7902-1400 or 020/7902-1500, www.shakespearesglobe.com.

Visiting the Globe: The complex has four parts: the Globe theater itself, the box office, a museum (the Exhibition), and the new Sam Wanamaker Playhouse (an indoor Jacobean theater). The Globe Exhibition ticket includes both a tour of the Globe theater and the Exhibition.

Exhibition: You browse on your own (with the included audioguide) through displays of Elizabethan-era costumes and makeup, music, script-printing, and special effects (the displays change). There are early folios and objects that were dug up on site. Videos and scale models help put Shakespearean theater within the context of the times. (The Globe opened one year after England mastered the seas by defeating the Spanish Armada. The debut play was Shakespeare's *Julius Caesar*.) You'll also learn how they built the replica in modern times, using Elizabethan materials and techniques. Take advantage of the touch screens to delve into specific topics.

Theater: You must tour the theater at the time stamped on your ticket, but you can come back to the Exhibition museum

afterward; tickets are good all day. A guide (usually an actor) leads you into the theater to see the stage and the various seating areas for the different classes of people. You take a seat and learn how the new Globe is similar to the old Globe (open-air performances, standing-room by the stage, no curtain) and how it's different (female actors today, lights for night performances, concrete floor). It's not a backstage tour—you don't see dressing rooms or costume shops or sit in on rehearsals, though you may see workers building sets for a new production. You mostly sit and listen. The guides are energetic, theatrical, and knowledgeable, bringing the Elizabethan period to life.

When matinee performances are going on, you can't tour the theater. But you can see the Exhibition museum, or possibly tour the nearby Rose Theatre (occasionally open and less interesting).

Sam Wanamaker Playhouse: The indoor Jacobean theater, which is attached to the back of the Globe complex, allows performances to continue through the winter. The intimate venue is horseshoe-shaped, seats fewer than 350, and is designed to use authentic candle-lighting for period performances. The repertoire focuses less on Shakespeare and more on the work of his contemporaries (Jonson, Marlow, Fletcher), as well as concerts. (For details on getting tickets, go to www.shakespearesglobe .com.) There may be tours of this new theater, but—as at the Globe itself—tours always come second to the performance schedule.

Eating: The Swan at the Globe café offers a sit-down restaurant (for lunch and dinner, reservations recommended, tel. 020/7928-9444), a drinks-and-plates bar, and a sandwich-and-coffee cart (daily 9:00-closing, depending on performance times).

Vinopolis

While it seems illogical to have a huge wine museum in beer-loving London, Vinopolis makes a good case for itself. Built over a Roman wine store and filling the massive vaults of an old wine warehouse, the museum offers interactive exhibits that give a light yet earnest history of wine to accompany your sips of various mediocre reds and whites, ports, and champagnes. A few varieties of spirits help keep it interesting. Your visit starts with a 15-minute wine-tasting lesson, then you're let loose. Ticket prices vary according to how many virtual "tokens" you load onto a card, which you use to dispense your samples through their "enomatic" machines (most wines cost 1-4 tokens). Tapas-style snacks are available, in addition to the five restaurants on site. Booking ahead for Friday and Saturday nights is smart.

Cost and Hours: Self-guided tour options range from £27 (7 tokens) to £38 (16 tokens); also offer packages that include a meal, Wed 18:00-21:30, Thu-Fri 14:00-21:30, Sat 12:00-21:30, Sun 12:00-16:00, closed Mon-Tue, last entry 2 hours before closing, between Shakespeare's Globe and Southwark Cathedral at 1 Bank End, Tube: London Bridge, tel. 020/7940-3000, www.vinopolis.co.uk.

The Clink Prison Museum

Proudly known as the "original clink," this was, until 1780, where law-abiding citizens threw Southwark troublemakers. Today, it's a low-tech torture museum filling grotty old rooms with papier-mâché gore. Unfortunately, there's little that seriously deals with the fascinating problem of law and order in Southwark, where 18th-century Londoners went for a good time.

Cost and Hours: Overpriced at £7.50; July-Sept daily 10:00-21:00; Oct-June Mon-Fri 10:00-18:00, Sat-Sun until 21:00, last entry 30 minutes before closing; 1 Clink Street, Tube: London Bridge, tel. 020/7403-0900, www.clink.co.uk.

Golden Hinde Replica

This is a full-size replica of the 16th-century warship in which Sir Francis Drake circumnavigated the globe from 1577 to 1580. Commanding the original ship (now long gone), Drake earned his reputation as history's most successful pirate. This replica, however, has logged more than 100,000 miles, including a voyage around the world. While the ship is fun to see, its interior is not worth touring.

Cost and Hours: £6, daily 10:00-17:30, last entry at 16:45, sometimes closed for private events, Tube: London Bridge, ticket office just up Pickfords Wharf from the ship, tel. 020/7403-0123, www.goldenhinde.com.

▲Southwark Cathedral

While made a cathedral only in 1905, it's been the neighborhood church since the 13th century, and comes with some interesting history. The enthusiastic docents give impromptu tours if you ask.

Cost and Hours: Free, but £4 donation requested (you'll likely be approached about the donation, so be prepared with at least £1 or a simple "No"), daily 8:00-18:30—though only the back of the nave is open to discreet sightseers during frequent services, last entry 30 minutes before closing, £3.50 guidebook, no photos without permission (£2), Tube: London Bridge. Tel. 020/7367-6700, http://cathedral.southwark.anglican.org.

Music: The cathedral hosts evensong Sun at 15:00, Tue-Fri 17:30, Sat at 16:00; they also host organ recitals Mon at 13:00 and music recitals Tue at 15:15 (call or check website to confirm times of evensong and recitals).

▲Old Operating Theatre Museum and Herb Garret

Climb a tight and creaky wooden spiral staircase to a church attic where you'll find a garret used to dry medicinal herbs, a fascinating exhibit on Victorian surgery, cases of well-described 19th-century medical paraphernalia, and a special look at "anesthesia, the defeat of pain." Then you stumble upon Britain's oldest operating theater, where limbs were sawed off way back in 1821.

Cost and Hours: £6.20, cash only, borrowable laminated descriptions, daily 10:30-16:45, closed Dec 15-Jan 5, £1 audioguide tries hard but is not quite worthwhile, 9a St. Thomas Street, Tube: London Bridge, tel. 020/7188-2679, www.thegarret.org.uk.

The Shard

Rocketing dramatically 1,020 feet above the south end of the London Bridge, this recent addition to London's skyline is by far the tallest building in Western Europe (for now). Designed by Renzo Piano (best known as the co-architect of Paris' Pompidou Center), the glass-clad pyramid shimmers in the sun and its prickly top glows like the city's nightlight after dark. Its uppermost floors are set aside as public viewing galleries, but the ticket price is as outrageously high as the building itself, especially given that it's a bit far from London's most exciting landmarks. For a list of cheaper view opportunities in London, see the sidebar on page 128.

Cost and Hours: £25 if booked at least a day in advance, £29 for same-day reservations, book as soon as you have reasonable chance of assuring decent weather, least crowded on weekday mornings, daily 9:00-22:00, last entry slot at 20:30, Tube: London Bridge—use London Bridge exit, tel. 0844-499-7111, www.theviewfromtheshard.com.

Ascending the Tower: From the entrance on Joiner Street (just off St. Thomas Street) you'll take a two-part elevator ride up to the 68th floor, then climb up one story to the main observation platform. It's equipped with cool telescopes that label major landmarks, and even let you see how the view from here would appear at other times of the day. From here you've got great views of St. Paul's, the Tower of London, Southwark Cathedral (straight down), and, in the distance, the 2012 Olympic stadium in one direction, and the Houses of Parliament in the other (find Buckingham Palace, just left of the Eye). On the clearest days, you can see 40 miles out, and a few people say they've been able to make out ships on the North Sea. Even in bad weather it's mesmerizing to watch the constant movement of the city's transit system, which looks like a model-train set from this height. Climbing up to the 72nd floor gets you to the open-air deck, where the wind roars over the glass enclosure. As you look up, try to picture Prince Andrew rappelling off the very top, which he and 40 others did in 2012 as a charity fundraising stunt.

HMS Belfast

"The last big-gun armored warship of World War II" clogs the Thames just upstream from the Tower Bridge. This huge vessel—now manned with wax sailors—thrills kids who always dreamed of sitting in a turret shooting off their imaginary guns. If you're into WWII warships, this is the ultimate. Otherwise, it's just lots of exercise with a nice view of the Tower Bridge.

Cost and Hours: £15 including 9 percent voluntary donation, includes audioguide, kids under 15 free, daily March-Oct 10:00-18:00, Nov-Feb 10:00-17:00, last entry one hour before closing, Tube: London Bridge, tel. 020/7940-6300, www.iwm.org.uk /visits/hms-belfast.

City Hall

The glassy, egg-shaped building near the south end of Tower Bridge is London's City Hall, designed by Sir Norman Foster, the architect who worked on London's Millennium Bridge and Berlin's Reichstag. Nicknamed "the Armadillo," City Hall houses the office of London's mayor—the blond, flamboyant, conservative former journalist and author Boris Johnson. He consults here with the Assembly representatives of the city's 25 districts. An interior spiral ramp allows visitors to watch and hear the action below in the Assembly Chamber—ride the lift to floor 2 (the highest visitors can go) and spiral down. On the lower ground

floor is a large aerial photograph of London and a handy cafeteria. Next to City Hall is the outdoor amphitheater called The Scoop (see page 170).

Cost and Hours: Free, open to visitors Mon-Thu 8:30-18:00, Fri 8:30-17:30, closed Sat-Sun; Tube: London Bridge station plus 10-minute walk, or Tower Hill station plus 15-minute walk; tel. 020/7983-4000, www.london.gov.uk.

Sights in West London

▲▲Tate Britain

One of Europe's great art houses, Tate Britain specializes in British painting from the 16th century through modern times. This is peo-

ple's art, with realistic paintings rooted in the people, landscapes, and stories of the British Isles.

The recently renovated Tate shows off Hogarth's stage sets, Gainsborough's ladies, Blake's angels, Constable's clouds, Turner's tempests, the swooning realism of the Pre-Raphaelites, and the camera-eye portraits of Hockney and Freud. Even if these names are new to you, don't worry. You'll likely see a few "famous" works you didn't know were British and exit the Tate Britain with at least one new favorite artist.

Cost and Hours: Free but £4 donation requested, admission fee for (optional) temporary exhibits, map-£1 suggested donation, ask if audioguide is available; daily 10:00-18:00, sometimes Fri until 22:00 (check online or call to confirm), last entry 45 minutes before closing; free tours generally offered daily—ask at the information desk or call ahead; café and restaurant, tel. 020/7887-8888, www.tate.org.uk.

Getting There: It's on the Thames River, south of Big Ben and north of Vauxhall Bridge. Take the Tube to Pimlico, then walk seven minutes. Or hop on the Tate Boat museum ferry from the Tate Modern (for details, see page 81).

Hyde Park and Nearby

A number of worthwhile sights border this grand park, from Apsley House on the east to the newly renovated Kensington Palace on the west.

▲Apsley House (Wellington Museum)

Having beaten Napoleon at Waterloo, Arthur Wellesley, the First Duke of Wellington, was once the most famous man in Europe. He was given a huge fortune, with which he purchased London's ultimate address, #1 London. His refurbished mansion offers a nice interior, a handful of world-class paintings, and a glimpse at the life of the great soldier and two-time prime minister. The highlight is the large ballroom, the Waterloo Gallery, decorated with Anthony van Dyck's *Charles I on Horseback* (over the main fireplace), Diego Velázquez's earthy *Water-Seller of Seville* (to the left of Van Dyck), and Jan Steen's playful *Dissolute Household* (to the right). Just outside the door, in the Portico Room, is a large portrait of Wellington by Francisco Goya.

Those who know something about Wellington ahead of time will appreciate the place much more than those who don't, as there's scarce biographical information provided. The place is well-described by the included audioguide, which has sound bites from the current Duke of Wellington (who still lives at Apsley).

Cost and Hours: £6.70, free on June 18—Waterloo Day, April-Oct Wed-Sun 11:00-17:00, closed Mon-Tue; Nov-March Sat-Sun 10:00-16:00, closed Mon-Fri; no photos, 20 yards from Hyde Park Corner Tube station, tel. 020/7499-5676, www.english -heritage.org.uk.

Nearby: Hyde Park's pleasant rose garden is picnic-friendly. **Wellington Arch,** which stands just across the street, is open to the public (except closed Mon-Tue) but not worth the £4 charge (or £8.60 combo-ticket with Apsley House; elevator up, lousy views and boring exhibits).

▲Hyde Park and Speakers' Corner
London's "Central Park," originally Henry VIII's hunting grounds, has more than 600 acres of lush greenery, "Boris Bikes" rental stations, the huge man-made Serpentine Lake (with rental boats and a lakeside swimming pool), the royal Kensington Palace (described later), and the ornate Neo-Gothic Albert Memorial across from

the Royal Albert Hall (for more about the park, see www.royal parks.org.uk/parks/hyde-park). The western half of the park is known as Kensington Gardens. The park is huge—study a Tube map to choose the stop nearest to your destination.

On Sundays, from just after noon until early evening, **Speakers' Corner** offers soapbox oratory at its best (northeast corner of the park, Tube: Marble Arch). Characters climb their stepladders, wave their flags, pound emphatically on their sandwich boards, and share what they are convinced is their wisdom. Regulars have resident hecklers who know their lines and are always ready with a verbal jab or barb. "The grass roots of democracy" is actually a holdover from when the gallows stood here and the criminal was allowed to say just about anything he wanted to before he swung. I dare you to raise your voice and gather a crowd—it's easy to do.

The **Princess Diana Memorial Fountain** honors the "People's Princess," who once lived in nearby Kensington Palace. The low-key circular stream, great for cooling off your feet on a hot day, is in the south-central part of the park, near the Albert Memorial and Serpentine Gallery (Tube: Knightsbridge). A similarly named but different sight, the **Diana, Princess of Wales Memorial Playground,** is in the park's northwest corner and fun for kids (Tube: Queensway).

▲▲Kensington Palace

For nearly 150 years (1689-1837), Kensington was the royal resi-

dence, before Buckingham Palace became the official home of the monarch. Sitting primly on its pleasant parkside grounds, the palace is immaculately restored and creatively presented, with exhibits designed to appeal to adults and kids alike. It gives a fun glimpse into the lives of several important residents, especially Queen Victoria, who was born and raised here.

Cost and Hours: £16.50 (includes 10 percent optional donation), save £1 by booking online, daily 10:00-18:00, until 17:00 Nov-Feb, last entry one hour before closing, least crowded in mornings, £5 guidebook but friendly "explainers" will answer questions for free, lockers take £1 coin deposit, a 10-minute stroll through Kensington Gardens from either High Street Kensington or Queensway Tube stations, tel. 0844-482-7788, www.hrp.org.uk.

Background: After Queen Victoria moved the monarchy to Buckingham Palace, lesser royals bedded down at Kensington. Princess Diana lived here both during and after her marriage to Prince Charles (1981-1997). More recently, Will and Kate moved into the thoroughly renovated Apartment 1A (the southern flank of the palace complex, with four stories and 20 rooms). And Prince Harry lives in their old digs, a "cottage" on the other side of the main building. However—as many disappointed visitors discover—none of these more recent apartments are open to the public.

Visiting the Palace: After buying your ticket, head into the vestibule. From here, you can reach any of the three main exhibits. To see them chronologically, head to the right, starting with the **Queen's State Apartments** (with highly conceptual exhibits focusing on the later Stuart dynasty—William and Mary, and Mary's sister, Queen Anne). Then move on to the **King's State Apartments** (the grandest spaces, from Hanoverian times), and finish with the **"Victoria Revealed"** exhibit (telling the story, through quotes and artifacts, of Britain's longest-ruling monarch).

Nearby: Garden enthusiasts enjoy popping into the secluded Sunken Garden, 50 yards from the exit. Consider afternoon tea at the nearby Orangery (see page 211), built as a greenhouse for Queen Anne in 1704. On the south side of the palace are the golden gates that became famous in 1997 as the backdrop to the sea of flowers left here by Princess Diana's mourners.

▲▲▲Victoria and Albert Museum

The world's top collection of decorative arts (vases, stained glass, fine furniture, clothing, jewelry, carpets, and more), "the V&A" is a surprisingly interesting assortment of crafts from the West, as well as Asian and Islamic cultures. Highlights include Raphael's tapestry cartoons, a cast of Trajan's Column that depicts the emperor's conquests, one of Leonardo da Vinci's notebooks, ladies' underwear through the ages, a Chihuly chandelier, a life-size *David* with detachable fig leaf, Henry VIII's quill pen, and Mick Jagger's sequined jumpsuit. From the worlds of Islam and India, there are stunning carpets, the ring of the man who built the Taj Mahal, and a mechanical tiger that eats Brits. Best of all, the objects are all quite beautiful. You could spend days in the place. Pick up a museum map and wander at will.

Cost and Hours: Free, but £3 donation requested, sometimes pricey fees for (optional) special exhibits, £1 suggested donation for much-needed museum map, daily 10:00-17:45, some galleries open Fri until 22:00, free one-hour tours daily on the half-hour 10:30-15:30, on Cromwell Road in South Kensington, Tube: South Kensington, from the Tube station a long tunnel leads directly to museum, tel. 020/7942-2000, www.vam.ac.uk.

▲▲Natural History Museum

Across the street from Victoria and Albert, this mammoth museum is housed in a giant and wonderful Victorian, Neo-

Romanesque building. In the main hall, above a big dinosaur skeleton and under a massive slice of sequoia tree, Charles Darwin sits as if upon a throne overseeing it all. Built in the 1870s specifically for the huge collection (50 million specimens), the building has several color-coded "zones" that cover everything from life ("creepy crawlies," human biology, "our place in evolution," and awe-inspiring dinosaurs) to earth science (meteors, volcanoes, earthquakes, and so on). Use the helpful map (£1 suggested donation) to find your way through the collection. Exhibits are wonderfully explained, with lots of creative, interactive displays.

Cost and Hours: Free, but £3 donation requested, fees for (optional) special exhibits, daily 10:00-17:50, open later last Fri of the month, last entry 20 minutes before closing, long tunnel leads directly from South Kensington Tube station to museum, tel. 020/7942-5000, exhibit info and reservations tel. 020/7942-5011, www.nhm.ac.uk.

▲Science Museum

Next door to the Natural History Museum, this sprawling wonderland for curious minds is kid-perfect, with themes such as measuring time, exploring space, climate change, and the evolution of modern medicine. It offers hands-on fun, from moonwalks to deep-sea exploration, with trendy technology exhibits and a state-of-the-art IMAX theater (shows-£10, £8 for kids, £27 family ticket).

Cost and Hours: Free, daily 10:00-18:00, until 19:00 during school holidays, last entry 45 minutes before closing, Exhibition Road, Tube: South Kensington, tel. 0870-870-4868, www.science museum.org.uk.

LONDON

Sights in Greater London

East of London
▲▲The Docklands

Once the primary harbor for the Port of London, the Docklands has been transformed into a vibrant business center, with ultra-tall skyscrapers, subterranean supermalls, trendy pubs, and peaceful parks with pedestrian bridges looping over canals. While not full of the touristy sights that many are seeking in London, the Docklands offers a refreshing look at the British version of a 21st-century city. It's best at the end of the workday, when it's lively with office workers. It's ideal to see on your way back from Greenwich, since both line up on the same train tracks.

Getting to the Docklands from the City Center: Take the Tube's Jubilee Line to the Canary Wharf station (15 minutes from Westminster, frequent departures). Or catch the Thames Clippers boat to Canary Wharf Pier (£6.50 one-way, £15 all-day pass; boats leave every 20-30 minutes from major London docks; 10-30-minute trip).

Combining the Docklands with Greenwich: It's easy to connect the Docklands with Greenwich—by Docklands Light Rail (DLR) or by boat (for details, see "Getting to Greenwich" on page 232). You could sightsee Greenwich in the morning and early afternoon, then make a brief stop at the Docklands (Canary Wharf station) on your way back to the city center.

▲Museum of London Docklands

Illuminating the gritty and fascinating history of this site, this museum traces the story of what was London's primary harbor. You'll see fascinating models of Old London Bridge, crammed with little houses and shops (not unlike how Florence's Ponte Vecchio still looks); a reconstruction of a "Legal Quay," where cargo was processed; and a re-creation of the fuel pipeline that was laid under the English Channel to supply the Allies on the Continent during WWII. You'll also walk through gritty "Sailortown," listening to the salty voices of those who lived and worked in quarters like these.

Cost and Hours: Free, daily 10:00-18:00, last entry 30 minutes before closing, West India Quay, Tube: West India Quay or Canary Wharf, tel. 020/7001-9844, www.museumoflondon.org.uk/docklands.

West of London
▲▲Kew Gardens

For a fine riverside park and a palatial greenhouse jungle to swing through, take the Tube or the boat to every botanist's favorite escape, Kew Gardens. While to most visitors the Royal Botanic

Gardens of Kew are simply a delightful opportunity to wander among 33,000 different types of plants, to the hardworking organization that runs them, the gardens are a way to promote the understanding and preservation of the botanical diversity of our planet. From the Kew Tube station, cross the footbridge over the tracks, which drops you in a little community of plant-and-herb shops, a two-block walk from Victoria Gate (the main garden entrance). Pick up a map brochure and check at the gate for a monthly listing of best blooms.

Garden-lovers could spend days exploring Kew's 300 acres. For a quick visit, spend a fragrant hour wandering through three buildings: the Palm House, a humid Victorian world of iron, glass, and tropical plants that was built in 1844; a Waterlily House that Monet would swim for (see photo); and the Princess of Wales Conservatory, a meandering modern greenhouse with many different climate zones growing countless cacti, bug-munching carnivorous plants, and more. With extra time, check out the Xstrata Treetop Walkway, a 200-yard-long scenic steel walkway that puts you high in the canopy 60 feet above the ground. Young kids will love

the Climbers and Creepers indoor/outdoor playground and little zip line, as well as a slow and easy ride on the hop-on, hop-off Kew Explorer tram (£4 for narrated 40-minute ride, departs on the hour from 11:00 from near Victoria Gate, 2/hour in summer).

Cost: £16 (includes £1.50 voluntary donation), discounted to £14 45 minutes before glasshouses close, kids under 17 free.

Hours: April-Aug Mon-Fri 9:30-18:30, Sat-Sun 9:30-19:30, closes earlier Sept-March—check schedule online, last entry to gardens 30 minutes before closing, glasshouses close at 17:30 in high season—earlier off-season, free one-hour walking tours daily at 11:00 and 13:30, Tube: Kew Gardens, boats run April-Oct between Kew Gardens and Westminster Pier—see page 80, switchboard tel. 020/8332-5000, recorded info tel. 020/8332-5655, www.kew.org.

Eating: For a sun-dappled lunch or snack, walk 10 minutes from the Palm House to the Orangery Cafeteria (£4 sandwiches, £8-12 lunches, daily 10:00-17:30, until 15:15 in winter, closes early for events).

▲Hampton Court Palace

Fifteen miles up the Thames from downtown, the 500-year-old palace of Henry VIII is worth ▲▲ for palace aficionados.

Actually, it was originally the palace of his minister, Cardinal Wolsey. When Wolsey, a clever man, realized Henry VIII was experiencing a little palace envy, he gave the mansion to his king. The Tudor palace was also home to Elizabeth I and Charles I. Sections were updated by Christopher Wren for William and Mary. The stately palace stands overlooking the Thames and includes some impressive Tudor rooms, including a Great Hall with a magnificent hammer-beam ceiling. The industrial-strength Tudor kitchen was capable of keeping 600 schmoozing courtiers thoroughly—if not well—fed. The sculpted garden features a rare Tudor tennis court and a popular maze.

The palace tries hard to please, but it doesn't quite sparkle. From the information center in the main courtyard, you can pick up audioguides for self-guided tours of various wings of the palace (free but slow, aimed mostly at school-aged children). For more in-depth information, strike up a conversation with the costumed characters or docents posted in each room. The Tudor portions of the castle, including the rooms dedicated to the young Henry, are most interesting; the Georgian rooms are pretty dull. The maze in the nearby garden is a curiosity some find fun (maze free with palace ticket, otherwise £5).

Cost and Hours: £18, family-£45 (both prices include a 10 percent optional donation); online discounts, daily April-Oct 10:00-18:00, Nov-March 10:00-16:30, last entry one hour before closing, café, tel. 0844-482-7777 or 020/3166-6000, www.hrp.org.uk.

Getting There: The train (2/hour, 35 minutes, Oyster cards OK) from London's Waterloo Station drops you across the river from the palace (just walk across the bridge). Consider arriving at or departing from the palace by boat (connections with London's Westminster Pier, see page 80); it's a relaxing and scenic three- to four-hour cruise past two locks and a fun new/old riverside mix.

Kew Gardens/Hampton Court Blitz: Because these two sights are in the same general direction (about £20 for a taxi between the two), you can visit both in one day. Here's a game plan: Start your morning at Hampton Court, tour the palace and garden, and have a Tudor-style lunch in the atmospheric dining hall. After lunch, take bus #R68 from Hampton Court Station to Richmond (40 minutes), then transfer to bus #65, which will drop you off at the Kew Gardens gate (5 minutes). After touring the gardens, have tea in the Orangery, then Tube or boat back to London.

North of London
The Making of Harry Potter: Warner Bros. Studio Tour

A nirvana for Potterphiles, this attraction lets fans young and old see the actual sets and props that were used to create the Harry Potter films, video interviews with the actors and filmmakers, and exhibits about how the films' special effects were created. Visitors must book a time slot in advance—it's essential to reserve your visit online as far ahead as possible. Since it's located in Leavesden, a 20-minute train ride from London, and takes about three hours to experience, a visit here will eat up the better part of a day.

Cost and Hours: £29, kids ages 5 to 15—£21.50, family ticket for 2 adults and 2 kids—£85, audio/videoguide—£5; opening hours flex with season—first tour at 9:00 or 10:00, last tour as early as 16:00 or as late as 18:30; café, still photography allowed, tel. 0845-084-0900, www.wbstudiotour.co.uk.

Getting There: Reaching the studio requires a **train and shuttle bus** connection. First, take the frequent train from London Euston to Watford Junction (about 5/hour, 15-20 minutes). From there, you can take a Mullany's Coaches shuttle bus to the studio tour (2-4/hour, 15 minutes, arrive at Watford Junction at least 45 minutes before your tour entrance time, £1.50 one-way, £2 round-trip). Golden Tours runs three more direct (and more expensive) **buses** per day between their office near Victoria Station in central London and the studio (price includes round-trip bus and entrance: adults—£57, kids—£52; leaves London at 8:00, 11:00, and 14:00, tour begins 2 hours after bus departs, reserve ahead at www.goldentours.com).

Shopping in London

Most stores are open Monday through Saturday from roughly 10:00 to 18:00, and many close Sundays. Large department stores stay open later during the week (until 20:00 or 21:00) and are open shorter hours on Sundays. If you're looking for bargains, you can visit one of the city's many street markets.

Shopping Streets

London is famous for its shopping. The best and most convenient shopping streets are in the West End and West London (roughly between Soho and Hyde Park). You'll find mid-range shops along **Oxford Street** (running east from Tube: Marble Arch), and fancier shops along **Regent Street** (stretching south from Tube: Oxford Circus to Piccadilly Circus) and **Knightsbridge** (where you'll find Harrods and Harvey Nichols, described later; Tube: Knightsbridge). Other streets are more specialized, such as **Jermyn Street** for old-fashioned men's clothing (just south of Piccadilly Street) and **Charing Cross Road** for books. **Floral Street,** connecting Leicester Square to Covent Garden, is lined with fashion boutiques.

Fancy Department Stores in West London

Harrods

Harrods is London's most famous and touristy department store. With more than four acres of retail space covering seven floors, it's a place where some shoppers could spend all day. (To me, it's still just a department store.) Big yet classy, Harrods has everything from elephants to toothbrushes (Mon-Sat 10:00-20:00, Sun 11:30-18:00, pay lockers for big backpacks, on Brompton Road, Tube: Knightsbridge, tel. 020/7730-1234, www.harrods.com).

Harvey Nichols

Once Princess Diana's favorite, "Harvey Nick's" remains the department store *du jour* (Mon-Sat 10:00-20:00, Sun 11:30-18:00, near Harrods, 109-125 Knightsbridge, Tube: Knightsbridge, tel. 020/7235-5000, www.harveynichols.com).

Fortnum & Mason

The official department store of the Queen, Fortnum & Mason embodies old-fashioned, British upper-class taste. While some may find it too stuffy, you won't find another store with the same storybook atmosphere (Mon-Sat 10:00-20:00, Sun 12:00-18:00, elegant tea served in their Diamond Jubilee Tea Salon—see page 212, 181 Piccadilly, Tube: Green Park, tel. 020/7734-8040, www.fortnumandmason.com).

Liberty

Known for its gorgeous floral fabrics and well-stocked crafts department, Liberty is fun to stroll through just for a look at its hip, artful displays and castle-like interior (Mon-Sat 10:00-20:00, Sun 12:00-18:00, Great Marlborough St, Tube: Oxford Circus, tel. 020/7734-1234, www.liberty.co.uk).

Street Markets

Antiques buffs, people-watchers, and folks who brake for garage sales love London's street markets. There's good early-morning market activity somewhere any day of the week. The best markets—which combine lively stalls and a colorful neighborhood with cute and characteristic shops of their own—are Portobello Road and Camden Lock Market. Any London TI has a complete, up-to-date list. Hagglers will enjoy the no-holds-barred bargaining encouraged in London's street markets.

Warning: Markets attract two kinds of people—tourists and pickpockets.

In Notting Hill
Portobello Road Market
Arguably London's best street market, Portobello Road stretches for several blocks through the delightful, colorful, funky-yet-quaint Notting Hill neighborhood. Already charming streets lined with pastel-painted houses and offbeat antiques shops are enlivened on Saturdays with 2,000 additional stalls (8:30-19:00), plus food, live music, and more. (It's also extremely crowded.) If you start at Notting Hill Gate and work your way north, you'll find these general sections: antiques, new goods, produce, more new goods, and a flea market. While Portobello Road is best on Saturdays, it's enjoyable to stroll this street on most other days as well, since the quirky shops are fun to explore—but skip it on Sundays, when virtually everything is closed (Tube: Notting Hill Gate, near recommended accommodations, tel. 020/7727-7684, www.portobelloroad.co.uk).

In Camden Town
Camden Lock Market
This huge, trendy arts-and-crafts festival is divided into three areas, each with its own vibe. The main market, set alongside the

picturesque canal, features a mix of shops and stalls selling boutique crafts and artisanal foods. The market on the opposite side of Chalk Farm Road is edgier, with cheap ethnic food stalls, lots of canalside seating, and punk crafts. The Stables, a sprawling, incense-scented complex, is decorated with fun statues of horses and squeezed into tunnels under the old rail bridge just behind the main market. It's a little lowbrow and wildly creative, with cheap clothes, junk jewelry, and loud music (daily 10:00-18:00, busiest on weekends, Tube: Chalk Farm, bus #24 heads from Pimlico to Victoria Station to Trafalgar Square and then straight up to Camden—before continuing on to Hampstead Heath, tel. 020/7485-7963, www.camdenlockmarket.com).

Avoid the tacky, crowded area between the market and the Camden Town Tube station (which bills itself as "The Camden Market," but lacks the real one's canalside charm) by getting off at the Chalk Farm stop; better yet, consider arriving via a scenic waterbus ride from Little Venice (tel. 020/7482-2660, www.london waterbus.com).

In the East End

All three of these East End markets are busiest and most interesting on Sundays.

Spitalfields Market

This huge, mod-feeling market hall (pronounced "spittle-fields") combines a shopping mall with old brick buildings and sleek modern ones, all covered by a giant glass roof. While the shops and a rainbow of restaurant options are open every day, the open space between them is filled with stalls Tuesdays through Fridays. It's best on Sundays (9:00-17:00), when all stalls and shops are open; you'll find a lively organic food market, many ethnic eateries, crafts, trendy clothes, bags, and an antiques-and-junk market. It's quietest on Saturdays, when only the shops are open—no stalls (shops open daily 10:00-19:00, Tube: Liverpool Street; from the Tube stop, take Bishopsgate East exit, turn left, walk to Brushfield Street, and turn right; www.visitspitalfields.com).

Petticoat Lane Market

Just a block from Spitalfields Market, this line of stalls sits on the otherwise dull, glass-skyscraper-filled Middlesex Street; adjoining Wentworth Street is grungier and more characteristic. Expect budget clothing, leather, shoes, watches, jewelry, and crowds (Sun 9:00-14:00, sometimes later; smaller market Mon-Fri 8:00-16:00 on Wentworth Street only; closed Sat; Middlesex Street and Wentworth Street, Tube: Liverpool Street). The Columbia Road flower market is nearby (Sun 8:00-15:00, http://columbiaroad .info).

Brick Lane Markets

Housed in the former Truman Brewery, this cluster of markets is in the heart of the "Banglatown" Bangladeshi community. Of the three East End market areas, Brick Lane's markets are the grittiest and most avant-garde, selling handmade clothes and home decor as well as ethnic street food. The markets are in full swing on Sundays (roughly 10:00-17:00), though you'll still see some action on Saturdays (11:00-18:00). The Boiler House Food Hall and the Backyard Market (hipster arts & crafts) go all weekend—and the Vintage Market (clothes) even operates on Fridays (11:00-17:30). (Tube: Liverpool Street or Aldgate East, tel. 020/7770-6028, www.bricklanemarket.com).

In the West End
Covent Garden Market
Originally the convent garden for Westminster Abbey, the iron-and-glass market hall hosted a produce market until the 1970s (earning it the name "Apple Market"). Now it's a mix of fun shops, eateries, and markets. Mondays are for antiques, while arts and crafts dominate the rest of the week. Yesteryear's produce stalls are open daily (10:00-19:00), and on Thursdays, a food market brightens up the square (Tube: Covent Garden, tel. 0870-780-5001, www.coventgardenlondonuk.com). The **Jubilee Hall Market** to the south follows a similar schedule (antiques Mon 5:00-16:00, general market Tue-Fri 9:30-18:30, handcrafts Sat-Sun 9:30-17:30, tel. 020/7836-2139, www.jubileemarket.co.uk).

In South London
Borough Market
The Southwark neighborhood hosts a carnival of food under the Borough Bridge, with stalls selling produce, baked goods, cheeses, and other delicacies (Mon-Wed 10:00-15:00, Thu 11:00-17:00, Fri 12:00-18:00, Sat 8:00-17:00, closed Sun, Tube: London Bridge, tel. 020/7407-1002, www.boroughmarket.org.uk).

Brixton Market
This seedy neighborhood south of the Thames features yet another thriving market. Here the food, clothing, records, and hair-braiding throb with an Afro-Caribbean beat (stalls open Mon-Sat 8:00-18:00, Wed until 15:00, farmers market Sun 10:00-14:00 but otherwise dead on Sun; Tube: Brixton, www.brixtonmarket.net).

In Greenwich
With several sightseeing treats just a quick DLR ride from central London, Greenwich has its share of great markets, especially lively on weekends. For details, see page 233.

Entertainment in London

For the best list of what's happening and a look at the latest London scene, check www.timeout.com/london. (Unfortunately, the once-dominant print version of *Time Out London*, though free, is thin, paltry, and hard to find.) The free monthly *London Planner* covers sights, events, and plays, though generally not as well as *Time Out* does.

Theater (a.k.a. "Theatre")
London's theater scene rivals Broadway's in quality and usually beats it in price. Choose from 200 offerings—Shakespeare,

LONDON

London's Major Theaters

1. Adelphi
2. Aldwych
3. Ambassadors & St. Martin's
4. Apollo
5. Cambridge
6. Criterion
7. Dominion
8. Donmar Warehouse
9. Drury Lane
10. Duke of York's
11. Fortune
12. Garrick
13. Haymarket
14. Her Majesty's
15. Lyceum
16. Lyric
17. New London
18. Noël Coward
19. Novello
20. Palace
21. Phoenix
22. Playhouse
23. Prince Edward
24. Prince of Wales
25. Queen's & Gielgud
26. Savoy
27. Shaftesbury
28. Trafalgar Studios
29. Wyndham's

musicals, comedies, thrillers, sex farces, cutting-edge fringe, revivals starring movie celebs, and more. London does it all well.

Seating Terminology: Just like at home, London's theaters sell seats in a range of levels—but the Brits use different terms: stalls (ground floor), dress circle (first balcony), upper circle (second balcony), balcony (sky-high third balcony), slips (cheap seats on the fringes). For floor plans of the various theaters, see www.theatremonkey.com.

Big West End Shows

Nearly all big-name shows are hosted in the commercial (non-subsidized) theaters of the West End, clustering around Soho (especially along Shaftesbury Avenue) between Piccadilly and Covent Garden. With a centuries-old tradition of pleasing the masses, they present London theater at its grandest.

I prefer big, glitzy—even bombastic—musicals over serious chamber dramas, simply because London can deliver the lights, booming voices, dancers, and multimedia spectacle I rarely get back home. If that's not to your taste—or you already have access to similar spectacles at home—you might prefer some of London's more low-key offerings.

Well-known musicals may draw the biggest crowds, but the West End offers plenty of other crowd-pleasers, from revivals of classics to cutting-edge works by the hottest young playwrights. These productions tend to have shorter runs than famous musicals. A few relatively recent cinematic hits (including *The King's Speech* and *War Horse*) started out as London plays. Many productions star huge-name celebrities—London is a magnet for movie stars who want to stretch their acting chops.

You'll see the latest offerings advertised all over the Tube and elsewhere. The free *Official London Theatre Guide*, updated weekly, is a handy tool (find it at hotels, box offices, the City of London TI, and online at www.officiallondontheatre.co.uk). If you're picky, check the reviews at www.timeout.com/london.

Most performances are nightly except Sunday, usually with one or two matinees a week. The few shows that run on Sundays are mostly family fare (*Matilda, The Lion King,* and so on). Tickets range from about £15 to £65. Matinees are generally cheaper and rarely sell out.

Buying Tickets for West End Shows

For most visitors, it makes the most sense to simply buy tickets in London. But if your time in London is limited and you have your heart set on a particular show that's likely to sell out (usually the newest shows), you can buy peace of mind by pre-booking your tickets from home.

Before You Go

Once you know what show you want to see, buy your tickets directly from its theater's website (which may reroute you to a third-party ticket vendor such as Ticketmaster). You can also call the theater box office (which may ring through to a central ticketing office).

Whether you book online or over the phone, you'll pay with your credit card. A service charge of £3 per ticket is typical if you book direct with the theater. You may be offered the option of having your tickets emailed to you (you print them out); otherwise, arrive about 30 minutes before the show starts to pick up your tickets at Will Call.

Avoid buying tickets through third-party middleman agencies, which mark up their prices dramatically (explained in "Booking Through Other Agencies," later). See www.london theatretickets.org and www.timeout.com/london for even more cheap-ticket advice.

In London

Most shows have tickets available on short notice—likely at a discount. While very recent and/or popular shows sell out early (especially for weekend performances), nearly-as-popular shows may offer discounted tickets to fill seats.

You have two good options for booking tickets—the official discount tkts booth at Leicester Square and the theater's box office...and one bad option—a middleman ticket agency (only worthwhile if you're desperate). All three alternatives are described next.

Discount tkts Booth: This famous ticket booth at Leicester (LESS-ter) Square, run by the Society of London Theatre, sells discounted tickets for top-price seats to shows on the push list. Big-name shows frequently turn up on this list. Most tickets are around half-price; other shows are discounted 25 percent (in either case, you'll pay a £3 service charge per ticket). For some extremely popular shows, they sell full-price tickets without the service charge (so it costs the same as at the box office). For about half of the shows, discounted tickets are available only on the day of the performance, although theaters are beginning to offer discounted tickets through tkts up to a week ahead. Their website (www.tkts.co.uk) lists ticket availability and prices, and is updated throughout the day—but you must buy in person at their kiosk. A similar list is posted next to the kiosk—survey your options before you queue (or, if the line is long, while you're in the queue). It's smart to have two or three options in mind, just in case your first choice is sold out when you reach the counter. While the line forms early, it tends to move fast. Unless you have your heart set on a particular show that has only same-day tickets, consider dropping by later in the day, when it's a bit less crowded—many tickets will still be available (open Mon-Sat 9:00-19:00, Sun 10:30-16:30). Note: If tkts runs out of its ticket allotment for a certain show, it doesn't necessarily mean that the show is sold out—you can still try the theater's box office.

Warning: The real booth (with its prominent *tkts* sign) is a freestanding kiosk at the south edge of the garden in Leicester Square. Several dishonest outfits nearby advertise "official half-price tickets"—avoid these, where you'll rarely pay anything close to half-price.

Booking Direct (at the Theater's Box Office): While tkts generally has seats that are as cheap or cheaper than at the theater itself, the advantage of buying direct is that you may have access to deals that you can't get anywhere else. Most theaters offer cheap returned tickets, standing-room, matinee, senior or student standby deals, and more. (Discounted tickets, called "concessions," are indicated with a "conc" or "s" in the listings.) Picking up a late

What's On in the West End

Here are some of the perennial favorites that you're likely to find among the West End's evening offerings. If spending the time and money for a London play, I like a full-fledged, high-energy musical (which all of these are). Generally you can book tickets for free at the box office or for a £2-3 fee by phone or online. See the map on page 160 for locations.

Billy Elliot—This adaptation of the popular British film is part family drama, part story of a boy who just has to dance, set to a score by Elton John (£20-68, Mon-Sat 19:30, matinees Thu and Sat 14:30, Victoria Palace Theatre, Victoria Street, Tube: Victoria, tel. 0844-248-5000, www.billyelliotthemusical.com).

Jersey Boys—This fast-moving, easy-to-follow show tracks the rough start and rise to stardom of Frankie Valli and the Four Seasons. It's light, but the music is so catchy that everyone leaves whistling the group's classics (£20-68; Tue-Sat 19:30; matinees Tue and Sat 15:00, Sun 17:00; Prince Edward Theatre, Old Compton Street, Tube: Leicester Square, box office tel. 0844-482-5151, www.jerseyboyslondon.com).

Les Misérables—Claude-Michel Schönberg's musical adaptation of Victor Hugo's epic follows the life of Jean Valjean as he struggles with the social and political realities of 19th-century France. This inspiring mega-hit takes you back to the days of France's struggle for a just and modern society (£20-68, Mon-Sat 19:30, matinees Wed and Sat 14:30, Queen's Theatre, Shaftesbury Avenue, Tube: Piccadilly Circus, box office tel. 0844-482-5160, www.lesmis.com).

The Lion King—In this Disney extravaganza, Simba the lion learns about the delicately balanced circle of life on the savanna (£25-68; Tue-Sat 19:30; matinees Wed, Sat, and Sun 14:30; Lyceum Theatre, Wellington Street, Tube: Charing Cross or Covent Garden, theater info tel. 020/7420-8100, box office tel. 0844-871-3000, www.thelionking.co.uk).

LONDON

return can get you a great seat at a cheap-seat price.

A good plan for same-day deals is to arrive at the box office right when it opens (most open at 10:00; a few open at 9:00). For example, the popular show *Wicked* saves its front-row tickets to sell at half-price at 10:00 on the day of the show, but you must buy them in person at the box office...and on busy days, people line up early. (Restrictions may apply—for example, you may be limited to two half-price tickets, and even if you can buy more, the seats may not be together.) To find deals, look at the show's website, call the box office, or simply drop by (the theaters are mostly in highly trafficked tourist areas, so you're likely to pass your chosen theater at some point during your visit). Even if a show is "sold out," there's usually a way to get a seat. Call the theater box office and ask how,

Mamma Mia!—This energetic, spandex-and-platform-boots musical weaves together a slew of ABBA hits to tell the story of a bride in search of her real dad as her promiscuous mom plans her Greek Isle wedding. The production has the audience dancing in their seats (£15-68, Mon-Sat 19:30, matinees Thu and Sat 15:00, Prince of Wales Theatre, Coventry Street, Tube: Piccadilly Circus, box office tel. 0844-482-5115, www.mamma-mia.com).

Matilda—Based on the Roald Dahl children's book, this hit is a family favorite for its tale of a precocious young girl who's unappreciated by her parents (£20-68, Tue 19:00, Wed-Sat 19:30, matinees Wed and Sat 14:30 and Sun 15:00, Cambridge Theatre, Seven Dials, Tube: Covent Garden or Leicester Square, box office tel. 0844-412-4652, www.matildathemusical.com).

Phantom of the Opera—A mysterious masked man falls in love with a singer in this haunting Andrew Lloyd Webber musical about life beneath the stage of the Paris Opera (£21-65, Mon-Sat 19:30, matinees Thu and Sat 14:30, Her Majesty's Theatre, Haymarket, Tube: Piccadilly Circus or Leicester Square, US toll-free tel. 800-334-8457, box office tel. 0844-412-2707, www.the phantomoftheopera.com).

We Will Rock You—This musical tribute to Queen (more to the band than to Freddie Mercury) is an understandably popular celebration of their work (£32-64, Mon-Sat 19:30, matinees Wed and Sat 14:30, Dominion Theatre, Tottenham Court Road, Tube: Tottenham Court Road, Ticketmaster tel. 0844-847-1775, www.wewillrockyou.co.uk).

Wicked—This lively prequel to The Wizard of Oz examines how the Witch of the West met Glinda the Good Witch, and later became so, you know... (£15-65, Mon-Sat 19:30, matinees Wed and Sat 14:30, Apollo Victoria Theatre, just east of Victoria Station, Tube: Victoria, Ticketmaster tel. 0844-826-8000, www.wickedthemusical.co.uk).

or check www.timeout.com/London for show-by-show info on same-day tickets at West End theaters.

If you don't care where you sit, you can often buy the absolute cheapest seats at the box office; these tickets usually cost £20 or less. These seats tend to be either in the nosebleed rows and/or have a restricted view (behind a pillar or extremely far to one side), and are often available only as same-day tickets. (For smaller theaters where every seat's a decent one, tkts may indeed beat the best box-office price: Compare online before heading out.) After the lights go down, scooting up is less than a capital offense. Shakespeare did it.

Booking Through Other Agencies: Although booking through a middleman (such as your hotel or a ticket agency) is quick and easy, prices are inflated by a standard 25 percent fee. Ticket agencies (whether in the US or in London) are just scalpers with an address. As a rule of thumb, if anyone other than the box office charges you more than £75 per ticket, you're almost certainly getting ripped off. If you're buying from an agency, look at the ticket carefully (your price should be no more than 30 percent over the printed face value; the 20 percent VAT is already included in the face value) and understand where you're sitting according to the floor plan (if your view is restricted, it will state this on the ticket).

Agencies are worthwhile only if a show you've just got to see is sold out at the box office. They scarf up hot tickets, planning to make a killing after the show is sold out. US booking agencies get their tickets from another agency, adding to your expense by involving yet another middleman. Many tickets sold on the street are forgeries. Although some theaters use booking agencies to handle their advance sales, you'll likely save money by avoiding the middleman.

Beyond the West End

Tickets for lesser-known shows tend to be cheaper (figure £15-30), in part because most of the smaller theaters are subsidized. Remember that plays don't need a familiar title or famous actor to be a worthwhile experience—read up on the latest offerings online; Time Out's site is a great place to start.

Major Noncommercial Theaters: One particularly good venue is the **National Theatre,** which has a range of impressive options, often starring recognizable names; while ugly on the outside, the acts that play out upon its stage are beautiful—as are the deeply discounted tickets it commonly offers (looming on the South Bank by Waterloo Bridge, Tube: Waterloo, www.national theatre.org.uk). The **Barbican Centre** puts on high-quality, often experimental work (right by the Museum of London, just north of The City, Tube: Barbican, www.barbican.org.uk), as does the **Royal Court Theatre,** which has £10 tickets for its Monday shows (west of the West End in Sloane Square, Tube: Sloane Square, www.royalcourttheatre.com).

Royal Shakespeare Company: If you'll ever enjoy Shakespeare, it'll be in Britain. The RSC performs at various theaters around London and in Stratford-upon-Avon year-round (for details, see page 457 in the Stratford-upon-Avon chapter). To get a schedule, contact the RSC (Royal Shakespeare Theatre, Stratford-upon-Avon, tel. 0844-800-1110, www.rsc.org.uk).

Shakespeare's Globe: To see Shakespeare in a replica of the theater for which he wrote his plays, attend a play at the Globe. In this round, thatch-roofed, open-air theater, the plays are performed much as Shakespeare intended—under the sky, with no amplification.

The play's the thing from late April through early October (usually Mon 19:30, Tue-Sat 14:00 and 19:30, Sun either 13:00 and/or 18:30, tickets can be sold out months in advance). You'll pay £5 to stand and £15-39 to sit, usually on a backless bench. Because only a few rows and the pricier Gentlemen's Rooms have seats with backs, £1 cushions and £3 add-on back rests are considered a good investment by many. Dress for the weather.

The £5 "groundling" tickets—which are open to rain—are most fun. Scurry in early to stake out a spot on the stage's edge, where the most interaction with the actors occurs. You're a crude peasant. You can lean your elbows on the stage, munch a picnic dinner (yes, you can bring in food), or walk around. I've never enjoyed Shakespeare as much as here, performed as it was meant to be in the "wooden O." If you can't get a ticket, consider waiting around. Plays can be long, and many groundlings leave before the end. Hang around outside and beg or buy a ticket from someone leaving early (groundlings are allowed to come and go). A few non-Shakespeare plays are also presented each year. If you can't attend a show, you can take a guided tour of the theater and museum by day (see page 142).

In 2014, the Globe opens a new, indoor theater within the Globe complex. The Sam Wanamaker Playhouse allows Shakespearean-era plays and early-music concerts to be performed through the winter. Tickets for this more intimate venue are somewhat pricier than for the Globe (check online or call the Globe box office for details).

To reserve tickets for plays at the Globe, call or drop by the box office (Mon-Sat 10:00-18:00, Sun 10:00-17:00, open one hour later on performance days, New Globe Walk entrance, no extra charge to book by phone, tel. 020/7401-9919). You can also reserve online (www.shakespearesglobe.com, £2.50 booking fee). If the tickets are sold out, don't despair; a few often free up at the last minute. Try calling around noon the day of the performance to see if the box office expects any returned tickets. If so, they'll advise you to show up a little more than an hour before the show, when these tickets are sold (first-come, first-served).

The theater is on the South Bank, directly across the Thames over the Millennium Bridge from St. Paul's Cathedral (Tube: Mansion House or London Bridge). The Globe is inconvenient for public transport, but the courtesy phone in the lobby lets you get a minicab in minutes. (These minicabs have set fees—e.g., £8 to South Kensington—but generally cost less than a metered cab and provide fine and honest service.) During theater season, there's a regular supply of black cabs outside the main foyer on New Globe Walk.

Outdoor Theater in Summer: Enjoy Shakespearean drama and other plays under the stars at the Open Air Theatre, in leafy Regent's Park in north London. Food is allowed: You can bring your own picnic, order à la carte from the theater menu, or pre-order a picnic supper from the theater at least 48 hours in advance (season runs late May-mid-Sept, tickets available beginning in mid-Jan; book at www.openairtheatre.org or—for an extra booking fee—by calling 0844-826-4242; grounds open 1.5 hours prior to evening performances, one hour prior to matinees; 10-minute walk north of Baker Street Tube, near Queen Mary's Gardens within Regent's Park; detailed directions and more info at www .openairtheatre.org).

Fringe Theater: London's rougher evening-entertainment scene is thriving. Choose from a wide range of fringe theater and comedy acts (generally £12).

Music at Churches

For easy, cheap, or free concerts in historic churches, attend a **lunch concert** (listed on *Time Out*'s website). Good options include St. Bride's Church, with free half-hour lunch concerts twice a week at 13:15 (usually Tue and Fri—confirm in advance, church tel. 020/7427-0133, www.stbrides.com); St. James's at Piccadilly, with 50-minute concerts on Mon, Wed, and Fri at 13:10 (suggested £3.50 donation, info tel. 020/7381-0441, www.st-james-piccadilly .org); and St. Martin-in-the-Fields, offering concerts on Mon, Tue, and Fri at 13:00 (suggested £3 donation, church tel. 020/7766-1100, www.smitf.org).

St. Martin-in-the-Fields also hosts fine **evening concerts** by candlelight (£8-28, several nights a week at 19:30) and live jazz in its underground Café in the Crypt (£5.50 or £9, Wed at 20:00).

Evensong services are held at several churches, including St. Paul's Cathedral (see details on page 123), Westminster Abbey (see page 84), Southwark Cathedral (see page 145), and St. Bride's Church (Sun at 17:30, tel. 020/7427-0133, www.stbrides.com).

Free **organ recitals** are usually held on Sunday at 17:45 in Westminster Abbey (30 minutes, tel. 020/7222-5152). Many other churches have free concerts; ask for the *London Organ Concerts Guide* at the City of London TI.

Summer Evenings Along the South Bank

If you're visiting London in summer, consider hitting the South Bank neighborhood after hours.

Take a trip around the **London Eye** while the sun sets over the city (the wheel spins until late—last ascent at 21:00 April-June, 21:30 July-Aug, 20:30 Sept-March). Then cap your night with an evening walk along the pedestrian-only **Jubilee Walkway,** which

Evensong

One of my favorite experiences in England is to attend evensong at a great church. Evensong is an evening worship service that is typically sung rather than said (though some parts—including scripture readings, a few prayers, and a homily—are spoken). It follows the traditional Anglican service in the Book of Common Prayer, including prayers, scripture readings, canticles (sung responses), and hymns that are appropriate for the early evening—traditionally the end of the working day and before the evening meal. In major churches with resident choirs, this service is filled with quality, professional musical elements. A singing or chanting priest leads the service, and a choir—usually made up of both men's and boys' voices (to sing the lower and higher parts, respectively)—sings the responses. The choir often sings a cappella, or is accompanied by organ. While regular attendees follow the service from memory, visitors—who are welcome—are given an order of service or a prayer book to help them follow along. (If you're not familiar with the order of service, watch the congregation to know when to stand, sit, and kneel.)

The most impressive places for evensong include London (Westminster Abbey, St. Paul's, Southwark Cathedral, or St. Bride's Church), Cambridge (King's College Chapel), Canterbury Cathedral, Wells Cathedral, Oxford (Christ Church Cathedral), York Minster, and Durham Cathedral. While this list includes many of the grandest churches in England, be aware that evensong typically takes place in the small choir area—which is far more intimate than the main nave. (To see the full church in action, a concert is a better choice.) Evensong generally occurs daily between 17:00 and 18:00 (often two hours earlier on Sundays)—check with individual churches for specifics. At smaller churches, evensong is sometimes spoken, not sung.

Note that evensong is not a performance—it's a somewhat somber worship service. If you enjoy worshiping in different churches, attending evensong can be a trip-capping highlight. But if regimented church services aren't your thing, consider getting a different music fix. Most major churches also offer organ or choral concerts—look for posted schedules or ask at the information desk or gift shop.

runs east-west along the river. It's where Londoners go to escape the heat. This pleasant stretch of the walkway—lined with pubs and casual eateries—goes from the London Eye past Shakespeare's Globe to Tower Bridge (you can walk in either direction).

If you're in the mood for a movie, take in a flick at the **BFI Southbank,** located just across the river, alongside Waterloo Bridge. Run by the British Film Institute, the state-of-the-art theater shows mostly classic films, as well as art cinema (Tube: Waterloo or Embankment, check www.bfi.org.uk for schedules and prices).

Farther east along the South Bank is **The Scoop**—an outdoor amphitheater next to City Hall. It's a good spot for movies, concerts, dance, and theater productions throughout the summer—with Tower Bridge as a scenic backdrop. These events are free, nearly nightly, and family-friendly. For the latest event schedule, see www.morelondon.com and click on "The Scoop at More London" (next to City Hall, Riverside, The Queen's Walkway, Tube: London Bridge).

Sleeping in London

London is an expensive city for lodging. Cheaper rooms are relatively dumpy. Don't expect £130 cheeriness in a £70 room. For £70, you'll get a double with breakfast in a safe, cramped, and dreary place with minimal service and the bathroom down the hall. For £90, you'll get a basic, clean, reasonably cheery double with a private bath in a usually cramped, cracked-plaster building, or a soulless but comfortable room without breakfast in a huge Motel 6-type place. My London splurges, at £160-290, are spacious, thoughtfully appointed places good for entertaining or romancing.

Looking for Hotel Deals Online: Given London's high hotel prices, using the Internet can help you score a deal. Various websites list rooms in high-rise, three- and four-star business hotels. You'll give up the charm and warmth of a family-run establishment, and breakfast probably won't be included, but you might

---

Sleep Code

(£1 = about $1.60, country code: 44, area code: 020)
S = Single, **D** = Double/Twin, **T** = Triple, **Q** = Quad, **b** = bathroom, **s** = shower only. Unless otherwise noted, credit cards are accepted and breakfast is included.

To help you sort easily through these listings, I've divided the rooms into three categories based on the price for a standard double room with bath:

$$$ Higher Priced—Most rooms £125 or more.
$$ Moderately Priced—Most rooms between £75-125.
$ Lower Priced—Most rooms £75 or less.

Prices can change without notice; verify the hotel's current rates online or by email. For the best prices, always book direct.

London's Hotel Neighborhoods

PADDINGTON — Regent's Park — EUSTON/ ST. PANCRAS/ KING'S CROSS — NORTH LONDON

BAYSWATER

NOTTING HILL — MARBLE ARCH — BRITISH MUSEUM

Hyde Park — WEST END — TRAFALGAR SQUARE — THE CITY — TOWER OF LONDON

WEST LONDON — CENTRAL LONDON — ST. PAUL'S

VICTORIA STATION — WEST-MINSTER

SOUTH KENSINGTON — BIG BEN — SOUTH BANK

The Tube's Circle Line — LONDON EYE

Thames River — Hotel Neighborhoods

LONDON

find that the price is right.

Start by browsing the websites of several chains to get a sense of typical rates and online deals. For listings of no-frills, Motel 6-type places, see "Big, Good-Value, Modern Hotels," later.

Pricier London hotel chains include Millennium/Copthorne (www.millenniumhotels.com), Thistle (www.thistle.com), Inter-Continental/Holiday Inn (www.ichotelsgroup.com), Radisson (www.radisson.com), Hilton (www.hilton.com), and Red Carnation (www.redcarnationhotels.com).

Auction-type sites (such as www.priceline.com and www.hot wire.com) match flexible travelers with empty hotel rooms, often at prices well below the hotel's normal rates.

My readers report good experiences with these accommodation discount sites: www.londontown.com (an informative site with a discount booking service), http://athomeinlondon.co.uk and www.londonbb.com (both list central B&Bs), www.lastminute .com, www.visitlondon.com, http://roomsnet.com, and www.euro cheapo.com.

Victoria Station Neighborhood

The streets behind Victoria Station teem with little, moderately priced-for-London B&Bs. It's a safe, surprisingly tidy, and decent area without a hint of the trashy, touristy glitz of the streets in front of the station. I've divided these accommodations into two broad categories: Belgravia, west of the station, feels particularly posh, while Pimlico, to the east, is still upscale and dotted with colorful eateries. While I wouldn't go out of my way just to dine here, each area has plenty of good restaurants (see page 205). All of my

LONDON

Victoria Station Neighborhood

1. Lime Tree Hotel
2. Morgan House
3. Luna Simone Hotel
4. Bakers Hotel
5. New England Hotel
6. Best Western Victoria Palace
7. Jubilee Hotel
8. Cherry Court Hotel
9. easyHotel Victoria
10. Ebury Wine Bar
11. Jenny Lo's Tea House
12. La Bottega Deli
13. The Thomas Cubitt Pub
14. To The Duke of Wellington Pub
15. The Orange Pub & Daylesford Deli
16. Grumbles Restaurant
17. Pimlico Fresh
18. Seafresh Fish Restaurant
19. The Jugged Hare Pub
20. St. George's Tavern
21. Nando's
22. Grocery Stores (4)
23. To Launderette
24. Bus Tours – Day (2)
25. Bus Tours – Night
26. Tube, Taxis, City Buses
27. Green Line Coach Terminal
28. Buses to Luton & Stansted Airports

recommended hotels are within a five-minute walk of the Victoria Tube, bus, and train stations. On hot summer nights, request a quiet back room; most of these B&Bs lack air-conditioning and may front busy streets.

The nearest laundry option is **Pimlico Launderette,** on the east—Pimlico—side about five blocks southwest of Warwick Square. Low prices and friendly George brighten your chore (£7.40 same-day full service, £5-6 self-service, daily 8:00-19:00; 3

Westmoreland Terrace—go down Clarendon Street, turn right on Sutherland, and look for the launderette on the left at the end of the street; tel. 020/7821-8692).

Drivers like the 400-space Semley Place NCP **parking garage,** near the hotels on the west—Belgravia—side (£40/day, possible discounts with hotel voucher, just west of Victoria Coach Station at Buckingham Palace Road and Semley Place, tel. 0845-050-7080, www.ncp.co.uk).

West of Victoria Station (Belgravia)

Here in Belgravia, the prices are a bit higher and your neighbors include some of the world's wealthiest people. These two places sit nearly kitty-corner from each other on tranquil Ebury Street, two blocks over from Victoria Station (or a slightly shorter walk from the Sloane Square Tube stop). You can cut the walk from Victoria Station to nearly nothing by taking a short ride on frequent bus #C1 (leaves from Buckingham Palace Road side of Victoria Station and drops you off directly in front of Morgan House).

$$$ Lime Tree Hotel, enthusiastically run by Charlotte and Matt, is a gem, with 25 spacious, stylish, comfortable, thoughtfully decorated rooms, a helpful staff, and a fun-loving breakfast room (Sb-£99, Db-£160, larger superior Db-£185, Tb-£205, family room-£220, usually cheaper Jan-Feb, free guest computer and Wi-Fi, small lounge opens onto quiet garden, 135 Ebury Street, tel. 020/7730-8191, www.limetreehotel.co.uk, info@limetreehotel.co.uk, Alex manages the office).

$$ Morgan House, a great budget choice in this neighborhood, has 11 nicely decorated rooms with far more character than you'll find in other nearby hotels in this price range. It's also entertainingly run, with lots of travel tips and friendly chat from owner Rachel Joplin and her staff (S-£58, D-£84, Db-£108, T-£108, family suites: Tb-£148, Qb-£158, free Wi-Fi can be spotty, 120 Ebury Street, tel. 020/7730-2384, www.morganhouse.co.uk, morgan house@btclick.com).

East of Victoria Station (Pimlico)

This area is a bit less genteel-feeling than Belgravia, but still plenty inviting, with eateries and grocery stores. Most of these hotels are on or near Warwick Way, the main drag through this area. Generally the best Tube stop for this neighborhood is Victoria (though the Pimlico stop works equally well for the Luna Simone). Bus #24 runs right through the middle of Pimlico, connecting Tate Britain to the south with Victoria Station, the Houses of Parliament, Trafalgar Square, and much more to the north.

$$ Luna Simone Hotel rents 36 fresh, spacious, remodeled rooms with modern bathrooms. It's a smartly managed place, run for more than 40 years by twins Peter and Bernard—and Bernard's son Mark—and they still seem to enjoy their work (Sb-£75, Db-£110, Tb-£135, Qb-£165, these prices with cash and this book in 2014, free guest computer and Wi-Fi, at 47 Belgrave Road near the corner of Charlwood Street, handy bus #24 to Victoria Station and Trafalgar Square stops out front, tel. 020/7834-5897, www.lunasimonehotel.com, stay@lunasimonehotel.com).

$$ Bakers Hotel shoehorns 11 brightly painted rooms into a small building, but it's conveniently located and offers modest prices and a small breakfast (S-£45-55, Sb-£70-80, D-£70-85, Db-£85-90, T-£90, Tb-£110-120, family room-£135, can be about £5-8 cheaper per person off-season, discounts for stays of at least a week, ask for Rick Steves discount when booking direct, free Wi-Fi, 126 Warwick Way, tel. 020/7834-0729, www.bakershotel.co.uk, reservations@bakershotel.co.uk, Amin Jamani).

$$ New England Hotel, run by Jay and the Patel family, has rather worn public spaces and somewhat faded but well-priced rooms in a tight old corner building (small Sb-£69-79, Db-£89-99, Tb-£119-129, Qb-£129-139, prices soft during slow times, breakfast is very basic, pay Wi-Fi, 20 Saint George's Drive, tel. 020/7834-8351, www.newenglandhotel.com, mystay@newengland hotel.com).

$$ Best Western Victoria Palace offers modern business-class comfort compared to the other creaky old hotels listed here. Choose between the 43 rooms in the main building (Db-£120, Tb-£200, prices flex with demand—often around Db-£90/Tb-£160 off-season, includes breakfast, elevator, 60-64 Warwick Way), or pay about 20 percent less by booking a nearly identical room in one of the two annexes, each a half-block away—an excellent value for this neighborhood if you skip breakfast. All three buildings were recently renovated (annex Db-£85-90, breakfast-£12.50, air-con, no elevator). Book in advance for the best rates (free guest computer and Wi-Fi, 17 Belgrave Road and 1 Warwick Way, reception at main building, tel. 020/7821-7113, www.bestwesternvictoriapalace.co.uk, info@bestwesternvictoria palace.co.uk).

$$ Jubilee Hotel is a well-run slumbermill with 24 tiny, simple rooms and many tiny, neat beds. The cheapest rooms, which share bathrooms, are just below street level (S-£39-45, Sb-£59-65, tiny twin D-£55-65, Db-£79-89, T-£65, Tb-£89-95, Qb-£99-109, rates depend on season and length of stay, 5 percent discount for Rick Steves readers if you book direct, free guest computer, pay Wi-Fi, 31 Eccleston Square, tel. 020/7834-0845, www.jubilee hotel.co.uk, stay@jubileehotel.co.uk, Bob Patel).

$ Cherry Court Hotel, run by the friendly and industrious Patel family, rents 12 very small but bright and well-designed rooms in a central location. Considering London's sky-high prices, this is a fine budget choice (Sb-£60, Db-£68, Tb-£105, Quint/b family room-£130, these prices with this book in 2014, 5 percent fee to pay with credit card, fruit-basket breakfast in room, air-con, free guest computer and Wi-Fi, laundry, peaceful garden patio, 23 Hugh Street, tel. 020/7828-2840, www.cherrycourthotel.co.uk, info@cherrycourthotel.co.uk, daughter Neha answers emails and offers informed restaurant advice).

$ easyHotel Victoria, at 36 Belgrave Road, is part of the budget chain described on page 187.

"South Kensington," She Said, Loosening His Cummerbund

To stay on a quiet street so classy it doesn't allow hotel signs, surrounded by trendy shops and colorful restaurants, call "South Ken" your London home. Shoppers like being a short walk from Harrods and the designer shops of King's Road and Chelsea. When I splurge, I splurge here. Sumner Place is just off Old Brompton Road, 200 yards from the handy South Kensington Tube station (on Circle Line, two stops from Victoria Station; and on Piccadilly Line, direct from Heathrow). A handy **launderette** is on the corner of Queensberry Place and Harrington Road (Mon-Fri 8:00-20:00, Sat 9:00-19:00, Sun 10:00-18:00, last wash one hour before closing, bring 50p and £1 coins).

$$$ Aster House, well-run by friendly and accommodating Simon and Leonie Tan, has a cheerful lobby, lounge, and breakfast room. Its 13 rooms are comfy and quiet, with TV, phone, and air-conditioning. Enjoy breakfast or just lounging in the whisper-elegant Orangery, a glassy greenhouse. Simon and Leonie offer free loaner mobile phones to their guests (Sb-£125, Db-£190, bigger Db-£235 or £270, does not include 20 percent VAT; significant discount offered to readers of this book in 2014—up to 20 percent discount if you book three or more nights, up to 25 percent discount for five or more nights; additional 5 percent off when you pay cash, check website for specials, pay guest computer, free Wi-Fi, 3 Sumner Place, tel. 020/7581-5888, www.asterhouse.com, aster house@gmail.com).

$$$ Number Sixteen, for well-heeled travelers, packs over-the-top class into its 41 artfully imagined rooms, plush designer-chic lounges, and tranquil garden. It's in a labyrinthine building, with boldly modern decor—perfect for an urban honeymoon (Sb-from £180, "superior" Db-from £235—but soft, ask for discounted "seasonal rates," especially on weekends and in Aug—subject to availability, larger "luxury" Db-£285, breakfast buffet in the garden-£19 continental or £20 full English, elevator, free guest computer and Wi-Fi, 16 Sumner Place, tel. 020/7589-5232, US tel. 800-553-6674, www.numbersixteenhotel.co.uk, sixteen@firmdale .com).

$$$ The Pelham Hotel, a 51-room business-class hotel with crisp service and a pricey mix of pretense and style, is genteel, with low lighting and a pleasant drawing room among the many perks (Db-£190-290, rate depends on room size and season, breakfast-£15 continental or £19 full English, does not include 20 percent VAT, slightly lower prices on weekends and in Aug,

South Kensington Neighborhood

1. Aster House
2. Number Sixteen Hotel
3. The Pelham Hotel
4. Brompton Hotel
5. La Bouchée Bistro Café
6. Moti Mahal Indian Rest.
7. Bosphorus Kebabs & Beirut Express
8. The Anglesea Arms Pub
9. Rocca di Papa
10. Fernandez & Wells
11. Thai Square
12. Tesco Express
13. Launderette

Web specials can include free breakfast; air-con, elevator, free guest computer, pay Wi-Fi, fitness room, 15 Cromwell Place, tel. 020/7589-8288, US tel. 1-888-757-5587, www.pelhamhotel.co.uk, reservations@pelhamhotel.co.uk, Jamie will take good care of you).

$$ Brompton Hotel is a humble place with 26 rooms above a jumble of cafés and clubs. There's a noisy bar and some street noise, so ask for a room in the back if you want quiet. Since it has no public spaces, they serve breakfast in your room. However, its rates are reasonable for this upscale neighborhood (Sb-£100, Db-£110—but can fall to £75 when demand is down, Tb-£140-150, "deluxe" rooms are just like the others but with a tub, save a little by booking via their website, includes continental breakfast, free Wi-Fi, across from the South Kensington Tube station at 30 Old Brompton Road, tel. 020/7584-4517, www.bromhotel.com, book@bromhotel.com).

North of Kensington Gardens and Hyde Park

From the core of the tourist's London, the vast Hyde Park spreads west, eventually becoming Kensington Gardens. Three good accommodations neighborhoods line up side-by-side along the northern edge of the park: Bayswater (with the highest concentration of good hotels) anchors the area, and is bordered by Notting Hill to the west and Paddington to the east. This area has quick bus and Tube access to downtown, and, for London, is very "homely" (Brit-speak for cozy).

Bayswater

Most of my Bayswater accommodations flank a tranquil, tidy park called Kensington Gardens Square (not to be confused with the much bigger Kensington Gardens adjacent to Hyde Park), a block west of bustling Queensway, north of Bayswater Tube station. These hotels are quiet for central London, but the area feels a bit sterile, and the hotels here tend to be impersonal.

Popular with young international travelers, the Bayswater street called **Queensway** is a multicultural festival of commerce and eateries. The neighborhood does its dirty clothes at **Galaxy Launderette** (£6-8 self-service, £10-12 full-service, Mon-Sat 8:00-20:00, Sun 9:00-20:00, last wash at 19:00, staff on hand with soap and coins, 65 Moscow Road, near corner of St. Petersburgh Place and Moscow Road, tel. 020/7229-7771). For **Internet access,** you'll find several stops along busy Queensway, and a self-serve bank of computer terminals on the food-circus level—third floor—of Whiteleys Shopping Centre (long hours daily, corner of Queensway and Porchester Gardens—see page 210).

$$$ Vancouver Studios offers one of the best values in this neighborhood. Its 45 modern, tastefully furnished rooms come with fully equipped kitchenettes (utensils, stove, microwave, and fridge) rather than breakfast. It's nestled between Kensington Gardens Square and Princes Square, and has its own tranquil garden patio out back (Sb-£97, Db-£140, Tb-£179, extra bed-£20, 10 percent discount for seven or more nights, pay guest computer, free Wi-Fi, welcoming lounge, 30 Princes Square, tel. 020/7243-1270, www.vancouverstudios.co.uk, info@vancouverstudios.co.uk).

$$$ Garden Court Hotel is understated, with 37 simple, homey-but-tasteful rooms (prices vary seasonally with demand—these are normal/low-demand rates: Sb-£70-75/£50-65, D-£125, Db-£125/£75-90, Tb-£150/£105, Qb-£175/£120, all rooms can be £20 more when demand is especially high, breakfast-£5, elevator, pay guest computer, free Wi-Fi, 30-31 Kensington Gardens Square, tel. 020/7229-2553, www.gardencourthotel.co.uk, info @gardencourthotel.co.uk).

$$$ London House Hotel has 103 spiffy, modern cookie-cutter rooms on Kensington Gardens Square. Its rates are great considering the quality and fine location (rates fluctuate, but generally Db-£105 weekdays and £130 on weekends, expect to pay more during busiest times and less in winter, smaller rooms not facing the square are about £10-20 cheaper, basement family rooms-£140, check online for specific rates and last-minute deals, continental breakfast-£7, elevator, free Wi-Fi, 81 Kensington Gardens Square, tel. 020/7243-1810, www.londonhousehotels.com, reservations @londonhousehotels.com).

$$$ Phoenix Hotel, a Best Western modernization of a 125-room hotel, offers American business-class comforts; spacious, plush public spaces; and big, modern-feeling rooms. Its prices—which range from fine value to rip-off—are determined by a greedy computer program, with huge variations according to expected demand. Book online to save money (Sb-£80-110, Db-£110-140, Tb-£150-180, elevator, free guest computer and Wi-Fi, 1-8 Kensington Gardens Square, tel. 020/7229-2494, US tel. 800-528-1234, www.phoenixhotel.co.uk, info@phoenixhotel.co.uk).

$$ Princes Square Guest Accommodation is a crisp (if impersonal) place renting 50 businesslike rooms with pleasant, modern decor. It's well-located, practical, and a very good value, especially if you can score a good rate (prices fluctuate with demand, but generally Db-£80-90, £20 less for a single, £40 more for a triple; email to ask for best price, breakfast likely included if you book direct—ask, elevator, pay Wi-Fi, 23-25 Princes Square, tel. 020/7229-9876, www.princessquarehotel.co.uk, info@princes squarehotel.co.uk).

$$ Kensington Gardens Hotel laces 17 pleasant, slightly scuffed rooms together in a tall, skinny building (Ss-£59, Sb-£66, Db-£92, Tb-£115; book by phone or email for these special Rick

LONDON

North of Kensington Gardens & Hyde Park

LONDON

1. Vancouver Studios
2. Garden Court Hotel
3. London House Hotel
4. Phoenix & Kensington Gardens Hotels
5. Princes Square Guest Accommodation
6. Bayswater Inn Hotel
7. The Gate Hotel
8. London Vicarage Hotel
9. To Norwegian YWCA
10. Tudor Court Hotel
11. St. David's Hotels
12. Falcon Hotel
13. easyHotel
14. The Royal Park Hotel
15. Stylotel
16. Olympic House Hotel
17. Caring Hotel
18. Maggie Jones Restaurant
19. The Churchill Arms Pub & Thai Kitchen
20. Hereford Road Restaurant
21. The Prince Edward Pub
22. Café Diana
23. Royal China Restaurant
24. Wagamama
25. More Chain Eateries
26. Whiteleys Shopping Centre (Eateries, Grocery, Internet)
27. Tesco Grocery
28. Spar Market
29. The Orangery (Afternoon Tea)
30. Launderette

Steves prices—and if booking on their website be sure to ask for the Rick Steves discount under "Additional Information"; continental breakfast served at Phoenix Hotel, free Wi-Fi, 9 Kensington Gardens Square, tel. 020/7243-7600, www.kensingtongardens hotel.co.uk, info@kensingtongardenshotel.co.uk, Rowshanak).

$$ Bayswater Inn Hotel's 140 tidy, perfectly adequate rooms come with dated style, an impersonal feel, and outrageously high official rack rates. But rooms commonly go for much lower prices, making this a decent—sometimes great—budget option (if booked in advance roughly Sb-£60, Db-£90, Tb-£125, Qb-£150, stay for free on fifth consecutive night, elevator, pay guest computer and Wi-Fi, 8-16 Princes Square, tel. 020/7727-8621, www.bayswater innhotel.com, reservations@bayswaterinnhotel.com).

Notting Hill and Nearby

The Notting Hill neighborhood, just west of Bayswater (spreading out from the northwest tip of Kensington Gardens), is famous for two things: It's the site of the colorful Portobello Road Market (see "Shopping in London," earlier), and the setting of the 1999 Hugh Grant/Julia Roberts film of the same name. While the neighborhood is now a bit more upscale and less funky than the one seen in that film, it's still a pleasant place to stay.

$$ The Gate Hotel has seven cramped but decent rooms on a delightful curved street near the start of the Portobello Road Market, in the heart of charming Notting Hill. The lodgings are basic and could be cleaner, but the prices are low for this area and the romantic setting might be worth it for some (Sb-£60, Db-£85, bigger "luxury" Db-£95, Tb-£115; £10-20 more Fri-Sat; 5 percent fee to pay with credit card, continental breakfast in room, pay Wi-Fi, 6 Portobello Road, Tube: Notting Hill Gate, tel. 020/7221-0707, www.gatehotel.co.uk, bookings@gatehotel.co.uk, Jasmine).

West of Kensington Gardens: **$$$ London Vicarage Hotel** is family-run, understandably popular, and located in a quiet, classy neighborhood just south of the core of Notting Hill. It has 17 quality rooms, a modest TV lounge, a grand staircase, and facilities on each floor. Mandy and Monika maintain a homey atmosphere (S-£67, Sb-£112, D-£112, Db-£140, T-£143, Tb-£184, Q-£155, Qb-£205, 20 percent less in winter—check website, free Wi-Fi; 8-minute walk from Notting Hill Gate and High Street Kensington Tube stations, near Kensington Palace at 10 Vicarage Gate; tel. 020/7229-4030, www.londonvicaragehotel.com, vicarage hotel@btconnect.com).

Near Holland Park: **$ Norwegian YWCA (Norsk K.F.U.K.)**—where English is definitely a second language—is open to any Norwegian woman, and to non-Norwegian women under 30. (Men must be under 30 with a Norwegian passport.) Located on a quiet, stately street, it offers a study, TV room, piano lounge, and an open-face Norwegian ambience (goat cheese on Sundays!). They have mostly quads, so those willing to share with strangers are most likely to get a bed (July-Aug: Ss-£46, shared double-£45/bed, shared triple-£40/bed, shared quad-£37/bed, includes sheets and towels, includes breakfast year-round plus sack lunch and dinner Sept-June, £20 key deposit and £3 membership fee required, pay Wi-Fi, 52 Holland Park, Tube: Holland Park, tel. 020/7727-9346 or 020/7727-9897, www.kfukhjemmet.org.uk, kontor@kfukhjemmet.org.uk). With each visit, I wonder which is easier to get—a sex change or a Norwegian passport?

Paddington Station Neighborhood

Just to the east of Bayswater, the neighborhood around Paddington Station—while much less charming than the other areas I've recommended—is pleasant enough, and very convenient to the Heathrow Express airport train. The area is flanked by the Paddington and Lancaster Gate Tube stops. Most of my recommendations circle Norfolk Square, just two blocks in front of Paddington Station, yet are still quiet and comfortable. The main drag, London Street, is lined with handy eateries—pubs, Indian, Italian, Moroccan, Greek, Lebanese, and more—plus convenience stores and an Internet café. (Better restaurants are a short stroll to the west, near Queensway and Notting Hill—see page 208.) To reach this area, exit the station toward Praed Street (with your back to the tracks, it's to the left). Once outside, continue straight across Praed Street and down London Street; Norfolk Square is a block ahead on the left.

On Norfolk Square

These places (and many more on the same street) are similar; all offer small rooms at a reasonable price, in tall buildings with lots of stairs and no elevator. I've chosen the ones that offer the most reasonable prices and the warmest welcome.

$$ Tudor Court Hotel has 38 colorful rooms conscientiously run by Connan and the Gupta family. While the tiny rooms are tight (with prefab plastic bathrooms) and the rates are a bit high, this place distinguishes itself with its warm welcome and attention to detail. If you smell them cooking up a big batch of curry rice, the Guptas are getting ready to take it to the homeless shelter, where they volunteer each week (S-£54-63, Sb-£95-108, "compact" Db-£99-120, larger "standard" Db-£135-165, "compact" Tb-£144-180, larger "standard" Tb-£162-198, family room-£180-225, higher rates are for Fri-Sat and other busy times, pay Wi-Fi, 10-12

Norfolk Square, tel. 020/7723-5157, www.tudorcourtpaddington
.co.uk, reservations@tudorcourtpaddington.co.uk).

$$ St. David's Hotels, run by the Neokleous family, has 60
rooms in several adjacent buildings. The rooms are small—as is
typical for less-expensive hotels in London—and scruffy, with
minimal amenities, but the staff is friendly, and their non-en-
suite rooms are a workable budget option (S-£50-60, Sb-£70-85,
D-£70-85, Db-£90-120, Tb-£100-130, pay Wi-Fi in rooms, free
Wi-Fi in lobby, 14-20 Norfolk Square, tel. 020/7723-3856, www
.stdavidshotels.com, info@stdavidshotels.com).

$$ Falcon Hotel, a lesser value, has less personality and 19
simple, old-school, faded rooms (S-£59, Sb-£69, D-£85, Db-£95,
twin Db-£99, Tb-£139, Qb-£149, rates flex with demand, free
guest computer, pay Wi-Fi, 11 Norfolk Square, tel. 020/7723-
8603, www.falcon-hotel.com, info@falcon-hotel.com).

$ easyHotel, the budget chain described on page 187, has a
branch at 10 Norfolk Place.

Elsewhere near Paddington Station

To reach these hotels, follow the directions on the previous page,
but continue away from the station past Norfolk Square to the big
intersection with Sussex Gardens; the Royal Park is a couple of
blocks to the right, and the others are immediately to the left.

$$$ The Royal Park is the neighborhood's classy splurge,
with 48 plush rooms, polished service, a genteel lounge (free
champagne for guests nightly 19:00-20:00), and all the little
extras ("classic" Db-official rates-£189-279, but prepaid/nonre-
fundable offers are as low as £140-190, bigger "executive" Db for
£20 more, prices vary with demand, does not include 20 percent
VAT, breakfast-£14-18, elevator, free guest computer and Wi-Fi, 3
Westbourne Terrace, tel. 020/7479-6600, www.theroyalpark.com,
info@theroyalpark.com).

$$ Stylotel feels like the stylish, super-modern, aluminum-
clad big sister of the easyHotel chain. Instead of peeling wallpaper
and ancient carpets held together with duct tape, they've opted
for sleek styling in their 39 rooms, all with clean, hard surfaces—
hardwood floors, prefab plastic bathrooms, and metallic walls.
While rooms can be a little cramped, the beds have space for your
luggage underneath. You may feel like an astronaut in a retro sci-
ence-fiction film, but if you don't need ye olde doilies, this place
offers a good value (Sb-£65, Db-£95, Tb-£115, Qb-£135, prices go
up with demand—book early and direct to get these rates, elevator, pay Wi-Fi, 160-162 Sussex Gardens, tel. 020/7723-1026, www
.stylotel.com, info@stylotel.com, well-run by Andreas). They also
have eight fancier, pricier, air-conditioned suites across the street
(£180-220 for 2-4 people, kitchenettes, no breakfast).

$$ **Olympic House Hotel** has stark public spaces and a stern welcome, but its 38 business-class rooms offer predictable comfort and fewer old-timey quirks than many hotels in this price range (Sb-£75, Db-£105, Tb-£120, rates vary with demand, air-con in most rooms costs extra, elevator, pay Wi-Fi, 138-140 Sussex Gardens, tel. 020/7723-5935, www.olympichousehotel.co.uk, olympichousehotel@btinternet.com).

Between Paddington and Bayswater: About halfway between these two hotel neighborhoods, $$ **Caring Hotel,** plain but affordable, has 25 tidy, nondescript-bordering-on-depressingly dull rooms in a nice, quiet location just off Hyde Park (basic D-£75, Ds-£80, small Db-£90, standard Db-£100, extra bed-£15, these rates are approximate—prices change with demand, free Wi-Fi, 24 Craven Hill Gardens—it's the second road with this name as you come from the park, Tube: Queensway, tel. 020/7262-8708, www.caringhotel.co.uk, enquiries@caringhotel.co.uk).

Elsewhere in Central London

$$$ **The Sumner Hotel** rents 19 rooms in a 19th-century Georgian townhouse sporting a lounge decorated with fancy modern Italian furniture. This swanky place packs in all the extras and is conveniently located north of Hyde Park and near Oxford Street, a busy shopping destination—with a convenient Marks & Spencer (see page 195) within walking distance (queen Db-£178, king Db-£197, "deluxe" Db-£216, mention this book to get these Rick Steves rates, can be cheaper off-season, extra bed-£60, air-con, elevator, free Wi-Fi, 54 Upper Berkeley Street, a block and a half off Edgware Road, Tube: Marble Arch, tel. 020/7723-2244, www.thesumner.com, hotel@thesumner.com).

$$$ **The 22 York Street B&B** offers a casual alternative in the city center, renting 10 traditional, hardwood, comfortable rooms, each named for a notable London landmark (Sb-£95, Db-£129, free guest computer and Wi-Fi, inviting lounge; near Marylebone/Baker Street: from Baker Street Tube station, walk 2 blocks down Baker Street and take a right to 22 York Street—since there's no sign, just look for #22; tel. 020/7224-2990, www.22yorkstreet.co.uk, mc@22yorkstreet.co.uk, energetically run by Liz and Michael Callis).

$$ **Seven Dials Hotel**'s 18 no-nonsense rooms are plain and fairly tight, but also clean, reasonably priced, and incredibly well-located. Since their doubles all cost the same, request one of their larger rooms when you book (Sb-£95, Db-£105 but £10 more for twin beds, Tb-£130, Qb-£150, free Wi-Fi, 7 Monmouth Street, Tube: Leicester Square or Covent Garden—see map on page 194, tel. 020/7681-0791, www.sevendialshotellondon.com, info@sevendialshotel.co.uk, Hanna).

North London Accommodations

400 Meters
400 Yards

To Zoo

Regent's Park

Queen Mary's Gardens

SHERLOCK HOLMES MUSEUM & BEATLES STORE

Baker Street ⊖

York

MADAME TUSSAUDS WAXWORKS

WALLACE COLLECTION

MARYLEBONE

GEORGE ST.

UP. BERK.

Marble Arch ⊖

MARBLE ARCH

Hyde Park

SELFRIDGES

Bond St. ⊖

OUTER CIRCLE

ALBANY ST.

EVERSHOLT ST.

HAMPSTEAD ROAD

ST. PANCRAS INT'L STATION

KING'S CROSS STATION

❸

PENTONVILLE RD.

❺ To ❽

EUSTON STATION

❼

❻

EUSTON ROAD

BRITISH LIBRARY

❹

GRAY'S INN ROAD

Euston Square ⊖

WOBURN PLACE

FITZROVIA

Russell Square

GUILFORD STREET

BLOOMSBURY

Great Portland Street ⊖

Warren Street ⊖

CARD ST.

Regent's Park ⊖

MARYLEBONE ROAD

PORTLAND PL.

GREAT PORTLAND ST.

CHARLOTTE ST.

GOWER ST.

❾

POLLOCK'S TOY MUSEUM

GOODGE ST.

Goodge Street ⊖

Russell Square ⊖

MONT.

BRITISH MUSEUM

Bedford Square

CARTOON MUSEUM

SIR JOHN SOANE'S MUSEUM

THEOBALD'S RD.

❶❷

BAKER ST.

GLOUCESTER PLACE

WIGMORE ST.

PORTMAN ST.

PARK ST.

DUKE ST.

NEW BOND ST.

REGENT ST.

OXFORD STREET

Oxford Circus ⊖

Bond St. ⊖

NEW OXFORD ST.

Holborn ⊖

Lincoln's Inn Fields

Tottenham Court Rd. ⊖

CHARING CROSS RD.

NOEL

❿

SOHO

Soho Square

To Trafalgar Square

To Trafalgar Square

SHAFTESBURY

THE STRAND

To The City

❶❷

❶ The Sumner Hotel

❷ The 22 York Street B&B

❸ Premier Inn London King's Cross St. Pancras

❹ Premier Inn London Euston

❺ Travelodge London King's Cross

❻ Travelodge London Euston

❼ Ibis London Euston St. Pancras & Drummond Street Eateries

❽ To Jurys Inn Islington

❾ London Central Youth Hostel

❿ Oxford Street Youth Hostel

⓫ Salumeria Dino Italian Deli & Lantana OUT Take-Away

⓬ Various Chain Eateries (2)

Big, Good-Value, Modern Hotels

London has an abundance of modern, impersonal, American-style chain hotels. I've listed and briefly described a few of the dominant chains below, along with a quick rundown on their more convenient London locations. Many of these hotels sit on busy streets in dreary train-station neighborhoods, so use common sense after dark and wear your money belt. For a sneak preview, try looking up the "Street View" for the address in Google Maps.

Premier Inn's locations include a branch inside **London County Hall** (next door to the London Eye), at **Southwark/Borough Market** (near Shakespeare's Globe on the South Bank, 34 Park Street, Tube: London Bridge), **Southwark/Tate Modern** (on Great Suffolk Street), **London King's Cross St. Pancras** (across the street from the east end of King's Cross Station and near the Eurostar terminus at St. Pancras), **London Euston** (handy but noisy location at corner of Euston Road and Dukes

Road), **Kensington/Earl's Court** (11 Knaresborough Place, Tube: Earl's Court or Gloucester Road), **Victoria** (82-83 Eccleston Square, Tube: Victoria), and **Putney Bridge** (farther out, 3 Putney Bridge Approach). Avoid the **Tower Bridge** location, which is an inconvenient 15-minute walk from the nearest Tube stop. Book online at www.premierinn.com or call 0871-527-9222; from North America, dial 011-44-1582-567-890.

Travelodge has quite a few locations in London, including at **King's Cross** (200 yards in front of King's Cross Station, Grays Inn Road, Tube: King's Cross St. Pancras), **Kings Cross Royal Scot, Euston, Marylebone, Covent Garden, Liverpool Street,** and **Farringdon** (www.travelodge.co.uk).

Ibis has only two locations that are convenient to London's center: **Euston St. Pancras** (on a quiet street a block west of Euston Station, 3 Cardington Street, Tube: Euston) and **The City** (5 Commercial Street, Tube: Aldgate East); book at www.ibis hotel.com.

Jurys Inn's locations include **Islington** (near King's Cross Station, 60 Pentonville Road, Tube: Angel), **Chelsea** (Imperial Road, Tube: Imperial Wharf), and near **Heathrow Airport**; all bookable at www.jurysinns.com.

easyHotel: With several branches in good neighborhoods around London, easyHotel (www.easyhotel.com) has a unique business model inspired by its parent company, the easyJet budget airline. The generally tiny, super-efficient, no-frills rooms feel popped out of a plastic mold, down to the prefab ship's head-type "bathroom pod." Rates can be surprisingly low (with doubles as cheap as £30 if you book early enough)—but you'll be charged à la carte for add-ons that are included at most hotels, such as TV use, luggage storage, fresh towels, and daily cleaning (breakfast, if available, comes from a vending machine). If you go with the basic package, it's like hosteling with privacy—a hard-to-beat value. But you get what you pay for (walls can be thin, construction can be flimsy, fellow guests can be noisy, and so on). They're only a good deal if you book far enough ahead to get a good price, and skip the many extras...which add up fast. Locations include **Victoria** (34-40 Belgrave Road—see map on page 172, Tube: Victoria), **South Kensington** (14 Lexham Gardens, Tube: Earl's Court or Gloucester Road), **Earl's Court** (44-48 West Cromwell Road, Tube: Earl's Court), **Paddington** (10 Norfolk Place, Tube: Paddington), and **Heathrow** and **Luton** airports.

Hostels

Hostels can slash accommodation costs while meeting your basic needs. Prices listed here include sheets and lockers (bring your own lock), but you'll likely have to rent towels and pay a bit extra

LONDON

for breakfast. All of these places are open 24 hours, give members a £3 discount, and have guest computers and Wi-Fi (usually for a fee).

$ London Central Youth Hostel is the flagship of London's hostels, with 300 beds and all the latest in security and comfortable efficiency. Families and travelers of any age will feel welcome in this wonderful facility. You'll pay the same price for any bed in a four- to eight-bed single-sex dorm—with or without private bathroom—so try to grab one with a bathroom (£16-30/bunk depending on demand, twin D-£40-60, families welcome to book an entire room, members' kitchen, book long in advance, between Oxford Circus and Great Portland Street Tube stations at 104 Bolsover Street—see map on page 186, tel. 0845-371-9154, www .yha.org.uk, londoncentral@yha.org.uk).

$ Oxford Street Youth Hostel is right in the shopping and clubbing zone in Soho, with 90 beds (£20-30/bunk, twin D-£50-60, members' kitchen, 14 Noel Street, Tube: Oxford Street, tel. 0845-371-9133, www.yha.org.uk, oxfordst@yha.org.uk).

$ St. Paul's Youth Hostel, near St. Paul's Cathedral, is modern, friendly, well-run, and a bit scruffy. Most of the 210 beds are in shared, single-sex 3- to 11-bunk rooms (£20-30/bunk depending on demand, twin D-£50-60, cheap meals, 36 Carter Lane, Tube: St. Paul's, tel. 020/7236-4965 or 0845-371-9012, www.yha .org.uk, stpauls@yha.org.uk).

$ A cluster of three **St. Christopher's Inn** hostels, south of the Thames near London Bridge, have cheap dorm beds; one branch (the Oasis) is for women only. All have loud and friendly bars attached (£22-36, higher price is for weekends, less in off-season, D-£60 or thereabouts, small breakfast included, must be over 18 years old, free Wi-Fi, 161-165 Borough High Street, Tube: Borough or London Bridge, reservations tel. 020/8600-7500, www.st-christophers.co.uk).

Heathrow and Gatwick Airports
At or near Heathrow Airport

It's so easy to get to Heathrow from central London, I see no reason to sleep there. But if you do, here are some options. The Yotel is actually inside the airport, while the rest are a short bus or taxi ride away. In addition to public buses, the cutely named £4 "Hotel Hoppa" shuttle buses connect the airport to many nearby hotels (different routes serve the various hotels and terminals—may take a while to spot your particular bus at the airport).

$$ Yotel, at the airport inside Terminal 4, has small sleep dens good for a quick nap (four hours-£35-70), or an overnight stay (tiny "standard cabin"—£70/8 hours, "premium cabin"—£93/8 hours; cabins sleep 1-2 people; price is per cabin—not person, these prices include £3 credit-card fee). Prices vary by day, week, and time of year, so check their website. The windowless rooms are only slightly larger than a double bed, with weirdly purplish lighting, private bathrooms, and free guest computers and Wi-Fi (tel. 020/7100-1100, www.yotel.com, customer@yotel.com).

$$ Jurys Inn, another hotel chain, tempts tired travelers with 300-plus cookie-cutter rooms (Db-£55-105, cheapest when booked at least a week in advance, check website for deals, breakfast extra; on Eastern Perimeter Road, Tube: Hatton Cross plus 5-minute walk; take the Tube one stop from Terminals 1 or 3; or two stops from Terminals 4 or 5; or the Hotel Hoppa #H9 from Terminals 1 or 3, or #H53 or #H56 from Terminals 4 or 5; tel. 020/8266-4664, www.jurysinns.com).

$ easyHotel, your cheapest bet, is in a low-rent residential neighborhood a £5 taxi ride from the airport. Its 53 no-frills, pod-like rooms are on two floors (Db-£40-55 including 20 percent VAT, no breakfast, no elevator, pay guest computer and Wi-Fi, see page 187 for more on easyHotel, Brick Field Lane; take free local bus #140 from airport's Central Bus Station or the Hotel Hoppa #H8 from Terminals 1 or 3—or #H3 after 20:00, or ask the hotel to arrange a taxi; www.easyhotel.com, enquiries@heathrow.easy hotel.com).

$ Hotel Ibis London Heathrow offers predictable value (Db-£40-55, cheapest when booked 3 weeks ahead, website specials as low as £35, breakfast-£9, pay guest computer and Wi-Fi; 112-114 Bath Road, take free local bus #105, #111, #140, or #285 from airport's Central Bus Station or Terminal 4, or the Hotel Hoppa #H6 from Terminals 1 or 3—or #H56 from Terminals 4 or 5; tel. 020/8759-4888, www.ibishotel.com, h0794@accor.com).

At or near Gatwick Airport

$$ Yotel, with small rooms, has a branch right at the airport (Gatwick South Terminal; see prices and contact info in Heathrow listing, previous page).

$ Gatwick Airport Central Premier Inn rents cheap rooms 350 yards from the airport (Db-£45-65, breakfast-£5-9, £3 shuttle bus from airport—must reserve in advance, Longbridge Way, North Terminal, tel. 0871-527-8406, frustrating phone tree, www .premierinn.com). Five more Premier Inns are within a five-mile radius of the airport.

$ Gatwick Airport Travelodge has budget rooms about two miles from the airport (Db-£30-60, breakfast extra, pay Wi-Fi, Church Road, Lowfield Heath, Crawley, £3.20 shuttle bus to/ from airport, tel. 0871-984-6031, www.travelodge.co.uk).

Apartment Rentals

Consider the advantages that come with renting a furnished apartment—or "flat," as the British say. Complete with a small, equipped kitchen and living room, this option can also work for families or groups on shorter visits.

Cross-Pollinate is an online booking agency representing B&Bs and apartments in a handful of European cities, including London. Search their website for a listing you like, then submit your reservation online. If the place is available, you'll be charged a small deposit and emailed the location and check-in details. Policies vary from owner to owner, but in most cases you'll pay the balance on arrival in cash. London listings range from a Chelsea B&B room for two for £100 per night to a two-bedroom Marble Arch apartment sleeping four for £280 per night. Minimum stays vary from one to five nights (US tel. 800-270-1190, UK tel. 020/3514-0083, www.cross-pollinate.com, info@cross-pollinate .com).

Coach House Rentals offers a range of hand-selected apartments around the city, nearly all of them in real homes. As with any apartment rental, these can be an especially smart option if you're traveling as a group of four or more. Generally speaking, the more central the apartment, the more you pay (around £200/night for place in Pimlico, £425/night right by Westminster Abbey, £120-150/night farther afield). Each comes with a packet of neighborhood info, a "starter pack" of breakfast snacks, and usually either cable Internet access or Wi-Fi. A staff member meets you when you first arrive, and someone's always available over the phone (5-night minimum, £90 fee on top of quoted rental, tel. 020/8133-8332, http://rentals.chslondon.com, rentals@chslondon .com).

Many other organizations are ready to help; the following have been recommended by local guides and readers: www .perfectplaces.com, www.homefromhome.co.uk, www.london -house.com, www.gowithit.co.uk, www.aplacelikehome.co.uk, and www.regentsuites.com. You can also rent directly from the apartment owner (check reputable websites such as www.airbnb .com, www.HomeAway.com, and www.vrbo.com).

No matter whom you rent through, be very careful to avoid getting scammed: Follow all of the website's safety advice and use their internal payment procedures. Never wire money directly to an apartment owner, or you may find yourself with no place to stay—and no hope of getting your money back.

Read the rental conditions carefully and ask lots of questions. If a certain amenity is important to you (such as Wi-Fi or a washing machine in the unit), ask specifically about it and what to do if it stops working. Plot the location carefully (plug the address into http://maps.google.com), and remember to factor in travel time and costs from outlying neighborhoods to central London. Finally, it's a good idea to buy trip cancellation/interruption insurance, as many weekly rentals are nonrefundable.

Eating in London

With "modern English" cuisine on the rise, you could try a different cuisine for each meal in London and never eat "local" English food, even on a lengthy stay. The sheer variety of foods—from every corner of its former empire and beyond—is astonishing. You'll be amazed at the number of hopping, happening new restaurants of all kinds.

If you want to dine (as opposed to eat), drop by a London newsstand to get a weekly entertainment guide or an annual restaurant guide (both have extensive restaurant listings). Visit www.london-eating.co.uk or www.square meal.co.uk for more options.

The thought of a £50 meal in Britain generally ruins my appetite, so my London dining is limited mostly to easygoing, fun, moderately priced alternatives. I've listed places by neighborhood—handy to your sightseeing or hotel. Considering how expensive London can be, if there's any good place to cut corners to stretch your budget, it's by eating cheaply. Pub grub (at one of London's 7,000 pubs) and ethnic restaurants (especially Indian and Chinese) are good low-cost options. Of course, picnicking is the fastest and cheapest way to go. Good grocery stores and sandwich shops, fine park benches, and polite pigeons abound in Britain's most expensive city. Affordable chain restaurants (such as those noted in the sidebar) are another good option.

London (and all of Britain) is smoke-free. Expect restaurants and pubs that sell food to be non-smoking indoors, with smokers occupying patios and doorways outside. When ready to pay, Brits generally ask for the "bill" rather than the "check."

Central London

I've arranged these options by neighborhood, but they're all within about a 15-minute walk of each other. Survey your options before settling on a place.

Near Soho and Chinatown

London has a trendy scene that most Beefeater-seekers miss

London's Chain Restaurants

One good way to save money and still eat well is by dining at one of London's excellent chain restaurants. Most of the branches listed here open daily no later than noon (several at 8:00 or 9:00), and close sometime between 22:00 and midnight. Occasionally a place may close on Sundays or in the afternoon between lunch and dinner, but these are rare exceptions.

Busaba Eathai is a hit with Londoners for its snappy (sometimes rushed) service, boisterous ambience, and good, inexpensive Thai cuisine. Wedge yourself at one of the 16-person hardwood tables or at a two-person table by the window—with everyone in the queue staring at your noodles (£7-12 meals, www.busaba.com). New locations pop up often, with outlets in Soho, Covent Garden, near the British Museum, and across from the Bond Street Tube stop.

Thai Square is another dependable Thai option with a much swankier atmosphere (£8-10 salads, noodle dishes, and curries; £13-16 meat dishes, www:thaisquareserver.co.uk). Handy locations include Soho, Trafalgar Square, Covent Garden, the Strand, South Kensington, near Oxford Circus, and The City (one on The Strand at Fleet Street and another near the Mansion House Tube stop).

Masala Zone, serving accessible and Indian food, makes a predictable, good alternative to the many one-off, hole-in-the-wall Indian joints around town. Try a curry-and-rice dish, a *thali* (platter with several small dishes), or their street food specials. Each branch has its own personality (£8-12 meals, www.masalazone.com). Locations include Soho, Covent Garden, Bayswater, and in the Selfridges department store on Oxford Street.

Byron, an upscale-hamburger chain with hip interiors, is worth seeking out if you need a burger fix. While British burgers tend to be a bit overcooked by our standards, Byron's burgers are your best bet (£7-10 burgers, www.byronhamburgers.com). Locations are in Soho, Covent Garden, Leicester Square, between Piccadilly Circus and Trafalgar Square, near St. Paul's, Fitzrovia, South Kensington, Kensington, and Greenwich.

Other quality chain restaurants—which you'll also find across the UK—are **Wagamama Noodle Bar, Côte Brasserie, Byron, Gourmet Burger Kitchen (GBK), Loch Fyne Fish Restaurant, Nando's, Yo! Sushi, Ask, Pizza Express,** and **Jamie's Italian.** (For descriptions of these eateries, see page 34.)

entirely. Foodies who want to eat well skip the more staid and touristy zones near Piccadilly and Trafalgar Square, and head to Soho instead. Make it a point to dine in Soho at least once, to feel the pulse of London's eclectic urban melting pot of international flavors. These restaurants are scattered throughout a chic, creative, and borderline-seedy zone that teems with hipsters, theatergoers, and London's gay community. Even if you plan to have dinner elsewhere, it's a treat just to wander around Soho.

Note: While gentrification has mostly stripped this area (no pun intended) of its former "red light district" vibe, a few pockets of sex for sale survive. Beware of the extremely welcoming women standing outside the strip clubs (especially on Great Windmill Street). Enjoy the sales pitch—but know that only fools fall for the "£5 drink and show" lure.

On and near Wardour Street, in the Heart of Soho

Running through the middle of Soho, rumbling past what's left of the strip-club zone, Wardour Street is ground zero for creative restaurateurs hoping to break into the big leagues. Strolling up this street—particularly from Brewer Street northward—you can take your pick from a world of options: Thai, Indonesian, Vietnamese, Italian, French and even...English. Not yet tarnished by the corporatization creeping in from areas to the south, this drag still seems to hit the right balance between trendy and accessible. While I've listed several choices below (including some that are a block or two off Wardour Street), simply strolling the length of the street and following your appetite to the place that looks best is a great plan.

Princi is a vast, bright, efficient, wildly popular Italian deli/bakery with Milanese flair. Along one wall is a long counter with display cases offering a tempting array of pizza rustica, panini sandwiches, focaccia, a few pasta dishes, and desserts (look in the window from the street to see their wood-fired oven in action). Order your food at the counter, then find a space at a long shared table; or get it to go for an affordable and fast meal (£7-13 meals, Mon-Sat 8:00-24:00, Sun 8:30-22:00, 135 Wardour Street, tel. 020/7478-8888).

Bi Bim Bap is named for what it sells: *bibimbap* (literally "mixed rice"), a scalding stone bowl filled with rice and thinly sliced veggies, topped with a fried egg. Mix it up with your spoon, flavor it to taste with the two sauces, then dig in with your chopsticks. While purists go with the straightforward rice bowl, you can pay a few pounds extra to add other toppings—including chicken, *bulgogi* (marinated beef strips), and mushrooms. Though the food is traditional Korean, the stylish, colorful interior lets you know you're in Soho (£7-10 meals, Mon-Fri 12:00-15:00 & 18:00-23:00, Sat 12:00-23:00, closed Sun, 11 Greek Street, tel. 020/7287-3434).

Central London Eateries

1. Seven Dials Hotel
2. Princi Italian Deli
3. Bi Bim Bap
4. Mooli's
5. Bocca di Lupo
6. Gelupo Gelato
7. Yalla Yalla
8. Ducksoup
9. Y Ming Chinese Rest.
10. Jen Café
11. Wong Kei
12. Andrew Edmunds Restaurant
13. Mildred's Vegetarian Rest.; Fernandez & Wells
14. St. Martin-in-the-Fields Café in the Crypt
15. The Chandos Pub
16. Gordon's Wine Bar
17. The Harp Pub
18. The Wolseley
19. Criterion Restaurant

LONDON

20 Stockpot & Woodlands South Indian Vegetarian Restaurant
21 West End Kitchen
22 Joe Allen
23 Sofra Turkish Restaurant
24 Sitar Indian Restaurant
25 Belgo Centraal
26 Neal's Yard Eateries
27 Food for Thought Café
28 Union Jacks (2)

29 Masala Zone (2)
30 Busaba Eathai (3)
31 Byron (7)
32 Thai Square (5)
33 Nando's (3)
34 Wagamama Noodle Bar (5)
35 Yo! Sushi (3)
36 Loch Fyne Fish Restaurant
37 Côte Brasserie (4)
38 The Princess Louise Pub

Mooli's, which may close or move to a new location in 2014, is made-to-order for a quick, affordable, flavorful jolt of Indian street food. Their £5-6 *mooli* wraps, sort of like an Indian burrito, are filled with pork, chicken, beef, *paneer* (cheese), chickpea, or spicy goat. Top it with your choice of chutneys and Indian salsas. Eat in or grab one to go; their "mini" version makes a good £3.50 snack (Mon-Sat 8:30-23:30, closed Sun, 50 Frith Street, tel. 020/7494-9075).

Bocca di Lupo, a pricey and popular splurge, serves small portions of classic regional Italian food. Dressy and a bit snooty, it's a place where you're glad you made a reservation. The counter seating, on cushy stools with a view into the open kitchen, is particularly memorable. Most diners assemble a sampler meal with a series of £7-10 small plates—but be careful, because at these prices, your bill can add up. A short selection of more affordable £10-15 "one-dish meals" is available for lunch and until 19:00 (Mon-Sat 12:00-15:00 & 17:30-23:00, Sun 12:30-15:15 & 17:00-21:00, 12 Archer Street, tel. 020/7734-2223, www.boccadilupo.com).

Gelupo, Bocca di Lupo's sister gelateria across the street, has a wide array of ever-changing but always creative and delicious dessert favorites—ranging from popular standbys like the incredibly rich chocolate sorbet to fresh-mint *stracciatella* to hay (yes, hay). A £3 sampler cup or cone gets you two flavors (and little taster spoons are generously offered to help you choose). Everything is homemade, and the white subway-tile interior feels clean and bright. They also have espresso drinks and—at lunchtime—£5-6 deli sandwiches (daily 12:00 until late, 7 Archer Street, tel. 020/7287-5555).

Yalla Yalla is a hole-in-the-wall serving up high-quality Beirut street food—hummus, baba ghanoush, tabbouleh, and *shawarmas*. Stylish as you'd expect for Soho, it's tucked down a seedy alley across from a sex shop. Eat in the cramped and cozy interior or at one of the few outdoor tables, or get your food to go (£3-4 sandwiches, £4-6 mezes, £7 meze platter available until 17:00, £10-12 bigger dishes, Mon-Sat 10:00-23:00, Sun 10:00-22:00, 1 Green's Court—just north of Brewer Street, tel. 020/7287-7663).

Ducksoup, a short block over from Wardour Street, is an upscale-feeling yet cool and relaxed little bar, with a small but thoughtful menu of well-executed international and modern British dishes (£7 small plates, £14 big plates—sharing several items can add up). The menu is handwritten, the music is on vinyl, and the rough woodwork and cramped-but-convivial atmosphere give it the feeling of a well-loved wine bar. While a bit overpriced, the atmosphere is memorable (Mon-Sat 12:00-24:00, food served until 22:30, Sun 13:00-16:00, 41 Dean Street, tel. 020/7287-4599).

And for Dessert: In addition to the outstanding gelato at

Gelupo and the treats at **Princi** (both described above), several other places along Wardour Street boast window displays that tickle the sweet tooth. In just a couple of blocks, you'll see pastry shops, a *crêperie*, and a Hummingbird cupcake shop.

Soho Chain Restaurants: Some of Britain's most popular chain restaurants started out here in Soho, but in this fast-evolving neighborhood, they're now a little like stale sushi. While I wouldn't waste a Soho meal on one of these places, they're a convenient fallback: **Byron** (particularly appealing industrial-mod branch at 97-99 Wardour Street), **Busaba Eathai** (106 Wardour Street), **Thai Square** (27-28 St. Anne's Court, plus one near Trafalgar Square at 21-24 Cockspur Street), **Wagamama** (10A Lexington Street), **Masala Zone** (9 Marshall Street), **Côte** (124-126 Wardour Street), and **Nando's** (10 Frith Street).

LONDON

Authentic Chinese Food in and near Chinatown

The main drag of Chinatown (Gerrard Street, with the ornamental archways) is lined with touristy, interchangeable Chinese joints. But these places seem to have an edge.

Y Ming Chinese Restaurant—across Shaftesbury Avenue from the ornate gates, clatter, and dim sum of Chinatown—has dressy European decor, serious but helpful service, and authentic Northern Chinese cooking. London's food critics consider this well worth the short walk from the heart of Chinatown for food that's a notch above (good £12 meal deal offered 12:00-18:00, £8-12 plates, open Mon-Sat 12:00-23:45, closed Sun, turquoise corner shop at 35-36 Greek Street, tel. 020/7734-2721).

Jen Café, across the little square called Newport Place, is a humble Chinese corner eatery much loved for its homemade dumplings. It's just stools and simple seating, with fast service, a fun, inexpensive menu, and a devoted following (£6-8 plates, daily 10:30-21:00, cash only, 4 Newport Place, tel. 020/7287-9708).

Wong Kei Chinese restaurant, at the Wardour Street (west) end of the Chinatown drag, offers a bewildering variety of dishes served by notoriously brusque waiters in a setting that feels like a hospital cafeteria. Londoners put up with the abuse to enjoy one of the satisfying BBQ rice dishes or hot pots. Individuals and couples are usually seated at communal tables, while larger parties are briskly shuffled up or down stairs (£7-12 main dishes, £10-15 fixed-price meals, cash only, Mon-Sat 12:00-23:30, Sun 12:00-22:30, 41-43 Wardour Street, tel. 020/7437-8408).

Sedate and Upscale Options in Soho

Andrew Edmunds Restaurant is a tiny, candlelit space where you'll want to hide your camera and guidebook and not act like a tourist. This little place—with a jealous and loyal clientele—is the closest I've found to Parisian quality in a cozy restaurant in London. The extensive wine list, modern European cooking, and creative seasonal menu are worth the splurge (£5-7 starters, £12-20 main dishes, Mon-Sat 12:00-15:30 & 17:30-22:45, Sun 13:00-16:00 & 18:00-22:30, these are last-order times, come early or call ahead, request ground floor rather than basement, 46 Lexington Street, tel. 020/7437-5708, www.andrewedmunds.com).

Mildred's Vegetarian Restaurant, across from Andrew Edmunds, has cheap prices, an enjoyable menu, and a pleasant interior filled with happy eaters (£8-11 meals, Mon-Sat 12:00-23:00, closed Sun, vegan options, 45 Lexington Street, tel. 020/7494-1634).

Fernandez & Wells is a cozy, convivial, delightfully simple little wine, cheese, and ham bar. Drop in and grab a stool as you belly up to the big wooden bar. Share a plate of top-quality cheeses and/or Spanish, Italian, or French hams with fine bread and oil, while sipping a nice glass of wine (Mon-Fri 11:00-22:00, Sat-Sun 12:00-22:00, quality sandwiches at lunch, 43 Lexington Street, tel. 020/7734-1546).

Traditional Choices near Trafalgar Square

These places, all of which provide a more "jolly olde" experience than high cuisine, are within about 100 yards of Trafalgar Square.

St. Martin-in-the-Fields Café in the Crypt is just right for a tasty meal on a monk's budget—maybe even on a monk's tomb. You'll dine sitting on somebody's gravestone in an ancient crypt. Their enticing buffet line is kept stocked all day, serving breakfast, lunch, and dinner (£7-10 cafeteria plates, hearty traditional desserts, free jugs of water). They also serve a restful cream tea (£6, daily 14:00-18:00). You'll find the café directly under the St. Martin-in-the-Fields Church, facing Trafalgar Square—enter through the glass pavilion next to the church (Mon-Tue 8:00-20:00, Wed 8:00-22:30, Thu-Sat 8:00-21:00, Sun 11:00-18:00, profits go to the church, Tube: Charing Cross, tel. 020/7766-1158 or 020/7766-1100). Wednesday evenings at 20:00 come with a live jazz band (£5.50-9 tickets). While here, check out the concert schedule for the busy church upstairs (or visit www.smitf.org).

The Chandos Pub's Opera Room floats amazingly apart from the tacky crush of tourism around Trafalgar Square. Look for it opposite the National Portrait Gallery (corner of William IV Street and St. Martin's Lane) and climb the stairs (to the right of the pub entrance) to the Opera Room. This is a fine Trafalgar rendezvous point and wonderfully local pub. They serve £4 sandwiches and a better-than-average range of traditional pub meals for under £10—meat pies and fish-and-chips are their specialty. The ground-floor pub is stuffed with regulars and offers snugs (private booths), the same menu, and more serious beer drinking. Chandos proudly serves the local Samuel Smith beer at £4 a pint (kitchen open daily 11:00-19:00, Fri and Sun until 18:00, order and pay at the bar, 29 St. Martin's Lane, Tube: Leicester Square, tel. 020/7836-1401).

Gordon's Wine Bar, with a simple, steep staircase leading into a candlelit 15th-century wine cellar, is filled with dusty old bottles, faded British memorabilia, and nine-to-fivers. At the "English rustic" buffet, choose a hot meal or cold meat dish with a salad (figure around £7-8/dish); the £9 cheese plate comes with two cheeses, bread, and a pickle. Then step up to the wine bar and consider the many varieties of wine and port available by the glass (this place is passionate about port). The low carbon-crusted vaulting deeper in the back seems to intensify the Hogarth-painting atmosphere. Although it's crowded, you can normally corral two chairs and grab the corner of a table. On hot days, the crowd spills out onto a leafy back patio, where a barbecue cooks for a long line of tables (arrive before 17:00 to get a seat, Mon-Sat 11:00-23:00, Sun 12:00-22:00, 2 blocks from Trafalgar Square, bottom of Villiers Street at #47, Tube: Embankment, tel. 020/7930-1408, manager Gerard Menan).

Ales: **The Harp,** clearly a local favorite, is a crowded and cluttered little pub just a block above Trafalgar Square. While they serve no food, this is a good, central spot to nurse a fine ale and make a new friend with one of the Londoners crowded around the coaster-coated bar. This is a top choice for an après-work pint among nine-to-fivers, who stand in the dozens out front after the workday, sipping their beers (Mon-Sat 10:30-23:30, Sun 12:00-22:30, 47 Chandos Place, tel. 020/7836-0291).

Near Piccadilly

The first two places are upscale and snooty—but if you want something cheaper in this same area, you'll find plenty of other options.

Swanky Splurges

The Wolseley is the grand 1920s showroom of a long-defunct British car. The last Wolseley drove out with the Great Depression, but today this old-time bistro bustles with formal waiters serving traditional Austrian and French dishes in an elegant black-marble-and-chandeliers setting fit for its location next to the Ritz. Although the food can be unexceptional, prices are reasonable, and the presentation and setting are grand. Reservations are a must (£13-30 main courses; cheaper soup, salad, and sandwich "café menu" available; both menus available in all areas of restaurant, Mon-Fri 7:00-24:00, Sat 8:00-24:00, Sun 8:00-23:00, 160 Piccadilly—see map on page 194, tel. 020/7499-6996,

Pub Appreciation

The pub is the heart of the people's Britain, where all manner of folks have, for generations, found their respite from work and a home-away-from-home. Britain's classic pubs are national treasures, with great cultural value and rich history, not to mention good beer and grub.

The Golden Age for pub-building was in the late Victorian era (c. 1880-1905), when pubs were independently owned and land prices were high enough to make it worthwhile to invest in fixing up pubs. The politics were pro-pub as well: Conservatives, backed by Big Beer, were in, and temperance-minded Liberals were out.

Especially in class-conscious Victorian times, traditional pubs were divided into sections by elaborate screens (now mostly gone), allowing the wealthy to drink in a more refined setting, while commoners congregated on the pub's rougher side. These were really "public houses," featuring nooks (snugs) for groups and clubs to meet, friends and lovers to rendezvous, and families to get out of the house at night. Because many medieval pub-goers were illiterate, pubs were simply named for the picture hung outside (e.g., The Crooked Stick, The Queen's Arms—meaning her coat of arms).

Historic pubs still dot the London cityscape. The only place to see the very oldest-style tavern in the "domestic tradition" is at **Ye Olde Cheshire Cheese,** which was rebuilt in 1667 (after the Great Fire) from a 16th-century tavern (£5-10 pub grub, £9-14 meals in the restaurant, open daily, 145 Fleet Street, Tube: Blackfriars, tel. 020/7353-6170). Imagine this mazelike place, with three separate bars, in the pre-Victorian era: With no bar, drinkers gathered around the fireplaces, while tap boys shuttled tankards up from the cellar. (This was long before barroom taps were connected to casks in the cellar. Oh, and don't say "keg"— that's a gassy modern thing.)

Late-Victorian pubs are more common, such as the lovingly restored 1897 **Princess Louise** (daily midday until 23:00, lunch and dinner served in less atmospheric upstairs lounge Mon-Thu, Fri lunch only, no food Sat-Sun, 208 High Holborn, see map on page 194, Tube: Holborn, tel. 020/7405-8816). These places are fancy, often with heavy embossed wallpaper ceilings, decorative tile work, fine-etched glass, ornate carved stillions (the big central hutch for storing bottles and glass), and even urinals equipped with a place to set your glass.

London's best Art Nouveau pub is **The Black Friar** (c. 1900-1915), with fine carved capitals, lamp holders, and quirky phrases worked into the decor (£8-11 meals, daily 10:00-23:30, outdoor seating, 174 Queen Victoria Street, Tube: Blackfriars, tel. 020/7236-5474).

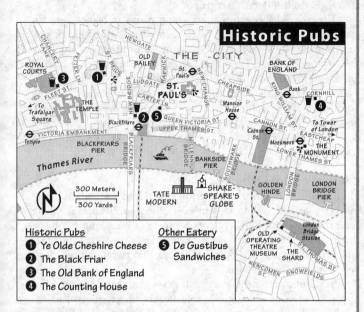

Historic Pubs

THE CITY

Historic Pubs
1. Ye Olde Cheshire Cheese
2. The Black Friar
3. The Old Bank of England
4. The Counting House

Other Eatery
5. De Gustibus Sandwiches

The "former-bank pubs" represent a more modern trend in pub-building. As banks increasingly go electronic, they're moving out of lavish, high-rent old buildings. Many of these former banks are being refitted as pubs with elegant bars and freestanding stillions, which provide a fine centerpiece. Three such pubs are **The Old Bank of England** (£7-10 meals, Mon-Fri 11:00-23:00, food served 12:00-21:00, closed Sat-Sun, 194 Fleet Street, Tube: Temple, tel. 020/7430-2255), **The Jugged Hare** (open daily, 172 Vauxhall Bridge Road—see map on page 172, Tube: Victoria, tel. 020/7828-1543, also see listing on page 207), and **The Counting House** (Mon-Fri 11:00-23:00, closed Sat-Sun, 50 Cornhill, Tube: Bank, tel. 020/7283-7123, see listing on page 210).

Go pubbing in the evening for a lively time, or drop by during the quiet late morning (from 11:00), when the pub is empty and filled with memories.

www.thewolseley.com). They're popular for their fancy cream or afternoon tea (for details, see page 211).

The palatial **Criterion** offers grand-piano ambience beneath gilded tiles and chandeliers in a dreamy Byzantine church setting from 1880. It's right on Piccadilly Circus but a world away from the punk junk. It's a deal for the visual experience during lunch and if you order the £19-23 fixed-price meal (except on Sun, when you must order from the expensive à la carte menu). At any hour, the service couldn't care less. Anyone can drop in for coffee or a drink (Mon-Sat 12:00-14:30 & 17:30-23:30, Sun 12:00-15:30 & 17:30-22:30, 224 Piccadilly, tel. 020/7930-0488, www.criterion restaurant.com).

Cheaper Options near Piccadilly

Hungry and broke in the theater district? Head for Panton Street (off Haymarket, two blocks southeast of Piccadilly Circus), where several hardworking little places compete, all seeming to offer a three-course meal for about £9. Peruse the entire block (vegetarian, Pizza Express, Moroccan, Chinese, and two famous diners) before making your choice.

Stockpot is a meat, potatoes, gravy, and mushy-peas kind of place, famous and rightly popular for its edible, cheap English meals (£6-12, daily 7:00-23:00, 38 Panton Street, tel. 020/7839-5142). The **West End Kitchen** (across the street at #5, same hours and menu) is a direct competitor that's also well-known and just as good (£5-11 meals). Vegetarians may prefer the **Woodlands South Indian Vegetarian Restaurant,** which serves an impressive £19 *thali* combination plate (otherwise £7 main courses, 37 Panton Street).

Good Chains near Piccadilly: **Busaba Eathai** (35 Panton Street), **Wagamama** (8 Norris Street and another in Leicester Square at 14 Irving Street), **Byron** (11 Haymarket), and **Nando's** (46 Glasshouse Street).

Near Covent Garden

Covent Garden bustles with people and touristy eateries. The area feels overrun, but if you must eat around here, you have some good choices.

Joe Allen, tucked in a brick cellar a block away from the market, serves modern international and American cuisine with both style and hubbub. Downstairs off a quiet street with candles and white tablecloths, it's comfortably spacious and popular with the theater crowd. It feels a bit old-fashioned and cluttered, but in a welcoming way (£7 starters, £10-22 main courses, £16 two-course specials and £20 three-course specials available at lunch and 17:00-

18:45, open Mon-Fri 12:00-24:00, Sat-Sun 10:00-24:00, piano music after 19:00, 13 Exeter Street, tel. 020/7836-0651).

Sofra Turkish Restaurant is good for quality Turkish with a touch of class. They have several menus: *meze* (Turkish tapas, £4-7), vegetarian, and £10 fixed-price meals (also £10-15 main dishes, daily 9:00-23:00, 36 Tavistock Street, tel. 020/7240-3773).

Sitar Indian Restaurant is a well-respected Indian/Bangladeshi place serving dishes from many regions, fine fish, and a tasty £15 vegetarian *thali* (combo plate). It's small and dressy, with snappy service (£10-17 main dishes, Mon-Fri 12:00-24:00, Sat-Sun 15:00-23:00, next to Somerset House at 149 Strand, tel. 020/7836-3730).

Belgo Centraal serves hearty Belgian specialties in a vast 400-seat underground lair. It's a mussels, chips, and beer emporium dressed up as a mod-monastic refectory—with noisy acoustics and waiters garbed as Trappist monks. The classy restaurant section is more comfortable and less rowdy, but usually requires reservations. It's often more fun just to grab a spot in the boisterous beer hall, with its tight, communal benches (no reservations accepted). Both sides have the same menu and specials. Belgians claim they eat as well as the French and as heartily as the Germans. This place, which offers a stunning array of dark, blonde, and fruity Belgian beers, actually makes Belgian things trendy—a formidable feat (£10-14 main dishes, open daily 12:00-23:00; Mon-Fri £5-6.30 "beat the clock" meal specials 17:00-18:30—the time you order is the price you pay—including main dishes and fries; no meal-splitting after 18:30, and you must buy food with beer; daily £8 lunch special 12:00-17:00; 1 kid eats free for each parent ordering a regular entrée; 1 block north of Covent Garden Tube station at 50 Earlham Street, tel. 020/7813-2233).

Neal's Yard is a surprisingly colorful courtyard full of cheap, hip, and healthy eateries near Covent Garden. The neighborhood is a tabbouleh of fun, hippie-type cafés. One of the best—nearby—is the venerable and ferociously vegetarian **Food for Thought,** packed with local health nuts (good £5 vegetarian meals, Mon-Sat 12:00-20:30, Sun 12:00-17:30, 2 blocks north of Covent Garden Tube station at 31 Neal Street, tel. 020/7836-9072).

Union Jacks, the latest venture of British celebrity chef Jamie Oliver, fuses traditional British ingredients to make inventive modern dishes. Jamie's wood-fired flatbreads are topped not with cheese and tomatoes, but roast pig shoulder or oxtail and brisket. While this sounds risky, he pulls it off with great flavors, plus fun "fizzy drinks." The more charming of its two London branches sits right inside the Covent Garden market hall; a second restaurant is several blocks away (past Neal's Yard in a glass office building across from St. Giles Church). Each dish costs a few pounds more at the Covent Garden restaurant—this kind of location doesn't come cheap (£5-7 small plates are very small, £10-13 flatbreads, £9-15 classic British dishes, daily 12:00-23:00, Covent Garden tel. 020/3640-7086, St. Giles tel. 020/3597-7888).

Good Chains near Covent Garden: This area seems to have a branch of nearly every London chain, including **Masala Zone** (particularly fun branch at the top end of the market has giant, colorful marionettes suspended from the ceiling, 48 Floral Street), **Côte** (17-21 Tavistock Street and one closer to Leicester Square at 50-51 St. Martin's Lane), **Busaba Eathai** (44 Floral Street), **Thai Square** (166-170 Shaftesbury Avenue, plus one next to Sitar Indian Restaurant at 148 The Strand), **Wagamama** (1 Tavistock Street), **Byron** (behind the London Transport Museum at 33-35 Wellington Street), **Loch Fyne** (a couple of blocks behind the square at 2 Catherine Street), and **Nando's** (66-68 Chandos Place).

Near the British Museum, in Fitzrovia

To avoid the touristy crush right around the museum (and just southwest, in Soho), Londoners head a few blocks west, to the Fitzrovia area. Here, tiny Charlotte Place is lined with small eateries (including the first two listed below); nearby, the much bigger Charlotte Street has several more good options. The higher street signs you'll notice on Charlotte Street are a holdover from a time when they needed to be visible to carriage drivers. This area is a short walk from the Goodge Street Tube station—convenient to the British Museum.

Salumeria Dino serves up hearty sandwiches, pasta, and Italian coffee. Dino, a native of Naples, has run his little shop for more than 30 years and has managed to create a classic Italian deli that's so authentic, you'll walk out singing "O Sole Mio" (£3-5 sandwiches, £1 take-away cappuccinos, Mon-Fri 9:00-17:00, closed Sat-Sun, 15 Charlotte Place, see map on page 186, tel. 020/7580-3938).

Lantana OUT, next door to Salumeria Dino, is an Australian coffee shop that sells modern soups, sandwiches, and salads at their take-away window (£3-7 meals, pricier sit-down café next door, Mon-Fri 7:30-15:00, café also open Sat-Sun 9:00-17:00, 13 Charlotte Place, see map on page 186, tel. 020/7637-3347).

Nearby Chains: Several recommended chain restaurants are a short walk from the museum, including **Busaba Eathai** (22 Store Street), **Wagamama** (4 Streatham Street and near Holborn Tube stop at 123 Kingsway), **Côte** (5 Charlotte Street), **Byron** (6 Store Street, with another at 6 Rathbone Place), and **Nando's** (9-10 Southampton Place).

West London
Near Victoria Station Accommodations

These restaurants are within a few blocks of Victoria Station—and all are places where I've enjoyed eating. As with the accommodations in this area, I've grouped them by location: east or west of the station (see the map on page 172).

Cheap Eats: For groceries, a handy **M&S Simply Food** is inside Victoria Station (Mon-Sat 7:00-24:00, Sun 8:00-23:00, near the front, by the bus terminus), along with a **Sainsbury's Local** (daily 6:00-23:00, at rear entrance, on Eccleston Street). A larger Sainsbury's is on Wilton Road near Warwick Way, a couple of blocks southeast of the station (Mon-Fri 7:00-23:00, Sat 7:00-22:00, Sun 11:00-17:00). A string of good ethnic restaurants lines Wilton Road, including this neighborhood's obligatory branch of **Nando's.** For affordable if forgettable meals, try the row of cheap little eateries on Elizabeth Street.

West of Victoria Station (Belgravia)

Ebury Wine Bar, filled with young professionals, provides a cut-above atmosphere (rumor has it that Prince William held his bachelor party here). In the delightful back room, the fancy menu features modern European cuisine with a French accent, including delicious £15-20 main dishes and a £19 two-course and £25 three-course special (available Mon-Fri at lunch and daily 18:00-20:00; three-course meal includes a glass of champagne that you're welcome to swap for house wine). At the wine bar, find a cheaper bar menu that's better than your average pub grub (£8-15 meals). This is emphatically a "traditional wine bar," with no beers on tap (restaurant open daily 12:00-15:00 & 18:00-22:30, wine bar open all day long, reservations smart, at intersection of Ebury and Elizabeth Streets, 139 Ebury Street, tel. 020/7730-5447, www.eburyrestaurant.co.uk).

Jenny Lo's Tea House is a simple budget place serving up a short menu of £8-9 eclectic Chinese-style meals to locals in the know. Jenny clearly learned from her father, Ken Lo, one of the most famous Cantonese chefs in Britain, whose fancy place is just around the corner (Mon-Fri 12:00-14:45 & 18:00-21:00, closed Sat-Sun, cash only, 14 Eccleston Street, tel. 020/7259-0399).

La Bottega is an Italian delicatessen that fits its upscale Belgravia neighborhood. It offers tasty, freshly cooked pastas (£6), lasagnas, and salads (£8 lasagna-and-salad meal), along with great sandwiches (£3) and a good coffee bar with pastries. While not cheap, it's fast (order at the counter), and the ingredients would please an Italian chef. Grab your meal to go, or enjoy the Belgravia good life with locals, either sitting inside or on the sidewalk (Mon-Fri 8:00-19:00, Sat 9:00-18:00, Sun 9:00-17:00, on corner of Ebury and Eccleston Streets, tel. 020/7730-2730, www.labottega65.com).

The Thomas Cubitt pub, named for the urban planner who designed much of Belgravia, is a trendy neighborhood gastropub packed with young professionals. It's pricey and a pinch pretentious, and prides itself on using sustainable ingredients in its modern English cooking. With a bright but slightly cramped interior and fine sidewalk seating, it's great for a drink or meal (£6 small plates, £14-17 main dishes, 44 Elizabeth Street). Upstairs is a more refined restaurant with the same kitchen, but an emphasis on finer technique and presentation (£8-11 starters, £17-25 main courses, reservations recommended, food served daily 12:00-22:00, tel. 020/7730-6060, www.thethomascubitt.co.uk).

The Duke of Wellington pub is a classic neighborhood place with forgettable grub, sidewalk seating, and an inviting interior. A bit more lowbrow than my other Belgravia listings, this may be your best shot at meeting a local (£5 sandwiches, £7-10 meals, food served Mon-Sat 12:00-15:00 & 18:00-21:00, Sun lunch only, 63 Eaton Terrace, tel. 020/7730-1782).

South End of Ebury Street: A five-minute walk down Ebury Street, where it intersects with Pimlico Road, you'll find a pretty square with a few more eateries to consider—including **The Orange,** a high-priced gastropub with the same owners and a similar menu to The Thomas Cubitt (described earlier); and **Daylesford,** the deli and café of an organic farm (£3-5 light meals to go—a good picnic option).

East of Victoria Station (Pimlico)

Grumbles brags it's been serving "good food and wine at nonscary prices since 1964." Offering a delicious mix of "modern eclectic French and traditional English," this unpretentious little place with cozy booths inside (on two levels, including a cellar) and four nice sidewalk tables is the best spot to eat well in this otherwise workaday neighborhood. Their traditional dishes are their forte (£10-16 plates, £11 early-bird specials 18:00-19:00, open Mon-Sat 12:00-14:30 & 18:00-23:00, Sun 12:00-22:30, reservations wise, half a block north of Belgrave Road at 35 Churton Street, tel. 020/7834-0149, www.grumblesrestaurant.co.uk).

Pimlico Fresh's breakfasts and lunches feature fresh, organic ingredients, served up with good coffee and/or fresh-squeezed juices. Choose from the dishes listed on the wall-sized chalkboard that lines the small eating area, then order at the counter. This place is heaven if you've slept through your hotel's breakfast hour, or if you just need a break from the bacon-eggs-beans routine (£5-10 meals, take-out lunches, plenty of vegetarian options; Mon-Fri 7:30-19:30, breakfast served until 15:00; Sat-Sun 9:00-18:00, breakfast until 17:00; 86 Wilton Road, tel. 020/7932-0030).

Seafresh Fish Restaurant is the neighborhood place for plaice—and classic and creative fish-and-chips cuisine. You can either take out on the cheap or eat in, enjoying a white fish ambience. Though Mario's father started this place in 1965, it feels like the chippie of the 21st century (meals-£5-8 to go, £12-17 to sit, Mon-Sat 12:00-15:00 & 17:00-22:30, closed Sun, 80-81 Wilton Road, tel. 020/7828-0747).

The Jugged Hare pub, a 10-minute walk from Victoria Station, sits in a lavish old bank building, with vaults replaced by tankards of beer and a fine kitchen. They have a fun, traditional menu with more fresh veggies than fries, and a plush, vivid pub scene good for a meal or just a drink (£6.50 sandwiches, £10 meals; Mon-Sat 11:00-23:00, food served 12:00-22:00; Sun 12:00-23:30, food served until 21:30; quiz night Wed at 19:00, 172 Vauxhall Bridge Road, tel. 020/7828-1543).

St. George's Tavern is the neighborhood's best pub for a full meal. They serve dinner from the same fun menu in three zones: on the sidewalk to catch the sun and enjoy some people-watching, in the ground-floor pub, and in a classier downstairs dining room. They're proud of their sausages and "toad in the hole." The scene is inviting for just a beer, too (£8-14 meals, food served Mon-Sat 10:00-22:00, Sun until 21:30, corner of Hugh Street and Belgrave Road, tel. 020/7630-1116).

South Kensington

Popular eateries line Old Brompton Road and Thurloe Street (Tube: South Kensington), and a good selection of cheap eateries are clumped around the Tube station. For locations, see the map on page 177.

La Bouchée Bistro Café is a classy hole-in-the-wall touch of France. This candlelit and woody bistro, with very tight seating, serves a special fixed-price meal (£14.50/2 courses, £16.50/3 courses) on weekdays during lunch and 17:00-19:00, and £15 *plats du jour* all *jour* (also £15-20 à la carte main courses). Reservations are smart in the evening (daily 12:00-15:00 & 17:00-23:00, 56 Old Brompton Road, tel. 020/7589-1929).

Moti Mahal Indian Restaurant, with minimalist-yet-upscale mod ambience and attentive service, serves mostly Bangladeshi cuisine that's delicious. Consider chicken *jalfrezi* if you like spicy food, and buttery chicken if you don't (£8-21 main courses, daily 12:00-15:00 & 17:30-23:00, 3 Glendower Place, tel. 020/7584-8428).

Bosphorus Kebabs is the student favorite for a quick, fast, and hearty Turkish dinner. While mostly for take-away, they have a few tight tables indoors and on the sidewalk (£5-6 meals, Turkish kebabs, daily 10:30-24:00, 59 Old Brompton Road, tel. 020/7584-4048).

Beirut Express has fresh, well-prepared Lebanese cuisine. In the front, you'll find take-away service as well as barstools for quick service (£4.50 sandwiches). In the back is a sit-down restaurant with £14-16 plates and £5-8 *mezes* (daily 12:00-24:00, 65 Old Brompton Road, tel. 020/7591-0123).

The Anglesea Arms, with a great terrace surrounded by classy South Kensington buildings, is a destination pub that feels like the classic neighborhood favorite. It's a thriving and happy place, with a woody ambience and a mellow step-down back dining room a world away from any tourism. While the food is the main draw, this is also a fine place to just have a beer (£6-8 starters, £12-17 main dishes, meals served daily 12:00-15:00 & 18:00-22:00; from Old Brompton Road, turn left at Onslow Gardens and go down a few blocks to 15 Selwood Terrace; tel. 020/7373-7960).

Rocca di Papa is a bright and dressy Italian place with a heated terrace (£6-8 pizza, pasta, and salads; daily 11:30-23:30, 73 Old Brompton Road, tel. 020/7225-3413).

Fernandez & Wells has a second outpost just north of the South Kensington Tube station (8 Exhibition Road; similar menu and hours as Soho location—see listing on page 198). Just up Exhibition Road (at #19) is a branch of **Thai Square** (described on page 192).

Supermarket: **Tesco Express** is handy for picnics (daily 7:00-24:00, 50-52 Old Brompton Road).

Near Bayswater and Notting Hill Accommodations

For locations, see the map on page 180.

Maggie Jones's, a Charles Dickens-meets-Ella Fitzgerald splurge, is exuberantly rustic and very English, with a 1940s-jazz soundtrack. It's a longer walk than most of my recommendations, but worth the hike. You'll get solid English cuisine, including huge plates of crunchy vegetables, served by a young and casual staff. It's pricey, but the portions are huge (especially the meat-and-fish pies, their specialty). You're welcome to save lots by splitting your main course. The candlelit upstairs is the most romantic, while the basement is kept lively with the kitchen, tight seating, and lots of action. If you eat well once in London, eat here—and do it quick, before it burns down (lunch—£5 starters, £7 main dishes; dinner—£6-9 starters, £15-24 main dishes; daily 12:00-14:30 & 18:00-23:00, reservations recommended, 6 Old Court Place, just east of Kensington Church Street, near High Street Kensington Tube stop, tel. 020/7937-6462, www.maggie-jones.co.uk).

The Churchill Arms pub and **Thai Kitchen** (same location) are local hangouts, with good beer and a thriving old-English ambience in front, and hearty £8 Thai plates in an enclosed patio in the back. You can eat the Thai food in the tropical hideaway (table service) or in the atmospheric pub section (order at the counter and they'll bring it to you). They also serve basic English pub food at lunch (£3 sandwiches, £5-7 meals). The place is festooned with Churchill memorabilia and chamber pots (including one with Hitler's mug on it—hanging from the ceiling farthest from Thai Kitchen—sure to cure the constipation of any Brit during World War II). Arrive by 18:00 or after 21:00 to avoid a line. During busy times, diners are limited to an hour at the table (food served daily 12:00-22:00, 119 Kensington Church Street, tel. 020/7727-4242).

Hereford Road is a cozy, mod eatery tucked at the far end of Prince's Square. It's stylish but not pretentious, serving heavy, meaty English cuisine executed with modern panache. Cozy two-person booths face the open kitchen up top; the main dining room is down below. There are also a few sidewalk tables (£6-8 starters, £14-16 main courses, reservations smart, Mon-Sat 12:00-15:00 & 18:00-22:00, Sun 12:00-16:00 & 18:00-22:30, 3 Hereford Road, tel. 020/7727-1144, www.herefordroad.org).

The Prince Edward serves good grub in a plush, upscale-pub setting and at its sidewalk tables (£10-15 meals, Mon-Fri 10:30-23:00, Sat 10:00-23:30, Sun 10:00-22:30, family-friendly, 2 blocks north of Bayswater Road at the corner of Dawson Place and Hereford Road, 73 Prince's Square, tel. 020/7727-2221).

Café Diana is a healthy little eatery serving sandwiches, salads, and Middle Eastern food. It's decorated—almost shrine-like—with photos of Princess Diana, who used to drop by for pita sandwiches. You can dine in the simple interior, or order some food from the counter to go (£3-5 sandwiches, £6-10 meat dishes, daily 8:00-23:00, cash only, 5 Wellington Terrace, on Bayswater Road, opposite Kensington Palace Garden Gates, where Di once lived, tel. 020/7792-9606, Abdul).

On Queensway: The road called Queensway is a multiethnic food circus, lined with lively and inexpensive eateries—browse the options along here and choose your favorite. For a cut above, head for **Royal China Restaurant**—filled with London's Chinese, who consider this one of the city's best eateries. It's dressed up in black, white, and gold, with candles and brisk waiters. While it's pricier than most neighborhood Chinese restaurants, the food is noticeably better (£9-13 dishes, Mon-Sat 12:00-23:00, Sun 11:00-22:00, dim sum until 17:00, 13 Queensway, tel. 020/7221-2535). For a lowbrow alternative, **Whiteleys Shopping Centre Food Court**—at the top end of Queensway—offers a fun selection of ethnic and fast-food chain eateries among Corinthian columns, and a multiscreen theater in a delightful mall (most restaurants daily 12:00-23:00, some eateries open shorter hours; options include Yo! Sushi, good salads at Café Rouge, pizza, Starbucks, and a coin-op Internet place; third floor, corner of Porchester Gardens and Queensway).

Supermarkets: Tesco is a half-block from the Notting Hill Gate Tube stop (Mon-Fri 7:00-24:00, Sat 7:00-23:00, Sun 12:00-.00, near intersection with Pembridge Road, 114-120 Notting Hill Gate). Queensway is home to several supermarkets, including the smaller **Spar Market** at #18 (Mon-Sat 7:00-24:00, Sun 8:00-24:00). Nearby, **Marks & Spencer** can be found in Whiteleys Shopping Centre (Mon-Sat 8:30-22:00, Sun 12:00-18:00).

Elsewhere in London

Between St. Paul's and the Tower: **The Counting House,** formerly an elegant old bank, offers great £7-11 meals, nice homemade £10-11 meat pies, fish, and fresh vegetables. The fun "nibbles menu," with £3-6 snacks, is available starting in the early evening until 22:00 (or until 21:00 on Mon; open Mon-Fri 11:00-23:00, gets really busy with the buttoned-down 9-to-5 crowd after 12:15 especially Thu-Fri, closed Sat-Sun, near Mansion House in The City, 50 Cornhill—see map on page 201, tel. 020/7283-7123).

Near St. Paul's: **De Gustibus Sandwiches** is where an artisan bakery meets the public, offering fresh, you-design-it sandwiches, salads, and soups. Communication can be difficult, but it's worth the effort. Just one block below St. Paul's, it has simple seating or take-out picnic sacks for lugging to one of the great nearby parks (£4-8 sandwiches, £6 hot dishes, Mon-Fri 7:00-17:00, closed Sat-Sun, from church steps follow signs to youth hostel a block downhill—see map on page 201, 53-55 Carter Lane, tel. 020/7236-0056; another outlet is inside the Borough Market in Southwark).

Near the British Library: Drummond Street (running just west of Euston Station—see map on page 186) is famous for cheap and good Indian vegetarian food (£5-10 dishes, £7 lunch buffets). For a good *thali* (combo plate) consider **Chutneys** (124 Drummond, tel. 020/7388-0604) and **Ravi Shankar** (133-135 Drummond, tel. 020/7388-6458, both open long hours daily).

Near the Tower of London: In **The Medieval Banquet**'s underground, brick-arched room, costumed wenches bring you a tasty four-course medieval-themed meal (includes ale and red wine) as minstrels, knights, jesters, and contortionists perform. If you enjoy an act, pound on the table. Reserve in advance online or by phone (adult-£50, child-£30, family deal for 2 adults and 2 kids-£110—Sun-Thu only, 15 percent discount for Rick Steves readers—can't combine with family deal, Mon-Sat around 20:00, Sun around 18:00, veggie option possible, rentable medieval garb, The Medieval Banquet Ivory House, St. Katharine Docks, enter docks off East Smithfield Street, Tube: Tower Hill, tel. 020/7480-5353, www.medievalbanquet.com).

Taking Tea in London

Once the sole province of genteel ladies in fancy hats, afternoon tea has become more democratic in the 21st century. While some tearooms—such as the wallet-draining £42-a-head tea service at the Ritz and the finicky Fortnum & Mason—still require a jacket and tie (and a bigger bank account), most happily welcome tourists in jeans and sneakers.

Tea Terms

The cheapest "tea" on the menu is generally a "cream tea"; the most expensive is the "champagne tea." **Cream tea** is simply a pot of tea and a homemade scone or two with jam and thick clotted cream. (For maximum pinkie-waving taste per calorie, slice your scone thin like a miniature loaf of bread.) **Afternoon tea**—what many Americans would call "high tea"—generally is a cream tea plus a tier of three plates holding small finger foods (such as cucumber sandwiches) and an assortment of small pastries. **Champagne tea** includes all of the goodies, plus a glass of bubbly. **High tea** to the British generally means a more substantial late-afternoon or early-evening meal, often served with meat or eggs.

Tearooms, which often also serve appealing light meals, are usually open for lunch and close about 17:00, just before dinner. At all the places listed below, it's perfectly acceptable for two people to order one afternoon tea and one cream tea (at about £5) and share the afternoon tea's goodies.

Places to Sip Tea

The Wolseley serves a good afternoon tea between their meal service. Split one with your companion and enjoy two light meals at a great price in classic elegance (£10 cream tea, £22.50 afternoon tea, served Mon-Fri 15:00-18:30, Sat 15:30-17:30, Sun 15:30-18:30, see full listing on page 199).

The Orangery at Kensington Palace serves a £20 "Orangery tea" and a £25-30 champagne tea in its bright white hall near Princess Di's former residence. You can also order treats à la carte. The portions aren't huge, but who can argue with eating at a princess' orangery or on the terrace? (Tea served 14:00-18:00, until 17:00 Nov-Feb, no reservations taken; a 10-minute walk through Kensington Gardens from either Queensway or High Street Kensington Tube stations to the orange brick building, about 100 yards from Kensington Palace—see map on page 180; tel. 020/3166-6113, www.hrp.org.uk.)

The Capital Hotel, a luxury hotel a half-block from Harrods, caters to weary shoppers with its intimate five-table, linen-table-cloth tearoom. It's where the ladies-who-lunch meet to decide whether to buy that Versace gown they've had their eye on. Even so, casual clothes, kids, and sharing plates are all OK (£30 afternoon tea, daily 14:30-17:30, call to book ahead—especially on weekends, 22 Basil Street—see map on page VI, Tube: Knightsbridge, tel. 020/7591-1202, www.capitalhotel.co.uk).

The **Fortnum & Mason** department store offers tea at several different restaurants within its walls. You can "Take Tea in the Parlour" for £18 (including ice-cream cakes; Mon-Sat 10:00-20:00, Sun 11:30-18:00), or try the all-out "Gallery Tea" for £26 (daily 15:00-18:00). But the pièce de resistance is their Diamond Jubilee Tea Salon, named in honor of the Queen's 60th year on the throne (and, no doubt, to remind visitors of Her Majesty's visit for tea here in 2012 with Camilla and Kate). At these royal prices, consider it dinner (£40-44, Mon-Sat 12:00-21:00, Sun 12:00-20:00, dress up a bit—no shorts, "children must be behaved," 181 Piccadilly—see map on page 194, smart to reserve online or by phone at least a week in advance, tel. 0845-602-5694, www.fortnumandmason.com).

Other Places Serving Good Tea: **The National Dining Rooms,** within the National Gallery on Trafalgar Square, offers a £17 afternoon tea (served 14:30-16:30, in Sainsbury Wing of National Gallery, Tube: Charing Cross or Leicester Square, tel. 020/7747-2525, www.peytonandbyrne.co.uk). **The National Café,** at the other end of the building, is a bit cheaper (£15 afternoon tea served 14:30-17:30). **The Café at Sotheby's,** on the ground floor of the auction giant's headquarters, gives shoppers a break from fashionable New Bond Street (£8-23, tea served Mon-Fri only 15:00-16:45, reservations smart, 34-35 New Bond Street—see map on page 194, Tube: Bond Street or Oxford Circus, tel. 020/7293-5077, www.sothebys.com/cafe).

Cheaper Options: Taking tea is not just for tourists and the wealthy—it's a true English tradition. If you want the teatime experience but are put off by the price, most department stores on Oxford Street (including those between Oxford Circus and Bond Street Tube stations) offer an afternoon tea. **John Lewis'** mod third-floor brasserie serves a nice afternoon tea platter from 15:30 (£12, on Oxford Street one block west of the Bond Street Tube station, tel. 020/7629-7711, www.johnlewis.com). Many museums and bookstores have cafés serving afternoon tea goodies à la carte, where you can put together a spread for less than £10—**Waterstones'** fifth-floor café and the **Victoria and Albert Museum** café are two of the best. **Teapod,** a modern place near the Tower Bridge, serves cream tea for £5.50 and afternoon tea for £13.50 (Mon-Fri 8:00-18:00, Sat-Sun 10:00-19:00, 31 Shad Thames, tel. 020/7407-0000).

In Bath: **The Pump Room** is reason enough to put off tea in London—assuming you'll be visiting the city of Bath. This historic, elegant Georgian hall with live music lets anyone enjoy the ritual of tea in grand style (see page 287).

London Connections

By Plane

London has six airports; I've focused my coverage on the two most widely used—Heathrow and Gatwick—with a few tips for using the others (Stansted, Luton, London City, and Southend).

Phone numbers and websites for major airlines are listed in the appendix. For accommodations at or near the major airports, see page 189. A number of discount airlines fly into and out of London's smaller airports, making London a great jumping-off point for other destinations (see "Cheap Flights" on page 1024).

Heathrow Airport

Heathrow Airport is one of the world's busiest airports. Think about it: 70 million passengers a year on 470,000 flights from

190 destinations riding 85 airlines, like some kind of global maypole dance. For Heathrow's airport, flight, and transfer information, call the switchboard at 0844-335-1801, or visit the helpful website at www.heathrowairport.com (airport code: LHR).

Heathrow has five terminals, numbered T-1 through T-5 (though T-2 is closed for renovation through mid-2014). Each terminal is served by different airlines and alliances; for example, T-5 is exclusively for British Air and Iberia Air flights, while T-1 serves mostly Star Alliance flights, such as United and Lufthansa. Screens posted throughout the airport identify which terminal each airline uses; this information should also be printed on your ticket or boarding pass.

To navigate, read signs and ask questions. You can walk between T-1, T-2 (when it's open), and T-3. From this central hub (called "Heathrow Central"), T-4 and T-5 split off in opposite directions (and are not walkable). To travel between the T-1/T-2/T-3 cluster and either T-4 or T-5, you can take a shuttle bus (free, serves all terminals), or the Tube (requires a ticket, serves all terminals). You can also connect T-1/T-2/T-3 and T-5 by Heathrow Express train (free, every 15-20 minutes, does not serve T-4).

If you're flying out of Heathrow, it's critical to confirm which terminal your flight will use (look carefully at your ticket/boarding pass, check online, or call your airline in advance)—because if

London's Airports

Luton
Luton
Stansted
Not to Scale
#757
Southend
ST. PANCRAS
Reading
PADDINGTON
LIVERPOOL STREET
Windsor
#71 & #77
Rail Air Link
Tube
D.L.R.
Southend
To Bath
Heathrow
VICTORIA COACH STN.
VICTORIA
London City
London
EUROSTAR
Thames
Guildford
Gatwick
Ashford
To Paris

Rail
Eurostar Rail
Tube & D.L.R.
Bus

ALL BUSES ARE NATIONAL EXPRESS UNLESS NOTED

To Brighton

English Channel

it's T-4 or T-5, you'll need to allow extra time. Taxi drivers generally know which terminal you'll need based on the airline, but bus drivers may not.

Services: Each terminal has an airport information desk (generally daily 5:00-22:00), car-rental agencies, exchange bureaus, ATMs, a pharmacy, a VAT refund desk (tel. 0845-872-7627, you must present the VAT claim form from the retailer here to get your tax rebate on items purchased in Britain—see page 18 for details), room-booking services, and baggage storage (£5/item for up to 4 hours, £8.50/item for 24 hours, daily 6:00-23:00, opens 30-60 minutes earlier in some terminals, www.excess-baggage .co.uk). Get online 24 hours a day at Heathrow's Internet access points (at each terminal—T-4's is up on the mezzanine level). Pay Wi-Fi is available throughout the airport (provided by Boingo, www.boingo.com). A post office is on the first floor of T-3 (departures area). Each terminal has cheap eateries.

Heathrow's small **"TI"** (tourist info shop), even though it's a for-profit business, is worth a visit if you're nearby and want to pick up free information: a simple map, the *London Planner,* and brochures (daily 6:30-22:00, 5-minute walk from T-3 in Tube station, follow signs to Underground; bypass queue for transit info to reach window for London questions).

Getting to London from Heathrow Airport

You have five basic options for traveling the 14 miles between Heathrow Airport and downtown London: Tube (£5.50/person), bus (£6-9/person), direct shuttle bus (£18/person), express train with connecting Tube or taxi (including connecting Tube fare, about £12/person for slower train, £23/person for faster train), or taxi (about £70/group).

By Tube (Subway): The Tube takes you from any Heathrow terminal to downtown London in 50-60 minutes on the Piccadilly

Line (6/hour, buy ticket at Tube station ticket window or self-service machine). Depending on your destination in London, you may need to transfer (for example, if headed to the Victoria Station neighborhood, transfer at Earl's Court to the District line and ride two more stops). If you plan to use the Tube for transport in London, it may make sense to buy a Travelcard or pay-as-you-go Oyster card at the airport's Tube station ticket window. (For details on these passes, see page 60.) If your Travelcard covers only Zones 1-2, it does not include Heathrow (Zone 6); however, you can pay a small supplement for the initial trip from Heathrow to downtown.

If you're taking the Tube from downtown London *to* the airport, note that Piccadilly Line trains don't stop at every terminal. Trains either stop at T-4, then T-1/T-2/T-3 (also called Heathrow Central), in that order; or T-1/T-2/T-3, then T-5. When leaving central London on the Tube, allow extra time if going to T-4 or T-5; to ensure you get on a train going to your terminal, carefully check the destination before you board.

By Bus: Most buses depart from the outdoor common area called the Central Bus Station, located a five-minute walk from the T-1/T-2/T-3 complex. To connect between T-4 or T-5 and the Central Bus Station, use Heathrow's free shuttle buses; to reach T-5 only, you can ride the free Heathrow Express train.

National Express has regular service from Heathrow's Central Bus Station to Victoria Coach Station in downtown London, near several of my recommended hotels. While slow, the bus is affordable and convenient for those staying near Victoria Station (£6-9, 1-2/hour, less frequent from Victoria Station to Heathrow, 45-75 minutes depending on time of day, tel. 0871-781-8178, www.nationalexpress.com). A less-frequent National Express bus goes from T-5 directly to Victoria Coach Station.

By Shuttle: **Heathrow Shuttle** is an economical shuttle-bus service that goes to/from your hotel and your terminal at Heathrow. You'll share a minivan with other travelers who are also being picked up or dropped off, so it's not much of a time savings over taking the Tube (£18/person, progressive discounts for groups of two or more, 1 child under age 10 travels free with 2 adults, runs daily 4:00-18:00, book at least 24 hours in advance, office open daily 7:00-20:00, tel. 0845-257-8068, www.heathrowshuttle.com, info@heathrowshuttle.com). The rival **Hotel by Bus** service is pricey in comparison (£22.50/person).

By Train: Two different trains run between Heathrow Airport and London's Paddington Station. At Paddington Station, you're in the thick of the Tube system, with easy access to any of my recommended neighborhoods—my Paddington hotels are just outside the front door, and Notting Hill Gate is just two Tube stops away. The **Heathrow Connect** train is the slightly slower, much cheaper option, serving T-1/T-2/T-3 at a single station called Heathrow Central; use free transfers if you're coming from either T-4 or T-5 (£9.50 one-way, £19 round-trip, 2/hour Mon-Sat, 1-2/hour Sun, 40 minutes, tel. 0845-678-6975, www.heathrow connect.com). The **Heathrow Express** train is fast and runs more frequently, but it's pricey (£20 one-way, £34 round-trip, £5 more if you buy ticket on board, 4/hour; 15 minutes to downtown from T-1/T-2/T-3, 21 minutes from T-5; transfer by shuttle required from T-4; covered by BritRail pass, daily 5:10-23:25, tel. 0845-600-1515, www.heathrowexpress.co.uk). At the airport, you can use the Heathrow Express as a free transfer between T-1/T-2/T-3 and T-5 (but not T-4).

By Taxi: Taxis from the airport cost £45-75 to west and central London (one hour). For four people traveling together, this can be a reasonable option. Hotels can often line up a cab back to the airport for about £40. For the cheapest taxi to the airport, don't order one from your hotel. Simply flag down a few and ask them for their best "off-meter" rate. Locals refer to hired cars that do the trip off-meter as "mini-cabs." These are reliable and generally cost about what you'd pay for a taxi in good traffic, but—with a fixed price—they can save you money when taxis are snarled in congestion with the meter running.

Getting to Bath from Heathrow Airport

Heathrow is well-connected by train to London, but it isn't tied directly into the regional rail network. You have several options for reaching Bath: train via London (fastest but expensive without a railpass), direct bus (cheaper but slower and relatively infrequent), train-and-bus combination (more frequent and sometimes shorter than the direct bus, can be cheaper than the direct train), or tour-company minibus. For details on all of these, see "Bath Connections" on page 313.

Gatwick Airport

More and more flights land at Gatwick Airport, which is half-way between London and the south coast (airport code: LGW, tel. 0844-892-0322, www.gatwickairport.com). Gatwick has two terminals, North and South, which are easily connected by a free monorail (two-minute trip, runs 24 hours daily). Note that boarding passes say "Gatwick N" or "Gatwick S" to indicate your terminal. British Airways flights generally use Gatwick North. The Gatwick Express trains (described next) stop only at Gatwick South. Schedules in each terminal show only arrivals and departures from that terminal.

Getting to London: Gatwick Express trains are clearly the best way into London from this airport. They shuttle conveniently between Gatwick South and London's Victoria Station, with many of my recommended hotels close by (£20 one-way, £35 round-trip, at least 10 percent cheaper if purchased online, 4/hour, 30 minutes, runs 5:00-24:00 daily, a few trains as early as 3:30, tel. 0845-850-1530, www.gatwickexpress.com). If you buy your tickets at the station before boarding, ask about their deal where three or four adults travel for the price of two. (If you see others in the ticket line, suggest buying your tickets together—you'll save up to 50 percent.) When going *to* the airport, at Victoria Station note that Gatwick Express has its own ticket windows right by the platform (tracks 13 and 14).

A train also runs between Gatwick South and **St. Pancras International Station** (£10, 3-5/hour, 45-60 minutes, www.first capitalconnect.co.uk)—useful for travelers taking the Eurostar train (to Paris or Brussels) or staying in the St. Pancras/King's Cross neighborhood.

Even slower, but cheap and handy to the Victoria Station neighborhood, you can take the **bus** (1.5 hours). National Express runs a bus from Gatwick direct to Victoria Station (£8, at least hourly, tel. 0871-781-8178, www.nationalexpress.com); easyBus has one going to near the Earls Court Tube stop (£2-10 depending on how far ahead you book, 2-3/hour, www.easybus.co.uk).

Getting to Bath: To get to Bath from Gatwick, you can go by train via Reading, or by bus via Heathrow. For details see page 313.

London's Other Airports

Stansted Airport: If you're using Stansted (airport code: STN, tel. 0844-335-1803, www.stanstedairport.com), you have several options for getting into or out of London. Two different **buses** connect the airport and London's Victoria Station neighborhood: National Express (£7-10, every 20 minutes, 1.75 hours, runs 24 hours a day, picks up and stops throughout London, ends at Victoria Coach Station, tel. 0871-781-8178, www.nationalexpress .com) and Terravision (£9, 2-3/hour, 1.25 hours, ends at Green Line Coach Station just south of Victoria Station). Or you can take the faster, pricier Stansted Express **train** (£23.50, connects to London's Tube system at Tottenham Hale and Liverpool Street, 4/hour, 45 minutes, 4:30-23:00, www.stanstedexpress.com). Stansted is expensive by **cab**; figure £100-120 one-way from central London.

Luton Airport: For Luton (airport code: LTN, airport tel. 01582/405-100, www.london-luton.co.uk), there are two choices into or out of London. The fastest way to go is by **train** to London's St. Pancras International Station (£9.50-13.50 one-way, 1-5/hour, 25-45 minutes—check schedule to avoid slower trains, tel. 0845-712-5678, www.eastmidlandstrains.co.uk); catch the 10-minute shuttle bus (every 10 minutes, £1.50) from outside the terminal to the Luton Airport Parkway Station. The Green Line express **bus** #757 runs to Buckingham Palace Road, just south of Victoria Station, and stops en route near the Baker Street Tube station—best if you're staying near Paddington Station or in North London (£17, small discount for easyJet passengers who buy online, 2-4/hour, 1-1.5 hours, runs 24 hours, tel. 0844-801-7261, www.green line.co.uk). If you're sleeping at Luton, consider easyHotel (see listing on page 187).

Other Airports: There's a slim chance you might use **London City Airport** (airport code: LCY, tel. 020/7646-0088, www .londoncityairport.com). To get into London, take the Docklands Light Railway (DLR) to the Bank Tube station, which is one stop east of St. Paul's on the Central Line (less than £5 one-way, covered by Travelcard, a bit cheaper with an Oyster card, 22 minutes, www.tfl.gov.uk/dlr). Some easyJet flights land even farther out, at **Southend Airport** (airport code: SEN, tel. 01702/608-100, www .southendairport.com). Trains connect this airport to London's Liverpool Street Station (£15 one-way, 3-8/hour, 55 minutes, www.greateranglia.co.uk).

Connecting London's Airports by Bus

A handy **National Express bus** runs between Heathrow, Gatwick, Stansted, and Luton airports—easier than having to cut through the center of London—although traffic can be bad and can increase travel times (tel. 0871-781-8178, www.nationalexpress.com).

From Heathrow Airport to: Gatwick Airport (1-6/hour, about 1.25 hours—but allow at least three hours between flights,

£25), **Stansted Airport** (1-2/hour, about 1.5 hours, £25), **Luton Airport** (roughly hourly, 1-1.5 hours, £21).

By Train

Britain is covered by myriad rail systems (owned by different companies), which together are called National Rail. London, the country's major transportation hub, has a different train station for each region. There are nine main stations (see the map):

Euston—Serves northwest England, North Wales, and Scotland.

St. Pancras International—Serves north and south England, plus the Eurostar to Paris or Brussels (see "Crossing the Channel," later).

King's Cross—Serves northeast England and Scotland, including York and Edinburgh.

Liverpool Street—Serves east England, including Essex and Harwich.

London Bridge—Serves south England, including Brighton.

Waterloo—Serves south England, including Salisbury and Southampton.

Victoria—Serves Gatwick Airport, Canterbury, Dover, and Brighton.

Paddington—Serves south and southwest England, including Heathrow Airport, Windsor, Bath, South Wales, and the Cotswolds.

Marylebone—Serves southwest and central England, including Stratford-upon-Avon.

In addition, London has several smaller train stations that you're less likely to use, such as **Charing Cross** (serves southeast England, including Dover) and **Blackfriars.**

Any train station has schedule information, can make reservations, and can sell tickets for any destination. Most stations offer a baggage-storage service (£8.50/bag for 24 hours, look for *left luggage* signs); because of long security lines, it can take a while to check or pick up your bag (www.excess-baggage.com). For more details on the services available at each station, see www.national rail.co.uk/stations.

For tips on buying train tickets—as well as your railpass options—see "Trains" on page 1010 of the Appendix.

Train Connections from London

To Points West

From Paddington Station to: Bath (2/hour, 1.5 hours; also consider a guided Evan Evans tour by bus—see page 222), **Windsor** (2-3/hour, 30-40 minutes, easy change at Slough; or slower but direct from Waterloo Station, 2/hour, 50 minutes), **Oxford** (2/hour

London's Major Train Stations

direct, 1 hour, more possible with transfer in Reading), **Penzance** (every 1-2 hours, 5-5.5 hours, possible change in Plymouth), and **Cardiff** (2/hour, 2 hours).

To Points North

From King's Cross Station: Trains run at least hourly, stopping in **York** (2 hours), **Durham** (3 hours), and **Edinburgh** (4.5 hours). Trains to **Cambridge** also leave from here (2/hour, 45 minutes-1.25 hours).

From Euston Station to: **Conwy** (nearly hourly, 3.5 hours, transfer in Chester), **Liverpool** (at least hourly, 2 hours, more with transfer), **Blackpool** (hourly, 3-3.5 hours, transfer at Preston), **Keswick** (hourly, 4-4.5 hours, transfer to bus at Penrith), and **Glasgow** (1-2/hour, 4.5-5 hours).

From London's Other Stations

Trains run between London and **Canterbury**, leaving from St. Pancras International Station and arriving in Canterbury West (1-2/hour, 1 hour), as well as from London's Victoria Station and arriving in Canterbury East (2/hour, 1.25 hours).

Public Transportation near London

Direct trains leave for **Stratford-upon-Avon** from Marylebone Station, located near the southwest corner of Regent's Park (5/day direct, more with transfers, 2.25 hours).

To Other Destinations: Dover (hourly, 1.25 hours, from St. Pancras International Station; also 2/hour, 2 hours, direct from Victoria Station or Charing Cross Station), **Brighton** (4-5/hour, 1 hour, from Victoria Station and London Bridge Station), **Portsmouth** (5/hour, 1.5-2 hours, most from Waterloo Station, a few from Victoria Station), and **Salisbury** (1-2/hour, 1.25 hours, from Waterloo Station).

By Bus

Buses are slower but considerably cheaper than trains for reaching destinations around Britain, and beyond. Most depart from **Victoria Coach Station,** which is one long block south of Victoria Station (near many recommended accommodations and Tube: Victoria). Inside the station, you'll find basic eateries, kiosks, and a helpful information desk stocked with schedules and ready to point you to your bus or answer any questions. Watch your bags carefully—luggage thieves thrive at the station.

Most domestic buses are operated by **National Express** (tel. 0871-781-8178, www.nationalexpress.com); their international departures are called **Eurolines** (www.eurolines.co.uk).

A smaller company called **Megabus** undersells National Express with deeply discounted promotional fares—the farther ahead you buy, the less you pay (some trips for just £1.50, toll tel. 0900-160-0900, www.megabus.com). While Megabus can be much cheaper than National Express—even half the price—they tend to be slower than their competitor and their routes mainly connect cities, not smaller towns. They also sell discounted train tickets on selected routes.

Try to avoid bus travel on Friday and Sunday evenings, when weekend travelers are more likely to make buses sell out.

To ensure getting a ticket—and to save money with special promotions—you can book your ticket in advance online (National Express charges a £1 fee) or over the phone (£2 surcharge). The cheapest pre-purchased tickets can be changed (for a £5 fee), but they're usually nonrefundable within 72 hours of travel. If you have a British mobile phone, you can order online and have a "text ticket" sent right to your phone.

Ideally you'll buy your tickets online. But if you must buy one at the station, try to arrive an hour before the bus departs—or drop by the day before. Ticketing machines are scattered around the station (separate machines for National Express/Eurolines and Megabus; you can buy either for today or for tomorrow); there's also a ticket counter near gate 21.

To Bath: The National Express bus leaves from Victoria Coach Station (nearly hourly, 3.5 hours, sample fares: one-way-£7-25, round-trip-£12-34). To get to Bath via Stonehenge, consider taking a guided bus tour from London to Stonehenge, Salisbury, and Bath, and abandoning the tour in Bath (confirm that Bath is the last stop on that particular tour; you can stow your bag in a compartment under the bus). **Evan Evans'** tour leaves from Victoria Coach Station every morning, stops in Salisbury (for a look at its magnificent cathedral) and Stonehenge, and then stops in Bath before returning to London (offered year-round—but order of stops can vary per day of week; they also offer another tour to Stonehenge and Bath via Windsor Castle; www.evanevanstours.co.uk). **Golden Tours** also runs a Stonehenge-Bath tour (departs from Fountain Square, located across from Victoria Coach Station, www.goldentours.com).

To Other Destinations: National Express buses go to **Oxford** (2/hour, about 2 hours), **Cambridge** (every 60-90 minutes, 2-2.5 hours), **Canterbury** (about hourly, 2-2.5 hours), **Dover** (about hourly, 2.5-3.25 hours), **Brighton** (hourly, 2.5 hours), **Penzance** (5/day, 8.5-10 hours, overnight available), **Cardiff** (hourly, 3.25 hours), **Stratford-upon-Avon** (3/day, 3.5 hours), **Liverpool** (8/day direct, 5.25-6 hours, overnight available), **Blackpool** (4/

day direct, 6.25-7 hours, overnight available), **York** (4/day direct, 5.25 hours), **Durham** (3/day direct, 6.5-7.5 hours, train is better), **Glasgow** (2-4/day direct, 8-9 hours, train is a much better option), **Edinburgh** (2/day direct, 8.75-9.75 hours, go by train instead).

To Dublin, Ireland: This bus/boat journey, operated by National Express, takes 10-12 hours (£52, 1/day, departs Victoria Coach Station at 18:00, check in with passport one hour before). Consider a cheap 1.25-hour Ryanair flight instead (www.ryanair.com).

To the Continent: Especially in summer, buses run to destinations all over Europe, including Paris, Amsterdam, Brussels, and Germany (sometimes crossing the Channel by ferry, other times through the Chunnel). For any international connection, you need to check in with your passport one hour before departure. For details, call 0871-781-8178 or visit www.eurolines.co.uk. For information on crossing the Channel by bus, see "By Bus and Boat," later.

Crossing the Channel
By Eurostar Train

The fastest and most convenient way to get from Big Ben to the Eiffel Tower is by rail. Eurostar is the speedy passenger train that zips you (and up to 800 others in 18 sleek cars) from downtown London to downtown Paris or Brussels (1-2/hour, 2.5 hours) faster and more easily than flying. The train goes 190 mph both before and after the English Channel crossing. The actual tunnel crossing is a 20-minute, silent, 100-mile-per-hour nonevent. Your ears won't even pop. Get ready for more high-speed connections: Germany's national railroad is negotiating to run bullet trains between Frankfurt, Amsterdam, and London by 2016.

Eurostar Fares

Unlike most trains in Western Europe, Eurostar is not covered by railpasses and always requires a separate, reserved train ticket. Eurostar fares (essentially the same between London and Paris or Brussels) vary depending on how far ahead you reserve, whether you can live with restrictions, and whether you're eligible for any discounts.

A **one-way, full-fare ticket** (with no restrictions on refundability) runs about $460 for first class and $300 for second class.

Discounts can lower fares substantially (figure $60-160 for second class, one-way, usually not refundable or changeable) for children under age 12, youths under age 26, seniors age 60 or older, adults booking months ahead or traveling roundtrip, and railpass holders. The early bird gets the best price in each category. If you're ready to commit, you can book tickets as early as 4-9 months in advance at www.eurostar.com.

A tour company called BritainShrinkers sells one- or two-day tours to Paris, Brussels, or Bruges, enabling you to side-trip to these cities from London for less than most train tickets alone. For example, you'll pay £129 for a one-day Paris "tour" (unescorted Mon-Sat day trip with Métro pass; tel. 020/7404-5100, www .britainshrinkers.com). This can be a particularly good option if you need to get to Paris from London on short notice, when only the costliest Eurostar fares are available.

Buying Eurostar Tickets

Because only the most expensive (full-fare) ticket is fully refundable, don't reserve until you're sure of your plans. But if you wait too long, the cheapest tickets will get bought up.

Once you're confident about the time and date of your crossing, you can check and book fares by phone or online. Ordering online through Eurostar or major agents offers a print-at-home eticket option. You can also order by phone through Rail Europe at US tel. 800-387-6782 for home delivery before you go, or through Eurostar (tel. 0843-218-6186, priced in euros) and pick up your ticket at the train station. In Britain, tickets can be issued only at the Eurostar office in St. Pancras International Station. In continental Europe, you can buy your Eurostar ticket at any major train station in any country or at any travel agency that handles train tickets (expect a booking fee). You can purchase passholder discount tickets at Eurostar departure stations, through US agents, or by phone with Eurostar, but they may be harder to get at other train stations and travel agencies, and are a discount category that can sell out.

Remember that Britain's time zone is one hour earlier than France and Belgium's. Times listed on tickets are local times (departure from London is British time, arrival in Paris is French time).

Taking the Eurostar

Eurostar trains depart from and arrive at London's St. Pancras International Station. Check in at least 30 minutes in advance for your Eurostar trip. It's very similar to an airport check-in: You pass through airport-like security, show your passport to customs officials, and find a TV monitor to locate your departure gate. There are a few airport-like shops, newsstands, horrible snack bars, and cafés (bring food for the trip from elsewhere), pay-Internet terminals, and a currency-exchange booth with rates about the same as you'll find on the other end.

Crossing the Channel Without Eurostar

For speed and affordability, look into cheap flights. The old-fashioned ways of crossing the Channel are cheaper than Eurostar (taking the bus is cheapest). They're also twice as romantic, complicated, and time-consuming.

LONDON

By Plane

Check with budget airlines for cheap round-trip fares to Paris or Brussels (see "Cheap Flights" on page 1024).

By Train and Boat

For additional European ferry info, visit www.aferry.to. For UK train and bus info, go to www.traveline.org.uk.

To Paris: You'll take a train from London to the port of Dover (trains depart hourly from London's St. Pancras International Station to Dover's Priory Station, 1.25 hours), then catch a ferry to Calais, France, before boarding another train for Paris. P&O Ferries sail from Dover to Calais (up to 2/hour, 1.5 hours, www.poferries.com); TGV trains run from Calais to Paris.

To Amsterdam: Stena Line's Dutchflyer service combines train and ferry tickets between London and Amsterdam via the ports of Harwich and Hoek van Holland. Trains go from London's Liverpool Street Station to **Harwich** (hourly, 1.75 hours, most transfer in Manningtree). From Harwich, Stena Line ferries sail to Hoek van Holland (8 hours), where you can catch a train to Amsterdam (book ahead for best price, 13 hours total travel time, www.stenaline.co.uk, Dutch train info at www.ns.nl).

By Bus and Boat

You can take the bus from London direct to **Paris** (4/day, 8.25-9.75 hours), **Brussels** (4/day, 9 hours), or **Amsterdam** (4/day, 12 hours) from Victoria Coach Station (via ferry or Chunnel, day or overnight). Prices are the same to Paris, Brussels, or Amsterdam (around £60-70 one-way, cheaper in advance, tel. 0870-514-3219, www.eurolines.co.uk).

London's Cruise Ports

Many cruises begin, end, or call at one of several English ports offering easy access to London. Cruise lines favor two ports in particular: **Southampton**, 80 miles southwest of London; and **Dover**, 80 miles southeast of London (each one within about a 1.5-hour drive or train ride into the city).

While London offers plenty of public-transportation connections for getting you from your ship into town (explained below), most cruise lines offer an **"On Your Own" excursion** that includes an unguided bus trip from your ship to downtown London (usually Piccadilly Circus), then back again at an appointed time. While a bit pricey (usually around £65, compared to about £40 round-trip by train from Southampton, or about £36 from Dover), this can be efficient and avoids the potential stress of doing it on your own. Ask your cruise line for details.

Southampton Cruise Port

An important English port city for centuries, Southampton is best known for three ships that set sail from here and gained fame for very different reasons: the *Mayflower* in 1620, the *Titanic* in 1912, and the *Queen Mary* in 1936. Like many port cities, Southampton was badly damaged by WWII bombs, obliterating whatever cobbled charm it once had. These days, if Southampton is known for anything, it's for cruising. In 2012, 1.4 million cruise passengers passed through here.

Services: With 240,000 people, Southampton is a sprawling port town with a relatively compact downtown core. Everything is, to a point, walkable—though most of the cruise terminals (described later) are a long walk from the train station. The main drag stretching up from the waterfront, High Street (which becomes Above Bar higher up), is the easiest place to find ATMs, Wi-Fi hotspots, and a Boots pharmacy.

Transit Within Town: To reach the train station from your cruise ship, the easiest solution is to take a **taxi** (figure £5-8; around £125 one-way into central London). To save a bit of money, you can walk partway or all the way to the station; to shave some time off the walk, consider the free **Citylink bus,** which goes from the public ferry dock at Town Quay (between the two cruise port areas, where High Street meets the water, in front of the Red Funnel ticket office) up to the train station about every 15 minutes. As this bus doesn't stop at the cruise terminals themselves, you must walk to meet it: Figure 10 minutes from the Ocean Cruise Terminal, 15 minutes from the City Cruise Terminal, and even farther from the other terminals (from those, I'd take a taxi instead).

Cruise Terminals: Within Southampton's sprawling port

(www.cruisesouthampton.com), cruises use two separate dock areas, each with two different terminals. All four terminal buildings have WCs, a rack of tourist brochures and maps, a basic café, a taxi stand out front, and possibly Wi-Fi (ask for the password). Most don't have ATMs or TIs.

Eastern Docks: The long piers jabbing straight out from Southampton have two cruise terminals (accessed through Dock Gate 4): **Ocean Cruise Terminal** at the near end (Berth 46, about a 5-minute walk to the mainland), and **QEII Cruise Terminal** at the tip (Berth 38/39, about a 15-minute walk to the mainland). From the QEII Terminal, I'd take a taxi; from Ocean Cruise Terminal, the walk-plus-bus combo is worth considering, though it takes longer: Walk down the pier and through Dock Gate 4, turn left, and follow the busy road (with the port on your left) about five more minutes to the Citylink bus stop at Town Quay.

Western Docks: This gloomy industrial zone, accessed through Dock Gate 8 (closer to town) or 10 (closer to the train station), hugs Southampton's coastline west of downtown. Shuffled between the endless parking lots and container shipping berths are two cruise terminals: **City Cruise Terminal,** close to the town center (Berth 101); and **Mayflower Cruise Terminal,** farther out (Berth 106). As Mayflower is a distant and dreary walk from the port gate, I'd spring for a taxi. From City Cruise Terminal, the walk-plus-bus combo may be worth considering: Exit the terminal to the right, then continue straight about 10 minutes through Dock Gate 8 and along the port to Town Quay and the free Citylink bus.

Trains to London: From Southampton Central Station, trains depart every 30 minutes to London's **Waterloo Station** (1.25 hours; additional departures require a change in Basingstoke and take 1.5 hours; slower trains go to London's Victoria Station in 2.5 hours). A same-day return (round-trip) ticket to London costs £39; a one-way ticket costs £34.10.

When returning to Southampton, be sure to get off at **Southampton Central Station**; the stop called Southampton Airport Parkway is much farther from the cruise port.

Sights in Southampton: While most people will make a beeline for London, the port city does have one sight worth considering: its excellent **SeaCity Museum**, with a beautifully presented exhibit about the *Titanic*. "Southampton's *Titanic* Story" explores every facet of the ill-fated ocean liner that set sail from here on April 10, 1912, and sank in the North Atlantic a few days later. Three-quarters of the *Titanic*'s 897 crew members lived in Southampton (£8.50, daily 10:00-17:00, last entry at 15:00, next to the Civic Centre along Havelock Road, tel. 023/8083-3007, www .seacitymuseum.co.uk).

Dover Cruise Port

For generations, Dover—with its easy ferry connections across the English Channel to the Continent—was the place where many travelers first set foot in Britain. But since the advent of cheap flights and the high-speed Eurostar train beneath the Channel, Dover is most useful these days for its cruise port. If you'd rather stick around Dover, you can tour its impressive castle, described below.

Services: Like much of southern England, Dover sits on a foundation of chalk; its famous white cliffs are visible from your cruise ship. The workaday city center is anchored by Market Square, with a handy **TI** (inside the Dover Museum). Across the square begins the mostly pedestrianized (but not particularly charming) main shopping drag, Cannon Street/Biggin Street, with ATMs, Wi-Fi hotspots, and a Boots pharmacy.

Cruise Terminals: Little Dover has a huge port, and cruises put in at its far western edge—at the **Western Docks,** along the extremely long Admiralty Pier (www.whitecliffscountry.org.uk). Near the port gate at the base of the pier, Terminal 1 is a converted old railway station; farther out at the tip, Terminal 2 is a modern facility.

Getting into Town: From either terminal, the best way into town (or to the train station) is by shuttle bus or taxi.

The bright-blue **shuttle bus** makes a loop connecting the cruise terminals, Market Square, and Dover Castle (bus costs £3 one-way into town; add £1 to continue up to the castle; www.open topbus.co.uk). From Market Square, it's a 15-minute walk to the train station: Head up Cannon Street (directly across the square from the TI) for three blocks, turn left onto Priory Street, continue straight through the big roundabout, and head slightly uphill on Folkestone Road; a half-block after the gas station, watch for *Dover Priory* signs on the right marking the station.

For more than two people, it's cheaper to take a **taxi**, which will run you about £7-8 whether you're going downtown, to the train station, or up to Dover Castle (figure around £150 one-way to central London).

I'd avoid the long, dreary, 30-minute **walk** from the cruise terminals into town (you'll have to go down the entire length of the pier to the mainland, turn right along the busy road, and trudge the rest of the way into town; to reach the train station, turn left up York Street, then left again on Folkestone Road).

Trains to London: From Dover Priory Station, you can choose between the faster "Javelin" train (hourly, 1.25 hours to London's **St. Pancras International Station;** £38.10 one-way, £40.60 same-day return, £71.20 anytime return) and the slower train (hourly to **Victoria Station** or hourly to **Charing Cross Station**, each 2 hours; £31.20 one-way, £31.40 same-day return). When choosing a train, consider this: St. Pancras International and Victoria Stations are both well-connected to any point in the city by Tube or bus (and St. Pancras International is right next to the British Library), but Charing Cross Station is within easy walking distance of the sights many first-timers want to see (Trafalgar Square, National Gallery, West End, Whitehall, Houses of Parliament)—so the extra time spent on that train could save you time commuting to your sightseeing in London.

Returning to Dover, you'll get off at the **Dover Priory** train station.

Sights in Dover: Most arriving cruisers will want to head straight into London. But if you're lingering in town, Dover Castle is well worth a look. Perched upon chalk cliffs, peering across the English Channel to France, it has sprawling grounds, a historic keep with a fine museum, and—its highlight—a chance to tour the WWII-era Secret Wartime Tunnels, where you'll hear the story of Operation Dynamo, a harrowing rescue operation across the English Channel (£16.50; April-Sept daily 10:00-18:00, from 9:30 in Aug; Oct daily 10:00-17:00; Nov-March Sat-Sun 10:00-16:00, closed Mon-Fri; tel. 01304/211-067, www.english-heritage.org.uk /dovercastle).

LONDON

GREENWICH, WINDSOR & CAMBRIDGE

Three of the best day-trip possibilities near London are Greenwich, Windsor, and Cambridge. Greenwich, which actually lies within London's city limits, is England's maritime capital; Windsor, west of the city, has a very famous castle; and Cambridge, an hour to the north, is England's best university town.

Other worthwhile destinations within day-tripping range of London include Stonehenge, Salisbury, and Bath—all covered in other chapters in this book.

Getting Around

By Train: If day-tripping from London, take advantage of British Rail's discounts. The "off-peak day return" ticket is a round-trip fare that costs virtually the same as one-way, provided you depart London outside rush hour (usually after 9:30 on weekdays and anytime Sat-Sun). Be sure to specifically ask for the "day return" ticket (round-trip within a single day) rather than the more expensive standard "return." You can also save a little money if you purchase tickets before 18:00 the day before your trip.

By Train Tour: London Walks offers a variety of "Daytrips from London" tours year-round by train, including a Cambridge itinerary (£16 plus transportation and admissions costs, pick up their brochure at the TI or hotels, tel. 020/7624-3978, www.walks.com).

London Day Trips

50 Kilometers

50 Miles

ENGLAND

WALES

Cambridge

Luton ✈

✈ Stansted

Southend

London ✈

✈ London City

North Sea

Greenwich

Bath •

Windsor ✈

Heathrow

STONEHENGE

BUS •

Salisbury

✈ Gatwick

CHANNEL TUNNEL

To Paris & Brussels

English ⛵ Channel

GREENWICH

Greenwich

Tudor kings favored the palace at Greenwich (GREN-ich). Henry VIII was born here. Later kings commissioned architects Inigo

Jones and Christopher Wren to beautify the town and palace, and William and Mary built a grand hospital to care for retired seamen (which later became a college for training naval officers).

Greenwich is England's maritime capital. Visitors come here for all things salty, including the *Cutty Sark* clipper ship, the area's premier attraction. The town is synonymous with timekeeping and astronomy, and at the Royal Observatory Greenwich, you can learn how those pursuits relate to seafaring. Greenwich also has stately Baroque architecture, appealing markets, a fleet of nautical shops, plenty of parks, kid-friendly museums, and hordes of tourists. Since many of the major sights here are free to enter, and you can travel between central London and Greenwich on a cheap Tube ticket, it's a wonderfully inexpensive day out. And where else can you set your watch with such accuracy?

Planning Your Time

Note that the town's popular market is closed Monday. Before or after the *Cutty Sark,* stroll to the Discover Greenwich exhibit and

TI, drop into the grand buildings of the Old Royal Naval College, and walk the shoreline promenade. Greenwich's parks are picnic-perfect: Consider gathering picnic supplies before heading to the National Maritime Museum, and on through the park to the Royal Observatory Greenwich.

If you like to mix and match public transit, I'd suggest taking the boat to Greenwich for the scenery and commentary, and the Docklands Light Railway (DLR) back, especially if you want to stop at the Docklands on the way home. To visit the Docklands—the glittering forest of skyscrapers rising from a once-derelict port—hop off the train at the Canary Wharf stop for a quick stroll (see page 152).

Getting to Greenwich

It's a joy by boat or a snap by DLR.

By Boat: From central London, you can cruise scenically down the Thames to Greenwich. Various tour boats—with commentary and open-deck seating up top—leave from the piers at Westminster, Waterloo, and the Tower of London (2/hour, 1-1.25 hours); most boats have commentary only on the way to Greenwich, not on the way back.

Thames Clippers offers faster trips, with no commentary and only a small deck at the stern (departs every 20-30 minutes from several piers in central London, 40 minutes). Thames Clippers also connects Greenwich to the Docklands' Canary Wharf Pier (2-3/hour, 10 minutes).

For cruising details, see page 80.

By DLR Train: From Bank Station in central London (also accessible from the Monument Tube station), take the DLR to Cutty Sark Station in central Greenwich; it's one stop before the main—but less central—Greenwich Station (departs at least every 10 minutes, 20 minutes, all in Zone 2, covered by any Tube pass). Many DLR trains terminate at Canary Wharf, so make sure you get on one that continues to Lewisham or Greenwich.

Some DLR trains terminate at Island Gardens—you can generally catch another train to Greenwich's Cutty Sark Station within a few minutes. Or, disembark at Island Gardens for the unique experience of walking under the Thames into Greenwich: To reach the pedestrian tunnel, exit the station, cross the street and follow signs to *Island Gardens* for a good photo op. Then enter the red-brick Greenwich Foot Tunnel (opened in 1902), descend 86 spiral stairs (or ride the lift), hold your breath, and re-emerge on dry land at the bow of the *Cutty Sark.*

By Train: Mainline trains also go from London (Cannon Street and London Bridge stations) several times an hour to Greenwich Station (10-minute walk from the sights). Although the train is fast and cheap, the DLR is preferable because it drops you right in the heart of town.

By Bus: Catch bus #188 from Russell Square near the British Museum (about 45 minutes to Greenwich).

Orientation to Greenwich

Still well within the city limits of London, the Royal Borough of Greenwich—a title bestowed by the Queen in honor of her

Diamond Jubilee—feels like a small town all its own. Covered markets and outdoor stalls make for lively weekends. Save time to browse the town. Wander beyond the touristy Church Street and Greenwich High Road to where flower stands spill onto the side streets and antique shops sell brass nautical knickknacks. King William Walk, College Approach, Nelson Road, and Turnpin Lane (all in the vicinity of Greenwich Market) are all worth a look. If you need pub grub, Greenwich has almost 100 pubs, with some boasting that they're mere milliseconds from the prime meridian.

Markets: Thanks to its markets, Greenwich throbs with day-trippers on weekends. The **Greenwich Market** is an entertaining mini-Covent Garden, located in the middle of the block between the Cutty Sark DLR station and the Old Royal Naval College—right on your way to the sights (Tue-Sun 10:00-17:30, closed Mon; farmers market, arts and crafts, and food stands; antiques-only on Thu, www.greenwichmarket.net). The **Clocktower Market** sells old odds and ends at high prices on Greenwich High Road, near the post office (Sat-Sun and bank holidays only 10:00-17:00, www.clocktowermarket.co.uk).

Tourist Information

The TI is inside the Discover Greenwich visitors center (described later, under "Sights in Greenwich"), right next to the *Cutty Sark* entrance. From the DLR station, turn left, pass under the brick archway, cross the street, and continue straight ahead to the monumental gateway for the Old Royal Naval College complex; Discover Greenwich is just inside the gate on the left (daily 10:00-17:00, Pepys House, 2 Cutty Sark Gardens, tel. 0870-608-2000, www.visitgreenwich.org.uk).

Guided walks, which depart from the TI, offer an overview of the town and go past most of the big sights (£8, daily at 12:15 and 14:15, 1.5 hours; the only sights you enter are the Painted Hall

Greenwich

GREENWICH

- - - Recommended Walks

To Canary Wharf & The Docklands

ISLE OF DOGS

WEST FERRY ROAD

Island Gardens (DLR)

Island Gardens

Thames River

PEDESTRIAN TUNNEL

To London

GREENWICH PIER

TUNNEL ENTRANCE

DISCOVER GREENWICH

CUTTY SARK

CREEK RD.

CHURCH ST.

COLLEGE APPROACH

Cutty Sark (DLR)

NELSON

ST. ALFEGE'S CHURCH

ROAN ST.

GREENWICH STATION

GREENWICH HIGH RD.

To London

BURNEY ST.

STOCKWELL

KING WILLIAM WALK

FIVE FOOT WALK

CRANE ST.

TRINITY HOSPITAL

OLD WOOLWICH RD.

To O2 Arena

PARK ROW

TRAFALGAR ROAD

OLD ROYAL NAVAL COLLEGE

CHAPEL

PAINTED HALL

GREENWICH UNIVERSITY

ROMNEY ROAD

COLONNADES

QUEEN'S HOUSE

NATIONAL MARITIME MUSEUM

Greenwich Park

PRIME MERIDIAN

THE AVENUE

CROOM'S HILL

THE AVENUE

KING GEORGE ST.

FLAMSTEED HOUSE

ROYAL OBSERVATORY GREENWICH

BLACKHEATH

PETER HARRISON PLANETARIUM

WELLER ASTRONOMY GALLERIES

200 Meters

200 Yards

1 Greenwich Market
2 Clocktower Market
3 Trafalgar Tavern
4 Marks & Spencer Simply Food
5 The Old Brewery

and Chapel of St. Peter and St. Paul, and only on the 14:15 tour; the 12:15 tour leaves you at the door of the Naval Observatory).

Sights in Greenwich

I've organized these listings as a handy sightseeing walk through town, starting near the Cutty Sark DLR station.

▲▲Cutty Sark

The Scottish-built *Cutty Sark* was the last of the great China tea clippers and the queen of the seas when first launched in 1869. She

was among the fastest clippers ever built, the culmination of centuries of ship design. With 32,000 square feet of sail—and favorable winds—she could travel 300 miles in a day. But as a new century dawned, steamers began to outmatch sailing ships for speed, and by the mid-1920s the *Cutty Sark*

was the world's last operating clipper ship. After a stint as a training ship, she was retired and turned into a museum in the 1950s.

Following a five-year-long restoration, interrupted by a devastating fire, the ship reopened to the public in the spring of 2012. The spectacular new display space has one major drawback: The glass building obscures the elegant lines of the hull that gave the *Cutty Sark* her record-breaking speed (one critic groused that the ship now "looks like it has run aground in a giant greenhouse"). On the plus side, the building allows visitors to walk directly below the ship, which has been raised 11 feet above her dry dock. Above deck, the ship's rigging has been restored to original specifications, while below deck, displays explore the *Cutty Sark*'s 140-year history and the cargo she carried—everything from tea to wool to gunpowder—as she raced between London and ports all around the world.

Cost and Hours: £12, includes voluntary 10 percent donation, kids ages 5-15-£6.50, free for kids under age 5, family tickets available; daily 10:00-17:00 but occasionally closed Mon, may stay open until 18:00 at busiest times; last entry one hour before closing; £5 guidebook available but hardly necessary, reservation tel. 020/8312-6608, www.rmg.co.uk/cuttysark.

Crowd-Beating Tips: The ship can get busy on school holidays and on weekends. To skip the line, you can reserve ahead online or by phone, or just try showing up around 13:00, when there's often a lull in visitors.

Visiting the *Cutty Sark*: The first deck you'll visit harkens back to the ship's days in the Chinese tea trade...which didn't last long, as the Suez Canal soon opened, allowing steam-powered ships to reach China much faster than sailboats. The *Cutty Sark* turned to trading wool with Australia, as explored on the next deck up. This "Tween Deck" is full of not-quite-gimmicky displays that mostly succeed in making the ship's history come alive, even for adults. Find the fun video game that lets you attempt to beat Captain Woodget's record voyage sailing a wool-laden *Sark* from Sydney to London. Sit on the tilting benches of tea crates for a seaborne feel, try your hand at some knots, enjoy the oddly mesmerizing video at the stern, and get the figurehead's take on *Sark* history in the bow.

Sailing fans will like the gorgeously restored top deck best. Notice how pathetic the crew's mattresses were, and don't miss the video showing the rigger's-eye-view as he climbs high above the deck. Your visit ends down below, where you can take a coffee break directly under the shiny stern (it may gleam like gold, but the hull's covering is actually an alloy of copper and zinc). Near the bow is a colorful collection of figureheads from other ships. On the floor directly under the front of the hull, note the compass rose that shows how many days at sea it'd take to reach major ports from here.

Discover Greenwich

This visitors center is located at the corner of the Old Royal Naval College closest to the *Cutty Sark*. While it's hardly a museum, it offers a decent introduction to Greenwich and some fun exhibits for kids. In the center, a model of the town lights up to tell its history. Surrounding the model are displays and artifacts from various people who have left their mark on the town, along with exhibits about the architecture and construction of Greenwich's fine buildings. Tours of the Royal Naval College (described next) leave from the reception desk. Adjoining Discover Greenwich are the TI and a recommended pub, The Old Brewery.

Cost and Hours: Free, daily 10:00-17:00, tel. 020/8269-4799, www.oldroyalnavalcollege.org.

▲Old Royal Naval College

The college was originally a hospital founded by Queen Mary II and King William III in 1692 as a charity to care for retired or injured naval officers (called pensioners). William and Mary spared no expense, hiring the great Christopher Wren to design the complex (though other architects completed it). Its days as a hospital ended in 1869, and it served as a college for training naval officers from 1873 to 1998. Now that the Royal Navy has moved out, the public is invited to view the college's elaborate Painted Hall and Chapel of St. Peter and St. Paul, which are in symmetrical buildings that face each other overlooking a broad riverfront park.

Cost and Hours: Free, daily 10:00-17:00, sometimes closed for private events, service Sun at 11:00 in chapel—all are welcome, www.ornc.org.

Tours: Guides give one-hour tours covering the hall and chapel, along with other areas not open to the general public (£5, daily at 14:00, departs from Discover Greenwich, call ahead to check availability, tel. 020/8269-4799).

Self-Guided Tour: Each building sells a descriptive guide (50p-£1), or you can buy the fun *Nasty Naval College* brochure, with offbeat facts about the place (£1). Volunteers are often standing by to answer questions.

Painted Hall: Originally intended as a dining hall for pensioners, this sumptuously painted room was deemed too glorious (and, in the winter, too cold) for that purpose. So almost as soon as it was completed, it became simply a place to impress visitors.

Enter the hall, climb the stairs, and gape up at one of the largest painted ceilings in Europe—112 feet long. It's a big propaganda scene, glorifying the building's founders, Queen Mary II and King William III (who, as a Protestant monarch, had recently trounced the Catholic French King Louis XIV in a pivotal bat-

tle). Crane your neck—or use the clever wheeled mirrors—to examine the scene. In the center are William and Mary. Under his foot, William is crushing a dark figure with a broken sword... Louis XIV. William is handing a red cap (representing liberty) to the woman on the right, who holds the reins of a white horse (symbolizing Europe). On the left, a white-robed woman hands him an olive branch, a sign of peace. The message: William has granted Europe liberty by saving it from the tyranny of Louis XIV. Below the royal couple, the Spirit of Architecture shows them the plans for this very building (commemorating the sad fact that Mary died before its completion). Ringing the central image are the four seasons (represented by Zodiac signs), the four virtues, and—at the top and bottom—a captured Spanish galleon and a British man-of-war battleship.

Up the steps at the end of the room, along the wall of the **upper hall,** is a portrait of the family of King George I. On the right is the artist who spent 19 years of his life painting this hall, James Thornhill (he finally finished it in 1727). He's holding out his hand—reportedly, he didn't feel he was paid enough for this Sistine-sized undertaking.

• *Exit the hall, and cross the field to enter the...*

Chapel of St. Peter and St. Paul: Not surprisingly, you'll sense a nautical air in this fine chapel. Notice the rope motif in the floor tiles down the aisle. The painting above the altar, by American Benjamin West, depicts the shipwreck of St. Paul on the island of Malta. According to the Bible, Paul disturbed a poisonous viper but managed to throw it in a fire, miraculously without being harmed. Soon after the chapel was completed, it was gutted by a fire and had to be redecorated all over again. The plans

were too ambitious, so the designers cut corners. Some of the columns and capitals are fake, and the "sculptures" lining the nave high above are actually *trompe l'oeil*—3-D paintings meant to look real. But some items, such as the marble frame around the main door, are finely crafted from expensive materials.

• *Leave the chapel, and walk straight down to the water—enjoying the sweeping views across to the Docklands. When you hit the river, turn right for a quick...*

Riverside Stroll

Looking back toward the Old Royal Naval College, notice how it's split into two parts; reportedly, Queen Mary didn't want the view from the Queen's House blocked. The college's twin-domed towers (one giving the time, the other the direction of the wind) frame the Queen's House, and the Royal Observatory Greenwich crowns the hill beyond.

Wander east along the Thames on Five Foot Walk (named for the width of the path). From here you can see the big, white, spiky **O2** dome a mile downstream. This stadium languished for nearly a decade after its controversial construction and brief life as the Millennium Dome. Intended to be a world's fair-type site and the center of London's year 2000 celebration, it ended up as the topic of heated debates about cost overruns and its controversial looks. The site was finally bought by a developer a few years ago and rechristened "The O2" (a telecommunications company paid for the naming rights). Today it hosts sporting events and concerts. Next to the O2 are the towers of the Emirates Air Line aerial gondola, which ferries passengers between the O2 and across the Thames to, essentially, nowhere.

Continuing downstream, just past the college, you'll find the recommended **Trafalgar Tavern.** Dickens knew the pub

well, and he used it as the setting for the wedding breakfast in *Our Mutual Friend.* Built in 1837 in the Regency style to attract Londoners downriver, the upstairs Nelson Room is still used for weddings. Its formal moldings and elegant windows with balconies over the Thames are a step back in time and worth a peek.

• *From the Trafalgar Tavern, walk two long blocks up Park Row. After crossing busy Romney Road, turn right (through the gate near the corner) into the park. The palatial buildings in the middle of the park are the Queen's House and the National Maritime Museum; the Royal Observatory Greenwich is on the hilltop beyond. Together, this trio is known as the Royal Museums of Greenwich.*

GREENWICH

Queen's House
This building, the first Palladian-style villa in Britain, was designed in 1616 by Inigo Jones for James I's wife, Anne of Denmark. All traces of the queen are long gone, and the Great Hall and Royal Apartments now serve as an art gallery for the National Maritime Museum. Predictably, most of the art is nautical-themed, with plenty of paintings of ships and sea battles, and portraits of admirals and captains. Among these is the great J. M. W. Turner painting *The Battle of Trafalgar* (1824), the artist's only royal commission. The painting is often out on loan, so ask at the entry before you look for it. If you're short on time or energy, skip this sight.

Cost and Hours: Free, daily 10:00-17:00, last entry 30 minutes before closing, tel. 020/8858-4422, www.rmg.co.uk.

Tours: Skip the free (and outdated) audioguide and instead ask about the daily tour (free, 2-3/day).

• *Exiting the Queen's House, walk toward the hill and turn right. About 300 yards farther on you'll find the...*

▲National Maritime Museum
Great for anyone interested in the sea, this museum holds everything from a giant working paddlewheel to the uniform Admiral Horatio Nelson wore when he was killed at Trafalgar (look for the bullet hole, in the left shoulder). A big glass roof tops three levels

of slick, modern, kid-friendly exhibits about all things seafaring.

Cost and Hours: Free, daily 10:00-17:00, ground floor until 20:00 on Thu, last entry 30 minutes before closing, tel. 020/8858-4422, www.rmg.co.uk. The museum hosts frequent family-oriented events—singing, treasure hunts, and storytelling—particularly on weekends; ask at the desk. Inside, listen for announcements alerting visitors to free tours on various topics.

Visiting the Museum: The Explorers exhibit covers early expeditions and an ill-fated Arctic trip, complete with a soundtrack of creaking wooden ships and crashing waves. One room displays stained-glass windows honoring members of London's Baltic Exchange (an important shipping consortium) killed in World War I, while the somber Atlantic Worlds hall thoughtfully

describes how the movements of goods, ideas, and enslaved people shaped the 17th to 19th centuries. Kids like the All Hands and Bridge galleries, where they can send secret messages by Morse code and operate a miniature dockside crane. Along with displays of lighthouse technology and a whaling cannon, you'll see model ships, nautical paintings, and various salty odds and ends. While some parts of the museum are closed for ongoing renovation, there's still plenty to see.

• *The final sight in town—the Royal Observatory Greenwich—is at the top of the hill just behind the National Maritime Museum. To reach it, cross through the colonnade connecting the museum and the Queen's House, then follow the crowds as they huff up the steep hill (allow 10-15 minutes).*

*As you hike up, look along the observatory's roof for the red **Time Ball** (also visible from the Thames), which drops daily at 13:00.*

▲▲Royal Observatory Greenwich

Located on the prime meridian (0° longitude), the observatory is famous as the point from which all time is measured. The observatory's early work, however, had nothing to do with coordinating the world's clocks to Greenwich Mean Time (GMT). The observatory was founded in 1675 by Charles II for the purpose of improving navigation by more accurately charting the night sky. Today, the Greenwich time signal is linked with the BBC (which broadcasts the famous "pips" worldwide at the top of the hour). A visit here gives you a taste of the sciences of astronomy, time-keeping, and seafaring—and how they all meld together—along with great views over Greenwich and the distant London skyline. The Royal Observatory grounds are made up of the observatory

The Longitude Problem

Around 1700, as the ships of seafaring nations began to venture farther from their home bases, the alarming increase in the number of shipwrecks made it clear that navigational tools had to be improved. Determining latitude—the relative position between the equator and the North or South Pole—was straightforward; sailors needed only to measure the angle of the sun at noon. But figuring out longitude, or their east-west position, was not as easy without a fixed point (such as the equator) from which to measure.

In 1714, the British government offered the £20,000 Longitude Prize. Two successful solutions emerged, and both are tied to Greenwich.

The first approach was to observe the position of the moon, which moves in relation to the stars. Sailors would compare the night sky they saw with the sky over Greenwich by consulting a book of tables prepared by Greenwich astronomers. This told them how far they were from Greenwich—their longitude. Visitors to the Royal Observatory can still see the giant telescopes—under retractable roofs—that were used to carefully chart the heavens to create these meticulous tables.

The second approach was to create a clock that would remain completely accurate on voyages—no easy feat back then, when turbulence and changes in weather and humidity made timepieces notoriously unreliable at sea. John Harrison spent 45 years working on this problem, finally succeeding in 1760 with his fourth effort, the H4 (which won him the Longitude Prize). All four of his attempts are on display at the Royal Observatory.

So, how can a clock determine longitude? Every 15° of longitude equals an hour when comparing the difference in sunrise or sunset times between two places. For example, the time gap between Greenwich and New York City is five hours, which translates into a longitudinal difference of 75°. Equipped with an accurate timepiece set to Greenwich Mean Time, sailors could figure out their longitude by comparing sunset time at their current position with sunset time back in Greenwich.

Notice that both approaches use Greenwich as a baseline—either on an astral map or on a clock. That's why, to this day, the prime meridian and official world time are both centered in this unassuming London suburb.

(with the prime meridian and three worthy exhibits), the Weller Astronomy Galleries, and the Peter Harrison Planetarium.

If your only interest in the Royal Observatory is the famous prime meridian line, you can enter through the iron gate near the entrance for a free, more simplistic (and significantly less crowded) display of the prime meridian. Under the analog clock just outside the courtyard, see how your foot measures up to the foot where the public standards of length are cast in bronze.

Observatory: £7, ticket good for re-entry for one year, £11.50 combo-ticket with planetarium saves money if you visit both, audioguide-£3.50, 1 hour; daily 10:00-17:00, later in summer—can be as late as 19:00, last entry 30 minutes before closing.

Weller Astronomy Galleries: Free, daily 10:00-17:00, last entry at 16:30.

Peter Harrison Planetarium: £6.50, £11.50 combo-ticket with observatory; 30-minute shows generally run every hour (usually Mon-Fri 13:00-16:00, Sat-Sun 11:00-16:00, fewer shows in winter, schedule can change from day to day). Confirm times by calling ahead, checking online, or picking up a flier (which you'll see around the observatory). As these shows can sell out, consider calling ahead to order tickets.

Information: Tel. 020/8858-4422, www.rmg.co.uk.

GREENWICH

❸ **Self-Guided Tour:** Entering the complex, you're directed

either to the observatory entrance or the Weller Astronomy Galleries. Since the observatory is more interesting, do that first (but note that the Weller Galleries won't let you in after 16:30).

• *After purchasing your ticket, enter the courtyard.*

Running through the middle of this space is The Line—the **prime meridian.** Visitors wait patiently to have their pho-

tographs taken as they straddle the line in front of the monument, with one foot in each hemisphere. While watching all this fuss over a little line, consider that—unlike the equator—the placement of the prime meridian is totally arbitrary. It could well have been at my house, in Timbuktu, or just a few feet over—as, for a time, it was (the trough along the building's roofline shows where one astronomer had placed it). While waiting for your turn, set your wristwatch to the digital clock showing GMT to a tenth of a second.

Three different attractions are scattered around this court-yard. First, hiding in a corner is a **camera obscura.** This thrillingly low-tech device projects a live image from Greenwich onto a flat disc in a darkened room simply by manipulating light, without electricity or machinery (although the image can be pretty dim on cloudy days). Imagine how astonishing it was in the days before television.

The smaller building is the **Flamsteed House,** named for John Flamsteed, the first king-appointed Astronomer Royal (in 1675). It contains the apartments that he lived in and the Wren-designed Octagon Room, where he carried out some of his work. Downstairs is a fascinating exhibit on the "Longitude Problem" and how it was solved (see sidebar). Also on display are all four of John Harrison's sea clocks. Compared to his other contraptions, the fourth and final attempt looks like an oversized pocket watch. But, in terms of its impact, this little timepiece is right up there with the printing press, the cotton gin, the telegraph, and the money belt on the scale of human achievement.

The **Telescopes Exhibition,** in the larger house, has a wide assortment of historical telescopes, including a couple of room-sized ones. Upstairs from the gift shop, a skippable exhibit explores the role of timekeeping in our society.

• *Now head out back.*

Walk past the giant rusted-copper cone top of the planetarium. The building beyond houses the **Weller Astronomy Galleries,** where interactive, kid-pleasing displays allow you to guide a space mission and touch a 4.5-billion-year-old meteorite. You can also buy tickets for and enter the state-of-the-art, 120-seat **Peter Harrison Planetarium** from here.

Before you leave the observatory grounds, enjoy the **view** from the overlook—the symmetrical royal buildings, the Thames, and the Docklands and its busy cranes (including the prominent

Canary Wharf Tower, with its pyramid cap). You may be able to see—poking up between buildings—the white stadium and red Orbit tower in Queen Elizabeth Olympic Park. To the right is the huge O2 dome and the towers of the

Emirates Air Line gondola. To the left lies the square-mile City of London, with skyscrapers and the dome of St. Paul's Cathedral. The Shard is to the far left. At night (17:00-24:00), look for the green laser beam the observatory projects into the sky (best viewed in winter), which extends along the prime meridian for 15 miles.

Eating in Greenwich

The colorful **Greenwich Market** hosts food stalls, great for assembling a picnic (Tue-Sun 10:00-17:30, closed Mon, down the street from Cutty Sark DLR station). Another handy place to pick up ready-made food is **Marks & Spencer Simply Food,** between the DLR station and the *Cutty Sark* dry dock (Mon-Sat 8:00-20:30, Sun 9:30-20:30, 55 Greenwich Church Street).

The Trafalgar Tavern, with a casual pub and elegant ground-floor dining room, is a historical place for an overpriced meal (£12-17 main courses in restaurant, food served Mon-Sat 12:00-22:00, Sun 12:00-16:00, Park Row, tel. 020/8858-2909).

The Old Brewery, in the Discover Greenwich center on the Old Royal Naval College grounds, is an upscale gastropub decorated with all things beer. An adjacent café serves cheap lunches. A brewery on this site once provided the daily ration of four pints of beer for pensioners at the hospital. Today it's a microbrewery offering 50 different beers, while a beer sommelier suggests the right pairings with food on the menu (£4 bar snacks, £12 lunches, part of the pub becomes a fancier restaurant in the evenings with £5-10 starters and £10-17 main courses; daily 10:00-23:00, lunch 12:00-17:00, dinner from 18:00, tel. 020/3327-1280).

Windsor

Windsor, a compact and easy walking town of about 30,000 people, originally grew up around the royal residence. In 1070, William the Conqueror continued his habit of kicking Saxons out of their various settlements, taking over what the locals called "Windlesora" (meaning "riverbank with a hoisting winch")—which eventually became "Windsor." William built the first fortified castle on a chalk hill above the Thames; later kings added on to his early designs, rebuilding and expanding the castle and surrounding gardens.

By setting up their primary residence here, modern monarchs increased Windsor's popularity and prosperity—most notably, Queen Victoria, whose stern statue glares at you as you approach the castle. After her death, Victoria rejoined her beloved husband, Albert, in the Royal Mausoleum at Frogmore House, a mile south of the castle in a private section of the Home Park (house and mausoleum rarely open). The current Queen considers Windsor her primary residence, and the one where she feels most at home. She generally hangs her crown here on weekends, using it as an escape from her workaday grind at Buckingham Palace in the city. You can tell if Her Majesty is in residence by checking to see which flag is flying above the round tower: If it's the royal standard (a red, yellow, and blue flag) instead of the Union Jack, the Queen is at home.

While 99 percent of visitors just come to tour the castle and go, some enjoy spending the night. Daytime crowds trample Windsor's charm, which is most evident when the tourists are gone. Consider overnighting here—parking and access to Heathrow Airport are easy, and an evening at the horse races (on Mondays) is hoof-pounding, heart-thumping fun.

Getting to Windsor

By Train: Windsor has two train stations—Windsor & Eton Central (5-minute walk to palace; TI in adjacent shopping center) and Windsor & Eton Riverside (5-minute walk to palace and TI). First Great Western trains run between London's Paddington Station and Windsor & Eton Central (2-3/hour, 30-40 minutes, easy change at Slough; £9.50 one-way standard class, £10-13 same-day return, www.firstgreatwestern.co.uk). South West Trains run between London's Waterloo Station and Windsor & Eton Riverside (2/hour, 50 minutes; £9.50 one-way standard class, £10-17.50 same-day return, info tel. 0845-748-4950, www.nationalrail .co.uk). If deciding between these, notice that while Waterloo is more central within London and has a direct connection, it takes nearly twice as long as the alternative from Paddington.

If you're day-tripping into London *from* Windsor, ask at the train station about combining a same-day return train ticket with a One-Day Travelcard—you'll end up with one ticket that covers rail transportation to and from London and doubles as an all-day Tube and bus pass in town (£13-22, lower price for travel after 9:30, rail ticket also qualifies you for some half-price London sightseeing discounts—ask or look for brochure at station, or go to www.daysoutguide.co.uk).

By Bus: Green Line buses #701 and #702 run from London's Victoria Colonnades (between the Victoria train and coach stations) to the Parish Church stop on Windsor's High Street, before continuing on to Legoland (1-2/hour, 1.5 hours to Windsor, £5.50-9.50 one-way, £9-16 round-trip, prices vary depending on time of day, tel. 01753/524-144, www.rainbowfares.com).

By Car: Windsor is about 20 miles from London and just off Heathrow Airport's landing path. The town (and then the castle and Legoland) is well-signposted from the M-4 motorway. It's a convenient first stop if you're arriving at and renting a car from Heathrow, and saving London until the end of your trip.

From Heathrow Airport: Buses #71 and #77 run between Terminal 5 and Windsor, dropping you in the center of town on Peascod Street (about £8, 1-3/hour, 50 minutes, tel. 01753/524-144). London black cabs can (and do) charge whatever they like from Heathrow to Windsor; avoid them by calling a local cab company, such as Windsor Radio Cars (£25, tel. 01753/677-677, www.windsorcars.com).

Orientation to Windsor

Windsor's pleasant pedestrian shopping zone litters the approach to its famous palace with fun temptations. You'll find most shops and restaurants around the castle on High and Thames Streets, and down the pedestrian Peascod Street (PESS-cot), which runs perpendicular to High Street.

Tourist Information

The TI is immediately adjacent to Windsor & Eton Central Station, in the Windsor Royal Shopping Centre's Old Booking Hall (May-Sept Mon-Sat 10:00-17:00, Sun 10:00-16:00; Oct-April Sun-Fri 10:00-16:00, Sat 10:00-17:00; tel. 01753/743-900, www.windsor.gov.uk). The TI sells discount tickets to Legoland (see "More Sights in Windsor," later).

Arrival in Windsor

By Train: The train to Windsor & Eton Central Station from Paddington (via Slough) spits you out into the Windsor Royal shopping pavilion (which houses the TI), only a few minutes' walk from the castle. If you arrive instead at Windsor & Eton Riverside Station (from Waterloo Station), you'll see the castle as you exit—just follow the wall to the castle entrance.

By Car: Follow signs from the M-4 motorway for pay-and-display parking in the center. River Street Car Park is closest to the castle, but pricey and often full. The cheaper, bigger Alexandra Car Park (near the riverside Alexandra Gardens) is farther west. To walk to the town center from the Alexandra Car Park, head east through the tour-bus parking lot toward the castle. At the

Windsor

To Heathrow Airport & London via M-4

- - - Changing of the Guard Route

To Slough & London (Paddington Station)

ETON COLLEGE

To London (Waterloo Station)

Home Park (Public)

POST

Thames River

BOAT TRIPS

WINDSOR BRIDGE (PEDESTRIAN)

RIVERSIDE STATION

NORMAN GATE

ST. GEORGE'S CHAPEL

STATE APARTMENTS

BIKE RENTAL

Alexandra Gardens

CENTRAL STATION

Middle Ward

ROUND TOWER

Upper Ward

Lower Ward

WINDSOR CASTLE

To Royal Windsor Racecourse

CASTLE HILL

CASTLE TICKETS

SHOPPING CENTER

GUILDHALL & MUSEUM

ST. JOHN

QUEEN VICTORIA STATUE

POST

BACH ACRE

GUARD BARRACKS

Home Park (Private)

200 Meters

200 Yards

To Legoland &

To Ascot via A-332

❶ Mercure Windsor Castle Hotel
❷ Langton House B&B
❸ To Park Farm B&B
❹ Dee & Steve's B&B
❺ 76 Duke Street B&B
❻ Crown & Cushion Rooms
❼ Bel & The Dragon
❽ Cornucopia Bistro
❾ The Duchess of Cambridge Pub
❿ The Crooked House Teahouse
⓫ Meimo Restaurant
⓬ Saffron Restaurant
⓭ Library (Internet Access)
⓮ Grocery Stores (2)
⓯ Legoland Bus Stops (2)

WINDSOR

souvenir shop, walk up the stairs (or take the elevator) and cross the overpass to Windsor & Eton Central Station. Just beyond the station, you'll find the TI in the Windsor Royal Shopping Centre. Yet another, even cheaper option is the King Edward VII Avenue car-park-and-ride, east of the castle on B-470, which includes a shuttle bus into town.

Helpful Hints

Festivals: In addition to the Royal Ascot horse races (described later, under "Beyond Windsor"), Windsor hosts a tattoo for four days in May, when troops march in military regalia at the public Home Park, just northeast of the castle.

Internet Access: Get online at the **library,** located on Bachelors' Acre, between Peascod and Victoria Streets (£1.50/30 minutes, free Wi-Fi, Mon and Thu 9:30-17:00, Tue 9:30-20:00, Wed 14:00-17:00, Fri 9:30-19:00, Sat 9:30-15:00, closed Sun, tel. 01753/743-940, www.rbwm.gov.uk).

Supermarkets: Pick up picnic supplies at **Marks & Spencer** (Mon-Sat 8:00-19:00, closed Sun, 130 Peascod Street, tel. 01753/852-266) or at **Waitrose** (Mon-Fri 8:00-21:00, Sat 8:00-20:00, Sun 11:00-17:00, King Edward Court Shopping Centre, just south of Windsor & Eton Central Station, tel. 01753/860-565). Just outside the castle, you'll find long benches near the statue of Queen Victoria—great for people-watching while you munch.

Bike Rental: Extreme Motion, near the river in Alexandra Gardens, rents 21-speed mountain bikes as well as helmets (£12.50/4 hours, £18/day, helmets-£1-1.50, £150 credit-card deposit required, bring passport as ID, summer daily 10:00-18:00, only open Sat-Sun off-season, tel. 01753/830-220).

Sights in Windsor

▲▲Windsor Castle

Windsor Castle, the official home of England's royal family for 900 years, claims to be the largest and oldest occupied castle in the world. Thankfully, touring it is simple. You'll see sprawling grounds, lavish staterooms, a crowd-pleasing dollhouse, a gallery of Michelangelo and Leonardo da Vinci drawings, and an exquisite Perpendicular Gothic chapel.

Cost: If everything is open, a ticket costs £18.50

(family-£48); on (relatively rare) days that the Queen is hosting special events in her state rooms, the price is reduced to £10 (family-£26) to make up for the closure. Either ticket is valid for one year of re-entry if you get it stamped at the exit.

Crowd Control: Ticket lines can be long in summer; avoid the wait by purchasing tickets in advance online at www.royal collection.org.uk or in person at the Buckingham Palace ticket office in London. Tickets in hand, you'll go in through a fast-entry door. There's nowhere in Windsor to buy advance tickets, so once you're here, the ticketless have to stand in line.

Hours: Grounds and most interiors open daily March-Oct 9:45-17:15, Nov-Feb 9:45-16:15, except St. George's Chapel, which is closed Sun to tourists (but open to worshippers). Last entry to grounds and St. George's Chapel 75 minutes before closing. Last entry to State Apartments and Queen Mary's Dolls' House 45 minutes before closing.

Possible Closures: If the queen is entertaining, the State Apartments may be closed—a big disappointment if you're not expecting it, but at least the ticket is cheaper (explained earlier). The entire palace occasionally closes for special events (such as the Garter Service in mid-June). It's smart to call ahead or check the website to make sure everything is open when you want to go. While you're at it, confirm the Changing of the Guard schedule.

Tours: As you enter, you'll pick up the dry, reverent, but informative audioguide, which covers both the grounds and interiors. For a good overview—and an opportunity to ask questions—consider the free 30-minute guided walks around the grounds (usually 2/hour, schedule posted next to audioguide desk). The official £5 guidebook is full of gorgeous images and makes a fine souvenir, but the information within is already covered by the audioguide and tour.

Information: Tel. 020/7766-7304, www.royalcollection .org.uk.

Changing of the Guard: The Changing of the Guard takes place Monday through Saturday at 11:00 (April-July) and on alternating days the rest of the year (check website to confirm schedule;

get there by 10:30, or earlier if you expect a line for tickets). There is no Changing of the Guard on Sundays or in very wet weather. The fresh guards, led by a marching band, leave their barracks on Sheet Street and march up High Street, hanging a right at Victoria, then a left into the castle's Lower Ward, arriving at about 11:00.

WINDSOR

The Order of the Garter

In addition to being the royal residence, Windsor is the home of the Most Noble Order of the Garter—Britain's most prestigious chivalrous order. The castle's history is inexorably tied to this order.

Founded in 1348 by King Edward III and his son (the "Black Prince"), the Order of the Garter was designed to honor returning Crusaders. This was a time when the legends of King Arthur and the Knights of the Round Table were sweeping England, and Edward III fantasized that Windsor could be a real-life Camelot. (He even built the Round Tower as an homage to the Round Table.)

The order's seal illustrates the story of the order's founding and unusual name: a cross of St. George encircled with a belt and a French motto loosely translated as "Shame be upon he who thinks evil of it." Supposedly while the king was dancing with a fair maiden, her garter slipped off onto the floor; in an act of great chivalry, he rescued her from embarrassment by picking it up and uttering those words.

The Order of the Garter continues to the present day as the single most prestigious honor in the United Kingdom. There can be only 24 knights at one time, plus the sitting monarch and the Prince of Wales (perfect numbers for splitting into two 12-man jousting teams). Aside from royals and the nobility, past Knights of the Garter have included Winston Churchill, Bernard "Monty" Montgomery, and Ethiopian Emperor Haile Selassie. In 2008, Prince William became only the 1,000th knight in the order's 660-year history.

The patron of the order is St. George, the namesake of the State Apartments' most sumptuous hall and of the castle's own chapel. Both of these spaces—the grandest in all of Windsor—are designed to celebrate and honor the Order of the Garter.

After about a half-hour, the tired guards march back the way they came. To watch the actual ceremony inside the castle, you'll need to have already bought your ticket, entered the grounds, and staked out a spot. Alternatively, you could wait for them to march by on High Street or on the lower half of Castle Hill.

Evensong: An evensong takes place in the chapel nightly at 17:15 (free for worshippers, line up at exit gate to be admitted).

Best View: While you can get great views of the castle from any direction, the classic views are from the long, wooded walkway called the Long Walk, which stretches south of the palace and is open to the public.

Eating: There are a few shops scattered around the premises, but none sell real food (unless you count gifty boxes of chocolates)—though bottles of water are available. If you'll want a snack during your long castle visit, plan ahead and pack one in from outside.

◑ Self-Guided Tour: After buying your ticket and going through the tight security checkpoint, head into the castle grounds to pick up your audioguide.

The Grounds: Turn right and head up the hill, enjoying the first of many fine castle views you'll see today. The tower-topped, conical hill on your left represents the historical core of the castle. William the Conqueror built this motte (artificial mound) and bailey (fortified stockade around it) in 1080—his first castle in England. Among the later monarchs who spiffed up Windsor were Edward III (flush with French war booty, he made it a palace fit for a 14th-century king), Charles II (determined to restore the monarchy properly in the 1660s), and George IV (Britain's "Bling King," who financed many such vanity projects in the 1820s). On your right, the circular bandstand platform has a seal of the Order of the Garter, which has important ties to Windsor (see sidebar).

Passing through the small gate, you approach the stately St. George's Gate. Peek through here to the Upper Ward's **Quadrangle,** surrounded by the State Apartments (across the field) and the Queen's private apartments (to the right).

Turn left and follow the wall. On your right-hand side, you enjoy great views of the **Round Tower** atop that original motte; running around the base of this artificial hill is the delightful, peaceful gar-
den of the castle governor. The unusual
design of this castle has not one "bailey"
(castle yard), but three, which today
make up Windsor's Upper Ward (where
the Queen lives, which we just saw),
Middle Ward (the ecclesiastical heart of
the complex, with St. George's Chapel,
which you'll soon pass on the left),
and Lower Ward (residences for castle
workers).

Continue all the way around
this mini-moat to the **Norman Gate,** which once held a prison. Walking under the gate, look up to see the bottom of the portcullis that could be dropped to seal off the inner courtyard. Three big holes are strategically situated to dump boiling goo or worse on whoever was being kept outside the gate. Past the gate are even finer views of the Quadrangle we just saw from the other side.

Do a 180 and head back toward the Norman Gate, but before you reach it, go down the staircase on the right. You'll emerge onto a fine **terrace** overlooking the flat lands all around. It's easy to understand why this was a strategic place to build a castle. That's Eton College across the Thames. Imagine how handy it's been for royals to be able to ship off their teenagers to an elite prep school so close that they could easily keep an eye on them...literally. The power-plant cooling towers in the distance mark the workaday burg of Slough (rhymes with "plow," immortalized as the setting for Britain's original version of *The Office*).

Turn right and wander along the terrace. You'll likely see two lines: one long and one short. The long line leads to Queen Mary's Dolls' House, then to the State Apartments. The short line skips the dollhouse and lets you proceed directly to the apartments. While the State Apartments are certainly worth seeing, the Dolls' House may not be worth a long wait; read the following descriptions and decide (or return at the end of your castle visit; the dollhouse line tends to ease up at the end of the day). You can see the Drawings Gallery and the China Museum either way.

Queen Mary's Dolls' House: This palace in miniature (1:12 scale, from 1924) is "the most famous dollhouse in the world." It was a gift for Queen Mary (the wife of King George V, and the current Queen's grandmother), who greatly enjoyed miniatures, when she was already a fully grown adult. It's basically one big, dimly lit room with the large dollhouse in the middle, executed with an astonishing level of detail. Each fork, knife, and spoon on the expertly set banquet table is perfect and made of real silver—and the tiny pipes of its plumbing system actually have running water. But you're kept a few feet away by a glass wall, and are constantly jostled by fellow sightseers in this crowded space, making it difficult to fully appreciate. Unless you're a dollhouse devotee, it's probably not worth waiting a half hour for a five-minute peek at this, but if the line is short it's definitely worth a look.

Drawings Gallery and China Museum: Positioned at the exit of the Dolls' House, this collects a changing array of pieces from the Queen's collection—usually including some big names, such as Michelangelo and Leonardo. The China Museum features items from the Queen's many exquisite settings for royal shindigs.

State Apartments: Dripping with chandeliers, finely furnished, and strewn with history and the art of a long line of kings and queens, they're the best I've seen in Britain. This is where the

Queen wows visiting dignitaries. The apartments are even more remarkable considering that many of these grand halls were badly damaged in a fire on November 20, 1992. They've been immaculately restored since. Take advantage of the talkative docents in each room, who are happy to answer your questions.

You'll climb the Grand Staircase up to the **Grand Vestibule,** decorated with exotic items seized by British troops during their missions to colonize various corners of the world. The **Waterloo Chamber** memorializes Wellington and others (from military officers to heads of state to Pope Pius VII) who worked together to defeat Napoleon. You'll pass through various bedchambers, dressing rooms, and drawing rooms of the king and queen (who traditionally maintained separate quarters). Many rooms are decorated with fine canvases by some of Europe's top artists, including Rubens, Van Dyck, and Holbein. Finally you emerge into **St. George's Hall,** decorated with emblems representing the knights of the prestigious Order of the Garter (see sidebar, earlier). This is the site of some of the most elaborate royal banquets—imagine one long table stretching from one end of the hall to the other, seating 160 VIPs. From here, you'll proceed into the rooms that were the most damaged by the 1992 fire, including the "Semi-State Apartments." The **Garter Throne Room** is where new members of the Order of the Garter are invested (ceremonially granted their titles).

Now head down to the opposite end of the terrace, and hook left back into the Middle Ward. From here, you're just above the chapel, with its buttresses; the entrance is about two-thirds of the way down.

St. George's Chapel: Housing numerous royal tombs, this chapel is an exquisite example of Perpendicular Gothic (dating

from about 1500), with classic fan-vaulting spreading out from each pillar and with nearly every joint capped with an elaborate and colorful roof boss. Most of these emblems are associated with the Knights of the Garter, which considers St. George's their "mother church." Under the upper stained-glass windows, notice the continuous frieze of 250 angels, lovingly carved with great detail, ringing the church.

In the corner, take in the melodramatic monument to the popular Princess Charlotte, the only child of King George IV. Heir to the throne, her death in 1817 (at 21, in childbirth) devastated the nation. Farther along, find the simple chapel containing the tombs of the current Queen's parents, King George VI and "Queen Mum" Elizabeth; the ashes of her younger sister, Princess

Margaret, are also kept here (see the marble slab against the wall).

Stepping into the choir area, you're immediately aware that you are in the inner sanctum of the Order of the Garter. The banners lining the nave represent the knights, as do the fancy helmets and half-drawn swords at the top of each wood-carved seat. These symbols honor only living knights; on the seats are some 800 golden panels memorializing departed knights. As you walk up the aisle, notice the marker in the floor: You're walking over the burial site of King Henry VIII and his favorite wife, Jane Seymour (perhaps because she was the only one who died before he could behead her). The body of King Charles I, who was beheaded by Oliver Cromwell's forces at the Banqueting House (see page 98), was also discovered here...with its head sewn back on.

On your way out, you can pause at the door of the sumptuous 13th-century **Albert Memorial Chapel,** redecorated in 1861 after the death of Prince Albert (Queen Victoria's husband) and dedicated to his memory.

Lower Ward: You'll exit the chapel into the castle's Lower Ward. This area is a living town where some 160 people who work for the Queen reside; they include clergy, military, and castle administrators. Just below the chapel, you may be able to enter a tranquil little horseshoe-shaped courtyard ringed with residential doorways—all of them with a spectacular view of the chapels' grand entrance.

Back out in the yard, look for the guard posted at his pillbox. Like those at Buckingham Palace, he's been trained to be a ruthless killing machine...just so he can wind up as somebody's photo op. Click!

More Sights in Windsor
Legoland Windsor

Paradise for Legomaniacs under 12, this huge, kid-pleasing park has dozens of tame but fun rides (often with very long lines) scattered throughout its 150 acres. The impressive Miniland has 40 million Lego pieces glued together to create 800 tiny buildings and a minitour of Europe; the Creation Centre boasts an 80 percent scale-model Boeing 747 cockpit, made of two million bricks. Several of the more exciting rides involve getting wet, so dress accordingly or buy a cheap disposable poncho in the gift shop. While you may be tempted to hop on the Hill Train at the entrance, it's faster and more convenient to walk down into the park. Food is available in

WINDSOR

the park, but you can save money by bringing a picnic.

Cost: Adults-£46, children-£37, about 10 percent cheaper if you book online or buy tickets at Windsor TI, free for ages 3 and under; optional Q-Bot ride-reservation gadget allows you to bypass lines (£15-70 depending on when you go and how much time you want to save); coin lockers-£1.

Hours: Convoluted schedule, but generally mid-March-late July and Sept-Oct Mon-Fri 10:00-17:00, Sat-Sun 10:00-18:00, often closed Tue-Wed; late July-Aug daily 10:00-19:00; closed Nov-mid-March. Call or check website for exact schedule, tel. 0871-222-2001, www.legoland.co.uk.

Getting There: A £4.80 round-trip shuttle bus runs from opposite Windsor's Theatre Royal on Thames Street, and from the Parish Church stop on High Street (2/hour). If day-tripping from London, ask about rail/shuttle/park admission deals from Paddington or Waterloo train stations. For drivers, the park is on B-3022 Windsor/Ascot road, two miles southwest of Windsor and 25 miles west of London. Legoland is clearly signposted from the M-3, M-4, and M-25 motorways. Parking is easy (£3).

Eton College

Across the bridge from Windsor Castle you'll find many post-castle tourists filing toward the most famous "public" (the equivalent of our "private") high school in Britain. Eton was founded in 1440 by King Henry VI; today it educates about 1,300 boys (ages 13-18), who live on campus. Eton has molded the characters of 19 prime ministers as well as members of the royal family, most recently princes William and Harry. The college is sparse on sights, but the public is allowed (via guided tour) into the school-yard, chapel, cloisters, and the Museum of Eton Life.

Cost and Hours: £7.50, access only by one-hour guided tour at 14:00 and 15:15; tours available late March-Sept, usually Wed and Fri-Sun but daily during spring and summer holiday; closed Oct-late March and about once a month for special events—call ahead; no photos in chapel, no food or drink allowed; tel. 01753/671-177, www.etoncollege.com.

Eton High Street

Even if you're not touring the college, it's worth the few minutes it takes to cross the pedestrian bridge and wander straight up Eton's High Street. A bit more cutesy and authentic-feeling than Windsor (which is given over to shopping malls and chain stores), Eton has a charm that's fun to sample.

Windsor and Royal Borough Museum

Tucked into a small space beneath the Guildhall (where Prince Charles remarried), this little museum does its best to give some insight into the history of Windsor and the surrounding area. They also have lots of special activities for kids. Ask at the desk if tours are running to the Guildhall itself (visits are only possible with a guide); if not, it's probably not worth the admission.

Cost and Hours: £3, includes audioguide, Tue-Sat 10:00-16:00, Sun 12:00-16:00, closed Mon, located in the Guildhall on High Street, tel. 01628/685-686, www.rbwm.gov.uk.

Boat Trips
Cruise up and down the Thames River for classic views of the castle, the village of Eton, Eton College, and the Royal Windsor Racecourse. Choose from a 40-minute or two-hour tour, then relax onboard and nibble a picnic. Boats leave from the riverside promenade adjacent to Barry Avenue.

Cost and Hours: 40-minute tour—£5.70, family pass from £14.25, mid-Feb-Oct 1-2/hour daily 10:00-17:00, Nov hourly Sat-Sun 10:00-16:00; 2-hour tour—£9, family pass from £22.50, late March-Oct only, 1-2/day; closed Dec-mid-Feb; tel. 01753/851-900, www.boat-trips.co.uk.

Horse Racing
The horses race near Windsor every Monday at the Royal Windsor Racecourse (£12-25 entry, online discounts, those under 18 free with an adult, April-Aug and Oct, no races in Sept, sporadic in Aug, off A-308 between Windsor and Maidenhead, tel. 01753/498-400, www.windsor-racecourse.co.uk). The romantic way to get there from Windsor is by a 10-minute shuttle boat (£6 round-trip, www.frenchbrothers.co.uk). The famous Ascot Racecourse (described below) is also nearby.

Near Windsor
Ascot Racecourse
Located seven miles southwest of Windsor and just north of the town of Ascot, this royally owned track is one of the most famous horse-racing venues in the world. The horses first ran here in 1711, and the course is best known for June's five-day Royal Ascot race meeting, attended by the Queen and 299,999 of her loyal subjects. For many, the outlandish hats worn on Ladies Day (Thu) are more interesting than the horses. Royal Ascot is usually the third week in June (June 17-21 in 2014, June 16-20 in 2015). The pricey tickets go on sale the preceding November; while the Friday and Saturday races tend to sell out far ahead, tickets for the other days are often available close to the date (see website). In addition to Royal Ascot, the racecourse runs the ponies year-round—funny hats strictly optional.

Cost: Regular tickets generally £18-30—some may be available at a discount from the TI, Royal Ascot £12-75, online discounts, kids ages 17 and under free; parking £6-8, more for special races; dress code enforced in some areas and on certain days, tel. 0870-722-7227, www.ascot.co.uk.

Sleeping in Windsor

(area code: 01753)

Most visitors stay in London and do Windsor as a day trip. But here are a few suggestions for those staying the night.

$$$ Mercure Windsor Castle Hotel, with 108 business-class rooms and elegant public spaces, is as central as can be, just down the street from Her Majesty's weekend retreat (official rates: Db-£129-169, breakfast-£17; but you'll likely pay around Db-£150 on weekdays and £140 on weekends including breakfast; £30-40 extra for fancy four-poster beds, nonrefundable online deals, air-con, free Wi-Fi, free parking, 18 High Street, tel. 01753/851-577, www.mercure.com, h6618@accor.com).

$$ Langton House B&B is a stately Victorian home with five spacious, well-appointed rooms lovingly maintained by Paul and Sonja Fogg (S-£73, Sb-£83, D/Db-£103, huge four-poster Db-£113, Tb-£139, Qb-£155, 5 percent extra if paying by credit card, prices can be soft—especially off-season, family-friendly, guest kitchen, free guest computer, free Wi-Fi, 46 Alma Road, tel. 01753/858-299, www.langtonhouse.co.uk, paul@langtonhouse .co.uk).

$$ Park Farm B&B, bright and cheery, is most convenient for drivers. But even if you're not driving, this beautiful place is such a good value, and the welcome is so warm, that you're unlikely to mind the bus ride into town (Sb-£65, Db-£85, Tb-£105, Qb-£120, ask about family room with bunk beds, cash only—credit card solely for reservations, free Wi-Fi, access to shared fridge and microwave, free off-street parking, 1 mile from Legoland on St.

Sleep Code

(£1 = about $1.60, country code: 44)

S = Single, **D** = Double/Twin, **T** = Triple, **Q** = Quad, **b** = bathroom, **s** = shower only. Unless otherwise noted, credit cards are accepted and breakfast is included.

To help you sort through these listings easily, I've divided the rooms into three categories based on the price for a standard double room with bath:

$$$ Higher Priced—Most rooms £100 or more.
$$ Moderately Priced—Most rooms between £60-100.
$ Lower Priced—Most rooms £60 or less.

Prices can change without notice; verify the hotel's current rates online or by email. For the best prices, always book direct.

Leonards Road near Imperial Road, 5-minute bus ride or 1-mile walk to castle, £5 taxi ride from station, tel. 01753/866-823, www .parkfarm.com, stay@parkfarm.com, Caroline and Drew Youds).

$$ Dee and Steve's B&B is a friendly four-room place above a window shop on a quiet residential street about a 10-minute walk from the castle and station. The rooms are cozy, Dee and Steve are pleasant hosts, and breakfast is served in the contemporary kitchen/lounge (S-£40, Sb-£55-60, Db-£75, free Wi-Fi, 169 Oxford Road, tel. 01753/854-489, www.deeandsteve.com, dee @deeandsteve.com).

$$ 76 Duke Street has two nice rooms, but only hosts one set of guests at a time. While the bathroom is (just) outside your bedroom, you have it to yourself (Db-£80, £5 more for one-night stay, free Wi-Fi, 15-minute walk from station at—you guessed it—76 Duke Street, tel. 01753/620-636, www.76dukestreet.co.uk, bandb@76dukestreet.co.uk, Julia).

$ Crown and Cushion is a good budget option on Eton's High Street, just across the pedestrian bridge from Windsor's waterfront (a short uphill walk to the castle). While the pub it's situated over is worn and drab, you're right in the heart of charming Eton, and the eight creaky rooms—with uneven floors and old-beam ceilings—are nicely furnished (S-£45, Db-£59, Tb-£79, free Wi-Fi, free parking, 84 High Street in Eton, tel. 01753/641-494, info@crownandcushioneton.com, www.crownandcushion eton.co.uk).

Eating in Windsor

Elegant Spots with River Views

Several places flank Windsor Bridge, offering romantic dining after dark. The riverside promenade, with cheap take-away stands scattered about, is a delightful place for a picnic lunch or dinner with the swans. If you don't see anything that appeals, continue up Eton's High Street, which is also lined with characteristic eateries.

In the Tourist Zone Around the Palace

Strolling the streets and lanes around the palace entrance—especially in the shopping zone near Windsor & Eton Station—you'll find countless trendy and inviting eateries. The central area also has a sampling of dependable British chains (including a Wagamama, Gourmet Burger Kitchen, Thai Square, and Nando's). Residents enjoy a wide selection of unpretentious little eateries (including a fire station turned pub-and-cultural center) just past the end of pedestrian Peascod Street.

Bel & The Dragon is the place to splurge on high-quality, classic British food in a charming half-timbered building with an upscale-rustic dining space (£16-25 mains, food served Mon-Fri 12:00-15:00 & 18:00-22:00, Sat-Sun 10:30-15:00 & 18:00-22:00, afternoon tea served between lunch and dinner, also serves basic pub grub, bar open longer hours, on Thames Street near the bridge to Eton, tel. 01753/866-056).

Cornucopia Bistro, with a cozy, woody atmosphere, serves tasty international dishes (£12 two-course meals available after 19:00 except on Fri-Sat, £12-15 main courses, daily 12:00-14:30 & 18:00-21:30, Fri-Sat until 22:00, closed Sun night, 6 High Street, tel. 01753/833-009).

The Duchess of Cambridge's friendly staff serves up the normal grub in a pub that's right across from the castle walls, and with an open fireplace to boot (£9-12 meals, daily 9:30-22:30 or later, 3-4 Thames Street, tel. 01753/864-405). While the pub predates Kate, it was named in her honor following a recent remodel, and has the photos to prove her endorsement.

The Crooked House is a touristy 17th-century timber-framed teahouse, serving fresh, hearty £8-10 lunches and £8.50 cream teas in a tipsy interior or outdoors on its cobbled lane (daily 10:30-18:00, Wed-Sat until 22:00, in winter daily 11:00-17:00, 51 High Street, tel. 01753/857-534).

Meimo offers "Moroccan/Mediterranean" cuisine in a nicely subdued dining room (£9-14 main dishes, several fixed-price meal options, daily 10:00-22:00, 69-70 Peascod Street, tel. 01753/862-222).

Saffron Restaurant, while a fairly long walk from the castle, is the local choice for South Indian cuisine, with a modern interior and attentive waiters who struggle with English but are fluent at bringing out tasty dishes. Their vegetarian *thali* is a treat (£8-12 dishes, daily 12:00-14:30 & 17:30-23:30, 99 St. Leonards Road, tel. 01753/855-467).

Cambridge

Cambridge, 60 miles north of London, is world-famous for its prestigious university. Wordsworth, Isaac Newton, Tennyson, Darwin, and Prince Charles are a few of its illustrious alumni. The university dominates—and owns—most of Cambridge, a historic town of 100,000 people. Cambridge is the epitome of a university town, with busy bikers, stately residence halls, plenty of bookshops, and proud locals who can point out where DNA was originally modeled, the atom first split, and electrons discovered.

In medieval Europe, higher education was the domain of the Church and was limited to ecclesiastical schools. Scholars lived

Visiting Highclere Castle

If you're a fan of *Downton Abbey*, consider a day trip from London to Highclere Castle, the stately house where much of the show is filmed. Though the hugely popular TV series is set in Yorkshire, the actual house is located in Hampshire, about an hour's train ride west of London. Highclere has been home to the Earls of Carnarvon since 1679 (and the current residents enjoy watching the TV show), but the present, Jacobean-style house was rebuilt in the 1840s by Sir Charles Berry, who also designed London's Houses of Parliament. Noted landscape architect Capability Brown laid out the traditional gardens in the mid-18th century. The castle's Egyptian exhibit features artifacts collected by Highclere's fifth Earl, George Herbert, a keen amateur archaeologist. When Howard Carter discovered King Tut's tomb in 1922, he waited three weeks for his friend and patron Herbert to join him before looking inside. The Earl died unexpectedly a few months later, giving birth to the legend of a "mummy's curse."

Cost and Hours: Entrance is by timed-entry ticket, best bought in advance online (although last-minute afternoon-entry tickets sometimes available—call ahead); £18 for castle, garden, and Egyptian exhibit; £11 for castle and garden only, or Egyptian exhibit and garden only; garden only-£5; July-mid-Sept Sun-Thu 10:30-17:00, closed Fri-Sat and mid-Sept-June except open sporadically April-early June, last entry at 15:30; tickets available online several months ahead—sales begin as early as Feb for following summer; no photos inside, 24-hour info tel. 01635/253-204, www.highclerecastle.co.uk.

Getting There: Highclere is six miles south of Newbury, about 70 miles west of London, off A-34.

By Train and Taxi: First Great Western trains run from London's Paddington Station to Newbury (1-2/hour, 50-70 minutes, £22-50 same-day return, tel. 0845-748-4950, from North America call 011-44-20-7278-5240). From Newbury train station, you'll have to take a taxi (£15-22 one-way, higher price is for Sun, taxis wait outside station or call 01635/33333) or reserve a car and driver (must arrange in advance, £12.50/person round-trip; £25 minimum, WebAir, tel. 07818/430-095, mapeng@msn.com).

By Tour: Brit Movie Tours offer an all-day bus tour of *Downton Abbey* filming locations, including Highclere Castle and the fictional village of Downton (sells out early, £85, includes transport and castle/garden entry, £5 extra for Egyptian exhibit, 9 hours, depart London from outside Gloucester Road Tube Station, reservations required, tel. 0844-247-1007 or 020/7118-1007, http://britmovietours.com).

in "halls" on campus. This academic community of residential halls, chapels, and lecture halls connected by peaceful garden courtyards survives today in the colleges that make up the universities of Cambridge and Oxford. By 1350 (Oxford is roughly 100 years older), Cambridge had eight colleges, each with a monastic-type courtyard, chapel, library, and lodgings. Today, Cambridge has 31 colleges, each with its own facilities. In the town center, these grand old halls date back centuries, with ornately decorated facades that try to one-up each other. While students' lives revolve around their independent colleges, the university organizes lectures, presents degrees, and promotes research.

The university schedule has three terms: Lent term from mid-January to mid-March, Easter term from mid-April to mid-June, and Michaelmas term from early October to early December. During exam time (roughly the month of May), the colleges are closed to visitors, which can impede access to all the picturesque little corners of the town. But the main sights—King's College Chapel and Trinity Library—stay open, and Cambridge is never sleepy.

Planning Your Time

Cambridge is worth most of a day. Start by taking the TI's walking tour, which includes a visit to the town's only must-see sight, the King's College Chapel (first tour at 11:00, later on Sun, call ahead to confirm and reserve—see "Tours in Cambridge," later). Spend the afternoon touring the Fitzwilliam Museum (closed Mon), or simply enjoying the ambience of this stately old college town.

Getting to Cambridge

By Train: It's an easy trip from London and less than an hour away. Catch the train from London's King's Cross Station (2/hour, trains leave King's Cross at :15 and :45 past the hour, 45 minutes, £22 one-way standard class, £23 same-day return after 9:30, operated by First Capital Connect, tel. 0845-748-4950, www.firstcapital connect.co.uk or www.nationalrail.co.uk). Direct trains also run from London's Liverpool Street Station, but take longer (2/hour, 1.25 hours).

By Bus: National Express coaches run from London's Victoria Coach Station to the Parkside stop in Cambridge (every 60-90 minutes, 2-2.5 hours, £11.60, £6 advance fares sometimes available online, tel. 0871-781-8178, www.nationalexpress.co.uk).

Orientation to Cambridge

Cambridge is congested but small. Everything is within a pleasant walk. There are two main streets, separated from the Cam River by the most interesting colleges. The town center, brimming with tearooms, has a TI and a colorful open-air market square. The train station is about a mile to the southeast.

Tourist Information

Cambridge's TI is well run and well signposted, just off Market Square in the town center. They book rooms for £5, offer walking tours (see "Tours in Cambridge," later), and sell bus tickets and a £1.50 map/guide (Mon-Sat 10:00-17:00, Easter-Sept also Sun 11:00-15:00—otherwise closed Sun, phones answered from 9:00, Peas Hill, tel. 0871-226-8006, room-booking tel. 01223/457-581, www.visitcambridge.org). In the same building as the TI, you can duck into a former courtroom to catch a free video overview of the town and its history.

Arrival in Cambridge

By Train: Cambridge's train station doesn't have baggage storage, but you can pay to leave your bags at the nearby bike-rental shop (see "Helpful Hints," later). The station does not have a TI, but it does offer free maps and other brochures on an interior wall just before the turnstiles.

To get from the station to downtown Cambridge, you can **walk** for about 25 minutes (exit straight ahead on Station Road, bear right at the war memorial onto Hills Road, and follow it into town); take public **bus** #1, #3, #7, or #8 (buses are referred to as "Citi 1," "Citi 3," and so on in print and online, but only the number is marked on the bus; £1.50, pay driver, runs every 5-10 minutes, turn left when exiting station to find bus stop, get off at Emmanuel Street stop—look for Grand Arcade shopping mall on the left); pay about £6 for a **taxi;** or ride a City Sightseeing **bus tour** (described later).

By Car: To park in the middle of town, follow signs from the M-11 motorway to any of the handy and central short-stay parking lots. Or you can leave the car at one of five park-and-ride lots outside the city, then take the shuttle into town (free parking, shuttle costs £2.50 round-trip if you buy ticket from machine, or £2.80 from driver).

Helpful Hints

Festival: The **Cambridge Folk Festival** gets things humming and strumming in late July (tickets go on sale several months

Cambridge

Note: Many roads are pedestrian or restricted

200 Meters
200 Yards

1. Hotel du Vin
2. Lensfield Hotel
3. The Eagle Pub
4. Michaelhouse Café
5. Café Carringtons
6. Marks & Spencer
7. Sainsbury's
8. Trinity Punt
9. Scudamore's Punts (2)
10. Bus from Train Station
11. Bus to Train Station

CAMBRIDGE

ahead and often sell out quickly; www.cambridgefolkfestival
.co.uk).

Bike Rental: Station Cycles, located about a block to your
right as you exit the station, rents bikes (£7/4 hours, £10/
day, helmets-£1, £60 deposit, cash or credit card) and stores
luggage (£3-4/bag depending on size; Mon-Fri 8:00-18:00,
Wed until 19:00, Sat 9:00-17:00, Sun 10:00-17:00, tel.
01223/307-125, www.stationcycles.co.uk). A second location
is near the center of town (inside the Grand Arcade shopping
mall, same hours, tel. 01223/307-655).

Tours in Cambridge

▲▲Walking Tour of the Colleges

A walking tour is the best way to understand Cambridge's mix of
"town and gown." The walks can be more educational (read: dry)
than entertaining. But they do provide a good rundown of the historic and scenic highlights of the university, some fun local gossip,
and plenty of university trivia. For example, why are entering students called "undergraduates"? Because long ago, new students at
Cambridge were assigned to a mentor who already had a degree...
so they were "under" the supervision of a "graduate."

The TI offers **daily walking tours** that include the King's
College Chapel, as well as another college—usually Queen's
College (£17.50, 2 hours, includes admission fees; July-Aug daily
at 11:00, 12:00, 13:00, and 14:00, no 11:00 tour on Sun; Sept-June
Mon-Sat at 11:00, 13:00, Sun only at 13:00; tel. 01223/457-574,
www.visitcambridge.org). It's smart to call ahead to reserve a spot
(they'll take your credit-card number), or you can drop by in person
(try to arrive 30 minutes before the tour). Notice that the 12:00 tour
overlaps with the limited opening times of the Wren Library—so
you'll miss out on the library if you take the noon tour.

Private guides are available through the TI (basic 1-hour
tour-£4.25/person, £64 minimum; 1.5-hour tour-£4.75/person,
£72 minimum; 2-hour tour-£5.25/person, £79 minimum; does not
include individual college entrance fees, tel. 01223/457-574, tours
@cambridge.gov.uk).

Walking and Punting Ghost Tour

If you're in Cambridge on the weekend, consider a £6 ghost-walk
to where spooky sightings have been reported, Friday evenings
at 18:00, or a creepy £18.50 trip on the River Cam followed by a
walk, most Saturdays at dusk (20:00 in summer; book ahead for
either tour, organized by the TI, tel. 01223/457-574).

Bus Tours

City Sightseeing hop-on, hop-off bus tours are informative and
cover the outskirts, including the American WWII Cemetery. But

keep in mind that buses can't go where walking tours can—right into the center (£14, 80 minutes for full 20-stop circuit, buy ticket with credit card at the bus-stop kiosk—or pay cash to driver when you board, departs every 20 minutes in summer, every 40 minutes in winter, first bus leaves train station at 10:06, last bus around 17:30, recorded commentary, tel. 01223/423-250, www.city-sight seeing.com). If arriving by train, you can buy your ticket from the kiosk directly in front of the station, then ride the bus into town.

Sights in Cambridge

Cambridge has many impressive old college buildings to explore, with fancy facades and tranquil grassy courtyards. I've featured the two most interesting (King's and Trinity), but feel free to wander beyond these. You might notice several bricked-up windows on the old buildings around town. This practice dates from a time when taxes were calculated per window...so filling them in saved money.

▲King's Parade and Nearby

The lively street in front of King's College, called King's Parade, seems to be where everyone in Cambridge gathers. Looming

across the street from the college is **Great St. Mary's Church,** with a climbable bell tower (£3.50, Mon-Sat 9:30-16:30, Sun 12:30-16:00, 123 stairs). On the street out front, students hawk punting tours on the Cam River (see "Punting on the Cam," later).

Behind the church is the thriving **Market Hill Square.** The big market is on Sunday (9:30-16:30) and features produce, arts, and crafts. On other days, you'll find mostly clothes and food (Mon-Sat roughly 9:30-16:00).

The imposing Neoclassical building at the top (north) end of King's Parade is the **Senate House,** the meeting place of the university's governing body. In June, you might notice green boxes lining the front of this house. Traditionally, at the end of the term students would come to these boxes to see whether or not they'd earned their degree; if a name was not on the list, the student had flunked. Amazingly, until 2010 this was the only notification students received about their status. (Now they also get an email.)

In the opposite direction (south), at Benet Street, look for the strikingly modern **Corpus Clock.** Designed and commissioned by alum John Taylor, the clock was ceremonially unveiled by Stephen Hawking in 2008. It uses concentric golden dials with blue LED lights to tell the time, but it's precise only every five minutes; its otherwise-irregular timekeeping mimics the unpredictability of life. Perched on top is Chronophage, the "eater of time"—a grotesque giant grasshopper that keeps the clock moving and periodically winks at passersby. Creepy and disturbing? Exactly, says Taylor...so is the passage of time.

Just down Benet Street on the left is the recommended **Eagle Pub**—Cambridge's oldest pub and a sight in itself; it's worth poking into the courtyard to learn about its dynamic history, even if you don't eat or drink here. Across the street from the pub stands the oldest surviving building in Cambridgeshire, **St. Benet's Church.** The Saxons who built the church included circular holes in its bell tower, to encourage owls to roost there and keep the mouse population under control.

▲▲King's College Chapel

Built from 1446 to 1515 by Henrys VI through VIII, England's best example of Perpendicular Gothic architecture is the single most impressive building in town.

Cost and Hours: £7.50, erratic hours depending on school schedule and events; during academic term usually Mon-Fri 9:30-15:30, Sat 9:30-15:15, Sun 13:15-14:30; during breaks (see page 261) usually daily 9:30-16:30; recorded info tel. 01223/331-1212, www.kings.cam.ac.uk/chapel.

Evensong: When school's in session, you're welcome to enjoy an evensong service in this glorious space, with a famous choir made up of men and boys (free, Mon-Sat at 17:30, Sun at 15:30; for more on evensong, see page 169).

Getting There: You'll see the regal front facade of King's College along King's Parade. To enter the chapel, curl around the back: Facing the college on King's Parade, head right and take the first left possible (just after the Senate House, on Senate House passage); at the end, bear left on Trinity Lane to reach the gate where you can pay to enter the chapel.

◆ **Self-Guided Tour:** Stand inside, look up, and marvel, as

Christopher Wren did, at what was then the largest single span of **vaulted roof** anywhere—2,000 tons of incredible fan vaulting, held in place by the force of gravity (a careful balancing act resting delicately on the buttresses visible outside the building).

While Henry VI—who began work on the chapel—wanted it to be austere, his descendants decided it should glorify the House of Tudor (of which his son, Henry VII, was the first king). Lining the walls are giant **Tudor coats-of-**

arms. The shield includes a fleur-de-lis because an earlier ancestor, Edward III, woke up one day and—citing his convoluted lineage—somewhat arbitrarily declared himself king of France. The symbols on the left (a rose and the red dragon of Wales, holding the shield) represent the Tudors, the family of Henry VII's father. On the right, the greyhound holding the shield and the portcullis (the iron grate) symbolize the family of Henry VII's mother, Lady Margaret Beaufort, who prodded her son for years to complete this chapel.

The 26 **stained-glass windows** date from the 16th century. It's the most Renaissance stained glass anywhere in one spot. (Most of

the stained glass in English churches dates from Victorian times, but this glass is much older.) The lower panes show scenes from the New Testament, while the upper panes feature corresponding stories from the Old Testament. Considering England's turbulent history, it's miraculous that these windows have survived for nearly half a millennium in such a pristine state. After Henry VIII separated from the Catholic Church in 1534, many such windows and other Catholic features around England were destroyed. (Think of all those ruined abbeys dotting the English countryside.) However, since Henry had just paid for these windows, he couldn't bear to get rid of them. A century later, in the days of Oliver Cromwell, another wave of iconoclasm destroyed more windows around England. Though these windows were slated for removal, they stayed put. (Historians speculate that Cromwell's troops, who were garrisoned in this building, didn't want the windows removed in the chilly wintertime.) Finally, during World War II, the windows were taken out and hidden away to keep them safe, and then painstakingly replaced after the war ended.

The **choir screen** that bisects the church was commissioned by King Henry VIII to commemorate his marriage to Anne Boleyn. By the time it was finished, so was she (beheaded). But it was too late to remove her initials, which were carved into the screen (look on the far left for *R.A.*, for *Regina Anna*—"Queen Anne").

Behind the screen is the **choir** area, where the King's College

Choir performs a daily evensong. On Christmas Eve, a special service is held here and broadcast around the world on the BBC—a tradition near and dear to British hearts.

Walk to the altar and admire Rubens' masterful *Adoration of the Magi* (1634). It's actually a family portrait: The admirer in the front (wearing red) is a self-portrait of Rubens, Mary looks an awful lot like his much-younger wife, and the Baby Jesus resembles their own newborn at the time.

Finally, pop through the door to the left of the altar to find an exhibit with a basic history of the chapel, a nice model showing how the fan vaults were constructed, and an explanation of how the chapel has managed to hang together after all these years.

▲▲Trinity College and Wren Library

More than a third of Cambridge's 83 Nobel Prize winners have come from this richest and biggest of the town's colleges, founded in 1546 by Henry VIII. The college has three sights to see: the entrance gate, the grounds, and the magnificent Wren Library.

Cost and Hours: Grounds—£3, often free off-season, daily 10:00-16:30, last entry 45 minutes before closing; library—free, Mon-Fri 12:00-14:00, Nov-mid-June also Sat 10:30-12:30, closed Sun year-round; only small groups allowed in at a time, tel. 01223/338-400, www.trin.cam.ac.uk.

To see the Wren Library without paying for the grounds, access it from the riverside entrance: Head toward the Garret Hostel Bridge, and, if the gate's open, pass through the parking lot to your right immediately before the bridge. If the gate is not open, it's a long walk across the bridge and around the field to the path that leads back to the college.

Trinity Gate: You'll notice gates like these adorning facades of colleges around town. Above the door is a statue of **King Henry VIII,** who founded Trinity because he feared that Cambridge's existing colleges were too cozy with the Church. Notice Henry's right hand holding a chair leg instead of the traditional crown jewels scepter. This is courtesy of Cambridge's Night Climbers, who first replaced the scepter a century ago, and continue to periodically switch it out for other items. According to campus legend, decades ago some of the world's most talented mountaineers enrolled at Cambridge...in one of the flattest parts of England. (Cambridge was actually a seaport until Dutch engineers

drained the surrounding swamps.) Lacking opportunities to practice their skill, they began scaling the frilly facades of Cambridge's college buildings under cover of darkness (if caught, they'd have been expelled). In the 1960s, climbers actually managed to haul an entire automobile onto the roof of the Senate House. The university had to bring in the army to cut it into pieces and remove it. Only 50 years later, at a class reunion, did the guilty parties finally fess up.

In the little park to the right, notice the lone **apple tree.**

Supposedly, this tree is a descendant of the very one that once stood in the garden of Sir Isaac Newton (who spent 30 years at Trinity). According to legend, Newton was inspired to investigate gravity when an apple fell from the tree onto his head. This tree stopped bearing fruit long ago; if you do see apples, they've been tied on by mischievous students.

• *If you like, head through the gate into the...*

Trinity Grounds: The grounds are enjoyable to explore, if not quite worth the cost of admission. Inside the **Great Court,** the

clock (on the tower on the right) double-rings at the top of each hour. It's a college tradition to take off running from the clock when the high noon bells begin (it takes 43 seconds to clang 24 times), race around the courtyard, touching each of the four corners without setting foot on the cobbles, and try to return to the same spot by the time the ringing ends. Supposedly only one student (a young lord) ever managed the feat—a scene featured in *Chariots of Fire* (but filmed elsewhere).

The **chapel** (entrance to the right of the clock tower)—which pales in comparison to the stunning King's College Chapel—feels like a shrine to thinking, with statues honoring great Trinity minds both familiar (Isaac Newton, Alfred Lord Tennyson, Francis Bacon) and unfamiliar. Who's missing? The poet Lord Byron, who was such a hell-raiser during his time at Trinity that a statue of him was deemed unfit for Church property; his statue stands in the library instead.

Wren Library: Don't miss the 1695 Christopher Wren-designed library, with its wonderful carving and fascinating original manuscripts. Just outside the library entrance, Sir Isaac Newton clapped his hands and timed the echo to measure the speed of sound as it raced down the side of the cloister and back. In the library's 12 display cases (covered with cloth that you flip back), you'll see handwritten works by Sir Isaac Newton and John Milton, alongside A. A. Milne's original *Winnie the Pooh* (the real Christopher Robin attended Trinity College).

▲▲Fitzwilliam Museum

Britain's best museum of antiquities and art outside of London is the Fitzwilliam, housed in a grand Neoclassical building a 10-minute walk south of Market Square. The Fitzwilliam's broad collection is like a mini-British Museum/National Gallery rolled into one; you're bound to find something you like. Helpful docents—many with degrees or doctorates in art history—are more than willing to answer questions about the collection. The ground floor features an extensive range of antiquities and applied arts—everything from Greek vases, Mesopotamian artifacts, and Egyptian sarcophagi to Roman statues, fine porcelain, and suits of armor.

Upstairs is the painting gallery, with works that span art history: Italian Venetian masters (such as Titian and Canaletto), a worthy English section (featuring Gainsborough, Reynolds, Hogarth, and others), and a notable array of French Impressionist art (including Monet, Renoir, Pissarro, Degas, and Sisley). Rounding out the collection are old manuscripts, including some musical compositions from Handel. Watch your step—in 2006, a visitor tripped and accidentally smashed three 17th-century Chinese vases. Amazingly, the vases were restored (with donations from the community) and are now on display in Gallery 17...in a protective case.

Cost and Hours: Free, £5 donation suggested, Tue-Sat 10:00-17:00, Sun 12:00-17:00, closed Mon except bank holidays, no photos, Trumpington Street, tel. 01223/332-900, www.fitzmuseum.cam.ac.uk.

Museum of Classical Archaeology

Although this museum contains no originals, it offers a unique chance to study accurate copies (19th-century casts) of virtually every famous ancient Greek and Roman statue. More than 450 statues are on display. If you've seen the real things in Greece, Istanbul, Rome, and elsewhere, touring this collection is like a high school reunion..."Hey, I know you!" But since it takes some time to get here, this museum is best left to devotees of classical sculpture.

Cost and Hours: Free, Mon-Fri 10:00-17:00, Sat 10:00-13:00 during term, closed Sun, Sidgwick Avenue, tel. 01223/330-402, www.classics.cam.ac.uk/museum.

Getting There: The museum is a five-minute walk west of Silver Street Bridge; after crossing the bridge, continue straight until you reach a sign reading *Sidgwick Site*. The museum is in the long building on the corner to your right; the entrance is on the opposite side, and the museum is upstairs.

▲Punting on the Cam

For a little levity and probably more exercise than you really want, try hiring one of the traditional flat-bottom punts at the river and

pole yourself up and down (or around and around, more likely) the lazy Cam. Once you get the hang of it, it's a fine way to enjoy the scenic side of Cambridge. It's less crowded in late afternoon (and less embarrassing).

Several companies rent punts and offer tours. Hawkers try to snare passengers in the thriving people zone in front of King's College. Prices are soft in slow times—try talking them down a bit before committing.

Trinity Punt, just north of Garret Hostel Bridge, is run by Trinity College students (£14/hour, £40 deposit, 45-minute tours-£40/boat, can share ride and cost with up to 2 others, cash only, ask for quick and free lesson, Easter-mid-Oct Mon-Fri 11:00-17:30, Sat-Sun 10:00-17:30, return punts by 18:30, no rentals mid-Oct-Easter, tel. 01223/338-483).

Scudamore's has two locations: Mill Lane, just south of the central Silver Street Bridge, and the less convenient Quayside at Magdalene Bridge, at the north end of town (£16-20/hour, credit-card deposit required; 45-minute tours-£16/person, discount if you book at TI; open daily June-Aug 9:00-22:00 or later, Sept-May at least 10:00-17:00, weather permitting, tel. 01223/359-750).

Near Cambridge
Imperial War Museum Duxford

This former airfield, nine miles south of Cambridge, is nirvana for aviation fans and WWII buffs. Wander through seven exhibition halls housing 200 vintage aircraft (including Spitfires, B-17 Flying Fortresses, a Concorde, and a Blackbird) as well as military land vehicles and special displays on Normandy and the Battle of Britain. On many weekends, the museum holds special events, such as air shows (extra fee)—check the website for details.

Cost and Hours: £17.50 (includes small donation), show local bus ticket for discount, daily mid-March-late Oct 10:00-18:00, late Oct-mid-March 10:00-16:00, last entry one hour before closing; Concorde interior open until 17:00, 15:00 off-season; tel. 01223/835-000, http://duxford.iwm.org.uk.

Getting There: The museum is located off A-505 in Duxford. From Cambridge, take bus #7 from the train station (45 minutes) or from Emmanuel Street's Stop A (55 minutes, 2-3/hour daily, www.stagecoachbus.com).

CAMBRIDGE

Sleeping in Cambridge

(area code: 01223)

While Cambridge is an easy side-trip from London, its subtle charms might convince you to spend the night. Cambridge has very few accommodations in the city center, and none in the tight maze of colleges and shops where you'll spend most of your time. These recommendations are about a 10- to 15-minute walk south of the town center, toward the train station.

$$$ Hotel du Vin blends France, England, and wine. This worthwhile splurge has 41 comfortable, spacious rooms with all the amenities above a characteristic bistro that offers good deals for guests and non-guests alike. This mod place manages to be classy yet unpretentious (Db-£150-190, fancier suites available, check online for special offers, breakfast-£13-15, air-con, elevator, free Wi-Fi, just down the street from the Fitzwilliam Museum at Trumpington Street 15-18, tel. 01223/227-330 or 0844-736-4253, www.hotelduvin.com, reception.cambridge@hotelduvin.com).

$$$ Lensfield Hotel, popular with visiting professors, has 30 old-fashioned rooms (Sb-£72, Db-£110, Tb-£136, newer "deluxe" Db-£150, pricier suites available, free Wi-Fi, spa and fitness room, 53 Lensfield Road, tel. 01223/355-017, www.lensfieldhotel.co.uk, enquiries@lensfieldhotel.co.uk).

Eating in Cambridge

While picnicking is scenic and saves money, the weather may not always cooperate. Here are a few ideas for fortifying yourself with a lunch in central Cambridge.

The Eagle, near the TI, is the oldest pub in town, and a Cambridge institution with a history so rich that a visit here practically qualifies as sightseeing. Find your way into the delightful courtyard, with outdoor seating and a good look at the place's past. The second-floor windows once lit guest rooms, back when this was a coachman's inn as well as a pub. Notice that the window on the right end is open; any local will love to tell you why. Follow the signs into the misnamed "RAF Bar," where US Army Air Corps pilots signed the ceiling while stationed here during World War II. Science fans can celebrate the discovery of DNA—Francis Crick and James Watson first announced their findings here in 1953 (£5-8 lunches, £8-11 dinners, food served daily 10:00-22:00, drinks until 23:00, 8 Benet

Street, tel. 01223/505-020).

The **Michaelhouse Café** is a heavenly respite from the crowds, tucked into the repurposed St. Michael's Church, just north of Great St. Mary's Church. At lunch, choose from salads, soups, and sandwiches, as well as a few hot dishes and a variety of tasty baked goods (£7-10 light meals, Mon-Sat 8:00-17:00, breakfast served 8:00-11:00, lunch served 11:30-15:30, hot drinks and baked goods always available, closed Sun, Trinity Street, tel. 01223/309-147). Between 14:30 and 15:30 you can pay £4 to fill your plate with whatever they have left.

Café Carringtons is a cozy cafeteria that serves traditional British food at reasonable prices, including a Sunday roast lunch (£6-8 meals, £5 sandwiches, Mon-Sat 8:00-17:00, Sun 10:00-16:00, down the stairs at 23 Market Street, tel. 01223/361-792).

Supermarkets: There's a **Marks & Spencer Simply Food** at the train station (Mon-Fri 7:00-23:00, Sat 7:00-22:00, Sun 9:00-21:00) and a larger Marks & Spencer department store on Market Hill Square (Mon-Thu 8:00-18:00, Wed until 20:00, Fri-Sat 8:00-19:00, Sun 11:00-17:00, tel. 01223/355-219). **Sainsbury's** supermarket has longer hours (Mon-Sat 8:00-23:30, Sun 11:00-17:00, 44 Sidney Street, at the corner of Green Street).

A good picnic spot is Laundress Green, a grassy park on the river, at the end of Mill Lane near the Silver Street Bridge punts. There are no benches, so bring something to sit on. Remember, the college lawns are private property, so walking or picnicking on the grass is generally not allowed. When in doubt, ask at the college's entrance.

Cambridge Connections

From Cambridge by Train to: York (hourly, 2.5 hours, transfer in Peterborough), **Oxford** (2-3/hour, 2.5-3 hours, change in London involves Tube transfer between train stations), **London** (King's Cross Station: 2/hour, 45 minutes; Liverpool Street Station: 2/hour, 1.25 hours). Train info: Tel. 0845-748-4950, www.national rail.co.uk.

By Bus to: London (every 60-90 minutes, 2-2.5 hours), **Heathrow Airport** (hourly, 2-3 hours). Bus info: Tel. 0871-781-8178, www.nationalexpress.com.

BATH

The best city to visit within easy striking distance of London is Bath—just a 1.5-hour train ride away. Two hundred years ago, this city of 85,000 was the trendsetting Hollywood of Britain. If ever a city enjoyed looking in the mirror, Bath's the one. It has more "government-listed" or protected historic buildings per capita than any other town in England. The entire city, built of the creamy warm-tone limestone called "Bath stone," beams in its cover-girl complexion. An architectural chorus line, it's a triumph of the Neoclassical style of the Georgian era—named for the four Georges who sat as England's kings from 1714 to 1830. Proud locals remind visitors that the town is routinely banned from the "Britain in Bloom" contest to give other towns a chance to win. Bath's narcissism is justified. Even with its mobs of tourists (2 million per year) and greedy prices, Bath is a joy to visit.

Bath's fame began with the allure of its (supposedly) healing hot springs. Long before the Romans arrived in the first century, Bath was known for its warm waters. Romans named the popular spa town Aquae Sulis, after a local Celtic goddess. The town's importance carried through Saxon times, when it had a huge church on the site of the present-day abbey and was considered the religious capital of Britain. Its influence peaked in 973 with King Edgar's sumptuous coronation in the abbey. Later, Bath prospered as a wool town.

Bath then declined until the mid-1600s, wasting away to just a huddle of huts around the abbey, with hot, smelly mud and 3,000 residents, oblivious to the Roman ruins 18 feet below their dirt floors. In fact, with its own walls built upon ancient ones, Bath was no bigger than that Roman town. Then, in 1687, Queen Mary, fighting infertility, bathed here. Within 10 months, she gave birth to a son...and a new age of popularity for Bath.

The revitalized town boomed as a spa resort. Ninety percent of the buildings you'll see today are from the 18th century. The classical revivalism of Italian architect Andrea Palladio inspired a local father-and-son team—both named John Wood (the Elder and the Younger)—to build a "new Rome." The town bloomed in the Neoclassical style, and streets were lined not with scrawny sidewalks but with wide "parades," upon which women in their stylishly wide dresses could spread their fashionable tails.

Beau Nash (1673-1762) was Bath's "master of ceremonies." He organized the daily social regimen of aristocratic visitors, and he made the city more appealing by lighting the streets, improving security, banning swords, and opening the Pump Room. Under his fashionable baton, Bath became a city of balls, gaming, and concerts—the place to see and be seen in England. This most civilized place became even more so with the great Neoclassical building spree that followed.

These days, modern tourism has stoked the local economy, as has the fast morning train to London. (A growing number of Bath-based professionals catch the 7:13 train to Paddington Station every morning.) With renewed access to Bath's soothing hot springs at the Thermae Bath Spa, the venerable waters are in the spotlight again, attracting a new generation of visitors in need of a cure or a soak.

BATH

Planning Your Time

Bath deserves two nights even on a quick trip. On a three-week British getaway, spend three nights in Bath, with one day for the city and one day for side-trips (see next chapter). Ideally, use Bath as your jet-lag recovery pillow, and do London at the end of your trip.

Consider starting your British vacation this way:

Day 1: Land at Heathrow. Connect to Bath either by train via London Paddington, direct bus, or bus/train combination via Reading (for details, see page 313). You can also consider flying into Bristol. While you don't need or want a car in Bath, those who land early and pick up their cars at the airport can visit Windsor Castle (near Heathrow) and/or Stonehenge on their way to Bath. If you have the evening free in Bath, take a walking tour.

Day 2: 9:00—Tour the Roman Baths; 10:30—Catch the free city walking tour; 12:30—Picnic on the open deck of a tour bus; 14:00—Free time in the shopping center of old Bath; 15:30—Tour the Fashion Museum or Museum of Bath at Work. At night, consider seeing a play, take the evening walking tour (unless you did last night), enjoy the Bizarre Bath comedy walk, consider seeing a play, or go for an evening soak in the Thermae Bath Spa.

Day 3 (and possibly 4): By car, explore nearby sights. Without a car, consider a one-day Avebury/Stonehenge/cute towns mini-bus tour from Bath (Mad Max tours are best; see "Tours in Bath," later).

Orientation to Bath

Bath's town square, three blocks in front of the bus and train station, is a cluster of tourist landmarks, including the abbey, Roman and Medieval Baths, and the Pump Room. Bath is hilly. In general, you'll gain elevation as you head north from the town center.

Tourist Information

The TI is in the abbey churchyard (Mon-Sat 9:30-17:30, Sun 10:00-16:00, pricey toll tel. 0906-711-2000—50p/minute, www.visitbath.co.uk). The TI sells various visitor guides and maps—survey your options before buying one (£1-1.50). The TI also books rooms with no extra fee (booking tel. 0844-847-5256). If you're a Jane Austen fan, ask about the walking tours that leave from the abbey churchyard on weekends. Entertainment listings from the local paper are posted on the bulletin board.

Arrival in Bath

The Bath Spa **train station** has a staffed ticket desk, ticket machines, and a privately run travel agency masquerading as a TI. Directly in front of the train station is the SouthGate Bath shopping center. To get from the train station to the TI, exit straight ahead and continue up Manvers Street for about five minutes, then turn left at the triangular "square" overlooking the riverfront park, following the small TI arrow on a signpost. The **bus station** is immediately west of the train station, along Dorchester Street.

Helpful Hints

Festivals: The **Bath Literature Festival** is an open book in early March (www.bathlitfest.org.uk). The **Bath International Music Festival** bursts into song in late May (classical, folk, jazz, contemporary; www.bathmusicfest.org.uk), overlapped by the eclectic **Bath Fringe Festival** (theater, walks, talks, bus trips; generally similar dates to the Music Festival, www.bathfringe.co.uk). The **Jane Austen Festival** unfolds genteelly in late September (www.janeausten.co.uk/festivalhome). And for three weeks in December, the squares around the abbey are filled with a **Christmas market.**

Bath's festival **box office** sells tickets for most events (but not for those at the Theatre Royal), and can tell you exactly what's on tonight (housed inside the TI, tel. 01225/463-362, www.bathfestivals.org.uk). The city's weekly paper, the *Bath Chronicle*, publishes a "What's On" events listing each Thursday (www.thisisbath.com).

Internet Access: Plenty of cafés offer free Wi-Fi (as do most of my recommended hotels and B&Bs). You can also get online at the Bath **library** (£1.20/20 minutes, Mon 9:30-18:00, Tue-Thu 9:30-19:00, Fri-Sat 9:30-17:00, Sun 13:00-16:00, 19 Northgate Street near Pulteney Bridge, tel. 01225/394-041, www.bathnes.gov.uk).

Bookstore: Topping & Company, an inviting bookshop, has posters in its windows advertising frequent author readings, free coffee and tea for browsers, a good selection of maps, and tables filled with tidy stacks of carefully selected volumes, including lots of books on Bath and this region (daily 9:00-20:00, near the bottom of the street called "The Paragon"—where it meets George Street, tel. 01225/428-111, www.toppingbooks.co.uk).

Laundry: The **Spruce Goose Launderette** is between the Circus and the Royal Crescent, on the pedestrian lane called Margaret's Buildings. Bring lots of £1 coins for washing and £0.20 coins for drying, as there are no change machines (self-service: about £4-5/load, daily 8:00-20:00, last load at 19:30; full-service: £13.50/load, Mon and Wed-Fri 8:00-12:00 only; tel. 01225/483-309). **Speedy Wash** can pick up your laundry anywhere in town on weekdays before 11:00 for same-day service (£12/small bag, Mon-Fri 7:30-17:30, Sat 8:30-13:00 but no pickup, closed Sun, no self-service, most hotels work with them, 4 Mile End, London Road, tel. 01225/427-616).

Car Rental: Enterprise provides a pickup service for customers to and from their hotels (extra fee for one-way rentals, at Lower Bristol Road outside Bath, tel. 01225/443-311, www.enterprise.com). Other companies include **Thrifty** (pickup service and one-way rentals available, in the Burnett Business Park in Keynsham—between Bath and Bristol, tel. 01179/867-997, www.thrifty.co.uk), **Hertz** (one-way rentals possible, at Windsor Bridge, tel. 0843-309-3004, www.hertz.co.uk), and **National/Europcar** (one-way rentals available, £7 by taxi from the train station, at Brassmill Lane—go west on Upper Bristol Road, tel. 0871-384-9985, www.europcar.co.uk). Skip **Avis**—it's a mile from the Bristol train station; you'd need to

WESTON RD.

CRESCENT LN.

To Lansdown Crescent

MORFORD

JULIAN RD.

RIVERS ST.

ROYAL CRESCENT

RUSSELL ST.

MUSEUM OF BATH AT WORK

MARLBOROUGH GARDENS

UPPER CHURCH ST.

CIRCUS MEWS

R.C. HOTEL

BENNETT ST.

FASHION MUSEUM & ASSEMBLY ROOMS

GEORGIAN HOUSE MUSEUM

BROCK ST.

THE CIRCUS

ALFRED ST.

BARTLETT

Royal

THE CIRCUS

Victoria

Park

ROYAL AVE.

GAY ST.

GEORGE

MARLBOROUGH LN.

To Bristol & Cardiff

P

JANE AUSTEN CENTRE

(A-4)

B #14

UPPER BRISTOL RD.

CHARLOTTE STREET

P

Queen Square

JOHN ST.

WOOD

QUEEN

CRESCENT GDNS.

CHARLOTTE ST.

PRINCES ST.

BARTON ST.

TRIM ST.

MONMOUTH PL.

NEW KING ST.

BEAUFORD SQ.

SAW CL.

BRIDEWELL

River

Avon

CHARLES ST.

MONMOUTH

THEATRE ROYAL

JOHN'S ST.

WESTGATE ST.

FARMERS' MARKET

Kingsmead Square

NEW ST.

AVON ST.

WESTGATE BLDGS.

CHANDOS

PINES WAY

MIDLAND BRIDGE RD.

JAMES ST. WEST

MILK ST.

AVON ST.

N

LOWER BRISTOL ROAD (A-36)

GREEN PARK ROAD

CORN ST.

River Avon

200 Meters

200 Yards

LOWER OLDFIELD PARK

WELLS ROAD (A-367)

BATH

One-way streets →

Traffic barriers

To Wells & Glastonbury

Bath

To M-4 & London

GUINEA LN.

LONDON RD.

To Boats

POWLETT RD.

FORESTER RD.

BATHWICK ST.

BUILDING OF BATH COLLECTION

THE PARAGON

LANSDOWN ROAD

ST.

River Avon

HENRIETTA RD.

HENRIETTA ST.

HENRIETTA GARDENS

Henrietta Park

SUTTON ST.

SYDNEY PL.

Sydney Gardens

HENRIETTA MEWS

GREAT PULTENEY ST.

See "Bath Town Center" detail map

BROAD ST.

WALCOT ST.

GROVE ST.

MILSOM ST.

GREEN ST.

NEW BOND ST.

PULTENEY BRIDGE

ARGYLE ST.

Laura Place

BOATS

BRIDGE

Victoria Art Gallery

PULTENEY ROAD (A-36)

To American Museum

UPPER BOROUGH WALLS

NORTH-UMBER-LAND

UNION ST.

HIGH ST.

PARSONAGE

CORRIDOR

GUILDHALL MARKET

ORANGE GROVE

Rugby Ground

WESTGATE ST.

CHEAP ST.

GRAND PARADE

Parade Gardens

CROSS BATH

ROMAN BATHS & PUMP ROOM

ABBEY

BATH ST.

YORK ST.

PIERREPONT ST.

SPORTS & LEISURE CENTER

N. PARADE RD.

THERMAE BATH SPA

BEAU ST.

Abbey Green

ABBEY GATE

OLD ORCHARD

DUKE ST.

LOWER BOROUGH

NEW ORCHARD

HENRY ST.

S. PARADE

FERRY LN.

PULTENEY GARDENS

ST. JAMES' PARADE

AMERY LN.

SOUTH GATE

MAN VERS ST.

ST. JOHN'S

To Bathampton

ARBURY

SOUTHGATE SHOPPING CENTER

SOUTHGATE PARKING

DORCHESTER ST.

RAIL STATION

BUS STATION

CLAVERTON ST.

FOOTBRIDGE

ROSSITER RD. (A-36)

Kennet & Avon Canal

CLAVERTON RD.

BATH

rent a car to get there. Most offices close Saturday afternoon and all day Sunday, which complicates weekend pickups. Ideally, take the train or bus from downtown London to Bath, and rent a car as you leave Bath.

Parking: As Bath becomes increasingly pedestrian-friendly, street parking in the city center is disappearing. Most short-term lots fill up fast (£1.60/hour, 2-4-hour maximum). You'll pay less per hour in long-stay lots. The SouthGate Bath shopping center lot on the corner of Southgate and Dorchester streets is a five-minute walk from the abbey (£4.30/up to 3 hours, £13/24 hours, cash or credit card, open 24/7); the Charlotte Street car park is also handy. For more info on parking, visit the "Travel and Maps" section of http://visitbath.co.uk.

Tours in Bath

▲▲▲Walking Tours

Free two-hour tours are led by **The Mayor's Corps of Honorary Guides,** volunteers who want to share their love of Bath with its many visitors (as the city's mayor first did when he took a group on a guided walk back in the 1930s). These chatty, historical, and gossip-filled walks are essential for your understanding of this town's amazing Georgian social scene. How else would you learn that the old "chair ho" call for your sedan chair evolved into today's "cheerio" farewell? Tours leave from outside the Pump Room in the abbey churchyard (free, no tips, year-round Sun-Fri at 10:30 and 14:00, Sat at 10:30 only; additional evening walks May-Sept Tue and Thu at 19:00; tel. 01225/477-411, www.bathguides.org.uk). Tip for theatergoers: When your guide stops to talk outside the Theatre Royal, skip out for a moment, pop into the box office, and see about snaring a great deal on a play for tonight.

For a **private tour,** call the local guides' bureau, Bath Parade Guides (£85/2 hours, tel. 01225/337-111, www.bathparadeguides .co.uk, bathparadeguides@yahoo.com). For **Ghost Walks** and **Bizarre Bath** tours, see "Nightlife in Bath," later.

▲▲City Bus Tours

City Sightseeing's hop-on, hop-off bus tours zip through Bath. Jump on a bus anytime at one of 17 signposted pickup points, pay the driver, climb upstairs, and hear recorded commentary about Bath. City Sightseeing has two 45-minute routes: a city tour and a "Skyline" route outside town. Try to get one with a live guide (usually at :15 and :45 past the hour for the city tour, and on the hour for the Skyline route); otherwise, bring your own earbuds if you've got 'em (the audio recording on the other buses is barely intelligible with the headsets provided). On a sunny day, this is a multitasking tourist's dream come true: You can munch a sandwich, work on a tan, snap great photos, and learn a lot, all at the same time. Save money by doing the bus tour first—ticket stubs get you minor discounts at many sights (£13, ticket valid for 24 hours and both tour routes, generally 4/hour daily in summer 9:30-18:30, in winter 10:00-15:00, tel. 01225/330-444, www.city-sightseeing.com).

Taxi Tours

Local taxis, driven by good talkers, go where big buses can't. A group of up to four can rent a cab for an hour (about £40; try to negotiate) and enjoy a fine, informative, and—with the right cabbie—entertaining private joyride. It's probably cheaper to let the meter run than to pay for an hourly rate, but ask the cabbie for advice.

To Stonehenge, Avebury, and the Cotswolds

Bath is a good launch pad for visiting Wells, Avebury, Stonehenge, and more.

Mad Max Minibus Tours

Operating daily from Bath, Maddy offers thoughtfully organized, informative tours run with entertaining guides and limited to 16 people per group. Book ahead—as far ahead as possible in summer—for these popular tours. The **Stone Circles and Villages** full-day tour covers 110 miles and visits Stonehenge, the Avebury Stone Circles, photogenic Lacock (LAY-cock)—featured in parts of the BBC's *Pride and Prejudice* and the Harry Potter movies—and Castle Combe, the southernmost Cotswold village (£35 plus Stonehenge entry fee, tours depart daily at 8:45 and return at 16:30, arrive 15 minutes early, leaves early to beat the Stonehenge hordes). Three days a week (Sun, Tue, Thu) Mad Max offers three-hour tours that skip Stonehenge: a **Villages** tour that includes Lacock and Castle Combe (£16, departs at 11:00), and an **Avebury Mini-Tour** (£16, departs at 14:00). If you combine these as a full-day tour (£30), you get a long lunch break in Lacock, with time to visit its abbey. Their full-day **Cotswold Explorer** tour visits Chipping Campden and other villages, and their full-day **Somerset Explorer** tour includes Wells, Glastonbury, and a rural farm (€35 each, April-Sept only; see website for departure times).

All tours depart from outside the Abbey Hotel on Terrace Walk in Bath, a one-minute walk from the abbey. Arrive 15 minutes before your departure time and bring cash (or book online with a credit card at least 48 hours in advance, 10 percent cash refund on second tour for Rick Steves readers who book two full-day tours; tel. 07990/505-970, phone answered daily 8:00-18:00, www.madmaxtours.co.uk, maddy@madmaxtours.co.uk). Please honor or cancel your seat reservation.

Bath at a Glance

▲▲▲Walking Tours Free top-notch tours, helping you make the most of your visit, led by The Mayor's Corps of Honorary Guides. **Hours:** Sun-Fri at 10:30 and 14:00, Sat at 10:30 only; additional evening walks offered May-Sept Tue and Thu at 19:00. See page 280.

▲▲▲Roman and Medieval Baths Ancient baths that gave the city its name, tourable with good audioguide. **Hours:** Daily July-Aug 9:00-22:00, March-June and Sept-Oct 9:00-18:00, Nov-Feb 9:30-17:30 except Sat until 18:00. See page 284.

▲▲Bath Abbey 500-year-old Perpendicular Gothic church, graced with beautiful fan vaulting and stained glass. **Hours:** Mon-Sat 9:00-18:00 except Nov-March until 16:30, Sun 13:00-14:30 & 16:30-17:30. See page 288.

▲▲The Circus and the Royal Crescent Stately Georgian (Neoclassical) buildings from Bath's late-18th-century glory days. **Hours:** Always viewable. See page 290.

▲▲Georgian House at No. 1 Royal Crescent Just reopened after an extensive renovation, this is your best look at the interior of one of Bath's high-rent Georgian beauties. **Hours:** Mon 12:00-17:30, Tue-Sun 10:30-17:30. See page 291.

▲Pump Room Swanky Georgian hall, ideal for a spot of tea or a taste of unforgettably "healthy" spa water. **Hours:** Daily 9:30-12:00 for coffee and breakfast, 12:00-14:30 for lunch, 14:30-17:00 for afternoon tea (open 18:00-21:00 for dinner July-Aug and Christmas holidays only). See page 287.

BATH

Lion Tours

This well-run outfit gets you to Stonehenge on a half-day tour: Their **Stonehenge and Lacock** tour leaves daily at 12:15 and returns at 17:15 (£20 plus Stonehenge entry). In summer this tour also leaves at 9:00 and returns at 13:30, and can be combined with their **Afternoon Villages** tour of Lacock, Biddestone and Castle Combe (£15, £12.50 with morning Stonehenge tour, departs at 13:45, returns at 16:45; runs Mon, Wed, Fri, and Sat). They also offer a **Stonehenge, Wells & Glastonbury** tour (info on website), and a full-day **Cotswold Discovery** tour with stops in Castle Combe, Bibury, Stow-on-the-Wold, Tetbury, the Coln Valley, and The Slaughters (£37.50; runs Sun, Tue, and Thu 8:45-17:30; arrive 15 minutes early). If you ask in advance, you can bring your luggage

▲**Pulteney Bridge and Parade Gardens** Shop-strewn bridge and relaxing riverside gardens. **Hours:** Bridge—always open; gardens—Easter-Sept daily 11:00-17:00, shorter hours off-season. See page 289.

▲**Victoria Art Gallery** Paintings from the late 17th century to today. **Hours:** Tue-Sat 10:00-17:00, Sun 13:30-17:00, closed Mon. See page 290.

▲**Fashion Museum** 400 years of clothing under one roof, plus the opulent Assembly Rooms. **Hours:** Daily March-Oct 10:30-18:00, Nov-Feb 10:30-17:00. See page 291.

▲**Museum of Bath at Work** Gadget-ridden circa-1900 engineer's shop, foundry, factory, and office. **Hours:** April-Oct daily 10:30-17:00, Nov and Jan-March weekends only, closed in Dec. See page 292.

▲**American Museum** Insightful look primarily at colonial/early-American lifestyles, with 18 furnished rooms and eager-to-talk guides. **Hours:** Mid-March-Oct Tue-Sun 12:00-17:00, closed Mon except in Aug, closed Nov-mid-March. See page 294.

▲**Thermae Bath Spa** Relaxation center that put the bath back in Bath. **Hours:** Daily 9:00-21:30. See page 295.

Jane Austen Centre Exhibit on 19th-century Bath-based novelist, best for her fans. **Hours:** Mid-March-mid-Nov daily 9:45-17:30, July-Aug Thu-Sat until 19:00; mid-Nov-mid-March Sun-Fri 11:00-16:30, Sat 9:45-18:00. See page 293.

BATH

along and use this tour to get to Stow or, for £5 extra, Moreton-in-Marsh (easy train connections to Oxford and bus connections to Chipping Campden). Lion's tours depart from the same stop as Mad Max Tours—see above (mobile 07769-668-668, book online with a credit card, www.liontours.co.uk).

Other Tour Options
Scarper Tours runs a minibus tour to Stonehenge (£15, doesn't include £8 Stonehenge entry fee, departs from behind the abbey; daily mid-June-Aug at 9:00, 12:30, and 16:00; mid-March-mid-June and Sept-Oct at 10:00 and 14:00; Nov-mid-March at 13:00; tel. 07739/644-155, www.scarpertours.com). The three-hour tour (two hours there and back, an hour at the site) includes driver narration en route.

Celtic Horizons, run by retired teacher Alan Price, offers tours from Bath to a variety of destinations, such as Stonehenge, Avebury, and Wells. Alan can provide a convenient transfer service (to or from London, Heathrow, Bristol Airport, the Cotswolds, and so on), with or without a tour itinerary en route. Allow about £25/hour for a group (his comfortable minivans seat 4, 6, or 8 people) and £150 for Heathrow-Bath transfers (1-4 persons). It's best to make arrangements and get pricing information by email at alan@celtichorizons.com (cash only, tel. 01373/461-784, www.celtichorizons.com).

Sights in Bath

In the Town Center
▲▲▲Roman and Medieval Baths

In ancient Roman times, high society enjoyed the mineral springs at Bath. From Londinium—and throughout the empire—Romans

traveled so often to Aquae Sulis, as the city was called, to "take a bath" that finally it became known simply as Bath. Today, a fine museum surrounds the ancient bath. With the help of a great audioguide, you'll wander past well-documented displays, Roman artifacts, a temple pedi-

ment with an evocative bearded face, a bronze head of the goddess Sulis Minerva, excavated ancient foundations, and the actual mouth of the spring. At the end, you'll have a chance to walk around the big pool itself, where Romans once lounged, splished, splashed, and thanked the gods for the gift of naturally hot water.

Cost and Hours: £13.50 (50p more July-Aug), includes audioguide, £18 combo-ticket includes Fashion Museum, family ticket available, daily July-Aug 9:00-22:00, March-June and Sept-Oct 9:00-18:00, Nov-Feb 9:30-17:30 except Sat until 18:00, last entry one hour before closing, tel. 01225/477-785, www.romanbaths.co.uk.

Crowd-Beating Tips: Long lines for tickets typically form on Saturdays and every day in the summer. You can avoid them by either getting your ticket online or, if you'll be visiting the Fashion Museum anyway, buying your combo-ticket there. With voucher or combo-ticket in hand, enter through the "fast track" lane, to the left of the general admission line. On any day, the least crowded time to visit is before 11:00; peak time is between 13:00 and 15:00. If you're here in July or August, the best time is after 19:00, when the baths are romantic, gas-lit, and all yours.

Bath Town Center

To the Circus & Royal Crescent

JANE AUSTEN CENTRE

100 Meters
100 Yards

Laura Place

Queen Square

JOHN ST.

MILSOM ST.

BROAD ST.

WALCOT ST.

GREEN ST.

ST. MICHAEL'S

PULTENEY BRIDGE

GROVE ST.

ARGYLE ST.

POST

BOATS

WOOD ST.

NEW BOND ST.

BRIDGE ST.

VICTORIA ART GALLERY

PRINCES ST.

BEAUFORD

BARTON ST.

TRIM ST.

UPPER BOROUGH WALLS

GRAND PARADE

River Avon

MONMOUTH ST.

SAW CL.

PARSONAGE

UNION ST.

UNION PASSAGE

NORTH-UMBER

HIGH ST.

GUILDHALL MARKET

THEATRE ROYAL

BRIDEWELL

ST. JOHN'S

WESTGATE ST.

CORRIDOR

ORANGE GROVE

USTINOV THEATRE & THE EGG

CHEAP ST.

ABBEY

Parade Gardens

Kingsmead Square

NEW ST.

AVON ST.

WESTGATE BLDGS.

CHANDOS

BATH ST.

CROSS BATH

ROMAN BATHS & PUMP ROOM

TERRACE

PIERREPONT ST.

SPORTS & LEISURE CENTER

JAMES ST. WEST

MILK ST.

THERMAE BATH SPA

HET.

STALL ST.

YORK ST.

WALK

Abbey Green

BEAU ST.

SPA MUSEUM

ABBEYGATE

OLD ORCHARD

MAN VERS ST.

S. PARADE

LOWER BOROUGH

HENRY ST.

P

Traffic barriers

One-way streets

Pedestrian-friendly areas

NEW ORCHARD

AMERY LN.

SOUTHGATE SHOPPING CENTER

BATH

Tours: Take advantage of the included, essential **audio-guide,** which makes your visit easy and informative. In addition to the basic commentary, look for posted numbers to key into your audioguide for specialty topics—including a kid-friendly tour and musings from American expat writer Bill Bryson. For those with a big appetite for Roman history, in-depth **guided tours** leave from the end of the museum at the edge of the actual bath (included

with ticket, on the hour, a poolside clock is set for the next departure time, 20-40 minutes depending on the guide). You can revisit the museum after the tour.

➋ **Self-Guided Tour:** Follow the one-way route through the bath and museum complex. This self-guided tour offers a basic overview; for more in-depth commentary, make ample use of the included audioguide.

Begin by walking around the upper **terrace,** overlooking the Great Bath. This terrace—lined with sculptures of

VIRs (Very Important Romans)—evokes ancient times but was built in the 1890s. The ruins of the bath complex sat undisturbed for centuries before finally being excavated and turned into a museum in the late 19th century.

Head inside to the **museum,** where exhibits explain the dual purpose of the buildings that stood here in Roman times: a bath complex, for relaxation and for healing; and a temple dedicated to the goddess Sulis Minerva, who was believed to be responsible for the mysterious and much-appreciated thermal springs. Cut-away diagrams and models resurrect both parts of this complex and help establish your bearings among the remaining fragments and foundations.

Peer down into the **spring,** where little air bubbles remind you that 240,000 gallons of water a day emerge from the earth— magically, it must have seemed to Romans—at a constant 115°F. The water you see now, heated more than a mile below the earth's surface, first fell to earth as rain onto nearby hills about 10,000 years ago...making the Romans seem relatively recent.

Go downstairs to get to know the Romans who built and enjoyed these baths. The fragments of the **temple pediment**—

carved by indigenous Celtic craftsmen but with Roman themes—represent a remarkable cultural synthesis. Sit and watch for a while, as a slide projection fills in historians' best guesses as to what once occupied the missing bits. The identity of the circular face in the middle puzzles researchers. (God? Santa Claus?) It could be the head of the Gorgon monster after it was slain by Perseus—are those snakes peeking through its hair and beard? And yet, the Gorgon was traditionally depicted as female. Perhaps instead it's Neptune, the god of water—appropriate for this aquatic site.

The next exhibits examine the importance of Aquae Sulis (the settlement here) in antiquity. Much like the pilgrimage sites of the Middle Ages, this spot exerted a powerful pull on people from all over the realm, who were eager to partake in its healing waters and to worship at the religious site. You'll see some of the small but extremely heavy carved-stone tables that pilgrims hauled here as an offering to the gods.

As you walk through the temple's original foundations, keep an eye out for the sacrificial altar. The gilded-bronze head of the goddess **Sulis Minerva** (in the display case) once overlooked a flaming cauldron inside the temple, where only priests were allowed to enter. Similar to the Greek goddess Athena, Sulis Minerva was considered to be a life-giving mother goddess. The next room displays some of the requests (inscribed on sheets of pewter or iron) that visitors made of the goddess. Take time to read some of these—many are comically spiteful and petty, offering a warts-and-all glimpse into day-to-day Roman culture.

Engineers enjoy a close-up look at the spring overflow and the original **drain system**—built two millennia ago—that still carries excess water to the River Avon. Marvel at the cleverness and durability of Roman engineering, created in (what we usually imagine to be) a "primitive" time. A nearby exhibit on pulleys and fasteners lets you play with these inventions.

Head outside to the **Great Bath** itself (where you can join one of the included guided tours—look for the clock with the next start time). Take a slow lap (by foot) around the perimeter, imagining the frolicking Romans who once immersed themselves up to their necks in this five-foot-deep pool. (On busy days, when costumed characters hang out by the bath, you may not have to imagine.) The water is greenish because of algae—don't drink it. The best views are from the west end, looking back toward the abbey. Nearby is a giant chunk of roof span, from a time when this was a cavernous covered swimming hall. At the corner, you'll step over a small canal where hot water still trickles into the main pool. Nearby, find a length of original lead pipe, remarkably well preserved since antiquity.

Symmetrical bath complexes branch off at opposite ends of the Great Bath (perhaps dating from a conservative period when the Romans maintained separate facilities for men and women). The **East Baths** show off changing rooms and various bathing rooms, each one designed for a special therapy or recreational purpose (immersion therapy tub, sauna-like heated floor, and so on), as described in detail by the audioguide.

When you're ready to leave, head for the **West Baths** (including a sweat bath and a *frigidarium*, or "cold plunge" pool) and take another look at the spring and more foundations. After returning your audioguide, pop over to the fountain for a free taste of the spa water. Then pass through the gift shop, past the convenient public WCs (which use plain old tap water), and exit through the **Pump Room**—or stay for a spot of tea.

▲Pump Room

For centuries, Bath was forgotten as a spa. Then, in 1687, the previously barren Queen Mary bathed here, became pregnant, and bore a male heir to the throne. A few years later, Queen Anne found the water eased her painful gout. Word of its wonder waters spread, and Bath earned its way back on the aristocratic map. High society soon turned the place into one big pleasure palace. The Pump Room, an elegant Georgian hall just above the Roman Baths, offers visitors their best chance to raise a pinky in Chippendale grandeur. Above the newspaper table and sedan chairs, a statue of Beau Nash himself sniffles down at you. Come for a light meal, or to try a famous (but forgettable) "Bath bun" with your spa water (the same water that's in the fountain at the end of the baths tour; also free in the Pump Rooms if you present your ticket). The spa water is served by an appropriately-attired waiter, who will tell you the water is pumped up from nearly 100 yards deep and marinated in 43 wonderful minerals. Or for just the price of a coffee, drop in anytime—except during lunch—to enjoy live music and the atmosphere.

Cost and Hours: Daily 9:30-12:00 for coffee and £6-15 breakfast, 12:00-14:30 for £11-16 lunches, 14:30-17:00 for £18.50 traditional afternoon tea (last orders at 16:00), tea/coffee and pastries also available in the afternoons; open 18:00-21:00 for dinner July-Aug and Christmas holidays only; live music daily—string trio or piano, times vary; tel. 01225/444-477.

BATH

▲▲Bath Abbey

The town of Bath wasn't much in the Middle Ages, but an important church has stood on this spot since Anglo-Saxon times.

King Edgar I was crowned here in 973, when the church was much bigger (before the bishop packed up and moved to Wells). Dominating the town center, today's abbey—the last great medieval church built in England—is 500 years old and a fine example of the Late Perpendicular Gothic style, with breezy fan vaulting and enough stained glass to earn it the nickname "Lantern of the West."

Cost and Hours: £2.50 suggested donation; April-Oct Mon-Sat 9:00-18:00 except Nov-March until 16:30, Sun 13:00-14:30 & 16:30-17:30; handy flier narrates a self-guided 19-stop tour, schedule of events—including concerts, services, and evensong—posted on the door and online, tel. 01225/422-462, www.bathabbey.org.

Visiting the Abbey: The facade (c. 1500, but mostly restored) is interesting for some of its carvings. Look for the angels going down the ladder. The statue of Peter (to the left of the door) lost its head to mean iconoclasts; it was re-carved out of Peter's once supersized beard. Take a moment to appreciate the abbey's architecture from the Abbey Green square.

Going inside is worth the small suggested contribution. The glass, red-iron gas-powered lamps, and the heating grates on the floor are all remnants of the 19th century. The window behind the altar shows 52 scenes from the life of Christ. A window to the left of the altar shows Edgar's coronation.

Climbing the Tower: You can reach the top of the tower but only with a worthwhile, 50-minute guided tour. You'll hike up 212 steps for views across the rooftops of Bath and a peek down into the Roman and Medieval Baths. In the rafters, you walk right up behind the clock face on the north transept, and get an inside-out look at the fan vaulting. Along the way, you'll hear a brief town history as you learn all about the tower's bells. If you've always wanted to clang a huge church bell for all the town to hear, this is your chance—it's oddly satisfying (£6, sporadic schedule but generally at the top of each hour when abbey is open, more often during busy times; Mon-Sat April-Oct 10:00-16:00, Nov-March 11:00-15:00, these are last tour-departure times; today's tour times usually posted outside abbey entrance, no tours Sun, buy tickets in abbey gift shop).

▲Pulteney Bridge, Parade Gardens, and Cruises

Bath is inclined to compare its shop-lined Pulteney Bridge to

Florence's Ponte Vecchio. That's pushing it. But to best enjoy a sunny day, pack a picnic lunch and pay £1.20 to enter the Parade Gardens below the bridge (Easter-Sept daily 11:00-17:00, shorter hours off-season, includes deck chairs, ask about concerts held some Sun at 15:00 in summer, entrance a block south of bridge).

Relaxing peacefully at the riverside provides a wonderful break (and memory).

Across the bridge at Pulteney Weir, tour boat companies run **cruises** (£4 each way, up to 12/day if the weather's good, one hour to Bathampton and back, WCs on board, tel. 01225/312-900). Just take whatever boat is running—all stop in Bathampton—allowing you to hop off and walk back (about 45-60 minutes; for details on the walk, see "Activities in Bath," later). Boats come with picnic-friendly sundecks.

Guildhall Market

The little, old-school shopping mall located across from Pulteney Bridge is a frumpy time warp in this affluent town. It's fun for browsing and picnic shopping, and its recommended Market Café is a cheap place for a bite.

▲Victoria Art Gallery

This gallery, next to Pulteney Bridge, has two parts: The ground floor houses temporary exhibits, while the upstairs is filled with paintings from the late 17th century to the present (find *Bath from the East*—left wall, just below eye level—for a nice look at pre-industrial Bath), along with a small collection of decorative arts.

Cost and Hours: £2 suggested donation, temporary exhibits-£2-4, Tue-Sat 10:00-17:00, Sun 13:30-17:00, closed Mon, WC, tel. 01225/477-233, www.victoriagal.org.uk.

Northwest of the Town Center

Several worthwhile public spaces and museums can be found a slightly uphill 10-minute walk away.

▲▲The Circus and the Royal Crescent

If Bath is an architectural cancan, these are its knickers. These first Georgian "condos"—built in the mid-18th century by the father-and-son John Woods (the Circus by the Elder, the Royal Crescent by the Younger)—are well explained by the city walking tours. "Georgian" is British for "Neoclassical." These two building complexes, conveniently located a block apart from each other, are quintessential Bath.

Circus: True to its name, this is a circular housing complex. Picture it as a coliseum turned inside out. Its Doric, Ionic, and Corinthian capital decorations pay homage to its Greco-Roman origin, and are a reminder that Bath (with its seven hills) aspired to be "the Rome of England." The frieze above the first row of columns has hundreds of different panels representing the arts, sciences, and crafts. The ground-floor entrances were made large enough that aristocrats could be carried right through the door in their sedan chairs, and women could enter without disturbing their sky-high hairdos. The tiny round windows on the top floors were the servants' quarters. While the building fronts are uniform, the backs are higgledy-piggledy, infamous for their "hanging loos" (bathrooms added years later). Stand in the middle of the Circus among the grand plane trees, on the capped old well. Imagine the days when there was no indoor plumbing, and the servant girls gathered here to fetch water—this was gossip central. If you stand on the well, your clap echoes three times around the circle (try it).

Royal Crescent: A long, graceful arc of buildings—impossible to see in one glance unless you step way back to the edge of the big park in front—evokes the wealth and gentility of Bath's glory days. As you cruise the Crescent, pretend you're rich. Then pretend you're poor. Notice the "ha ha fence," a drop-off in the front yard that acted as a barrier, invisible from the windows, for keeping out sheep and peasants. The refined and stylish **Royal Crescent Hotel** sits unmarked in the center of the Crescent (with the giant rhododendron growing over the door). You're welcome to (politely) drop in to explore its fine ground-floor public spaces and back garden, where a gracious and traditional tea is served (£14.50 cream tea, £25 afternoon tea, daily 15:00-17:00, sharing is OK, reserve a day in advance, tel. 01225/823-333, www.royalcrescent .co.uk).

▲▲Georgian House at No. 1 Royal Crescent

This museum (corner of Brock Street and Royal Crescent) just reopened after an extensive renovation. It takes visitors behind one of those classy Georgian facades, offering your best look into a period house. Take the time to talk with the docents stationed in each room and you'll learn all the fascinating details of Georgian life...like how high-class women shaved their eyebrows and pasted on carefully trimmed strips of furry mouse skin in their place. Look for a bowl of black beauty marks and a head-scratcher from those pre-shampoo days. Fido spent his days on the kitchen treadmill powering the rotisserie.

Cost and Hours: £8.50, Mon 12:00-17:30, Tue-Sun 10:30-17:30, last entry at 16:30, tel. 01225/487-713, www.bath-preservation -trust.org.uk.

▲Fashion Museum

Housed underneath Bath's Assembly Rooms, this museum displays four centuries of fashion on one floor. It's small, but the fact-filled, included audioguide can stretch a visit to an informative and enjoyable hour. Like fashion itself, the exhibits change all the time. A major feature is the "Dress of the Year" display, for which a fashion expert anoints a new frock each year. Ongoing since 1963, it's a chance to view nearly a half-century of fashion trends in one sweep of the head. (The menswear version—awarded sporadically—shows a bit less variation, but has flashes of creativity.) Many of the exhibits are organized by theme (bags, shoes, underwear, wedding dresses). You'll see how fashion evolved—just like architecture and other arts—from one historical period to the next: Georgian, Regency, Victorian, the Swinging '60s, and so on. If you're intrigued by all those historic garments, go ahead and lace up your own trainer corset (which looks more like a lifejacket) and try on a hoop underdress.

Cost and Hours: £8, includes entry to Assembly Rooms when open, £18 combo-ticket also covers Roman Baths, family ticket available, daily March-Oct 10:30-18:00, Nov-Feb 10:30-17:00, last entry one hour before closing, self-service café, Bennett Street, tel. 01225/477-789, www.fashionmuseum.co.uk.

Assembly Rooms

Above the Fashion Museum, these grand, empty rooms—where card games, concerts, tea, and dances were held in the 18th century (before the advent of fancy hotels with grand public spaces made them obsolete)—evoke images of dashing young gentlemen mingling with elegant ladies in a who's who of high society. Note the extreme symmetry (pleasing to the aristocratic eye) and the high windows (assuring privacy). After the Allies bombed the historic and well-preserved German city of Lübeck, the Germans picked up a Baedeker guide and chose a similarly lovely city to bomb: Bath. The Assembly Rooms—gutted in this wartime tit-for-tat by WWII bombs—have since been restored to their original splendor. (Only the chandeliers are original.)

Cost and Hours: Free with Fashion Museum entry, otherwise £2; same hours and contact information as Fashion Museum.

Nearby: Below the Assembly Rooms and Fashion Museum (to the left as you exit, 20 yards away at the door marked *14* and *Alfred House*) is one of the few surviving sets of **iron house hardware.** "Link boys" carried torches through the dark streets, lighting the way for big shots in their sedan chairs as they traveled from one affair to the next. The link boys extinguished their torches in the black conical "snuffers." The lamp above was once gas-lit. The crank on the left was used to hoist bulky things to various windows (see the hooks). Few of these sets survived the dark days of the WWII Blitz, when most were collected and melted down, purportedly to make weapons to feed the British war machine. (Not long ago, these well-meaning Brits finally found out that all of their patriotic extra commitment to the national struggle had been for naught, since the metal ended up in junk heaps.)

Shoppers head down **Bartlett Street,** just below the Fashion Museum, to browse the boutique shops.

▲Museum of Bath at Work

This modest but lovable place explains the industrial history of Bath. The museum is a vivid reminder that there's always been a grimy, workaday side to this spa town. The core of the museum

BATH

is the well-preserved, circa-1900 fizzy-drink business of one Mr. Bowler. It includes a Dickensian office, engineer's shop, brass foundry, essence room lined with bottled scents (see photo), and factory floor. It's just a pile of meaningless old gadgets—until the included audioguide resurrects Mr. Bowler's creative genius. Each item has its own story to tell.

Upstairs are display cases featuring other Bath creations through the years, including a 1914 Horstmann car, wheeled sedan chairs (this *is* Bath, after all), and versatile plasticine (colorful proto-Play-Doh—still the preferred medium of Aardman Studios, creators of the stop-motion animated *Wallace and Gromit* movies). At the snack bar, you can buy your own historic fizzy drink (a descendant of the ones once made here). On your way out, don't miss the intriguing collection of small exhibits on the ground floor, featuring cabinetmaking, the traditional methods for cutting the local "Bath stone," a locally produced six-stroke engine, and more.

Cost and Hours: £5, includes audioguide, April-Oct daily 10:30-17:00, Nov and Jan-March weekends only, closed Dec, last entry at 16:00, Julian Road, 2 steep blocks up Russell Street from Assembly Rooms, tel. 01225/318-348, www.bath-at-work.org.uk.

Sightseeing Tip: Notice the proximity of this museum to the very different Fashion Museum (described earlier). Museum attendants told me that—while open-minded spouses appreciate both places—it's standard for husbands to visit the Museum of Bath at Work while their wives are touring the Fashion Museum. Maybe it's time to divide and conquer?

Jane Austen Centre

This exhibition focuses on Jane Austen's tumultuous, sometimes troubled, five years in Bath (circa 1800, during which time her father died) and the influence the city had on her writing. There's little of historic substance here. You'll walk through a Georgian townhouse that she didn't live in (one of her real addresses in Bath was a few houses up the road, at 25 Gay Street), and you'll see mostly enlarged reproductions of things associated with her writing, but none of that seems to bother the steady stream of happy Austen fans touring through the house.

The museum does describe various places from two novels set in Bath (*Persuasion* and *Northanger Abbey*). Guides give an intro talk (on the first floor, 15 minutes, 3/hour, on the hour and at :20 and :40 past the hour) about the romantic but down-to-earth Austen, who skewered the silly, shallow, and arrogant aristocrats' world, where "the doing of nothing all day prevents one from doing anything." They also show a 15-minute video; after that, you're free to wander through the rest of the exhibit. The well-stocked gift shop—with "I love Mr. Darcy" tote bags and Colin Firth's visage emblazoned on teacups, postcards, and more—is a shopping spree in the making for Austen fans.

Cost and Hours: £8; mid-March-mid-Nov daily 9:45-17:30, July-Aug Thu-Sat until 19:00; mid-Nov-mid-March Sun-Fri 11:00-16:30, Sat 9:45-18:00; these are last tour times, between Queen's Square and the Circus at 40 Gay Street, tel. 01225/443-000, www.janeausten.co.uk.

Tea: Upstairs, the award-winning **Regency Tea Rooms** (free entrance) hits the spot for Austenites, with costumed waitstaff and themed teas (£6-10), including the all-out "Tea with Mr. Darcy" for £15 (also £6 sandwiches, same hours as the center, last order taken one hour before closing).

Sightseeing Tip: Jane Austen-themed **walking tours** of the city begin at the KC Change shop near the abbey churchyard and end at the Centre (£8, buy tickets at KC Change shop, 1.5 hours, Sat-Sun at 11:00, no reservation necessary).

Building of Bath Collection

This unique collection offers a geographic introduction to Bath and an intriguing behind-the-scenes look at how the Georgian city was actually built. The interactive model toward the back of the museum traces expansion from the 17th century forward, highlighting town sights. Compare the 1694 Gilmore map, one of Bath's first tourist maps, with the map beside it created 100 years later, which labels Barton's Field as a public space "never to be built upon"...and is now a parking lot.

Cost and Hours: £5, mid-Feb-Nov Tue-Fri 14:00-17:00, Sat-Sun 10:30-17:00, closed Mon and Dec-mid-Feb, last entry 30 minutes before closing, 20-minute film runs upon request or whenever enough people gather, a short walk north of the city center on a street called "The Paragon," tel. 01225/333-895, www.bath-preservation-trust.org.uk.

Outer Bath

▲American Museum

I know, you need this in Bath like you need a Big Mac. The UK's sole museum dedicated to American history, this may be the only place that combines Geronimo and Groucho Marx. It has thoughtful exhibits on the history of Native Americans and the Civil War, but the museum's heart is with the decorative arts and cultural artifacts that reveal how Americans lived from colonial times to the mid-19th century. Each of the 18 completely furnished rooms (from a plain 1600s Massachusetts dining/living room to a

Rococo Revival explosion in a New Orleans bedroom) is hosted by eager guides waiting to fill you in on the everyday items that make domestic Yankee history surprisingly interesting. (In the Lee Room, look for the original mouse holes, strategically backlit in the floorboards.) One room is a quilter's nirvana. It's interesting to see your own country through British eyes—but on a nice day, the surrounding gardens, and view of the hills, might be the best reasons to visit. You could easily spend an afternoon here, enjoying the gardens, arboretum, and trails.

Cost and Hours: £9, mid-March-Oct Tue-Sun 12:00-17:00, closed Mon except in Aug, closed Nov-mid-March, last entry one hour before closing, at Claverton Manor, tel. 01225/460-503, www.americanmuseum.org.

Getting There: The museum is outside of town, but a free hourly shuttle gets you there in 15 minutes (leaves at :15 past the hour from Terrace Walk, just behind the abbey; show up at least 5 minutes early, as shuttle schedule is a little erratic, and the official stop is often blocked by big tour buses—keep your eye out for a white van with the museum's name on it).

Activities in Bath

▲Thermae Bath Spa

After simmering unused for a quarter-century, Bath's natural thermal springs once again offer R&R for the masses. The state-

of-the-art spa is housed in a complex of three buildings that combine historic structures with controversial (and expensive) new glass-and-steel architecture.

Is the Thermae Bath Spa worth the time and money? The experience is pretty pricey and humble compared to similar German and Hungarian spas. The tall, modern building in the city center lacks a certain old-time elegance. Jets in the pools are very limited, and the only water toys are big foam noodles. There's no cold plunge—the only way to cool off between steam rooms is to step onto a small, unglamorous balcony. The Royal Bath's two pools are essentially the same, and the water isn't particularly hot in either—in fact, the main attraction is the rooftop view from the top one (best with a partner or as a social experience).

All that said, this is the only natural thermal spa in the UK and your one chance to bathe in Bath. Bring your swimsuit and come for a couple of hours (Fri night and all day Sat-Sun are most crowded). Consider an evening visit, when—on a chilly day—Bath's twilight glows through the steam from the rooftop pool.

Cost: The cheapest spa pass is £26 for two hours, which gains you access to the Royal Bath's large, ground-floor "Minerva Bath"; four steam rooms and a waterfall shower; and the view-filled, open-air, rooftop thermal pool. Longer stays are £36/4 hours and £56/day (towel, robe, and slippers are an extra £9). If you arrived in Bath by train, your used rail ticket will score you a four-hour session for the price of two hours (£26, Mon-Fri). The much-hyped £42 Twilight Package includes three hours and a meal (one plate, drink, robe, towel, and slippers). The appeal of this package is not the mediocre meal, but being on top of the building at a magical hour (which you can do for less money at the regular rate).

Thermae has all the "pamper thyself" extras: massages, mud wraps, and various healing-type treatments, including "watsu"—water shiatsu (£40-90 extra). Book treatments in advance by phone.

Hours: Daily 9:00-21:30, last entry at 19:00. No kids under age 16 are allowed.

Information: It's 100 yards from the Roman and Medieval Baths, on Beau Street (tel. 01225/331-234, www.thermaebathspa.com). There's a salad-and-smoothies café for guests.

The Cross Bath: Operated by Thermae Bath Spa, this renovated, circular Georgian structure across the street from the main spa provides a simpler and less-expensive bathing option. It has a hot-water fountain that taps directly into the spring, making its water hotter than the spa's (£16/1.5 hours, daily 10:00-20:00, last entry at 18:00, check in at Thermae Bath Spa's main entrance across the street and you'll be escorted to the Cross Bath, changing rooms, no access to Royal Bath, no kids under 12).

Spa Visitors Center: Also across the street, in the Hetling Pump Room, this free, one-room exhibit explains the story of the spa (Mon-Sat 10:00-17:00, Sun 11:00-16:00, audioguide-£2).

Walking

The Bath Skyline Walk is a six-mile wander around the hills surrounding Bath (leaflet at TI). Plenty of other scenic paths are described in the TI's literature. For additional options, get *Country Walks around Bath*, by Tim Mowl (£4.50 at TI or bookstores).

Hiking the Canal to Bathampton

An idyllic towpath leads two miles from the Bath Spa train station, along the Kennet and Avon Canal, to the sleepy village of Bathampton. Immediately behind the station in Bath, cross the footbridge, turn left, and find where the canal hits the River Avon. Head northeast along the small canal, noticing the series of Industrial Age locks and giving thanks that you're not a horse pulling a barge. After the path crisscrosses the canal a few times, you'll mostly walk with the water on your right. You'll be in Bathampton in less than an hour, where The George, a classic pub, awaits with a nice meal and cellar-temp beer (reservations smart, tel. 01225/425-079).

Boating

The Bath Boating Station, in an old Victorian boathouse, rents rowboats, canoes, and punts.

Cost and Hours: £7/person for first hour, then £4/additional hour; all day for £18; Easter-Sept daily 10:00-18:00, closed off-season, intersection of Forester and Rockcliffe roads, one mile northeast of center, tel. 01225/312-900, www.bathboating.co.uk.

Swimming and Kids' Activities

The Bath Sports and Leisure Centre has a fine pool for laps as well as lots of waterslides. Kids have entertaining options in the mini-gym "Active Club" area, which includes a rock wall and a "Zany Zone" indoor playground.

Cost and Hours: Swimming—£4 for adults, £2.60 for kids, family discounts, Mon-Fri 6:30-22:00, Sat 6:30-19:00, Sun 8:00-20:00, kids' hours limited, call for open-swim times, just across the bridge on North Parade Road, tel. 01225/486-905, www.aqua terra.org.

Shopping

There's great browsing between the abbey and the Assembly Rooms (Fashion Museum). Shops close at about 17:30, and many are open on Sunday (11:00-16:00). Explore the antique shops around Bartlett Street, below the Fashion Museum.

BATH

Nightlife in Bath

For an up-to-date list of events, pick up the local weekly newspaper, the *Bath Chronicle,* which includes a "What's On" schedule (www.thisisbath.com). Younger travelers may enjoy the party-ready bar, club, and nightlife recommendations at www.itchybath .co.uk.

▲▲Bizarre Bath Street Theater

For an entertaining walking-tour comedy act "with absolutely no history or culture," follow Dom or Noel Britten on their creative and lively Bizarre Bath walk. This 1.5-hour "tour," which combines stand-up comedy with cleverly executed magic tricks, plays off unsuspecting passersby as well as tour members. It's a belly laugh a minute.

Cost and Hours: £10, £8 if you show this book, April-Oct nightly at 20:00, smaller groups Mon-Thu, promises to insult all nationalities and sensitivities, just racy enough but still good family fun, leaves from The Huntsman pub near the abbey, confirm at TI or call 01225/335-124, www.bizarrebath.co.uk.

▲Theatre Royal Performance

The 18th-century, 800-seat Theatre Royal, recently restored and one of England's loveliest, offers a busy schedule of London West End-type plays, including many "pre-London" dress-rehearsal runs. The Theatre Royal also oversees performances at two other theaters around the corner from the main box office: Ustinov Studio (edgier, more obscure titles, many of which are premier runs in the UK) and "the egg" (for children, young people, and families).

Cost and Hours: £20-40, shows generally start at 19:30 or 20:00, matinees at 14:30, box office open Mon-Sat 10:00-20:00, Sun 12:00-20:00 if there's a show, £3 extra to book online or by phone with a credit card, on Saw Close, tel. 01225/448-844, www.theatreroyal.org.uk.

Ticket Deals: Forty nosebleed spots on a bench (misnamed "standbys") go on sale at noon Monday through Saturday for that day's evening performance in the main theater (£6, 2 tickets maximum, can book ahead but subject to £3 fee; no fee if bought at box office but cash only). If the show is sold out, same-day "standing places" go on sale at 18:00 (12:00 for matinees) for £4 (2 tickets maximum, cash only). Also at the box office, you can snatch up any "last minute" seats for £15-20 a half-hour before "curtain up" (cash only). Shows in the Ustinov Theatre go for around £20, with no cheap-seat deals.

Sightseeing Tip: During the free Bath walking tour, your guide stops here. Pop into the box office, ask what's playing, and see if there are many seats left for that night. If the play sounds good and plenty of seats remain unsold, you're fairly safe to come back 30 minutes before curtain time to buy a ticket at the cheaper price. Oh...and if you smell jasmine, it's the ghost of Lady Grey, a mistress of Beau Nash.

Evening Walks

Take your choice: comedy (Bizarre Bath, described earlier), history, or ghost tour. The free **city history walks** (a daily standard described on page 280) are offered on some summer evenings (2 hours, May-Sept Tue and Thu at 19:00, leave from Pump Room). **Ghost Walks** are a popular way to pass the after-dark hours (£7, cash only, 1.5 hours, year-round Thu-Sat at 20:00, leave from The Garrick's Head pub—to the left and behind Theatre Royal as you face it, tel. 01225/350-512, www.ghostwalksofbath.co.uk). The cities of York and Edinburgh—which have houses thought to be actually haunted—are better for these walks.

Pubs

Most pubs in the center are very noisy, catering to a rowdy twentysomething crowd. But on the top end of town, you can still find some classic old places with inviting ambience and live music.

These are listed in order from closest to farthest away:

The Old Green Tree, the most convenient of all these pubs, is a rare traditional pub right in the town center (locally brewed real ales, no children, 12 Green Street; also recommended for lunch—see "Eating in Bath," later).

The Star Inn is much appreciated by local beer-lovers for its fine ale and "no machines or music to distract from the chat." It's a spit 'n' sawdust place, and its long bench, nicknamed "death row," still comes with a complimentary pinch of snuff from tins on the ledge. Try the Bellringer Ale, made just up the road (Mon-Fri 12:00-14:30 & 17:30-late, Sat-Sun 12:00-late, no food served, 23 The Vineyards, top of The Paragon/A-4 Roman Road, tel. 01225/425-072, generous and friendly welcome from Paul, who runs the place).

The Bell has a jazzy, pierced-and-tattooed, bohemian feel, but with a mellow older crowd. Some kind of activity is brewing nearly every night, usually live music (Mon-Sat 11:30-23:00, Sun 12:00-22:30, 103 Walcot Street, tel. 01225/460-426, www.thebell innbath.co.uk).

Summer Nights at the Baths

In July and August, you can stretch your sightseeing day at the Roman Baths, open nightly until 22:00 (last entry 21:00), when the gas lamps flame and the baths are far less crowded and more atmospheric. To take a dip yourself, consider popping over to the Thermae Bath Spa (last entry at 19:00).

Sleeping in Bath

Bath is a busy tourist town. Accommodations are expensive, and low-cost alternatives are rare. By far the best budget option is the YMCA—it's central, safe, simple, very well-run, and has plenty of twin rooms available. To get a good B&B, make a telephone reservation in advance. Competition is stiff, and it's worth asking any of these places for a weekday, three-nights-in-a-row, or off-season deal. Friday and Saturday nights are tightest (with many rates going up by about 25 percent)—especially if you're staying only one night, since B&Bs favor those lingering longer. If staying only Saturday night, you're very bad news to a B&B hostess. If you're driving to Bath, stowing your car near the center will cost you (though some less-central B&Bs have parking)—see "Parking" on page 280, or ask your hotelier. Almost every place provides free Wi-Fi to its guests.

Near the Royal Crescent

These listings are all a 5-10-minute walk from the town center, and an easy 15-minute walk from the train station. With bags in tow

Sleep Code

(£1 = about $1.60, country code: 44, area code: 01225)
S = Single, **D** = Double/Twin, **T** = Triple, **Q** = Quad, **b** = bathroom, **s** = shower only. Unless otherwise noted, credit cards are accepted and breakfast is included.

To help you sort easily through these listings, I've divided the rooms into three categories based on the price for a standard double room with bath:

$$$ Higher Priced—Most rooms £100 or more.
$$ Moderately Priced—Most rooms between £60-100.
$ Lower Priced—Most rooms £60 or less.

Prices can change without notice; verify the hotel's current rates online or by email. For the best prices, always book direct.

you may want to either catch a taxi (£5-6) or (except for Brocks Guest House) hop on bus #14 or #14A (direction: Weston, catch bus inside bus station, pay driver £2.50, get off at the Comfortable Place stop—just after the car dealership on the left, cross street and backtrack 100 yards).

Marlborough, Brooks, and Cornerways all face a busy arterial street; while the noise is minimal by urban standards and these B&Bs have well-insulated windows, those sensitive to traffic noise should request a rear- or side-facing room.

$$$ Marlborough House, exuberantly run by hands-on owner Peter, mixes modern style with antique furnishings and features a welcoming breakfast room with an open kitchen. Each of the six rooms comes with a sip of sherry (Sb-£75-105, Db-£95-145, Tb-£105-155, rates can vary with demand, mention this book for Rick Steves discount, £5 additional discount when you pay cash, air-con, mini-fridges, organic vegetarian breakfasts and toiletries, free Wi-Fi, free parking, 1 Marlborough Lane, tel. 01225/318-175, www.marlborough-house.net, mars@manque.dircon.co.uk).

$$$ Brooks Guesthouse is the biggest and most polished of the bunch, albeit the least personal, with 21 modern rooms and classy public spaces, including an exceptionally pleasant breakfast room. It's smart to reconfirm your booking a day or two ahead (Sb-£60-90, Db/Tb-£80-120, rates vary with room size and season/demand, great breakfasts with non-traditional and vegetarian options, free Wi-Fi, shared guest fridge, limited parking-£8/day, 1 Crescent Gardens, Upper Bristol Road, tel. 01225/425-543, www.brooksguesthouse.com, info@brooksguesthouse.com).

$$$ Brocks Guest House has six rooms in a Georgian townhouse built by John Wood in 1765. Located between the prestigious Royal Crescent and the courtly Circus, it has been redone in a way that would make the great architect proud. Each room is themed for a famous Bath resident (standard Db-£99, superior Db-£109-119, Db suite-£129, family room-£179, free Wi-Fi, little top-floor library, airport transfers, 32 Brock Street, tel. 01225/338-374, www.brocksguesthouse.co.uk, brocks@brocksguesthouse.co.uk, Karen and Rachel).

$$ Parkside Guest House has five large, thoughtfully appointed Edwardian rooms. It's tidy, clean, homey, and well priced—and has a spacious back garden (Sb-£68, Db-£85, these prices for Rick Steves readers, free Wi-Fi, limited free parking, 11 Marlborough Lane, tel. 01225/429-444, www.parksidebandb.co.uk, post@parksidebandb.co.uk, kind Inge Lynall).

$$ Cornerways B&B, just a few blocks from the town center, is simple and pleasant, with three rooms and old-fashioned homey touches (Sb-£45-55, Db-£65-75, 15 percent discount with this book and 3-night stay, free Wi-Fi, DVD library, free parking, 47 Crescent Gardens, tel. 01225/422-382, www.cornerwaysbath.co.uk, info@cornerwaysbath.co.uk, Sue Black).

East of the River

These listings are a 5-10-minute walk from the city center. From the train station, it's best to take a taxi, as there are no good bus connections.

$$$ The Kennard, with 12 rooms immaculately maintained by proud owners Giovanni and Mary Baiano, is a short walk through a genteel neighborhood from the Pulteney Bridge. Each of the rooms is different, but all are colorfully and elaborately decorated (prices are for Sun-Thu/Fri-Sat: S-£65/£70, Sb-£89/£120, Db-£110/£130, superior Db-£140/£160, Tb-£150/£170, free Wi-Fi, free street parking permits, thoughtfully planned Georgian garden out back, 11 Henrietta Street, tel. 01225/310-472, www.kennard.co.uk, reception@kennard.co.uk).

$$$ Villa Magdala rents 20 stately yet modern rooms in a freestanding Victorian townhouse opposite a park. In a city that's so insistently Georgian, it's fun to stay in a mansion that's Victorian (Db-£120-150 depending on size and demand, about £20 more Fri-Sun, family rooms, inviting lounge, free Wi-Fi, free parking when booked direct, in quiet residential area on Henrietta Street, tel. 01225/466-329, www.villamagdala.co.uk, enquiries@villamagdala.co.uk).

$$$ The Ayrlington, next door to a lawn-bowling green, has 16 attractive rooms, each thoughtfully decorated either in classical or contemporary style and sprinkled with Asian decor. Though

BATH

Map legend:
- One-way streets →
- Traffic barriers

1. Marlborough House
2. Brooks Guesthouse
3. Brocks Guest House
4. Parkside Guest House
5. Cornerways B&B
6. The Kennard
7. Villa Magdala
8. The Ayrlington
9. Apple Tree Guesthouse
10. Three Abbey Green Guest House
11. Harington's Hotel
12. Abbey House Apartments
13. Pratt's Hotel
14. The Henry Guest House
15. YMCA
16. The White Hart
17. St. Christopher's Inn
18. Launderette
19. Library (Internet Access)
20. Topping & Company Bookstore

BATH

Bath Accommodations

To M-4 & London

GUINEA LN.

LONDON RD.

BUILDING OF BATH MUSEUM

LANSDOWN ROAD

THE PARAGON

ST.

20

15

MILSOM PLACE

BROAD ST.

WALCOT ST.

17

MILSOM ST.

GREEN ST.

NEW BOND ST.

UPPER BOROUGH WALLS

PARSONAGE LN.

UNION PASS.

NORTH-UMBER. PL.

CORRIDOR

UNION ST.

HIGH ST.

WESTGATE ST.

CHEAP ST.

CROSS BATH

ROMAN BATHS & PUMP ROOM

ABBEY

BATH ST.

THERMAE BATH SPA

BEAU ST.

STALL ST.

YORK ST.

LOWER BOROUGH

ST. JAMES PARADE

AMERY LN.

ARBURY

SOUTH GATE

SOUTHGATE SHOPPING CENTER

NEW ORCHARD

ABBEY GATE

OLD ORCHARD

10

12

Abbey Green

14

HENRY ST.

S. PARADE

13

DUKE ST.

PIERREPONT ST.

N. PARADE RD.

Parade Gardens

ST. JOHN'S

MANVERS ST.

GRAND PARADE

GUILDHALL MARKET

ORANGE GROVE

19

BRIDGE ST.

PULTENEY BRIDGE

BOATS

VICTORIA ART GALLERY

ARGYLE ST.

Laura Place

6

GROVE ST.

7

River Avon

200 Meters

200 Yards

HENRIETTA ST.

Henrietta Park

HENRIETTA RD.

HENRIETTA GARDENS

SUTTON ST.

HENRIETTA MEWS

GREAT PULTENEY ST.

POWLETT RD.

FORESTER RD.

BATHWICK ST.

To Boats

SYDNEY PL.

Sydney Gardens

PULTENEY ROAD (A-36)

To American Museum

Rugby Ground

8

FERRY LN.

9

PULTENEY GARDENS

To Bathampton

RAIL STATION

P

DORCHESTER ST.

BUS STATION

WELLS RD.

ROSSITER RD. (A-36)

CLAVERTON RD.

16

Kennet & Avon Canal

To M-4 & London

BATH

this well-maintained hotel fronts a busy street, it's reasonably quiet and tranquil, hinting of a more genteel time. Rooms in the back have pleasant views of sports greens and Bath beyond. For the best value, request a standard top-floor double with a view of Bath (prices are for Mon-Thu/Fri-Sun: twin or standard Db-£110/£130, superior Db-£140/£170, big deluxe Db-£150/£190, extra person-£40, free Wi-Fi, fine garden, free and easy parking, 24-25 Pulteney Road, tel. 01225/425-495, www.ayrlington.com, mail @ayrlington.com, Ling Roper).

$$ At **Apple Tree Guesthouse,** friendly Les and Lynsay offer six comfortable rooms near a shady canal. You'll think you've clicked your ruby heels three times (Sb-£60-66, Db-£90-110, family/Tb-£135-149, 2-night minimum Fri-Sat nights, free Wi-Fi, free parking, 7 Pulteney Gardens, tel. 01225/337-642, www.apple treeguesthouse.com, enquiries@appletreeguesthouse.co.uk).

In the Town Center

You'll pay a premium to sleep right in the center. And, since Bath is so pleasant and manageable by foot, a downtown location isn't essential. Still, these are particularly well located.

$$$ **Three Abbey Green Guest House,** with 10 rooms, is bright, cheery, and located in a quiet, traffic-free courtyard only 50 yards from the abbey and the Roman Baths. Its spacious rooms are a fine value (Db-£90-140, four-poster Db-£140-180, family rooms-£140-220, price depends on season and size of room, 2-night minimum on weekends, 3-night minimum on Bank Holiday weekends, free Internet access and Wi-Fi, nice breakfast, limited free parking, 2 ground-floor rooms work well for those with limited mobility, tel. 01225/428-558, www.threeabbeygreen.com, stay@three abbeygreen.com, Sue, Derek, and daughter Nicola). They also rent self-catering apartments (Db-£140-160, Qb-£170-250, 2-night minimum).

$$$ **Harington's Hotel** rents 13 fresh, modern rooms on a quiet street in the town center. This stylish place feels like a boutique hotel, but with a friendlier, laid-back vibe (Sb-£78-155, Db-£98-148, large superior Db-£108-168, Tb-£130-198, prices vary substantially with demand—always highest on weekends, free Wi-Fi, hot tub, parking-£11/day, 8-10 Queen Street, tel. 01225/461-728, www.haringtonshotel.co.uk, post@haringtons hotel.co.uk, manager Julian). Owners Melissa and Peter offer a 5 percent discount with this book for two-night stays except on Fridays, Saturdays, and holidays. They also rent two self-catering apartments down the street—one can sleep up to three (Db-£125, Tb-£145, higher on weekends), and the other can sleep up to eight (prices on request; for apartments: 2-night minimum on weekdays, 3-night minimum on weekends).

BATH

$$$ At **Abbey House Apartments,** "Goddess of Rock" Laura watches over five flats on Abbey Green and several others scattered around town—including a former residence of Jane Austen. The apartments called Abbey Green (which comes with a washer and dryer), Abbey View, and Abbey Studio have views of the abbey from their nicely equipped kitchens. These are especially practical and economical if you plan on cooking. Laura provides everything you need for simple breakfasts, and it's fun and cheap to stock the fridge or get take-away for a meal in your flat. When Laura meets you to give you the keys, you become a local (Sb-£90, Db-£100-175, price depends on size, 2-night minimum, rooms can sleep four with Murphy and sofa beds, apartments clearly described on website, free Wi-Fi, Abbey Green, tel. 01225/464-238, www.laurastownhouseapartments.co.uk, bookings@lauras townhouseapartments.co.uk).

$$$ **Pratt's Hotel** is as proper and olde English as you'll find in Bath, offering 46 comfy rooms. Its creaks and frays are aristocratic, and even its public places make you want to sip a brandy. Since it's near a busy street, it can occasionally get noisy—request a quiet room, away from the taxi stand and street (Sb-£60-100, Db-£80-150, price depends on size and demand, breakfast-£10, check website for current rates and specials, children under 15 free with 2 adults, elevator, pay Wi-Fi, attached restaurant-bar, 4-6 South Parade, tel. 01225/460-441, www.forestdalehotels.com, pratts@forestdale.com).

$$ **The Henry Guest House** is a simple, vertical place, renting seven clean rooms. It's friendly, well run, and just two blocks from the train station (Sb-£75-85, Db-£80-105, premier Db-£95-120, extra bed-£20, family/Tb-£145-165, 2-night minimum on weekends, free Wi-Fi, 6 Henry Street, tel. 01225/424-052, www.thehenry.com, stay@thehenry.com). Liz also rents two self-catering apartments nearby that sleep up to eight with roll-away beds and a sleeper couch (email for rates).

Bargain Accommodations

Bath's Best Budget Beds: **$** The **YMCA,** centrally located on a leafy square, has 210 beds in industrial-strength rooms—all with sinks and minimal furnishings. Although it smells a little like a gym, this place is a godsend for budget travelers—safe, secure, quiet, and efficiently run. With lots of twin rooms and a few double beds, this is the only easily accessible budget option in downtown Bath (rates for Sun-Thu/Fri-Sat: S-£32/£36, twin D-£56/£60, D-£60/£64, T-£69/£75, Q-£88/£96, dorm beds-£21/£23, WCs and showers down the hall, includes continental breakfast, cooked breakfast-£3.50, free linens, rental towels, lockers, pay guest computer, free Wi-Fi in lobby, laundry facilities, down a tiny alley

off Broad Street on Broad Street Place, tel. 01225/325-900, www
.bathymca.co.uk, stay@bathymca.co.uk).

$ White Hart is a friendly and colorful place, offering adults
and families good, cheap stays in one of four private rooms, or
in one of the two- to six-bed dorms (£15/bed, S-£25, D-£40,
Db-£50-70, Wi-Fi, kitchen, fine garden out back, 5-minute walk
behind the train station at Widcombe—where Widcombe Hill
hits Claverton Street, tel. 01225/313-985, www.whitehartbath
.co.uk). The White Hart also has a pub with a reputation for good,
although not cheap, food.

$ St. Christopher's Inn, in a prime central location, is part
of a chain of low-priced, high-energy hubs for backpackers looking for beds and brews. Their beds are so cheap because they know
you'll spend money on their beer. The inn sits above the lively,
youthful Belushi's pub, which is where you'll find the reception
(54 beds in 6- to 12-bed rooms-£15-25, S-£50-55, D-£110, higher
prices are for weekends and walk-ins—it's always cheaper to book
online, check website for specials, no guests under 18, free Wi-Fi,
laundry facilities, lounge, 9 Green Street, tel. 01225/481-444,
www.st-christophers.co.uk).

Eating in Bath

Bath is bursting with eateries. There's something for every appetite
and budget—just stroll around the center of town. A picnic dinner of deli food or take-out fish-and-chips in the Royal Crescent
Park or down by the river is ideal for aristocratic hoboes. The restaurants I recommend are small and popular—reserve a table on
Friday and Saturday evenings. Most pricey little bistros offer big
savings with their two- and three-course lunches and "pre-theatre"
specials. Restaurants advertise their early-bird specials, and as long
as you order within the time window, you're in for a cheap meal.

Romantic, Upscale French and English

Tilleys Bistro serves sophisticated French, English, and vegetar-
ian/gluten-free dishes with candlelit ambience. Owners Dawn
and Dave make you feel as if you are guests at a dinner party in
their elegant living room. Their menu lets you build your own
meal: Start by sharing a couple of small plates, then choose a
main course and add sides. Cap things off with homemade desert and a glass of the house port, a passion of Dave's. While it's
pricey and the portions are modest, this is a memorable splurge
(£6-9 small plates, £10-20 main courses; lunch specials: £6 cream
tea, £13.50/2 courses, £16/3 courses, also available 18:00-19:30;
open Mon-Sat 12:00-14:30 & 18:00-22:30, Sun 18:00-21:00 only,
reservations smart, 3 North Parade Passage, tel. 01225/484-200,

www.tilleysbistro.co.uk).

The Circus Café and Restaurant is a relaxing little eatery serving well-executed English cuisine with European flair. Choose between the modern interior—with seating on the main floor or in the cellar—and the four tables on the peaceful street connecting the Circus and the Royal Crescent (£9-13 lunches; set lunch menu: £16/2 courses, £20/3 courses; £7 starters and £15-17 main courses at dinner, open Mon-Sat 10:00-24:00, closed Sun, reservations smart, 34 Brock Street, tel. 01225/466-020, www.thecircuscafe andrestaurant.co.uk).

The Garrick's Head is an elegantly simple gastropub right around the corner from the Theatre Royal, with a pricey restaurant on one side and a bar serving affordable snacks on the other. You're welcome to eat from the bar menu, even if you're in the fancy dining room or outside enjoying some great people-watching. The word on the street: The fish-and-chips here are the best in town (£7-12 pub grub, £11-17 main courses on the fancier menu; lunch and pre-theater specials: £15/2 courses, £18/3 courses; food served daily 12:00-14:30 & 17:30-20:00, drinks until later, 8 St. John's Place, tel. 01225/318-368).

Casanis French Bistro-Restaurant is a local hit. Chef Laurent, who hails from Nice, cooks "authentic Provençal cuisine" from the south of France, while his wife, Jill, serves. The decor matches the cuisine—informal, relaxed, simple, and top quality. The intimate Georgian dining room upstairs is a bit nicer and more spacious than the ground floor (early dinner specials: £18/2 courses, £22/3 courses; similar specials £2 cheaper at lunchtime; open Tue-Sat 12:00-14:00 & 18:00-22:00, closed Sun-Mon, immediately behind the Assembly Rooms at 4 Saville Row, tel. 01225/780-055).

BATH

Casual Alternatives

Whether ethnic food or vegetarian, there are plenty of ways to get some fun culinary variation in this town.

Demuths Vegetarian Restaurant is highly rated and ideal for the well-heeled vegetarian. Its tight, understated interior comes with a vegan vibe (£5-11 lunches, £8 starters and £16 main courses at dinner; dinner specials: £16/2 courses, £19/3 courses, £4 cheaper at lunchtime; daily 12:00-15:00 & 17:30-21:30, 2 North Parade Passage, tel. 01225/446-059).

Yen Sushi is your basic little sushi bar—plain and sterile, with stools facing a conveyor belt that constantly tempts you with a variety of freshly made delights on color-coded plates. When you're done, the waitstaff will tally your plates and give you the bill (£2-5 plates, you can fill up for £14 or so, daily 12:00-15:00 & 17:30-22:30, 11 Bartlett Street, tel. 01225/333-313).

1 Tilleys Bistro & Demuths Vegetarian Restaurant
2 The Circus Café & Rest.
3 The Garrick's Head
4 Casanis French Bistro-Rest.
5 Yen Sushi
6 Martini Restaurant
7 Rajpoot Tandoori
8 Rustico Bistro Italiano
9 Thai Balcony
10 Yak Yeti Yak
11 Hoi Faan
12 Milsom Place Eateries
13 Wagamama
14 Ask
15 Loch Fyne
16 Crystal Palace Pub
17 The Old Green Tree
18 The Star Inn
19 The Bell
20 Boston Tea Party
21 Chandos Deli
22 Seafoods Fish & Chips
23 The Cornish Bakehouse (2)
24 Guildhall Market
25 Waitrose Supermarket
26 M&S Kitchen & Café Revive
27 Sainsbury's Local
28 Royal Crescent Hotel (Tea)

BATH

Bath Restaurants

To M-4 & London
GUINEA LN
LONDON RD.
POWLETT RD.
FORESTER RD.
BATHWICK ST.
To Boats
SYDNEY PL.

200 Meters
200 Yards

18
19
BUILDING OF
BATH MUSEUM

THE PARAGON
LANSDOWN ROAD
River Avon

HENRIETTA RD.

Sydney
Gardens

HENRIETTA ST.
HENRIETTA GARDENS
SUTTON ST.

Henrietta
Park

5
ST.
13
14

HENRIETTA MEWS

GREAT PULTENEY ST.

12
MILSOM
PLACE
BROAD ST.
WALCOT ST.
MILSOM ST.
GREEN ST.
17
NEW BOND ST.

PULTENEY
BRIDGE
7
25
GROVE ST.
ARGYLE ST.
Laura
Place

To
American
Museum

BOATS
BRIDGE
HIGH ST.
VICTORIA ART GALLERY

UPPER BOROUGH WALLS
UNION ST.
UNION PASS.
PARSONAGE
CORRIDOR
23
24
GUILDHALL
MARKET
GRAND PARADE
ORANGE
GROVE

Rugby
Ground

PULTENEY ROAD (A-36)

WESTGATE ST.
CHEAP ST.
CROSS
BATH
ROMAN
BATHS &
PUMP ROOM
ABBEY
BATH ST.
i
1
Parade
Gardens

One-way streets
Traffic barriers

THERMAE
BATH SPA
BEAU ST.
YORK ST.
STALL ST.
16
Abbey
Green
PIERREPONT ST.
N. PARADE RD.
DUKE ST.

BATH

LOWER BOROUGH
11
23
ABBEY
GATE
26
NEW
ORCHARD
OLD ORCHARD
HENRY ST.
10
S. PARADE
MAN VERS ST.
FERRY LN.

PULTENEY
GARDENS

ST. JAMES' PARADE
AMERY LN.
SOUTH GATE
P
ST.
JOHN'S

To
Bathampton

ARBURY
SOUTHGATE
SHOPPING
CENTER
27
DORCHESTER ST.
RAIL
STATION

BUS
STATION

WELLS RD.
ROSSITER RD. (A-36)
CLAVERTON RD.

Kennet &
Avon Canal

Martini Restaurant, a hopping, purely Italian place, has class and jovial waiters (£11-13 pastas and pizzas, £16-21 meat and fish dishes, daily 12:00-14:30 & 18:00-22:30, open all day long on Sat, veggie options, daily fish specials, extensive wine list, reservations smart on weekends, 9 George Street, tel. 01225/460-818, www .martinirestaurant.co.uk; Nunzio, Franco, and chef Luigi).

Rajpoot Tandoori serves—by all assessments—the best Indian food in Bath. You'll hike down deep into a sprawling cellar, where the plush Indian atmosphere and award-winning cooking make paying the extra pounds palatable. The seating is tight and the ceilings low, but it's air-conditioned (£9 three-course lunch special, £9-16 main courses; figure £20 per person with rice, naan, and drink; daily 12:00-14:30 & 18:00-23:00, 4 Argyle Street, tel. 01225/466-833, Ali).

Rustico Bistro Italiano, nestled between the Circus and the Royal Crescent, is precisely what its name implies. Franco and his staff are kept busy by a local crowd (£9-11 pastas, £14-19 *secondi,* no pizza, check chalkboard for specials, Tue-Sun 12:00-14:30 & 18:00-22:00, closed Mon, just off Brock Street at 2 Margaret's Buildings, tel. 01225/310-064).

Thai Balcony Restaurant's open, spacious interior is so plush, it'll have you wondering, "Where's the Thai wedding?" While residents debate which of Bath's handful of Thai restaurants serves the best food or offers the lowest prices, there's no doubt that Thai Balcony's fun and elegant atmosphere makes for a memorable and enjoyable dinner (£10 two-course lunch special, early dinner specials also available, £8-13 plates, daily 12:00-14:00 & 18:00-22:00, Fri-Sat until 22:30, reservations smart on weekends, Saw Close, tel. 01225/444-450, www.thai-balcony.com).

Yak Yeti Yak is a fun Nepalese restaurant with both Western and sit-on-the-floor seating. Sera and his wife, Sarah, along with their cheerful, hardworking Nepali team, cook up great traditional food (including plenty of vegetarian plates) at prices that would delight a Sherpa (£7-9 lunches, £5-6 veggie plates, £8-9 meat plates; lunch served daily 12:00-14:00; dinner served Mon-Thu 18:00-22:30, Fri-Sat 17:00-22:30, Sun 17:00-22:00; downstairs at 12 Pierrepont Street, tel. 01225/442-299).

Family-run **Hoi Faan** draws an international crowd by dishing up large portions of traditional Hong Kong-style Chinese food in a bare space. There are plenty of options; if you can't make up your mind, survey nearby tables and point to what looks good (£7 lunch specials include starter and main dish, £7-10 sharable main courses, daily 12:00-23:00, 41-42 St. James Parade, tel. 01225/318-212).

Chain Restaurants

With so many homegrown favorites, I see little reason to frequent a chain restaurant in Bath—but if you're a fan, you'll find plenty of decent choices. **Milsom Place** is a pleasant hidden courtyard with several dependable eateries, including a branch of **Yo! Sushi** and the French-themed **Côte Brasserie**.

Nearby, **Wagamama** specializes in pan-Asian cuisine (£8-11 meals, Mon-Sat 12:00-23:00, Sun 11:30-22:00, 1 York Buildings, corner of George and Broad streets, tel. 01225/337-314) and, just around the corner, **Ask** dishes up Italian comfort food (£8-12 pizzas and pastas, good salads, £11 2-course meal or £14 3-course meal available after 17:00 Sun-Thu, Mon-Sat 11:30-23:00, Sun until 22:00, George Street but entrance on Broad Street, tel. 01225/789-997).

Loch Fyne, a bright, youthful, high-energy place, serves fresh fish at reasonable prices in what was once a lavish bank building (£10-18 meals, £10 two-course special from lunch until 18:00, £5 more after 18:00, daily 12:00-22:00, 24 Milsom Street, tel. 01225/750-120).

Pubs

Bath is not a good pub-grub town, and with so many other tempting options, eating at a pub here isn't as appealing as elsewhere. For the best pub grub, head for **The Garrick's Head** gastropub (described earlier). But if you're looking for a more traditional, lowbrow place, consider these options.

Crystal Palace is an inviting place just a block away from the abbey, facing the delightful little Abbey Green. With a focus on food rather than drink, they serve "pub grub with a Continental flair" in three different spaces, including an airy back patio out back. Be sure to congratulate Toby on completing university (£9-12 meals, food served Mon-Fri 11:00-21:00, Sat 11:00-20:00, Sun 12:00-20:00, last orders for drinks at 22:45, 10-11 Abbey Green, tel. 01225/482-666).

The Old Green Tree, in the old town center, serves satisfying lunches to locals in a characteristic pub setting (real ales on tap, daily for drinks 11:00-23:00 except from 12:00 on Sun, no children, weekend nights can be crowded, 12 Green Street, tel. 01225/448-259).

For a pub to drink and hang out in, rather than eat at, check out **The Star Inn** or **The Bell** (described on page 299).

Simple Options

For a fast, handy, and tasty meal on the go, try one of these easy places. If you get take-away (possible at most of these), you can munch your picnic while watching street musicians from a bench

BATH

in the abbey churchyard.

The **Boston Tea Party** chain is what Starbucks aspires to be—the neighborhood coffeehouse and hangout. Its extensive breakfasts, light lunches, and salads are fresh and healthy. The outdoor seating overlooks a busy square. Their walls are decorated with works by local artists (£4-7 breakfasts, £5-7 lunches, Mon-Sat 7:30-19:30, Sun 9:00-19:00, free Wi-Fi, 19 Kingsmead Square, tel. 01225/314-826).

Chandos Deli has good coffee, breakfast pastries, and tasty £3-5 sandwiches made on artisan breads plus meats, cheese, baguettes, and wine for assembling a gourmet picnic. Upscale yet casual, this place satisfies dedicated foodies who don't want to pay too much (Mon-Fri 8:00-17:30, Sat 9:00-5:30, Sun 11:00-17:00, 12 George Street, tel. 01225/314-418).

Seafoods Fish & Chips is respected by lovers of greasy fried fish in Bath. There's diner-style and outdoor seating, or you can get your food to go for a bit less (£4-6 take-away meals, Mon-Wed 11:30-21:00, Thu-Sat 11:30-22:00, closed Sun, 38 Kingsmead Square, tel. 01225/465-190).

The Cornish Bakehouse has freshly baked £3 take-away pasties (Mon-Sat 8:30-17:30, Sun 10:00-17:00, kitty-corner from Marks & Spencer at 1 Lower Borough Walls, second location off High Street at 11A The Corridor, tel. 01225/780-432).

Produce Market and Café: **Guildhall Market,** across from Pulteney Bridge, has produce stalls with food for picnickers. At its inexpensive **Market Café,** you can munch on a homemade meat pie or sip a tea while surrounded by stacks of used books, bananas on the push list, and honest-to-goodness old-time locals (£3-5 traditional English meals including fried breakfasts all day, Mon-Sat 8:00-17:00, closed Sun, tel. 01225/461-593 a block north of the abbey, on High Street).

Supermarkets: **Waitrose** is great for picnics and has a good salad bar (Mon-Fri 7:30-21:00, Sat 7:30-20:00, Sun 11:00-17:00, just west of Pulteney Bridge and across from post office on High Street). **Marks & Spencer,** near the bottom end of town, has a grocery at the back of its department store and two eateries: **M&S Kitchen** on the ground floor and the pleasant, inexpensive **Café Revive** on the top floor (Mon-Sat 8:00-19:00, Sun 11:00-17:00, 16-18 Stall Street). **Sainsbury's Local,** across the street from the bus station, has the longest hours (daily 7:00-23:00, 2-4 Dorchester Street).

Bath Connections

Bath's train station is called Bath Spa (tel. 0845-748-4950). The National Express bus station is just west of the train station (bus info tel. 0871-781-8178, www.nationalexpress.com). For all public bus services in southwestern England, see www.travelinesw.com.

From Bath to London: You can catch a **train** to London's Paddington Station (2/hour, 1.5 hours, best deals for travel after 9:30 and when purchased in advance, www.firstgreatwestern .co.uk), or save money—but not time—by taking the National Express **bus** to Victoria Coach Station (direct buses nearly hourly, 3-3.5 hours, avoid those with layover in Bristol, one-way-£7-25, round-trip-£12-34, cheapest to purchase online several days in advance).

Connecting Bath with London's Airports: To get to or from **Heathrow,** it's fastest and most pleasant to take the **train via London;** with a Britrail pass, it's also the cheapest option, as the whole trip is covered. Without a railpass, it's the most expensive way to go (£50 total for off-peak travel without railpass, £5-10 cheaper bought in advance, up to £60 more for full-fare peak-time ticket; 2/hour, 2-2.25 hours depending on airport terminal, easy change between First Great Western train and Heathrow Express at London's Paddington Station). The **National Express bus** is direct, and often much cheaper for those without a railpass, but it's relatively infrequent, and can take nearly twice as long as the train (10/day, 2.5-4 hours, £22-44 one-way depending on time of day, tel. 0871-781-8178, www.nationalexpress.com). Doing a **train-and-bus combination** via the town of Reading can make sense for non-railpass holders, as it's more frequent, can take less time than the direct bus, and can be much cheaper than the train via London (train to Reading: 2/hour, 1 hour, RailAir Link shuttle bus from there: 2/hour, 45 minutes; allow 2.5 hours total; £26-40 for off-peak, nonrefundable travel booked in advance—but up to £72 for peak-time trains; tel. 0118-957-9425, buy bus ticket from www.railair.com, train ticket from www.firstgreatwestern.co.uk). Another option is the **minibus** operated by recommended tour company Celtic Horizons (see page 284).

You can get to **Gatwick** by train with a transfer in Reading (hourly, 2.5-3 hours, £50-75 one-way depending on time of day, cheaper in advance; avoid transfer in London, where you'll have to change stations; www.firstgreatwestern.co.uk) or by bus with a transfer at Heathrow (8/day, 3.5-4.5 hours, £30 one-way, transfer at Heathrow Airport, www.nationalexpress.com).

Connecting Bath and Bristol Airport: Located about 20 miles west of Bath, this airport is closer than Heathrow, but they haven't worked out good connections to Bath yet. From Bristol

Airport, your most convenient options are to take a taxi (£40) or call Alan Price (see "Celtic Horizons" on page 284). Otherwise, at the airport you can hop aboard the Bristol Airport Flyer (bus #A1), which takes you to the Temple Meads train station in Bristol (£7, 3/hour, 30 minutes, buy bus ticket at airport info counter or from driver, tell driver you want the Temple Meads train station). At the Temple Meads Station, check the departure boards for trains going to the Bath Spa train station (4/hour, 15 minutes, £7). To get from Bath to Bristol Airport, take the train to Temple Meads, then catch the Bristol Airport Flyer bus.

From Bath by Train to: Salisbury (1-2/hour, 1 hour), **Portsmouth** (hourly, 2.25 hours), **Exeter** (1-2/hour, 1.5-2 hours, transfer in Bristol or Westbury), **Penzance** (1-2/hour, 4.5-5 hours, one direct, most 1-2 transfers), **Moreton-in-Marsh** (hourly, 2.5-3 hours, 1-2 transfers), **York** (hourly with transfer in Bristol, 4.5 hours, more with additional transfers), **Oxford** (hourly, 1.5 hours, transfer in Didcot), **Cardiff** (hourly, 1-1.5 hours), **Birmingham** (2/hour, 2 hours, transfer in Bristol), and **points north** (from Birmingham, a major transportation hub, trains depart for Blackpool, Scotland, and North Wales; use a train/bus combination to reach Ironbridge Gorge and the Lake District).

From Bath by Bus to: Salisbury (hourly, 2.75 hours, transfer in Warminster or Devizes; or 1/day direct at 17:05, 1.5 hours on National Express #300), **Portsmouth** (1/day direct, 3 hours), **Exeter** (4/day, 3.5-4 hours, transfer in Bristol), **Penzance** (2/day, 7-8 hours, transfer in Bristol), **Cheltenham** or **Gloucester** (4/day, 2.5 hours, transfer in Bristol), **Stratford-upon-Avon** (1/day, 4 hours, transfer in Bristol), and **Oxford** (1/day direct, 2 hours, more with transfer). For bus connections to **Glastonbury, Avebury,** and **Wells**, see the next chapter.

NEAR BATH

Glastonbury • Wells • Avebury • Stonehenge • Salisbury • South Wales

Ooooh...mystery, history. The countryside surrounding Bath holds some of England's most goose-pimply prehistoric sites, as well as two particularly fine cathedral towns. Glastonbury, also known as Avalon, is the ancient resting place of King Arthur, and home (maybe) to the Holy Grail. Nearby, medieval Wells gathers around its grand cathedral, where you can enjoy an evensong service. Then get Neolithic at every druid's favorite stone circles, Avebury and Stonehenge. Salisbury is known for its colorful markets and soaring cathedral.

An hour west of Bath, at St. Fagans National History Museum, you'll find South Wales' story vividly told in a park full of restored houses. Relish the romantic ruins and poetic wax of Tintern Abbey and the lush Wye River Valley.

Planning Your Time

In England: Avebury, Glastonbury, and Wells make a wonderful day out from Bath. With a car, you can do all three in a day if you're

selective with your sightseeing in each town (no lingering). If you want to squeeze a little less into each day, choose either the sights to the west (Wells and Glastonbury), or those to the east (Avebury, Stonehenge, and Salisbury). Ideally, try to see Stonehenge on your way from London, saving your Bath side-tripping day for the other sights.

Sights near Bath

Everybody needs to see **Stonehenge**, but I'll tell you now: It looks just like it looks. You'll know what I mean when you pay to get in and rub up against the rope fence that keeps tourists at a distance. **Avebury** is the connoisseur's stone circle: more subtle and welcoming.

Wells is simply a cute small town, much smaller and more medieval than Bath, with a uniquely beautiful cathedral that's best experienced at the 17:15 evensong service (Sun at 15:00)—though the service isn't usually held in July and August.

Glastonbury can be covered well in two to three hours: See the abbey, climb the Tor, and ponder your hippie past (and where you are now).

Just an hour from Bath, **Salisbury** makes a pleasant stop, particularly on a market day (Tue, Sat, and every other Wed), though its cathedral is striking anytime. Salisbury is also the logical launch pad for visiting nearby Stonehenge (particularly if you lack a car).

In Wales: Think of the South Wales sights as a different grouping. Ideally, they fill the day you leave Bath for the Cotswolds. Anyone interested in Welsh culture can spend four hours in St. Fagans National History Museum. Castle lovers and romantics will want to consider seeing Tintern Abbey and the castles of Caerphilly, Cardiff, and Chepstow (Caerphilly is best).

For a great day in South Wales, consider this schedule:

Near Bath at a Glance

Glastonbury

▲▲**Glastonbury Abbey** Once a leading Christian pilgrimage destination, now a lush park with some of England's finest abbey ruins—along with the purported gravesite of Arthur and Guinevere. **Hours:** Daily June-Aug 9:00-20:00, Sept-Nov and March-May 9:00-17:00, Dec-Feb 9:00-16:00. See page 324.

▲**Glastonbury Tor** Holy hill topped with the remnants of a church tower and worth climbing for its sweeping views. **Hours:** Always open. See page 327.

Wells

▲▲**Wells Cathedral** England's first wholly Gothic cathedral, with an ornate facade and heavenly evensong service (except July-Aug). **Hours:** Daily Easter-Sept 7:00-19:00, Oct-Easter 7:00-18:00. See page 330.

▲**Bishop's Palace** Home of the Bishop of Bath and Wells, with spectacular gardens. **Hours:** Daily April-Oct 10:00-18:00, Nov-March 10:00-16:00, often closed on Sat for special events. See page 335.

Avebury

▲▲**Avebury Stone Circle** Giant stone circle, 16 times the size of Stonehenge—but with a fraction of the tourists. **Hours:** Always open. See page 340.

▲**Ritual Procession Way** Double line of stones that once served as a route for ritual processions. **Hours:** Always open. See page 342.

▲**Silbury Hill** Pyramid-shaped chalk mound—and the largest man-made object from prehistoric Europe. **Hours:** Always open. See page 342.

Stonehenge and Salisbury

▲▲**Stonehenge** England's most famous stone circle, unique for its horizontal stones. **Hours:** Daily June-Aug 9:00-20:00, mid-

March-May and Sept-mid-Oct 9:30-19:00, mid-Oct-mid-March 9:30-17:00. See page 345.

▲▲**Salisbury Cathedral** Architecturally harmonious Gothic cathedral, boasting the tallest spire in England, surrounded by a huge, peaceful green. **Hours:** April-Oct Mon-Sat 9:00-17:00, Sun 12:00-16:00; Nov-March daily 9:00-17:00. See page 354.

▲**Salisbury and South Wiltshire Museum** Random collection of costumes, art, ceramics, and other historical items, plus a fine exhibit about Stonehenge. **Hours:** Mon-Sat 10:00-17:00, Sun 12:00-17:00 except closed Sun Oct-May. See page 357.

South Wales
▲**Cardiff Castle** Sumptuous castle with a fanciful Victorian-era makeover, plus WWII tunnels, museum, and expansive walled grounds. **Hours:** Daily March-Oct 9:00-18:00, Nov-Feb 9:00-17:00. See page 366.

▲▲**Cardiff Bay** People-friendly, rejuvenated harborfront brimming with major attractions, striking architecture, entertainment, and dining options. **Hours:** Public areas always open. See page 368.

▲▲**St. Fagans National History Museum** One hundred acres dedicated to Welsh folk life, including a museum, castle, and more than 40 reconstructed houses demonstrating bygone Welsh ways. **Hours:** Daily 10:00-17:00. See page 370.

▲▲**Caerphilly Castle** Britain's second-largest castle, featuring a leaning tower inhabited by a heartbroken ghost. **Hours:** March-Oct daily 9:30-17:00, July-Aug until 18:00; Nov-Feb Mon-Sat 10:00-16:00, Sun 11:00-16:00. See page 373.

▲▲**Tintern Abbey** Remains of a Cistercian abbey that once inspired William Wordsworth and J. M. W. Turner. **Hours:** March-Oct daily 9:30-17:00, July-Aug until 18:00; Nov-Feb Mon-Sat 10:00-16:00, Sun 11:00-16:00. See page 378.

9:00	Leave Bath for South Wales.
10:30	Tour St. Fagans.
14:30	Leave for Tintern Abbey and/or a castle of your choice, then drive to the Cotswolds.
18:00	Set up in your Cotswolds home base.

Getting Around the Region

By Car: Drivers can do a 133-mile loop, from Bath to Avebury (25 miles) to Stonehenge (30 miles) to Glastonbury (50 miles) to Wells (6 miles) and back to Bath (22 miles). A loop from Bath to South Wales is 100 miles, mostly on the 70-mph motorway. Each of the Welsh sights is just off the motorway.

By Bus and Train: Wells and Glastonbury are both easily accessible by bus from Bath. Bus #173 goes direct from Bath to **Wells** (nearly hourly, less frequent on Sun, 1.25 hours), where you can continue on to **Glastonbury** by catching bus #375 toward Bridgewater, #377 toward Yeovil, or #29 toward Taunton (3-4/ hour, 25 minutes to Glastonbury, drops off directly in front of abbey entrance on Magdalene Street). Note that there are no direct buses between Bath and Glastonbury. First Bus Company offers a £7 day pass that covers all their routes—a good deal if you plan on connecting Glastonbury and Wells from your Bath home base. Wells and Glastonbury are also connected to each other by a 9.5-mile foot and bike path (though only Glastonbury has bike rental).

Many different buses run between Bath and **Avebury,** all requiring one or two transfers (hourly, 2.25 hours, transfer at Trowbridge or Devizes). There is no bus between Avebury and Stonehenge.

A one-hour train trip connects Bath to **Salisbury** (1-2/hour). With the best public transportation of all these towns, Salisbury is a good jumping-off point for Stonehenge or Avebury by bus or car. The Stonehenge Tour runs buses between Salisbury, Old Sarum, and Stonehenge (see page 354). Buses also run from Salisbury to Avebury (hourly, 2-2.5 hours; Wilts & Dorset bus #4 leaves from bus station on Endless Street and also from St. Paul's Church on Fisherton Street, near the train station; transfer in Devizes to Stagecoach's bus #49 to Avebury; other combinations possible, some with 2 transfers).

Various bus companies run these routes, including Stagecoach, Bodmans Coaches, the First Bus Company, and Wilts & Dorset. To find fare information, check with Traveline South West, which combines all the information from these companies into an easy-to-use website that covers all the southwest routes (www .travelinesw.com, tel. 0871-200-2233). Buses run much less frequently on Sundays.

To get to **South Wales** from Bath, take a train to Cardiff, then connect by bus (or train) to the sights.

By Tour: From Bath, if you don't have a car, the most convenient and quickest way to see Avebury and Stonehenge is to take an all-day bus tour, or a half-day tour just to Stonehenge. Mad Max is the liveliest of the tours leaving from Bath (see "Tours in Bath" on page 281).

Glastonbury

Marked by its hill, or "tor," and located on England's most powerful line of prehistoric sites, the town of Glastonbury gurgles with history and mystery.

In A.D. 37, Joseph of Arimathea—Jesus' wealthy uncle—reputedly brought vessels containing the blood of Jesus to Glastonbury, and with him, Christianity came to England. (Joseph's visit is plausible—long before Christ, locals traded lead and tin to merchants from the Levant.)

While this story is "proven" by fourth-century writings and accepted by the Church, the King-Arthur-and-the-Holy-Grail legends it inspired are not. Those medieval tales came when England needed a morale-boosting folk hero for inspiration during a war with France. They pointed to the ancient Celtic sanctuary at Glastonbury as proof enough of the greatness of the fifth-century warlord Arthur. In 1191, after a huge fire, Arthur's supposed remains (along with those of Queen Guinevere) were dug up from the abbey garden. Reburied in the abbey choir, Arthur and Guinevere's gravesite is a shrine today. Many think the Grail trail ends at the bottom of the Chalice Well, a natural spring at the base of the Glastonbury Tor.

By the 10th century, Glastonbury Abbey was England's most powerful and wealthy, and was part of a nationwide network of monasteries that by 1500 owned one-quarter of all English land and had four times the income of the Crown. Then Henry VIII dissolved the abbeys in 1536. He was particularly harsh on Glastonbury—he not only destroyed the abbey but also hung and quartered the abbot, sending the parts of his body on four different national tours...at the same time. This was meant as a warning to other religious clerics, and it worked.

But Glastonbury rebounded. In an 18th-century tourism campaign, thousands signed affidavits stating that they'd been healed by water from the Chalice Well, and once again Glastonbury was on the tourist map. Today, Glastonbury and its Tor are a center for "searchers"—too creepy for the mainstream Church but just right for those looking for a place to recharge their crystals. Glastonbury is also synonymous with its music and arts festival, an annual long-hair-and-mud Woodstock recreation that's a rite of passage for young music lovers.

Part of the fun of a visit to Glastonbury is just being in a town where every other shop and eatery is a New Age place. Locals who are not into this complain that on High Street, you can buy any kind of magic crystal or incense—but not a roll of TP. But, as this counterculture is their town's bread and butter, they do their best to sit in their pubs and go "Ommmmm."

Orientation to Glastonbury

Tourist Information

The TI is on High Street—as are many of the dreadlocked folks who walk it. It occupies a fine 15th-century townhouse called The Tribunal (Mon-Sat 10:00-16:00, closed Sun, pay Internet terminal, 9 High Street, tel. 01458/832-954, www.glastonburytic.co.uk). The TI sells several booklets about cycling and walking in the area, including the *Glastonbury and Street Guide*, with local listings and a map (£1); and the *Glastonbury Millennium Trail* pamphlet, which sends visitors on a historical scavenger hunt, following 20 numbered marble plaques embedded in the pavement throughout the town (£1). The TI also offers sporadic walking tours (£5, call ahead for schedule).

Above the TI is the marginally interesting **Lake Village Museum**, with two humble rooms featuring tools made of stones, bones, and antlers. Preserved in and excavated from the local peat bogs, these tools offer a look at the lives of marshland people in pre-Roman times (£2.50, extensive descriptions, same hours as TI, tel. 01458/832-954).

Helpful Hints

Market Day: Tuesday is market day for crafts, knickknacks, and local produce on the main street. There's also a country market Tuesday mornings in the Town Hall.

Glastonbury Festival: Nearly every summer (around the June solstice), the gigantic Glastonbury Festival—billing itself as the

Glastonbury

↑ TO WELLS VIA A-39 OR BIKE PATH

1/4 MILE
400 METERS

Ⓣ TAXI STAND
--- PATH
Ⓟ PARKING
Ⓑ BUS STOP

MANOR HOUSE RD.
NORTHLOAD ST.
POST
HIGH STREET
LAMBROOK ST.
POD LANE
THORN TREES
MUSEUM
ENTER→
MAG-DALENE ST.
TOWN HALL
CHURCH-YARD
KITCHEN
BERE LANE
BUTLEIGH RD.
← ABBEY RUINS
CHALICE WELL
CHILKWELL ST.
WELLHOUSE LANE
TOR TRAIL-HEAD
GLASTONBURY TOR
≥ξ≤ GREAT VIEW !
SOMERSET RURAL LIFE MUSEUM
TO BATH VIA A-361 →
DCH

❶ Rainbow's End Café
❷ Burns the Bread Bakery (2)
❸ Knights Fish & Chips Rest.
❹ The George & Pilgrims
❺ Tor Bus Stop & St. Dunstan's Parking
❻ Glastonbury Cycles

"largest music and performing arts festival in the world"—brings all manner of postmodern flower children to its notoriously muddy "Healing Fields." Music fans and London's beautiful people make the trek to see the hottest English and American bands. If you're near Glastonbury during the festival, anticipate increased traffic and crowds (especially on public transportation; more than 165,000 tickets generally sell out), even though the actual music venue is six miles east of town (www.glastonburyfestivals.co.uk).

Bike Rental: Try **Glastonbury Cycles**, at the top of High Street (£10/day, includes lock and tire repair kit, helmets-£2; Mon-Fri 9:30-18:00, Sat 9:30-17:00, closed Sun; deposit required—either cash, credit card, or passport; must return bikes in Glastonbury, 67 High Street, tel. 01458/830-639).

Sights in Glastonbury

I've listed these sights in the order you'll reach them, moving from the town center to the Tor.

▲▲Glastonbury Abbey

The massive and evocative ruins of the first Christian sanctuary in the British Isles stand mysteriously alive in a lush 36-acre park.

Because it comes with a small museum, a dramatic history, and enthusiastic guides dressed in period costume, this is one of the most engaging to visit of England's many ruined abbeys.

Cost and Hours: £6, daily June-Aug 9:00-20:00, Sept-Nov and March-May 9:00-17:00, Dec-Feb 9:00-16:00, last entry 30 minutes before closing.

Getting There: Enter the abbey from Magdalene Street (around the corner from High Street, near the St. Dunstan's parking lot). Pay parking is nearby.

Information: Tel. 01458/832-267, www.glastonburyabbey.com.

Tours and Demonstrations: Costumed guides offer tours and presentations throughout the day (all included with your ticket). These include a fun medieval kitchen demo (described later) and earnest, costumed "Living History" re-enactments (generally daily March-Oct on the hour from 10:00). As you enter, confirm these times, and ask about other tour and show times. Or, if you're coming on a slow day (off-season weekdays), call ahead to get the schedule.

Eating: Picnicking is encouraged—bring something from one of the shops in town (see "Eating in Glastonbury," later), or buy food at the small café on site (open May-Sept).

Background: The space that these ruins occupy has been sacred ground for centuries. The druids used it as a pagan holy site, and during Joseph of Arimathea's supposed visit here, he built a simple place of worship. In the 12th century—because of that legendary connection—Glastonbury was the leading Christian pilgrimage site in all of Britain. The popular abbey grew powerful and very wealthy, employing a thousand people to serve the needs of the pilgrims. Then, in 1171, Thomas Becket was martyred at Canterbury and immediately canonized by the pope (who thanked God for the opportunity to rile up the Christian public in England against King Henry II). This was a classic church-state power struggle. The king was excommunicated. In order to redeem himself, he had to crawl through the streets of London on his knees and submit to a whipping from each bishop in England. Religious pilgrims abandoned Glastonbury for Canterbury, leaving Glastonbury suddenly a backwater.

In 1184, there was a devastating fire in the monastery, and

in 1191, the abbot here "discovered"—with the help of a divine dream—the tomb and bodies of King Arthur and Queen Guinevere. Of course, this discovery rekindled the pilgrim trade in Glastonbury, and the new revenues helped to rebuild the abbey.

Then, in 1539, King Henry VIII ordered the abbey's destruction. When Glastonbury Abbot Richard Whiting questioned the king's decision, he was branded a traitor, hung at the top of Glastonbury Tor (after carrying up the plank that would support his noose), and his body cut into four pieces. His head was stuck over the gateway to the former abbey precinct. After this harsh example, the other abbots accepted the king's dissolution of England's abbeys, with many returning to monastic centers in France. Glastonbury Abbey fell into ruin.

Today, the abbey attracts people who find God within and the curious traveler alike. Tie-dyed, starry-eyed pilgrims seem to float through the grounds, naturally high. Others lie on the grave of King Arthur, whose burial site is marked off in the center of the abbey ruins.

❍ Self-Guided Tour: After buying your ticket, tour the informative **museum** at the entrance building. A model shows the abbey in its pre-Henry VIII splendor, and exhibits tell the story of a place "grandly constructed to entice the dullest minds to prayer." Knowledgeable, costumed guides are eager to share the site's story and might even offer an impromptu tour.

Then head out to explore the green park, dotted with bits of the **ruined abbey.** You come face-to-face with the abbey's west (entrance) end. The abbey was long and skinny, but vast. Measuring 580 feet, it was the longest in Britain (larger than York Minster is today) and the largest building north of the Alps.

Before poking around the ruins, circle to the left behind the entrance building to find the two **thorn trees.** According to legend, when Joseph of Arimathea came here, he climbed nearby Wearyall Hill and stuck his staff into the soil. A thorn tree sprouted, and its descendant still stands there today; these are its offspring. In 2010, vandals hacked off the branches of the original tree on Wearyall Hill, but miraculously, the stump put out small green shoots the following spring. The trees inside the abbey grounds bloom twice a year, at Easter and at Christmas. If the story seems far-fetched to you, don't tell the Queen—a blossom from the abbey's trees sits proudly on her breakfast table every Christmas morning.

Ahead and to the left of the trees, inside what was the north wall, look for two trap doors in the ground. Lift up the doors to see surviving fragments of the abbey's original tiled floor.

Now hike along the ruins, walking through the remains of the extensive cloisters, to the far end of the abbey. You can stand and, from what was once the altar, look down at what was the nave. In this area, you'll find the tombstone (formerly in the floor of the church's choir) marking the spot where the supposed relics of **Arthur and Guinevere** were interred.

Continue around the far side of the abbey ruins, feeling free to poke around the park. Head back toward the front of the

church, noticing all of the foundation rubble in the field adjoining the abbey; among these were the former church-yard, where Arthur and Guinevere's bones were originally found.

Head for the only surviving intact building on the grounds—the abbot's conical **kitchen.** Here, you'll often find Matilda the pilgrim (or another costumed docent) demonstrating life in the abbey kitchen in a kind of medieval cooking show.

Near Glastonbury Tor

These sights are about a 15-minute walk from the town center, toward the Tor (see "Getting There," on next page).

Somerset Rural Life Museum

Exhibits in this free and extremely kid-friendly museum include peat digging and cider- and cheese-making. The abbey farmhouse now houses a collection of domestic and work mementos that illustrate the life of Victorian farm laborer John Hodges "from the cradle to the grave." The fine 14th-century tithe barn (one of 30 such structures that funneled tithes to the local abbey), with its beautifully preserved wooden ceiling, is filled with Victorian farm tools and enthusiastic schoolchildren.

Cost and Hours: Free, Tue-Sat 10:00-17:00, closed Sun-Mon, last entry 30 minutes before closing; parking-£1/2 hours, £2/day; at intersection of Bere Lane and Chilkwell Street, tel. 01823/278-805, www.somerset.gov.uk/museums.

Chalice Well

According to tradition, Joseph of Arimathea brought the chal-

ice from the Last Supper to Glastonbury in A.D. 37. Supposedly it ended up in the bottom of a well, which is now the centerpiece of a peaceful and inviting garden. Even if the chalice is not in the bottom of the well (another legend says it made the trip to Wales), and the water is red from iron ore and not Jesus' blood, the tranquil setting is one where nature's harmony is a joy to ponder. To find the well itself, follow the well-marked path uphill alongside the gurgling stream, passing several places to drink from or wade in the healing water, as well as areas designated for silent reflection. The stones of the well shaft date from the 12th century and are believed to have come from the church in Glastonbury Abbey (which was destroyed by fire). During the 18th century, pilgrims flocked to Glastonbury for the well's healing powers. Have a drink or take some of the precious water home—they sell empty bottles to fill.

Cost and Hours: £3.80, daily April-Oct 10:00-18:00, Nov-March 10:00-16:30, last entry 30 minutes before closing, on Chilkwell Street/A-361, drivers park at Rural Life Museum and walk 5 minutes—see instructions below, tel. 01458/831-154, www.chalicewell.org.uk.

▲Glastonbury Tor

Seen by many as a Mother Goddess symbol, the Tor—a natural plug of sandstone on clay—has an undeniable geological charisma. Climbing the Tor is the essential activity on a visit to Glastonbury. A fine Somerset view rewards those who hike to its 520-foot summit.

Getting There: The Tor is a steep hill at the southeastern edge of the town (it's visible from just about everywhere). The base of the Tor is a 20-minute **walk** from the TI and town center. From the base, a trail leads up to the top (figure another 15-20 uphill minutes, if you keep a brisk pace). While you can hike up the Tor from either end, the less-steep approach (which most people take) starts next to the Chalice Well.

If you have a **car,** drive to the Somerset Rural Life Museum, where you can park, then walk five minutes to the trailhead (walk up the lane between the parking lot and the museum, turn right onto Chilkwell Street, and watch on the left for the Chalice Well, then signs for the trailhead).

If you're without a car and don't want to walk to the Tor trailhead, you have two options: The **Tor Bus** shuttles visitors from the town center to the base of the Tor. If you ask, the bus will also stop at the Somerset Rural Life Museum and the Chalice Well (£3 round-trip, 2/hour, on the half-hour, Easter-Sept daily 9:30-12:30 & 14:00-19:00, doesn't run Oct-Easter, catch bus at St. Dunstan's parking lot in the town center—to the right as you face the abbey entrance, pick up schedule at TI). A **taxi** to the Tor trailhead costs about £5 one-way—an easier and more economical choice for couples or groups. Remember, these take you only to the bottom of the Tor; to reach the top, you have to hike.

Climbing the Tor: Hiking up to the top of the tor, you can survey a former swamp, inhabited for 12,000 years, that is still below sea level at high tide. The ribbon-like man-made drainage canals that glisten as they slice through the farmland are the work of Dutch engineers—Huguenot refugees imported centuries ago to turn the marshy wasteland into something usable.

Looking out, find Glastonbury (at the base of the hill) and Wells (marked by its cathedral) to the right. Above Wells, a TV tower marks the 996-foot high point of the Mendip Hills. It was lead from these hills that attracted the Romans (and, perhaps, Jesus' uncle Joe) so long ago. Stretching to the left, the Mendip Hills define what was the coastline before those Dutch engineers arrived.

The Tor-top tower is the remnant of a chapel dedicated to St. Michael. Early Christians often employed St. Michael, the warrior angel, to combat pagan gods. When a church was built upon a pagan holy ground like this, it was frequently dedicated to Michael. But apparently those pagan gods fought back: St. Michael's Church was destroyed by an earthquake in 1275.

Eating in Glastonbury

Rainbow's End is one of several fine, healthy, vegetarian lunch cafés for hot meals (different every day), salads, herbal teas, soups, yummy homemade sweets, and New Age people-watching. If you're looking for a midwife or a male-bonding tribal meeting, check their notice board (£6-8 meals, cheaper salads sold by the portion, vegan and gluten-free options, counter service, daily 10:00-16:00, free Wi-Fi, a few doors up from the TI, 17 High Street, tel. 01458/833-896).

Burns the Bread has two locations in town, making hearty pasties (savory meat pies) as well as fresh pies, sandwiches, delicious cookies, and pastries. Ask for a sample of the Torsy Moorsy Cake (a type of fruitcake made with cheddar), or try a gingerbread man made with real ginger. Grab a pasty and picnic with the ghosts of Arthur and Guinevere in the abbey ruins (£1.80 pasties and pastries, £2-3 sandwiches, Mon-Sat 6:00-17:00, Sun 11:00-17:00, two locations: 14 High Street and in St. Dunstan's parking lot next to the abbey, tel. 01458/831-532).

Knights Fish and Chips Restaurant has been in the same family since 1909 and is the town's top chippy. It's another fine option for a picnic at the abbey (£6 to go, about £1 more for table service, Mon-Fri 12:00-14:15 & 17:00-21:30, Sat 17:00-21:30 only, closed Sun, 5 Northload Street, tel. 01458/831-882).

The George & Pilgrims Hotel's wonderfully Old World pub might be exactly what the doctor ordered for visitors suffering a New Age overdose. The local owners serve up a traditional pub-grub menu (£5 sandwiches, £8-11 meals, Mon-Sat 11:00-23:00, Sun 12:00-22:30, food served 12:00-14:45 & 18:00-20:45, 1 High Street, tel. 01458/831-146). They also rent rooms (Db-£80, family rooms-£85).

Glastonbury Connections

The nearest train station is in Bath. Local buses are run by First Bus Company (tel. 0845-602-0156, www.firstgroup.com).

From Glastonbury by Bus to: Wells (3-4/hour, 20 minutes, bus #375/#377 or #29), **Bath** (nearly hourly, allow 2 hours, take bus #375/#377 or #29 to Wells, transfer to bus #173 to Bath, 1.25 hours between Wells and Bath). Buses are sparse on Sundays (generally one bus every other hour). If you're heading to points west, you'll likely connect through **Taunton** (which is a transfer point for westbound buses from Bristol).

Wells

Because this well-preserved little town has a cathedral, it can be called a city. It's England's smallest cathedral city (pop. 9,400), with one of its most interesting cathedrals and a wonderful evensong service (generally not offered July-Aug). Wells has more medieval buildings still doing what they were originally built to do than any town you'll visit. Market day fills the town square on Wednesday (farmers' market) and Saturday (general goods).

NEAR BATH

Orientation to Wells

Tourist Information

The TI is in the lobby of the Wells Museum, across the green from the cathedral. It has useful information about the town's sights and nearby cheese factories (April-Oct Mon-Sat 10:00-17:00, Nov-March Mon-Sat 11:00-16:00, closed Sun year-round, 8 Cathedral Green, tel. 01749/671-770, www.visitsomerset.co.uk). The TI sells town maps for £0.50 and provides information on trails nearby; consider the *Wells City Trail* booklet for £0.60. It also offers a one-hour walking tour of town for £4 on Wednesdays and Saturdays at 11:00 (Easter-Sept only).

Arrival in Wells

If you're coming by **bus,** you can get off in the city center at the Sadler Street stop, around the corner from the cathedral. Or you can disembark at the big, well-organized bus station/parking lot (staffed Mon-Fri 9:00-16:30, closed Sat-Sun), about a five-minute walk from the town center, at the bottom of High Street. (The big church tower you see is *not* the cathedral.) Find the Wells map at the head of the stalls to get oriented; the signpost at the main exit directs you downtown.

Drivers will find pay parking right on the main square, but because of confusing one-way streets, it's hard to reach; instead, it's simpler to park at the Princes Road lot near the bus station (enter on Priory Road) and walk five minutes to the cathedral.

Helpful Hints

Local Guide: Edie Westmoreland, an official cathedral guide, offers town walks in the summer by appointment (£15/group of 2-5 people, £4/person for 8 or more, 1.5-hour tours usually start at Penniless Porch on town square, book three days in advance, tel. 01934/832-350, mobile 07899-836-706, ebwestmoreland@btinternet.com).

Best Views: It's hard to beat the grand views of the cathedral from the green in front of it...but the reflecting pool tucked inside the Bishop's Palace grounds tries hard. For a fine cathedral-and-town view from your own leafy hilltop bench, hike 10 minutes up Tor Hill.

Sights in Wells

NEAR BATH

▲▲Wells Cathedral

The city's highlight is England's first completely Gothic cathedral (dating from about 1200). Locals claim this church has the largest collection of medieval statuary north of the Alps. It certainly has one of the widest and most elaborate facades I've seen, and unique figure-eight ("scissors arch") that supports in the nave.

Cost and Hours: Free but £6 donation requested—not intended to keep you out, daily Easter-Sept 7:00-19:00, Oct-Easter 7:00-18:00, daily evensong service (except July-Aug)—described later.

Information: Good shop, handy Chapter Two restaurant, tel. 01749/674-483, www.wellscathedral.org.uk.

Tours: Free one-hour tours run April-Oct Mon-Sat at 10:00, 11:00, 13:00, 14:00, and 15:00; Nov-March Mon-Sat usually at 12:00 and 14:00—unless other events are going on in the cathedral.

Photography: To take pictures, pay the £3 photography fee at the info desk or at a coin-op machine inside the cathedral. No

Wells

1. Swan Hotel
2. The Old Farmhouse
3. To Baytree House B&B
4. West Cornwall Pasty Co.
5. The Fountain Inn
6. Chapter Two Restaurant
7. The Old Spot Restaurant

flash is allowed in the choir.

Self-Guided Tour: Begin on the vast, inviting **green** in front of the cathedral. In the Middle Ages, the cathedral was enclosed within "The Liberty," an area free from civil jurisdiction until the 1800s. The Liberty included the green on the west side of the cathedral, which, from the 13th to the 17th centuries, was a burial place for common folk, including 17th-century plague victims. During the Edwardian period, a local character known as Boney Foster used to dig up the human bones and sell them to tourists. The green later became a cricket pitch, then a field for grazing animals and picnicking people. Today, it's the perfect setting for an impressive cathedral.

Peer up at the magnificent **facade.** The west front displays almost 300 original 13th-century carvings of kings and the Last Judgment. The bottom row of niches is empty, too easily reached by Cromwell's men, who were hell-bent on destroying "graven images." Stand back and imagine it as a grand Palm Sunday welcome with a cast of hundreds—all gaily painted back then, choristers singing boldly from holes above the doors and trumpets tooting through the holes up by the 12 apostles.

Now head **inside.** Most of the time, visitors enter by going to the right, through the door under the small spire into the lobby and welcome center. (At certain times—generally 7:00-9:00 and 17:00-19:00—you can enter through the cathedral's main door.)

At the **welcome center,** you'll be warmly greeted and reminded how expensive it is to maintain the cathedral. Pay the donation, buy a photo-permission sticker (if you want to take photos), and pick up a map of the cathedral's highlights. Then head

through the cloister and into the cathedral.

At your first glance down the nave, you're immediately struck by the general sense of light and the unique "scissors" or hourglass-shaped **double arch** (added in 1338 to transfer weight from the south—where the foundations were sinking under the tower's weight—to the east, where they were firm). The warm tones of the stone interior give the place a modern feel. Until Henry VIII and the Reformation, the interior was opulently painted in golds, reds, and greens. Later it was whitewashed. Then, in the 1840s, the church experienced the Victorian "great scrape," as locals peeled moldy whitewash off and revealed the bare stone we see today. The floral ceiling painting is based on the original medieval design: A single pattern was discovered under the 17th-century whitewash and repeated throughout.

Small, ornate 15th-century pavilion-like chapels flank the altar, carved in lacy Gothic for wealthy townsmen. The **pulpit** features a post-Reformation, circa-1540 English script—rather than the standard Latin (see where the stonemason ran out of space when carving the inscription). Since this was not a monastery church, the Reformation didn't destroy it as it did the Glastonbury Abbey church.

We'll do a quick clockwise spin around the cathedral's interior. First walk down the left aisle until you reach the north transept. The medieval **clock** does a silly but much-loved joust on the quarter-hour. If you get to watch the show, notice how—like clockwork—the same rider gets clobbered, as he has for hundreds of years. The clock's face, which depicts the earth at the center of the universe, dates from 1390. The outer ring shows hours, the middle ring shows minutes, and the inner ring shows the dates of the month and phases of the moon. Beneath the clock, the fine **crucifix** (1947) was carved out of a yew tree by English

sculptor Estcourt James Clack. Also in the north transept is the door with well-worn steps leading up to the grand, fan-vaulted **Chapter House**—an inspiring architectural achievement and intimate place for the theological equivalent of a huddle among church officials.

Now continue down the left aisle. On the right is the entrance to the **choir** (or "quire," the central zone where the daily services are sung). Go in and take a close look at the embroidery work on the cushions, which celebrate the hometowns of important local church leaders. Up above the east end of the choir is "Jesse's Window," depicting Jesus' family tree. It's also called the "Golden Window," because it's bathed in sunlight each morning.

Head back out to the aisle the way you came in, and continue to the end of the church. In the apse you'll find the **Lady Chapel.** Examine the medieval stained-glass windows. Do they look jumbled? In the 17th century, Puritan troops trashed the precious original glass. Much was repaired, but many of the broken panes were like a puzzle that was never figured out. That's why today many of the

windows are simply kaleidoscopes of colored glass.

Next to the chapel is the oldest piece of wooden furniture in England: a **"cope chest,"** which is still used to store the clergy's garments. It is so large it can't be moved out through any of the cathedral's doors. Historians believe the chest is older than the existing building, and was originally installed around A.D. 800, in the Saxon church that predated the cathedral.

Now circle around and head up the other aisle. As you walk, notice that many of the black **tombstones** set in the floor have decorative recesses that aren't filled with brass (as they once were). After the Reformation in the 1530s, the church was short on cash, so they sold the brass to raise money for roof repairs.

Once you reach the south transept, you'll find several items of

interest. The **old font** survives from the previous church (A.D. 705) and has been the site of Wells baptisms for more than a thousand years. In the far end of this transept, a little of the original green and red wall painting, that wasn't white-washed, survives.

Nearby, notice the **carvings** at the tops of the pillars, which depict medieval life. On the first pillar, notice the man with a toothache and another man with a thorn in his foot. The second

pillar tells a story of medieval justice: On the left, we see thieves stealing grapes; on the right, the woodcut-ter (with an ax) is warning the farmer (with the pitchfork) what's happening. Circle around to the back of the pillar for the rest of the story: On the left, the farmer chases one of the thieves, grabbing him by the ear. On the right, he clobbers the thief over the head with his pitchfork—so hard the farm-er's hat falls off.

Also in the south transept, you'll find the entrance to the cathedral **Reading Room** (free, £0.50 donation requested, April-Oct Fri-Sat 14:30-16:30 only; might also be possible to step in for a quick look on weekday mornings and afternoons). Housing a few old manuscripts, it offers a peek into a real 15th-century library. At the back of the Reading Room, peer through the doors and notice the irons chaining the books to the shelves—a reflec-tion perhaps of the trust in the clergy at that time.

The south transept is where you'll exit the cathedral: Head out into the cloister, then cross the courtyard back to the welcome center, shop, Chapter Two restaurant, and exit. Go in peace.

More Cathedral Sights
▲▲Cathedral Evensong Service
The cathedral choir takes full advantage of heavenly acoustics with a nightly 45-minute evensong service. You'll sit right in the old

"quire" as you listen to a great pipe organ and the world-famous Wells Cathedral choir.

Cost and Hours: Free, Mon-Sat at 17:15, Sun at 15:00, generally no service when school is out July-Aug unless a visiting choir performs, to check call 01749/674-483 or visit www.wellscathedral .org.uk. At 17:05 (Sun at 14:50), the verger ushers visitors to their seats. There's usually plenty of room.

Returning to Bath after the Evensong: On weekdays and Saturdays, if you need to catch the 17:40 bus to Bath, request a seat on the north side of the presbytery, so you can slip out the side door without disturbing the service (10-minute walk from cathedral to station, bus also departs from The Liberty stop—a 4-minute walk away—at 17:42; or go at 18:15 via Bristol—explained later, under "Wells Connections").

Other Cathedral Concerts: The cathedral also hosts several evening concerts each month (£10-26, most about £20, generally Thu-Sat at 19:00 or 19:30, buy tickets by phone or at box office in cathedral gift shop; Mon-Sat 10:00-16:30, Sun 11:00-16:30; tel. 01749/672-773). Concert tickets are also available at the TI, along with pamphlets listing what's on.

Vicars Close

Lined with perfectly pickled 14th-century houses, this is the oldest

continuously occupied complete street in Europe (since 1348; just a block north of the cathedral—go under the big arch and look left). It was built to house the vicar's choir, and it still houses church officials and choristers (and one of the places, #14, can be rented for a weeklong holiday—from £509; find details on 14 Vicars Close at the cathedral's website, www .wellscathedral.org.uk).

▲Bishop's Palace

Next to the cathedral stands the moated Bishop's Palace, built in the 13th century and still in use today as the residence of the

Bishop of Bath and Wells. While the interior of the palace itself is dull, the grounds and gardens surrounding it are spectacular—the most tranquil and scenic spot in Wells, with wonderful views of the cathedral. It's just the place for a relaxing walk in the park. Watch the swans ring the bell when they have an attack of the munchies.

Cost and Hours: £7, daily April-Oct 10:00-18:00, Nov-March 10:00-16:00, often closed on Sat for special events—call to confirm, last entry one hour before closing,

Information: Tel. 01749/988-111, www.bishopspalace.org.uk.

Audioguide: A multimedia guide is available for £3.

Visiting the Palace and Gardens: The palace's spring-fed moat was built in the 14th century to protect the bishop during squabbles with the borough. Bishops would generously release this potable water into the town during local festivals (strangely, nobody asks why the freshwater springs were walled in to start with). Now the moat serves primarily as a pool for mute swans. The bridge was last drawn in 1831. Crossing that bridge, you'll buy your ticket and enter the grounds (past the old-timers playing a proper game of croquet—daily after 13:30). On your right, pass through the evocative ruins of the Great Hall (which was deserted and left to gradually deteriorate), and stroll through the chirpy south lawn. If you're feeling energetic, hike up to the top of the ramparts that encircle the property.

Circling around the far side of the mansion, walk through a door in the rampart wall, cross the wooden bridge, and follow a path to a smaller bridge and the wells (springs) that gave the city its name. Surrounding a reflecting pool with the cathedral towering overhead, these flower-bedecked pathways are idyllic. Nearby are an arboretum, picnic area, and sweet little pea-patch gardens.

After touring the gardens, the mansion's interior is a letdown—despite the borrowable descriptions that struggle to make the dusty old place meaningful. Have a spot of tea in the café (with outdoor garden seating), or climb the creaky wooden staircase to wander long halls lined with portraits of bishops past.

Near Wells

The following stops are best for drivers.

Cheddar Cheese

If you're in the mood for a picnic, drop by any local aromatic cheese shop for a great selection of tasty Somerset cheeses. Real farmhouse cheddar puts Velveeta to shame. The **Cheddar Gorge Cheese Company,** eight miles west of Wells, gives guests a chance to see the cheese-making process and enjoy a sample (£1.95, daily 10:00-15:30; take the A-39, then the A-371 to Cheddar Gorge; tel. 01934/742-810, www.cheddargorgecheeseco.co.uk).

Scrumpy Farms

Scrumpy is the wonderfully dangerous hard cider brewed in this part of England. You don't find it served in many pubs because of the unruly crowd it attracts. Scrumpy, at 8 percent alcohol, will rot your socks. "Scrumpy Jack," carbonated mass-produced cider, is not real scrumpy. The real stuff is "rough farmhouse cider." This is potent stuff. It's said some farmers throw a side of beef into the vat, and when fermentation is done only the teeth remain. (Some use a pair of old boots, for the tannin from the leather.)

TIs list cider farms open to the public, such as **Mr. Wilkins' Land's End Cider Farm,** a great Back Door travel experience (free, Mon-Sat 10:00-20:00, Sun 10:00-13:00; west of Wells in Mudgley, take the B-3139 from Wells to Wedmore, then the B-3151 south for 2 miles, farm is a quarter-mile off the B-3151—tough to find, get close and ask locals; tel. 01934/712-385, www.wilkinscider.com).

Apples are pressed from August through December. Hard cider, while not quite scrumpy, is also typical of the West Country, but more fashionable, "decent," and accessible. You can get a pint of hard cider at nearly any pub, drawn straight from the barrel—dry, medium, or sweet.

Nunney Castle

The centerpiece of the charming and quintessentially English village of Nunney (between Bath and Glastonbury, off the A-361) is a striking 14th-century castle surrounded by a fairy-tale moat. Its rare, French-style design brings to mind the Paris Bastille. The year 1644 was a tumultuous one for Nunney. Its noble family was royalist (and likely closet Catholics). They defied Parliament, so Parliament ordered their castle "slighted" (deliberately destroyed) to ensure that it would threaten the order of the land no more. Looking at this castle, so daunting in the age of bows and arrows, you can see how it was no match for the modern cannon. The pretty Mendip village of Nunney, with its little brook, is also worth a wander.

Cost and Hours: Free, visitable at "any reasonable time," tel. 01373/465-757, www.english-heritage.org.uk.

Sleeping in Wells

Wells is a pleasant overnight stop, with a handful of agreeable B&Bs. The first three places are within a short walk of the cathedral.

$$ Swan Hotel, a Best Western facing the cathedral, is a big, comfortable 48-room hotel. Prices for their Tudor-style rooms vary based on whether you want extras like a four-poster bed or a view of the cathedral. They also rent five apartments in the village (Sb-£110-124, Db-£144-160, superior Db-£169-179, deluxe

Sleep Code

(£1 = about $1.60, country code: 44)
S = Single, **D** = Double/Twin, **T** = Triple, **Q** = Quad, **b** = bathroom, **s** = shower only. Unless otherwise noted, credit cards are accepted and breakfast is included.

To help you sort easily through these listings, I've divided the accommodations into two categories based on the price for a standard double room with bath:

$$ **Higher Priced**—Most rooms £90 or more.
$ **Lower Priced**—Most rooms less than £90.

Prices can change without notice; verify the hotel's current rates online or by email. For the best prices, always book direct.

Db-£190-207, apartments-£119-155, ask about weekend deals, free Wi-Fi, Sadler Street, tel. 01749/836-300, www.swanhotelwells .co.uk, info@swanhotelwells.co.uk).

$$ The Old Farmhouse, a five-minute walk from the town center, welcomes you with a secluded front garden and two tastefully decorated rooms (Db-£85-90, 2-night minimum, free Wi-Fi, secure parking, next to the gas station at 62 Chamberlain Street, tel. 01749/675-058, www.wellsholiday.com, theoldfarmhouse wells@hotmail.com, charming owners Felicity and Christopher Wilkes).

$ Baytree House B&B is a modern and practical home at the edge of town (on a big road, a 10-minute walk to the bus station) renting five fresh, bright, and comfy rooms. Amanda and Paulo Bellini run the place with Italian enthusiasm (Db-£64-80, Tb-£75-90, two rooms have private bathrooms on the hall, free Wi-Fi, plush lounge, free parking, near where Strawberry Way hits the A-39 road to Cheddar at 85 Portway, tel. 01749/677-933, mobile 07745-287-194, www.baytree-house.co.uk, stay@baytree -house.co.uk).

Eating in Wells

Downtown Wells is tiny. A fine variety of eating options is within a block or two of its market square, including classic pubs, little delis and bakeries serving light meals, and a branch of **West Cornwall Pasty Company,** selling good savory pasties to go (Mon-Sat 8:30-17:00, Sun 10:00-16:30, 1a Sadler Street, tel. 01749/671-616).

The Fountain Inn, on a quiet street 50 yards behind the cathedral, serves good pub grub (£7-14 lunches, £10-14 dinners, daily 12:00-14:00 & 18:00-21:30, pub open until later, St. Thomas Street, tel. 01749/672-317).

Chapter Two, the modern restaurant in the cathedral welcome center, offers a handy if not heavenly lunch (£6-7 lunches, Mon-Sat 10:00-17:00, Sun 11:00-17:00, may close earlier in winter, tel. 01749/676-543).

The Old Spot is a dressy, modern place with a cathedral view. The food is elegant and well-prepared, although pricey (£20-23 fixed-price lunch, £6-7 starters, £14-19 main courses, Tue 19:00-22:30, Wed-Fri and Sat 12:30-14:30 & 19:00-22:30, Sun 12:30-14:30, closed Mon, 12 Sadler Street, tel. 01749/689-099, www.theoldspot.co.uk).

Wells Connections

The nearest train station is in Bath. The bus station in Wells is at a well-organized bus parking lot at the intersection of Priory and Princes roads. Local buses are run by First Bus Company (for Wells, tel. 0845-602-0156, www.firstgroup.com), while buses to and from London are run by National Express (tel. 0871-781-8178, www.nationalexpress.com).

From Wells by Bus to: Bath (nearly hourly, less frequent on Sun, 1.25 hours, last bus #173 leaves at 17:40—except Sun, when there are also buses at 18:46 and 20:03; if you miss the Mon-Sat 17:40 bus to Bath, catch the 18:15 bus to Bristol, then a 15-minute train ride to Bath, arriving 19:35), **Glastonbury** (3-4/hour, 20 minutes, bus #375/#377 or #29), **London**'s Victoria Coach Station (£21-30, 1/day direct, departs Wells at 6:55, arrives London at 11:20; otherwise hourly with a change in Bristol, 4 hours).

Avebury

Avebury is a prehistoric open-air museum, with a complex of fascinating Neolithic sites all gathered around the great stone henge

(circle). Because the area sports only a thin skin of topsoil over chalk, it is naturally treeless (similar to the area around Stonehenge). Perhaps this unique landscape—where the land connects with the big sky—made it the choice of prehistoric societies for their religious monuments. Whatever the case, Avebury dates to 2800 b.c.—six centuries older than

Stonehenge. This complex, the St. Peter's Basilica of Neolithic civilization, makes for a fascinating visit. Many enjoy it more than Stonehenge.

Orientation to Avebury

Avebury, just a little village with a big stone circle, is easy to reach by car, but difficult by public transportation (see "Getting Around the Region," page 320).

Tourist Information: The town's TI recently closed due to budget cuts. In the center of the village are signboards with some information provided by the National Trust. For more information on the Avebury sights, see the websites of the English Heritage (www.english-heritage.org.uk) and the National Trust (www .nationaltrust.org.uk).

Arrival by Car: You must pay to park in Avebury, and your only real option is the flat-fee National Trust parking lot, a three-minute walk from the village (£5, £3 after 15:00, £2 in winter; open summer 9:30-18:30, off-season 9:30-16:30). No other public parking is available in the village.

Sights in Avebury

All of Avebury's prehistoric sights are free to visit and always open.

▲▲Avebury Stone Circle

The stone circle at Avebury is bigger (16 times the size), less touristy, and for many, more interesting than Stonehenge. You're free to wander among 100 stones, ditches, mounds, and curious patterns from the past, as well as the village of Avebury, which grew up in the middle of this fascinating 1,400-foot-wide Neolithic circle.

In the 14th century, in a frenzy of ignorance and religious paranoia, Avebury villagers buried many of these mysterious pagan stones. Their 18th-century descendants hosted social events in which they broke up the remaining pagan stones (topple, heat up, douse with cold water, and scavenge the broken stones as building blocks). In modern times, the buried stones were dug up and re-erected. Concrete markers show where the missing broken-up stones once stood.

To make the roughly half-mile walk around the circle, you'll hike along an impressive earthwork henge—a 30-foot-high outer bank surrounding a ditch 30 feet deep, making a 60-foot-high rampart. This earthen rampart once had stones standing around the perimeter, placed about every 30 feet, and four grand causeway entries. Originally, two smaller circles made of about 200 stones stood within the henge.

Stone Circles: The Riddle of the Rocks

Britain is home to roughly 800 stone circles, most of them rudimentary, jaggedly sparse boulder rings that lack the

iconic upright-and-lintel form of Stonehenge. But their misty, mossy settings provide curious travelers with an intimate and accessible glimpse of the mysterious people who lived in prehistoric Britain.

Bronze Age Britain (2000-600 B.C.) was populated by farming folk who had mastered the craft of smelting heated tin and copper together to produce bronze, which was used to make more durable tools and weapons. Late in the Bronze Age, many of these primitive, clannish communities also chose to put considerable time and effort into gathering huge rocks and arranging them into ceremonial circles for use in rituals with long-forgotten meanings. Some scholars believe that these circles may have been used as solar observatories, to calculate solstices and equinoxes as they planned life-sustaining seasonal crop-planting cycles. Archaeologists have discovered a few ancient remains in the center of some circles, but their primary use seems to have been ceremonial rather than as burial sites. And without any written records, we can only make educated guesses as to their exact purpose.

The superstitious people of the Middle Ages, who hadn't quite perfected their carbon-dating techniques, came up with colorful explanations for the circles. Stonehenge, for example, was believed to have been arranged by giants (makes sense to me). Later, several circles were thought to be petrified partiers who had dared to dance on the Sabbath; nearby standing stones were supposedly the frozen figures of the pipers who had been playing the dance tunes.

Britain's stone circles generally lie in Scotland, Wales, and at the fringes of England, clustering mostly in the southwest (particularly on the Cornwall peninsula) and in the hills north of Manchester, and on the east side of Scotland (near Aberdeen). Dedicated travelers seeking stone circles will find them marked in the Ordnance Survey atlas and signposted along rural roads. Ask a local farmer for directions—and savor the experience (wear shoes impervious to grass dew and sheep doo). I've highlighted my favorites in this book: **Stonehenge** and **Avebury** (both described in this chapter), **Castlerigg** (in the Lake District, near Keswick—see page 549), and Scotland's **Clava Cairns,** just outside Inverness (see page 960).

Avebury

- —— ROAD
- ‑‑‑‑ FOOTPATH
- **P** PARKING
- ∙∙∙∙∙ STANDING STONES

TO SWINDON

Direction of Summer Sunrise

AVEBURY MANOR & GARDEN

ALEXANDER KEILLER MUSEUM

EARTHEN RAMPARTS

GREEN ST.

2

1

TO CALNE

HIGH ST.

P

AVEBURY STONE CIRCLE

RITUAL PROCESSION WAY

B-4003

TO CHERHILL HORSE & BATH

A-4

A-4361

BECKHAMPTON RD.

SILBURY HILL

A-4

A-361

TO DEVIZES

ROMAN ROAD

B-4003

TO MARL-BOROUGH

A-4

½ MILE
800 METERS

1 Circle Café
2 The Red Lion Pub

RIVER KENNET

WEST KENNET LONG BARROW

THE SANCTUARY "WOOD HENGE"

Direction of Winter Sunrise

DCH

NEAR BATH

▲Ritual Procession Way

Also known as West Kennet Avenue (one of four streets leaving the circle), this double line of stones provided a ritual procession way leading from Avebury to a long-gone wooden circle dubbed "The Sanctuary." This "wood henge," thought to have been 1,000 years older than everything else in the area, is considered to have been the genesis of Avebury and its big stone circle. Most of the stones standing along the procession way today were reconstructed in modern times.

▲Silbury Hill

This pyramid-shaped hill (reminiscent of Glastonbury Tor) is a 130-foot-high, yet-to-be-explained mound of chalk just outside of Avebury. More than 4,000 years old, this mound is considered the largest man-made object in prehistoric Europe (with the surface area of London's Trafalgar Square and the height of the Nelson Column). It's a reminder that we've only just scratched the surface of England's mysterious and ancient religious landscape.

Inspired by a legend that the hill hid a gold statue in its cen-

ter, locals tunneled through Silbury Hill in 1830, undermining the structure. Work is currently underway to restore the hill, which remains closed to the public. Archaeologists (who date things like this by carbon-dating snails and other little critters killed in its construction) figure Silbury Hill took only 60 years to build, in about 2200 B.C. This makes Silbury Hill the last element built at Avebury and contemporaneous with Stonehenge. Some think it may have been an observation point for all the other bits of the Avebury site. You can still see evidence of a spiral path leading up the hill and a moat at its base.

The Roman road detoured around Silbury Hill. (Roman engineers often used features of the landscape as visual reference points when building roads. Their roads would commonly kink at the crest of hills or other landmarks, where they realigned with a new visual point.) Later, the hill sported a wooden Saxon fort, which likely acted as a lookout for marauding Vikings. And in World War II, the Royal Observer Corps stationed men up here to count and report Nazi bombers on raids.

West Kennet Long Barrow

A pullout on the road just past Silbury Hill marks the West Kennet Long Barrow (a 15-minute walk from Silbury Hill). This burial chamber, the best-preserved Stone Age chamber tomb in the UK, stands intact on a ridge. It lines up with the rising sun on the summer solstice. You can walk inside the barrow, or sit on its roof and survey the Neolithic landscape around you.

Cherhill Horse

Heading west from Avebury on the A-4 (toward Bath), you'll see an obelisk (a monument to some important earl) above you on the downs, or chalk hills, near the village of Cherhill. You'll also see a white horse carved into the chalk hillside. Above it are the remains of an Iron Age hill fort known as Oldbury Castle—described on an information board at the roadside pullout. There is one genuinely prehistoric white horse in England (the Uffington White Horse); the Cherhill Horse, like all the others, is just an 18th-century creation. Prehistoric discoveries were all the rage in the 1700s, and it was a fad to make your own fake ones. Throughout southern England, you can cut into the thin layer of topsoil and find chalk. Now, so they don't have to weed, horses like this are cemented and painted white.

Alexander Keiller Museum

This museum, named for the archaeologist who led excavations at Avebury in the late 1930s, is housed in two buildings. The 17th-century Barn Gallery has an interactive exhibit, while the Stables Gallery, across the farmyard, holds artifacts from past digs.

Cost and Hours: £4.90, daily April-Oct 10:00-18:00, Nov-March 10:00-16:00, last entry one hour before closing, tel. 01672/539-250.

Avebury Manor and Garden

Archaeologist Alexander Keiller's former home was the subject of *The Manor Reborn*, a 2011 BBC documentary on the refurbishment of the 500-year-old estate by a team of historians and craftspeople. Nine rooms were decorated in five different styles showing the progression of design, from a Tudor wedding chapel to a Queen Anne-era bedroom to an early-20th-century billiards room. The grounds were also spruced up, with a topiary and a Victorian kitchen garden.

Cost and Hours: £9, limited number of timed tickets sold per day, April-Oct Thu-Tue 11:00-17:00, Nov-mid-Dec and mid-Feb-March Thu-Tue 11:00-15:30, closed Wed and mid-Dec-mid-Feb, last entry one hour before closing, buy tickets at Alexander Keiller Museum's Barn Gallery (listed above) or reserve online in advance (£1 booking fee), tel. 01672/539-250, www.nationaltrust.org.uk.

Eating in Avebury

The pleasant **Circle Café** serves healthy, hearty à la carte lunches, including vegan and gluten-free dishes, and cream teas on most days (daily April-Oct 10:00-17:30, Nov-March 10:00-16:00, no hot food after 14:30, next to National Trust store and the Alexander Keiller Museum, tel. 01672/539-250).

The Red Lion has inexpensive, traditional pub grub; a creaky, well-worn, dart-throwing ambience; and a medieval well in its dining room (£6-12 meals, daily 11:00-21:00, High Street, tel. 01672/539-266).

Stonehenge

As old as the pyramids, and older than the Acropolis and the Colosseum, this iconic stone circle amazed medieval Europeans, who figured it was built by a race of giants. And it still impresses visitors today. As one of Europe's most famous sights, Stonehenge, worth ▲▲, does a valiant job of retaining an air of mystery and majesty (partly because cordons, which keep hordes of tourists from trampling all over it, foster the illusion that it stands alone in a field). Although some people are underwhelmed by Stonehenge, most of its almost one million annual visitors find that it's worth the trip.

The ancient site continues to reveal its mysteries: A laser survey in 2011 found prehistoric carvings on the stones, excavations in 2008 showed that the Romans were active at Stonehenge, and an archaeological dig nearby in 2007 uncovered homes where the circle's builders may have lived.

Expect Changes: A new visitors center/museum and large parking lot opened 1.5 miles to the west of the stone circle in December of 2013. You'll park at the visitors center and ride a shuttle bus or walk to the stones. The highway that previously ran adjacent to the stones has closed, and the old parking lot and ticket booth near the circle are slated for demolition. Call ahead or check the website for updates.

Getting to Stonehenge

Stonehenge is about 90 miles southwest of central London, a two-hour drive.

By Public Transportation: Catch a train to Salisbury, then go by bus or taxi to Stonehenge (for details, see page 354). There is no public transportation between Avebury and Stonehenge.

By Car: Stonehenge is well-signed just off the A-303. It's about 15 minutes north of Salisbury, an hour east of Glastonbury, and an hour south of Avebury. From Salisbury, head north on the A-360 (Devizes Road) for 8.5 miles (13.6 km) to the intersection at Airman's Corner. Watch for signs to the visitors center and parking lot.

By Bus Tour: For tours of Stonehenge from Bath, see page 281 (Mad Max is best); for tours from Salisbury, see page 354.

Orientation to Stonehenge

Cost: £14.90, save £1 if you buy in advance online, covered by English Heritage Pass (see page 21). Entry includes a worthwhile 45-minute audioguide, entry to the visitors center/museum, and the shuttle bus ride to the stone circle. Parking is free with entry to the site (otherwise £3).

Reservations: While not required, buying a ticket in advance online at www.english-heritage.org.uk/stonehenge gives you a guaranteed 30-minute arrival window. Advance ticketholders also have the option of downloading the audio tour directly to their own mobile device.

Hours: Daily June-Aug 9:00-20:00, mid-March-May and Sept-mid-Oct 9:30-19:00, mid-Oct-mid-March 9:30-17:00. Note that last entry is two hours before closing. Expect shorter hours and possible closures June 20-22 due to huge, raucous solstice crowds.

Information: Tel. 0870-333-1181, www.english-heritage.org.uk/stonehenge.

Services: The new visitors center has WCs, a café, and a gift shop. Services at the circle itself are limited to emergency WCs.

Visiting the Inner Stones: Special one-hour access to the stones' inner circle may be available for an extra fee (outside regular visiting hours, no touching allowed, must be reserved well in advance). Details are on the English Heritage website (go to "Visit Stonehenge," then click "Stone Circle Access"), or call 01722/343-834.

Self-Guided Tour

The entrance fee includes a good audioguide, but this commentary will help make your visit even more meaningful. Allow at least two hours to see everything.

Visitors Center: The visitors center and museum are set 1.5 miles away from the circle itself. The new facilities are designed to blend in with the landscape and help make the stone circle feel more pristine.

Once you've bought your ticket and picked up an audioguide, tour the visitors center to learn more about the site and the people who built it. Stand inside a 360-degree projection showing the stones as they are today—and as they were when the monument was first built. The archaeological gallery features objects excavated from Stonehenge and other sites nearby, models of the circle, and videos about the site's history. Back outside, you can visit a reconstruction of the prehistoric homes recently unearthed near Stonehenge.

Be sure to use the WCs here, as there are only emergency WCs at the circle.

Stone Circle: Shuttle buses to the stones leave from the back of the visitors center (every 5 minutes, more frequent on busy days, 10-minute trip). You can disembark from the shuttle halfway and walk the remaining 20 minutes to the stones. It's also possible to walk the entire 1.5 miles to the circle.

As you approach the massive structure, walk right up to the knee-high cordon and let your fellow 21st-century tourists melt away. It's just you and the druids...although it was not the druids that built the stone circle (they probably didn't even use it).

England has hundreds of stone circles, but Stonehenge—which literally means "hanging stones"—is unique. It's the only one that has horizontal cross-pieces (called lintels) spanning the vertical monoliths, and the only one with stones that have been made smooth and uniform by human craftsmen. What you see here is a bit more than half the original structure—the rest was carted off centuries ago for use in other buildings.

Now do a slow clockwise spin around the monument, and ponder the following points. As you walk, mentally flesh out the missing pieces and re-erect the rubble. Knowledgeable guides posted around the site are happy to answer your questions.

It's now believed that Stonehenge, which was built in phases between 3000 and 1500 B.C., was originally used as a cremation cemetery. But that's not the end of the story, as the monument was expanded over the millennia. This was a hugely significant location to prehistoric peoples. There are several hundred burial mounds within a three-mile radius of Stonehenge—some likely belonging to kings or chieftains. Some of the human remains were of people from far away, and others show signs of injuries—evidence that Stonehenge may have been used as a place of medicine or healing.

Whatever its original purpose, Stonehenge still functions as a celestial calendar. As the sun rises on the summer solstice (June 21), the "heel stone"—the one set apart from the rest, near the road—lines up with the sun and the altar at the center of the stone circle. A disputed study of more than 300 similar circles in Britain found that each could have been used to calculate the movement of the sun, moon, and stars, and to predict eclipses in order to help early societies know when to plant, harvest, and party—just one of many plausible ideas as to the circles' significance. Even in modern times, as the summer solstice sun sets in just the right slot at Stonehenge, pagans arrive to boogie.

Some believe that Stonehenge is built at the precise point where six "ley lines" intersect. Ley lines are theoretical lines of magnetic or spiritual power that crisscross the globe, often connecting ancient sites. Belief in the power of these lines has gone in and out of fashion. If they were important to prehistoric peoples, they were largely ignored until the early 20th century, when the English writer Alfred Watkins popularized them (to the scorn of serious scientists). More recently, the concept has been embraced by the New Age movement. Without realizing it, you follow these ley lines all the time: Many of England's modern highways, following prehistoric paths, and churches, built over prehistoric monuments, are located where ley lines are thought to intersect. If you're a skeptic, ask one of the guides at Stonehenge to explain the mystique of this paranormal tradition; it's creepy and convincing.

Notice that two of the stones (facing the entry passageway) appear blemished. At the base of one monolith, it looks like someone has pulled back the stone to reveal a concrete skeleton. This is a repair job to fix damage done long ago by souvenir seekers, who actually rented hammers and chisels to take home a piece of Stonehenge. Look to the right of the repaired stone: The back of another stone is missing the same thin layer of protective lichen that covers the others. The lichen—and some of the stone itself—was sandblasted off to remove graffiti. (No wonder they've got Stonehenge roped off now.) The repairs were intentionally done in a different color, so as not to appear like the original stone.

Stonehenge's builders used two different types of stone. The tall, stout monoliths and lintels are sandstone blocks called sarsen stones. Most of the monoliths weigh about 25 tons (the largest is 45 tons), and the lintels are about seven tons apiece. These sarsen stones were brought from "only" 20 miles away. The shorter stones in the middle, called bluestones, came from the south coast of Wales—240 miles away (close if you're taking a train, but far if you're packing a megalith). Imagine the logistical puzzle of floating six-ton stones across Wales' Severn Estuary and up the River Avon, then rolling them on logs about 20 miles to this position...an impressive feat, even in our era of skyscrapers. We know the stones came from Wales because geologists have chemically matched the bluestones to specific outcrops there.

Why didn't the builders of Stonehenge use what seem like perfectly adequate stones nearby? This, like many other questions about Stonehenge, remains shrouded in mystery. Think again about the ley lines. Ponder the fact that many experts accept none of the explanations of how these giant stones were transported. Then imagine congregations gathering here 5,000 years ago, raising thought levels, creating a powerful life force transmitted along the ley lines. Maybe a particular kind of stone was essential for maximum energy transmission. Maybe the stones were levitated here. Maybe psychics really do create powerful vibes. Maybe not. It's as unbelievable as electricity used to be.

Salisbury

Salisbury, set in the middle of the expansive Salisbury Plain, is a favorite stop for its striking cathedral and intriguing history.

Salisbury was originally settled during the Bronze Age, possibly as early as 600 B.C., and later became a Roman town called Sarum. The modern city of Salisbury developed when the old settlement outgrew its boundaries, prompting the townspeople to move the city from a hill to the river valley below. Most of today's visitors come to marvel at the famous Salisbury Cathedral, featuring England's tallest spire and largest cathedral green. Collectors, bargain-hunters, and foodies will savor Salisbury's colorful market days. And archaeologists will dig the region around Salisbury, with England's highest concentration of ancient sites. The town itself is pleasant and walkable, and is a convenient base camp for visiting the ancient sites of Stonehenge and Avebury, or for exploring the countryside.

Orientation to Salisbury

Salisbury (pop. 45,000) stretches along the River Avon in the shadow of its huge landmark cathedral. The heart of the city clusters around Market Square, which is also a handy parking lot on non-market days. High Street, a block to the west, leads to the medieval North Gate of the Cathedral Close. Shoppers can explore the quirkily named streets south of the square. The area north of Market Square is generally residential, with a few shops and pubs.

Tourist Information

The TI, just off Market Square, hands out free city maps, books local rooms for no fee, sells train tickets with a £1.50 surcharge, and offers free Wi-Fi (April-Sept Mon-Sat 10:00-16:00, Sun 10:00-14:00; Oct-March Mon-Sat 9:00-17:00, closed Sun; Fish Row, tel. 01722/342-860, www.visitwiltshire.co.uk).

Ask the TI about 1.5-hour **walking tours** (£5, April-Oct daily at 11:00, Nov-March Sat-Sun only, depart from TI; other itineraries available, including £5 Ghost Walk May-Sept Fri at 20:00; tel. 07873/212-941, www.salisburycityguides.co.uk).

Arrival in Salisbury

By Train: From the train station, it's a 10-minute walk into the town center. Leave the station to the left, and walk about 50 yards down South Western Road. Passing The Railway Tavern on your right, continue onto Mill Road and then onto Fisherton Street. Following signs to the city center, walk up the right side of Fisherton over the river and all the way to High Street. Market Square and the TI are ahead on Queen Street, and it's another two short blocks north (left) on Queen Street to the bus station. The Salisbury Cathedral and recommended Exeter Street B&Bs are to the south (right), down St. John Street (which becomes Exeter Street).

By Bus: The bus station is located in the town center, just off Market Square on Endless Street.

By Car: Drivers will find several pay parking lots in Salisbury—simply follow the blue *P* signs. The "Central" lot, behind the giant red-brick Sainsbury's store, is within a 10-minute walk of the TI or cathedral and is best for overnight stays (enter from Churchill Way West or Castle Street, lot open 24 hours). The "Old George Mall" parking garage is closer to the cathedral and has comparable daytime rates (£1.50/1 hour, £2.20/2 hours, cash only, 1 block north of cathedral, enter from New Street; garage open Mon-Sat 7:00-20:00, Sun 10:00-17:00). Limited parking is available at the cathedral, on the corner of High Street and North Walk (£6/day).

Helpful Hints

Market Days: For centuries, Salisbury has been known for its lively markets. On Tuesdays and Saturdays, Market Square hosts the charter market, with general goods. Every other Wednesday is the farmers' market. There are also special markets, such as one with French products. Ask the TI for a current schedule.

Festivals: The **Salisbury International Arts Festival** runs for just over two weeks at the end of May and beginning of June (www.salisburyfestival.co.uk).

Internet Access: The library has terminals on the first floor for visitors, who can use them free of charge for 30 minutes (Mon 10:00-19:00, Tue and Fri 9:00-19:00, Wed-Thu and Sat 9:00-17:00, closed Sun, show ID at desk to sign in for access number, computers turned off 10 minutes before closing, Market

Salisbury

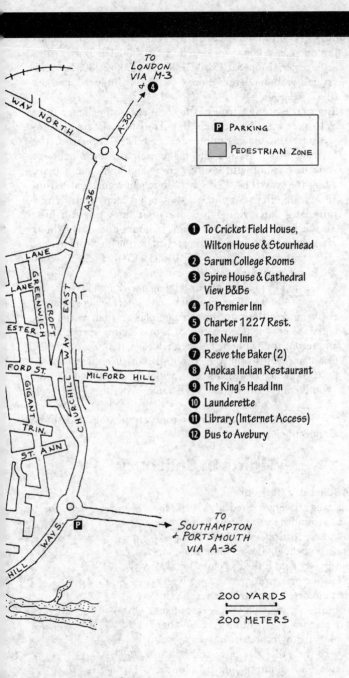

P Parking

Pedestrian Zone

1 To Cricket Field House, Wilton House & Stourhead
2 Sarum College Rooms
3 Spire House & Cathedral View B&Bs
4 To Premier Inn
5 Charter 1227 Rest.
6 The New Inn
7 Reeve the Baker (2)
8 Anokaa Indian Restaurant
9 The King's Head Inn
10 Launderette
11 Library (Internet Access)
12 Bus to Avebury

TO LONDON VIA M-3 & 4

WAY NORTH

A-30

A-36

GREENWICH LANE

LANE

ESTER

FORD ST.

GIGANT

TRIN.

ST. ANN

CROFT

CHURCHILL WAY

EAST

MILFORD HILL

WAY SOUTH

HILL

TO SOUTHAMPTON & PORTSMOUTH VIA A-36

200 YARDS
200 METERS

NEAR BATH

Place, tel. 01722/324-145).

Laundry: Washing Well has full-service (£8-15/load depending on size, 2-hour service, Mon-Sat 8:30-17:30) as well as self-service (Mon-Sat 15:30-21:00, Sun 7:00-21:00, last self-service wash one hour before closing; 28 Chipper Lane, tel. 01722/421-874).

Getting to the Stone Circles: You can get to Stonehenge from Salisbury on **The Stonehenge Tour** bus. Their distinctive red-and-black double-decker buses leave from the Salisbury train station and make a circuit to Stonehenge and Old Sarum, with lovely scenery and light commentary along the way (£12, £20 with Stonehenge and Old Sarum admission, tickets good all day, buy ticket from driver, June-Aug daily 9:30-17:00, 1-2/hour, may not run June 21 due to solstice crowds, shorter hours and only 1/hour off-season, 30 minutes from train station to Stonehenge, also stops at bus station, tel. 01983/827-005, check www.thestonehengetour.info for timetable).

A **taxi** from Salisbury to Stonehenge can make sense for groups (£40-50, call or email for exact price, includes round-trip from Salisbury to Stonehenge plus an hour at the site, entry fee not included, 5-6 people maximum, reserve ahead and reconfirm by phone a day in advance, tel. 01722/339-781, briantwort@ntlworld.com, Brian). Brian also offers a three-hour Stonehenge visit for £80, which includes Old Sarum, Woodhenge, Durrington Walls, and Woodford's thatched cottages.

For buses to Avebury's stone circle, see "Salisbury Connections," later.

Sights in Salisbury

▲▲Salisbury Cathedral

This magnificent cathedral, visible for miles around because of its huge spire (the tallest in England at 404 feet), is a wonder to behold. The surrounding enormous grassy field (called a "close") makes the Gothic masterpiece look even larger. What's more impressive is that all this was built in a mere 38 years—astonishingly fast for the Middle Ages. When the old hill town of Sarum was moved down to the valley, its cathedral had to be replaced in a hurry. So, in 1220, the townspeople began building, and in 1258

Salisbury Cathedral

COLUMNS

NAVE

SHOP

ENTRY ➤

TRANSEPT

CHOIR

❶

❷

DCH

CLOISTER

❸

CHAPTER HOUSE

Ⓝ

50 YARDS

50 METERS

❶ Morning Chapel
❷ Trinity Chapel
❸ Chapter House & Magna Carta

their sparkling-new cathedral was ready for ribbon-cutting. Since the structure was built in just a few decades, its style is uniform, rather than the patchwork of styles common in cathedrals of the time (which often took centuries to construct).

Cost and Hours: £5.50 suggested donation; April-Oct Mon-Sat 9:00-17:00, Sun 12:00-16:00; Nov-March daily 9:00-17:00; Chapter House usually open Mon-Sat 9:30-16:30, Sun 12:45-15:45, closes entirely for special events; choral evensong Mon-Sat at 17:30, Sun at 15:00. This working cathedral opens early for services: Be respectful if you arrive when one is in session.

Information: Tel. 01722/555-120, recorded info tel. 01722/555-113, www.salisburycathedral.org.uk.

Tower Tours: Imagine building a cathedral on this scale before the invention of cranes, bulldozers, or modern scaffolding. An excellent tower tour (1.5-2 hours) helps visitors understand how it was done. You'll climb in between the stone arches and the roof to inspect the vaulting and trussing; see a medieval winch that was used in the construction; and finish with the 332-step climb up the narrow tower for a sweeping view of the Wiltshire countryside (£10; early April-Sept Mon-Sat at 11:15, 12:15, 13:15, 14:15, and 15:15, Sun at 13:00 and 14:30; fewer off-season but usually one at 13:15, no tours in Dec except Christmas week; maximum 12 people, can reserve by calling 01722/555-156).

Eating: The cathedral's cafeteria is excellent.

❷ **Self-Guided Tour:** Entering the church, you'll instantly feel the architectural harmony. Volunteer guides posted strategically throughout the church stand ready to answer your questions. (Free guided tours of the cathedral nave are offered every hour or so, when enough people assemble.)

As you look down the **nave,** notice how the stone columns march identically down the aisle, like a thick gray forest of tree trunks. The arches overhead soar to grand heights, helping church-goers appreciate the vast and amazing heavens. Now imagine the interior surfaces painted in red, blue, green, and gold, as they would have been prior to the English Reformation.

From the entrance, head to the far wall (the back-left corner). You'll find an interesting **model** showing how this cathedral was built so quickly in the 13th century. Next to that is the "oldest working clock in existence," dating from the 14th century (the hourly bell has been removed, so as not to interrupt worship services). On the wall by the clock is a bell from the decommissioned ship HMS *Salisbury*. Look closely inside the bell to see the engraved names of crew members' children who were baptized on the ship.

Wander down the aisle past monuments and knights' tombs, as well as tombstones set into the floor. When you get to the transept, examine the **columns** where the arms of the church cross. These posts were supposed to support a more modest bell tower, but when a heavy tower was added 100 years later, the columns bent under the enormous weight, causing the tower to lean sideways. Although the posts were later reinforced, the tower still tilts about two and a half feet.

Continue down the left side of the choir and dip into the **Morning Chapel.** At the back of this chapel, find the spectacular glass prism engraved with images of Salisbury—donated to the church in memory of a soldier who died at the D-Day landing at Normandy.

The oldest part of the church is at the apse (far end), where construction began in 1220: the **Trinity Chapel.** The giant, modern stained-glass window ponders the theme "prisoners of conscience."

After you leave the nave, pace the cloister and follow signs to the medieval **Chapter House.** All English cathedrals have a chapter house, so called because it's where the daily Bible verse, or chapter, is read. These spaces often served as gathering places for conducting church or town business. Here you can see a modest display of cathedral items, plus one must-see: the best preserved of the four original copies of the Magna Carta. This document is as important to the English as the Constitution is to Americans. This "Great Charter," dating from 1215, settled a dispute between the slimy King John and some powerful barons. Revolutionary for limiting the monarch's power, the Magna Carta constitutionally guaranteed that the monarch was not above the law. This was one of the first major victories in the long tug-of-war between monarchs and nobles.

▲Cathedral Close

The enormous green surrounding the cathedral is the largest in England, and one of the loveliest. It's cradled in the elbow of the

River Avon and ringed by row houses, cottages, and grand mansions. The church owns the houses on the green and rents them to lucky people with holy connections. A former prime minister, Edward Heath, lived on the green, not because of his political influence, but because he was once the church organist.

The benches scattered around the green are an excellent place for having a romantic moonlit picnic or for gazing thoughtfully at the leaning spire. Although you may be tempted to linger until it's late, don't—this is still private church property...and the heavy medieval gates of the close shut at about 23:00.

A few houses are open to the public, such as the overpriced Mompesson House and the medieval Wardrobe. The most interesting attraction is the...

▲Salisbury and South Wiltshire Museum

Occupying the building just opposite the cathedral entry, this eclectic and sprawling collection was heralded by American expat travel writer Bill Bryson as one of England's best. While that's a stretch, the museum does offer a little something for everyone, including exhibits on local archaeology and social history, a costume gallery, the true-to-its-name "Salisbury Giant" puppet once used by the tailors' guilds during parades, some J. M. W. Turner paintings of the cathedral interior, and a collection of exquisite Wedgwood china and other ceramics. The highlight is the Stonehenge Gallery, with informative and interactive exhibits explaining the prehistoric structure.

Cost and Hours: £8 (includes small donation), Mon-Sat 10:00-17:00, Sun 12:00-17:00 except closed Sun Oct-May, check with desk about occasional tours, 65 The Close, tel. 01722/332-151, www.salisburymuseum.org.uk.

NEAR BATH

Sleeping in Salisbury

(area code: 01722)

Salisbury's town center has very few affordable accommodations, and I've listed them below—plus a couple of good choices a little farther out. The town gets particularly crowded during the arts festival (late May through early June).

$$ Cricket Field House, outside of town on the A-36 toward Wilton, overlooks a cricket pitch and golf course. It has 17 clean, comfortable rooms, its own gorgeous garden, and plenty of parking (Sb-£50-75, Db-£75-99, deluxe Db-£135, Tb-£75-118, price depends on season, Wilton Road, tel. 01722/322-595, www.cricket fieldhouse.co.uk, cricketfieldcottage@btinternet.com; Brian, Margaret, and Andrew James). While this place works best for drivers, it's just a 20-minute walk from the train station or a five-minute bus ride from the city center.

$$ Sarum College is a theological college that rents 40 rooms in its building right on the peaceful Cathedral Close. Much of the year, it houses visitors to the college, but it usually has rooms for tourists as well—except the week after Christmas, when it closes. The slightly institutional but clean rooms share hallways with libraries, bookstores, and offices, and the five attic rooms come with grand cathedral views (Sb-£64, Db-£99 depending on size, meals available at additional cost, elevator, 19 The Close, tel. 01722/424-800, www.sarum.ac.uk, hospitality@sarum.ac.uk).

$ Cathedral View B&B, with four rooms, offers a good value in an outstanding location just off the Cathedral Close (Db-£85, Tb-£90-105, cash only, 2-night minimum on weekends, no kids under age 10, free Wi-Fi, 83 Exeter Street, tel. 01722/502-254, www.cathedral-viewbandb.co.uk, info@cathedral-viewbandb .co.uk, Wenda and Steve).

$ Spire House B&B, next door, is similar. The four bright, surprisingly quiet rooms come with busy wallpaper, and two have canopied beds (Db-£80-90, Tb-£90-100, no kids under age 8, optional breakfast-£5, free Wi-Fi, 84 Exeter Street, tel. 01722/339-213, www.salisbury-bedandbreakfast.com, spire.enquiries@bt internet.com, friendly Lois and John).

$ Premier Inn, two miles from the city center, offers dozens of prefab and predictable rooms ideal for drivers and families (Db-£70-85, more during special events, 2 kids ages 15 and under sleep free, breakfast-£5-8, pay Wi-Fi, possible noise from nearby trains, off roundabout at A-30 and Pearce Way, tel. 0871-527-8956, www .premierinn.com).

NEAR BATH

Eating in Salisbury

There are plenty of atmospheric pubs all over town. For the best variety of restaurants, head to the Market Square area. Many places offer great "early bird" specials before 20:00.

Charter 1227, an upstairs eatery overlooking Market Square, is a handy place for a nice meal (£10 two-course lunch, open Tue-Sat 12:00-14:30 & 18:00-21:30, closed Sun-Mon, dinner reservations smart, 6 Ox Row, tel. 01722/333-118, www.charter1227.co.uk).

Reeve the Baker, with a branch just up the street from the TI, crafts an array of high-calorie delights and handy pick-me-ups for a fast and affordable lunch. The long cases of pastries and savory treats will make you drool (Mon-Sat 7:00-17:00, Sun 10:00-16:00, cash only, one location is next to the TI at 2 Butcher Row, another much smaller one is at the corner of Market and Bridge streets at 61 Silver Street, tel. 01722/320-367).

Anokaa is a classy splurge that's highly acclaimed for its updated Indian cuisine. You won't find the same old chicken *tikka* here, but clever newfangled variations on Indian themes, dished up in a dressy contemporary setting (£12-19 main dishes, £9 lunch buffet, daily 12:00-14:00 & 17:30-23:00, 60 Fisherton Street, tel. 01722/414-142, www.anokaa.com).

The New Inn serves inventive, game-centered dishes alongside classic pub fare in a 13th-century house rumored to have a tunnel leading directly into the cathedral—perhaps dug while the building housed a brothel? (£5 starters and baguettes, £8-12 main courses, daily 11:00-24:00, food served 12:00-15:00 & 18:00-21:00, 41-43 New Street, tel. 01722/326-662).

The King's Head Inn is a chain pub with an extensive menu, modern interior, and outdoor seating overlooking the pretty little River Avon. It's a bit tired, and so are its servers (£5-6 sandwiches, £5-12 main courses, daily 9:00-24:00, food served until 22:00, kids welcome but must order by 20:30, free Wi-Fi, 1 Bridge Street, tel. 01722/342-050).

Salisbury Connections

From Salisbury by Train to: London's Waterloo Station (1-2/hour, 1.25 hours), **Bath** (1-2/hour, 1 hour), **Oxford** (1-2/hour, 2 hours, transfer in Basingstoke and sometimes also Reading), **Portsmouth** (1/hour direct, 1.5 hours), **Exeter** (1-2/hour, 2 hours, some require transfers), **Penzance** (about hourly, 5.5-6 hours, 1-2 transfers). Train info: tel. 0845-748-4950, www.nationalrail.co.uk.

By Bus to: Bath (hourly, 2.75 hours, transfer in Warminster or Devizes, www.travelinesw.com; or one direct bus/day at 10:35, 1.5 hours on National Express #300, tel. 0871-781-8181, www .nationalexpress.com), **Avebury** (hourly, 2-2.5 hours, transfer in Trowbridge and Devizes, www.travelinesw.com), **Portsmouth** (evenings only at 18:25, 1.5 hours on National Express). Many of Salisbury's long-distance buses are run by Wilts & Dorset (tel. 01722/336-855 or 01983/827-005, www.salisburyreds.co.uk).

Near Salisbury

Old Sarum

Right here, on a hill overlooking the plain below, is where the original town of Salisbury was founded many centuries ago. While little remains of the old town, the view of the valley is amazing...and a little imagination can transport you back to *very* olde England. This is one of the most historically important sites in southern England. Uniquely, it combined both a castle and a cathedral within an Iron Age fortification.

Human settlement in this area stretches back to the Bronze Age, and the Romans, Saxons, and Normans all called this hill-top home. From about 500 B.C. through A.D. 1220, Old Sarum flourished, giving rise to a motte-and-bailey castle, a cathedral, and scores of wooden homes along the town's outer ring. The town grew so quickly that by the Middle Ages, it had outgrown its spot on the hill. In 1220, the local bishop successfully petitioned to move the entire city to the valley below, where space and water was plentiful. So, stone by stone, Old Sarum was packed up and shipped to New Sarum, where builders used nearly all the rubble from the old city to create a brand-new town with a magnificent cathedral.

Old Sarum was eventually abandoned altogether, leaving only a few stone foundations. The grand views of Salisbury from here have in-"spired" painters for ages and provided countless picnickers with a scenic backdrop: Grab a sandwich or snacks from one of the grocery stores in Salisbury or at the excellent Waitrose supermarket at the north end of town—just west of where the A-36 meets the A-345.

Cost and Hours: £3.90, daily July-Aug 9:00-18:00, April-June and Sept 10:00-17:00, Oct and March 10:00-16:00, Nov-Jan 11:00-15:00, Feb 11:00-16:00, last entry 30 minutes before closing, tel. 01722/335-398, www.english-heritage.org.uk.

Getting There: It's two miles north of Salisbury off the A-345, accessible by Wilts & Dorset bus #X5 or via The Stonehenge Tour bus (see page 354). Drivers will find free parking 200 yards from the entrance (on the slope of the original castle's outer bailey).

Near Salisbury

DORSET JOYRIDE

🏰 CASTLE

20 MILES
30 KM

TO BATH

LONDON

SHREWTON · STONEHENGE
B-390
STONEHENGE VISITORS CTR.
TO BATH
A-360
TO LONDON
A-303
WILTON HOUSE
A-345
OLD SARUM
A-36
STOURHEAD
B-3092
SALISBURY
TO WELLS & BATH
A-371
A-350
SHAFTESBURY
A-30
A-354
A-338
YEOVIL
A-30
A-350
B-3081
TO EXETER
A-37
A-352
SHERBORNE
D O R S E T
CERNE ABBAS GIANT →
MILTON ABBAS
BLANDFORD FORUM
TO PORTSMOUTH
CERNE ABBAS
PIDDLE-TRENT-HIDE
WINTERBORNE WHITECHURCH
TO LYME REGIS
CHESEL-BOURNE
A-35
POOLE
BOURNEMOUTH
A-35
A-37
DORCHESTER
HARDY'S COTTAGE
BERE REGIS
A-354
MORETON
WAREHAM
FERRY
OLD HARRY ROCKS
DCH
A-352
A-351
CORFE CASTLE
DURDLE DOOR
SWANAGE
CHESIL BEACH
WEYMOUTH
E N G L I S H   C H A N N E L

Wilton House

This sprawling estate, with a grand mansion and lush gardens, has been owned by the Earls of Pembroke since King Henry VIII's time. Long before that, this was the site of a ninth-century nunnery, and later, a Benedictine abbey. Inside the mansion, you'll find a collection of paintings by Rubens, Rembrandt, Van Dyck, and Brueghel, along with quirky odds and ends, such as a lock of Queen Elizabeth I's hair. The perfectly proportioned Double Cube Room has served as everything from a 17th-century state dining room to a secret D-Day planning room during World War II... if only the portraits could talk. The Old Riding School houses a skippable 20-minute film that dramatizes the history of the family. Outside, classic English gardens feature a river lazily winding its way through grasses and under Greek-inspired temples. Jane Austen fans particularly enjoy this stately home, where parts of

2005's Oscar-nominated *Pride and Prejudice* were filmed. But, alas, Mr. Darcy has checked out.

Cost and Hours: House and gardens-£14, gardens only-£5.50; house open Easter weekend and May-Aug Sun-Thu 11:30-17:00, closed Fri-Sat except holiday weekends, closed Sept-April; gardens open May-Aug daily 11:00-17:30, Sept Sat-Sun 11:00-17:30, closed Oct-April; last entry 30 minutes before closing, recorded info tel. 01722/746-729, tel. 01722/746-714, www.wiltonhouse.com.

Getting There: It's five miles west of Salisbury via the A-36 to Wilton's Minster Street; or bus #R3 from Salisbury to Wilton.

Stourhead

For a serious taste of a traditional English landscape and miles of footpaths, don't miss this 2,650-acre delight. Stourhead, designed by owner Henry Hoare II in the mid-18th century, is a wonderland of rolling hills, meandering paths, placid lakes, and colorful trees, punctuated by classically inspired bridges and monuments. It's what every other English estate aspires to be—like nature, but better.

Cost and Hours: House and garden-£12.50, or £7.70 to see just one; house open mid-March-Oct Fri-Tue 11:00-17:00, closed Wed-Thu; garden open year-round daily 9:00-19:00; last entry 30 minutes before closing, tel. 01747/841-152, www.nationaltrust.org.uk.

Getting There: It's 28 miles (40 minutes) west of Salisbury off the B-3092 in the town of Stourton (3 miles northwest of Mere).

Nearby: Drivers or ambitious walkers can visit nearby **King Alfred's Tower** and climb its 205 steps for glorious views of the estate and surrounding countryside (£3 to climb tower, same opening times as house, 2.5 miles northwest of Stourhead, off Tower Road).

Dorset Countryside Joyride

The region of Dorset, just southwest of Salisbury, is full of rolling fields, winding country lanes, footpaths, quaint cottages, and villages stuffed with tea shops. Anywhere you go in the area will take you someplace charming, so consider this tour only a suggestion and feel free to get pleasantly lost in the English countryside. You'll be taking some less-traveled roads, so bring along a good map.

Starting in Salisbury, take the A-354 through Blandford Forum to Winterborne Whitechurch. From here, follow signs and small back roads to the village of **Bere Regis,** where you'll find some lovely 15th-century buildings, including one with angels carved on the roof. Follow the A-35 and the B-3075 to Wareham, where T. E. Lawrence (a.k.a. Lawrence of Arabia) lived; he's buried in nearby Moreton. Continue south on the A-351 to the dramatic and romantic **Corfe Castle.** This was a favorite residence for medieval kings until it was destroyed by a massive gunpowder blast during a 17th-century siege (£7.70, daily 10:00-18:00, last entry 30 minutes before closing, tel. 01929/481-294, www.national trust.org.uk). Retrace the A-351 to Wareham, and then take the A-352 to Dorchester.

Just northeast of Dorchester on the A-35, near the village of Stinsford, novelist Thomas Hardy was born in 1840; you'll find **Hardy's family's cottage** nearby, in Higher Bockhampton (£5.50, March-Oct Wed-Sun 11:00-17:00, closed Mon-Tue and Nov-Feb, last entry 30 minutes before closing, tel. 01305/262-366, www .nationaltrust.org.uk). While Hardy's heart is buried in Stinsford with his first wife, Emma, the rest of him is in Westminster Abbey's Poets' Corner. Take the A-35 back to Dorchester. Just west of Dorchester, stay on the A-35 until it connects to the A-37; then follow the A-352 north toward Sherborne.

About eight miles north of Dorchester, on the way to Sherborne, you'll find the little town of **Cerne Abbas** (surn AB-iss), named for an abbey in the center of town. There are only two streets to wander down, so take this opportunity to recharge with a cup of tea and a scone. Abbots Tea Room has a nice cream tea (pot of tea, scone, jam, and clotted cream, 7 Long Street, tel. 01300/341-349). Up the street, you can visit the abbey and its well, reputed to have healing powers.

Just outside of town, a large chalk figure, the **Cerne Abbas Giant,** is carved into the green hillside. Chalk figures such as this one can be found in many parts of the region. Because the soil is only a few inches deep, the overlying grass and dirt can easily be removed to expose the bright white chalk bedrock beneath, creating the outlines. While nobody is sure exactly how old this figure is, or what its original purpose was, the giant is faithfully maintained by the locals, who mow and clear the fields at least once a year. This particular figure, possibly a fertility god, looks friendly...maybe a little too friendly. Locals claim that if a woman who's having trouble getting pregnant sleeps on the giant for one night, she will soon be able to conceive a child. (A few years back, controversy surrounded this giant, as a 180-foot-tall, donut-hoisting Homer Simpson was painted onto the adjacent hillside. No kidding.)

Leaving Cerne Abbas on country roads toward Piddletrenthide (on the aptly named River Piddle), continue through Cheselbourne to **Milton Abbas.** (This area, by the way, has some of the best town names in the country, such as Droop, Plush, Pleck, Folly, and of course, Piddle.) The village of Milton Abbas looks overly perfect. In the 18th century, a wealthy man bought up the town's large abbey and estate. His new place was great...except for the neighbors, a bunch of vulgar villagers with houses that cluttered his view from the garden. So, he had the town demolished and rebuilt a mile away. What you see now is probably the first planned community, with identical houses, a pub, and a church. The estate is now a "public school," which is what the English call an expensive private school. From Milton Abbas, signs lead you back to Winterborne Whitechurch, and the A-354 to Salisbury.

South Wales

Although the best bits of Wales lie to the north (see the North Wales chapter), the southern part of the country, not far from Bath, has some worthwhile sights (see map on page 316). Perhaps the most notable is the famous Tintern Abbey. Frequently immortalized in verse and on canvas, it's the most spectacular of Britain's many ruined abbeys. Cardiff, the Welsh capital, is a recently spiffed-up city with a welcoming urban core, a fun-to-tour castle, and a waterfront that combines modern architecture and lowbrow amusements. Just outside the city, St. Fagans open-air museum celebrates the unheralded Welsh culture. And two more towns—Chepstow and Caerphilly—have castles that, while not as dramatically situated or well-presented as the best ones in the north, still provide a good dose of the many stout castles designed by the British to keep the natives of this feisty little country in line. Note that many of the sights mentioned here—including Caerphilly Castle, Chepstow Castle, and Tintern Abbey—are included in Wales' Explorer Pass (described on page 21).

Cardiff and Nearby

The Welsh capital of Cardiff (pop. 345,000) comes with a fine castle, a freshly revitalized pedestrian core, a smattering of museums, and an impressively modern waterfront. While rugby and soccer fans know it as the home of Millennium Stadium, and sci-fi fans know it as the place where *Doctor Who* is filmed, the Welsh proudly view it as their political and cultural capital. You'll notice immediately that this place just feels different from England.

The Welsh capital was largely shaped by imported Scottish nobility, the Crichton-Stuart clan (a.k.a. the Marquesses of Bute), who married into a wealthy local family and adopted the city as their own. Over many generations, the Crichton-Stuarts invested in Cardiff's development. In the late 18th century, they funded the city's docklands (at today's Cardiff Bay), which spurred its growth as the natural export point for the many products of industrious Wales: Metals, coal, slate, and other fruits of hardworking Welsh ways passed through here on their way throughout Europe and beyond. The city peaked during the Industrial Age, when English and Irish workers flocked here seeking employment. As the market for Welsh coal (the city's main export) dried up following World War I, the port—and the city—faltered, though it was named the capital of Wales in 1955. Like many blue-collar British towns, Cardiff's economy slumped severely in the 1970s and 1980s with the closure of steelworks and other heavy industry. But the city also experienced the same rebounding effect through the 1990s and 2000s, enjoying the shared prosperity of Britain's new economic model.

While once a gloomy wasteland, Cardiff's docklands have been revitalized with state-of-the art facilities (such as the impressive Wales Millennium Centre for the performing arts) side-by-side with restored historic buildings. The formerly traffic-choked downtown streets have been largely pedestrianized and filled with modern shopping centers. Cardiff's 21st-century transformation is yet another in a long list of cities in Britain and beyond (Liverpool, Birmingham, Antwerp, Hamburg, and so on) that have emerged from dark days into a brighter future. But here, it comes with a lilting Welsh accent.

Planning Your Time

Unless you're a Welsh patriot, Cardiff isn't worth lingering in. Its best sights—the castle and Cardiff Bay waterfront zone—can be easily seen in a few hours. But the best sights are actually just outside Cardiff: St. Fagans National History Museum (open-air folk museum) to the west, and Caerphilly (with its stout castle) to the north.

Drivers connecting Bath to the Cotswolds via Cardiff can try this: Get an early start, and head directly to St. Fagans (or, with more time, swing through Caerphilly en route to St. Fagans). Then head into Cardiff for a tour of the castle and quick visit to Cardiff Bay. If not spending the night here, leave in the afternoon to visit Tintern Abbey (about one hour east of Cardiff) on the way to the Cotswolds (about 1.5 hours beyond Tintern Abbey).

Orientation to Cardiff

Tourist Information

Cardiff's helpful main TI is located in the Old Library—in the pedestrianized core of town, just behind the big church. It's a five-minute walk from Cardiff Castle and a 10-minute walk from the train station (Mon-Sat 9:30-17:30, Sun 10:00-16:00, The Hayes,

NEAR BATH

tel. 02920/873-573, www.visitcardiff.com). They have Internet access (£1/30 minutes), a room-booking service, info on events and walking tours (see schedule at www.cardiffonfoot.com), and storage lockers (£3.50-7.50 depending on size, requires £3 deposit, lockers open Mon-Sat 9:30-17:30, Sun 10:00-15:30). The same building hosts The Cardiff Story (free local history museum—see later). A branch TI is at Cardiff Bay, inside the Wales Millennium Centre.

Sights in Cardiff

Downtown

▲Cardiff Castle (Castell Caerdydd)

Most Welsh castles are partially ruined and mostly empty. But Cardiff's is another story: Completely overhauled in the late 19th century by a noble local clan, it's an over-the-top Victorian fantasy of the Middle Ages, its rooms slathered with gilded, Romantic visions of an idealized feudal past. You can also tour the expansive walled grounds—a bit more typical of other castles in Wales, with an original Norman keep—and visit its museum and the tunnels that protected locals during World War II. While you can see most of the castle on your own (with the included audioguide), it's well worth paying a few pounds extra for a detailed tour of the sumptuous interior.

Cost and Hours: £14 "premium" ticket includes 45-minute tour of Great Hall, £11 "essential" ticket doesn't include tour or cover admission to some of the Great Hall rooms; tours depart at the top of each hour; both tickets include audioguide covering the grounds; daily March-Oct 9:00-18:00, Nov-Feb 9:00-17:00, last tour and entry one hour before closing, café, tel. 029/2087-8100, www.cardiffcastle.com.

Visiting the Castle: With its ornate clock tower, the castle is the latest in a series of fortresses erected on the site by Romans, Normans, and assorted British lords.

In the building where you buy your ticket, explore the "Firing Line" exhibition (Welsh military history), see a fragment of a Roman wall (this was the site of a Roman castle nearly 2,800 years ago), and watch the film before heading out to explore. The included audioguide leads you around the grounds: As you step into the vast yard, the original **keep** is straight ahead—a classic, Norman motte-and-bailey construction, with a stout fortress on top of a manmade hill (a wooden forerunner of this castle was built by William the Conqueror in 1081 on his way back from a pilgrimage to St. David's—a cathedral and town in west Wales). Along the right wall are the **battlements walk** (stroll along the top of the fortified wall) and the entrance to the **Wartime Tunnels,** which were turned into air-raid shelters during World War II.

But the highlight of the complex is the **Great Hall,** to the left as you enter the yard. The "premium" ticket includes a guided tour of 10 of the rooms here; on your own you can see about half that many. John Crichton-Stuart, 3rd Marquess of Bute—whose income from the thriving coal trade flowing through his docklands made him Europe's wealthiest man—decided to spruce up this castle in 1865. He spared no expense. With his funds and architect William Burges' know-how, the castle was turned into a whimsical, fantastical take on the Middle Ages. It's the Welsh equivalent of "Mad" King Ludwig's fairy-tale castles in Bavaria. In 1957, the family decided to donate the whole shebang to the city of Cardiff. Every surface is covered in the highly detailed, gilded imagery of medieval symbolism. The glittering Arab Room is slathered in gold, including a gold-leaf stalactite ceiling. The breathtaking Banqueting Hall evokes the age of chivalry, right down to the raised minstrel's gallery (where musicians could perform, unseen and overhead). The small dining room has a table designed to allow a grapevine to grow right up through a hole in the middle—allowing guests to pick their own dessert. The library boasts rows of leather-bound books and desks that double as radiators. The "Premium" tour adds a few more rooms, including the nursery, decorated with every imaginable nursery rhyme and children's tale; the rooftop garden; and the Marquess' bedroom and bathroom, oozing masculine charisma.

Nearby: Stretching behind the castle, between the River Taff and North Road, is the sprawling park called **Coopers Field** (and, just over the river, **Coach Park**)—an enjoyable place for a walk.

The Cardiff Story

This free museum, sharing the Old Library building with the TI, is small but impressively high-tech. On the main floor, the "Cardiff in Context" exhibit uses engaging, often interactive exhibits to trace the city's history. Downstairs, the City Lab is for hands-on learning, with children's activities and computer terminals where you can learn more about the city. Don't miss the colorfully tiled historic corridor, hiding just past the museum entrance on the ground floor.

Cost and Hours: Free, Mon-Sat 10:00-17:00, Sun 11:00-16:00, The Hayes, tel. 029/2078-8334, www.cardiffstory.com.

More Sights

With more time in Cardiff, you can explore the recently pedestrianized and rejuvenated **downtown core**, dominated by the enormous St. David's shopping mall. Just north of this zone (and east of the castle), facing Gorsedd Gardens, is a row of three stately buildings (left to right): Crown Court (law courts), City Hall, and National Museum. Behind City Hall is the manicured Alexandra

Gardens. The **National Museum** focuses not on Welsh culture and history—that's at St. Fagans—but on art (with a particularly strong Impressionist collection), natural history (dinosaurs and mammoths), and archaeology (scant fragments of prehistoric Wales; museum free, Tue-Sun 10:00-17:00, closed Mon, Cathays Park, tel. 029/2057-3000, www.museumwales.ac.uk/cardiff).

Just west of downtown, between the pedestrian zone and the river, is **Millennium Stadium**. Nicknamed "The Dragon's Den" (after the symbol and mascot of Wales), it serves as the home pitch of the Welsh national rugby team (WRU) and soccer team, hosted soccer matches during the 2012 London Summer Olympics, and is *the* place for big rock concerts in Wales. Even if you don't join 74,500 screaming spectators for a match, you can pay for a guided tour of the building (details at www.millenniumstadium.com).

▲▲Cardiff Bay

The Welsh capital's harborfront zone recently enjoyed an extensive rejuvenation that has left it gleaming—packed with sparkling, bold architecture, major sightseeing attractions, and fun entertainment. It's worth the short bus ride from downtown to see how a once-flailing city can right the ship.

Getting to Cardiff Bay: From the Kingsway stop downtown (in front of the Hilton Hotel, across the street from the side wall of Cardiff Castle), catch bus #6 or the "Baycar" in the direction of Porth Teigr (£1.70, exact change only, about every 10 minutes, trip takes 10-15 minutes). Hop off at the East Bute Street stop, just behind the Wales Millennium Centre; for the return trip, you can catch the bus at the more convenient Millennium Centre stop, facing Roald Dahl Plass.

Background: During the Industrial Age, Cardiff was a hugely successful maritime port, rivaling Liverpool and London. But its fortunes collapsed in the 20th century, leaving it a derelict wasteland for decades. But in the late 1980s, city leaders hatched a scheme for the "Cardiff Bay Barrage," designed to seal off the mouth of the port and create a permanent high-tide waterline. Their goal was to attract developers with the promise of an inviting new waterfront people zone. It worked. Through the 1990s and 2000s, the bayfront has been transformed into a thriving entertainment, dining, residential, and working zone.

Visiting Cardiff Bay: Visitors congregate on the expansive, bowl-shaped plaza called **Roald Dahl Plass** (named in honor of the Cardiff-born children's author with many fans worldwide). As this area was once a coal port, it angles down to the water. The pillars are illuminated with a light show after dark, and the 70-foot-tall silver water tower is always trickling. (The Norwegian term *plass*—"square"—honors Dahl's Norwegian ancestry.)

On one side of the square, the enormous **Wales Millennium Centre** (opened in 2004) anchors the entire Cardiff Bay area. Its facade, dominated by slate and metal (two important Welsh resources that have kept this little country humming), is carved with the words of Welsh national poet Gwyneth Lewis: the English phrase "In these stones horizons sing," and the Welsh phrase *Creu gwir fel gwydr o ffwrnais awen* ("Creating truth like glass from the furnace of inspiration"). It's a cutting-edge venue for opera, theater, and other performances; inside are shops, eateries, and a TI (www.wmc.org.uk).

Facing the Wales Millennium Centre across the square is **Mermaid Quay,** an inviting outdoor-dining zone loaded with mostly chain restaurants.

Out along the harborfront, the red **Pierhead** building looks out over the port whose commerce it once oversaw. Sometimes called the "Welsh Big Ben," this landmark is a symbol of the city; inside is a history exhibit (www.pierhead.org).

Just behind the Pierhead, with the huge overhanging roof, is the **Senedd** building—home of the National Assembly of Wales (essentially the Welsh capitol). While Wales—like Scotland and Northern Ireland—have a degree of autonomy from the United Kingdom, many matters are still decided in London. The National Assembly (not quite a "parliament") was created in 1999, moved into these new digs in 2006, and gained more authority in 2007. The building, with vast walls of glass symbolizing the ideal of an open and transparent government, was designed by prominent architect Richard Rogers (best known for London's Millennium Dome and Lloyd's Building, and—with frequent collaborator Renzo Piano—Paris' Pompidou Centre).

Looking out at the horizon, you can see the "barrage" (tidal barrier) that made all of this development possible. Looking around the left side of the harbor, you'll see a shiplap church that would be more at home on a fjord. This **Norwegian Church** was built as a seamen's mission by the Norwegian merchant marine, in properly austere Lutheran style, during Cardiff's Industrial Age boom time. Originally it sat where the Wales Millennium Centre is today, but in the 1970s and 1980s—when the docklands were a dangerous, derelict no-man's land—the church was literally disassembled and mothballed for future use. Over the last couple of decades, it has been reassembled, reconsecrated, refurbished, and repurposed as a successful arts center (www.norwegianchurch cardiff.com).

Beyond the church is the Tardis-blue curve of the giant **Doctor Who Experience.** Honoring the astoundingly long-running BBC science fiction series—which celebrated its 50th anniversary in 2013 (with a decade-and-a-half break before its highly successful reboot in 2005)—this interactive exhibit is a must for fans...but totally lost on those who don't know a Dalek from a Sontaran (for details, see www.doctorwhoexperience.com). *Doctor Who* is one of many BBC shows filmed here in Cardiff; behind the museum, on Roath Lock, sprawls the **BBC Drama Village**, a studio lot where many popular series—including *Torchwood, Casualty,* and the 2010-2012 version of *Upstairs Downstairs*—have been filmed.

While those are the main landmarks, there's much more to see and do here: bike and boat rental, harbor boat tours, an old-fashioned carousel, a hands-on science museum (Techniquest), a tourable ship with a built-in lighthouse (the Lightship), an open-air exhibit of boats from around the world, a multiplex (with Wales' only IMAX screen), the nearby International Sports Village (with an ice arena and swimming pool), and more.

Near Cardiff
▲▲St. Fagans National History Museum/Amgueddfa Werin Cymru (Museum of Welsh Life)

The best look anywhere at traditional Welsh folk life, St. Fagans (rhymes with "Bilbo Baggins") is a 100-acre park with more than

40 carefully reconstructed and fully furnished old houses from all corners of this little country, as well as a "castle" (actually a Tudor-era manor house) that offers a glimpse of how the other half lived. Workshops feature busy craftsmen eager to demonstrate their skills, and each house comes equipped with a local expert warming up beside a toasty fire, happy to tell you anything you want to know about life in this old cottage. Ask questions.

Cost and Hours: Free, parking-£3.50, daily 10:00-17:00, tel. 029/2057-3500, www.museumwales.ac.uk/en/stfagans.

Information: Be sure to pick up the essential £0.30 map, which helps you navigate your way through the park. Plaques by each building do an exceptional job of succinctly explaining where the building came from, its role in Welsh culture, and how it came to be here, all illustrated by a helpful timeline. Docents posted throughout can tell you more. But if you want more detail, buy the £3 museum guidebook.

Expect Changes: The main entrance building (which usually houses the indoor part of the museum) is closed for renovation through at least 2016. When it reopens, its much-expanded exhibit will offer more to keep visitors occupied on not-uncommon rainy days. In the meantime, the services usually housed inside (ticket desk, WCs, café, restaurant, gift shop) will be relocated to other areas throughout the park. If you're looking for something, ask one of the many docents. Don't be surprised if the changes displace some of the exhibits mentioned below.

Getting There: To get from the Cardiff train station to the museum, catch bus #32 (which stops right at the museum entrance; buses #322 or #320 take you to St. Fagans village, a 5-minute walk to the museum; buses run hourly, 25 minutes, tel. 0871-200-2233, www.traveline-cymru.info). Drivers leave the M-4 at Junction 33 and follow the signs. Leaving the museum, jog left on the freeway, take the first exit, and circle back, following signs to the M-4.

Getting Around: While large, the sprawling grounds are walkable. But if you want to take it easy, a small train trundles among the exhibits from Easter to October (five stops, £0.50/stop, whole circuit takes 45 minutes).

Eating at St. Fagans: Within the park are plenty of snack stands, as well as two bigger eateries: the Gwalia Tea Room in the heart of the traditional building zone, and The Buttery inside the castle. (There may also be a temporary café and/or restaurant set up somewhere in the park during the renovation.) Back in the real world, The Plymouth Arms pub, just outside the museum, serves the best food.

Visiting the Museum: Buy the £0.30 map and pick up the list of today's activities. Once in the park, you'll find most of the traditional buildings to your left, while to the right are the castle and its surrounding gardens. Here's a rough framework for seeing the highlights:

First, head left and do a clockwise spin around the traditional buildings, starting with the circa 1800, red-and-white **Kennixton Farmhouse**. Then swing left, go down past the corn mill, and hook left again down the path to the **Lywyn-yr-eos Farmhouse.** Along with the castle, this is the only building at the museum that stands in its original location. It's furnished as it would have been at the end of World War I—complete with "welcome home" banner and patriotic portraits of stiff-upper-lip injured troops.

Head back up the main path and continue deeper into the park, turning left at the fork (toward *Church* and *Y Garieg Fawr*). Passing another farmhouse, then a small mill (used for grinding gorse—similar to scotch broom—into animal feed) and a Tudor-era trader's house, continue through the woods to **St. Teilos' Church,** surrounded by a whitewashed stone fence. The interior has been restored to the way it looked around 1520—including vibrantly colorful illustrations of Bible stories on all the walls.

Leaving the church, continue ahead to the **Oakdale Workmen's Institute**—basically a leisure club and community center for hardworking miners and their families. Poking around the building—from the library, reading room, and meeting hall downstairs to the concert hall upstairs—you can imagine how a space like this provided a humble community with a much-needed social space.

Next up are the **Gwalia Stores,** a village general store where you could buy just about anything imaginable (poke around to see what locals may have browsed for here). One section of the store still sells canned goods, local cheeses, sweets, and ice cream; upstairs is a full-service tearoom.

Pass the gimmicky portrait studio on your way up to the museum's highlight, the **Rhyd-y-Car** terrace of row houses, which displays ironworker cottages as they might have looked in 1805, 1855, 1895, 1925, 1955, and 1985—offering a fascinating zip through Welsh domestic life from hearths to microwaves. Notice the pea patches in front, and the chicken coops in the back.

This loop covers the top stops, but there's lots more to see in this part of the park (check your map to be sure you haven't missed something that interests you). When you're ready to move on, continue along more houses back to the entrance. Step into the one-room **St. Mary's Board Schoolhouse**, where the docent can explain the various items used to punish ill-behaved kids in the late 19th century. What looks like a wooden version of brass knuckles was used to force lefties to write right. The "Welsh not" was worn as a badge of shame by any student heard speaking Welsh rather than the required English. Students could pass it on to other kids they heard speaking Welsh, and whoever was wearing it at day's end was caned. (On the day of my visit, I overheard a present-day schoolkid loudly complaining that his teachers force him to speak *Welsh* instead of English. The more things change....) Also nearby are a **saddler's workshop** and a **blacksmith's shop**, where you can sometimes watch traditional craftmakers in action. And the field up above often hosts an array of old-timey **carnival rides**.

Head back past the entrance area and continue to the castle and gardens. You'll dip down past a series of terraced ponds, then climb steeply up to the misnamed **"castle"**—so-called because it was built on the remains of a real, Norman-era castle that once stood here. This circa-1580 Elizabethan manor house boasts a stately interior decorated with antique, period furnishing. It feels like the perfect setting for a murder mystery or a ghost tale. Pick up the information paddles in each room, and ask the docents if you have any questions. Entering, you'll walk through The Hall (a reception room for visitors), The Study (where the master of the house carried out his business), and The Drawing Room (where the ladies would convene for a post-dinner chat, a la *Downton Abbey*). Climb the funhouse stairs up to the long gallery, where you can dip into a series of bedrooms.

Leaving the castle, if it's nice out, turn left and explore the expansive, manicured **gardens** that stretch out across the grounds. Near the far end is a woolen mill.

▲▲Caerphilly Castle

The impressive but gutted old castle, surrounded by lakes, gently rolling hills, and the town of Caerphilly, is the most visit-worthy I've seen in South Wales.

Cost and Hours: £4.75; March-Oct daily 9:30-17:00, July-Aug until 18:00; Nov-Feb Mon-Sat 10:00-16:00, Sun 11:00-16:00; last entry 30 minutes before closing, tel. 029/2088-3143, www.cadw.wales.gov.uk.

Information: Scant explanations are offered by a few posted plaques; if you want the full story, invest in the £3.75 guidebook. Across the moat, Caerphilly's helpful town **TI** happily answers questions. It also has free Wi-Fi with comfortable seating overlooking the castle, and sells a variety of locally sourced, un-tacky Welsh souvenirs, from hand-carved heart spoons to gifty edibles (daily 10:00-17:30, tel. 029/2088-0011, www.visitcaerphilly.com).

Getting There: The castle is located right in the center of the town of Caerphilly, nine miles north of Cardiff. To get there, take the train from Cardiff to Caerphilly (4/hour Mon-Sat, every 2 hours Sun, 20 minutes) and walk five minutes. It's 20 minutes by car from St. Fagans (exit 32, following signs from the M-4). Once in town, follow signs to park in the pay lot right next to the TI (described above), facing the castle.

Background: Spread over 30 acres, Caerphilly is the second-largest castle in Britain after Windsor. English Earl Gilbert de

Clare erected this squat behemoth to try to establish a stronghold in Wales. With two concentric walls, it was considered to be a brilliant arrangement of defensive walls and moats. Attackers had to negotiate three drawbridges and four sets of doors and portcullises just to reach the main entrance. For the record, there were no known successful enemy forays beyond the current castle's inner walls. Later, this evocative castle understandably became a favorite of Romantics, who often painted it in the shimmering Welsh mist. And in modern times, during the Great Depression of the 1920s, de Clare's descendant undertook a restoration of the then-mostly ruined structure (as a sort of private stimulus package), restoring it at least partway to its previous glory. Today it's surrounded by a picturesque, picnic-perfect park.

Visiting the Castle: Cross the first moat and enter the outer gate to buy your ticket. Then head across the second moat to reach the central keep of the castle. You'll enter through the **Inner East Gatehouse**, with interactive touchscreens on the ground floor, and upstairs, unfurnished but still stately residential halls. The top-floor terrace offers great views between the crenellations of the castle complex and the town. On the way up and down, look for the little bathrooms. No need to flush—the chute beneath the hole drops several stories directly into the moat below. (Just one more disincentive for would-be attackers thinking of crossing that moat.)

From there, head into the **Inner Ward**—the central yard (or "bailey") that's ringed by thick walls and stout towers. The tower across the Inner Ward to the right features an entertaining, animated 12-minute **video presentation** that attempts to make a much-abbreviated version of the castle's grisly history accessible to kids.

To the left as you enter the Inner Ward is the restored, cavernous **Great Hall**, with thick stony walls, a wood-beam ceiling, and a man-sized fireplace. This space helps you imagine a great medieval feast. (If you'd like to do more than imagine, you can rent out the hall for a banquet of your own.)

Hiding behind the Great Hall is the icon of the castle—a half-destroyed, listing **tower** (which, they like to brag, "outleans Pisa's"). Following the English Civil War, the Parliament decreed that many castles like this one be destroyed as a preventive measure; this tower was a victim. Some believe that the adjacent **Braose Gallery** has a resident ghost: Legend has it that de Clare, after learning of his wife Alice's infidelity, exiled her back to France and had her lover killed. Upon discovering her paramour's fate, Alice died of a broken heart. Since then, the "Green Lady," named for her husband's jealousy, has reportedly roamed the ramparts.

Explore the rest of the castle. You could stroll here endlessly, climbing up to the ramparts and wandering the parks on either side of the moat. Before leaving, be sure to visit the strip of yard that stretches out in front of the ticket office (along the inner moat). The first tower has a replica (complete with sound effects) of the **latrines** that were used by the soldiers—again, these dumped right into the moat. Just beyond that tower is a collection of life-size replica **siege engines**—ingenious catapult-like devices and oversized crossbows designed to deter attackers (each one is well described).

Sleeping in Cardiff

(area code: 029)

To overnight here, the basic choice is between a chain hotel downtown (which can be deeply discounted when it's not busy—check hotel-booking sites for deals) or a more characteristic B&B, most of which line Cathedral Road, a one-mile walk or quick bus ride from the city center. Parking along Cathedral Road is free, but tight; some places offer private parking. Here are just a few of the seemingly dozens of choices along Cathedral Road.

$$ Beaufort House, with 10 rooms, boasts abundant decoration, a palatial breakfast room, and an inviting winter-garden lounge (Sb-£55-60, Db-£82-98, price depends on demand, free Wi-Fi, private parking, 65 Cathedral Road, tel. 029/2023-7003, www.beauforthousecardiff.co.uk, paul@beauforthousecardiff.co.uk, Paul).

$ Cathedral House, run by Liz, offers five good-value rooms with clean, tidy, modern style that's less cutesy than the old-fashioned neighboring places (Sb-£45, Db-£70, free Wi-Fi, two parking spaces, 146 Cathedral Road, tel. 029/2023-2872, www.cathedralhousecardiff.co.uk, beds@cathedralhousecardiff.co.uk).

$ The Town House has eight nondescript rooms in a classy old townhouse with a big, shared breakfast table (Sb-£50, Db-£70, free Wi-Fi, 70 Cathedral Road, tel. 029/2023-9399, www.thetownhousecardiff.co.uk, thetownhouse@msn.com, Charles and Paula).

Cardiff Connections

From Cardiff by Train to: Caerphilly (2-4/hour, 20 minutes), **Bath** (hourly, 1-1.5 hours), **Birmingham** (1/hour direct, more with change in Bristol, 2 hours), **London**'s Paddington Station (2/hour, 2 hours), **Chepstow** (every 1-2 hours, 40 minutes; then bus #69 to **Tintern**—runs every 1-2 hours, 20 minutes). Train info: tel. 0871-200-2233, www.traveline-cymru.info.

By Car: For driving directions from Bath to Cardiff, see "Route Tips for Drivers," at the end of this chapter.

The Wye Valley

From Chepstow, on the mouth of the River Severn, the River Wye cuts north, marking the border between Wales (Monmouthshire, on the west bank) and England (Gloucestershire, on the east bank). While technically in Wales, everything covered here is within sight of England—just over the river. If you've always dreamed of visiting the fabled Tintern Abbey—and wouldn't mind a quick taste of a stout castle and a couple of charming Welsh towns—the riverside road (A-466) that traces the Wye is a detour between Bath and the Cotswolds that's worth considering (adding about an hour of driving compared with the less scenic, more direct route).

This land is lush, mellow, and historic. Local tourist brochures explain the area's special dialect, its strange political autonomy, and its oaken ties to Trafalgar and Admiral Nelson (who harvested timbers for his ships in the Forest of Dean). While the valley itself is only gently pretty, it's home to the justifiably legendary Tintern Abbey, the ruined skeleton of a glorious church that's well worth a quick stop. The abbey sits partway between two pleasant, worka-day towns with interesting sights of their own: Chepstow (with a fine castle) and Monmouth (a market town with some quirky sights). Just to the east of the river, in England, is the romantic-sounding but disappointing Forest of Dean.

While drivers can take a more direct route between Bath and the Cotswolds, the sights listed here aren't too far out of the way and are certainly worthwhile if you're connecting those two areas via a South Wales detour. I've listed these sights in the order you'll reach them as you move north up the Wye.

Chepstow

This historic burg enjoys a strategic location, for the same reason it's your first stop in Wales: It marks the natural boundary between England and Wales. Driving into town, you'll pass through the town gate, where in medieval times, folks arriving to sell goods or livestock were hit up for tolls. The town's main attractions and ser-vices—TI, castle, museum, and free WCs—cluster around a large pay parking lot just up from the river, making things easy for visi-tors. Everything worth seeing is within a short walk. To explore more of the town, buy the £3 *Chepstow Town Trail* guide at the TI or Chepstow Museum; you can also print out more basic walking instructions from the TI website (go to www.chepstowtowncrier .org.uk and click on "Things to Do," then "Walking").

The **TI** is helpful, with lots of free brochures and maps, many more for purchase, and an inviting seating area in the back where you can access their free Wi-Fi and plan your River Wye day (Easter-early Oct daily 9:30-17:00, off-season until 15:30, Bridge Street, tel. 01291/623-772, www.chepstowtowncrier.org.uk).

Chepstow Castle

Perched on a riverside ridge overlooking the pleasant village of Chepstow on one side and the River Wye on the other, this cas-tle is worth a short stop for drivers heading for Tintern Abbey, or it's a 10-minute walk from the Chepstow train station (follow signs; uphill going back). The stone-built Great Tower, dating from 1066, was among the first castles the Normans plunked down to secure their turf in Wales, and it remained in use through 1690. While many castles of the time were built first in wood, Chepstow, then a key foothold on the England-Wales border, was built from stone from the start for durability. You'll work your way up through various towers and baileys (inner yards); a few posted plaques provide details, but you're mostly on your own. As you clamber along the battlements (with great views to town, and over the river to England), you'll find architectural evidence of military renovations through the centuries, from Norman to Tudor right up through Cromwellian additions. You can tell which parts date from Norman days—they're the ones built from yellow sandstone instead of the grayish limestone that makes up the rest of the castle. While the castle would benefit from more exhibits (it's basically an empty shell), with a little imagination you can resurrect the skeletons of buildings and appreciate how formidable and strategic it must have been in its heyday.

Cost and Hours: £4.50; March-Oct daily 9:30-17:00, July-Aug until 18:00; Nov-Feb Mon-Sat 10:00-16:00, Sun 11:00-16:00; last entry 30 minutes before closing, guidebook-£4.50, in Chepstow village a half-mile from train station, tel. 01291/624-065, www.cadw.wales.gov.uk.

Chepstow Museum

Highlighting Chepstow's history, this museum is in an 18th-century townhouse across the street from the castle. Endearingly earnest, jammed with artifacts, and well-presented, it says just about everything that could possibly be said about this small town.

Cost and Hours: Free; July-Sept Mon-Sat 10:30-17:30, Sun 14:00-17:30; March-June and Oct Mon-Sat 11:00-17:00, Sun 14:00-17:00; Nov-Feb Mon-Sat 11:00-16:00, Sun 14:00-16:00; tel. 01291/625-981.

Riverfront Park

From the TI and parking lot, walk one block down Bridge Street to the River Wye. The river is spanned by a graceful white cast-iron bridge. If you walk across it to the ornate decorations in the middle, you can stand with one foot in Wales and the other in England (notice the *Gloucestershire* sign across the bridge). From the bridge, you'll also have great views back to the castle. Beneath your feet, the River Wye's banks and water are muddy because this is a tidal river, which can rise and fall about 20 feet twice a day.

Back in Wales, stroll along the riverside park (with the river on your left), noticing that the English bank sits on a chalk cliff—

into which has been painted a Union Jack (to celebrate King George V's Silver Jubilee in 1935). Near the standing stones is a large, circular plaque marking the beginning of the Welsh Coast Path; from here, you can walk 870 miles all the way along the coast of Wales. Nearby is the 176-mile Offa's Dyke Path, which roughly traces the border between Wales and England. Together, these two paths go almost all the way around the country.

▲▲Tintern Abbey

Inspiring monks to prayer, William Wordsworth to poetry, J. M. W. Turner to a famous painting, and rushed tourists to a thoughtful moment, this verse-worthy ruined-castle-of-an-abbey merits a five-mile detour off the motorway. Founded in 1131 on a site chosen by Norman monks for its tranquility, it functioned as an austere Cistercian abbey until its dissolution in 1536. The monks followed a strict schedule. They rose several hours after midnight for the first of eight daily prayer sessions and spent the rest of their time studying, working the surrounding farmlands, and meditating. Dissolved under Henry VIII's Act of Suppression in 1536, the magnificent church moldered in relative obscurity until tourists in the Romantic era (mid-18th century) discovered the wooded Wye Valley and abbey ruins. J. M. W. Turner made his first sketches in 1792, and William Wordsworth penned "Lines Composed a Few Miles Above Tintern Abbey..." in 1798.

With all the evocative ruined abbeys dotting the British landscape, why all the fuss about this one? Because few are as big, as remarkably intact, and as picturesquely situated. Most of the external walls of the 250-foot-long, 150-foot-wide church still stand, along with the exquisite window tracery and outlines of the sacristy, chapter house, and dining hall. The daylight that floods through the roofless ruins highlights the Gothic decorated arches—in those days a bold departure from Cistercian simplicity. While the guidebook (described below) narrates a very detailed, architecture-oriented tour, the best visit is to simply stroll the cavernous interior and let your imagination roam, like the generations of Romantics before you.

In summer, the abbey is flooded with tourists, so visit early or late to miss the biggest crowds. The shop sells Celtic jewelry and other gifts. Take an easy 15-minute walk up to St. Mary's Church (on the hill above town) for a view of the abbey, River Wye, and England just beyond.

Cost and Hours: £4.50; March-Oct daily 9:30-17:00, July-Aug until 18:00; Nov-Feb Mon-Sat 10:00-16:00, Sun 11:00-16:00; last entry 30 minutes before closing, occasional summertime concerts in the cloisters (check website for schedule or ask at the TI), tel. 01291/689-251, www.cadw.wales.gov.uk.

NEAR BATH

Information: Sparse informational plaques clearly identify and explain each part of the complex. The dry, extensive £4.50 guidebook may be too much information—but if you're looking to redeem your £3 parking fee (see next), it brings the cost down to just £1.50.

Getting There: Drivers park in the pricey pay lot right next to the abbey (£3, but refundable if you buy anything in the official shop or at The Anchor restaurant). By public transportation from Cardiff, catch a 40-minute train to Chepstow; from there, hop on bus #69 (runs every 1-2 hours, 20 minutes) or take a taxi to the abbey (figure about £10 one-way).

Near Tintern Abbey: The villages of **Tintern** and **Tintern Parva** cluster in wide spots along the main riverside road, just north of the abbey. A couple of miles north, just beyond the last of the inns, you'll find the **Old Station**—a converted train station with old rail cars that house a regional TI, gift shop, and an exhibit on the local railway (daily April-Oct 10:30-17:30, closed Nov-March,

pay parking lot, tel. 01291/689-566, www.visitwyevalley.com). Surrounding the train cars are a fine riverside park, a café, and a few low-key, kid-friendly attractions.

Eating: For a couple of mealtime ideas near Tintern Abbey, see "Eating in the Wye Valley," later.

Monmouth

Another bustling market town—bookending the valley of the River Wye with Chepstow—Monmouth has a pleasant square, a few offbeat museums, and an impressive roster of past residents. The main square is called **Agincourt Square**, after the famous battle won by a king who was born right here: Henry V (you'll see a statue of him in the niche on the big building). The stately building on that square, which houses the TI, is **Shire Hall**, the historic home of the courts and town council. This was the site of a famous 1840 trial of John Frost, a leader of the Chartist movement (championing the rights of the working class in Victorian Britain).

Standing in front of Shire Hall is a statue of **Charles Rolls** (1877-1910), contemplating a model airplane. This descendant of a noble Monmouth family was a pioneer of ballooning and aviation, and—together with his business partner, Frederick Royce—revolutionized motoring with the creation of their company, Rolls-Royce. The airplane he's holding, which he purchased from the

NEAR BATH

Wright Brothers, helped him become the first person to fly over the English Channel and back, in 1910. (Just over a month later, he also became the first British person to die in a plane crash, when that same Wright Flyer lost its tail mid-flight.)

Across the street from Shire Hall, angle right up the lane to the Regimental Museum and the scant ruins of **Monmouth Castle,** where Henry V was born in 1386. While there's not much to see, the site may wring out a few goose bumps for historians.

A block up Priory Street is the endearing **Nelson Museum** (a.k.a. Monmouth Museum). Admiral Horatio Nelson, who was considered in Victorian times (and, by many, still today) to be the savior of England for his naval victories in the Napoleonic Wars, was a frequent visitor to Monmouth. This remarkable collection of Nelson-worship began as the personal collection of local noblewoman, Lady Georgiana Llangattock, who was also the mother of Charles Rolls. You'll see several of Nelson's personal effects, a replica of his uniform, the actual sword he wore in the Battle of Trafalgar (as well as the two swords surrendered by the French and Spanish commanders), and some 800 letters by or to him (pull out the drawers to see them). There are also a few small exhibits about other aspects of town history, including the Rolls family (free, Mon-Sat 11:00-13:00 & 14:00-17:00, Sun 14:00-17:00 only, until 16:00 Nov-Feb, tel. 01600/710-630, www.monmouthshire .gov.uk).

A few blocks downhill in the opposite direction (down Monnow Street from Agincourt Square) is the picturesque, 13th-century **Monnow Bridge,** with its graceful arches and stout defensive tower in the middle.

Forest of Dean

East of Monmouth and the River Wye is this heavily promoted, 43-square-mile patch of rare "ancient woodland" (what Americans call "old-growth forest"). While the name alone is enough to conjure fantasies of primeval forests, King Arthur, and Robin Hood, the reality is underwhelming if you come from a region with a forested area of any significant size. You could drive to the visitors center at Beechenhurst Lodge to pay too much for parking and get advice for a local hike, but I'd rather skip this forest entirely. Both England and Wales have far more interesting natural areas that are deserving of your time.

Sleeping in the Wye Valley

If you're seduced into spending the night in this charming area, you'll find plenty of B&Bs near Tintern Abbey or in the castle-crowned town of Chepstow, located just down the road (a one-hour drive from Bath). I've listed a few accommodations that are near the abbey.

$ The Florence is snuggled in the lower Wye Valley north of Tintern on the way to Monmouth. Four rooms are in the 17th-century main hotel building, with four more in the former gardener's cottage. All of the rooms are nicely maintained and a great value. On a nice day, hotel guests can eat on the garden terrace and share the scenery with the cows lazing along the riverbanks (Sb-£40, Db-£80, all with river view, £17 two-course dinners available by arrangement, no kids under 10, free Wi-Fi in main building, tel. 01594/530-830, www.florencehotel.co.uk, enquiries@florence hotel.co.uk, kind owners Dennis and Kathy). The B&B is along the main road between Tintern Abbey and Monmouth, about a 12-minute drive north of the abbey (just after the road forks off for St. Briavels).

$ Parva Farmhouse, a lesser value, has eight old-fashioned rooms in a 400-year-old building right along the main road through Tintern. While a bit dated, it comes with Welsh charm and is within walking distance of the abbey, village, and local pubs (Sb-£52-60, Db-£72-78, a few pounds more on weekends, Monmouth Road, tel. 01291/689-411, www.parvafarmhouse.co .uk, Peter and Angela).

For a medieval night, check into the **$ St. Briavels Castle Youth Hostel.** An 800-year-old Norman castle used by King John in 1215 (the year he signed the Magna Carta), the hostel is comfortable (as castles go), friendly, and in the center of the quiet village of St. Briavels just north of Tintern Abbey. Non-guests are welcome to poke around the courtyard; if you're in town and the gates are open, step inside (70 beds, £23-25 beds in 8- to 16-bed dorms, members-£3 less, breakfast-£5, private 4- to 8-bed rooms available, Nov-March open to groups only, reception open daily 8:00-10:00 & 17:00-23:00, hostel closed to guests daily 10:00-17:00, curfew at 23:30, modern kitchen and medieval lounge, brown-bag lunches and evening meals available, pay Wi-Fi, tel. 0845-371-9042, www.yha.org.uk, stbriavels @yha.org.uk). The village of St. Briavels sits in a forest high above the river. From Tintern, head north on A-466, the main Monmouth road; just after the road crosses the river, watch for the St. Briavels turnoff on the right, and switchback up the steep road into town.

Eating in the Wye Valley

Chepstow and Monmouth both have the usual range of pubs and other eateries. But assuming you're sleeping near Tintern Abbey, here are a few suggestions.

Near Tintern Abbey

While culinary offerings here are more functional than memorable, there are a few good pub options. **The Anchor,** across the parking lot from the abbey, has a pub, restaurant, and tearoom. While it feels like a slick and modern tourist trap, the food is good (if overpriced), and their Garden Room is a glassed-in winter garden with great views of the abbey (£10-16 meals, food served Mon-Sat 12:00-14:45 & 18:00-21:00, Sun 12:00-16:00 & 17:30-19:30, tel. 01291/689-582). A short drive or longish walk up the road (toward Monmouth), **The Moon and Sixpence** has a friendly, cozy, pubby atmosphere (£8-14 meals, food served Wed-Sat 12:00-14:30 & 18:30-21:00, Sun 12:00-16:00 only, closed Sun for dinner and all day Mon-Tue; parking across the road, tel. 01291/689-284).

In St. Briavels

St. Briavels Castle B&B/Youth Hostel (in the town of St. Briavels, high above the River Wye—for directions, see above) hosts medieval banquets regularly during holidays and weekends. While mostly intended for guests, they often let non-guests join the feast—if you contact them a few days in advance (£10, see hostel listing above for contact info).

The George, "just down the path and up the snicket" from the hostel, is a pub with decent food (£10-16 main dishes, food served daily 12:00-15:00 & 18:00-21:00, until 19:45 on Sun, High Street, tel. 01594/530-228).

South Wales Connections

Route Tips for Drivers

Bath to Cardiff and St. Fagans: Leave Bath following signs for the A-4, then the M-4. It's 10 miles north (on the A-46 past a village called Pennsylvania) to the M-4 freeway. Zip westward, crossing a huge suspension bridge over the Severn, into Wales (£6.20 toll westbound only). Stay on the M-4 (not the M-48) past Cardiff, take exit 33, and follow the brown signs south to *St. Fagans National History Museum/Amgueddfa Werin Cymru/Museum of Welsh Life*.

Bath to Tintern Abbey: Follow the directions above to the M-4. Take the M-4 to exit 21 and get on the M-48. The abbey is six miles (up the A-466, follow signs to *Chepstow*, then *Tintern*) off the M-48 at exit 2, right where the northern bridge (£6.20 toll) across the Severn hits Wales.

Cardiff to the Cotswolds via Forest of Dean: On the Welsh side of the big suspension bridge, take the Chepstow exit and follow signs up the A-466 to *Tintern Abbey* and the *Wye River Valley*. Carry on to Monmouth, and follow the A-40 and the M-50 to the Tewkesbury exit, where small roads lead to the Cotswolds.

THE COTSWOLDS

Chipping Campden • Stow-on-the-Wold
• Moreton-in-Marsh • Blenheim Palace

The Cotswold Hills, a 25-by-90-mile chunk of Gloucestershire, are dotted with enchanting villages and graced with England's greatest countryside palace, Blenheim. As with many fairy-tale regions of Europe, the present-day beauty of the Cotswolds was the result of an economic disaster. Wool was a huge industry in medieval England, and Cotswold sheep grew the best wool. A 12th-century saying bragged, "In Europe the best wool is English. In England the best wool is Cotswold." The region prospered. Wool money built fine towns and houses. Local "wool" churches are called "cathedrals" for their scale and wealth. Stained-glass slogans say things like "I thank my God and ever shall, it is the sheep hath paid for all."

With the rise of cotton and the Industrial Revolution, the woolen industry collapsed. Ba-a-a-ad news. The wealthy Cotswold towns fell into a depressed time warp; the homes of impoverished nobility became gracefully dilapidated. Today, visitors enjoy a harmonious blend of man and nature—the most pristine of English countrysides decorated with time-passed villages, rich wool churches, tell-me-a-story stone fences, and "kissing gates" you wouldn't want to experience alone. Appreciated by throngs of 21st-century Romantics, the Cotswolds are enjoying new prosperity.

The north Cotswolds are best. Two of the region's coziest towns, Chipping Campden and

Stow-on-the-Wold, are eight and four miles, respectively, from Moreton-in-Marsh, which has the best public transportation connections. Any of these three towns makes a fine home base for your exploration of the thatch-happiest of Cotswold villages and walks.

Planning Your Time

The Cotswolds are an absolute delight by car and, with patience, enjoyable even without a car. On a three-week countrywide trip, I'd spend at least two nights and a day in the Cotswolds. The Cotswolds' charm has a softening effect on many uptight itineraries. You could enjoy days of walking from a home base here.

Home Bases: Chipping Campden and **Stow-on-the-Wold** are quaint without being overrun, and both have good accommodations. Stow has a bit more character for an overnight stay and offers the widest range of choices. The plain town of **Moreton-in-Marsh** is the only one of the three with a train station, and only worth visiting as a transit hub. While Moreton has the most convenient connections, non-drivers can also make it work to home-base in Chipping Campden or Stow—especially if you don't mind sorting through bus schedules or springing for the occasional taxi to connect towns. (This becomes even more challenging on Sundays, when there is essentially no bus service.) With a car, consider really getting away from it all by staying in one of the smaller villages.

Nearby Sights: England's top countryside palace, **Blenheim,** is located at the eastern edge of the Cotswolds, between Moreton and Oxford (see end of this chapter); for drivers, Blenheim fits well on the way into or out of the region. If you want to take in some Shakespeare, note that Stow, Chipping Campden, and Moreton are only a 30-minute drive from **Stratford**, which offers a great evening of world-class entertainment (see next chapter).

One-Day Driver's 100-Mile Cotswold Blitz: Use a good map and reshuffle this plan to fit your home base:

9:00	Browse through Chipping Campden, following my self-guided walk.
10:30	Joyride through Snowshill, Stanway, and Stanton.
12:30	Have lunch in Stow-on-the-Wold, then follow my self-guided walk there.
15:00	Drive to the Slaughters, Bourton-on-the-Water, and Bibury; or, if you're up for a hike instead of a drive, walk from Stow to the Slaughters to Bourton, then catch the bus back to Stow.
18:00	Have dinner at a countryside gastropub (reserve in advance by phone), then head home; or drive 30 minutes to Stratford-upon-Avon for a Shakespeare play.

Cotswold Appreciation 101

History can be read into the names of the area. *Cotswold* could come from the Saxon phrase meaning "hills of sheep's cotes" (shelters for sheep). Or it could mean shelter ("cot" like cottage) on the open upland ("wold").

In the Cotswolds, a town's main street (called High Street) needed to be wide to accommodate the sheep and cattle being marched to market (and today, to park tour buses). Some of the most picturesque cottages were once humble row houses of weavers' cottages, usually located along a stream for their waterwheels (good examples in Bibury and Lower Slaughter). The towns run on slow clocks and yellowed calendars. An entire village might not have a phone booth.

Fields of yellow (rapeseed) and pale blue (linseed) separate pastures dotted with black and white sheep. In just about any B&B, when you open your window in the morning you'll hear sheep baa-ing. The decorative "toadstool" stones dotting front yards throughout the region are medieval staddle stones, which buildings were set upon to keep the rodents out.

Cotswold walls and roofs are made of the local limestone. The limestone roof tiles hang by pegs. To make the weight more bearable, smaller and lighter tiles are higher up. An extremely strict building code keeps towns looking what many locals call "overly quaint."

Two-Day Plan by Public Transportation: This plan is best for any day except Sunday—when virtually no buses run—and assumes you're home-basing in Moreton-in-Marsh.

Day 1: Take the morning bus (likely around 9:30) to Chipping Campden to explore that town. If you want to stretch your legs, hike 30 minutes (each way) into Broad Campden. Then take the bus from Chipping Campden to Moreton and transfer to a Stow-bound bus. After poking around Stow, hike from Stow through the Slaughters to Bourton-on-the-Water (about 3 hours at a relaxed pace), then return by bus or taxi to Moreton for dinner. (For less walking and more time for an early dinner in Stow, do just part of the hike, or take the bus from Stow to Bourton and back.)

Day 2: Take a day trip to Blenheim Palace via Oxford (train to Oxford, bus to palace—explained on page 438); or rent a bike and ride to Chastleton House; or take a daylong countryside walk (best to bus to Stow or Chipping Campden and walk from there).

While you'll still see lots of sheep, the commercial wool industry is essentially dead. It costs more to shear a sheep than the 50 pence the wool will fetch. In the old days, sheep lived long lives, producing lots of wool. When they were finally slaughtered, the meat was tough and eaten as "mutton." Today, you don't find mutton much because the sheep are raised primarily for their meat, and slaughtered younger. When it comes to Cotswold sheep these days, it's lamb (not mutton) for dinner (not sweaters).

Towns are small, and everyone seems to know everyone. The area is provincial yet ever-so-polite, and people commonly rescue themselves from a gossipy tangent by saying, "It's all very...mmm...yaaa."

In contrast to the village ambience are the giant manors and mansions whose private, gated driveways you'll drive past. Many of these now belong to A-list celebrities, who have country homes here. If you live in the Cotswolds, you can call Madonna, Elizabeth Hurley, and Kate Moss your neighbors.

This is walking country. The English love their walks and vigorously defend their age-old right to free passage. Once a year the Ramblers, Britain's largest walking club, organizes a "Mass Trespass," when each of the country's 50,000 miles of public footpaths is walked. By assuring that each path is used at least once a year, they stop landlords from putting up fences. Any paths found blocked are unceremoniously unblocked.

Questions to ask locals: Do you think foxhunting should have been banned? Who are the Morris men? What's a kissing gate?

Tourist Information

Local TIs stock a wide array of helpful resources. Ask for the *Cotswold Lion*, the biannual newspaper, which includes suggestions for walks and hikes (spring/summer); the monthly *Cotswold Events* guide; bus schedules for the routes you'll be using; and the *Attractions and Events Guide* (with updated prices and hours for Cotswold sights). Each village also has its own assortment of brochures about the place itself, and the surrounding countryside, often for a small fee (£0.50-1). While paying for these items seems chintzy, realize that Cotswold TIs have lost much of their funding and are struggling to make ends meet (some are run by volunteers).

Getting Around the Cotswolds

By Bus

The Cotswolds are so well-preserved, in part, because public transportation to and within this area has long been miserable. Fortunately, larger towns are linked by trains, and a few key buses

The Cotswolds

TO WORCESTER

A-44

A-46

TO M-5

B-4084

EVESHAM

HIDCOTE MANOR GARDEN

B-4632

MICKLETON

CHIPPING CAMPDEN

A-44

BROADWAY

A-44

B-4081

BROAD CAMPDEN

STANTON

⑪

SNOWS-HILL

⑩

⑫

BLOCKLEY

TO TEWKES-BURY

①

②

⑦

A-44

STANWAY

STANWAY HOUSE

A-424

WINCHE-COMBE

FORD

⑥

B-4077

UPPER SWELL

B-4632

COTSWOLD FARM PARK

LOWER SWELL

COTSWOLD WAY FOOTPATH

B-4068

TO CHELTENHAM

UPPER + LOWER SLAUGHTER

⑨

A-436

A-429

— MAJOR ROAD
— MINOR ROAD
--- FOOTPATH

NOTE: NOT ALL ROADS OR SHEEP ARE SHOWN

TO ❸, BIBURY, NORTHLEACH & CIRENCESTER

COTSWOLDS

TO STRATFORD-UPON-AVON

A-34

1 The Vine B&B
2 Sheepscombe House B&B
3 To The William Morris B&B
4 The Horse and Groom Village Inn (Upper Oddington)
5 The Fox Inn (Lower Oddington)
6 The Plough Inn
7 Horse and Groom (Bourton-on-the-Hill)
8 The Fox Inn (Broadwell)
9 "Slaughter Pike" Bus Stop
10 Broadway Tower
11 Cotswolds Riding Centre
12 Cotswold Lavender
13 Cotswold Falconry Centre & Batsford Arboretum

ILMINGTON

A-3035

B-4479

A-429

SHIPSTON-ON-STOUR

5 MILES

5 KM

MORETON-IN-MARSH

CHASTLETON HOUSE

A-44

A-34

N

13

8

A-436

4 5

CHIPPING NORTON

TO OXFORD & BLENHEIM PALACE

STOW-ON-THE-WOLD

B-4450

BOURTON-ON-THE-WATER

A-424

TO OXFORD

TO BURFORD & OXFORD

DCH

LONDON

COTSWOLDS

connect the more interesting villages. Centrally located Moreton-in-the-Marsh is the region's transit hub—with the only train station and several bus lines.

To explore the towns, use the bus routes that hop through the Cotswolds about every 1.5 hours, lacing together main stops and ending at rail stations. In each case, the entire trip takes about an hour. Individual fares are around £2-3.

The TI hands out easy-to-read bus schedules for the key lines described below (or check www.traveline.org.uk, or call the Traveline info line, tel. 0871-200-2233). Put together a one-way or return trip by public transportation, making for a fine Cotswold day. If you're traveling one-way between two train stations, remember that the Cotswold villages—generally pretty clueless when it comes to the needs of travelers without a car—have no official baggage-check services. You'll need to improvise; ask sweetly at the nearest TI or business.

Note that no single bus connects the three major towns described in this chapter (Chipping Campden, Stow, and Moreton); to get between Chipping Campden and Stow, you'll have to change buses in Moreton. Since buses can be unreliable and connections aren't timed, it may be better to call a driver or taxi to go between Chipping Campden and Stow.

The following bus lines are operated by Johnsons Coaches (tel. 01564/797-070, www.johnsonscoaches.co.uk): Buses **#21** and **#22** run from Moreton-in-Marsh to Batsford to Bourton-on-the-Hill to Blockley, then either to Broadway (#21) or Broad Campden (#22) on their way to Chipping Campden, and pass through Mickleton before ending at Stratford-upon-Avon. Note that this route is the only one that goes all the way through to Chipping Campden. Bus **#23** goes from Moreton-in-Marsh to Shipston-on-Stour to Stratford-upon-Avon.

The following buses are operated by Pulham & Sons Coaches (tel. 01451/820-369, www.pulhamscoaches.com): Bus **#801** goes from Moreton-in-Marsh to Stow-on-the-Wold to Bourton-on-the-Water; most continue on to Northleach and Cheltenham (limited service on Sun in summer). Bus **#855** goes from Northleach to Bibury to Cirencester and then (in the morning and afternoon) on to the Kemble train station.

Warning: Unfortunately, the buses described here aren't particularly reliable—it's not uncommon for them to show up late, early, or not at all. Leave yourself a huge cushion if using buses to make another connection (such as a train to London), and always have a backup plan (such as the phone number for a few taxis/drivers or for your hotel, who can try calling someone for you). Remember that bus service is essentially nonexistent on Sundays.

By Bike

Despite narrow roads, high hedgerows (blocking some views), and even higher hills, bikers enjoy the Cotswolds free from the constraints of bus schedules. For each area, TIs have fine route planners that indicate which peaceful, paved lanes are particularly scenic for biking. In summer, it's smart to book your rental bike a couple of days ahead.

In **Chipping Campden,** you have two options: **Cycle Cotswolds,** right in town at the Volunteer Inn pub, is the most convenient (£12/day, £15/24 hours, daily 7:00-dusk, Lower High Street, tel. 01789/720-193, www.cyclecotswolds.co.uk). Otherwise, try **Cotswold Country Cycles** (£15/day, tandem-£30/day, includes helmets and route maps, delivery for a fee, daily 9:30-dusk Easter-Sept only, 2 miles north of town at Longlands Farm Cottage, call in advance—tel. 01386/438-706, www.cotswoldcountrycycles .com); they also offer self-led bike tours of the Cotswolds and surrounding areas (2-7 days, see website for details).

In **Moreton-in-Marsh,** the nice folks at the **Toy Shop** rent mountain bikes. You can stop in the shop to rent a bike, or call ahead to pick up or drop off at other times—they're flexible (£15/day with route maps, bike locks, and helmets; shop open Mon and Wed-Fri 9:00-17:00, Sat 10:00-17:00, closed Sun and Tue, High Street, tel. 01608/650-756).

Stow-on-the-Wold does not have any bike-rental shops.

By Foot

Walking guidebooks and leaflets abound, giving you a world of choices for each of my recommended stops (choose a book with clear maps). If you're doing any hiking whatsoever, get the excellent Ordnance Survey Explorer OL #45 map, which shows every road, trail, and ridgeline (£8 at local TIs). Nearly every hotel and B&B has a box or shelf of local walking guides and maps, including Ordnance Survey #45. Don't hesitate to ask for a loaner. For a quick circular hike from a particular village, peruse the books and brochures offered by that village's TI. Villages are generally no more than three miles apart, and most have pubs that would love to feed and water you. For a list of guided walks, ask at any TI for the free *Cotswold Lion* newspaper. The walks range from 2 to 12 miles, and often involve a stop at a pub or tearoom (*Lion* newspaper also online at www.cotswoldsaonb.org.uk—click on "Publications"). Another option is to leave the planning to a company such as Cotswold Walking Holidays, which can provide

The Cotswolds at a Glance

Chipping Campden and Nearby

▲▲**Chipping Campden** Picturesque market town with finest High Street in England, accented by a 17th-century Market Hall, wool-tycoon manors, and a characteristic Gothic church. See page 396.

▲▲**Stanway House** Grand, aristocratic home of the Earl of Wemyss, with the tallest fountain in Britain and a 14th-century tithe barn. **Hours:** June-Aug Tue and Thu only 14:00-17:00, closed Sept-May. See page 408.

▲**Stanton** Classic Cotswold village with flower-filled exteriors and 15th-century church. See page 410.

▲**Snowshill Manor** Eerie mansion packed to the rafters with eclectic curiosities collected over a lifetime. **Hours**: July-Aug Wed-Mon 11:30-16:30, closed Tue; April-June and Sept-Oct Wed-Sun 12:00-17:00, closed Mon-Tue; closed Nov-March. See page 411.

▲**Hidcote Manor Garden** Fragrant garden organized into color-themed "outdoor rooms" that set a trend in 20th-century garden design. **Hours:** May-Aug daily 9:00-19:00; mid-March-April and Sept Sat-Wed 10:00-18:00, closed Thu-Fri; Oct Sat-Wed 10:00-17:00, closed Thu-Fri; Nov-Dec and mid-Feb-mid-March Sat-Sun 11:00-16:00, closed Mon-Fri; closed Jan-mid-Feb. See page 413.

▲**Broad Campden, Blockley, and Bourton-on-the-Hill** Trio of villages with sweeping views and quaint homes, far from the madding crowds. See page 414.

Stow-on-the-Wold and Nearby

▲▲**Stow-on-the-Wold** Convenient Cotswold home base with charming shops and pubs clustered around town square, plus popular day-hikes. See page 415.

▲**Lower and Upper Slaughter** Inaptly named historic villages—home to a working waterwheel, peaceful churches, and a folksy museum. See page 426.

COTSWOLDS

route instructions and maps, transfer your bags, and arrange lodging (www.cotswoldwalks.com).

There are many options for hikers, ranging from the "Cotswold Way" path that leads 100 miles from Chipping Campden all the way to Bath, to easy loop trips to the next village. Serious hikers enjoy doing a several-day loop, walking for several hours each day and sleeping in a different village each night. One popular route

▲**Bourton-on-the-Water** The "Venice of the Cotswolds," touristy yet undeniably striking, with petite canals and impressive Motor Museum. See page 427.

▲**Cotswold Farm Park** Kid-friendly park with endangered breeds of native British animals, farm demonstrations, and tractor rides. **Hours:** Mid-Feb-mid-Dec daily 10:30-17:00, closed mid-Dec-mid-Feb. See page 429.

▲**Keith Harding's World of Mechanical Music** Tiny museum brimming with self-playing musical instruments, demonstrations, and Victorian music boxes. **Hours:** Daily 10:00-17:00. See page 430.

▲**Bibury** Village of antique weavers' cottages, ideal for outdoor activities like fishing and picnicking. See page 431.

▲**Cirencester** Ancient 2,000-year-old city noteworthy for its crafts center and museum, showcasing artifacts from Roman and Saxon times. See page 431.

Moreton-in-Marsh and Nearby

▲**Moreton-in-Marsh** Relatively flat and functional home base with the best transportation links in the Cotswolds and a bustling Tuesday market. See page 432.

▲**Chastleton House** Lofty Jacobean-era home with a rich family history. **Hours:** April-Sept Wed-Sat 13:00-17:00; mid- to late March and Oct Wed-Sat 13:00-16:00; closed Nov-mid-March and Sun-Tue year-round. See page 436.

▲▲▲**Blenheim Palace** Fascinating, sumptuous, still-occupied aristocratic abode—one of Britain's best. **Hours:** Mid-Feb-Oct daily 10:30-17:30, Nov-mid-Dec Wed-Sun 10:30-17:30, park open but palace closed Nov-mid-Dec Mon-Tue and mid-Dec-mid-Feb. See page 438.

COTSWOLDS

is the **"Cotswold Ring"**: Day 1—Moreton-in-Marsh to Stow-on-the-Wold to the Slaughters to Bourton-on-the-Water (12 miles); Day 2—Bourton-on-the-Water to Winchcombe (13 miles); Day 3—Winchcombe to Stanway to Stanton (7 miles), or all the way to Broadway (10.5 miles total); Day 4—On to Chipping Campden (just 5.5 miles, but steeply uphill); Day 5—Chipping Campden to Broad Campden, Blockley, Bourton-on-the-Hill or Batsford, and back to Moreton (7 miles).

Realistically, on a short visit, you won't have time for that much hiking. But if you have a few hours to spare, consider venturing across the pretty hills and meadows of the Cotswolds. Each of the home-base villages I recommend has several options. Stow-on-the-Wold, immersed in pleasant but not-too-hilly terrain, is within easy walking distance of several interesting spots and is probably the best starting point. Chipping Campden sits along a ridge, which means that hikes from there are extremely scenic, but also more strenuous. Moreton—true to its name—sits on a marsh, offering flatter and less picturesque hikes.

Here are a few hikes to consider, in order of difficulty (easiest first). I've selected these for their convenience to the home-base towns and because the start and/or end points are on bus lines, allowing you to hitch a ride back to where you started (or on to the next town) rather than backtracking by foot.

Stow, the Slaughters, and Bourton-on-the-Water: Walk from Stow to Upper and Lower Slaughter, then on to Bourton-on-the-Water (which has bus service back to Stow on #801). One big advantage of this walk is that it's mostly downhill (4 miles, about 2-3 hours one-way). For details, see page 419.

Chipping Campden, Broad Campden, Blockley, and Bourton-on-the-Hill: From Chipping Campden, it's an easy mile walk into charming Broad Campden, and from there, a more strenuous hike to Blockley and Bourton-on-the-Hill (which are both connected by buses #21 and #22 to Chipping Campden and Moreton). For more details, see page 397.

Winchcombe, Stanway, Stanton, and Broadway: You can reach the charming villages of Stanway and Stanton by foot, but it's tough going—lots of up and down. The start and end points (Winchcombe and Broadway) have decent bus connections, and in a pinch some buses do serve Stanton (but carefully check schedules before you set out).

Broadway to Chipping Campden: The hardiest hike of those I list here, this takes you along the Cotswold Ridge. Attempt it only if you're a serious hiker (5.5 miles).

Bibury and the Coln Valley are pretty, but limited bus access makes hiking there less appealing.

By Car

Joyriding here truly is a joy. Winding country roads seem designed to spring bucolic village-and-countryside scenes on the driver at every turn. Distances here are wonderfully short—but only if you invest in the Ordnance Survey map of the Cotswolds, sold locally at TIs and newsstands (the £8 Explorer OL #45 map is excellent but almost too detailed for drivers; a £5 tour map covers a wider area in less detail). Here are driving distances from Moreton: **Stow-on-the-Wold** (4 miles), **Chipping Campden** (8 miles), **Broadway** (10 miles), **Stratford-upon-Avon** (17 miles), **Warwick** (23 miles), **Blenheim Palace** (20 miles).

Car hiking is great. In this chapter, I cover the postcard-perfect (but discovered) villages. With a car and the local Ordnance Survey map, you can easily ramble about and find your own gems. The problem with having a car is that you are less likely to walk. Consider taking a taxi or bus somewhere, so that you can walk back to your car and enjoy the scenery (see suggestions earlier).

Car Rental: Two places near Moreton-in-Marsh rent cars by the day. **Value Self Drive,** based in Shipston-on-Stour (about six miles north of Moreton) and run by Steve Bradley, has affordable rates (£23-35/day plus tax, includes insurance, cheaper for longer rentals; open Mon-Sat 8:15-17:30, Sun by appointment only; call ahead to arrange, mobile 07974-805-485, stevebradleycars @aol.com). Conveniently, Steve will pick you up in Moreton (£8) or Stratford-upon-Avon (£12), and bring you back to Shipston to get your car. **Robinson Goss Self Drive,** also six miles north of Moreton-in-Marsh, is a bit more expensive and won't bring the car to you in Moreton (£31-52/day including everything but gas, Mon-Thu 8:30-17:00, Fri 8:30-17:30, Sat 8:30-12:00, closed Sun, tel. 01608/663-322, www.robgos.co.uk).

By Taxi or Private Driver

Two or three town-to-town taxi trips can make more sense than renting a car. While taking a cab cross-country seems extravagant, the distances are short (Stow to Moreton is 4 miles, Stow to Chipping Campden is 10), and one-way walks are lovely. If you call a cab, confirm that the meter will start only when you are actually picked up. Consider hiring a private driver at the hourly "touring rate" (generally around £30), rather than the meter rate. For a few more bucks, you can have a joyride peppered with commentary. Whether you book a taxi or a private driver, expect to pay about £20-23 between Chipping Campden and Stow and about £18-20 between Chipping Campden and Moreton.

Note that the drivers listed here are not typical city taxi services (with many drivers on call), but are mostly individuals—it's smart to call ahead if you're arriving in high season, since they can be booked in advance on weekends.

To scare up a taxi in Moreton, try Stuart and Stephen at **ETC,** "Everything Taken Care of" (toll-free tel. 0800/955-8584, cotswoldtravel.co.uk) or **Iain Taxis** (mobile 07789-897-966, iain taxis@bpinternet.com); for more options, see the list of taxi phone numbers posted outside the Moreton train station office. In Stow, try Iain (above) or **Tony Knight** (mobile 07887-714-047).

In Chipping Campden, call Iain (above), Paul at **Cotswold Private Hire** (mobile 07980-857-833), Barry Roberts at **Chipping Campden Private Hire** (also does tours, mobile 07774-224-684, cotswoldpersonaltours.com), or **Les Proctor**, who offers village tours and station pick-ups (mobile 07580-993-492, Les co-runs Cornerways B&B—see page 405). Tim Harrison at **Tour the Cotswolds** specializes in tours of the Cotswolds and its gardens, but will also do tours outside the area (mobile 07779-030-820, www.tourthecotswolds.co.uk; Tim co-runs Sheepscombe House B&B—see page 413).

By Tour

Departing from Bath, **Lion Tours** offers a Cotswold Discovery full-day tour, and can drop you and your luggage off in Stow at no extra charge or in Moreton-in-Marsh for £2.50/person. If you want to get back to London in time for a show, then ask to be dropped off at Kemble Station; it's best to arrange these drop-offs in advance (see page 282 of the Bath chapter).

While none of the Cotswold towns offer regularly scheduled walks, many have voluntary warden groups who love to meet visitors and give walks for a small donation (see specific contact information for Chipping Campden on next page).

Chipping Campden

Just touristy enough to be convenient, the north Cotswold town of Chipping Campden (CAM-den) is a ▲▲ sight. This market town, once the home of the richest Cotswold wool merchants, has some incredibly beautiful thatched roofs. Both the great British historian G. M. Trevelyan and I call Chipping Campden's High Street the finest in England.

Orientation to Chipping Campden

To get your bearings, walk the full length of High Street; its width is characteristic of market towns. Go around the block on both ends. On one end, you'll find impressively thatched homes (out Sheep Street, past the public WC, and right on Westington Street). Walking north on High Street, you'll pass the Market Hall, the

COTSWOLDS

wavy roof of the first great wool mansion, a fine and free memorial garden, and, finally, the town's famous 15th-century Perpendicular Gothic "wool" church. (This route is the same as my self-guided town walk.)

Tourist Information

Chipping Campden's TI is tucked away in the old police station on High Street. Get the £1.50 town guide, which includes a map (April-Oct daily 9:30-17:00; Nov-March Mon-Thu 9:30-13:00, Fri-Sun 9:30-16:00; tel. 01386/841-206, www.chippingcampden online.org).

Helpful Hints

Festivals: Chipping Campden's biggest festival is the **Cotswold Olimpicks,** a series of tongue-in-cheek countryside games (such as competitive shin-kicking) atop Dover's Hill, just above town (first Fri-Sat after Late May Bank Holiday, www .olimpickgames.co.uk). They also have a **music festival** in May and an **open gardens festival** the third weekend in June.

Internet Access: Try the occasionally open **library** (closed Thu and Sun; High Street, tel. 08452/305-420) or **Butty's at the Old Bakehouse,** a casual eatery and Internet café (£1.50/15 minutes, £2.50/30 minutes, £4/hour, free Wi-Fi, see page 407 for hours, Lower High Street, tel. 01386/840-401).

Bike Rental: Call **Cycle Cotswolds** or **Cotswold Country Cycles** (see page 391).

Taxi: Try **Cotswold Private Hire, Chipping Campden Private Hire,** or **Tour the Cotswolds** (for contact info, see previous page).

Parking: Find a spot anywhere along High Street and park for free with no time limit. There's also a pay-and-display lot on High Street, across from the TI (1.5-hour maximum). If those are full, there is free parking on the street called Back Ends.

Tours: The local members of the **Cotswold Voluntary Wardens** would be happy to show you around town for a small donation to their conservation society (suggested donation-£3/person, 1-hour walk, walks June-Sept Tue at 14:30 and Thu at 10:00, meet at Market Hall). Tour guide and coordinator Ann Colcomb can help arrange for a walk on other days as well (tel. 01386/832-131).

Walks and Hikes from Chipping Campden: Since this is a particularly hilly area, long-distance hikes are challenging. The easiest and most rewarding stroll is to the thatch-happy hobbit village of **Broad Campden** (about a mile, mostly level). From there, you can walk or take the bus (#22) back to Chipping Campden.

COTSWOLDS

Or, if you have more energy, continue from Broad Campden up over the ridge and into picturesque **Blockley**—and, if your stamina holds out, all the way to **Bourton-on-the-Hill** (Blockley and Bourton-on-the-Hill are also connected by buses #21 and #22 to Chipping Campden and Moreton).

Alternatively, you can hike up to **Dover's Hill,** just north of the village. Ask locally about this easy circular one-hour walk that takes you on the first mile of the 100-mile-long Cotswold Way (which goes from here to Bath).

For more about hiking, see "Getting Around the Cotswolds—By Foot" on page 391.

Self-Guided Walk

Welcome to Chipping Campden

This stroll through "Campden" (as locals call their town) takes you from the Market Hall west to the old silk mill, and then back east the length of High Street to the church. It takes about an hour.

Market Hall: Begin at Campden's most famous monument—the Market Hall. It stands in front of the TI, marking the town center. The Market Hall was built in 1627 by the 17th-century Lord of the Manor, Sir Baptist Hicks. (Look for the Hicks family coat of arms in the building's facade.) Back then, it was an elegant—even over-the-top—shopping hall for the townsfolk who'd come here to buy their produce. In the 1940s, it was almost sold to an American, but the townspeople heroically raised money to buy it first, then gave it to the National Trust for its preservation.

The timbers inside are true to the original. Study the classic Cotswold stone roof, still held together with wooden pegs nailed in from underneath. (Tiles were cut and sold with peg holes, and stacked like waterproof scales.) Buildings all over the region still use these stone shingles. Today, the hall, which is rarely used, stands as a testimony to the importance of trade to medieval Campden.

Adjacent to the Market Hall is the sober WWI monument—a reminder of the huge price paid by every little town. Walk around it, noticing how 1918 brought the greatest losses.

The TI is just across the street, in the old police courthouse. If it's open, you're welcome to climb the stairs and peek into the **Magistrate's Court** (free, same hours as TI, ask at TI to go up).

Under the open-beamed courtroom, you'll find a humble little exhibit on the town's history.

• *Walk west until you reach the Red Lion Inn. Across High Street (and a bit to the right), look for the house with a sundial, called...*

"Green Dragons": The house's decorative black cast-iron fixtures once held hay and functioned much like salad bowls for horses. Fine-cut stones define the door, but "rubble stones" make up the rest of the wall. The pink stones are the same limestone but have been heated, and likely were scavenged from a house that burned down.

• *At the Red Lion, leave High Street and walk a block down Sheep Street. Just past the public loo, on the right-hand side, is the old...*

Silk Mill: The tiny Cam River powered a mill here since about 1790. Today it houses the handicraft workers guild and some interesting history. In 1902, Charles Robert Ashbee (1863-1942) revitalized this sleepy hamlet of 2,500 by bringing a troupe of London artisans and their families (160 people in all) to town. Ashbee was a leader in the romantic Arts and Crafts movement—craftspeople repulsed by the Industrial Revolution who idealized handmade crafts and preindustrial ways. Ashbee's idealistic craftsmen's guild lasted only until 1908, when most of his men grew bored with their small-town, back-to-nature ideals. Today, the only shop surviving from the originals is that of **silversmith David Hart.** His grandfather came to town with Ashbee, and the workshop (upstairs in the mill building) is an amazing time warp—little changed since 1902. Mr. Hart is a gracious man as well as a fine silversmith, and he welcomes browsers six days a week (Mon-Fri 9:00-17:00, Sat 9:00-12:00, closed Sun, tel. 01386/841-100). (While you could continue 200 yards farther to see some fine thatched houses, this walk doesn't.)

• *Return to High Street, turn right, and walk through town.*

High Street: Chipping Campden's High Street has changed

little architecturally since 1840. (The town's street plan and property lines survive from the 12th century.) Notice the harmony of the long rows of buildings. While the street comprises different styles through the centuries, everything you see was made of the same Cotswold stone—the only stone allowed today.

To remain level, High Street arcs with the contour of the hillside. Because it's so wide, you know this was a market town. In past centuries, livestock and packhorses laden with piles of freshly shorn fleece would fill the streets. Campden was a sales and

COTSWOLDS

Chipping Campden

Self-Guided Walk
A Market Hall
B Magistrate's Court (above TI)
C "Green Dragons" House
D Silk Mill & Silversmith Workshop
E High Street
F Grevel House
G Ernest Wilson Memorial Garden
H Baptist Hicks Land, Ruined Mansion & St. James Church

Hotels & Restaurants
1 Noel Arms Hotel
2 The Lygon Arms Hotel & Pub
3 Badgers Hall Tea Room/B&B
4 Bantam Tea Rooms
5 Cornerways & Stonecroft B&Bs
6 The Old Bakehouse & Butty's (Internet Café)
7 Cherry Trees B&B
8 The Chance B&B & Bramley House
9 Eight Bells Pub
10 Michael's Restaurant
11 Maharaja Indian Restaurant & Cycle Cotswolds
12 La Tradition
13 Co-op Grocery

COTSWOLDS

distribution center for the wool industry, and merchants from as far away as Italy would come here for the prized raw wool.

High Street has no house numbers: Locals know the houses by their names. In the distance, you'll see the town church (where this walk ends). Notice that the power lines are buried underground, making the scene delightfully uncluttered.

As you stroll High Street, you'll find the finest houses on the uphill side—which gets more sun. You'll pass several old sundials as you wander. Decorative features (like the Ionic capitals near the TI) are added for non-structural touches of class. Most

To Hidcote Manor Garden

To Stratford-Upon-Avon

B-4035

B-4081

MBE LANE

ASTON RD.

8

7

BACK ENDS

CIDERMILL

STATION ROAD

C

10 MARKET HALL

START

F

G

ALMS-HOUSES

9

P

A

E

HIGH STREET

CHURCH LANE

H

ST. JAMES

BAPTIST HICKS LAND

12 1

13 3

4

2

CALF LANE

COURT BARN MUSEUM

5

B

GEORGE LANE

COTSWOLD WAY FOOTPATH

OOT

P PARKING

SELF-GUIDED WALK

NOT TO SCALE

COTSWOLDS

High Street buildings are half-timbered, but with cosmetic stone facades. You may see some exposed half-timbered walls. Study the crudely beautiful framing, made of hand-hewn oak (you can see the adze marks) and held together by wooden pegs.

Peeking down alleys, you'll notice how the lots are narrow but very deep. Called "burgage plots," this platting goes back to 1170. In medieval times, rooms were lined up long and skinny like train cars: Each building had a small storefront, followed by a workshop, living quarters, staff quarters, stables, and a pea patch-type garden at the very back. Now the private alleys that still define many of these old lots lead to comfy gardens. While some of today's buildings are wider, virtually all the widths are exact multiples of that basic first unit (for example, a modern building may be three times wider than its medieval counterpart).

• *Hike up High Street toward the church, to just before the first intersection, to find a house with gargoyles hanging out above. This is the....*

Grevel House: In 1367, William Grevel built what's considered Campden's first stone house (on the left). Sheep tycoons had big homes. Imagine back then, when this fine building was surrounded by humble wattle-and-daub huts. It had newfangled chimneys, rather than a crude hole in the roof. (No more rain inside!) Originally a "hall house" with just one big, tall room, it got its upper floor in the 16th century. The finely carved central bay window is a good early example of the Perpendicular Gothic style. The gargoyles scared away bad spirits—and served as rain spouts. The boot scrapers outside each door were fixtures in that muddy age—especially in market towns, where the streets were filled with animal dung.

• *Continue up High Street for about 100 yards. Go past Church Street (which we'll walk up later). On the right, you'll find a small Gothic arch leading into a garden.*

Ernest Wilson Memorial Garden: Once the church's vegetable patch, this small and secluded garden is a botanist's delight today. Pop inside if it's open. The garden is filled with well-labeled plants that the Victorian botanist Ernest Wilson brought back to England from his extensive travels in Asia. There's a complete history of the garden on the board to the left of the entry.

• *Backtrack to Church Street. Turn left, walk past the recommended Eight Bells Inn, and hook left with the street. Along your right-hand side stretches...*

Baptist Hicks Land: Sprawling adjacent to the town church, the area known as Baptist Hicks Land held Hicks' huge estate and manor house. This influential Lord of the Manor was from "a family of substance," who were merchants of silk and fine clothing as well as moneylenders. Beyond the ornate gate (which you'll see ahead, near the church), only a few outbuildings and the charred corner of his **mansion** survive.

The mansion was burned by Royalists in 1645 during the Civil War—notice how Cotswold stone turns red when burned. Hicks housed the poor, making a show of his generosity, adding a long row of almshouses (with his family coat of arms) for neighbors to see as they walked to church. These almshouses (lining Church Street on the left) house pensioners today, as they have since the 17th century.

On the right, filling the old **Court Barn,** is a museum about crafts and designs from the Arts and Crafts movement, with works by Ashbee and his craftsmen (£4, April-Sept Tue-Sun 10:00-17:00, Oct-March Tue-Sun 10:00-16:00, closed Mon year-round, tel. 01386/841-951, www.courtbarn.org.uk).

• *Next to the Court Barn, a scenic, tree-lined lane leads to the front door of the church. On the way, notice the 12 lime trees, one for each of the apostles, that were planted in about 1760 (sorry, no limes).*

St. James Church: One of the finest churches in the Cotswolds, St. James Church graces one of its leading towns. Both the town and the church were built by wool wealth. Go inside. The church is Perpendicular Gothic, with lots of light and strong verticality. Notice the fine vestments and altar hangings (intricate c. 1460 embroidery) behind protective blue curtains (near the back of the church). Tombstones pave the floor in the chancel (often under protective red carpeting)—memorializing great wool merchants through the ages.

At the altar is a brass relief of William Grevel, the first owner

of the Grevel House (described earlier), and his wife. But it is Sir Baptist Hicks who dominates the church. His huge, canopied tomb is the ornate final resting place for Hicks and his wife, Elizabeth. Study their faces, framed by fancy lace ruffs (trendy in the 1620s). Adjacent—as if in a closet—is a statue of their daughter, Lady Juliana, and her husband, Lutheran Yokels. Juliana commissioned the statue in 1642, when her husband died, but had it closed until *she* died in 1680. Then, the doors were opened, revealing these two people holding hands and living happily ever after—at least in marble. The hinges were likely used only once.

As you leave the church, look immediately around the corner to the left of the door. A small tombstone reads "Thank you Lord for Simon, a dearly loved cat who greeted everyone who entered this church. RIP 1980."

Sleeping in Chipping Campden

(area code: 01386)

In Chipping Campden—as in any town in the Cotswolds—B&Bs offer a better value than hotels. Try to book well in advance, as rooms are snapped up early in the spring and summer by happy hikers heading for the nearby Cotswold Way. Rooms are also

Sleep Code

(£1 = about $1.60, country code: 44)
S = Single, **D** = Double/Twin, **T** = Triple, **Q** = Quad, **b** = bathroom,
s = shower only. Unless otherwise noted, credit cards are
accepted and breakfast is included.

To help you sort easily through these listings, I've divided
the accommodations into three categories based on the price
for a standard double room with bath:

$$$ Higher Priced—Most rooms £100 or more.
$$ Moderately Priced—Most rooms between £75-100.
$ Lower Priced—Most rooms £75 or less.

Prices can change without notice; verify the hotel's current rates online or by email. For the best prices, always book
direct.

generally tight on Saturdays (when many charge a bit more and are
reluctant to rent to one-nighters) and in September, another peak
month. Parking is never a problem. Always ask for a discount if
staying longer than one or two nights.

On or near High Street

Located on the main street (or just off of it), these places couldn't
be more central.

$$$ Noel Arms Hotel, the characteristic old hotel on the
main square, has welcomed guests for 600 years. Its lobby was
remodeled in a medieval-meets-modern style, and its 28 rooms are
well-furnished with antiques (standard Db-£120, bigger Db-£140,
fancier 4-poster Db-£160-180, deluxe king Db-£180, £10 less for
singles, prices are lower midweek or off-season, some ground-floor
doubles, free Wi-Fi in lobby, attached restaurant/bar and café,
free parking, High Street, tel. 01386/840-317, www.noelarmshotel
.com, reception@noelarmshotel.com).

$$$ The Lygon Arms Hotel (pronounced "lig-un"), attached
to the popular pub of the same name, has small public areas and
10 cheery, open-beamed rooms (one small older Db-£80-85, huge
"superior" Db-£115-120, lovely courtyard Db-£145-165, lower
prices are for midweek or multi-night stays, family deals, free
Wi-Fi, free parking, High Street, go through archway and look
for hotel reception on the left, tel. 01386/840-318, www.lygonarms
.co.uk, sandra@lygonarms.co.uk, Sandra Davenport).

$$$ Badgers Hall Tea Room, also listed later under "Eating
in Chipping Campden," rents three pricey rooms (small low-

ceilinged Db-£95, larger Db-£98-115, 2-night minimum, includes breakfast and tea, no kids under age 10, free Wi-Fi, High Street, tel. 01386/840-839, www.badgershall.com, badgershall@talk21 .com, Karen).

$$ Cornerways B&B is a fresh, bright, and comfy home (not "oldie worldie") a block off High Street. It's run by the delightful Carole Proctor, who can "look out the window and see the church where we were married." The two huge, light, airy loft rooms are great for families. If you're happy to exchange breakfast for more space, ask about the cottage across the street (Db-£80, Tb-£110, Qb-£130, 2-night minimum; cottage Db-£75, 3-night minimum; cash only, free Wi-Fi, off-street parking, George Lane, just walk through the arch beside Noel Arms Hotel, tel. 01386/841-307, www.cornerways.info, carole@cornerways.info). For a fee, Les can pick you up from the train station, or take you on village tours.

$$ Stonecroft B&B, next to Cornerways (listed above), has three polished, well-maintained rooms (one with low, slanted ceilings—unfriendly to tall people). The lovely garden with a patio and small stream is a tranquil place for meals or an early-evening drink (Sb-£62, Db-£73, Tb-£110, Qb-£146, no kids under 10, free Wi-Fi, George Lane, tel. 01386/840-486, www.stonecroft -chippingcampden.co.uk, info@stonecroft-chippingcampden.co .uk, Roger and Lesley Yates).

$$ The Old Bakehouse, run by energetic young mom Zoe, rents two small but pleasant twin-bedded rooms in a 600-year-old home with a plush fireplace lounge (Sb-£65, Db-£80, discount for multiple nights, cash only, free Wi-Fi, Lower High Street, near intersection with Sheep Street, tel. 01386/840-979, mobile 07717/330-838, www.theoldbakehouse.org.uk, zoegabb@yahoo .co.uk).

A Short Walk from Town on Aston Road

The B&Bs below are a 10-minute walk from Market Hall. They are listed in the order you would find them when strolling from town (if arriving by bus, ask to be dropped off at Aston Road).

$$ Cherry Trees B&B, set well off the road, is bubbly Angie's spacious, modern home, with two king rooms and one slanty-roof twin room (Sb-£65, Db-£85, discount for multiple nights, free Wi-Fi, free parking, Aston Road, tel. 01386/840-873, www.cherrytreescampden.com, sclrksn7@tiscali.co.uk).

$$ The Chance B&B—a modern home with Cotswold charm—has three tastefully decorated rooms, a small lounge area, and a breakfast room that opens onto a patio. The super-king room has a private garden entry. They also offer a self-catering "Crafty Cottage" in town, next to the silk mill (Sb-£70, Db-£75, super-king

Db-£90, call for cottage prices, discounts for stays of 5 nights or longer, cash only, free Wi-Fi, free parking, 1 Aston Road, tel. 01386/849-079, www.the-chance.co.uk, enquiries@the-chance .co.uk, Sally and Paul).

$$ Bramley House, which backs up to a farm, has three rooms including a spacious garden suite with a private outdoor patio and lounge area (bathroom downstairs from bedroom). Crisp white linens and simple country decor give the place a light and airy feel (standard Db-£70-75, king Db-£80-85, garden suite Db-£90-95, 2-night minimum, homemade cake with tea or coffee on arrival, locally sourced/organic breakfast, free Wi-Fi, 6 Aston Road, tel. 01386/840-066, www.bramleyhouse.co.uk, bramleybb @btinternet.com, Jane Povey).

Eating in Chipping Campden

This town—filled with wealthy residents and tourists—comes with many choices. I've listed some local favorites below. If you have a car, consider driving to one of the excellent countryside pubs mentioned in the sidebar on page 424.

The Eight Bells pub is a charming 14th-century inn on Leysbourne with a classy and woody restaurant and a more colorful pub. For more than a decade now, Neil and Julie have enjoyed keeping their seasonal menu as locally sourced as possible. They serve a daily special, are proud of their fish dishes, and always have a good vegetarian dish. As this is rightly considered the best deal going in town for top-end pub dining with warm service, reservations are smart (£8-12 lunches, £14-20 dinners, Mon-Thu 12:00-14:00 & 18:30-21:00, later Fri-Sat, Sun 12:00-21:00, tel. 01386/840-371, www.eightbellsinn.co.uk).

The Lygon Arms pub is cozy and inviting, with a good, basic bar menu. You can order from the same menu in the colorful pub or the more elegant dining room across the passage (£7 sandwiches, £8-15 meals, daily 11:30-14:30 & 18:00-22:00, tel. 01386/840-318).

Michael's, a fun Mediterranean restaurant on High Street, serves hearty portions and breaks plates at closing every Saturday night. Michael, who runs his place with a contagious passion and love of life, is from Cyprus: The forte here is Greek, with plenty of *mezes*—small dishes for £6-10 (also £15-21 larger dishes, £7 *meze* lunch platter, Tue-Sat 11:00-14:30 & 19:00-22:00, Sun 12:00-15:00, closed Mon, tel. 01386/840-826).

Maharaja Indian Restaurant in the Volunteer Inn, while forgettable, is the only Indian place in town (£10-15 meals, daily 17:30-22:30, grassy courtyard out back, Lower High Street, tel. 01386/849-281).

Light Meals

If you want a quick, takeaway sandwich, consider these options. Munch your lunch on the benches on the little green near the Market Hall.

Butty's at the Old Bakehouse offers tasty £3-4 sandwiches and wraps made to order (Mon-Fri 7:30-14:30, Sat 8:00-14:00, closed Sun, Lower High Street, tel. 01386/840-401). They also have Internet access (see "Helpful Hints," earlier).

La Tradition is a hardworking French bakery that serves sausage rolls, quiches, filled croissants, and Cornish pasties (Tue-Sat 8:30-17:00, closed Sun-Mon, 6 High Street, tel. 01386/840-766).

Picnic: The **Co-op** grocery store is the town's small "supermarket" (Mon-Sat 7:00-22:00, Sun 8:00-22:00, next to TI on High Street).

Tearooms

To visit a cute tearoom, try one of these places, located in the town center.

Badgers Hall Tea Room is great for a wide selection of savory dishes and desserts. A tempting table of homemade cakes, crumbles, and scones just inside the door lures passersby into its delightful half-timbered dining room. Along with light lunches, they serve a generous afternoon tea—a tall and ritualistic tray of dainty sandwiches, pastries, and scones with tea—at £14, that's half the London price (£9-13 lunches, daily 10:00-16:30, possibly later in summer, High Street).

Bantam Tea Rooms, near the Market Hall, is also a good value (£8 teas, £6 sandwiches, Mon-Sat 10:00-16:00, Sun 10:30-16:00, slightly shorter hours Nov-March, High Street, tel. 01386/840-386).

Near Chipping Campden

Because the countryside around Chipping Campden is particularly hilly, it's also especially scenic. This is a very rewarding area to poke around and discover little thatched villages.

West of Chipping Campden

Due west of Chipping Campden lies the famous and touristy town of Broadway. Just south of that, you'll find my nominations for the cutest Cotswold villages. Like marshmallows in hot chocolate, Stanway, Stanton, and Snowshill nestle side by side, awaiting your arrival. (Note the Stanway House's limited hours when planning your visit.)

COTSWOLDS

Broadway

This postcard-pretty town, a couple of miles west of Chipping Campden, is filled with inviting shops and fancy teahouses. With a "broad way" indeed running through its middle, it's one of the bigger towns in the area. This means you'll likely pass through at some point if you're driving—but, since all the big bus tours seem to stop here, I usually give Broadway a miss. However, with a new road that allows traffic to skirt the town, Broadway has gotten cuter than ever. Broadway has good bus connections with Chipping Campden (on bus #21).

Just outside Broadway, on the road to Chipping Campden, you might spot signs for the **Broadway Tower,** which looks like a turreted castle fortification stranded in the countryside without a castle in sight. This 55-foot-tall observation tower is a "folly"—a uniquely English term for a quirky, outlandish novelty erected as a giant lawn ornament by some aristocrat with more money than taste. If you're also weighted down with too many pounds, you can relieve yourself of £4.80 to climb to its top for a view over the pastures (daily 10:00-17:00).

Stanway

More of a humble crossroads community than a true village, sleepy Stanway is worth a visit mostly for its manor house, which offers an intriguing insight into the English aristocracy today. If you're in the area when it's open, it's well worth visiting.

▲▲Stanway House

The Earl of Wemyss (pronounced "Weemz"), whose family tree charts relatives back to 1202, opens his melancholy home and grounds to visitors just two days a week in the summer. Walking through his house offers a unique glimpse into the lifestyles of England's eccentric and fading nobility.

Cost and Hours: £7 ticket covers house and fountain, £9 ticket also includes watermill; both tickets include audioguide, narrated by the lordship himself; June-Aug Tue and Thu only 14:00-17:00, closed Sept-May, tel. 01386/584-469, www.stanwayfountain.co.uk.

Getting There: By car, leave B-4077 at a statue of (the Christian) George slaying the dragon (of pagan superstition); you'll round the corner and see the manor's fine 17th-century Jacobean gatehouse. There's no public transportation to Stanway.

Visiting the Manor: Start with the grounds, then head into the house.

The Earl restored "the tallest **fountain** in Britain" on the grounds —300 feet tall, gravity-powered, and quite impressive (fountain spurts for 30 minutes at 14:45 and 16:00 on opening days).

The bitchin' **Tithe Barn** (near where you enter the grounds) dates to the 14th century, and predates the manor. It was originally where monks—in the days before money— would accept one-tenth of whatever the peasants produced. Peek inside: This is a great hall for village hoedowns. While the Tithe Barn is no longer used to greet motley peasants and collect their feudal "rents," the lord still gets rent from his vast landholdings, and hosts community fêtes in his barn.

Stepping into the obviously very lived-in **manor,** you're free to wander around pretty much as you like, but keep in mind that a family does live here. His lordship is often roaming about as well. The place feels like a time warp. Ask a staff member to demonstrate the spinning rent-collection table. In the great hall, marvel at the one-piece oak shuffleboard table and the 1780 Chippendale exercise chair (half an hour of bouncing on this was considered good for the liver).

The manor dogs have their own cutely painted "family tree," but the Earl admits that his last dog, C. J., was "all character and no breeding." Poke into the office. You can psychoanalyze the lord by the books that fill his library, the DVDs stacked in front of his bed (with the mink bedspread), and whatever's next to his toilet.

The place has a story to tell. And so do the docents stationed in each room—modern-day peasants who, even without family trees, probably have relatives going back just as far in this village. Really. Talk to these people. Probe. Learn what you can about this side of England.

A working **watermill**, which produces flour from wheat grown on the estate, is about 100 yards from the house (requires higher-priced ticket to enter).

From Stanway to Stanton: These towns are separated by a row of oak trees and grazing land, with parallel waves echoing the furrows plowed by medieval farmers. Centuries ago, farmers were allotted long strips of land called "furlongs." The idea was to dole out good and bad land equitably. (One square furlong equals 10 acres.) Over centuries of plowing these, furrows were formed. Let someone else drive, so you can hang out the window under a canopy of oaks, passing stone walls and sheep. Leaving Stanway

COTSWOLDS

on the road to Stanton, the first building you'll see (on the left, just outside Stanway) is a thatched cricket pavilion overlooking the village cricket green. Dating only from 1930, it's raised up (as medieval buildings were) on rodent-resistant staddle stones. Stanton is just ahead; follow the signs.

▲Stanton

Pristine Cotswold charm cheers you as you head up the main street of the village of Stanton. Go on a photo safari for flower-bedecked doorways and windows. (A scant few buses serve Stanton, but they're unpredictable—inquire locally.)

Stanton's **Church of St. Michael** (with the pointy spire) betrays a pagan past. It's safe to assume any church dedicated to St. Michael (the archangel who fought the devil) sits upon a sacred pagan site. Stanton is actually at the intersection of two ley lines (a line connecting prehistoric or ancient sights). You'll see St. Michael's well-worn figure (and, above that, a sundial) over the door as you enter. Inside, above the capitals in the nave, find the pagan symbols for the sun and the moon (see photo). While the church probably dates back to

the ninth century, today's building is mostly from the 15th century, with 13th-century transepts. On the north transept (far side from entry), medieval frescoes show faintly through the 17th-century whitewash. (Once upon a time, these frescoes were considered too "papist.") Imagine the church interior colorfully decorated through-

out. Original medieval glass is behind the altar. The list of rectors (at the very back of the church, under the organ loft) goes back to 1269. Finger the grooves in the back pews, worn away by sheepdog leashes. (A man's sheepdog accompanied him everywhere.)

Horse Riding: Anyone can enjoy the Cotswolds from the saddle. Jill Carenza's **Cotswolds Riding Centre,** set just outside Stanton village, is in the most scenic corner of the region. The facility's horses can take anyone from rank beginners to more experienced riders on a scenic "hack" through the village and into the high country (per-hour prices: £30/person for a group hack, £40/person for a semi-private hack, £50 for a private one-person hack; lessons, longer rides, rides for experts, and pub tours available; tel. 01386/584-250, www.cotswolds riding.co.uk, info@cotswoldsriding.co.uk). From Stanton, head toward Broadway and watch for the riding center on your right after about a third of a mile.

Sleeping in Stanton: **$$$ The Vine B&B** has five rooms in a characteristic old Cotswold house near the center of town, next to the Cricket Pitch. It's owned by no-nonsense Jill, whose daughter, Sarah Jane, welcomes you to their large, lovingly worn family home. While it suffers from absentee management, the Vine is the best option in Stanton and convenient if you want to ride all day (Ss-£60-80, twin Ds-£80, attic Db-£80, most rooms with 4-poster beds, some stairs; for contact info, see listing for riding center, above).

Eating in Stanton: High on a hill at the far end (nearest to Broadway) of Stanton's main drag, the aptly name **Mount Inn** serves up pricey, upscale meals on its big, inviting terrace, with grand views of Stanton rooftops and the Cotswold Hills (£14-17 meals, food served daily 12:00-14:00 & 18:00-21:00, may be closed Mon off-season, Old Snowshill Road, tel. 01386/584-316).

Snowshill
Another nearly edible little bundle of cuteness, the village of Snowshill (SNOWS-hill) has a photogenic triangular square with a characteristic pub at its base.

▲Snowshill Manor
Dark and mysterious, this old palace is filled with the lifetime collection of Charles Paget Wade. It's one big, musty celebration of craftsmanship, from finely carved spinning wheels to frightening samurai armor to tiny elaborate figurines carved by prisoners from the bones of meat served at dinner. Taking seriously his family motto, "Let Nothing Perish," Wade dedicated his life and fortune to preserving

COTSWOLDS

things finely crafted. The house (whose management made me promise not to promote it as an eccentric collector's pile of curiosities) really shows off Mr. Wade's ability to recognize and acquire fine examples of craftsmanship. It's all very...mmm...yaaa.

Cost and Hours: £10.40; manor house open July-Aug Wed-Mon 11:30-16:30, closed Tue; April-June and Sept-Oct Wed-Sun 12:00-17:00, closed Mon-Tue; closed Nov-March; gardens and ticket window open at 11:00, last entry one hour before closing, restaurant, tel. 01386/852-410, www.nationaltrust.org.uk/snowshillmanor.

Getting There: The manor overlooks the town square, but there's no direct access from the square; instead, the entrance and parking lot are about a half-mile up the road toward Broadway. Park there and follow the long walkway through the garden to get to the house. A golf-cart-type shuttle to the house is available for those who need assistance.

Getting In: This popular sight strictly limits the number of entering visitors by doling out entry times. No reservations are possible; to get a slot, you must report to the ticket desk. It can be up to an hour's wait—even more on busy days, especially weekends (when they can sell out for the day as early as 14:00). Tickets go on sale and the gardens open at 11:00. Therefore, a good strategy is to arrive close to the opening time, and if there's a wait, enjoy the gardens (it's a 10-minute walk to the manor). If you have more time to kill, head into the village of Snowshill itself (a half-mile away) to wander and explore—or get a time slot for later in the day, and return in the afternoon.

Cotswold Lavender

In 2000, farmer Charlie Byrd realized that tourists love lavender. He planted his farm with 250,000 plants, and now visitors come to wander among his 53 acres, which burst with gorgeous lavender blossoms from mid-June through late August. His fragrant fantasy peaks late each July. Lavender—so famous in France's Provence—is not indigenous to this region, but it fits the climate and soil just fine. A free flier in the shop explains the variations of blooming flowers. Farmer Byrd produces lavender oil (an herbal product valued since ancient times for its healing, calming, and fragrant qualities) and sells it in a delightful shop, along with many other lavender-themed items. In the café, enjoy a pot of lavender-flavored tea with a lavender scone.

Cost and Hours: Free to enter shop and café, £2.50 to walk through the fields and the distillery; generally open June-Aug daily 10:00-17:00; closed Sept-May; schedule changes annually depending on when the lavender blooms—call ahead or check their website, tel. 01386/854-821, www.cotswoldlavender.co.uk.

Getting There: It's a half-mile out of Snowshill on the road toward Chipping Campden (easy parking). Entering Snowshill from the road to the manor (described above), take the left fork, then turn left again at the end of the village.

Sleeping near Snowshill: The pretty, one-pub village of Snowshill holds a gem of a B&B. **$$$ Sheepscombe House B&B** is a clean and pristine home on a working sheep farm. It's immersed in the best of Cotswold scenery, with plenty of sheep in the nearby fields. Jacki and Tim Harrison rent two modern, spacious, and thoughtfully appointed rooms. They also offer a holiday cottage (Db-£100-120, call for cottage price, folding cots available, free Wi-Fi, just a third of a mile south of Snowshill—look for signs, tel. 01386/853-769, www.broadway-cotswolds.co.uk/sheeps combe.html, reservations@snowshill-broadway.co.uk). Tim, who's happy to give you a local's perspective on this area, also runs Tour the Cotswolds car service (see page 396).

East of Chipping Campden

Hidcote Manor Garden is just northeast of Chipping Campden, while Broad Campden, Blockley, and Bourton-on-the-Hill lie roughly between Chipping Campden and Stow (or Moreton)— handy if you're connecting those towns.

▲Hidcote Manor Garden

This is less "on the way" between towns than the other sights in this section—but the grounds around this manor house are well

worth a detour if you like gardens. Hidcote is where garden designers pioneered the notion of creating a series of outdoor "rooms," each with a unique theme (such as maple room, red room, and so on) and separated by a yew-tree hedge. The garden's design, mostly inspired by the Arts and Crafts movement, is most formal near the house and becomes more pastoral as it approaches the countryside. Ogle the gigantic, 350-year-old cedar tree, then follow your nose through a clever series of small gardens that lead delightfully from one to the next. Among the best in England, Hidcote Gardens are at their fragrant peak from May through August. But don't expect much indoors— the manor house has only a few rooms open to the public.

COTSWOLDS

Cost and Hours: £10.50; May-Aug daily 9:00-19:00; mid-March-April and Sept Sat-Wed 10:00-18:00, closed Thu-Fri; Oct Sat-Wed 10:00-17:00, closed Thu-Fri; Nov-Dec and mid-Feb-mid-March Sat-Sun 11:00-16:00, closed Mon-Fri; closed Jan-mid-Feb; last entry one hour before closing, café, restaurant, tel. 01386/438-333, www.nationaltrust.org.uk/hidcote.

Getting There: If you're driving, it's four miles northeast of Chipping Campden—roughly toward Ilmington. Both gardens are accessible by bus and a 45-minute country walk. Buses #21 and #22 take you to Mickleton (one stop past Chipping Campden), where a footpath begins next to the churchyard. Continuing more or less straight, the path leads uphill through sheep pastures and ends at Hidcote's driveway.

Nearby: Gardening enthusiasts will want to also stop at **Kiftsgate Court Garden,** just across the road from Hidcote. While not as impressive, these private gardens are a fun contrast since they were designed at the same time and influenced by Hidcote (£7.50; May-July Sat-Wed 12:00-18:00, except Aug opens at 14:00, closed Thu-Fri; April and Sept Sun-Mon and Wed only 14:00-18:00; closed Oct-March; tel. 01386/438-777, www.kiftsgate.co.uk).

▲Broad Campden, Blockley, and Bourton-on-the-Hill

This trio of pleasant villages lines up along an off-the-beaten-path road between Chipping Campden and Moreton or Stow. **Broad Campden,** just on the outskirts of Chipping Campden, has some of the cutest thatched-roof houses I've seen. **Blockley,** nestled higher in the picturesque hills, is a popular setting for films. The same road continues on to **Bourton-on-the-Hill** (pictured), with fine views looking down into

a valley and an excellent gastropub (Horse and Groom, described on page 424). All three of these towns are connected to Chipping Campden by bus #22 (#21 goes only to Bourton and Blockley), or you can walk (easy to Broad Campden, more challenging to the other two—see page 397).

COTSWOLDS

Stow-on-the-Wold

Located 10 miles south of Chipping Campden, Stow-on-the-Wold—with a name that means "meeting place on the uplands"—

is the highest point of the Cotswolds. Despite its crowds, it retains its charm, and it merits ▲▲. Most of the tourists are day-trippers, so nights—even in the peak of summer—are peaceful. Stow has no real sights other than the town itself, some good pubs, antiques stores, and cute shops draped seductively around a big town square. Visit the church, with its evocative old door guarded by ancient yew trees and the tombs of wool tycoons. A visit to Stow is not complete until you've locked your partner in the stocks on the village green.

Orientation to Stow-on-the-Wold

Tourist Information

There isn't an official TI in Stow—the nearest is in Moreton-in-Marsh (see page 432). But, you could check in with Andy, who runs Stowi (Stow Info) and Grace Tea & Coffee, located on the ground floor of the Cricket Museum on Sheep Street. He's happy to answer basic questions and hand out brochures (Tue-Sun 9:30-17:00, closed Mon, free Wi-Fi, WC, tel. 01451/830-341, stowinfo. co.uk).

Helpful Hints

Internet Access: Try the erratically open **library** in St. Edwards Hall on the main square (closed Sun, tel. 08452/305-420), or the **youth hostel** (open long hours daily).

Taxi: See "Getting Around the Cotswolds—By Taxi" (page 395).

Parking: Park anywhere on Market Square free for two hours, or overnight between 16:00 and 11:00 (free 18:00-9:00 plus any 2 hours—they note your license, so you can't just move to another spot; £50 tickets for offenders). You can park for free on some streets farther from the center (such as Park Street and Well Lane) for an unlimited amount of time. A pay-and-display lot for longer stays is at the bottom of town (toward the Oddingtons), and there is a free long-stay lot 400 yards north of the town square at the Tesco supermarket (follow the signs).

COTSWOLDS

Self-Guided Walk

Welcome to Stow-on-the-Wold

This little four-stop walk covers about 500 yards and takes about 45 minutes.

Start at the **Stocks on the Market Square.** Imagine this village during the era when people were publicly ridiculed here as

a punishment. Stow was born in pre-Roman times; it's where three trade routes crossed at a high point in the region (altitude: 800 feet). This square was the site of an Iron Age fort, and then a Roman garrison town. This main square hosted an international fair starting in 1107, and people came from as far away as Italy for the wool fleeces. This grand square was a vast, grassy expanse. Picture it in the Middle Ages (before the buildings in the center were added): a public commons and grazing ground, paths worn through the grass, and no well. Until the late 1800s, Stow had no running water; women fetched water from the "Roman Well" a quarter-mile away.

With as many as 20,000 sheep sold in a single day, this square was a thriving scene. And Stow was filled with inns and pubs to keep everyone housed, fed, and watered. A thin skin of topsoil covers the Cotswold limestone, from which these buildings were made. The **Stow Lodge** (next to the church) lies a little lower than the church; the lodge sits on the spot where locals quarried stones for the church. That building, originally the rectory, is now a hotel. The church (where we'll end this little walk) is made of Cotswold stone, and marks the summit of the hill upon which the town was built. The stocks are a great photo op (lock dad up for a great family Christmas card).

• *Walk past the youth hostel and The White Hart Inn to the market, and cross to the other part of the square. Notice how locals seem to be part of a tight-knit little community.*

For 500 years, the **Market Cross** stood in the market reminding all Christian merchants to "trade fairly under the sight of God." Notice the stubs of the iron fence in the concrete base—a reminder of how countless wrought-iron fences were cut down and given to the government to be melted down during World War II. (Recently, it's been disclosed that all that

Stow-on-the-Wold

TO BROADWAY & CHIPPING CAMPDEN

TO MORETON-IN-MARSH, STRATFORD-UPON-AVON, WARWICK

NOT TO SCALE

A-424

B-4077

A-429

TO UPPER SWELL, FORD & STANWAY

Tesco Supermkt

P Free

PATH TO BROADWELL

BUS STOP

HIGH ST.

PARSON'S CORNER

N

FOSSE WAY

WC

Stocks

START

P PARKING

SELF-GUIDED WALK

THE SQUARE

ELM LANE

CHURCH

TO LOWER SWELL

POST

CHURCH

SHEEP

B-4068

MARKET CROSS

DIGBETH ST.

PARK ST.

TO UPPER & LOWER ODDINGTON

WC

P TO

Pay + Display

"Go Stow"

FLEECE ALLEY

BACK WALLS

DCH

CEM.

SPRING GARDENS

TO LOWER SLAUGHTER/ BOURTON DAY HIKE

A-424

TO BOURTON-ON-THE-WATER & THE SLAUGHTERS

1 The Stow Lodge Hotel & Rest.
2 The Kings Arms Hotel & Pub; Co-op Grocery
3 The Old Stocks Hotel & Rest.
4 Number Nine B&B; Park Street Eateries
5 Cross Keys Cottage
6 Chure House
7 The Pound B&B

8 Youth Hostel & Café
9 To Little Broom B&B
10 The Bell at Stow
11 The Queen's Head Pub
12 The Talbot Restaurant
13 The Coffee House
14 St. Edwards Hall & Library (Internet)

COTSWOLDS

iron ended up in junk heaps—frantic patriotism just wasted.) The plaque on the cross honors the Lord of the Manor, who donated money back to his tenants, allowing the town to finally finance running water in 1878.

Scan the square for a tipsy shop that locals call the "wonky house" (next to The Kings Arms). Because it lists (tilts) so severely, it's a listed building—the facade is protected (but the interior is modern and level). The Kings Arms, with its great gables and scary chimney, was once where travelers parked their horses before spending the night. In the 1600s, this was considered the premium "posting house" between London and Birmingham. Today, The Kings Arms cooks up pub grub and rents rooms upstairs.

During the English Civil War, which pitted Parliamentarians against Royalists, Stow-on-the-Wold remained staunchly loyal to the king. (Charles I is said to have eaten at The Kings Arms before a great battle.) Because of its allegiance, the town has an abundance of pubs with royal names (King's This and Queen's That).

The stately building in the center of the square with the wooden steeple is **St. Edwards Hall.** Back in the 1870s, a bank couldn't locate the owner of an account containing a small fortune, so it donated the funds to the town to build this civic center. It serves as a city hall, library, and meeting place. When it's open for some local event, you can wander around upstairs to see the largest collection of Civil War portrait paintings in England.

• *Walk past The Kings Arms down Digbeth Street to the little triangular park located in front of the Methodist Church and across from the Royalist Hotel. This hotel—along with about 20 others—claims to be the oldest in England, dating from 947.*

Just beyond the small grassy triangle with benches was the place where locals gathered for bloody cockfights and bearbaiting (watching packs of hungry dogs tear at bears). Today this is where—twice a year, in May and October—the Stow Horse Fair attracts nomadic Roma (Gypsies) and Irish Travellers from far and wide. They congregate down the street on the Maugersbury Road. Locals paint a colorful picture of the Roma, Travellers, and horses inundating the town. The young women dress up because the fair also functions as a marriage market.

• *Hook right and hike up the wide street.*

As you head up **Sheep Street,** you'll pass a boutique-filled former brewery yard (on the left). Notice its fancy street-front office, with a striking flint facade. Sheep Street was originally not a street, but a staging place for medieval sheep markets. The sheep would be gathered here, then paraded into the Market Square down narrow alleys—just wide enough for a single file of sheep to walk down, making it easier to count them. You'll see several of these so-called "fleece alleys" as you walk up the street.

• *Make a right onto Church Street, which leads past the best coffee shop in town (The Coffee House), and find the church.*

Before entering the **church,** circle it. On the back side, a door is flanked by two ancient yew trees. While many view it as the Christian "Behold, I stand at the door and knock" door, J. R. R. Tolkien fans see something quite different. Tolkien hiked the Cotswolds, and had a passion for sketching evocative trees such as this. *Lord of the Rings* enthusiasts are convinced this must be the inspiration for the door into Moria.

While the church (open daily—apart from services— 9:00-18:00) dates from Saxon times, today's structure is from the 15th century. Its history is played up in leaflets and plaques just inside the door. The floor is paved with the tombs of big shots who made their money from wool and are still boastful in death. (Find the tombs crowned with the bales of wool.) Most of the windows are traditional Victorian designs (19th-century), but the two sets high up in the clerestory are from the dreamier Pre-Raphaelite school.

On the right wall as you approach the altar, a monument remembers the many boys from this small town who were lost in World War I (50 out of a population of 2,000). There were far fewer in World War II. The biscuit-shaped plaque remembers an admiral from Stow who lost four sons defending the realm. It's sliced from an ancient fluted column (which locals believe is from Ephesus, Turkey).

During the English Civil War (1615), the church was ransacked, and more than 1,000 soldiers were imprisoned here. The tombstone in front of the altar remembers the Royalist Captain Francis Keyt. His long hair, lace, and sash indicate he was a "cavalier," and true-blue to the king (Cromwellians were called "round heads"—named for their short hair). Study the crude provincial art—childlike skulls and (in the upper corners) symbols of his service to the king (armor, weapons).

Finally, don't miss the kneelers tucked in the pews. These are made by a committed band of women known as "the Kneeler Group." They meet most Tuesday mornings (except sometimes in summer) at 10:30 in the Church Room to needlepoint, sip coffee, and enjoy a good chat. (The vicar assured me that any tourist wanting to join them would be more than welcome. The help would be appreciated and the company would be excellent.)

Hiking from Stow

Stow/Lower Slaughter/Bourton Day Hike

Stow is made-to-order for day hikes. The most popular is the downhill stroll to Lower Slaughter (3 miles), then on to Bourton-on-the-Water (about 1.5 miles more). It's a two-hour walk if you keep up a brisk pace and don't stop, but dawdlers should allow three to four hours. At the end, from Bourton-on-the-Water, a bus can bring you back to Stow. While those with keen eyes can follow this walk by spotting trail signs, it can't hurt to bring a map

COTSWOLDS

(ask to borrow one at your B&B). Note that these three towns are described in more detail starting on page 426.

To reach the trail, find the cemetery (from the main square, head down Church Street, turn left on Sheep Street, right into

Fleece Alley, right onto Back Walls, and left onto Spring Gardens). Walk past the community's big pea patch, then duck right through the cemetery to the far end. Here, go through the gate and walk down the footpath that runs alongside the big A-429 road for about 200 yards, then cross the road and catch the well-marked trail (gravel road with green sign noting *Public Footpath/Gloucestershire Way,* next to Quarwood Cottage). Follow this trail for a delightful hour across farms, through romantic gates, across a fancy driveway, and past Gainsborough-painting vistas. You'll enjoy an intimate backyard look at local farm life. Although it seems like you might lose the trail, tiny, easy-to-miss signs (yellow *Public Footpath* arrows—sometimes also marked *Gloucestershire Way* or *The Monarch's Way*—usually embedded in fence posts) keep you on target—watch for these very carefully to avoid getting lost. Finally, passing a cricket pitch, you reach **Lower Slaughter,** with its fine church and a mill creek leading up to its mill.

Hiking from Lower Slaughter up to **Upper Slaughter** is a worthwhile one-mile detour each way, if you have the time and energy.

From Lower Slaughter, it's a less-scenic 25-minute walk into the bigger town of **Bourton-on-the-Water.** Leave Lower Slaughter along its mill creek, then follow a bridle path back to A-429 and into Bourton. Walking through Bourton's burbs, you'll pass two different bus stops for the ride back to Stow; better yet, to enjoy some time in Bourton itself, continue all the way into town and—when ready—catch the bus from in front of the Edinburgh Woolen Mill shop (bus #801 departs roughly hourly, none on Sun except May-Aug when it runs about 2/day, 10-minute ride, £1.40).

Sleeping in Stow

(area code: 01451)

$$$ The Stow Lodge Hotel fills the historic church rectory with lots of old English charm. Facing the town square, with its own sprawling and peaceful garden, this lavish old place offers 21 large, thoughtfully appointed rooms with soft beds, stately public spaces, and a cushy-chair lounge (slippery rates but generally Db-£130, £10 extra on Sat, cheaper Nov-April, closed Jan, free Wi-Fi, free off-street parking, The Square, tel. 01451/830-485, www.stowlodge.co.uk, enquiries@stowlodge.co.uk, helpful Hartley family).

$$$ **The Kings Arms,** with 10 rooms above a pub, manages to keep its historic Cotswold character while still feeling fresh and modern in all the right ways (standard Db-£100, superior Db-£120, steep stairs, three "cottages" out back, free Wi-Fi, free off-street parking, Market Square, tel. 01451/830-364, www.kingsarmsstow.co.uk, info@kingsarmsstow.co.uk, Lucinda and Felicity).

$$ **The Old Stocks Hotel,** facing the town square, is a good value, even though the building itself is classier than its 18 big, simply furnished rooms. It's friendly and family-run, yet professional as can be. With man-killer beams and all beds equipped with footboards, it's a challenge for anyone over six feet tall (Sb-£45, standard Db-£90, deluxe Db-£100, refurbished "superior" Db-£110, Tb-£120, each room £10 extra on Sat, ground-floor room, free Wi-Fi in common areas, attached bar and restaurant, garden patio, free off-street parking, The Square, tel. 01451/830-666, www.oldstockshotel.co.uk, info@oldstockshotel.co.uk, Allen family).

$$ **Number Nine** has three large, bright, refurbished, and tastefully decorated rooms. This 200-year-old home comes with watch-your-head beamed ceilings and beautiful old wooden doors (Sb-£45-55, Db-£80, guest computer, free Wi-Fi, 9 Park Street, tel. 01451/870-333, mobile 07779-006-539, www.number-nine.info, enquiries@number-nine.info, James and Carol Brown and their dog Snoop).

$$ **Cross Keys Cottage** offers four smallish but smartly updated rooms—some bright and floral, others classy white—with modern bathrooms. Kindly Margaret and Roger Welton take care of their guests in this 360-year-old beamed cottage (Sb-£55-65, Db-£70-85, 5 percent Rick Steves discount if you book by phone or email, free Wi-Fi, Park Street, tel. 01451/831-128, www.crosskeys cottage.co.uk, rogxmag@hotmail.com).

$$ **Chure House** is a new home, built to look as if it's always been there. Tucked off Sheep Street, chatty Kiwi Jill has three light, comfy double rooms and a splendid little garden that begs for a cup of tea (Sb-£60, Db-£80-115, higher rates on weekends and in summer, no children under age 6, free Wi-Fi, limited parking, tel. 01451/832-185, www.bedandbreakfast-stowonthewold.co.uk, churehouse@googlemail.com).

$ The Pound is the quaint, 500-year-old, slanty, cozy, and low-beamed home of Patricia Whitehead. She offers two bright, inviting, twin-bedded rooms and a classic old fireplace lounge (D-£55-65, T-£95, cash only, downtown on Sheep Street next to the Grapevine Bar, tel. 01451/830-229, patwhite head1@live.co.uk).

$ *Hostel:* The **Stow-on-the-Wold Youth Hostel,** on Stow's main square, is the only hostel in the Cotswolds. It has 48 beds in nine rooms, a kitchen, and a friendly atmosphere (dorm bed-£18, £3 less for members, includes sheets, some family rooms with private bathrooms, evening meals, pay guest computer and Wi-Fi, reserve long in advance—especially family rooms, tel. 01451/830-497, www.yha.org.uk, stow@yha.org.uk, manager Kayleigh).

Near Stow

$$ Little Broom B&B hides out in the neighboring hamlet of Maugersbury, which enjoys the peace Stow once had. It rents three cozy rooms that share a lush garden and pool (S-£30, Sb-£45-65, D-£55, Db-£60-75, apartment Db-£75 for two people plus £15 for each extra person, cash only, free Wi-Fi, tel. 01451/830-510, www.cotswolds.info/webpage/little-broom.htm, brendarussell1@hotmail.co.uk). Brenda has racehorses, and her greenhouse keeps the pool warm throughout the summer (guests welcome). It's an easy eight-minute walk from Stow: Head east on Park Street and stay right toward Maugersbury. Turn right into Chapel Street and take the first right uphill to the B&B.

Eating in and near Stow

While Stow has several good dining options, consider venturing out of town for a meal. You can walk to the pub in nearby Broadwell, or—better yet—drive to one of the many enticing gastropubs in the surrounding villages (see sidebar on page 424).

In Stow

These places are all within a five-minute walk of each other, either on the main square or downhill on Queen and Park streets. For dessert, consider munching a treat or fruit (there's plenty for sale at the late-hours grocery on the square) under the trees on the square's benches and watching the sky darken, the lamps come on, and visitors having their photo fun in the stocks.

Restaurants and Pubs

The Stow Lodge is the choice of the town's proper ladies. There are two parts: The formal but friendly bar serves fine pub grub (hearty £9-12 lunches and dinners, daily 12:00-14:00 & 19:00-20:30). The restaurant serves a popular £26 three-course dinner (nightly, veggie options, good wines, just off main square, tel. 01451/830-485, Val). On a sunny day, the pub serves lunch in the well-manicured garden, where you'll feel quite aristocratic.

The Old Stocks Hotel Restaurant, which might at first glance seem like a tired and big hotel dining room, is actually a classy place to dine. With attentive service and an interesting menu, they provide tasty and well-presented food. It's good, basic pub grub at pub prices served in a fancy dining room with views of the square. In good weather, the garden out back is a hit (£5-10 lunches, £10-14 dinners, dinner served Sun-Thu 18:30-20:30, Fri-Sat 18:30-21:00, reservations recommended on weekends, tel. 01451/830-666, www.oldstockshotel.co.uk).

The Bell at Stow, at the end of Park Street, serves up classic English dishes with a lighter, sometimes Asian twist. Produce and fish are locally sourced (£7-15 lunches, £12-15 dinners, veggies extra, Mon-Sat full menu served 12:00-14:30 & 18:30-21:30, lighter menu in between, Sun 12:00-21:00, reservations recommended, tel. 01451/870-916, www.thebellatstow.com).

The Queen's Head faces the Market Square, next to the Stow Lodge. With a classic pub vibe, it's a great place to bring your dog and watch the eccentrics while you eat pub grub and drink the local Cotswold brew, Donnington Ale (£5-7 sandwiches, £8-10 lunches, £9-13 dinners, beer garden out back, Mon-Fri 12:00-14:30 & 18:30-21:00, Sat-Sun 12:00-21:00, tel. 01451/830-563, John).

The Talbot has a more contemporary feel, with creative, modern dishes (£6-8 lunches, £12-15 dinners). They serve drinks until midnight or later (lunch served Mon-Sat 12:00-14:30, Sun 12:30-15:30; dinner served Sun-Thu 18:30-21:00, Fri-Sat 18:30-21:30). On Friday and Saturday evenings after 22:00, they crank up the music, making it the liveliest place in town (The Square, tel. 01451/870-934).

Cheaper Options and Ethnic Food

Head to the grassy triangle where Digbeth hits Sheep Street; there you'll find take-out fish-and-chips, Chinese, and Indian food. You can picnic at the triangle, or on the benches by the stocks on Market Street.

Greedy's Fish and Chips, on Park Street, is a favorite with locals for takeout. There's no seating, but they do have benches in front (£5 fish-and-chips, Mon 12:00-14:00 & 16:30-20:30, Tue-Sat

Great Country Gastropubs

These places—known for their high-quality meals and fine settings—are very popular. Arrive early or phone in a reservation. (If you show up at 20:00, it's unlikely that they'll be able to seat you for dinner if you haven't called first.) These pubs allow "well-behaved children," and are practical only for those with a car. If you have wheels, make a point to dine at one (or more) of these—no matter where you're sleeping. In addition to these fine choices, other pubs serving worth-a-trip food are **The Eight Bells** in Chipping Campden (described on page 406) and **The Wheatsheaf Inn** in Northleach (see page 430).

Near Stow

The first two (in Oddington, about three miles from Stow) are more trendy and fresh, yet still in a traditional pub setting. The Plough (in Ford, a few miles farther away) is your jolly olde dark pub.

The Fox Inn, a different Fox Inn than the one in Broadwell (see "Pub Dinner Hike from Stow"), has a long history but a fresh approach. It's a popular choice among local foodies for its delicately prepared, borderline-pretentious but still reasonably priced updated pub classics and more-creative dishes. They've perfected their upmarket, rustic-chic vibe, with a genteelly Old World interior and a delightful back terrace and garden (£15-21 main dishes, daily 12:00-14:00 & 18:30-21:30, in Lower Oddington, tel. 01451/870-555). They also rent three rooms (Db-£75-95, www.foxinn.net).

The Horse and Groom Village Inn in Upper Oddington is a smart place in a 16th-century inn, serving modern English and Continental food with a good wine list (38 wines by the glass) and serious beer (lunch: £7-10 sandwiches, £10-15 main dishes; dinner: £16-20 main dishes; lunch served daily 12:00-14:00; dinner served Mon-Sat 18:30-21:00, Sun 19:00-21:00, tel. 01451/830-584).

12:00-14:00 & 16:30-21:00, closed Sun, tel. 01451/870-821).

Jade Garden Chinese Take-Away is appreciated by locals who don't want to cook (£3-6 dishes, Wed-Mon 17:00-23:00, closed Tue, 15 Park Street, tel. 01451/870-288).

The Prince of India offers good Indian food to take out or eat in (£8-12 main dishes, nightly 18:00-23:30, 5 Park Street, tel. 01451/830-099).

The Coffee House provides a nice break from the horses-

Between Stow and Chipping Campden

The Plough Inn, in the hamlet of Ford, fills a fascinating old building, once an old coaching inn and later a courthouse. Ask the

bar staff for some fun history—like what "you're barred" means. Eat from the same traditional English menu in the restaurant, bar, or garden. They are serious about their beer, and serve up heaping portions of stick-to-your-ribs pub-grub classics—a bit more traditional and less refined than others listed here (£11-19 meals, food served daily 12:00-14:00 & 18:00-21:00, all day long Fri-Sun and June-Aug, 6 miles from Stow on the road to Tewkesbury, reservations smart, tel. 01386/584-215, www.theploughinnford.co.uk).

Near Moreton-in-Marsh, in Bourton-on-the-Hill

The hill-capping Bourton—about a five-minute drive (or two-mile uphill walk) above Moreton—offers sweeping views over the Cotswold countryside. Perched at the top of this steep, picturesque burg is an enticing destination pub.

Horse and Groom melds a warm welcome with a tempting menu of delicious modern English fare. Of the pubs listed here, they seem to hit the best balance of old and new, combining unassumingly delicious food with a convivial spit-and-sawdust spirit. Choose between the lively, light, spacious interior or—in good weather—the terraced picnic-table garden out back (£13-19 meals, food served Mon-Thu 12:00-14:00 & 19:00-21:00, Fri-Sat 12:00-14:00 & 19:00-21:30, Sun 12:00-14:30 only, tel. 01386/700-413). They also rent rooms (Db-£120-170 depending on size, www.horseandgroom.info, greenstocks@horseandgroom.info). Don't confuse this with The Horse and Groom Village Inn in Upper Oddington, near Stow (described earlier).

COTSWOLDS

and-hounds traditional cuisine found elsewhere. You can get your food to go, or eat here—there's pleasant garden seating out back (£5 soups, £9-10 salads and sandwiches, good coffee; April-Sept Mon-Wed 9:00-17:00, Thu-Sat 9:00-21:00, Sun 10:00-16:30; off-season Mon-Sat 9:30-17:00, Sun 10:00-16:00; Church Street, tel. 01451/870-802).

The **Youth Hostel Café** (facing the Market Square) serves drinks and meals all day and is family-friendly, with great prices and tables in the backyard garden (£5 breakfast, £7-8 dinner, tel. 01451/830-497).

Even Cheaper: Small grocery stores face the main square (the **Co-op** is open Mon-Sat 7:00-22:00, Sun 8:00-22:00; next to The Kings Arms), and a big **Tesco** supermarket is 400 yards north of town.

Pub Dinner Hike from Stow

From Stow, consider taking a half-hour countryside walk to the village of Broadwell, where you'll find a traditional old pub serving good basic grub in a convivial atmosphere. **The Fox Inn** serves pub dinners and draws traditional ales—including the local Donnington ales (£8-10 meals, food served Mon-Sat 11:30-14:00 & 18:30-21:00, Sun 12:00-14:00 only, outdoor tables in garden out back, on the village green, tel. 01451/870-909, Mike and Carol).

Getting There: If you walk briskly, it's just 20 minutes downhill from Stow. While the walk is not particularly scenic (it's one-third paved lane, and the rest on an arrow-straight bridle path), it is peaceful, and the exercise is a nice way to start and finish your meal. The trail is poorly marked, but it's hard to get lost: Leave Stow at Parson's Corner, continue downhill, pass the town well, follow the bridle path straight until you hit the next road, then turn right at the road and walk downhill into the village of Broadwell. You can often hitch a ride with someone from the pub back to Stow after you eat.

Near Stow-on-the-Wold

These sights are all south of Stow: Some are within walking distance (the Slaughters and Bourton-on-the-Water), and one is 20 miles away (Cirencester). The Slaughters and Bourton are tied together by the countryside walk described on page 419.

▲Lower and Upper Slaughter

"Slaughter" has nothing to do with lamb chops. It comes from the sloe tree (the one used to make sloe gin).

Lower Slaughter is a classic village, with ducks, a charming little church, a working water mill, and usually an artist busy at her easel somewhere. The Old Mill Museum is a folksy ensemble with a tiny museum, shop, and cafe complete with a delightful terrace overlooking the mill pond, enthusiastically run by Gerald and his daughter Laura, who just can't resist giving generous tastes of their homemade ice cream (£2.50, March-Oct daily 10:00-18:00, Nov-Feb daily 10:00-dusk, tel. 01451/822-127, www.oldmill -lowerslaughter.com). Just behind the Old Mill, two kissing gates lead to the path that goes to nearby Upper Slaughter (a 15-minute walk or 2-minute drive away). And if you follow the mill creek downstream, a bridle path leads to Bourton-on-the-Water (described next).

In **Upper Slaughter,** walk through the yew trees (sacred in pagan days) down a lane through the raised graveyard (a buildup of centuries of graves) to the peaceful church. In the back of the fine graveyard, the statue of a wistful woman looks over the tomb of an 18th-century rector (sculpted by his son).

Getting There: Though the stop is not listed on schedules, you should be able to reach these towns on bus #801 (from Moreton or Stow) by requesting the "Slaughter Pike" stop (along the main road, near the villages). Confirm with the driver before getting on. If driving, the small roads from Upper Slaughter to Ford and Kineton (and the Cotswold Farm Park, described later) are some of England's most scenic. Roll your window down and joyride slowly.

▲Bourton-on-the-Water

I can't figure out whether they call this "the Venice of the Cotswolds" because of its quaint canals or its miserable crowds. Either way, it's very pretty. This town—four miles

south of Stow and a mile from Lower Slaughter—gets overrun by midday and weekend hordes. Surrounding Bourton's green are sidewalks jammed with disoriented tourists wearing nametags. If you can avoid them, it's worth a drive-through and maybe a short

stop. While it can be mobbed with tour groups during the day, it's pleasantly empty in the early evening and after dark.

Getting There: It's conveniently connected to Stow and Moreton by bus #801.

Parking: Finding a spot here is predictably tough. Even during the busy business day, rather than park in the pay-and-display lot a five-minute walk from the center, drive right into town and wait for a spot on High Street just past the village green (where the road swings left, turn right to go down High Street; there's a long row of free two-hour spots in front of the Edinburgh Woolen Mills shop, on the right).

Tourist Information: The TI is tucked across the stream a

COTSWOLDS

short block off the main drag, on Victoria Street, behind Village Hall (Mon-Fri 9:30-17:00, Sat 9:30-17:30, Sun 10:00-14:00 except closed Sun Oct-April, closes one hour earlier Nov-March, tel. 01451/820-211, www.bourtoninfo.com).

Sights: Bourton's attractions are tacky tourist traps, but the three listed below might be worth considering. All are on High Street in the town center. In addition to these, consider Bourton's **leisure center** (big pool and sauna, 5-minute walk from town center off Station Road, open daily, Mon-Fri 6:30-22:00, Sat-Sun 8:00-20:00, tel. 01451/824-024).

▲Motor Museum

Lovingly presented, this good, jumbled museum shows off a lifetime's accumulation of vintage cars, old lacquered signs, threadbare toys, and prewar memorabilia. If you appreciate old cars, this

is nirvana. Wander the car-and-driver displays, from the automobile's early days to the stylish James Bond era. Don't miss the back door (marked *Village Life Exhibition*), which leads to old carriage houses filled with even more cars. Talk to an elderly Brit who's touring the place for some personal memories.

Cost and Hours: £4.75, mid-Feb-early Dec daily 10:00-18:00, closed off-season, in the mill facing the town center, tel. 01451/821-255, www.cotswoldmotor museum.co.uk.

Model Railway Exhibition

This exhibit of three model railway layouts is impressive only to train buffs.

Cost and Hours: £2.75, June-Aug daily 11:00-17:30; Sept-Dec and Feb-May Sat-Sun 11:00-17:00, closed Mon-Fri; closed Jan; located in the back of a hobby shop, in the center of town, tel. 01451/820-686, www.bourtonmodelrailway.co.uk.

Model Village

This light but fun display re-creates the town on a 1:9 scale in a tiny outdoor park, and has an attached room full of tiny models showing off various bits of British domestic life.

Cost and Hours: £3.60 for the park, £1 more for the model room; daily 10:00-18:00, until 16:00 in winter, last entry 15 minutes before closing; at the edge of town, behind The Old New Inn, tel. 01451/820-467.

Walk to the Slaughters

From Bourton-on-the-Water, it's about a 30-minute walk (or a two-minute drive) to Upper and Lower Slaughter (described previously); taken together, they make for an easy two-hour round-trip walk from Bourton. (You could also walk from Stow through the Slaughters to Bourton—hike described on page 419.)

▲Cotswold Farm Park

Here's a delight for young and old alike. This park is the private venture of the Henson family, who are passionate about preserving rare and endangered breeds of native British animals. While it feels like a kids' zone (with all the family-friendly facilities you can imagine), it's actually a fascinating chance for anyone to get up close and (very) personal with piles of mostly cute animals, including the sheep that made this region famous—the big and woolly Cotswold Lion. The "listening posts" deliver audio information on each rare breed.

A busy schedule of demonstrations gives you a look at local farm life—check the events board as you enter for times for the milking, "farm safari," shearing, and well-done "sheep show." Join the included 20-minute tractor ride, with live narration. Buy a bag of seed (£0.60) upon arrival, or have your map eaten by munchy goats as I did. Tykes love the little tractor rides, maze, and zip line, but the "touch barn" is where it's at for little kids.

Cost and Hours: £8.50, kids-£7.50, family ticket for 2 adults and 2 kids-£29, mid-Feb-mid-Dec daily 10:30-17:00, closed mid-Dec-mid-Feb, last entry 30 minutes before closing, good guidebook (small fee), decent cafeteria, tel. 01451/850-307, www.cotswoldfarmpark.co.uk.

Getting There: It's well-signposted about halfway between Stow and Stanway (15 minutes from either) just off Tewkesbury Road (B-4077, toward Ford from Stow). A visit here makes sense if you're traveling from Stow to Chipping Campden.

Northleach

One of the "untouched and untouristed" Cotswold villages, Northleach is worth a short stop. The town's impressive main square and church attest to its position as a major wool center in the Middle Ages. Park in the square called The Green or the adjoining Market Place. The town has no TI, but you can pick

COTSWOLDS

up a free town map and visitor guide at Keith Harding's World of Mechanical Music (described next) or at the post office on the Market Place (Mon-Fri 9:00-13:00 & 14:00-17:30, Sat 9:00-12:30, closed Sun) and at other nearby shops. Information: www.north leach.gov.uk.

Getting There: Northleach is nine miles south of Stow, down A-429. Bus #801 connects it to Stow and Moreton.

▲Keith Harding's World of Mechanical Music

In 1962, Keith Harding, tired of giving ad-lib "living room tours," opened this delightful little one-room place. It offers a unique opportunity to listen to 300 years of amazing self-playing musical instruments. It's run by people who are passionate about the restoration work they do on these musical marvels. The curators delight in demonstrating about 20 of the museum's machines with each hour-long tour. You'll hear Victorian music boxes and the earliest polyphones (record players) playing cylinders and then discs—all from an age when music was made mechanically, without the help of electricity. The admission fee includes an essential hour-long tour.

Cost and Hours: £8, daily 10:00-17:00, last entry at 16:00, tours go constantly—join one in progress, High Street, Northleach, tel. 01451/860-181, www.mechanicalmusic.co.uk.

Church of Saints Peter and Paul

This fine Perpendicular Gothic church has been called the "cathedral of the Cotswolds." It's one of the Cotswolds' two fin-

est "wool" churches (along with Chipping Campden's), paid for by 15th-century wool tycoons. Find the oldest tombstone. The brass plaques on the floor memorialize big shots, showing sheep and sacks of wool at their long-dead feet, and inscriptions mixing Latin and the old English.

Eating in Northleach: Tucked along unassuming Northleach's main drag is a foodies' favorite, **The Wheatsheaf Inn.** With a pleasantly traditional dining room and a gorgeous, sprawling garden, it serves up an intriguing, eclectic menu of modern English cuisine. They pride themselves on offering a warm welcome, relaxed service, and a take-your-time approach to top-quality food. Reservations are smart (£16-19 meals, daily, on West End, tel. 01451/860-244, www.cotswoldswheatsheaf.com).

COTSWOLDS

▲Bibury

Six miles northeast of Cirencester, this village is a favorite with British picnickers fond of strolling and fishing. Bibury (BYE-

bree) offers some relaxing sights, including a row of very old weavers' cottages, a trout farm, a stream teeming with fat fish and proud ducks, and a church surrounded by rosebushes, each tended by a volunteer of the parish. A protected wetlands area on the far side of the stream hosts

newts and water voles. Walk up the main street, then turn right along the old weavers' Arlington Row and back on the far side of the marsh, peeking into the rushes for wildlife.

For a closer look at the fish, cross the little bridge to the 15-acre **Trout Farm,** where you can feed them—or catch your own (£4 to walk the grounds, fish food-£0.50; daily March-Oct 8:00-18:00, Nov-Feb 8:00-16:00; catch-your-own only on weekends March-Oct 10:00-17:00, no fishing in winter, call or email to confirm fishing schedule, tel. 01285/740-215, www.biburytroutfarm.co.uk).

Drivers will enjoy exploring the scenic **Coln Valley** from A-429 to Bibury through the enigmatic villages of Coln St. Dennis, Coln Rogers, Coln Powell, and Winson.

Getting There: Bus #801 goes from Moreton-in-Marsh and Stow to Northleach. From there, you can transfer to bus #855 to reach Bibury.

Sleeping in Bibury: If you'd like to spend the night in tiny Bibury, consider **$$ The William Morris B&B,** named for the 19th-century designer and writer (small Db-£85, big Db-£95, 2 rooms, tearoom, 200 yards from the bridge toward the church at 11 The Street, tel. 01285/740-555, www.thewilliammorris.com, ian @ianhowards.wanadoo.co.uk).

▲Cirencester

Almost 2,000 years ago, Cirencester (SIGH-ren-ses-ter) was the ancient Roman city of Corinium. It's 20 miles from Stow down A-429, which was called Fosse Way in Roman times.

Tourist Information: The TI, in the shop at the Corinium Museum (described next), answers questions and sells a £0.50 town map and a £1.20 town walking-tour brochure (same

COTSWOLDS

hours as museum, tel. 01285/654-180).

Getting There: If traveling by bus, take #801 from Moreton-in-Marsh or Stow to Northleach, then transfer to bus #855 to Cirencester. Drivers follow *Town Centre* signs and try to find parking right on the market square; if it's parked up, retreat to the Waterloo pay-and-display lot (a five-minute walk away).

Sights: In Cirencester, stop by the impressive **Corinium Museum** to find out why they say, "If you scratch Gloucestershire, you'll find Rome."

The museum chronologically displays well-explained artifacts from the town's rich history, with a focus on Roman times—when Corinium was the second-biggest city in the British Isles (after Londinium). You'll see column capitals and fine mosaics, before moving on to the Anglo-Saxon and Middle Ages exhibits (£5; Mon-Sat 10:00-17:00, Sun 14:00-17:00, until 16:00 Nov-March; Park Street, tel. 01285/655-611, www.corinium museum.org).

Cirencester's church is the largest of the Cotswold "wool" churches. The cutesy New Brewery Arts crafts center entertains visitors with traditional weaving and potting, workshops, an interesting gallery, and a good coffee shop. Monday and Friday are general-market days, Friday features an antiques market, and a crafts market is held on most Saturdays.

Moreton-in-Marsh

This workaday town—worth ▲—is like Stow or Chipping Campden without the touristy sugar. Rather than gift and

antiques shops, you'll find streets lined with real shops: ironmongers selling cottage nameplates and carpet shops strewn with the remarkable patterns that decorate B&B floors. A traditional market of 100-plus stalls fills High Street each Tuesday, as it has for the last 400 years (8:00-15:30, handicrafts, farm produce, clothing, books, and people-watching; best if you go early). The Cotswolds has an economy aside from tourism, and you'll feel it here.

Moreton-in-Marsh

TO WORCESTER

TO STRATFORD-UPON-AVON VIA A-429

TO BATSFORD

BATSFORD

TODENHAM RD.

VICTORIA PARK

HIGH ST.

TRAIN STATION

TO BATSFORD

PATH

NEW

Post

LONDON ROAD

TO CHASTLETON HOUSE & OXFORD VIA A-44

OXFORD ST.

WC

EAST ST.

BOURTON ROAD

TO BROADWAY VIA A-44

TO OXFORD & LONDON

CHURCH ST.

LIBRARY

DCH

P PARKING

NOT TO SCALE

- ❶ Manor House Hotel
- ❷ The Swan Inn
- ❸ Treetops B&B
- ❹ Acacia B&B
- ❺ The Marshmallow Restaurant
- ❻ The Black Bear Inn
- ❼ Hassan Balti Rest.
- ❽ Tilly's Tea House & Mermaid Fish Shop
- ❾ Ask Restaurant
- ❿ Co-op & Tesco Express
- ⓫ Budgens Supermarket
- ⓬ Launderette
- ⓭ Toy Shop Bike Rental

COTSWOLDS

Orientation to Moreton-in-Marsh

Moreton has a tiny, sleepy train station two blocks from High Street, lots of bus connections, and the best **TI** in the region. The TI offers a room-booking service, pay Internet access, and discounted tickets for major sights (such as Blenheim Palace and Warwick Castle). Peruse the racks of fliers, confirm rail and bus schedules, and consider the £0.50 *Town Trail* self-guided walking tour leaflet (Mon 8:45-16:00, Tue-Thu 8:45-17:15, Fri 8:45-16:45,

Sat 10:00-13:00—or until 12:30 in winter, closed Sun, good public WC, tel. 01608/650-881).

Helpful Hints

Internet Access: It's available for £0.50/15 minutes at the **TI** and free at the erratically open **library** (down High Street where it becomes Stow Road, tel. 0845-230-5420).

Baggage Storage: While there is no formal baggage storage in town, the **Black Bear Inn** (next to the TI) might let you leave bags there—especially if you buy a drink.

Laundry: The handy launderette is a block in front of the train station on New Road (daily 7:00-19:00, last wash at 18:00, £4-5 self-service wash, £2-3 self-service dry, or drop off Mon-Fri 8:00-11:00 for £3 extra and same-day service—pick up by 17:00, tel. 01608/650-888).

Bike Rental, Taxis, and Car Rental: See "Getting Around the Cotswolds" (page 387).

Parking: It's easy—anywhere on High Street is fine any time, as long as you want, for free (though there is a 2-hour parking limit for the small lot in the middle of the street). On Tuesdays, when the market makes parking tricky, you can park at the **Budgens** supermarket for £3—refundable if you spend at least £5 in the store (2-hour limit).

Hikes and Walks from Moreton-in-Marsh: As its name implies, Moreton-in-Marsh sits on a flat, boggy landscape, making it a bit less appealing for hikes; I'd bus to Chipping Campden or to Stow, both described earlier, for a better hike (this is easy, since Moreton is a transit hub). If you do have just a bit of time to kill in Moreton, consider taking a fun and easy walk a mile out to the arboretum and falconry center in **Batsford** (described later).

Sleeping in Moreton-in-Marsh

(area code: 01608)

$$$ Manor House Hotel is Moreton's big old hotel, dating from 1545 but sporting such modern amenities as toilets and electricity. Its 35 classy-for-the-Cotswolds rooms and its garden invite relaxation (Sb-£120, standard Db-£158, superior Db-£178, four-poster Db-£200, family suite-£220, £40 more for Sat night, rates are soft—often a bit less, includes breakfast, elevator, free Wi-Fi, log fire in winter, attached restaurants, free parking, on far end of High Street away from train station, tel. 01608/650-501, www .cotswold-inns-hotels.co.uk, info@manorhousehotel.info).

$$ The Swan Inn is wonderfully perched on the main drag, with eight en suite rooms. Though the halls look a bit worn and you enter through a bar/restaurant (that can be noisy on weekends), the renovated rooms themselves are classy and the bathrooms modern (Sb-£60, standard Db-£70-110, four-poster Db-£90-130, free Wi-Fi, free parking, restaurant gives guests 10 percent discount, High Street, tel. 01608/650-711, www.swanmoreton.co.uk, info @swanmoreton.co.uk, Sara and Terry Todd and their two sons). Terry can pick up guests from the train station and is willing to drive carless guests to various destinations within 20 miles if no public transport is available.

$ Treetops B&B is plush, with seven spacious, attractive rooms, a sun lounge, and a three-quarter-acre backyard. Liz and Ben (the family dog) will make you feel right at home—if you meet the two-night minimum on weekends (large Db-£70, gigantic Db-£75, two wheelchair-accessible ground-floor rooms have patios, free Wi-Fi, set far back from the busy road, London Road, tel. 01608/651-036, www.treetopscotswolds.co.uk, treetops1@talk 21.com, Liz and Brian Dean). It's an eight-minute walk from town and the train station (exit station, keep left, go left on bridge over train tracks, look for sign, then long driveway).

$ Acacia B&B, on the short road connecting the train station to the town center, is a convenient budget option. Dorothy has four small rooms: one is en suite, the other three share one bathroom. The public spaces are a bit tired, but the rooms are bright and tidy, and most overlook a lovely garden (S-£40, D-£55, Db-£60, tel. 01608/650-130, 2 New Road, www.acaciainthecotswolds.co.uk, acacia.guesthouse@tiscali.co.uk).

Eating in Moreton-in-Marsh

A stroll up and down High Street lets you survey your small-town options.

The Marshmallow is relatively upscale but affordable, with a menu that includes traditional English dishes as well as lasagna and salads (£9-11 main dishes, £13 high tea, Mon 8:30-18:00, Tue 10:00-18:00, Wed-Sat 8:30-20:00, Sun 10:30-18:00, closed for dinner Jan, reservations smart, shady back garden for dining, tel. 01608/651-536, www.marshmallow-tea-restaurant.co.uk).

The Black Bear Inn offers traditional English food. As you enter, choose between the dining room on the left or the pub on the right (£8-14 meals and daily specials, restaurant open daily 12:00-14:00 & 18:30-21:00, pub open daily 10:30-23:30, tel. 01608/652-992).

Hassan Balti, with tasty Bangladeshi food, is a fine value for sit-down or takeout (£7-11 meals, daily 12:00-14:00 & 17:30-23:30, tel. 01608/650-798).

Tilly's Tea House serves fresh soups, salads, sandwiches, and pastries for lunch in a cheerful spot on High Street across from the TI (£5-7 light meals, good cream tea-£4.50, Mon-Sat 9:00-17:00, Sun 10:00-16:00, tel. 01608/650-000).

Ask, a chain restaurant across the street, has decent pastas, pizzas, and salads, and a breezy, family-friendly atmosphere (£9-12 pizzas, daily 11:30-23:00, takeout available, tel. 01608/651-119).

Mermaid fish shop is popular for its take-out fish and tasty selection of traditional savory pies (£5 fish-and-chips, £2 pies, Mon-Sat 11:30-14:00 & 17:00-22:30, closed Sun, tel. 01608/651-391).

Picnic: There's a small **Co-op** grocery on High Street in the town center (Mon-Sat 7:00-20:00, Sun 8:00-20:00), and a **Tesco Express** two doors down (Mon-Fri 6:00-23:00, Sat-Sun 7:00-23:00). The big **Budgens** supermarket is indeed super (Mon-Sat 8:00-22:00, Sun 10:00-16:00, far end of High Street). You can picnic across the busy street, in pleasant Victoria Park (with a playground for kids).

Nearby: The excellent **Horse and Groom** gastropub in Bourton-on-the-Hill is a quick drive or uphill two-mile walk away (see page 424).

Moreton-in-Marsh Connections

Moreton, the only Cotswold town with a train station, is also the best base for exploring the region by bus (see "Getting Around the Cotswolds," page 387).

From Moreton by Train to: London's Paddington Station (one-way-£32-33, every 1-2 hours, 1.5-2 hours), **Bath** (hourly, 2.5-3 hours, 1-2 transfers), **Oxford** (every 1-2 hours, 40 minutes), **Ironbridge Gorge** (hourly, 2.5-3 hours, 2 transfers; arrive Telford, then catch bus or cab 7 miles to Ironbridge Gorge—see page 489), **Stratford-upon-Avon** (almost hourly, 2.5-3 hours, 2-3 transfers, slow and expensive, better by bus). Train info: Tel. 0845-748-4950, www.nationalrail.co.uk.

From Moreton by Bus to: Stratford-upon-Avon (#21 and #22 go via Chipping Campden: Mon-Sat 8/day, none on Sun, 1-1.25 hours; #23 goes via Shipston-on-Stour: Mon-Sat 2/day, none on Sun, 1 hour; Johnsons Coaches, tel. 01564/797-070, www.johnsonscoaches.co.uk).

Near Moreton-in-Marsh

▲Chastleton House

This stately home, located about five miles southeast of Moreton-in-Marsh, was actually lived in by the same family from 1607 until 1991. It offers a rare peek into a Jacobean gentry house. (Jacobean, which comes from the Latin for "James," indicates the style from the time of King James I—the early 1600s.) Built, like most Cotswold palaces, with wool money, it gradually declined with the fortunes of its aristocratic family until, according to the last lady of the house, it was "held together by cobwebs." It came to the National Trust on condition that they would maintain its musty Jacobean ambience. Wander on creaky floorboards, many of them original, and chat with volunteer guides stationed in each room. It's an uppity place that doesn't encourage spontaneity. The docents are proud to play on one of the best croquet teams in the region (the rules of croquet were formalized in this house in 1868). Page through the early 20th-century family photo albums in the room just off the entry.

Cost and Hours: £9.50; April-Sept Wed-Sat 13:00-17:00; mid- to late March and Oct Wed-Sat 13:00-16:00; closed Nov-mid-March and Sun-Tue year-round; ticket office opens at 12:30, last entry one hour before closing; recorded info tel. 01494/755-560, www.nationaltrust.org.uk/chastleton.

Getting In: Only 180 visitors a day are allowed into the home (25 people every 30 minutes), and reservations are not possible—it's first-come, first served. At the busiest times, you might have to wait a bit to enter the house. Wednesday and Thursday are the quietest days, with the shortest wait times.

Getting There: Chastleton House is well-signposted, about a 10-minute drive southeast of Moreton-in-Marsh off A-44. It's a five-minute hike to the house from the free parking lot.

Batsford

This village has two side-by-side attractions that might appeal if you have a special interest or time to kill.

Getting There: Batsford is an easy 45-minute, one-mile country walk west of Moreton-in-Marsh. It's also connected to Moreton by buses #21 and #22.

Cotswold Falconry Centre

Along with the Cotswolds' hunting heritage comes falconry—and this place, with dozens of specimens of eagles, falcons, owls, and other birds, gives a sample of what these deadly birds of prey can do. You can peruse the cages to see all the different birds, but the demonstration, with vultures or falcons swooping inches over your head, is what makes it fun.

Cost and Hours: £8, ticket good for 10 percent discount at Batsford Arboretum; daily mid-Feb-mid-Nov 10:30-17:30, mid-Nov–mid-Feb 10:30-16:30, last entry 30 minutes before closing; flying displays at 11:30, 13:30, and 15:00, plus in summer at 16:30; Batsford Park, tel. 01386/701-043, www.cotswold-falconry.co.uk.

Batsford Arboretum

This sleepy grove, with 2,800 trees from around the world, pales in comparison to some of the Cotswolds' genteel manor gardens. But it's next door to the Falconry Centre, and handy to visit if you'd enjoy strolling through a diverse wood. The arboretum's café serves lunch and tea on a terrace with sweeping views of the Gloucestershire countryside.

Cost and Hours: £7, ticket good for 10 percent discount at Falconry Centre, daily 10:00-18:00, last entry at 16:45, tel. 01386/701-441, www.batsarb.co.uk.

Blenheim Palace

Conveniently located halfway between the Cotswolds and Oxford, Blenheim Palace is one of Britain's best—worth ▲▲▲. Too many

palaces can send you into a furniture-wax coma, but everyone should see Blenheim. The Duke of Marlborough's home—the largest in England—is still lived in, which is wonderfully obvious as you prowl through it. The 2,000-acre yard, well-designed by Lancelot "Capability" Brown, is as majestic to some as the palace itself. The view just past the outer gate as you enter is a classic. Even if you're in a hurry, you'll need two hours to see the basic sights—but if you have more time, you could spend all day here. Note: Americans who pronounce the place "blen-HEIM" are the butt of jokes. It's "BLEN-em."

Cost and Hours: £21, discount tickets that save £2.50-3 are available at TIs in surrounding towns—including Oxford and Moreton-in-Marsh—or on the #S3 bus from Oxford; family ticket for two adults and two kids-£55, £5 guidebook; open mid-Feb–Oct daily 10:30-17:30, last entry at 16:45; Nov–mid-Dec Wed-Sun 10:30-17:30; park open but palace closed Nov–mid-Dec Mon-Tue and mid-Dec–mid-Feb.

Information: Tel. 01993/810-530, recorded info toll-free tel. 0800-849-6500, www.blenheimpalace.com.

Getting There: Blenheim Palace sits at the edge of the cute cobbled town of Woodstock. The train station nearest the palace

(Hanborough, 1.5 miles away) has no taxi or bus service.

If you're coming from the **Cotswolds,** your easiest train connection is from Moreton-in-Marsh to Oxford, where you can catch the bus to Blenheim (explained next; note that bus #S3 doesn't always stop at the Oxford train station—you may have to walk five minutes to the bus station).

From **Oxford,** take bus #S3 (2/hour, 30 minutes; bus tel. 01865/772-250, www.stagecoachbus.com). Catch it from the bus station at Gloucester Green (usually stops at Oxford's train station as well; may also pick up in the center on George Street—ask). It stops twice near Blenheim Palace: the "Blenheim Palace Gates" stop is along the main road about a half-mile walk to the palace itself; the "Woodstock/Marlborough Arms" stop puts you right in the heart of the village of Woodstock (handy if you want to poke around town before heading to the palace; this adds just a few more minutes' walking than the other bus stop). The Woodstock gate also offers the most spectacular view of the palace and lake.

Drivers head for Woodstock (from the Cotswolds, follow signs for *Oxford* on A-44); the palace is well-signposted once in town, just off the main road. Buy your ticket at the gate, then drive up the long driveway to park near the palace.

Background: John Churchill, first duke of Marlborough, defeated Louis XIV's French forces at the Battle of Blenheim in 1704. This pivotal event marked a turning point in the centuries-long struggle between the English and the French, and some historians claim that if not for his victory, we'd all be speaking French today. (They're probably exaggerating, but *qui sait?*) A thankful Queen Anne rewarded Churchill by building him this nice home, perhaps the finest Baroque building in England (designed by playwright-turned-architect John Vanbrugh). Ten dukes of Marlborough later, it's as impressive as ever. (The current, 11th duke considers the would-be 12th more of an error than an heir, and has largely disowned him.) In 1874, a later John Churchill's daughter-in-law, Jennie Jerome, gave birth at Blenheim to another historic baby in that line...and named him Winston. The history continues.

⮕ **Self-Guided Tour:** From the parking lot, you'll likely enter at the recently opened East Courtyard Visitors' Center (with café). Pick up a free map and head through the small courtyard. You'll emerge into a grand courtyard in front of the palace's columned yellow facade. Most of the attractions are reached by going through the palace's main entry.

You'll enter into the truly great **Great Hall.** Before taking the well-organized tour, spend some time on your own in the fine **Winston Churchill Exhibition,** which displays letters, paintings, and other artifacts of the great statesman who was born here. The highlight is the bed in which Sir Winston was born in 1874 (prematurely...his mother went into labor suddenly while attending a party here).

When you've had your fill of Churchill, catch the 45-minute guided tour of the **state rooms**—the fancy halls the dukes use to impress visiting dignitaries (tours leave every 10 minutes, included with ticket, last one at 16:45). This fascinating tour lets visitors ogle some of the most sumptuous rooms in the palace, ornamented with fine porcelain, gilded ceilings, portraits of past dukes, photos of the present duke's family, and "chaperone" sofas designed to give courting couples just enough privacy...but not *too* much. When the palace is really busy (most likely on Sun), they dispense with guided tours and go "free flow," allowing those with an appetite for learning to strike up conversations with docents in each room.

Enjoy the series of 10 Brussels tapestries that commemorate military victories of the First Duke of Marlborough, including the Battle of Blenheim. After winning that pivotal conflict, he scrawled a quick note on the back of a tavern bill notifying the queen of his victory (you'll see a replica). The tour offers insights into the quirky ways of England's fading nobility—for example, in exchange for this fine palace, the duke still pays "rent" to the Queen in the form of one ornamental flag per year (called "quitrent standard").

The palace items come with tales of past dukes of Marlborough and their families. You'll learn about Consuelo Vanderbilt—of the New York Vanderbilts—who was forced against her will to marry into this aristocratic family. She was miserable, but dutifully produced two sons (whom she dubbed "the heir and the spare") before the marriage fell apart after 10 years.

Finish with the remarkable "long library"—with its tiers of books and stuccoed ceilings—before exiting through the chapel, near the entrance to the gardens (described later). But before taking off to explore the gardens, consider two more attractions inside the main palace.

The Untold Story (to the left as you enter the Great Hall) is a modern, 45-minute, multimedia "visitors' experience" (15 people go in every 3 minutes, included in your ticket). You'll travel from room to room—as doors open and close behind you—guided through 300 years of history by a maid named Grace Ridley. (If you have limited time to spend at the palace, this is skippable.)

For a more extensive visit, follow up the general tour with a 30-minute guided walk through the **private apartments** of the duke. Tours leave at the top and bottom of each hour; however, since you'll see where the duke's family actually resides today, tours are cancelled if His Grace is in his jammies (£4.50, irregular schedule but generally daily 12:00-16:30, most likely to be open in summer, tickets are limited, buy from table in library or at main entry, enter in corner of courtyard to left of grand palace entry).

The palace's expansive **gardens** stretch nearly as far as the eye can see in every direction. Access them from the courtyard, by going through the little door near the "Churchill Shop" (as you face the main palace entrance, it's to the right). You'll emerge into the Water Terraces; from there, you can loop around to the left, behind the palace, to see (but not enter) the Italian Garden. Or, head down to the lake to walk along the waterfront trail; going left takes you to the rose gardens and arboretum, while turning right brings you to the Grand Bridge. You can explore on your

own (using the map and good signposting), or rent a £3 audioguide that outlines three different walks around the property (40-90 minutes depending on tour; rent it in the "Churchill Shop" next to the door to the gardens). A café sits at the garden exit for basic lunch and teatime treats.

Finally, in the "stables block" (under the gateway to the right, as you face the main palace entrance) is the **Churchill's Destiny exhibit,** which traces the military leadership of two great men who shared that name: John, who defeated Louis XIV at the Battle of Blenheim in the 18th century, and in whose honor this palace was built; and Winston, who was born in this palace, and who won the Battle of Britain and helped defeat Hitler in the 20th century. The exhibit offers a painstaking, blow-by-blow account of each of the battles. It's remarkable that arguably two of the most important military victories in the nation's history were overseen by distant cousins—England is a small island indeed. (Winston Churchill fans can visit his tomb, just over a mile away to the south in the Bladon town churchyard—the church is faintly visible from inside the palace. Look for the footpath across from The White House pub.)

The final attraction is actually on the way out of the palace complex: the kid-friendly **pleasure garden,** where a lush and humid greenhouse flutters with butterflies. A kid zone includes a few second-rate games and the "world's largest symbolic hedge maze." The maze is worth a look if you haven't seen one and want some exercise. If you have a car, you'll pass these gardens as you drive down the road toward the exit; otherwise, you can take the tiny train from the palace parking lot to the garden (2/hour).

Sleeping near Blenheim Palace

(area code: 01993)

These accommodations near Blenheim Palace are in the town of Woodstock.

$$ Blenheim Guest House, charming and 200 years old, has six rooms in the town center. A bit musty, it's located above a tearoom literally next door to the gateway into the palace grounds (Sb-£65, Db-£80-90 depending on size, free Wi-Fi, 17 Park Street, tel. 01993/813-814, www.theblenheim.co.uk, theblenheim@aol.com).

$$ The Blenheim Buttery has six modern, comfortable rooms fitted into a half-timbered, slanted-floor building (Sb-£69-115, Db-£89-125, lower prices are for off-season, free cable Internet, 7 Market Place, tel. 01865/811-950, www.theblenheimbuttery.co.uk, info@theblenheimbuttery.co.uk).

STRATFORD-UPON-AVON

Stratford is Shakespeare's hometown. To see or not to see? Stratford is a must for every big bus tour in England, and one of the most popular side-trips from London. English majors and actors are in seventh heaven here. Sure, it's touristy, and non-literary types might find it's much ado about nothing. But nobody back home would understand if you skipped Shakespeare's house.

Shakespeare connection aside, the town's riverside and half-

timbered charm, coupled with its hardworking tourist industry, make Stratford a fun stop. But the play's the thing to bring the Bard to life—and you've arrived just in time to see the Royal Shakespeare Company (the world's best Shakespeare ensemble) making the most of their

state-of-the-art theater complex. If you'll ever enjoy a Shakespeare performance, it'll be here...even if you flunked English Lit.

Planning Your Time

If you're just passing through Stratford, it's worth a half-day—stroll the charming core, visit your choice of Shakespeare sights (Shakespeare's Birthplace is best and easiest), and watch the swans along the river. But if you can squeeze it in, it's worth it to stick around to see a play; in this case, you'll need to spend the night here or drive in from the nearby Cotswolds (doable—just 30 minutes away; see previous chapter).

By Train or Bus: It's easy to stop in Stratford for a wander or

Stratford-upon-Avon

TO WORCESTER VIA A-46

TRAIN STATION

ALCESTER RD.

ARDEN ST.

GREENHILL

WIND---

- ③
- ⑧
- ⑰
- ⑨

PEDESTRIAN ZONE

Ⓟ PARKING

Ⓣ TAXI

-- FOOTPATH

TO ANNE HATHAWAY'S COTTAGE

SHOTTERY

EVESHAM PL.

GROVE L.

ROTHER

MARKET PLACE

ELY

- ①
- ⑬

NASH'S HOUSE

BROAD WALK

CHESTNUT

CHURCH

T.O.P (FORMER COURTYARD THEATRE)

- ⑰
- ⑩

HALL'S CROFT

OLD TOWN

SOUTHERN

TO OXFORD VIA A-439

RIVER

HOLY TRINITY CHURCH (SHAKESPEARE'S GRAVE)

① Ambleside, Woodstock, Adelphi & Salamander Guest Houses

② Mercure Shakespeare Hotel

③ The Emsley Guest House

④ To Hemmingford House Hostel

⑤ Le Bistro Pierre

⑥ Lambs, The Opposition & Barnaby's Fish & Chips

⑦ The Vintner Restaurant

⑧ Avon Spice Restaurant

⑨ The Old Thatch Tavern

⑩ The Windmill Inn

⑪ The Garrick Tavern

TO MARY ARDEN'S FARM

BIRM. ROAD

200 YARDS
200 METERS

SHAKESPEARE'S BIRTHPLACE

TO WARWICK VIA A-439

WARWICK ROAD

BUS STATION

SOR

MEER

WOOD

HENLEY

GUILD ST.

PAYTON

Post T

BRIDGE

HIGH

Bridgefoot

P

BRIDGEWAY

11

TUDOR WORLD

WATERSIDE

BRIDGEFOOT

19

i

PARK

2

SHEEP

7

6

CHAPEL

18

TRAMWAY BRIDGE

25

23

AVON

LANE

21

20

TIDDINGTON RD.

TO 4

22

SWAN THEATRE

Boat House

SWAN'S NEST

21

CLOPTON BR.

5

SHIPSTON RD

BANBURY RD

ROYAL SHAKESPEARE THEATRE

TO OXFORD VIA A-3400 & THE COTSWOLDS

DCH

⑫ Henley Street Tea Rooms & Bensons House of Tea
⑬ Kingfisher Fish & Chips
⑭ Marks & Spencer
⑮ Sainsbury's Local
⑯ Library (Internet)
⑰ Launderettes (2)
⑱ Swan Fountain (Town Walks)

⑲ City Bus Tours
⑳ River Cruises
㉑ Boat Rentals (2)
㉒ Chain Ferry
㉓ Cox's Yard
㉔ MAD Museum
㉕ Gower Memorial

an overnight. Stratford is well-connected by train to London and Oxford, and linked by bus and train to nearby towns (Warwick and Coventry to the north, and Moreton in the Cotswolds to the south).

By Car: Stratford, conveniently located at the northern edge of the Cotswolds, is made-to-order for drivers connecting the Cotswolds with points north (such as Ironbridge Gorge or North Wales). If you're driving north after you visit Stratford, you're within easy reach of two more worthwhile stop-offs: the impressive Warwick Castle and the evocative ruined cathedral at Coventry (both covered in the next chapter). Speedy travelers squeeze in all three of these towns (Stratford, Warwick, and Coventry) on a one-day drive-through: Leave the Cotswolds early, spend the morning exploring Stratford, have lunch and tour the castle in Warwick, visit Coventry's cathedral at the end of the day (it closes Mon-Sat at 16:30; Sun evensong at 16:00), and drive in the evening to your next stop (you'll find driving tips at the end of this chapter). If you're more relaxed, see a play and stay in Stratford, then stop at Warwick and/or Coventry the following morning en route to your next destination.

Orientation to Stratford

Stratford, with 26,500 people, has a compact old town, with the TI and theater along the riverbank, and Shakespeare's Birthplace a few blocks inland; you can easily walk to everything except Mary Arden's place. The core of the town is lined with half-timbered houses. The River Avon has an idyllic yet playful feel, with a park along both banks, paddleboats, hungry swans, and a fun old crank-powered ferry.

Tourist Information

The TI is in a small brick building on Bridgefoot, where the main street hits the river (Mon-Sat 9:00-17:30, Sun 10:00-16:00, tel. 01789/264-293, www.discover-stratford.com). It has a café and a couple of Internet terminals (£1/12 minutes, £5/hour).

Combo-Tickets: The TI sells the Shakespeare Birthplace Trust Five House combo-ticket at a discount, as well as a special any-three combo-ticket, which gives you entry into your pick of three of the five Trust sights (see "Shakespearean Sights," later, for details).

Arrival in Stratford

By Train: Don't get off at the Stratford Parkway train station—you want Stratford-upon-Avon. Once there, exit straight ahead from the train station, bear right up the hill (alongside the parking lot), and follow the main drag straight to the river. (For the Grove Road B&Bs, turn right at the first big intersection.) If you need to buy a picnic for your return train trip, stop at the Morrison's grocery store nearby (you can see it across the tracks). Unfortunately, Stratford (as of this writing) does not have baggage storage—but ask the TI to see if any options have opened up.

By Car: If you're sleeping in Stratford, ask your B&B for arrival and parking details (many have a few free parking spaces, but it's best to reserve ahead). If you're just here for the day, and coming from the south (i.e., the Cotswolds), cross the big bridge and veer right for the best parking, following *Through Traffic, P,* and *Wark* (Warwick Road) signs. Go around the block—turning right and right and right—and enter the multistory Bridgefoot garage; first hour free, £6/9 hours, £10/24 hours, you'll find no place easier or cheaper. The City Sightseeing bus stop and the TI are a block away. Parking is free at the park-and-ride near the Stratford Parkway train station, just off the A-46—but it's less convenient because you have to ride a shuttle bus into town (£1.70 round-trip, 4/hour during the day, 2/hour in the evening, drops off near the river on Bridge Street).

Helpful Hints

Name That Stratford: If you're coming by train or bus, be sure to request a ticket for "Stratford-upon-Avon," not just "Stratford" (to avoid a mix-up with Stratford Langthorne, near London, which hosted the 2012 Olympics and now boasts a huge park where the games were held).

Festival: Every year on the weekend nearest to Shakespeare's birthday (traditionally considered to be April 23—also the day he died), Stratford celebrates. The town hosts free events, including activities for children.

Internet Access: Get online at the **TI** (described earlier) or the **library** (£2.50/30 minutes; Mon-Fri 10:00-17:00, Sat 10:00-15:00, closed Sun; if all computers are in use, reserve a time at the desk; tel. 01789/292-209).

Laundry: Silly Suds, on the road between the train station and the river, is run by kindly Jane. You can do self-service (wash-£3.60, dryer-£1/10 minutes, daily 8:00-21:00, last wash at 18:45), or pay Jane £12 to do the wash for you in a few hours (daily 9:00-16:00; if you're in a pinch, she may even be able to pick up or drop off at your B&B; 34 Greenhill Street, tel. 01789/417-766, mobile 07710-192-704). The other option in town is **Sparklean**, a 10-minute walk from the city center, or about five minutes from the Grove Road B&Bs (same self-serve prices as above, no full-service option, daily 8:00-21:00, last wash at 20:00, 74 Bull Street, tel. 01789/269-075).

Taxis: Try **007 Taxis** (tel. 01789/414-007) or the taxi stand on Woodbridge, near the intersection with High Street. To arrange for a private car and driver, contact **Platinum Cars** (£25/hour, tel. 01789/264-626, www.platinum-cars.co.uk).

Tours in Stratford

Stratford Town Walks

These entertaining, award-winning two-hour walks introduce you to the town and its famous playwright. Tours run daily year-round, rain or shine. Just show up at the Swan fountain (on the waterfront, opposite Sheep Street) in front of the Royal Shakespeare Theatre and pay the guide (£5, kids-£2, ticket stub offers discounts to some sights and shops, Fri-Wed at 11:00, Fri-Sun also at 14:00, mobile 07855/760-377, www.stratford townwalk.co.uk). They also run an evening ghost walk led by a professional magician (£6, kids-£4, Mon and Thu-Sat at 19:30, 1.5 hours, must book in advance).

City Sightseeing Bus Tours

Open-top buses constantly make the rounds, allowing visitors to hop on and hop off at all the Shakespeare sights. Given the far-flung nature of two of the Shakespeare sights, and the value of the fun commentary provided, this tour makes the town more manageable. The full 11-stop circuit takes about an hour and comes with a steady and informative commentary (£12.50, discount with town walk ticket stub, buy tickets on bus or as you board, ticket good for 24 hours, buses leave from the TI every 20 minutes in high season from about 9:30-17:00, every 30 minutes and shorter hours off-season; buses alternate between recorded commentary and live guides—for the best tour, wait for a live guide; tel. 01789/412-680, www.citysightseeing-stratford.com).

Shakespearean Sights

Stratford's five biggest Shakespeare sights are run by the same organization, the Shakespeare Birthplace Trust (www.shakes peare.org.uk). While these sights are promoted as if they were tacky tourist attractions—and are designed to be crowd-pleasers rather than to tickle academics—they're well-run and genuinely interesting. Shakespeare's Birthplace, Nash's House, and Hall's Croft are in town; Mary Arden's Farm and Anne Hathaway's Cottage are just outside Stratford. Each has a tranquil garden and helpful, eager docents who love to tell a story; and yet, each is quite different, so visiting all five gives you a well-rounded look at the Bard.

If you're here for Shakespeare sightseeing—and have time to venture to the countryside sights—you might as well buy the "Five House" combo-ticket and drop into them all. If your time is more limited, visit only Shakespeare's Birthplace, which is the most convenient to reach (right in the town center) and offers the best historical introduction to the playwright.

Combo-Tickets: Admission to the three Shakespeare Birthplace Trust sights in town—Shakespeare's Birthplace, Hall's Croft, and Nash's House—requires a combo-ticket; no individual tickets are sold. To visit only these three sights, get the £14.95 **Shakespeare Birthplace combo-ticket**, which is sold at the participating sights. To add Anne Hathaway's Cottage and Mary Arden's Farm, you can buy the £22.50 **Shakespeare Five House combo-ticket** (sold at participating sights, good for one year; also available at a discount—£19.20—at the TI). You can also buy individual tickets for Anne Hathaway's Cottage and Mary Arden's Farm (see "Just Outside Stratford," later). Both tickets also include Holy Trinity Church, with Shakespeare's grave, which usually requests a £2 donation.

Another option is the £16.50 **any-three combo-ticket,** sold only at the TI. This ticket lets you choose which trio of sights you want to see—for instance, the birthplace, Anne Hathaway's Cottage, and Mary Arden's Farm (buy at TI; you'll get a receipt, then show it at the first sight you visit to receive your three-sight card).

Discounts: If you've taken a Stratford town walk (described under "Tours in Stratford," earlier), show your ticket stub to receive a 50 percent discount off any combo-ticket you buy at the sights. Also, ask your B&B owner if they have any discount vouchers—they often do.

Closing Times: What the Shakespeare sights list as their "closing time" is actually their last-entry time. If you show up at the closing time I've noted below, you'll still be able to get in, but with limited time to enjoy the sight (since they start closing things down soon after).

In Stratford
▲▲Shakespeare's Birthplace
Touring this sight, you'll experience a modern exhibit before seeing Shakespeare's actual place of birth. While the birthplace itself is a bit underwhelming, the exhibit, helpful docents, and sense that Shakespeare's ghost still haunts these halls make it a good introduction to the Bard.

William Shakespeare
(1564-1616)

To many, William Shakespeare is the greatest author, in any language, period. In one fell swoop, he expanded and helped define modern English—the unrefined tongue of everyday people—and granted it a beauty and legitimacy that put it on par with Latin. In the process, he gave us phrases like "one fell swoop," which we quote without knowing that no one ever said it before Shakespeare wrote it.

Shakespeare was born in Stratford-upon-Avon in 1564 to John Shakespeare and Mary Arden. Though his parents were probably illiterate, Shakespeare is thought to have attended Stratford's grammar school, finishing his education at age 14. When he was 18, he married a 26-year-old local girl, Anne Hathaway (she was three months pregnant with their daughter Susanna).

The very beginnings of Shakespeare's writing career are shrouded in mystery: Historians have been unable to unearth any record of what he was up to in his early 20s. We only know that seven years after his marriage, Shakespeare was living in London as a budding poet, playwright, and actor. He soon hit the big time, writing and performing for royalty, founding (along with his troupe) the Globe Theatre (a functioning replica of which now stands along the Thames' South Bank—see page 142), and raking in enough dough to buy New Place, a swanky mansion back in his hometown. Around 1611, the rich-and-famous playwright retired from the theater, moving back to Stratford, where he died at the age of 52.

With plots that entertained both the highest and the lowest minds, Shakespeare taught the play-going public about human nature. His tool was an unrivaled linguistic mastery of English. Using borrowed plots, outrageous puns, and poetic language,

Cost and Hours: Covered by combo-tickets, daily April-Oct 9:00-17:00, July-Aug until 18:00, Nov-March 10:00-16:00, café, in town center on Henley Street, tel. 01789/204-016.

Visiting Shakespeare's Birthplace: You'll begin by touring an exhibit that provides an entertaining and easily digestible introduction (or, for some, review) about what made the Bard so great. The new exhibit, planned to open in early 2014, is expected to include movie clips of his works and information about his upbringing in Stratford, his family life, and his career in London. Likely on display will be actual historic artifacts, including an

Shakespeare wrote comedies (c. 1590—*Taming of the Shrew*, *As You Like It*), tragedies (c. 1600—*Hamlet*, *Othello*, *Macbeth*, *King Lear*), and fanciful combinations (c. 1610—*The Tempest*), exploring the full range of human emotions and reinventing the English language.

Perhaps as important was his insight into humanity. His father was a glove-maker and wool merchant, and his mother was the daughter of a landowner from a Catholic family. Some scholars speculate that Shakespeare's parents were closet Catholics, practicing their faith during the rise of Protestantism. It is this tug-of-war between two worlds, some think, that helped enlighten Shakespeare's humanism. Think of his stock of great characters and great lines: Hamlet ("To be or not to be, that is the question"), Othello and his jealousy ("It is the green-eyed monster"), ambitious Mark Antony ("Friends, Romans, countrymen, lend me your ears"), rowdy Falstaff ("The better part of valor is discretion"), and the star-crossed lovers Romeo and Juliet ("But soft, what light through yonder window breaks"). Shakespeare probed the psychology of human beings 300 years before Freud. Even today, his characters strike a familiar chord.

The scope of his brilliant work, his humble beginnings, and the fact that no original Shakespeare manuscripts survive raise a few scholarly eyebrows. Some have wondered if Shakespeare had help on several of his plays. After all, they reasoned, how could a journeyman actor with little education have written so many masterpieces? And he was surrounded by other great writers, such as his friend and fellow poet, Ben Jonson. Most modern scholars, though, agree that Shakespeare did indeed write the plays and sonnets attributed to him.

His contemporaries had no doubts about Shakespeare—or his legacy. As Jonson wrote in the preface to the First Folio, "He was not of an age, but for all time!"

original 1623 First Folio of Shakespeare's work. (If you're in a hurry, look for an express route—designed for groups—that lets you skip the main exhibit and head more directly for the garden and house.)

You'll exit the exhibit into the garden, where you can follow signs to the **birthplace,** a half-timbered Elizabethan building where young William grew up. I find the old house a bit disappointing, as if millions of visitors have rubbed it clean of anything authentic. It was restored in the 1800s, and, while the furnishings seem tacky and modern, they're supposed to be true to 1575, when William was 11. To liven up the otherwise dead-feeling house, chat up the well-versed, often-costumed attendants posted here and there, eager to answer your questions. You'll be greeted by a guide who offers an introductory talk, then set free to explore on your own. Look for the window etched with the names of decades of important visitors, from Water Scott to actor Henry Irving.

Shakespeare's father, John—who came from humble beginnings, but bettered himself by pursuing a career in glove-making (you'll see the window where he sold them to customers on the street)—provided his family with a comfortable, upper-middle-class existence. The guest bed in the parlor was a major status symbol: They must have been rich to afford such a nice bed that wasn't even used every day. This is also the house where Shakespeare and his bride, Anne Hathaway, began their married life together. Upstairs are the rooms where young Will, his siblings, and his parents slept (along with their servants). After Shakespeare's father died and William inherited the building, the thrifty playwright converted it into a pub to make a little money.

Exit into the fine **garden.** The ugly modern building in the middle of the complex houses a café and sometimes hosts temporary exhibits upstairs. If you hear a commotion, it's likely Shakespearean **actors,** who perform brief scenes in the garden (they may even take requests). Pull up a bench and listen, imagining the playwright as a young boy stretching his imagination in this very place.

Nash's House
Nash was the first husband of Shakespeare's granddaughter...not exactly a close connection. However, this house is next to the garden that was once the site of New Place, the house where Shakespeare retired. The sight features the dull parlor of Nash's House, along with the pretty Knott Garden and behind it, what was once Shakespeare's orchard. Upstairs are temporary exhibits, often featuring items that archaeologists have excavated in the adjacent New Place site.

Cost and Hours: Covered by combo-ticket; daily April-Oct 10:00-17:00, Nov-March 11:00-16:00; Chapel Street, tel. 01789/292-325.

Hall's Croft
This former home of Shakespeare's eldest daughter, Susanna, is in the Stratford town center. A fine old Jacobean house, it's the fanciest of the group. Since she married a doctor, the exhibits here are

focused on 17th-century medicine. If you have time to spare and one of the combo-tickets, it's worth a quick pop-in. To make the exhibits interesting, ask the docent for the 15- to 20-minute introduction, which helps bring the plague—and some of the bizarre remedies of the time—to life.

Cost and Hours: Covered by combo-ticket, same hours as Nash's House, on-site tearoom, between Church Street and the river on Old Town Street, tel. 01789/292-107.

Shakespeare's Grave

To see his final resting place, head to the riverside Holy Trinity Church. Shakespeare was a rector for this church when he died.

While the church is surrounded by an evocative graveyard, the Bard is entombed in a place of honor, right in front of the altar inside. The church marks the ninth-century birthplace of the town, which was once a religious settlement.

Cost and Hours: £2 donation, not covered by combo-ticket (but included in individual tickets to Anne Hathaway's Cottage or Mary Arden's Farm), April-Sept Mon-Sat 8:30-17:40, Sun 12:30-16:40; Oct-March until 16:40 or 15:40, 10-minute walk past the theater—see its graceful spire as you gaze down the river, tel. 01789/266-316, www.stratford-upon-avon.org.

Just Outside Stratford

To reach either of these sights, it's best to drive or take the hop-on, hop-off bus tour (see "Tours in Stratford," earlier)—unless you're staying at one of the Grove Road B&Bs, which are an easy 20-minute walk from Anne Hathaway's Cottage. Both sights are well-signposted (with brown signs) from the major streets and ring roads around Stratford. If driving between the sights, ask for directions at the sight you're leaving.

▲▲Mary Arden's Farm

Along with Shakespeare's Birthplace, this is my favorite of the Shakespearean sights. Famous as the girlhood home of William's mom, this homestead is in Wilmcote (about three miles from Stratford). Built around two historic farmhouses, it's an open-air folk museum depicting 16th-century farm life...which happens to

Stratford Thanks America

Residents of Stratford are thankful for the many contributions Americans have made to their city and its heritage. Along with pumping up the economy day in and day out with tourist visits, Americans paid for half the rebuilding of the Royal Shakespeare Theatre after it burned down in 1926. The Swan Theatre renovation was funded entirely by American aid. Harvard University inherited—you guessed it—the Harvard House, and it maintains the house today. London's much-loved theater, Shakespeare's Globe, was the dream (and gift) of an American. And there's even an odd but prominent "American Fountain" overlooking Stratford's market square on Rother Street, which was given in 1887 to celebrate the Golden Jubilee of the rule of Queen Victoria.

have ties to Shakespeare. The Bard is basically an afterthought here.

Cost and Hours: £10, also covered by certain combo-tickets—see page 446, daily April-Oct 10:00-17:00, visitors must leave by 17:30, closed Nov-March, tel. 01789/293-455.

Getting There: The most convenient way to get here is by car (free parking) or the hop-on, hop-off bus tour, but it's also easy to reach by train. The Wilmcote train station is up the street, about a five-minute walk from Mary Arden's Farm (£1.80 round-trip fare, two stops from Stratford-upon-Avon on Birmingham- and London-bound trains, 1-2/hour, 5-minute trip, call London Midland to confirm departure time—tel. 0844-811-0133, www.londonmidland.com).

Visiting Mary Arden's Farm: The museum hosts many special **events,** including the falconry show described below. The day's events are listed on a chalkboard by the entry, or you can call ahead to find out what's on. There are always plenty of activities to engage kids: It's an active, hands-on place.

Follow the Tudor roses from building to building, through farmhouses with good displays about farm life. Throughout the complex, you'll see period interpreters in Tudor costumes. They'll likely be going through the day's chores as people back then would have done—activities such as milking the sheep and cutting wood to do repairs on the house. They're there to answer questions and provide fun, gossipy insight into what life was like at the time.

The first building, **Palmer's farm** (mistaken for Mary Arden's home for hundreds of years, and correctly identified in 2000), is furnished as it would have been in Shakespeare's day.

Mary Arden actually lived in the neighboring **farmhouse,** covered in brick facade and seemingly less impressive. The house is filled with kid-oriented activities, including period dress-up clothes, board games from Shakespeare's day, and a Tudor alphabet so kids can write their names in fancy lettering.

Of the many events here, the most enjoyable is the **falconry demonstration,** with lots of mean-footed birds (daily, usually at 11:30, 13:30, and 15:30). Chat with the falconers about their methods for earning the birds' trust. The birds' hunger sets them to flight (a round-trip earns the bird a bit of food; the birds fly when hungry—but don't have the energy if they're *too* hungry). Like Katherine, the wife described as "my falcon" in *The Taming of the Shrew,* these birds are tamed and trained with food as a reward. If things are slow, ask if you can feed one.

▲Anne Hathaway's Cottage

Located 1.5 miles out of Stratford (in Shottery), this home is a 12-room farmhouse where the Bard's wife grew up. William

courted Anne here—she was 26, he was only 18—and his tactics proved successful. (Maybe a little too much, as she was several months pregnant at their wedding.) Their 34-year marriage produced two more children, and lasted until his death in 1616 at age 52. The Hathaway family lived here for 400 years, until 1911, and much of the family's 92-acre farm remains part of the sight.

Cost and Hours: £9, also covered by certain combo-tickets—see page 446, daily April-Oct 9:00-17:00, Nov-March 10:00-16:00, tel. 01789/292-100.

Getting There: It's a 30-minute walk from central Stratford (20 minutes from the Grove Road B&Bs), a stop on the hop-on, hop-off tour bus, or a quick taxi ride from downtown Stratford (around £5). Drivers will find it well-signposted entering Stratford from any direction, with easy £1 parking.

Visiting Anne Hathaway's Cottage: After buying your ticket, turn left and head down through the garden to the thatch-roofed **cottage,** which looks cute enough to eat. The house offers

The Look of Stratford

There's much more to Stratford than Shakespeare sights. Take time to appreciate the look of the town itself. While the main street goes back to Roman times, the key date for the city was 1196, when the king gave the town "market privileges." Stratford was shaped by its marketplace years. The market's many "departments" were located on logically named streets, whose names still remain: Sheep Street, Corn Street, and so on. Today's street plan—and even the 57' 9" width of the lots—survives from the 12th century. (Some of the modern storefronts in the town center are still that exact width.)

Starting in about 1600, three great fires gutted the town, leaving very few buildings older than that era. After those fires, tinderbox thatch roofs were prohibited—the Old Thatch Tavern on Greenhill Street is the only remaining thatch roof in town, predating the law and grandfathered in.

The town's main drag, Bridge Street, is the oldest street in town, but looks the youngest. It was built in the Regency style—a result of a rough little middle row of wattle-and-daub houses being torn down in the 1820s to double the street's width. Today's Bridge Street buildings retain that early 19th-century style: Regency.

Throughout Stratford, you'll see striking black-and-white, half-timbered buildings, as well as half-timbered structures that were partially plastered over and covered up in the 19th century. During Victorian times, the half-timbered style was considered low-class, but in the 20th century—just as tourists came, preferring ye olde style—timbers came back into vogue, and the plaster was removed on many old buildings. But any black and white you see is likely to be modern paint. The original coloring was "biscuit yellow" and brown.

an intimate peek at life in Shakespeare's day. In some ways, it feels even more authentic than his birthplace, and it's fun to imagine the writer of some of the world's greatest romances wooing his favorite girl right here during his formative years. Docents are posted in the first and last rooms to provide meaning and answer questions; while most tourists just stampede through, you'll have a more informative visit if you pause to listen to their commentary. (If the place shakes, a tourist has thunked his or her head on the low beams.)

Maybe even more interesting than the cottage are the **gardens,** which have several parts (including a prizewinning "traditional cottage garden"). If you head uphill, to the right from the entry, you'll find a "Woodland Walk" (look for the Singing Tree—touch it to hear a tune), along with a fun sculpture garden littered with modern interpretations of Shakespearean characters (such as Falstaff's mead gut, and a great photo-op statue of the British Isles sliced out of steel). From April through June, the gardens are at their best, with bulbs in bloom and a large sweet-pea display. You'll also find a music trail, a butterfly trail, and—likely—rotating exhibits, generally on a gardening theme.

The Royal Shakespeare Company

The Royal Shakespeare Company (RSC), undoubtedly the best Shakespeare company on earth, performs year-round in Stratford and in London. Seeing a play here in the Bard's birthplace is a must for Shakespeare fans, and a memorable experience for anybody. Between its excellent acting and remarkable staging, the RSC makes Shakespeare as accessible and enjoyable as it gets.

The RSC makes it easy to take in a play, thanks to their very user-friendly website (www.rsc.org.uk), painless ticket-booking system, and chock-a-block schedule that fills the summer with mostly big-name Shakespeare plays (plus a few more obscure titles to please the die-hard aficionados). Except in January and February, there's almost always something playing.

The RSC is enjoying new popularity after the 2011 opening of its cutting-edge Royal Shakespeare Theatre. Even if you're not seeing a play, exploring this cleverly designed theater building is well worth your time. The smaller, attached Swan Theatre hosts plays on a more intimate scale, with only about 400 seats.

▲▲▲Seeing a Play

Performances take place most days (Mon-Sat generally at 19:15 for the Royal Shakespeare Theatre or 19:30 at the Swan, matinees around 13:15 at the RST or 13:30 at the Swan, sporadic Sun shows). Shows generally last three hours or more, with one intermission; for an evening show, don't count on getting back to your B&B much before 23:00. There's no strict dress code—and people dress casually (nice jeans and short-sleeve shirts are fine)—but shorts are discouraged. You can buy a program for £4. If you're feeling bold, buy a £5 standing ticket and then slip into an open seat as the lights dim—if nothing is available during the play's first half, something might open up after intermission.

Getting Tickets: Tickets range from £5 (standing) to £60, with most around £40. Saturday evening shows—the most popular—are most expensive. You can book tickets as you like it: online (www.rsc.org.uk), by phone (tel. 0844-800-1110), or in person at the box office (Mon-Sat 10:00-20:00, Sun 10:00-17:00). Pay by credit card, get a confirmation number, then pick up your tickets at the theater 30 minutes before "curtain up." Because it's so easy to get tickets online or by phone, it makes absolutely no sense to pay extra to book tickets through any other source.

Tickets go on sale months in advance. Saturdays and very famous plays (such as *Romeo and Juliet* or *Hamlet*)—or any play with a well-known actor—sell out the fastest; the earlier in the week the performance is, the longer it takes to sell out (Thursdays sell out faster than Mondays, for example). Before your trip, check the schedule on their website, and consider buying tickets if something strikes your fancy. But demand is difficult to predict, and some tickets do go unsold. On a recent visit, on a sunny Friday in June, the riverbank was crawling with tourists. I stepped into the RSC on a lark to see if they had any tickets. An hour later, I was watching King Lear lose his marbles.

Even if there aren't any seats available, you may be able to buy a returned ticket on the same day of an otherwise sold-out show. Also, the few standing-room tickets in the main theater are sold only on the day of the show. While you can check at the box office anytime during the day, it's best to go either when it opens at 10:00 (daily) or between 17:30 and 18:00 (Mon-Sat). Be prepared to wait.

Visiting the Theaters
▲▲The Royal Shakespeare Theatre

The RSC's main venue reopened in 2011 after it was updated head to toe, with both a respect for tradition and a sensitivity to the

needs of contemporary theater-goers. You need to take a guided tour (explained later) to see the backstage areas, but you're welcome to wander the theater's public areas anytime the building is open. Interesting tidbits of theater history and easy-to-miss special exhibits make this one of Stratford's most fascinating sights. If you're seeing a play here, come early to poke around the building. Even if you're not, step inside and explore.

Cost and Hours: Free entry, Mon-Sat 10:00-20:00, Sun 10:00-17:00.

Guided Tours: Well-informed RSC volunteers lead entertaining, one-hour building tours. Some cover the main theater while others take you into behind-the-scenes spaces, such as the space-age control room (try for a £7.50 behind-the-scenes tour, but if those aren't running, consider a £5.50 front-of-the-house tour—which skips the backstage areas; tour schedule varies by day, depending on performances, but there's often one at 9:15—call, check online, or go to box office to confirm schedule; best to book ahead, tel. 0844-800-1110, www.rsc.org.uk).

Background: The recently remodeled flagship theater of the RSC has an interesting past. The original, Victorian-style theater was built in 1879 to honor the Bard, but it burned down in 1926. The big Art Deco-style building you see today was erected in 1932 and outfitted with a stodgy Edwardian "picture frame"-style stage, even though a more dynamic "thrust"-style stage—better for engaging the audience—was the actors' choice. (It's would also have been closer in design to Shakespeare's original Globe stage, which jutted into the crowd.)

The latest renovation addressed this ill-conceived design, adding an updated, thrust-style stage. They've left the shell of the 1930s theater, but given it an unconventional deconstructed-industrial style, with the seats stacked at an extreme vertical pitch. Though smaller, the redesigned theater can seat about the same size audience as before (1,048 seats), and now there's not a bad seat in the house—no matter what, you're no more than 50 feet from the stage (the cheapest "gallery" seats look down right onto Othello's bald spot). Productions are staged to play to all of the seats throughout the show. Those sitting up high appreciate different details from those at stage level, and vice versa.

Visiting the Theater: From the main lobby and box office/gift shop area, there's plenty to see. First head left. In the circular **atrium** between the brick wall of the modern theater and fragments of the previous theater, notice the ratty old floorboards. These were pried up from the 1932 stage and laid down here—so as you wait for your play, you're treading on theater history. Upstairs on level 2, find the **Paccar Room**, with generally excellent temporary exhibits assembled from the RSC's substantial collection of historic costumes, props, manuscripts, and other theater memorabilia. Continue upstairs to level 3 to the Rooftop Restaurant (described later). High on the partition that runs through the restaurant, facing the brick theater wall, notice the four **chairs** affixed to the wall. These are original seats from the earlier theater, situated where the back row used to be (90 feet from the stage)—illustrating how much more audience-friendly the new design is.

Back downstairs, pass through the box office/gift shop area to find the **Swan Gallery**—an old, Gothic-style Victorian space that survives from the original 1879 Memorial Theatre. Just past the bar, the Victorian reading room comes with borrowable binders filled with newspaper reviews of several decades of RSC performances. Upstairs is the Ferguson Room, with additional special exhibits.

Back outside, across the street from the theater, notice the building with the steep gable and huge door (marked *CFE 1887*). This was built as a **workshop** for building sets, which could be moved in large pieces to the main theater. To this day, all of the sets, costumes, and props are made here in Stratford. The row of **cottages** to the right is housing for actors. The RSC's reputation exerts enough pull to attract serious actors from all over the UK and beyond, who live here for the entire season. The RSC uses a repertory company approach, where the same actors appear in multiple shows concurrently. Today's Lady Macbeth may be tomorrow's Rosalind.

Tower View: For a God's-eye view of all of Shakespeare's houses, ride the elevator to the top of the RSC's **tower** (£2.50, buy ticket at box office, daily 10:00-19:00). Aside from a few sparse exhibits, the main attraction here is the 360-degree view over the theater building, the Avon, and the lanes of Stratford.

The Food's the Thing: The main theater has a casual café with a terrace overlooking the river (£3 sandwiches, daily 10:00-21:00), as well as the fancier Rooftop Restaurant, which counts the Queen as a patron (£11.50 lunch menu; dinner—£17.50 two-course meal, £22.50 three-course meal; Mon-Sat 11:30 until late, Sun 12:00-18:00, dinner reservations smart, tel. 01789/403-449).

The Swan Theatre

Adjacent to the RSC Theatre is the smaller (about 400 seats), Elizabethan-style Swan Theatre, named not for the birds that fill the park out front, but for the Bard's nickname—the "sweet swan of Avon." This galleried playhouse opened in 1986, thanks to an extremely generous donation from an American theater lover. It has a vertical layout (with a thrust stage) similar to the RSC Theatre, but its wood trim and railings give it a cozier, more traditional feel. The Swan is used for lesser-known Shakespeare plays and alternative works. Occasionally, the lowest level of seats is removed to accommodate "groundling" (standing-only) tickets, much like at the Globe Theatre in London.

The Courtyard Theatre

A two-minute walk down Southern Lane from the original Royal Shakespeare Theatre, this theater (affectionately called the "rusty shed" by locals) was built as a replacement venue while the Royal Shakespeare Theatre was being renovated. It was used as a prototype for the main theater—a testing ground for the lights, seats, and structure of its big brother. Now it's being converted into an alternative, studio theater-type venue called The Other Place (TOP), which will showcase new writing and experimental works. Part of the building is also used for rehearsal space and a costume shop.

Other Stratford Sights

Avon Riverfront

The River Avon is a playground of swans and canal boats. The swans have been the mascots of Stratford since 1623, when, seven years after the Bard's death, Ben Jonson's poem in the First Folio dubbed him "the sweet swan of Avon." Join in the bird-scene fun and buy **swan food** to feed swans and ducks (sold at the TI for £1, and possibly by other vendors—ask around). Don't feed the Canada geese, which locals disdain (they say the geese are vicious and have been messing up the eco-balance since they were imported by a king in 1665).

The **canal boats** saw their workhorse days during the short window of time between the start of the Industrial Revolution and the establishment of the railways. Today, they're mostly pleasure boats. The boats are long and narrow, so two can pass in the slim canals. There are 2,000 miles of canals in England's Midlands, built to connect centers of industry with seaports and provide vital

transportation during the early days of the Industrial Revolution. Stratford was as far inland as you could sail on natural rivers from Bristol; it was the terminus of the man-made Birmingham Canal, built in 1816. Even today, you can motor your canal boat all the way to London from here. Along the embankment, look for the signs indicating how many hours it'll take—and how many locks you'll traverse—to go by barge to various English cities.

For a little bit of mellow river action, rent a **rowboat** (£5/hour per person) or, for more of a challenge, pole yourself around on a Cambridge-style **punt** (canal is poleable—only 4 or 5 feet deep; same price as the rowboat and more memorable/embarrassing if you do the punting—don't pay £10/30 minutes per person for a waterman to do the punting for you). You can rent these boats at the Swan's Nest Boathouse across the Tramway Footbridge; another rental station, along the river, next to the theater, has higher prices but is more conveniently located. Take a short stop on your lazy tour of the English countryside, and moor your canal boat at Stratford's Canal Basin.

You can also try a sleepy 40-minute **river cruise** (£5.50,

includes commentary, Avon Boating, board boat in Bancroft Gardens near the RSC theater, tel. 01789/267-073, www.avon-boating.co.uk), or jump on the oldest surviving **chain ferry** (c. 1937) in Britain (£0.50), which shuttles people across the river just beyond the theater.

Cox's Yard, a riverside timber yard until the 1990s, is a rare physical remnant of the days when Stratford was an industrial port. Today, Cox's has been taken over by the pricey, sprawling Lazy Cow restaurant complex, with a pricey steakhouse, a burger stand, a milkshake shop, lots of outdoor seating, and occasional live music. Upstairs is the Attic Theatre, which puts on fringe theater acts (www.treadtheboardstheatre.co.uk).

In the riverfront park, roughly between Cox's Yard and the TI, the **Gower Memorial** honors the Bard and his creations. Named for Lord Ronald Gower, the man who paid for and sculpted the memorial, this 1888 work shows Shakespeare up top ringed by four of his most indelible creations, each representing a human pursuit: Hamlet (philosophy), Lady Macbeth (tragedy), Falstaff (comedy), and Prince Hal (history). Originally located next to the theater, it was moved here after the 1932 fire.

▲MAD Museum

A refreshing change of pace in Bard-bonkers Stratford, this museum's name stands for "Mechanical Art and Design." It celebrates machines as art, showcasing a changing collection of skillfully constructed robots, gizmos, and Rube-Goldberg machines that spring to entertaining life with the push of a button. Engaging for kids, riveting for engineers, and enjoyable to anybody, it's pricey but conveniently located near Shakespeare's Birthplace.

Cost and Hours: £6.80, daily April-Sept 10:30-17:30, Oct-March 11:00-17:00, 45 Hanley Street, tel. 01789/269-356, www.themadmuseum.co.uk.

Tudor World at the Falstaff Experience

This attraction is tacky, gimmicky, and more about entertainment than education. (And, while it's named for a Shakespeare

character, the exhibit isn't about the Bard.) Filling Shrieve's House Barn with mostly kid-oriented exhibits (mannequins and descriptions, but few real artifacts), it sweeps through Tudor history from the plague to Henry VIII's privy chamber to a replica 16th-century tavern. If you're into ghost-spotting, their nightly ghost tours may be your best shot.

Cost and Hours: Museum-£5.50, daily 10:30-17:30, last entry 30 minutes before closing; ghost tours-£7.50, daily at 18:00, additional tours may be available Fri-Sat; Sheep Street, tel. 01789/298-070, www.falstaffexperience.co.uk.

Sleeping in Stratford

If you want to spend the night after you catch a show, options abound. Ye olde timbered hotels are scattered through the city

center. Most B&Bs are a short walk away on the fringes of town, right on the busy ring roads that route traffic away from the center. (The recommended places below generally have double-paned windows for rooms in the front, but still get some traffic noise.)

In general, the weekend on or near Shakespeare's birthday (April 23) is particularly tight, but Fridays and Saturdays are busy throughout the season. This town is so reliant upon the theater for its business that some B&Bs have secondary insurance covering their loss if the Royal Shakespeare Company ever stops performing in Stratford.

On Grove Road

These accommodations are at the edge of town on busy Grove Road, across from a grassy park. From here, it's about a 10-minute walk either to the town center or to the train station (opposite directions).

$$$ Adelphi Guest House is run by Shakespeare buffs Sue and Simon, who pride themselves on providing a warm welcome, homemade cakes, and original art in every room (S-£40-50, Db-£80-95, Tb-£130, Qb-£160, 2 percent surcharge on credit cards, 10 percent discount off these prices if you stay at least 2 nights—mention this book when you reserve, free Wi-Fi, free parking if booked in advance, 39 Grove Road, tel. 01789/204-469, www.adelphi-guesthouse.com, info@adelphi-guesthouse.com).

$$ Ambleside Guest House is run with quiet efficiency and attentiveness by owners Peter and Ruth. Each of the seven rooms has been completely renovated, including the small but tidy bathrooms. The place has a homey, airy feel, with no B&B clutter (S-£35-40, Db-£60-80, Tb-£85-115, Qb-£100-140, ground-floor rooms, free Wi-Fi, free parking, 41 Grove Road, tel. 01789/297-239, www.amblesideguesthouse.com, peter@amblesideguesthouse.com—include your phone number in your request, since they like to call you back to confirm with a personal touch).

Sleep Code

(£1 = about $1.60, country code: 44, area code: 01789)
S = Single, **D** = Double/Twin, **T** = Triple, **Q** = Quad, **b** = bathroom, **s** = shower only. Unless noted otherwise, credit cards are accepted and breakfast is included.

To help you sort easily through these listings, I've divided the accommodations into three categories based on the price for a standard double room with bath:

$$$ Higher Priced—Most rooms £90 or more.
$$ Moderately Priced—Most rooms between £60-90.
$ Lower Priced—Most rooms £60 or less.

Prices can change without notice; verify the hotel's current rates online or by email. For the best prices, always book direct.

$$ Woodstock Guest House is a friendly, frilly, family-run, and flowery place with five comfortable rooms (Sb-£35-48, Db-£60-85, Tb-£90-120, can accommodate 4 people—ask, get Rick Steves discount if you stay 2 or more nights—mention this book when you reserve, 5 percent surcharge on credit cards, ground-floor room, free Wi-Fi, free parking, 30 Grove Road, tel. 01789/299-881, www.woodstock-house.co.uk, jackie@woodstock-house.co.uk, owners Denis and bubbly Jackie).

$ Salamander Guest House, run by gregarious Frenchman Pascal and his wife, Anna, rents eight simple rooms that are a bit cheaper than their neighbors (S-£39, Db-£50-65, Tb-£70-85, Qb-£80-95, free Wi-Fi, free on-site parking, 40 Grove Road, tel. 01789/205-728, www.salamanderguesthouse.co.uk, p.delin@btinternet.com).

Elsewhere in Stratford

$$$ Mercure Shakespeare Hotel, centrally located in a black-and-white building just up the street from Nash's House, has 78 business-class rooms, each one named for a Shakespearean play or character. Some of the rooms are old-style Elizabethan higgledy-piggledy (with modern finishes), while others are contemporary style—note your preference when you reserve (Sb-£80-100, standard Db-£110-140, deluxe Db-£140-170, prices soft depending on demand, breakfast-£15.50/person, free Wi-Fi, parking-£10/day, Chapel Street, tel. 01789/294-997, www.mercure.com, h6630-re@accor.com).

$$ The Emsley Guest House holds five bright, modern rooms named after different counties in England. It's conscientiously run by Melanie and Ray Coulson, who give it a homey and inviting atmosphere (Db-£70-90, Qb or Quint/b-£100-130, 5-person family room with extra bathroom, no kids under 5, free Wi-Fi, free off-street parking, 5 minutes from station at 4 Arden Street, tel. 01789/299-557, www.theemsley.co.uk, mel@theemsley.co.uk).

$ *Hostel:* **Hemmingford House,** with 134 beds in 2- to 6-bed rooms (half of them en suite), is a 10-minute bus ride from town (from £15/bed, breakfast-£5; take bus #15, #18, or #18A two miles to Alveston; tel. 01789/297-093 or 0845-371-9661, stratford@yha .org.uk).

Eating in Stratford

Restaurants

Stratford's numerous restaurants vie for your pre-theater business, with special hours and meal deals. (Most offer light two- and three-course menus before 19:00.) You'll find many hardworking places on Sheep Street and Waterside. Unfortunately, post-theater dinners are more challenging, as most places close early.

Le Bistro Pierre, across the river near the boating station, is a French eatery that's been impressing Stratford residents. They have indoor or outdoor seating and slow service (£11 two-course lunches; £14 two-course meals before 18:45, otherwise £13-17 main courses; Mon-Fri 12:00-15:00 & 17:00-22:30, Sat 12:00-16:00 & 17:00-23:00, Sun 12:30-16:30 & 18:00-22:00, Swan's Nest, Bridgefoot, tel. 01789/264-804). They also have a pub with a different menu.

Sheep Street Eateries: The next three places, part of the same chain, line up along Sheep Street, offering trendy ambience and modern English cuisine at relatively high prices (all three have pre-theatre menus before 19:00—£13.50 two-course meal, £17 for three courses): **Lambs** is intimate and serves meat, fish, and veggie dishes with panache. The upstairs feels dressy, under low, half-timbered beams (£12-17 main courses, Mon-Fri 17:00-21:00, Wed-Fri also 12:00-14:00, Sat 12:00-21:30, Sun 12:00-15:00 & 18:00-21:00, 12 Sheep Street, tel. 01789/292-554). **The Opposition,** next door, has a less formal "bistro" ambience (£8-10 light meals, £13-16 main courses; Mon-Thu 12:00-14:00 & 17:00-21:00, Fri-Sat until 22:30, closed Sun, tel. 01789/269-980; book in advance if you want to have a post-theater dinner here on Fri or Sat). **The Vintner,** just up the street, has the best reputation and feels even trendier than its siblings, but still with old style. They're known for their £11 burgers (£7-11 light meals, £12-16 main courses, daily 9:30-21:00, until 22:00 Fri-Sat, 4-5 Sheep Street, tel. 01789/297-259).

Indian: **Avon Spice** has a good reputation and good prices (£7-9 main courses, daily 17:00-23:30, until later Fri-Sat, 7 Greenhill Street, tel. 01789/267-067).

Pubs

The Old Thatch Tavern is, according to natives, the best place in town for beer, serving up London-based Fuller's brews. The atmosphere is cozy, and the food is a cut above what you'll get in the other pubs; enjoy it either in the bar, in the tight, candlelit restaurant, or out on the quiet patio (£9-12 main courses, food served Mon-Sat 12:00-21:00, Sun 12:00-15:00, on Greenhill Street overlooking the market square, tel. 01789/295-216).

The Windmill Inn serves decent, modestly priced fare in a 17th-century inn. It combines old and new styles, and—since it's a few steps beyond the heart of the tourist zone—actually attracts some locals as well. Order drinks and food at the bar, settle into a comfy chair or head out to the half-timbered courtyard, and wait for your meal (£8-10 pub grub, food served daily 11:00-21:45, Church Street, tel. 01789/297-687).

The Garrick Inn bills itself as the oldest pub in town, and comes with a cozy, dimly lit restaurant vibe. Choose between the pub or table-service section; either way, you'll dine on bland, pricey pub grub (£9-13 dishes, food served daily 12:00-22:00, Sun until 21:00, 25 High Street, tel. 01789/292-186).

Picnics

With its sprawling and inviting riverfront park, Stratford is a particularly pleasant place to picnic. Choose a bench with views of the river or vacation houseboats, and munch your meal while tossing a few scraps into the river to attract swans. It's a fine way to spend a midsummer night's eve. For groceries or prepared foods, find **Marks & Spencer** on Bridge Street (Mon-Sat 9:00-18:00, Sun 10:30-16:30, small coffee-and-sandwiches café upstairs, tel. 01789/292-430). Across the street, **Sainsbury's Local** stays open later than other supermarkets in town (daily 7:00-22:00).

For fish-and-chips, you have a couple of options: **Barnaby's** is a greasy fast-food joint near the waterfront—but it's convenient if you want to get takeout for the riverside park just across the street (£4-7 fish-and-chips, daily 11:00-20:00, at Sheep Street and Waterside). For better food (but a less convenient location—closer to my recommended B&Bs than to the park), queue up with the locals at **Kingfisher,** then ask for the freshly battered haddock (£6-7 fish-and-chips, Mon 11:30-13:45 & 17:00-21:30, Tue-Sat 11:30-13:45 & 17:00-22:00, closed Sun, a long block up at 13 Ely Street, tel. 01789/292-513).

Tearoom

Henley Street Tea Rooms, across the street from Shakespeare's Birthplace, has indoor seating, outdoor tables right on the main pedestrian mall, and friendly service (£4.25 cream tea, £11 afternoon tea, teas available all day, daily 9:00-17:30, Sept-March until 17:00, 40 Henley Street, tel. 01789/415-572). The same people run Bensons House of Tea & Gift Shop, just down the street (at #33).

Stratford Connections

Remember: When buying tickets or checking schedules, ask for "Stratford-upon-Avon," not just "Stratford." Notice that a single train (running about every 2 hours) connects most of these destinations: Warwick, Leamington Spa (change for Coventry or Oxford), then London.

From Stratford-upon-Avon by Train to: London (5/day direct, more with transfers, 2.25 hours, to Marylebone Station), **Warwick** (10/day, 30 minutes), **Coventry** (at least hourly, 1.75 hours, change in Leamington Spa or Birmingham), **Oxford** (every 2 hours, 1.5 hours, change in Leamington Spa, Birmingham, or Banbury), **Moreton-in-Marsh** (almost hourly, 2.5-3 hours, 2-3 transfers, slow and expensive, better by bus). Train info: tel. 0845-748-4950, www.nationalrail.co.uk.

By Bus to: Cotswolds towns (bus #21 or #22, Mon-Sat 8/day, none on Sun, 35 minutes to **Chipping Campden,** 1-1.25 hours to **Moreton-in-Marsh;** also stops at Broadway, Blockley, and Bourton-on-the-Hill; Johnsons Coaches, tel. 01564/797-070, www.johnsonscoaches.co.uk), **Warwick** (#16 is fastest, hourly, 20 minutes, tel. 01788/535-555, www.stagecoachbus.com), **Coventry** (hourly, 1.25 hours, same bus as Warwick). A direct bus runs to **Oxford** once a day (National Express, tel. 0871-781-8181, www.nationalexpress.com); otherwise 4/day with change in Chipping Norton (train is better). Most intercity buses stop on Stratford's Bridge Street (a block up from the TI). For bus info that covers all the region's companies, call Traveline at tel. 0871-200-2233 (www.travelinemidlands.co.uk).

By Car: Driving is easy and distances are short: **Stow-on-the-Wold** (22 miles), **Warwick** (8 miles), **Coventry** (19 miles).

Route Tips for Drivers

These tips assume you're heading north from Stratford and considering visits to Warwick and/or Coventry (both described in the next chapter).

Stratford to Points North via Warwick and Coventry: Leaving the Bridgefoot garage in downtown Stratford (see map on page 444), circle to the right around the same block, but stay on "the Wark" (Warwick Road, A-439). Warwick is eight miles away. The castle is just south of town on the right. (For parking advice, see page 473.) When you're trying to decide whether to stop in Coventry or not, factor in Birmingham's rush hour—try to avoid driving through that city between 14:00-20:00, if you can (worst on Fri-Sun; on Mon-Thu it generally gets better earlier, around 18:30).

If You're Including Coventry: After touring Warwick Castle, carry on through the center of Warwick town and follow signs to Coventry (still the A-439, then the A-46). If you're stopping in Coventry, follow signs painted on the road to the *City Centre,* and then to *Cathedral Parking.* Grab a place in the high-rise parking lot. Leaving Coventry, follow signs to *Nuneaton* and *M6 North* through lots of sprawl, and you're on your way. (See below.)

If You're Skirting Coventry: Take the M-69 (direction: Leicester) and follow the M-6 as it threads through giant Birmingham.

Once You're on the M-6: The highway divides into the free M-6 and an "M-6 Toll" road (designed to help drivers cut through the Birmingham traffic chaos). Take the toll road—£5.50 is a small price to pay to avoid all the nasty traffic (www.m6toll.co.uk).

When battling through sprawling Birmingham, keep your sights on the M-6. If you're heading for any points north—Ironbridge Gorge (Telford), North Wales, Liverpool, Blackpool, or the Lakes (Kendal for the South Lake District, Keswick for the North Lake District)—just stay relentlessly on the M-6 (direction: North West). Each destination is clearly signed directly from the M-6. For specifics on getting to Ironbridge Gorge, see page 490.

WARWICK AND COVENTRY

Just north of Stratford, you'll find England's single most spectacular castle: Warwick. This medieval masterpiece, which has been turned into a virtual theme park, is extremely touristy—but it's also historic and fun, and may well be Britain's most kid-friendly experience. The town of Warwick, huddled protectively against the castle walls, is a half-timbered delight—enjoyable for a lunch or dinner, or even for an overnight.

A bit farther north sits the decidedly *not* cute city of Coventry—a blue-collar burg that was notoriously obliterated by the Nazi Luftwaffe in World War II. While today's Coventry, having been rebuilt modern and drab, offers little charm, it does feature one of Britain's most poignant WWII sights: the charred husk of its once-grand cathedral, now left as a monument, with the inspiring new cathedral just next door. A few other intriguing museums round out Coventry's appeal.

Planning Your Time

Warwick and Coventry are both ideal on-the-way destinations—lash them onto your itinerary as you head north from Stratford. Warwick Castle deserves at least three hours for a quick visit, but it can be an all-day outing for families. Coventry's cathedral can be seen quickly—in about an hour, if that's all the time you have—though the city's other sights could fill an additional couple of hours. If you're prioritizing, Warwick is (for most) the better stop, with its grand castle and charming town; Coventry is worthwhile primarily for its iconic cathedral ruins and for the chance to see a real, struggling, industrial Midlands city.

Warwick and Coventry

TO TELFORD &
IRONBRIDGE
GORGE

TO
YORK
VIA M-1

TO
CAMBRIDGE
VIA A-14

M-6

M-42

M-6

A-444

A-45

TO
BIRMINGHAM

M-42

COVENTRY

A-435

M-40

A-3400

A-46

A-445

A-45

WARWICK

LEAMINGTON
SPA

A-425

A-423

MARY
ARDEN'S
FARM

A-46

A-439

M-40

A-46

ANNE
HATHAWAY'S
COTTAGE

STRATFORD-
UPON-AVON

B-439

AVON   RIVER

B-4632

A-3400

A-422

A-429

B-4100

MICKLETON

TO
BROADWAY

HIDCOTE
MANOR
GARDEN

BANBURY

TO
OXFORD
& LONDON

N

CHIPPING
CAMPDEN

C O T S W O L D S

MORETON-
IN-MARSH

TO
STOW-
ON-THE-WOLD

TO
OXFORD
& LONDON

- MOTORWAY
- OTHER ROAD
- CASTLE

5 MILES

5 KM

LONDON

DCH

Warwick and Coventry are both reachable by public transportation, but easier for drivers. For tips on splicing Warwick and/ or Coventry into your northbound drive out of Stratford, see that chapter's "Planning Your Time" on page 443 and "Route Tips for Drivers" on page 467.

Warwick

The pleasant town of Warwick ("WAR-ick") is home to England's finest medieval castle, which dominates the banks of the River Avon just upstream from Stratford. The castle is impressive in itself, but its lineup of theme-park-type experiences makes it particularly entertaining, especially for kids. The castle-related attractions, while pricey, offer something for everyone, and on a sunny day the grounds are a treat to explore.

Meanwhile, Warwick town—with a fine market square and some good eateries—goes about its business almost oblivious to the busloads of tourists passing through. While handy for an overnight, Warwick offers relatively little to see beyond its castle.

Orientation to Warwick

With about 24,000 people, Warwick is small and manageable. The castle and old town center sit side by side, with the train station about a mile to the north. From the castle's main gate, a lane leads into the old town center a block away, where you'll find the TI, plenty of eateries (see "Eating in Warwick," later), and a few minor sights.

Tourist Information

Warwick's TI sells same-day tickets to Warwick Castle for £15, an £8 savings over buying them at the castle (Mon-Fri 9:30-16:30, Sat 10:30-16:00, Sun 10:30-15:30, closes 30 minutes earlier Oct-May, The Court House, Jury Street, tel. 01926/492-212, www.visit warwick.co.uk, info@visitwarwick.co.uk). The TI has computers with Internet access (£0.50 to get online for a few minutes) and a room-booking service (pay 10 percent here and the rest at your B&B).

Warwick

P PARKING Ⓑ BUS STOP
ʌ VIEW → ONE-WAY

TO COVENTRY VIA A-429

TRAIN STATION

TO WARWICK PARKWAY TRAIN STN.

SALTISFORD

CAPE RD.

THE ROCK

PRIORY PARK

STATION ROAD

COVENTRY ROAD

ST. JOHNS RD.

TO ②

PRIORY ROAD

BARRACK

NORTHGATE ST.

THE BUTTS

CHAPEL ST.

SMITH

CASTLE HILL

ST. NICH.

ST. NICH. CHURCH ST.

BANBURY RD.

THEATRE

Post

ST. NICHOLAS

MARKET PLACE

④

③

BOWL GR.

LINEN

MKT.

⑥

Ⓑ

BROOK

SWAN ST.

⑤

⑦

CHURCH ST.

JURY ST.

CASTLE LANE

ⓘ

LOCKERS

Stables P

MILL ST.

MILL GARDEN

LORD LEYCESTER HOSPITAL

HIGH ST.

CASTLE ST.

GATE

THE MOUND

WARWICK CASTLE

MILL

FRIARS ST.

WEST GATE

CONSERVATORY

RIVER ISLAND

TO BANBURY & M-40

AVON RIVER

TO HILL CLOSE GDNS.

WEST ST.

TO STRATFORD VIA A-429, A-46 ①

JOUSTING

DCH

200 YARDS

200 METERS

① To Park Cottage
② To Agincourt Lodge
③ The Rose and Crown Pub
④ The Lazy Cow
⑤ The Pot & Fin
⑥ Saffron Gold
⑦ The Art Kitchen

Arrival in Warwick

By Train: Warwick has two train stations; you want the one called simply "Warwick" (Warwick Parkway Station is farther from the castle). Day-trippers might be able to leave bags at the train station's Castle Cars taxi office for an extortionate £10 a day (tel. 01926/494-989). It's much cheaper to carry your bags into town and use the £1 lockers near the castle (at the entrance to the Stables Car Park; if lockers are all taken—unlikely but possible—try asking very nicely at the castle information desk).

A **taxi** from the station to the castle or town center costs about £5. It's a 15-minute, one-mile **walk** from the station to the castle or town center: Exit straight ahead down the street, then bear right onto Coventry Road, where you'll start to see signs for the castle. From here, at the traffic light, turn right onto St. John's Road. At the three-way fork, take Smith Street (the middle fork), which leads you through the old gateway straight up Warwick's High Street. After a long block, the TI appears on your left, with the main castle gate just beyond (up Castle Street). To reach the market square and restaurants from the TI, go one more block and turn right.

By Car: The main Stratford-Coventry road cuts right through Warwick. Coming from Stratford (8 miles to the south), you'll hit the castle parking lots first (£6, buy token from machine to exit lot; if these are full, lurk until a few cars leave and they'll let you in). The four castle lots are expensive, and three of them are a 10- to 15-minute walk from the actual castle; the closest one, just off Castle Lane, is the Stables Car Park, which costs more (£10). Street parking in the town center is cheaper (less than £2), but there's a two- to three-hour maximum—not enough time to fully experience the castle.

Sights in Warwick

▲▲Warwick Castle

Almost too groomed and organized, this theme park of a castle gives its crowds of visitors a decent value for the stiff entry fee. The

cash-poor but enterprising Earl of Warwick hired the folks at Merlin Entertainments (which owns many other big-name British attractions) to wring maximum tourist dollars out of his castle. They've made the place entertaining indeed, and packed it with lively exhibits...but also watered down the history a bit, and added several layers of gift shops, overpriced concessions, and nickel-and-dime add-ons. The greedy feel of the place can be a little annoying, considering the already-steep admission. But—especially for kids—there just isn't a better medieval castle experience in Britain. With a lush, green, grassy moat and fairy-tale fortifications, Warwick Castle will entertain you from dungeon to lookout.

The castle is a 14th- and 15th-century fortified shell, holding an 18th- and 19th-century royal residence, surrounded by another

one of dandy "Capability" Brown's land-scape jobs (like at Blenheim Palace). You can tour the sumptuous staterooms, climb the towers and ramparts for the views, stroll through themed exhibits populated by aristocratic wax figures, explore the sprawling grounds and gardens, and—best of all—interact with costumed docents who explain the place and perform fantastic demonstrations of medieval weapons and other skills.

Cost: Steep £23 entry fee (£16 for kids under age 12, £17 for seniors) includes gardens and most castle attractions except for the gory Castle Dungeon (£9) and the *Merlin: The Dragon Tower* show (£4). Combo-tickets are available. English Heritage members get a 50 percent discount at the door.

Hours: Open daily April-Sept 10:00-18:00, Oct-March 10:00-17:00.

Advance Tickets: Booking in advance at www.warwick-castle.com saves substantial money and time waiting in the ticket line (even better, advance tickets bought at the Warwick TI let you avoid the line, and save you £8).

Audioguides and Guidebooks: The dry, nine-stop audio-guide leads you through the state rooms (£2.50; £4/2 people), but the posted information is more concise and interesting. The £5 guidebook gives you nearly the same script in souvenir-booklet form. (A children's audioguide, called "A Knight's Tale," is £1.50.) The audioguides and the guidebook are available at the gift shop near the entrance (not the ticket booth). If you tour the castle without help, pick the brains of the earnest and talkative docents.

Information: Recorded info tel. 0871-265-2000, or call 01926/495-421 Mon-Fri 9:00-17:00, www.warwick-castle.com.

Demonstrations and Events: It's the well-presented demos and other events that make this castle particularly worthwhile. These can include jousting competitions, archers showing off their longbow skills, sword fights, jester acts, falconry shows, and dem-onstrations of the trebuchet (like a catapult) and ballista (a type of giant slingshot). They're offered year-round, but most frequently in summer and on weekends and school holidays. When you buy your castle ticket, be sure to pick up the daily events flier and plan your day around these events.

Eating at the Castle: Consider bringing your own picnic to enjoy at the gorgeous grounds. Otherwise you'll be left with overpriced concessions stands serving variations on the same mass-produced food. The stands are scattered around the castle grounds (and marked on the map you get with your ticket). **The Coach House** has cafeteria fare and grungy seating (located just before the turnstiles). **The Undercroft** has a sandwich buffet line (located inside, in basement of palace); you can sit under medieval vaults or escape with your food and picnic outside. The **riverside pavilion** sells sandwiches and fish-and-chips, and has fine outdoor seating (in park just before the bridge, behind castle). Fortunately, just 100 yards from the castle turnstiles—through a tiny gate in the wall—is Warwick town's workaday commercial district, with several better (and better-value) lunch options. It's worth the walk (see "Eating in Warwick," later).

 Self-Guided Tour: Buy your ticket and head through the turnstile into the moat area, where you'll get your first view of the dramatic castle. In good weather, this lawn-like zone is filled with tents populated by costumed docents demonstrating everyday medieval lifestyles.

From the moat, two different entrance gateways lead to the

castle's **inner courtyard.** Within these mighty walls, there's something for every taste (described below); look for signs for where to enter each one.

The bulge of land at the far end of the courtyard, called **The Mound**, is where the original Norman castle of 1068 stood. Under this "motte," the wooden stockade (the "bailey") defined the courtyard in the way the castle walls do today. You can climb up to the top for a view down into the castle courtyard (do this at the end, since you can exit down the other side, toward the riverbank).

The main attractions are in the largest buildings along the side of the courtyard: the Great Hall, five lavish staterooms, and the chapel. Progressing through these rooms, you'll see how the castle complex evolved over the centuries, from the militarized Middle Ages to civilized Victorian times, from a formidable defensive fortress to a genteel manor home.

Enter through the cavernous **Great Hall,** decorated with suits of equestrian armor. Adjoining the Great Hall is the state dining room, with portraits of English kings and princes. Then follow the

one-way route through the **staterooms,** keeping ever more esteemed company as you go—the rooms closest to the center of the complex were the most exclusive, reserved only for those especially close to the Earl of Warwick. You'll pass through a series of three drawing rooms (abbreviated from "withdrawing," from a time when these provided a retreat into a more intimate area after a to-do in the larger, more public rooms): first, one decorated in a deep burgundy; then the cedar drawing room, with intricately carved wood paneling, a Waterford crystal chandelier, and a Carrara marble fireplace; and finally the green drawing room, with a beautiful painted coffered ceiling and wax figures of Henry VIII and his six wives. The sumptuous Queen Anne Room was decorated in preparation for a planned 1704 visit by the monarch (unfortunately, Queen Anne never came—she got wind that one of her ladies-in-waiting, with whom she was fiercely competitive, was also coming, so she canceled at the last minute). Finally comes the blue boudoir, an oversized closet decorated in blue silk wallpaper. The portrait of King Henry VIII over the fireplace faces a clock once owned by Marie-Antoinette.

On your way out, you'll pass the earl's private **chapel.** The earl's family worshipped in the pews in front of the stone screen, while the servants would stand behind it. Notice the ornate woodcarved relief depicting a scene of the Greeks fighting the Amazons, based on a painting by Peter Paul Rubens. The organ in the back of the chapel was powered by a hand-pumped bellows.

Back out in the courtyard, to the left of the staterooms, are the entrances to two other, less impressive exhibits. The **Kingmaker** exhibit (set in 1471) uses mannequins, sound effects, and smells to show how medieval townsfolk prepared for battle—from the blacksmiths and armory, to the wardrobe, to the final rallying cry, with costumed docents standing by. The **Secrets and Scandals of the Royal Weekend Party** exhibit lets you explore staterooms staged as they appeared in 1898, but with an added narrative element: The philandering Daisy Maynard Greville, Countess of Warwick—considered the most beautiful woman in Victorian England—is throwing a party, and big-name aristocrats are in attendance, including a young Winston Churchill. Among the guests is the Prince of

Wales (the future King Edward VII), with whom Daisy reportedly also had a long-time affair. Gossipy "servants" clue you in on who's flirting with whom. The rooms are populated by eerily convincing Madame Tussauds-style wax figures, and posted information and soundtracks loosely narrate the scandal. Unfortunately, it's more dry than titillating, and a bit hard to follow unless you're versed in the ins and outs of late-19th-century aristocratic intrigue.

You can climb up onto the **ramparts and tower**—a one-way, no-return route that leads you up and down (on very tight spiral stairs) the tallest tower, leaving you at a fun perch from which to fire your imaginary longbow. The halls and stairs can be very crowded with young kids, and—as the signs warn—it takes 530 steep steps (both up and down) to follow the whole route; claustrophobes should consider it carefully.

The **Princess Tower** offers children (ages 3-8) the chance to dress up as princesses and princes for a photo op. While it's included in the castle ticket, those interested must first sign up for a 15-minute time slot at the information tent in the middle of the courtyard, near the staterooms.

Two other pricey and skippable add-on attractions can also be entered from the courtyard (if you didn't buy a combo-ticket at the entrance, you can buy individual tickets at the information tent near the staterooms). **The Castle Dungeon,** a gory, tacky knock-off of the London Dungeon, features a series of costumed hosts who entertain and spook visitors on a 45-minute tour. *Merlin: The Dragon Tower,* a 20-minute live-action stage show with special effects, is based on a popular BBC television series.

Outside of the inner courtyard area are additional diversions. Surrounding everything is a lush, peacock-patrolled, picnic-perfect park, complete with a Victorian rose garden. The castle grounds are often enlivened by a knight in shining armor on a horse or a merry band of musical jesters. The grassy moat area is typically filled with costumed characters and demonstrations, including archery and falconry. Near the entrance to the complex is the **Pageant Playground,** with medieval-themed slides and climbing areas for kids. Down by the river is a bridge across to River Island, and—tucked around the back of the castle—a restored **mill and engine house,** with an exhibit that explains how the castle was electrified in 1894.

More Sights in Warwick

While Warwick has a few attractions beyond the castle, most are not that exciting.

The most photogenic building in town (aside from the castle) is the **Lord Leycester Hospital,** a gaggle of adjoining 14th-cen-

tury half-timbered houses next to the southern gate of High Street. Converted into a "hospital" (rest home for the elderly or ill) in 1571, it has a chapel, great hall, maze of old rooms, and pretty garden (overpriced at £5, borrow self-guided tour brochure at entry, Tue-Sun 10:00-17:00, until 16:30 in winter, closed Mon year-round except Bank Holidays, 60 High Street, tel. 01926/491-422, www.lordleycester.com).

Garden fans will find three good ones in Warwick. Most appealing is the **Mill Garden,** down the quaint and half-timbered Mill Street from the castle gate; this small garden, which adjoins the castle property, has fantastic views of the River Avon and castle (£2, April-Oct daily 9:00-18:00, closed Nov-March, 55 Mill Street, tel. 01926/492-

877). **Hill Close Gardens,** at the other end of town near the racecourse, has 16 small Victorian garden plots and an erratically open café (£3.50, April-mid-Oct Mon-Thu 10:30-15:30, Fri 10:30-17:00, Sat 11:00-17:00, Sun 14:00-17:00; shorter hours and closed Sat-Sun off-season, Bread and Meat Close, tel. 01926/493-339, www .hillclosegardens.com). The garden at the **Lord Leycester Hospital** (described above) rounds out your options.

Sleeping in Warwick

(area code: 01926)

$$ Park Cottage fills a creaky 1521 half-timbered house (once the dairy for the castle) with seven rooms and teddy-on-the-beddy touches. It's on the main road at the opposite end of town from the train station (near the racecourse and the castle), but Stuart and Janet will pick you up if their schedule allows (Sb-£65, Db-£75-85, family room-£12.50 extra per child, free Wi-Fi, free parking, 113 West Street/A-429, tel. 01926/410-319, www.parkcottagewarwick .co.uk, janet@parkcottagewarwick.co.uk).

Several B&Bs line Emscote Road (A-445) at the train-station end of town. The closest to town—and best—is **$$ Agincourt Lodge,** renting six comfortable rooms in an 1854 Victorian house (S-£45, Sb-£50-58 depending on size, D with private b in the hall-£65, Db-£73, larger Db with four-poster bed-£83, Tb-£85, Qb-£95, free Wi-Fi, free parking, 36 Coten End, tel. 01926/499-399, www.agincourtlodge.co.uk, enquiries@agincourtlodge.co.uk, Mike and Marisa).

Eating in Warwick

All of these are on or within a short stroll of Market Place.

The Rose and Crown is a popular gastropub serving English food with a modern twist. Enjoy the cozy but not claustrophobic interior (order food at the bar, or dine in the table-service area), or sit outside (lunch—£5-7 light meals, £11-13 larger dishes; dinner—£11-18 main courses, £3 sides; food served daily 8:00-22:00, open longer for drinks, 30 Market Place, tel. 01926/411-117).

The Lazy Cow, a newer competitor a few doors down, is a bit more trendy and pricey, with a focus on steaks (in the open kitchen, see the aging cabinet and the indoor barbecue). Vegetarians may be put off by both the meat-heavy menu and the cow-themed decor (£6-8 starters, £10-20 main courses, open Mon-Thu 7:00-23:00, Fri-Sat until 24:00, Sun until 22:30, food served in bar until 19:00 Fri-Sat, in sit-down restaurant until closing, 10 Theatre Street, tel. 08451-200-666, www.thelazycowwarwick.co.uk).

The Pot & Fin serves up excellent fish-and-chips in a charming, rustic cottage setting a block off of Market Place (toward the castle). Everything is made fresh in-house. If you order takeaway (£4-7), you can grab one of the tables; or head upstairs for the pricier table-service menu, with £8 main courses (Tue-Sat 12:00-14:00 & 17:00-21:00, 48 Brook Street, tel. 01926/492-426).

Saffron Gold is a well-regarded Indian restaurant serving tasty £7-13 meals in an upscale setting with good service (Sun-Thu 17:30-23:30, Fri-Sat 17:30-24:00, just a block off Market Square but tricky to find—in drab Westgate House building near the Marks & Spencer, on Market Street, tel. 01926/402-061).

The Art Kitchen, right on the main pedestrian shopping street, is a mod Thai bistro surrounding a bar (£6-8 lunches, £8-17 dinners, daily 12:00-23:00, 7 Swan Street, tel. 01926/494-303).

Warwick Connections

Warwick is on the train line between Birmingham's Moor Street Station and London's Marylebone Station; most other connections require a change in the adjacent town of Leamington Spa.

From Warwick by Train to: Leamington Spa (about 2/hour, 3-10 minutes), **Stratford** (10/day, 30 minutes—buses are better, see below), **Coventry** (2/hour, 30-60 minutes, transfer in Leamington Spa), **Oxford** (2/hour, 50-70 minutes, transfer in Leamington Spa), **London**'s Marylebone Station (2/hour direct, 1.5 hours). Train info: Tel. 0845-748-4950, www.nationalrail.co.uk.

By Bus to: Stratford-upon-Avon (hourly, 20 minutes, bus #X17, also slower #15/ #18), **Coventry** (10/day, 1 hour, bus #X17, www.stagecoachbus.com).

Coventry

Coventry was bombed to smithereens in 1940 by the Nazi Luftwaffe (air force). From that point on, the German phrase for "to really blast the heck out of a place" was (roughly) "to coventrate" it. But Coventry rose from its ashes, and its message to our world is one of forgiveness, reconciliation, and the importance of peace.

Before it was infamous as a victim of World War II, Coventry had an illustrious history. According to legend, Coventry's most

famous hometown girl, Lady Godiva, rode bareback and barenaked through the town in the 11th century to convince her stubborn husband to lower taxes. You'll see her bronze statue on the market square a block from the cathedral, and a fun exhibit about her in the Herbert Museum.

The cloth trade made Coventry one of England's leading cities in the Middle Ages. Its fortunes rose and fell over time, and by the 20th century it had become a major industrial center—first as Britain's main bicycle manufacturer, later as its top car-making city, and eventually as a major center of armaments and aircraft assembly (making it a key target for the Nazis' Luftwaffe bombers). The city was utterly devastated by the Blitz; aside from the human toll, its greatest loss was its proud and famous St. Michael's Cathedral, which burned to the ground—the only English cathedral destroyed by the Nazis. Tellingly, Coventry's sister cities include two other places synonymous with horrific WWII destruction: Dresden, Germany, and Volgograd (formerly Stalingrad), Russia.

Today's Coventry isn't pretty. While many other WWII-damaged English towns were rebuilt quaint and cobbled, Coventry is all characterless modern concrete. But its cathedral—combining the still bombed-out shell of the old building, and a highly symbolic, starkly modern new one—is poignant and inspiring, and its other museums are quite good (and free). While I wouldn't go out of my way to visit Coventry, if you're passing by, consider stopping off to browse through a bit of normal, everyday, urban England.

Orientation to Coventry

Coventry is a big city—with about 310,000 people—but everything of interest to visitors is in the small central core, which is bound by a busy ring road. You can walk from one end of the ring to the other in about 15 minutes. The train station is just south of the ring; the cathedral, TI, St. Anne's Guildhall, and Herbert Museum are in the northeastern part of the ring; and the Transport Museum is about a 10-minute walk west of the cathedral.

Tourist Information

The TI, at the base of the cathedral tower, hands out free maps and brochures (April-Sept Mon-Fri 10:00-17:00, Sat 10:00-16:30, Sun 10:00-12:30 & 13:30-16:30, closes 30 minutes earlier Oct-March, may move in 2014—check online for location or call; tel. 024/7622-5616, www.visitcoventryandwarwickshire.co.uk, tic@coventry.gov.uk).

Arrival in Coventry

If you're passing through Coventry by public transportation, baggage storage is a problem—there's none at the train station. The cathedral and Transport Museum will store your bags while you visit each sight, but otherwise you're stuck. If your train route takes you through Birmingham's New Street Station (a transit hub for the area), consider using the left luggage desk there.

By Train: From the train station (which sits just outside the ring road), it's about a 15-minute walk to the cathedral. Exit straight ahead and find the blue line in the pavement, which leads you through the confusing maze of ring road overpasses to the edge of downtown; from there, simply follow signs for the cathedral (or the Transport Museum) through the modern shopping district. The cathedral is the taller of the two pointy spires.

By Car: Use the pay parking lot on Cox Street (just off of Fairfax Street), near the cathedral. From the ring road, take junction (exit) 2. The parking lot is basically under the ring road, across from the Coventry Sports and Leisure Centre.

Sights in Coventry

▲▲St. Michael's Cathedral

The symbol of Coventry is the bombed-out hulk of its old cathedral, with the huge new one adjoining it. This inspiring complex welcomes visitors.

Cost and Hours: The ruins of the old cathedral are free to enter (gates open daily roughly 9:00-17:00), though you'll pay to climb the tower (see below). Entering the new cathedral costs a hefty £8; consider it a donation to a worthwhile cause (Mon-Sat 10:00-17:00, Sun 12:00-16:00, last entry one hour before closing). During the afternoon service or evensong, admission is free (Mon-Fri at 17:15, Sat-Sun at 16:00, evensong predictable only on Sun, otherwise service may be spoken). The museum and café are closed on Sundays.

Services: The front desk will hold your bags while you visit.

Information: Tel. 024/7652-1200, www.coventrycathedral.org.uk.

Tower Climb: You can walk 181 steps up to the top of the tower for views over the cathedral complex and city. Buy your ticket and enter at the TI, at the base of the tower (£2.50, open same hours as TI, last entry 30 minutes before closing).

◐ Self-Guided Tour: A visit to the cathedral complex has two parts: First explore the ruins of the original building, then head into the new cathedral. You can pick up the free *Guide to the Ruined Cathedral* pamphlet at the TI; the new cathedral also hands out a floor plan that includes both the old and new churches.

Old Cathedral Ruins: Coventry's grand Perpendicular Gothic cathedral was the second to stand on this spot (built 1373-1460). Its towering, 303-foot-tall steeple—the third-highest in England—was a symbol for the city. On the night of November 14, 1940, Nazi Luftwaffe bombers filled the skies above Coventry. They dropped incendiary devices (firebombs) to light up the ground so they could see their targets. One of these hit the roof of the cathedral, which was quickly consumed in flames. (The tower survived.) Today the footprint and surviving walls stand as a testament to the travesty of war.

At the apse of the ruined structure (far end from tower) is a replica of the **charred cross;** the original is inside the new cathe-

dral. While surveying the wreckage after the bombing, workers found these beams lying on the ground in the shape of a cross—so they lashed them together and erected it here. The message "Father Forgive" (spoken by Christ on the cross) makes it clear that this is a symbol not of anger, but of reconciliation. Every Friday at 12:00, the Coventry Litany of Reconciliation is said in these ruins—asking forgiveness for the seven deadly sins.

Various **monuments** are scattered around the ruins. Directly to the left of the charred cross is the bronze memorial to an early 20th-century bishop. In a chilling bit of irony, there's a swastika on his headband—dating from a time when this was just a good-luck symbol, before it had been appropriated by Hitler and painted on the planes that destroyed this place. Closer to the tower, you'll see the modern *Ecce Homo* sculpture (depicting Christ before Pilate) and a reconciliation monument, showing two people embracing across a gulf.

Before going inside the new cathedral building, head out to the plaza just beyond the complex and look back at it: old and new cathedrals, set perpendicular to each other, creating a continuous ensemble of worship. The large sculpture on the side of the new cathedral depicts St. Michael triumphing over the devil, as foretold by the Book of Revelation.

The cathedral's visitors center is to the right; in this undercroft is a museum about the history of all three cathedrals that have stood on this site, with artifacts from each one. (Also notice, to your left, the glassy entrance to the Herbert Art Gallery and Museum—a good post-cathedral stop, it's described later.)

• *Now head into the new cathedral interior. If the main door (up the stairs) is open, head inside and buy a ticket; otherwise, enter through the visitors center.*

New Cathedral: By the morning after the cathedral burned, the people of Coventry had already decided to rebuild it. The architect Basil Spence won the contest to design this re-imagining of the important church: The ruined old cathedral represents death and sacrifice, while the new structure—part of the same continuum—represents resurrection. While at first the cold gray walls inside the building make it feel gloomy and uninspired—almost (perhaps appropriately) like a giant bomb shelter—its highly symbolic design reveals itself to those who take the time to explore it.

Stand at the top of the main nave, on the giant letters that create a **gathering area** for the congregation. In the center of the nave near these letters, look for the maple leaf embedded in the floor—a thank-you to the Canadians whose donations helped fund this building. Looking down the nave, notice that the cathedral follows the same basic traditional layout of much older churches (long nave, choir area, high altar and apse at the far end) but features decidedly modern designs and decorations.

Turn right to take in the gigantic and gorgeous stained-glass window of the **baptistery**—a starburst with intensely warm colors at the center, cool colors at the perimeter. Beneath this is the baptismal font, which is carved into a chunk of rock from the hills near Bethlehem. Looking down the nave, notice that otherwise, the cathedral has relatively little stained glass...from here, at least.

Across the nave from the baptistery, walk up the stairs into the **Chapel of Unity.** With its circular shape and floor mosaics depicting the five continents, this chapel preaches understanding among all Christian faiths—an ecumenism that echoes the cathedral's mission of reconciliation.

Back out in the main nave, walk down the central aisle. Notice the well-worn **copper coins** embedded in the floor. Dating from 1962 (when the cathedral was consecrated), these help choir members keep a straight line as they process into the church.

Pause in front of the **choir**, with its modern, dramatically prickly canopy, designed to evoke Jesus' crown of thorns—or possibly birds in flight. The Christmas-tree-shaped tower marks the seat of the bishop.

The green artwork that fills the far wall is not a fresco but a 74-foot-by-38-foot **tapestry** that depicts Jesus in a Byzantine Pantocrator ("creator of all") pose, surrounded by symbols of the four evangelists. Notice the faint outline of a small human being standing protected between Jesus' feet.

Turn around and look back down the **nave.** Remember how stained glass seemed in short supply from the far end of the church? From this direction, you can clearly see how the sawtooth-shaped design allows for row after row of colorful glass to be seen by worshippers as they return to their seats after taking communion. At the far end, notice that instead of a wall sealing off the church, there's a giant glass window—to emphasize the connection between this new cathedral and the old one just outside. Both buildings also use the same local red sandstone. This is intended to be one big, unified space.

Now circle around the left side of the choir, to the back-left corner of the church, where stairs lead down to WCs, the church museum, and a café. Hanging at the top of the stairwell is the **original charred cross** that was found in the ruins of the cathedral after the bombing.

Now cross toward the other side of the church. Right in the middle, you'll pass a misshapen cross above the main altar; in its center is a smaller cross consisting of three nails from the medieval church, which were also found in the wreckage. This **"cross of nails"** has become a symbol worldwide for postwar reconciliation. Several such crosses have been made, many of them given to other cities that were devastated by the war; one stands above the high altar of the rebuilt Frauenkirche in Dresden, Germany. (You can buy a small replica of the cross of nails in the cathedral shop, across from the main door.)

Continue to the far side of the church. You'll pass the **Chapel of Gethsemane,** with a crown of thorns-shaped screen around the window. Beyond that, walk down the hallway and into the **Chapel of Christ the Servant.** The clear (rather than stained-glass) windows remind worshippers to extend their faith and stewardship outside the walls of this building. Also displayed here are fragments of the old cathedral's original stained-glass windows.

Near the Cathedral

▲Herbert Art Gallery and Museum

This expanded, impressive museum complex and cultural center combines town history exhibits and art collections. Since it's free and directly behind the cathedral, it's well worth dropping in if you have some time to spare. As there are several different exhibits—both permanent and temporary—be sure to explore the entire building (ask for a floor plan).

Cost and Hours: Free, Mon-Sat 10:00-16:00, Sun 12:00-16:00, Jordan Well, tel. 024/7683-2386, www.theherbert.org.

Visiting the Gallery: Near the entrance is the History Gallery, with enjoyable interactive exhibits that trace the city's story from its beginnings to the Blitz to today. You'll see actual artifacts from the Blitz and hear locals describe living through it. Beyond the information desk are small exhibits on peace and reconciliation (Coventry has understandably become a very pacifist city), and the small but entertaining Discover Godiva exhibit, which examines the legend (and possible fact) of Lady Godiva. Her husband, Earl Leofric, increased taxes dramatically on his subjects. She pleaded with him for a tax cut, and he agreed—provided that she ride naked through town on horseback. A fun animated video shows how the legend evolved, with each generation of storytellers adding their own flourishes. One popular version says that the townspeople respectfully averted their eyes, except for one "Peeping Tom"—who was struck blind for his voyeurism. You'll also see paintings of the Lady, clips from movies about her, and companies that have appropriated her as a mascot. Upstairs is the museum's modest but enjoyable gallery of sculpture, Old Masters, modern and contemporary artwork, and temporary exhibits.

▲St. Mary's Guildhall

The origins of this fine half-timbered building, sitting next to the cathedral, are rooted in the fascinating history of England's often-overlooked King Henry VI (r. 1422-1461). Afflicted with what today would be diagnosed as catatonic schizophrenia, Henry seemed to his medieval subjects to exist between our world and another—he'd drift into a trance and be unreachable for days or weeks at a time, and emerge reporting the vibrant visions he'd had. During the Wars of the Roses, Henry briefly moved the capital of England to Coventry, creating a special bond with the city. After his death, Henry's corpse reportedly bled in front of observers, leading them to conclude that he was miraculous. A cult of followers sprang up around Henry, centered here in Coventry. People began to pray for divine intervention from the man they came to call "Saint Henry." One young girl, who had been crushed under a wagon wheel, was miraculously healed when her mother prayed to Henry. (The pope sent delegates to verify some 300 reported miracles, and Henry would likely have been formally canonized—if his son, Henry VII, hadn't refused to pay the hefty sum for sainthood. By the time his grandson, Henry VIII, broke away from the Vatican, all bets were off.) The local businessmen's guilds of Coventry built this fine hall to venerate their favorite king and unofficial saint.

Cost and Hours: Free, £0.50 pamphlet, £1 detailed descriptions, Easter-early Oct Sun-Thu 10:00-16:00, closed Fri-Sat, during events, and off-season, tel. 024/7683-3328, www.coventry.gov.uk/stmarys.

Visiting the Guildhall: While it's fun and a bit spooky to explore the maze of tight old rooms, the highlight here is the great

hall. The semicircular stained-glass window traces Henry VI's royal lineage—that's him in the center, flanked by his supposed ancestors, William the Conqueror, King Arthur, and the Roman emperor Constantine (notice that Constantine's cross is bigger than the others'—his mother, St. Helen, supposedly discovered Jesus' "true cross"). Below the window is a remarkable, if faded, 14th-century tapestry that also honors Henry (ask the attendants to briefly turn on the light to see it better). More than 500 years old, this tapestry is still in situ—in the location for which it was intended. The hall is staffed by knowledgeable attendants who love to explain its history. If you dare, also ask them about the constant ghost sightings in this building—so frequent they've become routine.

▲Coventry Transport Museum

A 10-minute walk from the cathedral, this good museum pays homage to Coventry's car-making heritage. For much of the 20th century, Coventry was the main auto production center of Britain, and in the 1950s and '60s, more than a third of the city's population built cars. On two floors of a sprawling modern building, you can see the first, fastest, and most famous cars that came from this "British Detroit." The museum also shows off a collection of tractors, bicycles, motorcycles, and tanks...if it had wheels, they made it here. For car lovers, it's worth ▲▲.

Cost and Hours: Free, good £5 souvenir guidebook, £1 lockers for use only while on the premises, daily 10:00-17:00, tel. 024/7623-4270, www.transport-museum.com.

Visiting the Museum: The exhibit focuses on local production (Daimler, Standard, Mandslay, and others), but a few famous non-Coventry cars are also included, such as Monty's staff car, Princess Di's modest Austin Metro car (a gift from Prince Charles before they married), a DeLorean, a 1949 Land Rover, and Ewan McGregor's motorcycle from the BBC series *Long Way Round*. Aside from the cars, you'll find the "Landmarques Show" (re-created streets of old-

time Coventry, circa 1868-1948), the "Coventry Blitz Experience" (a low-tech, walk-through simulation of war-torn Coventry with sound and light effects), and—upstairs—the thought-provoking "Ghost Town?" exhibit (tracing the decline of the Coventry auto industry from 1980 to 2010).

Coventry Connections

From Coventry by Train to: Warwick (2/hour, 30-60 minutes, change in Leamington Spa), **Stratford-upon-Avon** (at least hourly, 1.75 hours, change in Leamington Spa or Birmingham), **Oxford** (hourly, 50 minutes), **London**'s Euston Station (6/hour, 1-2 hours), **Telford Central** (near Ironbridge Gorge; 2/hour, 1.5 hours, change in Birmingham). Train info: Tel. 0845-748-4950, www.nationalrail.co.uk.

IRONBRIDGE GORGE

The Industrial Revolution was born in the Severn River Valley. In its glory days, this valley (blessed with abundant deposits of iron ore and coal, and a river for transport) gave the world its first iron wheels, steam-powered locomotive, and cast-iron bridge (begun in 1779). The museums in Ironbridge Gorge, which capture the flavor of the Victorian Age, take you back into the days when Britain was racing into the modern era, and pulling the rest of the West with her.

Near the end of the 20th century, the valley went through a second transformation: Photos taken just 30 years ago show an industrial wasteland. Today the Severn River Valley is lush and lined with walks and parklands. Even its bricks, while still smoke-stained, seem warmer and more inviting.

Planning Your Time

Without a car, Ironbridge Gorge isn't worth the headache. Drivers can slip it in between the Cotswolds/Stratford/Warwick and points north (such as the Lake District or North Wales). Speed demons zip in for a midday tour of the Blists Hill Victorian Town, look at the famous Iron Bridge and quaint Industrial Age town that sprawls around it, and head out. For an overnight visit, arrive in the early evening to browse the town, see the bridge, and walk along the river. Spend the morning touring the Blists Hill Victorian Town, have lunch there, and head to your next destination.

With more time—say, a full month in Britain—I'd spend two nights and a leisurely day: 9:30-Iron Bridge and the town; 10:30-Museum of the Gorge; 11:30-Coalbrookdale Museum of

Iron; 14:30-Blists Hill Victorian Town; then dinner at the recommended Golden Ball Inn.

Orientation to Ironbridge Gorge

The town is just a few blocks gathered around the Iron Bridge, which spans the peaceful, tree-lined Severn River. While the smoke-belching bustle is long gone, knowing that this wooded, sleepy river valley was the "Silicon Valley" of the 19th century makes wandering its brick streets almost a pilgrimage. The actual museum sites are scattered over three miles. The modern cooling towers (for coal, not nuclear energy) that loom ominously over these red-brick remnants seem strangely appropriate.

Tourist Information

The TI is in the Museum of the Gorge, just west of the town center. It has lots of booklets for sale, including pamphlets describing nearby walks (daily 10:00-17:00, tel. 01952/433-424, www.iron bridge.org.uk or www.ironbridgeguide.info).

Getting Around Ironbridge Gorge

By Bus: Gorge Connect buses link the various museums, running every 30 minutes on weekends and Bank Holidays from Easter through October—and every day in late July and August (£1.50/ride, £2 day ticket, free with Passport Ticket—described on page 492; runs 9:30-17:00, no buses Nov-Easter; see schedule at www.telford.gov.uk—search site for "Gorge Connect"; tel. 01952/200-005).

If you're waiting for the Gorge Connect bus on the main road by the bridge, or at a stop for one of the less-popular museums, make sure the driver sees you or the bus may not stop. For connections from the Telford train or bus stations to the sights, see the end of this chapter.

Bus **#88**, operated by Arriva, connects the Museum of Iron (stop: Coalbrookdale School Road) and the TI in Ironbridge, but it runs infrequently (roughly 1/hour).

By Car: Routes to the attractions are well-signed, so driving should be a snap (museum parking described later).

By Taxi: Taxis will pick up at the museums, making this a good option if you don't have a car and the bus is not convenient. Call Central Taxis at tel. 01952/501-050.

By Bike: An eight-mile, relatively flat, circular bike path connects all of the museums except the Broseley Pipeworks. You can rent a bike from **The Bicycle Hub**, five miles north of Ironbridge in Telford (£15/day, helmet-£1, lock-£1; Mon-Sat 9:00-18:00, closed Sun; smart to book ahead, especially in nice weather—£25 refundable booking fee; international travelers must leave passport; within the Telford Town Park Visitor Centre—follow Hinkshay Road to Dark Lane, free parking at the Wonderland kiddie park, then 3-minute walk; tel. 01952/883-249; www.the bicyclehub.co.uk). If you're tempted to test a tandem, try their sister shop, **Bicycles by Design.** It's next to the Jackfield Tile Museum, about a mile from the bridge (£40/day; Mon-Fri 10:00-17:00, Sat 9:00-17:00, closed Sun; must leave passport, Church Road, tel. 01952/459-900, www.bicycles-by-design.co.uk).

Sights in Ironbridge Gorge

▲▲Iron Bridge

While England was at war with her American colonies, this first cast-iron bridge was built in 1779 to show off a wonderful new

building material. Lacking experience with cast iron, the builders erred on the side of sturdiness and constructed it as if it were made out of wood. Notice that the original construction used traditional timber-jointing techniques rather than rivets. (Any rivets are from later repairs.) The valley's centerpiece is free, open all the time, and thought-provoking. Walk across the bridge to the tollhouse. Inside, read the fee schedule and notice the subtle slam against royalty. (England was not immune to the revolutionary sentiment brewing in the colonies at this time.) Pedestrians paid half a penny to cross; poor people crossed cheaper by coracle—a crude tub-like wood-and-canvas shuttle ferry. Cross back to the town and enjoy a pleasant walk downstream along the towpath. Where horses once dragged boats laden with Industrial Age cargo, locals now walk their dogs.

Ironbridge Gorge Museums

Ten museums located within a few miles of each other focus on the Iron Bridge and all that it represents. Not all the sights are worth your time. The Blists Hill Victorian Town is by far the best. The Museum of the Gorge attempts to give a historical overview, but the displays are humble—its most interesting feature is the 12-minute video. The Coalbrookdale Museum of Iron tells the story of iron—interesting to metalheads. Enginuity is just for kids. And the original Abraham Darby Furnace (free to view, located across from the Museum of Iron), is a shrine to 18th-century technology. Before visiting any of these places, it helps to see the introductory movie at the Museum of the Gorge, to put everything

Ironbridge Gorge

1. Library House Guest House
2. Tontine Hotel
3. Calcutts House
4. Coalport Youth Hostel
5. To Wilderhope Manor Youth Hostel
6. Restaurant Severn
7. Pondicherry Restaurant
8. Da Vinci's Restaurant
9. The Golden Ball Inn
10. The Coalbrookdale Inn
11. The Malt House Bar & Rest.
12. Bike Rentals (2)
13. Swimming Pool

Ⓑ BUS STOP
— ROAD
◉ ROUNDABOUTS
Ⓟ PARKING
--- PATH

1 MILE
1 KILOMETER

into context.

Cost: This group of widely scattered sights has varied admission charges (most sights £4-9; Blists Hill is £16); the £24 **Passport Ticket** (families-£65) covers admission to all of them and the Gorge Connect bus. If you're visiting the area's top three sights—Blists Hill Victorian Town, the Museum of the Gorge, and the Coalbrookdale Museum of Iron—you'll save about £4 with the Passport Ticket.

Hours: Unless otherwise noted, the sights share the same opening hours: daily 10:00-17:00.

Parking: To see the most significant sights by car, you'll park three times: once in town (either in the pay-and-display lot just over the bridge or at the Museum of the Gorge—the Iron Bridge and Gorge Museum are connected by an easy, flat walk); once at the Blists Hill parking lot; and once outside of the Coalbrookdale Museum of Iron (Enginuity is across the lot, and the Darby Houses are a three-minute uphill hike away). While you'll pay separately to park at the Museum of the Gorge, a single ticket is good for both pay-and-display lots at the Coalbrookdale Museum and Blists Hill.

Information: Tel. 01952/433-424, www.ironbridge.org.uk.

Museum of the Gorge

Orient yourself to the valley here in the Old Severn Warehouse. The 12-minute introductory movie (on a continuous loop) lays the groundwork for what you'll see in the other museums. Check out the exhibit and the model of the gorge in its heyday. Farther upstream from the museum parking lot is the fine riverside Dale End Park, with picnic areas and a playground.

Cost: £4, 500 yards upstream from the bridge, parking-£1.50 (3-hour maximum).

▲▲Blists Hill Victorian Town

Save most of your time and energy for this wonderful town—an immersive, open-air folk museum. You'll wander through 50 acres of Victorian industry, factories, and a re-created community from the 1890s. Pick up the Blists Hill guidebook for a good step-by-step rundown.

Cost and Hours: £16, closes at 16:00 Nov-March.

Visiting Blists Hill: The map you're given when entering is very important—it shows which stops in the big park are staffed with lively docents in Victorian dress. Pop in to say hello to the banker, the lady in the post office, the blacksmith, and the girl in the candy shop. Maybe the boys are singing in the pub. It's fine to take photos. Asking questions and chatting with the villagers is encouraged. What's a shilling? How was the pay? What about health care in the 1800s?

Stop by the pharmacy and check out the squirm-inducing setup of the dentist's chair—it'll make you appreciate the marvel of modern dental care. Check the hands-on activities in the barn across the way. Down the street, kids like watching a costumed candle-maker at work, as he explains the process and tells how candles were used back in the day.

Just as it would've had in Victorian days, the village has a working pub, a greengrocer's shop, a fascinating squatter's cottage, and a snorty, slippery pigsty. Don't miss the explanation of the "winding engine" at the Blists Hill Mine (demos throughout the day).

At the back of the park, you can hop aboard a train and enter a clay mine, complete with a sound and light show illustrating the dangers of working in this type of environment (£2, 10 minutes). Nearby, the Hay Inclined Plane was used to haul loaded tub boats between the river and the upper canal. Today, a passenger-operated lift hauls visitors instead (just press the button to call for it). At the top, you can walk along the canal back to the town.

Eating in Blists Hill: Several places serve lunch: a café near the entrance, the New Inn Pub for beer and pub snacks, a traditional fish-and-chips joint, and the cafeteria near the children's old-time rides.

▲Coalbrookdale Museum of Iron and Abraham Darby's Old Furnace

The Coalbrookdale neighborhood is the birthplace of modern technology—the place where locals like to claim that mass production was invented. The museum and furnace are located on either side of a parking lot.

Cost: Museum—£8.25, £9 combo-ticket includes the Darby Houses—listed later; furnace—free, volunteer tour guides sometimes lead free guided walks to the furnace (ask at museum info desk for times).

Museum: While old-school, this museum does a fine job of explaining the original iron-smelting process and how iron (which makes up 95 percent of all industrial metal) changed our world. But compared to the fun and frolicking Blists Hill village, this museum is sleepy. There's a café inside the museum.

Abraham Darby Furnace: Across from the museum, standing like a shrine to the Industrial Revolution, is Darby's blast furnace, sitting inside a big glass pyramid and surrounded by evocative Industrial Age ruins (info sheets on the furnace available at museum). It was here that, in 1709, Darby first smelted iron, using coke as fuel. To me, "coke" is a drink, and "smelt" is the past tense of smell...but around here, these words recall the event that kicked off the modern Industrial Age.

All the ingredients of the recipe for big industry were here in abundance—iron ore, top-grade coal, and water for power and shipping. Wander around Abraham Darby's furnace. Before this furnace was built, iron ore was laboriously melted by charcoal. With huge waterwheel-powered bellows, Darby burned top-grade coal at super-hot temperatures (burning off the impurities to make "coke"). Local iron ore was dumped into the furnace and melted. Impurities floated to the top, while the pure iron sank to the bottom of a clay tub in the bottom of the furnace. Twice a day, the plugs were knocked off, allowing the "slag" to drain away on the top and the molten iron to drain out on the bottom. The low-grade slag was used locally on walls and paths. The high-grade iron trickled into molds formed in the sand below the furnace. It cooled into pig iron (named because the molds look like piglets suckling their mother). The pig-iron "planks" were broken off by sledgehammers and shipped away. The Severn River became one of Europe's busiest, shipping pig iron to distant foundries, where it was melted again and made into cast iron (for projects such as the Iron Bridge), or to forges, where it was worked like toffee into wrought iron.

Enginuity

Enginuity is a hands-on funfest for kids. Riffing on Ironbridge's engineering roots, this converted 1709 foundry is full of entertaining-to-kids water contraptions, pumps, magnets, and laser games. Build a dam, try your hand at earthquake-proof construction, navigate a water maze, operate a remote-controlled robot, or power a turbine with your own steam.

Cost: £8.50, across the parking lot from the Coalbrookdale Museum of Iron.

Darby Houses

The Darby family, Quakers who were the area's richest residents by far, lived in these two homes located just above the Coalbrookdale Museum.

The 18th-century Darby mansion, **Rosehill House,** features a collection of fine china, furniture, and trinkets from various family members. It's decorated in the way the family home would have been in 1850. If the gilt-framed mirrors and fancy china seem a little ostentatious for the normally wealth-shunning Quakers, keep in mind that these folks were rich beyond reason, and—as docents will assure you—considering their vast wealth, this was relatively modest.

Skip the adjacent **Dale House.** Dating from the 1780s, it's older than Rosehill, but almost completely devoid of interior furniture, and its exhibits are rarely open.

Cost and Hours: £5, £9 combo-ticket includes Coalbrookdale Museum of Iron, closed Nov-March for lack of light.

Coalport China Museum, Jackfield Tile Museum, and Broseley Pipeworks

Housed in their original factories, these showcase the region's porcelain, decorated tiles, and clay tobacco pipes. These industries were developed to pick up the slack when the iron industry shifted away from the Severn Valley in the 1850s. Each museum features finely decorated pieces, and the china and tile museums offer low-energy workshops.

Cost and Hours: £5-8.25 each; Broseley Pipeworks open afternoons only late spring through summer (mid-May-mid-Sept 13:00-17:00, closed mid-Sept-mid-May).

Near Ironbridge
Ironbridge Open-Air Museum of Steel Sculpture

This park is a striking tribute to the region's industrial heritage. Stroll the 10-acre grounds and spot works by Roy Kitchin and other sculptors stashed in the forest and perched in rolling grasslands.

Cost and Hours: £3, March-Nov Tue-Sun 10:00-17:00, closed Mon except Bank Holidays, closed Dec-Feb, free parking, 2 miles from Ironbridge, Moss House, Cherry Tree Hill, Coalbrookdale, Telford, tel. 01952/433-152).

Skiing and Swimming

There's a small, brush-covered **ski and snowboarding slope** with two Poma lifts at Telford Snowboard and Ski Center in Madeley, two miles from Ironbridge Gorge; you'll see signs for it as you drive into Ironbridge Gorge (£13/hour including gear, less for kids, open practice times vary by day—schedule posted online, tel. 01952/382-688, www.telford.gov.uk/skicentre). A public **swimming pool** is in Madeley (5-minute drive from town on Ironbridge Road, Abraham Darby Sports and Leisure Centre, tel. 01952/382-770).

Royal Air Force (RAF) Museum Cosford

This Red Baron-magnet displays more than 80 aircraft, from warplanes to rockets. Get the background on ejection seats and a primer on the principles of propulsion.

Cost and Hours: Free, daily March-Oct 10:00-18:00, Nov-Feb 10:00-17:00, last entry one hour before closing, parking-£2.50/3 hours, Shifnal, Shropshire, on the A-41 near junction with the M-54, tel. 01902/376-200, www.rafmuseum.org.uk/cosford.

More Sights

If you're looking for reasons to linger in Ironbridge Gorge, these sights are all within a short drive: the medieval town of Shrewsbury, the abbey village of Much Wenlock, the scenic Long Mynd gorge at Church Stretton, the castle at Ludlow, and the steam railway at the river town of Bridgnorth. Shoppers like Chester (en route to points north).

Sleeping in Ironbridge Gorge

$$$ Library House Guesthouse is *Better Homes and Gardens*-elegant. Located in the town center, a half-block downhill from the bridge, it's a classy, friendly gem that actually used to be the village library. Each of its four rooms is a delight. The Chaucer Room, which includes a small garden, is the smallest and least expensive. Lizzie Steel offers a complimentary drink upon arrival (small Db-£85, larger Db-£95, twin Db-£105, take £10 off these prices for Sb, DVD library, free Wi-Fi, free parking just up the road, 11 Severn Bank, Ironbridge Gorge, tel. 01952/432-299, www.library house.com, info@libraryhouse.com). Lizzie may be able to pick you up from the Telford train station if you request it in advance.

$$ Tontine Hotel is the town's big, 12-room, musty, Industrial Age hotel. Check out the historic photos in the bar (S-£30, Sb-£45, D-£46, Db-£62, Tb-£70, Qb-£80, if booking in advance ask about discount with this book, restaurant, The Square, tel. 01952/432-127, www.tontine-hotel.com, tontinehotel@tiscali .co.uk).

Sleep Code

(£1 = about $1.60, country code: 44, area code: 01952)
S = Single, **D** = Double/Twin, **T** = Triple, **Q** = Quad, **b** = bathroom,
s = shower only. Unless otherwise noted, credit cards are
accepted and breakfast is included.

To help you sort easily through these listings, I've divided
the accommodations into three categories based on the price
for a standard double room with bath during high season:

$$$ Higher Priced—Most rooms £65 or more.
  $$ Moderately Priced—Most rooms between £45-65.
    $ Lower Priced—Most rooms £45 or less.

Prices can change without notice; verify the hotel's current rates online or by email. For the best prices, always book
direct.

Outside of Town

$$$ Calcutts House rents seven rooms in their 18th-century
ironmaster's home and adjacent coach house. Rooms in the main
house are elegant, while the coach-house rooms are bright, mod-
ern, and less expensive. Their inviting garden is a plus. Ask the
owners, James and Sarah Pittam, how the rooms were named
(Db-£55-95, price depends on room size, free Wi-Fi, Calcutts
Road, tel. 01952/882-631, www.calcuttshouse.co.uk, info@calcutts
house.co.uk). From Calcutts House, it's a delightful 15-minute
stroll down a former train track into town.

$ Coalport Youth Hostel, plush for a hostel, fills an old fac-
tory at the China Museum in Coalport (£13-22 bunks in mostly
4-bed dorms, bunk-bed Db-£36-48, £3 less for members, includes
sheets, reception open 7:30-23:00, no lockout, kitchen, restaurant,
self-service laundry, High Street, tel. 01952/588-755 or 0845-371-
9325, www.yha.org.uk, coalport@yha.org.uk). Don't confuse this
hostel with another area hostel, Coalbrookdale, which is only
available for groups.

$ Wilderhope Manor Youth Hostel, a beautifully remote
Elizabethan manor house from 1586, is one of Europe's best hos-
tels—and recently refurbished (it even has a bridal suite). On
Wednesday and Sunday afternoons, tourists actually pay to see
what hostelers get to sleep in (£18.50-25 bunks, under 18-£17-19,
£3 less for members, single-sex dorms, family rooms available,
reservations recommended, reception closed 10:00-15:00, restau-
rant open 18:00-20:30, laundry, kitchen, tel. 01694/771-363 or
0845-371-9149, www.yha.org.uk, wilderhope@yha.org.uk). It's in

Longville-in-the-Dale, six miles from Much Wenlock, down the B-4371 toward Church Stretton.

Eating in Ironbridge Gorge

Restaurant Severn is the local favorite for a place with style that serves contemporary dishes. Choose from a £24-27 two-course fixed-price meal or a £26-29 three-course offering (evenings Wed-Sat, lunch only on Sun, closed Mon-Tue, across from the Iron Bridge in the town center, reservations smart—especially on weekends, 33 High Street, tel. 01952/432-233, www.restaurant seven.co.uk).

Pondicherry, in a renovated former police station, serves delicious Indian curries and a few British dishes to keep the less adventurous happy. The mixed vegetarian sampler is popular even with meat-eaters. The basement holding cells are now little plush lounges—a great option if you'd like your pre-dinner drink "in prison" (£10-16 plates, daily 17:00-23:00, starts to get hopping after 19:00, 57 Waterloo Street, tel. 01952/433-055).

Da Vinci's serves good, though pricey, Italian food and has a dressy ambience (£15-20 main courses, Tue-Sat 19:00-22:00, closed Sun-Mon, 26 High Street, tel. 01952/432-250).

The Golden Ball Inn, a brewery back in the 18th century, is a popular pub known for its quality food and great atmosphere. You can dine with the friendly local crowd in the "bar," eat in back with the brewing gear in the more quiet—and formal—dining room, or munch on the lush garden patio. This place is serious about their beer, listing featured ales daily (£10-15 meals, food served Mon-Fri 12:00-14:30 & 18:00-21:00, Sat 12:00-21:00, Sun 12:00-19:45, reservations smart on weekends, 8-minute hike up Madeley Road from the town roundabout, 1 Newbridge Road, tel. 01952/432-179).

The Coalbrookdale Inn is filled with locals enjoying excellent ales and good food. This former "best pub in Britain" has a tradition of offering free samples from a lineup of featured beers. Ask which real ales are available (daily 12:00-24:00, food served only until 16:00) lively ladies' loo, across street from Coalbrookdale Museum of Iron, 1 mile from Ironbridge, 12 Wellington Road, tel. 01952/432-166).

The Malt House, located in an 18th-century beer house, is a very popular scene with the local twentysomething gang (£9-20 main courses, bar menu at their Rock Bar, food served daily 12:30-22:00, near Museum of the Gorge, 5-minute walk from center, The Wharfage, tel. 01952/433-712). For nighttime action, The Malt House is *the* vibrant spot in town, with live rock music and a fun crowd (generally Thu-Sat).

IRONBRIDGE GORGE

Ironbridge Gorge Connections

Ironbridge Gorge is five miles southwest of Telford, which has the nearest train station.

Getting between Telford and Ironbridge Gorge: To go by **bus** from Telford's train station to the center of Ironbridge Gorge, you'll first have to zip over to the Telford bus station—any north-bound bus that stops at the train station will take you there (every 5-10 minutes; some buses drive by without stopping—don't be alarmed—just wait for one that stops). From the Telford bus station, take bus #77, #88, or #99 into Ironbridge (roughly 1/hour, usually at :30 or :45 after the hour, 30 minutes, none on Sun). The Telford bus station is attached to a large modern mall, making it an easy place to wait—ask at the info office when the next bus is leaving and from which door. The bus drops you off in Ironbridge at the TI or the bridge—tell the driver which stop you want (pay per leg or buy "Day Saver" pass—only cost-effective if you take the bus at least three times). Buses are run by Arriva (www.arriva bus.co.uk), but you can also call Traveline for departure times and other information (tel. 0871-200-2233, www.traveline.org.uk).

If the Gorge Connect bus is running (generally April-Oct on weekends and Bank Holidays, plus some weeks in summer; see page 490) you can take bus #44 (2-5/hour) direct from the Telford train station to High Street in the town of Madeley. This is where the Gorge Connect bus originates and ends. Hop on it to ride to one of the museums, the TI, or the bridge.

A **taxi** from Telford train station to Ironbridge costs about £10.

By Train from Telford to: Birmingham (2/hour, 30-50 minutes), **Stratford-upon-Avon** (roughly hourly, 2.5 hours, 1-2 changes), **Moreton-in-Marsh** (hourly, 2.5-3 hours, 2 transfers), **Conwy** in North Wales (10/day, 2.5-3 hours, some change in Chester or Shrewsbury), **Blackpool** (hourly, 2.5 hours, 2 changes), **Keswick/Lake District** (hourly, 4 hours total; 3 hours to Penrith with 1-2 changes, then catch a bus to Keswick—see page 566), **Edinburgh** (hourly, 4-5 hours, 1-2 changes). **Train info:** Tel. 0845-748-4950, www.nationalrail.co.uk.

Route Tips for Drivers

From the South to Ironbridge Gorge: From the Cotswolds and Stratford, take the M-40 to Birmingham, then the M-6 (direction northwest) through Birmingham. Be aware that traffic north-bound through Birmingham is miserable from 14:00 to 20:00, especially on Fridays. Take one of two M-6 options: free with traffic through the city center; or the M-6 Toll, which, for around £5.50, skirts you north of the center with nearly no traffic—a very good bet during rush hour.

After Birmingham, follow signs to *Telford* via the M-54 (if on toll road, it'll be via the A-5). Leave the M-54 at the Telford/Ironbridge exit (Junction 4). Follow the brown *Ironbridge* signs through several roundabouts to Ironbridge Gorge. (Note: On maps, Ironbridge Gorge is often referred to as "Iron Bridge" or "Iron-Bridge.")

From Ironbridge Gorge to North Wales: The drive is fairly easy, with clear signs and good roads all the way. From Ironbridge Gorge, follow signs to the M-54. Get on the M-54 in the direction of Telford, and then Shrewsbury, as the M-54 becomes the A-5; then follow signs to North Wales. In Wales, the A-483 (direction Wrexham, then Chester) takes you to the A-55, which leads to Conwy.

LIVERPOOL

Wedged between serene North Wales and the even-more-serene Lake District, Liverpool provides an opportunity to sample the "real" England. It's the best look at urban England outside of London.

Beatles fans flock to Liverpool to learn about the Fab Four's early days, but the city has much more to offer—most notably, a wealth of free and good museums, a pair of striking cathedrals, a dramatic skyline mingling old red-brick maritime buildings and glassy new skyscrapers, and—most of all—the charm of the Liverpudlians.

Sitting at the mouth of the River Mersey in the metropolitan county of Merseyside, Liverpool has long been a major shipping center. Its port played a key role in several centuries of world history—as a point in the "triangular trade" of African slaves, a gateway for millions of New World-bound European emigrants, and a staging ground for the British Navy's Battle of the Atlantic against the Nazi's U-boat fleet. But Liverpool was devastated physically by WWII bombs, then economically by the advent of container shipping in the 1960s. Liverpudlians looked on helplessly as England's postwar recovery resources were steered elsewhere, the city's substantial wartime contributions seemingly ignored.

Despite the pride and attention garnered in the 1960s by a certain quartet of favorite sons, Liverpool continued to decline through the 1970s and '80s. The Toxteth Riots of 1981, sparked by the city's dizzyingly high unemployment, brought worldwide attention to Liverpool's troubles.

But finally, things started looking up. The city's status as the 2008 European Capital of Culture spurred major gentrification, EU funding, and a cultural renaissance. And, with some 50,000

On the Scouse

Nicknamed "Scousers" (after a traditional local stew, originally brought here by Norwegian immigrants), the people of Liverpool have a reputation for being relaxed, easygoing, and welcoming to visitors. The Scouse dialect comes with a distinctive lilt and quick wit (the latter likely a means of coping with long-term hardship)—think of the Beatles' familiar accents, and all their famously sarcastic off-the-cuff remarks, and you get the picture. Many Liverpudlians attribute these qualities to the Celtic influence here: Liverpool is a melting pot of not only English culture, but also loads of Irish and Welsh immigrants, as well as newer arrivals from all over Europe and beyond (Liverpool's diverse population includes many of African descent). Liverpudlians are also famous for their passion for football (i.e., soccer), and the two Liverpool-based teams, Liverpool FC and Everton FC, have a friendly-but-fierce rivalry.

LIVERPOOL

students attending three universities in town, Liverpool is also a youthful city, with a pub or nightclub on every corner. Anyone who still thinks of Liverpool as a depressed industrial center is behind the times.

Planning Your Time

Liverpool deserves at least a few hours, but those willing to give it a full day or more won't be disappointed.

For the quickest visit, focus your time at the Albert Dock, home to The Beatles Story, Merseyside Maritime Museum, Tate Gallery (for contemporary art lovers), and Museum of Liverpool. If time allows, consider a Beatles bus tour (departs from the Albert Dock).

A full day buys you time either to delve into the rest of the city (the rejuvenated urban core, the cathedrals, and the Walker Art Gallery near the train station), to binge on more Beatles sights (the boyhood homes of John and Paul), or a bit of both.

If you're here just for the Beatles, you can easily fill a day with Fab Four sights: Do the tour of John and Paul's homes in

Liverpool

A-59 TO PRESTON & BLACKPOOL

TO SOUTHPORT

BATH ST

A-565

NEW QUAY

SCOTLAND ROAD

LEEDS ROAD

MARYBONE

TITHE BARN

CHAPEL

VERNON

DALE

WORLD MUSEUM BLDG.

CHUR

22

Moor-fields

6

TUNNEL ENTRANCE

QUEEN SQ.

B

24 23 M

WATER

20

5

RICH.

TOWER

VICTORIA

28

MATHEW St.

2

WHITECHAPEL

PARADISE

PARKER

25

Royal Liver Bldg.

PIER HEAD FERRY TERMINAL

Cunard Bldg.

LORD

CHURCH

RICH

MERSEY FERRIES DOCK

Port. Bldg.

M

James Street

STRAND

Liverpool One Mall

HANOVER

6

Central Stn.

ROPE

21

B

18

DUKE ST.

ARGYLE

MUSEUM OF LIVERPOOL

MARITIME & SLAVERY MUSEUMS

i

ALBERT DOCK

PARK LANE

WAPPING

BLUNDELL ST.

JAMAICA

CHALONER

PA

TATE GALLERY LIVERPOOL

7 6

27

THE BEATLES STORY

R I V E R

M E R S E Y

26

Arena & Convention Centre

P

Legend

B BUS HUB
M MERSEYRAIL SUBWAY STOP
P PARKING
PEDESTRIAN SHOPPING ZONE

LIVERPOOL

400 YARDS

400 METERS

Hotels

1. Hope Street Hotel
2. Hard Day's Night Hotel
3. Aachen Guest Accom.
4. Best Western Feathers Hotel
5. Sir Thomas Hotel
6. Premier Inns (3)
7. Holiday Inn Express
8. Internat'l Inn Hostel & Cocoon Pod Hotel

Restaurants & Pubs

9. The Quarter Rest.
10. HOST
11. The Side Door
12. 60 Hope Street
13. Yuet Ben
14. Tokyou
15. The Philharmonic Dining Rooms Pub
16. The Fly in the Loaf Pub
17. Alma de Cuba
18. Liverpool One Bridewell
19. Duke Street Eateries
20. Delifonseca
21. Liverpool One Eateries
22. The Ship and Mitre Pub
23. Thomas Rigby's Pub
24. Ye Hole in Ye Wall Pub
25. The Globe Pub

Other

26. National Trust Beatles Tour Pick-Up Point
27. Magical Mystery Big Bus Tour Pick-Up Point
28. Cavern Quarter (Mathew Street & Site of Original Cavern Club)

the morning, then return to the Albert Dock to visit The Beatles Story. Take an afternoon bus tour from the Albert Dock to the other Beatles sights in town, winding up at the Cavern Quarter to enjoy a Beatles cover band in the reconstructed Cavern Club. (Beatles bus tours zip past the John and Paul houses from the outside, but visiting the interiors takes more time and should be reserved well in advance.)

International Beatles Week, celebrated in late August, is a very busy time in Liverpool, with lots of live musical performances.

Orientation to Liverpool

With nearly a half-million people, Liverpool is Britain's fifth-biggest city. But for visitors, most points of interest are concentrated in the generally pedestrian-friendly downtown area. You can walk from one end of this zone to the other in about 25 minutes. Since interesting sights and colorful neighborhoods are scattered throughout this area, it's enjoyable to connect your sightseeing on foot. (Beatles sights, however, are spread far and wide—it's much easier to connect them with a tour.)

Tourist Information

Liverpool's TI is at the **Albert Dock** (daily April-Oct 10:00-17:30, Nov-March 10:00-17:00, just inland from The Beatles Story, tel. 0151/707-0729, www.visitliverpool.com). Pick up the free, good city map and the comprehensive *Liverpool Visitor Guide,* crammed with updated lists of museums, hotels, restaurants, shops, and more.

Arrival in Liverpool

By Train: Most trains use the main **Lime Street train station.** The station has eateries, shops, and baggage storage (per item: £3/3 hours, £5/6 hours, £7/24 hours, Mon-Thu 7:00-21:00, Fri-Sun 7:00-23:00; most bus tours and private minivan/car tours are able to accommodate people with luggage). Note that regional trains also arrive at the much smaller, confusingly named **Central Station,** located just a few blocks south.

Getting to the Albert Dock: From Lime Street Station to the Albert Dock is about a 20-minute walk or a quick trip by bus, subway, or taxi.

To **walk,** exit straight out the front door. On your right, you'll see the giant, Neoclassical St. George's Hall; the Walker Art Gallery is just beyond it. To reach the Albert Dock, go straight ahead across the street, then head down the hill between St. George's Hall (on your right) and the big blob-shaped mall (on your left). This brings you to Queen Square Centre, a hub for buses. (The round pavilion with the "i" symbol is a transit info center—see "Getting Around Liverpool," later.) From here, you can continue by bus (see below) or take a pleasant walk through Liverpool's spiffed-up central core: Head around the right side of the transit-info pavilion, then turn left onto Whitechapel Street, which soon becomes a slick pedestrian zone lined with shopping malls. Follow this all the way down to the waterfront, where you'll see the big red-brick warehouses of the Albert Dock.

To ride the **bus,** walk to Queen Square Centre (see directions above); for the most direct route to the Albert Dock, take bus #C5 from stall 9 (2/hour—see schedule posted next to stall, bus prices vary—from about £1.10/ride, £3.60 for all-day ticket).

You can also take a **subway** from Lime Street Station to James Street Station, then walk about five minutes to the Albert Dock (about £2, also covered by BritRail pass). Note that some regional trains may pass through James Street Station before reaching Lime Street Station; if so, you can hop out here rather than riding to Lime Street.

A **taxi** from Lime Street Station to the Albert Dock costs about £5. Taxis wait outside either of the side doors of the station.

By Plane: From Liverpool John Lennon Airport (code: LPL, tel. 0871-521-8484, www.liverpoolairport.com) is about eight miles southeast of downtown, along the river. Buses into town depart regularly from the bus stalls just outside the main terminal doors. Bus #500 to the city center is quickest, stopping at Queen Square Centre, Liverpool One bus hub, and Lime Street Station (2/hour, 35 minutes, about £3, covered by all-day ticket). Buses #80A, #82A, and #86A also go from the airport to the Liverpool One bus hub, but these take a bit longer.

By Car: Drivers approaching Liverpool first follow signs to *City Centre* and *Waterfront*, then brown signs to *Albert Dock*, where you'll find a huge pay parking lot at the dock. If coming from Wales, take the toll tunnel under the River Mersey (£1.60) and follow signs for *Albert Dock*.

Getting Around Liverpool

The city is walkable (and fun to explore), so you may not need to take advantage of the local bus network. But if your feet need a rest, several city center buses swing around Liverpool, stopping at major sights. Of these, the most useful is #C3, which loops from the Albert Dock, up the hill to Chinatown and the Liverpool

Cathedral, down Hope Street (with many recommended restaurants) to the Metropolitan Cathedral, past Lime Street Station and Queen Square Centre bus hub, and through the downtown area and the Beatles-focused Cavern Quarter (#C1 does a similar circle in the opposite direction). For more public-transit information, visit a Merseytravel center—there's one at the main bus hub on Queen Square Centre (near Lime Street Station) and another at the Liverpool One bus station (1 Canning Place), across the busy street from the Albert Dock (both open Mon-Sat 8:30-18:00, Sun 10:00-17:00, tel. 0871-200-2233, www.merseytravel.gov.uk).

Tours in Liverpool

Beatles Bus Tours

If you want to see as many Beatles-related sights as possible in a short time, these tours are the way to go. Each drives by the houses where the Fab Four grew up (exteriors only), places they performed, and spots made famous by the lyrics of their hits ("Penny Lane," "Strawberry Fields," the Eleanor Rigby graveyard, and so on). Even lukewarm fans will enjoy the commentary and seeing the shelter on the roundabout, the barber who shaves another customer, and the banker who never wears a mack in the pouring rain. (Very strange.)

Magical Mystery Big Bus Tour

Beatles fans enjoy loading onto this old, psychedelically painted bus for a spin past Liverpool's main Beatles landmarks, with a few photo ops off the bus. With an enthusiastic live commentary and Beatles tunes cued to famous landmarks, it leaves people happy (£16, daily year-round at 14:00; also at 11:30 daily April-Oct, off-season weekends, and school holidays; often at other times as well—ask TI, call, or check online for schedule; 1.75 hours, buses depart from the Albert Dock near The Beatles Story and TI, tel. 0151/236-9091, www.cavernclub.org). As these tours often fill up, you'd be wise to book at least a day ahead by phone or through the TI (tel. 0151/707-0729).

Phil Hughes Minibus Beatles and Liverpool Tours

For something more extensive, fun, and intimate, consider a four-hour minibus Beatles tour from Phil Hughes. It's longer because it includes information on historic Liverpool, along with the Beatles stuff and a couple of *Titanic* and *Lusitania* sights. Phil organizes his tour to fit your schedule and will do his best to accommodate you (£20/person, private group tour with 5-person minimum, can coordinate tour to include pickup from end of National Trust tour of Lennon and McCartney homes or drop-off for late-day tour starting at Speke Hall, 8-seat minibus, tel. 0151/228-4565, mobile 07961-511-223, www.tourliverpool.co.uk, tourliverpool@hotmail .com).

Jackie Spencer Private Tours
To tailor a visit to your schedule and interests, Jackie Spencer is at your service...just say when and where you want to go (up to 5 people in her chauffeur-driven minivan-£150, 2.5 hours, longer tours available, will pick you up at hotel or train station, mobile 0799-076-1478, www.beatleguides.com, jackie@beatleguides.com).

Other Tours

City Bus Tour
Two different hop-on, hop-off bus tours cruise around town, offering a quick way to get an overview that links all the major sights. The options are **City Sightseeing** (£10, buy ticket from driver, valid 24 hours, recorded commentary, 14 stops, April-Oct Mon-Sat 10:00-17:00, 3/hour, less frequent Sun and Nov-March, tel. 0151/203-3920, www.citysightseeingliverpool.com) and **City Explorer** (£8, buy ticket from driver, valid 24 hours, live guides, 13 stops; April-Aug daily 10:00-16:30, 2/hour; Sept-March generally daily 10:00-16:00, until 15:00 in winter, 1-2/hour; tel. 0151/933-2324, www.cityexplorerliverpool.co.uk).

Ferry Cruise
Mersey Ferries offers narrated cruises that depart from the Pier Head ferry terminal, an easy five-minute walk north of the Albert Dock. The 50-minute cruise makes two brief stops on the other side of the river; you can hop off and catch the next boat back (£8 round-trip, ask about £4.80 All-Areas Saveaway ticket if you plan to get off, runs year-round, Mon-Fri 10:00-15:00, Sat-Sun 10:00-18:00, leaves Pier Head at top of hour, café, WCs onboard, tel. 0151/330-1000, www.merseyferries.co.uk).

Sights in Liverpool

On the Waterfront

In its day, Liverpool was England's greatest seaport, but trade declined after 1890, as the port wasn't deep enough for the big new ships. The advent of mega container ships in the 1960s put the final nail in the port's coffin, and by 1972 it was closed entirely.

But over the last couple of decades, this formerly derelict and dangerous area has been the focus of the city's rejuvenation efforts. Liverpool's waterfront is now a venue for some of the city's top attractions. Three zones interest tourists (from south to north): the Wapping Dock area, with Liverpool's futuristic new arena,

Liverpool at a Glance

▲▲Museum of Liverpool Three floors of intriguing exhibits, historical artifacts, and fun interactive displays tracing the port city's history, culture, and contributions to the world. **Hours:** Daily 10:00-17:00. See page 516.

▲▲Liverpool Cathedral Huge Anglican house of worship—the largest cathedral in Great Britain—with cavernous interior and tower climb. **Hours:** Daily 8:00-18:00. See page 523.

▲Lennon and McCartney Homes The 1950s boyhood homes of Beatles John Lennon and Paul McCartney, with restored interiors viewable on a National Trust minibus tour. Advance reservations smart. **Hours:** Tours run four times a day Wed-Sun in summer. See page 525.

▲The Beatles Story Well-done if overpriced exhibit about the Fab Four, with a great audioguide narrated by John Lennon's sister, Julia Baird. **Hours:** Daily May-Sept 9:00-19:00, Oct-April 10:00-18:00. See page 511.

▲Merseyside Maritime Museum and International Slavery Museum Duo of thought-provoking museums exploring Liverpool's seafaring heritage and the city's role in the African slave trade. **Hours:** Daily 10:00-17:00. See page 514.

▲Walker Art Gallery Enjoyable, easy-to-appreciate collection of European paintings, sculptures, and decorative arts. **Hours:** Daily 10:00-17:00. See page 519.

▲Metropolitan Cathedral of Christ the King Striking, daringly modern Catholic cathedral with a story as fascinating as the building itself. **Hours:** Daily 8:00-18:00, until 17:00 on Sun in winter; after 17:15 (during Mass), you can't walk around. See page 521.

Tate Gallery Liverpool Prestigious modern art gallery with a rotating collection of 20th-century statues and paintings. **Hours:** Daily 10:00-18:00, except closes at 17:00 Nov-Easter. See page 516.

World Museum Family-oriented museum with five floors of kid-friendly exhibits, including dinosaurs and an aquarium. **Hours:** Daily 10:00-17:00. See page 520.

conference center, and adjacent Ferris wheel; the red-brick Albert Dock complex, with some of the city's top museums and lively restaurants and nightlife; and Pier Head, with the Museum of Liverpool, ferries across the River Mersey, and buildings both old/stately and new/glassy. Below are descriptions of the main sights at the Albert Dock and Pier Head.

At the Albert Dock

Opened in 1852 by Prince Albert, and enclosing seven acres of water, the Albert Dock is surrounded by five-story brick warehouses. A half-dozen trendy eateries are lined up here, protected from the rain by arcades and padded by lots of shopping mall-type distractions. There's plenty of pay parking.

▲The Beatles Story

It's sad to think the Beatles are stuck in a museum. Still, this exhibit—while overpriced and a bit small—is well-done, the story's

a fascinating one, and even an avid fan will pick up some new information. The Beatles Story has two parts: the original, main exhibit at the south end of the Albert Dock; and a much smaller branch in the Pier Head ferry terminal, near the Museum of Liverpool just to the north. A free shuttle runs between the two locations every 30 minutes.

Cost and Hours: £13 covers both parts, tickets good for 48 hours, includes audioguide, daily May-Sept 9:00-19:00, Oct-April 10:00-18:00, last entry at 17:00 year-round, tel. 0151/709-1963, www.beatlesstory.com.

Visiting the Museum: Start in the **main exhibit** with a chronological stroll through the evolution of the Beatles, focusing on their Liverpool years: meeting as schoolboys, performing at (and helping decorate) the Casbah Coffee Club, making a name for themselves in Hamburg, meeting their manager Brian Epstein, and the advent of worldwide Beatlemania (with some help from Ed Sullivan). There are many actual artifacts (from George Harrison's first boyhood guitar to John Lennon's orange-tinted "Imagine" glasses), as well as large dioramas celebrating landmarks in Beatles lore (a reconstruction of the Cavern Club, a life-size

The Beatles in Liverpool

The most iconic rock-and-roll band of all time was made up of four Liverpudlians who spent their formative years amid the bombed-out shell of WWII-era Liverpool. The city has become a pilgrimage site for Beatlemaniacs, but even those with just a passing interest in the Fab Four are likely to find themselves humming their favorite tunes around town. Most Beatles sights in Liverpool relate to their early days, before the psychedelia, transcendental meditation, Yoko, and solo careers. Because these sights are so spread out, the easiest way to connect all of them in one go is by tour (see "Tours in Liverpool").

All four of the Beatles were born in Liverpool, and any tour of town glides by the **home** most identified with each one's childhood: John Lennon at "Mendips," Paul McCartney at 20 Forthlin Road, George Harrison at 12 Arnold Grove, and Ringo Starr (a.k.a. Richard Starkey) at 10 Admiral Grove.

Behind John's house at Mendips is a wooded area called **Strawberry Field** (he added the "s" for the song). This surrounds a Victorian mansion that was, at various times, a Salvation Army home and an orphanage. John enjoyed sneaking into the trees around the mansion to play. Today visitors pose in front of Strawberry Field's red gate (a replica of the original).

During the Beatles' formative years in the mid-1950s, skiffle music (American-inspired rockabilly/folk) swept through Liverpool. As a teenager, John formed a skiffle band called the Quarrymen. Paul met John for the first time when he saw the Quarrymen on July 6, 1957, at **St. Peter's Church** in Woolton. After the show, in the social hall across the street, Paul noted that John played only banjo chords (his mother had taught him to play on a banjo rather than a guitar—he didn't even know how to tune a guitar), and improvised many lyrics. John, two years older, realized he was a better improviser than a musician, so he was impressed when Paul borrowed a guitar, tuned it effortlessly, and played a note-perfect rendition of Eddie Cochran's "Twenty Flight Rock." Before long, Paul had joined the band.

In the St. Peter's Church graveyard is a headstone for a woman named **Eleanor Rigby.** But to this day, Paul swears that he never saw it, and made up the name for that famous song. Either he's lying, the name crept into his subconscious, or it's a truly remarkable coincidence.

The boys went to school on **Mount Street** in the center of Liverpool (near Hope Street, between the two cathedrals). John and his friend Stuart Sutcliffe attended the Liverpool College of Art, and Paul and his pal George Harrison went to Liverpool Institute High School for Boys. (When Paul introduced George to John as a possible new member for the band, John dismissed him as being too young...until he heard George play. He immediately became the lead guitarist.) Paul later bought his old school building and turned it into the Liverpool Institute for Performing Arts (LIPA)—nicknamed the "Fame Academy" for the similar school on the American TV series.

As young men, the boys rode the bus together to school—waiting at a bus stop in the **Penny Lane** neighborhood. Later they wrote a nostalgic song about the things they would observe while waiting there: the shelter by the roundabout, the barbershop, and so on. (While they also sing about the fireman with the clean machine, the firehouse itself is not actually on Penny Lane, but around the corner.)

After a series of lineup shuffles, by 1960 the group had officially become The Beatles: John Lennon, Paul McCartney,

George Harrison, and...Pete Best and Stu Sutcliffe. The quintet gradually built a name for themselves in Liverpool's "Merseybeat" scene, performing at local clubs. While the famous **Cavern Club** is gone (the one you see advertised is a reconstruction, but does offer similar ambience and good cover bands), the original **Casbah Coffee Club**—which the group felt more attached to—still exists and is open for tours (3.5 miles northwest of downtown in Pete Best's former basement, prebook by calling the TI at tel. 0151/707-0729 or online at www.petebest.com).

The group went to Hamburg, Germany, to cut their teeth in the thriving music scene there. They wound up performing as the backing band for Tony Sheridan's single "My Bonny." When this caught on back in Liverpool, promoter Brian Epstein took note, and signed the act. His shrewd management would eventually propel the Beatles to superstardom.

Many different people could be considered the "Fifth Beatle." John's friend Stu, who performed with the group in Hamburg, left to pursue his own artistic interests. Pete Best was the band's original drummer, but he was a loner and producers questioned his musical chops, so he was replaced with Ringo Starr. (John later said, "Pete Best was a great drummer, but Ringo was a Beatle.") Brian Epstein, the manager who marketed the Beatles brilliantly before his untimely death, is another candidate. But—in terms of long-term musical influence—it's hard to ignore the case for George Martin, who produced all of the Beatles' albums except *Let It Be,* and was instrumental in both forging and developing the Beatles sound.

By 1963, the Beatles were already world-famous—but, as evidenced by their songs about Penny Lane and Strawberry Fields, they never forgot their Merseyside home.

re-creation of the *Sgt. Pepper* album cover, and a walk-through yellow submarine). The last rooms trace the members' solo careers, and the final few steps are reserved for reverence about John's peace work, including a replica of the white room he used while writing "Imagine." Rounding out the exhibits are a "Discovery Zone" for kids and (of course) the "Fab 4 Store," with an impressive pile of Beatles buyables.

The great audioguide, narrated by Julia Baird (John Lennon's little sister), captures the Beatles' charm and cheekiness in a way the stiff wax mannequins can't. You'll hear clips of interviews from the actual participants in the Beatles' story—their families, friends, and collaborators. Cynthia Lennon, John's first wife, still marvels at the manic power of Beatlemania.

While this is a fairly sanitized look at the Fab Four (LSD and Yoko-related conflicts are glossed over), the exhibits remind listeners of all that made the group earth-shattering—and even a little edgy—at the time. For example, performing before the Queen Mother, John Lennon famously quips: "Will the people in the cheaper seats clap your hands? And the rest of you, if you'll just rattle your jewelry."

The **Pier Head exhibit** is less interesting, but since it's included with the ticket, it's worth dropping into if you have the time. You'll find it upstairs in the Pier Head ferry terminal— a quick trip on the free shuttle bus (runs every 30 minutes) or about a 10-minute walk north (at the opposite end of the Albert Dock, then another 5-minute walk across the bridge and past the Museum of Liverpool). The main attraction here is a corny "Fab 4D Experience," an animated movie that strings together Beatles tunes into something resembling a plot while mainly offering an excuse to play around with 3-D effects and other surprises (such as the smell of strawberries when you hear "Strawberry Fields Forever"). The Hidden Gallery displays recently rediscovered early photos of the moptops by then-teenaged photographer Paul Berriff. Through fall of 2014, the museum also features the temporary exhibit Elvis and Us, about the relationship between the Beatles and their fellow 1960s music icon (£3 extra).

▲Merseyside Maritime Museum and International Slavery Museum

These museums tell the story of Liverpool, once the second city of the British Empire. The third floor covers slavery, while the first, second, and basement handle other maritime topics.

Cost and Hours: Free, donations accepted, daily 10:00-17:00, café, tel. 0151/478-4499, www.liverpoolmuseums.org.uk.

Background: Liverpool's port prospered in the 18th century as one corner of a commerce triangle with Africa and America. British shippers profited greatly through exploitation: About 1.5

million enslaved African people passed through Liverpool's docks (that's 10 percent of all African slaves). From Liverpool, the British exported manufactured goods to Africa in exchange for enslaved Africans; the slaves were then shipped to the Americas, where they were traded for raw material (cotton, sugar, and tobacco); and the goods were then brought back to Britain. While the merchants on all three sides made money, the big profit came home to England (which enjoyed substantial income from customs, duties, and a thriving smugglers' market). As Britain's economy boomed, so did Liverpool's.

After participation in the slave trade was outlawed in Britain in the early 1800s, Liverpool kept its port busy as a transfer point for emigrants. If your ancestors came from Scandinavia, Ukraine, or Ireland, they likely left Europe from this port. Between 1830 and 1930, nine million emigrants sailed from Liverpool to find their dreams in the New World.

Visiting the Museums: Begin by riding the elevator up to floor 3—we'll work our way back down.

On floor 3, three galleries make up the **International Slavery Museum.** First is a description of life in West Africa, which re-creates traditional domestic architecture and displays actual artifacts. Then comes a harrowing exhibit about enslavement and the Middle Passage. The tools of the enslavers—chains, muzzles, and a branding iron—and the intense film about the Middle Passage sea voyage to America drive home the horrifying experience of being abducted from your home and taken in wretched, life-threatening conditions thousands of miles away to toil for a wealthy stranger. Finally, the museum examines the legacy of slavery—both the persistence of racism in contemporary society and the substantial positive impact that people of African descent have had on European and American cultures. Walls of photos celebrate important people of African descent, and a music station lets you sample songs from a variety of African-influenced genres.

Continue down the stairs to the **Maritime Museum,** on floor 2. This celebrates Liverpool's shipbuilding heritage and displays actual ship components, model boats, and a gallery of nautical paintings.

Floor 1 shows footage and artifacts of three big Liverpool-related **shipwrecks:** the *Lusitania*, the *Empress of Ireland,* and the *Titanic* (all of which were destroyed—by a German U-boat, accidental collision with a coal freighter, and iceberg, respectively—in a tragically short span of time between 1912 and 1915). Also on this floor, an extensive exhibit traces the **Battle of the Atlantic** (during World War II, Nazi U-boats attacked merchant ships bringing supplies to Britain, in an attempt to cripple this island nation). You'll see how crew members lived aboard merchant ships. The

Hello Sailor! exhibit explains how gay culture flourished at sea at a time where it was taboo in almost every other walk of British life.

Make your way to the basement, where exhibits describe the tremendous wave of **emigration** through Liverpool's port. And the **Seized!** exhibit looks at the legal and illegal movement of goods through that same port, including thought-provoking displays on customs, taxation, and smuggling.

Tate Gallery Liverpool

This prestigious gallery of modern art is near the Maritime Museum. It won't entertain you as well as its London sister, the Tate Modern, but if you're into modern art, any Tate's great. Its two airy floors, dedicated to the rotating collection of statues and paintings from the 20th century, are free; the top and ground floors are devoted to special exhibits. The Tate also has an inexpensive, recommended café.

Cost and Hours: Free, donations accepted, £7-13 for special exhibits, daily Easter-Oct 10:00-18:00, Nov-Easter 10:00-17:00, tel. 0151/702-7400, www.tate.org.uk/liverpool.

At Pier Head, North of the Albert Dock

A five-minute walk across the bridge north of the Albert Dock takes you to the Pier Head area, with the following sights.

▲▲Museum of Liverpool

This museum, which opened in 2011 in the blocky white building just across the bridge north of the Albert Dock, does a good job of fulfilling its goal to "capture Liverpool's vibrant character and demonstrate the city's unique contribution to the world." The museum is full of interesting items, fun interactive displays (great for kids), and fascinating facts that bring a whole new depth to your Liverpool experience.

Cost and Hours: Free, donations accepted, daily 10:00-17:00, guidebook-£1, café, Mann Island, Pier Head, tel. 0151/478-4545, www.liverpoolmuseums.org.uk/mol.

Visiting the Museum: First, stop by the information desk to check on the show times for the museum's various videos. If you have kids age six and under, you can also get a free timed-entry ticket for the hands-on Little Liverpool exhibit on the ground floor.

Ground Floor: On this level, **The Great Port** details the story of Liverpool's defining industry and how it developed through the Industrial Revolution. On display is an 1838 steam locomotive that was originally built for the Liverpool and Manchester Railway.

The **Global City** exhibit focuses on how Liverpool's status as a major British shipping center made it the gateway to a global empire and features a 20-minute video, *Power and the Glory*, about Liverpool's role within the British Empire.

First Floor: Don't miss the **Liverpool Overhead Railway** exhibit, which features the only surviving car from this 19th-century elevated railway. You can actually jump aboard and take a seat to watch 1897 movie footage shot from the train line. A huge interactive model shows the railway's route. Also on this floor is the **History Detectives** exhibit, which covers Liverpool's history and archaeology.

Second Floor: If you're short on time, spend most of it here. The **People's Republic** exhibit examines what it means to be a Liverpudlian (a.k.a. "Scouser") and covers everything from housing and health issues to military and religious topics. As industrialized Liverpool has long been a hotbed of the labor movement, exhibits here also detail the political side of the city, including child labor issues and women's suffrage.

One fascinating display is the re-creation of Liverpool's 19th-century court housing, which consisted of a series of tiny dwellings bunched around a narrow courtyard. With more than 60 people sharing two toilets, this was some of the most overcrowded and unsanitary housing in Britain at the time.

Next, the exhibit skips to religion and the centerpiece of this room: a 10-foot-tall model of Liverpool's Catholic cathedral that was never built. In 1932, Archbishop Richard Downey and architect Sir Edwin Lutyens commissioned this model to showcase their grandiose plans for constructing the world's second-largest cathedral. Their vision never came to fruition, and the Metropolitan Cathedral was built instead (for more on what happened, see page 521).

On the other side of the floor, the **Wondrous Place** exhibit celebrates the arts, cultural, and sporting side of Liverpool. An exhibit on the city's famous passion for soccer features memorabilia and the 17-minute video *Kicking and Screaming*, about the rivalry between the Everton and Liverpool football teams and the sometimes tragic history of the sport (such as when 96 fans were crushed to death at a Liverpool match).

Music is the other big focus here, with plenty of fun, interactive stops that include music quizzes, a karaoke booth, and listening stations featuring artists with ties to Liverpool (from Elvis Costello to Echo & the Bunnymen). And, of course, you'll see plenty of Beatles mania, including their famous suits, the original stage from St. Peter's Church (where John Lennon was performing the first time Paul McCartney laid eyes on him; located in the theater), and an eight-minute film on the band.

LIVERPOOL

Finally, in the **Skylight Gallery,** look for Ben Johnson's painting *The Liverpool Cityscape, 2008*, a remarkable and fun-to-examine melding of old and new art styles. At first glance, it's a typical skyline painting, but Johnson used computer models to create perfect depictions of each building before he put brush to canvas. This method allows for a photorealistic, highly detailed, but completely sanitized portrait of a city. Notice there are no cars or people.

The Three Graces

Three towering buildings near the Museum of Liverpool, remnants of a time of great seafaring prosperity, are known collectively

as Liverpool's Three Graces: the double-clock-towered **Royal Liver Building,** with spires topped by the city's mythical mascot, the "Liver birds"; the relatively dull and boxy **Cunard Building;** and the domed **Port of Liverpool Building,** which strains to evoke memories of St. Paul's Cathedral in London. A 2002 plan to create a Fourth Grace—a metallic, glassy, and yellow blob called The Cloud—never panned out, and that site is now home to the Museum of Liverpool (described previously). While you can see the Three Graces from along the embankment—which is also lined with monuments to important Liverpudlians—the best views are from across the River Mersey (see page 509 for details on riding the ferry; note that the Pier Head ferry terminal also hosts some exhibits from The Beatles Story).

Downtown

Beatles Sights in the Cavern Quarter

The narrow, bar-lined Mathew Street, right in the heart of downtown, is ground zero for Beatles fans. The Beatles frequently performed in their early days together at the original Cavern Club, deep in a cellar along this street. While that's long gone, a mock-up of the historic nightspot (built with many of the original bricks) lives on a few doors down. Still billed as "the **Cavern Club,**" this is worth a visit to see the reconstructed cellar that's often filled by Beatles cover bands. While touristy, dropping by in the afternoon for a live Beatles tribute act in the Cavern Club somehow just feels right. You'll have Beatles songs stuck in your head all day anyway, so you might as well see a wannabe John and Paul strumming and harmonizing a close approximation of the original (open daily 10:00-24:00, later Thu-Sat; live music daily from 14:00, Sat from 12:00, cover charge Thu-Fri and Sun after 20:00 and Sat after 14:00, tel. 0151/236-9091, www.cavernclub.org).

Across the street and run by the same owners, the **Cavern Pub** lacks its sibling's troglodyte aura, but makes up for it with walls lined with old photos and memorabilia from the Beatles and other bands who've performed here. Like the Cavern Club, the pub features frequent performances by Beatles cover bands and other acts (no cover, Mon-Wed 11:00-24:00, later Thu-Sun, tel. 0151/236-4041).

Out front is the Cavern's **Wall of Fame,** with a too-cool-for-school bronze John Lennon leaning up against a wall of bricks engraved with the names of musical acts that have graced the Cavern stage.

At the corner is the recommended **Hard Day's Night Hotel,** decorated inside and out to honor the Fab Four. Notice the statues of John, Paul, George, and Ringo on the second-story corners, and the Beatles gift shop (one of many in town) on the ground floor.

Museums near the Train Station

Both of these museums are just a five-minute walk from the Lime Street train station.

▲Walker Art Gallery

Though it has few recognizable works, Liverpool's main art gallery offers an enjoyable walk through an easy-to-digest collection of European (mostly British) paintings, sculpture, and decorative arts. There's no audioguide, but many of the works are well-explained by posted descriptions.

Cost and Hours: Free, donations accepted, daily 10:00-17:00, William Brown Street, tel. 0151/478-4199, www.liverpoolmuseums.org.uk.

Visiting the Museum: The ground floor has an information desk, café, children's area, small decorative arts collection, and sculpture gallery focusing on British Neoclassical works from the 19th century. The sculpture gallery has many works by John

Gibson, a Welshman who grew up in Liverpool, and later studied under the Italian master Antonio Canova. Gibson's *Tinted Venus* (in the case in the middle) was considered scandalous to Victorian mores because of the nude sculpture's lifelike pinkish tint.

Upstairs is a concise 15-room painting gallery. For a general chronological spin, from the top of the stairs head straight back

to find Room 1. Because of various special exhibits that rotate in and out, the following paintings may be located in other rooms or not on display.

Room 1 (actually two adjoining rooms) has a famous Nicholas Hilliard portrait of Queen Elizabeth I (nicknamed "The Pelican," for her brooch) and a well-known royal portrait of Henry VIII by Hans Holbein. Room 3 has bombastic Baroque works by Rubens and Murillo, Room 4 features a Rembrandt self-portrait, while Room 5 focuses on 18th-century English

painting, including canvases by Gainsborough, Hogarth (find the painting of the great actor David Garrick in the role of Richard III), and lots of George Stubbs. Rooms 6-8 showcase a delightful array of Pre-Raphaelite works, among them Millias' evocative portrait of Isabella (Room 6). You'll find some Turners (a mushy landscape and a more sharp-focus Linlithgow Castle) in Room 7.

For a counterpoint to the lyrical, mystical Pre-Raphaelite works, step into Room 9, with very literal Victorian narrative paintings depicting slices of English life, such as Sadler's *Friday* (showing Dominican monks feasting on fish) and Yeams' *And When Did You Last See Your Father?* On this chilling canvas, showing a scene from the English Civil War, authorities are slyly interrogating a naive, cherubic boy while his family watches from behind, terrified that the child will reveal where his father is hiding.

Room 10 makes the transition to the 20th century and Impressionism, while modern British art dominates the rest of the gallery. In Room 11, Bernard Fleetwood-Walker's *Amity* shows a pair of chaste but (apparently) sexually charged teenagers relaxing in the grass.

World Museum

This catch-all family museum offers five floors of kid-oriented exhibits. You'll see dinosaurs, an aquarium, artifacts from the ancient world, a planetarium and theater (get free tickets at the info desk in the lobby for these), and more.

Cost and Hours: Free, donations accepted, daily 10:00-17:00, William Brown Street, tel. 0151/478-4393, www.liverpoolmuseums .org.uk.

Cathedrals

Liverpool has not one but two notable cathedrals—one Anglican, the other Catholic. (As the Spinners song puts it, "If you want a cathedral, we've got one to spare.") Both are huge, architecturally significant, and well worth visiting. Near the eastern edge of downtown, they're connected by a 10-minute, half-mile walk on pleasant Hope Street, which is lined with theaters and good restaurants (see "Eating in Liverpool," later).

Liverpudlians enjoy pointing out that they have not only the world's only Catholic cathedral designed by a Protestant architect, but also the only Protestant one designed by a Catholic. With its large Irish-immigrant population, Liverpool suffered from tension between its Catholic and Protestant communities for much of its history. But during the city's darkest stretch of the depressed 1970s, the bishops of each church—Anglican Bishop David Sheppard and Catholic Archbishop Derek Worlock—came together and worked hard to reconcile the two communities for the betterment of Liverpool. (Liverpudlians nicknamed this dynamic duo "fish and chips" because they were "always together, and always in the newspaper.") It worked: Liverpool is a bold new cultural center, and relations between the two faiths remain healthy here. Join in this ecumenical spirit by visiting both of their main churches.

▲Metropolitan Cathedral of Christ the King (Catholic)

This daringly modern building, a cone topped with a crowned cylinder, seems almost out of place in its workaday Liverpool neighborhood.

But the cathedral you see today bears no resemblance to Sir Edwin Lutyens' original 1930s plans for a stately Neo-Byzantine cathedral, which was to take 200 years to build and rival St. Peter's Basilica in Vatican City. (Lutyens was desperate to one-up the grandiose plans of Sir Giles Gilbert Scott, who was building the Anglican Cathedral down the street.) The crypt for the ambitious church was excavated in the 1930s, but World War II (during which the crypt was used as an air-raid shelter) stalled progress for decades. In the 1960s, the plans were scaled back, and this smaller (but still impressive) house of worship was completed in 1967.

Cost and Hours: Cathedral—free entry but donations accepted, daily 8:00-18:00 (until 17:00 on Sun in winter)—but after 17:15 (during Mass), you won't be able to walk around; crypt—£3, Mon-Sat 10:00-16:00, closed Sun, last entry 45 minutes before closing, enter from inside church near organ; visitors center/café/ gift shop—Mon-Sat 9:00-17:30, Sun 9:00-16:00; Mount Pleasant,

LIVERPOOL

tel. 0151/709-9222, www.liverpoolmetrocathedral.org.uk.

Visiting the Cathedral: On the stepped plaza in front of the church, you'll see the entrance to the cathedral's visitors center and café (on your right). You're standing on a big concrete slab that provides a roof to the humongous Lutyens Crypt, underfoot. The existing cathedral occupies only a small part of the would-be cathedral's footprint. Imagine what might have been—"the greatest building never built." Because of the cathedral's tent-like appearance and ties to the local Irish community, some Liverpudlians dubbed it "Paddy's Wigwam."

Climb up the stairs to the main doors, step inside, and let your eyes adjust to this magnificent, dimly lit space. Unlike a typical nave-plus-transept cross-shaped church, this cathedral has a round footprint, with seating for a congregation of 3,000 fully surrounding the white marble altar. Like a theater in the round, it was designed to involve worshippers in the service. Suspended above the altar is a stylized crown of thorns.

Spinning off from the round central sanctuary are 13 smaller chapels, many of them representing different stages of Jesus' life. Each chapel is different. Explore, tuning into the symbolic details in each one. Also keep an eye out for the 14 exquisite bronze Stations of the Cross by local artist Sean Rice (on the wall).

The massive **Lutyens Crypt** (named for the ambitious original architect)—the only part of the originally planned cathedral to be completed—is massive, with huge vaults and vast halls lined with six million bricks. The crypt contains a chapel—with windows by Lutyens—that's still used for Sunday Mass, the tombs of three archbishops, a treasury, and an exhibit about the cathedral's construction.

Hope Street

The street connecting the cathedrals is the main artery of Liverpool's "uptown," a lively and fun-to-explore district loaded with dining and entertainment options. In addition to well-respected theaters, this street is home to the Philharmonic and its namesake pub (see "Eating in Liverpool," later). At the intersection with Mount Street is a monument consisting of concrete suitcases; just down this street are the high schools that Paul, George, and John attended (for details, see "The

Beatles in Liverpool" sidebar, earlier).

▲▲Liverpool Cathedral (Anglican)

The largest cathedral in Great Britain, this gigantic house of worship hovers at the south end of downtown. Tour its cavernous interior and consider scaling its tower.

Cost and Hours: Free, £3 suggested donation, daily 8:00-18:00; £5 ticket includes tower climb (2 elevators and 108 steps), audioguide, and 10-minute "Great Space" film; tower—Mon-Fri 10:00-16:30 (last ascent), Thu until sunset March-Oct, Sat 9:00-16:30, Sun 12:00-15:30 (changes possible depending on bell-ringing schedule); film—Mon-Sat 9:00-15:45 (last showing), Sun 12:00-13:30 (depending on services); St. James Mount, tel. 0151/709-6271, www.liverpoolcathedral.org.uk.

◐ Self-Guided Tour: Over the main door is a modern *Risen Christ* statue by Elisabeth Frink. Liverpudlians, not thrilled with the featureless statue and always quick with a joke, have dubbed it **"Frinkenstein."**

Stepping inside, pick up a floor plan at the information desk, go into the main hall, and take in the size of the place. When Liverpool was officially designated a "city" (seat of a bishop), they wanted to build a huge house of worship as a symbol of Liverpudlian pride. Built in bold Neo-Gothic style (like London's Parliament), it seems to trumpet with modern bombast the importance of this city on the Mersey. Begun in 1904, the cathedral's construction was interrupted by the tumultuous 20th century, and not completed until 1973.

Go to the big, circular tile in the very center of the cathedral, under the highest tower. This is a plaque for the building's architect, **Sir Giles Gilbert Scott** (1880-1960). While the church you're surrounded by may seem like his biggest legacy, he also designed an icon that's synonymous with Britain: the classic red telephone box. Flanking this aisle, notice the highly detailed sandstone carvings.

Take a counterclockwise spin around the church interior. Head up the right aisle until you find the **model** of the original plan for the cathedral (press the button to light it up). Scott was a very young architect, and received the commission with the agreement that

LIVERPOOL

he work closely under the wing of his more established mentor, George Bodley. These two architects' visions clashed, and Bodley usually won...until he died early in the planning stages, leaving Scott to pursue his own muse. If Bodley had survived, the cathedral would probably look more like this model. As it was, only one corner of the complex (the Lady Chapel, which we're about to see) was completed before Giles changed plans and created the version you see today.

Nearby, the **"whispering arch"** spanning over the sarcophagus has remarkable acoustics, carrying voices from one end to the other. Try it.

Continuing down the church, notice the very colorful, mod-

ern painting of *The Good Samaritan* (by Adrian Wiszniewski, 1995), high above on the right. The naked crime victim (who has been stabbed in his side, like the Crucifixion wound of Jesus) has been ignored by the well-dressed yuppies in the foreground, but the female Samaritan is finally taking notice. The canvas is packed with symbolism (for example, the Swiss Army knife, in a pool of blood in the left foreground, is open in the 3 o'clock position—the time that Jesus was crucified). This contemporary work of art demonstrates that this is a new, living church. But the congregation has its limits. This painting used to hang closer to the front of the church, but now they've moved it here, out of sight.

Proceeding to the corner, you'll reach the entrance to the oldest part of the church (1910): the **Lady Chapel,** with stained-glass

windows celebrating important women. (Sadly, the original windows were destroyed in World War II; these are replicas.)

Back up in the main part of the church, continue behind the main altar, to the **Education Centre,** with a fun, sped-up video showing all of the daily work it takes to make this cathedral run.

Circling around the far corner of the church, you'll pass the children's chapel and chapterhouse, and then pass under another modern Wiszniewski painting *(The House Built on Rock)*. Across from that painting, go into the choir to get a good look at the Last Supper altarpiece above the **main altar.**

Continuing back up the aisle, you'll come to the **war chapel.** At its entrance is a book listing Liverpudlians lost in war. Battle flags fly high on the wall above.

You'll wind up at the gift shop, where you can buy a ticket to climb up to the top of the tower. The cathedral's café is up the stairs, above the gift shop.

▲Lennon and McCartney Homes

John and Paul's boyhood homes are now owned by the National Trust and have both been restored to how they looked during the lads' 1950s childhoods. While some Beatles bus tours stop here for photo ops, only the National Trust minibus tour gets you inside the homes. This isn't Graceland—you won't find an over-the-top rock-and-roll extravaganza here. If you don't know the difference between John and Paul, you'll likely be bored. But for die-hard Beatles fans who want to get a glimpse into the time and place that created these musical masterminds, the National Trust tour is worth ▲▲▲.

Because the houses are in residential neighborhoods—and still share walls with neighbors—the National Trust runs only four tours per day (Wed-Sun) in summer, limited to 15 or so Beatlemaniacs each.

Cost and Reservations: Tickets are £20. Because so few people are allowed on each tour, it's strongly advised to make a reservation ahead of time, especially in summer and on weekends or holidays. It's a good idea to book as soon as you know your Liverpool plans (or at least two weeks ahead)—though at times, you may be able to get tickets a couple of days in advance. (On the flip side, tours can be booked up months in advance, such as during Beatles week in August.) You can reserve online (www .nationaltrust.org.uk/beatles) or by calling 0151/427-7231. If you haven't reserved ahead, you can try to book a same-day tour (for the morning tours, call 0151/707-0729). The last tour is less likely to be full because it takes 30 minutes (by car or taxi) to reach the tour's starting point from central Liverpool—see below.

Tour Options: A minibus takes you to the homes of John and Paul, with about 45 minutes inside each. From late Feb-Nov, tours run from the Albert Dock Wed-Sun at 10:00, 11:00, and 14:15 (no tours Mon-Tue or Dec-late Feb). They depart from the Jurys Inn (south across the bridge from The Beatles Story, near the Ferris wheel) and follow a route that includes a quick pass by Penny Lane.

From mid-March-Oct, an additional tour leaves at 15:00 from Speke Hall, an out-of-the-way National Trust property located eight miles southeast of Liverpool. Drivers should allow 30 minutes from the city center to Speke Hall—follow the brown *Speke Hall* signs through dozens of roundabouts, heading in the general direction of the airport. If you don't have a car, hop in a taxi.

From either starting point, the entire visit takes about 2.5 hours.

Guides: Each home has a live-in caretaker who acts as your guide. These folks give an entertaining, insightful-to-fans 20- to 30-minute talk, and then leave you time (10-15 minutes) to wander through the house on your own. Ask lots of questions if their spiel peters out early—these docents are a wealth of information.

Mendips (John Lennon's Home)

Even though he sang about being a working-class hero, John grew up in the suburbs of Liverpool, surrounded by doctors, lawyers,

and—beyond the back fence—Strawberry Field.

This was the home of John's Aunt Mimi, who raised him in this house from the time he was five years old and once told him, "A guitar's all right, John, but you'll never earn a living by it." (John later bought Mimi a country cottage with those fateful words etched over the fireplace.) John moved out at age 23, but his first wife, Cynthia, bunked here for a while when John made his famous first trip to America. Yoko Ono bought the house in 2002 and gave it as a gift to the National Trust (generating controversy among the neighbors). The house's stewards make this place come to life.

On the surface, it's just a 1930s house carefully restored to how it would have been in the past. But delve deeper. It's been lovingly cared for—restored to be the tidy, well-kept place Mimi would have recognized (down to her apron hanging in the kitchen). It's a lucky quirk of fate that the house's interior remained mostly unchanged after the Lennons left: The bachelor who owned it decades after them didn't upgrade much, so even the light switches are true to the time.

If you're a John Lennon fan, it's fun to picture him as a young boy drawing and imagining at his dining room table. It also makes for an interesting comparison to Paul's humbler home, which is the second part of the tour.

20 Forthlin Road (Paul McCartney's Home)

In comparison to Aunt Mimi's house, the home where Paul grew up is simpler, much less "posh," and even a little ratty around the edges. Michael, Paul's brother, wanted it that way—their mother, Mary (famously mentioned in "Let It Be"), died when the boys were young, and it never had the tidiness of a woman's touch. It's been intentionally scuffed up around the edges to preserve the

LIVERPOOL

historical accuracy. Notice the differences—Paul has said that John's house was vastly different and more clearly middle class; at Mendips, there were books on the bookshelves.

More than a hundred Beatles songs were written in this house (including "I Saw Her Standing There") during days Paul and John spent skipping school. The photos from Michael, taken in this house, help make the scene of what's mostly a barren interior much more interesting.

Nightlife in Liverpool

Liverpool hops after hours, especially on weekends. The most happening zone is the area called **Ropewalks,** just east of the downtown shopping district and Albert Dock. Part of the protected historic area of Liverpool's docklands, the Ropewalks area has been redeveloped over the last few years and is now filled mostly with trendy pubs, nightclubs, and lounges—some of them rough around the edges, others posh and sleek. While this area is aimed primarily at the college-age crowd, it's still worth a stroll, and has a few eateries worth considering.

Pubs

The "Eating in Liverpool" section, later, lists several pubs good for either a drink or a meal. Liverpool also has a wide range of watering holes best for serious drinkers and beer aficionados. The food at these palaces, all in the city center, is an afterthought, but they're a great spot for a pint: **The Ship and Mitre,** overlooking an off-ramp at the edge of downtown, has perhaps Liverpool's best selection of beers—with 30-plus types on tap—as well as frequent beer festivals; it can get very crowded (133 Dale Street, tel. 0151/236-0859, see festival schedule at www.theshipandmitre.com). **Thomas Rigby's** has hard-used wooden floors that spill out into a rollicking garden courtyard (21 Dale Street). Around the corner and much more sedate, **Ye Hole in Ye Wall** brags that it's Liverpool's oldest pub, from 1726. Notice the men's room on the ground floor—the women's room, required by law to be added in the 1970s, is upstairs (just off Dale Street on Hackins Hey). A few blocks over, right in the heart of downtown and surrounded by modern mega-malls, is **The Globe**—a tight, cozy, local-feeling pub with five real ales and sloping floors (17 Cases Street).

Sleeping in Liverpool

Your best budget options in this thriving city are the boring, predictable, and central chain hotels—though I've listed a couple of more colorful options also worth considering. Many hotels, including the ones listed below, charge more on weekends (particularly Sat), especially when the Liverpool FC soccer team plays a home game. Rates shoot up even higher two weekends a year: during the Grand National horse race (long weekend in April) and during Beatles Week in late August—avoid these times if you can. Prices plummet on Sunday nights.

$$$ Hope Street Hotel is a class act that sets the bar for Liverpool's hotels. Located across from the Philharmonic on Hope Street (midway between the cathedrals, in an enticing dining neighborhood), this stylish and contemporary hotel has 89 luxurious rooms with lots of hardwood, exposed brick, and elegant little extras (standard Db-officially £190, but often £120-160 Fri-Sat and £87-107 Sun-Thu; fancier and pricier deluxe rooms and suites available, breakfast-£10 if you prebook, elevator, free Wi-Fi, parking-£10, 40 Hope Street, tel. 0151/709-3000, www.hopestreet hotel.co.uk, sleep@hopestreethotel.co.uk).

$$$ Hard Day's Night Hotel is the ideal splurge for Beatles pilgrims. Located in a carefully restored old building smack in the heart of the Cavern Quarter, its decor is purely Beatles, from its public spaces (lobby, lounge, bar, restaurant) to its 110 rooms, each with a different original Beatles portrait by New York artist Shannon. What could have been a tacky travesty is instead tasteful, with a largely black-and-white color scheme and subtle nods

---

Sleep Code

(£1 = about $1.60, country code: 44, area code: 0151)
S = Single, **D** = Double/Twin, **T** = Triple, **Q** = Quad, **b** = bathroom, **s** = shower only. Unless noted otherwise, credit cards are accepted.

   To help you sort easily through these listings, I've divided the accommodations into three categories based on the price for a standard double room with bath:

   $$$ Higher Priced—Most rooms £90 or more.
   $$ Moderately Priced—Most rooms between £45-90.
   $ Lower Priced—Most rooms £45 or less.

   Prices can change without notice; verify the hotel's current rates online or by email. For the best prices, always book direct.

to the Fab Four (standard Db-£90-150, deluxe Db-£20 more, prices can spike dramatically during peak times, especially busy for Sat weddings in their own wedding chapel/reception hall, breakfast-£10 if you prebook, air-con, elevator, Internet-enabled TVs with music playlists, free Wi-Fi, Central Building, North John Street, tel. 0151/236-1964, www.harddaysnighthotel.com, enquiries @harddaysnighthotel.com).

$$ Aachen Guest Accommodations has 15 modern, straightforward rooms in an old Georgian townhouse on a pleasant street just uphill from the heart of downtown (Sb-£45-55, D-£49-75, Db-£59-85, Tb-£95-125, rates depend on demand—higher price is usually for weekends, includes breakfast, free Wi-Fi, 89-91 Mount Pleasant, tel. 0151/709-3477, www.aachenhotel.co.uk, enquiries @aachenhotel.co.uk).

$$ Best Western Feathers Hotel, nearly next door in a stately old Georgian building, has tight hallways and 82 small rooms with mod decor and amenities (Db-generally around £69-79 Sun-Thu, £99-109 Fri, £149-159 Sat, breakfast-£10 if you prebook, no elevator and six floors, guest computer, free Wi-Fi, parking-£10, 115-125 Mount Pleasant, tel. 0151/709-9655, www.feathers.uk.com, feathershotel@feathers.uk.com).

$$ Sir Thomas Hotel is a centrally located hotel that was once a bank. The lobby has been redone in trendy style, and the 39 rooms are comfortable. As windows are thin and it's a busy neighborhood, ask for a quieter room (Db-£69-85 Sun-Thu, £91-151 Fri-Sat, little difference between "standard" and "superior" rooms, one stately "luxury" room with heavy decor available, some rates include breakfast—otherwise £4, elevator, free Wi-Fi, 10-minute walk from station, 24 Sir Thomas Street at the corner of Victoria Street, tel. 0151/236-1366, www.sirthomashotel.co.uk, reservations @sirthomashotel.co.uk).

$$ Premier Inn, which has 186 pleasant, American-style rooms and a friendly staff, is inside the giant converted warehouses on the Albert Dock; many rooms have exposed brick from the original structure (Db-£68-140, averages £70-80 on weekdays, check website for specific rates and special deals, breakfast-£8.25, elevator, pay Wi-Fi, discounted parking in nearby garage-£7.50/day, next to The Beatles Story, tel. 0151/702-6320, www.premierinn.com). There's also a second, downtown **$$ Premier Inn** with 165 rooms. While it's farther from the Albert Dock sights, it's just a 10-minute walk from the Lime Street train station and handy to downtown (Db-£53-141, Vernon Street, just off Dale Street, tel. 0151/242-7650). A third location is on Hanover Street, near the Liverpool One mall. These places can fill up quickly on weekends.

$$ Holiday Inn Express has a branch at the Albert Dock, next door and nearly identical to the Premier Inn described above. Its 135 rooms are a smidge more basic—and cheaper—than the Premier Inn's; you might as well check both hotels' websites to see which has the better deal going (Db-generally around £70-100 Sun-Thu, £125-135 Fri-Sat, includes buffet breakfast, pay Wi-Fi, nearby parking-£7.50/day, beyond The Beatles Story at the Albert Dock, tel. 0844-875-7575, www.holidayinnexpressliverpool.com, enquiries@exliverpool.com).

$ International Inn Hostel, run by the daughter of the Beatles' first manager, rents 100 budget beds in a former Victorian warehouse (Db-£38-47, bed in 2- to 10-bed room-£17-22, includes sheets, all rooms have bathrooms, guest kitchen with free toast and tea/coffee available 24 hours, free Wi-Fi, laundry room, game room/TV lounge, video library, 24-hour reception, café next door has pay Internet access, 4 South Hunter Street, tel. 0151/709-8135, www.internationalinn.co.uk, info@internationalinn.co.uk).

In the hostel's basement is the **$$ Cocoon Pod Hotel,** offering 32 small, no-nonsense, modern rooms for people who have outgrown hosteling. As all the rooms are underground, there are no windows, which can make rooms a bit stuffy, though very quiet (except on weekends, when the hotel attracts some rowdy stag and hen parties). Choose either two twins or a king (Sb or Db-£45 Sun-Thu, £55 Fri-Sat; 1- and 3-bedroom apartments from £65; same location, amenities, and contact info as hostel; 2-night minimum on weekends; www.cocoonliverpool.co.uk). From the Lime Street Station, the hostel/Cocoon Pod are an easy 15-minute walk; if taking a taxi, tell them it's on South Hunter Street near Hardman Street.

Eating in Liverpool

Liverpool has an exciting and quickly evolving culinary scene; as a rollicking, youthful city, it's a magnet for creative chefs as well as upscale chain restaurants. I've arranged my listings by neighborhood. Consider my suggestions, but also browse the surrounding streets. This is a city where restaurant-finding is a joy rather than a chore.

On and near Hope Street

Hope Street, which connects the two cathedrals, is also home to several excellent restaurants. The Quarter, HOST, and 60 Hope Street—which cluster near the corner of Hope and Falkner streets—are owned by brothers.

The Quarter serves up Mediterranean food at rustic tables that sprawl through several connected houses. It's trendy but cozy. They also serve breakfast and have carryout coffee, cakes, pasta, and sandwiches in their attached deli (£4-7 starters, £7-10 pizzas and pastas, chalkboard specials, Mon-Fri 8:00-23:00, Sat 9:00-23:00, Sun 9:00-22:30, 7 Falkner Street, tel. 0151/707-1965).

HOST (short for "Hope Street") features Asian fusion dishes in a casual, colorful, modern atmosphere (£4-6 small plates, £10-13 big plates, Mon-Sat 11:00-23:00, Sun 11:00-22:00, 31 Hope Street, tel. 0151/708-5831).

The Side Door is a tight, upscale, and inviting little one-room bistro with a constantly changing menu of highly regarded modern English food. While this place is pricey, their "pre-theatre menu" is a good value (£17-19 two-course meals, £19-21 three-course meals, available before 18:30; open Mon-Sat 12:00-14:30 & 17:00-21:30, closed Sun, 29a Hope Street, tel. 0151/707-7888).

60 Hope Street has modern English cuisine made with "as locally sourced as possible" ingredients in an upscale atmosphere. While the prices are high (£8-9 starters, £19-30 main dishes), their fixed-price meals are a good deal (£20/two courses, £25/three courses, prices include half-carafe of wine on Mon-Thu; open Mon-Sat 12:00-14:30 & 17:00-22:30, Sun 12:00-20:00, reservations smart—especially on weekends, 60 Hope Street, tel. 0151/707-6060, www.60hopestreet.com).

Chinatown: A few blocks southwest of Hope Street is Liverpool's thriving Chinatown neighborhood, with the world's

biggest Chinese arch. Lots of enticing options dishing up Chinese grub line up along Berry Street in front of the arch and Cornwallis Street behind it. Among these, **Yuet Ben** is one of the most established (Tue-Sun 17:00-23:00, until 24:00 Fri-Sat, closed Mon, facing the arch at 1 Upper Duke Street, tel. 0151/709-5772). Or you can line up with the Liverpudlians at **Tokyou**, featuring tasty £5 noodle and rice dishes (Cantonese, Japanese, Malaysian, etc.), with service that's fast and furious (daily 12:30-23:00, 7 Berry Street, tel. 0151/445-1023).

Pubs near Hope Street

The Philharmonic Dining Rooms, kitty-corner from the actual Philharmonic, is actually a pub—but what a pub. This place wins the "atmosphere award" for its old-time elegance. The bar is a work of art, the marble urinals are downright genteel, and the three sitting

LIVERPOOL

areas on the ground floor (including the giant hall) are an enticing place to sip a pint. This is a better place to drink than to eat, as food is usually served in the less-atmospheric upstairs (Mon-Fri evenings and all day Sat-Sun, £6-11 pub grub). John Lennon once said that his biggest regret about fame was "not being able to go to the Phil for a drink" (open for drinks daily 11:00-24:00, corner of Hope and Hardman streets, tel. 0151/707-2837).

The Fly in the Loaf has a classic pub exterior and interior, with efficient service, eight hand pulls for real ales, and good food (£3-4 sandwiches, £6-7 meals, open daily 12:00-23:00; food served Tue-Sat until 19:00, Sun until 17:00, no food on Mon; 13 Hardman Street, tel. 0151/708-0817).

Ropewalks

While primarily a nightlife zone (see "Nightlife in Liverpool," earlier), this gentrified area also has a smattering of unique restaurants—including one in a former church, and another in a former police station.

Alma de Cuba is housed in the former Polish Catholic Church of St. Peter's with a trendy bar (downstairs, in the nave and altar

area) and restaurant (upstairs, looking down into the nave). While the food (an eclectic international mix) is an afterthought, the "hedonists' church" atmosphere is nothing short of remarkable—at least, to those who don't find it all a bit sacrilegious (£3-7 starters, £10-18 main dishes; food served daily 12:00-22:00, Fri-Sat until 23:00, bar stays open later; live music Thu from 22:30, live DJ with flower-petal shower and samba dancers Fri-Sat from 23:00, gospel brunch with small gospel choir Sun 13:30-17:00; Seel Street, tel. 0151/702-7394).

Liverpool One Bridewell pub fills a circa-1850 police station with a lively pub atmosphere. Downstairs, past the bar, several jail cells have been converted into cozy seating areas, while another bar and dining area sprawl upstairs (£7-10 meals; open daily 12:00-23:00, until 24:00 Fri-Sat; food served Tue-Sat until 21:00, Sun-Mon until 18:00; 1 Campbell Square, Argyle Street, tel. 0151/709-7000).

On Duke Street: A few big, modern, popular, chain-feeling restaurants—Japanese, Mexican, Italian, and more—line up along Duke Street in the heart of the Ropewalks area (concentrated on the block between Kent Street and the Chinatown arch). While not high cuisine, these crowd-pleasers are close to the nightlife action.

Downtown

Delifonseca is a trendy delicatessen with two parts. In the cellar is the picnic-perfect deli counter, with prepared salads sold by weight, a wide range of meats and cheeses, and made-to-order £3 sandwiches. Upstairs is a casual bistro serving British, Mediterranean, and international cuisine (£7-10 sandwiches and salads, £10-13 chalkboard main dishes). While not cheap, the food here is high-quality (both open Mon-Sat 8:00-21:00, closed Sun, 12 Stanley Street, tel. 0151/255-0808).

Liverpool One: This shopping center, right in the heart of town, is nirvana for British chain restaurants. The upper Leisure Terrace has a row of some popular chains—including **Café Rouge** (French), **Wagamama Noodle Bar, Gourmet Burger Company, Pizza Express,** and more—all with outdoor seating. If you want to dine on predictable mass-produced food, you'll have a wide selection here.

At the Albert Dock

The eateries at the Albert Dock aren't high cuisine, but they're handy to your sightseeing. A slew of trendy restaurants come alive with club energy at night, but are sedate and pleasant in the afternoon and early evening. For lunch near the sights, consider the café in the **Tate Gallery** (£3-4 sandwiches and soups, £6-9 main dishes, daily 10:00-17:30 except closes at 16:30 Nov-March).

Liverpool Connections

By Train

Note that many connections from Liverpool transfer at the Wigan North Western Station, which is on a major north-south train line.

From Liverpool by Train to: Blackpool (1/hour direct, 1.5 hours), **Keswick/Lake District** (train to Penrith—roughly hourly with change in Wigan and possibly elsewhere, 2.25 hours; then bus to Keswick), **York** (1/hour direct, 2.25 hours, more with transfer), **Edinburgh** (1-2/hour, 3.5-4.5 hours, most change in Wigan or Manchester), **Glasgow** (1/hour, 3.5-4.5 hours, change in Wigan and possibly elsewhere), **London**'s Euston Station (1/hour direct, 2 hours, more with changes), **Crewe** (2/hour, 45 minutes), **Chester** (4/hour, 45 minutes). Train info: tel. 0845-748-4950, www.national rail.co.uk.

By Ferry

By Ferry to Dublin, Republic of Ireland: P&O Irish Sea Ferries runs a car ferry only—no foot passengers (1-3/day, 8-hour trip, prices vary widely—roughly £150 for car and 2 passengers, overnight ferry includes berth and meals, 20-minute drive north of the city center at Liverpool Freeport—Gladstone dock, check in 1-2 hours before departure, tel. 0871-664-4777, www.poirishsea .com). Those without cars can take a ferry to Dublin via the Isle of Man (www.steam-packet.com), or ride the train to North Wales, and catch the Dublin ferry from Holyhead (www.stenaline.co.uk).

By Ferry to Belfast, Northern Ireland: Ferries sail from nearby Birkenhead roughly twice a day (8 hours, fares vary widely, tel. 0871-230-0330, www.stenaline.co.uk). Birkenhead's dock is a 15-minute walk from Hamilton Square Station on Merseyrail's Wirral Line.

THE LAKE DISTRICT

*Keswick • North Lake District • Ullswater Lake
• South Lake District*

In the pristine Lake District, William Wordsworth's poems still shiver in trees and ripple on ponds. Nature rules this land, and humanity keeps a wide-eyed but low profile. Relax, recharge, take a cruise or a hike, and maybe even write a poem. Renew your poetic license at Wordsworth's famous Dove Cottage.

The Lake District, about 30 miles long and 30 miles wide, is nature's lush, green playground. Explore it by foot, bike, bus, or car. While not impressive in sheer height (Scafell Pike, the tallest peak in England, is only 3,206 feet), there's a walking-stick charm about the way nature and the culture mix here. Locals are fond of declaring that their mountains are older than the Himalayas and were once as tall, but have been worn down by the ages. Walking along a windblown ridge or climbing over a rock fence to look into the eyes of a ragamuffin sheep, even tenderfeet get a chance to feel very outdoorsy. The tradition of staying close to the land remains true—albeit in an updated form—in the 21st century; you'll see restaurants serving organic food as well as stickers advocating for environmental causes in the windows of homes.

Dress in layers, and expect rain mixed with brilliant "bright spells" (pubs offer atmospheric shelter at every turn). Drizzly days can be followed by delightful evenings.

Plan to spend the majority of your time in the unspoiled North Lake District. In this chapter, I focus on the town of Keswick, the lake called Derwentwater, and the vast, time-passed Newlands Valley. The North Lake District works great by car or by bus (with easy train access via Penrith), delights nature lovers, and has good accommodations to boot.

The South Lake District—slightly closer to London—is

famous primarily for its Wordsworth and Beatrix Potter sights, and gets the promotion, the tour crowds, and the tackiness that comes with them. While the slate-colored towns (Ambleside, Windermere, Bowness-on-Windermere, and so on) are cute, they're also touristy—which means crowded and overpriced. I strongly recommend that you buck the trend and focus on the north. Ideally, enter the region from the north, via Penrith. Make your home base in or near Keswick, and side-trip from here into the South Lake District only if you're interested in the Wordsworth and Beatrix Potter sights. Dipping into the South Lake District also works well en route if you're driving between Keswick and points south.

Planning Your Time

I'd suggest spending two days and two nights in this area. Penrith is the nearest train station, just 45 minutes by bus or car from Keswick. Those without a car will use Keswick as a springboard: Cruise the lake and take one of the many hikes in the Catbells area. Non-hikers can hop on a minibus tour. If great scenery is commonplace in your life, the Lake District can be more soothing (and rainy) than exciting. If you're rushed, you could make this area a one-night stand—or even a quick drive-through. But since the towns themselves are unexceptional, a visit here isn't worth it unless you have time to head up into the hills or out on the water at least once.

Two-Day Driving Plan: Here's the most exciting way for drivers coming from the south—who'd like to visit South Lake District sights en route to the North Lake District—to max out their time here:

Day 1: Get an early start, aiming to leave the motorway at Kendal by 10:30; drive along Windermere, the lake, and through the town of Ambleside.

11:30   Tour Dove Cottage and the Wordsworth Museum.

13:00   Backtrack to Ambleside, where a small road leads up and over the dramatic Kirkstone Pass (far more scenic northbound than southbound—get out and bite the wind) and down to Glenridding on Lake Ullswater.

15:00   Catch the next Ullswater boat and ride to Howtown. Hike six miles (3-4 hours) from Howtown back to Glenridding. Or, for a shorter Ullswater experience, hike up to the Aira Force waterfall (1 hour) or up and around Lanty's Tarn (2-2.5 hours).

19:00   Drive to your Keswick hotel or farmhouse B&B near Keswick, with a stop as the sun sets at Castlerigg Stone Circle.

Day 2: Spend the morning (3-4 hours) splicing the Catbells high-ridge hike into a circular boat trip around Derwentwater.

In the afternoon, make the circular drive from Keswick through the Newlands Valley, Buttermere, Honister Pass, and Borrowdale. You could tour the Honister Slate Mine en route (last tour at 15:30) and/or pitch-and-putt nine holes in Keswick before a late dinner.

Getting Around the Lake District

With a Car

Nothing is very far from Keswick and Derwentwater. Pick up a good map (any hotel can loan you one), get off the big roads,

and leave the car, at least occasionally, for some walking. In summer, the Keswick-Ambleside-Windermere-Bowness corridor (A-591) suffers from congestion. Back lanes are far less trampled and lead you through forgotten villages, where sheep outnumber people and stone churchyards are filled with happily permanent residents.

To **rent a car** here, try Enterprise in Penrith. They'll pick you up in Keswick and drive you back to their office to get the car, and also drive you back to Keswick after you've dropped it off (Mon-Fri 8:00-18:00, Sat 9:00-12:00, closed Sun, requires drivers license and second form of ID, reserve a day in advance, tel. 01768/893-840). Larger outfits are more likely to have a branch in Carlisle, which is a bit to the north but well-served by train (on the same Glasgow-Birmingham line as Penrith) and only a few minutes farther from the Keswick area.

Parking is tight throughout the region. It's easiest to park in the pay-and-display lots (generally about £3/2-3 hours, £5/4-5 hours, and £7/12 hours; have coins on hand, as most machines don't make change). If you're parking for free on the roadside, don't block vital turnouts. Never park on double yellow lines.

Without a Car

Those based in Keswick without a car manage fine. Because of the region's efforts to "green up" travel and cut down on car traffic, the bus service is quite efficient for hiking and sightseeing. (Consider leaving your car in town and using the bus for many sightseeing and hiking agendas.)

By Bus: Keswick has no real bus station; buses stop at a turn-out in front of the Booths Supermarket. Local buses take you quickly and easily (if not always frequently) to all nearby points of interest. Check the schedule carefully to make sure you can catch the last bus home. The *Lakes Connection* booklet explains the schedules (available at TIs or on any bus). On board, you can

The Lake District

SEE DETAIL MAPS

TO GLASGOW & OBAN

M-6

COCKER-MOUTH A-66 BASSENTHWAITE LAKE

B-5292 PENRITH

A-66

KESWICK

CRUMMOCK-WATER NEWLANDS VALLEY HAWES END CASTLERIGG STONE CIRCLE AIRA FORCE WATER-FALL POOLEY BRIDGE

CATBELLS HIKE DERWENT-WATER ULLS-WATER

BUTTER-MERE HIGH BRANDELHOW STRIDING EDGE WALK HOWTOWN

BUTTER-MERE (LAKE) HONISTER PASS BORROW-DALE SEATOLLER SEATHWAITE HELVELLYN THIRLMERE GLENRIDDING PATTERDALE

A-591 A-592

GRASMERE DOVE COTTAGE KIRKSTONE PASS

RYDAL

HARD KNOTT PASS AMBLESIDE BROCKHOLE

TO RAVENGLASS CONISTON TARN HOWS WINDERMERE

M-6

5 MILES HAWKS-HEAD BOWNESS
5 KM CONISTON-WATER HILL TOP FARM KENDAL OXENHOLME

A-591 A-65

WINDERMERE LAKE

AQUARIUM NEWBY BRIDGE
TO ULVERSTON A-592

TO LIVERPOOL & LONDON

LONDON

DCH

THE LAKE DISTRICT

purchase an Explorer pass that lets you ride any Stagecoach bus throughout the area (£10.30/1 day, £22/3 days), or you can get one-day passes for certain routes. For bus and rail info, visit www .traveline.org.uk.

Buses **#X4** and **#X5** connect Penrith train station to Keswick (hourly Mon-Sat, every 2 hours Sun, 45 minutes, £6.20).

Bus **#77/#77A**, the Honister Rambler, makes the gorgeous circle from Keswick around Derwentwater, over Honister Pass, through Buttermere, and down the Whinlatter Valley (4/day clockwise, 4/day "anticlockwise," daily Easter-Oct, 1.5-hour loop, £7 Honister & Borrowdale Dayrider all-day pass).

Bus **#78,** the Borrowdale Rambler, goes topless in the summer, affording a wonderful sightseeing experience in and of itself, heading from Keswick to Lodore Hotel, Grange, Rosthwaite, and Seatoller at the base of Honister Pass (nearly hourly, more frequent late July-Aug, 30 minutes each way, £7 Honister & Borrowdale Dayrider all-day pass).

Buses **#108** and **#508**, the Kirkstone Rambler, run between Penrith and Glenridding (near the bottom of Ullswater), stopping in Pooley Bridge (4/day, 45 minutes). On weekends and in late July-Aug, bus #508 also connects Glenridding and Windermere (4/day, 1 hour). The £14.80 Ullswater Bus & Boat all-day pass covers buses #108 and #508 as well as steamers on Ullswater.

Bus **#505,** the Coniston Rambler, connects Windermere with Hawkshead (about hourly, daily Easter-Oct, 35 minutes).

Bus **#555** connects Keswick with the south (hourly, more frequent in summer, one hour to Windermere).

Bus **#599,** the open-top Lakeland Experience, runs along the main Windermere corridor, connecting the big tourist attractions in the south: Grasmere and Dove Cottage, Rydal Mount, Ambleside, Brockhole, Windermere, and Bowness Pier (3/hour Easter-late Sept, 2/hour late Sept-Oct, 50 minutes each way, £7 Central Lakes Dayrider all-day pass).

By Bike: Keswick works well as a springboard for several fine days out on a bike; consider a three-hour loop trip up Newlands Valley, following the Railway Path up a former train track (now a biking path), and returning via Castlerigg Stone Circle.

Several shops in Keswick rent road bikes and mountain bikes. Bikes come with helmets, touring maps, and advice for good trips. Try **Whinlatter Bikes** (£15/day, daily 10:00-17:00, 82 Main Street, tel. 017687/73940, www.whinlatterbikes.com) or **Keswick Bikes** (from £12/half-day, £15/day, daily 9:00-17:30, 133 Main Street, tel. 017687/73355, www.keswickbikes.co.uk).

By Boat: A circular boat service glides you around Derwentwater, with several hiker-aiding stops along the way (for a cruise/hike option, see "Derwentwater Lakeside Walk" on page 550).

By Foot: Hiking information is available everywhere. Don't hike without a good, detailed map (wide selection at Keswick TI and at the many outdoor gear stores, or borrow one from your B&B). Helpful fliers at TIs and B&Bs describe the most popular routes. For an up-to-date weather report, ask at a TI or call 0844-846-2444. Wear suitable clothing and footwear (you can rent boots in town; B&Bs can likely loan you a good coat or an umbrella if weather looks threatening). Plan for rain. Watch your footing. Injuries are common. Every year, several people die while hiking in the area (some from overexertion; others are blown off ridges).

By Tour: For organized bus tours that run the roads of the Lake District, see "Tours in Keswick," later.

The Lake District at a Glance

North Lake District
In Keswick

▲▲Theatre by the Lake Top-notch theater a pleasant stroll from Keswick's main square. **Hours:** Shows generally at 20:00 in summer, possibly earlier fall through spring; box office open daily 9:30-20:00. See page 557.

▲Derwentwater Lake immediately south of Keswick, with good boat service and trails. See page 547.

▲Pencil Museum Paean to graphite-filled wooden sticks. **Hours:** Daily 9:30-17:00. See page 548.

▲Pitch-and-Putt Golf Cheap, easygoing nine-hole course in Keswick's Hope Park. **Hours:** Daily from 10:00, last start at 18:00 but possibly later in summer, closed Nov-Feb. See page 549.

Near Keswick

▲▲▲Scenic Circle Drive South of Keswick Hour-long drive through the best of the Lake District's scenery, with plenty of fun stops (including the fascinating Honister Slate Mine) and short side-trip options. See page 554.

▲▲Castlerigg Stone Circle Evocative and extremely old (even by British standards) ring of Neolithic stones. See page 549.

▲▲Catbells High Ridge Hike Two-hour hike along dramatic ridge southwest of Keswick. See page 550.

▲▲Buttermere Hike Four-mile, low-impact lakeside loop in a gorgeous setting. See page 551.

▲▲More Hikes from Keswick Scenic hikes with varying degrees of difficulty: Latrigg Peak, Railway Path, and Walla Crag. See page 554.

▲Honister Slate Mine Tour A 1.5-hour guided hike through a 19th-century mine at the top of Honister Pass. **Hours:** Daily at 10:30, 12:30, and 15:30; also at 14:00 in summer; Dec-Jan 12:30 tour only. See page 555.

Ullswater Lake Area

▲▲Ullswater Hike and Boat Ride Long lake best enjoyed via steamer boat and seven-mile walk. **Hours:** Boats generally daily 9:45-16:45, 6-9/day April-Oct, fewer off-season. See page 567.

▲▲Lanty's Tarn and Keldas Hill Moderately challenging 2.5-mile loop hike from Glenridding with sweeping views of Ullswater. See page 567.

▲Aira Force Waterfall Easy uphill hike to thundering waterfall. See page 568.

South Lake District

▲▲Dove Cottage and Wordsworth Museum The poet's humble home, with a museum that tells the story of his remarkable life. **Hours:** Daily March-Oct 9:30-17:30, Nov-Feb 9:30-16:30 except closed Jan. See page 570.

▲Rydal Mount Wordsworth's later, more upscale home. **Hours:** March-Oct daily 9:30-17:00; Nov-Dec and Feb Wed-Sun 11:00-16:00, closed Mon-Tue; closed Jan. See page 573.

▲Hill Top Farm Beatrix Potter's painstakingly preserved cottage. **Hours:** June-Aug Sat-Thu 10:00-17:30, April-May and Sept-Oct Sat-Thu 10:30-16:30, mid-Feb-March Sat-Thu 10:30-15:30, closed Nov-mid-Feb and Fri year-round, often a long wait to visit—call ahead. See page 574.

▲Beatrix Potter Gallery Collection of artwork by and background on the creator of Peter Rabbit. **Hours:** April-Oct Sat-Thu 10:30-17:00, mid-Feb-March Sat-Thu 10:30-15:30, closed Fri (except possibly in summer) and Nov-mid-Feb. See page 575.

The World of Beatrix Potter Touristy exhibition about the author. **Hours:** Daily April-Sept 10:00-18:00, Oct-March 10:00-17:00. See page 575.

Brockhole National Park Visitors Centre Best place to gather info on Lake Windermere and the surrounding area, grandly situated in a lakeside mansion. **Hours:** Daily April-Oct 10:00-17:00, Nov-March 10:00-16:00. See page 576.

Keswick and the North Lake District

As far as touristy Lake District towns go, Keswick (KEZ-ick, population 5,000) is far more enjoyable than Windermere, Bowness, or Ambleside. Many of
the place names around Keswick
have Norse origins, inherited
from the region's 10th-century
settlers. Notice that most lakes
in the region end in either *water*
(e.g., Derwentwater) or *mere* (e.g.,
Windermere), which is related to
the German word for lake, *Meer*.

An important mining center
for slate, copper, and lead through the Middle Ages, Keswick
became a resort in the 19th century. Its fine Victorian buildings
recall those Romantic days when city slickers first learned about
"communing with nature." Today, the compact town is lined
with tearooms, pubs, gift shops, and hiking-gear shops. The lake
called Derwentwater is a pleasant 10-minute walk from the town
center.

Orientation to Keswick

Keswick is an ideal home base, with plenty of good B&Bs, an
easy bus connection to the nearest train station at Penrith, and a
prime location near the best lake in the area, Derwentwater. In
Keswick, everything is within a 10-minute walk of everything else:
the pedestrian town square, the TI, recommended B&Bs, grocery
stores, the wonderful municipal pitch-and-putt golf course, the
main bus stop, a lakeside boat dock, the post office (with Internet
access upstairs), and a central parking lot. Thursdays and Saturdays
are market days in the town square, but the square is lively every
day throughout the summer.

Keswick town is a delight for wandering. Its centerpiece,
Moot Hall (meaning "meeting hall"), was a 16th-century copper
warehouse upstairs with an arcade below (closed after World War
II; most Lake District towns and villages have similar meeting
halls). "Keswick" means "cheese farm"—a legacy from the time
when the town square was the spot to sell cheese. When the town
square went pedestrian-only, locals were all abuzz about people
tripping over the curbs. (The English, seemingly thrilled by ever-

present danger, are endlessly warning visitors to "watch your head," "duck or grouse," "watch the step," and "mind the gap.")

Keswick and the Lake District are popular with English holiday makers who prefer to bring their dogs with them on vacation. The town square in Keswick can look like the Westminster Dog Show, and the recommended Dog and Gun pub, where "well-behaved dogs are welcomed," is always full of patient pups. If you are shy about connecting with people, pal up to an English pooch—you'll often find they're happy to introduce you to their owners.

Tourist Information

The National Park Visitors Centre/TI is in Moot Hall, right in the

middle of the town square (daily Easter-Oct 9:30-17:30, Nov-Easter 9:30-16:30, tel. 017687/72645, www.lakedistrict.gov.uk and www.keswick.org). Staffers are pros at advising you about hiking routes. They can also help you figure out public transportation to outlying sights, book rooms (you'll pay a £4 booking fee; it's cheaper to call B&Bs direct), and tell you about the region's various adventure activities.

The TI sells theater tickets, Keswick Launch tickets (at a £1 discount), fishing licenses, and brochures and maps that outline nearby hikes (£0.60-2, including a very simple and driver-friendly £2 *Lap Map* featuring sights, walks, and a mileage chart). The TI also has books and maps for hikers, cyclists, and drivers (more books are sold at shops all over town).

Check the boards inside the TI's foyer for information about walks, talks, and entertainment. You can also pick up the *Events and Guided Walks* guide. The daily weather forecast is posted just outside the front door (weather tel. 0844-846-2444). For information about the TI's guided walks, see "Tours in Keswick," later.

Helpful Hints

Book in Advance: Keswick hosts a variety of festivals and conventions, especially during the summer, so it's smart to book ahead. Please honor your bookings—the B&B proprietors here lose out on much-needed business if you don't show up.

A sampling of events: The Keswick Jazz Festival mellows out the town in early May (www.keswickjazzfestival.co.uk), followed immediately by the Mountain Festival (www.keswickmountainfestival.co.uk), then a beer festival in early June (www.keswickbeerfestival.co.uk). The Keswick

THE LAKE DISTRICT

Keswick

1 Stanger Street B&Bs
2 Howe Keld & Parkfield House
3 Hazeldene Hotel
4 Burleigh Mead B&B; Brundholme Guest House
5 Allerdale House
6 Keswick Youth Hostel
7 To Derwentwater Hostel
8 The Dog and Gun
9 To The Pheasant
10 Star of Siam
11 Abraham's Tea Room
12 The Lakeland Pedlar
13 Bryson's Bakery & Tea Room
14 Pumpkin Café
15 Station Rd. Eateries
16 Supermarket
17 The Oddfellows Arms
18 Post Office & Internet Café
19 Bike Rentals (2)
20 Theatre by the Lake
21 Cinema
22 Keswick Launch Cruises
23 Cricket Pitch
24 Lawn Bowling, Tennis, Putting Green
25 Photo Fun with Sheep
26 Launderette

P PARKING

PEDESTRIAN ZONE

TO NEWLANDS VALLEY B&Bs

HIGH HILL

RIVER GRETA

CAMPING

DCH

TO NICHOL END PIER ←

DERWENTWATER

TO ASHNESS GATE PIER

TO ⑨ & A-66

PATH TO LATRIGG PEAK

CROSTHWAITE

PATH

PATH TO THRELKELD

BRUNDHOLME

PENCIL MUSEUM

FITZ PARK ㉓

PLAYGROUND

POOL

ART MUSEUM

OLD RAIL STN.

MAIN

⑲

BUS STOP

⑲

& ⑯

STANGER

①

㉖

P

⑥

STATION ROAD

㉔

PENRITH ROAD

TO PENRITH

HEADLANDS

⑩

BANK

⑱

P

⑬

⑫

VICTORIA

STN. ST.

HEADS RD.

MARKET

⑰

PL.

⑧

LAKE

⑭

DER.

㉑

i

⑮

SOUTHEY

ST. JOHNS

BLEN.

HELV.

CHURCH

ACORN

ESKIN

⑤

THE HEADS

④ ③

②

LAKE RD.

⑪

ⓗ

AMBLESIDE

TO CASTLERIGG STONE CIRCLE & WINDERMERE VIA A-591

PITCH + PUTT GOLF

HOPE PARK

㉕

LAKE ROAD

HEADS ROAD

BORROWDALE ROAD

P

⑳

DOCK

㉒

TO BUTTERMERE VIA B-5289

LAKE PATH

TO ⑦

¼ MILE

400 METERS

THE LAKE DISTRICT

Convention packs the town with 4,000 evangelical Christians for three weeks each summer (sometime in July-Aug, www.keswickministries.org).

Several Bank Holiday Mondays in spring and summer (May 5, May 26, and Aug 25 in 2014; May 4, May 25, and Aug 31 in 2015) draw vacationers from all over the island for three-day weekends.

If you have trouble finding a room (or a B&B that accepts small children), try www.keswick.org to search for available rooms.

Internet Access: U-Compute, located above the store that contains the post office, provides computer terminals and Wi-Fi (same price no matter how you connect—£2/30 minutes, £3/hour, unused time valid for 2 weeks, Mon-Sat 9:00-17:30, closed Sun, corner of Main and Bank streets, tel. 017687/75127). The **launderette** listed next also has Wi-Fi.

Laundry: The town's launderette is on Bank Street, just up the side street from the post office (self-service Mon-Fri 8:00-19:00, Sat-Sun 9:00-18:00, about £6/load wash and dry, coin-op soap dispenser; full-service for a reasonable additional £1.40-2.80 fee depending on load size; tea and Wi-Fi for £2, see map on page 544, tel. 017687/75448).

Midges: Tiny biting insects called midges—similar to no-see-ums—might bug you in this region from late May through September, particularly at dawn and dusk. The severity depends on the weather since wind and sunshine can deter them, and insect repellant fends them off: Ask the locals what works if you'll be hiking.

Local Candy: Kendal mint cakes are advertised throughout this area. Basically a big, flat, mint-flavored sugar cube, these sweet, refreshing treats are worth sampling.

Tours in Keswick

Guided Walks

KR Guided Walks offers hikes of varying levels of difficulty. They depart several times a week at 9:00 or 10:00 from the Keswick TI (check their calendar of planned hikes online). They're led by local guides, leave regardless of the weather, and sometimes incorporate a bus ride into the outing (£20/day, Easter-Oct, wear suitable clothing and footwear, bring lunch and water, full-day tours return by 17:00, must book in advance, tel. 017687/71302, mobile 0709-176-5860, www.keswickrambles.org.uk, booking@keswickrambles.org.uk). The guides are also available for private tours throughout the year.

TIs throughout the region also offer **free walks** led by

"Voluntary Rangers" several times a month in summer (depart from Keswick TI; check schedule in the *Events and Guided Walks* guide).

Bus Tours

These are great for people with bucks who'd like to wring maximum experience out of their limited time and see the area without lots of hiking or messing with public transport. For a cheaper alternative, take public buses.

Mountain Goat Tours is the region's dominant tour company. Unfortunately, they run their minibus tours out of Windermere, with pick-ups in Bowness, Ambleside, and sometimes in Grasmere. For those based in Keswick, add about an extra hour of driving or bus riding, round-trip, if you join their tours in Windermere, though they may be able to arrange tours from Keswick if you contact them in advance (tours run daily, £28/half-day, £39/day, year-round if there are sufficient sign-ups, minimum 4 people to a maximum of 16 per hearty bus, book in advance by calling 015394/45161, www.mountain-goat.com, enquiries @mountain-goat.com).

Show Me Cumbria Private Tours runs personalized tours all around the Lake District, and can pick you up in Keswick and other locations. They charge per hour, not per person, so their tours are a fine value for small groups (£30/hour, 1-6 people per tour, room for 2 small children in built-in child seats, tel. 01768/864-825, mobile 0780-902-6357, based in Penrith, www.showmecumbria .co.uk, andy@showmecumbria.co.uk).

Sights in Keswick

▲Derwentwater

One of Cumbria's most photographed and popular lakes, Derwentwater has four islands, good circular boat service, and

plenty of trails. The pleasant town of Keswick is a short stroll from the shore, near the lake's north end. The roadside views aren't much, and while you can walk around the lake (fine trail, floods in heavy rains, 9 miles, 4 hours), much of the walk is boring. You're better off mixing a hike and boat ride (see "Hikes and Drives in the North Lake District," later), or simply enjoy the circular boat tour of the lake.

Boating on Derwentwater: Keswick Launch runs two **cruises** an hour, alternating clockwise and "anticlockwise" (boats depart on the half-hour, daily 10:00-16:30, July-Aug until 17:30, in winter 5-6/day generally weekends and holidays only, at end of Lake Road, tel. 017687/72263, www.keswick-launch.co.uk). Boats make seven stops on each 50-minute round-trip (may skip some stops or not run at all if the water level is very high—such as after a heavy rain). The boat trip costs about £2 per segment (cheaper the more segments you buy) or £9.50 per circle (£1 less if you book through TI) with free stopovers; you can get on and off all you want, but tickets are collected on the boat's last leg to Keswick, marking the end of your ride. If you want to be picked up at a certain stop, stand at the end of the pier Gilligan-style, or the boat may not stop. Keswick Launch also rents **rowboats** for up to three people (£8/30 minutes, £12/hour, open Easter-Oct, larger rowboats and motor boats available). Keswick Launch also has a delightful **evening cruise** (see page 557).

▲Pencil Museum

Graphite was first discovered centuries ago in Keswick. A hunk of the stuff proved great for marking sheep in the 15th century. In 1832, the first crude Keswick pencil factory opened, and the rest is history (which is what you'll learn about here). While you can't actually tour the 150-year-old factory where the famous Derwent pencils were made, you can enjoy the smell of thousands of pencils getting sharpened for the first time. The adjacent charming and kid-friendly museum is a good way to pass a rainy hour; you may even catch an artist's demonstration. Take a look at the exhibit on "war pencils," which were made for WWII bomber crews (filled with tiny maps and compasses). Relax in the theater with a 10-minute video on the pencil-manufacturing process, followed by a sleepy animated-snowman short (drawn with Rexel Cumberland pencils).

Cost and Hours: £4.25, daily 9:30-17:00, last entry one hour before closing, humble café, 3-minute walk from the town center, signposted off Main Street, tel. 017687/73626, www.pencil museum.co.uk.

Fitz Park

An inviting, grassy park stretches alongside Keswick's tree-lined, duck-filled River Greta. There's plenty of room and a playground for kids to burn off energy. Consider an after-dinner stroll on the footpath. You may catch men in white (or frisky schoolboys in uniform) playing a game of cricket. There's the serious bowling green (where you're welcome to watch the experts play and enjoy the cheapest cuppa—i.e., tea—in town), and the public one where tourists are welcome to give lawn bowling a go (£3.50/person per hour). You can try tennis on a grass court (£7/hour for 2 people, includes rackets) or enjoy the putting green (£2.80/person).

Find the rental pavilion across the road from the art gallery (open daily Easter-Sept 10:00-17:30, longer hours July-Aug, mobile 07976/573-785).

▲Golf

A lush nine-hole pitch-and-putt golf course near the gardens in Hope Park separates the town from the lake and offers a classy, cheap, and convenient chance to golf near the birthplace of the sport. This is a great, fun, and inexpensive experience—just right after a day of touring and before dinner (£4.50 for pitch-and-putt, £2.80 for putting, £3.10 for 18 tame holes of "obstacle golf," daily from 10:00, last round starts around 18:00, possibly later in summer, café, tel. 017687/73445).

Swimming

While the leisure center doesn't have a serious adult pool, it does have an indoor pool kids love, with a huge waterslide and wave machine (swim times vary by day and by season—call or check website, no towels or suits for rent, lockers-£1 deposit, 10-minute walk from town center, follow Station Road past Fitz Park and veer left, tel. 017687/72760, www.carlisleleisure.com).

Near Keswick

▲▲Castlerigg Stone Circle

For some reason, 70 percent of England's stone circles are here in Cumbria. Castlerigg is one of the best and oldest in Britain, and an easy stop for drivers. The circle—90 feet across and 5,000 years old—has 38 stones mysteriously laid out on a line between the two tallest peaks on the horizon. They served as a celestial calendar for ritual celebrations. Imagine the ambience here, as ancient people filled this

clearing in spring to celebrate fertility, in late summer to commemorate the harvest, and in the winter to celebrate the winter solstice and the coming renewal of light. Festival dates were dictated by how the sun rose and set in relation to the stones. The more that modern academics study this circle, the more meaning they find in the placement of the stones. The two front stones face due north, toward a cut in the mountains. The rare-for-stone-circles "sanctuary" lines up with its center stone to mark where the sun rises on May Day. (Party!) For maximum "goose pimples" (as they say here), show up at sunset (free, open all the time, 1-mile hike from town; by car it's a 3-mile drive east of Keswick—follow brown signs, 3 minutes off the A-66, easy parking).

Hikes and Drives in the North Lake District

From Keswick

Derwentwater Lakeside Walk

A trail runs all along Derwentwater, but much of it (especially the Keswick-to-Hawes End stretch) is not that interesting. The best hour-long section is the 1.5-mile path between the docks at High Brandelhow and Hawes End in Keswick, where you'll stroll a level trail through peaceful trees. This walk works best in conjunction with the lake boat (see "Boating on Derwentwater," earlier).

▲▲Catbells High Ridge Hike

For a great "king of the mountain" feeling, 360-degree views, and a close-up look at the weather blowing over the ridge, hike above

Derwentwater about two hours from Hawes End up along the ridge to Catbells (1,480 feet) and down to High Brandelhow. Because the mountaintop is basically treeless, you're treated to dramatic panoramas the entire way up. From High Brandelhow, you can catch the boat back to Keswick or take the easy path along the shore of Derwentwater to your Hawes End starting point. (Extending the hike farther around the lake to Lodore takes you to a waterfall, rock climbers, a fine café, and another boat dock for a convenient return to Keswick—see page 556.) Note: When the water level is very high (for example, after a heavy rain), boats can't stop at Hawes End—ask at the TI or boat dock before setting out.

Catbells is probably the most dramatic family walk in the area (but wear sturdy shoes, bring a raincoat, and watch your footing). From Keswick, the lake, or your farmhouse B&B, you can see silhouetted figures hiking along this ridge.

Getting There: To reach the trailhead from Keswick, catch the "anticlockwise" boat (see "Boating on Derwentwater," earlier) and ride for 10 minutes to the second stop, Hawes End. (You can also ride to High Brandelhow and take this walk in the other direction, but I don't recommend it—two rocky scrambles along the way are easier and safer to navigate going uphill from Hawes End.) Note the schedule for your return boat ride. Drivers can park free at Hawes End, but parking is limited and the road can be hard to find—get very clear directions in town before heading out. (Hardcore hikers can walk to the foot of Catbells from Keswick via Portinscale, which takes about 40 minutes—ask your B&B

or the TI for directions). The Keswick TI sells a *Catbells* brochure about the hike (£1).

The Route: The path is not signposted, but it's easy to fol-

low, and you'll see plenty of other walkers. From Hawes End, walk away from the lake, through a kissing gate to the turn just before the car park. Then turn left and go up, up, up. After about 20 minutes, you'll hit the first of two short scrambles (where the trail vanishes into a cluster of steep

rocks), which leads to a bluff. From the first little summit (great for a picnic break), and then along the ridge, you'll enjoy sweeping views of the lake on one side and of Newlands Valley on the other. The bald peak in the distance is Catbells. Broken stones crunch under each step, wind buffets your ears, clouds prowl overhead, and the sheep baa comically. To anyone looking up from the distant farmhouse B&Bs, you are but a stick figure on the ridge. Just below the summit, the trail disintegrates into another short, steep, scramble. Your reward is just beyond: a magnificent hilltop perch.

After Catbells summit, descend along the ridge to a saddle ahead. The ridge continues much higher, and while it may look like your only option, at its base a small, unmarked lane with comfortable steps leads left. Unless you're up for extending the hike (see "Longer Catbells Options," next), take this path down to the lake. To get to High Brandelhow Pier, take the first left fork you come across down through a forest to the lake. When you reach Abbot's Bay, go left through a swinging gate, following a lakeside trail around a gravelly bluff, to the idyllic High Brandelhow Pier, a peaceful place to wait for your boat back to Keswick. (You can pay your fare when you board.)

Longer Catbells Options: Catbells is just the first of a series of peaks, all connected by a fine ridge trail. Hardier hikers continue up to nine miles along this same ridge, enjoying valley and lake views as they arc around the Newlands Valley toward (and even down to) Buttermere. After High Spy, you can descend an easy path into Newlands Valley. The ultimate, very full day-plan would be to take a bus to Buttermere, climb Robinson, and follow the ridge around to Catbells and back to Keswick.

▲▲Buttermere Hike

The ideal little lake with a lovely, circular four-mile stroll offers nonstop, no-sweat Lake District beauty. If you're not a hiker (but kind of wish you were), take this walk. If you're very short on time, at least stop here and get your shoes dirty.

Buttermere is connected with Borrowdale and Derwentwater

Derwentwater & Newlands Valley

Accommodations
1. Uzzicar Farm
2. Ellas Crag Guest House
3. Gill Brow Farm
4. Keskadale Farm
5. Bridge Hotel
6. Buttermere Hostel
7. Ashness Farm
8. Seatoller Farm B&B
9. Borrowdale Hostel

1 MILE
1 KM

Derwentwater Piers
A. Keswick Launch Pier
B. Ashness Gate Pier
C. Lodore Pier
D. High Brandelhow Pier
E. Low Brandelhow Pier
F. Hawes End Pier
G. Nichol End Pier

TO COCKERMOUTH
B-5292
(B) 77
WHIN-LATTER PASS
BRAITH-WAITE
PORTIN-SCALE
A-66
STAIR
SKEL-GILL
NEWLANDS VALLEY
TO COCKERMOUTH
NEWLANDS PASS
CRUMMOCK WATER
B-5289
LITTLE TOWN
CATBELLS RIDGE HIKE
GRANGE
BRIDGE
BUTTERMERE VILLAGE
(B) 77
BUTTER-MERE
GATESGARTH FARM
SEATOLLER
(B) 78
(END POINT)
B-5289
HONISTER PASS
SLATE MINE
SEATHWAITE

THE LAKE DISTRICT

THE LAKE DISTRICT

by a great road that runs over rugged Honister Pass. Buses #77/#77A make a 1.5-hour round-trip loop between Keswick and Buttermere that includes a trip over this pass. The two-pub hamlet of Buttermere has a pay-and-display parking lot, but many drivers park free along the side of the road. There's also a pay parking lot at the Honister Pass end of the lake (at Gatesgarth Farm). The Syke Farm in Buttermere is popular for its homemade ice cream (tel. 01768/77022).

▲▲More Hikes from Keswick

The area is riddled with wonderful hikes. B&Bs all have good advice, but consider these as well:

Latrigg Peak: For the easiest mountain-climbing sensation around, take the short drive to the Latrigg Peak parking lot just north of Keswick, and hike 15 minutes to the top of the 1,200-foot-high hill, where you'll be rewarded with a commanding view of the town, lake, and valley, all the way to the next lake over (Bassenthwaite). At the traffic circle just outside of Keswick, take the A-591 Carlisle exit, then an immediate right (direction: Ormathwaite/Underscar). Take the next right, a hard right, at the *Skiddaw* sign, where a long, steep, one-lane road leads to the Latrigg car park at the end of the lane. With more time, you can walk all the way from your Keswick B&B to Latrigg and back (it's a popular evening walk for locals). Or extend it even farther with the walk described next.

Railway Path: Right from downtown Keswick, this flat, easy, four-mile trail follows an old train track and the river to the village of Threlkeld (with two pubs). You can either walk back along the same path, or loop back via the Castlerigg Stone Circle (described earlier, roughly seven miles total). The Railway Path starts behind the leisure center (as you face the center, head right and around back; pick up £1 map/guide from TI).

Walla Crag: From your Keswick B&B, a fine two-hour walk to Walla Crag offers great fell (mountain) walking and a ridge-walk experience without the necessity of a bus or car. Start by strolling along the lake to the Great Wood parking lot (or drive to this lot), and head up Cat Ghyl (where "fell runners"—trail-running enthusiasts—practice) to Walla Crag. You'll be treated to great panoramic views over Derwentwater and surrounding peaks. You can do a shorter version of this walk from the parking lot at Ashness Packhorse Bridge.

▲▲▲Car Hiking: A Scenic Circle Drive South of Keswick

This hour-long drive, which includes Newlands Valley, Buttermere, Honister Pass, and Borrowdale, gives you the best scenery you'll find in the North Lake District. (To do a similar route without a car from Keswick, take loop bus #77/#77A.) Distances are short, roads are narrow and have turnouts, and views are rewarding. Get a good map and ask your B&B host for advice.

From Keswick, leave town on Crosthwaite Road, then, at the roundabout, head west on Cockermouth Road (A-66, following *Cockermouth* and *Workington* signs). Don't take the first Newlands Valley exit, but do take the second one (through Braithwaite), and follow signs up the majestic Newlands Valley (also signed for *Buttermere*).

If the **Newlands Valley** had a lake, it would be packed with tourists. But it doesn't—and it isn't. The valley is dotted with

500-year-old family-owned farms. Shearing day is reason to rush home from school. Sons get school out of the way ASAP and follow their dads into the family business. Neighbor girls marry those sons and move in.

Grandparents retire to the cottage next door. With the price of wool depressed, most of the wives supplement the family income by running B&Bs (virtually every farm in the valley rents rooms). The road has one lane, with turnouts for passing. From the Newlands Pass summit, notice the glacial-shaped wilds, once forested, now not.

From the parking lot at **Newlands Pass,** at the top of Newlands Valley (unmarked, but you'll see a waterfall on the left), an easy 300-yard hike leads to a little waterfall. On the other side of the road, an easy one-mile hike climbs up to **Knottrigg,** which probably offers more TPCB (thrills per calorie burned) than any walk in the region. If you don't have time for even a short hike, at least get out of the car and get a feel for the setting.

After Newlands Pass, descend to **Buttermere** (scenic lake, tiny hamlet with pubs and an ice-cream store—see "Buttermere Hike," earlier), turn left, drive the length of the lake, and climb over rugged **Honister Pass**—strewn with glacial debris, remnants from the old slate mines, and curious, shaggy Swaledale sheep (looking more like goats with their curly horns). The U-shaped valleys you'll see are textbook examples of those carved out by glaciers. Look high on the hillsides for "hanging valleys"—small glacial-shaped scoops cut off by the huge flow of the biggest glacier, which swept down the main valley.

The **Honister Slate Mine,** England's last still-functioning slate mine (and worth ▲), stands at the summit of Honister Pass. The youth hostel next to it was originally built to house miners in the 1920s. The mine offers worthwhile tours (perfect for when it's pouring outside): You'll put on a hardhat, load onto a bus for a short climb, then hike into a shaft to learn about the region's slate industry. It's a long, stooped hike into the mountain, made interesting by the guide and punctuated by the sound of your helmet scraping against low bits of the shaft. Standing deep in the mountain, surrounded by slate scrap and the beams of thirty headlamps fluttering around like

fireflies, you'll learn of the hardships of miners' lives and how "green gold" is trendy once again, making the mine viable. Even if you don't have time to take the tour, stop here for its slate-filled shop (café and nice WCs, £10, 1.5-hour tour; departs daily at 10:30, 12:30, and 15:30; additional tour at 14:00 in summer; Dec-Jan 12:30 tour only; call ahead to confirm times and to book a spot, helmets and lamps provided, wear good walking shoes and bring warm clothing—even in summer, tel. 017687/77230, www.honister-slate-mine.co.uk).

After stark and lonely Honister Pass, drop into sweet and homey **Borrowdale,** with a few lonely hamlets and fine hikes from Seathwaite. Circling back to Keswick past Borrowdale, the B-5289 (a.k.a., the Borrowdale Valley Road) takes you past the following popular attractions.

A set of stairs leads to the top of the house-size **Bowder Stone** (signposted, a few minutes' walk off the main road). For a great lunch or snack, including tea and homemade quiche and cakes, drop into the much-loved **High Lodore Farm Café** (Easter-Oct daily 9:00-18:00, closed Nov-Easter, short drive uphill from the main road and over a tiny bridge, tel. 017687/77221). Farther along, **Lodore Falls** is a short walk from the road, behind Lodore Hotel (a nice place to stop for tea and beautiful views). **Shepherds Crag,** a cliff overlooking Lodore, was made famous by pioneer rock climbers. (Their descendants hang from little ridges on its face today.) This is serious climbing, with several fatalities a year.

A very hard right off the B-5289 (signposted *Ashness Bridge, Watendlath*) and a steep half-mile climb on a narrow lane takes

you to the postcard-pretty **Ashness Packhorse Bridge**, a quintessential Lake District scene (parking lot just above on right). A half-mile farther up, park the car and hop out (parking lot on left, no sign). You'll be startled by the "surprise view" of Derwentwater—great for a lakes photo op. Continuing from here, the road gets extremely narrow en route to the hamlet of **Watendlath,** which has a tiny lake and lazy farm animals.

Return to the B-5289 and head back to Keswick. If you have yet to see it, cap your drive with a short detour from Keswick to the Castlerigg Stone Circle (described earlier).

Nightlife in Keswick

▲▲Theatre by the Lake
Keswickians brag that they enjoy "London theater quality at Keswick prices." Their theater offers events year-round and a wonderful rotation of six plays from late May through October (plays vary throughout the week, with music concerts on Sun in summer). There are two stages: The main one seats 400, and the smaller "studio" theater seats 100 (and features edgier plays that may involve rough language and/or nudity). Attending a play here is a fine opportunity to enjoy a classy night out.

Cost and Hours: £10-32, discounts for old and young, shows generally at 20:00, possibly earlier fall through spring, café, restaurant (pre-theater dinners must be booked 24 hours ahead by calling 017687/81102), smart to buy tickets in advance, parking at the adjacent lot is free after 19:00, tel. 017687/74411; book at box office (daily 9:30-20:00), by phone, at TI, or at www.theatrebythelake .com.

▲▲Evening Activities
For a small and remote town, Keswick has lots going on in the evening. Remember, at this latitude it's light until 22:00 in midsummer.

In Hope Park: Along with the Theatre by the Lake (described above), you can do some early evening **golfing** (fine course, pitch-and-putt, goofy golf, or just enjoy the putting green—see "Golf" under "Sights in Keswick," earlier) or **walk** among the grazing sheep as the sun gets ready to set (between the lake and the golf course, access from just above the beach, great photo ops on balmy evenings).

Keswick Launch's **evening lake cruise** comes with a glass of wine and a mid-lake stop for a short commentary. You're welcome to bring a picnic dinner and munch scenically as you cruise (£9.50, £23.50 family ticket, 1 hour, daily mid-July-Aug at 18:30 and 19:30—weather permitting and if enough people show up).

In the Town Center: To socialize with locals, head to a pub for one of their special evenings: There's **quiz night** at The Dog and Gun (21:30 on most Thu; £1, proceeds go to Keswick's Mountain Rescue team, which rescues hikers and the occasional sheep). At a quiz night, tourists are more than welcome. Drop in, say you want to join a team, and you're in. If you like trivia, it's a great way to get to know people here.

The Oddfellows Arms has free **live music** (often classic rock) just about every night in summer (April-Oct, from 21:30).

The **Keswick Street Theatre**—a theatrical walk through Keswick and its history—takes place on Tuesday evenings in summer (£3, 1.5 hours, usually starts at 19:30, weekly late May-early July, details at TI). Or you could catch a **movie** at the Lonsdale Alhambra Cinema (St. Johns Street, tel. 017687/72195, www .keswick-alhambra.co.uk), a restored old-fashioned movie theater a few minutes' walk from the town center.

Sleeping in Keswick

The Lake District abounds with attractive B&Bs, guesthouses, and hostels. It needs them all when the summer hordes threaten the serenity of this Romantic mecca.

Reserve your room in advance in high season. From November through March, you should have no trouble finding a room. But to get a particular place (especially on Saturdays), call ahead. If you're using public transportation, you should sleep in Keswick. If you're driving, staying outside Keswick is your best chance for a remote farmhouse experience. Lakeland hostels offer inexpensive beds and come with an interesting crowd of all ages.

For Keswick, I've featured B&Bs and small hotels mainly on two streets, each within three blocks of the bus station and town square. Stanger Street, a bit humbler but quiet and handy, has smaller homes and more moderately priced rooms. "The Heads" is a classier area lined with proud Victorian houses, close to the lake

---

Sleep Code

(£1 = about $1.60, country code: 44, area code: 017687)

S = Single, **D** = Double/Twin, **T** = Triple, **Q** = Quad, **b** = bathroom, **s** = shower only. Unless otherwise noted, credit cards are accepted and breakfast is included.

To help you sort easily through these listings, I've divided the accommodations into three categories based on the price for a double room with bath:

$$$ Higher Priced—Most rooms £80 or more.
  $$ Moderately Priced—Most rooms between £60-80.
    $ Lower Priced—Most rooms £60 or less.

Prices can change without notice; verify the hotel's current rates online or by email. For the best prices, always book direct.

and theater, overlooking the golf course. In addition to these two streets, Keswick abounds with many other options that are equally good; for example, the southeast area of the town center (around Eskin, Blencathra, and Helvellyn streets) is a few minutes' walk farther out, but has several B&Bs with easier parking.

Many of my Keswick listings charge extra for a one-night stay. Most won't book one-night stays on weekends (but if you show up and they have a bed free, it's yours) and don't welcome young children (generally under ages 8-12). Owners are enthusiastic about offering plenty of advice to get you on the right walking trail. Most accommodations have inviting lounges with libraries of books on the region and loaner maps. Take advantage of these lounges to transform your humble B&B room into a suite.

This is still the countryside—expect huge breakfasts (often with a wide selection, including vegetarian options), no phones in the rooms, and shower systems that might need to be switched on to get hot water. Parking is pretty easy (each place has a line on parking).

On Stanger Street

This street, quiet but just a block from Keswick's town center, is lined with B&Bs situated in Victorian slate townhouses. Each of these places is small and family-run. They are all good, offering comfortably sized rooms and a friendly welcome.

$$ Ellergill Guest House has five spic-and-span rooms with an airy, contemporary feel—several with views (Db-£65-80 depending on room size, 1 with private bath down the hall, 2 percent surcharge for credit cards, 2-night minimum, no children under age 10, free Wi-Fi, private parking, 22 Stanger Street, tel. 017687/73347, www.ellergill.co.uk, stay@ellergill.co.uk, Clare and Robin Pinkney).

$$ Badgers Wood B&B, at the top of the street, has six modern, bright, un-frilly view rooms, each named after a different tree (Sb-£40, Db-£74-78, cash only, 2-night minimum, no children under age 10, special diets accommodated, free Wi-Fi, free parking, 30 Stanger Street, tel. 017687/72621, www.badgers-wood .co.uk, enquiries@badgers-wood.co.uk, Andrew and Anne).

$$ Dunsford Guest House rents four recently updated rooms at a good price. Stained glass and wooden pews give the blue-and-cream breakfast room a country-chapel vibe (Db-£70, this price promised with this book when you book direct, cash only, free Wi-Fi, parking, 16 Stanger Street, tel. 017687/75059, www.dunsford .net, enquiries@dunsford.net, Deb and Keith).

$$ Abacourt House, with a daisy-fresh breakfast room, has five pleasant doubles (Db-£74-78, 3 percent surcharge for credit cards, no children, free Wi-Fi, £5 sack lunches available, 26

Stanger Street, tel. 017687/72967, www.abacourt.co.uk, abacourt.keswick@btinternet.com, John and Heather).

On The Heads

These B&Bs are in an area known as The Heads. This area is classier, with bigger and grander Victorian architecture and great views overlooking the pitch-and-putt range and out into the hilly distance. The golf-course side of The Heads has free parking, if you can snare a spot (easy at night). A single yellow line on the curb means you're allowed to park there for free, but only overnight (16:00-10:00).

$$$ Howe Keld has the polished feel of a boutique hotel, but offers all the friendliness of a B&B. Its 14 contemporary-posh rooms, two on the ground floor, are spacious and tastefully decked out in native woods and slate. It's warm, welcoming, and family-run, with one of the best breakfasts I've had anywhere in England (Sb-£55-65, standard Db-£95-110, superior Db-£100-125, cash and 2-night minimum preferred, discount for 2 or more nights, family deals, free Wi-Fi, tel. 017687/72417 or toll-free 0800-783-0212, www.howekeld.co.uk, david@howekeld.co.uk, run with care by David and Valerie Fisher).

$$$ Parkfield House, thoughtfully run and decorated by John and Susan Berry, is a big Victorian house with a homey lounge. Its six rooms, some with fine views, are bright and classy (Sb-£70, Db-£80, superior king Db-£95-100, these prices promised with this book, 2-night minimum, no children under age 16, free Wi-Fi, free parking, tel. 017687/72328, www.parkfield-keswick.co.uk, parkfieldkeswick@hotmail.co.uk).

$$$ Burleigh Mead B&B is a slate mansion from 1892 with wild carpeting. Gill (pronounced "Jill," short for Gillian) rents seven lovely rooms and offers a friendly welcome, as well as a lounge and peaceful front-yard sitting area that's perfect for enjoying the view (north-facing Db with lesser views-£78-84, south-facing Db with grander views-£82-90, Db suite-£96-106, rate depends on length of stay, cash only, no children under age 8, free Wi-Fi, tel. 017687/75935, www.burleighmead.co.uk, info@burleighmead.co.uk).

$$$ Hazeldene Hotel, on the corner of The Heads, rents 10 spacious rooms, many with commanding views. It's run with care by delightful Helen and Howard (Db-£75-100 depending on view, Tb-£120, free guest computer, free Wi-Fi, free parking, tel.

017687/72106, www.hazeldene-hotel.co.uk, info@hazeldene-hotel
.co.uk).

$$ Brundholme Guest House has four bright and comfy rooms, most with sweeping views—especially from the front side—and a friendly and welcoming atmosphere (Db-£70, free Wi-Fi, tel. 017687/73305, mobile 0773-943-5401, www .brundholme.co.uk, bazaly@hotmail.co.uk, Barry and Allison Thompson).

On Eskin Street

The area just southeast of the town center has several streets lined with good B&Bs, and is still within easy walking distance of downtown and the lake.

$$ Allerdale House, a classy, nicely decorated stone mansion, holds six rooms and is well-run by Barbara and Paul (Sb-£39.50, standard Db-£79, superior Db-£93, these prices promised with this book, cash only, free Wi-Fi, private parking, 1 Eskin Street, tel. 017687/73891, www.allerdale-house.co.uk, reception @allerdale-house.co.uk).

Hostels in and near Keswick

The Lake District's inexpensive hostels, mostly located in great old buildings, are handy sources of information and social fun.

$ Keswick Youth Hostel, with 85 beds in a converted old mill that overlooks the river, has a big lounge and great riverside balcony. Travelers of all ages feel at home here, but book ahead—family rooms can be especially hard to come by from July through September (£13-22 beds in mostly 3- to 6-bed rooms, members pay £3 less, breakfast-£5, family rooms, includes sheets, pay guest computer, pay Wi-Fi, kitchen, laundry, café, bar, office open 7:00-23:00, center of town just off Station Road before river, tel. 017687/72484, www.yha.org.uk, keswick@yha.org.uk).

$ Derwentwater Hostel, in a 220-year-old mansion on the shore of Derwentwater, is two miles south of Keswick and has 88 beds (£19-21 beds in 4- to 22-bed rooms, family rooms, breakfast-£5.25, free Wi-Fi, kitchen, laundry, 23:00 curfew; follow B-5289 from Keswick—entrance is 2 miles along the Borrowdale Valley Road about 150 yards after Ashness exit—look for cottage and bus stop at bottom of the drive; tel. 017687/77246, www .derwentwater.org, contact@derwentwater.org).

West of Keswick, in the Newlands Valley

If you have a car, drive 10 minutes past Keswick down the majestic Newlands Valley (described earlier, under "Car Hiking: Scenic Circle Drive South of Keswick"). This valley is studded with

THE LAKE DISTRICT

500-year-old farms that have been in the same family for centuries and now rent rooms to supplement the family income. Each place offers easy parking, grand views, and perfect tranquility. Most of these rooms tend to be plainer and generally more dated than the B&Bs in town, and come with steep and gravelly roads, plenty of dogs, and an earthy charm. Traditionally, farmhouses lacked central heating, and while they are now heated, you can still request a hot-water bottle to warm up your bed.

Getting to the Newlands Valley: Leave Keswick via the roundabout at the end of Crosthwaite Road, and then head west on Cockermouth Road (A-66). Take the second Newlands Valley exit through Braithwaite, and follow signs through Newlands Valley (drive toward Buttermere). All of my recommended B&Bs are on this road: Uzzicar Farm (under the shale field, which local kids love hiking up to glissade down; a 10-minute drive from Keswick), Ellas Crag Guest House, then Gill Brow Farm, and finally—the last house before the stark summit—Keskadale Farm (about four miles before Buttermere at the top of the valley, about a 15-minute drive from Keswick). The one-lane road has turnouts for passing.

$$ Uzzicar Farm is a big, rustic place with two comfy guest rooms in a low-ceilinged, 16th-century farmhouse—watch out for ducks. It's a particularly intimate and homey setting, where you'll feel like part of the family (Db-£70-80, family rooms, cash or check only, tel. 017687/78026, www.uzzicarfarm.co.uk, stay @uzzicarfarm.co.uk, Helen, David, and three daughters).

$$ Ellas Crag Guest House, with three rooms—each with a great view—is a comfortable stone house with a contemporary feel and tranquil terrace overlooking the valley. This homey B&B offers a good mix of modern and traditional decor, including beautifully tiled bathrooms (Sb-£55-65, Db-£68-72, these prices good with this book, singles available Mon-Thu only, cash only, 2-night minimum, local free-range meats and eggs for breakfast, sack lunches available, huge DVD library, laundry-£10/load, tel. 017687/78217, www.ellascrag.co.uk, info@ellascrag.co.uk, Jane and Ed Ma and their children).

$$ Keskadale Farm is another good farmhouse experience, with Ponderosa hospitality. One of the valley's oldest, the house—with two guest rooms and a cozy lounge—is made from 500-year-old ship beams. This working farm is an authentic slice of Lake District life and is your chance to get to know lots of curly-horned sheep and the dogs that herd them. Now that her boys are old enough to help Dad in the fields, Margaret Harryman runs the B&B (Db-£70-80, £2 extra for one-night stays, cash only, closed Dec-Feb, sack lunches available, tel. 017687/78544, www.keskadalefarm.co.uk, info@keskadalefarm.co.uk). They also rent a two-bedroom apartment (£450/week).

$ Gill Brow Farm is a rough-hewn, working farmhouse more than 300 years old where Anne Wilson rents two simple but fine rooms, one with an en-suite bathroom, the other with a private bathroom down the hall (Db-£64, discount with 3-night stay, self-catering cottage also available, tel. 017687/78270, www.gillbrow -keswick.co.uk, info@gillbrow-keswick.co.uk).

Southwest of Keswick, in Buttermere

$$$ Bridge Hotel, just beyond Newlands Valley at Buttermere, offers 21 beautiful rooms—most of them quite spacious—and a classic Old World countryside-hotel experience. On Fridays and Saturdays, dinner is required (standard Db-£90-130 Sun-Thu, £130-180 Fri-Sat with dinner, fancier rooms for £10-20 more, apartments available, check website for specials, minimum 2-night stay on weekends, free Wi-Fi in lobby, tel. 017687/70252, www .bridge-hotel.com, enquiries@bridge-hotel.com). There are no shops within 10 miles—only peace and quiet a stone's throw from one of the region's most beautiful lakes. The hotel has a dark-wood pub/restaurant on the ground floor.

$ Buttermere Hostel, a quarter-mile south of Buttermere village on Honister Pass Road, has good food, 70 beds, family rooms, and a peacefully rural setting (£15-22 beds in mostly 4- to 6-bed rooms, members pay £3 less, breakfast-£5, inexpensive dinners and packed lunches, laundry, office open 8:30-10:00 & 17:00-22:30, 23:00 curfew, reservation tel. 0845-371-9508, hostel tel. 017687/70245, www.yha.org.uk, buttermere@yha.org.uk).

South of Keswick, near Borrowdale

$$$ Ashness Farm sits alone, ruling its valley high above Derwentwater. If you want to be immersed in farm sounds and lakeland beauty, this is the place. On this 750-acre working farm, now owned by the National Trust, people have raised sheep and cattle for centuries. Today Anne and her family are "tenant farmers," keeping this farm operating and renting five rooms to boot (Sb-£56-58, Db-£82-94, discount with stays of 2 or more nights, cozy lounge, eggs and sausage literally fresh off the farm for breakfast, sack lunches available, just above Ashness Packhorse Bridge, tel. 017687/77361, www.ashnessfarm.co.uk, enquiries@ashness farm.co.uk).

$$ Seatoller Farm B&B is a rustic 16th-century house on another working farm owned by the National Trust. Christine Simpson rents three rooms in her B&B, one of five buildings in this hamlet. The old windows are small, but the abundant flower boxes keep things bright (Db-£78, discount with stays of 2 or more nights, cottage available, closed mid-Dec-mid-Jan, tel. 017687/77232, www.seatollerfarm.co.uk, info@seatollerfarm.co.uk).

THE LAKE DISTRICT

$ Borrowdale Hostel, in secluded Borrowdale Valley just south of Rosthwaite, is a well-run place surrounded by many ways to immerse yourself in nature. The hostel offers cheap dinners and sack lunches (86 beds—mostly bunks, £18-23 beds in mostly 2- to 6-bed dorms, D-£50-60, members pay £3 less, family rooms, breakfast-£5, pay guest computer, pay Wi-Fi, laundry, office open 7:00-23:00, 23:00 curfew, reservation tel. 0845-371-9624, hostel tel. 017687/77257, www.yha.org.uk, borrowdale@yha.org.uk). To reach this hostel from Keswick by bus, take #78, the Borrowdale Rambler. Note that the last bus from Keswick departs around 17:00-17:30 most of year (see page 537 for bus details).

Eating in Keswick

Keswick has a huge variety of eateries catering to its many visitors, but I've found nothing particularly enticing at the top end; the places listed here are just good, basic values. Most stop serving by 21:00.

The Dog and Gun serves good pub food (I love their rump of lamb) with great pub ambience. Upon arrival, muscle up to the bar to order your beer and/or meal. Then snag a table as soon as one opens up. Mind your head, and tread carefully: Low ceilings and wooden beams loom overhead, while paws poke out from under tables below, as Keswick's canines wait patiently for their masters to finish their beer (£6–10 meals, food served daily 12:00–21:00, goulash, no chips and proud of it, dog treats, 2 Lake Road, tel. 017687/73463).

The Pheasant is a walk outside town, but locals trek here regularly for the food. The menu offers Lake District pub standards (fish pie, Cumbrian sausage, guinea fowl), as well as more inventive choices. Check the walls for caricatures of pub regulars, sketched at these tables by a Keswick artist. While they have a small restaurant section, I much prefer eating in the bar (£9-13 meals, daily 12:00-14:00 & 18:00-21:00, light bites served 14:00-16:00 on spring and summer weekends, Crosthwaite Road, tel. 017687/72219). From the town square, walk past the Pencil Museum, hang a right onto Crosthwaite Road, and walk 10 minutes. For a more scenic route, cross the river into Fitz Park, go left along the riverside path until it ends at the gate to Crosthwaite Road, turn right, and walk five minutes.

Star of Siam serves authentic Thai dishes in a tasteful dining room (£8-11 plates, daily 12:00-14:30 & 17:30-22:30, 89 Main Street, tel. 017687/71444).

Abraham's Tea Room, popular with townspeople, is a fine value for lunch. It's tucked away on the upper floor of the giant George Fisher outdoor store (£4-8 soups, salads, and sandwiches;

Mon-Fri 10:00-17:00, Sat 9:30-17:00, Sun 10:30-16:30, on the corner where Lake Road turns right, tel. 017687/71811).

The Lakeland Pedlar, a wholesome, pleasant café, serves freshly baked vegan, gluten-free, and vegetarian fare, including soups, organic bread, and daily specials. Their interior is cute. Outside tables face a big parking lot (£8 meals, Sun-Wed 9:00-17:00, Thu-Sat 9:00-20:30, Hendersons Yard, find the narrow walkway off Market Street between pink Johnson's sweet shop and The Golden Lion, tel. 017687/74492).

Bryson's Bakery and Tea Room has an enticing ground-floor bakery, with sandwiches and light lunches. The upstairs is a popular tearoom. Order lunch to go from the bakery, or for a few pence more, eat there, either sitting on stools or at a couple of sidewalk tables. Consider their £22.50 two-person Cumberland Cream Tea, which is like afternoon tea in London, but cheaper, and made with local products. Sandwiches, scones, and little cakes are served on a three-tiered platter with tea (£4-8 meals, daily 9:00-17:00, 42 Main Street, tel. 017687/72257).

Pumpkin has a small café space but a huge following, and is known for its fresh ingredients. Stop by for a light snack of homemade muffins and an espresso, or try a lamb burger (prices higher if you eat in, Mon-Sat 8:30-16:00, Sun 10:00-16:00, 19 Lake Road, tel. 017687/75973).

Eateries on Station Road: The street leading from the town square to the leisure center has several restaurants, including **Casa Bella**, a popular and packed Italian place that's good for families—reserve ahead (£8-11 pizzas and pastas, daily 17:00-21:15, 24 Station Street, tel. 017687/75575).

Picnic: The fine **Booths supermarket** is right where all the buses arrive (Mon-Sat 8:00-21:00, Sun 9:30-16:00, The Headlands). The recommended **Bryson's Bakery** does good sandwiches to go (described earlier). **The Old Keswickian,** on the town square, serves up old-fashioned fish-and-chips to go (Sun-Thu 11:00-22:30, Fri-Sat 11:00-23:30, closes at 22:00 in winter, upstairs restaurant closes earlier). Just around the corner, **The Cornish Pasty** offers an enticing variety of fresh meat pies to go (£2-3 pies, daily 9:00-17:30 or until the pasties are all gone, across from The Dog and Gun on Borrowdale Road, tel. 017687/72205).

In the Newlands Valley

The farmhouse B&Bs of Newlands Valley don't serve dinner, so their guests have two good options: Go into Keswick, or take the lovely 10-minute drive to Buttermere for an evening meal at **The Fish Inn** pub, which has fine indoor and outdoor seating, but takes no reservations (£8-10 meals, food served daily 12:00-14:00 & 18:00-21:00, family-friendly, good fish and daily specials with fresh vegetables, tel. 017687/70253). The neighboring **Bridge Hotel Pub** is a bit cozier and serves "modern-day nibbles and good classic pub grub" (£10-12 meals, food served daily 9:30-21:30, tel. 017687/70252).

Keswick Connections

The nearest train station to Keswick is in Penrith (ticket window open Mon-Sat 5:30-21:00, Sun 11:30-21:00, no lockers). For train and bus info, check at a TI, visit www.traveline.org.uk, or call 0845-748-4950 (for train), or 0871-200-2233. Most routes run less frequently on Sundays.

From Keswick by Bus: For connections, see page 537.

From Penrith by Bus to: Keswick (hourly Mon-Sat, every 2 hours on Sun, 45 minutes, £6.20, pay driver, Stagecoach bus #X4 or #X5), **Ullswater** and **Glenridding** (4/day, 45 minutes, bus #108 or #508). The Penrith bus stop is just outside the train station (bus schedules posted inside and outside station).

From Penrith by Train to: Blackpool (nearly hourly, 2 hours, change in Preston), **Liverpool** (nearly hourly, 2.25 hours, change in Wigan or Preston), **Birmingham**'s New Street Station (5/day direct, more with transfer, 2.5-3 hours), **Durham** (hourly, 3 hours, change in Carlisle and Newcastle), **York** (roughly 2/hour, 3.5-4 hours, 1-2 transfers), **London**'s Euston Station (4/day direct, more with transfer, 3-4 hours), **Edinburgh** (9/day direct, 1.75 hours), **Glasgow** (roughly hourly direct, 1.75 hours), **Oban** (2/day, 6 hours, transfer in Glasgow).

Route Tips for Drivers

From Points South (such as Liverpool or North Wales) to the Lake District: The direct, easy way to Keswick is to leave the M-6 at Penrith, and take the A-66 motorway for 16 miles to Keswick. For a scenic sightseeing drive through the south lakes to Keswick, exit the M-6 on the A-590/A-591 through the towns of Kendal and Windermere to reach Brockhole National Park Visitors Centre. From Brockhole, the A road to Keswick is fastest, but the high road—the tiny road over Kirkstone Pass to Glenridding and lovely Ullswater—is much more dramatic.

Coming from (or Going to) the West: Only 1,300 feet above sea level, Hard Knott Pass is still a thriller, with a narrow, winding, steeply graded road. Just over the pass are the scant but evocative remains of the Hard Knott Roman fortress. The great views can come with miserable rainstorms, and it can be very slow and frustrating when the one-lane road with turnouts is clogged by traffic. Avoid it on summer weekends.

Ullswater Lake

For advice on the Ullswater area, visit the **TI** at the pay parking lot in the heart of the lakefront village of Glenridding (daily 9:30-17:30, tel. 017684/82414, www.visiteden.co.uk).

▲▲Ullswater Hike and Boat Ride

Long, narrow Ullswater, which some consider the loveliest lake in the area, offers eight miles of diverse and grand Lake District

 scenery. While you can drive it or cruise it, I'd ride the boat from the south tip halfway up (to Howtown—which is nothing more than a dock) and hike back. Or walk first, then enjoy an easy ride back.

An old-fashioned **"steamer" boat** (actually diesel-powered) leaves Glenridding regularly for Howtown (departs daily generally 9:45-16:45, 6-9/day April-Oct, fewer off-season, 40 minutes; £6.20 one-way, £9.80 round-trip, £13.20 round-the-lake ticket lets you hop on and off, covered by £14.80 Ullswater Bus & Boat day pass, family rates, drivers can use safe pay-and-display parking lot, by public transit take bus #108 or #508 from Penrith, café at dock, £4 walking route map, tel. 017684/82229, www.ullswater-steamers.co.uk).

From Howtown, spend three to four hours hiking and dawdling along the well-marked path by the lake south to Patterdale, and then along the road back to Glenridding. This is a serious seven-mile walk with good views, varied terrain, and a few bridges and farms along the way. For a shorter hike from Howtown Pier, consider a three-mile loop around Hallin Fell. A rainy-day plan is to ride the covered boat up and down the lake to Howtown and Pooley Bridge at the northern tip of the lake (£13.20, 2.25 hours). Boats don't run in really bad weather—call ahead if it looks iffy.

▲▲Lanty's Tarn and Keldas Hill

If you like the idea of an Ullswater-area hike, but aren't up for the long huff from Howtown, consider this shorter (but still moderately challenging and plenty scenic) loop that leaves right from the TI's pay parking lot in Glenridding (about 2.5 miles, allow 2-2.5 hours; before embarking, buy the well-described leaflet for this walk in the TI).

From the parking lot, head to the main road, turn right to cross the river, then turn right again immediately and follow the river up into the hills. After passing a row of cottages, turn left, cross the wooden bridge, and proceed up the hill through the swing gate. Just before the next swing gate, turn left (following *Grisedale* signs) and head to yet another gate. From here you can see the small lake called Lanty's Tarn.

While you'll eventually go through this gate and walk along the lake to finish the loop, first you can detour to the top of the adjacent hill, called Keldas, for sweeping views over the near side of Ullswater (to reach the summit, climb over the step gate and follow the faint path up the hill). Returning to—and passing through—the swing gate, you'll walk along Lanty's Tarn, then begin your slow, steep, and scenic descent into the Grisedale Valley. Reaching the valley floor (and passing a noisy dog breeder's farm), cross the stone bridge, then turn left and follow the road all the way back to the lakefront, where a left turn returns you to Glenridding.

▲Aira Force Waterfall

At Ullswater, there's a delightful little park with parking, a ranger trailer, and easy trails leading half a mile uphill to a powerful 60-foot-tall waterfall. You'll read about how Wordsworth was inspired to write three poems here...and after taking this little walk, you'll know why. The pay-and-display car park is just where the Troutbeck road from the A-66 hits the lake, on the A-592 between Pooley Bridge and Glenridding.

Helvellyn

Considered by many the best high-mountain hike in the Lake District, this breathtaking round-trip route from Glenridding includes the spectacular Striding Edge—about a half-mile along the ridge. Be careful; do this six-hour hike only in good weather, since the wind can be fierce. While it's not the shortest route, the Glenridding ascent is best. Get advice from the Ullswater TI in Glenridding or look for various books on this hike at any area TI.

South Lake District

The South Lake District has a cheesiness that's similar to other popular English resort destinations. Here, piles of low-end vacationers suffer through terrible traffic, slurp ice cream, and get candy floss caught in their hair. The area around Windermere is worth a drive-through if you're a fan of Wordsworth or Beatrix Potter, but you'll still want to spend the majority of your Lake District time (and book your accommodations) up north.

South Lake District

Getting Around

By Car: Driving is your best option to see the small towns and sights clustered in the South Lake District; consider combining your drive with the bus trip mentioned below. If you're coming to or leaving the South Lake District from the west, you could take the Hard Knott Pass for a scenic introduction to the area.

By Bus: Buses are a fine and stress-less way to lace together this gauntlet of sights in the congested Lake Windermere neighborhood. The open-top Lakeland Experience bus #599 stops at Bowness Pier (lake cruises), Windermere (train station), Brockhole (National Park Visitors Centre), Ambleside, Rydal Mount, and Grasmere (Dove Cottage). Consider leaving your car at Grasmere and enjoying the breezy and extremely scenic ride, hopping off and on as you like (3/hour Easter-late Sept, 2/hour late Sept-Oct, 50 minutes each way, £7 Central Lakes Dayrider all-day pass). Bus #555 runs between Windermere and Keswick.

Sights in the South Lake District

Wordsworth Sights

William Wordsworth was one of the first writers to reject fast-paced city life. During England's Industrial Age, hearts were muzzled and brains ruled. Science was in, machines were taming nature, and factory hours were taming humans. In reaction to these brainy ideals, a rare few—dubbed Romantics—began to embrace untamed nature and undomesticated emotions.

Back then, nobody climbed a mountain just because it was there—but Wordsworth did. He'd "wander lonely as a cloud" through the countryside, finding inspiration in "plain living and high thinking." He soon attracted a circle of like-minded creative friends.

The emotional highs the Romantics felt weren't all natural. Wordsworth and his poet friends Samuel Taylor Coleridge and Thomas de Quincey got stoned on opium and wrote poetry, combining their generation's standard painkiller drug with their tree-hugging passions. Today, opium is out of vogue, but the Romantic movement thrives as visitors continue to inundate the region.

▲▲Dove Cottage and Wordsworth Museum

For poets, this two-part visit is the top sight of the Lake District. Take a short tour of William Wordsworth's humble cottage, and

be inspired in its excellent museum, which displays original writings, sketches, personal items, and fine paintings.

The poet whose appreciation of nature and a back-to-basics lifestyle put this area on the map spent his most productive years (1799-1808) in this well-preserved stone cottage on the edge of Grasmere. After functioning as the Dove and Olive Bow pub for almost 200 years, it was bought by his family. This is where Wordsworth got married, had kids, and wrote much of his best poetry. Still owned by the Wordsworth family, the furniture was his, and the place comes with some amazing artifacts, including the poet's passport and suitcase (he packed light). Even during his lifetime, Wordsworth was famous, and Dove Cottage was turned into a museum in 1891—predating even the National Trust, which protects the house today.

Cost and Hours: £7.50, daily March-Oct 9:30-17:30, Nov-Feb 9:30-16:30 except closed Jan, last entry 30 minutes before closing,

Wordsworth at Dove Cottage

William Wordsworth (1770-1850) was a Lake District home-boy. Born in Cockermouth (in a house now open to the public), he was schooled in Hawkshead. In adulthood, he married a local girl, settled down in Grasmere and Ambleside, and was buried in Grasmere's St. Oswald's churchyard.

But the 30-year-old man who moved into Dove Cottage in 1799 was not the carefree lad who'd once roamed the district's lakes and fields. At Cambridge University, he'd been a C student, graduating with no job skills and no interest in a nine-to-five career. Instead, he and a buddy hiked through Europe, where Wordsworth had an epiphany of the "sublime" atop Switzerland's Alps. He lived a year in France, watching the Revolution rage. It stirred his soul. He fell in love with a Frenchwoman who bore his daughter, Caroline. But lack of money forced him to return to England, and the outbreak of war with France kept them apart.

Pining away in London, William hung out in the pubs and coffeehouses with fellow radicals, where he met poet Samuel Taylor Coleridge. They inspired each other to write, edited each other's work, and jointly published a groundbreaking book of poetry.

In 1799, his head buzzing with words and ideas, William and his sister (and soul mate) Dorothy moved into the white-washed, slate-tiled former inn now known as Dove Cottage. He came into a small inheritance, and dedicated himself to poetry full time. In 1802, with the war over, William returned to France to finally meet his daughter. (He wrote of the rich experience: "It is a beauteous evening, calm and free.../Dear child! Dear Girl! that walkest with me here,/If thou appear untouched by solemn thought,/Thy nature is not therefore less divine.")

Having achieved closure, Wordsworth returned home to marry a former kindergarten classmate, Mary. She moved into Dove Cottage, along with an initially jealous Dorothy. Three of their five children were born here, and the cottage was also home to Mary's sister, the family dog Pepper (a gift from Sir Walter Scott; see Pepper's portrait), and frequent houseguests who bedded down in the pantry: Scott, Coleridge, and Thomas de Quincey, the Timothy Leary of opium.

After almost nine years here, Wordsworth's family and social status had outgrown the humble cottage. They moved first to a house in Grasmere before settling down in Rydal Hall. Wordsworth was changing. After the Dove years, he would write less, settle into a regular government job, quarrel with Coleridge, drift to the right politically, and endure criticism from old friends who branded him a sellout. Still, his poetry—most of it written at Dove—became increasingly famous, and he died honored as England's Poet Laureate.

Wordsworth's Poetry at Dove

At Dove Cottage, Wordsworth was immersed in the beauty of nature and the simple joy of his young, growing family. It was here that he reflected on both his idyllic childhood and his troubled twenties. The following are select lines from two well-known poems from this fertile time.

Ode: Intimations of Immortality
There was a time when meadow, grove, and stream,
The earth, and every common sight, to me did seem
Apparelled in celestial light, the glory and the
    freshness of a dream.
It is not now as it hath been of yore; turn
    wheresoe'er I may, by night or day,
The things which I have seen I now can see no more.
Now while the birds thus sing a joyous song...
To me alone there came a thought of grief...
Whither is fled the visionary gleam?
Where is it now, the glory and the dream?
Our birth is but a sleep and a forgetting:
The Soul...cometh from afar...
Trailing clouds of glory do we come
From God, who is our home.

I Wandered Lonely as a Cloud
I wandered lonely as a cloud
That floats on high o'er vales and hills,
When all at once I saw a crowd,
A host, of golden daffodils;
Beside the lake, beneath the trees,
Fluttering and dancing in the breeze...
For oft, when on my couch I lie
In vacant or in pensive mood,
They flash upon that inward eye
Which is the bliss of solitude;
And then my heart with pleasure fills,
And dances with the daffodils.

café, bus #555 from Keswick, bus #555 or #599 from Windermere, tel. 015394/35544, www.wordsworth.org.uk. Parking costs £1 in the Dove Cottage lot off the main road (A-591), 50 yards from the site.

Visiting the Cottage and Museum: Even if you're not a fan, Wordsworth's appreciation of nature, his Romanticism, and the ways his friends unleashed their creative talents with such abandon are appealing. The 25-minute cottage tour (which departs regularly—you shouldn't have to wait more than 30 minutes) and adjoining museum, with lots of actual manuscripts handwritten by

Wordsworth and his illustrious friends, are both excellent. In dry weather, the garden where the poet was much inspired is worth a wander. (Visit this after leaving the cottage tour, and pick up the description at the back door. The garden is closed when wet.) Allow 1.5 hours for this visit.

Poetry Readings: On some Tuesday evenings in summer, the Wordsworth Trust puts on poetry readings, where national poets read their own works. They're hoping to continue the poetry tradition of the Lake District. Readings are held in Grasmere Village either at St. Oswald's Church or at the Daffodil Hotel (£8 at the door, £7 if prebooked, every other Tue at 19:30, generally May-mid-Oct, same contact info as above).

▲Rydal Mount

Located just down the road from Dove Cottage, this sight is worthwhile for Wordsworth fans. The poet's final, higher-class

home, with a lovely garden and view, lacks the humble charm of Dove Cottage, but still evokes the time and creative spirit of the literary giant who lived here for 37 years. His family repurchased it in 1969 (after a 100-year gap), and his great-great-great-granddaughter still calls it home on occasion, as shown by recent family photos sprinkled throughout the house. After a short intro by the attendant, you'll be given an explanatory flier and are welcome to roam. Wander through the garden William himself designed, which has changed little since then. Surrounded by his nature, you can imagine the poet enjoying them with you. "O happy gardens! Whose seclusion deep, so friendly to industrious hours; and to soft slumbers, that did gently steep our spirits carry with them dreams of flowers, and wild notes warbled among leafy bowers."

Cost and Hours: £6.75; March-Oct daily 9:30-17:00; Nov-Dec and Feb Wed-Sun 11:00-16:00, closed Mon-Tue; closed Jan, occasionally closed for private functions—check website, tearoom, 1.5 miles north of Ambleside, well-signed, free and easy parking, bus #555 from Keswick, tel. 015394/33002, www.rydalmount.co.uk.

Beatrix Potter Sights

Of the many Beatrix Potter commercial ventures in the Lake District, there are two serious Beatrix Potter sights: her farm (Hill Top Farm) and her husband's former office, which is now the Beatrix Potter Gallery, filled with her sketches and paintings. The sights are two miles apart, in or near Hawkshead, a 20-minute drive south of Ambleside. If you're coming from Windermere,

Beatrix Potter
(1866-1943)

As a girl growing up in London, Beatrix Potter vacationed in the Lake District, where she became inspired to write her popular children's books. Unable to get a publisher, she self-published the first two editions of *The Tale of Peter Rabbit* in 1901 and 1902. When she finally landed a publisher, sales of her books were phenomenal. With the money she made, she bought Hill Top Farm, a 17th-century cottage, and fixed it up, living there from 1905 until she married in 1913. Potter was more than a children's book writer; she was a fine artist, an avid gardener, and a successful farmer. She married a lawyer and put her knack for business to use, amassing a 4,000-acre estate. An early conservationist, she used the garden-cradled cottage as a place to study nature. She willed it—along with the rest of her vast estate—to the National Trust, which she enthusiastically supported.

take bus #505 to Hawkshead or catch the little 15-car ferry from Bowness (runs constantly except when it's extremely windy, 10-minute trip, £4.30 car fare includes all passengers, £3.80 if you buy ticket at TI). If you have questions, call the Hawkshead TI at tel. 015394/36946. Note that both of the major sights are closed on Friday (though the Beatrix Potter Gallery may be open on Fridays in summer—call ahead).

On busy summer days, the wait to get into Hill Top Farm can last several hours (only 8 people are allowed in every 5 minutes, and the timed-entry tickets must be bought in person). If you like cutesy tourist towns (Hawkshead), this can be a blessing. Otherwise, you'll wish you were in the woods somewhere with Wordsworth.

▲Hill Top Farm

A hit with Beatrix Potter fans (and skippable for others), this dark and intimate cottage, swallowed up in the inspirational and rough nature around it, provides an enjoyable if quick experience. The six-room farm was left just as it was when she died in 1943. At her request, the house is set as if she had just stepped out—flowers on the tables, fire on, low lights. While there's no printed information here, guides in each room are eager to explain things. Call the farm for the current tour-wait times (if no one answers, leave a message for the administrator; someone will call you back).

Cost and Hours: Farmhouse-£8.50, tickets often sell out by 14:00 or even earlier during busy times; gardens-free; June-Aug Sat-Thu 10:00-17:30, April-May and Sept-Oct Sat-Thu 10:30-16:30, mid-Feb-March Sat-Thu 10:30-15:30, closed Nov-mid-Feb and Fri year-round; last entry 30 minutes before closing, tel. 015394/36269, www.nationaltrust.org.uk/hill-top.

Getting There: The farm is located in Near Sawrey village, 2 miles south of Hawkshead. Mountain Goat Tours runs a shuttle bus from across from the Hawkshead TI to the farm every 40 minutes (tel. 015394/45161). Drivers can take the B-5286 and B-5285 from Ambleside or the B-5285 from Coniston. Park and buy tickets 150 yards down the road, and walk back to tour the place.

▲Beatrix Potter Gallery

Located in the cute but extremely touristy town of Hawkshead, this gallery fills Beatrix's husband's former law office with the wonderful and intimate drawings and watercolors that she did to illustrate her books. Each year the museum highlights a new theme and brings out a different set of her paintings, drawings, and other items. The best of the Potter sights, the gallery has plenty of explanation about her life and work, including touchscreen displays and information panels. Even non-Potter fans will find this museum rather charming and her art surprisingly interesting.

Cost and Hours: £4.80, April-Oct Sat-Thu 10:30-17:00, mid-Feb-March Sat-Thu 10:30-15:30, closed Fri except possibly in summer (June-Aug; call or check online), closed Nov-mid-Feb, last entry 30 minutes before closing, Main Street, drivers use the nearby pay-and-display lot and walk 200 yards to the town center, tel. 015394/36355, www.nationaltrust.org.uk/beatrix-potter-gallery.

Hawkshead Grammar School Museum

The town of Hawkshead is engulfed in Potter tourism, and the extreme quaintness of it all is off-putting. Just across from the pay-and-display parking lot is the interesting Hawkshead Grammar School Museum, founded in 1585, where William Wordsworth studied from 1779 to 1787. It shows off old school benches and desks whittled with penknife graffiti.

Cost and Hours: £2.50 includes guided tour; April-Sept Mon-Sat 10:00-12:30 & 13:30-17:00, Sun 13:00-17:00; Oct until 16:30, closed Nov-March, tel. 015394/36735, www.hawksheadgrammar.org.uk.

The World of Beatrix Potter

This tour, a hit with children, is a gimmicky exhibit with all the historical value of a Disney ride. The 45-minute experience features a four-minute video trip into the world of Mrs. Tiggywinkle and company, a series of Lake District tableaux starring the same imaginary gang, and an all-about-Beatrix section, with an eight-minute video biography.

Cost and Hours: £7, kids-£3.65, daily April-Sept 10:00-18:00, Oct-March 10:00-17:00, last entry 30 minutes before closing, tearoom, on Crag Brow in Bowness-on-Windermere, tel. 08445-041-233, www.hop-skip-jump.com.

More Sights at Lake Windermere

Brockhole National Park Visitors Centre

Look for a stately old lakeside mansion between Ambleside and Windermere on the A-591. Set in a nicely groomed lakeside park, the center offers a free video on life in the Lake District, an information desk, organized walks (see the park's free *Visitor Guide*), exhibits, a shop (excellent selection of maps and guidebooks), a cafeteria, gardens, and nature walks. It's also a great place to bring kids for its free indoor play space, six-foot-tall climbing wall, and fun adventure playground with slides, swings, zip lines, nets, and swinging bridges. Other family activities, including an aerial treetop trek, mini-golf, and pony rides, have a fee.

Cost and Hours: Free, pay-when-you-leave parking (coins only); daily April-Oct 10:00-17:00, Nov-March 10:00-16:00, bus #555 from Keswick, bus #599 from Windermere, tel. 015394/46601, www.lakedistrict.gov.uk.

Cruise: For a joyride around famous Lake Windermere, you can catch the Brockhole "Green" cruise here (£7.40, runs daily 10:00-16:00, 2/hour mid-July-Aug, hourly April-mid-July and Sept-Oct, 45-minute circle, scant narration, tel. 015394/43360, www.windermere-lakecruises.co.uk).

Lakes Aquarium

This aquarium gives a glimpse of the natural history of Cumbria. Exhibits describe the local wildlife living in lake and coastal environments, including otters, eels, pike, and sharks. A rainforest exhibit features reptiles and marmoset monkeys. Experts give various talks throughout the day.

Cost and Hours: £9, £6 for kids under age 16, cheaper online, family deals, daily 9:00-18:00, until 17:00 in winter, last entry one hour before closing, in Lakeside, one mile north of Newby Bridge, at south end of Lake Windermere, tel. 015395/30153, www.lakes aquarium.co.uk.

Hayes Garden World

This extensive gardening center, a popular weekend excursion for locals, offers garden supplies, a bookstore, a playground, and gorgeous grounds. Gardeners could wander this all afternoon. Upstairs is a fine cafeteria-style restaurant.

Cost and Hours: Mon-Sat 9:00-18:00, Sun 10:00-17:00, at south end of Ambleside on main drag, see *Garden Centre* signs, located at north end of Lake Windermere, tel. 015394/33434, www.hayesgardenworld.co.uk.

YORK

Historic York is loaded with world-class sights. Marvel at the York Minster, England's finest Gothic church. Ramble The Shambles, York's wonderfully preserved medieval quarter. Enjoy a walking tour led by an old Yorker. Hop a train at one of the world's greatest railway museums, travel to the 1800s in the York Castle Museum, head back 1,000 years to Viking times at the Jorvik Viking Centre, or dig into the city's buried past at the Yorkshire Museum. And to get a taste of scenically desolate countryside, side-trip to the North York Moors.

York has a rich history. In A.D. 71, it was Eboracum, a Roman provincial capital—the northernmost city in the empire. Constantine was proclaimed emperor here in A.D. 306. In the fifth century, as Rome was toppling, the Roman emperor sent a letter telling England it was on its own, and York—now called Eoforwic—became the capital of the Anglo-Saxon kingdom of Northumbria.

The city's first church was built here in 627, and the town became an early Christian center of learning. The Vikings later took the town, and from the 9th through the 11th centuries, it was a Danish trading center called Jorvik. The invading and conquering Normans destroyed and then rebuilt the city, fortifying it with a castle and the walls you see today.

Medieval York, with 9,000 inhabitants, grew rich on the wool trade and became England's second city. Henry VIII used the city's fine Minster as the northern capital of his Anglican Church. (In today's Anglican Church, the Archbishop of York is second only to the Archbishop of Canterbury.)

In the Industrial Age, York was the railway hub of northern

England. When it was built, York's train station was the world's largest. During World War II, Hitler chose to bomb York by picking the city out of a travel guidebook (not this one).

Today, York's leading industry is tourism. It seems like everything that's great about Britain finds its best expression in this manageable town. While the city has no single claim to fame, York is more than the sum of its parts. With its strollable cobbles and half-timbered buildings, grand cathedral and excellent museums, thriving restaurant scene and welcoming locals, York delights.

Planning Your Time

After London, York is the best sightseeing city in England. On even a 10-day trip through Britain, it deserves two nights and a day. For the best 36 hours, follow this plan: Arrive early enough to catch the 17:15 evensong service at the Minster, then take the free city walking tour at 18:45 (evening tours offered June-Aug only). Splurge on dinner at one of the city's creative bistros. The next morning at 9:00, take my self-guided walk, interrupting it midway with a tour of the Minster. Finish the walk and grab lunch near The Shambles. To fill your afternoon, choose among the town's many important sights (such as the York Castle Museum—open until 17:00; or great Railway Museum—open until 18:00). Spend the evening enjoying a ghost walk of your choice (they depart at different times between 18:45 and 20:00) and another memorable dinner.

It's not worth going out of your way to visit the North York Moors (described at the end of this chapter), but it's handy to zip through that area if you're traveling between York and Durham.

This is a packed day; as you review this chapter, you'll see that there are easily two days of sightseeing fun in York.

Orientation to York

York has roughly 195,000 people; about one in ten is a student. But despite the city's size, the sightseer's York is small. Virtually everything is within a few minutes' walk: sights, train station, TI, and B&Bs. The longest walk a visitor might take (from a B&B across the old town to the York Castle Museum) is about 25 minutes.

Bootham Bar, a gate in the medieval town wall, is the hub of your York visit. (In York, a "bar" is a gate and a "gate" is a street. Blame the Vikings.) At Bootham Bar and on Exhibition Square, you'll find the starting points for most walking tours and bus tours, handy access to the medieval town wall, a public WC, and Bootham Street (which leads to my recommended B&Bs). To find your way around York, use the Minster's towers as a navigational landmark, or follow the strategically placed signposts, which point out all places of interest to tourists.

Tourist Information

York's TI, a block in front of the Minster, sells a £1 *York Map and Guide*. Ask for the free monthly *What's On* guide and the *York MiniGuide,* which includes a map (Mon-Sat 9:00-17:00, Sun 10:00-16:00, 1 Museum Street, tel. 01904/550-099, www.visityork .org). The TI books rooms for a £4 fee and has an Internet terminal (£1.50/30 minutes). A screen lists upcoming events.

York Pass: The TI sells an expensive pass that covers most sights in York, along with a few regional sights, including the North Yorkshire Moors Railway and Castle Howard (both described later under "Near York: North York Moors); it also gives discounts on the City Sightseeing hop-on, hop-off bus tours. You'd have to be a very busy sightseer to make this pass worth it (£36/1 day, £48/2 days, £58/3 days, www.yorkpass.com).

Arrival in York

By Train: The train station is a 10-minute walk from town. Day-trippers can store baggage at the window next to the Europcar office on platform 1 (£5/24 hours, baggage window open Mon-Sat 8:00-20:30, Sun 9:00-20:30).

Recommended B&Bs are a 5- to 15-minute walk (depending on where you're staying) or a £6 taxi ride from the station. For specific walking directions to the B&Bs, see page 611.

To walk downtown from the station, turn left down Station Road, veer through the gap in the wall and then left across the river, and follow the crowd toward the Gothic towers of the Minster. After the bridge, a block before the Minster, you'll come upon the TI on your right.

By Car: Driving and parking in York is maddening. Those day-tripping here should follow signs to one of the several park-and-ride lots ringing the perimeter. At these lots, parking is free, and cheap shuttle buses go every 10 minutes into the center.

If you're sleeping here, park your car where your B&B advises and walk. As you near York (and your B&B), you'll hit the A-1237 ring road. Follow this to the A-19/Thirsk roundabout (next to river on northeast side of town). From the roundabout, follow signs for *York,* traveling through Clifton into Bootham. All recommended B&Bs are four or five blocks before you hit the medieval city gate (see neighborhood map on page 612). If you're approaching York

York

200 YARDS
200 METERS

TO A-19 & THIRSK ↑

Access Stairs to Wall
Pedestrian Zone
P Parking
--- Footpath

CLIFTON
BOOTH CRES.
QUEEN ANNES
BOOTHAM TERR.
GROS TERR.
SYCAMORE
ST MARYS
LONGFIELD
FREDERIC
MARGATE
EARLS

RIVER

Railway Museum

LEEMAN

P

ROAD

WALKING PATH TO B&Bs

STATION RD.

Train Station

TOFT GREEN
BARKER
MICKLE

QUEEN

NUNNERY

BLOSSOM

MICKLEGATE BAR

TO A-64 & LEEDS

① Start of Welcome to York Walk
② Multangular Tower (Roman Wall)
③ Start of Ouse Riverside Walk or Bike Ride
④ Antiques Centre York
⑤ Red House Antiques Centre
⑥ Cavendish Antiques & Jewellers
⑦ Charity Shops
⑧ King's Square & Chocolate Museum
⑨ York Brewery
⑩ City Screen Cinema
⑪ Bike Rentals (2)

DCH

from the south, take the M-1 until it becomes the A-1M, exit at junction 45 onto the A-64, and follow it for 10 miles until you reach York's ring road (A-1237), which allows you to avoid driving through the city center. If you have more time, the A-19 from Selby is a slower and more scenic route into York.

Helpful Hints

Festivals: Book a room well in advance during festival times and on weekends any time of year. The **Viking Festival** features *lur* horn-blowing, warrior drills, and re-created battles in mid-February (www.jorvik-viking-centre.co.uk). The **Early Music Festival** (medieval minstrels, Renaissance dance, and so on) zings its strings in early July (www.ncem.co.uk/yemf .shtml). York claims to be the "Ascot of the North," and the town fills up on horse-race weekends (once a month May-Oct, check schedules at www.yorkracecourse.co.uk); it's especially busy during the **Ebor Races** in mid-August. (Many avoid York during this period, as prices go up and the streets are filled with drunken revelers. Others find that attractive.) The **York Food and Drink Festival** takes a bite out of late September (www.yorkfoodfestival.com). And the St. Nicholas Fayre Christmas market jingles its bells in late November. For a complete list of festivals, see www.yorkfestivals.com.

Internet Access: The **TI** has one Internet terminal (see "Tourist Information," earlier). **Evil Eye Lounge** has six terminals in a hip bar (£1/30 minutes, free Wi-Fi, Mon-Sat 10:00-23:00, Sun 11:00-23:00, upstairs at 42 Stonegate, tel. 01904/640-002). The **York Public Library**'s reference desk, on the first floor up, provides computer terminals for visitors (£1/2 hours, free Wi-Fi, Mon-Thu 9:00-20:00, Fri 9:00-18:00, Sat 9:00-17:00, Sun 11:00-16:00, Museum Street, tel. 01904/552-828).

Laundry: The nearest place is **Haxby Road Launderette,** a long 15-minute walk north of the town center (self-service-about £6/load, about £1.50 more for drop-off service, Mon-Wed and Fri 9:00-17:45, Thu 10:00-18:00, Sat 9:00-17:00, Sun 9:00-16:00, start last loads 1.5 hours before closing, drop off 3 hours before closing, 124 Haxby Road, tel. 01904/623-379). Some B&Bs will do laundry for a reasonable charge.

Bike Rental: With the exception of the pedestrian center, the town's not great for biking. But there are several fine countryside rides from York, and the riverside New Walk bike path is pleasant. **Giant York** is just outside Monk Bar (£15/day, helmet and map free with this book, Mon-Sat 9:00-18:00, closed Sun, 13-15 Lord Mayor's Walk, tel. 01904/622-868, www .giant-york.co.uk). **Cycle Heaven** is at the train station (£10/ half-day, £15/day, Mon-Fri 8:30-17:30, Sat 9:00-18:00, Sun

11:00-16:00, closed Sun off-season, to the left as you face the main station entrance from outside, tel. 01904/622-701). For locations, see the map on page 580.

Taxi: From the train station, taxis zip new arrivals to their B&Bs for £6. Queue up at the taxi stand, or call 01904/638-833; cabbies don't start the meter until you get in.

Car Rental: If you're nearing the end of your trip, consider dropping your car upon arrival in York. The money saved by turning it in early just about pays for the train ticket that whisks you effortlessly to London. In York, you'll find these agencies: **Avis** (3 Layerthorpe, tel. 0844-544-6117); **Hertz** (at train station, tel. 01904/500-193); **Budget** (near the National Railway Museum behind the train station at 75 Leeman Road, tel. 01904/644-919); and **Europcar** (train station platform 1, tel. 0844-846-4003). Beware: Car-rental agencies close early on Saturday afternoons and all day Sunday—when dropping off is OK, but picking up is only possible by prior arrangement (and for an extra fee).

Updates to this Book: For news about changes to this book's coverage since it was published, see www.ricksteves.com/update.

Tours in York

▲▲▲Walking Tours
Free Walks with Volunteer Guides

Charming locals give energetic, entertaining, and free two-hour walks through York (April-Oct daily at 10:15 and 14:15, June-Aug also at 18:45; Nov-March daily at 10:15 and also at 13:15 on weekends; depart from Exhibition Square in front of the art gallery, tel. 01904/550-098, www.avgyork.co.uk). These tours often go long because the guides love to teach and tell stories. You're welcome to cut out early—but let them know, or they'll worry, thinking they've lost you.

Yorkwalk Tours

These are more serious 1.5- to 2-hour walks with a history focus. They do four different walks—Essential York, Roman York, Secret York, and The Snickelways of York—as well as a variety of "special walks" on more specific topics (£6, Feb-Nov daily at 10:30 and 14:15, Dec-Jan weekends only, depart from Museum Gardens Gate, just show up, tel. 01904/622-303, www.yorkwalk.co.uk—check website, ask TI, or call for schedule). Tours go rain or shine, with as few as two participants.

Ghost Walks

Each evening, the old center of York is crawling with creepy ghost walks. These are generally 1.5 hours long, cost £5, and go every evening, rain or shine. There are no reservations (you simply show

York at a Glance

▲▲▲**York Minster** York's pride and joy, and one of England's finest churches, with stunning stained-glass windows, textbook Decorated Gothic design, and glorious evensong services. **Hours:** Open for worship daily from 7:00 and for sightseeing Mon-Sat 9:00-18:30, Sun 12:30-18:30; shorter hours for tower and undercroft; evensong services Tue-Sat at 17:15, Sun at 16:00, occasionally on Mon at 17:15. See page 591.

▲▲**Yorkshire Museum** Sophisticated archaeology and natural history museum with York's best Viking exhibit, plus Roman, Saxon, Norman, and Gothic artifacts. **Hours:** Daily 10:00-17:00. See page 598.

▲▲**Jorvik Viking Centre** Entertaining and informative Disney-style exhibit/ride exploring Viking lifestyles and artifacts. **Hours:** Daily April-Oct 10:00-17:00, Nov-March until 16:00. See page 601.

▲▲**York Castle Museum** Far-ranging collection displaying everyday objects from Victorian times to the present. **Hours:** Daily 9:30-17:00. See page 604.

▲▲**National Railway Museum** Train buff's nirvana, tracing the history of all manner of rail-bound transport. **Hours:** Daily 10:00-18:00. See page 605.

▲**The Shambles** Atmospheric old butchers' quarter, with colorful, tipsy medieval buildings. **Hours:** Always open. See page 590.

▲**Ouse Riverside Walk** Bucolic path along river to a mod pedestrian bridge. **Hours:** Always open. See page 607.

▲**York Brewery** Honest, casual tour through an award-winning microbrewery with the guy who makes the beer. **Hours:** Mon-Sat at 12:30, 14:00, 15:30, and 17:00. See page 607.

▲**Fairfax House** Glimpse into an 18th-century Georgian family house, with enjoyably chatty docents. **Hours:** Tue-Sat 10:00-17:00, Sun 12:30-16:00, Mon by tour only at 11:00 and 14:00, closed Jan-mid-Feb. See page 603.

YORK

up) and no tickets (just pay at the start). At the advertised time and place, your black-clad guide appears, and you follow him or her to the first stop. Your guide gives a sample of the entertainment you have in store, humorously collects the "toll," and you're off.

You'll see fliers and signboards all over town advertising the many ghost walks. Companies come and go, but I find there are three general styles of walks: historic, street theater, and storytelling. Here are three reliably good walks, one for each style. Each gives a £1 discount (limit two "victims" per book) off full price for Rick Steves readers with this book:

The **Terror Trail Walk** is more historic, "all true," and a bit more intellectual (18:45, meet at The Golden Fleece at bottom of The Shambles, www.yorkterrortrail.co.uk).

The **Ghost Hunt** is comedic street theater produced and usually performed by Andy Dextrous, who introduces himself by saying, "My name is...unimportant" (19:30, meet at the bottom of The Shambles, www.ghosthunt.co.uk).

The **Original Ghost Walk** was the first of its kind, dating back to the 1970s, and is more classic, spooky storytelling rather than comedy (20:00, meet at The Kings Arms at Ouse Bridge, www.theoriginalghostwalkofyork.co.uk).

▲City Bus Tours

City Sightseeing's half-enclosed, double-decker, hop-on, hop-off buses circle York, taking tourists past secondary sights that the city walking tours skip—the mundane perimeter of town. While you can hop on and off all day, York is so compact that these have no real transportation value. If taking a bus tour, I'd catch either one at Exhibition Square (near Bootham Bar) and ride it for an orientation all the way around. Consider getting off at the National Railway Museum, skipping the last five minutes. Once or twice an hour, they run a "Heritage Tour" route with a live guide (£12, £13.50 combo-ticket with York Boat cruise—described next, pay driver, cash only, ticket valid 24 hours, Easter-Oct departs every 10-15 minutes, daily 9:00-17:30, less frequent off-season, about 1 hour, tel. 01904/633-990, www.yorkbus.co.uk).

Boat Cruise

York Boat does a lazy, narrated 45-minute lap along the River Ouse (£7.50, £13.50 combo-ticket with City Sightseeing bus tours—see above, April-Sept runs every 30 minutes, daily 10:30-15:00, off-season 4/day; leaves from Lendal Bridge and King's Staith landings, near Skeldergate Bridge; also 1.25-hour evening cruise at 21:15 for £9.50, leaves from King's Staith; tel. 01904/628-324, www.yorkboat.co.uk).

Self-Guided Walk

Welcome to York

Get a taste of Roman and medieval York on this easy stroll. The walk begins in the gardens just in front of the Yorkshire Museum, covers a stretch of the medieval city walls, and then cuts through the middle of the old town. Start at the ruins of St. Mary's Abbey in the Museum Gardens.

St. Mary's Abbey: This abbey dates to the age of William the Conqueror—whose harsh policies (called the "Harrowing of the North") consisted of massacres and destruction, including the burning of York's main church. His son Rufus, who tried to improve relations in the 11th century, established a great church here. The church became an abbey that thrived from the 13th century until the Dissolution of the Monasteries in the 16th century. The Dissolution, which accompanied the Protestant Reformation and break with Rome, was a power play by Henry VIII. The king wanted much more than just a divorce: He wanted the land and riches of the monasteries. Upset with the pope, he demanded that his subjects pay him taxes rather than give the Church tithes. (For more information, see the sidebar on page 132.)

As you gaze at this ruin, imagine magnificent abbeys like this scattered throughout the realm. Henry VIII destroyed most

of them, taking the lead from their roofs and leaving the stones to scavenging townsfolk. Scant as they are today, these ruins still evoke a time of immense monastic power. The one surviving wall was the west half of a very long, skinny nave. The tall arch marked the start of the transept. Stand on the plaque that reads *Crossing beneath central tower,* and look up at the air that now fills the space where a huge tower once stood. (Fine carved stonework from the ruined abbey is on display in a basement room of the adjacent Yorkshire Museum.)

Beyond the abbey, laid out like a dozen stone eggs, are 12 ancient **Roman sarcophagi** that were excavated at the train station. You'll also see a bowling green and the abbey's original wall (not part of the city walls).

• *With your back to the abbey, see the fine Neoclassical building housing the* **Yorkshire Museum** *(well worth a visit and described later, under "Sights in York"). Walk past this about 30 yards to a corner of the city's* **Roman wall.** *A tiny lane through the garden (past a yew tree) leads through a small arch, giving a peek into the ruined tower.*

Multangular Tower: This 12-sided tower (c. A.D. 300) was likely a catapult station built to protect the town from enemy river traffic. The red ribbon of bricks was a Roman trademark—both structural and decorative. The lower stones are Roman, while the upper, bigger stones are medieval. After Rome fell, York suffered through two centuries of a dark age. Then, in the ninth century, the Vikings ruled. They built with wood, so almost nothing from that period remains. The Normans came in 1066 and built in stone, generally atop Roman structures (like this wall). The wall that defined the ancient Roman garrison town worked for the Norman town, too. But after the English Civil War in the 1600s and Jacobite rebellions in the 1700s, fortified walls were no longer needed in England's interior.

• *Now, return 10 steps down the lane and turn right, walking between the museum and the Roman wall. Continuing straight, the lane goes between the abbot's palace and the town wall. This is a "snickelway"—a small, characteristic York lane or footpath. The snickelway pops out on...*

Exhibition Square: With Henry VIII's Dissolution of the Monasteries, the abbey was destroyed and the Abbot's Palace became the **King's Manor** (from the snickelway, make a U-turn to the left and through the gate). Enter the building under the coat of arms of Charles I, who stayed here during the English Civil War in the 1640s. Today, the building is part of the University of York. Because the northerners were slow to embrace the king's reforms, Henry VIII came here to enforce the Dissolution. He stayed 17 days in this mansion and brought along 1,000 troops to make his determination clear. You can wander into the grounds and building. The Refectory Café serves cheap cakes, soup, and sandwiches

to students, professors, and visitors like you (Mon-Fri 9:30-15:30, closed Sat-Sun).

Exhibition Square is the departure point for various walking and bus tours. You can see the towers of the Minster in the distance. Travelers in the Middle Ages could see the Minster from miles away as they approached the city. Across the street is a public WC and **Bootham Bar**—one of the fourth-century Roman gates in York's wall—with access to the best part of the city walls (free, walls open 8:00-dusk).

• *Climb up the bar.*

Walk the Wall: Hike along the top of the wall behind the Minster to the first corner. York's 13th-century walls are three miles long. This stretch follows the original Roman wall. Norman kings built the walls to assert control over northern England. Notice the pivots in the crenellations (square notches at the top of a medieval wall), which once held wooden hatches to provide cover for archers. The wall was extensively renovated in the 19th century (Victorians added Romantic arrow slits).

At the corner with the benches—**Robin Hood's Tower**— you can lean out and see the moat outside. This was originally the Roman ditch that surrounded the fortified garrison town. Continue walking for a fine view of the Minster, with its truncated main tower and the pointy rooftop of its chapter house.

• *Continue on to the next gate...*

Monk Bar: This fine medieval gatehouse is the home of the quirky **Richard III Museum.** Run by eccentric enthusiasts of the last king of England's Plantagenet dynasty (the Tudors took over after Richard was killed in 1485), it's filled with high-schoolish exhibits and lacks any historic artifacts. But with fun architecture to explore, it's mildly entertaining. Especially since the sensational discovery of Richard III's remains in Leicester in 2013, this king— demonized as a hunchbacked monster by Shakespeare—fascinates the English (£3, daily 9:00-17:00, Monk Bar, tel. 01904/634-191, www.richardiiimuseum.co.uk).

• *Descend the wall at Monk Bar, and step past the portcullis (last lowered in 1953 for the Queen's coronation) to emerge outside the city's protective wall. Take 10 paces and gaze up at the tower. Imagine 10 archers behind the arrow slits. Keep an eye on the 17th-century guards, with their stones raised and primed to protect the town.*

Return through the city wall. After a short block, turn right on Ogleforth. ("Ogle" is the Norse word for owl, hence our word "ogle"—to look at something fiercely.)

York's Old Town: Walking down Ogleforth, ogle (on your left) a charming little brick house called the **Dutch House**. Designed by an apprentice architect who was trying to show off for his master, it's from the 17th century. It was the first entirely brick house in town, a sign of opulence. Next, also of brick, is a former brewery, with a 19th-century, industrial feel.

Ogleforth jogs left and becomes **Chapter House Street**, passing the Treasurer's House to the back side of the Minster. Circle around the left side of the church, past the stonemasons' lodge (where craftsmen are chiseling local limestone for the church, as has been done here since the 13th century), to the statue of Roman Emperor Constantine and an ancient Roman column.

Step up to lounging **Constantine**. Five emperors visited York when it was the Roman city of Eboracum. Constantine was here when his father died. The troops declared him the Roman emperor in A.D. 306 at this site, and six years later, he went to Rome to claim his throne. In A.D. 312, Constantine legalized Christianity, and in A.D. 314, York got its first bishop. The thought-provoking plaque reads: "His rec-ognition of the civil liberty of his

Christian subjects and his personal conversion established the reli-gious foundation of Western Christendom."

The **ancient column,** across the street from Constantine, is a reminder that the Minster sits upon the site of the Roman head-quarters, or *principia*. The city placed this column here in 1971, just before celebrating the 1,900th anniversary of the founding of Eboracum—a.k.a. York.

• If you want to visit **York Minster** now, find the entrance on its west side (see description on page 591). Otherwise, head into the town center. From opposite the Minster's south transept door (by Constantine), take a narrow pedestrian walkway—which becomes Stonegate—into the tan-gled commercial center of medieval York. Walk straight down Stonegate, a street lined with fun and inviting cafés, pubs, and restaurants. Just before the Ye Olde Starre Inne banner hanging over the street, turn left down the snickelway called Coffee Yard. (It's marked by a red devil.) Enjoy strolling York's...

"Snickelways": This is a made-up York word combining "snicket" (a passageway between walls or fences), "ginnel" (a nar-row passageway between buildings), and "alleyway" (any narrow passage)—snickelway. York—with its population packed densely inside its protective walls—has about 50 of these public passages. In general, when exploring the city, you should duck into these, both for the adventure and to take a shortcut. While some of York's history has been bulldozed by modernity, bits of it hide and survive in the snickelways.

Coffee Yard leads past Barley Hall, popping out at the corner of Grape Lane and Swinegate. Medieval towns named streets for the business done there. Swinegate, a lane of pig farmers, leads to the market. Grape Lane is a polite version of that street's original, crude name, Gropec*nt Lane. If you were here a thousand years

YORK

ago, you'd find it lined by brothels. Throughout England, streets for prostitutes were called by this graphic name. Today, if you see a street named Grape Lane, that's usually its heritage.

Skip Grape Lane and turn right down Swinegate to a market (which you can see in the distance). The frumpy **Newgate Market,** popular for cheap produce and clothing, was created in the 1960s with the demolition of a bunch of colorful medieval lanes.

• *In the center of the market, tiny "Little Shambles" lane (on the left) dead-ends into the most famous lane in York.*

The Shambles: This colorful old street (rated ▲) was once the "street of the butchers." The name is derived from "shammell"— a butcher's bench upon which he'd cut and display his meat. In

the 16th century, this lane was dripping with red meat. Look for the hooks under the eaves; these were once used to hang rabbit, pheasant, beef, lamb, and pigs' heads. Fresh slabs were displayed on the fat sills, while people lived above the shops. All the garbage and sewage flushed down the street to a mucky pond at the end—a favorite hangout for the town's cats and dogs. Tourist shops now fill these fine, half-timbered Tudor buildings. Look above the modern crowds and storefronts to appreciate the classic old English architecture. Unfortunately, the soil here isn't great for building; notice how the structures have settled in the absence of a solid foundation.

Turn right and slalom down The Shambles. At the Mr. Sandwich shop, pop into the snickelway and look for very old **woodwork.** Study the 16th-century carpentry—mortise-and-tenon joints with wooden plugs rather than nails.

Next door (on The Shambles) is the **shrine of St. Margaret Clitherow,** a 16th-century Catholic crushed by Protestants under her own door (as was the humiliating custom when a city wanted to teach someone a lesson). She was killed for hiding priests in her home here. Stop into the tiny shrine for a peaceful moment to ponder Margaret who, in 1970, was sainted for her faith.

At the bottom of The Shambles is the cute, tiny **St. Crux Parish Hall,** which charities use to raise funds by selling light meals (see "Eating in York," later). Take some time to chat with the volunteers.

With blood and guts from The Shambles' 20 butchers all draining down the lane, it's no wonder The Golden Fleece, just below, is considered the most haunted pub in town.

• *Your town walk is finished. From here, you're just a few minutes from plenty of fun: street entertainment and lots of cheap eating options on King's Square, good restaurants on Fossgate, the York Castle Museum (a few blocks farther downhill), and the starting point for my Ouse Riverside Walk.*

Sights in York

▲▲▲York Minster

The pride of York, this largest Gothic church north of the Alps (540 feet long, 200 feet tall) brilliantly shows that the High Middle Ages were far from dark. The word "minster" means an important church chartered with a mission to evangelize. As it's the seat of a bishop, York Minster is also a cathedral. While Henry VIII destroyed England's great abbeys, this was not part of a monastery and was therefore left standing. It seats 2,000 comfortably; on Christmas and Easter, at least 4,000 worshippers pack the place. Today, more

than 250 employees and 500 volunteers work to preserve its heritage and welcome 1.3 million visitors each year.

Cost: £10 includes guided tour, undercroft museum, and crypt; free for kids under age 16; tower climb-£5.

Hours: The cathedral is open for sightseeing Mon-Sat 9:00-18:30, Sun 12:30-18:30. It opens for worship daily at 7:00. Closing time flexes with activities, but last entry is generally at 17:30—call or look online to confirm. Sights within the Minster have shorter hours (listed below). The Minster may close for special events (check calendar on website).

Information: Pick up the worthwhile *Welcome to the York Minster* flier. Helpful Minster guides stationed throughout are happy to answer your questions. Tel. 01904/557-217 or 0844-393-0011, www.yorkminster.org.

Tower Climb: It costs £5 for 30 minutes of exercise (275 steps) and forgettable views. The tower opens at 10:00 (later on Sun), with ascents every 45 minutes; the last ascent is generally at 16:00—later in peak season and earlier in winter (no children under 8, not good for acrophobes, closes in extreme weather). Be

York Minster

50 YARDS
50 METERS

WHEELCHAIR ENTRY/EXIT

NAVE
TRANSEPT
CHOIR

WC

ENTRY → TICKETS

SHOP →

EXIT

MINSTER STONE YARD ■

■ CONSTANTINE STATUE

■ ROMAN COLUMN

1 Great West Doors
2 Nave
3 Central Tower & View of Great West Window
4 Dragon
5 South Transept
6 Undercroft Museum & Tower Climb

7 Choir
8 North Transept & "Five Sisters"
9 Astronomical Clock
10 Chapter House
11 East End & Great East Window
12 Crypt

YORK

sure to get your ticket upon arrival, as only 50 visitors are allowed up at once; you'll be assigned an entry time. It's a tight, spiraling, claustrophobic staircase with an iron handrail. You'll climb about 150 steps to the top of the transept, step outside to cross a narrow walkway, then go back inside for more than 100 steps to the top of the central tower. From here (while caged in), you can enjoy views of rooftops and the flat countryside.

Undercroft Museum: This new museum focuses on the history of the site and its origins as a Roman fortress (Mon-Sat 10:00-17:00, Sun 12:30-16:00).

Tours: Free guided tours depart from the ticket desk every hour on the hour (Mon-Sat 10:00-15:00, can be more frequent during busy times, none on Sun, one hour, they go even with just one or two people). You can join a tour in progress, or if none is scheduled, request a departure.

Stained-Glass Tours: Glass enthusiasts can take a special behind-the-scenes tour to learn about the restoration of the Minster's glass masterpiece, the Great East Window (£7.50; Mon, Wed, and Fri at 14:00; one hour, 15-person maximum).

Evensong: To experience the cathedral in musical and spiritual action, attend an evensong (Tue-Sat at 17:15, Sun at 16:00). On Mondays, visiting choirs fill in about half the time (otherwise it's a spoken service, also at 17:15). Visiting choirs also perform when the Minster's choir is on summer break (mid-July-Aug, confirm at church or TI). Arrive 15 minutes early and wait just outside the choir in the center of the church. You'll be ushered in and can sit in one of the big wooden stalls. As evensong is a worship service, attendees enter the church free of charge. For more on evensong, see page 169.

Church Bells: If you're a fan of church bells, you'll experience ding-dong ecstasy daily except Mon (Sun morning about 10:00, Tue practice 19:30-21:30, and Tue-Sat at 16:45 to announce evensong). These performances are especially impressive, as the church holds a full carillon of 35 bells (it's the only English cathedral to have such a range). Stand in front of the church's west portal and imagine the gang pulling on a dozen ropes (halfway up the right tower—you can actually see the ropes through a little window) while one talented carillonneur plays 22 more bells with a keyboard and foot pedals.

◉ Self-Guided Tour: Enter the great church through the west portal (under the twin towers). Upon entering, decide if you're climbing the tower. If so, get a ticket (with an assigned time).

• *Entering the church, turn 180 degrees and look back at the...*

Great West Doors: These are used only on special occasions. Flanking the doors is a list of archbishops (and other church

officials) that goes unbroken back to the 600s. The statue of Peter with the key and Bible is a reminder that the church is dedicated to St. Peter, and the key to heaven is found through the word of God. While the Minster sits on the remains of a Romanesque church (c. 1100),

today's church was begun in 1220 and took 250 years to complete. Up above, look for the female, headless "semaphore saints," using semaphore flag code to spell out a message with golden discs: "Christ is here."

• *Grab a chair and enjoy the view down the...*

Nave: Your first impression might be of its spaciousness and brightness. One of the widest Gothic naves in Europe, it was built between 1280 and 1360—the middle period of the Gothic

England's Anglican Church

The Anglican Church (a.k.a. the Church of England) came into existence in 1534 when Henry VIII declared that he, and not Pope Clement VII, was the head of England's Catholics. The pope had refused to allow Henry to divorce his wife to marry his mistress Anne Boleyn (which Henry did anyway, resulting in the birth of Elizabeth I). Still, Henry regarded himself as a faithful Catholic—just not a *Roman* Catholic—and made relatively few changes in how and what Anglicans worshipped.

Henry's son, Edward VI, later instituted many of the changes that Reformation Protestants were bringing about in continental Europe: an emphasis on preaching, people in the pews actually reading the Bible, clergy being allowed to marry, and a more "Protestant" liturgy in English from the revised Book of Common Prayer (1549). The next monarch, Edward's sister Mary I, returned England to the Roman Catholic Church (1553), earning the nickname of "Bloody Mary" for her brutal suppression of Protestant elements. When Elizabeth I succeeded Mary (1558), she soon broke from Rome again. Today, many regard the Anglican Church as a compromise between the Catholic and Protestant traditions. In the US, Anglicans split off from the Church in England after the American Revolution, creating the Episcopal Church that still thrives today.

Ever since Henry VIII's time, the York Minster has held a special status within the Anglican hierarchy. After a long feud over which was the leading church, the archbishops of Canterbury and York agreed that York's bishop would have the title "Primate of England" and Canterbury's would be the "Primate of All England," directing Anglicans on the national level.

style, called "Decorated Gothic." Rather than risk a stone roof, builders spanned the space with wood. Colorful shields on the arcades are the coats of arms of nobles who helped tall and formidable Edward I, known as "Longshanks," fight the Scots in the 13th century.

The coats of arms in the clerestory (upper-level) glass represent the nobles who helped his son, Edward II, in the same fight. There's more medieval glass in this building than in the rest of England combined. This precious glass survived World War II—hidden in stately homes throughout Yorkshire.

Walk to the very center of the church, under the **central tower**. Look up. An exhibit in the undercroft explains how gifts and skill saved this 197-foot tower from collapse. Use the neck-saving mirror to marvel at it.

Look back at the west end to marvel at the **Great West**

Window, especially the stone tracery. While its nickname is the "Heart of Yorkshire," it represents the sacred heart of Christ, meant to remind people of his love for the world.

Find the **dragon** on the right of the nave (two-thirds of the way up the wall). While no one is sure of its purpose, it pivots and has a hole through its neck—so it was likely a mechanism designed to raise a lid on a baptismal font.

• *Facing the altar, turn right and head into the...*

South Transept: Look up. The new "bosses" (carved medallions decorating the point where the ribs meet on the ceiling) are a reminder that the roof of this wing of the church was destroyed by fire in 1984, caused when lightning hit an electricity box. Some believe the lightning was God's angry response to a new bishop, David Jenkins, who questioned the literal truth of Jesus' miracles. (Jenkins had been interviewed at a nearby TV studio the night before, leading locals to joke that the lightning occurred "12 hours too late, and 17 miles off-target.") Regardless, the entire country came to York's aid. *Blue Peter* (England's top kids' show) conducted a competition among their young viewers to design new bosses. Out of 30,000 entries, there were six winners (the blue ones—e.g., man on the moon, feed the children, save the whales).

Two other sights can be accessed through the south transept: the **Undercroft Museum** (explained later) and the **tower climb** (explained earlier). But for now, stick with this tour; we'll circle back to the south transept at the end, before exiting the church.

• *Head back into the middle of the nave and face the front of the church. You're looking at the...*

Choir: Examine the choir screen—the ornate wall of carvings separating the nave from the choir. It's lined with all the English kings from William I (the Conqueror) to Henry VI (during whose reign it was carved, in 1461). Numbers indicate the years each reigned. It is indeed "slathered in gold leaf," which sounds impressive, but the gold is very thin...a nugget the size of a sugar cube is pounded into a sheet the size of a driveway.

Step into the choir, where a service is held daily. All the carving was redone after an 1829 fire, but its tradition of glorious evensong services (sung by choristers from the Minster School) goes all the way back to the eighth century.

• *To the left as you face the choir is the...*

North Transept: In this transept, the grisaille windows—dubbed the **"Five Sisters"**—are dedicated to British servicewomen

YORK

who died in wars. Made in 1260, before colored glass was produced in England, these contain more than 100,000 pieces of glass.

The 18th-century **astronomical clock** is worth a look (the sign helps you make sense of it). It's dedicated to the heroic Allied aircrews from bases here in northern England who died in World War II (as Britain kept the Nazis from invading in its "darkest hour"). The Book of Remembrance below the clock contains 18,000 names.

• *A corridor leads to the Gothic, octagonal...*

Chapter House: This was the traditional meeting place of the governing body (or chapter) of the Minster. On the pillar in the middle of the doorway, the Virgin holds Baby Jesus while standing on the devilish serpent. The Chapter House, without an interior support, is remarkable (almost frightening) for its breadth. The fanciful carvings decorating the canopies above the stalls date from 1280 (80 percent are originals) and are some of the Minster's finest. Stroll slowly around the entire room and imagine that the tiny sculpted heads are a 14th-century parade—a fun glimpse of medieval society. Grates still send hot air up robes of attendees on cold winter mornings. A model of the wooden construction illustrates the impressive 1285 engineering.

The Chapter House was the site of an important moment in England's parliamentary history. Fighting the Scots in 1295, Edward I (the "Longshanks" we met earlier) convened the "Model Parliament" here, rather than down south, in London. (The Model Parliament is the name for its early version, back before the legislature was split into the Houses of Commons and Lords.) The government met here through the 20-year reign of Edward II, before moving to London during Edward III's rule in the 14th century.

• *Go back out into the main part of the church, turn left, and continue all the way down the nave (behind the choir) to the...*

East End: This part of the church is square, lacking a semicircular apse, typical of England's Perpendicular Gothic style (15th century). Monuments (almost no graves) were once strewn throughout the church, but in the Victorian Age, they were gathered into the east end, where you see them today.

The **Great East Window,** the size of a tennis court, is currently under restoration. Under it, three exhibits—"Stone by Stone," "Let There Be Light," and "The Orb"—give an intimate look at Gothic stone and glass work.

"Let There Be Light" explains the significance of the window and the scope of the conservation project. It illustrates the painstaking process of removing, dismantling, cleaning, and restoring each of the 311 panels. Interactive computers let you zoom in on each panel, read about the stories depicted in them, and explore the codes and symbols that are hidden in the window.

"The Orb," a futuristic dome that seems out of place in a medieval cathedral, offers a close-up look at several restored and exquisite stained-glass panels. Photos show what the windows looked like before, and information boards explain the challenges involved in restoring each one. This is a unique opportunity to see how exquisitely detailed the panels are. When they're back in their proper location, their minute features will be invisible from the floor of the church and therefore will be "for God's eyes only."

Because of the Great East Window's immense size, the east end has an extra layer of supportive stonework, parts of it wide enough to walk along. In fact, for special occasions, the choir has been known to actually sing from the walkway halfway up the window. But just as the window has deteriorated over time, so too has the stone. Nearly 3,500 stones need to be replaced or restored (as explained in the "Stone by Stone" exhibit). On some days, you may even see masons in action in the stone yard behind the Minster.

· *Below the choir (on either side), steps lead down to the...*

Crypt: Here you can view the boundary of the much smaller, but still huge, Norman church from 1100 that stood on this spot (look for the red dots, marking where the Norman church ended, and note how thick the wall was). You can also see some of the old columns and additional remains from the Roman fortress that once stood here, the tomb of St. William of York (actually a Roman sarcophagus that was reused), and the modern concrete save-the-church foundations (much of this church history is covered in the undercroft museum).

· *You'll exit the church through the south transept. If you've yet to climb the **tower**, the entrance is in the south transept. Also before leaving, look for the entrance to the...*

Undercroft Museum: Well-described exhibits follow the history of the site from its origins as a Roman fortress to the founding of an Anglo-Saxon/Viking church, the shift to a Norman place of worship, and finally the construction of the Gothic structure that stands today. Videos re-create how the fortress and Norman structure would have been laid out, and various artifacts and remains provide an insight into each period. The museum fills a space that was excavated following the near collapse of the central tower in 1967.

Highlights include the actual remains of the Roman fort's basilica, which are viewable through a see-through floor. There are also patches of Roman frescoes from what was the basilica's anteroom. One remarkable artifact is the Horn of Ulf: an intricately carved elephant's tusk presented to the Minster in 1030 by Ulf, a Viking nobleman, as a symbol that he was dedicating his land to God and the Church. Also on view is the York Gospels manuscript, a thousand-year-old text containing the four gospels. Made by Anglo-Saxon monks at Canterbury, it's the only book in the Minster's collection that dates from prior to the Norman Conquest. It is still used to this day to swear in archbishops. Your last stop in the undercroft is a small and comfortable theater where you can enjoy three short videos (10 minutes total) showing the Minster in action.

• *This finishes your visit. Before leaving, take a moment to just be in this amazing building. Then, go in peace.*

Nearby: As you leave through the south transept, notice the people-friendly plaza created here and how effectively it ties the church in with the city that stretches before you. To your left are the Roman column from the ancient headquarters, which stood where the Minster stands today (and from where Rome administered the northern reaches of Britannia 1,800 years ago); a statue of Emperor Constantine; and the covered York Minster Stone Yard, where masons are chiseling stone—as they have for centuries—to keep the religious pride-and-joy of York looking good.

Other Sights Inside York's Walls

I've listed these roughly in geographical order, from near the Minster at the northwest end of town to the York Castle Museum at the southeast end.

Note that several of York's glitzier and most heavily promoted sights (including Jorvik Viking Centre, Dig, and Barley Hall) are run by the York Archaeological Trust (YAT). While rooted in real history, YAT attractions are geared primarily for kids and work hard (some say too hard) to make the history entertaining. If you like their approach and plan to visit several, ask about the various combo-ticket options.

▲▲Yorkshire Museum

Located in a lush, picnic-perfect park next to the stately ruins of St. Mary's Abbey (described in the self-guided walk, earlier), the Yorkshire Museum is the city's serious "archaeology of York" museum. You can't dig a hole in York without hitting some remnant of the city's long past, and most of what's found ends up here. While the hordes line up at Jorvik Viking Centre, this museum has no crowds and provides a broader historical context, with more real artifacts. The three main collections—Roman, medieval, and natural history—are well-described, bright, and kid-friendly.

Cost and Hours: £7.50, kids under 16 free with paying adult, £13 combo-ticket with York Castle Museum, daily 10:00-17:00, within Museum Gardens, tel. 01904/687-687, www.yorkshire museum.org.uk.

Visiting the Museum: At the entrance, you're greeted by an original, early fourth-century A.D. Roman statue of the god Mars. If he could talk, he'd say, "Hear me, mortals. There are three sections here: Roman (on this floor), medieval (downstairs), and natural history (a kid-friendly wing on this floor). Start first with the 10-minute video for a sweeping history of the city."

The **Roman** collection surrounds a large map on the floor of the Roman Empire. You'll see slice-of-life exhibits about Roman baths, a huge floor mosaic, and skulls accompanied by artists' renderings of how the people originally looked. (One man was apparently killed by a sword blow to the head—making it graphically clear that the struggle between Romans and barbarians was a violent one.) These artifacts are particularly interesting when you consider that you're standing in one of the farthest reaches of the Roman Empire.

The **medieval** collection is in the basement. During the Middle Ages, York was England's second city. One large room is dominated by ruins of the St. Mary's Abbey complex (described on page 586; one wall still stands just out front—be sure to see it before leaving). You'll also see old weapons, glazed vessels, and a well-preserved 13th-century leather box.

The museum's prized pieces are in this section: a helmet and a pendant. The eighth-century Anglo-Saxon helmet (known as the York Helmet or the Coppergate Helmet) shows a bit of barbarian refinement. Examine the delicate carving on its brass trim. The exquisitely etched 15th-century pendant—called the Middleham Jewel—is considered the finest piece of Gothic jewelry in Britain. The noble lady who wore this on a necklace believed that it helped her worship and protected her from illness. The back of the pendant, which rested near her heart, shows the Nativity.

The front shows the Holy Trinity crowned by a sapphire (which people believed put their prayers at the top of God's to-do list).

In addition to the Anglo-Saxon pieces, the Viking collection is one of the best in England. Looking over the artifacts, you'll find that the Vikings (who conquered most of the Anglo-Saxon lands) wore some pretty decent shoes and actually combed their hair. The Cawood Sword, nearly 1,000 years old, is one of the finest surviving swords from that era.

The **natural history** exhibit (titled "Extinct") is back upstairs, showing off skeletons of the extinct dodo and ostrich-like moa birds, as well as an ichthyosaurus.

Barley Hall

Uncovered behind a derelict office block in the 1980s, this medieval house has been restored to replicate a 1483 dwelling. It's designed to resurrect the Tudor age for visiting school groups, but feels soulless to adults.

Cost and Hours: £5, includes audioguide, kids under 5-free, combo-tickets with Jorvik Viking Centre and/or Dig, daily April-Oct 10:00-17:00, Nov-March 10:00-16:00, 2 Coffee Yard off Stonegate, tel. 01904/615-505, www.barleyhall.org.uk.

Holy Trinity Church

Built in the late Perpendicular Gothic style, this church has windows made of precious glass—both clear and stained—from the 13th to 15th centuries. It holds rare box pews, which rest atop a floor that is sinking as bodies rot and coffins collapse. Enjoy its peaceful picnic-friendly gardens.

Cost and Hours: Free, Tue-Sat 10:00-16:00, Sun-Mon 12:00-16:00, 70 Goodramgate, tel. 1904/613-451, www.holytrinityyork.org.

King's Square

This lively people-watching zone, with its inviting benches, once hosted a church. Then it was the site for the town's gallows. Today, it's prime real estate for buskers and street performers. Just hanging out here can be very entertaining. Just beyond is the most characteristic and touristy street in old York: The Shambles. Within sight of this lively square are plenty of cheap eating options (for tips, see "Eating in York," later).

Chocolate: York's Sweet Story

Though known mainly for its Roman, Viking, and medieval past, York also has a rich history in chocolate-making. Throughout the 1800s and 1900s, York was home to three major confectionaries—including Rowntree's, originators of the venerable Kit Kat.

However, this chocolate "museum" is childish and overpriced. The building has no significance, and there are almost no historic artifacts. If you come, the visits are by tour only; your guide gives you lots of chocolate as you learn of York's confectionary past and watch brief videos.

Cost and Hours: £10, 30-minute tours run every 15 minutes daily 10:00-17:00 (last tour at 17:00), King's Square, tel. 0845-498-9411, www.yorksweetstory.com.

Dig

This hands-on, kid-oriented archaeological site gives young visitors an idea of what York looked during Roman, Viking, medieval, and Victorian eras. Sift through "dirt" (actually, shredded tires), dig up reconstructed Roman wall plaster, and take a look at what archaeologists have found recently. Entry is possible only with a one-hour guided tour (departures every 30 minutes); pass any waiting time by looking at the exhibits near the entry. The exhibits fill the haunted old St. Saviour's Church.

Cost and Hours: £5.50, kids under 5-free, combo-tickets with Jorvik Viking Centre and/or Barley Hall, daily 10:00-17:00, last tour departs one hour before closing, Saviourgate, tel. 01904/615-505, www.digyork.com.

Merchant Adventurers' Hall

Claiming to be the finest surviving medieval guildhall in Britain (from 1357-1361), this vast half-timbered building with marvelous

exposed beams contains about 15 minutes' worth of interesting displays about life and commerce in the Middle Ages. You'll see three original, large rooms that are still intact: the great hall itself, where meetings took place; the undercroft, which housed a hospital and almshouse; and a chapel. Several smaller rooms are filled with exhibits about old York. Sitting by itself in its own little park, this classic old building is worth a stop even just to see it from the outside. Remarkably, the hall is still owned by the same Merchant Adventurers society that built it 650 years ago (now a modern charitable organization).

Cost and Hours: £6, includes audioguide, March-Oct Mon-Thu 9:00-17:00, Fri-Sat 9:00-15:30, Sun 11:00-16:00, shorter hours and closed Sun off-season, south of The Shambles between Fossgate and Piccadilly, tel. 01904/654-818, www.theyorkcompany.co.uk.

▲▲Jorvik Viking Centre

Take the "Pirates of the Caribbean," sail them northeast and back in time 1,000 years, sprinkle in some real artifacts, and you get

Jorvik (YOR-vik)—as much a ride as a museum. Between 1976 and 1981, more than 40,000 artifacts were dug out of the peat bog right here in downtown York—the UK's largest archaeological dig of Viking-era artifacts. When the archaeologists were finished, the dig site was converted into this attraction. Innovative in 1984, the commercial success of Jorvik inspired copycat ride/museums all over England. Some love Jorvik, while others call it gimmicky and overpriced. If you think of it as Disneyland with a splash of history, Jorvik's fun. To me, Jorvik is a commercial venture designed for kids, with too much emphasis on its gift shop. But it's also undeniably entertaining, and—if you take the time to peruse its exhibits—it can be quite informative.

Cost and Hours: £10, various combo-tickets with Dig and/or Barley Hall, daily April-Oct 10:00-17:00, Nov-March until 16:00, these are last-entry times, tel. 01904/615-505, www.jorvik-viking-centre.co.uk.

Crowd-Beating Tips: This popular attraction can come with long lines. At the busiest times (roughly 11:00-15:00), you may have to wait an hour or more—especially on school holidays. For £1 extra, you can book a slot in advance, either over the phone or on their website. Or you can avoid the worst lines by coming early or late in the day (when you'll more likely wait just 10-15 minutes).

Visiting Jorvik: First you'll walk down stairs (marked with the layers of history you're passing) and explore a small **museum.** Under the glass floor is a re-creation of the archaeological dig that took place right here. Surrounding that are a few actual artifacts (such as a knife, comb, shoe, and cup) and engaging videos detailing the Viking invasions, longships, and explorers, and the history of the excavations. Next to where you board your people-mover is the largest Viking timber found in the UK (from a wooden building on Coppergate). Don't rush through this area: These exhibits offer historical context to your upcoming journey back in time. Viking-costumed docents are happy to explain what you're seeing.

When ready, board a theme-park-esque **people-mover** for a 12-minute trip through the re-created Viking street of Coppergate. It's the year 975, and you're in the village of Jorvik. You'll glide past reconstructed houses and streets that sit atop the actual excavation site, while the recorded commentary tells you about everyday life in Viking times. Animatronic characters jabber at you in Old Norse, as you experience the sights, sounds, and smells of yore. Everything is true to the original dig—the face of one of the mannequins was computer-modeled from a skull dug up here.

Finally, you'll disembark at the **hands-on area,** where you can actually touch original Viking artifacts. You'll see several skeletons, carefully laid out and labeled to point out diseases and injuries, along with a big gob of coprolite (fossilized feces that offer archaeologists invaluable clues about long-gone lifestyles). Next, a gallery of everyday items (metal, glass, leather, wood, and so on) provides intimate glimpses into that redheaded culture. Take advantage of the informative touchscreens. The final section is devoted to swords, spears, axes, and shields. You'll also see bashed-in skulls (with injuries possibly sustained in battle) and a replica of the famous Coppergate Helmet (the original is in the Yorkshire Museum).

▲Fairfax House

This well-furnished home, supposedly the "first Georgian townhouse in England," is perfectly Neoclassical inside. Each room is staffed by wonderfully pleasant docents eager to talk with you. They'll explain how the circa-1760 home was built as the dowry for an aristocrat's daughter. The house is compact and bursting with stunning period furniture (the personal collection of a local chocolate magnate), gorgeously restored woodwork, and lavish stucco ceilings that offer clues as to each room's purpose. For example, stuccoed philosophers look down on the library, while the goddess of friendship presides over the drawing room. Taken together, this house provides fine insights into aristocratic life in 18th-century England.

Cost and Hours: £6, Tue-Sat 10:00-17:00, Sun 12:30-16:00, Mon by guided tour only at 11:00 and 14:00—the one-hour tours are worthwhile, closed Jan-mid-Feb, near Jorvik Viking Centre at 29 Castlegate, tel. 01904/655-543, www.fairfaxhouse.co.uk.

Clifford's Tower

Perched high on a knoll across from the York Castle Museum, this ruin is all that's left of York's 13th-century castle—the site

of the gruesome 1190 mass-suicide of local Jews (they locked themselves inside and set the castle afire rather than face death at the hands of the bloodthirsty townspeople; read the whole story on the sign at the base of the hill). If you go inside, you'll see a model of the original castle complex as it looked in the Middle Ages, and you can climb up to enjoy fine city views from the top of the ramparts—but neither is worth the cost of admission.

Cost and Hours: £4.20, daily April-Sept 10:00-18:00,

closes earlier off-season, last entry 15 minutes before closing, tel. 01904/646-940.

▲▲York Castle Museum

This fascinating museum is a Victorian home show, possibly the closest thing to a time-tunnel experience England has to offer.

The one-way plan assures that you'll see everything, including remakes of rooms from the 17th to 20th centuries, a re-creation of a Victorian street, interesting military exhibits, and some eerie prison cells.

Cost and Hours: £8.50, kids under 16 free with paying adult, £13 combo-ticket with Yorkshire Museum, daily 9:30-17:00, cafeteria at entrance, tel. 01904/687-687, www.yorkcastlemuseum .org.uk. It's at the bottom of the hop-on, hop-off bus route. The museum can call you a taxi (worthwhile if you're hurrying to the National Railway Museum, across town).

Information: The museum's £4 guidebook isn't necessary, but it makes a fine souvenir. The museum proudly offers no audioguides, as its roaming guides are enthusiastic about talking—engage them.

⊘ Self-Guided Tour: The exhibits are divided between two wings: the North Building (to the left as you enter) and the South Building (to the right).

Follow the one-way route through the complex, starting in the **North Building.** You'll first visit the Period Rooms, illuminating Yorkshire lifestyles during different time periods (1600s-1950s) and among various walks of life. The excellent From Cradle to Grave exhibit traces the rites of passage of a typical lifetime during the Victorian Age. For example, most women mourned their husbands for two and a half years, reflected by the color of their clothes. (Queen Victoria, who was famously an extra-credit mourner, dressed in black for four decades after the death of her beloved Prince Albert; for more on Victoria, see sidebar on page

980.) The Hearth and Home exhibit showcases fireplaces and kitchens from the 1600s to the 1980s, and the Barn Gallery explains farming in Yorkshire.

Next, stroll down the museum's re-created Kirkgate, a street from the Victorian era, when Britain was at the peak of its power. It features old-time shops and storefronts, including a pharmacist, sweet shop, school, and grocer for the working class, along with roaming live guides in period dress. Around the back is a slum area depicting how the poor lived in those times.

Circle back to the entry and cross over to the **South Building**. A new World War I exhibit marks the war's centennial. Because of the reorganization, parts of the following exhibits may be closed, in flux, or missing. The military section includes displays about the Merchant Adventurers (traders and buccaneers on the high seas), Elizabethan soldiers of York, Yorkshire's role in the English Civil War (tracing the events of 1642-1651), and a powerful exhibit called Seeing It Through in York, explaining both the military and civilian experience here during World War II. The Costume Gallery features 250 years of clothes and textiles, and the Toy Gallery takes you from dollhouses to Transformers.

Exit outside and cross through the castle yard. A detour to the left leads to a flour mill (open sporadically). Otherwise, your

tour continues through the door on the right, where you'll find another reconstructed historical street, this one capturing the spirit of the swinging 1960s—"a time when the cultural changes were massive but the cars and skirts were mini." Slathered with DayGlo colors, this street scene examines fashion, music, and television (including clips of beloved kids' shows and period news reports).

Finally, head into the York Castle Prison, which recounts the experiences of actual people who were thrown into the clink here. Videos, eerily projected onto the walls of individual cells, show actors telling tragic stories about the cells' one-time inhabitants.

Across the River
▲▲National Railway Museum

If you like model railways, this is train-car heaven. The thunderous museum shows 200 illustrious years of British railroad history. This biggest and best railroad museum anywhere is interesting even to people who think "Pullman" means "don't push."

Cost and Hours: Free but £3 suggested donation, daily 10:00-18:00, café, restaurant, tel. 0844-815-3139, www.nrm.org.uk.

Getting There: It's about a 15-minute walk from the Minster (southwest of town, up the hill behind the train station). From the train station itself, the fastest approach is to go all the way to the back of the station (using the overpass to cross the tracks), exit out the back door, and turn right up the hill. To skip the walk, a cute little "road train" shuttles you more quickly between the Minster and the Railway Museum (£2 each way, runs daily Easter-Oct, leaves museum every 30 minutes 11:00-16:00 at :00 and :30 past each hour; leaves town—from Duncombe Place, 100 yards in front of the Minster—at :15 and :45 past each hour).

Visiting the Museum: Pick up the floor plan to locate the various exhibits, which sprawl through several gigantic buildings on both sides of the street. Throughout the complex, red-shirted "explainers" are eager to talk trains.

The museum's most impressive room is the **Great Hall** (head right from the entrance area; it's across the street). Fanning out

from this grand roundhouse is an array of historic cars and engines, starting with the very first "stage-coaches on rails," with a crude steam engine from 1830. You'll trace the evolution of steam-powered transportation, from the Flying Scotsman (the first London-Edinburgh express rail service), to the era of the aero-dynamic Mallard (famous as the first train to travel at a startling two miles per minute—a marvel back in 1938) and the striking Art Deco-style Duchess of Hamilton. (The Flying Scotsman and other trains may not be on display, as they are sometimes on loan or under maintenance—ask an explainer if you can't find something.) The collection spans to the present day, with a replica of the Eurostar (Chunnel) train and the Shinkansen Japanese bullet train. Other exhibits include a steam engine that's been sliced open to show its cylinders, driving wheels, and smoke box, as well as a working turntable that's put into action twice a day. The Mallard Experience simulates a ride on the Mallard.

The Works is an actual workshop where engineers scurry about, fixing old trains. Live train switchboards show real-time rail traffic on the East Coast Main Line. Next to the diagrammed screens, you can look out to see the actual trains moving up and down the line. **The Warehouse** is loaded with more than 10,000 items relating to train travel (including dinnerware, signage, and actual trains). Exhibits feature dining cars, post cars, sleeping cars, train posters, and more info on the Flying Scotsman.

Crossing back to the entrance side, continue to the **Station Hall**, with a collection of older trains, including ones that the royals have used to ride the rails (including Queen Victoria's lavish royal car). Behind that are the South Yard and the Depot, with actual, working trains in storage.

YORK

▲York Brewery

This intimate, tactile, and informative 45-minute-long tour gives an enjoyable look at how this charming little microbrewery produces 5,500 pints per batch. Their award-winning Ghost Ale is strong, dark, and chocolaty. You can drink their beer throughout town, but to get it as fresh as possible, drink it where it's birthed, in their cozy Tap Room.

Cost and Hours: £6, includes a pint of the best beer—ale not lager—in town; tours Mon-Sat at 12:30, 14:00, 15:30, and 17:00—just show up; cross the river on Lendal Bridge and walk 5 minutes to Toft Green just below Micklegate, tel. 01904/621-162, www.york-brewery.co.uk.

Outside of Town

▲Ouse Riverside Walk or Bike Ride

The New Walk is a mile-long, tree-lined riverside lane created in the 1730s as a promenade for York's dandy class to stroll, see, and be seen—and is a fine place for today's visitors to walk or bike. This hour-long walk is a delightful way to enjoy a dose of countryside away from York. It's paved, illuminated in the evening, and a popular jogging route any time of day.

Start from the riverside under Skeldergate Bridge (near the York Castle Museum), and walk south away from town for a mile. Notice modern buildings across the river, with their floodwalls. Shortly afterwards, you cross the tiny Foss River on Blue Bridge, originally built in 1738. The easily defended confluence of the Foss and the Ouse is the reason the Romans founded York in A.D. 71. Look back to see the modern floodgate (built after a flood in 1979) designed to stop the flooding Ouse from oozing up the Foss. At the bridge, a history panel describes this walk to the Millennium Bridge.

Stroll until you hit the striking, modern **Millennium Bridge.** Sit a bit on its reclining-lounge-chair fence and enjoy the vibrations of bikes and joggers as they pass. There's a strong biking trend in Britain these days. In recent Olympics, the British have won most of the gold medals in cycling. In 2012, Bradley Wiggins became Sir Bradley Wiggins by winning the Tour de France; his countryman, Chris Froome, won it in 2013. You'll see lots of locals riding fancy bikes and wearing high-tech gear while getting into better shape. (Energetic bikers can continue past the Millennium Bridge 14 miles to the market town of Selby.)

Cross the river and walk back home, passing **Rowntree Park.** After the skateboard court, enter the park through its fine old gate. This park was financed by Joseph Rowntree, a wealthy chocolate baron with a Quaker ethic of contributing to his community. In the 19th century, life for the poor was a Charles Dickens-like struggle. A rich man building a park for the working class, which even had a swimming pool, was quite progressive. Victorian England had a laissez-faire approach to social issues. Then, like now, many wealthy people believed things would work out for the poor if the government just stayed out of it. However, others, such as the Rowntree family, felt differently. Their altruism contributed to the establishment of a society that now takes much better care of its workers and poor.

Walk directly into the park toward the evocative Industrial Age housing complex capping the hill beyond the central fountain. In the park's brick gazebo are touching memorial plaques to WWI and WWII deaths. Rowntree gave this park to York to remember those lost in the "Great War." Stroll along the delightful, duck-filled pond near the Rowntree Park Café, return to the riverside lane, and continue back into York. You're almost home.

Shopping in York

With its medieval lanes lined with classy as well as tacky little shops, York is a hit with shoppers. I find two kinds of shopping in York particularly interesting: antique malls and charity shops.

Antiques Malls: Three places within a few blocks of each other are filled with stalls and cases owned by antiques dealers from the countryside (all open daily). The malls, a warren of rooms on three floors with cafés buried deep inside, sell the dealers' bygones on commission. Serious shoppers do better heading for the country, but York's shops are a fun browse: The **Antiques Centre York** (41 Stonegate, www.theantiquescentreyork.co.uk), the **Red House Antiques Centre** (a block from the Minster at Duncombe Place, www.redhouseyork.co.uk), and **Cavendish Antiques and Jewellers** (44 Stonegate, www.cavendishjewellers .co.uk).

Charity Shops: In towns all over Britain, it seems one low-rent street is lined with charity shops, allowing locals to both donate their junk and buy the junk of others in the name of a good cause. (Talk about a win-win.) It's great for random shopping. And, as the people working there are often volunteers involved in that cause, it can lead to some interesting conversations. In York, on Goodramgate (stretching a block or so in from the town wall), you'll find "thrift shops" run by the British Heart Foundation, Save the Children, Mind, and Oxfam. Good deals abound on clothing, purses, accessories, children's toys, books, CDs, and maybe even a guitar. If you buy something, you're getting a bargain and at the same time helping the poor, mentally ill, elderly, or even a pet in need of a vet (stores generally open between 9:00 and 10:00 and close between 16:00 and 17:00, with shorter hours on Sun).

Nightlife in York

Pubs

Even more than chocolate, York likes its beer. It has its own award-winning microbrewery, the York Brewery (which offers fine tours daily—see page 607), along with countless atmospheric pubs for memorable and convivial eating or drinking. Many pubs serve inexpensive plates at lunch, then focus on selling beer in the evening. Others offer lunch and early dinner. You can tell by their marketing how enthusiastic they are about cooking versus drawing pints.

The York Brewery Tap Room, a private club, feels like a fraternity of older men. But if you drop in, you can be an honorary guest. It's right at the microbrewery, with five beloved varieties on tap as fresh as you'll find anywhere (14 Toft Green, just below Micklegate, tel. 01904/621-162, www.york-brewery.co.uk).

The Maltings, just over Lendal Bridge, has classic pub ambience and serves good meals at lunch only. Local beer purists swear by this place (£6-7 pub lunches, open for drinks nightly, cross the bridge and look down and left to Tanners Moat, tel. 01904/655-387).

The Blue Bell is one of my favorites for old-school York vibes. This tiny, traditional establishment with a time-warp Edwardian interior is the smallest pub in York. It has two distinct and inviting little rooms (limited food served at lunch only, east end of town at 53 Fossgate, tel. 01904/654-904).

The House of the Trembling Madness is another fine watering hole with a cozy atmosphere above a "bottle shop" selling a stunning variety of beers by the bottle to go (48 Stonegate; also described later, under "Eating in York").

Evil Eye Lounge, a hit with York's young crowd, is a creaky, funky, hip space famous for its strong cocktails and edgy ambience. There are even beds to drink in. You can order downstairs at the bar (with a small terrace out back), or head upstairs (42 Stonegate; also a restaurant—described later, under "Eating in York").

The Golden Fleece is a sloppy, dingy place with tilty floors that make you feel drunk even if you aren't. Its wooden frame has survived without foundations for 500 years. Originally owned by wool traders, it's considered the oldest and most haunted coaching inn in York (16 Pavement, across the street from the southern end of The Shambles, tel. 01904/625-171).

The Last Drop is a solid, basic pub—no music, no game machines, no children. It's owned by the York Brewery, so it always has their ales on tap (27 Colliergate facing King's Square, tel. 01904/621-951).

Student Pub Crawl: The **"Micklegate Run"** is a ritual for students all over Yorkshire. As this pub crawl starts just below the train station, students ride the train into York and then have a pint in each pub or club along Micklegate. You'll pass at least eight pubs as the street runs downhill from Micklegate Bar to the river. It can be lowbrow and sloppy. You'll see lots of hen-party and stag-party spectacles, and what local guys rudely call "mutton dressed as lamb"—older women trying to look young.

Riverside Eating and Drinking: On sunny days, there are several pubs with riverside tables just below Ouse Bridge, starting with **The Kings Arms**, which boasts flood marks inside its door and has a rougher local crowd than other recommended pubs (3 King's Staith, tel. 01904/659-435).

Entertainment
Theatre Royal
A full variety of dramas, comedies, and works by Shakespeare entertain the locals in either the main theater or the little 100-seat theater-in-the-round (£10-22, usually Tue-Sat at 19:30, tickets easy to get, on St. Leonard's Place near Bootham Bar and a 5- to 10-minute walk from recommended B&Bs, booking tel. 01904/623-568, www.yorktheatreroyal.co.uk). Those under 25 and students of any age can get tickets for only £8.

Ghost Tours
You'll see fliers, signs, and promoters hawking a variety of entertaining after-dark tours. For a rundown on this scene, see page 583.

Movies
The centrally located **City Screen Cinema,** right on the river, plays both art-house and mainstream flicks. They also have an enticing café/bar overlooking the river that serves good food (13 Coney Street, tel. 0871-902-5726).

Sleeping in York

I've listed peak-season, book-direct prices; July through October are the busiest (and usually most expensive) months. B&Bs often charge more for weekends and sometimes turn away one-night bookings, particularly for peak-season Saturdays. (York is worth two nights anyway.) Prices may spike up for horse races and Bank Holidays (about 20 nights a season). Remember to book ahead during festival times (see "Helpful Hints," page 582) and weekends year-round.

B&Bs and Small Hotels
These B&Bs are all small and family-run. They come with plenty of steep stairs (and no elevators) but no traffic noise. Rooms can be

Sleep Code

(£1 = about $1.60, country code: 44, area code: 01904)
S = Single, **D** = Double/Twin, **T** = Triple, **Q** = Quad, **b** = bathroom,
s = shower only. Unless otherwise noted, credit cards are
accepted and breakfast is included.

To help you sort easily through these listings, I've divided
the accommodations into three categories based on the price
for a standard double room with bath (during high season):

$$$ **Higher Priced**—Most rooms £100 or more.
  $$ **Moderately Priced**—Most rooms between £75-100.
   $ **Lower Priced**—Most rooms £75 or less.

Prices can change without notice; verify the hotel's current rates online or by email. For the best prices, always book
direct.

tight; if maneuverability is important to you, say so when booking.
For a good selection, contact them well in advance. B&B owners
will generally hold a room with an email or phone call and work
hard to help their guests sightsee and eat smartly. Most have per-
mits to lend for street parking. Please honor your bookings—the
B&B proprietors here lose out on much-needed business if you
don't show up.

The handiest B&B neighborhood is the quiet residential
area just outside the old town wall's Bootham gate, along the
road called Bootham. All of these are within a 10-minute walk
of the Minster and TI, and a 5- to 15-minute walk or £6 taxi ride
from the station. If driving, head for the cathedral and follow the
medieval wall to the gate called Bootham Bar. The street called
Bootham leads away from Bootham Bar.

Getting There: Here's the most direct way to walk to this
B&B area from the train station: Head to the north end of the
station, to the area between platforms 2 and 4. Shoot through the
gap between the men's WC and the York Tap pub, into the short-
stay parking lot. Walk to the end of the lot to a pedestrian ramp,
and zigzag your way down. At the bottom, head left, following
the sign for the riverside route. When you reach the river, cross
over it on the footbridge. At the far end of the bridge, the Abbey
Guest House is a few yards to your right, facing the river. To reach
The Hazelwood and Ardmore Guest House (closer to the town
wall), walk from the bridge along the river until just before the
short ruined tower, then turn inland up onto Marygate. For other
B&Bs, at the bottom of the footbridge, turn left immediately onto
a path that skirts the big parking lot (parallel to the train tracks).

YORK

York Accommodations

1 Hedley House Hotel
2 Abbeyfields Guest House
3 St. Raphael Guesthouse
4 Arnot House
5 Amber House & Number 34
6 Bootham Guest House
7 Queen Annes Guest House
8 Abbey Guest House
9 Number 23 St. Mary's B&B
10 Crook Lodge B&B
11 Airden House
12 The Hazelwood
13 Ardmore Guest House
14 Dean Court Hotel
15 Grays Court Hotel
16 Premier Inns (2)
17 Travelodge York Central
18 Travelodge York Central Micklegate
19 Ace York Hostel
20 Internet Café
21 Library (Internet)
22 To Launderette

TO A-19 & THIRSK

CLIFTON
BOOTH. CRES.
GROS. TERR.
QUEEN ANNES
BOOTHAM TERR.
SYCAMORE
ST. MARYS
LONGFIELD
FREDERIC
MARYGATE
EARLS

RAILWAY MUSEUM

RIVER

LEEMAN

ROAD

WALKING PATH TO B+Bs

STATION RD.

TRAIN STATION

TOFT GREEN
BARKER
MICKLE

QUEEN

BLOSSOM

NUNNERY

MICKLEGATE BAR

TO A-64 & LEEDS

200 YARDS
200 METERS

ACCESS STAIRS TO WALL
PEDESTRIAN ZONE
P PARKING
--- FOOTPATH

YORK

YORK

At the end of the parking lot, you'll turn depending on your B&B: for the places on or near Bootham Terrace, turn left and go under the tracks; for B&Bs on St. Mary's Street, take the short stairway on your right.

On or near Bootham Terrace

$$$ Hedley House Hotel, well-run by a wonderful family, has 30 clean and spacious rooms. The outdoor hot tub/sauna is a fine way to end your day (Sb-£75-105, standard Db-£80-135, larger Db-£90-155, rates depend on demand, ask for a deal with stay of 3 or more nights, family rooms, good two-course evening meals from £18, free Wi-Fi, in-house massage and beauty services, free parking, 3 Bootham Terrace, tel. 01904/637-404, www.hedley house.com, greg@hedleyhouse.com, Greg and Louise Harrand). They also have nine luxury studio apartments—see their website for details.

$$ Abbeyfields Guest House has eight comfortable, bright rooms. This doily-free place lacks B&B clutter and has been designed with care (Sb-£55; Db-£84 Sun-Thu, £89 Fri-Sat; these prices good if you mention this book when reserving direct, home-made bread, free Wi-Fi, free parking, 19 Bootham Terrace, tel. 01904/636-471, www.abbeyfields.co.uk, enquire@abbeyfields.co .uk, charming Al and Les).

$$ At St. Raphael Guesthouse, young, creative, and ener-getic Dom and Zoe (and son Ollie) understand a traveler's needs. You'll be instant friends. Dom's graphic design training brings a dash of class to their seven comfy rooms, each themed after a dif-ferent York street, and each lovingly accented with a fresh rose (Sb-£75 Sun-Thu, £85 Fri-Sat; Db-£82 Sun-Thu, £94 Fri-Sat; these prices promised if you mention this book when reserving direct, free drinks in their guests' fridge, family rooms, guest computer, free Wi-Fi, 44 Queen Annes Road, tel. 01904/645-028, www .straphaelguesthouse.co.uk, info@straphaelguesthouse.co.uk).

$$ Arnot House, run by a hardworking daughter-and-mother team, is old-fashioned, homey, and lushly decorated with Victorian memorabilia. The three well-furnished rooms even have little libraries (Db-£80-85 if you book direct, 2-night minimum stay unless it's last-minute, no children, free Wi-Fi, huge DVD library, 17 Grosvenor Terrace, tel. 01904/641-966, www.arnot houseyork.co.uk, kim.robbins@virgin.net, Kim).

$ Amber House is a small place with three breezy and well-tended rooms (one Asian-inspired). It's homey, but with some elegant touches—a bit more tasteful and upscale-feeling than oth-ers in this price range (Db-£66 Sun-Thu, £74 Fri-Sat; Tb-£93; mention this book when reserving direct for these prices, free Wi-Fi, free parking, 36 Bootham Crescent, tel. 01904/620-275, www.amberhouse-york.co.uk, amberhouseyork@hotmail.co.uk, John and Linda).

$ Bootham Guest House features gregarious and welcoming Emma. Public spaces are ho-hum, but the eight rooms (six are en-suite, two share a bath) are cheery and stylish (S-£40, Sb-£50, D-£65, Db-£75, Tb-£95, mention this book when reserving direct for these prices, free Wi-Fi, 56 Bootham Crescent, tel. 01904/672-123, www.boothamguesthouse.com, boothamguesthouse1@hotmail.com).

$ Number 34, run by hardworking Amy and Jason, has five simple, light, and airy rooms at fair prices. It's a bit masculine-feeling, with modern decor (Sb-£35-45, Db-£60-66, Tb-£85-90, price depends on season and day of week, mention Rick Steves when reserving to get best rates, ground-floor room, free Wi-Fi, 34 Bootham Crescent, tel. 01904/645-818, www.number34york.co.uk, enquiries@number34york.co.uk).

$ Queen Annes Guest House has eight basic rooms in two adjacent houses at some of the best prices in the neighborhood. While it doesn't have the plushest beds or richest decor, this is a respectable, affordable, and clean place to sleep (S-£35, Db-£72, Tb-£108, 10 percent discount if you mention this book and reserve direct, cheaper if you stay 2 nights, family room, free Wi-Fi, lounge, 24 and 26 Queen Annes Road, tel. 01904/629-389, www.queen-annes-guesthouse.co.uk, info@queen-annes-guesthouse.co.uk, Phil).

On the River
$$ Abbey Guest House is a peaceful refuge overlooking the River Ouse, with five cheerful, beautifully updated, contemporary-style rooms and a cute little garden (Db-£78, four-poster Db with river view-£83, ask for Rick Steves discount when you book direct, free Wi-Fi, free parking, £7 laundry service, 13-14 Earlsborough Terrace, tel. 01904/627-782, www.abbeyghyork.co.uk, info@abbeyghyork.co.uk, delightful couple Gill—pronounced "Jill"—and Alec Saville, and a dog aptly named Loofah).

On St. Mary's Street
$$ Number 23 St. Mary's B&B is extravagantly decorated. Chris and Julie Simpson have done everything just right and offer nine spacious and tastefully comfy rooms, a classy lounge, and all the doily touches (Sb-£50-60, Db-£80-100 depending on room size and season, discount for longer stays, family room, honesty box for drinks and snacks, free Wi-Fi, 23 St. Mary's, tel. 01904/622-738, www.23stmarys.co.uk, stmarys23@hotmail.com).

$$ Crook Lodge B&B, with seven tight but elegantly charming rooms, serves breakfast in an old Victorian kitchen.

YORK

The 21st-century style somehow fits this old house (Db-£75-80, cheaper off-season, check for online specials, one ground-floor room, guest computer, free Wi-Fi, parking, quiet, 26 St. Mary's, tel. 01904/655-614, www.crooklodge.co.uk, crooklodge@hotmail .com, Brian and Louise Aiken).

$ **Airden House** rents 10 nice, mostly traditional rooms, though the two basement-level rooms are more mod. One comes with a sauna, and the other, decorated in bright, feminine hues, has a space-age-looking Jacuzzi and a separate room with twin bed (standard Db-£68-72, traditional Db-£74-78, sauna Db-£78-82, Jacuzzi Db-£84-92, Tb-£94-100, these prices with 2-night minimum if you mention this book when reserving, higher prices are for weekends, lounge, free Wi-Fi, free parking, 1 St. Mary's, tel. 01904/638-915, www.airdenhouse.co.uk, info@airdenhouse.co.uk, Emma and Heather).

Closer to the Town Wall

$$$ **The Hazelwood**, more formal than a B&B, rents 14 rooms. The "standard" rooms have bright, cheery decor and small bathrooms, while the bigger "superior" rooms come with newer bathrooms and handcrafted furniture. Ask about their bright top-floor two-bedroom apartment good for families (Sb-£70, standard Db-£80-100, superior Db-£100-130, price depends on season and day of week, guest computer, free Wi-Fi, homemade biscuits on arrival, free laundry service for Rick Steves readers, free parking, garden patio; fridge, ice, and travel library in pleasant basement lounge; 24 Portland Street, tel. 01904/626-548, www.thehazel woodyork.com, reservations@thehazelwoodyork.com; Ian and Carolyn, along with Sharon and Emma).

$ **Ardmore Guest House** is a fine little three-room place enthusiastically run by Irishwoman Vera. It's about 15 minutes' walk from the station, but only five minutes from Bootham Bar (Sb-£40, smaller Db-£60, larger Db-£75, Tb-£75, discount off-season for 3 or more nights, cash only, free Wi-Fi, parking, 31 Claremont Terrace, tel. 01904/622-562, mobile 0793-928-3588, www.ardmoreyork.co.uk, ardmoreguesthouse@crwprojects.co.uk).

Large Hotels

$$$ **Dean Court Hotel**, a Best Western facing the Minster, is a big, stately hotel with classy lounges and 37 comfortable rooms. A few have views for no extra charge—try requesting one (Sb-£115, small Db-£150, standard Db-£180, superior Db-£210, spacious deluxe Db-£230; cheaper midweek, off-season, and on Sun—check specific rates online; elevator, guest computer, free Wi-Fi, bistro, restaurant, Duncombe Place, tel. 01904/625-082, www .deancourt-york.co.uk, sales@deancourt-york.co.uk).

YORK

$$$ Grays Court Hotel is a historic mansion—the home of dukes and archbishops since 1091—that now rents seven rooms to tourists. While its public spaces and gardens are lavish, its rooms are elegant yet modest. The creaky, historic nature of the place makes for a memorable stay. If it's too pricey for lodging, consider coming here for its tearoom—described later, under "Eating in York" (Db-£160-200, free Wi-Fi, Chapter House Street, tel. 01904/612-613, www.grayscourtyork.com).

$$$ Premier Inn offers 200 rooms in two side-by-side hotels that I hate to recommend, but it's a workable option if York's B&Bs have filled up, or if you can score a deep advance discount. They have little character (at one, you enter through a coffee shop), but they offer industrial-strength efficiency and a decent value (Db-£75-141, usually £80-95 Sun-Thu, £90-141 Fri-Sat; check for specials online—occasional deals as low as £29 if you book far enough ahead; up to 2 kids stay free, continental breakfast-£5.25, full breakfast-£8.25, elevator in one building, pay guest computer, pay Wi-Fi, parking-£8.50/24 hours, 5-minute walk to train station, 20 and 28-40 Blossom Street, tel. 0871-527-9194 and 0871-527-9196, www.premierinn.com).

$$ Travelodge York Central offers 93 affordable, recently renovated rooms near the York Castle Museum. If you book long in advance on their website, this can be amazingly cheap. River views make some rooms slightly less boring—after booking online, call the front desk to try to arrange a view (rates vary wildly depending on demand—as cheap as £19 for a fully prepaid "saver rate" 21 days ahead; for best rates, book online; cheapest rates are first-come, first-served; continental breakfast-£4.50, elevator, pay guest computer, pay Wi-Fi, parking-£7.50/24 hours and a 5-minute walk away, 90 Piccadilly, central reservations tel. 0871-984-8484, front desk tel. 0203-195-4978, www.travelodge.co.uk). A second location, **Travelodge York Central Micklegate,** has 104 rooms at the train station end of the Ouse Bridge (similar rates, Micklegate, tel. 0203-195-4976).

Hostel

$ Ace York is a boutique hostel on a rowdy street, which can be very noisy late at night on Fridays and Saturdays. It's in a big, old Georgian house that provides a much-needed option for backpackers. They rent 158 beds in 2- to 14-bed rooms, with great views, private prefab "pod" bathrooms, and reading lights for each bed. They also offer fancier, hotel-quality doubles (£16-25/bed, twin Db-£60-68, king Db-£80-84, family room for up to four-£120-128, rates depend on day and size of room, includes continental breakfast; four floors, no elevator, air-con, free Wi-Fi, self-service laundry-£3, TV lounge, game room, bar, lockers, no curfew, 5-minute

walk from train station at 88 Micklegate, tel. 01904/627-720, www
.acehotelyork.co.uk, reception@ace-hotelyork.co.uk, Brian).

Eating in York

York is touting its new reputation as a foodie city. It claims to be
rated "#5 in Europe" by some social media—but that's a stretch.
Still, the local high-tech industry and university—combined with
all the tourists—build a demand that sustains lots of creative and
fun eateries. There's also a wide range of ethnic food (including several good choices for Indian, Thai, Italian, Spanish tapas,
and so on). While there's plenty of decent pub grub served in the
bars, York still has no great gastropubs. (For pubbing advice, see
"Nightlife in York," earlier.)

If you're in a hurry or on a tight budget, picnic and light-
meals-to-go options abound, and it's easy to find a churchyard,
bench, or riverside perch upon which to munch cheaply. On
a sunny day, perhaps the best picnic spot in town is under the
evocative 12th-century ruins of St. Mary's Abbey in the Museum
Gardens (near Bootham Bar).

Upscale Bistros: As these trendy, pricey eateries are a York
forte, I've listed four of my favorites: Café No. 8, Café Concerto,
The Blue Bicycle, and Ambience Café Bistro. These places are each
romantic, laid-back, and popular with locals (so reservations are
wise for dinner). They also have good-quality, creative vegetarian
options. Most offer economical lunch specials and early dinners.
After 19:00 or so, main courses cost £15-25 and fixed-price meals
(two or three courses) go for around £25. On Friday and Saturday
evenings, many offer special, more expensive menus.

Cheap Eats Around King's Square

King's Square is about as central as can be for sightseers. And
from here, you can actually see several fine quick-and-cheap lunch
options. After buying your take-out food, sit on the square and
enjoy the street entertainers. Or, for a peaceful place to munch
more prayerfully, find the Holy Trinity Church yard, with benches
amid the old tombstones on Goodramgate (half a block to the
right of York Roast Company).

York Roast Company is a local fixture, serving delicious
and hearty £4-6 pork sandwiches with apple sauce, stuffing, and
"crackling" (roasted bits of fat and skin). Other meats are also
available. You can even oversee the stuffing of your own Yorkshire
pudding (£6-7). If Henry VIII wanted fast food, he'd eat here
(corner of Low Petergate and Goodramgate, order at counter then
dine upstairs or take away, daily 10:00-23:00, 74 Low Petergate,
tel. 01904/629-197).

Drakes Fish-and-Chips, across the street from York Roast Company, is a local favorite chippy (daily 11:00-22:30, 97 Low Petergate, tel. 01904/624-788).

The Cornish Bakery, facing King's Square, cooks up £3 pasties to eat in or take away (30 Colliergate, tel. 01904/671-177).

The Newgate Market, just past The Shambles, has several stalls offering fun and nutritious light meals. On The Shambles, **Mr. Sandwich** is famous for its £1 sandwiches.

St. Crux Parish Hall is a medieval church now used by a medley of charities that sell tea, homemade cakes, and light meals. They each book the church for a day, often a year in advance (usually open Tue-Sat 10:00-16:00, closed Sun-Mon, at bottom of The Shambles at its intersection with Pavement, tel. 01904/621-756).

For a nice finish, consider the **Harlequin Café**, a charming place loved by locals for its good coffee and homemade cakes, as well as its light meals. It's up a creaky staircase overlooking the square (daily 10:00-16:00, 2 King's Square, tel. 01904/630-631).

On or near Swinegate

Strolling this street, you can just take your pick of the various tempting bars and eateries. Some are trendy, with thumping music, while others are tranquil; some have elaborately decorated dining rooms, while others emphasize heated courtyards. This corner of town has two similar, fiercely competitive, American-style bar/brasserie/lounges (both open daily and serving £8-12 meals): **Oscar's,** right on Swinegate, has a mod interior and good burgers; **Stonegate Yard,** around the corner on Little Stonegate, in a delightful, ivy-covered courtyard. Others enjoy the courtyard and Mediterranean food at **Lucia** (£4 small plates, £10-15 meals, daily, 12-13 Swinegate).

Vegetarian: **El Piano Restaurant,** just off Swinegate on charming Grape Lane, is a popular place serving only vegan, gluten-free, and low-sodium dishes. Their meals are made with locally sourced ingredients and Indian/Asian/Middle Eastern/East African flavors. The inside ambience is bubble gum with blinking lights. If you don't want to feel that you're eating inside a sombrero, they also have a pleasant patio out back (£3 starters, £10 meals, £30 two-or-three-person sampler, Mon-Sat 11:00-23:00, Sun 12:00-21:00, between Low Petergate and Swinegate at 15-17 Grape Lane, tel. 01904/610-676). Save money at the take-away window (£4-5 boxes).

On Stonegate

The House of the Trembling Madness, considered by some to be the best pub in town, is easy to miss. Enter through The Bottle, a ground-floor shop selling an astonishing number of different

YORK

York Restaurants

1. King's Square Eateries
2. York Roast Co.
3. Drakes Fish & Chips
4. Newgate Market
5. St. Crux Parish Hall Café
6. Swinegate Eateries
7. Stonegate Yard
8. El Piano Restaurant
9. The House of the Trembling Madness & Bottle Shop
10. Evil Eye Lounge
11. Café Concerto
12. Café No. 8
13. Ambience Café Bistro
14. The Exhibition Hotel Pub
15. Sainsbury's Local Grocery
16. Rustique French Bistro
17. The Blue Bicycle
18. Melton's Too
19. Mumbai Lounge
20. Il Paradiso del Cibo Rist. Pizzeria
21. Ristorante Bari
22. Mamma Mia
23. Ask Restaurant
24. Bettys Café Tea Rooms
25. Grays Court Tea Rooms
26. York Brewery Tap Room
27. The Maltings Pub
28. The Blue Bell Pub
29. The Golden Fleece Pub
30. The Last Drop Pub
31. "Micklegate Run" Pub Crawl
32. The Kings Arms Pub

TO A-19 & THIRSK

CLIFTON
BOOTH CRES.
QUEEN ANNES
BOOTHAM TERR.
GROS. TERR.
ST. MARY'S
SYCAMORE
LONGFIELD
FREDERIC
MARGATE
EARLS.

RAILWAY MUSEUM

RIVER

P

LEEMAN

ROAD

WALKING PATH TO B+Bs

TRAIN STATION

STATION RD.

TOFT GREEN
MICKLE
BARKER
26
31

QUEEN

BLOSSOM

NUNNERY

MICKLEGATE BAR

TO A-64 & LEEDS

ACCESS STAIRS TO WALL

PEDESTRIAN ZONE

P PARKING

--- FOOTPATH

YORK

YORK

take-away beers (called a "bottle shop" in England). Climb the stairs to find a small but cozy pub beneath a high, airy timbered ceiling. It's youthful and a bit fashion-forward, yet still accessible to all ages. The food tries to be locally sourced and is far more creative than standard York pub grub (£3-6 snacks, £8-10 meals, daily 10:00-24:00, 48 Stonegate, tel. 01904/640-009).

Evil Eye Lounge serves large portions of delicious, authentic Southeast Asian cuisine. But the hipster space may be a bit too much for some. There's food and drinks on several levels (£8 meals, food served Mon-Fri 12:00-21:00, Sat 12:00-19:00, 42 Stonegate, tel. 01904/640-002).

Near Bootham Bar and Recommended B&Bs

Café Concerto, a casual and cozy bistro with wholesome food and a charming musical theme, has an understandably loyal following. The fun menu features updated English favorites with some international options (£4-8 starters; £9-12 soups, sandwiches, and salads; £12-17 main dishes; vegetarian and gluten-free options; daily 9:00-21:00, weekends until 22:00, smart to reserve for dinner—try for a window seat, also offers take-away, facing the Minster at 21 High Petergate, tel. 01904/610-478, http://cafeconcerto.biz).

Café No. 8 feels like Café Concerto but is more romantic, with jazz, modern art, candles, and hardworking Martin bringing it all together. Grab one of the tables in front or in the sunroom, or enjoy a shaded little garden out back if the weather's good. Chef Chris Pragnell uses what's fresh in the market to shape his menu. The food—mod cuisine with veggie options—is simple, elegant, and creative (£6-10 lunches, £16.50 two-course dinners, £22 three-course dinners, about £5 more Fri-Sat; daily 10:00-22:00, 8 Gillygate, tel. 01904/653-074, www.cafeno8.co.uk).

Ambience Café Bistro serves modern English and international dishes with seven cute tables in front. You can also dine in its delightful garden under the town wall out back. Chef Guy Whapples serves lunch daily and dinners—with a fancier "bistro" menu—only two nights a week (£7 lunch plates, daily 12:00-17:00; £21 two-course and £24 three-course dinners, a bit less if you come before 19:00, dinner served Thu-Fri only 18:00-20:30; 40 Gillygate, tel. 01904/652-500, www.ambiencecafebistro .co.uk).

The Exhibition Hotel pub has a classic pub interior, as well as a glassed-in conservatory and beer garden out back that's great for kids. While the food is nothing special, it's conveniently located near my recommended B&Bs (£8-11 pub grub, daily 12:00-23:00, until 24:00 on weekends, facing Bootham Bar at 19 Bootham Street, tel. 01904/641-105).

YORK

Supermarket: **Sainsbury's Local** grocery store is handy and open late (daily 6:00-24:00, 50 yards outside Bootham Bar, on Bootham).

At the East End of Town

This neighborhood is across town from my recommended B&Bs, but still central (and a short walk from the York Castle Museum). These places are all hits with local foodies; reservations are smart for all.

Rustique French Bistro has one big room of tight tables and walls decorated with simple posters. The place has good prices and is straight French—right down to the welcome (£6 starters, £15 main dishes, £13 two-course and £15 three-course meals available except after 19:00 Fri-Sat, open Mon-Sat 12:00-22:00, Sun 12:00-19:00, across from Fairfax House at 28 Castlegate, tel. 01904/612-744, www.rustiqueyork.co.uk).

The Blue Bicycle is no longer a brothel (but if you explore downstairs, you can still imagine when the tiny privacy-snugs needed their curtains). Today, it is passionate about fish. The energy of its happy eaters, its charming canalside setting, and its tasty Anglo-French cuisine make it worth the splurge. It's a velvety, hardwood scene, a little sultry but fresh...like its fish. The basement, while *très romantique*, may be a bit hot and stuffy (£6-12 starters, £16-24 main dishes, vegetarian and meat options, daily 18:00-21:30, also open for lunch Thu-Sun 12:00-14:30, 34 Fossgate, tel. 01904/673-990, www.thebluebicycle.com).

Melton's Too is a fun and casual place to eat. This homey, spacious, youthful restaurant (combining old timbers and plastic chairs) serves up elegantly simple traditional and international meals and a nice a selection of £5-8 tapas, all with a focus on local ingredients. The seating sprawls on several floors: ground-floor pub, upstairs bistro, and top-floor loft (£7 lunches, £11-14 dinners, £11.50 two-course and £13 three-course meals; Mon-Sat 10:30-22:30, Sun 10:30-21:30, just past Fossgate at 25 Walmgate, tel. 01904/629-222).

Mumbai Lounge (named for its top-floor lounge) is considered the best place in town for Indian food, so it's very popular. The space is big and high-energy, with a hardworking team of waiters in black T-shirts. I'd call to reserve a table on the ground floor—but avoid the basement (£10 plates, £7 lunch special, daily 12:00-14:30 & 17:30-23:30, 47 Fossgate, tel. 01904/654-155, www.mumbailoungeyork.co.uk).

Ethnic on Walmgate: The emerging bohemian-chic street called Walmgate has several quality little restaurants within a few steps of each other. Each is small, feels real, and has a local, untouristy energy: **Il Paradiso del Cibo Ristorante Pizzeria** (described next), **Khao San Thai Bistro** (52 Walmgate, tel. 01904/635-599), and **The Barbakan Polish Restaurant** (58 Walmgate, tel. 01904/672-474).

Italian

Il Paradiso del Cibo Ristorante Pizzeria just feels special. It's a small place with tight seating, no tourists, and a fun bustle, run by a Sardinian with attitude (£7 pastas and pizzas, £15 main dishes, £7 lunch/early dinner special Mon-Fri only, open daily 12:00-15:00 & 18:00-22:00 except closed Sun off-season, 40 Walmgate, tel. 01904/611-444).

Ristorante Bari has perhaps the most touristy location in York, right in the middle of The Shambles—but it also has a loyal local following that has kept it in business for more than 50 years. This family-run place has red rustic chairs and an accessible menu of Italian classics (£8-11 pizzas and pastas, £12-20 main dishes, daily 11:30-14:30 & 18:00-22:00, The Shambles, tel. 01904/633-807).

Mamma Mia is another popular choice for functional, affordable Italian. The casual, garlicky eating area features a tempting gelato bar, and in nice weather the back patio is *molto bello* (£8-10 pizza and pasta, daily 11:30-14:00 & 17:30-23:00, 20 Gillygate, tel. 01904/622-020).

Ask Restaurant is a cheap and cheery Italian chain, similar to those found in historic buildings all over Britain. But York's

version lets you dine in the majestic Neoclassical yellow hall of its Grand Assembly Rooms, lined with Corinthian marble columns. The food may be Italian-chain dull—but the atmosphere is 18th-century deluxe (£9-12 pizza, pastas, and salads; Sun-Wed 11:00-22:00, Thu-Sat 11:00-23:00, Blake Street, tel. 01904/637-254). Even if you're just walking past, peek inside to gape at the interior.

Tearooms

York is famous for its elegant teahouses. These two places serve traditional afternoon tea as well as light meals in memorable settings. In both cases, the food is pricey and comes in small portions—I'd come here at 16:00 for tea and cakes, but dine elsewhere. It's permissible for travel partners on a budget to enjoy the experience for about half the price by having one person order "full tea" (with enough little sandwiches and sweets for two to share) and the other a simple cup of tea.

Bettys Café Tea Rooms is a destination restaurant for many ladies. You pay £9 for a Yorkshire Cream Tea (tea and scones with clotted Yorkshire cream and strawberry jam) or £18 for a full traditional English afternoon tea (tea, delicate sandwiches, scones, and sweets). Your table is so full of doily niceties that the food is served on a little three-tray tower. While you'll pay a little extra here (and the food's nothing special), the ambience and people-watching are hard to beat. When there's a line, it moves quickly (except at dinnertime). They'll offer to seat you sooner in the bigger and less atmospheric basement, but I'd be patient and wait for a place upstairs—ideally by the window (daily 9:00-21:00, "afternoon tea" served all day; on weekends the special £26 afternoon tea includes fresh-from-the-oven scones served 12:30-17:00 in upstairs room with pianist; piano music nightly 18:00-21:00 and Sun 10:00-13:00, tel. 01904/659-142, St. Helen's Square, fine view of street scene from a window seat on the main floor). Near the WC downstairs is a mirror signed by WWII bomber pilots—read the story. For those just wanting to buy a pastry to go, it's fine to go directly to the bakery counter.

Grays Court, tucked away behind the Minster, holds court over its own delightful garden just inside the town wall. (You'll look down into its inviting oasis as you walk along the top of the wall.) For centuries, this was the residence of the Norman Treasurers of York Minster. Today it's home to a pleasant tea-room, small hotel, and bar. In summer, you can either sit outside, at tables scattered in the pleasant garden; or inside, in their elegant dining room or Jacobean gallery—a long wood-paneled hall with comfy sofas (£37 for 2-person "afternoon tea" served all day, £6 sandwiches, £6-11 light meals, daily 9:00-17:00, Chapter House Street, tel. 01904/612-613).

York Connections

From York by Train to: Durham (3-4/hour, 45 minutes), **London's** King's Cross Station (2/hour, 2 hours), **Bath** (hourly with change in Bristol, 4.5 hours, more with additional transfers), **Oxford** (1/hour direct, 3.5 hours), **Cambridge** (roughly 2/hour, 2.5-3 hours, 1-2 transfers), **Birmingham** (2/hour, 2-2.5 hours), **Keswick/Lake District** (train to Penrith: roughly 2/hour, 3.5-4 hours, 1-2 transfers; then bus, allow about 4.5 hours total), **Manchester Airport** (2/hour, 1.75 hours), **Edinburgh** (2/hour, 2.5 hours). Train info: tel. 0845-748-4950, www.nationalrail.co.uk.

Connections with London's Airports: Heathrow (allow 3 hours minimum; from airport take Heathrow Express train to London's Paddington Station, transfer by Tube to King's Cross, train to York—2/hour, 2 hours; for details on cheaper but slower

Tube or bus option from airport to London King's Cross, see page 215), **Gatwick** (allow 3 hours minimum; from Gatwick South, catch First Capital Connect train to London's St. Pancras Station; from there, walk to neighboring King's Cross Station, and catch train to York—2/hour, 2 hours).

North York Moors

In the lonesome North York Moors, sheep seem to outnumber people. Upon this high, desolate-feeling plateau, with spongy and inhospitable soil, bleating flocks jockey for position against scrubby heather for control of the terrain. Although the 1847 novel *Wuthering Heights* was set 60 miles to the southwest, you can almost imagine the mysterious Heathcliff plodding across this countryside. As you pass through this haunt-ing landscape, crisscrossed by

only a few roads, notice how the gloomy brown heather—which blooms briefly with purple flowers at summer's end—is actually burned back by wardens to clear the way for new growth. The vast, undulating expanses of nothingness are punctuated by greener, sparsely populated valleys called dales. Park your car and take a hike across the moors on any small road. You'll come upon a few tidy villages and maybe even old Roman roads.

For information on the moors, you can stop at the TI in Pickering (at the south end) and/or the excellent Moors Centre (near Danby, at the north end). Pick up the annual magazine *Out and About in the North York Moors*. Either place can give you hik-ing tips and sell you essential maps. Popular walks include a 5.5-mile loop near the Hole of Horcum, the 4.5-mile walk between Goathland and Grosmont, or the brief stroll to the waterfall near Goathland. Most villages have at least one general store where you can buy a basic brochure suggesting local hikes.

Getting Around the North York Moors

If you're **driving**, the easiest route across the moors is the A-169, which roughly parallels the steam-train line north to Grosmont; it passes the Hole of Horcum and comes close to Grosmont, before heading east to Whitby. To the west, smaller roads head north through Hutton-le-Hole (with its folk museum) and the village of Rosedale Abbey. While less straightforward—you'll need a very good map and an even better navigator—this western zone really gets you deep into the moors.

Those relying on **public transportation** will primarily use the North Yorkshire Moors Railway (explained later) and the sporadic, made-for-hikers **Moorsbus.** The Moorsbus offers various handy routes to middle-of-nowhere hiking destinations in the North York Moors and out-of-the-way sights such as the Ryedale Folk Museum; however, funding cuts have dramatically reduced its frequency and it may stop running completely by October of 2013 (in 2012, it was running Sun and Bank Holiday Mondays only April-Oct). Check the most recent schedules carefully when planning your trip (tel. 01845-597-000, www.northyorkmoors .org.uk/moorsbus). Various companies operate Yorkshire buses; for most connections, use the route planner at www.yorkshiretravel .net.

Sights on the Moors

These locations are listed roughly from south to north (as you'd approach them coming from York).

Pickering

This functional town, the southern gateway to the North York Moors, is a major crossroads and a proud hub for this region's meager public transit. Pickering's two-hour parking lot, train station, and TI all cluster on the same block. The helpful **TI** can provide advice for driving and hiking on the moors, and has a room-booking service (March-Oct Mon-Sat 9:30-17:00, Sun until 16:00; Nov-Feb Mon-Sat 9:30-16:00, closed Sun; tel. 01751/473-791, www.discovernorthyorkshire.co.uk, pickeringtic@btconnect.com).

The main reason to visit Pickering is to catch the **North Yorkshire Moors Railway** steam train into the moors (described next). Pickering is also the jumping-off point for various Moorsbus lines into the moors (lines #M6, #M7, and #M8; for more on this infrequent service, see above). Otherwise, you can browse its Monday market (produce, knickknacks) and consider its rural-life museum (Hutton-le-Hole's is better)—but don't bother visiting Pickering unless you're passing through anyway.

With more time, consider stopping by Pickering's ruined 13th-century Norman **castle,** built on the site of a wooden castle from William the Conqueror's 11th-century heyday. Appreciate its textbook motte-and-bailey (stone fort on a grassy hilltop) design, and climb to the top to understand its strategic location (£4; April-Sept Thu-Mon 10:00-17:00, closed Tue-Wed except open daily July-Aug; closed Oct-March, on the ridge above town, tel. 01751/474-989, www.english-heritage.org.uk).

Getting There: Drivers find Pickering right on the A-169, 25 miles north of York (en route to the coast). Or you can catch Coastliner bus #840 from York (every 1-2 hours Mon-Sat, fewer on Sun, 1.5 hours, www.coastliner.co.uk); you can shave a few minutes off the trip by taking the train to Malton, then catching bus #840 from there.

▲North Yorkshire Moors Railway

This 18-mile, one-hour steam-engine ride between Pickering and Grosmont (GROW-mont) runs almost hourly through some of the best parts of the moors. Sometimes the train continues from Grosmont on to the seaside town of Whitby; otherwise, you might be able to transfer in Grosmont to another, non-steam train to reach Whitby—check schedules as you plan your trip. (For details on getting to Pickering, see previous paragraph.)

Even with the small and dirty windows (try to wipe off the outside of yours before you roll), and with the track situated mostly in a scenic gully, it's a good ride. You can stop along the way for a walk on the moors (or at the appealing village of Goathland) and catch the next train (£17 round-trip to Grosmont, £23 round-trip to Whitby, includes hop-on, hop-off privileges; runs daily late March-Oct, and some Dec weekends, no trains Nov and Jan-late March, schedule flexes with season but first train generally departs Pickering at 9:00, last train departs Grosmont about 18:30; trip takes about one hour one-way to Grosmont, allow about 2.75 hours round-trip to come back on the same train; tel. 01751/472-508—press 1 for 24-hour timetable info, www.nymr.co.uk). There's no baggage storage at any stop on the steam-train line (but you can leave your bag for free at the Pickering TI until 17:00)—pack light if you decide to hike.

▲Hutton-le-Hole

This postcard-pretty town, lining up along a river as if posing for its close-up, is an ideal springboard for a trip into the North York Moors. It has some touristy shops and inviting picnic benches, but Hutton-le-Hole's (pronounced "HOO-ton le hole") biggest attraction is its engaging folk museum.

The **Ryedale Folk Museum** illustrates farm life in the moors

through reconstructed and furnished 18th-century buildings. At this open-air complex, you'll wander along a line of shops, including a village store—one-stop shopping (the original Costco) to save locals the long trek into the closest market town.

Then you'll come to a humble cluster of traditional, lived-in-feeling thatch-roof cottages. If the beds are unmade, notice the "mattress" is made of rope stretched across a frame, which could be tightened for a firmer night's sleep (giving us the phrase "sleep tight"). The museum is most worthwhile during frequent special weekends, when lively costumed docents explain what you're seeing along the way—check the online schedule or call ahead (£7; mid-March-late Oct daily 10:00-17:30, last entry at 16:30; late Oct-mid-March 10:00-dusk, closes early Dec-mid-Jan; tel. 01751/417-367, www.ryedalefolkmuseum.co.uk).

Getting There: Drivers find it just north of the A-170. From Hutton-le-Hole, you can plunge northward directly into the North York Moors (which begin suddenly as you leave town). Non-drivers will rely on the sporadic Moorsbus to reach Hutton-le-Hole (#M3 from Helmsley, Sun and Bank Holiday Mondays only April-Oct, schedules change frequently—confirm before you set out, www.northyorkmoors.org.uk/moorsbus).

In the Heart of the Moors
The Hole of Horcum
This huge sinkhole was supposedly scooped out by a giant. While not too exciting, it offers a good excuse to get out of your car and appreciate the moorland scenery (at the Saltergate car park).

Rosedale Abbey
A tranquil village on the west side of the moors (north of Hutton-le-Hole and far from the Hole of Horcum and Goathland), Rosedale Abbey offers a good dose of small-town moor life. Nestled between hills, it also provides pleasing moor views.

Goathland
This village, huddled along a babbling brook, is worth consider-

ing for a sleepy stopover, either on the steam-train trip or for drivers (it's an easy detour from the A-169). Movie buffs will enjoy Goathland's train station, which was used to film scenes at "Hogsmeade Station" for the early Harry Potter movies (for more on Harry Potter sights, see page 1028). But Brits know and love Goathland as the setting for the beloved, long-running TV series *Heartbeat*, about a small Yorkshire town in the 1960s. You'll see TV sets intermingled with real buildings, and some shops are even labeled "Aidensfield," for the TV town's fictional name.

▲The Moors Centre

This expanded and refurbished visitors center near Danby provides the best orientation for exploring North York Moors National Park. (Unfortunately, it's at the northern end of the park—not as convenient if you're coming from York.) The grand old lodge offers excellent exhibits on various moorland topics, informative films about the landscape, an art gallery showcasing works by local artists inspired by these surroundings, a children's play area, an information desk, plenty of books and maps, guided nature walks, brass rubbing, a cheery cafeteria, and brochures on several good walks that start right outside the front door.

Cost and Hours: Free entry, parking-£2.20/up to 2 hours, £4/day; March-Oct daily 10:00-17:00; Nov-Feb Sat-Sun 11:00-16:00, closed Mon-Fri; café, tel. 01439/772-737, www.northyorkmoors.org.uk.

Getting There: The Moors Centre is three-fourths of a mile from Danby in Esk Valley, in the northern part of the park (follow signs from Danby, which is a short drive from the A-171, running along the northern edge of the park). Danby is where the Moorsbus system (routes #M2, #M3, and #M4) meets the rail network (Danby is on the Northern Line #5, with connections to Grosmont—the terminus for the North Yorkshire Moors Railway described earlier—and Whitby; trains run along here 4/day, less often Sun off-season, 20 minutes from Danby to Grosmont, 40 minutes from Danby to Whitby, www.northernrail.org).

DURHAM AND NORTHEAST ENGLAND

Durham • Beamish Museum • Hadrian's Wall
• Holy Island • Bamburgh Castle

Northeast England harbors some of the country's best historical sights. Go for a Roman ramble at Hadrian's Wall, a reminder that Britain was an important Roman colony 2,000 years ago. Make a pilgrimage to Holy Island, where Christianity gained its first toehold in Britain. Marvel at England's greatest Norman church—Durham's cathedral—and enjoy an evensong service there. At the excellent Beamish Museum, travel back in time to the 18th and 19th centuries.

Planning Your Time

For **train** travelers, Durham is the most convenient overnight stop in this region. But it's problematic to see en route to another destination, since there's no baggage storage in Durham: Either stay overnight, or do Durham as a day trip from York. If you like Roman ruins, visit Hadrian's Wall (tricky but doable by public transportation—see page 658). The Beamish Museum is an easy day trip from Durham (less than an hour by bus).

By **car,** you can easily visit everything in this chapter. Spend a night in Durham and a night near Hadrian's Wall. With a car, you can easily visit Beamish Museum on the way to Hadrian's Wall.

For the best quick visit to Durham, arrive by mid-afternoon, in time to tour the cathedral and enjoy the evensong service (Tue-Sat at 17:15, Sun at 15:30; limited access and no tours during June graduation ceremonies). Sleep in Durham. Visit Beamish the next morning before continuing on to your next destination.

Durham

Without its cathedral, Durham would hardly be noticed. But this magnificently situated structure is hard to miss (even if you're zooming by on the train). Seemingly happy to go nowhere, Durham sits along the tight curve of its river, snug below its castle and famous church. It has a medieval, cobbled atmosphere and a scraggly peasant's indoor market just off the main square. Durham is the home to England's third-oldest university, with a student vibe jostling against its lingering working-class mining-town feel. You'll see tattooed and pierced people in search of job security and a good karaoke bar. Yet Durham has a youthful liveliness and a small-town warmth that shines—especially on sunny days, when most everyone is out licking ice cream cones.

Orientation to Durham

As it has for a thousand years, tidy little Durham (pop. 30,000) clusters everything safely under its castle, within the protective hairpin bend of the River Wear. Because of the town's hilly topography, going just about anywhere involves a lot of up and down... and back up again. The main spine through the middle of town (Framwellgate Bridge, Silver Street, and Market Place) is level to moderately steep, but walking

in any direction from that area involves some serious uphill climbing. Take advantage of the handy Cathedral Bus to avoid the tiring elevation changes—especially up to the cathedral and castle area, or to the train station (perched high on a separate hill).

Tourist Information

Due to funding cuts, Durham no longer has a physical TI, but the town does maintain a call center and website (calls answered Mon-Sat 9:30-17:30, Sun 11:00-16:00, tel. 03000-262-626, www.thisisdurham.com, visitor@thisisdurham.com).

Though not an official TI, the Durham World Heritage Site Visitor Centre, near the Palace Green, can offer some guidance, including brochures on things to see and a 12-minute video on the town. They also sell tickets to tour the castle (center open daily April-Sept 9:30-17:00, until 18:00 July-Aug, Oct-March 9:30-16:30, 7 Owengate, tel. 0191/334-3805, www.durhamworldheritage site.com). You can also ask for advice at your B&B or hotel.

Durham

TO **16** &
A-167 & A-691
(BEAMISH
& HEXHAM)

300 YARDS
300 METERS

N

WESTERN/ALBERT
FRAMWELL
NORTH ROAD
GATEPETH

1
5
WADD

TRAIN STATION

PED BRIDGE
ALEX CRES.
NEVILLE
NORTH ROAD
BUS STN.
ALLERGATE
HAWTER
THE AVE
CROSSGATE
MARGERY LANE

2
3

TO
A-690
TO
A-68
(HEXHAM)

MILBURNGATE
FRAMWELL GATE BRIDGE
Post
MKT. PLACE
SILVER
17
15
14
7
Boats
SADDLER
ELVET BRIDGE
LEAZES ROAD
CLAYPATH
6
8
11
12
TO A-1 (BEAMISH)
ROAD
A-690

4
13
9
10
PARK
OLD ELVET
NEW ELVET

CASTLE
PALACE GREEN
SOUTH BAILEY
NORTH BAILEY
PATH
VIEW

CATHEDRAL

GROVE
QUARRY HEADS
PREBENDS BRIDGE

SEE DETAIL MAP

RIVER   WEAR

HALGARTH STREET
CHURCH STREET

STOCKTON ROAD
TO A-1 MOTORWAY
LANE
TO A-167 (YORK)

P PARKING

1. Victorian Town House B&B
2. Castleview Guest House
3. To Farnley Tower B&B
4. Durham Marriott Hotel Royal County
5. Kingslodge Hotel & Rest.
6. Premier Inn Durham City Center
7. Durham Castle Rooms
8. Oldfields Restaurant
9. The Court Inn Pub
10. The Dun Cow
11. Claypath Deli
12. The Capital Indian Rest.
13. Zen Restaurant
14. Café Rouge & Bella Italia
15. Bells Fish & Chips
16. To Bistro 21
17. Marks & Spencer; Tesco Metro

DURHAM & NE ENGLAND

Arrival in Durham

By Train: From the train station, the fastest and easiest way to reach the cathedral is to hop on the convenient **Cathedral Bus** (described later, under "Getting Around Durham"). But the town's setting—while steep in places—is enjoyable to stroll through (and you can begin my self-guided walk halfway through, at the Framwellgate Bridge).

To **walk** into town from the station, follow the walkway along the road downhill to the second pedestrian turnoff (within sight of the railway bridge), which leads almost immediately over a bridge above the busy road called Alexander Crescent. From here, you can walk to some of my recommended accommodations (using this chapter's map—and the giant rail bridge as a handy landmark); to reach other hotels—or the river and cathedral—take North Road down into town.

By Car: Drivers simply surrender to the wonderful 400-space Prince Bishops Shopping Centre parking lot (coming from the M-1 exit, you'll run right into it at the roundabout at the base of the old town). It's perfectly safe, with 24-hour access. An elevator deposits you right in the heart of Durham (£2.10/up to 2 hours, £3.30/up to 4 hours, £11.50/over 6 hours, £1.50/overnight 18:00-8:00; a short block from Market Place, tel. 0191/375-0416, www.princebishops.co.uk).

Helpful Hints

Markets: The main square, known as Market Place, has an indoor market (generally Mon-Sat 9:00-17:00, closed Sun) and hosts outdoor markets (Sat retail market generally 9:30-16:30, farmers' market third Thu of each month 9:30-15:30, tel. 0191/384-6153, www.durhammarkets.co.uk).

Internet Access: The **Clayport Library,** set on huge Millennium Place, has about 40 terminals with free Internet access (Mon-Fri 9:30-19:00, Sat 9:00-17:00, closed Sun, tel. 03000/265-524).

Laundry: Durham has none within walking distance; ask your B&B host for recommendations if you're willing to drive or take a taxi.

Tours: Blue Badge guides offer 1.5-hour city walking tours on weekends in peak season (£4, usually May-Sept Sat-Sun at 14:00, meet outside Town Hall in Market Square, contact TI call center to confirm schedule, tel. 03000-262-626). **David Butler,** the town historian, gives excellent private tours (reasonable prices, tel. 0191/386-1500, www.dhent.co.uk, dhent @dhent.fsnet.co.uk) as well as a weekly Durham Ghost Tour in summer (£5, July-Sept Mon at 19:00).

Getting Around Durham

While all my recommended hotels, eateries, and sights are doable by foot, if you don't feel like walking Durham's hills, hop on the convenient **Cathedral Bus**. Bus #40A runs between the train station, Market Place, and the Palace Green (£1 all-day ticket, those over 60 ride free most of the day; daily 3/hour Mon-Fri about 8:30-17:00, from 9:00 on Sat, none on Sun; tel. 0191/372-5386, www.thisisdurham.com). A different bus #40A goes from Freeman's Place (near the Premier Inn) to Market Place and the Palace Green (2/hour Mon-Sat about 10:00-15:45). Confirm the route when you board.

Taxis zip tired tourists to their B&Bs or back up to the train station (about £5 from city center, wait on west side of Framwellgate Bridge at the bottom of North Road or on the east side of Elvet Bridge).

Self-Guided Walk

Welcome to Durham

• *Begin at Framwellgate Bridge (down in the center of town, halfway between the train station and the cathedral).*

Framwellgate Bridge was a wonder when it was built in the 12th century—much longer than the river is wide and higher than

seemingly necessary. It was well-designed to connect stretches of solid high ground and to avoid steep descents toward the marshy river. Note how elegantly today's Silver Street (which leads toward town) slopes into the Framwellgate Bridge. (Imagine that until the 1970s, this people-friendly lane was congested with traffic and buses.)

• *Follow Silver Street up the hill to the town's main square.*

Durham's **Market Place** retains the same plotting the prince bishop gave it when he moved villagers here in about 1100. Each long and skinny plot of land was the same width (about eight yards), maximizing the number of shops that could have a piece of the Market Place action. Find today's distinctly narrow buildings (Thomas Cook, Whittard, and Thomson)—they still fit the 900-year-old plan. The widths of the other buildings fronting the square are multiples of that original shop width.

Examine the square's **statues.** Coal has long been the basis of this region's economy. The statue of Neptune was part of an ill-fated attempt by a coal baron to bribe the townsfolk into embracing a canal project that would make the shipment of his coal more efficient. The statue of the fancy guy on the horse is Charles Stewart Vane, the Third Marquess of Londonderry. He was an Irish aristocrat and a general in Wellington's army who married a local coal heiress. A clever and aggressive businessman, he managed to create a vast business empire by controlling every link in the coal business chain—mines, railroads, boats, harbors, and so on.

In the 1850s throughout England, towns were moving their markets off squares and into Industrial Age iron-and-glass market halls. Durham was no exception, and today its funky 19th-century **indoor market** (which faces Market Place) is a delight to explore (closed Sun). There are also outdoor markets here on Saturdays and the third Thursday of each month.

Do you enjoy the sparse traffic in Durham's old town? It was the first city in England to institute a "congestion fee." When drivers enter, a camera snaps a photo of each car's license plate, and mails them a bill for £5. This has cut downtown traffic by more than 50 percent. Locals brag that London (which now has a similar congestion fee) was inspired by their success.

• *Head up the hill on Saddler Street toward the cathedral, stopping where you reach the chunk of wall at the top of a stairway. On the left, you'll see a bridge.*

A 12th-century construction, **Elvet Bridge** led to a town market over the river. Like Framwellgate, it's very long (17 arches) and designed to avoid riverside muck and steep inclines. Even today, Elvet Bridge leads to an unusually wide road—once swollen to accommodate the market action. Shops lined the right-hand side of Elvet Bridge in the 12th century, as they do today. An alley separated the bridge from the buildings on the left. When the bridge was widened, it met the upper stories of the buildings on the left, which became "street level."

Turn back to look at the chunk of **wall** by the top of the stairs—a reminder of a once-formidable fortification. The Scots, living just 50 miles from here, were on the rampage in the 14th century. After their victory at Bannockburn in 1314, they pushed farther south and actually burned part of Durham. Wary of this

Central Durham

TO TRAIN STN.

TO BUS STN.

FRAMWELL

FREEMAN

PROV. ROW

GILESGATE

CLAYPATH

MILLENNIUM PLACE

LIB.

MILLBURNGATE BRIDGE

ST. NICH.

LEAZES RD.

A-690

HIGH ST.

INDOOR MKT.

MARKET PLACE

PRINCE BISHOP'S SHOPPING CENTRE

START

POST

SILVER

SADDLER

BOATS

ELVET BRIDGE

NORTH RD.

FRAMWELLGATE BRIDGE

SADDLERS YARD

CASTLE

NEW ELVET

CROSSGATE

ST. MARG.

PIMLICO

SOUTH STREET

PALACE GREEN LIBRARY

PALACE GREEN

OWENGATE

DURHAM HERITAGE CENTRE

DUNCOW

END

BOW LANE

KINGSGATE BR.

NORTH BAILEY

OLD MILL

CATHEDRAL

SOUTH BAILEY

WEIR

ST. OSWALD'S

CHURCH ST.

PREBENDS BR.

DCH

RIVER WEAR

N

VIEW

FOOTPATH

P PARKING

PEDESTRIAN ZONE

100 YARDS

100 METERS

DURHAM & NE ENGLAND

new threat, Durham built thick city walls. As people settled within the walls, the population density soared. Soon, open lanes were covered by residences and became tunnels (called "vennels"). A classic vennel leads to Saddlers Yard, a fine little 16th-century courtyard (opposite the wall). While the vennels are cute today, centuries ago they were Dickensian nightmares—the filthiest of hovels.

• *Continue up Saddler Street. Just before the fork at the top of the street, duck through the purple door below the* Georgian Window *sign. You'll see a bit of the medieval wall incorporated into the brickwork of a newer building and a turret from an earlier wall. Back on Saddler Street, you can see the ghost of the old wall. (It's exactly the width of the building now housing the Salvation Army.) Veer right at Owengate as you continue uphill to the Palace Green. (The Durham World Heritage Site Visitor Centre is near the top of the hill, on the left.)*

The **Palace Green** was the site of the original 11th-century Saxon town, filling this green between the castle and an earlier church. Later, the town made way for 12th-century Durham's defenses, which now enclose the green. With the threat presented by the Vikings, it's no wonder people found comfort in a spot like this.

The **castle** still stands—as it has for a thousand years—on its motte (man-made mound). Like Oxford and Cambridge, Durham University is a collection of colleges scattered throughout the town, and even this castle is

now part of the school. Look into the old courtyard from the castle gate. It traces the very first and smallest bailey (protected area). As future bishops expanded the castle, they left their coats of arms as a way of "signing" the wing they built. Because the Norman kings appointed prince bishops here to rule this part of their realm, Durham was the seat of power for much of northern England. The bishops had their own army and even minted their own coins. You can enter the castle only with a 45-minute guided tour, which includes the courtyard, kitchens, great hall, and chapel (£5, open most days when school is in session—but schedule varies so call ahead, buy tickets at Durham World Heritage Site Visitor Centre or Palace Green Library—described next, tel. 0191/334-

Durham's Early Years

Durham's location, tucked inside a tight bend in the River Wear, was practically custom-made for easy fortifications. But it wasn't settled until A.D. 995, with the arrival of St. Cuthbert's body (buried in Durham Cathedral). Shortly after that, a small church and fortification were built upon the site of today's castle and church to house the relic. The castle was a classic "motte-and-bailey" design (with the "motte," or mound, providing a lookout tower for the stockade encircling the protected area, or "bailey"). By 1100, the prince bishop's bailey was filled with villagers—and he wanted everyone out. This was *his* place! He provided a wider protective wall, and had the town resettle below (around today's Market Place). But this displaced the townsfolk's cows, so the prince bishop constructed a fine stone bridge (today's Framwellgate) to connect the new town to grazing land he established across the river. The bridge had a defensive gate, with a wall circling the peninsula and the river serving as a moat.

2932, www.dur.ac.uk/university.college/tours).

• *Turning your back to the castle and facing the cathedral, on the right is the university's Palace Green Library.*

The **Palace Green Library** hosts rotating exhibits on everything from rare books to robots in its Wolfson Gallery and Dunelm Gallery. Pop in or check online for current exhibits (generally £3, Tue-Sun 10:00-16:45, closed Mon, Palace Green, tel. 0191/334-2932, www.dur.ac.uk/library/asc).

• *This walk ends at Durham's stunning **cathedral**, described next.*

Sights in Durham

▲▲▲Durham's Cathedral

Built to house the much-venerated bones of St. Cuthbert from Lindisfarne (known today as Holy Island), Durham's cathedral offers the best look at Norman architecture in England. ("Norman" is British for "Romanesque.") In addition to touring the cathedral,

try to fit in an evensong service.

Cost: Entry to the cathedral itself is free, though a donation is requested, and you must pay to climb the tower and possibly to enter the Treasures of St. Cuthbert exhibit (if open).

Hours: The cathedral is open to visitors Mon-Sat 9:30-18:00,

Durham's Cathedral

① Information Desk
② Modern Window
③ Black Marble Strip
④ Galilee Chapel &
   Tomb of the Venerable Bede
⑤ Chapel of the Nine Altars
⑥ LAWSON – Pietà

⑦ Tomb of St. Cuthbert
⑧ Tower Entry
⑨ Miners' Memorial
⑩ Cloister Entry
⑪ Stairs to Monks' Dormitory
⑫ Monastic Great Kitchen
   (Treasures of St. Cuthbert)

Sun 12:30-18:00, daily until 20:00 mid-July-Aug, sometimes closes for special services, opens daily at 7:15 for worship and prayer. Access is limited for a few days in June, when the cathedral is used for graduation ceremonies (check online).

Information: The £1 pamphlet, *A Short Guide to Durham Cathedral*, is informative but dull. Tel. 0191/386-4266, www.durhamcathedral.co.uk.

Tours: Regular tours run Monday through Saturday. If one is already in session, you're welcome to join (£5; tours start at 10:30, 11:00, and 14:00; fewer in winter, call or check website to confirm schedule).

Services: A shop, café, and WC are tucked away in the cloister.

Photography: No photos, videos, or mobile phones are allowed inside the cathedral.

Evensong: For a thousand years, this cradle of English

Christianity has been praising God. To really experience the cathedral, attend an evensong service. Arrive early and ask to be seated in the choir. It's a spiritual Oz, as the choristers (12 men and 40 youngsters—now girls as well as boys) sing psalms—a red-and-white-robed pillow of praise, raised up by the powerful pipe organ. If you're lucky and the service goes well, the organist will run a spiritual musical victory lap as the congregation breaks up (Tue-Sat at 17:15, Sun at 15:30, 1 hour, sometimes sung on Mon; visiting choirs nearly always fill in when choir is off on school break mid-July-Aug; tel. 0191/386-4266). For more on evensong, see page 169.

Organ Recitals: The organ plays most Wednesday evenings in July and August (£8, 19:30).

Tower Climb: The view from the tower will cost you 325 steps and £5 (Mon-Sat 10:00-16:00, closes at 15:00 in winter, sometimes open Sun outside of services, last entry 30 minutes before closing; closed during services, events, and bad weather; must be at least 4'3" tall, no backless shoes; enter through south transept).

❷ Self-Guided Tour: Begin your visit outside the cathedral. From the Palace Green, notice how this fortress of God stands boldly opposite the Norman keep of Durham's fortress of man.

Look closely: The **exterior** of this awe-inspiring cathedral has a serious skin problem. In the 1770s, as the stone was crumbling, they crudely peeled it back a few inches. The scrape marks give the cathedral a bad complexion to this day. For proof of this odd "restoration," study the masonry 10 yards to the right of the door. The L-shaped stones in the corner would normally never be found in a church like this—they only became L-shaped when the surface was cut back.

At the cathedral **door,** check out the big, bronze, lion-faced knocker (this is a replica of the 12th-century original, which should be in the Treasures of St. Cuthbert exhibit when reopened). The knocker was used by criminals seeking sanctuary (read the explanation).

Inside, purple-robed church attendants are standing by to happily answer questions. Ideally, follow a church tour. A handy information desk is at the back (right) end of the nave.

Notice the **modern window** with the novel depiction of the Last Supper (above and to the left of the entry door). It was given to the church by the local Marks & Spencer department store in 1984. The shapes of the apostles represent worlds and persons of every kind, from the shadowy Judas to the brightness of Jesus. This window is a good reminder that the cathedral remains a living part of the community.

Spanning the nave (toward the altar from the info desk), the **black marble strip** on the floor was as close to the altar as women were allowed in the days when this was a Benedictine church (until 1540). Sit down (ignoring the black line) and let the fine proportions of England's best Norman nave—and arguably Europe's best Romanesque nave—stir you. All the frilly woodwork and stonework were added in later centuries.

The architecture of the **nave** is particularly harmonious because it was built in a mere 40 years (1093-1133). The round

arches and zigzag-carved decorations are textbook Norman. The church was also proto-Gothic, built by well-traveled French masons and architects who knew the latest innovations from Europe. Its stone and ribbed roof, pointed arches, and flying buttresses were revolutionary in England. Notice the clean lines and simplicity. It's not as cluttered as other churches for several reasons: For centuries—out of respect for St. Cuthbert— no one else was buried here (so it's not filled with tombs). During Reformation times, sumptuous Catholic decor was removed. Subsequent fires and wars destroyed what Protestants didn't.

Head to the back of the nave and enter the **Galilee Chapel** (late Norman, from 1175). Find the smaller altar just to the left of the main altar. The paintings of St. Cuthbert and St. Oswald (seventh-century king of Northumbria) on the side walls of the niche are rare examples of Romanesque (Norman) paintings. Facing this altar, look above to your right to see more faint paintings on the upper walls above the columns. On the right side of the chapel, the upraised tomb topped with a black slab contains the remains of the **Venerable Bede,** an eighth-century Christian scholar who wrote the first history of England. The Latin reads, "In this tomb are the bones of the Venerable Bede."

Back in the main church, stroll down the nave to the center, under the highest **bell tower** in Europe (218 feet). Gaze up. The ropes turn wheels upon which bells are mounted. If you're stirred by the cheery ringing of church bells, tune in to the cathedral on Sunday (9:15-10:00 & 14:30-15:30) or Thursday (19:30-21:00 practice, trained bell ringers welcome, www.durhambellringers.org .uk) when the resounding notes tumble merrily through the entire town.

Continuing east (all medieval churches faced east), enter the **choir.** Monks worshipped many times a day, and the choir in the center of the church provided a cozy place to gather in this vast, dark, and chilly building. Mass has been said daily here, in the heart of the cathedral, for 900 years. The fancy wooden benches are from the 17th century. Behind the altar is the delicately carved Neville Screen from 1380 (made of Normandy stone in London, shipped to Newcastle by sea, then brought here by wagon). Until the Reformation, the niches contained statues of 107 saints. Exit the choir from the far right side (south). Look for the stained-glass window (to your right) that commemorates the church's 1,000th anniversary in 1995. The colorful scenes depict England's history, from coal miners to cows to computers.

Step down behind the high altar into the east end of the church, which contains the 13th-century **Chapel of the Nine Altars.** Built later than the rest of the church, this is Gothic—taller, lighter, and relatively more extravagant than the Norman nave. On the right, see the powerful modern *pietà* made of driftwood, with brass accents by local sculptor Fenwick Lawson.

Climb a few steps to the **tomb of St. Cuthbert.** An inspirational leader of the early Christian Church in north England, St. Cuthbert lived in the Lindisfarne monastery (100 miles north of Durham, today called Holy Island—see page 667). He died in 687. Eleven years later, his body was exhumed and found to be miraculously preserved. This stoked the popularity of his shrine, and pilgrims came in growing numbers. When Vikings raided Lindisfarne in 875, the monks fled with his body (and the famous illuminated Lindisfarne Gospels, now in the British Library in London). In 995, after 120 years of roaming, the monks settled in Durham on an easy-to-defend tight bend in the River Wear. This cathedral was built over Cuthbert's tomb.

Throughout the Middle Ages, a shrine stood here and was visited by countless pilgrims. In 1539, during the Reformation—whose proponents advocated focusing on God rather than saints—the shrine was destroyed. But pilgrims still come, especially on St. Cuthbert's feast day (March 20).

Turn around and walk back the way you came. In the **south transept** (to your left) is the entrance to the tower (described earlier), as well as an astronomical clock and the Chapel of the Durham Light Infantry, a regiment of the British Army (1881-1968). The old flags and banners hanging above were actually carried into battle.

Return along the left side of the nave toward the entrance. Across from the entry is the door to the cloister. Along the wall by the door to the cloister, notice the **memorial honoring coal miners** who died, and those who "work in darkness and danger in those pits today." (This message is a bit dated—Durham's coal mines closed down in the 1980s.) The nearby book of remembrance lists mine victims. As an ecclesiastical center, a major university town and a gritty, blue-collar coal-mining town, Durham's population has long been a complicated mix: priests, academics, and the working class.

Sights in the Cloister: The following sights are within the cloister (which provides a fine view back up to the church towers—made briefly famous in the Harry Potter films, described on page 1028).

Enter the cloister, go through a door on the right and up some stairs to the **Monks' Dormitory,** a long, impressive room that stretches out under an original 14th-century timber roof. Formerly the monks' sleeping quarters, the room now holds a library with a small exhibit of Anglo-Saxon stones such as old Celtic crosses (donation suggested, Mon-Sat 10:00-16:00, Sun 13:00-16:00).

The reshuffled **Treasures of St. Cuthbert** collection recently moved to the Monastic Great Kitchen. It may be reopened by the time you visit. Filled with medieval bits and holy pieces, it contains the actual relics from St. Cuthbert's tomb—his coffin, vestments, and cross—as well as items from the Norman/medieval period (when the monks of Durham busily copied manuscripts), the Reformation, and the 17th century (check exhibit status, prices and times at info desk or by calling the cathedral).

In the newly renovated undercroft, you'll find a **shop** and a **café** (daily 10:00-16:30, tel. 0191/386-3721).

More Sights in Durham

There's little to see in Durham beyond its cathedral, but it's a pleasant place to go for a stroll and enjoy its riverside setting.

Durham Heritage Centre Museum

Situated in the old Church of St. Mary-le-Bow near the cathedral, this modest, somewhat hokey, but charming little museum does its best to illuminate the city's history, and is worthwhile on a rainy day. The exhibits, which are scattered willy-nilly throughout the old nave, include a reconstructed Victorian-era prison cell; a look at Durham industries past and present, especially coal mining (in Victorian times, the river was literally black from coal); and a 10-minute movie about 20th-century Durham. In the garden on the side of the church are two modern sculptures by local artist Fenwick Lawson, whose work you'll also see in the cathedral.

Cost and Hours: £2; July-Sept daily 11:00-16:30; June daily 14:00-16:30; April-May and Oct Sat-Sun 14:00-16:30, closed Mon-Fri; closed Nov-March; corner of North Bailey and Bow Lane, tel. 0191/384-5589, www.durhamheritagecentre.org.uk.

Riverside Path

For a 20-minute woodsy escape, walk Durham's riverside path from busy Framwellgate Bridge to sleepy Prebends Bridge.

Boat Cruise and Rental

Hop on the *Prince Bishop* for a relaxing one-hour narrated cruise of the river that nearly surrounds Durham (£7, Easter-Oct; for schedule, call 24-hour info line at 0191/386-9525, check their website or go down to dock at Brown's Boat House at Elvet Bridge, just east of old town; www.princebishoprc.co.uk). Sailings vary based on weather and tides. For some exercise with identical scenery, you can rent a rowboat at the same pier (£5/hour per person, £10 deposit, late-March-Oct daily 10:00-18:00, last rental at 17:00, tel. 0191/386-3779).

Sleeping in Durham

(area code: 0191)

Close-in pickings are slim in Durham. Because much of the housing is rented to students, there are only a handful of B&Bs. Otherwise, there are a few hotels within easy walking distance of the town center. During graduation (typically the last two weeks of June), everything books up well in advance and prices increase dramatically. Rooms can be tight on weekends any time of year. If the B&Bs are full, Durham could be a good place to resort to a bigger chain hotel (Premier Inn or Marriott).

B&Bs

$$$ **Victorian Town House B&B** offers three spacious, boutique-like rooms in an 1853 townhouse. It's in a nice residential area just down the hill from the train station and is handy to the town center (Sb-£55-65, Db-£85-90, family room for up to 4 people-£85-120, cash only, 2-night minimum preferred April-Oct, some view rooms, free Wi-Fi, check-in 16:00-19:00 or by prior arrangement, 2 Victoria Terrace, 10-minute walk from train or bus station, tel. 0191/370-9963, www.durhambedandbreakfast.com, stay@durhambedandbreakfast.com, friendly Jill and Andy).

$$$ **Castleview Guest House** rents five airy, restful rooms in a well-located, 250-year-old guesthouse next door to a little church. Located on a charming cobbled street, it's just above Silver Street and the Framwellgate Bridge (Sb-£70, Db-£100, cash preferred, guest computer, free Wi-Fi, free street-parking permit, 4 Crossgate, tel. 0191/386-8852, www.castle-view.co.uk, info @guesthousesdurham.co.uk, Anne and Mike Williams).

$$ **Farnley Tower,** a decent but impersonal B&B, has 13 large rooms and a quirky staff. On a quiet street at the top of a hill, it's a 15-minute hike up from the town center. Though you

Sleep Code

(£1 = about $1.60, country code: 44)

S = Single, **D** = Double/Twin, **T** = Triple, **Q** = Quad, **b** = bathroom, **s** = shower only. Unless otherwise noted, credit cards are accepted and breakfast is included.

To help you sort easily through these listings, I've divided the accommodations into three categories based on the price for a standard double room with bath (during high season):

$$$ Higher Priced—Most rooms £90 or more.
$$ Moderately Priced—Most rooms between £50-90.
$ Lower Priced—Most rooms £50 or less.

Prices can change without notice; verify the hotel's current rates online or by email. For the best prices, always book direct.

won't find the standard B&B warmth and service, this is a suitable alternative when the central hotels are booked (Sb-£65, Db-£85, superior Db-£95—some with cathedral view, family room-£120, 2 percent fee for credit cards, free Wi-Fi, phones in rooms, easy free parking, inviting yard, The Avenue—hike up this steep street and look for the sign on the right, tel. 0191/375-0011, www.farnley-tower.co.uk, enquiries@farnley-tower.co.uk, Raj and Roopal Naik). The Naiks also run the inventive Gourmet Spot fine-dining restaurant, in the same building.

Hotels

$$$ Durham Marriott Hotel Royal County scatters its 150 posh, four-star, but slightly scruffy, rooms among several buildings sprawling across the river from the city center. The Leisure Club has a pool, sauna, Jacuzzi, spa, and fitness equipment (prices vary, standard Db-about £94-114, supreme Db with separate seating area-about £119-129, check website for exact prices and deals, breakfast included in some rates but otherwise £15.50 extra, elevator, pay guest computer, free Wi-Fi in public areas, pay Wi-Fi in rooms, restaurant, bar, parking-£5/overnight, Old Elvet, tel. 0191/386-6821 or tel. 0870-400-7286, www.marriott.co.uk).

$$ Kingslodge Hotel & Restaurant is a slightly worn but comfortable 21-room place with charming terraces, an attached restaurant, and a pub. Located in a pleasantly wooded setting, it's convenient for train travelers (Sb-£60-65, Db-£75-85, family room-£109-115, free Wi-Fi, free parking, Waddington Street, Flass Vale, tel. 0191/370-9977, www.kingslodge.info, kingslodgehotel@yahoo.co.uk).

$$ Premier Inn Durham City Center, squeezed between Clayport Library and the river, has 103 cookie-cutter purple rooms in a very convenient central location (Sb/Db-generally around £70-95, check online for prepaid deals as low as £29, continental breakfast-£5.25, full English breakfast-£8.25, air-con, elevator, pay guest computer, pay Wi-Fi, validated parking for guests at Walkergate car park behind hotel-£7.70/24 hours, Freemans Place, tel. 0871-527-8338 or 0191/374-4400, www.premierinn.com).

$$ *Student Housing Open to Anyone:* Durham Castle, a student residence actually on the castle grounds facing the

cathedral, rents rooms during the summer break (generally July-Sept). Request a room in the stylish main building, which is more appealing than the modern dorm rooms (S-£36.50, Sb-£61, Db-£92, fancier Db-£150-200, elegant breakfast hall, Palace Green, tel. 0191/334-4106, www.dur.ac.uk/university.college, durham.castle@durham.ac.uk). Note that the same office also rents rooms in other university buildings, but most are far less convenient to the city center—make sure to request the Durham Castle location when booking.

Eating in Durham

Durham is a university town with plenty of lively, inexpensive eateries, but there's not much to get excited about. Especially on weekends, the places downtown are crowded with noisy college kids and rowdy townies. Stroll down North Road, across Framwellgate Bridge, up through Market Place, and up Saddler Street, and consider the options suggested below. The better choices are about a five-minute walk from this main artery and worth the short trek.

Updated British Food: **Oldfields** serves pricey, updated British classics made from locally sourced ingredients. The inviting dining room feels upscale but not snooty, and there's another, more traditional dining room upstairs. While the service can be spotty and some locals wonder if this place is resting on its laurels, it remains one of the best options in town (£5-7 starters, £13-18 main dishes; lunch and early bird specials—£12/two courses, £15/three courses; Mon-Sat 12:00-22:00, Sun 12:00-21:00, 18 Claypath, tel. 0191/370-9595).

Pubs Across the Elvet Bridge: Two good options are within a five-minute walk of the Elvet Bridge (just east of the old town). **The Court Inn** offers an eclectic menu of pub grub and an open, lively atmosphere (£4-6 sandwiches, £8-12 meals, Spanish-style tapas, food served daily 11:00-22:00; cross the Elvet Bridge, turn right, walk several blocks, and then look left; Court Lane, tel. 0191/384-7350). For beer and ales, locals favor **The Dun Cow.** There's a cozy "snug bar" up front and a more spacious lounge in the back. Read the legend behind the pub's name on the wall along the outside corridor. More sedate than the student-oriented places in the town center, this pub serves only snacks and light meals (£2-4)—come here to drink and nibble, not to feast (Mon-Sat 11:00-23:00, Sun 12:00-23:00; from the Elvet Bridge, walk five minutes straight ahead to Old Elvet 37; tel. 0191/386-9219).

Deli Lunch: **Claypath Delicatessen** is worth the five-minute uphill walk above Market Place. Not just any old sandwich shop, this creative place assembles fresh ingredients into tasty sandwiches, salads, sampler platters, and more. While carryout is possible, most people eat in the casual, comfortable café setting (£4-6 light meals, Tue-Sat 10:00-17:00, closed Sun-Mon; from Market Place, cross the bridge and walk up Claypath to #57; tel. 0191/340-7209).

Indian: **The Capital,** a five-minute uphill walk above Market Place (and across the street from Claypath Deli), has well-executed Indian food in a contemporary setting (£8-12 meals, daily 18:00-23:30, 69 Claypath, tel. 0191/386-8803).

Thai: **Zen** is a trendy, modern, dark-wood place serving curries, noodles, fried rice, and other Asian fare. It's popular with students, so it's best to book a table or go early and sit in the bar (£9-11 meals, daily 12:00-22:00, Court Lane, tel. 0191/384-9588, www.zendurham.co.uk).

Chain Restaurants with a Bridge View: Two chain places (that you'll find in every British city) are worth considering in Durham only because of their delightful setting right at the Old Town end of the picturesque Framwellgate Bridge. **Café Rouge** has French-bistro food and decor (£5-9 starters and light meals, £11-14 main dishes, Mon-Sat 9:00-22:30, Sun 10:00-22:00, 21 Silver Street, tel. 0191/384-3429). **Bella Italia,** next door and down the stairs, has a terrace overlooking the river and surprisingly good food (£5-6 starters, £7-10 pizzas and pastas, Tue-Sat 10:00-23:00, Sun-Mon 10:00-22:30, reservations recommended, 20 Silver Street, tel. 0191/386-1060).

Fish-and-Chips: **Bells,** just off Market Place toward the cathedral, is a standby for carryout fish-and-chips. I'd skip their fancier dining room (£5-7, hours vary but likely Mon-Thu 11:00-21:00, Fri-Sat 11:00-2:00 in the morning, Sun 12:00-16:00).

Splurge Outside Town: **Bistro 21,** an untouristy splurge serving modern French/Mediterranean fare and good seafood, is one of Durham's top restaurants. Unfortunately, it's about 1.5 miles out of Durham—practical only for drivers (£6-7 starters, £15-22 main dishes; dinner special available Mon-Sat 17:30-19:00—£16.50/two courses, £19/three courses; open Mon-Sat 12:00-14:00 & 17:30-22:00, Sun 12:00-15:00, northwest of town, Aykley Heads, tel. 0191/384-4354).

Supermarket: **Marks & Spencer** is in the old town, just off Market Place (Mon-Sat 8:00-18:00, Sun 11:00-17:00, 4 Silver Street, across from post office). Next door is a **Tesco Metro** (Mon-Sat 7:00-22:00, Sun 11:00-17:00). You can **picnic** on Market Place, or on the benches and grass outside the cathedral entrance (but not on the Palace Green, unless the park police have gone home).

Durham Connections

From Durham by Train to: York (3-4/hour, 45 minutes), **Keswick/Lake District** (train to Penrith—hourly, 3 hours, change in Newcastle and Carlisle; then bus to Keswick), **London** (1/hour direct, 3 hours, more with changes), **Hadrian's Wall** (take train to Newcastle—4/hour, 15 minutes, then a bus or a train/bus combination to near Hadrian's Wall—see "Getting Around Hadrian's Wall" on page 657), **Edinburgh** (1/hour direct, 2 hours, more with changes, less frequent in winter). **Train info:** tel. 0845-748-4950, www.nationalrail.co.uk.

Route Tips for Drivers

As you head north from Durham on the A-1 motorway, you'll pass a famous bit of public art: **The Angel of the North,** a modern, rusted-metal angel standing 65 feet tall with a wingspan of 175 feet (wider than a Boeing 757). While initially controversial when it was erected in 1998, it has since become synonymous with Northeast England, and is a beloved local fixture.

Beamish Museum

This huge, 300-acre open-air museum, which re-creates the years 1825 and 1913 in northeast England, is England's best museum of its type. It takes at least three hours to explore its four sections: Pit Village (a coal-mining settlement with an actual mine), The Town (a 1913 street lined with actual shops), Pockerley Old Hall (a "gentleman farmer's" manor house), and Home Farm (a preserved farm and farmhouse). This

DURHAM & NE ENGLAND

Near Durham

TO EDINBURGH

A-1

BERWICK

HOLY ISLAND (LINDISFARNE)

N

BEAL

SCOTLAND

BAMBURGH CASTLE

JEDBURGH

BORDERS

A-68

NORTH SEA

HOUSESTEADS ROMAN FORT

HADRIAN'S WALL

GREEN HEAD

B-6318

A-69

NEWCASTLE

TO CARLISLE + LAKE DISTRICT

A-69

VINDOLANDA ROMAN FORT

HALT-WHISTLE

HEXHAM

ANGEL OF THE NORTH

TO AMSTER-DAM

SEE DETAIL MAP

A-693

BEAMISH MUSEUM

DURHAM

A-691

A-167

A-1

ENGLAND

20 MILES

20 KM

TO YORK & LONDON

DCH

isn't a wax museum. If you touch the exhibits, they may smack you. Attendants at each stop happily explain everything. In fact, the place is only really interesting if you talk to the attendants—who make it worth ▲▲▲.

Cost and Hours: £17.50, children 5-16-£10, under 5-free, 25 percent discount with bus ticket—see below; to visit over several days, choose the "Beamish Unlimited Pass" at no extra charge (makes your ticket valid for a year); Easter-Oct open daily 10:00-17:00; Nov-Easter only The Town and Pit Village are open but vintage trams still run, Tue-Thu and Sat-Sun 10:00-16:00, closed Mon and Fri, half-price on weekdays; check events schedule on chalkboard as you enter, last tickets sold at 15:00 year-round, tel. 0191/370-4000, www.beamish.org.uk.

Getting There: By **car,** the museum is five minutes off the A-1/M-1 motorway (one exit north of Durham at Chester-le-Street/Junction 63, well-signposted, 12 miles, 25-minute drive northwest of Durham).

Getting to Beamish from Durham by **bus** is a snap on peak-season Saturdays via direct bus #128 (£3.70 day pass, 8/day, 30 minutes, runs April-Oct only, stops at Durham train and bus stations). Otherwise, catch bus #21 or #50 from the Durham bus station (£3.70 day pass, 3-4/hour, 25 minutes) and transfer at Chester-le-Street to bus #28 or #28A, which will take you right to the museum entrance (2/hour Mon-Sat, hourly Sun, 15 minutes, leaves from central bus kiosk a half-block away, tel. 0845-606-0260, www.simplygo.com). Show your bus ticket for a 25 percent museum discount.

Getting Around the Museum: Pick up a free map at the entry to help navigate the four different zones; while some are side-by-

side, others are up to a 15-minute walk apart. Vintage trams and cool, circa-1910 double-decker buses shuttle visitors around the grounds, and their attendants are helpful and knowledgeable. Signs on the trams advertise a variety of 19th-century products, from "Borax, for washing everything" to "Murton's Reliable Travelling Trunks."

Eating at Beamish: There are several eateries scattered around Beamish, including a pub and tearooms (in The Town), a fish-and-chips stand (in the Pit Village), and various cafeterias and snack stands. Or bring a picnic.

⊙ Self-Guided Tour: I've described the four areas in counterclockwise order from the entrance.

From the entrance building, bear left along the road, then watch for the turnoff on the right to the **Pit Village.** This is a com-

pany town built around a coal mine, with a schoolhouse, a Methodist chapel, and a row of miners' homes with long, skinny pea-patch gardens out front. Poke into some of the homes to see their modest interiors. In the Board School, explore

the different classrooms, and look for the interesting poster with instructions for avoiding consumption (a.k.a. tuberculosis, a huge public-health crisis back then).

Next, cross to the adjacent **Colliery** (coal mine) where you can take a fascinating—if claustrophobic—20-minute tour into the drift mine (check in at the "lamp camp"—tours depart when enough people gather, generally every 5-10 minutes). Your guide will tell you stories about beams collapsing, gas exploding, and flooding; after that cheerful speech, you'll don a hard hat as you're led into the mine. Nearby (across the tram tracks) is the fascinating **engine works,** where you can see the actual steam-powered winding engine used to operate the mine elevator. The "winderman" demonstrates how he skillfully eases both coal and miners up and down the tight shaft of the mine. This delicate, high-stakes job was one of the most sought-after at the entire Colliery—passed down from father to son—and the winderman had to stay in this building for his entire shift (the seat of his chair flips up to reveal a built-in WC).

A path leads through the woods to Georgian-era **Pockerley,** which has two parts. First you'll see the **Waggonway,** a big barn filled with steam engines, including the re-created, first-ever passenger train from 1825. (Occasionally this train takes modern-day visitors for a spin on its 1825 tracks—a hit with railway buffs.)

Then, climb the hill to **Pockerley Old Hall,** the manor house of a gentleman farmer and his family. The house dates from the

1820s, and—along with the farmhouse described later—is Beamish's only vintage building still on its original site (other buildings at Beamish were relocated from elsewhere and reconstructed here). While not extremely wealthy, the farmer who lived here owned large tracts of land and could afford to hire help to farm it for him. This rustic home is no palace, but it was comfortable for the period. Costumed docents in the kitchen often bake delicious cookies from old recipes...and hand out samples.

The small garden terrace out front provides beautiful views across the pastures. From the garden, turn left and locate the narrow stairs up to the "old house." Actually under the same roof as the gentleman farmer's family, this space consists of a few small rooms that were rented by some of the higher-up workers to shelter their entire families of up to 15 children (young boys worked on the farm, while girls were married off early). While the parents had their own bedroom, the children all slept in the loft up above (notice the ladder in the hall).

From the manor house, hop on a vintage tram or bus, or walk 10 minutes, to the Edwardian-era **The Town** (c. 1913). This bustling

street features several working shops and other buildings that are a delight to explore. In the Masonic Hall, ogle the grand, high-ceilinged meeting room, and check out the fun old metal signs inside the garage. Across the street, poke into the courtyard to find the stables, which are full of carriages. The heavenly smelling candy store sells old-timey sweets, and has an actual workshop in back with trays of free samples. The newsagent sells stationery, cards, and old toys, while in the grocery, you can see old packaging and the scales used for weighing out products. Other buildings include a clothing store, a working pub (The Sun Inn, Mon-Sat 11:00-16:30, Sun 12:00-16:30, tel. 01913/702-908), Barclays Bank, and a hardware store featuring a variety of "toilet sets" (not what you think).

For lunch, try the Tea Rooms cafeteria (upstairs, daily 10:00-16:00). Or, if the weather is good, picnic in the grassy park with the gazebo next to the tram stop. The row of townhouses includes both homes and offices (if the dentist is in, chat with him to hear some harrowing stories about pre-Novocain tooth extraction). At the circa-1913 railway station at the far end of The Town, you can stand on the bridge over the tracks to watch old steam engines go back and forth—along with a carousel of "steam gallopers." Nearby, look for the "Westoe netty," a circa 1890 men's public urinal. This loo became famous in 1972 as the subject in a nostalgic Norman Rockwell-style painting of six miners and a young boy doing their business while they read the graffiti.

Finally, walk or ride a tram or bus to the **Home Farm.** (This is the least interesting section—if you're running short on time, it's skippable.) Here you'll get to experience a petting zoo and see a "horse gin" (a.k.a. "gin gan")—where a horse walking in a circle turned a crank on a gear to amplify its "horsepower," helping to replace human hand labor. Near the cafeteria, you can cross a busy road (carefully) to the old farmhouse, still on its original site, where attendants sometimes bake goodies on a coal fire.

DURHAM & NE ENGLAND

Hadrian's Wall

Cutting across the width of the isle of Britain, this ruined Roman wall is one of England's most thought-provoking sights. Once a

towering 20-foot-tall fortification, these days "Hadrian's Shelf," as some cynics call it, is only about three feet wide and three to six feet high. (The conveniently pre-cut stones of the wall were carried away by peasants during the post-Rome Dark Ages and now form the foundations of many local churches, farmhouses, and other structures.) In most places, what's left of the wall has been covered over by centuries of sod...making it effectively disappear into the landscape. But for those intrigued by Roman history, Hadrian's Wall provides a fine excuse to take your imagination for a stroll. Pretend you're a legionnaire on patrol in dangerous and distant Britannia, at the empire's northernmost frontier... with nothing but this wall protecting you from the terrifying, bloodthirsty Picts just to the north.

Today, several chunks of the wall, ruined forts, and museums thrill history buffs. While a dozen Roman sights cling along the wall's route, I've focused my coverage on an easily digestible six-mile stretch right in the middle, where you'll find the best museums and some of the most enjoyable-to-hike stretches of the wall. Three top sights are worth visiting: Housesteads Roman Fort shows you where the Romans lived; Vindolanda's museum shows you how they lived; and the Roman Army Museum explains the empire-wide military organization that brought them here.

A breeze for drivers, this area can also be seen fairly easily in summer by bus for those good at studying timetables (see "Getting Around Hadrian's Wall," later).

Hadrian's Wall is in vogue as a destination for multi-day hikes through the pastoral English countryside. The Hadrian's Wall National Trail runs 84 miles, following the wall's route from coast to coast (for details, go to www.nationaltrail.co.uk/HadriansWall). Through-hikers (mostly British) can walk the wall's entire length in four to ten days. You'll see them bobbing along the ridgeline, drying out their socks in your B&B's mudroom, and recharging at local pubs in the evening. For those with less time, the brief ridge walk next to the wall from Steel Rigg to Sycamore Gap to Housesteads Roman Fort gives you a perfect taste of the scenery and history.

The History of Hadrian's Wall

In about A.D. 122, during the reign of Emperor Hadrian, the Romans constructed this great stone wall. Stretching 73 miles coast to coast across the narrowest stretch of northern England, it was built and defended by some 20,000 troops. Not just a wall, it was a military complex that included forts, ditches, settlements, and roads. At every mile of the wall, a castle guarded a gate, and two turrets stood between each castle. The mile-castles are numbered. (Eighty of them cover the 73 miles, because a Roman mile was slightly shorter than our mile.)

In cross-section, Hadrian's Wall consisted of a stone wall—around 15 to 20 feet tall—with a ditch on either side. The

flat-bottomed ditch on the south side of the wall, called the vallum, was flanked by earthen ramparts and likely demarcated the "no-man's land" beyond which civilians were not allowed to pass. Between the vallum and the wall ran a service road called the Military Way. Another less-elaborate ditch ran along the north side of the wall. In some areas—including the region that I describe—the wall was built upon a volcanic ridgeline that provided a natural fortification.

The wall's actual purpose is still debated. While Rome ruled Britain for 400 years, it never quite ruled its people. The wall may have been used for any number of reasons: to protect Roman Britain from invading Pict tribes from the north (or at least cut down on pesky border raids); to monitor the movement of people as a show of Roman strength and superiority; or to simply give an otherwise bored army something to do. (Emperors understood that nothing was more dangerous than a bored army.) Or perhaps the wall represented Hadrian's tacit admission that the empire had reached its maximum extent; Hadrian was known for consolidating his territory, in some cases giving up chunks of land that had been conquered by his predecessor, Trajan, to create an easier-to-defend (if slightly smaller) empire. His philosophy of "defense before expansion" is embodied by the impressive wall that still bears his name.

Hadrian's Wall

1. Once Brewed National Park Visitor Centre & Youth Hostel
2. Vallum Lodge
3. The Twice Brewed Inn
4. Milecastle Inn
5. Gibbs Hill Farm B&B & Hostel
6. Ashcroft Guest House
7. To High Reins B&B
8. To Bessiestown Farm Country Guest House

--- WALL HIKE

NOT TO SCALE

ROMAN ARMY MUSEUM

HADRIA

TO CATLOWDY

B-6318
MILITARY ROAD

A-69

TO CARLISLE

GREEN-HEAD

HALTWHISTLE

DCH

Orientation to Hadrian's Wall

The area described in this section is roughly between the mid-size towns of Bardon Mill and Haltwhistle, which are located along the busy A-69 highway. Each town has a train station and some handy B&Bs, restaurants, and services. However, to get right up close to the wall, you'll need to head a couple of miles north to the adjacent villages of Once Brewed and Twice Brewed (along the B-6318 road).

Tourist Information

Portions of the wall are in Northumberland National Park. The **Once Brewed National Park Visitor Centre** lies along the Hadrian's Wall bus #AD122 route and has information on the area, including walking guides to the wall. (Note that this center may undergo a major renovation and could be in a temporary location when you visit). The TV, set in front of a cozy couch, plays a variety of interesting movies about the wall and the surrounding landscape—ideal for a rainy day (Easter-Oct daily 9:30-17:00; Nov-Easter 10:00-15:00 Sat-Sun only, closed Mon-Fri; parking-

DURHAM & NE ENGLAND

£4/day, Military Road/B-6318, tel. 01434/344-396, www.north umberlandnationalpark.org.uk, tic.oncebrewed@nnpa.org.uk).

The helpful **TI** in Haltwhistle, a block from the train station inside the library, has a good selection of maps and guidebooks, and schedule information for the Hadrian's Wall bus #AD122 (Easter-Oct Mon-Sat 10:00-13:00 & 13:30-16:30, closed Sun and Nov-Easter, The Library, Westgate, tel. 01434/322-002, www .hadrians-wall.org).

Getting Around Hadrian's Wall

Hadrian's Wall is anchored by the big cities of Newcastle to the east and Carlisle to the west. Driving is the most convenient way to see Hadrian's Wall. If you're coming by train, consider renting a car for the day at either Newcastle or Carlisle; otherwise, you'll need to rely on the bus to connect the sights. If you're just passing through for the day using public transportation, it's challenging to stop and see more than just one or two of the sights—study the bus schedule carefully and prioritize. Non-drivers who want to see everything—or even hike part of the wall—will need to stay at least one night along the bus route.

By Car

Zip to this "best of Hadrian's Wall" zone on the speedy A-69; when you get close, head a few miles north and follow the B-6318, which parallels the wall and passes several viewpoints, minor sights, and "severe dips." (These road signs add a lot to a photo portrait.) Buy a good local map to help you explore this interesting area more easily and thoroughly. Official Hadrian's Wall parking lots (including the Once Brewed National Park Visitor Centre, Housesteads Roman Fort, and the trailhead at Steel Rigg) are covered by a single one-day £4 parking pass (coin-op pay-and-display machines at all lots).

By Public Transportation

To reach the Roman sights without a car, take the made-for-tourists Hadrian's Wall **bus #AD122** (named for the year the wall was built; runs only in peak season—see below). Essential resources for navigating the wall by public transit include the *Hadrian's Wall Country Map*, the bus #AD122 schedule, and a local train timetable for Northern Line #4—all available at local visitors centers and train stations (also see www.visithadrianswall.co.uk). If you arrive by train during the off-season, you'll need to rely on taxis or long walks to visit the wall (see "Off-Season Options," later).

By Bus: Bus #AD122 connects the Roman sights (and several recommended accommodations) with the following train stations, listed west to east: **Carlisle, Haltwhistle, Hexham,** and **Newcastle** (from £2/ride, £9 unlimited Day Rover ticket, buy tickets on board, Day Rover also available at TI, tel. 01434/322-002).

Due to funding cuts, the bus schedule has been scaled back. It runs most frequently between Haltwhistle and Hexham (7/day in each direction late-May-Aug, less frequent and possibly weekends only Easter-late-May and Sept-Oct, no service Nov-Easter). From Carlisle, it runs three times a day late May-Aug (less frequently outside those times). From Newcastle, the bus leaves just once a day (at 9:30—if you miss this bus, take the train to Haltwhistle and pick up the bus there). If you're planning to take this bus, it's smart to confirm online whether it'll be running during your visit (www.visithadrianswall.co.uk).

By Train: Northern Line's train route #4 runs parallel to and a few miles south of the wall much more frequently than the bus. While the train stops at stations in larger towns—including (west to east) **Carlisle, Haltwhistle, Hexham,** and **Newcastle**—it doesn't take you near the actual Roman sights. You can catch bus #AD122 at all four stations, though bus service is best from Hexham and Haltwhistle (no bus service off-season; train runs daily 1/hour; Carlisle to Haltwhistle—30 minutes; Haltwhistle to Hexham—20 minutes; Hexham to Newcastle—40 minutes;

www.northernrail.org). Note: To get to or from Newcastle on this line, you must transfer in Hexham.

By Taxi: These Haltwhistle-based taxi companies can help you connect the dots: Melvin's Taxi (tel. 01434/320-632, mobile 07903-760-230), Sprouls (tel. 01434/321-064, mobile 07712-321-064), or Diamond (mobile 07597/641-222). It costs about £11 one-way from Haltwhistle to Housesteads Roman Fort (arrange for return pickup or have museum staff call a taxi). Note that on school days, all of these taxis are busy shuttling rural kids to class in the morning (about 8:00-10:00) and afternoon (about 14:30-16:30), so you may have to wait.

Off-Season Options: Bus #AD122 doesn't run off-season (Nov-Easter) and may operate only on weekends in spring and fall, so you can only get as far as the train will take you (i.e., Haltwhistle)—from there, you'll have to take a taxi (described above) to the sights. Or, if you're a hardy hiker, take the Northern Line train to Bardon Mill, then walk about two miles to Vindolanda and another 2.5 miles to Housesteads Roman Fort.

Baggage Storage: It's difficult to bring your luggage along with you. If you're day-tripping, you can store your luggage in **Carlisle** (across the street from the train station at Bar Solo, £2/bag per day, daily 9:00-22:30, tel. 01228/631-600) or possibly at the **Newcastle** train station left-luggage office (may be closed; if open, £5/bag per day, Mon-Sat 8:00-20:00, Sun 9:00-20:00, platform 12; call or email Newcastle TI to confirm if it's open—tel. 01912/778-000, visitorinfo@ngi.org.uk). If you must travel with luggage, Housesteads Roman Fort and Vindolanda will most likely let you leave your bags at the sight entrance while you're inside. If you want to walk the wall, various baggage-courier services will send your luggage ahead to your next B&B in the region for about £5 per bag (contact Hadrian's Haul, mobile 07967-564-823, www.hadrianshaul.com; or Walkers', tel. 0871-423-8803, www.walkersbags.co.uk).

By Private Tour

Peter Carney, a former history teacher, leads guided walks and tours around Hadrian's Wall, including an all-day walk that starts at the Roman Army Museum and then connects Vindolanda and Housesteads via a seven-mile hike (£100/person, £125 for 2 people, £150 for up to 6 people, does not include museum admission). His Roman Fort Tour includes the same sights but without the hike (£80/person, £90 for 2 people, £100 for up to 6 people). He can also customize tours to suit your time frame and interests (£50/half-day or £90/day for 2 people, happy to pick you up from your B&B or hotel, mobile 07585/139-016, 07810-665/733, or 07757/420-672, www.hadrianswall-walk.com, petercarney@hadrianswall-walk.com).

Sights at Hadrian's Wall

▲▲Hiking the Wall

It's enjoyable to hike along the wall speaking Latin, even if only for a short stretch. Note that park rangers forbid anyone from

actually walking on top of the wall, except along a very short stretch at Housesteads. On the following hikes, you'll walk alongside the wall.

For a good, craggy, three-mile, up-and-down walk along the wall, hike between Steel Rigg and Housesteads Roman Fort. For a shorter stretch, begin at Steel Rigg (where there's a handy parking lot) and walk a mile to Sycamore Gap, then back again (described next; the Once Brewed National Park Visitor Centre hands out a free sheet outlining this walk). These hikes are moderately strenuous and are best for those in good shape and with sturdy shoes.

To reach the trailhead for the short hike from **Steel Rigg to Sycamore Gap,** take the little road across from the Once Brewed

National Park Visitor Centre and park in the pay-and-display parking lot on the right at the crest of the hill. Walk through the gate to the shoulder-high stretch of wall, go to the left, and follow the wall running steeply down the valley below you. Ahead of you are dramatic cliffs, creating a natu-

ral boundary made-to-order for this Roman fortification. Walk down the steep slope into the valley, then back up the other side (watch your footing on the stone stairs). Following the wall, you'll do a similar up-and-down routine three more times, like a slow-motion human roller coaster. In the second gap is one of the best-preserved milecastles, #39 (called Castle Nick because it sits in a

nick in a crag).

Soon after, you'll reach the third gap, called Sycamore Gap for the large symmetrical tree in the middle. (Do you remember the 1991 Kevin Costner movie *Robin Hood: Prince of Thieves*? Locals certainly do—this tree was featured in it, and tourists frequently ask for directions to the "Robin Hood Tree.") You can either hike back the way you came, or cut down toward the main road to find the less strenuous Roman Military Way path, which skirts the bottom of the ridge (rather than following the wall); this leads back to the base of the Steel Rigg hill, where you can huff back up to your car.

▲▲Housesteads Roman Fort

With its recently revamped museum, powerful scenery, and the best-preserved segment of the wall, this is your best single stop

 at Hadrian's Wall. It requires a steep hike up from the parking lot, but once there it's just you, the bleating sheep, and memories of ancient Rome.

Cost and Hours: £6.20 for site and museum; April-Sept daily 10:00-18:00; Oct daily 10:00-17:00; Nov-March Sat-Sun 10:00-16:00, closed Mon-Fri though visitors center may be open during the week; last entry 45 minutes before closing, parking-£4/day, same parking ticket also good for the Once Brewed National Park Visitor Centre and Steel Rigg parking lots, bus #AD122 stops here.

Information: Museum tel. 01434/344-363, info tel. 0870-333-1181, gift shop tel. 01434/344-525, www.english-heritage.org.uk/housesteads.

Services: At the car park is a visitors center with WCs, a snack bar, and a gift shop. They sell a £3.50 guidebook about the fort or a £5 guidebook covering the entire wall. If you're traveling by bus and want to leave your luggage, ask at the visitors center if they'll stow it for a bit.

Visiting the Museum and Fort: From the visitors center, head outside and hike about a half-mile uphill to the fort. At the top of the hill, duck into the **museum** (on the left) before touring the site. While smaller and housing fewer artifacts than the museum at Vindolanda (explained next), it's interesting nonetheless. Look for the giant Victory statue, which once adorned the fort's East Gate; her foot is stepping on a globe, serving as an intimidating reminder to outsiders of the Romans' success in battle. A good seven-minute film shows how Housesteads (known back then as Vercovicium) would have operated.

Artifacts offer more insights into those who lived here. A cooking pot from Frisia (Northern Holland) indicates the presence of women, showing that soldiers came with their families in tow. A tweezer, probe, spoons, and votive foot (that would have been offered to the gods in exchange for a cure for a foot ailment) reveal the type of medical care you could expect. And a weighted die and a coin mold—perhaps used to make counterfeit money—show what may have been the less-than-savory side of life at the fort.

After exploring the museum, head out to the sprawling ruins of the **fort.** Interpretive signs and illustrations explain what you're seeing. All Roman forts were the same rectangular shape and design, containing a commander's headquarters, barracks, and latrines (Housesteads has the best-preserved Roman toilets found anywhere—look for them at the lower-right corner). This fort even had a hospital. The fort was built right up to the wall, which runs along its upper end. (This is the one place along the wall where you're actually allowed to get up and walk on top of it for a photo op.) Visually trace the wall to the left to see how it disappears into a bank of overgrown turf.

▲▲Vindolanda

This larger Roman fort (which actually predates the wall by 40 years) and museum are just south of the wall. Although Housesteads has better ruins and the wall, Vindolanda has the more impressive museum, packed with artifacts that reveal intimate details of Roman life.

Cost and Hours: £6.50, £10 combo-ticket includes Roman Army Museum, guidebook-£4, daily April-Sept 10:00-18:00, mid-Feb-March and Oct 10:00-17:00, Nov 10:00-16:00, may be open on weekends Dec-mid-Feb, last entry 45 minutes before closing, call first during bad weather, free parking with entry, bus #AD122 stops here, café.

Information: Tel. 01434/344-277, www.vindolanda.com.

Tours: Guided tours run twice daily on weekends only (typically at 10:45 and 14:00); in high season, archaeological talks and tours may be offered on weekdays as well. Both are included in your ticket.

Archaeological Dig: The Vindolanda site is an active dig—from Easter through September, you'll see the excavation work in progress (usually Mon-Fri, weather permitting). Much of the work is done by volunteers, including armchair archaeologists from the US.

Visiting the Site and Museum: After entering, stop at the model of the entire site as it was in Roman times (c. 213-276). Notice that the site had two parts: the fort itself, and the town just outside that helped to supply it.

Head out to the **site,** walking through 500 yards of grassy parkland decorated by the foundation stones of the Roman fort and a full-size replica chunk of the wall. Over the course of 400 years, at least nine forts were built on this spot. The Romans, by lazily sealing the foundations from each successive fort, left modern-day archaeologists with a 20-foot-deep treasure trove of remarkably well-preserved artifacts: keys, coins, brooches, scales, pottery, glass, tools, leather shoes, bits of cloth, and even a wig. Many of these are now displayed in the museum, well-described in English, German, French, and...Latin.

At the far side of the site, pass through the pleasant riverside garden area on the way to the museum. The well-presented **museum** pairs actual artifacts with insightful explanations—such as a collection of Roman shoes with a description about what each one tells us about its wearer. The weapons (including arrowheads and spearheads) and fragments of armor are a reminder that Vindolanda was an important outpost on Rome's northern boundary—look for the Scottish skull stuck on a pike to discourage rebellion. You'll also see lots of leather; tools that were used for building and expanding the fort; locks and keys (the fort had a password that changed daily—jotting it on a Post-It note wasn't allowed); a large coin collection; items imported here from the far corners of the vast empire (such as fragments of French pottery and amphora jugs from the Mediterranean); beauty aids such as combs, tools for applying makeup, and hairpins; and religious pillars and steles.

But the museum's main attraction is its collection of writing tablets. A good video explains how these impressively well-preserved examples of early Roman cursive were discovered here in 1973. Displays show some of the actual letters—written on thin pieces of wood—alongside the translations. These letters bring Romans to life in a way that ruins alone can't. The most famous piece (described but not displayed here) is the first known example of a woman writing to a woman (an invitation to a birthday party).

Finally, you'll pass through an exhibit about the history of the excavations, including a case featuring the latest discoveries, on your way to the shop and cafeteria.

▲▲Roman Army Museum

This museum, a few miles farther west at Greenhead (near the site of the Carvoran Roman fort), was fully renovated in 2011. Its cutting-edge, interactive exhibit illustrates the structure of the Roman Army that built and monitored this wall, with a focus on the everyday lifestyles of the Roman soldiers stationed here. Bombastic displays, life-size figures, and several different films—but few actual artifacts—make this entertaining museum a good complement to the archaeological emphasis of Vindolanda. If visiting all three Roman sights, this is a good one to start at, as it sets the stage for what you're about to see.

Cost and Hours: £5.25, £10 combo-ticket includes Vindolanda, daily April-Sept 10:00-18:00, mid-Feb-March and Oct-mid-Nov 10:00-17:00, may be open on weekends mid-Nov-mid-Feb, last entry 30 minutes before closing, free parking with entry, bus #AD122 stops here.

Information: Tel. 01697/747-485; if no answer, call Vindolanda tel. 01434/344-277; www.vindolanda.com.

Visiting the Museum: In the first room, a video explains the complicated structure of the Roman Army—legions, cohorts, centuries, and so on. While a "legionnaire" was a Roman citizen, an "auxiliary" was a non-citizen specialist recruited for their unique skills (such as horsemen and archers). A video of an army recruiting officer delivers an "Uncle Caesar wants YOU!" speech to prospective soldiers. A timeline traces the history of the Roman Empire, especially as it related to the British Isles.

The good 20-minute *Edge of Empire* 3-D movie offers an evocative look at what life was like for a Roman soldier marking time on the wall, and digital models show reconstructions of the wall and forts. In the exhibit on weapons, shields, and armor (mostly replicas), you'll learn how Roman soldiers trained with lead-filled wooden swords, so that when they went into battle, their steel swords felt light by comparison. Another exhibit explains the story of Hadrian, the man behind the wall.

Sleeping and Eating near Hadrian's Wall

If you want to spend the night in this area, set your sights on the adjacent villages of Once Brewed and Twice Brewed, with a few accommodations options, a good pub, and easy access to the most important sights. I've also listed some other accommodations scattered around the region.

In and near Once Brewed and Twice Brewed
(area code: 01434)

These two side-by-side villages, each with a handful of houses, sit at the base of the volcanic ridge along the B-6318 road. (While the mailing address for these hamlets is "Bardon Mill," that town is actually about 2.5 miles away, across the busy A-69 highway.) The Twice Brewed Inn, Once Brewed Youth Hostel, and Milecastle Inn are reachable by Hadrian's Wall bus #AD122 (described earlier). Bus drivers can drop you off at Vallum Lodge by request (but they won't pick up).

$$ Vallum Lodge is a cushy, comfortable, nicely renovated base situated near the vallum (the ditch that forms part of the fortification a half-mile from the wall itself). Its six cheery rooms are all on the ground floor, and a separate guesthouse called the Snug has one bedroom and a kitchen. It's just up the road from The Twice Brewed Inn—a handy dinner option (Sb-£70, Db-£85, Db in Snug-£98, free Wi-Fi, lounge, Military Road, tel. 01434/344-248, www.vallum-lodge.co.uk, stay@vallum-lodge.co.uk, Clare and Michael).

$$ The Twice Brewed Inn, two miles west of Housesteads and a half-mile from the wall, rents 16 workable rooms, including en-suite rooms that have been recently renovated (S-£37, D-£59, Db-£76-90, ask for a room away from the road, free Wi-Fi, Military Road, tel. 01434/344-534, www.twicebrewedinn.co.uk, info@twicebrewedinn.co.uk). The inn's friendly **pub** serves as the community gathering place (free Wi-Fi), and is a hangout for hikers and the archaeologists digging at the nearby sites. It serves real ales and large portions of good pub grub (£9-12 meals, vegetarian options, fancier restaurant in back with same menu, food served daily 12:00-20:30, Fri-Sat until 21:00).

$ Once Brewed Youth Hostel is a comfortable, institutional place next door to the Once Brewed National Park Visitor Centre, though it may be closed for renovation when you visit (£18-22/bed with sheets in 2- to 6-bed rooms, private rooms available, members pay £3 less, breakfast-£5, packed lunch-£5.50, dinner-£7.50-12, reception open daily 8:00-10:00 & 16:00-22:00, must reserve ahead in Dec-Jan, guest kitchen, laundry, Military Road, tel. 01434/344-360 or 0845-371-9753, www.yha.org.uk, oncebrewed@yha.org.uk).

West of Once/Twice Brewed: **Milecastle Inn,** two miles to the west, cooks up all sorts of exotic game and offers the best dinner around, according to hungry national park rangers. You can order food at the counter and sit in the pub, or take a seat in the table-service area (£9-13 meals, food served daily Easter-Sept 12:00-20:45, Oct-Easter 14:30 & 18:00-20:30, smart to reserve in summer, North Road, tel. 01434/321-372).

Rural and Remote, North of the Wall: **$$ Gibbs Hill Farm B&B and Hostel** is a friendly working sheep-and-cattle farm set on 700 acres in the stunning valley on the far side of the wall (only practical for drivers). The B&B offers four big, airy double en-suite rooms in the main house, while the three six-bed dorm rooms are in a restored hay barn (hostel bed/bedding-£16, Sb-£50, Db-£75, packed lunch-£5, laundry facilities, 5-minute drive from Once Brewed National Park Visitor Centre, tel. 01434/344-030, www.gibbshillfarm.co.uk, val@gibbshillfarm.co.uk, warm Val). They also rent several cottages for two to six people by the week (£280-600).

In Haltwhistle
(area code: 01434)

The larger town of Haltwhistle has a train station, along with stops for Hadrian's Wall bus #AD122 (at the train station and a few blocks east, at Market Place). It also has a helpful TI (see "Tourist Information," on page 656), a launderette, several eateries, and a handful of B&Bs, including this one.

$$ Ashcroft Guest House, a large Victorian former vicarage, is 400 yards from the Haltwhistle train station and 200 yards from the Market Place bus stop. It has six big, luxurious rooms, huge terraced gardens, and views from the comfy lounge, along with a two-bedroom apartment with kitchen (Sb-£55, Db-£85, super king or four-poster Db-£95, ask about family deals, 2-night minimum for apartment, guest computer, free Wi-Fi, 1.5 miles from the wall, Lanty's Lonnen, tel. 01434/320-213, www.ashcroft guesthouse.co.uk, info@ashcroftguesthouse.co.uk, helpful Geoff and Christine James).

Near Hexham
(area code: 01434)

$$ High Reins offers four rooms in a stone house built by a shipping tycoon in the 1920s (Sb-£46, Db-£72, cash only, 2-bedroom apartment also available, lounge, 1 mile south of train station on the western outskirts of Hexham, Leazes Lane, tel. 01434/603-590, pwalton@highreins.co.uk, Jan and Peter Walton).

Near Carlisle
(area code: 01228)

$$$ Bessiestown Farm Country Guest House, located far northwest of the Hadrian sights, is convenient for drivers connecting the Lake District and Scotland. It's a quiet and soothing stop in the middle of sheep pastures, with four bedrooms in the main house and two 2-bedroom apartments in the former stables (Sb-£59, Db-£90, Tb-£120, honeymoon suite-£150, discount with 3-night stay; in Catlowdy, midway between Gretna Green and Hadrian's Wall, 14 miles—a 20-minute drive—north of Carlisle; tel. 01228/577-219, www.bessiestown.co.uk, info@bessiestown.co.uk, gracious Margaret and John Sisson).

Holy Island and Bamburgh Castle

This remote area is worthwhile only for those with a car. It's out of the way for most itineraries—unless you're driving between Durham and Edinburgh on the A-1 highway, in which case Holy Island and Bamburgh Castle (and Beamish Museum, described earlier) are easy stop-offs. If you're determined to reach these sights by public transportation, you can go to Newcastle, then take bus #501 to Bamburgh Castle (2-3/day, 2.5 hours); or bus #505 to Beal (6/day Mon-Sat, none direct on Sun, 2 hours), where you can walk a level six miles or catch Perrymans bus #477 to Holy Island (2/day Mon-Sat late-July-Aug, Wed and Sat only Sept-mid-July, none on Sun year-round, described under "Getting There," below).

Holy Island (Lindisfarne)

Twelve hundred years ago, this "Holy Island"—then known as Lindisfarne—was Christianity's tenuous toehold in England. In

the A.D. 680s, Holy Island was the home and original burial ground of St. Cuthbert (he's now in Durham). We know it as the source of the magnificent Lindisfarne Gospels (A.D. 698; now in London's British Library), decorated by monks with some of the finest art from Europe's "Dark Ages." By the ninth century, Viking raids forced the monks to take shelter in Durham, but they returned centuries later to re-establish a church on this holy site.

Today Holy Island—worth ▲▲—makes a pleasant stop for modern-day pilgrims: You'll cross a causeway to a quiet town with a striking castle and the ruins of an evocative priory that was originally founded in 635.

Getting There: Holy Island is reached by a two-mile causeway that's cut off twice a day by high tides. Safe crossing times are posted at each end of the causeway (and at www.lindisfarne.org.uk), warning **drivers** when this holy place becomes Holy Island—and you become stranded. Once on the island, signs direct you to a well-marked, mandatory parking lot at the entrance to town (£2.40/3 hours).

It's also possible to reach Holy Island by **bus** from the nearby

DURHAM & NE ENGLAND

town of Beal, but it's not worth the effort unless you're a determined pilgrim (Perrymans bus #477, 2/day Mon-Sat late-July-Aug, Wed and Sat only Sept-mid-July, none on Sun year-round; if coming on the bus from Newcastle, get off at Beal to transfer to this bus—but carefully confirm schedule for the complete connection before you head out).

Getting Around Holy Island: From the parking lot, it's an easy 10-minute **walk** into town and to the priory; the castle is about a 20-minute walk away. To save time, ride the convenient **shuttle bus,** which makes a circuit from the parking lot to the village green (next to the priory entrance), then out to the castle, and back again (£1, 3/hour, runs only when castle is open).

Sights on Holy Island

The two main attractions on Holy Island are the ruins of the old priory and the castle outside of town. The town itself is a charming little community of about 150 residents.

Holy Island Town

The town has B&Bs and cafés catering to tourists, a tiny post office, a fire station (with no firefighters—they're helicoptered in when the need arises), a six-student schoolhouse, and a tiny winery offering free tastes of their Lindisfarne mead. There's no official TI, but the **Lindisfarne Centre**—with a well-presented, kid-friendly history exhibit—acts as an unofficial information point and is proudly staffed by native Holy Islanders (£3 to tour the exhibit, daily April-Sept 10:00-17:00, Oct 10:00-16:00, open sporadically Nov-March, Marygate, tel. 01289/389-004, www .lindisfarne.org.uk).

Lindisfarne Priory

The priory has an evocative field of ruined church walls and a tiny but instructive museum. (A priory—run by a prior rather than an abbot—is similar to an abbey, but smaller.)

Cost and Hours: £5.20 ticket includes both museum and priory ruins, guidebook-£4; April-Sept daily 10:00-18:00; Oct daily 10:00-16:00; Nov-March Sat-Sun 10:00-16:00, closed Mon-Fri, shorter winter hours possible; tel. 01289/389-200, www.english -heritage.org.uk/lindisfarne.

Visiting the Priory: In the **museum,** you'll see exhibits about Holy Island's Anglo-Saxon culture, from stonework to manuscripts—including the famous Lindisfarne Gospels. The Gospels' text was in Latin, the language of scholars ever since the Roman Empire, but the illustrations—with elaborate tracery and interwoven decoration—are a mix of Irish, classical, and even Byzantine forms. These Gospels are a reminder that Christianity almost didn't make it in Europe. After the fall of Rome (which had established Christianity as the Empire's official religion), much of Europe reverted to its pagan ways. In that chaotic era, Lindisfarne—an obscure monastery of Irish monks on a remote island—was one of the few beacons of light, tending the embers of civilization through the long night of the Dark Ages.

You can visit the adjacent church and churchyard without paying, but you need a ticket to get into the actual **priory ruins.**

The Lindisfarne monks fled the island in A.D. 875 to escape Viking raids. They made their way to Durham, and built a cathedral to hold the tomb of St. Cuthbert (see page 643). Centuries later, in 1082, the monks returned to Holy Island to re-found the priory and build a fine church in a Norman (Romanesque) style similar to the one in Durham. They fended off invasions by Picts and Scots throughout the 14th century, and fortified the great church. But when Henry VIII "dissolved" (destroyed) the monasteries in the 1530s, the priory was one of his victims. The forgotten ruins were later excavated in the 1850s as an important example of early English (Anglo-Saxon) history.

As you walk through this site, you're stepping on several layers of history: a ruined Norman church sitting on the ruins of an earlier Anglo-Saxon one (where Cuthbert served as bishop), next to the still-standing Parish Church of St. Mary's, where Holy Islanders worship today. The priory ruins are well-explained by posted plaques and floor plans that help resurrect the rubble.

Lindisfarne Castle

Faintly visible from the priory ruins, the dramatically situated Lindisfarne Castle is enticing from afar, and makes for a fine photo op. But inside, there's little of interest. Built in 1549—many centuries after the heyday of Cuthbert and the monks—the castle never really saw much action, and it was converted into a holiday home for an aristocratic publisher in the early 1900s. If you do visit, you'll wander through sparsely furnished rooms and stroll out onto the upper battery—an outdoor terrace with views of the priory ruins.

Cost and Hours: £6.50; mid-Feb-Oct Tue-Sun 10:00-15:00 or 12:00-17:00 depending on tides—confirm times at the National Trust shop on Marygate in town before heading out, closed Mon except on Bank Holidays and in Aug;

Jan-mid-Feb Sat-Sun 10:00-15:00 twice per month, closed Mon-Fri and every other weekend; also closed Nov-Dec; tel. 01289/389-244, www.nationaltrust.org.uk/lindisfarne.

Bamburgh Castle

About 10 miles south of Holy Island, this grand castle—worth ▲—dominates the Northumbrian countryside and over-looks Britain's loveliest beach.

Bamburgh (BOMB-ruh) was bought and passionately refurbished by Lord William George Armstrong, a wealthy industrialist, in the 1890s. While it's one of England's most dramatic castles from the outside, the interior (a 19th-century rebuild) lacks soul, barely cracking the country's top ten. But if you're passing by or visiting nearby Holy Island, Bamburgh may be worth a stop.

Cost and Hours: £9.75 includes staterooms and grounds, daily mid-Feb-Oct 10:00-17:00, winter Sat-Sun only 11:00-16:30, last entry one hour before closing, parking-£2, tel. 01668/214-515, www.bamburghcastle.com.

Touring the Castle: Bamburgh's main attraction is its staterooms; as you explore the rest of the grounds, you'll also have the chance to see several smaller exhibits. If arriving late in the day, go directly to the staterooms, which may close early. There's virtually no information inside the castle, aside from a few docents; to give meaning to your visit, either rent the £1 audioguide (with two hours of commentary) or buy the £1 guidebook.

The **staterooms** feel lived-in because they still are—with Armstrong family portraits and aristocratic-yet-homey knick-knacks hanging everywhere. You'll enter through the medieval

kitchen, with its three giant fireplaces, and work your way through smaller storage rooms to the King's Hall, with a fantastic teak ceiling and a J. M. W. Turner painting. At the far end of the great hall is a smaller (but still-grand) alcove separated by an archway, which could be sealed off by gigantic folding doors. Continuing through the stairwell, notice the *private apartment* signs.

The armory once had a very different purpose—you can still see the apse of what was once a chapel. In the keep is a 145-foot-deep Anglo-Saxon well. The scullery (a medieval utility room) includes a long row of sinks and an alcove where they make fresh fudge. You'll wind up in the gift shop; before leaving, check out the archaeology room, with exhibits about the castle's history; and the dungeon, with cheesy mannequins being tortured.

Exploring the **grounds,** you enjoy fine views over the sea and beach, and get a good look at the stout 12th-century keep that's

the castle's centerpiece. In the former stables is an art gallery displaying works by local artists. The Armstrong and Aviation Artefacts Museum features the inventions of the family that has owned the castle through modern times. Lord William George Armstrong (1810-1900) was a pioneer in aviation and a clever innovator, creating (among other things) the first all-steel aircraft structure, a method for in-flight refueling, and the ejector seat. You'll see several of his inventions, along with exhibits on cars, shipbuilding, and more. While the museum is fun for aviation-history buffs, it may be dull to others.

Nearby: The village of Bamburgh is pleasant enough, with tourist-oriented cafés and fine views over a manicured cricket pitch of the looming castle. Better yet, go for a walk on the beach: Crisscrossed by walking paths, rolling dunes lead to a vast sandy beach and lots of families on holiday.

WALES

WALES

Wales, a country the size of Massachusetts, is located on a peninsula on the west coast of the Isle of Britain, facing the Irish Sea. Longer than it is wide (170 miles by 60 miles), it's shaped somewhat like a miniature Britain. The north is mountainous, rural, and sparsely populated. The south, with a less-rugged topography, is where two-thirds of the people live (including 345,000 in the capital of Cardiff). The country has 750 miles of scenic, windswept coastline and is capped by Mount Snowdon, which, at 3,560 feet, is taller than any mountain in England.

Despite centuries of English imperialism, the Welsh language

(a.k.a. Cymraeg, pronounced kum-RAH-ig) remains alive and well—more so than its nearly dead Celtic cousin in Scotland, Gaelic. Though everyone in Wales speaks English, one in five can also speak the native tongue. In the northwest, well over half the population is fluent in Welsh and uses it in everyday life. Listen in.

Most certainly *not* a dialect of English, the Celtic Welsh tongue sounds to foreign ears like it might be Elvish from *The Lord of the Rings*. One of Europe's oldest languages, Welsh has been written down since about A.D. 600, and was spoken 300 years before French or German. Today, the Welsh language is protected by law from complete English encroachment—the country is officially bilingual, and signs always display both languages (e.g., *Cardiff/Caerdydd*). In schools, it's either the first or the required second language; in many areas, English isn't used in classes at all until middle school.

Though English has been the dominant language in Wales for many years (and most newspapers and media are in English), the Welsh people cherish their linguistic heritage as something that sets them apart. In fact, a line of the Welsh national anthem goes,

Speaking Welsh

Welsh pronunciation is tricky. The common "ll" combination sounds roughly like "thl" (pronounced as if you were ready to make an "l" sound and then blew it out). As in Scotland, "ch" is a soft, guttural k, pronounced in the back of the throat. The Welsh "dd" sounds like the English "th," f = v, ff = f, w = the "u" in "push," y = i. Non-Welsh people often make the mistake of trying to say a long Welsh name too fast, and inevitably trip themselves up. A local tipped me off: Slow down and say each syllable separately, and it'll come out right. For example, Llangollen is thlang-GOT-hlen.

Although there's no need to learn any Welsh (because everyone also speaks English), without too much effort you can make friends and impress the locals by learning a few polite phrases:

Hello	**Helo**	hee-LOH
Good-bye	**Hwyl**	hoo-il
Please	**Os gwelwch yn dda**	os GWELL-uck UN thah
Thank you	**Diolch**	dee-olkh
Wales	**Cymru**	KUM-ree
England	**Lloegr**	THLOY-ger

In a pub, toast the guy who just bought your drink with Diolch and Yeach-hid dah (YECH-id dah, "Good health to you").

"Oh, may the old language survive!"

Wales has some traditional foods worth looking for, particularly lamb dishes and leek soup *(cawl)*. In fact, the national symbol is the leek, ever since medieval warriors—who wore the vegetable on their helmets in battle—saved the land from Saxon invaders. Cheese on toast is known as "Welsh rarebit" (or "Welsh rabbit"; the name is a throwback to a time when the poor Welsh couldn't afford much meat in their diet). At breakfast, you might get some "Welsh cakes," basically a small squashed scone. Cockles and seaweed bread were once common breakfast items—but don't expect your hotel to serve them.

Wales' three million people are mostly white and Christian (Presbyterian, Anglican, or Catholic). Like their English and Scottish counterparts, they enjoy football (soccer), but rugby is the unofficial Welsh sport, more popular in Wales than in any country outside of New Zealand. Other big sports are cricket and snooker (similar to billiards).

The Welsh flag features a red dragon on a field of green and

Singing the Praises of Welsh Choirs

The Welsh love their choirs. Every town has a choir (men's or mixed) that practices weekly. Visitors are usually welcome to observe the session (lasting about 1.5-2 hours), and sometimes the choir heads to the pub afterward for a good old-fashioned, beer-lubricated sing-along that you can join.

As these choir rehearsals have become something of a tourist attraction, many choirs ask attendees for a small donation—fair enough. Note that some towns have more than one choir, and schedules are subject to change; confirm the schedule with a local TI or your B&B before making the trip. Additionally, many choirs regularly perform concerts—inquire for the latest schedule.

Here are choir practices that occur in or near towns I recommend visiting: **Llandudno Junction,** near **Conwy** (men's choir Mon at 19:30 except Aug, tel. 01248/681-159, www.maelgwn.co.uk); **Caernarfon** (men's choir Tue at 19:45, arrive by 19:30 in summer to guarantee a seat, no practice in Aug, in the Galeri Creative Enterprise Centre at Victoria Dock, tel. 01286/677-404, www.cormeibioncaernarfon.org/eng); **Ruthin** (mixed choir Thu at 20:00 except Aug at Pwllglas Village Hall, mobile tel. 07724/112-984, www.corrhuthun.co.uk); and **Llangollen** (men's choir Fri at 19:30 at Hand Hotel, 21:30 pub singsong afterward, hotel tel. 01978/860-303).

white. The dragon has been a symbol of Wales since at least the ninth century (maybe even from Roman days). According to legend, King Arthur's men carried the dragon flag to battle.

Welsh history stretches back into the mists of prehistoric Britain. When Roman armies arrived on the island of Britain, they conquered the Celtic tribes here, built forts and cities, and (later) introduced Christianity. As Rome fell, Saxon (Germanic) tribes like the Angles stepped into the power vacuum, conquering what they renamed "Angle-land"—but they failed to penetrate Wales. Brave Welsh warriors, mountainous terrain, and the 177-mile man-made ditch-and-wall known as Offa's Dyke helped preserve the country's unique Celtic/Roman heritage. In 1216, Wales' medieval kingdoms unified under Llywelyn Fawr ("the Great").

But just a few decades later, in 1282, King Edward I of England invaded and conquered, putting an end to Wales' one era as a unified, sovereign nation. To solidify his hold on the country,

Edward built a string of castles (at Caernarfon, Conwy, and many other places—see sidebar on page 688). He then named his son and successor the "Prince of Wales," starting the tradition of granting that ceremonial title to the heir to the English throne. Despite an unsuccessful rebellion in 1400, led by Owen Glendower (Owain Glyndwr), Wales has remained under English rule ever since Edward's invasion. In 1535, the annexation was formalized under Henry VIII.

By the 19th century, Welsh coal and iron stoked the engines of Britain's Industrial Revolution, and its slate was exported to shingle roofs throughout Europe. The stereotype of the Welsh as poor, grimy-faced miners continued into the 20th century. Their economy has been slow to transition from mining, factories, and sheep farming to the service-and-software model of the global world.

In recent decades, the Welsh have consciously tried to preserve their local traditions and language. In 1999, Wales was granted its own parliament, the National Assembly, with powers to distribute the national budget. Though still ruled by the UK government in London, Wales now has a measure of independence and self-rule.

Less urbanized and less wealthy than England, Wales consists of miles of green land where sheep graze (because the soil is too poor for crops). It makes for wonderful hillwalking, but hikers should beware of midges. From late May through September, these tiny, biting insects are very interested in dawn, dusk, dampness, and you—pack insect repellent along on any hike.

Because Wales is an affordable weekend destination for many English, the country is becoming popular among avid English drinkers, who pour over the border on Friday nights for the cheap beer before stumbling home on Sunday. Expect otherwise-sleepy Welsh border towns to be rowdy on Saturday nights.

I've focused my coverage of Wales on the north, which has the highest concentration of castles, natural beauty, and attractions. A few South Wales sights that are convenient to visit from Bath are covered in the Near Bath chapter.

Try to connect with Welsh culture in your itinerary. Clamber over a castle, eat a leek, count sheep in a field, catch a rugby match, or share a pint of bitter with a baritone. Open your ears to the sound of words as old as the legendary King Arthur. "May the old language survive!"

NORTH WALES

Conwy • Caernarfon • Snowdonia National Park • Blaenau Ffestiniog • Ruthin

Wales' top historical, cultural, and natural wonders are found in its north. From towering Mount Snowdon to lush forests to desolate moor country, North Wales is a poem written in landscape. For sightseeing thrills and diversity, North Wales is Britain's most interesting slice of the Celtic crescent.

Wales is wonderful, but smart travelers sort through their options carefully. The region's economy is poor, and the Welsh tourism industry keeps busy trying to wring every possible pound out of the tourist trade—be careful not to be waylaid by the many gimmicky sights and bogus "best of" lists.

This chapter covers only my favorite Welsh stopovers. Conwy and Caernarfon offer two of Wales' top castles, which hover in the mist as mysterious reminders of the country's hard-fought history. Each castle adjoins a pleasant town; Conwy, the more charming of the two, makes the region's best home base, with appealing B&Bs and restaurants, a fun-to-explore townscape within mighty walls, and manageable connections to many nearby sights. Nearby, Snowdonia National Park plunges you into some of Wales' top scenery—you can ride a train from Llanberis to the top of Mount Snowdon, learn more about the local industry at Llanberis' National Slate Museum, and explore the huggable villages of Beddgelert and Betws-y-Coed. The tongue-twisting industrial town of Blaenau Ffestiniog invites you to tour an actual slate mine, while appealing Ruthin—on the way back toward England—has a relaxing market-town vibe. Rounding out your options are the sumptuous Bodnant Garden (near Conwy), plenty more imposing castles (I particularly like Beaumaris), and the canal-straddling town of Llangollen.

Planning Your Time

On a three-week Britain trip, give North Wales two nights and a day. It'll give you mighty castles, a giant slate mine, and some of Britain's most beautiful scenery. Many visitors are charmed and decide to stay an extra day...or longer.

Drivers staying in Conwy who have just one day can follow this ambitious plan:

9:30	Leave after breakfast
10:00	Visit Bodnant Garden
12:00	Pop into Trefriw Woolen Mills
13:00	Lunch in Llanberis and tour the National Slate Museum, then drive to Caernarfon
16:00	Catch the 16:00 Caernarfon Castle tour (castle open until 18:00 July-Aug)
18:00	Browse the town of Caernarfon
19:00	Drive back to Conwy to follow my self-guided town walk and have dinner

For those relying on **public transportation**, Conwy is a good home base, as it's a hub for many of the area's buses and trains. If you have just one day, leave Conwy in the morning for a loop through the Snowdonia sights (possibly including Betws-y-Coed, Beddgelert, or Llanberis, depending on bus and train schedules—check timetables and plan your route before heading out), then return to Conwy in the evening for the town walk and dinner. To see more in your limited time, consider hiring a local guide for a private driving tour.

With a second day, slow down and consider the region's other sights: the train from Llanberis up Mount Snowdon, the slate-mine tour in Blaenau Ffestiniog, Beaumaris Castle and jail, and the town of Ruthin. With more time and a desire to hike, consider using the mountain village of Beddgelert as your base.

Getting Around North Wales

By Public Transportation: North Wales (except Ruthin) is surprisingly well covered by a combination of buses and trains (though you'll want to get an early start to allow ample time to visit several destinations).

A main **train** line runs along the north coast from Chester to Holyhead via Llandudno Junction, Conwy, and Bangor, with nearly hourly departures (tel. 0845-748-4950, www.nationalrail.co.uk or www.arrivatrainswales.co.uk). From Llandudno Junction, the Conwy Valley line goes scenically south to Betws-y-Coed and Blaenau Ffestiniog (5/day Mon-Sat, 3/day on Sun in summer, no Sun trains in winter, www.conwy.gov.uk/cvr). And the old-fashioned Welsh Highland Railway steam train goes from Caernarfon to Beddgelert (2-3 trips/day, most days late March-Oct, 1.5 hours), continuing on to Porthmadog.

Public **buses** (run by various companies) pick up where the trains leave off. Get the *Public Transport Information* booklet at any local TI. Certain bus lines—dubbed "Sherpa" routes (the bus numbers begin with #S)—circle Snowdonia National Park with the needs of hikers in mind (www.gwynedd.gov.uk, search on "Snowdon Sherpa" for timetables).

Schedules get sparse late in the afternoon and on Sundays; plan ahead and confirm times carefully at local TIs and bus and train stations. For any questions about public transportation, call the Wales Travel Line at tel. 0871-200-2233, or check www.traveline-cymru.info.

Your choices for money-saving public-transportation **passes** are confusing. The Red Rover Ticket—the simplest and probably the best bet for most travelers—covers all buses west of Llandudno, including Sherpa buses (£6.40/day, buy from driver). The North Wales Rover Ticket covers trains and certain buses within a complex zone system (£9.50-26/day, depending on how many zones you need; buy on bus or train, www.taith.gov.uk).

By Private Tour: Mari Roberts, a Welsh guide based in

Ruthin, leads driving tours of the area tailored to your interests. Tours in her car are generally out of Conwy, but she will happily pick you up in Ruthin or Holyhead (£20/hour, 4-hour minimum, £160/day, tel. 01824/702-713, marihr@talktalk.net). **Donna Goodman** leads private day trips of North Wales and walking tours of Conwy, Caernarfon, or Beaumaris, including the castles (from £180/day, book in advance, tel. 01286/677-059, mobile 07946-163-906, www.turnstone-tours.co.uk, info@turnstone-tours.co.uk).

By Car: Driving and parking throughout North Wales is easy and allows you to cover more ground. If you need to rent a car after your arrival, see "Conwy Helpful Hints," later.

Conwy

Along with Conwy Castle, this garrison town was built in the 1280s to give Edward I a toehold in Wales. As there were no real

cities in 13th-century Wales, this was an English town, planted with settlers for the king's political purposes. What's left today are the best medieval walls in Britain, surrounding a humble town, crowned by the bleak and barren hulk of a castle that was awesome in its day (and still is). Conwy's charming High Street leads down to a fishy harbor that permitted Edward to restock his castle safely. Because the highway was tunneled under the town, Conwy has a strolling ambience.

Orientation to Conwy

Conwy is an enjoyably small community of 4,000 people. The walled old town center is compact and manageable. Lancaster Square marks the center, where you'll find the bus "station" (a blue-and-white bus shelter), the unstaffed train station (the little white hut at the end of a sunken parking lot), and the start of the main drag, High Street—and my self-guided walk.

Tourist Information

Conwy's TI is located across from the castle's short-stay parking lot on Rosehill Street (Mon-Sat 9:30-17:00, Sun 9:30-16:30, tel. 01492/577-566, www.visitllandudno.org.uk). Because Conwy's train and bus "stations" are unstaffed, ask at the TI about train or bus schedules for your departure. Don't confuse the TI with the uninformative Conwy Visitors Centre, a big gift shop near the station.

Arrival in Conwy

Whether taking the bus or train, you need to tell the driver or conductor you want to stop at Conwy. Milk-run trains stop here only upon request; major trains don't stop here at all (instead, they stop at nearby Llandudno Junction—see below). Consider getting train times and connections for your onward journey at a bigger station before you come here. In Conwy, train schedules are posted above the platforms. For train info in town, ask at the TI, call tel. 0871-200-2233, or see www.traveline-cymru.info.

For more frequent trains, use **Llandudno Junction,** visible a mile away beyond the bridges (from Conwy, catch the bus, take a £5 taxi, or simply walk a mile). Make sure to ask for trains that stop at Llandudno Junction, not Llandudno proper, which is a seaside resort farther from Conwy.

Helpful Hints

Festivals: The town is eager to emphasize its medieval history, with several events and festivals annually. These are some popular ones: the pirate festival (May, www.conwypirates.co.uk), the bluegrass festival (early July, www.northwalesbluegrass.co.uk), the River Festival (a week in Aug, www.conwyriverfestival .org) and a food festival, which includes a laser light show projected onto the castle (a weekend in Oct, www.conwyfeast .co.uk). Ask at the TI or at your B&B to see what's going on during your visit.

Internet Access: Get online at the **library** at the intersection of High and Castle streets (free guest computers and Wi-Fi, Mon and Thu-Fri 10:00-17:30, Tue 10:00-19:00, Sat 10:00-13:00, closed Wed and Sun, tel. 01492/596-242).

Car Rental: A dozen car-rental agencies in the city of Llandudno (a mile north of Llandudno Junction) offer cars and can generally deliver to you in Conwy; the Conwy TI has a list. The closest ones, in Llandudno Junction, are **Avis,** a 10-minute walk from Conwy (113a Conwy Road, tel. 0844-544-6075) and **Enterprise** (tel. 01492/593-380). Both close early on Saturday and all day Sunday.

Harbor Cruise: Two tour boats depart nearly hourly from the Conwy harborfront (£6 for 30 minutes, £8.50 for 1 hour, pay on boat, runs early Feb-Oct daily 10:30-17:00 or 18:00 depending on tides, longer trips available, mobile 07917-343-058, www.sightseeingcruises.co.uk).

Self-Guided Walk

Welcome to Conwy

This brief orientation walk introduces you to the essential Conwy in about an hour. As the town walls are open late, you can do this walk at any time—evening is a fine time. If you want a shorter stroll, skip ahead to the harborfront's promenade, which is perfect for a peaceful half-mile shoreline walk (start at the Smallest House in Great Britain—listed later, under "Harborfront").

• *Start at the top of High Street on the main square.*

❶ **Lancaster Square:** The square's centerpiece is a **column** honoring the town's founder, the Welsh prince Llywelyn the Great. Looking downhill, past the blue-and-white bus stop, find the cute pointed archway built into the medieval wall so the train could get through. Looking uphill, you can see Bangor Gate, built by the British engineer Thomas Telford in 1826 to accommodate traffic from his suspension bridge.

• *Walk uphill past Alfredo Restaurant to the end of the lane.*

❷ **Slate Memorials:** This wall of memorials recalls the 1937 coronation of King George VI (the father of today's Queen Elizabeth II). Notice the Welsh-language lesson here, given to the town by a citizen who never learned to read and wanted to inspire others to avoid his fate. It lists, in Welsh, the counties (shires, or *sir*), months (a few are vaguely recognizable), days, numbers, and alphabet with its different letters. Much has changed since this memorial was posted. Today more people are speaking Welsh, and all children are taught Welsh in school until age 12.

• *Turn left and walk uphill all the way to the wall, where steps lead to the ramparts. At the top of the stairs, head left and continue climbing to the very top of the town's tallest turret.*

❸ **Tallest Tower and Walls:** You're standing atop the most complete set of medieval town walls in Britain. In 1283, workers started to build them in conjunction with the castle. Four years later, they sent a message to London declaring, "Castle habitable, town defensible." Edward then sent in English settlers. Enjoy the view from the top. From here, guards could spot ships approaching by sea.

• *Heading left, walk two turrets downhill along the ramparts.*

The turrets were positioned about every 50 yards, connected by ramparts, and each one had a drawbridge that could be raised to bottle up any breach. Passing the second turret, notice that its wall is cracked. When they tunneled underneath this turret for the train, the construction accidentally undermined the foundation, effectively taking the same tactic that invading armies would have. The huge crack makes plain why undermining was such a popular

Welcome to Conwy Walk

N

TO BANGOR &
CAERNARFON

PARK

TOWN DITCH ROAD

BANGOR ROAD

1 Lancaster Square
2 Slate Memorials
3 Tallest Tower & Walls
4 The Walls (from Outside)
5 Carmel Church
6 Royal Cambrian Academy
7 High Street
8 Harborfront
9 Bridges
10 The Knight Shop
11 View of Conwy Castle

BANGOR
GATE

P

MOUNT PLEASANT

UPPER GATE ST.

CHAPEL

2

5 ✝

CROWN

6
PLAS
MAWR

HIGH

LANCASTER
SQUARE

1

START

P

CHURCH

3

ROSE

TALLEST
TOWER

UPPER
GATE

TRAIN
STATION

B

TOWN
WALLS

← SELF-GUIDED WALK
P PARKING
🹏 VIEW

TO
BETWS-Y-COED & ←
BLAENAU FFESTINIOG

technique in medieval warfare. (Unlike the town walls, Conwy Castle was built upon solid rock, so it couldn't be undermined.)

• At the first opportunity (just after walking above Bangor Gate), take the steps back down to street level. Then leave the old town by passing through Bangor Gate, heading downhill, and crossing the street for the best wide view of the walls.

4 The Walls (from Outside): You are walking down Town Ditch Road, named for the dry moat that was the first line of defense from the highest tower down to the riverbank. As was the case with most walled towns, there was a clear swath of "dead ground" outside the walls, so no one could sneak up. Once England centralized and consolidated its rule, all the walls and castles in Britain were pretty useless. Most fell into disrepair—ravaged by time and by scavengers who used them as quarries. During the Napoleonic Wars, English aristocrats were unable to make their Grand Tour of the Continent, so they explored the far reaches of their own land. That's when ruined castles such as this one were "discovered" and began to be appreciated for their romantic allure.

• *Stroll downhill to the bottom of Town Ditch Road. At the elderly-crossing sign (which also serves as a reminder to stand up straight), re-enter the old town, crossing through a hole cut in the wall by a modern mayor who wanted better access from his land, and walk down Berry Street. Originally called "Burial Street," it was a big ditch for mass burials during a 17th-century plague. After one block, turn right, climbing up Chapel Street to an austere stone structure.*

❺ Carmel Church: This Presbyterian church is a fine example of stark "statement architecture"—stern, no-frills, and typical of churches built in the early 20th century. Even very small Welsh towns tend to have churches for several Christian denominations. (The Welsh have a reputation for nonconformity, even contentiousness—as the saying goes, "Get two Welshmen together, and you'll have an argument. Get three together, and you'll have a fight.") In the 18th and 19th centuries, Welsh Christians who didn't want to worship in the official, English-style Anglican Church joined "nonconformist" congregations, such as Methodists, Congregationalists, Quakers, or Presbyterians. You could say "nonconformist" is to "Anglican" as "Protestant" is to "Catholic." Religious affiliation is closely tied to politics in Wales, where the Anglican Church, a.k.a. "The Church of England," goes by the more politically appealing "The Church in Wales." Still, many Welsh say, "The Anglican Church is the Conservative Party at prayer, and the nonconformist churches are the Labour Party at prayer."

• Just beyond the church (on the left, just past Seaview Terrace), in a modern building, is...

❻ The Royal Cambrian Academy: This art academy, showing off two floors of contemporary Welsh painting, gives a fine glimpse into the region and its people through art (free, most paintings are for sale, Tue-Sat 11:00-17:00, closed Sun-Mon and for one week before each exhibition; on Crown Lane just above Plas Mawr, tel. 01492/593-413, www.rcaconwy.org).

*• Continue on Crown Lane downhill past **Plas Mawr**. The first Welsh house built within the town walls, it dates from the time of Henry VIII (well worth touring, and described later, under "Sights in Conwy").*

Turn left onto...

❼ High Street: Wander downhill, enjoying this slice-of-Welsh-life scene—tearooms, bakery, butcher, newsstand, and old timers. All the colorful flags you see have no meaning—merchants are flying them simply to pump up the town's medieval feel. **Aberconwy House** marks the bottom of High Street. One of the oldest houses in town, it's a museum (not worth touring).

Conwy was once a garrison town filled with half-timbered build-ings just like this one. At end of High Street, 20 yards to the right at 4 Castle Street, is the **Penny Farthing Sweet Shop**—filled with old-fashioned candy.

• *Follow High Street through the gate and to the harbor.*

❽ **Harborfront:** The Harbor Gate, one of three original gates in the town walls, leads to the waterfront. The harbor dates from the 13th century, when it served Edward's castle and town. (The harborfront street is still called King's Quay.) Conwy was once a busy slate port. Slate, barged downstream to here, was loaded onto big three-masted ships and transported to the Continent. Back when much of Europe was roofed with Welsh slate, Conwy was a boomtown. All the mud is new—the modern bridge caused this part of the river to silt up.

The actions of the European Union have had a mixed effect on this waterfront. EU money helped pay for the recently built promenade, but hygiene laws have forced Conwy's fishermen out: Now that fish must be transported in refrigerated vehicles, the fishermen had to set up shop a few miles away (refrigerator trucks can't fit through the stone gate).

Conwy's harbor is now a laid-back area that locals treat like a town square. On summer evenings, the action is on the quay (pronounced "key"). The scene is mellow, multigenerational, and perfectly Welsh. It's a small town, and everyone is here enjoying the local cuisine—"chips," ice cream, and beer—and savoring that great British pastime: torturing little crabs. (If you want to do more than photograph the action, rent gear from the nearby life-boat house. Mooch some bacon from others for bait, and join in. It's catch-and-release.)

The Liverpool Arms pub was built by a captain who ran a ferry service to Liverpool in the 19th century. Today it remains a salty and characteristic hangout—one of the few thriving pubs in town. In 1900, Conwy had about 40 pubs. Back when this harbor was busy with quarrymen shipping their slate, mussel men carting their catch, and small farmers with their goods, Conwy's pubs were all thriving. Today, times are tough on the pubs, and this one depends on tourism.

• *Facing the harbor in front of The Liverpool Arms, turn left and walk along the promenade.*

It's easy to miss the **Smallest House in Great Britain.** It's red, 72 inches wide, 122 inches high, and worth £1 to pop in and listen to the short audioguide tour.

King Edward's Castles

In the 13th century, the Welsh, unified by two great princes named Llywelyn, created a united and independent Wales. The English king Edward I fought hard to end this Welsh sovereignty. In 1282, Llywelyn the Last was killed (and went to "where everyone speaks Welsh"). King Edward spent the next 20 years building or rebuilding 17 great castles to consolidate his English foothold in troublesome North Wales. The greatest

of these (such as Conwy Castle) were masterpieces of medieval engineering, with round towers (tough to undermine), castle-within-a-castle defenses (giving defenders a place to retreat and wreak havoc on the advancing enemy...or just wait for reinforcements), and sea access (safe to restock from England).

These castles were English islands in the middle of angry Wales. Most were built with a fortified grid-plan town attached and then filled with English settlers. (With this blatant abuse of Wales, you have to wonder, where was Greenpeace 700 years ago?) Edward I was arguably England's best monarch. By establishing and consolidating his realm (adding Wales to England), he made his kingdom big enough to compete with the other rising European powers.

Castle lovers will want to visit each of Edward's five greatest castles (see map on page 713). With a car and two days, this

No WC—but it did have a bedpan (April-Oct daily 10:00-16:00, closed Nov-March, mobile 07925/049-786).

• *Turn around and walk along the promenade toward the bridges and castle. On your right, you'll find a processing plant.*

Mussels, historically a big "crop" for Conwy, are processed "in the months with an R" at the **Conwy Mussel Museum.** In the other months, it's open to visitors (free, Easter-Aug generally daily 10:30-16:30, on the quay, tel. 01492/592-689).

The nearby **lifeboat house** also welcomes visitors. Each coastal town has a house like this one, outfitted with a rescue boat suited to the area—in the shallow waters around Conwy, inflatable boats work best. You'll see *Lifeboats* stickers around town, marking homes of people who donate to the valuable cause of the Royal National Lifeboat Institution (RNLI)—Britain's all-volunteer and totally donation-funded answer to the Coast Guard.

Check out the striking **sculpture** on the quay—a giant clump of mussels carved from dark-gray limestone. The benches are great for a picnic (two recommended fish-and-chips shops are back makes one of Europe's best castle tours (all the castles except for Criccieth—listed below—have the same opening hours: March-Oct daily 9:30-17:00, July-Aug until 18:00; Nov-Feb Mon-Sat 10:00-16:00, Sun 11:00-16:00; last entry 30 minutes before closing). I'd rate them in this order:

Conwy is attached to the cutest medieval town and has the best public transport (see page 681).

Caernarfon is the most entertaining and best presented (see page 703).

Harlech is the most dramatically situated, on a hilltop (£4.25, tel. 01766/780-552, TI open March-Oct, www.harlech .com).

Beaumaris, surrounded by a moat, is the last, largest, and most romantic (see page 701).

Criccieth (KRICK-ith), built in 1230 by Llywelyn and later renovated by Edward, is also dramatic and remote (£3.50, April-Oct daily 10:00-17:00, Nov-March Fri-Sat 9:30-16:00, Sun 11:00-16:00, closed Mon-Thu, tel. 01766/522-227).

Cadw, the Welsh version of England's National Trust, sells a three-day Explorer Pass that covers many sights in Wales. If you're planning to visit at least three of the above castles, the pass will probably save you money (3-day pass: £15.20 for 1 person, £23.50 for 2 people, £32 for a family; 7-day pass also available; buy at castle ticket desks). For photos and more information on the castles, as well as information on Welsh historic monuments in general, check www.cadw.wales.gov.uk.

through the gate) or a visit with the noisy gulls.

• *Walk past the sculpture and a giant red-and-white buoy, and head up the stairs to the big street for a view of the castle and bridges. You can cross the road for a closer look at the...*

❾ **Bridges:** Three bridges cross the river, side by side. Behind the modern 1958 highway bridge is the historic 1826 Telford Suspension Bridge. This was an engineering marvel in its day, part of a big infrastructure project to better connect Ireland with the rest of the realm (and, as a result, have more control over Ireland). In those days, Dublin was the number-two city in all of Britain. These two major landmarks—the castle and 19th-century bridge—are both symbols of English imperialism. Just beyond that is Robert Stephenson's tube bridge for the train line (built in 1848). These days, 90 percent of traffic passes Conwy underground, unseen and unheard, in a modern tunnel.

• *On the town side of the big road, follow the sidewalk away from the water, past the ivy and through an arch, to a tiny park around a well. Facing that square is...*

⑩ The Knight Shop: If you're in the market for a battleaxe or perhaps some chainmail, pop into The Knight Shop. Even if you're not, it's a fun place to browse. The manager, Toby, is evangelical about mead, an ancient drink made from honey. Most travelers just get the cheap stuff at tourist shops, but Toby offers free tastes so you can appreciate quality mead (daily 10:00-17:00, Castle Square, tel. 01492/596-142, www.theknightshop.co.uk).

• *Now, with a belly full of mead, set your bleary eyes on the...*

⑪ View of Conwy Castle: Imagine this when it was newly built. Its eight mighty drum towers were brightly whitewashed, a statement of power from the English king to the Welsh—who had no cities and little more than bows and arrows to fight with. The castle is built upon solid rock—making it impossible for invaders to tunnel underneath the walls. The English paid dearly for its construction, through heavy taxes. And today, with the Welsh flag proudly flying from its top, the English pay again just to visit. Notice the remains of the castle entry, which was within the town walls. There was once a steep set of stairs (designed so no horse could approach) up to the drawbridge. The castle is by far the town's top sight (described next).

Sights in Conwy

▲▲Conwy Castle

Dramatically situated on a rock overlooking the sea with eight line-backer towers, this castle has an interesting story to tell. Finished in just four years, it had a water gate that allowed safe entry for English boats in a land of hostile Welsh subjects. At the back, beyond the 91-foot-deep spring-fed well, is a tower containing the chapel (with reconstructed stained-glass windows) and the king's "watching chamber" (for observing chapel services by himself—complete with toilet). In one of the towers, you'll also find a scale model of the town as it might have looked around the year 1312.

Cost and Hours: £5.75, or £8 combo-ticket with Plas Mawr; guidebook-£4.50; March-Oct daily 9:30-17:00, July-Aug until 18:00; Nov-Feb Mon-Sat 10:00-16:00, Sun 11:00-16:00; last entry 30 minutes before closing, tel. 01492/592-358, www.cadw.wales .gov.uk.

▲City Walls

Most of the walls, with 22 towers and castle and harbor views, can be walked for free. Start at Upper Gate (the highest point) or Berry

Street (the lowest), or you can do the small section at the castle entrance. (My favorite stretch is described on my "Welcome to Conwy" walk, earlier.) In the evening, most of the walkways stay open, though the section located near the castle closes 30 minutes before the castle does.

▲Plas Mawr

A rare house from 1580, built during the reign of Elizabeth I, Plas Mawr was the first Welsh home to be built within Conwy's walls. (The Tudor family had Welsh roots—and therefore relations between Wales and England warmed.) Billed as "the oldest house in Wales," it offers a delightful look at 16th-century domestic life. Historically accurate household items bring the rooms to life, as does the refreshing lack of velvet ropes—you're free to wander as you imagine life in this house.

Cost and Hours: £5.75, or £8 combo-ticket with Conwy Castle, includes audioguide, April-Sept Tue-Sun 9:00-17:00, Oct Tue-Sun 9:30-16:00, closed Mon and Nov-March, last entry 45 minutes before closing, tel. 01492/580-167, www.cadw.wales .gov.uk.

Visiting the House: At the entry, pick up the included audioguide or an info sheet. Docents, who are posted in some rooms, are happy to answer your questions.

Guests stepping into the house in the 16th century were wowed by the heraldry over the fireplace. This symbol, now repainted in its original bright colors, proclaimed the family's rich lineage and princely stock. The kitchen came with all the circa-1600 conveniences: hay on the floor to add a little warmth and soak up spills; a hanging bread cage to keep food safe from wandering critters; and a good supply of fresh meat in the pantry (take a whiff). Inside the parlor, an interactive display lets you take a closer virtual look at the different parts of the house.

Upstairs, the lady of the house's bedroom doubled as a sitting room—with a finely carved four-poster bed and a foot warmer by the chair. At night, the bedroom's curtains were drawn to keep in warmth. In the great chamber next door, hearty evening feasting was followed by boisterous gaming, dancing, and music. And fixed above all of this extravagant entertainment was...more heraldry, pronouncing those important—if unproven—family connections and leaving a powerful impact on impressed guests. On the same floor is a well-done exhibit on health and hygiene in medieval Britain—you'll be grateful you were born a few centuries later.

St. Mary's Parish Church

Sitting lonely in the town center, Conwy's church was the centerpiece of a Cistercian abbey that stood here a century before the town or castle. The Cistercians were French monks who built their abbeys in places "far from the haunts of man." Popular here because they were French—that is, not English—the Cistercians taught locals farming and mussel-gathering techniques. Edward moved the monks 12 miles upstream but kept the church for his town. Find the tombstone of a survivor of the 1805 Battle of Trafalgar who died in 1860 (two feet left of the north transept). On the other side of the church, a tomb containing seven brothers and sisters is marked "We Are Seven." It inspired William Wordsworth to write his poem of the same name. The slate tombstones look new even though many are hundreds of years old; slate weathers better than marble.

Cost and Hours: Free, church generally open May-Sept Mon-Fri 10:00-12:00 & 14:00-16:00, closed Sat-Sun though you can try visiting before or after the Sunday services at 8:00 and 11:00; if the church isn't open, you may be able to obtain the key next door from the vicarage (generally available Mon-Fri 10:00-17:00); tel. 01492/593-402.

Near Conwy
Llandudno
This genteel Victorian beach resort, a few miles away, is bigger and better known than Conwy. It was built after the advent of railroads, which made the Welsh seacoast easily accessible to the English industrial heartland. In the 1800s, the notion that bathing in seawater was good for your health was trendy, and the bracing sea air was just what the doctor ordered. These days, Llandudno remains popular with the English, but you won't see many other foreigners strolling its long pier and line of old-time hotels.

Hill Climb
For lovely views across the bay to Llandudno, take a pleasant walk (40 minutes one-way) along the footpath up Conwy Mount (follow Sychnant Pass Road past the Bryn B&B, look for fields on the right and a sign with a stick figure of a walker).

Nightlife in Conwy

No one goes to Conwy for wild nightlife. But you will find some typically Welsh diversions here.

In Town: The **Conwy Folk Music Club** plays at the Royal British Legion Club off Church Street Mondays at 20:30 (free, doors open at 20:00, www.conwyfolkclub.org.uk).

To sample local brews, including some made in Conwy, head to the **Albion.** Managed by a coalition of four local breweries, the Albion has real ales and a fun communal pub atmosphere (Sun-Thu 12:00-23:00, Fri-Sat 12:00-24:00, Upper Gate Street, tel. 01492/582-484, www.conwybrewery.co.uk).

Near Conwy: For an authentic Welsh experience, catch a performance of the **local choir**. The Maelgwn men's choir from nearby Llandudno Junction rehearses weekly, and visitors are welcome to watch (free, Mon 19:30-21:00 except Aug, at Maelgwn School in Llandudno Junction, tel. 01248/681-159, www.maelgwn .co.uk).

Several churches in Llandudno hold regular **choir concerts** each summer featuring a rotation of visiting choirs. These include St. John's Church (£6, May-Oct Tue and Thu at 20:00, between the two Marks & Spencer stores at 53-55 Mostyn Street, tel. 01492/860-439, www.stjohnsllandudno.org) and Holy Trinity Church (£6, late May-Sept Sun at 20:00, corner of Mostyn Street and Trinity Square, www.llandudno-parish.org.uk). The Llanddulas Choir performs weekly concerts at Gloddaeth Church (£5, April-Sept most Tue at 20:00, corner of Chapel Street and Gloddaeth Street, www.llanddulaschoir.co.uk).

Llandudno also has the **beach fun** you'd expect at a Coney-Island-type coastal resort.

Sleeping in Conwy

(area code: 01492)

Conwy's hotels are overpriced, but its B&Bs include some good-value gems. Nearly all have free parking (ask when booking), and most are happy to accommodate dietary needs in their breakfast offers (the local butcher, who supplies many of these B&Bs, even makes gluten-free sausages). There's no launderette in town.

Sleep Code

(£1 = about $1.60, country code: 44)
S = Single, **D** = Double/Twin, **T** = Triple, **Q** = Quad, **b** = bathroom, **s** = shower only. Unless otherwise noted, credit cards are accepted and breakfast is included.

To help you sort easily through these listings, I've divided the accommodations into three categories based on the price for a standard double room with bath:

$$$ Higher Priced—Most rooms £80 or more.
$$ Moderately Priced—Most rooms between £55-80.
$ Lower Priced—Most rooms £55 or less.

Prices can change without notice; verify the hotel's current rates online or by email. For the best prices, always book direct.

Conwy Hotels & Restaurants

1. Castle Hotel & Dawson's Cuisine
2. Gwynfryn B&B
3. The Town House B&B
4. Castlebank Hotel
5. Bryn B&B
6. Llys Llewelyn B&B
7. To Conwy Hostel
8. To Glan Heulog Guest House
9. To Whinward House B&B
10. Watson's Bistro
11. Alfredo Restaurant
12. Conwy Pantry
13. Anna's Tea Rooms & Conwy Outdoor Shop
14. The Galleon Fish & Chips
15. Fisherman's Fish & Chips
16. Archway Fish & Chips
17. Spar Grocery
18. The Liverpool Arms Pub
19. The Albion Pub
20. Library (Internet)
21. The Knight Shop
22. Royal British Legion (Concerts)
23. Bus to Caernarfon
24. Bus to Betws & Llandudno

P PARKING

⟋ VIEW

Inside Conwy's Walled Old Town

$$$ Castle Hotel, along the main drag, rents 28 elegant rooms where Old World antique furnishings mingle with modern amenities. Peter and Bobbi Lavin, along with sons Joe and Gareth, are eager to make your stay comfortable (Sb-£85-95, Db-£140-180, rates vary depending on room size and day of the week, prices lower in off-season—check website, 10 percent discount if you show this book at check-in, free Wi-Fi, High Street, tel. 01492/582-800, www.castlewales.co.uk, mail@castlewales.co.uk). The hotel has a recommended restaurant and a bar.

$$ Gwynfryn B&B rents five bright, airy rooms, each with eclectic decor, a DVD player, and access to a DVD library. The location is dead center in Conwy. It has a plush lounge, and out back there's a small patio for pleasant breakfasts in good weather (D with private bath across the hall-£65-75, standard Db-£65-75, king-size Db-£75-85, price depends on season, £5 extra for 1-night stays, no children under 12, fridges in rooms, free guest computer, free Wi-Fi, self-catering cottage for 4 also available, 4 York Place, on the lane off Lancaster Square, tel. 01492/576-733, mobile 07947-272-821, www.gwynfrynbandb.co.uk, info@gwynfrynbandb.co.uk, energetic Monica and Colin). This B&B recently expanded into the adjacent former chapel; additional accommodations and a café should be open in 2014.

$$ The Town House B&B is a colorful place renting five tidy, bright, updated rooms near train and bus stops, with the old city walls just across the street (S-£45, D-£65, Db-£70-75, Tb-£95, £5 extra for 1-night stays, no children under 12, free Wi-Fi, DVD library, free parking, 18 Rosehill Street, tel. 01492/596-454, mobile 07974-650-609, www.thetownhousebb.co.uk, thetownhouse@hotmail.co.uk, Julie and Mark Poole).

Just Outside the Wall

The first three options are a two-minute walk from Conwy's old town wall; the hostel is about 10 minutes beyond.

$$$ Castlebank Hotel is a cozy hotel with nine spacious rooms, a small bar, and an inviting lounge with a wood-burning fireplace that makes the Welsh winter warmer. Owners Jo and Henrique have done a heroic job of rehabilitating a formerly dumpy hotel into a dolled-up and comfortable home-away-from-home (S with private bath down the hall-£40, Sb-£55-85, Db-£75-95, Tb-£95, price depends on season, 10 percent discount with this book for 2 or more nights—except on Bank Holiday and festival weekends, check website for deals, dinner available Fri-Sat by reservation, family rooms, free guest computer, free Wi-Fi, DVD library, easy parking, closed first 3 weeks in Jan, just outside town wall at Mount Pleasant, tel. 01492/593-888, www.castlebankhotel.co.uk, bookings@castlebankhotel.co.uk).

$$ Bryn B&B offers four large, clutter-free rooms (and one small one) with castle or mountain views in a big 19th-century house with the city wall literally in the backyard. Owner Alison Archard runs the place with style and energy, providing all the thoughtful touches—a library of regional guides and maps; a glorious garden; fresh, organic food for breakfast; and a very warm welcome (small Sb-£45, Sb-£55-60, Db-£75-80, Tb-£95-100, £5 extra for 1-night stays, ground-floor room available, free Wi-Fi, private parking in back, B&B located on the right just outside upper gate of wall on Sychnant Pass Road, tel. 01492/592-449, www.bryn.org.uk, stay@bryn.org.uk).

$ Llys Llewelyn B&B has five basic budget rooms in need of a little TLC. But the great prices—along with the humor and pleasant nature of Alan Hughes, who's in his 70s and still a top-notch ski coach—make this a fine value (Sb-£35, top-floor D-£40, Db-£50, 10 percent discount with this book, includes continental breakfast, free Wi-Fi, cash only, easy parking, Mount Pleasant, tel. 01492/593-257, www.llewelynbandb.co.uk, llewelynbandb@yahoo.co.uk).

$ Conwy Hostel, welcoming travelers of any age, has super views from all 24 of its rooms and a spacious garden. Rooms are equipped with bunk beds, sleep two to four people, and have a full bathroom. The airy dining hall and glorious rooftop lounge and deck make you feel like you're in the majestic midst of Wales (beds in 4-bed rooms-£16-24/person, Db-£35-38, Qb family room-£55-58, price depends on season, members pay £3 less, breakfast-£5, pay guest computer, pay Wi-Fi, laundry, lockers, sack lunches, dinners, bar, elevator, parking, no lock-out times but office closed 10:30-14:00, check-in at 15:00, Sychnant Pass Road in Larkhill, tel. 01492/593-571, www.yha.org.uk, conwy@yha.org.uk). It's a 10-minute uphill walk from the upper gate of Conwy's wall.

Beyond the Old Town

$$ Glan Heulog Guest House offers six fresh, bright rooms and a pleasant, enclosed sun porch (Sb-£40-45, standard Db-£60-65, superior Db-£68-73, Tb-£85-90, free Wi-Fi, will pick up from train station, a 10-minute walk from town on Llanrwst Road on the way to Betws-y-Coed, tel. 01492/593-845, www.conwy-bedand breakfast.co.uk, glanheulog@no1guesthouse.freeserve.co.uk, Richard and Jenny Nash).

$$ Whinward House, a half-mile west of Conwy's town walls, works well for drivers. Because their three rooms lack any B&B formality—and because Chris and Janis quickly make you feel at home—staying here feels like sleeping in the spare room of old friends. Guests are encouraged to relax in the sunlit living room and the large garden. Hiking trails, two pubs, a marina, and a golf course are all within a short walk (Sb-£70, Db-£80, free Wi-Fi, laundry service available, DVD library, will pick up from train station, Whinacres, tel. 01492/573-275, www.whinwardhouse.co.uk, whinwardhouse@aol.com). From the north gate in Conwy's town wall, head straight out along Bangor Road; after a minute's drive, turn right just before an overhead railroad bridge. Turn immediately right again onto Whinacres. It's up about 200 yards on the left.

Eating in Conwy

All of these places are inside Conwy's walled old town. For dinner, consider strolling down High Street, comparing the cute teahouses and workaday eateries. Most pubs serve food, but none in town is currently worth recommending for a meal.

Watson's Bistro, tucked away on Chapel Street, serves freshly prepared modern and traditional Welsh cuisine in a warm wood-floor-and-exposed-beam setting. Dishes on the inventive menu are made from locally sourced ingredients and well worth the splurge (£9-13 lunches, £16-20 dinners; Easter-Sept lunch served Tue-Sun

12:00-14:00, closed for lunch on Mon, dinner served daily 17:30-20:00, later Fri-Sat; off-season closed Mon all day and Tue lunch; reservations smart, tel. 01492/596-326, www.watsonsbistroconwy .co.uk).

Dawson's Cuisine, in the recommended Castle Hotel, is a hit with locals. The hotel bar has the same menu with a cozier and less formal ambience (£14-19 main courses, food served daily in the bar 12:00-21:30, restaurant open for lunch Sat-Sun 12:00-15:30 and daily for dinner 18:30-21:30, reservations smart for both bar and restaurant—especially on weekends, High Street, tel. 01492/582-800, www.castlewales.co.uk/dawsons-restaurant.aspx).

Alfredo Restaurant, a thriving and family-friendly place right on Lancaster Square, serves solid, reasonably priced Italian food (£8-10 pizzas and pastas, £15-20 main courses, daily 18:00-22:00, Sun until 21:30, reservations recommended on weekends, York Place, tel. 01492/592-381, Christine).

Conwy Pantry dishes up cheap, hearty daily specials, salads, and homemade sweets in a cheery setting (£4-7 lunches, daily 9:00-17:00, until 16:30 in winter, 26 High Street, tel. 01492/596-445).

Anna's Tea Rooms, a frilly, doily, very feminine-feeling eatery located upstairs in the masculine-feeling Conwy Outdoor Shop, is popular with locals (£5-8 lunches, daily 10:00-17:00, 9 Castle Street, tel. 01492/580-908).

Fish-and-Chips: At the bottom of High Street, on the intersecting Castle Street, are two chippies—**The Galleon** (mid-March-Oct Mon-Fri 12:00-15:00, Sat-Sun 12:00-19:00; mid-July-mid-Sept daily until 19:00, closed Nov-mid-March, mobile 07899-901-637) and **Fisherman's** (daily May-Nov 11:30-20:00, July-Aug until 21:00, Dec-April 11:30-14:30, Fri-Sun until 19:00, tel. 01492/593-792). **Archway Fish & Chips,** at the top of town just inside Bangor Gate, is open later and has both a restaurant and a to-go operation (take-out open daily 11:30-22:00, restaurant open daily 11:30-20:30, 10-14 Bangor Road, tel. 01492/592-458). Consider taking your fish-and-chips down to the harbor and sharing it with the noisy seagulls.

Picnics: The **Spar** grocery is conveniently located and well-stocked (daily 7:00-22:00, middle of High Street). Several other shops on High Street—including the bakery and the butcher nearby—sell meat pies and other microwaveables that can quickly flesh out a sparse picnic.

Conwy Connections

If you want to leave Conwy by train, be sure the schedule indicates the train can stop there, and then wave as it approaches; for more frequent trains, go to Llandudno Junction (see "Arrival in Conwy,"

earlier). For train info, call 0871-200-2233, or see www.traveline
-cymru.info. If hopping around by bus, simply buy the £6.40 Red
Rover Ticket from the driver, and you're covered for the entire day
on all Arriva buses. Remember, all connections are less frequent
on Sundays.

From Conwy by Bus to: Llandudno Junction (4/hour, 5
minutes), **Caernarfon** (2-4/hour, some may require transfer,
1.25 hours), **Betws-y-Coed** (hourly, 45 minutes, fewer on Sun),
Blaenau Ffestiniog (8/day, none on Sun, 1.25 hours, transfer in
Llandudno Junction to bus #X1, also stops in Betws-y-Coed; train
is better—see below), **Beddgelert** (7/day Mon-Sat, 2/day on Sun,
1.75 hours total, transfer in Caernarfon).

From Conwy by Train to: Llandudno Junction (nearly
hourly, 5 minutes), **Chester** (nearly hourly, 1 hour), **Holyhead**
(nearly hourly, 1 hour), **Llangollen** (hourly, 2 hours; take train to
Ruabon, then change to bus), **London's Euston Station** (nearly
hourly, 3.5 hours, transfer in Chester).

From Llandudno Junction by Train to the Conwy Valley:
Take the train to Llandudno Junction, where you'll board the
scenic little Conwy Valley line, which runs up the pretty Conwy
Valley to **Betws-y-Coed** and **Blaenau Ffestiniog** (5/day Mon-Sat,
3/day on Sun in summer, no Sun trains in winter, 30 minutes to
Betws-y-Coed, 1 hour to Blaenau Ffestiniog, www.conwy.gov.uk
/cvr). If your train from Conwy to Llandudno Junction is late and
you miss the Conwy Valley connection, tell a station employee at
Llandudno Junction, who can arrange a taxi for you. Your taxi is
free, as long as the missed connection is the Conwy train's fault
and the next train doesn't leave for more than an hour (common on
the infrequent Conwy Valley line).

From Llandudno Junction by Train to: Chester (2-3/
hour, 1 hour), **Birmingham** (1-2/hour, 2.5-3 hours, 1-2 transfers),
London's Euston Station (4/day direct, 3 hours, many more with
changes in Chester and/or Crewe).

Between Conwy and Snowdonia

These two attractions are south of Conwy, on the route to Betws-
y-Coed and Snowdonia National Park. Note that Bodnant Garden
is on the east side of the River Conwy, on the A-470, and Trefriw
is on the west side, along the B-5106. To see them both, you'll
drive about 20 minutes and cross the river at Tal-y-Cafn.

▲Bodnant Garden

This sumptuous 80-acre display of floral color six miles south of
Conwy is one of Britain's best gardens. Originally the private garden of the stately Bodnant Hall, this lush landscape was donated

by the Aberconway family (who still live in the house) to the National Trust in 1949. The map you receive upon entering suggests a handy walking route. The highlight for many is the famous Laburnum Arch—a 180-foot-long canopy made of bright-yellow laburnum, hanging like stalactites over the heads of garden lovers who stroll beneath it (just inside the entry, blooms late May through early June). The garden is also famous for its mag-

nolias, rhododendrons, camellias, and roses—and for the way that the buildings of the estate complement the carefully planned landscaping. The wild English-style plots seem to spar playfully with the more formal, Italian-style gardens. Consider your visit an extravagantly beautiful nature hike, and walk all the way to the old mill and waterfall.

Cost and Hours: £8.45, March-Oct daily 10:00-17:00, possibly open later on some summer days, tickets are cheaper and hours are shorter off-season, last entry 30 minutes before closing, café, WCs in parking lot and inside garden, best in spring, check online to see what's blooming and a schedule of guided walks, tel. 01492/650-460, www.nationaltrust.org.uk/bodnant-garden.

Getting There: To reach the garden by public transportation from Conwy, first head to the Llandudno Junction train station, then catch bus #25 (hourly Mon-Sat; on Sun, take bus #84—just 2/day) toward Eglwysbach, which takes you right to the garden in about 20 minutes.

Nearby: About 1.5 miles south of Bodnant Garden off A-470, the **Bodnant Welsh Food Centre** is a fun stop for foodies with a farm shop mostly selling food produced in Wales, a restaurant, a tearoom, and a cooking school (tel. 01492/651-100, www.bodnant -welshfood.co.uk). It's also the home of the National Beekeeping Centre, which features an interesting exhibit on bees and honey production and offers paid tours of its beehives in nice weather (tel. 01492/651-106, http://beeswales.co.uk).

Trefriw Woolen Mills

At Trefriw (TREV-roo), five miles north of Betws-y-Coed, you can peek into a working woolen mill. It's surprisingly interesting and rated ▲ if the machines are running (weekdays Easter-Oct).

This mill buys wool from local farmers and turns it into scarves, sweaters, bedspreads, caps, and more. You can peruse the finished products in the **shop** (daily April-Oct 9:30-17:30, Nov-March Mon-Sat 10:00-17:00, closed Sun). The whole complex creates its own hydroelectric power; the **"turbine house"** in the cellar lets you take a peek at the enormous, fiercely spinning turbines, dating from the 1930s and 1940s, powered by streams that flow down the hillside above the mill (same hours as shop). The **weaving looms,** with bobbin-loaded shuttles flying to and fro, allow you to watch a bedspread being created before your eyes (mid-Feb-mid-Dec Mon-Fri 10:00-13:00 & 14:00-17:00).

The highlight is the **mill museum,** which follows the 11 stages of wool transformation: blending, carding, spinning, doubling, hanking, spanking, warping, weaving, and so on. Follow a matted glob of fleece on its journey to becoming a fashionable cap or scarf. It's impressive that this Rube Goldberg-type process was so ingeniously designed and coordinated in an age before computers (mostly the 1950s and 1960s)—each machine seems to "know" how to do its rattling, clattering duty with amazing precision (some but not all machines are likely running at any one time; Easter-Oct Mon-Fri 10:00-13:00 & 14:00-17:00, closed Sat-Sun, closed Nov-Easter because they don't heat it in winter). In the summer, the **hand-spinning house** (next to the WC) has a charming spinster and yarn and knitted goods for sale (June-Sept only, Tue-Thu 10:00-17:00, closed Fri-Mon).

The grade school next door is busy with rambunctious Welsh-speaking kids—fun to listen to at recess.

Cost and Hours: Free, variable hours for the different parts of the mill (see above); tel. 01492/640-462, www.t-w-m.co.uk.

Getting There: Bus #19 goes from Conwy and Llandudno Junction right to Trefriw (hourly Mon-Sat, fewer on Sun, 30 minutes).

Between Conwy and Caernarfon: Beaumaris

Charming little Beaumaris is on the Isle of Anglesey ("Ynys Môn" in Welsh), about a 40-minute drive from Conwy, and a short detour from the route to Caernarfon. (The otherwise sleepy island has been in the news since Prince William and Kate moved to the Royal Air Force base here for his job as a search-and-rescue helicopter pilot.) The town of Beaumaris originated, like other castle towns, as an English "green zone" in the 13th century surrounded by Welsh guerrillas. Today, it feels workaday Welsh, with a fine harborfront, lots of colorful shops and eateries, a fascinating

Victorian prison (now a museum), and the remains of an idyllic castle. Around the castle are putt-putt-type amusements for the family and a moat.

Beaumaris has no official tourist information center, but you may find volunteers staffing a small tourist-info kiosk on the main street. The island's official **TI** is in the town of Llanfairpwll, where the modern A-55 bridge crosses the strait. This is just a nickname; the town's real name is (no kidding) Llanfairpwllgwyngyllgogery-chwyrndrobwllllantysiliogogogoch—the second-longest place name in the world. Town signs make for good photo ops...if you have a wide-angle lens (TI open Mon-Sat 9:30-17:00, July-Aug until 17:30, Sun 9:30-16:30, Holyhead Road, tel. 01248/713-177, www.visitanglesey.co.uk).

Getting There: If driving, simply follow signs toward *Holyhead*, and immediately after crossing the big bridge onto the island, take the small coastal A-545 highway for 10 minutes into Beaumaris.

Sights in Beaumaris

Beaumaris Gaol

The jail opened in 1829 as a result of new laws designed to give prisoners more humane treatment; it remained in use until 1878. Under this "modern" ethic, inmates had their own cells, women prisoners were kept separate and attended by female guards, and prisoners worked to pay for their keep rather than suffer from jailers bilking their families for favors. This new standard of incarceration is the subject of this fascinating museum, where you'll see the prisoners' quarters, work yard, punishment cells, whipping rack, treadmill, and chapel.

Cost and Hours: £4.60, includes audioguide, Easter-Sept Sat-Thu 10:30-17:00, closed Fri, weekends only in Oct, closed most days in off-season, last entry one hour before closing; it's on Bunkers Hill—coming down the main street from the castle, go right on Steeple Lane then left on Bunkers Hill; tel. 01248/810-921.

▲Beaumaris Castle

Begun in 1295, Beaumaris was the last link in King Edward's "Iron Chain" of castles to enclose Gwynedd, the rebellious former kingdom of North Wales. The site has no natural geological constraints like those that encumbered the castle designers at Caernarfon and Conwy, so its wall-within-a-wall design is almost perfectly concentric. The result is one of Britain's most beautiful castles. While Beaumaris shows medieval castle engineering at its best—four rings of defense, a moat, and a fortified dock—problems in Scotland changed the king's priorities. Construction stopped in 1330, and the castle was never finished. It looks ruined (and rather squat), but it was never ransacked or destroyed—it's simply unfinished. The site was overgrown until the last century yet today it's like a park. Look for information boards explaining the architect's vision and an exhibit on the history of the castle.

Cost and Hours: £4.50; March-Oct daily 9:30-17:00, July-Aug until 18:00; Nov-Feb Mon-Sat 10:00-16:00, Sun 11:00-16:00; last entry 30 minutes before closing, tel. 01248/810-361, www.beaumaris.com.

Near Beaumaris
Menai Suspension Bridge
The Isle of Anglesey is connected to the mainland by one of the engineering marvels of its day, the Menai Suspension Bridge. Designed by Thomas Telford and finished in 1826, at 580 feet it was the longest bridge of its day. It was built to be 100 feet above sea level at high tide—high enough to let Royal Navy ships sail beneath. With the Act of Union of 1800, London needed to be better connected to Dublin. And, as the economy of the island of Anglesey was mainly cattle farming (cows had to literally swim the Straits of Menai to get to market), there was a local need for this bridge. When it opened, the bridge cut the travel time from London to Holyhead from 36 to 27 hours. Most drivers today take the modern A-55 highway bridge, but the historic bridge still handles local traffic.

Caernarfon

The small, lively little town of Caernarfon (kah-NAR-von) is famous for its striking castle—the place where the Prince of Wales is "invested" (given his title). Like Conwy, it has an Edward I gar-

rison town marching out from the castle; it still follows the original, medieval grid plan laid within its well-preserved ramparts.

Caernarfon is mostly a 19th-century town. At that time, the most important thing in town wasn't the castle but the area that

NORTH WALES

Conwy or Caernarfon?

Trying to decide between these two walled towns and their castles?

The town of Conwy is more quaint, with a higgledy-piggledy medieval vibe and a modern, workaday heart and soul—both of which feel diluted in busier, although more Welsh-feeling, Caernarfon. Conwy also has more accommodations and good eateries than Caernarfon. All this makes Conwy the better home base, which also means its castle is more convenient to see. Conwy's castle is a bit more ruined and less slickly presented than Caernarfon's—with fewer fancy exhibits—but some think that makes it more evocative. While Caernarfon's castle is the most famous in Wales, I find Conwy's to be more exciting.

sprawls below the castle (now a parking lot). This was once a booming slate port, shipping tidy bundles of slate from North Wales mining towns to roofs all over Europe.

The statue of local boy David Lloyd George looks over the town square. A member of Parliament from 1890 to 1945, he was the most important politician Wales ever sent to London, and ultimately became Britain's prime minister during the last years of World War I. Young Lloyd George began his career as a noisy nonconformist Liberal advocating Welsh rights. He ended up an eloquent spokesperson for the nation of Great Britain, convincing his slate-mining constituents that only as part of the Union would their industry boom.

Caernarfon bustles with shops, cafés, and people. Market-day activities fill its main square on Saturdays year-round; a smaller, sleepier market yawns on Monday from late May to September. The charming town is worth a wander.

Orientation to Caernarfon

The small, walled old town of Caernarfon spreads out from its waterfront castle, its outer flanks fringed with modern sprawl (pop. 10,000). The main square, called Castle Square ("Y Maes" in Welsh), is fronted by the castle (with the TI across from its entry on Castle Street) and a post office. Public WCs are off the main square, on the road down to the riverfront and parking lot, where you'll find a bike-rental shop.

Tourist Information

The TI, facing the castle entrance, has a wonderful, free town map/guide (with a good self-guided town walk) and train and bus schedules. The staff dispenses tips about all the North Wales attractions, sells hiking books and maps, and books rooms here and elsewhere for a £2 fee (April-Oct daily 9:30-16:30; Nov-March Mon-Sat 10:00-15:30, closed Sun; tel. 01286/672-232, www.visit snowdonia.info).

Arrival in Caernarfon

If you arrive by **bus**, walk straight ahead up to the corner at Bridge Street, turn left, and walk two short blocks until you hit the main square and the castle. **Drivers** can park in the lot along the riverfront quay below the castle (£4/day) or follow signs as you enter town to a covered garage. The big lot under the Morrisons Supermarket (near Victoria Dock) has free parking.

Helpful Hints

Internet Access: Get wired at the public **library** (£1/30 minutes for terminals, free Wi-Fi, Mon-Tue and Thu-Fri 9:30-19:00, Wed and Sat 9:30-13:00, closed Sun, just around the corner from Bridge Street—between the castle and the recommended Celtic Royal Hotel, tel. 01286/679-463, www.gwynedd.gov.uk/library).

Laundry: **Pete's Launderette** hides at the end of Skinner Street, a narrow lane branching off the main square (same-day full-service-£7-8/load, Mon-Thu 9:00-18:00, Fri-Sat 9:00-17:30, Sun 11:00-16:00, tel. 01286/678-395, Pete and Monica).

Bike Rental: **Beics Menai Cycles** rents good bikes on the riverfront, near the start of a handy bike path (£15/2 hours, £17/4 hours, £19/6 hours, £22/8 hours; includes helmet, lock, and map of suggested routes; daily 9:00-17:00, closed off-season Sun-Mon, 1 Slate Quay—across the parking lot from the lot's payment booth, tel. 01286/676-804, mobile 07770-951-007). One of their suggested routes is 12 miles down an old train track—now a bike path—through five villages to Bryncir and back (figure 4 hours for the 24-mile round-trip).

Harbor Cruise: Narrated cruises on the **Queen of the Sea** run daily in summer (£6; May-Oct 11:00 or 12:00 until 17:00 or 18:00—depending on weather, tides, and demand; 40 minutes, castle views, tel. 01286/672-772, mobile 07979-593-483, www.menaicruises.co.uk).

Welsh Choir: If you're spending a Tuesday night here, drop by the weekly practice of the local men's choir (Tue at 19:45 in Galeri Creative Enterprise Centre at Victoria Dock, no practice in Aug, arrive by 19:30 in summer since practices can be crowded, just outside the old town walls, tel. 01286/677-404, www.cormeibioncaernarfon.org/eng; best to call ahead or complete web form if you want to attend).

Caernarfon

1 Celtic Royal Hotel
2 Caer Menai B&B
3 Victoria House B&B
4 Totters Hostel
5 Hole-in-the-Wall Street Eateries
6 Palace Street Eateries
7 J&C's Fish & Chips
8 Spar Supermarket
9 Iceland Supermarket
10 Morrisons Supermarket
11 The Anglesey Arms
12 Library (Internet)
13 Launderette
14 Bike Rental
15 Na-Nog Shop
16 Harbor Cruises
17 Bus Stop to/from Conwy

VICTORIA DOCK

GALERI

BANK QUAY

NORTH.

THE PROMENADE

CHURCH

HIGH ST.

MARKET

PALACE

MENAI STRAIT

SHIREHALL

CASTLE

CASTLE DITCH

CASTLE

RAMPARTS

ABER BRIDGE

P PARKING

100 YARDS

100 METERS

SEIONT RIVER

DCH

A Taste of Wales: For a store selling all things Welsh—books, movies, music, and more—check out **Na-Nog** on the main square (Mon-Sat 9:00-17:00, closed Sun, 16 Castle Square, tel. 01286/676-946).

Crabs on the Quay: As is the case in neighboring harbor towns, a popular family activity is capturing, toying with, then releasing little crabs (under the castle, along the harbor).

Sights in Caernarfon

▲▲Caernarfon Castle

Edward I built this impressive castle 700 years ago to establish English rule over North Wales. Rather than being purely defensive, it also had elements of a palace—where Edward and his family could stay on visits to Wales. Modeled after the striped, angular walls of ancient Constantinople, the castle, though impressive, was never finished and never really used. From the inner courtyard, you can see the notched walls ready for more walls—which were never built.

The castle's fame derives from its physical grandeur and its association with the Prince of Wales. Edward got the angry Welsh to agree that if he presented them with "a prince, born in Wales, who spoke not a word of English," they would submit to the Crown. In time, Edward had a son born in Wales (here in Caernarfon), who spoke not a word of English, Welsh, or any other language—as an infant. In modern times, as another political maneuver, the Prince of Wales has been "invested" (given his title) here. This "tradition" actually dates only from the 20th century, and only two of the 21 Princes of Wales (Prince Charles, the current prince, and King Edward VIII) have taken part.

Cost and Hours: £6; March-Oct daily 9:30-17:00, July-Aug until 18:00; Nov-Feb Mon-Sat 10:00-16:00, Sun 11:00-16:00; last entry 30 minutes before closing, tel. 01286/677-617, www.cadw.wales.gov.uk.

Tours: To bring the stones to life, catch the £3 **guided tour** (50-minute tours leave on the hour—and occasionally, with demand, on the half-hour—from the courtyard steps just beyond the ticket booth; if you're late, ask to join one in progress). Local guide **Martin de Lewandowicz** gives mind-bending tours of the castle (tel. 01286/674-369).

Visiting the Castle: Despite its unfinished state, the castle is fun to climb around. In the huge **Eagle Tower** (to the far right as you enter), see the ground-floor "Prospect of Caernarfon" history exhibit (look for the model of the original castle); watch the

23-minute movie (*The Eagle and the Dragon,* a broad mix of Welsh legend and history enthusiastically enacted by an elfin narrator, shown upstairs on the hour and half-hour); and climb the tower for a great view.

The **Chamberlain's Tower** and **Queen's Tower** (ahead and to the right as you enter the castle) house the mildly interesting Museum of the Royal Welsh Fusiliers—a military branch made up entirely of Welshmen. The museum shows off medals, firearms, uniforms, and information about various British battles and military strategies. The **Northeast Tower,** at the opposite end of the castle (to the left as you enter), has a "Princes of Wales" exhibit highlighting the investiture of Prince Charles in 1969.

Near Caernarfon
Narrow-Gauge Steam Train
The Welsh Highland Railway steam train billows scenically through the countryside south from Caernarfon along the original line that served a slate quarry, crossing the flanks of Mount Snowdon en route. The trip to Beddgelert makes a fine joyride; to save time, ride the train one-way, look around, and catch bus #S4 back to Caernarfon. But steam-train enthusiasts will want to ride all the way to Porthmadog and can even loop from there back up to Conwy with a ride on the Ffestiniog Railway steam train from Porthmadog to Blaenau Ffestiniog and then the Conwy Valley line from Blaenau Ffestiniog to Conwy—check schedules online (Caernarfon to Beddgelert—£17.40 one-way, £26 round-trip, 1.5 hours; Caernarfon to Porthmadog—£22.70 one-way, £34 round-trip, 2.5 hours; trains run 2-3 times per day on most days late March-Oct, tel. 01766/516-000, www.festrail.co.uk).

Segontium Roman Fort
Dating from A.D. 77, this ruin is the westernmost Roman fort in Britain. It was manned for more than 300 years to keep the Welsh and the coast quiet. Little is left but foundations (the stone was plundered to help build Edward I's castle at Caernarfon), and any artifacts that are found end up in Cardiff.

Cost and Hours: Free, gate generally unlocked daily 12:30-16:30, 20-minute walk from town, atop a hill on A-4085, drivers follow signs to Beddgelert, www.cadw.wales.gov.uk.

Horseback Riding
To ride a pony or horse, try **Snowdonia Riding Stables** (£20/hour, £45/half-day mountain ride, must book in advance, 3 miles from Caernarfon, off the road to Beddgelert, bus #S4 from Caernarfon, tel. 01286/650-342, www.snowdoniaridingstables.co.uk, info@snowdoniaridingstables.co.uk).

Sleeping in Caernarfon

(area code: 01286)

My listings favor traditional hotels and B&Bs, but if you're looking for a big hotel with cheap rooms, consider Caernarfon's branches of Premier Inn (www.premierinn.com) and Travelodge (www.travelodge.co.uk).

$$$ Celtic Royal Hotel rents 110 large, comfortable rooms and includes a restaurant, gym, pool, hot tub, and sauna; some top-floor rooms have castle views. Its grand, old-fashioned look comes with modern-day conveniences—but it's still overpriced (Sb-£86, Db-£120, extra bed-£20, discounts for 2 or more nights, free Wi-Fi, bar, restaurant, on Bangor Street, tel. 01286/674-477, www.celtic-royal.co.uk, reservations@celtic-royal.co.uk).

$$ Caer Menai B&B ("Fort of the Menai Strait") rents seven classy rooms one block from the harbor (Sb-£30-45, Db-£50-68, family room-£78-85, ask for seaview room, free guest computer, free Wi-Fi, 15 Church Street, tel. 01286/672-612, www.caermenai.co.uk, info@caermenai.co.uk, Karen and Mark). Church Street is two blocks from the castle and the TI; with your back to the TI, turn right at the nearest corner and walk down Shirehall Street, which becomes Church Street after one block.

$$ Victoria House B&B, next door to the Caer Menai, rents four airy, fresh, large-for-Britain rooms with nice natural-stone bathrooms. Generous breakfasts are served in a pleasant, woody room, and the lounge has a fridge stocked with free soft drinks. Stairs from the courtyard lead to the top of the castle wall for a fine view (Db-£75-85, £5 discount for 2 or more nights, free guest laptop, free Wi-Fi, 13 Church Street, tel. 01286/678-263, mobile 07748-098-928, www.thevictoriahouse.co.uk, jan@thevictoriahouse.co.uk, friendly Jan Baker). For directions, see previous listing.

$ Totters Hostel is a creative little hostel well-run by Bob and Henryette (28 beds in 5 dorm rooms, £17/bed with sheets, includes continental breakfast, cash only, couples can have their own twin room when available-£40, beautiful and large top-floor Db-£48, open all day, lockers, welcoming cellar game room, inviting living room, DVD library, kitchen, a block from castle and sea at 2 High Street, tel. 01286/672-963, www.totters.co.uk, totters.hostel@googlemail.com). They also own a three-bedroom house across the street (£100/4 people, £120/6 people—perfect for families, 2-night minimum).

Eating in Caernarfon

The streets near Caernarfon's castle teem with inviting eateries. Rather than recommending a particular one, I'll point you in the direction of several good streets with reasonable options.

"**Hole-in-the-Wall Street**" (between Castle Square and TI) is lined with several charming cafés and bistros. Nearby, on **Palace Street,** you'll find plenty of casual eateries. The pedestrianized but grubby **Pool Street** offers several budget options, including the popular **J&C's** fish-and-chips joint. In nice weather, several places on the **main square** have outside tables from which you can watch the people scene while munching your toasted sandwich.

Picnic: For groceries, you'll find a small **Spar** supermarket on the main square, an **Iceland** supermarket near the bus stop, and a huge **Morrisons** supermarket a five-minute walk from the city center on Bangor Street.

Pub Grub and Fun: **The Anglesey Arms** is a rough, old, characteristic pub serving basic lunches; it has picnic benches on the harborfront. The place is lively in the evening with darts, pool, and well-lubricated locals, hosting live folk on some Fridays from about 21:00 (Harbour Front, tel. 01286/672-158).

Caernarfon Connections

Caernarfon is a handy hub for buses into Snowdonia National Park (such as to Llanberis, Beddgelert, and Betws-y-Coed). Bus info: tel. 0871-200-2233, www.gwynedd.gov.uk/bwsgwynedd. And the narrow-gauge steam train provides both sightseeing and transport from Caernarfon to **Beddgelert** (described earlier).

From Caernarfon by Bus to: Conwy (2-4/hour, some may require transfer, 1.25 hours), **Llanberis** (2/hour, 20 minutes, bus #88), **Beddgelert** (7/day Mon-Sat, 2/day on Sun, 30 minutes, bus #S4), **Betws-y-Coed** (hourly, 1-1.5 hours, 1 transfer), **Blaenau Ffestiniog** (hourly, 1.5 hours, change in Porthmadog).

Snowdonia National Park

This is Britain's second-largest national park, and its centerpiece—the tallest mountain in Wales or England—is Mount Snowdon (www.eryri-npa.gov.uk). Each year, half a million people ascend one of seven different paths to the top of the 3,560-foot mountain. Hikes take from five to seven hours; if you're fit and the weather's good, it's an exciting day. Trail info abounds (local TIs sell maps and guidebooks, including the small £3 book *The Ascent of Snowdon,* by E. G. Bowland, which describes the routes). As you explore, notice the slate roofs—the local specialty.

Betws-y-Coed

The resort center of Snowdonia National Park, Betws-y-Coed (BET-oos-uh-coyd), bursts with tour buses and souvenir shops.

 This picturesque town is cuddled by wooded hills, made cozy by generous trees, and situated along a striking, waterfall-rippled stretch of the River Conwy. It verges on feeling overly manicured, with uniform checkerboard-stone houses yawning at each other from across a broad central green. There's little to do here except wander along the waterfalls (don't miss the old stone bridge—just up the river from the green—with the best waterfall views), have a snack or meal, and go for a walk in the woods.

Stop by Betws-y-Coed's good **National Park Centre/TI,** which books rooms for a £2 fee and sells the handy £3 *Forest Walks* map, outlining five different hikes you can do from here. They show a free 13-minute video with bird's-eye views of the park (daily Easter-Oct 9:30-17:00, Nov-Easter 9:30-12:30 & 13:30-16:30, tel. 01690/710-426, www.snowdonia-npa.gov.uk). If you have an iPhone, you can download a free audioguide tour of the park from their website (with maps and navigational aids). In summer, you might be able to catch some live entertainment in the TI's courtyard.

Snowdonia Area

HOLY- MTN. RAIL
OTHER RAIL
CASTLE

IRISH SEA

LLANDUDNO
Conwy LLANDUDNO JUNCTION
TO CHESTER & RUTHIN

TO HOLY-HEAD (FERRY TO IRELAND)
Menai Suspension Bridge
Beaumaris
BODNANT GARDEN
BODNANT WELSH FOOD CENTRE
A-55
Llanfair P.G.
BANGOR
TREFRIW WOOLEN MILLS
CAERNARFON
Llanberis
A-5
CAPEL CURIG
BETWS-Y-COED
Dinas
PEN-Y-PASS
Pen-y-Gwryd Hotel Pub
MT. SNOWDON
A-5 TO LLANGWN, RUTHIN & LLANGOLLEN
BEDDGELERT
LLECHWEDD SLATE MINE
PORTH-MADOG
BLAENAU FFESTINIOG
CRICCIETH
FFESTINIOG
PORTMEIRION
5 MILES
5 KM
HARLECH
To ABERYSTWYTH

Arrival in Betws-y-Coed: Drivers can follow signs for *National Park* and *i* to find the main parking lot by the TI. **Trains** and **buses** arrive at the village green; with your back to the station, the TI is to the right of the green.

Nearby: If you drive west out of town on the A-5 (toward Beddgelert or Llanberis), after two miles you'll see the parking lot for scenic **Swallow Falls,** a pleasant five-minute walk from the road (£1.50 entry). A half-mile past the falls on the right is **The Ugly House** (with a café), built overnight to take advantage of a 15th-century law that let any quickie building avoid fees and taxes.

Betws-y-Coed Connections

Betws-y-Coed is connected to **Llandudno Junction** near Conwy (north, 30 minutes) and **Blaenau Ffestiniog** (south, 30 minutes) by the Conwy Valley train line (5/day Mon-Sat, 3/day Sun in summer, no Sun trains in winter). Buses connect Betws-y-Coed with **Conwy** (hourly, 45 minutes, fewer on Sun), **Llanberis** (7/day, more in summer, 40 minutes), **Beddgelert** (4/day, 1-1.5 hours, 1 transfer), **Blaenau Ffestiniog** (8/day, none on Sun, 20 minutes; usually bus #X1), and **Caernarfon** (hourly, 1-1.5 hours, 1 transfer).

Beddgelert

This is the quintessential Snowdon village, rated ▲▲ and packing a scenic mountain punch without the tourist crowds (17 miles from Betws-y-Coed). Beddgelert (BETH-geh-lert) is a cluster of stone houses lining a babbling brook in the shadow of Mount Snowdon and her sisters. Cute as a hobbit, Beddgelert will have you looking for The Shire around the next bend. Thanks to the

fine variety of hikes from its doorstep and its decent bus service, Beddgelert makes a good stop for those wanting to experience the peace of Snowdonia.

The village doesn't have real "sights," but it's a starting place for some great **walks**—ask any local for tips. Here are several to consider: You can follow the lane along the river (3 miles round-trip); trek along the cycle path that goes from the center of Beddgelert, through the forest to the village of Rhyd-Ddu (4.5 miles); walk down the river and around the hill (3 hours, 6 miles, 900-foot gain, via Cwm Bychan); hike along (or around) Llyn Gwynant Lake and four miles back to Beddgelert (ride the bus to the lake); or try the dramatic ridge walks on Moel Hebog (Hawk Hill).

The **Welsh Highland Railway** serves Beddgelert. This narrow-gauge joyride (12 miles and 1.5 hours to or from Caernarfon) is a popular excursion. Most people ride the train one-way and return by bus (described under "Sights in Caernarfon," earlier).

Orientation to Beddgelert

Beddgelert clusters around its triple-arch stone bridge. The recommended B&Bs line up single-file along one side of the brook, while the hotels, most eateries, and the TI are on the other side.

The **National Park Centre/TI** is at the far end of town. If you're walking from the bridge, it's several blocks up, on your right. They can suggest tips for walks and hikes (Easter-Oct daily 9:30-17:00; Nov-Easter Fri-Sun 9:30-16:00—but closes for lunch, closed Mon-Thu; tel. 01766/890-615, www.snowdonia-npa.gov .uk). For info on the town, see www.beddgelerttourism.com.

Helpful Hints: There's **Internet** access inside the TI (£2/ hour). For **mountain-bike rental,** try Beddgelert Bikes (directly under Welsh Highland Railway station, tel. 01766/890-434, www .beddgelertbikes.co.uk).

Sleeping in Beddgelert

(area code: 01766)
The three recommended B&Bs all line up in a row at the bridge. They're quite different from each other—each seems to fill its own niche. The larger inn (listed first) is across the river.

$$$ Tanronnen Inn has seven hotelesque rooms above a pub that's been well-renovated from its interior medieval timbers to its exterior stone walls (Sb-£55, Db-£100, discount for 2 or more nights, tel. 01766/890-347, www.tanronnen.co.uk, guestservice @tanronnen.co.uk).

$$$ Plas Tan y Graig Guest House has seven thoughtfully updated, calming, uncluttered rooms run with care and contemporary style by Tony and Sharon (Sb-£60, Db-£86-90 depending on season, 2-night minimum stay, family rooms, fine lounge, free Wi-Fi, beautiful breakfast terrace overlooking the village, homemade bread and jam, packed lunches offered, tel. 01766/890-310, www.plas-tanygraig.co.uk, plastanygraig@googlemail.com).

$$ Plas Gwyn Guest House rents six rooms in a cozy, cheery, 19th-century townhouse with a comfy lounge (S-£35, Db-£75, 10 percent discount with this book if you stay 2 or more nights, cash only, packed lunch-£6, free Wi-Fi, tel. 01766/890-215, mobile 07815-549-708, www.plas-gwyn.com, stay@plas-gwyn.com).

$$ Colwyn Guest House has five tight but slick and new-feeling rooms (S with private bath next door-£35, Db-£70, 2-night minimum on weekends, 10 percent discount with this book, cash only, free guest computer in lounge, free Wi-Fi, tel. 01766/890-276, mobile 07774-002-637, www.beddgelertguesthouse.co.uk, colwynguesthouse@tiscali.co.uk, Colleen).

Near Beddgelert

Mountaineers appreciate that Sir Edmund Hillary and Sherpa Tenzing Norgay practiced here before the first successful ascent of Mount Everest. They slept at **$$$ Pen-y-Gwryd Hotel,** at the base of the road leading up to the Pen-y-Pass by Mount Snowdon, and today the bar is strewn with fascinating memorabilia from Hillary's 1953 climb. The 16 rooms, with dingy old furnishings and crampon ambience, are a poor value—aside from the impressive history (S-£42, Sb-£70, D-£84, Db-£100-104, old-time-elegant public rooms, some double rooms share museum-piece Victorian tubs and showers, natural pool and sauna for guests, £25 three-course dinners, £30 grand five-course dinners, tel. 01286/870-211, www.pyg.co.uk, escape@pyg.co.uk).

Eating in Beddgelert

Lyn's Café, just across the bridge from the B&Bs, serves nicely done home cookin' at good prices in a cozy one-room bistro (£3-7 lunches, £9-12 dinners, daily Easter-mid-Sept 9:00-20:30, mid-Sept-Easter 10:00-18:00, closed Jan, tel. 01766/890-374).

The **Tanronnen Inn** serves up tasty food in an inviting pub setting, with several cozy, atmospheric rooms (£5-7 sandwiches, £9-14 meals, tel. 01766/890-347).

And for Dessert: The **Glaslyn Homemade Ice Cream** shop (up the road from the Tanronnen Inn) offers good quality and selection.

Beddgelert Connections

Beddgelert is connected to **Caernarfon** by the scenic Welsh Highland Railway (2-3/day on most days late March-Oct, 1.5 hours) and handy bus #S4 (7/day Mon-Sat, 2/day Sun, 30 minutes). Bus connections to **Betws-y-Coed** are much less convenient (4/day, 1-1.5 hours, 1 transfer). To reach **Conwy,** it's generally easiest to transfer in Caernarfon (7/day Mon-Sat, 2/day Sun, 1.75 hours total). Buses to **Blaenau Ffestiniog** involve one or two transfers (7/day Mon-Sat, fewer on Sun, 1-2.5 hours).

Llanberis

A town of 2,000 people with as many tourists on a sunny day, Llanberis (THLAN-beh-ris) is a popular base for Snowdon activities. Most people prefer to take the train from here to the summit, but Llanberis is also loaded with hikers, as it's the launchpad for the longest (five miles) but least strenuous hiking route to the

Snowdon summit. (Routes from the nearby Pen-y-Pass, between here and Beddgelert, are steeper and even more scenic.)

Orientation to Llanberis

Llanberis is a long, skinny, rugged, and functional town that feels like a frontier village. Drivers approaching Llanberis will find pay

parking lots all throughout town, including one next to the Electric Mountain/TI and another along the lake (prices vary but generally are £2/2-4 hours and £4/4 hours-full day).

Tourist Information: The TI, located in the Electric Mountain, sells maps and offers tips for ascending Snowdon (Easter-Sept Fri-Tue 10:00-16:00, closed Wed-Thu and Oct-Easter, tel. 01286/870-765, www.visitsnowdonia.info).

Sights in Llanberis

▲▲Snowdon Mountain Railway

This is the easiest and most popular ascent of Mount Snowdon. You'll travel five miles from Llanberis to the summit on Britain's only rack-and-pinion railway (from 1896), climbing a total of 3,500 feet. On the way up, you'll hear a constant narration on legends, geology, and history. A mountaintop visitors' center includes a café. On the way down, there's only engine noise. You can take a diesel or steam train: The diesel-powered train with a 70-person car takes 2.5 hours, including a 30-minute stop at the top, while the steam train, carrying 34 passengers in a rebuilt Victorian carriage, takes 3 hours with a full hour at the summit.

Don't confuse this with the Welsh Highland Railway (described on page 709) or the Llanberis Lake Railway, a different (and far less appealing) "Thomas the Tank Engine"-type steam train that fascinates kids and runs to the end of Padarn Lake and back.

Cost and Hours: Diesel train—£27 round-trip, £21 early-bird special for 9:00 departure (must book in advance); steam train—£35 round-trip. The first departure is often at 9:00, and the last trip can be as late as 17:30 during peak season (July-Aug). While the schedule flexes with weather and demand, they try to run several trips each day late-March through October and up to 10/day in peak season (steam train 1-2/day). Until May (or in bad weather), the train may not run all the way to the summit. In that case, tickets are partially refunded or sold at a reduced rate.

Buying Tickets: On sunny summer days—especially in July and August—trains fill up fast. Originally designed for Victorian gentry, these days the train is overrun with commoners, and it's smart to reserve ahead. You can buy tickets in advance either by going online or calling the booking line after 13:00 (£3.50 reservation fee per party, tel. 0844-493-8120, www.snowdonrailway .co.uk). If you're trying to buy same-day tickets, show up early—the office opens at 8:30, and on very busy days, tickets can be sold out by midmorning; even if you get one, you may have to wait until afternoon for your scheduled departure time.

Getting There: The train departs from Llanberis Station, along the main road at the south end of Llanberis' town center. The closest parking lots are the pay-and-display lot located behind the station (off Victoria Terrace) or the pricier car park at Royal Victoria Hotel (across the street from the station). You can also park at one of the other pay lots in town (cheaper, about a 10-minute walk).

▲▲National Slate Museum

Across the lake from Llanberis yawns a giant slate quarry. To learn more, venture across to this free museum. The well-presented exhibit, displayed around the 19th-century workshop that was used until 1969 to support the giant slate mine above, explains various aspects of this local industry. In addition to a giant water-wheel and the slate-splitting demo (lasts 30 minutes, starts at :15 past

each hour), the museum has a little row of modest quarrymen's houses from different eras, offering a thought-provoking glimpse into their hardy lifestyle. The big, 50-foot-high waterwheel turns a shaft that runs throughout the workshop, powering all the various belt-driven machinery. Historic photo galleries and a 12-minute video re-create what was—until the last generation—a thriving industry employing 3,000 workers. While not as in-depth (literally) as the Llechwedd Slate Caverns in Blaenau Ffestiniog, this is as interesting and more convenient.

Cost and Hours: Free, Easter-Oct daily 10:00-17:00; Nov-Easter Sun-Fri 10:00-16:00, closed Sat; last entry one hour before closing, pay-and-display parking, tel. 02920/573-700, www .museumwales.ac.uk/en/slate.

Electric Mountain

This attraction offers tours into a power plant burrowed into Elidir Mountain, across the lake from town. After a 10-minute video, you'll load onto a bus and venture underground into Europe's biggest hydroelectric power station for a one-hour guided tour.

Cost and Hours: Visitors center-free, tour-£7.75, daily June-Aug 9:30-17:30, Sept-May 10:00-16:30, tours run Easter-Oct about hourly (every 30 minutes when busy), 3-5 tours/day off-season—call or check online for times, wear warm clothes and sturdy shoes, make advance reservations online, no children under 4, no photos, café, tel. 01286/870-636, www.electricmountain.co.uk.

Llanberis Connections

Llanberis is easiest to reach from **Caernarfon** (2/hour, 20 minutes, bus #88) or **Betws-y-Coed** (7/day, more in summer, 40 minutes); from **Conwy,** transfer in one of these towns (Caernarfon is generally best). While it's a quick 30-minute drive from Llanberis to **Beddgelert,** the bus connection is more complicated, requiring a transfer at Caernarfon or Pen-y-Pass, on the high road around Mount Snowdon (9/day, 1-1.5 hours).

Blaenau Ffestiniog

Blaenau Ffestiniog (BLEH-nigh FES-tin-yog) is a quintessential Welsh slate-mining town, notable for its slate-mine tour and its old steam train. The town seems to struggle on, oblivious to the tourists who nip in and out. Though it's tucked amidst a pastoral Welsh landscape, Blaenau Ffestiniog is surrounded by a gunmetal-gray wasteland of "tips," huge mountain-like piles of excess slate.

Take a walk. The shops are right out of the 1950s. Long rows of humble "two-up and two-down" houses (four rooms) feel a bit grim. The train station, bus stop, and parking lot all cluster along a one-block stretch in the heart of town. There's no TI.

Getting There: Blaenau Ffestiniog is conveniently connected to **Betws-y-Coed** and **Conwy** both by the Conwy Valley train line (5/day Mon-Sat, 3/day Sun in summer, no Sun trains in winter, 30 minutes to Betws-y-Coed, 1 hour to Conwy via Llandudno Junction) and by bus #X1 (8/day, none Sun, 20 minutes to Betws-y-Coed, 1 hour to Llandudno Junction near Conwy). By bus, it's possible to connect with **Beddgelert** (7/day Mon-Sat, fewer on Sun, 1-2.5 hours, 1-2 transfers) or **Caernarfon** (hourly, 1.5 hours, transfer in Porthmadog).

Sights in Blaenau Ffestiniog

▲▲Llechwedd Slate Caverns

Slate mining played a blockbuster role in Welsh heritage, and this working slate mine on the northern edge of Blaenau Ffestiniog does a fine job of explaining the mining culture of Victorian Wales. The Welsh mined and split most of the slate roofs of Europe. For every ton of usable slate found, 10 tons were mined. You can wander around its re-created mining town or join one of two different guided tours. Dress warmly—I mean it. You'll freeze underground without a sweater. Lines are longer when rain drives in the hikers.

Cost and Hours: Tours-£10.50 for one, £17 for both, free entry to mining town; daily April-Dec 9:30-18:00, Jan-March Wed-Sun 10:00-16:00, closed Mon-Tue; in peak season (July-Aug), mine tours may run as often as every 10-15 minutes, tram tours every 30-45 minutes, depends on demand, first tour usually at 10:30, last tour generally at 16:45; cafeteria, pub, tel. 01766/830-306, www.llechwedd-slate-caverns.co.uk.

Getting There: The slate mine is about a mile from the town center. Bus #X1 leaves from the Blaenau Ffestiniog rail station and drops you off near the mine (8/day Mon-Sat, none on Sun, Express Motors). If you don't want to wait for a bus, you can walk 30 minutes to the mine or take a taxi (about £5, reserve in advance, tel. 01766/762-465).

Visiting the Mine: Two different 30-minute tours take you into the mine. You can do just one or get a combo-ticket for both. The **miners' tramway tour** is a level half-mile train ride with three stops, not much walking, and a live guide. It focuses on working life and traditional mining techniques. The **deep mine tour** descends nearly 500 feet deep into the mountain for an audiovisual dramatization, set in the 1860s and centered around a young boy who works in the mine with his dad. The tour requires a half-mile of walking through tunnels and caves with 60-plus stairs and some uneven footing. The tours overlap slightly, but the combo-ticket makes doing both worth considering.

The re-created Victorian mining town, with a pub, bank, candy shop, and other stops, is free and open for anyone to explore. A highlight is the interesting slate-splitting demonstration. While the demonstration is generally timed to coincide with the end of the tramway tour, anyone is welcome to watch. Don't miss this—ask when the next one is scheduled.

Near Blaenau Ffestiniog
▲Ffestiniog Railway

This 13-mile narrow-gauge train line was built in 1836 for small horse-drawn wagons to transport the slate from the Ffestiniog mines to the port of Porthmadog. In the 1860s, horses gave way to steam trains. Today, hikers and tourists enjoy these tiny titans (tel. 01766/516-000, www.festrail.co.uk). This line connects to the narrow-gauge Welsh Highland Railway from Caernarfon via Porthmadog (see page 709). This is a novel steam-train experience, but the full-size Conwy Valley line from Llandudno to Blaenau Ffestiniog is more scenic and works a little better for hikers (see page 699).

Portmeirion

Ten miles southwest of Blaenau Ffestiniog, this "Italian Village" was the life's work of a rich local architect who began building it in 1925. Set idyllically on the coast just beyond the poverty of the slate-mine towns, this flower-filled fantasy is extravagant. Surrounded by lush Welsh greenery and a windswept mudflat at low tide, the village is an artistic glob of palazzo arches, fountains, gardens, and promenades filled with cafés, tacky shops, a hotel, and local tourists who always wanted to go to Italy. Fans of the cultish British 1960s TV series *The Prisoner*, which was filmed here, will recognize the place.

Cost and Hours: £10, cheaper if you buy online, daily 9:30-19:30, tel. 01766/770-000 www.portmeirion-village.com.

Ruthin

Ruthin (RITH-in; "Rhuthun" in Welsh) is a low-key market town whose charm is in its ordinary Welshness. The town (pop. 5,200)

is situated atop a gentle hill surrounded by undulating meadows. Simple streets branch out from the central roundabout (at the former medieval marketplace, St. Peter's Square) like spokes on a wheel. It's so untouristy that it has no TI. The market square, jail, museum, bus station, and in-town accommodations are all within five blocks of one another. Ruthin is as Welsh as can be, making it a distinctive stopover on your way to northern England. The people are the sights, and admission is free if you start the conversation.

Ruthin has poor transportation connections to just about everywhere. Skip it unless you have a car.

Sights in Ruthin

▲Ruthin Gaol

Get a glimpse into crime and punishment in 17th- to early-20th-century Wales in this 100-cell prison. Explore the "dark" and

condemned cells, give the dreaded hand-crank a whirl, and learn about the men, women, and children who did time here before the prison closed in 1916. The audioguide—partly narrated by a jovial "prisoner" named Will—is very good, informative, and engaging. You'll find out why prison kitchens came with a cat, why the bathtubs had a severe case of ring-around-the-tub, how they got prisoners to sit still for their mug shots (and why these photos often included the prisoners' hands), and why the prison was renovated in the "panopticon" style in the late 19th century.

Cost and Hours: £3.90, family-£10, April-Sept Wed-Sun 10:00-17:00, closed Tue and Oct-March, last entry 1 hour before closing, audioguide-£0.50, Clwyd Street, tel. 01824/708-281, www.ruthingaol.co.uk.

Nantclwyd y Dre

This Elizabethan-era "oldest timbered townhouse in Wales"—a white-and-brown half-timbered house between the castle and the market square—underwent an award-winning £600,000 renovation (funded partly by the EU) to convert it into a museum. Seven decorated rooms give visitors a peek into the history of the house, which was built in 1435.

Cost and Hours: £3.90, family-£10, April-Sept Fri-Sun 10:30-17:00, possibly open Mon-Tue mid-July-Aug, otherwise closed Mon-Thu and Oct-March, last entry 45 minutes before closing, Castle Street, tel. 01824/709-822, www.denbighshire.gov.uk.

Walks

For a scenic and interesting one-hour walk, try the Offa's Dyke Path to Moel Famau (the "Jubilee Tower," a 200-year-old war memorial on a peak overlooking stark moorlands). The trailhead is a 10-minute drive east of Ruthin on the A-494.

▲▲Welsh Choir

The Côr Rhuthun mixed choir usually rehearses weekly at the Pwllglas Village Hall (Thu at 20:00 except Aug, Well Street, call or email in advance to confirm practice, mobile 07724/112-984, www.corrhuthun.co.uk, cor@corrhuthun.co.uk).

Ruthin

① Manorhaus Hotel & Rest.
② On the Hill Restaurant
③ Leonardo's Delicatessen
④ Finn's Fish-and-Chips
⑤ To Offa's Dyke Path

P PARKING

Sleeping in Ruthin

(area code: 01824)

For cheap sleeps, you'll have to stay at the youth hostels in Conwy or Caernarfon. Or, if you're driving, keep an eye out for rustic hostel-like "bunkhouses" that dot the North Wales countryside.

$$$ Manorhaus, filling a Georgian building, is Ruthin's classiest sleeping option. Its eight rooms are impeccably appointed with artsy-contemporary decor, and the halls serve as gallery space for local artists. Guests enjoy use of the sauna, steam room, library, and mini-cinema in the cellar. In fact, you could have a vacation and never leave the place. It's run by Christopher (who played piano for years in London's West End theaters) and Gavin (an architect and former mayor of Ruthin)—together, it seems, they've brought Ruthin a splash of fun and style (Sb-£83-133, standard Db-£135, superior Db-£155, pricier Db suite-£180, check website for deals, no children under 12, free Wi-Fi, recommended restaurant, Well Street, tel. 01824/704-830, www.manorhaus.com, post@manorhaus.com).

NORTH WALES

Eating in Ruthin

On the Hill serves hearty £10-16 lunches and £12-20 dinners—mostly made with fresh, local ingredients—to an enthusiastic crowd. The Old World decor complements the good cuisine (lunch served Tue-Sat 12:00-14:00, closed for lunch Sun-Mon, dinner served Mon-Sat 18:30-21:00, Sun 17:00-21:00, 1 Upper Clwyd Street, tel. 01824/707-736).

Manorhaus is the town splurge in a recommended hotel (described above), with updated Welsh and British dinners served in a mod art-gallery space. Eating here—especially when in the care of Christopher or Gavin—is an evening in itself (£26 for two courses, £33 for three courses, dinner served daily 18:30-21:00, reservations recommended, Well Street, tel. 01824/704-830).

Leonardo's Delicatessen is *the* place to buy a top-notch gourmet picnic (made-to-order sandwiches, small salad bar, Mon-Sat 9:00-16:30, closed Sun, 4 Well Street, just off the main square, tel. 01824/707-161).

Finn's is the local favorite for take-away fish-and-chips (£3-5, daily 11:30-13:45 & 16:30-21:30 except closed Sun for lunch, near Ruthin Gaol at the bottom of Clwyd Street, tel. 01824/702-518).

Near Ruthin: Llangollen

Worth a stop if you have a car, Llangollen (thlang-GOTH-lehn) is a red-brick riverside town that's equal parts blue collar and touristy. The town is famous for its weeklong **International Musical Eisteddfod,** a very popular and crowded festival held every July, with dance competitions and evening concerts (tel. 01978/862-001, www.international-eisteddfod.co.uk). The enthusiastic **TI** has the details on these events, scenic

steam-train trips, and other attractions (daily July-Aug 9:30-17:30, Sept-June 9:30-17:00, Castle Street, tel. 01978/860-828, www.llangollen.org.uk).

The **men's choir** practices traditional Welsh songs weekly on Friday nights (19:30 at the Hand Hotel on Bridge Street, 21:30 pub sing-along afterward, hotel tel. 01978/860-303).

Llangollen's most interesting attraction is the **Llangollen Canal,** a narrow, shallow waterway up the hill and across the bridge from the town center. You can stroll along the canal or take a boat ride from Llangollen Wharf. Options include a 45-minute horse-drawn boat that goes for a spin around the wharf (£6.50, daily Easter-Oct, 2/hour 11:00-16:30 in July-Aug, shorter hours and less frequent rest of the year—call or check online to confirm schedule; tel. 01978/860-702, www.horsedrawnboats.co.uk); a two-hour, motorized canal-boat trip that goes across the remarkable Pontcysyllte aqueduct (£12.50, Easter-Oct daily at 12:15 and 13:45, sometimes also at 10:00 or 11:30, smart to book ahead); or, on weekends, a two-hour horse-drawn boat that floats down to Horseshoe Falls (£11, Easter-Oct Sat-Sun at 11:30).

If you take a walk, you'll reach the lovely 13th-century Cistercian **Valle Crucis Abbey** (£3.50, April-Oct daily 10:00-17:00, last entry 30 minutes before closing, closed but free access to grounds Nov-March, tel. 01978/860-326, www.llangollen.com /valle.html). An even older cross, **Eliseg's Pillar,** is nearby.

Sleeping in Llangollen: **$$ Glasgwm B&B** rents four spacious rooms in a Victorian townhouse (Sb-£40, Db-£65-75, price depends on size of room, evening meals available by advance request, packed lunches-£5.50, Abbey Road, tel. 01978/861-975, www.glasgwm-llangollen.co.uk, glasgwm@llangollen.co.uk, John and Heather). **$$$ Manorhaus** is a luxurious boutique option in Llangollen, with six rooms and suites, run by the same owners of the recommended Manorhaus hotel in Ruthin (standard Db-£115, superior Db-£145, Db suite-£180, robes and slippers, free Wi-Fi, restaurant, Hill Street, tel. 01978/860-775, www.manorhaus llangollen.com, post@manorhaus.com).

Llangollen Connections: To reach **Conwy,** it's quickest to take the bus to Ruabon and then transfer to a train (hourly, 2 hours for entire journey).

North Wales Connections

Two major transfer points out of (or into) North Wales are Crewe and Chester. Figure out your complete connection at www.national rail.co.uk.

From Crewe by Train to: London's Euston Station (2/ hour direct, 1.75 hours), Bristol, near **Bath** (2/hour, 2.75 hours, 1 transfer), **Cardiff** (1/hour direct, 2.75 hours), **Holyhead** (hourly, 2-2.5 hours, most with 1 transfer), **Blackpool** (hourly, 1.5 hours, 1 transfer), **Keswick** in the Lake District (hourly, 1.5-2.5 hours to Penrith, some with 1 transfer; then bus to Keswick, 45 minutes), **Birmingham** (3/hour direct, 1 hour), **Glasgow** (hourly, 3-4 hours, some with 1 transfer).

From Chester by Train to: London's Euston Station (2/hour, 2 hours, some with 1 transfer), **Liverpool** (4/hour direct, 45 minutes), points in North Wales via **Llandudno Junction** (2-3/hour, 1 hour).

Ferry Connections Between North Wales and Ireland

Two companies make the crossing between Holyhead (in North Wales, beyond Caernarfon) and Ireland. Some boats go to Dublin, while others head for Dublin's southern suburb of Dun Laoghaire (pronounced "Dun Leary"). **Stena Line** sails from Holyhead to Dublin (4/day including 2 at night, 3.25 hours) and also to Dun Laoghaire (1/day, 2.25 hours, runs late March-early Sept, can book up long in advance on summer weekends, British tel. 0844-770-7070, or book online at www.stenaline.co.uk). **Irish Ferries** sails to Dublin (4/day—2 slow, 2 fast; slow boat takes 3.25 hours and includes 1 night sailing, fast boat takes 2 hours; reserve online for best fares; Britain tel. 0818-300-400, www.irishferries.com).

Sleeping near Holyhead Dock: On the island of Anglesey, the fine **$$ Monravon B&B** has five rooms a 15-minute uphill walk from the dock (Sb-£35, Db-£55, family deals, includes continental breakfast, cooked breakfast-£4, free Wi-Fi, Porth-Y-Felin Road, tel. 01407/762-944, www.monravon.co.uk, monravon@yahoo.co.uk, John and Joan).

Sleeping En Route to Holyhead, Between Liverpool and Conwy: **$$ Celyn Villa B&B** is a lovely mid-19th-century house on the mainland, with three rooms with views of the Dee estuary (Sb-£50, Db-£70, family room-£85, 10 percent discount if you stay 2 or more nights, 2-night minimum July-Aug, free Wi-Fi, dinner available, Carmel Road, tel. 01352/710-853, www.celynvilla.co.uk, celynvilla@gmail.com, Paulene and Les).

Route Tips for Drivers

From North Wales to Liverpool (40 miles): From Ruthin or the A-55, follow signs to the town of *Mold*, then *Queensferry*, then *Manchester M-56*, then *Liverpool M-53*, which tunnels under the River Mersey (£1.60).

SCOTLAND

SCOTLAND

The country of Scotland makes up about a third of Britain's geographical area (30,400 square miles), but has less than a tenth of its population (just under 5.3 million). This sparsely populated chunk of land stretches to Norwegian latitudes. Its Shetland Islands, at about 60°N (similar to Anchorage, Alaska), are the northernmost point in Britain.

The southern part of Scotland, called the Lowlands, is relatively flat and urbanized. The northern area—the Highlands—fea-

tures a wild, severely undulating terrain, punctuated by lochs (lakes) and fringed by sea lochs (inlets) and islands. The Highland Boundary Fault that divides Scotland geologically also divides it culturally. Historically, there was a big difference between grizzled, kilt-wearing Highlanders in the northern wilderness and the more refined Lowlanders in the southern flatlands and cities. The Highlanders spoke and acted like "true Scots," while the Lowlanders often seemed more "British" than Scottish.

Although this division has faded over time, some Scots still cling to it today—city slickers down south think that Highlanders are crude and unrefined, and those who live at higher latitudes grumble about the soft, pampered urbanites in the Lowlands.

The Lowlands are dominated by a pair of rival cities: Edinburgh, the old royal capital, teems with Scottish history and is the country's best tourist attraction. Glasgow, once a gloomy industrial city, is becoming a hip, laid-back city of today, known for its modern architecture. The medieval university town and golf mecca of St. Andrews, the whisky village of Pitlochry, and the historic city of Stirling are my picks as the Lowlands' highlights.

The Highlands provide your best look at traditional Scotland. The sights are subtle, but the warm culture and friendly people are engaging. There are a lot of miles, but they're scenic, the roads are

Scotland

••• FERRY ROUTES
(NOT ALL SHOWN)

ATLANTIC OCEAN

ORKNEY

STROMNESS · · · · · KIRKWALL

THURSO   JOHN
O'GROATS

LEWIS

50 MILES

30 KM

ULLAPOOL

NORTH
UIST

KYLE OF
LOCHALSH

MORAY FIRTH

SOUTH
UIST

SKYE

CULLODEN

PORTREE·
KYLEAKIN·

HIGHLANDS

INVERNESS

RUM

CALEDONIAN CANAL

LOCH
NESS

ABERDEEN ·

MALLAIG

FORT AUGUSTUS

COLL

▲ BEN NEVIS

PITLOCHRY

NORTH

TIREE

Ft. WILLIAM

SEA

GLENCOE

MULL

Perth

DUNDEE

IONA

OBAN

LOCH
LOMOND

St. ANDREWS
EAST NEUK

JURA

STIRLING

FIRTH OF FORTH

ISLAY

BANNOCK-
BURN

GLASGOW

EDINBURGH

CAMPBELTOWN ·

· TROON

BERWICK-
UPON-
TWEED

ARRAN

AYR

LOWLANDS

ENGLAND

NORTHERN
IRELAND

CAIRNRYAN
STRANRAER

CARLISLE - - - -

LARNE

BELFAST·

IRISH
SEA

TO
DUBLIN

HADRIAN'S
WALL

NEW-
CASTLE

TO LAKE
DISTRICT

TO YORK +
LONDON

DCH

good, and the traffic is light. Generally, the Highlands are hungry
for the tourist dollar, and everything overtly Scottish is exploited to
the kilt. You'll need more than a quick visit to get away from that.
But if you only have two days, you can get a feel for the area with
a quick drive to Oban, through Glencoe, then up the Caledonian
Canal to Inverness. With more time, the Isles of Iona and Mull (an
easy day trip from Oban), the Isle of Skye, and countless brooding
countryside castles will flesh out your Highlands experience.

The Highlands are more rocky and harsh than other parts of
the British Isles. It's no wonder that many of the exterior scenes
of Hogwarts' grounds in the Harry Potter movies were filmed in
this moody, sometimes spooky landscape (see page 1028). Though

Scotland's "hills" are technically too short to be called "mountains," they do a convincing imitation. Scotland has 282 hills over 3,000 feet. A list of these was first compiled in 1891 by Sir Hugh Munro, and to this day the Scots still call their high hills "Munros." (Hills from 2,500-3,000 feet are known as "Corbetts," and those from 2,000-2,500 are "Grahams.") According to the Munro Society, more than 5,000 intrepid hikers can brag that they've climbed all of the Munros.

In this northern climate, cold and drizzly weather isn't uncommon—even in midsummer. The blazing sun can quickly be covered over by black clouds and howling wind. Scots warn visitors to prepare for "four seasons in one day." Because Scots feel personally responsible for bad weather, they tend to be overly optimistic about forecasts. Take any Scottish promise of "sun by the afternoon" with a grain of salt—and bring your raincoat.

In the summer, the Highlands swarm with tourists...and midges. These tiny biting insects—like "no-see-ums" in some parts of North America—are bloodthirsty and determined. They can be an annoyance from late May through September, depending on the weather. Hot sun or a stiff breeze blows the tiny buggers away, but they thrive in damp, shady areas. Locals suggest blowing or brushing them off, rather than swatting them—since killing them only seems to attract more (likely because of the smell of fresh blood). Scots say, "If you kill one midge, a million more will come to his funeral." Even if you don't usually travel with bug spray, consider bringing or buying some for a summer visit—or your most vivid memory of your Scottish vacation might be itchy arms and legs.

Keep an eye out for another Scottish animal: shaggy Highland

cattle—those adorable "hairy coos" with their hair falling in their eyes. With a heavy coat to keep them insulated, hairy coos graze on sparse vegetation that other animals ignore. And of course, Scotland's not short on sheep.

The major theme of Scottish history is the drive for independence, especially from England. (Scotland's rabble-rousing national motto is *Nemo me impune lacessit*—"No one provokes me with impunity.") Like Wales, Scotland is a country of ragtag Celts sharing an island with wealthy and powerful Anglo-Saxons. Scotland's Celtic culture is a result of its remoteness—the invading Romans were never able to conquer this rough-and-tumble people, and even built Hadrian's Wall to lock off this distant corner of their empire. The Anglo-Saxons, and their descendants the English, fared little better than the Romans did. Even King Edward I—who so successfully dominated Wales—was unable to hold on to Scotland for long, largely thanks to the relentlessly rebellious William Wallace (a.k.a. "Braveheart").

Failing to conquer Scotland by the blade, England eventually absorbed it politically. In 1603, England's Queen Elizabeth I died without an heir, so Scotland's King James VI took the throne, becoming King James I of England. It took another century or so of battles, both military and diplomatic, but the Act of Union in 1707 definitively (and controversially) unified the Kingdom of Great Britain. In 1745, Bonnie Prince Charlie attempted to reclaim the Scottish throne on behalf of the deposed Stuarts, but his army was slaughtered at the Battle of Culloden (described in the Inverness and the Northern Highlands chapter). This cemented English rule over Scotland, and is seen by many Scots as the last gasp of the traditional Highlands clan system.

Scotland has been joined—however unwillingly—to England ever since, and the Scots have often felt oppressed by their English countrymen (see the sidebar on page 748). During the Highland Clearances in the 18th and 19th centuries, landowners (mostly English) decided that vast tracks of land were more profitable as grazing land for sheep than as farmland for people. Many Highlanders were forced to abandon their traditional homes and lifestyles and seek employment elsewhere. Large numbers ended up in North America, especially parts of eastern Canada, such as Prince Edward Island and Nova Scotia (literally, "New Scotland").

Today, Americans and Canadians of Scottish descent enjoy coming "home" to Scotland. If you're Scottish, your surname will tell you which clan your ancestors likely belonged to. The prefix "Mac" (or "Mc") means "son of"—so "MacDonald" means the same thing as "Donaldson." Tourist shops everywhere are happy

to help you track down your clan's tartan, or distinctive plaid pattern—many clans have several.

Is Scotland really a country? It's not a sovereign state, but it is a "nation" in that it has its own traditions, ethnic identity, languages (Gaelic and Scots), and football league. To some extent, it even has its own government:

Robert Burns
(1759–1796)

Robert Burns, Scotland's national poet, holds a unique place in the heart of Scottish people—a heart that's still beating loud and proud thanks, in large part, to Burns himself.

Born on a farm in southwestern Scotland, Robbie, as he's still affectionately called, was the oldest of seven children. His early years were full of literally backbreaking farm labor, which left him with a lifelong stoop. Though much was later made of his ascendance to literary acclaim from a rural, poverty-stricken upbringing, he was actually quite well-educated (per Scottish tradition), equally as familiar with Latin and French as he was with hard work.

He started writing poetry at 15, but didn't have any published until age 28—to finance a voyage to the West Indies (which promised better farming opportunities). When that first volume, *Poems, Chiefly in the Scottish Dialect*, became a sudden and overwhelming success, he reconsidered his emigration. Instead, he left his farm for Edinburgh, living just off the Royal Mile. He spent a year and a half in the city, schmoozing with literary elites, who celebrated this "heaven taught" farmer from the hinterlands as Scotland's "ploughman poet."

His poetry, written primarily in the Scots dialect, drew on his substantial familiarity with both Scottish tradition and Western literature. By using the language of the common man to create works of beauty and sophistication, he found himself wildly popular among both rural folk and high society. Hearty poems such as "To a Mouse," "To a Louse," and "The Holy Fair" exalted the virtues of physical labor, romantic love, friendship, natural beauty, and drink—all of which he also pursued with vigor in real life. This further endeared him to most Scots, though consider-

Recently, Scotland has enjoyed its greatest measure of political autonomy in centuries—a trend called "devolution." In 1999, the Scottish parliament opened its doors in Edinburgh for the first time in almost 300 years. Though the Scottish parliament's powers are limited (most major decisions are still made in London), the Scots are enjoying the refreshing breeze of increased independence. However, with the power (at the moment) ultimately in Westminster, some locals, especially the younger generation, view the British democracy as two wolves and one sheep deciding what to have for lunch—and Scotland is the sheep.

ably less so to Church fathers, who were particularly displeased with his love life (of Burns' dozen children, nine were by his eventual wife, the others by various servants and barmaids).

After achieving fame and wealth, Burns never lost touch with the concerns of the Scottish people, championing such radical ideas as social equality and economic justice. Burns bravely and loudly supported the French and American revolutions, which inspired one of his most beloved poems, "A Man's a Man for A' That," and even an ode to George Washington—all while other writers were being shipped off to Australia for similar beliefs. While his social causes cost him some aristocratic friends, it cemented his popularity among the masses, and not just within Scotland (he became, and remains, especially beloved in Russia).

Intent on preserving Scotland's rich musical and lyrical traditions, Burns traveled the countryside collecting traditional Scottish ballads. If it weren't for Burns, we'd have to come up with a different song to sing on New Year's Eve—he's the one who found, reworked, and popularized "Auld Lang Syne." His championing of Scottish culture came at a critical time: England had recently and finally crushed Scotland's last hopes of independence, and the Highland clan system was nearing its end. Burns lent the Scots dialect a new prestige, and the scrappy Scottish people a reinvigorated identity.

Burns died at 37 of a heart condition likely exacerbated by so much hard labor (all the carousing probably hadn't helped, either). By that time, his fortune was largely spent, but his celebrity was going strong—around 10,000 people attended his burial. Even the Church eventually overcame its disapproval, installing a window in his honor at St. Giles' Cathedral. In 2009, his nation voted Burns "Greatest Ever Scot" in a TV poll. And every January 25 (the poet's birthday), on Burns' Night, Scots gather to recite his songs and poems, tuck into some haggis ("chieftain o' the puddin' race," according to Burns), and raise their whisky to friendship, and Scotland.

In September of 2014, the Scottish people vote on an independence referendum answering the yes-or-no question: "Should Scotland be an independent country?" While Scottish ministers (and many nationals) support the bid for independence, a number of Scots remain uncertain—perhaps afraid of change. What this will mean for Scotland's people, infrastructure, or banks is anyone's guess. The current government is holding fast to the notion that time, and the people who choose to live in Scotland, will pioneer the nation's fate. One thing is sure—the debate is starting to get interesting.

Scotland even has its own currency. While Scots use the same coins as England, Scotland also prints its own bills (with Scottish rather than English people and landmarks). Just to confuse tourists, three different banks print Scottish pound notes, each with a different design. In the Lowlands (around Edinburgh and Glasgow), you'll receive both Scottish and English pounds from ATMs and in change. But in the Highlands, you'll almost never see English pounds. Though most merchants in England accept Scottish pound notes, a few might balk—especially at the rare one-pound note, which their cash registers don't have a slot for. (They are, however, legally required to accept your Scottish currency.)

The Scottish flag—a diagonal, X-shaped white cross on a blue field—represents the cross of Scotland's patron saint, the Apostle Andrew (who was crucified on an X-shaped cross). You may not realize it, but you see the Scottish flag every time you look at the Union Jack: England's flag (the red St. George's cross on a white field) superimposed on Scotland's (a blue field with a white diagonal cross). The diagonal red cross (St. Patrick's cross) over Scotland's white one represents Northern Ireland. (Wales gets no love on the Union Jack.)

Scots are known for their inimitable burr, but they are also proud of their old Celtic language, Scottish Gaelic (pronounced "gallic"; Ireland's closely related Celtic language is spelled the same but pronounced "gaylic"). Gaelic thrives only in the remotest corners of Scotland. In major towns and cities, virtually nobody speaks Gaelic every day, but the language is kept on life-support by a Scottish population keen to remember their heritage. New Gaelic schools are opening all the time, and Scotland has passed a law to replace road signs with new ones listing both English and Gaelic spellings (e.g., *Edinburgh/Dùn Èideann*).

Scotland has another language of its own, called Scots (a.k.a. "Lowland Scots," to distinguish it from Gaelic). Aye, you're likely already a wee bit familiar with a few Scots words, ye lads and lassies. As you travel, you're sure to pick up a bit more (see sidebar) and enjoy the lovely musical lilt as well. Many linguists argue that Scots is technically an ancient dialect of English, rather than a distinct language. These linguists have clearly never heard a Scot read aloud the poetry of Robert Burns, who wrote in unfiltered (and often unintelligible) Scots. (Opening line of "To a Louse": "Ha! Whaur ye gaun, ye crowlin ferlie?") Fortunately, you're unlikely to meet anyone quite that hard to understand; most Scots speak Scottish-accented standard English, peppered with their favorite Scots phrases. If you have a hard time understanding someone, ask them to translate—you may take home some new words as souvenirs.

Scottish Words

Scotch may be the peaty drink the bartender serves you, but the nationality of the bartender is **Scots** or **Scottish.** Here are some other Scottish words that may come in handy during your time here:

aye: yes
auld: old
ben: mountain
blether: talk
bonnie: beautiful
brae: slope, hill
burn: creek or stream
cairn: pile of stones
close: an alley leading to a courtyard or square
craig: rock, cliff
firth: estuary
innis: island
inver: mouth of a river

ken: to know
kirk: church
kyle: strait
loch: lake
nae: no (as in "nae bother"— you're welcome)
neeps: turnips
ree: king, royal ("righ" in Gaelic)
tattie: potato
wee: small
wynd: tight, winding lane connecting major streets

A sharp intake of breath (like a little gasp), sometimes while saying "aye," means "yes."

Scottish cuisine is down-to-earth, often with an emphasis on local produce. Both seafood and "land food" (beef and chicken) are common. One Scottish mainstay—eaten more by tourists than by Scots these days—is the famous haggis (see sidebar in this chapter), tastier than it sounds and worth trying...even before you've tucked into the whisky.

The "Scottish Breakfast" is similar to the English version, but they often add a potato scone (like a flavorless, soggy potato pancake) and haggis (best when served with poached eggs and HP brown sauce).

Breakfast, lunch, or dinner, the Scots love their whisky—and touring one of the country's many distilleries is a sightseeing treat. The Scots are fiercely competitive with the Irish when it comes to this peaty spirit. Scottish "whisky" is distilled twice, whereas Irish "whiskey" adds a third distillation (and an extra *e*). Grain here is roasted over peat fires, giving it a smokier flavor than its Irish cousin. Also note that what we call "scotch"—short for "scotch whisky"—is just "whisky" here. I've listed several of the most convenient and interesting distilleries to visit, but if you're a whisky connoisseur, make a point of tracking down and touring your favorite.

Another unique Scottish flavor to sample is the soft drink called Irn-Bru (pronounced "Iron Brew"). This bright-orange

Haggis: Not Just for Peasants (or Tourists) Anymore

Haggis began as a peasant food: Waste-conscious cooks wrapped sheep's heart, liver, and lungs in stomach lining and boiled these scraps to create a hearty meal that's slightly palatable (thanks to added spices and oats). Traditionally served with "neeps and tatties" (turnips and potatoes), haggis turned a corner and was forever immortalized thanks to Robbie Burns' *Address to a Haggis*, which extolled the dish's virtues.

For generations, haggis was served as a staple in peasant diets; today it's been refined, almost to the point of high cuisine. Cooking methods range from plain deep-fried to "haute and oat" (a term for Scottish fine dining). Instead of using spices to take away the taste, butchers use their own unique mix to complement it. (Good luck getting one to tell you what his secret is.)

You're likely to find haggis on many menus, including at breakfast (often served with blood pudding). You can dress it up with anything from a fine whisky cream sauce to your basic HP brown sauce. The trick to appreciating this iconic Scottish dish is to think of how it tastes, not what it's made of—just like with other favorites such as foie gras, caviar, or hot dogs.

beverage tastes not like orange soda, but like bubblegum with a slightly bitter aftertaste. (The diet version is even more bitter.) While Irn-Bru's appeal eludes non-Scots, it's hugely popular here, even outselling Coke. As the label states, "Bru'd in Scotland to a secret recipe for over 100 years"—they must be doing something right.

Whether toasting with beer, whisky, or Irn-Bru, enjoy meeting the Scottish people. It's easy to fall in love with the irrepressible spirit and beautiful landscape of this faraway corner of Britain.

EDINBURGH

Edinburgh is the historical, cultural, and political capital of Scotland. For nearly a thousand years, Scotland's kings, parliaments, writers, thinkers, and bankers have called Edinburgh home. Today, it remains Scotland's most sophisticated city.

Edinburgh (ED'n-burah—only tourists pronounce it like "Pittsburgh") is Scotland's showpiece and one of Europe's most entertaining cities. It's a place of stunning vistas—nestled among craggy bluffs and studded with a prickly skyline of spires, towers, domes, and steeples. Proud statues of famous Scots dot the urban landscape. The buildings are a harmonious yellow-gray, all built from the same local sandstone.

Culturally, Edinburgh has always been the place where Lowland culture (urban and English) met Highland style (rustic and Gaelic). Tourists will find no end of traditional Scottish clichés: whisky tastings, kilt shops, bagpipe-playing buskers, and gimmicky tours featuring Scotland's bloody history and ghost stories.

Edinburgh is two cities in one. The Old Town stretches along a narrow ridge. Promenade down the Royal Mile through Old Town from the grand castle on top to the palace on the bottom. Along the way, medieval skyscrapers stand shoulder to shoulder, hiding peaceful courtyards. This colorful labyrinth of cobbled streets and narrow lanes is the tourist's Edinburgh.

A few hundred yards north of the Old Town lies the New Town. It's a magnificent planned neighborhood (from the 1700s) laid out in a grid plan. Here, you'll enjoy upscale shops, broad boulevards, straight streets, square squares, circular circuses, and

EDINBURGH

Greater Edinburgh

TO PERTH & INVERNESS

FORTH BRIDGE

FIRTH OF FORTH

BRITANNIA

ROYAL BOTANIC GARDEN

LEITH

SEE EDINBURGH CENTER MAPS

AIRPORT

QUEENSFERRY RD.

M-9

CORSTORPHINE ROAD

SEE DALKEITH RD. NEIGHBORHOOD MAP

HOLYROOD PARK

TO BERWICK-UPON-TWEED

TO GLASGOW M-8

A-70

A-720

COMISTON ROAD

DALKEITH RD.

GILMERTON

A-1

A-68

TO NEWCASTLE & DURHAM

A-7

HILLEND

MIDLOTHIAN SKI CENTRE

A-720

N

ROSSLYN CHAPEL

4 MILES

6 KM

A-702

A-703

TO CARLISLE

DCH

---

elegant Georgian mansions decked out in Greek-style columns and statues.

Today's Edinburgh is a thriving city of a half-million. It's big in banking, scientific research, and scholarship at its four universities. Since 1999, when Scotland regained a measure of self-rule, Edinburgh reassumed its place as home of the Scottish Parliament. The city hums with life. Students and professionals pack the pubs and art galleries. It's especially lively in August, when the Edinburgh Festival takes over the town. Historic, monumental, fun, and well organized, Edinburgh is a tourist's delight.

Planning Your Time

While the major sights can be seen in a day, I'd give Edinburgh two days and three nights.

Day 1: Tour the castle (open from 9:30). Then consider catching one of the city bus tours for a one-hour loop (departing from a block below the castle at the Hub/Tolbooth Church; you could munch a sandwich from the top deck if you're into multitasking). Back near the castle, take my self-guided Royal Mile walk or catch the 14:15 Mercat Tours walk (1.5 hours, leaves from Mercat Cross on the Royal Mile). Spend the remainder of your day enjoying the Royal Mile's shops and museums, or touring the Palace of Holyroodhouse (at the bottom of the Mile).

Day 2: Visit the National Museum of Scotland. After lunch, stroll through the Princes Street Gardens and the Scottish National Gallery. Then wander through the New Town, visiting the Georgian House and Scottish National Portrait Gallery, or squeeze in a quick tour of the good ship *Britannia* (last entry at 16:30).

Evenings: Options include various "haunted Edinburgh" walks, literary pub crawls, or live music in pubs. Sadly, traditional folk shows are just about extinct, surviving only in excruciatingly schmaltzy variety shows put on for tour-bus groups. Perhaps the most authentic evening out is just settling down in a pub to sample the whisky and local beers while meeting the locals...and attempting to understand them through their thick Scottish accents (see "Nightlife in Edinburgh," page 803).

Orientation to Edinburgh

A Verbal Map

Scotland's Old Town stretches across a ridgeline slung between two bluffs. From west to east, this "Royal Mile" runs from Castle Hill—which is visible from anywhere—to the base of the 822-foot dormant volcano called Arthur's Seat. For most tourists, this east-west axis is the center of the action. North of the Royal Mile ridge is the New Town, a neighborhood of grid-planned streets and elegant Georgian buildings. South of the Royal Mile are the university and the National Museum of Scotland.

In the center of it all, in a drained lake bed between the Old and New Towns, sit the Princes Street Gardens park and Waverley Bridge, where you'll find the Waverley train station, TI, Princes Mall, bus info office (starting point for most city bus tours), Scottish National Gallery, and a covered dance-and-music pavilion.

Tourist Information

The crowded TI is as central as can be atop the Princes Mall and Waverley train station (Mon-Sat 9:00-18:00, Sun 10:00-18:00, July-Aug daily until 19:00, tel. 0131-473-3868, www.edinburgh .org). The staff is knowledgeable and eager to help, but much of their information—including their assessment of museums—is skewed by tourism payola. The TI at the airport is more helpful (on the main concourse, tel. 0131-344-3120).

At either TI, pick up a free map or buy the excellent *Collins Discovering Edinburgh* map (which comes with opinionated commentary and locates almost every major shop and sight). If you're interested in late-night music, ask for the free monthly entertainment *Gig Guide*. (The best monthly entertainment listing, *The List*, sells for a few pounds at newsstands.) The free *Essential Guide to Edinburgh*, while not truly essential, lists additional sights and services (when it's in stock).

The TIs sell the mediocre **Edinburgh Pass,** which provides a ticket for the Airlink airport bus and entry to dozens of B-list sights (£30/1 day, £40/2 days, £50/3 days, doesn't include Edinburgh Castle, Holyroodhouse, or *Britannia*, www.edinburgh.org/pass).

Also at the TI, consider buying a three-day **Explorer Pass**—you'll save money if you visit the castles at both Edinburgh and Stirling, and could save much more if you plan to see many sights (a less-useful 7-day pass is also available, can also buy online or at most participating sites, www.historic-scotland.gov.uk/explorer).

Arrival in Edinburgh

By Train: Arriving by train at Waverley Station puts you in the city center and below the TI. Taxis queue almost trackside; the ramp they come and go on leads to Waverley Bridge. If this taxi lane is closed (due to construction), hike up the ramp and hail one on the street. From the station, *Way Out–1–Princes Street* signs lead up to the TI and the city bus stop (for bus directions from here to my recommended B&Bs, see "Sleeping in Edinburgh," later). For picnic supplies, an **M&S Simply Food** is near platform 2.

By Bus: Scottish Citylink, Megabus, and National Express buses use the bus station (with luggage lockers) in the New Town, two blocks north of the train station on St. Andrew Square.

By Plane: Edinburgh's slingshot of an airport is located eight miles northwest of the center. Airport flight info: Tel. 0844-481-8989, www.edinburghairport.com.

Taxis between the airport and the city center are pricey (£20-25, 20 minutes to downtown or to Dalkeith Road B&Bs). Fortunately, the airport is well connected to central Edinburgh by the convenient, frequent, cheap Lothian **Airlink bus #100** (£3.50, £6 round-trip, 6/hour, 30 minutes, buses run all day and 2/hour through the night, tel. 0131/555-6363, www.flybybus.com). The bus drops you at the center of Waverley Bridge. From here, to reach my recommended B&Bs near Dalkeith Road, you can either take a taxi (about £7), or hop on a city bus (£1.50; for bus directions to recommended B&Bs, see "Sleeping in Edinburgh," later).

If you're headed *to* the airport, you can take this same Airlink bus: To get from the Dalkeith Road B&Bs to the Airlink stop downtown, you can ride a city bus to North Bridge, get off, turn left at the grand Balmoral Hotel and walk a short distance down Princes Street to the next bridge, Waverley, where you'll find the

Airlink bus stop. Or, rather than riding a £25 taxi all the way to the airport, take a £7 taxi to this stop, then hop the bus to the airport.

By Car: If you're arriving from the north, rather than drive through downtown Edinburgh to the recommended B&Bs, circle the city on the A-720 City Bypass road. Approaching Edinburgh on the M-9, take the M-8 (direction: Glasgow) and quickly get onto the A-720 City Bypass (direction: Edinburgh South). After four miles, you'll hit a roundabout. Ignore signs directing you into *Edinburgh North* and stay on the A-720 for 10 more miles to the next and last roundabout, named *Sheriffhall*. Exit the roundabout at the first left (A-7 Edinburgh). From here it's four miles to the B&B neighborhood. After a while, the A-7 becomes Dalkeith Road (you'll pass the Royal Infirmary hospital complex). If you see the huge Royal Commonwealth Pool, you've gone a couple of blocks too far (avoid this by referring to the map on page 808).

If you're driving in on A-68 from the south, take the A-7 Edinburgh exit off the roundabout and follow the directions above.

Helpful Hints

Sunday Activities: Many Royal Mile sights close on Sunday (except during August and the Edinburgh Festival), but other major sights and shops are open. Sunday is a good day to catch a guided walking tour along the Royal Mile or a city bus tour (buses go faster in light traffic). The slopes of Arthur's Seat, an extinct volcano, are lively with hikers and picnickers on weekends.

Festivals: August is a crowded, popular month to visit Edinburgh because of the multiple festivals hosted here, including the official **Edinburgh Festival** (Aug 8-31 in 2014, likely Aug 7-30 in 2015, www.edinburghfestivals.co.uk). Book ahead for hotels, events, and restaurant dinners if you'll be visiting during this month, and expect to pay significantly more for your accommodations. For all the details, see page 802.

Internet Access: Many B&Bs and coffee shops, including one at the **Hub,** offer free Wi-Fi. You can also get online at the TI (£1/20 minutes).

Baggage Storage: At the train station, you'll find pricey, high-security luggage storage near platform 2 (£9/24 hours, daily 7:00-23:00). It's cheaper to use the lockers at the bus station on St. Andrew Square, just two blocks north of the train station (£3-10 depending on size and duration—even smallest locker is plenty big, coins only, station open daily 6:00-24:00).

Laundry: The **Ace Cleaning Centre** launderette is located near the recommended B&Bs (£8 self-service, £9 drop-off, Mon-Fri 8:00-20:00, Sat 9:00-17:00, Sun 10:00-16:00, along the

Edinburgh at a Glance

▲▲▲**Royal Mile** Historic road—good for walking—stretching from the castle down to the palace, lined with museums, pubs, and shops. **Hours:** Always open, but best during business hours, with walking tours daily. See page 749.

▲▲▲**Edinburgh Castle** Iconic 11th-century hilltop fort and royal residence complete with crown jewels, Romanesque chapel, memorial, and fine military museum. **Hours:** Daily April-Sept 9:30-18:00, Oct-March 9:30-17:00. See page 761.

▲▲▲**National Museum of Scotland** Intriguing, well-displayed artifacts from prehistoric times to the 20th century. **Hours:** Daily 10:00-17:00. See page 783.

▲▲**Gladstone's Land** Sixteenth-century Royal Mile merchant's residence. **Hours:** Daily July-Aug 10:00-18:30, April-June and Sept-Oct 10:00-17:00, closed Nov-March. See page 771.

▲▲**St. Giles Cathedral** Preaching grounds of Calvinist John Knox, with spectacular organ, Neo-Gothic chapel, and distinctive crown spire. **Hours:** Mon-Sat 9:00-17:00 (until 19:00 Mon-Fri May-Sept), Sun 13:00-17:00. See page 775.

▲▲**Scottish Parliament Building** Striking headquarters for parliament, which returned to Scotland in 1999. **Hours:** If parliament's in session—Mon, Fri-Sat 10:00-17:00, Tue-Thu 9:00-18:30; if parliament's recessed—Mon-Sat 10:00-17:00; closed Sun year-round. See page 781.

▲▲**Georgian New Town** Elegant late 18th-century subdivision spiced with trendy shops, bars, and eateries. **Hours:** Always open. See page 787.

▲▲**Georgian House** Intimate peek at upper-crust life in the late 1700s. **Hours:** Daily April-Oct 10:00-17:00, July-Aug until 18:00, March 11:00-16:00, Nov 11:00-15:00, closed Dec-Feb. See page 790.

▲▲**Scottish National Gallery** Choice sampling of European masters and Scotland's finest. **Hours:** Daily 10:00-17:00, Thu until 19:00, Fri-Wed in Aug until 18:00. See page 792.

▲▲ **Scottish National Portrait Gallery** Beautifully displayed *Who's Who* of Scottish history. **Hours:** Daily 10:00-17:00, Thu until 19:00. See page 796.

▲▲*Britannia* The royal yacht with a history of distinguished passengers, a 15-minute trip out of town. **Hours:** Daily July-Sept 9:30-16:30, April-June and Oct 9:30-16:00, Nov-March 10:00-15:30 (these are last entry times). See page 798.

▲**Writers' Museum at Lady Stair's House** Tribute to Scottish literary triumvirate: Robert Burns, Sir Walter Scott, and Robert Louis Stevenson. **Hours:** Mon-Sat 10:00-17:00, closed Sun except during Festival 12:00-17:00. See page 772.

▲**Mary King's Close** Underground street and houses last occupied in the 17th century, viewable by guided tour. **Hours:** April-Oct daily 10:00-21:00, Aug until 23:00; Nov-March daily 10:00-17:00, Fri-Sat until 21:00 (these are last tour times). See page 778.

▲**Museum of Childhood** Five stories of historic fun. **Hours:** Mon-Sat 10:00-17:00, Sun 12:00-17:00. See page 779.

▲**John Knox House** Reputed digs of the great 16th-century reformer. **Hours:** Mon-Sat 10:00-18:00, closed Sun except in July-Aug 12:00-18:00. See page 779.

▲**People's Story Museum** Everyday life from the 18th to 20th centuries. **Hours:** Mon-Sat 10:00-17:00, closed Sun except during Festival 12:00-17:00. See page 780.

▲**Museum of Edinburgh** Historic mementos, from the original National Covenant inscribed on animal skin to early golf balls. **Hours:** Mon-Sat 10:00-17:00, closed Sun except during Festival 12:00-17:00. See page 780.

▲**Palace of Holyroodhouse** The Queen's splendid home away from home, with lavish rooms, 12th-century abbey, and gallery with rotating exhibits. **Hours:** Daily April-Oct 9:30-18:00, Nov-March until 16:30, closed during royal visits. See page 782.

▲**Scott Monument** Climbable tribute to the famed novelist Sir Walter Scott. **Hours:** Daily April-Sept 10:00-19:00, Oct-March 10:00-16:00. See page 791.

EDINBURGH

bus route to the city center at 13 South Clerk Street, opposite Queens Hall, tel. 0131/667-0549). For a small extra fee, they collect and drop off laundry at the neighborhood B&Bs.

Bike Rental: The laid-back crew at **Cycle Scotland** offers bike tours and happily recommends good bike routes (£15/3 hours, £20/day, daily 10:00-18:00, just off Royal Mile at 29 Blackfriars Street, tel. 0131/556-5560, www.cyclescotland .co.uk).

Dress for the Weather: Weather blows in and out—bring your sweater and be prepared for rain. Locals say the bad weather is one of the disadvantages of living so close to England.

Car Rental: These places have offices both in the town center and at the airport: **Avis** (24 East London Street, tel. 0844-544-6059, airport tel. 0844-544-6004), **Europcar** (Waverley Station, tel. 0871-384-3453, airport tel. 0871-384-3406), **Hertz** (10 Picardy Place, tel. 0843-309-3026, airport tel. 0843-309-3025), and **Budget** (select Waverley Station pick-up; they will meet you at train station and take you to their office at 1 Murrayburn Road, tel. 0131/455-7314, airport tel. 0844-544-4605). Some downtown offices are closed on Sunday, but the airport locations tend to be open daily. If you're going to rent a car, pick it up on your way out of Edinburgh—you won't need it in town.

Blue Badge Local Guides: The following guides charge similar prices and offer half-day and full-day tours: **Jean Blair** (a delightful teacher and guide, £160/day, £380/day with car, tel. 0150/682-5930, mobile 0798-957-0287, www.travelthrough scotland.com, jean@travelthroughscotland.com); **Sergio La Spina** (an Argentinean who adopted Edinburgh as his home-town more than 20 years ago, £175/day, tel. 0131/664-1731, mobile 0797-330-6579, sergiolaspina@aol.com); **Ken Hanley** (who wears his kilt as if pants don't exist, £100/half-day, £150/day, extra charge if he uses his car—seats up to six, tel. 0131/666-1944, mobile 0771-034-2044, www.small-world -tours.co.uk, k.hanley@blueyonder.co.uk); and **Liz Everett** (£100/half-day, £150/day mobile 07821-683-837, liz.everett @live.co.uk).

Updates to this Book: For updates to this book, check www.rick steves.com/update.

Getting Around Edinburgh

Many of Edinburgh's sights are within walking distance of one another, but buses come in handy. Two companies handle the city routes: Lothian (which dominates) and First. Lothian sells a day pass valid only on their buses (£3.50, buy from driver). Buses run from about 6:00 (9:00 on Sun) to 23:00 (£1.50/ride, buy tickets on bus, exact change, Lothian Buses transit office at Old Town end of

Waverley Bridge has schedules and route maps, tel. 0131/555-6363, www.lothianbuses.com). Tell the driver where you're going, have change handy (buses require exact change—you lose any extra you put in), take your ticket as you board, and ping the bell as you near your stop. Double-deckers come with fine views upstairs.

The 1,300 **taxis** cruising Edinburgh's streets are easy to flag down (a ride between downtown and the B&B neighborhood costs about £7). They can turn on a dime, so hail them in either direction.

Tours in Edinburgh

Royal Mile Walking Tours
Edinburgh Tour Guides offers your best basic historical walk (without all the ghosts and goblins). The staff of committed guides heads out as long as they have at least two people. Their Royal Mile tour is a gentle two-hour downhill stroll from the castle to the palace (£12; daily at 9:30, 14:00, and 19:00; meet outside Gladstone's Land, near the top of the Royal Mile—see map on page 772, must call ahead to reserve, mobile 0785-888-0072, www .edinburghtourguides.com).

Mercat Tours offers 1.5-hour guided walks of the Mile that are more entertaining than intellectual (£11, daily at 14:15, leaves from Mercat Cross on the Royal Mile, tel. 0131/225-5445, www .mercattours.com). The guides, who enjoy making a short story long, ignore the big sights and take you behind the scenes with piles of barely historical gossip, bully-pulpit Scottish pride, and fun but forgettable trivia. These tours can move quickly, scaling the steep hills and steps of Edinburgh—wear good shoes. They also offer several ghost tours, as well as one focused on 18th-century underground vaults on the southern slope of the Royal Mile.

The **Voluntary Guides Association** offers free two-hour walks, but only during the Edinburgh Festival. You don't need a reservation, but it's a good idea to call the TI or drop by there to double-check details, such as departure point and time (daily at about 10:00 and 14:00, generally depart from City Chambers, opposite St. Giles Cathedral, www.edinburghfestivalguides.org).

Evening **ghost walks** and **pub tours** are described later, under "Nightlife in Edinburgh" on page 803.

Edinburgh Bus Tours
Five different one-hour hop-on, hop-off bus tour routes, all run by the same company, circle the town center, stopping at the major sights: **MacTours** (focuses on Old Town, most comprehensive, vintage bus), **Edinburgh Tour** (focuses on the wider city, more panoramic), **World Heritage** (explores historic heritage-listed sites), **City Sightseeing** (Old Town and Edinburgh Castle),

Edinburgh

Map labels: To Scottish Nat'l Gallery of Modern Art · Water of Leith · ¼ MILE · 400 METERS · MORAY PLACE · QUEEN ST. GARDENS · QUEEN · Georgian House · HILL · NEW · NAT'L PORT. GALL. · ST. ANDREW'S · CHARLOTTE SQ. · GEORGE · FREDERICK · ST. · HANOVER · ST. ANDREW SQ. · ROSE · TOWN · ST. DAVID · SCOTT MON. · PRINCES STREET · THE MOUND · WAVERLEY BRIDGE · SHANDWICK PLACE · PRINCES ST. GARDENS · NATIONAL GALLERY · LOTHIAN · To Haymarket Stn., A-8, Airport & Glasgow · EDINBURGH CASTLE · ESPLANADE · GEORGE IV · RO · MORRISON · BREAD · GRASSMARKET · GEORGE BRIDGE · ST. GILES · COW- · FOUNTAINBRIDGE · OLD TOWN · LAURISTON PL. · NATIONAL MUSEUM OF SCOTLAND

Legend:
- View
- See Detail Maps
- (B) Bus Stop for Dalkeith Road

Majestic Tour (longer route includes a stop at the *Britannia* and Royal Botanic Garden). The tours all have virtually the same route, cost, and frequency (pick-ups about every 10-15 minutes), but only the first three have live guides—the others use audioguides (£13/tour, £17 for all five tours, £30 family ticket covers two adults and up to three children, tickets give small discounts on most sights along the route, valid 24 hours, buy on bus or at kiosk on Waverley Bridge, tel. 0131/220-

0770, www.edinburghtour.com). Buses run daily year-round (Mac Tours runs only April-Aug); in peak season (April-Oct), they run roughly between 9:30 and 19:00 (last departure from Waverley Bridge at 17:30, later in July-Aug, hours shrink off-season). On sunny days they go topless (the buses), but come with increased traffic noise and exhaust fumes.

Busy sightseers might want to get the **Royal Edinburgh Ticket** (£45, www.edinburghtour.com/ticket-offers), which covers two days of unlimited travel on all five tour buses, as well as admission to Edinburgh Castle (£16), the Palace of Holyroodhouse (£11), and the *Britannia* (£12). If you plan to visit all these sights and to use a tour bus both days, the ticket will save you a few pounds

British, Scottish, and English

Scotland and England have been tied together for 300 years, since the Act of Union in 1707. For a century and a half afterward, Scottish nationalists rioted for independence in Edinburgh's streets and led rebellions in the Highlands. In this controversial union, history is clearly seen through two very different filters.

If you tour a British-oriented sight, such as the National War Museum Scotland, you'll find things told in a "happy union" way, which ignores the long history of Scottish resistance—from the ancient Picts through the time of Robert the Bruce. The official line: In 1706-1707, it was clear to England and some of Scotland (especially landowners from the Lowlands) that it was in their mutual interest to dissolve the Scottish government and fold it into Britain, to be ruled from London.

But talk to a cabbie or your B&B host, and you may get a different spin. Scottish independence is still a hot-button issue today. In 2007, the Scottish National Party (SNP) won a major election, and now has the largest majority in the fledgling Scottish parliament. Alex Salmond, SNP leader and the First Minister of Scotland, is pushing for Scotland to be recognized as an independent nation within the EU, and citizens will vote on this issue in September of 2014. (English leaders are obviously not in favor of breaking up the "united kingdom," though there's a like-minded independence movement in Wales, as well.)

The deep-seated rift shows itself in sports, too. While the English may refer to a British team in international competition as "English," the Scots are careful to call it "British." If a Scottish athlete does well, the English call him "British." If he screws up...he's a clumsy Scot.

(and, in the summer, help you bypass any lines). You can buy these tickets online, from the TI, or from the staff at the tour-bus pickup point on Waverley Bridge. If your main interest is seeing the *Britannia*, you'll save money by taking a regular bus instead (see page 798).

Day Trips from Edinburgh

Many companies run a variety of day trips to regional sights. Study the brochures at the TI's rack. (Several of the private guides listed above have cars, too.)

By far the most popular tour is the all-day **Highlands trip.** The standard Highlands tour gives those with limited time a chance to experience the wonders of Scotland's wild and legend-soaked Highlands in a single long day (about £35-45, roughly 8:00-

20:30). You'll generally see the vast and brutal Rannoch Moor; Glencoe, still evocative with memories of the clan massacre; views of Britain's highest mountain, Ben Nevis; Fort Augustus on Loch Ness (some tours have a 1.5-hour stop here with an optional £12 boat ride); and a 45-minute tea or pub break in the fine town of Pitlochry. You learn about the Loch Ness monster, and a bit about Edinburgh to boot as you drive in and out.

Various competing companies run these tours (each offering a slightly different combination of sights), including **Timberbush Highland Tours** (£41, 7- to 36-seat air-con buses, reliable, depart from entrance to Edinburgh Castle, tel. 0131/226-6066, www .timberbushtours.com); **Gray Line** (£41, tel. 0131/555-5558, www .graylinescotland.com); **Rabbie's Trail Burners** (£42-49, maximum 16 per tour, guaranteed departures, depart from their office at 207 High Street, tel. 0131/226-3133, www.rabbies.com); and **Heart of Scotland Tours** (£45, £3 Rick Steves discount on all their tours—mention when booking, departures daily at 8:00, leaves from opposite Apex Hotel on Waterloo Place near Waverley Station, tel. 01828/627-799, www.heartofscotlandtours.co.uk, run by Nick Roche). As Heart of Scotland is a small company, from November to March they may need to cancel if the requisite six people don't sign up. Be sure to leave a contact number so you can be notified. A final decision is made by 18:00 the night before.

Haggis Adventures runs cheap and youthful tours on 16- to 39-seat buses with a very Scottish driver/guide. Their day trips (£35-45) include a distillery visit and the Highlands, or Loch Lomond and the southern Highlands. Their overnight trips are designed for young backpackers, but they welcome travelers of any age who want a quick look at the countryside and are up for hosteling (2- to 10-day trips, office at 60 High Street, tel. 0131/557-9393, www.haggisadventures.com).

At **Discreet Scotland,** Matthew Wight and his partners specialize in tours of greater Edinburgh and Scotland in spacious SUVs—good for families (£335/9 hours, mobile 0798-941-6990, www.discreetscotland.com). Their 15 day-trips with driver/guides cover the Highlands, St. Andrews, royal castles, and more.

Self-Guided Walk

▲▲▲Royal Mile

The Royal Mile is one of Europe's most interesting historic walks. Start at Edinburgh Castle at the top and amble down to the Palace of Holyroodhouse. Along the way, the street changes names— Castlehill, Lawnmarket, High Street, and Canongate—but it's a straight, downhill shot totaling just over one mile. And nearly every step is packed with shops, cafés, and lanes leading to tiny squares.

The city was born on the easily defended rock at the top where the castle stands today. Celtic tribes (and maybe the Romans) once occupied this site. As the town grew, it spilled downhill along the sloping ridge that became the Royal Mile. Because this strip of land is so narrow, there was no place to build but up. So in medi-

eval times, it was densely packed with multistory "tenements"—large edifices under one roof that housed a number of tenants.

As you walk, you'll be tracing the growth of the city—its birth atop Castle Hill, its Old Town heyday in the 1600s, its expansion in the 1700s into the Georgian New Town (leaving the old quarter an overcrowded, disease-ridden Victorian slum), and on to the 21st century at the modern Scottish Parliament building (2004).

The way the Royal Mile is developing, it seems it's well on its way to becoming a touristic mall—all tartans, kilts, and short-bread. But the streets are packed with history, and if you push past the postcard racks into one of the many side alleys, you can still find a few surviving rough edges of the old city.

This walk covers the route, but skips the many museums and indoor attractions along the way. They (and other sights) are described in walking order after this self-guided walk. You can stay focused on the walk (which takes about 60 to 90 minutes, without stops) and return later to visit the various indoor attractions (many of which are free), or you can review the sights before-hand and pop in as you pass them.

• *We'll start at the Castle Esplanade, the big parking lot at the entrance to...*

Edinburgh Castle

Edinburgh was born on the bluff—a big rock—where the castle now stands. Since before history, people have lived on this strate-gic, easily-defended perch.

The **castle** is an imposing symbol of Scottish independence. Flanking the entryway are statues of the fierce warriors who bat-tled English invaders, William "Braveheart" Wallace (on the right) and Robert the Bruce (left). Between them is the Scottish motto, *Nemo me impune lacessit*—"No one messes with me and gets away with it." These fighting words are also engraved around the edge of the Scottish pound coin. (For a self-guided tour of Edinburgh Castle, see page 762.)

The esplanade—built as a military parade ground (1816)—is now the site of the annual Military Tattoo. This spectacular mass-

The Kilt

The kilt, Scotland's national dress, is intimately tied in with the country's history. It originated back in the 1500s as a multi-purpose robe, toga, tent, poncho, and ground cloth. A wearer would lay it on the ground to scrunch up pleats, then wrap it around the waist and belt it. Extra fabric was thrown over the shoulder or tucked into the belt, making a rucksack-like pouch.

The kilt was standard dress in the Highlands and came to be a patriotic statement during wars with England. After the tragic-for-Scotland Battle of Culloden in 1746, England wanted to end the Scottish clan system. Wearing the kilt, speaking Gaelic, and playing the bagpipe were all outlawed.

In 1782 kilts were permitted again, but the image of a kilt-dressed man had taken on an unrefined connotation, so most Scots no longer even wanted to wear it. The modern rehabilitation of the kilt really took off when King George IV visited Edinburgh in 1822. He wanted to show he was king of Scotland and needed to dress the part—so he wore a kilt. Scottish aristocrats ended up being charmed by the king's embrace of Scottish pageantry, and suddenly the kilt was in vogue again.

During the king's visit, Sir Walter Scott organized a Highland festival that also helped change the image of traditional Scottish culture, giving it a newfound respectability. A generation later, Queen Victoria raised the image of Scottish culture even higher. She loved Scotland and wallpapered her palace at Balmoral with "tartanry"—as the tartan patterns are called.

The colors and patterns of the original kilts were determined by what dyes were available and who wove them—not by clan patterns, as is commonly thought. The whole tartan thing (a certain pattern, or tartan, that told which clan the wearer was from) started as a scam by fabric salesmen in Victorian times. Since then, tartanry has been embraced as if it were historic.

In modern times the smaller kilt, or philibeg, replaced the big, heavy, and hot traditional kilt. While still heavy, the philibeg has less fabric and is little more than a wraparound skirt. Half the weight of the original old-style kilts, it's the more practical choice.

ing of regimental bands fills the square nightly for most of August. Fans watch from temporary bleacher seats to see kilt-wearing bagpipers marching against the spectacular backdrop of the castle. TV crews broadcast the spectacle to all corners of the globe.

When the bleachers aren't up, there are fine views in both directions from the esplanade. Facing north, you'll see the body of water called the Firth of Forth, and Fife beyond that. (The

Firth of Forth is the estuary where the Forth River flows into the North Sea.) Still facing north, find the lacy spire of the Scott Memorial and two Neoclassical buildings housing art galleries. Beyond them, the stately buildings of Edinburgh's New Town rise. Panning to the right, find the Nelson Monument and some fake Greek ruins atop Calton Hill.

The city's many bluffs, crags, and ridges were built up by volcanoes, then carved down by glaciers—a city formed in "fire and ice," as the locals say. So, during the Ice Age, as a river of glaciers swept in from the west (behind today's castle), it ran into the super-hard volcanic basalt of Castle Hill and flowed around it, cutting valleys on either side and leaving a tail that became the Royal Mile you're about to walk.

At the bottom of the esplanade (where the square hits the road, on the left), a plaque on the wall above the tiny witches' fountain memorializes 300 women who were accused of witchcraft and burned here. Below was the Nor' Loch, the swampy lake where those accused of witchcraft (mostly women) were tested. Bound up, they were dropped into the lake. If they sank and drowned, they were innocent. If they floated, they were guilty, and were burned here in front of the castle, providing the city folk a nice afternoon out. Scotland burned more witches per capita than any other country—17,000 souls between 1479 and 1722. The plaque shows two witches: one good and one bad. Tickle the serpent's snout to sympathize with the witches. (I just made that up.)

• Start walking down the Royal Mile. The first block is a street called...

Castlehill

You're immediately in the tourist hubbub. The big tank-like building on your left was the Old Town's reservoir. You'll see the well-heads it served all along this walk. While it once held 1.5 million gallons of water, today it's filled with the touristy Tartan Weaving Mill and Exhibition. If you want to peruse several floors of tartanry and Chinese-produced Scottish kitsch, pop in.

The tower ahead on the left has entertained visitors since the 1850s with its **camera obscura**, a darkened room where a mirror and a series of lenses capture live images of the city surroundings outside (described on page 770.) Giggle at the funny mirrors as you walk fatly by. Across the street, filling the old Castle Hill Primary School, is a gimmicky-if-intoxicating whisky-sampling exhibit called the Scotch Whisky Experience (a.k.a. "Malt Disney," described on page 771).

• Just ahead, in front of the church with the tall, lacy spire, is the old market square known as...

Lawnmarket

During the Royal Mile's heyday, in the 1600s, this intersection was bigger and served as a market for fabric (especially "lawn," a linen-like cloth). The market would fill this space with bustle, hustle, and lots of commerce. The round white hump in the middle of the roundabout is all that remains of the official weighing beam called the Butter Tron—where all goods sold were weighed for honesty and tax purposes.

Towering above Lawnmarket, with the tallest spire in the city, is the former **Tolbooth Church.** This impressive Neo-Gothic structure (1844) is now home to the Hub, Edinburgh's festival ticket and information center. The world-famous Edinburgh Festival fills the month of August with cultural action. The various festivals feature classical music, traditional and fringe theater (especially comedy), art, books, and more. Drop inside the building to get festival info (see also page 802). This is a handy stop for its WC and café (£5-8 lunches, free Wi-Fi).

In the 1600s, this, along with the next stretch, called High Street, was the city's main street. At that time, Edinburgh was bursting with breweries, printing presses, and banks. Tens of thousands of citizens were squeezed into the narrow confines of the Old Town. Here on this ridge, they built tenements (multiple-unit residences) similar to the more recent ones you see today. These tenements, rising up 10 stories and more, were some of the tallest domestic buildings in Europe. The living arrangements shocked class-conscious English visitors to Edinburgh because the tenements were occupied by rich and poor alike—usually the poor in the cellars and attics, and the rich in the middle floors.

Gladstone's Land (at #477b, on the left), a surviving original tenement, was acquired by a wealthy merchant in 1617. Stand in front of the building and look up. That's a centuries-old skyscraper. This design was standard on this street back then: a shop or shops on the ground floor, with columns and an arcade, and residences on the floors above. Because window glass was expensive, the lower halves of window openings were made of cheaper wood, which swung out like shutters for ventilation—and convenient for tossing out garbage. (For more on this sight, see page 771).

For a good Royal Mile photo, climb the curved stairway outside Gladstone's Land and look downhill. Notice the snoozing pig outside the front door. Just like every house has a vacuum cleaner today, in the good old days a snorting rubbish collector was a standard feature of any well-equipped house.

Branching off the spine of the Royal Mile are a number of narrow alleyways that go by various local names. A "wynd" (rhymes with "kind") is a narrow, winding lane. A "pend" is an

EDINBURGH

arched gateway. "Gate" is from an old Scandinavian word for street. And a "close" is a tiny alley between two buildings (originally with a door that "close"-ed it at night). A close usually leads to a "court," or courtyard.

To explore one of these alleyways, head into **Lady Stair's Close** (across the street, 10 steps downhill from Gladstone's Land). This alley pops out in a small courtyard, where you'll find the **Writers' Museum**. It's free and well worth a visit for fans of the city's holy trinity of writers (Robert Burns, Sir Walter Scott, and Robert Louis Stevenson), but it's also a glimpse of what a typical home might have looked like in the 1600s. You'll wind up steep staircases through a maze of rooms as you peruse first editions and keepsakes of these great writers. Burns actually lived for a while in this neighborhood, in 1786, when he first arrived in Edinburgh.

Opposite Gladstone's Land (at #322), another close leads to **Riddle's Court.** Wander through here and imagine Edinburgh in the 17th and 18th centuries, when tourists came here to marvel at its skyscrapers. Visualize the labyrinthine maze of the old city, with thousands of people scurrying through these back alleyways, buying and selling, and popping into taverns.

No city in Europe was as densely populated—or perhaps as filthy. Without modern hygiene, it was a living hell of smoke, smell, and noise, with the constant threat of fire, collapse, and disease. The dirt streets were soiled with sewage from bedpans emptied out windows. By the 1700s, the Old Town was rife with poverty and cholera outbreaks. The smoky home fires rising from tenements and the infamous smell (or "reek" in Scottish) that wafted across the city gave it a nickname which sticks today— "Auld Reekie."

• *Return to the Royal Mile and continue down it a few steps to take in some sights at the...*

Bank/High Streets Intersection

A number of sights cluster here, where Bank Street changes its

name to High Street and intersects with George IV Bridge.

Begin with **Deacon Brodie's Tavern.** Read the "Doctor Jekyll and Mister Hyde" story of this pub's notorious namesake on the wall facing Bank Street. Then, to see his spooky split personality, check out both sides of the hanging signpost. Brodie—a pillar of the community by day but a burglar by night—epitomizes the divided personality of

1700s Edinburgh. It was a rich, productive city—home to great philosophers and scientists, participants in the Enlightenment of that age. But the Old Town was riddled with crime and squalor. The city was scandalized when a respected surgeon—driven by a passion for medical research and needing corpses—was accused of colluding with two lowlifes to acquire (freshly murdered) corpses for dissection. (In the next century, in the late 1800s, novelist Robert Louis Stevenson would capture the dichotomy of Edinburgh's rich-poor society in his *Strange Case of Dr. Jekyll and Mr. Hyde.*)

In the late 1700s, Edinburgh's upper class moved out of the Old Town into a planned community called the New Town (a quarter-mile north of here). Eventually, most tenements were torn down and replaced with newer **Victorian buildings.** You'll see some at this intersection.

Look left down Bank Street to the green-domed **Bank of Scotland.** This was the headquarters of the bank, which had practiced modern capitalist financing since 1695. The building now houses the Museum on the Mound, a free exhibit on banking history (see page 774), and it's also the Scottish headquarters for Lloyds Banking Group—which swallowed up the Bank of Scotland after the financial crisis of 2008. The confusing array of mergers here, as in the USA, has led skeptics to see the bank crisis as intentionally created to make big banks "too big to fail."

• *If you **detour** left down the road toward the bank, you'll find the recommended Whiski Rooms Shop. If you head in the other direction down Bank Street (to your right), you'll reach some recommended eateries (The Elephant House and The Outsider), as well as the excellent National Museum of Scotland, the famous Greyfriars Bobby statue, and photogenic Victoria Street, which leads to the fun pub-lined Grassmarket square (all described later in this chapter).*

Otherwise, continue along the Royal Mile.

Across the street from Deacon Brodie's Tavern is a seated green statue of hometown boy **David Hume** (1711-1776)—one of the most influential thinkers not only of Scotland, but in all of Western philosophy. The atheistic Hume was one of the towering figures of the Scottish Enlightenment of the mid-1700s. Thinkers and scientists were using the experimental method to challenge and investigate everything, including religion. Hume questioned cause and effect in thought puzzles such as this: We can see that when one billiard ball strikes another, the second one moves, but how do we know the collision "caused" the movement? Notice his shiny toe: People on their way to trial (in the high court just behind the statue) or students on their way to exams (in the nearby university) rub it for good luck.

Follow David Hume's gaze to the opposite corner, where a

brass H in the pavement marks the site of the last public execution in Edinburgh in 1864. Deacon Brodie himself would have been hung about here (in 1788, on a gallows whose design he had helped to improve—smart guy).

• *From the brass H, continue down the Royal Mile, pausing just before the church square at a stone wellhead with the pyramid cap.*

All along the Royal Mile, **wellheads** like this (from 1835) provided townsfolk with water in the days before buildings had plumbing. This neighborhood well was served by the reservoir up at the castle. Imagine long lines of people in need of water standing here, gossiping and sharing the news. Eventually buildings were retrofitted with water pipes—the ones you see running along building exteriors.

• *Ahead of you (past the Victorian statue of some duke, about 10 steps in front of the church), near the street, embedded in the pavement, is a heart. Find it.*

The **Heart of Midlothian** marks the spot of the city's 15th-century municipal building and jail. In times past, in a nearby open space, criminals were hanged, traitors were decapitated, and witches were burned. Citizens hated the rough justice doled out here. Locals still spit on the heart in the pavement. Go ahead... do as the locals do—land one right in the heart of the heart. By the way, Edinburgh has two soccer teams—Heart of Midlothian (known as "Hearts") and Hibernian ("Hibs"). If you're a Hibs fan, spit again.

• *Make your way to the entrance of the church.*

St. Giles Cathedral

This is the flagship of the Church of Scotland (Scotland's largest denomination) and the historic home of Scottish Presbyterianism. These days the interior serves as a kind of Scottish Westminster Abbey, filled with monuments, statues, plaques, and stained-glass windows dedicated to great Scots and moments in history.

A church has stood on this spot since 854, though this structure is an architectural hodgepodge, dating mostly from the 15th through 19th century. In the 16th century, St. Giles was a kind of national stage on which the drama of the Reformation was played out. The reformer John Knox (1514-1572) was the preacher here. His fiery sermons helped turn once-Catholic Edinburgh into a bastion of Protestantism. During the Scottish Reformation, St. Giles was transformed from a Catholic cathedral to a Presbyterian church. The spacious interior is well worth a visit. (If it's open, you can splice a visit of the church into this tour now by following the self-guided tour on page 776.)

• *Walk around the front of the church to the right, into a parking lot.*

Sights Around St. Giles

The grand building next door to St. Giles is the **Old Parliament House.** Since the 13th century, the king had ruled a rubber-stamp parliament of nobles and bishops. But with the Reformation, Protestantism promoted democracy, and the parliament gained real power. From the early 1600s until 1707, this building evolved to become the seat of a true parliament of elected officials. In 1707 Scotland signed an Act of Union, joining what's known today as the United Kingdom and giving up their right to self-rule. (More on that later in the walk.) You can go inside the Old Parliament; it's free, but requires a pass through security (see page 778).

By the way, the great reformer **John Knox** is buried—with appropriate austerity—under parking lot spot #23. The statue among the cars shows King Charles II riding to a toga party back in 1685.

• *Continue on through the parking lot, around the back end of the church.*

Standard features of any Scottish burgh or town licensed by the king to trade were a "tolbooth" (basically a town hall, with a courthouse, meeting room, and jail); a "tron" (official weighing scale); and a "mercat" (or market) cross. The **market cross** standing just behind St. Giles Cathedral has a slender column decorated with a unicorn holding a flag with the cross of St. Andrew. Royal proclamations have been read at this market cross since the 14th century. In 1952, a town crier heralded the news that Britain had a new queen—three days after the actual event (traditionally the time it took for a horse to speed here from London). Today, Mercat Cross is the meeting point of various walking tours—both historic and ghostly.

• *Circle around to the street side of the church.*

The statue to **Adam Smith** honors the Edinburgh author of the pioneering *Wealth of Nations* (1776), in which he laid out the economics of free market capitalism. Smith theorized that there was an "invisible hand" that wisely guides the unregulated free market. Stand in front of Smith and imagine the intellectual energy of Edinburgh in the mid-1700s when it was Europe's most enlightened city. Adam Smith was right in the center of it. He and David Hume were good friends. James Boswell, the famed biographer of Samuel Johnson, took classes from Smith. James Watt, inventor of the steam engine, was another proud Scotsman of the age. With great intellectuals like these, Edinburgh helped create the modern world. The poet Robert Burns, geologist James Hutton (who's considered the father of modern geology), and the publishers of the first Encyclopedia Britannica all lived in Edinburgh. Steeped in the inquisitive mindset of the Enlightenment, they applied cool rationality and a secular approach to their respective fields.

• *Head on down the Royal Mile.*

More of High Street

A few steps downhill, at #188, is the **Police Information Center.** This place provides a pleasant police presence (say that three times) and a little local law-and-order history to boot. Ask the officer on duty about the impact of modern technology and budget austerity on police work today. Seriously—drop in and discuss whatever law-and-order issue piques your curiosity (free, open daily 10:00-17:30, Aug until 21:30).

Continuing down this stretch of the Royal Mile, which is traffic-free most of the day (notice the bollards that raise and lower for permitted traffic), you'll see the Fringe Festival office (at #180), street musicians, and another wellhead (with horse "sippies," dating from 1675).

Notice those three red boxes. In the 20th century, people used these to make telephonic calls to each other. These cast-iron booths are produced for all of Britain here in Scotland. As phone booths are gradually being decommissioned, they are showing up at British homes as nostalgic garden decorations.

On the left is **Cockburn Street** (pronounced "COE-burn"). This was cut through High Street's dense wall of medieval skyscrapers in the 1860s to give easy access to the Georgian New Town and the train station. Notice how the sliced buildings were thoughtfully capped with facades that fit the aesthetic look of the Royal Mile. In the Middle Ages, only tiny lanes (like Fleshmarket Lane just uphill from Cockburn Street) interrupted the long line of Royal Mile buildings. These days, Cockburn Street has a reputation for its eclectic independent shops and string of trendy bars and eateries.

• *When you reach the* **Tron Church** *(17th century, currently empty), you're at the intersection of* **North and South Bridge streets.** *These major streets lead left to Waverley Station and right to the Dalkeith Road B&Bs. Several handy bus lines run along here.*

This is the halfway point of this walk. Stand on the corner diagonally across from the church. Look up to the top of the Royal Mile at the Hub and its 240-foot spire. Notwithstanding its turret and 16th-century charm, the Radisson Blu Hotel just across the street is entirely new construction (1990), built to fit in. The city is protecting its historic look. The Bank Hotel next door was once a fancy bank with a lavish interior. As modern banks are moving away from city centers, sumptuous buildings like these are being converted into ornate pubs and restaurants.

In the next block downhill are three **characteristic pubs**, side by side, that offer free traditional Scottish and folk music in the evenings. Notice the chimneys. Tenement buildings shared stairways and entries, but held individual apartments, each with its own chimney. Take a look back at the spire of St. Giles Cathedral—inspired by the Scottish crown and the thistle, Scotland's national flower.

• *Go down High Street another block, passing near the* **Museum of Childhood** *(worth a stop; see page 779) and a fragrant* **fudge shop** *where you can sample various flavors as you would gelato (tempting you to buy a slab—£4). Directly across the street, just below another wellhead, is the...*

John Knox House

As mentioned earlier, Knox was a towering figure in Edinburgh's history, converting Scotland to a Calvinist style of Protestantism. His religious bent was "Presbyterianism"—in which parishes are governed by elected officials rather than appointed bishops. As this brand of Christianity was more democratic, it also spurred Scotland toward political democracy. If you're interested in Knox or the Reformation, this sight is worth a visit (see page 779). Full disclosure: It's not certain that Knox ever actually lived here.

• *A few steps farther down High Street, at the intersection with St. Mary's and Jeffrey streets, you'll reach...*

World's End

For centuries, a wall stood here, marking the end of the burgh of Edinburgh. For residents within the protective walls of the city, this must have felt like the "world's end," indeed. The area beyond was called Canongate, a monastic community associated with Holyrood Abbey. At the intersection, find the brass bricks in the street that trace the gate (demolished in 1764). Look down St. Mary's Street about 200 yards to see a surviving bit of that old wall, known as **Flodden Wall.** In the 1513 Battle of Flodden, the Scottish king James IV made the disastrous decision to invade northern England. James and 10,000 of his Scotsmen were killed. Fearing a brutal English counterattack, Edinburgh scrambled to reinforce its broken-down city wall.

The pub on the corner, No. 1 High Street, is a centrally located venue for live traditional music—pop in and see what's on tonight.

• *Continue down the Royal Mile—leaving old Edinburgh—as High Street changes names to...*

Canongate

About 10 steps down Canongate, look left down Cranston Street (past the train tracks) to a good view of the Calton Cemetery up on Calton Hill. The obelisk, called **Martyrs' Monument,** remembers a group of 18th-century patriots exiled by London to Australia for their reform politics. The round building to the left is the grave of philosopher David Hume. And the big, turreted building to the right was the jail master's house. Today, the main reason to go up Calton Hill is for the fine views.

• *A couple of hundred yards farther along the Royal Mile (on the right at #172) you reach a special shop, Cadenhead's, a serious place to sample and buy whisky (see page 780). About 30 yards farther along, you'll pass two worthwhile and free museums, the* **People's Story Museum** *(#163) and* **Museum of Edinburgh** *(#142; see page 780). But our next stop is the church just across from the Museum of Edinburgh.*

The 1688 **Canongate Church**—located not far from the royal residence of Holyroodhouse—is where Queen Elizabeth and her family worship whenever they're in town. (So don't sit in the front pew marked with her crown.) The gilded emblem at the top of the roof, high above the door, has the antlers of a stag from the nearby royal estate of Balmoral. The Queen's granddaughter married here in 2011.

Step inside the lofty blue and red interior, renovated with royal money; the church is filled with light and the flags of various Scottish regiments. In the narthex, peruse the photos of royal family events here, and find the list of priests and ministers of this parish—it goes back to 1143 (with a clear break with the Reformation in 1561).

Outside, in the graveyard, follow the cute little markers to the tomb of **Adam Smith,** the father of capitalism (his monument abuts the back of the People's Story Museum).

Just outside the churchyard, the statue on the sidewalk is of the poet **Robert Fergusson.** One of the first to write verse in Scottish, he so inspired Robert Burns that Burns paid for Fergusson's tombstone in the Canongate churchyard and composed his epitaph.

Now look across the street at the gabled house for shells put there in the 17th century to defend against the evil power of witches yet to be drowned.

• *Walk about 300 yards farther along. In the distance you can see the Palace of Holyroodhouse (the end of this walk) and soon, on the right, you'll come to the modern Scottish parliament building.*

Just opposite the parliament building is **White Horse Close** (in the white arcade). Step into this 17th-century courtyard. It was from here that the Edinburgh stagecoach left for London. Eight days later, the horse-drawn carriage would pull into its destination: Scotland Yard. Note that bus #35 leaves in two directions from here—downhill for the Royal Yacht *Britannia,* and uphill along the Royal Mile (as far as South Bridge) and on to the National Museum of Scotland.

• *Now walk up around the corner to the flagpoles (flying the flags of Europe, Britain, and Scotland) in front of the...*

Scottish Parliament Building

Finally, after centuries of history, we reach the 21st century. And finally, after three centuries of London rule, Scotland has a parliament building...in Scotland. When Scotland united with England in 1707, its parliament was dissolved. But the Scots won it back nearly three centuries years later.

In 1999, the Scottish parliament was re-established, and in 2004, moved into its striking new home. Notice how the eco-friendly building, by the Catalan architect Enric Miralles, mixes wild angles, lots of light, bold windows, oak, and native stone into a startling complex. From the front of the parliament building, look in the distance at the rocky Salisbury Crags, with people hiking the traverse up to the dramatic next summit called Arthur's Seat. Now look at the building in relation to the craggy cliffs. The architect envisioned the building as if were rising right from the base of Arthur's Seat, almost bursting from the rock.

Since it celebrates Scottish democracy, the architecture is not a statement of authority. There are no statues of old heroes. There's not even a grand entry. You feel like you're entering an office park. (For details on touring the building and seeing parliament in action, see page 781.)

• *Across the street is the Queen's Gallery, where she shares part of her amazing personal art collection in excellent revolving exhibits (see page 782). Finally, walk to the end of the road (Abbey Strand), and step up to the impressive wrought-iron gate of the Queen's palace. Look up at the stag with its holy cross, or "holy rood," on its forehead, and peer into the palace grounds. (The ticket office and palace entryway, a fine café, and a handy public toilet are just through the arch on the right.)*

Palace of Holyroodhouse

Since the 16th century, this palace has marked the end of the Royal Mile. An abbey—part of a 12th-century Augustinian monastery—originally stood in its place. While most of that old building is gone, you can see the surviving nave behind the palace on the left. It was named "holy rood" for a piece of the cross, brought here as a relic by Queen (and later Saint) Margaret. Because Scotland's royalty preferred living at Holyroodhouse to the blustery castle on the rock, the palace evolved over time. If the Queen's not visiting, the palace welcomes visitors (see page 782 for details).

Your walk—from the castle to the palace, with so much Scottish history packed in between—is complete. And, if your appetite is whetted for more, don't worry; you've just scratched the surface. Enjoy the rest of Edinburgh.

Sights in Edinburgh

▲▲▲Edinburgh Castle

The fortified birthplace of the city 1,300 years ago, this imposing symbol of Edinburgh sits proudly on a rock high above you.

The home of Scotland's kings and queens for centuries, the castle has witnessed royal births, medieval pageantry, and bloody sieges. Today it's a complex of various buildings linked by cobbled roads that survive from its more recent use as a military garrison. The

castle—with expansive views, plenty of history, and the stunning crown jewels of Scotland—is a fascinating and multifaceted sight that deserves several hours of your time.

Cost and Hours: £16, daily April-Sept 9:30-18:00, Oct-March 9:30-17:00, last entry one hour before closing, National War Museum Scotland closes one hour before rest of castle, tel. 0131/225-9846, www.edinburghcastle.gov.uk.

Avoiding Lines: The least crowded times are usually first thing in the morning and after 14:00. To avoid ticket lines (worst in August), book online and print your ticket at home, or pick up your prebooked ticket at the machines by the red phone boxes just inside the entrance.

Getting There: You can walk to the castle, catch a bus (which drops you off a short, uphill walk away), or take a taxi (taxis let you off a block below the esplanade at the Hub/Tolbooth Church).

Tours: Thirty-minute guided introductory tours are free with admission (2-4/hour, depart from Argyle Battery, see clock for next departure; fewer tours off-season). The informative audioguide provides four hours of descriptions, including the National War Museum Scotland (£3.50, slightly cheaper if purchased online with entry ticket).

Services: The clean WC at the entry routinely wins "British Loo of the Year" awards. For lunch, you have two choices. **The Red Coat Café and Jacobite Room**—located within Edinburgh Castle—is a big, bright, efficient cafeteria with great views (£8-

10 quick, healthy meals). Punctuate the two parts of your castle visit (the castle itself and the impressive National War Museum Scotland) with a smart break here. The **Tea Rooms,** in a building at the top of the hill, right across from the crown jewels, serves sit-down meals in its small, tight space (last orders 30 minutes before castle complex closes).

● **Self-Guided Tour:** From the ❶ **entry gate,** start winding your way uphill toward for the main sights—the crown jewels and the Royal Palace—located near

Edinburgh Castle

PRINCES ST. GARDENS

50 YARDS
50 METERS

CLIFFS

ESPLANADE

MIDDLE WARD

SHOP

START
ENTRY GATE

TO ROYAL MILE

CLIFFS

GARDENS

WALLS

CROWN SQUARE

WC

DCH

- → ROUTE FROM ENTRY GATE TO CROWN SQUARE
- ☐ MAIN BUILDINGS
- ☐ OTHER BUILDINGS
- ⚐ VIEW
- ⊞ STAIRS

Tour
1. Entry Gate & Tickets
2. Argyle Battery
3. One O'Clock Gun
4. St. Margaret's Chapel, Mons Meg & Dog Cemetery
5. Crown Square
6. Scottish Crown Jewels
7. Royal Palace & Great Hall
8. Scottish National War Memorial
9. National War Museum Scotland

Eateries
10. Red Coat Café & Jacobite Room
11. Tea Rooms

the summit. Since the castle was protected on three sides by sheer cliffs, the main defense had to be here at the entrance. During the castle's heyday in the 1500s, a 100-foot tower loomed overhead, facing the city.

• *Passing through the portcullis gate, you reach the...*

2 Argyle (Six-Gun) Battery, with View: These front-loading, cast-iron cannons are from the Napoleonic era (c. 1800), when the castle was still a force to be reckoned with.

From here, look north across the valley to the grid blocks of the New Town. The valley sits where the Nor' Loch once was; this lake was drained and filled in when the New Town was built in the late 1700s, its swamps replaced with gardens. Later the land provided sites for the Greek-temple-looking Scottish National Gallery and Waverley Station. Looking farther north, you can make out the port town of Leith with its high-rises and cranes, the Firth of Forth, the island of Inchkeith, and—in the far, far distance (to the east)—the cone-like mountain of North Berwick Law, a former volcano.

Now look down. The sheer north precipice looks impregnable. But on the night of March 14, 1314, 30 armed men silently scaled this rock face. They were loyal to Robert the Bruce and determined to capture the castle, which had fallen into English hands. They caught the English by surprise, took the castle, and—three months later—Bruce defeated the English at the Battle of Bannockburn. This was the last great Scottish military victory.

• *A little farther along, near the café, is the...*

❸ One O'Clock Gun: Crowds gather for the 13:00 gun blast, a tradition that gives ships in the bay something to set their navigational devices by. Before the gun, sailors set their clocks with help from the Nelson Monument—that's the tall pillar in the distance on Calton Hill. The monument has a "time ball" affixed to the cross on top, which dropped precisely at the top of the hour. But on foggy days, ships couldn't see the ball, so the cannon shot was instituted instead (1861). The tradition stuck, every day at 13:00—the frugal Scots don't fire it at high noon, as that would cost 11 extra rounds a day.

• *Continue uphill, winding to the left and passing through Foog's Gate. At the very top of the hill is...*

❹ St. Margaret's Chapel: This tiny stone chapel is Edinburgh's oldest building (1130) and sits atop its highest point (440 feet). It represents the birth of the city.

In 1057, Malcolm III murdered King Macbeth (of Shakespeare fame) and assumed the Scottish throne. Later, he married Princess Margaret, and the family settled atop this hill. Their marriage united Malcolm's Highland Scots with Margaret's Lowland Anglo-Saxons—the cultural mix that would define Edinburgh.

Step inside the tiny, unadorned church—a testament to Margaret's reputed piety. The style is Romanesque. The nave is wonderfully simple, with classic Norman zigzags decorating the round arch that separates the tiny nave from the sacristy. You'll see a facsimile of St. Margaret's 11th-century gospel book. The small (modern) stained-glass windows feature St. Margaret herself, St. Columba (who brought Christianity to Scotland via Iona), and William Wallace (the brave-hearted defender of Scotland). These days, the place is popular for weddings, and—as it seats only 20—it's particularly popular with brides' parents.

Margaret died at the castle in 1093, and her son King David I built this chapel in her honor (she was sainted in 1250). David expanded the castle and also founded Holyrood Abbey, across town. These two structures were soon linked by a Royal Mile of buildings, and Edinburgh was born.

Mons Meg, in front of the church, is a huge and once-upon-a-time frightening 15th-century siege cannon that fired 330-pound stones nearly two miles. Imagine. It was a gift from the Belgians, who shared a common enemy with the Scots—England—and were eager to arm Scotland. Nearby, belly up to the banister and look down to find the **Dog Cemetery,** a tiny patch of grass with a sweet little line of doggie tombstones, marking the graves of soldiers' faithful canines in arms.

• *Continue on, curving downhill into...*

❺ Crown Square: This courtyard is the center of today's Royal Castle complex. Get oriented. You're surrounded by the crown jewels, the Royal Palace (with its Great Hall), and the Scottish National War Memorial.

The castle has evolved over the centuries, and Crown Square is relatively "new." After the time of Malcolm and Margaret, the castle was greatly expanded by David II (1324-1371), complete with tall towers, a Great Hall, dungeon, cellars, and so on. This served as the grand royal residence for two centuries. Then, in 1571-1573, the Protestant citizens of Edinburgh laid siege to the castle and its Catholic/monarchist holdouts, eventually blasting it to smithereens. (You can tour the paltry remains of the medieval castle in nearby **David's Tower.**) The palace was rebuilt nearby—around what is today's Crown Square.

• *We'll tour the buildings around Crown Square. First up, the crown jewels. The main year-round entry to the jewels is on Crown Square. In summer, there's a second option that avoids the line: Head to the left as you face the main entrance and find another entry near the WCs. This route takes you through the Honors of Scotland exhibition—an interesting, if Disney-esque, series of displays (which often moves at a shuffle) telling the story of the crown jewels and how they survived the harrowing centuries.*

❻ Scottish Crown Jewels: For centuries, Scotland's monarchs were crowned in elaborate rituals involving three wondrous objects: a jewel-studded crown, scepter, and sword. These objects—along with the ceremonial Stone of Scone (pronounced "skoon")—are known as the "Honors." Scotland's crown jewels may not be as impressive as England's, but they're treasured by locals as a symbol of Scottish nationalism. They're also older than England's; while Oliver Cromwell destroyed England's jewels, the Scots managed to hide theirs.

History of the Jewels: The Honors of Scotland exhibit that leads up to the Crown Room traces the evolution of the jewels, the ceremony, and the often turbulent journey of this precious regalia.

In 1306, Robert the Bruce was crowned with a "circlet of gold" in a ceremony at Scone—a town 40 miles north of Edinburgh, which Scotland's earliest kings had claimed as their capital. Around 1500, King James IV added two new items to the

William Wallace
(c. 1270-1305)

In 1286, Scotland's king died without an heir, plunging the prosperous country into a generation of chaos. As Scottish nobles bickered over naming a successor, the English King Edward I—nicknamed "Longshanks" because of his height—invaded and assumed power (1296). He placed a figurehead on the throne, forced Scottish nobles to sign a pledge of allegiance to England (the "Ragman's Roll"), moved the British parliament north to York, and carried off the highly symbolic 336-pound Stone of Scone to London, where it would remain for the next seven centuries.

A year later, the Scots rose up against Edward, led by William Wallace (nicknamed "Braveheart"). A mix of history and legend portrays Wallace as the son of a poor-but-knightly family that refused to sign the Ragman's Roll. Exceptionally tall and strong, he learned Latin and French from two uncles, who were priests. In his teenage years, his father and older brother were killed by the English. Later, he killed an English sheriff to avenge the death of his wife, Marion. Wallace's rage inspired his fellow Scots to revolt.

In the summer of 1297, Wallace and his guerrillas scored a series of stunning victories over the English. On September 11, a large, well-equipped English army of 10,000 soldiers and 300 horsemen began crossing Stirling Bridge. Half of the army had made it across when Wallace's men attacked. In the chaos, the bridge collapsed, splitting the English ranks in two, and the ragtag Scots drove the confused English into the river. The Battle of Stirling Bridge was a rout, and Wallace was knighted and appointed guardian (a caretaker ruler) of Scotland.

All through the winter, King Edward's men chased Wallace, continually frustrated by the Scots' hit-and-run tactics. Finally, at the Battle of Falkirk (1298), they drew Wallace's men out onto the open battlefield. The English with their horses and archers easily destroyed the spear-carrying Scots. Wallace resigned in disgrace and went on the lam, while his successors negotiated truces with the English, finally surrendering unconditionally in 1304. Wallace alone held out.

In 1305, the English tracked him down and took him to London, where he was convicted of treason and mocked with a crown of oak leaves as the "King of Scotland." On August 23, they stripped him naked and dragged him to the execution site. There he was strangled to near death, castrated, and dismembered. His head was stuck on a stick atop London Bridge, while his body parts were sent on tour around the realm to spook would-be rebels. But Wallace's martyrdom only served to inspire his countrymen, and the torch of independence was picked up by Robert the Bruce (see sidebar on page 769).

coronation ceremony—a scepter (a gift from the pope) and a huge sword (a gift from another pope). In 1540, James V had the original crown augmented by an Edinburgh goldsmith, giving it the imperial-crown shape it has today.

These Honors were used to crown every monarch: nine-month-old Mary, Queen of Scots (she cried); her one-year-old son James VI (future king of England); and Charles I and II. But the days of divine-right rulers were numbered.

In 1649, the Parliament had Charles I (king of both England and Scotland) beheaded. Soon rabid English antiroyalists were marching on Edinburgh. Quick! Legend says two women scooped up the crown and sword, hid them in their skirts and belongings, and buried them in a church far to the northeast until the coast was clear.

When the monarchy was restored, the regalia were used to crown Scotland's last king, Charles II (1660). Then, in 1707, the Treaty of Union with England ended Scotland's independence. The Honors came out for a ceremony to bless the treaty, and were then locked away in a strongbox in the castle. There they lay for a century, until Sir Walter Scott—the writer and great champion of Scottish tradition—forced a detailed search of the castle in 1818. The box was found...and there the Honors were, perfectly preserved. Within a few years, they were put on display, as they have been ever since.

The crown's most recent official appearance was in 1999, when it was taken across town to the grand opening of the reinstated parliament, marking a new chapter in the Scottish nation. As it represents the monarchy, the crown is present whenever a new session of parliament opens. (And if Scotland secedes, you can be sure that crown will be in the front row.)

The Honors: Finally, you enter the Crown Room to see the regalia itself. The four-foot steel sword was made in Italy under orders of Pope Julius II (the man who also commissioned Michelangelo's Sistine Chapel and St. Peter's Basilica). The scepter is made of silver, covered with gold, and topped with a rock crystal and a pearl. The gem- and pearl-encrusted crown has an imperial arch topped with a cross. Legend says the band of gold in the center is the original crown that once adorned the head of Robert the Bruce.

The **Stone of Scone** (a.k.a. the "Stone of Destiny") sits plain and strong next to the jewels. It's a rough-hewn gray slab of sandstone, about 26 by 17 by 10 inches. As far back as the ninth century, Scotland's kings were crowned atop this stone, when it stood at the medieval capital of Scone. But in 1296, the invading army of Edward I of England carried the stone off to Westminster Abbey. For the next seven centuries, English (and subsequently British) kings and queens were crowned sitting on a coronation chair with the Stone of Scone tucked in a compartment underneath.

In 1950, four Scottish students broke into Westminster Abbey on Christmas Day and smuggled the stone back to Scotland in an act of foolhardy patriotism. But what could they do with it? After three months, they abandoned the stone, draped in Scotland's national flag. It was returned to Westminster Abbey, where (in 1953) Queen Elizabeth II was crowned atop it. Then in 1996, in recognition of increased Scottish autonomy, Elizabeth agreed to let the stone go home, on one condition: that it be returned to Westminster Abbey for all British coronations. One day, the next monarch of England—Prince Charles is first in line—will sit atop it, re-enacting a coronation ritual that dates back a thousand years.

• *Exit the crown jewel display and turn left before exiting back into the courtyard through a door that leads into the Royal Palace.*

❼ Royal Palace and Great Hall: Scottish royalty lived in the Royal Palace only when safety or protocol required it (they preferred the Palace of Holyroodhouse at the bottom of the Royal Mile). It has several historic but unimpressive rooms. In the smallest one, Mary, Queen of Scots (1542-1587), gave birth to James VI of Scotland, who later became King James I of England. The Presence Chamber leads into Laich Hall (Lower Hall), the dining room of the royal family.

The **Great Hall** (through a separate entrance on Crown Square) was built by James IV to host the castle's official banquets and meetings. It's still used for such purposes today. Most of the interior—its fireplace, carved walls, pikes, and armor—is Victorian. But the well-constructed wood ceiling is original. This hammer-beam roof (constructed like the hull of a ship) is self-supporting. The complex system of braces and arches distributes the weight of the roof outward to the walls, so there's no need for supporting pillars or long cross beams. Before leaving, find the big iron-barred peephole above the fireplace, on the right. This allowed the king to spy on his subjects while they partied.

• *Across the Crown Square courtyard is the...*

❽ Scottish National War Memorial: This commemorates the 149,000 Scottish soldiers lost in World War I, the 58,000 who died in World War II, and the nearly 800 (and counting) lost in British battles since. This is a somber spot (put away your camera, phone, etc.). Paid for by public donations, each bay is dedicated to a particular Scottish regiment. The main shrine, featuring a green Italian-marble memorial that contains the original WWI rolls of honor, sits—almost as if it were sacred—on an exposed chunk of the castle rock. Above you, the archangel Michael is busy slaying a dragon. The bronze frieze accurately shows the attire of various wings of Scotland's military. The stained glass starts with Cain

Robert the Bruce
(1274-1329)

In 1314, Robert the Bruce's men attacked Edinburgh's Royal Castle, recapturing it from the English. It was just one of many intense battles between the oppressive English and the plucky Scots during the wars of independence.

In this era, Scotland had to overcome not only its English foes but also its own divisiveness—and no one was more divided than Robert the Bruce. As earl of Carrick, he was born with blood ties to England and a long-standing family claim to the Scottish throne.

When England's King Edward I ("Longshanks") conquered Scotland in 1296, the Bruce family welcomed it, hoping Edward would defeat their rivals and put Bruce's father on the throne. They dutifully signed the "Ragman's Roll" of allegiance—and then Edward chose someone else as king.

Twenty-something Robert the Bruce (the "the" comes from his original family name of "de Bruce") then joined William Wallace's revolt against the English. Legend has it that it was he who knighted Wallace after the victory at Stirling Bridge. When Wallace fell from favor, Bruce became a guardian of Scotland (caretaker ruler in the absence of a king) and continued fighting the English. But when Edward's armies again got the upper hand in 1302, Robert—along with Scotland's other nobles—diplomatically surrendered and again pledged loyalty.

In 1306, Robert the Bruce murdered his chief rival and boldly claimed to be king of Scotland. Few nobles supported him. Edward crushed the revolt and kidnapped Bruce's wife, the church excommunicated him, and Bruce went into hiding on a distant North Sea island. He was now the king of nothing. Legend says he gained inspiration by watching a spider patiently build its web.

The following year, Bruce returned to Scotland and wove alliances with both nobles and the church, slowly gaining acceptance as Scotland's king by a populace chafing under English rule. On June 24, 1314, he decisively defeated the English (now led by Edward's weak son, Edward II) at the Battle of Bannockburn. After a generation of turmoil (1286-1314), England was finally driven from Scotland, and the country was united under Robert I, king of Scotland.

As king, Robert the Bruce's priority was to stabilize the monarchy and establish clear lines of succession. His descendants would rule Scotland for the next 400 years, and even today, Bruce blood runs through the veins of Queen Elizabeth II, Prince Charles, and princes William and Harry.

EDINBURGH

and Abel on the left, and finishes with a celebration of peace on the right. To appreciate how important this place is, consider that Scottish soldiers died at twice the rate of other British soldiers in World War I.

• *Our final stop is worth the five-minute walk to get there. Backtrack to the café (and One O'Clock Gun), then head downhill to the National War Museum Scotland (closes one hour before rest of castle complex).*

❾ **National War Museum Scotland:** This thoughtful museum covers four centuries of Scottish military history. Instead of the usual musty, dusty displays of endless armor, there's a compelling mix of videos, uniforms, weapons, medals, mementos, and eloquent excerpts from soldiers' letters.

Here you'll learn the story of how the fierce and courageous Scottish warrior changed from being a symbol of resistance against Britain to being a champion of that same empire. Along the way, these military men received many decorations for valor and did more than their share of dying in battle. But even when fighting for—rather than against—England, Scottish regiments still promoted their romantic, kilted-warrior image.

Queen Victoria fueled this ideal throughout the 19th century. She was infatuated with the Scottish Highlands and the culture's untamed, rustic mystique. Highland soldiers, especially officers, went to great personal expense to sport all their elaborate regalia, and the kilted men fought best to the tune of their beloved bagpipes. For centuries the stirring drone of bagpipes accompanied Highland soldiers into battle—inspiring them, raising their spirits, and announcing to the enemy that they were about to meet a fierce and mighty foe.

This museum shows the human side of war as well as the cleverness of government-sponsored ad campaigns that kept the lads enlisting. Two centuries of recruiting posters make the same pitch that still works today: a hefty signing bonus, steady pay, and job security with the promise of a manly and adventurous life—all spiked with a mix of pride and patriotism.

Stepping outside the museum, you're surrounded by cannons that no longer fire, stony walls that tell an amazing story, dramatic views of this grand city, and the clatter of tourists (rather than soldiers) on cobbles. Consider for a moment all the bloody history and valiant struggles, along with British power and Scottish pride, that have shaped the city over which you are perched.

• *There's only one way out—the same way you came in.*

Sights on and near the Royal Mile
Camera Obscura
A big deal when it was built in 1853, this observatory topped with a mirror reflected images onto a disc before the wide eyes of people

who had never seen a photograph or a captured image. Today, you can climb 100 steps for an entertaining 20-minute demonstration (3/hour). At the top, enjoy the best view anywhere of the Royal Mile. Then work your way down through five floors of illusions, holograms, and early photos. This is a big hit with kids, but sadly overpriced. (It's less impressive on cloudy days.)

Cost and Hours: £12, daily July-Aug 9:30-21:00, April-June and Sept-Oct 9:30-18:00, Nov-March 10:00-17:00, last demonstration one hour before closing, tel. 0131/226-3709, www.camera -obscura.co.uk.

Scotch Whisky Experience (a.k.a. "Malt Disney")

This gimmicky ambush is designed only to distill £13 out of your pocket. You kick things off with a slow-moving whisky-barrel train-car ride that goes to great lengths to make whisky production seem thrilling (things get pretty psychedelic when you hit the yeast stage). An informative lecture on whisky regions and production in Scotland includes sampling a wee dram and the chance to stand amid the world's largest Scotch whisky collection (almost 3,500 bottles). At the end, you'll find yourself in the bar, which is worth a quick look for its wall of unusually shaped whisky bottles. People do seem to enjoy this place, but that might have something to do with the sample. If you're visiting Oban, Pitlochry, or the Isle of Skye, you'll find cheaper, less hokey distillery tours there. Serious connoisseurs of the Scottish firewater will want to pop into the Whiski Rooms Shop off North Bank Street or Cadenhead's Whisky Shop at the bottom of the Royal Mile (both described later).

Cost and Hours: £13, daily 10:00-18:30, last tour at 17:30, tel. 0131/220-0441, www.scotchwhiskyexperience.co.uk.

▲▲Gladstone's Land

This is a typical 16th- to 17th-century merchant's "land," or tenement building. These multistory structures—in which merchants ran their shops on the ground floor and lived upstairs—were typi-

cal of the time (the word "tenement" didn't have the slum connotation then that it has today). Gladstone's Land comes complete with an almost-lived-in, furnished interior and guides in each room who love to talk. Keep this place in mind as you stroll the rest of the Mile, imagining other houses as if they still looked like this on the inside. (For a comparison of life in the Old Town versus the New Town, also visit the Georgian House—described later.)

Cost and Hours: £6.50, daily July-Aug 10:00-18:30, April-June and Sept-Oct

Edinburgh's Royal Mile

EDINBURGH

1. MacDonald Holyrood Hotel
2. Jurys Inn
3. Ibis Hotel
4. Holiday Inn Express Edinburgh Royal Mile
5. Travelodge Central
6. Smart City Hostel
7. High Street Hostel
8. Royal Mile Backpackers Hostel
9. Castle Rock Hostel
10. Brodie's Hostels & The World's End Pub
11. The Elephant House
12. The Outsider Restaurant
13. Grain Store, Maison Bleue & Oink
14. The Witchery by the Castle

10:00-17:00, last entry 30 minutes before closing, closed Nov-March, no photos allowed, tel. 0844-493-2100, www.nts.org.uk.

▲Writers' Museum at Lady Stair's House

This aristocrat's house, built in 1622, is filled with well-described manuscripts and knickknacks of Scotland's three greatest literary figures: Robert Burns, Sir Walter Scott, and Robert Louis Stevenson. If you'd like to see Scott's pipe and Burns' snuffboxes, you'll love this little museum. Edinburgh's high society gathered in homes like this in the 1780s to hear the great poet Robbie Burns read his work—it's meant to be read aloud rather than to oneself. In the Burns room, you can hear his poetry—worth a few minutes for anyone, and essential for fans.

Cost and Hours: Free, Mon-Sat 10:00-17:00, closed Sun

NOT TO SCALE -
CASTLE TO
PALACE OF HOLYROODHOUSE
IS ABOUT 1 MILE

+ WAVERLEY TRAIN STN.

JOHN KNOX HOUSE

PEOPLE'S STORY MUSEUM

CANONGATE CHURCH

WHITE HORSE CLOSE

QUEEN'S GALLERY

PALACE OF HOLYROOD-HOUSE

BOTTOM OF ROYAL MILE

CANONGATE

MUSEUM OF CHILDHOOD

MUSEUM OF EDINBURGH

SCOTTISH PARLIAMENT

HOLYROOD ROAD

DYNAMIC EARTH

QUEEN'S DRIVE

ST. MARYS ST.

TO DALKEITH ROAD B+Bs + A-7

TRAIL TO ARTHUR'S SEAT

DCH

HOLYROOD PARK

EDINBURGH

15 Deacon Brodie's Tavern
16 St. Giles Cathedral Café
17 Angels with Bagpipes
18 Piemaker Café
19 Dubh Prais Scottish Rest. & Folk Music Pubs
20 Wedgwood Restaurant
21 David Bann Restaurant

22 Clarinda's Tea Room
23 Sandy Bell's Pub
24 The Royal Oak Pub
25 Whistlebinkies Bar
26 No. 1 High Street Pub

except during Festival 12:00-17:00, no photos, tel. 0131/529-4901, www.edinburghmuseums.org.uk.

Whiski Rooms Shop

The knowledgeable, friendly staff in this shop just off the Royal Mile happily assists novices and experts alike to select the right bottle. Their bar usually has about 200 open bottles—and if you are a serious purchaser, you can get a sample. Even better, try one of their tasting flights, which include four tastes and a £5 voucher toward purchasing a bottle: Intro to Whisky (£17.50); Premium Tasting (£35—the really good stuff); Whisky and Chocolate or Whisky and Cheese (£22.50). Tastings are offered during store hours and last about an hour; call ahead to reserve, especially in peak season.

Scotland's Literary Greats

Edinburgh was home to Scotland's three greatest literary figures: Robert Burns, Robert Louis Stevenson, and Sir Walter Scott.

Robert Burns (1759-1796), quite possibly the most famous and beloved Scot of all time, moved to Edinburgh after achieving overnight celebrity with his first volume of poetry (staying in a house on the spot where Deacon Brodie's Tavern now stands). Even though he wrote in the rough Scots dialect and dared to attack social rank, he was a favorite of Edinburgh's high society, who'd gather in fine homes to hear him recite his works. For more on Burns, see the sidebar on page 732.

One hundred years later, **Robert Louis Stevenson** (1850-1894) also stirred the Scottish soul with his pen. An avid traveler who always packed his notepad, Stevenson created settings that are vivid and filled with wonder. Traveling through Scotland, Europe, and around the world, he distilled his adventures into Romantic classics, including *Kidnapped* and *Treasure Island* (as well as *The Strange Case of Dr. Jekyll and Mr. Hyde*). Stevenson, who was married in San Francisco and spent his last years in the South Pacific, wrote, "Youth is the time to travel—both in mind and in body—to try the manners of different nations." He said, "I travel not to go anywhere...but to simply go." Travel was his inspiration and his success.

Sir Walter Scott (1771-1832) wrote the *Waverley* novels, including *Ivanhoe* and *Rob Roy*. He's considered the father of the Romantic historical novel. Through his writing, he generated

Cost and Hours: Daily 10:00-19:00, later in Aug, 4-7 North Bank Street, tel. 0131/225-1532, www.whiskirooms.com.

Museum on the Mound

Located in the basement of the grand Bank of Scotland building (easily spotted from a distance), this exhibit tells the story of the bank, which was founded in 1695 (making it only a year younger than the Bank of England, and the longest operating bank in the world). Featuring displays on cash production, safe technology, and bank robberies, this museum struggles mightily, with some success, to make banking interesting (the case holding £1 million is cool). It's worth popping in if you have some time or find the subject appealing. But no matter how well the information is presented, it's still about...yawn...banking.

Cost and Hours: Free, Tue-Fri 10:00-17:00, Sat-Sun 13:00-17:00, closed Mon, down Bank Street from the Royal Mile—follow the street around to the left and enter through the gate, tel. 0131/243-5464, www.museumonthemound.com.

a worldwide interest in Scotland, and re-awakened his fellow countrymen's pride in their inheritance. His novels helped revive interest in Highland culture—the Gaelic language, kilts, songs, legends, myths, the clan system—and created a national identity. An avid patriot, he wrote, "Every Scottish man has a pedigree. It is a national prerogative, as unalienable as his pride and his poverty." Scott is so revered in Edinburgh that his towering Neo-Gothic monument dominates the city center. With his favorite hound by his side, Sir Walter Scott overlooks the city that he inspired, and that inspired him.

The best way to learn about and experience these literary greats is to visit the Writers' Museum at Lady Stair's House (see page 772) and to take Edinburgh's Literary Pub Tour (see page 803).

While just three writers dominate your Edinburgh sightseeing, consider also the other great writers with Edinburgh connections: J.K. Rowling (who captures the "Gothic" spirit of Edinburgh with her Harry Potter series); current resident Ian Rankin (with his "tartan noir" novels); J.M. Barrie (who attended University of Edinburgh and later created Peter Pan); Sir Arthur Conan Doyle (who was born in Edinburgh, went to medical school here, and is best known for inventing Sherlock Holmes); and James Boswell (who lived 50 yards away from the Writers' Museum, in James Court, and is revered for his biography of Samuel Johnson).

▲▲St. Giles Cathedral

This is Scotland's most important church. Its ornate spire—the Scottish crown steeple from 1495—is a proud part of Edinburgh's skyline. The fascinating interior contains nearly 200 memorials honoring distinguished Scots through the ages.

Cost and Hours: Free but donations encouraged, audioguide-£3, £2 to take photos; Mon-Sat 9:00-17:00 (until 19:00 Mon-Fri May-Sept), Sun 13:00-17:00; tel. 0131/225-9442, www.stgiles cathedral.org.uk.

Concerts: St. Giles' busy concert schedule includes organ recitals and visiting choirs (frequent free events at 12:15, concerts often Wed at 20:00 and Sun at 18:00, see schedule or ask for *Music at St. Giles* pamphlet in gift shop).

EDINBURGH

EDINBURGH

St. Giles Cathedral

TO EDINBURGH CASTLE ← HIGH STREET (ROYAL MILE) → TO HOLYROOD HOUSE

HEART OF MIDLOTHIAN ♥

SHOP

❾

❷ ❸

ENTRANCE →

❶ NAVE ❹ CHANCEL

❻ ❼

PARLIAMENT SQUARE

❺

CAFÉ

❽

MERCAT CROSS

KING CHARLES II STATUE

❿

50 FEET
10 METERS

PARKING LOT

DCH

❶ Robert Burns Window
❷ Pre-Raphaelite Window
❸ John Knox Statue
❹ Four Massive Central Pillars
❺ Organ
❻ Stained-Glass Window
❼ National Covenant
❽ Chapel of the Knights of the Thistle
❾ Down to Café & WC
❿ John Knox's Burial Spot

⊙ **Self-Guided Tour:** Today's facade is 19th-century Neo-Gothic, but most of what you'll see inside is from the 14th and 15th centuries. You'll also find cathedral guides trolling around, hoping you'll engage them in conversation. You'll be glad you did.

Just inside the entrance, turn around to see the modern stained-glass **Robert Burns window,** which celebrates Scotland's favorite poet (see page 732). It was made in 1985 by the Icelandic artist Leifur Breidfjord. The green of the lower level symbolizes the natural world—God's creation. The middle zone with the circle shows the brotherhood of man—Burns was a great internationalist. The top is a rosy red sunburst of creativity, reminding Scots of Burns' famous line, "My love is like a red, red rose"—part of a song near and dear to every Scottish heart.

To the right of the Burns window is a fine **Pre-Raphaelite window.** Like most in the church, it's a memorial to an important patron (in this case, John Marshall). From here stretches a great swath of war memorials.

As you walk along the north wall, find **John Knox's statue** (standing like a six-foot-tall bronze chess piece.) Look into his eyes for 10 seconds from 10 inches away, and think of the Reformation struggles of the 16th century. Knox, the great religious reformer and founder of austere Scottish Presbyterianism, first preached here in 1559. His insistence that every person should be able to personally read the word of God gave Scotland an educational system 300 years ahead of the rest of Europe (for more on Knox, see "The Scottish Reformation" on page 831). Thanks partly to Knox, it was Scottish minds that led the way in math, science, medicine, and engineering. Voltaire called Scotland "the intellectual capital of Europe."

Knox preached Calvinism. Consider that the Dutch and the Scots both embraced this creed of hard work, frugality, and strict ethics. This helps explain why the Scots are so different from the English (and why the Dutch and the Scots—both famous for their thriftiness and industriousness—are so much alike).

The oldest parts of the cathedral—the **four massive central pillars**—are Norman and date from the 12th century. They supported a mostly wooden superstructure that was lost when an invading English force burned in 1385. The Scots rebuilt it bigger and better than ever, and in 1495 its famous crown spire was completed.

During the Reformation—when Knox preached here (1559-1572)—the place was simplified and whitewashed. Before this, when the emphasis was on holy services provided by priests, there were lots of little niches. With the new focus on sermons rather than rituals, the grand pulpit took center stage.

Knox preached against anything that separated you from God, including stained glass (considered the poor man's Bible, as illiterate Christians could learn from its pictures). Knox had the church's fancy medieval glass windows replaced with clear glass, but 19th-century Victorians took them out and installed the brilliantly colored ones you see today.

Cross over to the **organ** (1992, Austrian-built, one of Europe's finest) and take in its sheer might.

Immediately to the right of the organ (as you're facing it) is a tiny chapel for silence and prayer. The dramatic **stained-glass window** above shows the commotion that surrounded Knox when

he preached. Bearded, fiery-eyed Knox had a huge impact on this community. Notice how there were no pews back then. The church was so packed, people even looked through clear windows from across the street. With his hand on the holy book, Knox seems to conduct divine electricity to the Scottish faithful.

To the left of the organ as you face it, in the next alcove, is a copy of the **National Covenant**. It was signed in blood in 1638 by Scottish heroes who refused to compromise their religion for the king's. Most who signed were martyred (their monument is nearby in Grassmarket).

Head toward the east (back) end of the church, and turn right to see the Neo-Gothic **Chapel of the Knights of the Thistle** (£2 donation requested) and its intricate wood carving. Built in two years (1910-1911), entirely with Scottish materials and labor, it is the private chapel of the Knights of the Thistle, the only Scottish chivalric order. It's used about once a year to inaugurate new members. Scotland recognizes its leading citizens by bestowing a membership upon them. The Queen presides over the ritual from her fancy stall, marked by her Scottish coat of arms—a heraldic zoo of symbolism. Are there bagpipes in heaven? Find the tooting angel at the top of a window to the left of the altar.

Downstairs (enter stairs near the chapel entry) is an inviting, recommended café, along with handy public toilets.

Old Parliament House

The building now holds the civil law courts, so you'll need to go through security first. Step in to see the grand hall, with its fine 1639 hammer-beam ceiling and stained glass. This space housed the Scottish parliament until the Act of Union in 1707. Find the big stained-glass depiction of the initiation of the first Scottish High Court in 1532. The building now holds the civil law courts and is busy with wigged and robed lawyers hard at work in the old library (peek through the door) or pacing the hall deep in discussion. The cleverly named Writz Café, in the basement, is literally their supreme court's restaurant (cheap, Mon-Fri 9:00-14:00, closed Sat-Sun).

Cost and Hours: Free, public welcome Mon-Fri 9:00-16:30, closed Sat-Sun, no photos, borrow info sheet at security for more information, enter behind St. Giles Cathedral; open-to-the-public trials are just across the street at the High Court—the doorman has the day's docket.

▲Mary King's Close

For an unusual peek at Edinburgh's gritty, plague-ridden past, join a costumed performer on an hour-long trip through an excavated underground street and buildings on the northern slope of the Royal Mile. Tours cover the standard goofy, crowd-pleasing ghost stories, but also provide authentic and historical insight into a part of town entombed by later construction. It's best to book (and pay) ahead by phone or on their website (or drop by in person for a same-day booking)—even though tours leave every 20 minutes, groups are small and the sight is popular.

Cost and Hours: £13; April-Oct daily 10:00-21:00, Aug until

23:00; Nov-March daily 10:00-17:00, Fri-Sat until 21:00; these are last tour times, no kids under 5, across from St. Giles at 2 Warriston's Close, tel. 0845-070-6244, www.realmarykingsclose .com.

▲Museum of Childhood

This five-story playground of historical toys and games is rich in nostalgia and history. Each well-signed gallery is as jovial as a Norman Rockwell painting, highlighting the delights and simplicity of childhood. The museum does a fair job of representing culturally relevant oddities, such as ancient Egyptian, Peruvian, and voodoo dolls, and displays early versions of toys it's probably best didn't make the final cut (a grim snake-centered precursor to the popular board game Chutes and Ladders is one example).

Cost and Hours: Free, Mon-Sat 10:00-17:00, Sun 12:00-17:00, last entry 15 minutes before closing.

▲John Knox House

Intriguing for Reformation buffs, this fine medieval house dates back to 1470 and offers a well-explained look at the life of the great

16th-century reformer. Although most contend he never actually lived here, preservationists called it "Knox's house" to save it from the wrecking ball in the 1840s.

Regardless, the place has good information on Knox and his intellectual sparring partner, Mary, Queen of Scots. Imagine—even though it likely never happened—

the Protestant firebrand John Knox and the devout Catholic Mary sitting face to face in these old rooms, discussing the most intimate matters of their spiritual lives as they decided the course of Scotland's religious future.

The house contains some period furniture, and on the top floor there's a fun photo op with a dress-up cape, hat, and feather pen.

Cost and Hours: £5, Mon-Sat 10:00-18:00, closed Sun except in July-Aug 12:00-18:00, 43 High Street, tel. 0131/556-9579, www .tracscotland.org.

Lickety Splits Gallery

This quirky shop is part art, part candy, and completely full of character. Naomi, who claims to specialize in all things sweet, stocks her shelves with traditional candies and local crafts, and shares fascinating historical tidbits on the origins of your favorite childhood treats—such as the scandal over how Chelsea Whoppers became Tootsie Rolls. Candy lovers can mix and match a little bag of goodies to go.

EDINBURGH

Cost and Hours: Free entry, Mon-Sat 11:00-17:30, Sun 12:00-16:00, mobile 0753-575-4299, 6 Jeffrey Street, www.licketysplits gallery.co.uk.

▲Cadenhead's Whisky Shop

The shop is not a tourist sight. Founded in 1842, this firm prides itself on bottling good whisky straight from casks at the distilleries, without all the compromises that come with profitable mass production (coloring with sugar to fit the expected look, watering down to lessen the alcohol tax, and so on). Those drinking from Cadenhead-bottled whiskies will enjoy the pure product as the distilleries' owners themselves do, not as the sorry public does.

Mark, Neil, and Alan happily explain the sometimes-complex whisky storyboard and talk you through flavor profiles. Mark is amazing with analogies (for example, "A single cask whisky is like a football team where all the players come from the same town."). Buy the right bottle to enjoy in your hotel room night after night (prices start around £13 for about 7 ounces). Unlike wine, whisky has a long shelf life after it's opened. The bottles are extremely durable—just ask the staff to demonstrate (but get a second cap and twist off carefully, as they can break). They host whisky tastings a couple of times a month (posted in the shop)—a hit with aficionados.

Cost and Hours: Free entry, Mon-Sat 10:30-17:30, closed Sun, 172 Canongate, tel. 0131/556-5864, www.wmcadenhead.com.

▲People's Story Museum

This interesting exhibition traces the working and social lives of ordinary people through the 18th, 19th, and 20th centuries. You'll see objects related to important Edinburgh trades (printing, brewing), tools and the finished products made with them, a wartime kitchen, and even a former jail, an original part of the historic building (the Canongate Tolbooth, built in 1591).

Cost and Hours: Free, Mon-Sat 10:00-17:00, closed Sun except during Festival 12:00-17:00, last entry 15 minutes before closing, 163 Canongate, tel. 0131/529-4057, www.edinburghmuseums.org.uk.

▲Museum of Edinburgh

Another old house full of old stuff, this one is worth a look for its early Edinburgh history and handy ground-floor WC. Be sure to see the original copy of the National Covenant (written in 1638 on an animal skin), sketches of pre-Georgian Edinburgh (which show a lake, later filled in to become Princes Street Gardens when the New Town was built), and early golf balls. A favorite Scottish say-it-aloud joke: "Balls," said the queen. "If I had two, I'd be king." The king laughed—he had to.

Cost and Hours: Free, same hours as People's Story Museum—listed above, 142 Canongate, tel. 0131/529-4143, www

.edinburghmuseums.org.uk.

▲▲Scottish Parliament Building

Scotland's parliament originated in 1293 and was dissolved when

Scotland united with England in 1707. But after the Scottish electorate and the British parliament gave their consent, in 1998 it was decided that there would be "a Scottish parliament guided by justice, wisdom, integrity, and compassion." Formally reconvened by Queen Elizabeth after elections in 1999, the Scottish parliament now enjoys self-rule (except for matters of defense, foreign policy, immigration, and taxation). The current government, run by the Scottish Nationalist Party, is pushing for more independence.

The innovative building, opened in 2004, brought together all the functions of the fledgling parliament in one complex. It's a people-oriented structure (conceived by Catalan architect Enric Miralles; for more on the building, see page 760). Signs are written in both English and Gaelic (the Scots' Celtic tongue).

For a peek at the building and a lesson in how the Scottish

parliament works, drop in, pass through security, and find the visitors' desk. You're welcome into the public parts of the building, including a viewing gallery overlooking the impressive Debating Chambers, and anyone can attend committee meetings.

Cost and Hours: Free; in-session hours: Mon, Fri-Sat 10:00-17:00, Tue-Thu 9:00-18:30, recess hours (including July-Aug and other holidays): Mon-Sat 10:00-17:00, closed Sun year-round; last entry 30 minutes before closing, www.scottish.parliament.uk. For a complete list of recess dates or to book tickets for debates, check their website or call their visitors services line at tel. 0131/348-5200.

Tours: Worthwhile hour-long tours by proud locals are offered (free, 2/hour, usually when parliament is recessed). While you can just drop in, it's best to call or check online for times and reserve a spot.

Seeing Parliament in Session: You can call or sign up online to witness the Scottish parliament's hugely popular debates (usually Tue-Thu 14:00-18:00). On Thursdays from 12:00-12:30 the First Minister is on the hot seat and has to field questions from members across all parties.

▲Palace of Holyroodhouse

Founded as a monastery in 1128, this palace was the true home, birthplace, and coronation spot of Scottish kings in their heyday (James IV, Mary, Queen of Scots, and Charles I). It's particularly memorable as the site of some dramatic moments from the short reign of Mary, Queen of Scots—including the murder of her personal secretary, David Rizzio, by agents of her jealous husband. Today, it's one of the Queen's official residences. She generally stops here on the way to vacationing at Balmoral Palace.

Consider touring the interior. The building, rich in history and decor, is filled with elegantly furnished Victorian rooms and a few darker, older rooms with glass cases of historic bits and Scottish pieces that locals find fascinating.

Bring the palace to life with the included one-hour audioguide. You'll learn which of the kings featured in the 110 portraits lining the Great Gallery are real and which are fictional, what touches were added to the bedchambers to flatter King Charles II, and why the exiled Comte d'Artois took refuge in the palace. You'll also hear a goofy reenactment of the moment when conspirators stormed into the chambers of Mary, Queen of Scots, and stabbed her male secretary 56 times.

Cost and Hours: £11 includes a quality audioguide, £15.50 combo-ticket includes Queen's Gallery—listed below, tickets sold in Queen's Gallery (see below), daily April-Oct 9:30-18:00, Nov-March until 16:30, last entry one hour before closing, tel. 0131/556-5100, www.royalcollection.org.uk. It's still a working palace, so it's closed when the Queen or other VIPs are in residence.

Palace Gardens: After exiting the palace, you're free to stroll through the ruined abbey (destroyed by the English during the time of Mary, Queen of Scots, in the 16th century) and the palace gardens (closed in winter). The Queen hosts a magnificent tea party here every July, with honored ladies sporting fancy hats. For a 30-minute guided tour of the garden, check at the ticket office on entry to the palace (£3.75, daily May-Sept 10:00-17:00).

Nearby: Hikers—note that the wonderful trail up Arthur's Seat starts just across the street from the gardens (see page 800 for details).

Queen's Gallery

This small museum features rotating exhibits of artwork from the royal collection. For more than five centuries, the royal family has amassed a wealth of art treasures. While the Queen keeps most in her many private palaces, she shares an impressive load of it here, with exhibits changing about every six months. Though the gallery occupies just a few rooms, its displays can be exquisite. The entry fee includes an excellent audioguide, written and read by the curator.

Cost and Hours: £6.25, £15.50 combo-ticket includes Palace of Holyroodhouse, daily April-Oct 9:30-18:00, Nov-March until 16:30, café, last entry one hour before closing, on the palace grounds, to the right of the palace entrance, www.royalcollection .org.uk. Buses #35 and #36 stop outside, and can save you a walk to or from Princes Street/North Bridge.

EDINBURGH

Sights South of the Royal Mile
▲▲▲ National Museum of Scotland

This huge museum has amassed more historic artifacts than every other place I've seen in Scotland combined. It's all wonderfully

displayed, with fine descriptions offering a best-anywhere hike through the history of Scotland.

The place gives you two museums in one. One wing houses a popular natural history collection, with everything from kid-friendly T-Rex skeletons to Egyptian mummies. But we'll focus on the other wing, which

sweeps you through Scottish history from prehistory until today, covering Roman and Viking times, Edinburgh's witch-burning craze and clan massacres, the struggle for Scottish independence, the Industrial Revolution, and right up to Scotland in the 21st century.

Cost and Hours: Free, daily 10:00-17:00; free one-hour "Highlights" tours daily at 11:00 and 15:00, themed tours at 13:00—confirm tour schedule at info desk or on TV screens; two long blocks south of St. Giles Cathedral and the Royal Mile, on Chambers Street off George IV Bridge, tel. 0131/247-4422, www .nms.ac.uk.

Eating: On the museum's top floor, the dressy and upscale **Tower restaurant** serves good food with a castle view (£16 two-course lunch special served 12:00-18:30, £16 afternoon tea 14:30-17:30, £33 three-course dinner special, fancy £18-25 meals, open daily 12:00-23:00—later than the museum itself, tel. 0131/225-3003).

⊖ Self-Guided Tour: Get oriented on level 1, in the impressive glass-roofed Grand Gallery. This part of the building houses the natural history collection. To reach the Scottish history wing, exit the Grand Gallery at the far right end, under the clock. Pause in the "Connect" hall long enough to find Dolly the sheep—the world's first cloned mammal—born in Edinburgh and now stuffed and on display.

Continue into Hawthornden Court (level 1), where our tour begins. (It's possible to detour downstairs from here to level -1 for Scotland's prehistoric origins—geologic formation, Celts, Romans, Vikings.)

Kingdom of the Scots (c.1300-1700): From its very start, Scotland was determined to be free. You're greeted with proud quotes from what's been called the Scottish Declaration of Independence—the Declaration of Arboath, a defiant letter written to the pope in 1320. As early as the ninth century, Scotland's patron saint, Andrew (see the small statue), had—according to legend—miraculously intervened to help the Picts of Scotland remain free by defeating the Angles of England. Andrew's X-shaped cross still decorates the Scottish flag today.

Turning right, enter the first room on your right, with swords, battle-axes, and objects related to Scotland's most famous patriots—William ("Braveheart") Wallace and Robert the Bruce. Bruce's family, the Stuarts (or "Stewarts"), went on to rule Scotland for the next 300 years. Eventually, James I (see his baby cradle) came to rule England as well.

In the next room, a big guillotine recalls the harsh justice meted out to criminals, witches, and "Covenanters" (politically active Protestants who didn't want to conform with the Church of England). Also check out the tomb (a copy) of Mary, Queen of Scots, the Stuart monarch who opposed those Protestants. Educated and raised in Renaissance France, Mary brought refinement to the Scottish throne. After she was imprisoned and then executed by the English in 1587, her countrymen rallied each other by

invoking her memory. Pendants and coins with her portrait stoked the irrepressible Scottish spirit. Near the replica of Mary's tomb are tiny cameos, pieces of jewelry, and coins with her image.

Browse the rest of level 1 to see everyday medieval objects—carved panels, cookware, and clothes.

• *Backtrack to Hawthornden Court and take the elevator to level 3.*

Scotland Transformed (1700s): You'll see artifacts related to Bonnie Prince Charlie and the Jacobite Rebellion as well as the ornate Act of Union document, signed in 1707 by the Scottish parliament. This act voluntarily united Scotland with England under the single parliament of Great Britain. For some Scots, this move was an inevitable step in connecting to the wider world, but for others it symbolized the end of Scotland's existence.

Union with England brought stability and investment to Scotland. In this same era, the advances of the Industrial Revolution were making a big impact on Scottish life. Mechanized textile looms (on display) replaced hand craftsmanship. The huge Newcomen steam-engine water pump helped the mining industry to develop sites with tricky drainage. (The museum puts the device in motion twice a day, around 11:15 and 14:15.) Nearby is a model of a coal mine (or "colliery"); coal-rich Scotland exploited this natural resource to fuel its textile factories.

How the parsimonious Scots financed these new, large-scale enterprises is explained in an exhibit on the Bank of Scotland. Powered by the Scottish work ethic and the new opportunities that came from the Industrial Revolution, the country came into relative prosperity. Education and medicine thrived. With the dawn of the modern age came leisure time, the concept of "healthful sports," and golf—a Scottish invention. The first golf balls, which date from about 1820, were leather stuffed with feathers.

• *Return to the elevator and journey up to level 5.*

Industry and Empire (1800s): Circle around to survey Scottish life in the 19th century. Industry had transformed the country. Highland farmers left their land to find work in Lowland factories and foundries. Modern inventions—the phonograph, the steam-powered train—revolutionized everyday life. Scotland was at the forefront of literature (Robert Burns, Sir Walter Scott, Robert Louis Stevenson, the first printing of the Encyclopedia Britannica) and world exploration (David Livingstone in Africa, Sir Alexander Mackenzie in Canada).

• *Climb the stairs to level 6.*

Scotland: A Changing Nation (1900s): The two world wars did a number on Scotland, decimating the population of this already wee nation. In addition, hundreds of thousands emigrated, especially to Canada (where one in eight Canadians has Scottish origins). The small country has made a big mark on the world: In the Sports Hall of Fame you'll see the pioneers of modern golf (Tom Morris, from St. Andrews), auto racing (Jackie Stewart and Jim Clark), and a signed baseball by Glasgow-born Bobby (1951 home run) Thomson. Finally, you'll learn how Scots have gone global in the world of entertainment, from early boy band Bay City Rollers to funk masters Average White Band to the Proclaimers ("I Would Walk 500 Miles") to actor-comedians Billy Connolly and Craig Ferguson.

• *Finish your visit on level 7, the rooftop.*

Garden Terrace: Don't miss the great views of Edinburgh from this well-described roof garden, growing grasses and heathers from every corner of Scotland.

Greyfriars Bobby

This famous statue of Edinburgh's favorite dog is across the street from the National Museum of Scotland. Every business nearby, it seems, is named for this Victorian Skye terrier, who is reputed to have stood by his master's grave in Greyfriars Cemetery for 14 years. The story was immortalized in a 1960s Disney flick, but recent research suggests that 19th-century businessmen bribed a stray to hang out in the cemetery to attract sightseers. If it was a ruse, it still works.

Grassmarket

Once Edinburgh's site for hangings (residents rented out their windows—above the rudely named "Last Drop" pub—for the view), today Grassmarket is being renovated into a people-friendly piazza. It was originally the city's garage, a depot for horses and cows (hence the name). It's rowdy here at night—a popular place for "hen" and "stag" parties. In the early evening, the literary pub tour departs from here (see page 803). Budget shoppers might want to look at W. Armstrong & Son, a fun vintage-clothing store. Victoria Street, built in the Victorian Age, is lined with colorful little shops and eateries.

Hiding in the blur of traffic is a monument to the "Covenanters." These strict 17th-century Scottish Protestants were killed for refusing to accept the king's Episcopalian prayer book. To this day, Scots celebrate their emphatically democratic church government. Rather than big-shot bishops (as in the Anglican or Roman Catholic churches), they have a low-key "moderator" who's elected each year.

Dynamic Earth

Located about a five-minute walk from the Palace of Holyroodhouse, this immense exhibit tells the story of our planet, filling

several underground floors under a vast, white Gore-Tex tent. It's pitched, appropriately, at the base of the Salisbury Crags. The exhibit is designed for younger kids and does the same thing an American science exhibit would do—but with a charming Scottish accent. Standing in a time tunnel, you watch the years rewind from Churchill to dinosaurs to the Big Bang. After viewing several short films on stars, tectonic plates, ice caps, and worldwide weather (in a "4-D" exhibit), you're free to wander past salty pools, a re-created rain forest, and various TV screens.

Cost and Hours: £11.50, daily 10:00-17:30, July-Aug until 18:00, Nov-March closed Mon-Tue, last admission at 16:00, on Holyrood Road, between the palace and mountain, tel. 0131/550-7800, www.dynamicearth.co.uk. Dynamic Earth is a stop on the hop-on, hop-off bus route.

Bonnie Wee Sights in the New Town

The New Town itself is worth a wander. Here's an overview, along with some of the sights you'll see as you stroll. Save energy for the two major museums—the Scottish National Gallery and the Scottish National Portrait Gallery—which are covered in the next section.

▲▲Georgian New Town

The grid-planned new town, laid out in 1776 when George III was king, was a model of urban planning in its day. And it came with a clear message: to celebrate the union of Scotland with England into the United Kingdom. St. Andrew Square (patron saint of Scotland) and Charlotte Square (George III's queen) bookend the New Town with its three main streets named for the royal family of the time (George, Queen, and Princes). Thistle and Rose streets are named for the national flowers of Scotland and England.

The plan for the New Town was the masterstroke of the 23-year-old urban designer James Craig. George Street—20 feet wider than the others (so a four-horse carriage could make a U-turn)—was the main drag. Running down the high spine of the area, it afforded grand, unobstructed views (thanks to the parks on either side) of the River Forth in one direction and the Old Town in the other.

While Princes Street—busy with buses and taxis—has gone down-market, George Street still maintains its old grace. Mostly pedestrianized Rose Street is famous for its rowdy pubs. Sprinkled with popular restaurants and bars, the stately New Town is turning trendy.

Jenners Department Store

As you're standing outside the venerable Jenners (on Rose Street, near St. Andrew Square and across from Sainsbury's supermarket), notice how statues of women support the building—just as real women support the business. The arrival of new fashions here was such a big deal in the old days that they'd announce it by flying flags on the Nelson Monument atop Calton Hill. Step inside. The central space—filled with a towering tree at Christmas—is classic Industrial Age architecture. The Queen's coat of arms high on the wall indicates she shops here.

Edinburgh's New Town

EDINBURGH

TO ROYAL BOTANIC GARDEN & BRITANNIA

1. To Holiday Inn Express Edinburgh City Centre & Central Youth Hostel
2. Travelodges (4)
3. The Bon Vivant Rest. & Le Café St. Honoré
4. Café Royal
5. The Dome Restaurant
6. St. Andrew's & St. George's Church Undercroft Café
7. Henderson's Salad Table
8. Hanover St. Ethnic Eateries
9. M&S Food Hall
10. Sainsbury's Supermarket

EDINBURGH

DRUMMOND PLACE

GREAT KING ST.

DUNDAS ST.

TOWN

ABERCROMBY PL.

GARDENS

Scottish National Portrait Gallery

STREET

YORK PL. TO 1

HANOVER ST.

STREET

DAVID ST.

THISTLE ST.

ST. AND.

STREET

SQUARE

ROSE STREET

JENNERS DEP'T STORE

PRINCES MALL

BUS STATION

LEITH ST.

WATERLOO PL.

HALF-PRICE HUT

THE MOUND

SCOTT MON.

WAVERLY BR.

AIRLINK #100 B

TATTOO TICKETS

BALMORAL HOTEL

CALTON RD.

NORTH BRIDGE

B TO DALKEITH ROAD

WAVERLEY TRAIN STN.

Scottish National Gallery

N. BANK

MARKET ST.

COCKBURN

ROYAL MILE

JEFFREY

EDINBURGH

St. Andrew Square

This green space is dedicated to the patron saint of Scotland. In the early 19th century, there were no shops around here—just fine residences; this was a private garden for the fancy people living here. Now open to the public, the square is a popular lunch hangout for workers. The Melville Monument honors a power-monger member of parliament who, for four decades (around 1800), was nicknamed the "uncrowned king of Scotland."

St. Andrew's and St. George's Church

Designed as part of the New Town in the 1780s, the church is a product of the Scottish Enlightenment. It has an elliptical plan (the first in Britain) so that all can focus on the pulpit. A fine leaflet tells the story of the church, and a handy cafeteria downstairs serves cheap and cheery lunches (see page 819).

Cost and Hours: Free entry, Mon-Fri 10:00-15:00, 13 George Street, tel. 0131/225-3847.

Charlotte Square

The building of New Town started cheap with St. Andrew Square, but finished well with this stately square. In 1791 the Edinburgh town council asked the prestigious Scottish architect Robert Adam to pump up the design for Charlotte Square. The council hoped that Adam's plan would answer criticism that the New Town buildings lacked innovation or ambition, and they got what they wanted. Adam's design, which raised the standard of New Town architecture to "international class," created Edinburgh's finest Georgian square.

▲▲Georgian House

This refurbished Neoclassical house, set on Charlotte Square, is a trip back to 1796. It recounts the era when a newly gentrified and well-educated Edinburgh was nicknamed the "Athens of the North." A volunteer guide in each of the five rooms shares stories and trivia—from the kitchen in the basement to the fully stocked medicine cabinet in the bedroom. Start your visit in the basement and view the interesting 16-minute video, which shows the life of the first family who owned this property and touches on the architecture of the Georgian period. A walk down George Street after your visit here can be fun for the imagination.

Cost and Hours: £6.50, daily April-Oct 10:00-17:00, July-Aug until 18:00, March 11:00-16:00, Nov 11:00-15:00, last entry 30 minutes before closing, closed Dec-Feb, 7 Charlotte Square, tel. 0844-493-2117, www.nts.org.uk.

Princes Street Gardens

The grassy park, a former lakebed, separates Edinburgh's New and Old Towns and offers a wonderful escape from the bustle of the city. Once the private domain of the wealthy, it was opened to the public around 1870—not as a democratic gesture, but because it was thought that allowing the public into the park would increase sales for the Princes Street department stores. Join the office workers for a picnic lunch break, and don't miss the oldest floral clock in the world.

In summer, you can watch or join in **Scottish country dancing** in the park (£4, May-July Mon 19:30-21:30, at Ross Bandstand, also ask about summer dances held Tue at St. Peter's Church on Lutton Place—near recommended Dalkeith Road B&Bs, tel. 0131/228-8616, www.princesstreetgardensdancing.org.uk).

The big lake, **Nor' Loch,** was drained around 1800 as part of the Georgian expansion of Edinburgh. Before that, the lake was the town's sewer, water reservoir, and a handy place for drowning witches. Much was written about the town's infamous stink (a.k.a. the "flowers of Edinburgh"). The town's nickname, "Auld Reekie," referred to both the smoke of its industry and the stench of its squalor. Although the loch is now long gone, memories of the countless women drowned as witches remain. With their thumbs tied to their ankles, they'd be lashed to dunking stools. Those who survived the ordeal were considered "aided by the devil" and burned as witches. If they died, they were innocent and given a good Christian burial. Until 1720, Edinburgh was Europe's witch-burning mecca—any perceived "sign," including a small birthmark, could condemn you.

The Mound

The Scottish National Gallery sits upon what's known as "the Mound." When the Georgian New Town was built, tons of rubble from the excavations were piled into the Mound (1781-1830), forming a dirt bridge that would connect the new development with the Old Town and allay merchant concerns about being disconnected from the future heart of the city. The two fine Neoclassical buildings here (which house museums) date from the 1840s. From the Mound, you can enjoy fine views of medieval Edinburgh, with its 10-story-plus "skyscrapers."

▲Scott Monument

Built in 1840, this elaborate Neo-Gothic monument honors the great author Sir Walter Scott, one of Edinburgh's many illustrious sons. When Scott died in 1832, it was said that "Scotland never owed so much to one man." Scott almost singlehandedly created the "Scotland" we know. Just as the country was in danger of being assimilated into England, Scott celebrated its songs, legends, myths, and kilts, thereby reviving the Highland culture and cementing a national identity. And, as the father of the Romantic historical novel, he contributed to Western literature in general.

The 200-foot monument shelters a marble statue of Scott and his favorite pet, Maida, a deerhound who was one of 30 canines this dog lover owned during his lifetime. They're surrounded by busts of 16 great Scottish poets and 64 characters from his books. Climbing the tight, stony spiral staircase of 287 steps earns you a peek at a tiny museum midway, a fine city view at the top, and intimate encounters going up and down.

Cost and Hours: £4; daily April-Sept 10:00-19:00, Oct-March 10:00-16:00, last entry 30 minutes before closing, tel. 0131/529-4068, www.edinburghmuseums.org.uk.

Museums in the New Town
▲▲ Scottish National Gallery

This delightfully small museum has Scotland's best collection of paintings. In a short visit, you can admire works by Old Masters

(Raphael, Rembrandt, Rubens), Impressionists (Monet, Degas, Gauguin), and underrated Scottish painters. Although there are no iconic masterpieces, it's a surprisingly enjoyable collection that's truly world class. There's no audioguide, but each painting is well described. If you can't find what you're looking for, ask one of the friendly tartan-sporting guards, or visit the info desk downstairs near the WCs and gallery shop.

Cost and Hours: Free, daily 10:00-17:00, Thu until 19:00, Fri-Wed in Aug until 18:00, photos OK unless noted, the Mound (between Princes and Market streets), tel. 0131/624-6200, www.nationalgalleries.org.

Next Door: The skippable **Royal Scottish Academy** hosts temporary art exhibits and is connected to the Scottish National Gallery at the garden level (underneath the gallery) by the Weston Link building (same hours as the gallery, fine café and restaurant).

◆ Self-Guided Tour: Start at the gallery entrance (at the north end of the building). Climb the stairs to the upper level (north end), and take a left. Ask the attendant to point out these three stars:

Van der Goes—*Trinity Altarpiece Panels* (c. 1478-1479): For more than five centuries, these panels have stood on this spot in Edinburgh—first in a church, then (when the church was leveled to build Waverley train station) in this museum. The panels likely flanked a central scene of the Virgin Mary that was destroyed by Protestant vandals during the Reformation.

In the left panel is the Trinity: God the Father, in a rich red robe, cradles a spindly, just-crucified Christ, while the dove of the Holy Spirit hovers between them. On the right, the church's director (the man who commissioned the painting from the well-known Flemish painter) kneels and looks on while an angel plays a hymn on the church organ. In typically medieval fashion, the details are meticulous—expressive faces, intricate folds in the robes, Christ's pallid skin, observant angels. The donor's face is a remarkable portrait, with realistic skin tone and a five-o'clock shadow. But the painting lacks true 3-D realism—God's gold throne is overly exaggerated, and Christ's cardboard-cutout body hovers weightlessly.

The flip side of the panels depicts Scotland's king and queen, who are best known to history as the parents of the boy kneeling alongside them. (You can ask the guard to open the panels.) He grew up to become James IV, the Renaissance king who made Edinburgh a cultural capital.

Botticelli—*The Virgin Adoring the Sleeping Christ Child* (c. 1490): Mary looks down at her baby, peacefully sleeping in a flower-filled garden. It's easy to appreciate Botticelli's masterful style: the precisely drawn outlines, the Virgin's pristine skin, the translucent glow. Botticelli creates a serene world in which no shadows are cast. The scene is painted on canvas—unusual at a time when wood panels were the norm. For the Virgin's rich cloak, Botticelli used ground-up lapis lazuli (a very pricey semiprecious stone), and her hem is decorated with gold leaf.

Renaissance-era art lovers would instantly catch the symbolism. Mary wears a wispy halo and blue cloak that recalls the sky blue of heaven. The roses without thorns and enclosed garden are both symbols of virginity, while the violet flowers (at bottom) represent humility. Darker symbolism hints at what's to come. The strawberries (lower right) signify Christ's blood, soon to be shed, while the roses—though thornless now—will become the Crown of Thorns. For now, Mary can adore her sleeping, blissful baby in a peaceful garden. But in a few decades she'll be kneeling again to weep over the dead, crucified Messiah.

Raphael—*Holy Family with a Palm Tree* (1506-1507): Mary, Joseph, and the Christ Child fit snugly within a round frame (a tondo), their pose symbolizing geometric perfection and the perfect family unit. Joseph kneels to offer Jesus flowers. Mary curves toward him. Baby Jesus dangles in between, linking the family together. Raphael also connects the figures through eye contact: Mary eyes Joseph, who locks onto Jesus, who gazes precociously back. Like in a cameo, we see the faces incised in profile, while their bodies bulge out toward us.

• *Back downstairs at ground level is the main gallery space. Again, ask the attendant to locate these three highlights:*

Rubens—*Feast of Herod* (c.1635-1638): All eyes turn to watch the dramatic culmination of the story of John the Baptist. Salome (standing in center) presents John's severed head on a platter to a horrified King Herod. Meanwhile, Herod's wife—who cooked up the nasty plot—pokes spitefully at John's head with a fork. A dog tugs at Herod's foot like a nasty conscience. The canvas—big, colorful, full of motion and drama—is totally Baroque. Some have suggested that the features of Herod's wife and Salome are those of Rubens' wife and ex-wives, and the head is Rubens himself.

Rembrandt—*Self-Portrait, Aged 51* (c. 1657): It's 1657, and 51-year-old Rembrandt has just declared bankruptcy. Besides financial hardship and the auctioning-off of his personal belongings, he's also facing social stigma and behind-the-back ridicule. Once Holland's most renowned painter, he's begun a slow decline into poverty and obscurity.

His face says it all. Holding a steady gaze, he stares with matter-of-fact acceptance, with his lips pursed. He's dressed in dark clothes against a dark background, with the only spot of light shining on the worry lines of his forehead. Get close enough to the canvas to see the thick paste of paint he used for the wrinkles around his eyes—a study in aging.

Gainsborough—*The Honorable Mrs. Graham* (1775-1777): The slender, elegant, lavishly dressed woman was the teenage bride of a wealthy Scottish landowner. She leans on a column, ostrich feather in hand, staring off to the side (thoughtfully? Determinedly? Haughtily?). Her faultless face and smooth neck stand out from the elaborately ruffled dress and background foliage. This 18th-century woman wears a silvery dress that echoes 17th-century style—Gainsborough's way of showing how, though she was young, she was classy. Thomas ("Blue Boy") Gainsborough—the product of a clothes-making father and a flower-painting mother—uses aspects of both in this lush portrait. The ruby brooch on her bodice marks the center of this harmonious composition.

• *Elsewhere on the ground floor, you'll find nice works by Bellini, Titian, Velázquez, and El Greco. Then climb the stairs to the upper level (south end) and turn right for the Impressionists and Post-Impressionists.*

Impressionist Collection: The gallery has a smattering of (mostly smaller-scale) works from all the main artists of the Impressionist and Post-Impressionist eras. You'll see Degas' ballet scenes, Renoir's pastel-colored family scenes, Van Gogh's peasants, and Seurat's pointillism.

Monet's *Poplars on the Epte* (1891) was part of the artist's famous "series" paintings. He set up several canvases in a floating studio near his home in Giverny. He'd start on one canvas in the morning (to catch the morning light), then move to the next as the light changed. This particular canvas captures a perfect summer day, showing both the poplars on the riverbank and their mirror image in the still water. The subject matter begins to dissolve into a pure pattern of color, anticipating abstract art.

Gauguin's *Vision of the Sermon* (1888) shows French peasant women imagining the miraculous event they've just heard preached about in church—when Jacob wrestles with an angel. The painting is a watershed in art history, as Gauguin throws out the rules of "realism" that had reigned since the Renaissance. The colors are surreal, there are no shadows, the figures are arranged almost randomly, and there's no attempt to make the wrestlers appear distant. The diagonal tree branch is the only thing separating the everyday world from the miraculous. Later, when Gauguin moved to Tahiti (see his *Three Tahitians* nearby), he painted a similar world, where the everyday and magical coexist, with symbolic power.

Sargent's *Lady Agnew of Lochnaw* (1892) is the work that launched the career of this American-born portrait artist. Lady Agnew—the young wife of a wealthy old Scotsman—lounges back languidly and gazes out self-assuredly. The Impressionistic smudges of paint on her dress and the chair contrast with her clear skin and luminous eyeballs. Her relaxed pose (one arm hanging down the side) contrasts with her intensity: head tilted slightly down while she gazes up, a corner of her mouth askew, and an eyebrow cocked seductively.

• *End your visit downstairs on the lower level, home to the...*

Scottish Collection: Though Scotland has produced few "name" painters, this small wing lets you sample some of the best. It's all in one room, designed to be toured chronologically (clockwise).

Allan Ramsay (son of the well-known poet Allan Ramsay) painted portraits of curly-wigged men of the Enlightenment era (the philosopher David Hume, King George III) as well as likenesses of his two wives. Ramsay's portrait of the duke of Argyll (founder of the Royal Bank of Scotland) appears on the Scottish 5-pound note.

Sir Henry Raeburn chronicled the next generation: Sir Walter Scott, the proud kilt-wearing Alastair Macdonell, and the ice-skating Reverend Robert Walker, minister of the Canongate Church.

Sir David Wilkie's forte was small-scale scenes of everyday life. *The Letter of Introduction* (1813) captures Wilkie's own experience of trying to impress skeptical art patrons in London; even the dog is sniffing the Scotsman out. *Distraining for Rent* (1815) shows the plight of a poor farmer about to lose his farm—a common occurrence during 19th-century industrialization.

Pause and swoon before **William Dyce's** *Francesca da Rimini* (1837). The star-crossed lovers—a young wife and her husband's kid brother—can't help but indulge their passion. The husband later finds out and kills her; at the far left, you see his ominous hand.

Finally, take in **William McTaggart's** impressionistic landscape scenes from the late 1800s for a glimpse of the unique light, powerful clouds, and natural wonder of the Highlands.

▲▲Scottish National Portrait Gallery

Put a face on Scotland's history by enjoying these portraits of famous Scots from the earliest times until today. From its Neo-Gothic facade to a grand entry hall featuring a *Who's Who* of Scotland, to galleries highlighting the great Scots of each age, this impressive museum will fascinate anyone interested in Scottish culture. The gallery also hosts temporary exhibits highlighting the work of more contemporary Scots.

Cost and Hours: Free, daily 10:00-17:00, Thu until 19:00—when occasionally there is live music at 18:00; good cafeteria serving £5-7 soups, sandwiches, and heartier fare, café closes 30 minutes before museum; 1 Queen Street, tel. 0131/624-6490, www.nationalgalleries.org.

Visiting the Gallery: In the **entrance hall** you'll see a frieze showing a parade of great Scots and murals depicting important events in Scottish history. (These are better viewed from the first floor and its mezzanine—described later). We'll start on the **second floor**, right into the thick of the struggle between Scotland and England over who should rule this land.

Reformation to Revolution (gallery 1): The collection starts with a portrait of **Mary, Queen of Scots** (1542-1587), her cross and rosary prominent. This controversial ruler set off two centuries of strife. Mary was born with Stuart blood (the ruling family of Scotland) and the Tudor blood of England's monarchs (Queen Elizabeth I was her cousin). Catholic and French-educated, Mary was unpopular in her own increasingly Protestant homeland. Then came a series of scandals: She married unpopular Lord Darnley, then (possibly) cheated on him, causing Darnley to (possibly) murder her lover, causing Mary to (possibly) murder Darnley, then run off with another man, and (possibly) plot against Queen Elizabeth.

Amid all that drama, Mary was forced by her own people to abdicate in favor of her infant son, **James VI.** Find his portraits as a child and as a grown-up. James grew up to rule Scotland, and when Queen Elizabeth (the Virgin Queen) died without an heir, he also became king of England (James I). But James' son, **Charles I,** after a bitter civil war, was arrested and executed in 1649 (see the large *Execution of Charles I* painting high on the far wall), his blood-dripping head displayed to the crowd. Charles II (see portrait as 12-year-old boy) briefly restored the Stuarts to power before they were sent into exile in France. There the Stuarts stewed, planning a return to power, waiting for someone to lead them in what would come to be known as the Jacobite Rebellion.

The Jacobite Cause (gallery 4): The biggest painting in the room is *The Baptism of Prince Charles Edward Stuart*. Born in 1720, this heir to the thrones of Great Britain and Ireland is better known to history as "Bonnie Prince Charlie." (See his bonnie features in various portraits nearby, as a child, young man, and grown man.) Charismatic Charles convinced France to invade Scotland and put him back on the throne there. In 1745, he entered Edinburgh in triumph. But he was defeated at the tide-turning Battle of Culloden (1746). The Stuart cause died forever, and Bonnie Prince Charlie went into exile, eventually dying drunk and wasted in Rome, far from the land he nearly ruled.

Citizens of the World (galleries 5-6): The two biggest paintings here are of King George III and Queen Charlotte (namesakes of the New Town's main street and square). In the late 18th century, Scotland was doing just fine being ruled from England. Paintings here show the confidence of this age, when the New Town of Edinburgh was designed and built. In the 1760s, Edinburgh was the center of Europe's Enlightenment, powered by philosophers such as David Hume and his economist friend Adam Smith. Before moving on, find the portrait of Hume (by Allan Ramsay, who also painted the likeness of George III) and a cameo medallion of Smith.

The Age of Improvement (gallery 7): The faces portrayed here belonged to a new society whose hard work and public spirit achieved progress with a Scottish accent. Social equality and the Industrial Revolution "transformed" Scotland—you'll see portraits of the great poet Robert Burns, the son of a farmer (Burns was heralded as a "heaven-taught ploughman" when his poems were first published) and the inventor of the steam engine, James Watt.

Sports (gallery 10): Lighten things up with a swing through old-time sports in Scotland, including early golf, curling, Highland Games (including "putting the stone"—similar to shot put), fox hunting, and croquet.

Central Atrium (first floor): Great Scots! The atrium is decorated in a parade of late 19th-century Romantic Historicism. The **frieze** (working counterclockwise) is a visual encyclopedia, from an ax-wielding Stone Age man and a druid, to the early mythical monarchs (Macbeth), to warriors William Wallace and Robert the Bruce, to many kings (James I, II, III, and so on), to great thinkers, inventors, and artists (Allan Ramsay, Flora MacDonald, David Hume, Adam Smith, James Boswell, James Watt), the three greatest Scottish writers (Robert Burns, Sir Walter Scott, Robert Louis Stevenson), and culminating with the poet Thomas Carlyle, who was the driving spirit (powered by the fortune of a local newspaper baron) behind creating this portrait gallery.

Best viewed from the first-floor mezzanine are the large-scale **murals** depicting great events in Scottish history, including the landing of St. Margaret at Queensferry in 1068, the Battle of Stirling Bridge in 1297, the Battle of Bannockburn in 1314, and the marriage procession of James IV and Margaret Tudor through the streets of Edinburgh in 1509.

The Modern Scot (gallery 11): Paintings on the first floor make it clear that Scotland continues to contribute. You'll see distinguished Scottish scientists such as physicist Peter Higgs, theorizer of the Higgs boson, the so-called God particle. He was researching at the University of Edinburgh in the 1960s when he speculated on the existence of a subatomic particle that might tie together many other theories on the structure of the universe. Nearby is the stirring *Three Oncologists,* a ghostly painting depicting the anxiety and terror of cancer and the dedication of those working so hard to conquer it.

Sights near Edinburgh
▲▲Britannia

This much-revered vessel, which transported Britain's royal family for more than 40 years on 900 voyages before being retired in 1997, is permanently moored at the Ocean Terminal Shopping Mall in Edinburgh's port of Leith. It's open to the public and worth the half-hour bus or taxi ride from the center; figure on spending about 2.5 hours total on the outing.

Cost and Hours: £12, daily July-Sept 9:30-16:30, April-June and Oct 9:30-16:00, Nov-March 10:00-15:30, these are last-entry times, tearoom, on Ocean Drive in Leith, tel. 0131/555-5566, www.royalyachtbritannia.co.uk.

Getting There: From central Edinburgh, catch Lothian bus #11, #22, or #35 at Waverley Bridge to Ocean Terminal. If you're doing a city bus tour, consider the Majestic Tour, which includes transportation to the *Britannia* (see page 746). Entrance to the museum is on the second floor at the north (right) end of the shopping center.

Visiting the Ship: Explore the museum, filled with engrossing royal-family-afloat history. Then, armed with your included 90-minute audioguide, you're welcome aboard.

This was the last in a line of royal yachts that stretches back to 1660. With all its royal functions, the ship required a crew of more than 200. The captain's bridge feels like it's been preserved from the day it was launched in 1953. Queen Elizabeth II, who enjoyed the ship for 40 years, said, "This is the only place I can truly relax." The Sunny Lounge, just off the back Veranda Deck, was the Queen's favorite, with Burmese teak and the same phone system she was used to in Buckingham Palace.

The back deck was the favorite place for outdoor entertainment. Ronald Reagan, Boris Yeltsin, Bill Clinton, and Nelson Mandela all sipped champagne here with the Queen. When she wasn't entertaining, the Queen liked it quiet. The crew wore sneakers, communicated in hand signals, and (at least near the Queen's quarters) had to be finished with all their work by 8:00 in the morning.

The state dining room, decorated with gifts given by the ship's many noteworthy guests, enabled the Queen to entertain a good-size crowd. The silver pantry was just down the hall. The drawing room, while rather simple, was perfect for casual relaxing among royals. Princess Diana played the piano, which is bolted to the deck. Royal family photos evoke the fine times the Windsors enjoyed on the *Britannia*. Visitors can also see the crew's quarters and engine room.

Rosslyn Chapel

Founded in 1446 by the Sinclair family, this church is a fascinating riot of carved iconography. The patterned ceiling and walls have left scholars guessing about its symbolism for centuries, particularly questioning if there's a link to the Knights Templar and the Masons. But much of the speculation, especially the *Da Vinci Code* connections, has been debunked.

Cost and Hours: £9, Mon-Sat 9:30-18:00, until 17:00 Oct-March, Sun 12:00-16:45 year-round, last entry 30 minutes before closing, no photos, located in Roslin Village, www.rosslynchapel.org.uk.

Getting There: Ride Lothian **bus** #15 from the station at St. Andrew Square (1-2/hour, 45 minutes). By **car,** take the A-701 to Penicuik/Peebles, and follow signs for *Roslin;* once you're in the village, you'll see signs for the chapel.

Royal Botanic Garden

Britain's second-oldest botanical garden (after Oxford) was established in 1670 for medicinal herbs, and this 70-acre refuge is now one of Europe's best.

Cost and Hours: Gardens free, greenhouse admission-£4.50, daily March-Sept 10:00-18:00, until 16:00 Nov-Jan, until 17:00 Feb and Oct, 1-hour tours April-Oct daily at 11:00 and 14:00 for £5, maps-£1, café, a mile north of the city center at Inverleith Row; tel. 0131/552-7171, www.rbge.org.uk.

Getting There: It's a 10-minute bus ride from the city center: Take Lothian bus #8 from North Bridge, #23 from the Mound, or #27 from George IV Bridge; Majestic Tour also stops here (see page 746).

Scottish National Gallery of Modern Art

This museum, set in a beautiful parkland, houses Scottish and international paintings and sculpture from 1900 to the present, including works by Matisse, Duchamp, Picasso, and Warhol. The grounds include a pleasant outdoor sculpture park and a café.

Cost and Hours: Free, daily 10:00-17:00, Aug until 18:00, 75 Belford Road, tel. 0131/624-6336, www.nationalgalleries.org.

Getting There: It's about a 20-minute walk west from the city center. Public transportation options aren't good, but a free shuttle bus runs about every half-hour between this museum and the Scottish National Gallery (daily 11:00-18:00, confirm times on website).

Activities in Edinburgh

▲▲Arthur's Seat Hike

A 45-minute hike up the 822-foot remains of an extinct volcano (surrounded by a fine park overlooking Edinburgh) starts from the parking lot below the Palace of Holyroodhouse. You can run up like they did in *Chariots of Fire*, or just stroll—at the summit, you'll be rewarded with commanding views of the town and surroundings. On May Day, be on the summit at dawn and wash your face in the morning dew to commemorate the Celtic holiday of Beltaine, the celebration of spring. (Morning dew is supposedly very good for your complexion.)

From the parking lot below the Palace of Holyroodhouse, there are two trailheads. Take the wide path on the left (easier grade, through the abbey ruins and "Hunter's Bog"). After making the summit, you can return along the other path (to the right, with the steps), which skirts the base of the cliffs.

Those staying at my recommended B&Bs can enjoy a pre-breakfast or late-evening hike starting from the other side (in June, the sun comes up early, and it stays light until nearly midnight). From the Commonwealth Pool, take Holyrood Park Road, turn right on Queen's Drive, and continue to a small parking lot. From here it's a 20-minute hike.

If you have a car, you can drive up most of the way from behind (follow the one-way street from the palace, park safely and for free by the little lake, and hike up).

More Hikes

You can hike along the river (called Water of Leith) through Edinburgh. Locals favor the stretch between Roseburn and Dean Village, but the 1.5-mile walk from Dean Village to the Royal

Botanic Garden is also good. For more information on these and other hikes, ask at the TI for the free *Walks In and Around Edinburgh* one-page flier (if it's unavailable, consider their £3 guide to walks).

Brush Skiing

If you like skiing, but not all that pesky snow, head a little south of town to Hillend, where the Midlothian Snowsports Centre has a hill with a chairlift, two slopes, a jump slope, and rentable skis, boots, and poles. It feels like snow-skiing on a slushy day, even though you're schussing over what seems like a million tooth-brushes. Beware: Doctors are used to treating an ailment called "Hillend Thumb"—thumbs dislocated when people fall here and get tangled in the brush. Locals say that skiing here is like falling on a carrot grater.

Cost and Hours: £12/first hour, then £5.30/hour, includes gear, beginners must take a lesson, generally Mon-Tue 18:30-22:00, Wed 13:00-20:00, Thu-Fri 18:00-21:00, Sat-Sun 14:00-19:00—but call to confirm before showing up, probably closes if it snows, 40 minutes away on Lothian bus #4 or #15 from Princes Street—garden side, tel. 0131/445-4433, www.midlothian.gov.uk.

Royal Commonwealth Pool

This indoor fitness and activity complex on Dalkeith Road—in the shadow of Arthur's Seat—includes a 50-meter pool (bring a suit and towel), gym/fitness studio, café, and kids' soft play zone.

Cost and Hours: Pool day pass-£5.80 for individual or £13.70 for families, gym pass-£7, £21 for family swim and soft play package; Mon-Fri 5:30-22:00, Sat 5:30-20:00, Sun 7:30-20:00; open swim nearly all the time but not Sat-Sun after 13:00; lockers available; tel. 0131/667-7211, www.edinburghleisure.co.uk.

Prestonfield Golf Club

The club has golfers feeling like they're in a country estate. A dress code is enforced—no jeans, shorts, T-shirts, sweats, or tennis shoes. It's at the foot of Arthur's Seat, a mile and a half from town (and easy walking distance from my recommended Dalkeith Road B&Bs).

Cost and Hours: £32-38/person plus £15-20 for clubs, cart-£3 (pull) or £22 (power); 6 Priestfield Road North, tel. 0131/667-9665, www.prestonfieldgolf.com.

Shopping

The streets to browse are Princes Street (the elegant old Jenners department store is close by on Rose Street, near St. Andrew Square), Victoria Street (antiques galore), Nicolson Street (south of the Royal Mile, line of secondhand stores), and the Royal Mile (touristy but competitively priced). Shops are usually open 10:00-18:00 (later on Thu). If you want to be sure you are taking home local merchandise, check if the labels read: "Made in Scotland." "Designed in Scotland" actually means "Made in China."

Experiences in Edinburgh

Edinburgh Festival

One of Europe's great cultural events, Edinburgh's annual festival turns the city into a carnival of the arts. There are enough music, dance, drama, and multicultural events to make even the most jaded traveler giddy with excitement. Every day is jammed with formal and spontaneous fun. A riot of festivals—official, fringe, book, and jazz and blues—rages simultaneously for about three weeks each August, with the Military Tattoo starting (and ending) a week earlier. The best overall website is www.edinburgh festivals.co.uk.

Many city sights run on extended hours, and those along the Royal Mile that normally close on Sunday are open in the afternoon. It's a glorious time to be in Edinburgh—if you have (and can afford) a room.

The official **Edinburgh International Festival** (Aug 8-31 in 2014, likely Aug 7-30 in 2015) is the original—it's more formal, and the most likely to get booked up. Major events sell out well in advance. The ticket office is at the Hub, located in the former Tolbooth Church, near the top of the Royal Mile (tickets-£5-75, booking from late March, office open Mon-Sat 10:00-17:00 or longer, in Aug 9:00-19:30 plus Sun 10:00-19:30, tel. 0131/473-2000, www.hubtickets.co.uk or www.eif.co.uk).

Pick up your ticket at the Hub office on the day of the show or at the venue before noon. Several publications—including the festival's official schedule, the *Edinburgh Festivals Guide Daily, The List, Fringe Program,* and *Daily Diary*—list and evaluate festival events.

The less formal **Fringe Festival,** featuring "on the edge" comedy and theater, is huge—with 2,000 shows (Aug 1-25 in 2014, ticket/info office just below St. Giles Cathedral on the Royal Mile, 180 High Street, bookings tel. 0131/226-0000, can book online from mid-May on, www.edfringe.com). Tickets may be available at the door, and half-price tickets for some events are sold on the day of the show at the Half-Price Hut, located at the Mound, near the Scottish National Gallery (daily 10:00-21:00).

The **Military Tattoo** is a massing of bands, drums, and bagpipes, with groups from all over the former British Empire. Displaying military finesse with a stirring lone-piper finale, this grand spectacle fills the Castle Esplanade nightly except Sunday, normally from a week before the festival starts until a week before it finishes (Aug 1-23 in 2014, Mon-Fri at 21:00, Sat at 19:30 and 22:30, £25-60, booking starts in Dec, Fri-Sat shows sell out first, all seats generally sold out by early summer, some scattered same-day tickets may be available; office open Mon-Fri 10:00-16:30, closed Sat-Sun, during Tattoo open until show time and Sat 10:00-22:30, closed Sun; 32 Market Street, behind Waverley Station, tel. 0131/225-1188, www.edintattoo.co.uk). The last day is filmed by the BBC and later broadcast as a big national television special.

The **Festival of Politics,** adding yet another dimension to Edinburgh's festival action, is held in August in the Scottish parliament building. It's a busy four days of discussions and lectures on environmentalism, globalization, terrorism, gender, and other issues (www.festivalofpolitics.org.uk).

Other summer festivals cover jazz and blues (early August, tel. 0131/467-5200, www.edinburghjazzfestival.co.uk), film (mid-June, tel. 0131/228-4051, www.edfilmfest.org.uk), and books (mid-late August, tel. 0131/718-5666, www.edbookfest.co.uk).

If you do plan to hit Edinburgh during a festival, book a room far in advance and extend your stay by a day or two. Once you know your dates, reserve tickets to any show you really want to see.

Nightlife in Edinburgh

▲▲Literary Pub Tour

This two-hour walk is interesting even if you think Sir Walter Scott was an Antarctic explorer. You'll follow the witty dialogue of two actors as they debate whether the great literature of Scotland was high art or the creative re-creation of fun-loving louts fueled by a love of whisky. You'll wander from the Grassmarket over the Old Town and New Town, with stops in three pubs as your guides share their takes on Scotland's literary greats. The tour meets at the Beehive pub on Grassmarket (£14, book online and save £2, May-Sept nightly at 19:30, March-April and Oct Thu-Sun, Nov-Feb Fri only, www.edinburghliterarypubtour.co.uk).

▲Ghost Walks

These walks are an entertaining and cheap night out (offered nightly, most around 19:00 and 21:00, easy socializing for solo travelers). The theatrical and creatively staged **Witchery Tours,** the most established outfit, offers two different walks: "Ghosts and Gore" (1.5 hours, April-Aug only) and "Murder and Mystery" (1.25 hours, year-round). The former is better suited for kids than the latter (either tour £8.50, includes book of stories, leaves from top of Royal Mile, outside the Witchery Restaurant, near Castle Esplanade, reservations required, tel. 0131/225-6745, www.witchery tours.com).

Auld Reekie Tours offers a scary array of walks daily and nightly (£9-12, 50-90 minutes, leaves from front steps of the Tron Church building on Cockburn Street, tel. 0131/557-4700, pick up brochure or visit www.auldreekietours.com). Auld Reekie focuses on the paranormal, witch covens, and pagan temples, taking groups into the "haunted vaults" under the old bridges "where it was so dark, so crowded, and so squalid that the people there knew each other not by how they looked, but by how they sounded, felt, and smelt." If you want more, there's plenty of it (complete with screaming Gothic "jumpers").

Scottish Folk Evenings

These £35-40 dinner shows, generally for tour groups intent on photographing old cultural clichés, are held in the huge halls of expensive hotels. (Prices are bloated to include 20 percent commissions.) Your "traditional" meal is followed by a full slate of swirling kilts, blaring bagpipes, and Scottish folk dancing with an old-time music hall emcee. If you like Lawrence Welk, you're in for a treat. But for most travelers, these are painfully cheesy variety shows. You can sometimes see the show without dinner for about two-thirds the price. The TI has fliers on all the latest venues.

Prestonfield House offers its kitschy "Taste of Scotland" folk evening—a plaid fantasy of smiling performers accompanied by electric keyboards—with or without dinner Sunday to Friday. For £45, you get the show with two drinks and a wad of haggis; £58 buys you the same, plus a three-course meal and a half-bottle of wine (be there at 18:45, dinner at 19:00, show runs 20:00-22:00, May-Oct only). It's in the stables of "the handsomest house in Edinburgh," which is now home to the recommended Rhubarb Restaurant (Priestfield Road, a 10-minute walk from Dalkeith Road B&Bs, tel. 0131/225-7800, www.scottishshow.co.uk).

Theater

Even outside festival time, Edinburgh is a fine place for lively and affordable theater. Pick up *The List* for a complete rundown of what's on (sold at newsstands for a few pounds; also online at www.list.co.uk).

▲▲Live Music in Pubs

Edinburgh used to be a better place for traditional folk music, but in the last few years, pub owners—out of economic necessity—are catering to college-age customers more interested in beer drinking. And several pubs that were famous for folk music have gone pop. But, if you know where to look, you'll still find pubs that can deliver a traditional folk-music fix. The monthly *Gig Guide* (free at TI, accommodations, and various pubs, www.gigguide.co.uk) lists 8 or 10 places each night that have live music, divided by genre (pop, rock, world, and folk).

South of High Street: **Sandy Bell's** is a tight little pub with live folk music nightly from 21:30 (just outside the tourist zone, a few minutes' walk from the Greyfriars Bobby statue and the National Museum of Scotland at 25 Forrest Road, tel. 0131/225-2751). Food is very simple (toasted sandwiches and soup), drinks are cheap, tables are small, and the vibe is local. They also have weekend

EDINBURGH

Sampling Whisky

While pub-hopping tourists generally think in terms of beer, many pubs are just as enthusiastic about serving whisky. If

you are unfamiliar with whisky (what Americans call "Scotch"), it's a great conversation starter. Many pubs (including Leslie's, described on next page) have lists of dozens of whiskies available. Lists include descriptions of their personalities (peaty, heavy iodine finish, and so on), which are much easier to discern than most wine flavors. A glass generally costs around £2.50. Let a local teach you how to drink it "neat," then add a little water. Learn how to swish it around and let your gums taste it, too. Keep experimenting until you discover "the nurse's knickers."

In Edinburgh you can peruse the selection at the Whiski Rooms Shop or Cadenhead's, join a whisky tasting, or stop in at the Scotch Whisky Experience (for details on each of these, see "Sights in Edinburgh," earlier). Outside Edinburgh, Luvians Bottle Shop in St. Andrews and the Pot Still in Glasgow are fine places to sample a wee dram. Authentic distillery tours abound in Oban or Pitlochry and on the Isle of Skye. (For more on these options, see their respective chapters in this book.)

But don't neglect the easiest and perhaps best option for sampling Scotland's national drink: Find a local pub with a passion for whisky that's filled with locals who share that passion. Make a friend, buy a few shots, and learn by drinking.

afternoon sessions (Sat-Sun at 14:00).

The Royal Oak is another good place for a dose of Celtic music (just off South Bridge opposite Chambers Road at 1 Infirmary Street, tel. 0131/557-2976).

The **Grassmarket** neighborhood (below the castle) bustles with live music and rowdy people spilling out of the pubs and into what was (once upon a time) a busy market square. While it used to be a mecca for Scottish folk music, today it's more youthful with a heavy-drinking, rockin' feel. It's fun to just wander through this area late at night and check out the scene. Thanks to the music and crowds, you'll know where to go...and where not to. Have a beer and follow your ear to places like **Biddy Mulligans** or **White Hart Inn** (both on Grassmarket). **Finnegans Wake** on Victoria Street (which leads down to Grassmarket) also has live folk and rock each night.

On High Street: Three characteristic pubs within a few steps of each other on High Street (opposite Radisson Hotel) offer a fun setting, classic pub architecture and ambience, and live music for the cost of a beer: **Whiski Bar** (trad and folk nightly at 22:00), **Royal Mile** (pop and folk, nightly at 22:00), and **Mitre Bar** (nightly at 21:00 or 21:30, trad on Tue and Thu). Just a block away (on South Bridge) is **Whistlebinkies Live Music Bar.** While they rarely do folk or Scottish trad, this is the most serious of the music pubs, with an actual stage and several acts nightly (schedule posted outside the door makes the genre clear: rock, pop, jazz or blues, music starts at 19:00 or earlier, young crowd, fun energy, no cover, tel. 0131/557-5114). **No. 1 High Street** is an accessible little pub with a love of folk and traditional music and free performances many nights from 21:00 (Scottish trad on Tue-Wed, bluegrass on Thu). Drop by during your sightseeing as you walk the lower part of the Royal Mile, and ask what's on tonight (across from World's End, 1 High Street, tel. 0131/556-5758).

In the New Town: All the beer drinkers seem to head for the pedestrianized Rose Street, famous for having the most pubs per square inch anywhere in Scotland—and plenty of live music.

Near Dalkeith Road B&Bs: The first three listed below are classic pubs (without a lot of noisy machines and rowdy twenty-somethings). They cluster within 100 yards of each other around the intersection of Duncan Street and Causewayside.

Leslie's Pub, sitting between a working-class and an upper-class neighborhood, has two sides. Originally, the gang would go in on the right to gather around the great hardwood bar, glittering with a century of *Cheers* ambience. Meanwhile, the more delicate folks would slip in on the left, with its discreet doors, plush snugs (cozy private booths), and ornate ordering windows. Since 1896, this Victorian classic has been appreciated for both its real ales and its huge selection of fine whiskies (listed on a lengthy menu). Dive into the whisky mosh pit on the right, and let them show you how whisky can become "a very good friend." (Leslie's is a block downhill from the next two pubs, at 49 Ratcliffe Terrace, daily 11:00-24:00, tel. 0131/667-7205.)

The Old Bell Inn, with a nostalgic sports-bar vibe, serves only drinks after 19:00 (see "Scottish Grub and Pubs" on page 821).

Swanny's Pub is not quite as welcoming, but it's a quintessential hangout for the working-class boys of the neighborhood, with some fun characters to get to know (Mon-Sat 11:00-24:00, Sun 12:30-late).

The Salisbury Arms Pub is an inviting place to mingle with locals, enjoy a three-ale sampler for around £3.50, or simply unwind over a few drinks after a long day of sightseeing (see "Scottish Grub and Pubs" on page 821).

Sleeping in Edinburgh

The advent of big, inexpensive hotels has made life more of a struggle for B&Bs, which are tending to go plush to compete. Still, book ahead, especially in August, when the annual Festival fills Edinburgh. Conventions, rugby matches, school holidays, and weekends can make finding a room tough at almost any time of year. For the best prices, skip middleman websites or the for-profit TI (which charges a higher room fee and levies a £4 booking fee) and book direct. "Standard" rooms, with toilets and showers a tissue-toss away, are cheaper than "en suite" rooms (with a private bathroom). At B&Bs, you can usually save some money by paying cash; although most B&Bs take credit cards, many add the card service fee to your bill (about three percent of the price).

B&Bs off Dalkeith Road

South of town near the Royal Commonwealth Pool, these B&Bs—just off Dalkeith Road—are nearly all top-end, sporting three or four stars. While pricey, they come with uniformly friendly hosts and great cooked breakfasts, and are a good value for people with enough money. At these not-quite-interchangeable places, character is provided by the personality quirks of the hosts.

Most listings are on quiet streets and within a two-minute walk of a bus stop. Though you won't find phones in the rooms, most have Wi-Fi and several offer guest computers. Most can provide triples or even quads for families.

Prices listed are for most of peak season; if there's a range, prices slide up with summer demand. During the Festival in

---

Sleep Code

(£1 = about $1.60, country code: 44, area code: 0131)
S = Single, **D** = Double/Twin, **T** = Triple, **Q** = Quad, **b** = bathroom, **s** = shower only. Unless otherwise noted, credit cards are accepted and prices include breakfast.

To help you sort easily through these listings, I've divided the accommodations into three categories based on the price for a standard double room with bath (during high season):

   $$$ Higher Priced—Most rooms £80 or more.
   $$ Moderately Priced—Most rooms between £60-80.
   $ Lower Priced—Most rooms £60 or less.

Prices can change without notice; verify the hotel's current rates online or by email. For the best prices, always book direct.

Edinburgh's Dalkeith Road Neighborhood

1/4 MILE

400 METERS

ⓑ BUS STOP

1 Hotel Ceilidh-Donia

2 AmarAgua Guest House & Aonach Mor B&B

3 Dunedin Guest House

4 Gil Dun Guest House

5 Gifford House

6 Ardenair Guest House

7 Ard-Na-Said Guest House

8 Kingsway Guest House

9 Kenvie Guest House

10 Priestville Guest House

11 Belford Guest House

12 23 Mayfield Guest House & Glenalmond House

13 Edinburgh Bakehouse, Il Positano Ristorante & Voujon

14 To Rhubarb Restaurant & Prestonfield House

15 To The Sheeps Heid Inn

16 The Old Bell Inn & Rest.

17 The Salisbury Arms Pub

18 Reverie Bar & Metropole Café

19 Hewat's Restaurant

20 Hellers Kitchen

21 Leslie's Pub

22 Swanny's Pub

23 Tesco Express Supermarket

24 Launderette

August, prices are higher; B&Bs also do not accept bookings for one-night stays during this time. Conversely, in winter, when demand is light, prices get really soft (less than what's listed here). These prices are for cash; expect a 3-5 percent fee for using your credit card.

Near the B&Bs, you'll find plenty of great eateries (see "Eating in Edinburgh," later) and several good, classic pubs (see "Nightlife in Edinburgh," earlier). A few places have their own private parking spots; others offer access to easy, free street parking (ask about it when booking—or better yet, don't rent a car for your time in Edinburgh).

If you bring in take-out food, your host would probably prefer you eat it in the breakfast area rather than muck up your room—ask. The nearest launderette is Ace Cleaning Centre (which picks up and drops off; see page 741).

Getting There: This comfortable, safe neighborhood is a 10-minute bus ride from the Royal Mile. From the train station, the nearest place to catch the bus (at least while tram construction is under way) is around the corner on North Bridge (exit the station onto Princes Street, turn right, cross the street, and walk up the bridge). If you're here after the Princes Street construction is finished, use the bus stop in front of the Marks & Spencer department store (£1.50, use exact change; catch Lothian bus #14, #30, or #33 or First bus #86). Tell the driver your destination is Dalkeith Road; about 10 minutes into the ride, after following South Clerk Street for a while, the bus makes a left turn, then a right—depending on where you're staying, you'll get off at the first or second stop after the turn (confirm specifics with your B&B). These buses also stop at the corner of North Bridge and High Street on the Royal Mile. Buses run from 6:00 (9:00 on Sun) to 23:00. Taxi fare between the train station or Royal Mile and the B&Bs is about £7. Taxis are easy to hail on Dalkeith Road if it isn't raining.

$$$ Hotel Ceilidh-Donia rents 17 contemporary rooms with a pleasant back deck, a quiet bar, a free DVD lending library, and your choice of full Scottish, English, American, or vegetarian breakfast (Sb-£50-66, Db-£70-120, more in Aug and for special events, less off-season, guest computer, free Wi-Fi, 14-16 Marchhall Crescent, tel. 0131/667-2743, www.hotelceilidh-donia .co.uk, reservations@hotelceilidh-donia.co.uk, Max and Annette).

$$$ AmarAgua Guest House is an inviting Victorian home away from home, with five welcoming rooms and a Japanese garden. It's given a little extra sparkle by its energetic proprietors, former entertainers Dawn-Ann and Tony Costa (Db-£70-85, Tb-£90-110, more for fancy four-poster rooms, 2-night minimum, guest computer and iPads, free Wi-Fi, 10 Kilmaurs Terrace, tel. 0131/667-6775, www.amaragua.co.uk, reservations@amaragua.co.uk).

$$$ Dunedin Guest House (dun-EE-din) is a fine value: bright, plush, and elegantly Scottish, with seven nice, airy rooms and a spacious breakfast room (S with private b on hall-£52-67, Db-£79-124, family rooms for up to 5, less off-season, free Wi-Fi, 8 Priestfield Road, tel. 0131/668-1949, www.dunedinguesthouse .co.uk, reservations@dunedinguesthouse.co.uk, David and Irene Wright).

$$$ Gil Dun Guest House, with eight rooms on a quiet cul-de-sac just off Dalkeith Road, is comfortable, pleasant, and managed with care by Gerry and Bill (Sb-£40-50, Db-£85-90, or £130 in Aug, great bathrooms, family deals, free Wi-Fi, pleasant garden, 9 Spence Street, tel. 0131/667-1368, www.gildun.co.uk, gildun.edin@btinternet.com).

$$$ Gifford House, on busy Dalkeith Road, is a bright, flowery, creaky-floor retreat with six surprisingly peaceful rooms, some with ornate cornices, super-king-size beds, and views of Arthur's Seat (Sb-£70-80, Db-£80-90, Tb-£114-120, Qb-£130-140, free Wi-Fi, street parking, 103 Dalkeith Road, tel. 0131/667-4688, www.giffordhouseedinburgh.com, giffordhouse@btinternet .com, David and Margaret).

$$ Airdenair Guest House, offering views and a friendly welcome, has five attractive rooms on the second floor with a lofty above-it-all feeling. Homemade scones and Jill's pulse on the latest neighborhood information are staples here (Sb-£40-45, Db-£70-80, Tb-£85-95, less off-season, free Wi-Fi, 29 Kilmaurs Road, tel. 0131/668-2336, www.airdenair.com, jill@airdenair.com, Jill and Doug McLennan).

$$ Ard-Na-Said B&B is an elegant 1875 Victorian house with a comfy lounge. It offers seven bright, spacious rooms with modern bathrooms—including one ground-floor room with a pleasant patio (Sb-£35-50, Db-£65-95, huge four-poster Db-£70-105, Tb-£90-120, prices depend on size of room as well as season, guest computer, free Wi-Fi, DVD players, free parking, 5 Priestfield Road, tel. 0131/667-8754, www.ardnasaid.co.uk, enquiries @ardnasaid.co.uk, Jim and Olive Lyons—or Olive and Jim Lyons, depending on whom you ask).

$$ Kingsway Guest House has seven high-quality, stylish, Scottish-modern rooms. Delightful owners Gary and Lizzie have thought of all the little touches, like take-away breakfast for early departures and bike and golf club rental (Sb-£45-65, Db-£60-85, Tb-£80-115, Qb-£90-125, 5 percent off these prices with cash and this book—mention Rick Steves when booking, free Wi-Fi, free parking, 5 East Mayfield, tel. 0131/667-5029, www.edinburgh -guesthouse.com, room@edinburgh-guesthouse.com).

$$ Aonach Mor B&B's eight plush rooms have views of either nearby Arthur's Seat or walled gardens (Db-£45-85, more in July-Aug, online specials, free Wi-Fi, 14 Kilmaurs Terrace, tel. 0131/667-8694, www.aonachmor.com, info@aonachmor.com, Tom and Fiona).

$$ Kenvie Guest House, expertly run by Dorothy Vidler, comes with five pleasant rooms (D-£64-68, Db-£72-78, these prices with cash and this book—but must claim when you reserve, family deals, guest computer, free Wi-Fi, 16 Kilmaurs Road, tel. 0131/668-1964, www.kenvie.co.uk, dorothy@kenvie.co.uk).

$$ Priestville Guest House is homey, with a dramatic skylight above the stairs, a sunny breakfast room, and cozy charm—not fancy, but more than workable, and great for families. The six rooms have Wi-Fi, VCRs, and a free video library (D-£50-64, Db-£56-80, Tb-£100, Q-£120, these prices when booked via email and paid in cash, discount for 2 or more nights, guest computer, free Wi-Fi, family rooms, 10 Priestfield Road, tel. 0131/667-2435, www.priestville.com, bookings@priestville.com, Trina and Colin Warwick).

$$ Belford Guest House is a tidy, homey place offering three basic rooms all with renovated en suite bathrooms (Sb-£45, Db-£70-75, family room, cheaper for longer stays, cash only, free parking, 13 Blacket Avenue—no sign out front, tel. 0131/667-2422, www.belfordguesthouse.com, tom@belfordguesthouse.com, Tom Borthwick).

Guesthouses on Mayfield Gardens

These two very well-run B&Bs come with a little street noise, but are bigger buildings with more spacious rooms, finer public lounges, and nice comforts (such as iPod-compatible bedside radios).

$$$ At **23 Mayfield Guest House,** Ross (and Grandma Mary) rent nine splurge-worthy, thoughtfully appointed rooms complete with high-tech bathrooms and a hot tub in the garden. Little extras—such as locally sourced gourmet breakfasts, an inviting guest lounge outfitted with Sir Arthur Conan Doyle books, an "honesty bar," and classic black-and-white movie screenings—make you feel like royalty (Sb-£65-95, Db-£80-110, bigger Db-£90-140, four-poster Db-£120-170, family room for up to 4, 7 percent Rick Steves discount if you pay with cash, guest computer, free Wi-Fi, swap library, free parking, 23 Mayfield Gardens, tel. 0131/667-5806, www.23mayfield.co.uk, info@23mayfield.co.uk). If you can't wait until tomorrow for another taste of Ross' delicious cuisine (or aren't lucky enough to book a room), stop by his Copper Coffee stand for a goat cheese and roasted red pepper *panini* (22a St. Patrick Square, just off the route to/from downtown Edinburgh).

$$$ Glenalmond House, run by Jimmy and Fiona Mackie, has 10 beautiful rooms with fancy modern bathrooms (Db-£80-100, bigger four-poster Db-up to £125, Tb-£80-120, Qb-£120-150, 5 percent Rick Steves discount off these prices if you book direct and pay cash, less off-season, discount for longer stays, guest computer, free Wi-Fi, free parking, 25 Mayfield Gardens, tel. 0131/668-2392, www.glenalmondhouse.com, enquiries@glen almondhouse.com).

Big, Modern Hotels

The first listing's a splurge. The rest are cheaper than most of the city's other chain hotels, and offer more comfort than character. In each case, I'd skip the institutional breakfast and eat out. To locate these hotels, see the maps on pages 746 and 816. You'll generally pay £10 a day to park near these hotels.

$$$ Macdonald Holyrood Hotel, my only fancy listing, is a four-star splurge, with 156 rooms up the street from the new Parliament building. With its classy marble-and-wood decor, fitness center, and pool, it's hard to leave. On a gray winter day in Edinburgh, this could be worth it, but some parts may be undergoing renovation in 2014. Prices can vary wildly (Db-£110-170, breakfast extra, check for specials online, family deals, near bottom of Royal Mile, across from Dynamic Earth, 81 Holyrood Road, tel. 0131/528-8000, www.macdonaldhotels.co.uk).

$$$ Jurys Inn offers a more enjoyable feeling than the Ibis and Travelodge (listed below). A cookie-cutter place with 186 dependably comfortable and bright rooms, it is capably run and well-situated a short walk from the station (Sb/Db/Tb-£99, less on weekdays, can be much cheaper off-season and for online bookings, much more in Aug, breakfast-£9-11, some views, pay Wi-Fi, laundry service, pub/restaurant, on quiet street just off Royal Mile, 43 Jeffrey Street, tel. 0131/200-3300, www.jurysinns.com).

$$$ Ibis Hotel, at the middle of the Royal Mile, is well-run and perfectly located. It has 99 soulless but clean and comfy rooms drenched in prefab American "charm." Room rates vary widely—book online to get their best offers (Db in June-Sept-£80-149, more during Festival, less off-season, breakfast-£8, pay guest computer and Wi-Fi, 6 Hunter Square, tel. 0131/240-7000, www.ibishotels.com, h2039@accor.com).

$$$ Holiday Inn Express Edinburgh Royal Mile rents 78 rooms with stark modern efficiency in a fine location, a five-minute walk from the train station (Db-£95-135 depending on day, generally most expensive on Fri-Sat, much more during Festival, cheaper off-season, for best rates book online, free Wi-Fi, just off the Royal Mile down St. Mary's Street, 300 Cowgate, tel. 0131/524-8400, www.hiexpressedinburgh.co.uk). Another Holiday Inn Express is on Picardy Place (Db-£95-135, 16 Picardy Place, tel. 0131/558-2300, www.hieedinburgh.co.uk).

$$ Travelodge Central has 193 well-located, no-nonsense rooms, all decorated in sky blue. All rooms are the same and suitable for two adults with two kids, or three adults. While sleepable, it has a cheap feel with a quickly revolving staff (Sb/Db/Tb-£60-70, weekend Db-£70-85, Aug Db-£150, cheaper off-season and when booked online in advance, breakfast-£8, 33 St. Mary's Street, a block off Royal Mile, tel. 0871-984-6137, www.travelodge.co.uk). They have four other locations in the New Town: at 37-43 Rose Street; on Meuse Lane off Princes Street; at 30-31 Queen Street; and at 3 Waterloo Place, on the east end of Princes Street. Book online for any location.

Hostels

Edinburgh has two five-star hostels with dorm beds for about £20, slick modern efficiency, and careful management. They offer the best cheap beds in town. These places welcome families—travelers of any age feel comfortable here. Anyone on a tight budget wanting a twin room should think of these as simple hotels. The alternative is one of Edinburgh's scruffy bohemian hostels, each of which offers a youthful, mellow ambience and beds for around £15.

$ Edinburgh Central Youth Hostel rents 300 beds in rooms with one to eight beds (all with private bathrooms and lockers). Guests can eat cheaply in the cafeteria, or cook for the cost of groceries in the members' kitchen. Prices include sheets; towel rental costs £2 extra (£18-29/person in 4- to 8-bed rooms, Sb-£43-57, Db-£71-88, Tb-£73-127, Qb-£100-158, depends on season, non-members pay £2 extra per night, single-sex dorms, cooked breakfast-£6, continental breakfast-£4.50, open 24/7, pay guest computer and Wi-Fi, laundry facilities, 15-minute downhill walk from Waverley Station—head down Leith Walk, pass through two roundabouts, hostel is on your left—or take Lothian bus #22 or #25 to Elm Rowe, 9 Haddington Place off Leith Walk, tel. 0131/524-2090, www.syha.org.uk).

$ Smart City Hostel is a godsend for backpackers and anyone looking for simple, efficient rooms in the old center for cheap. You'll pay £10-20 (depends on season) for a bed in an austere, industrial-strength 4- to 12-bed dorm—each with its own private bathroom. But it can get crazy with raucous weekend stag and hen parties. Bar 50 in the basement has an inviting lounge with cheap meals. Half of the rooms function as a university dorm during the school year, becoming available just in time for the tourists (620 beds, Db-£50-120, bunky Qb-£60-165, includes linens and towels, cooked breakfast-£5, usually some female-only rooms but can't guarantee in summer, lockers, kitchen, lots of modern and efficient extras, pay Wi-Fi, coin-op laundry, 50 Blackfriars Street, tel. 0131/524-1989, www.smartcityhostels.com, info@smartcity hostels.com).

Cheap and Scruffy Bohemian Hostels in the Center: These first three sister hostels—popular crash pads for young, hip back-packers—are beautifully located in the noisy center (£13.50-20 depending on time of year, twin D-£40-55, www.scotlandstop hostels.com): **High Street Hostel** (130 beds, 8 Blackfriars Street, just off High Street/Royal Mile, tel. 0131/557-3984); **Royal Mile Backpackers** (40 beds, dorms only—no private rooms, 105 High Street, tel. 0131/557-6120); and **Castle Rock Hostel** (300 beds, just below the castle and above the pubs, 15 Johnston Terrace, tel. 0131/225-9666). **Brodie's Hostels,** somewhere between spartan and dumpy in the middle of the Royal Mile, rents 130 cheap beds in 4- to 16-bed dorms (£10-13 beds, D-£55-65, Db-£65-75, includes linens, lockers-£1/day, kitchen, pay guest computer and Wi-Fi, laundry, 93 High Street, tel. 0131/556-2223, www.brodies hostels.co.uk).

Eating in Edinburgh

Reservations for restaurants are essential in August and on weekends, and a good idea anytime. Children aren't allowed in many of the pubs. All restaurants in Scotland are smoke-free.

Along the Royal Mile

Historic pubs and doily cafés with reasonable, unremarkable meals abound. Though the eateries along this most-crowded stretch of the city are invariably touristy, the scene is fun, and competition makes a well-chosen place a good value. Here are some handy, affordable options for a good bite to eat (listed roughly in downhill order; for locations, see map on page 816). Sprinkled in this list are some places a block or two off the main drag offering better values—and correspondingly filled with more locals than tourists.

The first two restaurants are in a cluster of pleasant eateries happily removed from the Royal Mile melee. Consider stopping at one of these on your way to the National Museum of Scotland, which is a half-block away.

The Elephant House, two blocks out of the touristy zone, is a comfy neighborhood coffee shop where relaxed patrons browse newspapers in the stay-awhile back room, listen to soft rock, enjoy the castle and cemetery vistas, and sip coffee or munch a light meal. During the day, you'll pick up food at the counter and grab your own seat; after 17:00, the café switches to table service. It's easy to imagine J. K. Rowling annoying waiters with her baby pram while spending long afternoons here writing the first Harry Potter book (£8 dinner plates, traditional meat pies, great desserts, daily 8:00-22:00, vegetarian options, 2 blocks south of Royal Mile near National Museum of Scotland at 21 George IV Bridge, tel. 0131/220-5355).

The Outsider, also without a hint of Royal Mile tourism, is a sleek spot serving creative and trendy cuisine (good fish and grilled meats and vegetables) in a minimalist, stylish, hardwood, candlelit castle-view setting. It's noisy with enthusiasm, and the service is crisp and youthful. As you'll be competing with yuppies, reserve for dinner (£7 lunch plates 12:00-19:00, £13-16 main dishes, always a vegetarian course, good wines by the glass, daily 12:00-23:00, 30 yards up from The Elephant House at 15 George IV Bridge, tel. 0131/226-3131).

Grain Store Restaurant, a dressy world of wood, stone, and candles tucked away above busy Victoria Street, has served Scottish produce with a French twist for more than two decades. While they have inexpensive £12.50 two-course lunch specials, dinner is à la carte (£10-14 starters, £18-28 main dishes, daily, reservations smart, 30 Victoria Street, tel. 0131/225-7635, www .grainstore-restaurant.co.uk).

Maison Bleue Restaurant is popular for their à la carte French/Scottish/North African menu and £15 dinner special from 17:00-19:00 (£7-9 starters, £15-27 main dishes, daily, 36 Victoria Street, tel. 0131/226-1900).

Oink, a short detour off the Royal Mile from the George IV Bridge, carves from a freshly roasted pig each afternoon for mouthwatering sandwiches that come in "oink" (160 grams-£3.60) or "grunter" (250 grams-£4.60) portions. Watch the pig shrink in the front window throughout the day (daily 11:00-18:00 or whenever they run out of meat, cash only, 34 Victoria Street, tel. 01890/761-355).

The Witchery by the Castle is set in a lushly decorated 16th-century building just below the castle on the Royal Mile, with wood paneling, antique candlesticks, tapestries, and opulent red leather upholstery. Frequented by celebrities, tourists, and locals out for a splurge, the restaurant's emphasis is on fresh—and pricey—Scottish meats and seafood (£16 two-course lunch specials 12:00-16:00, specials also good 17:30-18:30 & 22:30-23:30, £33 three-course dinner menu, £23-28 main dishes, daily 12:00-16:00 & 17:30-23:30, dress smart, reservations critical, tel. 0131/225-5613, www.thewitchery.com).

EDINBURGH

Royal Mile Accommodations & Eateries

Legend:

- Ⓑ BUS STOP
- ⚘ VIEW
- ▨ PEDESTRIAN ZONE

**Map labels:**
TO NEW TOWN ↑ • THE MOUND • MUSEUM ON THE MOUND • AIRLINK #100 • MARKET ST. • MOUND PL. • PRINCES STREET GARDENS • WRITERS' MUSEUM AT LADY STAIR'S HOUSE • GLADSTONE'S LAND • CAMERA OBSCURA • ST. GILES • BANK ST. • COCKBURN ST. • NORTH BRIDGE • WAVERLEY BR. • TO DALKEITH ROAD • CASTLE • TOP OF ROYAL MILE • ESPLANADE • LAWN MKT. • HIGH • JOHNSTON TERRACE • OLD PARLIAMENT HOUSE • TRON KIRK • GOOD RESTAURANTS + ANTIQUE SHOPS • VICTORIA • GEORGE IV BR. • COWGATE • SOUTH BRIDGE • CHAMBERS • GRASSMARKET • FOLK MUSIC PUBS • GREYFRIARS BOBBY STATUE • NATIONAL MUSEUM OF SCOTLAND

1. MacDonald Holyrood Hotel
2. Jurys Inn
3. Ibis Hotel
4. Holiday Inn Express Edinburgh Royal Mile
5. Travelodge Central
6. Smart City Hostel
7. High Street Hostel
8. Royal Mile Backpackers Hostel
9. Castle Rock Hostel
10. Brodie's Hostels & The World's End Pub
11. The Elephant House
12. The Outsider Restaurant
13. Grain Store, Maison Bleue & Oink
14. The Witchery by the Castle

Deacon Brodie's Tavern, at a dead-center location on the Royal Mile, is a sloppy pub on the ground floor with a sloppy restaurant upstairs serving basic £8-11 pub meals. While painfully touristy, it comes with a fun history and decent food (daily 10:00-22:00, hearty salads, kids' menu, kids welcome upstairs—but they're not allowed to enter after 20:00, tel. 0131/220-0317).

St. Giles Cathedral Café, hiding under the landmark church, is *the* place for paupers to munch prayerfully. Stairs on the back side of the church lead into the basement, where you'll find simple, light lunches from 11:30 and coffee with cakes all day (Mon-Sat 9:00-17:00, Sun 11:00-17:00, tel. 0131/225-5147).

Angels with Bagpipes, in the shadow of St. Giles Cathedral,

WAVERLEY TRAIN STN.

NOT TO SCALE –
CASTLE TO
PALACE OF HOLYROODHOUSE
IS ABOUT 1 MILE

JOHN KNOX HOUSE

PEOPLE'S STORY MUSEUM

CANONGATE CHURCH

WHITE HORSE CLOSE

QUEEN'S GALLERY

CANONGATE

ST.

MUSEUM OF CHILDHOOD

MUSEUM OF EDINBURGH

PALACE OF HOLYROOD-HOUSE

BOTTOM OF ROYAL MILE

HOLYROOD ROAD

DYNAMIC EARTH

SCOTTISH PARLIAMENT

QUEEN'S DRIVE

TO DALKEITH ROAD B+Bs & A-7

TRAIL TO ARTHUR'S SEAT

DCH

HOLYROOD PARK

15 Deacon Brodie's Tavern
16 St. Giles Cathedral Café
17 Angels with Bagpipes
18 Piemaker Café
19 Dubh Prais Scottish Rest. & Folk Music Pubs
20 Wedgwood Restaurant
21 David Bann Restaurant

22 Clarinda's Tea Room
23 Sandy Bell's Pub
24 The Royal Oak Pub
25 Whistlebinkies Bar
26 No. 1 High Street Pub

serves sophisticated Scottish staples in the plush interior (daily 12:00-22:00, £6-9 starters, £14-18 main dishes, 343 High Street, tel. 0131/220-1111).

Piemaker is a great place to grab a cheap and tasty meal, especially if you're in a hurry. Their meat pies and pastries—try the cherry—are "so fresh they'll pinch your bum and call you darlin'" (most everything under £3, daily 10:00-19:00, until 23:00 on Tue, Fri, and Sat, about 100 yards off the Royal Mile at 38 South Bridge, tel. 0131/556-8566).

Dubh Prais Scottish Restaurant (pronounced "DOO-prash") is a dressy nine-table place filling a cellar 10 steps and a world away from the High Street bustle. The owner-chef, James

, proudly serves Scottish "fayre" at its very best
urmet haggis). The daily specials are not printed, to
"zombie waiters." They like to get to know you a bit
by explaining things (£16-24 main dishes, open Tue-Sat 17:00-
22:30, closed Sun-Mon, reservations wise, opposite Radisson Blu
Hotel at 123b High Street, tel. 0131/557-5732, www.dubhprais
restaurant.com).

Wedgwood Restaurant is romantic, contemporary, chic, and
as gourmet as possible with no pretense. Paul Wedgwood cooks
while his wife Lisa serves with appetizing charm. The cuisine:
creative, modern Scottish with an international twist and a whiff
of Asia. The pigeon and haggis starter is scrumptious. Paul and
Lisa believe in making the meal the event of the evening—don't
come here to eat and run. I like the ground level with the Royal
Mile view, but the busy kitchen ambience in the basement is also
fine (£7-9 starters, £18-24 main courses, fine wine by the glass,
daily 12:00-15:00 & 18:00-22:00, Sun open at 12:30, reservations
advised, 267 Canongate on Royal Mile, tel. 0131/558-8737, www
.wedgwoodtherestaurant.co.uk).

The World's End Pub, a colorful old place, dishes up hearty
£9-11 meals from a creative menu in a fun, dark, and noisy space
(daily 12:00-22:00, 4 High Street, tel. 0131/556-3628).

David Bann, just a three-minute walk off the Royal Mile, is
a worthwhile stop for well-heeled vegetarians in need of a break
from the morning fry. While vegetarian as can be, there's not a
hint of hippie here. It's upscale (it has a cocktail bar), sleek, minimalist, and stylish (gorgeously presented dishes), serious about
quality, and organic—they serve polenta, tartlets, soups, and light
meals (£6 starters, £11-13 main dishes, decadent desserts, Mon-Fri
12:00-22:00, Sat-Sun 11:00-22:00, vegan options, 56-58 St. Mary's
Street, tel. 0131/556-5888).

Clarinda's Tea Room, near the bottom of the Royal Mile, is
charming and girlish—a fine and tasty place to relax after touring
the Mile or the Palace of Holyroodhouse. Stop in for a £5 quiche,
salad, or soup lunch. It's also great for sandwiches and tea and cake
anytime (Mon-Sat 8:30-16:45, Sun 9:30-16:45, 69 Canongate, tel.
0131/557-1888).

In the New Town

While most of your sightseeing will be along the Royal Mile, it's
important that your Edinburgh experience stretches beyond this
happy tourist gauntlet. Just a few minutes away, in the Georgian
town, you'll find a bustling world of office workers, students, and
pensioners doing their thing. And at midday, that includes eating. Simply hiking over to one of these places will give you a good
helping of modern Edinburgh. All these places are within a few

minutes' walk of the TI and main Waverley Bridge tour-bus depot.

The Bon Vivant is woody, youthful, and candlelit, with a rotating menu of eclectic Mediterranean/Asian dishes and a companion wine shop serving 50 wines by the glass. They have fun £1.50 tapas plates and heartier dishes (daily 12:00-22:00, 55 Thistle Street, tel. 0131/225-3275, www.bonvivantedinburgh.co.uk).

Le Café St. Honoré, tucked away like a secret bit of old Paris, is a charming place with friendly service and walls lined by tempting wine bottles. It serves French-Scottish cuisine in tight, Old World, cut-glass elegance to a dressy crowd (daily £18 two-course and £23 three-course lunch and dinner specials, open daily 12:00-14:00 & Mon-Fri 17:15-22:00, Sat-Sun 18:00-22:00, reservations smart—ask to sit upstairs, down Thistle Street from Hanover Street, 34 Northwest Thistle Street Lane, tel. 0131/226-2211, www.cafesthonore.com).

Café Royal is a movie producer's dream pub—the perfect fin de siècle setting for a coffee, beer, or light meal. (In fact, parts of *Chariots of Fire* were filmed here.) Drop in, if only to admire the 1880 tiles featuring famous inventors (daily 12:00-14:30 & 17:00-21:30, bar food available during the afternoon, two blocks from Princes Mall on 19 West Register Street, tel. 0131/556-1884). There are two eateries here: the noisy pub (£10-13 main dishes, Mon-Sat 11:00-21:30, Sun open at 12:30) and the dressier restaurant, specializing in oysters, fish, and game (£14-20 plates, daily 12:00-14:30 & 17:00-21:30, reserve for dinner—it's quite small and understandably popular).

The Dome Restaurant, in what was a fancy bank, serves decent, modern international cuisine around a classy bar and under the elegant 19th-century skylight dome. With soft jazz and chic, white-tablecloth ambience, it feels a world apart (£12-16 plates until 17:00, £14-20 dinners until 21:45, daily 12:00-23:00, reserve for dinner, open for a drink any time under the dome; the adjacent, more intimate Club Room serves food Mon-Sat 10:00-17:00, Thu-Sat until late, closed Sun; 14 George Street, tel. 0131/624-8634). As you leave, look up to take in the facade of this former bank building—the pediment is filled with figures demonstrating various ways to make money, which they do with all the nobility of classical gods.

St. Andrew's and St. George's Church Undercroft Café, in the basement of a fine old church, is the cheapest place in town for lunch—under £5 for a sandwich and soup. Your tiny bill helps support the Church of Scotland (Mon-Fri 10:00-14:00, closed Sat-Sun, at 13 George Street, just off St. Andrew Square, tel. 0131/225-3847).

Henderson's Salad Table and Wine Bar has fed a generation of New Town vegetarians hearty cuisine and salads. Even carnivores love this place for its delectable salads and desserts (two-course lunch for £10, Mon-Sat 8:00-22:00, Thu-Sat until 23:00, closed Sun except in Aug 11:00-19:00, strictly vegetarian, take-away available, pleasant live music nightly in wine bar—generally guitar or jazz; between Queen and George streets at 94 Hanover Street, tel. 0131/225-2131). Henderson's two different seating areas use the same self-serve cafeteria line. For the identical healthy food with more elegant seating and table service, eat at the attached **Henderson's Bistro** (daily 12:00-20:30, Thu-Sat until 21:30).

Fun Ethnic Eateries on Hanover Street: Hanover Street is lined with Thai, Greek, Turkish, Italian, and other restaurants. Stroll the block to eye your options.

Supermarkets: **Marks & Spencer Food Hall** offers an assortment of tasty hot foods, prepared sandwiches, fresh bakery items, a wide selection of wines and beverages, and plastic utensils at the checkout queue. It's just a block from the Scott Monument and the picnic-perfect Princes Street Gardens (Mon-Sat 8:00-19:00, Thu until 20:00, Sun 11:00-18:00, 4 Waverley Bridge—on Princes Street, separate stairway next to main M&S entrance leads directly to food hall, tel. 0131/225-2301). **Sainsbury's** supermarket, a block off Princes Street, also offers grab-and-go items for a quick lunch (Mon-Sat 7:00-22:00, Sun 9:00-20:00, on corner of Rose Street on St. Andrew Square, across the street from Jenners, the classy department store).

The Dalkeith Road Area, near B&Bs

Nearly all of these places (except for The Sheeps Heid Inn) are within a 10-minute walk of my recommended B&Bs. Most are on or near the intersection of Newington Road and East Preston Street. Reserve on weekends and during the Festival. For locations, see the map on page 808. The nearest grocery store is **Tesco Express** (daily 6:00-23:00, 158 Causewayside). Cameron Toll Shopping Centre, about a half-mile south, houses a **Sainsbury's** superstore for more substantial supplies (and gasoline), handy on your way out of town (Mon-Sat 7:30-22:00, Sun 8:00-20:00, 6 Lady Road, tel. 0131/666-5200). For a cozy drink after dinner, visit the recommended pubs in the area (see "Nightlife in Edinburgh," earlier).

Scottish/French Restaurants

At **Edinburgh Bakehouse**, award-winning baker James Lynch makes fresh breads, sweets, and meat pies from scratch in this laid-back, nondescript shop. Locals line up for his morning rolls—which earned him the title "baker of the year." Stop by to see the friendly staff and open kitchen in action and judge for yourself (£2-5, cash only, daily 7:00-18:00, 101 Newington Road).

Rhubarb Restaurant specializes in Old World elegance. It's in "Edinburgh's most handsome house"—a riot of antiques, velvet, tassels, and fringes. The plush dark-rhubarb color theme reminds visitors that this was the place where rhubarb was first grown in Britain. It's a 10-minute walk past the other recommended eateries behind Arthur's Seat, in a huge estate with big, shaggy Highland cattle enjoying their salads al fresco. At night, it's a candlelit wonder. While most spend a wad here (£20-34 plates), they have an £18 two-course lunch and a £33 three-course dinner (Sun-Thu 12:00-14:00 & 18:30-23:00, Fri-Sat 12:00-14:00 & 18:00-22:00, afternoon tea served daily 14:00-19:00, reserve in advance and dress up if you can, in Prestonfield House, Priestfield Road, tel. 0131/225-1333, www.prestonfield.com). For details on their schmaltzy Scottish folk evening, see "Nightlife in Edinburgh," earlier.

The Sheeps Heid Inn, Edinburgh's oldest public house, is equally notable for its history, date-night appeal, and hearty portions of affordable, classy dishes. Though it requires a cab ride, it is worth the fare to dine in this dreamy setting in the presence of past queens and kings (£7-9 starters, £11-17 main dishes; open Mon-Sat 12:00-22:00, Sun 12:30-21:30, 43-45 The Causeway, tel. 0131/661-7974, www.thesheepheidedinburgh.co.uk).

Scottish Grub and Pubs

The Old Bell Inn, with an old-time sports-bar ambience—fishing, golf, horses—serves simple £8 pub meals. This is a classic "snug pub"—all dark woods and brass beer taps, littered with evocative knickknacks. It comes with sidewalk seating and a mixed-age crowd (open daily until 24:00; food served Sun-Thu 12:00-21:00, Fri-Sat 12:00-19:30, 233 Causewayside, tel. 0131/668-1573). The fancier restaurant upstairs serves good Italian food in a wonderful ambience.

The Salisbury Arms Pub, with a nice garden terrace, serves upscale, pleasing traditional classics with yuppie flair in a space that exudes more Martha Stewart and Pottery Barn than traditional public house (£4-7 starters, £12-17 main dishes, evening specials, daily 12:00-22:00, pub open until 23:00, 58 Dalkeith Road, tel. 0131/667-4518).

Reverie Bar is just your basic, fun traditional pub with a focus on food rather than drinking, and free live music most nights from 21:30 (every other Sun-jazz, Mon-quiz night, Tue-traditional/folk, Thu-blues; £9-12 main dishes, food served daily 12:00-15:00 & 17:00-21:00, real ales, 1-5 Newington Road, tel. 0131/667-8870, http://thereverie.co.uk).

Hewat's Restaurant is the neighborhood hit. Sample Scottish cuisine or their popular steak dishes in this elegantly whimsical dining space (£10.25 dinner deals Mon-Thu until 19:30; pre-theater menu £15 for two courses, £18 for three courses until 18:45; midweek dinner menu £18.50 for two courses, £22.50 for three courses; open Mon-Sat 18:00-21:30, Fri-Sat 18:00-22:00, Wed-Sat also open for lunch 12:00-14:00, closed Sun, 19-21b Causeway, tel. 0131/466-6660, www.hewatsrestaurant.co.uk).

Hellers Kitchen is a casual blond-wood space specializing in dishes using local produce and fresh-baked breads. Check the big chalkboard to see what's on (£5-6 light bites and sandwiches, £7-10 main dishes, daily 12:00-15:00 & 17:00-22:00, next to post office at 15 Salisbury Place, tel. 0131/667-4654).

Metropole Café is a fresh, healthy eatery with a Starbucks ambience, serving light bites for £3-4, or 3/£8.50, and simple meals for £8 (Mon-Sat 8:00-20:00, Sun 9:00-18:00, always a good vegetarian dish, free Wi-Fi, 33 Newington Road, tel. 0131/668-4999).

Ethnic Options

Il Positano Ristorante has a spirited Italian ambience, as manager Donato injects a love of life and food into his little restaurant. The moment you step through the door, you know you're in for good, classic Italian cuisine (£7-10 pizzas and pastas, £11-15 plates, daily 12:00-14:00 & 17:00-23:00, 85-87 Newington Road, tel. 0131/662-9977).

Voujon Restaurant serves a fusion menu flaunting highlights of Bengali and Indian cuisines. Vegetarians delight at the expansive yet inexpensive offerings starting at £8 (lunch specials, dinner main dishes £11-17, daily 12:00-14:00 & 17:30-23:30, 107 Newington Road, tel. 0131/667-5046, www.voujonedinburgh .co.uk).

Edinburgh Connections

By Train or Bus

From Edinburgh by Train to: Glasgow (4/hour, 50 minutes), **St. Andrews** (train to Leuchars, 1-2/hour, 1 hour, then 10-minute bus into St. Andrews), **Stirling** (roughly 2/hour, 1 hour), **Pitlochry** (6/day direct, 2 hours), **Inverness** (every 1-2 hours, 3.5-4 hours, some with change in Perth), **Oban** (2/day, 4.25 hours, change in Glasgow), **York** (2/hour, 2.5 hours), **London** (1-2/hour, 4.5 hours), **Durham** (hourly direct, 2 hours, more with changes, less frequent in winter), **Newcastle** (2/hour, 1.5 hours), **Keswick/Lake District** (8-10/day to Penrith—some via Carlisle, 1.75 hours, then 40-minute bus ride to Keswick), **Birmingham** (at least hourly, 4-5 hours, some with change in Newcastle or York), **Crewe** (every 2 hours, 3 hours), **Bristol,** near Bath (hourly, 6-6.5 hours), **Blackpool** (roughly hourly, 3-3.5 hours, transfer in Preston). **Train info**: Tel.

0845-748-4950, www.nationalrail.co.uk.

By Bus to: Glasgow (4/hour, 1.25-1.5 hours), **Oban** (7/day Mon-Sat, 4-5 hours; 1 direct, rest with transfer in Glasgow), **Fort William** (7/day, 4-5 hours, 1 direct, rest with change in Glasgow or Tyndrum), **Portree** on the Isle of Skye (4/day, 7.5-8 hours, transfer in Inverness or Glasgow), **Inverness** (nearly hourly, 3.5-4.5 hours). For bus info, call Scottish Citylink (tel. 0871-266-3333, www.city link.co.uk) or National Express (expensive toll tel. 0871-781-8181, £1/minute; booking online is smarter—and free). Megabus also operates some long-distance routes (www.megabus.com). You can get info and tickets at the bus desk inside the Princes Mall TI or at the bus station.

Route Tips for Drivers

It's 100 miles south from Edinburgh to Hadrian's Wall; to Durham, it's another 50 miles.

To Hadrian's Wall: From Edinburgh, Dalkeith Road leads south and eventually becomes the A-68 (handy Cameron Toll supermarket with cheap gas is on the left as you leave Edinburgh Town, 10 minutes south of Edinburgh; gas and parking behind store). The A-68 road takes you to Hadrian's Wall in 2.5 hours. You'll pass Jedburgh and its abbey after one hour. (For one last shot of Scotland shopping, there's a coach tour's delight just before Jedburgh, with kilt makers, woolens, and a sheepskin shop.) Across from Jedburgh's lovely abbey is a free parking lot, a good visitors center, and public toilets (£0.20 to pee). The England/Scotland border is a fun, quick stop (great view, ice cream, and tea caravan). Just after the turn for Colwell, turn right onto the A-6079, and roller-coaster four miles down to Low Brunton. Then turn right onto the B-6318, and stay on it by turning left at Chollerford, following the Roman wall westward. (For information on Hadrian's Wall, see the Durham and Northeast England chapter.)

To Durham: If you're heading straight to Durham, you can take the scenic coastal route on the A-1 (a few more miles than the A-68, but similar time), which takes you near Holy Island and Bamburgh Castle; for details, see the end of the Durham and Northeast England chapter.

ST. ANDREWS

St. Andrews • The East Neuk

For many, St. Andrews is synonymous with golf. But there's more to this charming town than its famous links. Dramatically situated at the edge of a sandy bay, St. Andrews is the home of Scotland's most important university—think of it as the Scottish Cambridge. And centuries ago, the town was the religious capital of the country.

In its long history, St. Andrews has seen two boom periods. First, in the early Middle Ages, the relics of St. Andrew made the town cathedral one of the most important pilgrimage sites in Christendom. The faithful flocked here from all over Europe, leaving the town with a medieval all-roads-lead-to-the-cathedral street plan that survives today. But after the Scottish Reformation, the cathedral rotted away and the town became a forgotten backwater. A new wave of visitors arrived in the mid-19th century, when a visionary mayor named (appropriately enough) Provost Playfair began to promote the town's connection with the newly in-vogue game of golf. Most buildings in town date from this time (similar to Edinburgh's New Town).

Today St. Andrews remains a popular spot for students, golf devotees (including professional golfers and celebrities such as Scotsman Sean Connery, often seen out on the links), and occasionally Britain's royal couple, Will and Kate. With vast sandy beaches, golfing opportunities for pros and novices alike, playgrounds of ruins, a fun-loving student vibe, and a string of relaxing fishing villages nearby (the East Neuk), St. Andrews is an appealing place to take a vacation from your busy vacation.

Planning Your Time

St. Andrews, hugging the east coast of Scotland, is a bit off the main tourist track. But it's well-connected by train to Edinburgh (via bus from nearby Leuchars), making it a worthwhile day trip from the capital. Better yet, spend a night (or more, if you're a golfer) to enjoy this university town after dark.

If you're not here to golf, this is a good way to spend a day: Follow my self-guided walk, which connects the golf course, the university quad, the castle, and the cathedral. Dip into the Golf Museum, watch the golfers on the Old Course, and play a round at "the Himalayas" putting green. With more time, walk along the West Sands beach or take a spin by car or bus to the nearby East Neuk.

Orientation to St. Andrews

St. Andrews (pop. 16,000), situated at the tip of a peninsula next to a broad bay, retains its old medieval street plan: Three main streets (North, Market, and South) converge at the cathedral, which overlooks the sea at the tip of town. The middle street—Market Street—has the TI and many handy shops and eateries. North of North Street, the seafront street called The Scores connects the cathedral with the golf scene, which huddles along the West Sands beach at the base of the old town. St. Andrews is enjoyably compact: You can stroll across town—from the cathedral to the historic golf course—in about 15 minutes.

Tourist Information

St. Andrews' helpful TI is on Market Street, about two blocks in front of the cathedral (July-Aug Mon-Sat 9:15-18:00, Sun 10:00-17:00; April-June and Sept-mid-Oct Mon-Sat 9:15-17:00, Sun 11:00-16:00; mid-Oct-March Mon-Sat 9:15-17:00, Sun 10:00-17:00; 70 Market Street, tel. 01334/472-021, www.visitfife.com or www.visitscotland.com). Pick up their stack of brochures on the town and region, and ask about other tours (such as ghost walks or witches walks). They also have Internet access (£1/20 minutes) and can find you a room for a £4 fee.

Arrival in St. Andrews

By Train and Bus: The nearest train station is in the village of Leuchars, five miles away. From there, a 10-minute bus ride takes you right into St. Andrews (£2.75, buy ticket from driver, round-trip day tickets are cheaper; buses meet most trains, see schedule at bus shelter for next bus to St. Andrews; while waiting, read the historical info under the nearby flagpole). St. Andrews' bus station is near the base of Market Street—a short walk from most

St. Andrews

ST. ANDREWS

1. Cameron House & Glenderran Guest House
2. Lorimer Guest House
3. Doune Guest House
4. Arran House
5. Hoppity House B&B
6. St. Andrews Tourist Hostel & The Grill House Restaurant
7. Agnes Blackadder Hall
8. McIntosh Hall
9. The Doll's House Restaurant
10. The Glass House Restaurant

ST. ANDREWS

400 YARDS
400 METERS

← SELF-GUIDED WALK
P PARKING
↗ VIEW
PEDESTRIAN ZONE

NORTH SEA

N

MUSA
ST. SALVATOR'S COLLEGE
SCORES
WYND
BUTTS
NORTH STREET
ST. SALV. CHAPEL
UNION ST.
CHURCH ST.
CHURCH SQ.
MARKET STREET
W. BURN LANE
ST. MARY'S COLLEGE
QUEEN'S TERRACE
ABBEY ST.

CASTLE
PATH TO CASTLE SANDS
CLIFF WALK
CASTLE ST.
ST. ANDREW'S CATHEDRAL
LONG PIER
RUINS
EXHIBIT
ST. RULES TOWER
THE PENDS
EAST SANDS
ST. ANDREWS PRESERVATION TRUST MUSEUM

TO EAST NEUK VILLAGES, A-917 & EDINBURGH

11 The Seafood Restaurant
12 Aikmans Pub
13 The Central Pub
14 Ma Bells Pub
15 Greyfriars Pub

16 Fritto Fish & Chips
17 Fisher and Donaldson Pastries
18 B. Jannettas Ice Cream
19 Groceries (3)
20 Luvians Bottle Shop

B&Bs and the TI (follow the map). A taxi from Leuchars into St. Andrews costs about £12.

By Car: For a short stay, drivers can simply head into the town center and park anywhere along the street. Easy-to-use meters dispense stickers (£1/hour, coins only, 2-hour limit, monitored Mon-Sat 9:00-17:00). For longer stays, you can park for free along certain streets near the center (such as along The Scores), or use one of the long-stay lots near the entrance to town.

Helpful Hints

Golf Events: Every five years, St. Andrews is swamped with about 100,000 visitors when it hosts the British Open (called simply "The Open" around here; the next one is in 2015). The town also fills up every year in early October for the Alfred Dunhill Links Championship. Unless you're a golf pilgrim, avoid the town at these times (as room rates skyrocket).

School Term: The University of St. Andrews has two terms: spring semester ("Candlemas"), from mid-February through May; and fall semester ("Martinmas"), from mid-September until December. St. Andrews feels downright sleepy in summer, when most students leave and golfers take over the town.

Internet Access: You can get online for free at the **public library,** behind the church on South Street (photo ID required, Mon and Fri-Sat 9:30-17:00, Tue-Thu 9:30-19:00, closed Sun, tel. 01334/659-378). The TI also has two pay terminals (£1/20 minutes).

Self-Guided Walk

Welcome to St. Andrews

This walk links all of St. Andrews' must-see sights and takes you down hidden medieval streets. Allow a couple of hours or more if you detour for the sights along the way.

• *Start at the base of the seaside street called The Scores, overlooking the famous golf course. (There are benches with nice views by the Links Golf Shop for those with a sandwich to munch.)*

▲The Old Course

You're looking at the mecca of golf. The 18th hole of the world's first golf course is a few yards away, on your left (for info on playing the course, see "Golfing in St. Andrews," later).

The gray Neoclassical building to the right of the 18th hole is the **Royal and Ancient Golf Club** (or "R&A" for short), which is the world's governing body for golf (like the British version of the PGA). The R&A is a private club with membership by invitation only, and only men can be members. (In Scotland, men-only clubs lose tax benefits, which is quite costly, but they generally don't care about expenses because their membership is wealthy.) Women can enter the R&A building only during the Women's British Open on St. Andrew's Day (Nov 30). Anyone can enter the shop nearby, which is a great spot to buy a souvenir for the golf lover back home. Even if you're not golfing, watch the action for a while. (Serious fans can walk around to the low-profile stone bridge across the creek called Swilken Burn, with golf's single most iconic view: back over the 18th hole and the R&A.)

Overlooking the course is the big, red-sandstone **Hamilton Hall,** an old hotel long used as a university dormitory and now under renovation to become swanky apartments. According to town legend, the grand building was built to upstage the R&A by an American upset over being declined membership to the exclusive club.

Between Hamilton Hall and the beach is the low-profile **British Golf Museum** (described on page 839).

• *Now, turn your back to the golf course and walk through the park (along the street called The Scores) a few steps to the obelisk.*

Martyrs' Monument

This obelisk commemorates all those who died for their Protestant beliefs during the Scottish Reformation. Walk to the benches on the bluff for a good look at the cliffs on your right. For a time, the sea below was called "Witches' Lake" because of all the women and men pushed off the cliff on suspicion of witchcraft. The Victorian bandstand gazebo recalls the town's genteel heyday as a seaside resort, when the train line ran all the way to town.

The broad, two-mile-long sandy beach that stretches below the golf course is the West Sands (a.k.a. "Chariots of Fire beach"). It's a wonderful place for a relaxing and/or invigorating walk. Or do a slo-mo jog, humming the theme to *Chariots of Fire*. This is the beach on which the characters run in the movie's famous opening scene.

Just opposite the obelisk, across The Scores and next to the Alexander Restaurant, walk down the tiny **Gillespie Wynd alleyway.** It winds through the back gardens of the city's stone houses. Notice how the medieval platting gave landowners a little bit of street front and a long back garden. St. Andrews' street plan typifies that of a medieval pilgrimage town: All main roads lead to the cathedral; only tiny lanes, hidden alleys, and twisting "wynds" (rhymes with "minds") such as this one connect the main east-west streets.

• *The wynd pops you out onto North Street. Make like a pilgrim and head left toward the cathedral—look for its ruined façade in the distance. Walk about 100 yards to the small cinema from where you'll see* *the church tower with the red clock face (our next stop). It's on the corner of North Street and **Butts Wynd** (no joke). For some reason, this street sign often goes missing.*

At Butts Wynd, you're standing outside St. Salvator's Chapel and St. Salvator's College. If you're a student, be careful not to stand on the initials PH in the cobbles. They mark the spot where St. Andrews alum and professor Patrick Hamilton—the Scottish Reformation's most famous martyr—was burned at the stake. According to student legend, as he suffered in the flames, Hamilton threatened that any students who stood on this spot would fail their exams. (And you thought you had dramatic professors.)

Enter the grounds by walking through the arch under the tower with the red clock. (If the entrance is closed, you can go halfway down Butts Wynd and enter, or at least look, through the gate to the green square.)

St. Salvator's College

This grassy square, known to students as **Sally's Quad,** is the heart of the university. As most of the university's classrooms, offices, and libraries are spread out across the medieval town, this quad is the one focal point for student gatherings. It's where graduation is held every July, where the free-for-all food fight of Raisin Monday takes place in November (see sidebar on page 832), and where almost the entire student body gathered to celebrate the wedding day of their famous alumni couple—Prince William and Princess Kate—complete with military flybys.

On the outside wall of **St. Salvator's Chapel** are cases holding notices and university information; if you're here in spring, you might see students nervously clustered here, looking to see if they've passed their exams.

Go through the simple wooden door and into the chapel. Dating from 1450, this is the town's most beautiful medieval church. It's a Gothic gem, with a wooden ceiling, 19th-century stained glass, and (supposedly) the pulpit of reformer John Knox.

Stroll around Sally's Quad counterclockwise. If you're feeling curious, push a few doors (some seemingly off-limits university buildings, many marked by blue doors, are actually open to the public). On the east (far) side, stop to check out the crazy faces on the heads above the second-floor windows. Find the **university's shield** over the door marked *School Six*. The diamonds are from the coat of arms of the bishop who issued the first university charter in 1411; the crescent moon is a shout-out to Pope Benedict XIII, who gave the OK in 1413 to found the university (his given name was Peter de Luna); the lion is from the Scottish coat of arms; and the X-shaped cross is a stylized version of the Scottish flag (a.k.a. St.

The Scottish Reformation

It's easy to forget that during the 16th-century English Reformation—when King Henry VIII split with the Vatican and formed the Anglican Church (so he could get an officially recognized divorce)—Scotland was still its own independent nation. Like much of northern Europe, Scotland eventually chose a Protestant path, but it was more gradual and grassroots than Henry VIII's top-down, destroy-the-abbeys approach. While the English Reformation resulted in the Church of England (a.k.a. the Anglican Church, called "Episcopal" outside of England), with the monarch as its head, the Scottish Reformation created the Church of Scotland, which had groups of elected leaders (called "presbyteries" in church jargon).

One of the leaders of the Scottish Reformation was John Knox (1514-1572), who studied under the great Swiss Reformer John Calvin. Returning to Scotland, Knox hopped from pulpit to pulpit, and his feverish sermons incited riots of "born-again" iconoclasts who dismantled or destroyed Catholic churches and abbeys (including St. Andrew's Cathedral). Knox's newly minted Church of Scotland gradually spread from the Lowlands to the Highlands. The southern and eastern part of Scotland, around St. Andrews—just across the North Sea from the Protestant countries of northern Europe—embraced the Church of Scotland long before the more remote and Catholic-oriented part of the country to the north and west. Today about 40 percent of Scots claim affiliation with the Church of Scotland, compared with 20 percent who are Catholic (still mostly in the western Highlands). Glasgow and western Scotland are more Catholic, partly because of the Irish immigrants who settled here after fleeing the potato famine in the 1840s.

ST. ANDREWS

Andrew's Cross). On the next building to the left, facing the chapel, is St. Andrew himself (above door of building labeled *Upper & Lower College Halls*).

• *Exit the square at the west end, if the gate's open, and turn right into Butts Wynd (if the gate's closed, backtrack out the main gate and hang a right into Butts Wynd). When the alley ends, you're back at The Scores. Cross the street and head to the right. The turreted stone buildings along here are built in the Neo-Gothic Scots Baronial style, and most are academic departments. Head for the...*

Museum of the University of St. Andrews (MUSA)

This free museum is worth a quick stop. The first room has some well-explained medieval artifacts. Note the copy of the earliest-

Student Life in St. Andrews

Although most people associate St. Andrews with golf, it's first and foremost a university town—the home of Scotland's most prestigious university. Founded in 1411, it's the third-oldest in the English-speaking world; only Oxford and Cambridge have been around longer.

The U. of St. A. has about 6,000 undergrads and 1,000 grad students. Though Scots and most EU citizens attend for free, others (including students from England) must pay tuition. Some Scots resent the high concentration of upper-class English students (disparagingly dubbed "Yahs" for the snooty way they say "yes"), who treat St. Andrews as a safety school if rejected by Cambridge or Oxford. The school has even been called "England's northernmost university" because it has as many English students as Scottish ones. (Adding to the mix, about a quarter of the students come from overseas.) Its most famous recent graduate is Prince William (class of '05). Soon after he started here, the number of female applicants to study art history—his major—skyrocketed. (He later switched to geography.)

As with any venerable university, St. Andrews has its share of quirky customs—as if the university, like the town's street plan, insists on clinging to the Middle Ages. Most students own traditional red academic "gowns" (woolen robes). Today these are only worn for special occasions, such as graduation, but in medieval times, students were required to wear them always—supposedly so they could be easily identified in brothels and pubs. (In a leap of faith, divinity students—apparently beyond temptation—wear black.) The way the robe is worn indicates the student's progress toward graduation: First-year students (called

known map of the town, made in 1580—back when the town walls led directly to the countryside and the cathedral was intact. Notice that the street plan within the town walls has remained the same—but no golf course. The next room has some exhibits on student life. For a great view of the West Sands, climb to the rooftop terrace.

Cost and Hours: Free; April-Oct Mon-Sat 10:00-17:00, Sun 12:00-16:00; Nov-March Thu-Sun 12:00-16:00, closed Mon-Wed; 7 The Scores, tel. 01334/461-660, www.st-andrews.ac.uk/musa.

• *Leaving the museum, walk left toward the castle. The neighboring building is a fine example of that Neo-Gothic Scots Baronial style. About 100 yards farther along, the grand building (on the right, fronting The Scores) is St. Salvator's Hall, the most prestigious of the university residences and former dorm of Prince William. Just past St. Salvator's Hall, on a bluff overlooking the sea, are the remains of...*

"bejants") wear them normally, on the shoulders; second-years ("semi-bejants") wear them slightly off the shoulders; third-years ("tertians") wear them off one shoulder (right shoulder for "scientists" and left shoulder for "artists"); and fourth-years ("magistrands") wear them off both shoulders.

There's no better time to see these robes than during the Pier Walk on Sunday afternoons during the university term. After church services (around noon), students clad in their gowns parade out to the end of the lonesome pier beyond the cathedral ruins. The tradition dates so far back that no one's sure how it started (probably to bid farewell to a visiting dignitary). Today, students participate mostly because it's fun to be a part of the visual spectacle of a long line of red robes flapping in the North Sea wind.

St. Andrews also clings to an antiquated social-mentoring system, where underclassmen choose an "academic family." In mid-November comes Raisin Monday, named for the raisins traditionally given as treats to one's "parents" (but today students usually give wine to their "dad" and lingerie to their "mum"). After receiving their gifts, the upperclassmen "parents" dress up their "children" in outrageous costumes and parade them through town. The underclassmen are also obliged to carry around "receipts" for their gifts—often written on unlikely or unwieldy objects (e.g., plastic dinosaurs, microwave ovens, even refrigerators). Any upperclassmen they come across can demand a rendition of the school song in Latin. The whole scene invariably turns into a free-for-all food fight in St. Salvator's Quad (weapons include condiments, shaving cream, and, according to campus rumors, human entrails pilfered by med students).

ST. ANDREWS

▲St. Andrews Castle

Overlooking the sea, the castle is an evocative empty shell— another casualty of the Scottish Reformation. Built by a bishop to

entertain visiting diplomats in the late 12th century, the castle was home to the powerful bishops, archbishops, and cardinals of St. Andrews. In 1546, the cardinal burned a Protestant preacher at the stake in front of the castle. In retribution, Protestant Reformers took the castle and killed the cardinal. In 1547, the French came to attack the castle on behalf of their Catholic ally, Mary, Queen of Scots. During the ensuing siege, a young Protestant refugee named John Knox was captured and sent to France to row on a galley ship. Eventually he traveled to Switzerland and met the Swiss Protestant ringleader, John Calvin. Knox brought Calvin's ideas back home and became Scotland's greatest Reformer.

Your visit starts with a colorful, kid-friendly exhibit about the history of the castle. Afterward, head outside to explore. The most interesting parts are underground: the "bottle dungeon," where prisoners were sent, never to return (peer down into it in the Sea Tower); and the tight "mine" and even tighter "counter-mine" tunnels (follow the signs, crawling is required to reach it all; go in as far as your claustrophobia allows). This shows how the besieging French army dug a mine to take (or "undermine") the castle—but were followed at every turn by the Protestant counter-miners.

Just below the castle is a small beach called the Castle Sands, where university students take a traditional and chilly morning dip on May 1. Supposedly, doing this May Day swim is the only way to reverse the curse of having stepped on Patrick Hamilton's initials (explained earlier).

Cost and Hours: £5.50, £7.20 combo-ticket includes cathedral exhibit, daily April-Sept 9:30-17:30, Oct-March 9:30-16:30, last entry 30 minutes before closing, tel. 01334/477-196, www.historic-scotland.gov.uk.

• *Leaving the castle, turn left and continue along the bluff on The Scores, which soon becomes a pedestrian lane leading directly to the gate to the cathedral graveyard. Enter it to stand amid the tombstone-strewn ruins of...*

▲St. Andrew's Cathedral

Between the Great Schism and the Reformation (roughly the 14th-16th centuries), St. Andrews was the ecclesiastical capital of Scotland—and this was its showpiece church. Today the site features the remains of the cathedral and cloister (with walls and spires pecked away by centuries of scavengers), a graveyard, and a small exhibit and climbable tower.

Cost and Hours: Cathedral ruins-free; exhibit and tower-£4.50, £7.20 combo-ticket includes castle; daily April-Sept 9:30-17:30, Oct-March 9:30-16:30, last entry 30 minutes before closing, tel. 01334/472-563, www.historic-scotland.gov.uk.

Background: It was the relics of the Apostle Andrew that first put this town on the map and gave it its name. There are numerous legends associated with the relics. According to one version, in the fourth century, St. Rule was directed in a dream to bring the relics northward from Constantinople. When the ship wrecked offshore from here, it was clear that this was a sacred place. Andrew's bones (an upper arm, a kneecap, some fingers, and a tooth) were kept on this site, and starting in 1160, the cathedral was built and pilgrims began to arrive. Since St. Andrew had a direct connection to Jesus, his relics were believed to possess special properties, making them worthy of pilgrimages on par with St. James' relics in Santiago de Compostela, Spain (of Camino de Santiago fame). St. Andrew became Scotland's patron saint; in fact, the white "X" on the blue Scottish flag evokes the diagonal cross on which St. Andrew was crucified (he chose this type of cross because he felt unworthy to die as Jesus had).

> **Self-Guided Tour:** You can stroll around the cathedral **ruins**—the best part of the complex—for free. First walk between

the two ruined but still towering ends of the church, which used to be the apse (at the sea end, where you entered) and the main entry (at the town end). Visually trace the gigantic footprint of the former church in the ground, including the bases of columns—like giant sawed-off tree trunks. Plaques identify where elements of the church once stood.

Looking at the one wall that's still standing, you can see the architectural changes that were made over the 150 years the cathedral was built—from the rounded, Romanesque windows at the front to the more highly decorated, pointed Gothic arches near the back. Mentally rebuild the church, and try to imagine it in its former majesty, when it played host to pilgrims from all over Europe.

The church wasn't destroyed all at once, like all those ruined abbeys in England (demolished in a huff by Henry VIII when he broke with the pope). Instead, because the Scottish Reformation was more gradual, this church was slowly picked apart over time. First just the decorations were removed from inside the cathedral. Then the roof was pulled down to make use of its lead. Without a roof, the cathedral fell further and further into disrepair, and was quarried by locals for its handy precut stones (which you'll still find in the walls of many old St. Andrews homes). The elements—a big storm in the 1270s and a fire in 1378—also contributed to the cathedral's demise.

The surrounding **graveyard,** dating from the post-Reformation Protestant era, is much more recent than the cathedral. In this golf-obsessed town, the game even infiltrates the cemeteries: Many notable golfers from St. Andrews are buried here (such as Young Tom—or "Tommy"—Morris, four-time British Open winner).

ST. ANDREWS

Go through the surviving wall into the former **cloister,** marked by a gigantic grassy square in the center. You can still see the cleats up on the wall, which once supported beams. Imagine the cloister back in its heyday, its passages filled with strolling monks.

At the end of the cloister is a small **exhibit** (entry fee required), with a relatively dull collection of old tombs and other carved-stone relics that have been unearthed on this site. Your ticket also includes entry to the surviving **tower of St. Rule's Church** (the rectangular tower beyond the cathedral ruins that was built to hold the precious relics of St. Andrew about a thousand years ago). If you feel like hiking up the 157 very claustrophobic steps for the view over St. Andrews' rooftops, it's worth the price. Up top, you can also look out to sea to find the pier where students traditionally walk out in their robes (see sidebar on page 832).

• *Leave the cathedral grounds on the town side of the cathedral. Angling right, head down North Street. Just ahead, on the left, is the adorable...*

▲St. Andrews Preservation Trust Museum and Garden

Filling a 17th-century fishing family's house that was protected from developers, this museum is a time capsule of an earlier, simpler era. The house itself seems built for Smurfs, but once housed 20 family members. The ground floor features replicas of a grocer's shop and a "chemist's" (pharmacy), using original fittings from actual stores. Upstairs are temporary exhibits. (To mark the centennial of the start of World War I, one of the rotating exhibits in 2014 will feature The Great War—from the perspective of its social history and impact on St. Andrews.) Out back is a tranquil garden (dedicated to the memory of a beloved professor) with "great-grandma's washhouse," featuring an exhibit about the history of soap and washing. Lovingly presented, this quaint, humble house provides a nice contrast to the big-money scene around the golf course at the other end of town.

Cost and Hours: Free but donation requested, generally open late May-late Sept daily 14:00-17:00, closed off-season, 12 North Street, tel. 01334/477-629, www.standrewspreservationtrust.org.

• *From the museum, hang a left around the next corner to South Castle Street. At the top of Market Street, look for the tiny white house on your left, with the cute curved staircase. What's that chase scene on the roof?*

Turn right down Market Street (which leads directly to the town's center, but we'll take a curvier route). Notice how the streets and even the buildings are smaller at this oldest end of town, as if the whole city is shrinking as the streets close in on the cathedral. Passing an antique bookstore on your right, take a left onto Baxter Wynd, a.k.a. Baker

Lane (unmarked). You'll pass a tiny garden on your right before land-ing on South Street. Turn right and head down South Street. After 50 yards, cross the street and enter a gate marked by a cute gray facade and a university insignia.

St. Mary's College

This is the home of the university's School of Divinity (theology). If the gate's open, find the peaceful quad, with its gnarled tree, purportedly planted by Mary, Queen of Scots. To get a feel of stu-dent life from centuries past, try poking your nose into one of the old classrooms.

• *Back on South Street, continue to your left. Some of the plainest build-ings on this stretch of the street have the most interesting history—sev-eral of them were built to fund the Crusades. Turn right on Church Street. You can end this walk at charming Church Square, where you'll find the library (with Internet access; see "Helpful Hints," earlier) and recommended Fisher and Donaldson bakery (closed Sun).*

But if you want to do more exploring, head to nearby Market Street (just a few yards down Church Street) to find the TI, grocery store, and...

Luvians Bottle Shop

Run by three brothers (**Lu**igi, **Vi**ncenzo, and **An**tonio), this might be the friendliest place in Scotland to talk, taste, and purchase whisky. The brothers and staff are so well-regarded that distill-eries bottle unique single-cask vintages just for them to celebrate the British Open every five years (ask about the recent 17-year-old Glenfarclas, or the 21-year-old Springbank they are expecting in 2015 to commemorate the tournament). With nearly 50 bottles open, a map of Scotland's whisky regions, and more-than-helpful team members, if you don't leave the shop enjoying whisky, you never will.

Cost and Hours: Daily 10:00-22:00, Sun open at 12:30, 66 Market Street, tel. 01334/477-752, www.luvians.com.

• *About a five-minute walk away in Kinburn Park is...*

St. Andrews Museum

This small, modest museum, which traces St. Andrews' history "from A to Zed," is an enjoyable way to pass time on a rainy day. It's situated in an old mansion in Kinburn Park, a five-minute walk from the old town (walk east down Market Street and St. Mary's Place, then through the roundabout onto Doubledykes Road; the museum is ahead on the right).

Cost and Hours: Free, daily April-Sept 10:00-17:00, Oct-March 10:30-16:00, café, Doubledykes Road, tel. 01334/659-380.

Golfing in St. Andrews

St. Andrews is the Cooperstown and Mecca of golf. While St. Andrews lays claim to founding the sport (the first record of golf being played here was in 1553), nobody knows exactly where and when people first hit a ball with a stick for fun. In the Middle Ages, St. Andrews traded with the Dutch; some historians believe they picked up a golf-like Dutch game on ice, and translated it to the bonnie rolling hills of Scotland's east coast. Since the grassy beachfront strip just outside St. Andrews was too poor to support crops, it was used for playing the game—and, centuries later, it still is. Why do golf courses have 18 holes? Because that's how many fit at the Old Course in St. Andrews, golf's single most famous site.

The Old Course

The Old Course hosts the British Open every five years (next in 2015). At other times it's open to the public for golfing. Fortunately for women golfers, the men-only Royal and Ancient Golf Club (R&A) doesn't actually own the course, which is public and managed by the St. Andrews Links Trust. Drop by their clubhouse, overlooking the beach near the Old Course (hours roughly May-Aug daily 7:00-21:00, progressively shorter until 7:30-16:00 in Dec, www.standrews.org.uk).

Teeing Off at the Old Course: Playing at golf's pinnacle course is pricey (£155/person, less off-season), but accessible to the public—subject to lottery drawings for tee times and reserved spots by club members. You can play the Old Course only if you have a handicap of 24 (men) or 36 (women); bring along your certificate or card. If you don't know your handicap—or don't know what "handicap" means—then you're not good enough to play here (they want to keep the game moving, rather than wait for novices to spend 10 strokes on each hole). If you play, you'll do nine holes out, then nine more back in—however, all but four share the same greens.

Reserving a Tee Time: To ensure a specific tee time at the Old Course, it's smart to reserve a full year ahead. Call 01334/466-666 or email reservations@standrews.org.uk. Otherwise, some tee times are determined each day by a lottery called the "daily ballot." Call or visit in person by 14:00 two days before to put your name in (2 players minimum, 4 players max)—they post the results online at 16:00. Note that no advance reservations are taken on Saturdays or in September, and the courses are closed on Sundays—which is traditionally the day reserved for townspeople.

Other Courses: The trust manages six other courses (including two right next to the Old Course—the New Course and the Jubilee Course), plus the modern cliff-top Castle Course just outside the city. These are cheaper, and it's much easier to get a tee time (£70 for New and Jubilee, £120 for Castle Course, £15-45 for others). It's usually possible to get a tee time for the same day or next day (if you want a guaranteed reservation, make it at least 2 weeks in advance). The Castle Course has great views overlooking the town, but even more wind to blow your ball around.

▲The Himalayas

Named for its dramatically hilly terrain, "The Himalayas" is basically a very classy (but still relaxed) game of mini-golf. Technically the "Ladies' Putting Green," this cute little patch of undulating grass presents the perfect opportunity for non-golfers (female or male) to say they've played the links at St. Andrews—for less than the cost of a Coke. It's remarkable how the contour of the land can present even more challenging obstacles than the tunnels, gates, and distractions of a corny putt-putt course back home. Flat shoes are required (no high heels). You'll see it on the left as you walk toward the clubhouse from the R&A.

Cost and Hours: £2 for 18 holes. The putting green is open April-Oct daily 10:30-18:00 or 19:00, closed Nov-March. While most hours are reserved for members, non-members (tourists like you) are welcome to play Mon-Tue and Fri (10:30-17:00), Wed (10:30-12:00 & 16:00-18:00), Thu (11:00-18:00), and Sun (10:00-12:00). Tel. 1334/475-196.

British Golf Museum

This exhibit, which started as a small collection in the R&A across the street, is the best place in Britain to learn about the Scots' favorite sport. It's fascinating for golf lovers.

The compact, one-way exhibit reverently presents a meticulous survey of the game's history—from the monarchs who loved and hated golf (including the king who outlawed it because it was distracting men from church and archery practice), right up to the "Golden Bear" and a randy Tiger. A constant 2-hour loop film shows highlights of the British Open from 1923 to the present, and other video screens show scratchy black-and-white highlights from the days before corporate sponsorship. At the end, find items donated by the golfers of today, including Tiger Woods' shirt, hat, and glove.

Cost and Hours: £6.50, includes informative book about the history of golf; April-Oct Mon-Sat 9:30-17:00, Sun 10:00-17:00; Nov-March daily 10:00-16:00; last entry 45 minutes before closing; free 45-minute guided tours June-Sept daily at 11:15 and 15:45; Bruce Embankment, in the blocky modern building squatting behind the R&A by the Old Course, tel. 01334/460-046, www.britishgolfmuseum.co.uk.

Sleeping in St. Andrews

Owing partly to the high-roller golf tourists flowing through the town, St. Andrews' accommodations are expensive. During graduation week in June, hotels often require a four-night stay and book up quickly. Solo travelers are at a disadvantage, as many B&Bs don't have singles—and charge close to the double price for one person (I've listed "S" or "Sb" below for those that actually have single rooms). But the quality at my recommendations is high, and budget alternatives—including a hostel—are workable. All of these, except the hostel and the dorms, are on the streets called Murray Park and Murray Place, between North Street and The Scores in the old town. If you need to find a room on the fly, head for this same neighborhood, which has far more options than just the ones I've listed below.

$$ Cameron House has five old-fashioned, paisley, masculine-feeling rooms—including two nice singles that share one bathroom—around a beautiful stained-glass atrium (S-£45, Db-£90, discount for longer stays, prices soft and sometimes closed Nov-Easter, free Wi-Fi, lounge, 11 Murray Park, tel. 01334/472-306, www.cameronhouse-sta.co.uk, info@cameron house-sta.co.uk, Donna and Yvonne).

$$ Lorimer Guest House has five comfortable, tastefully decorated rooms, including one on the ground floor (Db-£88-104, deluxe Db-£94-120, higher prices are for July-Sept, ask about discount for longer stays, guest computer, free Wi-Fi, 19 Murray Park, tel. 01334/476-599, www.lorimerhouse.com, info@lorimer house.com, Mick and Chris Cordner).

$$ Doune Guest House is golfer-friendly, with six comfortable, plaid-heavy rooms. The helpful owners are happy to arrange early breakfasts and airport transfers (S-£40-49, Db-£80-98, price depends on season, cheaper off-season, cash only, guest computer, free Wi-Fi, 5 Murray Place, tel. 01334/475-195, www.dounehouse .com, info@dounehouse.com).

$$ Arran House has nine modern rooms, including a single with a private bathroom across the hall (S-£50, Sb-£60, Db-£85-90, three ground-floor rooms, two family rooms, free Wi-Fi, 5 Murray Park, tel. 01334/474-724, mobile 07768-718-237, www .arranhousestandrews.co.uk, info@arranhousestandrews.co.uk, Anne and Jim McGrory).

$$ Glenderran Guest House offers five plush rooms (including two true singles) and a few nice breakfast extras (Sb-£40-60, Db-£80-120, free Wi-Fi, same-day laundry-£10, 9 Murray Park, tel. 01334/477-951, www.glenderran.com, info@glenderran.com, Ray and Maggie).

Sleep Code

(£1 = about $1.60, country code: 44, area code: 01334)
S = Single, **D** = Double/Twin, **T** = Triple, **Q** = Quad, **b** = bathroom, **s** = shower only. Unless otherwise noted, credit cards are accepted and breakfast is included.

To help you sort easily through these listings, I've divided the accommodations into two categories based on the price for a standard double room with bath (during high season):

$$ Higher Priced—Most rooms £70 or more.
$ Lower Priced—Most rooms less than £70.

Prices can change without notice; verify the hotel's current rates online or by email. For the best prices, always book direct.

$$ Hoppity House is a bright and contemporary place, with neutral tones and built-in furniture that makes good use of space. You may find a stuffed namesake bunny or two hiding out among its six rooms. Golfers appreciate the golf-bag lockers on the ground floor (Sb-£45-55, Db-£75-90, deluxe Db-£90-110, family room, lower prices off-season, fridges in rooms, free Wi-Fi, 4 Murray Park, tel. 01334/461-116, mobile 07701-099-100, www.hoppity house.co.uk, enquiries@hoppityhouse.co.uk, helpful Gordon and Heather).

Hostel: **$ St. Andrews Tourist Hostel** has 44 beds in colorful 4- to 8-bed rooms about a block from the base of Market Street. The high-ceilinged lounge is a comfy place for a break, and the friendly staff is happy to recommend their favorite pubs (£16-20/bed, includes sheets, no breakfast, kitchen, free Wi-Fi, self-service laundry-£4, towels-£2, office open 7:00-23:00, office closed 15:00-18:00 outside of summer, no curfew, St. Mary's Place, tel. 01334/479-911, www.standrewshostel.com, standrewshostel @gmail.com).

University Accommodations

In the summer (mid-June-Aug), two of the University of St. Andrews' student-housing buildings are tidied up and rented out to tourists (website for both: www.discoverstandrews.com; pay when reserving).

$$ Agnes Blackadder Hall has double beds and private bathrooms; it's more comfortable, but also more expensive and less central (Sb-£39-59, Db-£68-85, family Qb-£89-102, includes breakfast, tel. 01334/467-000, agnes.blackadder@st-andrews.ac.uk).

$ McIntosh Hall is cheaper and more central, but it only has twin beds and shared bathrooms (S-£39, D-£68, tel. 01334/467-035, mchall@st-andrews.ac.uk). Because true single rooms are rare in St. Andrews' B&Bs, these dorms are a good option for solo travelers.

Eating in St. Andrews

The first three listings—owned by the same group—are popular and serve up reliably good international cuisine. Comparing their early-dinner specials may help you choose (www.houserestaurants .com).

The Doll's House offers cuisine with a French flair, with two floors of indoor seating and a cozy, colorful, casual atmosphere; the sidewalk seating out front is across from Holy Trinity Church (£7-11 lunches, £14-18 dinners, £12 two-course early-bird special 17:00-19:00, open daily 12:00-15:00 & 17:00-22:00, a block from the TI at 3 Church Square, tel. 01334/477-422).

The Glass House serves pizza, pasta, and salads in a two-story glass building with an open-style layout (£7 lunches 12:00-17:00, £9-11 dinners, £10 two-course early-bird special 17:00-18:30, open daily 12:00-22:00, second-floor outdoor patio, near the castle on 80 North Street, tel. 01334/473-673).

The Grill House offers Mexican-style food in a vibrantly colored space (£6 lunches 12:00-16:00, £11-17 dinners, £10 two-course early-bird special 16:00-18:30, open daily 12:00-22:00, St. Mary's Place, tel. 01334/470-500).

The Seafood Restaurant is St. Andrews' favorite splurge. Situated in a modern glassy building overlooking the beach near the Old Course, it's like dining in an aquarium. The place serves locally caught seafood to a room full of tables that wrap around the busy open kitchen. Dinner reservations are recommended (£13-26 lunches, £48.50 three-course dinner, daily 12:00-14:30 & 18:00-22:00, The Scores, tel. 01334/479-475, www.theseafoodrestaurant .com).

On Market Street: In the area around the TI, you'll find a concentration of good restaurants—pubs, grill houses, coffee shops, Asian food, fish-and-chips (see later), and more...take your pick. Also on Market Street, you can stock up for a picnic at **Greggs, Tesco,** and **Sainsbury's Local.**

Pubs: There's no shortage in this college town. **Aikmans,** run by Barbara and Malcolm (two graduates from the university who couldn't bring themselves to leave), features a cozy wood-table ambience, live music (traditional Scottish music upstairs once a month, other live music Fri-Sat) and simple soups, sandwiches, and snacks. This place knows its ales—it's been featured for the past quarter-century in the *Good Beer Guide* (£3-5 grub, open daily 11:00-24:00, 32 Bell Street, tel. 01334/477-425). **The Central** is a St. Andrews standby, with old lamps and lots of brass (£5 sandwiches, £8-10 burgers, Mon-Sat 11:00-23:45, Sun 12:30-23:45, food until 21:00, 77 Market Street, tel. 01334/478-296). **Ma Bells** is a sleek but friendly place that clings to its status as one of Prince William's favorites (£5-10 pub grub, pricier bistro meals, Mon-Sat 12:00-24:00, Sun 12:30-24:00, food served until 21:00, two blocks from the Old Course and R&A at 40 The Scores, tel. 01334/472-622). **Greyfriars** is in a classy, modern hotel near the Murray Park B&Bs (£5 light meals, £8-15 main dishes, daily 12:00-24:00, 129 North Street, tel. 01334/474-906).

Fish-and-Chips: **Fritto** is a local favorite for take-away fish-and-chips, centrally located on Market Street near the TI (£6 fish-and-chips, £4 burgers, daily 12:00-21:00, can be later Fri-Sat and when the weather's good, at the corner of Union and Market, tel. 01334/475-555). Brave souls will order a can of Irn-Bru with their fish (warning: It doesn't taste like orange soda—see page 735). For what's considered the country's best chippie, head for the Anstruther Fish Bar in the East Neuk (described at the end of this chapter).

Dessert: **Fisher and Donaldson** is beloved for its rich, affordable pastries and chocolates. Listen as the straw-hatted bakers chat with their regular customers, then try their Coffee Tower—like a giant cream puff filled with rich, lightly coffee-flavored cream—or their number-one seller, the fudge doughnut (£1-2 pastries, Mon-Fri 6:00-17:15, Sat until 17:00, closed Sun, just around the corner from the TI at 13 Church Street, tel. 01334/472-201). **B. Jannettas,** which has been around for more than a century, features a wide and creative range of 52 tasty ice-cream flavors (£1.60 single scoop, £2.90 double scoop, daily 9:00-22:00, 31 South Street, tel. 01334/473-285, www.jannettas.co.uk).

St. Andrews Connections

Trains don't go into St. Andrews—instead, use the Leuchars station (5 miles from St. Andrews, connected by buses coordinated to meet most trains, 2-4/hour, see "Arrival in St. Andrews" on page 825). The TI has useful train schedules, which also list bus departure times from St. Andrews.

From Leuchars by Train to: Edinburgh (1-2/hour, 1 hour), **Glasgow** (2/hour, 2 hours, transfer in Haymarket), **Inverness** (roughly hourly, 3.25-4 hours, 1-2 changes). Trains run less frequently on Sundays. Train info: Tel. 0845-748-4950, www.national rail.co.uk.

The East Neuk

On the lazy coastline meandering south from St. Andrews, the cute-as-a-pin East Neuk (pronounced "nook") is a collection of tidy fishing villages. While hardly earth-shattering, the East Neuk is a pleasant detour if you've got the time. The villages of Crail and Pittenweem have their fans, but Anstruther is worth most of your attention. The East

Neuk works best as a half-day side-trip (by either car or bus) from St. Andrews, though drivers can use it as a scenic detour between Edinburgh and St. Andrews.

Getting There: It's an easy **drive** from St. Andrews. For the scenic route, follow the A-917 south of town along the coast, past Crail, on the way to Anstruther and Pittenweem. For a shortcut directly to Anstruther, take the B-9131 across the peninsula (or return that way after driving the longer coastal route there). **Buses** connect St. Andrews to the East Neuk: Bus #95 goes hourly from St. Andrews to Crail and Anstruther (50 minutes to Anstruther, catch bus at St. Andrews bus station or from Church Street, around the corner from the TI). The hourly #X60 bus goes directly to Anstruther, then on to Edinburgh (25 minutes to Anstruther, 2.25 hours more to Edinburgh). Bus info: Tel. 0871-200-2233, www.travelinescotland.com.

▲Anstruther

Stretched out along its harbor, colorful Anstruther (AN-stru-ther; pronounced ENT-ster by locals) is the centerpiece of the East Neuk. The main parking lot and bus stop are both right on the harbor. Anstruther's handy **TI,** which offers lots of useful information for the entire East Neuk area, is located next door to the town's main sight, the Scottish Fisheries Museum (April-Oct Mon-Sat 10:00-17:00, Sun 11:00-16:00, closed Nov-March, tel. 01333/311-073, www.visitfife.com). Stroll the harborfront to the end, detouring inland around the little cove (or crossing the causeway at low tide) to reach some colorful old houses, including one encrusted with seashells.

Anstruther's **Scottish Fisheries Museum** is true to its slogan: "We are bigger than you think!" The endearingly hokey exhibit sprawls through several harborfront buildings, painstakingly tracing the history of Scottish seafaring from primitive dugout dinghies to modern vessels. You'll learn the story of Scotland's "Zulu" fishing boats and walk through vast rooms filled with boats. For a glimpse at humble fishing lifestyles, don't miss the Fisherman's Cottage, hiding upstairs from the courtyard (£7; April-Sept Mon-Sat 10:00-17:30, Sun 11:00-17:00; Oct-March Mon-Sat 10:00-16:30, Sun 12:00-16:30; last entry one hour before closing, tearoom, Harbourhead, tel. 01333/310-628, www.scotfishmuseum .org).

Eating in Anstruther: Anstruther's claim to fame is its fish-and-chips, considered by many to be Scotland's best. Though there are several good chippies in town, the famous one is the **Anstruther Fish Bar,** facing the harbor just a block from the TI and Fisheries Museum. As you enter, choose whether you want to get takeout or dine in for a few pounds more. While more expensive than most chippies, the food here is good—so good the place has officially been named "UK's Fish and Chip Shop of the Year" multiple times. For those who don't like fish, they also have pizza, burgers, and—for the truly brave—deep-fried haggis (£6-8 take-out, £8-11 to dine in, dine-in prices include bread and a drink, daily 11:30-21:30, until 22:00 for take-away, 42-44 Shore Street, tel. 01333/310-518).

GLASGOW

Glasgow (GLAS-goh)—astride the River Clyde—is a surprising city. A century ago it had 1.2 million people, twice the size (and importance) of today. It was an industrial powerhouse producing 25 percent of the world's oceangoing ships. In its heyday, Glasgow was one of Europe's biggest cities and the second-largest in Britain, right behind London. But in the mid-20th century, tough times hit Glasgow, giving it a rough edge and a run-down image.

Today Glasgow is on the rise again. Its industrial heritage, combined with its flair for art and its unpretentious friendliness, make it more popular than ever to visit. And the city is spiffing up its image and offering a warm welcome. You'll enjoy free admission to all city museums, and have your choice of more music venues than you'll find anywhere north of London. The shopping is great—Glasgow likes to brag that it's Britain's number two shopping town.

Yet there still is a rough side to the culture, and locals seem to come in two stripes: heavy-drinking football (soccer) fans...and the rest. Historically, you could get beat up for wearing the wrong football club colors into the wrong pub. The two rival Glasgow teams (sort of like the Cubs and White Sox in Chicago) each have a rabid following. But assaults on tourists are very rare.

In 2014, all eyes will be on Glasgow as it hosts the Commonwealth Games—something like the Olympics—for the 53 countries of the former British Empire. More than 6,000 athletes will compete from July 23 to August 3. Just as London did when choosing the site for its 2012 Olympics, Glasgow has chosen to invest in its poor East End. (In Industrial Age cities, the wealth-

When the Great Ships of the World Were "Clyde-Built"

Glasgow's River Clyde shipyards were the mightiest in the world, famed for building the largest moving manmade objects on earth. The shipyards, once 50 strong, have dwindled to just three. Yet a few giant cranes still stand to remind locals and visitors that from 1880 to 1950, a quarter of the world's ships were built here and "Clyde-built" meant reliability and quality. For 200 years, shipbuilding was Glasgow's top employer—as many as 100,000 workers at its peak, producing a new ship every two days. The glamorous Cunard ships were built here—from the *Lusitania* in 1906 (infamously sunk by a German U-boat in World War I, which brought the US into the war) to the *Queen Elizabeth II* in 1967. People still talk about the day when over 200,000 Glaswegians gathered for the launch, the queen herself smashed the Champagne bottle on the prow, and the magnificent ship slid into the harbor. To learn lots more about shipbuilding in Glasgow, visit the excellent Riverside Museum of Transport and Travel.

ier people lived upwind, while the poor lived in slums downwind of the factories.) Glasgow's struggling East End will come out of the games with a nice souvenir—a modernized infrastructure.

Glasgow is both a workaday Scottish city as well as a cosmopolitan destination, with an energetic dining and nightlife scene. It's also a pilgrimage site of sorts for architecture buffs, thanks to a cityscape packed with Victorian architecture, early 20th-century touches, and modern flair. Most beloved are the works by hometown boy Charles Rennie Mackintosh, the visionary—and now very trendy—architect who left his mark all over Glasgow during the turn of the 20th century.

Many more tourists visit Edinburgh, a short train trip away. And, even though Glasgow is bigger than Edinburgh, it lives forever in the shadow of its more popular neighbor. (In Edinburgh, people identify with the quality of the school they attended; in Glasgow, it's their soccer team allegiance.)

Edinburgh may have the royal aura, but Glasgow's down-to-earth appeal is captivating. One Glaswegian told me, "The people of Glasgow have a better time at a funeral than the people of Edinburgh have at a wedding." In Glasgow, there's no upper-crust history, and no one puts on airs. Locals call sanded and polished concrete "Glasgow marble." In this revitalized city, friendly locals do their best to introduce you to the fun-loving, laid-back Glaswegian (rhymes with "Norwegian") way of life.

Planning Your Time

While many visitors just blitz Glasgow as a day trip from Edinburgh (and a first day in Glasgow is certainly more exciting than a fourth day in Edinburgh), the city can easily fill two days of sightseeing. The sights and museums seem to represent a city greater than it is today—a reminder of its former industrial importance.

My self-guided walk of the city (described later) covers the core of Glasgow, tying together the most important sights in the center. The two-hour hop-on, hop-off bus tour is perfect for getting the bigger picture and visiting the three important sights away from the center (the Cathedral Precinct, the Riverside Museum of Transport and Travel, and the Kelvingrove Art Gallery and Museum).

If you're a fan of Art Nouveau and Charles Rennie Mackintosh, you can lace together a busy day's worth of sightseeing (the TI has a brochure laying it out). At a minimum, those interested in Mackintosh should tour the Glasgow School of Art (which he designed and is only open via tour) and see the Mackintosh exhibit at the Kelvingrove Gallery.

If you just have one evening in town, the West End is most enjoyable.

Day Trip from Edinburgh: For a full day, catch the 9:30 train to Glasgow (morning trains every 15 minutes; £13 same-day round-trip if leaving after 9:15 or on weekend); it arrives at Queen Street Train Station at 10:30. To fill your Glasgow hours smartly, I'd do the entire hop-on, hop-off bus tour circuit (two hours). Then I'd follow my self-guided walk (finishing with the Glasgow School of Art tour and the Tenement House).

The four major interiors to consider, depending on your interests and time limits, are: The Glasgow School of Art (one-hour tours need to be booked in advance); The Tenement House (last entry at 16:30); the Riverside Museum (closes at 17:00); and the Kelvingrove Gallery (closes at 17:00).

For dinner, consider heading out to the thriving West End restaurant scene, then hop the subway back to Queen Street Station (use the Buchanan Street stop) and catch the 21:00 train back to Edinburgh (evening trains depart every 30 minutes).

GLASGOW

Orientation to Glasgow

With a grid street plan, a downtown business zone, and more than its share of boxy office buildings, Glasgow feels more like a mid-sized American city than a big Scottish one—like Cleveland or Cincinnati with shorter skyscrapers, more sandstone, and more hills. (In fact, the film *Cloud Atlas,* set in San Francisco and starring Halle Berry, was filmed here.) The tourist's Glasgow has three main parts: the city center; the Cathedral Precinct (a cluster of minor sights near the cathedral in the east); and the West End restaurant/nightlife/shopping zone.

The easily walkable city center has two main drags, both lined with shops and crawling with shoppers: Sauchiehall Street (pronounced "Suckyhall," running west to east) and Buchanan Street (running north to south). These two pedestrian malls, part of what's nicknamed the Golden Zed (Golden Z), make a big zig and zag through the heart of town. Three streets make up the full Golden Zed: Sauchiehall Street is the top of the Z, Buchanan Street the middle part, and Argyle Street the bottom of the Z.

Tourist Information

The TI is outside Queen Street Station opposite the Buchanan Street subway station (at #170 Buchanan Street). They hand out an excellent free map, stock other Glasgow brochures, and can book you a room for a £4 fee plus 10 percent deposit. They also have information on the rest of Scotland (Mon-Sat 9:00-18:00, Sun 10:00-17:00, until 16:00 Oct-April, www.visitscotland.com).

Mackintosh Trail Ticket: Ask about this ticket at the TI. If it's available, it covers entry to all "Charles Rennie Mac" sights and public transportation to those outside the city limits (£16/day, www.crmsociety.com).

Arrival in Glasgow

By Train: Glasgow, a major Scottish transportation hub, has two main train stations, which are just a few blocks apart in the heart of town: **Central Station** (with a grand, genteel interior under a vast steel-and-glass Industrial Age roof) and **Queen Street Station** (more functional, with better connections to Edinburgh, and closer to the TI—take the exit marked *Dundas Street* and head one block straight ahead to Buchanan Street). Both stations have pay WCs and baggage storage (about £7 per bag). You can walk the five minutes between the stations or take the roundabout "RailLink" bus #398 (£0.80, or free if you have a ticket for a connecting train).

By Bus: Buchanan bus station is at Killermont Street, two blocks up the hill behind Queen Street train station.

By Car: The M-8 motorway, which slices through downtown Glasgow, is the easiest way in and out of the city. Ask your hotel for directions to and from the M-8, and connect with other highways from there.

By Air: For information on Glasgow's two airports, see "Glasgow Connections," at the end of this chapter.

Helpful Hints

Safety: The city center, which is packed with ambitious career types during the day, can feel deserted at night. Avoid the area near the River Clyde (hookers and thugs), and confine yourself to the streets north of Argyle Street if you're in the downtown quarter. The Merchant City area (east of the train stations) and the West End bustle with crowded restaurants well into the evening and feel well-populated in the wee hours.

If you've picked up a football (soccer) jersey or scarf as a souvenir, don't wear it in Glasgow; passions run very high, and most drunken brawls in town are between supporters of Glasgow's two rival soccer clubs: Celtic in green, and Rangers in blue and red. (For reasons no one can explain, the Celtic team name is pronounced "sell-tic"—like it is in Boston. In all other cases, such as when referring to music, language, or culture, this word is pronounced "kell-tic".)

Sightseeing: Glasgow's city-owned museums—including the big museums and the sights near the cathedral—are free, but request £1-3 donations (www.glasgowmuseums.com).

Sunday Travel: Bus and train schedules are dramatically reduced on Sundays—most routes have only half the departure times they have during the week. And trains run less frequently in the off-season; so if you want to get to the Highlands by bus on a Sunday in winter, forget it.

Internet Access: Many pubs and coffee shops offer free Wi-Fi. You'll see signs advertising Internet cafés around the city core (near Central Station and Buchanan Street).

Local Guides: Joan Dobbie, a native Glaswegian and registered Scottish Tourist Guide, will give you the insider's take on Glasgow's sights (£95/half-day, £140/day, tel. 01355/236-749, mobile 07773-555-151, joan.leo@lineone.net). Colin Mairs, who was the youngest licensed guide in town, is also good and is licensed to drive while guiding (£100/half-day, £150/day, more by car, mobile 07716-232-001, www.excursionscotland.com, colin_mairs@yahoo.co.uk).

Getting Around Glasgow

By City Bus: Most city-center routes are operated by First Bus Company (£1.90/ride, £4 for all-day ticket—good only on First buses, buy tickets from driver, exact change required). Buses run every few minutes down Glasgow's main thoroughfares (such as Sauchiehall Street) to the downtown core (train stations). If you're waiting at a stop and a bus comes along, put out your hand to signal it to stop. Ask the driver if the bus is headed to Central Station; chances are the answer is yes.

By Hop-On, Hop-Off Bus Tour: This tour connects Glasgow's far-flung historic sights in a two-hour loop and lets you hop on and off as you like for two days. Buses are frequent (every 15 to 20 minutes) and punctual, and alternate between live guide and recorded narration (both are equally good). It works great for Glasgow, covering the city very well, and the guide does a fine job of describing activities at each stop. While the first stop is on George Square, you can hop on and pay the driver anywhere along the route (£12, daily 9:30-16:00, July-Aug 4/hour, spring and fall 3/hour, winter 2/hour, tel. 0141/204-0444, www.citysightseeing glasgow.co.uk).

By Taxi: Taxis are affordable, plentiful, and often come with nice, chatty cabbies—all speaking in the impenetrable Glaswegian accent. (Scottish English is considered its own language—as you'll hear in a cab.) Just smile and nod. Most taxi rides in the downtown area cost about £5; to the West End about £7. Use taxis or public transport to connect Glasgow's more remote sights; splurge for a taxi (for safety) any time you're traveling late at night.

By Subway: Glasgow's cute little single-line subway system, nicknamed Clockwork Orange, makes a six-mile circle that has 15 stops. While simple today, when it opened in 1896 it was the bee's knees (it's the world's third-oldest subway system, after London and Budapest). Though the subway is essentially useless for connecting city-center sightseeing (Buchanan Street and St. Enoch are the only downtown stops), it's handy for reaching sights farther out, including the Kelvingrove Gallery (Kelvinhall stop) and West End restaurant/nightlife neighborhood (Hillhead stop; £1.40 single trip, £3.80 for all-day ticket, subway runs Mon-Sat 6:30-23:45, Sun 10:00-18:00, www.spt.co.uk/subway).

GLASGOW

Self-Guided Walk

Get to Know Glasgow

Glasgow isn't romantic, but it has an earthy charm, and architecture buffs love it. The longer you spend here, the more you'll feel the edgy, artsy vibe. The trick to sightseeing here is to always look up—above the chain restaurants and mall stores, you'll see a wealth of imaginative facades, complete with ornate friezes and expressive sculptures. These buildings transport you to the heady days around the turn of the 20th century—when the rest of Great

Glasgow Walk

1 Buchanan Street
2 Royal Exchange Square &
  Glasgow Gallery of Modern Art
3 George Square &
  Queen Victoria Statue
4 Nelson Mandela Place
5 More of the Golden Zed
6 Celtic Shop
7 Willow Tea Rooms (2)
8 Glasgow School of Art
9 Tenement House
10 Bus to Central Station

TO EDINBURGH
WEST
TENEMENT HOUSE
9
M-8
GARN.
HILL
RENFREW
FINISH
B
10
SAUCHIEHA
CHARING
CROSS
STN.
BATH
TO
KELVINGROVE
MUSEUM
M-8
MOTORWAY
NEWTON ST.
ELMBANK
HOLLAND
WEST
WEST
B
PITT
BOTH-
WATER-
CA
FOOT-
BRIDGE
A-814
ARGYLE
TO
RIVERSIDE
MUSEUM OF
TRANSPORT
KINGSTON BRIDGE
BROOMIE
RIVER
TO
AIRPORT & OBAN
VIA A-82

S SUBWAY STOP
B BUS STOP
P PARKING
  PEDESTRIAN ZONE

200 YARDS
200 METERS

GLASGOW

Britain was enthralled by Victorianism, but Glasgow set its own
course, thanks largely to the artistic bravado of Charles Rennie
Mackintosh and his friends (the "Glasgow Four"). This walking
tour takes a couple of hours—more if you tour the Glasgow School
of Art along the way.
• Start at the St. Enoch subway station, at the base of the pedestrian
shopping boulevard, Buchanan Street. (This is a short walk from the
Central Station, a longer walk or quick cab ride from Queen Street
Station.) Begin strolling up...

❶ Buchanan Street

The Golden Zed is the nickname for a Z-shaped pedestrian bou-levard made of three streets: Sauchiehall, Buchanan, and Argyle. Always coming up with marketing slogans to goose the shopping metabolism of the city, this district (with the top shops in town) is also called the "Style Mile." City officials have cleverly co-opted graffiti artists by sanctioning huge, fun, and edgy graffiti murals that you can see if you side-trip down alleys in the Style Mile.

Buchanan Street has a friendly Ramblas-style vibe with an

abundance of street musicians. As you stroll uphill, keep an eye out for: The **Argyll Arcade** (#30, opposite Frasers), dating from 1827, is the oldest arcade in town. It's filled with mostly jewelry and comes with security guards dressed in Victorian-era garb. Eager couples—whether they're engaged or about to be—can be heard to say, "Let's take a shortcut through here." **Frasers** (#45) is a vast and venerable department store, considered the Harrods of Glasgow. **Princes Square** (#48) is a classic old building dressed with a modern steel peacock and foliage. Step inside to see the delightfully modernized Art Nouveau atrium.

At #97 (on the left) is one of two Mackintosh-designed **Willow Tea Rooms** (other location described later in this walk).

• *Cross the street and leave the big pedestrian boulevard by turning down the second alley on the right, called Exchange Place. You'll pass windows full of old sewing machines on the left and the recommended Rogano restaurant on your right before emerging onto...*

❷ Royal Exchange Square

The centerpiece of this square—which marks the entrance to the shopping zone called Merchant City—is a stately, Neoclassical, bank-like building. This was once the **private mansion** of one of the tobacco lords, the super-rich businessmen who reigned here through the 1700s, stomping through the city with gold-tipped canes. During the port's heyday, these entrepreneurs helped Glasgow become Europe's sixth-biggest city—number two in the British Empire.

Today the mansion houses the **Glasgow Gallery of Modern Art,** nicknamed GoMA. Walk to the main entry (at the eques-

trian statue of the Duke of Wellington, often creatively decorated as Glasgow's favorite cone-head), and step back to take in the full Neoclassical facade. On the pediment, notice the funky, mirrored mosaic celebrating the miracles of St. Mungo—an example of how Glasgow refuses to take itself too seriously. The temporary exhibits inside GoMA are generally forgettable, but the museum does have an unusual charter: It displays only the work of living artists (free, £2 suggested donation, Mon-Wed and Sat 10:00-17:00, Thu 10:00-20:00, Fri and Sun 11:00-17:00, free guided tours Sat-Sun at 12:00 and 14:00, tel. 0141/287-3050).

• *Facing the fanciful GoMA facade, turn right onto Queen Street. Within a block, you'll reach...*

❸ George Square

This square, the centerpiece of Glasgow, is filled with statues and lined with notable buildings, such as the Queen Street train station

and the Glasgow City Chambers (the big Neoclassical building standing like a secular church to the east, open by tour, generally Mon-Fri 10:30 and 14:30, free). In front of the City Chambers stands a monument to Glaswegians killed fighting in the World Wars. The square is decorated with a *Who's Who* of statues depicting great Glaswegians. Find James Watt (who perfected the steam engine that helped power Europe into the Industrial Age), as well as Scotland's two top poets: Robert Burns and Sir Walter Scott (capping the tallest pillar in the center). The two equestrian statues are of Prince Albert and a surprisingly skinny **Queen Victoria**—a rare image of her in her more svelte youth.

• *If you're hungry, pop into Wetherspoon, a big, cheap pub with good basic meals that fills a former bank building facing the square. Next, just past skinny Vic and Robert Peel, turn left onto West George Street, and cross busy Buchanan Street to the tall church in the middle of...*

❹ Nelson Mandela Place

This is the first public space named for Nelson Mandela—honoring the man who, while still in prison, helped bring down apartheid in South Africa. Glasgow, nicknamed Red Clyde Side for its socialist politics and empathy for the working class, has been quick to jump on progressive causes—like ending apartheid.

The area around this church features some interesting bits of architectural detail. Standing along the left side of the church, look up across from the church to find the three circular friezes of the former **Stock Exchange** (built in 1875). These idealized heads represent the industries that made Glasgow prosperous during its heyday: building, engineering, and mining.

Around the back of the church find the Athenaeum, the sandy-colored building at #8 (notice the low-profile label over the door). Now a law office, this was founded in 1847 as a school and city library during Glasgow's Golden Age. (Charles Dickens gave the building's inaugural address.) Like Edinburgh, Glasgow was at the forefront of the 17th-century Scottish Enlightenment, a celebration of education and intellectualism. The Scots were known for their extremely practical brand of humanism; all members of society, including the merchant and working classes, were expected to be well-educated. (Tobacco lords, for example, often knew Latin and Greek.) Look above the door to find the symbolic statue of a reader sharing books with young children, an embodiment of this ideal.

• *Return to the big, busy pedestrianized Buchanan Street in front of the church. Just downhill, to the right, is a huge Apple Store in a grand old building. Turn left and start up...*

❺ Buchanan Street to Sauchiehall Street (More of the Golden Zed)

A short distance uphill is the glass entry to Glasgow's subway (from here you could ride directly to the Hillhead stop for the West End restaurant district; see "Eating in Glasgow," later). Across the street is the TI, with information on Glasgow and all of Scotland. And just up the street from the TI is the Buchanan Galleries, a big indoor mall (offering a refuge if it's raining).

At the top of Buchanan Street stands the Glasgow Royal Concert Hall. Its steps are a favorite perch where local office workers munch lunch and enjoy the street scene. The statue is of Donald Dewar, who served as Scotland's first ever "First Minister" after the Scottish Parliament reconvened in 1999 (previously they'd been serving in London—as part of the British Parliament—since 1707).

• *From here, the Golden Zed zags left, Buchanan Street becomes Sauchiehall Street, and the shopping gets cheaper and less elegant. While there's little of note to see, it's still an enjoyable stroll. Walk a few blocks and enjoy the people-watching. Just before the end of the pedestrian zone are two final attractions (both on the left): a sports club store and a tea house (at #217).*

❻ The Celtic Shop

This shop is extreme green. That's the color of Glasgow's dominant (for now) soccer team. It's hard to fathom the intensity of the rivalry between Glasgow's Celtic and Rangers. Celtic, founded by an Irish Catholic priest to raise money for poor Irish immigrants in the East End, is—naturally—green and favored by Catholics. The Rangers, with team colors of the Union Jack (red, white, and blue), are more likely to be supported by Unionist and Protestant families. Today Celtic is in the major league and the Rangers (wracked recently by scandals) have fallen into a lower division. Wander into the shop (minimizing or hiding any red or blue you might be wearing). Check out the energy in the photos and shots of the stadium filled with 60,000 fans. Walk to the back and look for red or blue. You're in a world where those colors don't exist.

• *The Willow Tea Rooms, a smartly designed, affordable restaurant, is next door.*

Charles Rennie Mackintosh
(1868-1928)

During his lifetime, Charles Rennie Mackintosh brought an exuberant Art Nouveau influence to the architecture of his hometown. His designs challenged the city planners of this otherwise practical, working-class port city to create beauty in the buildings they commissioned. A radical thinker, he freely shared credit with his artist wife, Margaret MacDonald. (He once famously said, "I have the talent...Margaret has the genius.")

When Mackintosh was a young student at the Glasgow School of Art, the Industrial Age dominated life here. Factories belched black soot into the city as they burned coal and forged steel. Mackintosh and his circle of artist friends drew their solace and inspiration from nature (just as the Romantics had before them) and created some of the original Art Nouveau buildings, paintings, drawings, and furniture.

As a student traveling abroad in Italy, Mackintosh ignored the famous Renaissance paintings inside the museum walls and set up his easel to paint the exteriors of churches and buildings instead. He rejected the architectural traditions of ancient Greece and Rome. In Venice and Ravenna, he fell under the spell of Byzantine design, and in Siena he saw a unified, medieval city design he would try to import—but with a Scottish flavor and Glaswegian palette—to his own hometown.

His first commission came in 1893, to design an extension to the Glasgow Herald building. More work soon followed, including the Glasgow School of Art and the Willow Tea Rooms 10 years later. Mackintosh envisioned a world without artistic borders, where an Islamic flourish could find its way onto a workaday building in a Scottish city. Inspired by the great buildings of the past and by his Art Nouveau peers, he in turn influenced others, such as painter Gustav Klimt and Bauhaus founder Walter Gropius. As is the fate of many artists, his vision was not as appreciated in his own time as it is now. When he died, he had only £88 to his name. But today, a century after Scotland's greatest architect set pencil to paper, his hometown is at last celebrating his unique vision.

❼ Willow Tea Rooms

This delightful black-and-white space is an Art Nouveau masterpiece by Charles Rennie Mackintosh. Visitors are welcome to browse.

Mackintosh made his living from design commissions, including multiple tearooms for businesswoman Kate Cranston. A well-known control freak, Mackintosh designed everything here—down to the furniture, lighting, and cutlery. He took his theme for the café from the name of the street it's on—*saugh* is Scots for willow, and *haugh* for meadow.

In the design of these tearooms, there was a meeting of the (very modern) minds. Cranston wanted a place for women to be

able to gather while unescorted, in a time when traveling solo could give a woman a less-than-desirable reputation. An ardent women's rights supporter, Cranston requested that the rooms be bathed in white, the suffragettes' signature color.

On the ground floor peruse the Mackintosh-inspired jewelry and the exhibit about his design in back. Then climb the stairs to find 20 tables run like a diner from a corner kitchen, serving simple meals to middle-class people—just as this place has since it opened in 1903. Then look for the almost-hidden Room de Luxe dining room (upstairs). While some parts of the Room de Luxe are reproductions (such as the chairs and the doors, which were too fragile to survive), the rest is just as it was in Mackintosh's day (same menu no matter where you eat: £5-9 meals, £13 tea, and more; Mon-Sat 9:00-17:00, Sun 11:00-16:15).

• *From here it's a five-minute, mostly uphill walk to the must-see Mackintosh sight in the town center. Continue a block and a half on Sauchiehall (with traffic), and make a right onto Dalhousie Street; the big, blond sandstone building on the left at the top of the hill is the Glasgow School of Art (described next). Tickets for the school tour are sold across the street in the new Reid Building (where tours start).*

If you have time to kill before your tour starts, consider eating lunch at the nearby **CCA Saramago Bar and Courtyard Café** *(on Sauchiehall, see page 870). Or, if you have an hour before your tour,*

you can head to the **Tenement House** *(listed at the end of this walk), a preserved home from the early 1900s—right when Mackintosh was doing his most important work.*

❽ Glasgow School of Art

A pinnacle of artistic and architectural achievement—worth ▲—the Glasgow School of Art presented a unique opportunity for Charles Rennie Mackintosh to design a massive project entirely to his own liking, down to every last detail. Those details—from a fireplace that looks like a kimono to windows that soar for multiple stories—are the beauty of the Glasgow School of Art.

Because the Glasgow School of Art is still a working school, the interior can only be visited by one-hour guided tour. The tour fees help fund the conservation of Mackintosh's work and, as a bonus, you get to meet and enjoy the accent of a smart, young Glasgow art student.

Each year in early June, the **Degree Show** opens the entire building to the public—for free—for a week. This is when tomorrow's stars in design—graduating art students—show their work. While there are no guided tours during this period, it is the best time to see the art school, with the building used as it was intended.

Cost and Hours: £10 guided tour, usually daily at 11:00, 13:00, and 15:00, hourly at busy times. Tip the starving student guides a pound or two if they give a good spiel. In the summer, tours run more frequently but fill up quickly (confirm times and reserve a spot by booking online, calling, or emailing the shop, open daily April-Sept 10:30-18:30, Oct-March 10:30-17:00; tel. 0141/353-4526—provide call-back number if leaving a message, www.gsa.ac.uk/visit-gsa/tours, tours@gsa.ac.uk). No photos are allowed on the tour. Serious admirers may also want to ask about the 2.5-hour Mackintosh-themed city walking tours given by students (£20, both tours £24, July-Aug only).

Visiting the School: Mackintosh loved the hands-on ideology of the Arts and Crafts movement, but he was also a practical Scot. Study the outside of the building. Those protruding wrought-iron brackets that hover outside the multi-paned windows were a new invention during the time of the Industrial Revolution; they reinforce the big, fragile glass windows, allowing natural light to pour in to the school. Mackintosh brought all the most recent technologies to this work and added them to his artistic palate—which also merged clean Modernist lines, Asian influences, and Art Nouveau flourishes.

When the building first opened, it was modern and minimalist. Other elements were added later, such as the lobby's tile mosaics depicting the artistic greats, including mustachioed Mackintosh (who hovers over the gift shop).

As you tour the school, you'll see how Mackintosh—who'd been a humble art student himself not too long before he designed this building—strove to create a space that was both artistically innovative and completely functional for students. The plaster replicas of classical sculptures lining the halls were part of Mackintosh's vision to inspire students by the greats of the past. You'll likely see students and their canvases lining the halls.

Linking these useable spaces are clever artistic patterns and puzzles that Mackintosh embedded to spur creative thought. If you notice a design that looks like it is repeated elsewhere, look again. No two motifs are exactly alike, just as nothing is exactly the same in nature.

Mackintosh cleverly arranged the school so that the cellar studios are bathed in intense natural light. And yet, as you climb to the top of the building—which you'd expect be the brightest, most light-filled area—the space becomes dark and gloomy, and the stairwell is encumbered by a cage-like structure.

During the tour, you'll be able to linger a few minutes in the major rooms, such as the remarkable forest-like library and the furniture gallery (including some original tables and chairs from the Willow Tea Rooms). Walking through the GSA, remember that this work was the Art Nouveau original, and that Frank Lloyd Wright, the Art Deco Chrysler Building, and everything that resembles it came well after Charles Rennie Mack's time.

• *To finish this walk, head north from the Glasgow School of Art on Scott Street. Just past the crest of the hill, make a left onto Buccleuch Street. After three blocks, the last house on the left is the...*

❾ Tenement House

Here's a chance to drop into a perfectly preserved 1930s-era middle-class residence. The National Trust for Scotland bought this otherwise ordinary row home, located in a residential neighborhood, because of the peculiar tendencies of Miss Agnes Toward (1886-1975). For five decades, she kept her home essentially unchanged. The kitchen calendar is still set for 1935, and canisters of licorice powder (a laxative) still sit on the bathroom shelf. It's a time-warp experience, where Glaswegian old-timers enjoy coming to reminisce about how they grew up.

Buy your ticket on the main floor, and poke around the little museum on the ground floor. You'll learn that in Glasgow, a "tenement" isn't a slum—it's simply an apartment house. In fact, tenements like these were typical for every class except the richest.

Head upstairs to the apartment, which is staffed by caring volunteers. Ring the doorbell to be let in. Ask them why the bed is in the kitchen or why the rooms still smell like natural gas. As you look through the rooms laced with Victorian trinkets—such as the ceramic dogs on the living room's fireplace mantle—consider how different they are from Mackintosh's stark, minimalist designs from the same period.

Cost and Hours: £6.50, £3.50 guidebook, March-Oct daily 13:00-17:00, last entry 30 minutes before closing, closed Nov-Feb, no photos allowed, 145 Buccleuch Street (pronounced "ba-KLOO") down off the top of Garnethill, tel. 0844-493-2197, www.nts.org.uk.

• *Our walk is finished. To get to Sauchiehall Street (with the nearest bus stop and taxis), exit the Tenement House, cross the street, go left, and follow the sidewalk down the hill toward the traffic noise. Pass under the pedestrian bridge and curve around to arrive at the far end of Sauchiehall.*

More Sights in Glasgow

Cathedral Precinct, with a Hint of Medieval Glasgow

Very little remains of medieval Glasgow, but when you visit the cathedral and the area around it, you're visiting the birthplace of the city. The first church was built here in the seventh century. Today's towering cathedral is mostly 13th-century—the only great Scottish church to survive the Reformation intact. In front you'll see an attention-grabbing statue of David Livingstone (1813-1873). Livingstone—the Scottish missionary/explorer/cartographer who discovered a huge waterfall in Africa and named it in honor of his queen, Victoria—was born eight miles from here.

Nearby, the Provand's Lordship is Glasgow's only secular building dating from the Middle Ages. The St. Mungo Museum of Religious Life and Art, built on the site of the old Bishop's Castle, is a unique exhibit covering the spectrum of religions. And the Necropolis, blanketing the hill behind the cathedral, provides an atmospheric walk through a world of stately Victorian tombstones. From there you can scan the city and look down on the brewery where Tennent's Lager (a longtime Glasgow favorite) has been made since 1885.

The four main sights, including the cathedral, are within close range of each other. As you face the cathedral, the St. Mungo Museum is on your right (with handy public WCs), the Provand's Lordship is across the street from St. Mungo, and the Necropolis is behind the cathedral and toward the right.

To reach these sights from the TI, head up Buchanan Street and turn right on Bath Street, which soon becomes Cathedral Street, and walk about 15 minutes (or hop a bus along the main drag—try bus #38, or #57, confirm with driver that the bus stops at the cathedral). If you'll be heading to the Kelvingrove Gallery after your visit: From the cathedral, walk two blocks up Castle Street and catch bus #19 (on the cathedral side) to the gallery.

▲Glasgow Cathedral

This blackened, Gothic cathedral is a rare example of an intact pre-Reformation Scottish cathedral. (It was once known as "the Pink Church" for the tone of its stone. But with Industrial Age soot and modern pollution, it blackened. Cleaning would damage the integrity of the stone structure so it was left black.) While the zealous Reformation forces of John Knox ripped out the stained glass and the ornate chapels of the Catholic age, they left the church standing. Look up to see the wooden barrel-vaulted ceiling, and take in the beautifully decorated section over the choir ("quire"). The choir screen is the only pre-Reformation screen surviving in Scotland. It divided the common people from the priests and big shots of the day, who got to worship closer to the religious action. Standing at the choir, turn around to look down the nave at the west wall, and notice how the right wall lists. (Don't worry; it's been listing—and still standing—for 800 years.) The cathedral's glass dates mostly from the 19th century. One window on the right side of the choir, celebrating the 14 trades of Glasgow, dates from 1951.

Step into the lower church (down stairs on right as you face the choir), where the central altar sits upon St. Mungo's tomb. Mungo was the seventh-century Scottish monk and mythical founder of Glasgow who established the first wooden church on this spot and gave Glasgow its name. Notice the ceiling bosses (decorative caps where the ribs come together) with their colorfully carved demons, dragons, and skulls.

Cost and Hours: Free, suggested donation £3; April-Sept Mon-Sat 9:30-17:30, Sun 13:00-17:00; Oct-March Mon-Sat 9:30-16:30, Sun 13:00-16:30, ask about free guided tours; last entry 30 minutes before closing, near junction of Castle and Cathedral Streets, tel. 0141/552-8198, www.glasgowcathedral.org.uk.

Necropolis

From the cathedral, a lane leads over the "bridge of sighs" into the park filled with grand tombstones. Glasgow's huge burial hill has a wistful, ramshackle appeal. A stroll among the tombstones of the eminent Glaswegians of the 19th century gives a glimpse of Victorian Glasgow and a feeling for the confidence and wealth of the second city of the British Empire in its glory days.

With the Industrial Age (in the early 1800s), Glasgow's population tripled to 200,000. The existing churchyards were jammed and unhygienic. The city needed a beautiful place in which to bury its beautiful citizens, so this grand necropolis was established. As Presbyterians are more into simplicity, the statuary is simpler than in a Catholic cemetery. Wandering among the disintegrating memorials to once important people, I thought about how, someday, everyone's tombstone will fall over and no one will care.

The highest pillar in the graveyard is a memorial to John Knox. The Great Reformer (who's actually buried in Edinburgh) looks down at the cathedral he wanted to strip of all art, and even tear down. (The Glaswegians rallied to follow Knox, but saved the church.) If the cemetery's main black gates are closed, see if you can get in and out through a gate off the street to the right.

▲St. Mungo Museum of Religious Life and Art

This interesting museum, next to the cathedral, aims to promote religious understanding. Built in 1990 upon the site of the old Bishop's Castle, it provides a handy summary of major and minor world religions, showing how each faith handles various rites of passage across the human life span: birth, puberty, marriage, death, and everything in between and after. Start with the 10-minute video overview on the first floor, and finish with a great view from the top floor of the cathedral and Necropolis.

Cost and Hours: Free, suggested donation £3, Tue-Thu and Sat 10:00-17:00, Fri and Sun 11:00-17:00, closed Mon, free WCs downstairs, cheap ground-floor café, 2 Castle Street, tel. 0141/276-1625, www.glasgowmuseums.com.

Provand's Lordship

With low beams and medieval decor, this creaky home—supposedly the "oldest house in Glasgow"—is the only secular building surviving in Glasgow from the Middle Ages. It displays the *Lifestyles of the Rich and Famous*...circa 1471. The interior, while sparse and stony, shows off a few pieces of furniture from the 16th, 17th, and 18th centuries. Out back, explore the St. Nicholas Garden, which was once part of a hospital that dispensed herbal remedies. The plaques in each section show the part of the body each plant is used to treat.

Cost and Hours: Free, small donation requested, Tue-Thu and Sat 10:00-17:00, Fri and Sun 11:00-17:00, closed Mon, across the street from St. Mungo Museum at 3 Castle Street, tel. 0141/552-8819, www.glasgowmuseums.com.

Away from the Center

▲▲Riverside Museum of Transport and Travel

Located along the River Clyde, this high-tech, extremely kid-friendly museum is dedicated to all things transportation-related. Named the European museum of the year in 2013, a visit here is a must for anyone interested in transportation and how it has shaped society. Highlights of its vast collection include the world's oldest bicycle, stagecoaches, locomotives, a re-creation of a circa-1900 street (with video clips of local seniors in time-warp shops reminiscing—like about the time the little girl noticed her daddy was selling things to the pawn shop to pay the rent).

A highlight is the shipping section, commemorating Glasgow's shipbuilding era. Exhilarating newsreels show that proud moment when "the band plays, the minister prays, the lady sponsor gives the name, the crowds cheer, and seconds later a new ship takes to the water for the first time."

Upon entering, find out about upcoming tours and activities (free, ask at info desk—to the right as you enter, near the shop—or listen for announcements). Be sure to pick up a map from the info desk, as the museum's open floor plan, spread over two levels and packed with original vehicles, can feel a bit like a traffic jam at rush hour.

Cost and Hours: Free, £1-2 suggested donation, Mon-Thu and Sat 10:00-17:00, Fri and Sun 11:00-17:00, restaurant (£6-9 meals, daily 12:00-16:00), first-floor coffee shop with basic drinks and snacks, 100 Pointhouse Place, tel. 0141/287-2720, www .glasgowmuseums.com.

Getting There: It's on the riverfront promenade, two miles west of the city center. **Bus #100** runs between the museum and George Square (2/hour, last departure from George Square at 15:02, operated by McColl's), or you can take a **taxi** (£6, 10-minute ride from downtown). The museum is also included on the **hop-on, hop-off sightseeing bus** route (described earlier, under "Getting Around Glasgow").

Nearby: The *Glenlee*, one of five remaining tall ships built in Glasgow in the 19th century, is moored just outside the museum on the River Clyde (free, daily 10:00-17:00, Nov-Feb until 16:00, tel. 01413/573-699, www.thetallship.com).

▲▲Kelvingrove Art Gallery and Museum

This museum is like a Scottish Smithsonian—with everything from a stuffed elephant to fine artwork by the great masters. The well-described contents are impressively displayed in a grand, 100-year-old, Spanish Baroque-style building. Purpose-built to house the city collection in 1902, it's divided into two sections. The "Life" section, in the West Court, features a menagerie of stuffed animals (including a giraffe, kangaroo, ostrich, and

moose) with a WWII-era Spitfire fighter plane hovering overhead. Branching off are halls with exhibits ranging from Ancient Egypt to "Scotland's First Peoples" to weaponry ("Conflict and Consequence"). The more serene "Expression" section, in the East Court, focuses on artwork, including Dutch, Flemish, French, and Scottish Colorists. On the second floor near the main hall, you'll find its most famous painting, Salvador Dalí's *Christ of St. John of the Cross,* which brought visitors to tears when it was first displayed here in the 1950s. This section also has exhibits on "Scottish Identity in Art" (letting you tour the country's scenic wonders and history on canvas) and on Charles Rennie Mackintosh and the Glasgow School. The Kelvingrove claims to be one of the most-visited museums in Britain—presumably because of all the field-trip groups you'll see here. Watching all the excited Scottish kids—their imaginations ablaze—is as much fun as the collection itself.

Cost and Hours: Free, suggested donation £3, Mon-Thu and Sat 10:00-17:00, Fri and Sun 11:00-17:00, free tours at 11:00 and 14:30, Argyle Street, tel. 0141/276-9599, www.glasgowmuseums .com.

Getting There: Ride the **subway** to the Kelvinhall stop; when you exit, turn left and walk five minutes. **Buses** #3, #7, and #19 all stop nearby—when you get off the bus, look for the huge red-brick building. It's also on the hop-on, hop-off bus route.

Organ Concerts: At the top of the main hall, the huge pipe organ booms with a daily recital at 13:00 (15:00 on Sunday, 30-45 minutes).

▲Burrell Collection

This eclectic art collection of a wealthy local shipping magnate is one of Glasgow's top destinations, but it's three miles outside the

city center. If you'd like to visit, plan to make an afternoon of it, and leave time to walk around the surrounding park, where Highland cattle graze. The diverse contents of this museum include sculptures (from Roman to Rodin), stained glass, tapestries, furniture, Asian and Islamic works, and halls of paintings—starring Cézanne, Renoir, Degas, and a Rembrandt self-portrait.

Cost and Hours: Free, Mon-Thu and Sat 10:00-17:00, Fri and Sun 11:00-17:00, Pollok Country Park, 2060 Pollokshaws Road, tel. 0141/287-2550, www.glasgowmuseums.com.

Getting There: From downtown, take **bus** #57 to Pollokshaws Road, or take a train to the Pollokshaws West train station; the entrance is a 10-minute walk from the bus stop and the train station. By **car**, follow the M-8 to exit at Junction 22 onto the M-77 Ayr; exit Junction 1 on the M-77 and follow signs.

Nightlife in Glasgow

Glasgow has a youthful vibe, and its nightlife scene is renowned. The city is full of live music acts and venues. Walking through the city center, you'll pass at least one club or bar on every block. For the latest, pick up a copy of *The List* (sold at newsstands) or the *Gig Guide*. For nightlife suggestions in the West End, see that section under "Eating in Glasgow," later.

Sleeping in Glasgow

Near the Glasgow School of Art

The area just west of the school has a few decent accommodations options, including a fine guesthouse in a church building (Adelaides), an Ibis chain hotel, and a buffet line of tired, basic B&Bs along Renfrew Street. From here you can walk downhill into the downtown core in about 10 to 15 minutes (or take a £5 taxi). If approaching by car, you can't drive down one-way Renfrew Street from the city center. Instead, from busy Sauchiehall Street, go up Scott Street or Rose Street, turn left onto Buccleuch Street, and circle around to Renfrew Street.

South of Sauchiehall Street

$$ Adelaides Guest House rents eight clean and cheerful rooms in a multitasking church building that also houses a theater and nursery school. Ted and Lisa run the place with warmth and quirky humor (S-£37, Sb-£55, Db-£69, family deals, includes very basic breakfast, £5.50 cooked breakfast available Mon-Fri, guest computer, 209 Bath Street, tel. 0141/248-4970, www.adelaides .co.uk, reservations@adelaides.co.uk).

$$ Ibis Glasgow, part of the modern hotel chain, has 141 cookie-cutter rooms with blond wood and predictable comfort (Sb/Db-£56 on weeknights, £69 on weekends, £85 "event rate" during festivals and in Aug, breakfast-£8, air-con, pay guest computer, free Wi-Fi in lobby, elevator, restaurant, hiding behind a big Novotel at 220 West Regent Street, tel. 0141/225-6000, www .ibishotel.com, h3139@accor.com).

North of Sauchiehall, on Renfrew Street

These places, all on Renfrew Street, offer instant immersion into Glasgow's working-class roots. Adjust your expectations: Each comes with tired public spaces, past-their-prime rooms, and a touch of indifference. But breakfast is included and the prices are competitive.

$$ Rennie Mackintosh Art School Hotel has 24 rooms— some redecorated—and hints of Glasgow's favorite architect (slippery rates change with demand, but generally Sb-£40-55; Db-£55-60 Sun-Thu, £55 Fri-Sat; family rooms around £100, free Wi-Fi, 218-220 Renfrew Street, tel. 0141/333-9992, www.rmg hotels.com, rennie@rmghotels.com).

$$ Victorian House Hotel is a crank-'em-out place with a friendly staff and 58 worn but workable rooms sprawling through several old townhouses (S-£32, Sb-£39, Db-£60, lots of stairs and no elevator, free Wi-Fi, 212 Renfrew Street, tel. 0141/332-0129, www.thevictorian.co.uk, info@thevictorian.co.uk).

Sleep Code

(£1 = about $1.60, country code: 44, area code: 0141)
S = Single, **D** = Double/Twin, **T** = Triple, **Q** = Quad, **b** = bathroom,
s = shower only. You can assume credit cards are accepted
unless otherwise noted.

To help you sort easily through these listings, I've divided
the accommodations into two categories based on the price
for a standard double room with bath (during high season):

$$ Higher Priced—Most rooms £50 or more.
$ Lower Priced—Most rooms less than £50.

Prices can change without notice; verify the hotel's cur-
rent rates online or by email. For the best prices, always book
direct.

GLASGOW

$$ Willow Guest House feels the most boutique, with 39
rooms—all with private bath (Sb-£40-45, Db-£60-70, family
rooms-£95, free Wi-Fi, 228 Renfrew Street, tel. 0141/332-2332,
www.willowguesthouseglasgow.com).

$$ Alba Lodge Guest House, at the end of the Renfrew row,
has 15 mostly en suite rooms and featureless common areas (Sb-
£35, Db-£52, Tb-£72, Qb-£89, free Wi-Fi, 232 Renfrew Street,
tel. 0141/332-2588, www.albalodge.co.uk, info@albalodge.co.uk).

$ Hampton Court Guest House, with 18 basic rooms (most
set up for families), drapes visitors in tartan. Run by the hard-
working Purewal family, who offer a warm welcome and friendly
respite, their house is the pearl on this oyster of a street (Sb-£36,
Db-£55-59, family rooms-£78-129, free Wi-Fi, 230 Renfrew
Street, tel. 0141/332-6623, info@hamptoncourtguesthouse.com).

Elsewhere in Central Glasgow

$$ Premier Inn George Square is a family-friendly chain hotel
in the Merchant City district, close to Queen Street Station (Sb/
Db-£61, Db for up to 2 adults and 2 kids-£69-100, cheaper midweek and in winter—see page 24 for tips on getting the best deal,
elevator, pay Wi-Fi, 187 George Street, tel. 08715-278-440, www
.premierinn.com).

$$ Babbity Bowster, named for a traditional Scottish dance,
is a pub and restaurant renting six simple, mod rooms up top.
It's located in the trendy Merchant City on the eastern fringe of
downtown, near several clubs and restaurants (Sb-£45, Db-£60,
breakfast-£6, lots of stairs and no elevator, 10-minute walk from
Central Station, 16-18 Blackfriars Street, tel. 0141/552-5055,

Central Glasgow Hotels & Restaurants

TO EDINBURGH

N

TENEMENT HOUSE

FOOT-BRIDGE

TO WEST END ↗ ⑬

TO KELVINGROVE MUSEUM

CHARING CROSS STN.

SAUCHIEHALL

School OF ART

Ⓢ Cowcaddens

COWCADDENS

RENFREW

STREET

200 YARDS
200 METERS

TO RIVERSIDE MUSEUM OF TRANSPORT

A-814

FOOT-BRIDGE

CENTRAL STATION

P

ARGYLE

BROOMIELAW

RIVER CLYDE

KINGSTON BRIDGE

TO AIRPORT & OBAN VIA A-82

TO BURRELL COLLECTION ↓

THE LIGHTHOUSE

Ⓢ St. Enoch

⑥

GLASGOW

www.babbitybowster.com, babbity@btinternet.com). The ground-floor pub serves £5-9 pub grub (daily 12:00-22:00); the first-floor restaurant, run by a French chef, offers £14-17 main dishes (Fri-Sat only 18:30-21:30, closed Sun-Thu).

$ **Euro Hostel** is the best bet for hostel beds in the city center. Part of a chain, this place is a lively hive of backpacker activity, with 364 beds on nine floors, plus pay guest computer, free Wi-Fi in the bar, a kitchen, and friendly staff (request a room on a higher floor and in the back for maximum quiet; very slippery rates, but figure £13-20 bunk in 4- to 14-bed dorm with bathroom, Sb-£29-40, Db-£36-52, couples should request a double or else end up with a bunk-bed, includes continental breakfast, elevator, laundry-£4/load, 318 Clyde Street, tel. 08455-399-956, www.euro-hostels.co.uk, reservations@euro-hostels.co.uk). It's on the busy

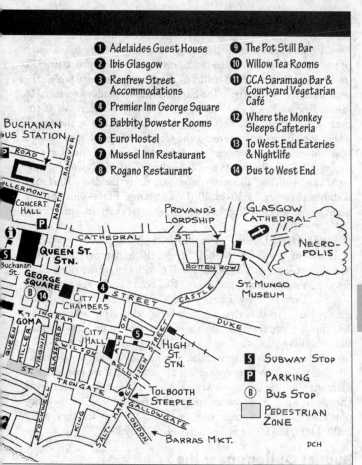

1. Adelaides Guest House
2. Ibis Glasgow
3. Renfrew Street Accommodations
4. Premier Inn George Square
5. Babbity Bowster Rooms
6. Euro Hostel
7. Mussel Inn Restaurant
8. Rogano Restaurant
9. The Pot Still Bar
10. Willow Tea Rooms
11. CCA Saramago Bar & Courtyard Vegetarian Café
12. Where the Monkey Sleeps Cafeteria
13. To West End Eateries & Nightlife
14. Bus to West End

S SUBWAY STOP
P PARKING
B BUS STOP
☐ PEDESTRIAN ZONE

main thoroughfare past Central Station, along the River Clyde, near some seedy areas.

Eating in Glasgow

Many of Glasgow's fancier eateries serve "pre-theatre menus"— affordable, fixed-price meals served before 19:00.

In the City Center

Mussel Inn offers light, good-value fish dinners and seafood plates in an airy, informal environment. The restaurant is a cooperative, owned and run by shellfish farmers. Their £10 "kilo pot" of Scottish mussels is popular with locals and big enough to share (£7-8 small grilled platters, £11-18 meals, Mon-Fri 12:00-14:30 &

17:00-22:00, Sat 12:00-22:00, Sun 12:30-22:00, 157 Hope Street, between St. Vincent and West George Streets, tel. 0141/572-1405).

Rogano is a time-warp Glasgow institution that retains much of the same classy Art Deco interior it had when it opened in 1935. You half-expect to see Bacall and Bogart at the next table. The restaurant has three parts. The bar in front has outdoor seating (£6 lunch sandwiches, £12-15 meals). The fancy dining room at the back of the main floor smacks of the officers' mess on the *Queen Mary*, which was built here on the Clyde during the same period (£20-24 meals with a focus on seafood). A more casual yet still dressy bistro in the cellar is filled with 1930s-Hollywood glamour (£11-14 meals, £15 afternoon tea; daily 12:00-21:30, fancy restaurant closed 14:30-18:00, 11 Exchange Place—just before giant archway from Buchanan Street, reservations smart, tel. 0141/248-4055).

And More: Dozens of restaurants line the main commercial areas of town: Sauchiehall Street, Buchanan Street, and the Merchant City area. Many are similar, with trendy interiors, Euro disco-pop soundtracks, and dinner for about £15-20 per person.

For Your Whisky: **The Pot Still** is an award-winning malt whisky bar from 1835 that boasts a formidable array of more than 300 choices. You'll see locals of all ages sitting in its leathery interior, watching football (soccer), and discussing their drinks. They have whisky aged in sherry casks, whisky preferred by wine drinkers, and whisky from every region of Scotland. Give the friendly bartenders a little background on your beverage tastes, and they'll narrow down a good choice for you from their long list (whisky runs £2-55 a glass, average price £4-5, £2.50 pasties and pies, daily 11:00-24:00, 154 Hope Street, tel. 0141/333-0980).

Budget Options near the Glasgow School of Art

The **Willow Tea Rooms,** designed by Charles Rennie Mackintosh, has a diner-type eatery and a classy Room de Luxe dining room (described on page 857 of the self-guided walk). The cheap and cheery menu covers both dining areas (£4-7 breakfasts, £5 sandwiches, £7-9 salads and main dishes, £13 afternoon tea served all day, gluten-free options, Mon-Sat 9:00-17:00, Sun 11:00-16:15, 217 Sauchiehall Street, tel. 0141/332-0521, www.willowtearooms.co.uk).

CCA Saramago Bar and Courtyard Vegetarian Café, located on the first floor of Glasgow's edgy contemporary art museum, charges art-student prices for its designer, animal-free food (such as tasty roast beetroot and avocado salads). An 18th-century facade, discovered when the site was excavated to build the gallery, looms over the courtyard restaurant (£3-4 small plates,

£7-9 main courses, food served Mon-Sat 12:00-22:00, closed Sun, free Wi-Fi, 350 Sauchiehall Street, tel. 0141/332-7959).

Where the Monkey Sleeps is the Glasgow School of Art's cheap student cafeteria. It's your chance to mingle with the city's next generation of artists and hear more of that lilting Glaswegian accent (if open, generally Sept-June Mon-Fri 8:00-17:00, closed Sat-Sun, tel. 0141/353-4728).

In the West End

The hip, lively residential neighborhood/university district called the West End is worth exploring, particularly in the evening. A collection of fun eateries and bars lines Ashton Lane, just off bustling Byres Road (the scene continues to the left along Cresswell Lane). It's a short 10-minute walk from the nearby Kelvingrove Gallery and convenient to downtown as it's right at the Hillhead subway station.

Before choosing a place, take a stroll and scout the whole scene. The subway station is on Byres Road. Across the street is Ruthven Lane (with two good restaurants) and around the corner is the popular, quaint, and cobbled Ashton Lane—lined with an array of restaurants and bars. Most have tables out front positioned nicely so you can watch the parade of people, and also have convivial gardens in the back.

Along Ashton Lane you'll find: **Ketchup** (an American-style diner), **Brel** (a Belgian beer bar), **The Wee Curry Shop** (£7-14 Scottish-Indian fusion main dishes, tel. 0141/357-5280), and **Jinty McGuinty's** Irish pub and beer garden.

Other favorites nearby include: The landmark **Ubiquitous Chip,** which has various pubs and restaurants sprawling through a deceptively large building (£5-9 pub grub, £6-9 starters, £16-28 restaurant meals, tel. 0141/334-5007), and **La Vallée Blanche,** which serves French cuisine with a Scottish twist, in a romantic dining area that resembles an upscale mountain lodge (£12 two-course early dinner specials, £11-18 main courses, closed Mon, 360 Byres Road, tel. 0141/334-3333).

On nearby Cresswell Lane, consider **Café Andaluz,** which offers £4-9 tapas and sangria behind lacy wooden screens, as the waitstaff clicks past on the cool tiles (2 Cresswell Lane, tel. 0141/339-1111).

Along Ruthven Lane (across Byre's Road from the subway station) are two fine options: one Scottish and one Vietnamese, both with inside and outside seating.

Bothy Restaurant offers tasty, traditional Scottish fayre and a warm welcome (mains £10-18, 11 Ruthven Lane, tel. 0141/334-4040).

The Hanoi Bike Shop, a rare Vietnamese restaurant (opened

2013), serves Asian tapas that are healthy and tasty, using local produce. With tight seating and friendly service, the place has a nice energy (small plates for around £5 each, homemade desserts, kitchen open daily 12:00-23:00, 8 Ruthven Lane, tel. 0141/334-7165).

West End Nightlife: **Òran Mòr,** a converted 1862 church overlooking a busy intersection, is one of Glasgow's most popular hangouts. It's a five-minute walk from the recommended restaurants (at the intersection of Byres and Great Western Road). In addition to hosting an atmospheric bar, outdoor beer garden, and brasserie, the building's former nave (now decorated with funky murals) has a downstairs nightclub featuring everything from rock shows to traditional Scottish music nights (brasserie serves £7-18 main dishes; pub with dressy conservatory or outdoor beer garden serves £3-10 pub grub; daily 9:00-very late, food served Mon-Wed 9:00-21:00, Thu-Sat 9:00-19:00, Sun 10:00-21:00, top of Byres Road at 731-735 Great Western Road, tel. 0141/357-6200).

Hillhead Bookclub Bar is a historic building cleared out to make room for fun, disco, pub grub, and lots of booze. It's a youthful and quirky art-school scene, with lots of beers on tap, creative cocktails, retro computer games, ping-pong, and theme evenings (just off Byres Road at 17 Vinicombe Street, tel. 0141/576-1700).

Getting to the West End: It's easiest to take the subway to Hillhead, which is a one-minute walk from Ashton Lane (exit the station to the left, then take the first left to find the lane). From the city center, you can also take a £5-6 taxi.

Glasgow Connections

Traveline Scotland has a journey planner that's linked to all of Scotland's train and bus schedule info. Go online (www.travelinescotland.com); call them at tel. 0871-200-2233; or use the individual websites listed below. If you're connecting with Edinburgh, note that the train is faster but the bus is cheaper.

By Train
From Glasgow's Central Station by Train to: Keswick in the Lake District (roughly hourly, 1.5 hours to Penrith, then catch a bus to Keswick, 45 minutes—see page 566), **Cairnryan** and ferry to Belfast (take train to Ayr, 2/hour, 1 hour; then ride bus to Cairnryan, 1 hour), **Blackpool** (hourly, 3.5-4 hours, transfer in Preston), **Liverpool** (1-2/hour, 3.5-4 hours, change in Wigan or Preston), **Durham** (2/hour, 3 hours, may require change in Edinburgh), **York** (2/hour, 3.5 hours, may require change in Edin-

burgh), **London** (1-2/hour, 4.5-5 hours direct). Train info: Tel. 0845-748-4950, www.nationalrail.co.uk.

From Glasgow's Queen Street Station by Train to: **Oban** (3-4/day, just 1/day Sun in winter, 3 hours), **Inverness** (10/day, 3 hours, 4 direct, the rest change in Perth), **Edinburgh** (4/hour, 50 minutes), **Stirling** (3/hour, 30-45 minutes), **Pitlochry** (9/day, 1.75-2 hours, some transfer in Perth).

By Bus

From Glasgow by Bus to: Edinburgh (4/hour, 1.25-1.5 hours), **Oban** (3-6/day, 2.75-3 hours, some with transfer in Tyndrum), **Fort William** (buses #914, #915, and #916; 8/day, 3 hours), **Glencoe** (buses #914, #915, and #916; 8/day, 2.5 hours), **Inverness** (7/day, 3.5-4.5 hours, some transfer in Perth), **Portree** on the Isle of Skye (buses #915 and #916, 3/day, 6.5-7.5 hours), **Pitlochry** (3/day, 2.25 hours, transfer in Perth). Bus info: Tel. 0871-266-3333, www.citylink.co.uk.

By Plane

Glasgow International Airport: Located eight miles west of the city, this airport (code: GLA) has currency-exchange desks, a TI, Internet access, luggage storage, and ATMs (tel. 0844-481-5555, www.glasgowairport.com). Taxis connect downtown to the airport for about £20. Your hotel can likely arrange a private taxi service for £14. Bus #500 zips to central Glasgow (daily at least 4/hour 5:00-23:00, then hourly through the night, £6/one-way, £8.50/round-trip, 15-20 minutes to both train stations, 25 minutes to the bus station, catch at bus stop #1).

Prestwick Airport: A hub for Ryanair (as well as the US military, which refuels planes here), this airport (code: PIK) is about 30 miles southwest of the city center (tel. 0871-223-0700, ext. 1006, www.gpia.co.uk). The best connection is by train, which runs between the airport and Central Station (Mon-Sat 3/hour, 45 minutes, half-price with Ryanair ticket). Stagecoach buses link the airport with Buchanan Street Station (£10, daily 4/hour plus a few nighttime buses, 45-60 minutes, check schedules at www.travelinescotland.com). If you're wondering about the Elvis Presley Bar, this airport is said to be the only piece of Britain that Elvis ever set foot upon. (Elvis' manager, the Dutch-born Colonel Tom Parker, had a legal problem with British immigration.)

Route Tips for Drivers

From England's Lake District to Glasgow: From Keswick, take the A-66 for 18 miles to the M-6 and speed north nonstop (via Penrith and Carlisle), crossing Hadrian's Wall into Scotland. The road becomes the M-74 just north of Carlisle. To slip through Glasgow quickly, leave the M-74 at Junction 4 onto the M-73, following signs to *M-8/Glasgow*. Leave the M-73 at Junction 2, exiting onto the M-8. Stay on the M-8 west through Glasgow, exit at Junction 30, cross Erskine Bridge, and turn left on the A-82, following signs to *Crianlarich* and *Loch Lomond*. (For a scenic drive through Glasgow, take exit 17 off the M-8 and stay on the A-82 toward Dumbarton.)

OBAN AND THE SOUTHERN HIGHLANDS

Oban • Islands of Mull and Iona
• Glencoe • Fort William

The area north of Glasgow offers a fun and easy dip into the southern part of the Scottish Highlands. Oban is a basket of Scottish traditions, with a handy pair of wind-bitten Hebrides islands (Mull and Iona) just a hop, skip, and jump away. Nearby, the evocative "Weeping Glen" of Glencoe aches with both history and natural beauty. Beyond that, Fort William anchors the southern end of the Caledonian Canal, offering a springboard to more Highlands scenery—this is where Britain's highest peak, Ben Nevis, keeps its head in the clouds, and where you'll find a valley made famous by a steam train carrying a young wizard named Harry.

Planning Your Time

Oban is a smart place to spend the night on a blitz tour of central Scotland; with more time to linger (and an interest in a day trip to the islands), spend two nights—Iona is worthwhile but adds a day to your trip. If you have a third night to spare, you can sleep in Iona and give yourself time to roam around Mull. Glencoe is worth considering as a very sleepy, rural overnight alternative to Oban, or if you have plenty of time and want a remote village experience on your way north.

Oban works well if you're coming from Glasgow, or even all the way from England's Lake District (for driving tips, see the end of this chapter). Assuming you're driving, here's an ambitious two-day plan for the Highlands (some of these sights are described in the next three chapters).

Day 1

Morning	Drive up from the Lake District, or linger in Glasgow.
11:30	Depart Glasgow.
12:00	Rest stop on Loch Lomond, then joyride on.
13:00	Lunch in Inveraray.
16:00	Arrive in Oban, tour whisky distillery (last tour earlier off-season), and drop by the TI.
20:00	Dine in Oban.

Day 2

9:00	Leave Oban.
10:00	Visit Glencoe museum and the valley's visitors center.
12:00	Drive to Fort William and follow the Caledonian Canal to Inverness, stopping at Fort Augustus to see the locks and along Loch Ness to search for monsters.
16:00	Visit the Culloden Battlefield (closes earlier off-season) near Inverness.
17:00	Drive south.
20:00	Arrive in Edinburgh.

With More Time

While you'll see the Highlands on the above itinerary, you'll whiz past them in a misty blur. With more time, head north from Fort William to the Isle of Skye, spend a night or two there, head over to Inverness via Loch Ness, and consider a stop in Pitlochry.

Getting Around the Highlands

By Car: Drivers enjoy flexibility and plenty of tempting stopovers. Barring traffic, you'll make great time on good, mostly two-lane roads. Be careful, but don't be too timid about passing; otherwise, diesel fumes and large trucks might be your main memory of driving in Scotland. As you drive along Loch Ness, antsy locals may ride your bumper. For step-by-step instructions, read the "Route Tips for Drivers" at the end of this chapter.

By Public Transportation: Glasgow is the gateway to this region (so you'll most likely have to transfer there if coming from Edinburgh). The **train** zips from Glasgow to Fort William, Oban, and Kyle of Lochalsh in the west; and up to Stirling, Pitlochry, and Inverness in the east. For more remote destinations (such as Glencoe), the bus is better.

Most of the **buses** you'll need are operated by Scottish Citylink. Pay the driver in cash when you board, or buy tickets in advance at local TIs or online at www.citylink.co.uk (during busy times, it's smart to buy your ticket ahead of time to guarantee a seat on the bus). The nondescript town of Fort William serves as a hub for Highlands buses. Note that bus frequency is substantially reduced on Sundays and off-season—during these times, always carefully confirm schedules locally. Unless otherwise noted, I've listed bus information for summer weekdays.

These buses are particularly useful for connecting the sights in this book:

Buses **#976** and **#977** connect Glasgow with Oban (3-6/day, 2.75-3 hours, some with transfer in Tyndrum).

Bus **#913** runs one daily direct route from Edinburgh to this region—stopping at Glasgow, Stirling, and Glencoe on the way to Fort William (allow 4 hours from Edinburgh to Fort William; 3/day with change in Glasgow on buses #900 and #914, 5 hours).

Bus **#978** connects Edinburgh with Oban, stopping in Stirling, but not Glencoe (1/day direct, 4 hours; 6 more/day with changes in Glasgow and/or Tyndrum, 5-5.5 hours).

Bus **#914** goes from Glasgow to Fort William, stopping at Glencoe (1/day, 3 hours).

Buses **#915** and **#916** follow the same route (Glasgow-Glencoe-Fort William), then continue all the way up to Portree on the Isle of Skye (3/day, 6.75 hours for the full run).

Bus **#918** goes from Oban to Fort William, stopping en route at Ballachulish near Glencoe (3/day in summer, 2/day off-season, never on Sun; 1 hour to Ballachulish, 1.5 hours total to Fort William).

Bus **#919** connects Fort William with Inverness (5/day, 2 hours).

Oban

Oban (pronounced "OH-bin") is called the "gateway to the isles." Equal parts functional and scenic, this busy little ferry-and-train

terminal has no important sights, but makes up the difference in character and a famous distillery. It's a low-key resort, with a winding promenade lined by gravel beaches, ice-cream stands, fish-and-chip joints, and a surprising diversity of good restaurants. When the rain clears, sun-starved Scots sit on benches along the Esplanade, leaning back to catch some rays. Wind, boats, gulls, layers of islands, and the promise of a wide-open Atlantic beyond give Oban a rugged charm.

Oban

1. Strathaven Terrace Accommodations
2. To Glenburnie House, The Barriemore & Kilchrenan House
3. The Rowantree Hotel
4. Backpackers Plus
5. Backpackers Plus Annexes (2)
6. SYHA Hostel
7. Jeremy Inglis' Hostel
8. Ee'usk & Piazza Restaurants
9. Coast Restaurant
10. Cuan Mòr Gastropub
11. Room 9 Restaurant
12. To Waypoint Bar & Grill (via Ferry)
13. Oban Fish & Chip Shop
14. The Oban Bay Fish & Chips; Skipinnish Ceilidh House
15. Shellfish Shack
16. The Kitchen Garden Deli & Café
17. Tesco Supermarket
18. Aulay's Bar
19. Great Western Hotel (Live Shows)
20. Cinema
21. Fancy That Shop (Internet)
22. West Coast Motors (Day Trips; Bag Storage)
23. Laundry
24. Bike Rental
25. Whisky Distillery
26. Oban War & Peace Museum

TO **2** & DUNLOLLIE CASTL

CORRAN

ST. COLUMBA

O B A N

B A Y

BOATS TO MULL & IONA

FERRY TERMINAL

SOUTH PIER

TO KERREA FERRY

100 YARDS

100 METERS

|||| STAIRS

P PARKING

OBAN

TO FORT WILLIAM & INVERNESS

LONGSDALE

Atlantis Sports & Leisure Centre

Oban Lawn Bowling Club

DUNOLLIE RD.

BREAD-ALBANE ST.

ALBERT LN.

DALRIACH ROAD

LAUREL RD.

McCAIG'S TOWER

DUNOLLIE TERR.

CORRAN ESPLANADE

GEORGE ST.

NURSERY

ALBERT RD.

CRAIGARD RD.

ARDCONNEL ROAD

ARDCONNEL TERR.

Post

North Pier

ROCKFIELD RD.

HILL ST.

STEVENSON ST.

TRAIN STN.

AIRDS CRES.

ARGYLL SQUARE

COMBE ST.

SHORE ST.

ALBANY

HIGH ST.

MKT. ST.

LIBRARY

DCH

OBAN

Orientation to Oban

Oban, with about 10,000 people, is where the train system of Scotland meets the ferry system serving the Hebrides islands. It's always been on the way to something. As "gateway to the isles," its center is not a square or market, but its harbor.

Oban seems dominated by Caledonian-MacBrayne, Scotland's biggest ferry company. CalMac's 30 ships serve 24 destinations and transport over 4 million passengers a year. The city's port has long been a lifeline to the islands.

With the arrival of the train in 1880, Oban became the unofficial capital of Scotland's west coast and a destination for tourists. Caledonian Hotel, the original terminus hotel that once served those train travelers, dominates the harborfront.

Herring was the first big industry, then came tobacco (imported from the American colonies), then whisky. It's rare to find a distillery in the middle of a town, but Oban grew up around its distillery. With the success of its whisky, the town enjoyed an invigorating confidence, optimism, and, in 1811, a royal charter. Today the big industry is tourism.

A dozen boats still fish commercially (the fish market is across the harbor). The local tourist board, in an attempt to entice people to stay, is trying to rebrand the town as a seafood capital rather than "gateway to the isles." As the ocean's supply has become depleted, most local fish is farmed. There's still plenty of shellfish.

At the height of the Cold War, Oban played a critical role when the world's first two-way transatlantic telephone cable was laid from Gallanach Bay to Newfoundland in 1956—a milestone in global communication. This technology provided the White House and the Kremlin with the "hotline" that was crucial in helping to resolve the Cuban Missile Crisis without a nuclear conflagration.

Oban's business action, just a couple of streets deep, stretches along the harbor and its promenade. Everything in Oban is close together, and the town seems eager to please its many visitors. There's live music nightly in several bars and restaurants; wool and tweed are perpetually on sale; and posters announce a variety of day tours to Scotland's wild and wildlife-strewn western islands.

Tourist Information

Oban's TI, located at the North Pier, sells bus and ferry tickets and has a fine bookshop. Stop by to get brochures and information on everything from bike rental to golf courses to horseback riding to rainy-day activities and more. They can also book you a room for a £4 fee (flexible hours, generally July-Aug daily 9:00-19:00; April-June Mon-Sat 9:00-17:30, Sun 10:00-17:00; Sept-Oct daily

10:00-17:00; Nov-March Mon-Sat 10:00-17:00, Sun 11:00-15:00; 3 North Pier, tel. 01631/563-122, www.oban.org.uk).

Events and Activities: Black-and-gold signboards around town show "What's On." Fun low-key activities may include open-mic, disco, or quiz theme nights in pubs; Scottish folk shows; pipe-band concerts; coffee meetings; accordion concerts; and—if you're lucky—duck races. There's often free live entertainment upstairs in the Great Western Hotel on the Esplanade (most nights at 20:30 year-round; Scottish Night with bagpipes and sometimes dancers generally Wed and Fri; call for details, tel. 01631/563-101). On Wednesday nights, the Oban Pipe Band plays in the town square. And the city hosts Highland Games every August (www.obangames.com).

Helpful Hints

Internet Access: There's free Wi-Fi all over town. **Fancy That** is a souvenir shop on the main drag with seven high-speed Internet terminals and Wi-Fi in the back room (£1/20 minutes, daily 9:30-17:00, until 22:00 July-Aug, 108 George Street, tel. 01631/562-996). To surf for free, get online at the **library** just above the ferry terminal; you can just show up, but it's smart to call ahead to book a 30-minute time slot (Mon and Wed 10:00-13:00 & 14:00-19:00, Thu until 18:00, Fri until 17:00, closed Sat afternoon and all day Tue and Sun, 77 Albany Street, tel. 01631/571-444).

Bookstore: Waterstones, a huge bookstore overlooking the harborfront, offers maps and a fine collection of books on Scotland (daily, 12 George Street, tel. 0843/290-8529).

Baggage Storage: The train station has luggage lockers (£3-5 depending on bag size). **West Coast Motors,** which sells bus tickets, has a pricey left-luggage service (£1/hour per piece, unsecured in main office, Mon-Fri 9:00-13:00 & 14:00-17:00, Sat 9:00-14:00, closed Sun, July-Sept open during lunch, can be sporadically closed Oct-May, at Queens Park Place, www.westcoastmotors.co.uk).

Laundry: You'll find **Oban Quality Laundry** tucked a block behind the main drag on Stevenson Street (£7-10/load for same-day drop-off service, no self-service, Mon-Fri 9:00-17:00, Sat 9:00-13:00, closed Sun, tel. 01631/563-554).

Supermarket: Tesco is a five-minute walk from the train station (Mon-Sat 6:00-24:00, Sun 8:00-20:00, WC in front by registers, inexpensive cafeteria; walk through Argyll Square and look for entrance to large parking lot on right, Lochside Street).

Bike Rental: Nevis Cycles is on the main drag (£10/half-day, £25/day, includes helmets, can pick up in Oban and drop off in Fort William or Inverness for extra charge, daily 10:00-17:00, 87 George Street, tel. 01631/566-033).

Bus Station: The "station" is just a pullout, marked by a stubby clock tower, at the roundabout just in front of the train station.

Cinema: The Phoenix Cinema closed down for two years and then was saved by the community. It's now volunteer-run and booming (140 George Street, www.obanphoenix.com).

Characteristic Pub: Aulay's Bar, with decor that shows off Oban's maritime heritage, has two sides, each with a different personality. Having a drink here invariably comes with a good "blether" (conversation), and the gang is local (8 Airds Crescent, just around the corner from the train station and ferry terminal).

Sights in Oban

▲West Highland Malt Scotch Whisky Distillery Tours

The 200-year-old Oban Whisky Distillery produces more than 16,000 liters a week and exports much of that to the US. They offer serious and fragrant one-hour tours explaining the process from start to finish, with two smooth samples (in the tasting room at the end of the tour, say "yes" when the guide asks if anyone is a whisky drinker and you may get a third taste), a whisky glass (normally sells for £6.50), and a discount coupon for the shop. This is the handiest whisky tour you'll see, just a block off the harbor and better than anything in Edinburgh. The exhibition that precedes the tour gives a quick, whisky-centric history of Scotland. In high season, these popular tours (which are limited to 16 people every 20-30 minutes) fill up quickly. Call, go online, or stop by in advance to reserve your time slot.

Cost and Hours: £7.50; July-Sept Mon-Fri 9:30-19:30, Sat-Sun 9:30-17:00; Easter-June and Oct daily 9:30-17:00; March-Easter and Nov Mon-Fri 10:00-17:00, closed Sat-Sun; Dec and Feb Mon-Fri 12:30-16:00, closed Sat-Sun; closed Jan; last tour 1.25 hours before closing, Stafford Street, tel. 01631/572-004, www.discovering-distilleries.com. Connoisseurs can ask about the new "vertical tasting" (sampling whisky by age) held in their warehouse (£30, 2 hours, likely July-Sept, Mon-Fri at 16:00 only).

Oban War & Peace Museum

Opened in 1995 on the 50th anniversary of Victory in Europe Day, this museum covers more than war and peace. Photos show Oban through the years, and a 15-minute looped video gives a simple tour around the region. Volunteer staffers love to chat about the exhibit—or anything else on your mind (free, daily 10:00-16:00, longer hours in summer, Corran Esplanade, next to Regent Hotel on the promenade, www.obanmuseum.org.uk).

Skipinnish Ceilidh House

On most nights mid-June through mid-September, you can stroll into Skipinnish on the main drag for Highland music, song, and dancing. The owners—professional musicians Angus and Andrew—invest in talented musicians and put on a good show, featuring live bands, songs sung in Gaelic, Highland dancing, and great Scottish storytelling. For many, the best part is the chance to learn some *ceilidh* (KAY-lee) dancing. These group dances are a lot of fun—wallflowers and bad dancers are warmly welcomed, and the staff is happy to give you pointers.

Cost and Hours: £10 music session, pricier for concerts with visiting big-name *ceilidh* bands, music four nights/week mid-June-mid-Sept usually starting around 20:30, 2 hours, check website for off-season show schedule, 34 George Street, tel. 01631/569-599, www.skipinnishceilidhhouse.com.

McCaig's Tower

The unfinished "colosseum" on the hill overlooking town was an employ-the-workers-and-build-me-a-fine-memorial project undertaken by an Oban tycoon in 1900. While the structure itself is nothing to see up close, a 10-minute hike through a Victorian residential neighborhood leads you to a peaceful garden and a commanding view. McCaig died before completing the structure, so his complete vision for it remains a mystery.

Atlantis Leisure Centre

This industrial-type sports center is a good place to get some exercise on a rainy day or let the kids run wild for a few hours. It has a rock-climbing wall, tennis courts, two playgrounds, and an indoor swimming pool with a big water slide. The center's outdoor playground is free and open all the time; the indoor "soft play centre" for children under five costs £3.60 per hour, per child.

Cost and Hours: Pool only-£4/adult, £2/child, no rental towels or suits, lockers-£0.20; day pass for everything-£12/adult, £8/child; Mon-Fri 7:00-22:00, Sat-Sun 9:00-18:00; open-swim pool hours vary by season—call or check online for exact times; on the north end of Dalriach Road, tel. 01631/566-800, www.atlantisleisure.co.uk.

Oban Lawn Bowling Club

The club has welcomed visitors since 1869. This elegant green is the scene of a wonderfully British spectacle of old men tiptoeing wishfully after their balls. It's fun to watch, and—if there's no match scheduled and the weather's dry—anyone can rent shoes and balls and actually play.

Cost and Hours: £4/person; informal hours, but generally daily 10:00-16:00 & 17:00 to "however long the weather lasts"; lessons at 13:45; just south of sports center on Dalriach Road, tel. 01631/570-808, www.obanbowlingclub.com.

OBAN

Dunollie Castle and Museum

In a park just a mile up the coast, this spartan, stocky castle with 10-foot walls is a delightful stroll from the town center. The ruins offer a commanding, windy view of the harbor, a strategic spot back in the days when transport was mainly by water. For more than a thousand years, clan chiefs ruled this region from this ancestral home of Clan MacDougall, but the castle was abandoned in 1746. The adjacent house, which dates from 1745, shows off the MacDougall clan's family heritage—much of it naval; docents explain the charming if humble exhibits.

While the castle and museum are, frankly, not much, the local pride in the display and the walk from town make the visit fun. To get there, stroll out of town along the harborfront promenade. At the war memorial (where there are inviting sea-view benches), cross the street. A gate leads to a little lane, lined with historic and nature boards along the way to the castle (£4, free Sun; April-Nov Mon-Sat 11:00-16:00, Sun 13:00-16:00; closed Dec-March, tel. 01631/570-625).

Near Oban
Isle of Kerrera

Functioning like a giant breakwater, the Isle of Kerrera (KEH-reh-rah) makes Oban possible. Just offshore from Oban, this stark but very green island offers a quick, easy opportunity to get that romantic island experience. While it has no proper roads, it offers nice hikes, a ruined castle, and a few sheep farms. You may see the Kerrera ferry filled with sheep heading for Oban's livestock market.

Although Kerrera dominates Oban's sea view, you'll have to head two miles south of town (follow the coast road past the ferry terminal) to catch the boat to the middle of the island (ferry-£4.50 round-trip, bikes free, 5-minute trip; Easter-Sept first ferry Mon-Sat at 8:45, then daily 2/hour 10:30-12:30 & 14:00-17:00, last ferry at 18:00; Oct-Easter 5-6/day, last ferry at 17:50 but changes with demand; at Gallanach's dock; tel. 01631/563-665, if no answer contact Oban TI for info; www.kerrera-ferry.co.uk). For an easier approach from the center of Oban, you can ride the free shuttle ferry between Oban's North Pier and the Kerrera Marina. The tiny boat is designed for customers of the recommended Waypoint Bar & Grill (must show your receipt on the way back). It's fine to just drop in for a drink after an island stroll to get your receipt.

Sleeping on Kerrera: To spend the night on the island, your only option is the **$ Kerrera Bunkhouse,** a newly refurbished 18th-century stable that can sleep up to eight people in four compartments (£15/person, £100 for the entire bunkhouse, includes bedding but not towels, cheaper for 2 nights or more, open year-round but must book ahead, kitchen, tel. 01631/566-367, www .kerrerabunkhouse.co.uk, info@kerrerabunkhouse.co.uk, Martin and Aideen). They also run a tea garden that serves meals (April-Sept daily 10:30-16:30, closed Oct-March).

Isle of Seil

Enjoy a drive, a walk, some solitude, and the sea. Drive 12 miles south of Oban on the A-816 to the B-844 to the Isle of Seil (pronounced "seal"), connected to the mainland by a bridge (which, locals like to brag, "crosses the Atlantic"...well, maybe a small part of it).

Just over the bridge on the Isle of Seil is a pub called **Tigh-an-Truish** ("House of Trousers"). After a 1745 English law forbade the wearing of kilts on the mainland, Highlanders on the island used this pub to change from kilts to trousers before they made the crossing. The pub serves great meals and good seafood dishes to those either in kilts or pants (pub open daily April-Oct 11:00-23:00—food served 12:00-14:00 & 18:00-20:30, Nov-March shorter hours and soup/sandwiches only, darts anytime, tel. 01852/300-242).

Seven miles across the island, on a tiny second island and facing the open Atlantic, is **Easdale,** a historic, touristy, windy little slate-mining town—with a slate-town museum and an incredibly tacky, egomaniac's "Highland Arts" shop (shuttle ferry goes the 300 yards). An overpriced direct ferry runs from Easdale to Iona; but, at twice the cost of the Mull-Iona trip, the same time on the island, and very little time with a local guide, it's hardly worth it. For a better connection to Iona, see page 892.

Tours from Oban

▲▲Nearby Islands

For the best day trip from Oban, tour the islands of Mull and Iona (offered daily Easter-Oct, described later)—or consider staying overnight on remote and beautiful Iona. With more time or other interests, consider one of many other options you'll see advertised.

Wildlife Tours

Those more interested in nature than church history will enjoy trips to the wildly scenic Isle of Staffa with Fingal's Cave (known for its basalt column formations—marking the Scottish end of the Giant's Causeway so famous in Northern Ireland). The journey to Treshnish Island brims with puffins, seals, and other sea critters. Several groups, including Sealife Adventures and SeaFari, run whale-watching tours that feature rare minke whales, basking sharks, bottlenose dolphins, and porpoises. Departures and options abound—check at the TI for information.

OBAN

Open-Top Bus Tours

If there's good weather and you don't have a car, take a spin out of Oban for views of nearby castles and islands, plus a stop near McCaig's Tower with a narration by the driver (£8, £7 if pre-booked online, valid for 24 hours, ticket also valid on regular service buses, late May-late Sept daily at 11:00 and 14:00, no tours off-season, 2.5 hours, departs from rail station, tel. 01412/040-444, www.city-sightseeing.com).

Caledonian MacBrayne Day Tours

Choose from an array of ferry and boat tours from Oban to the islands (daily 8:30-18:00, purchase at ferry terminal or at www.calmac.co.uk, tel. 0631/562-244).

Sleeping in Oban

B&Bs on Strathaven Terrace

Oban's B&Bs offer a better value than its hotels. None of these B&Bs accept credit cards; all have free Wi-Fi. The following B&Bs line up on a quiet, flowery street that's nicely located two blocks off the harbor, three blocks from the center, and a 10-minute walk from the train station. By car, as you enter town, turn left after King's Knoll Hotel, and take your first right onto Breadalbane Street. ("Strathaven Terrace" is actually just the name for this row of houses on Breadalbane Street.) The alley behind the buildings has parking for all of these places.

$$ Sandvilla B&B rents five fine rooms with sleek contemporary decor (Db-£60-70, Tb-£83-90, at #4, tel. 01631/562-803, www.holidayoban.co.uk, sandvilla@holidayoban.co.uk, Joyce and Scott).

$$ Gramarvin Guest House has four fresh and cheery rooms (Db-£55-70, £65 in Aug, Tb-£82-105, at #5, tel. 01631/564-622, www.gramarvin.co.uk, mary@gramarvin.co.uk, Mary).

$$ Raniven Guest House has five simple, tastefully decorated rooms and gracious, fun-loving hosts (Sb-£30-35, Db-£55-60, price depends on season, at #1, tel. 01631/562-713, www.raniven.co.uk, info@raniven.co.uk, Moyra and Stuart).

$$ Tanglin B&B, with five Grandma's house-homey rooms, comes with lively, chatty hosts Liz and Jim Montgomery, who create an easygoing atmosphere (S-£28, Db-£54-56, family room available, at #3, tel. 01631/563-247, mobile 0774/8305-891, jim tanglin@aol.com).

Guesthouses and Small Hotels

These options are a step up from the B&Bs—in terms of both amenities and price. Glenburnie House, Kilchrenan House, and The Barriemore are along the Esplanade, which stretches north

Sleep Code

(£1 = about $1.60, country code: 44, area code 01631)
S = Single, **D** = Double/Twin, **T** = Triple, **Q** = Quad, **b** = bathroom, **s** = shower only. Unless otherwise noted, you can assume credit cards are accepted at hotels and hostels—but not B&Bs—and breakfast is included.

To help you sort easily through these listings, I've divided the accommodations into three categories based on the price for a standard double room with bath (during high season):

$$$ Higher Priced—Most rooms £70 or more.
  $$ Moderately Priced—Most rooms between £30-70.
    $ Lower Priced—Most rooms £30 or less.

Prices can change without notice; verify the hotel's current rates online or by email. For the best prices, always book direct.

of town above a cobble beach (with beautiful bay views); they are a 5- to 10-minute walk from the center. The Rowantree is on the main drag in town.

$$$ Glenburnie House, a stately Victorian home, has an elegant breakfast room overlooking the bay. Its 12 spacious, comfortable, classy rooms feel like plush living rooms. There's a nice lounge and a tiny sunroom with a stuffed "hairy coo" head (Sb-£55, Db-£90-115, price depends on size and view, closed mid-Nov-March, free Wi-Fi, free parking, the Esplanade, tel. 01631/562-089, www.glenburnie.co.uk, stay@glenburnie.co.uk, Graeme).

$$$ Kilchrenan House, the turreted former retreat of a textile magnate, has 14 tastefully renovated, large rooms, most with bay views (Sb-£50, Db-£70-105, 2-night minimum, higher prices are for seaview rooms in June-Aug, lower prices are for back-facing rooms and Sept-May, stunning rooms #5, #9, and #15 are worth the few extra pounds, welcome drink of whisky or sherry, different "breakfast special" every day, closed Dec-Jan, a few houses past the cathedral on the Esplanade, tel. 01631/562-663, www.kilchrenanhouse.co.uk, info@kilchrenanhouse.co.uk, Colin and Frances).

$$$ The Rowantree Hotel is a group-friendly place with 24 renovated rooms reminiscent of a budget hotel in the US (complete with thin walls) and a central locale right on Oban's main drag (Sb-£60-90, Db-£100-160, includes breakfast, prices may be soft for walk-ins and off-season, easy parking, George Street, tel. 01631/562-954, www.rowantreehoteloban.co.uk).

$$$ **The Barriemore,** at the very end of Oban's grand waterfront Esplanade, comes with a nice patio, front sitting area, and well-appointed rooms. Some front-facing rooms have views; rooms in the modern addition in the back are cheaper (Sb-£65-75, Db-£90-110, Tb-£100-125, two ground-floor double mini suites with views-£130-165, less off-season, price depends on view, free Wi-Fi, the Esplanade, tel. 01631/566-356, www.barriemore-hotel .co.uk, reception@barriemore-hotel.co.uk, Sue and Jan).

Hostels

$ **Backpackers Plus** is the most central, laid-back, and fun, with a sprawling public living room, 48 beds, and a staff who is generous with travel tips (£17/bed, 6-12 bunks per room, includes breakfast, guest computer, free Wi-Fi, £4 laundry service for guests only, 10-minute walk from station, on Breadalbane Street, tel. 01631/567-189, www.backpackersplus.com, info@backpackersplus.com, Peter). Their bunkhouse across the street has several basic but cheerful private rooms that share a kitchen; a third property, at the top of the block, has seven private rooms, each with a bath (S-£17-23, Sb-£19-28, D-£46, Db-£54, T-£61-69, same contact info as hostel).

$ The HI-affiliated **SYHA hostel,** on the scenic waterfront Esplanade, is in a grand building with 98 beds and smashing views of the harbor and islands from the lounges and dining rooms. There are also some private rooms, including several that can usually be rented as twin rooms (£17.50-20/bed in 4- to 6-bed rooms with en-suite bathroom, bunk-bed Db-£46, Tb-£55-65, Qb-£75-88, price varies with demand, also has family rooms and 8-bed apartment with kitchen, £2/night more for nonmembers, breakfast-£4-6, dinner-£5.50-12, pay guest computer and Wi-Fi, great facilities, pay laundry, kitchen, tel. 01631/562-025, www.syha.org .uk, oban@syha.org.uk).

$ **Jeremy Inglis' Hostel** has 37 beds located two blocks from the TI and train station. This loosely run place feels more like a commune than a youth hostel...and it's cheap (£15/bed, S-£22, D-£30, cash only, includes linens, breakfast comes with Jeremy's homemade jam, free Wi-Fi, kitchen, no curfew, second floor at 21 Airds Crescent, tel. 01631/565-065, jeremyinglis@mctavishs .freeserve.co.uk).

Eating in Oban

Oban calls itself the "seafood capital of Scotland," and is passionate about good fish-and-chips. There are plenty of good fish places in town, but the two recommended fish-and-chips joints (listed at the end of this section) are the town favorites. Both have food to go and good seating inside.

OBAN

Ee'usk (a phonetic rendering of *iasg*, Scottish Gaelic for "fish") is a popular, stylish, family-run place on the waterfront. It has a casual-chic atmosphere, a bright and glassy interior, sweeping views on three sides, and fish dishes favored by both natives and tourists. Reservations are recommended every day in summer and on weekends off-season (£9-12 lunches, £13-20 dinners, daily 12:00-15:00 & 17:45-21:30, North Pier, tel. 01631/565-666, www.eeusk.com, MacLeod family).

Piazza, next door and also run by the MacLeods, has similar decor but serves Italian cuisine and offers a more family-friendly ambience. They have some outdoor seats and big windows facing the sea (£8-12 pizzas and pastas, daily 12:00-15:00 & 17:30-21:00, smart to reserve ahead July-Aug, tel. 01631/563-628).

Coast proudly serves fresh local fish, meat, and veggies in a mod pine-and-candlelight atmosphere. As everything is prepared and presented with care by husband-and-wife team Richard and Nicola—who try to combine traditional Scottish elements in innovative new ways—come here only if you have time for a slow meal (£10-13 lunches, £13-18 dinners, £13 two-course and £16 three-course specials, open daily 12:00-14:00 & 17:30-21:00, closed Sun for lunch, 104 George Street, tel. 01631/569-900).

Cuan Mòr is a popular gastropub that combines traditional Scottish with modern flair—both in its tasty cuisine and in its furnishings, made entirely of wood, stone, and metal scavenged from the beaches of Scotland's west coast (£6 lunches, £9-13 main courses, food served daily 12:00-22:00, brewery in the back, 60 George Street, tel. 01631/565-078).

Room 9 seats just 24 diners in one tiny light-wood room, and has a select menu of homemade nouvelle-cuisine dishes. It's owned and run with care by chef Michael (dinner only, £13-16 meals, Mon-Sat 17:30-21:30, closed Sun, reservations smart Fri-Sat, 9 Craigard Road, tel. 01631/564-200, www.room9oban.co.uk).

Waypoint Bar & Grill, just across the bay from Oban, is a laid-back patio at the Kerrera Marina with a no-nonsense menu of grilled seafood. It's not fancy, but the food is fresh and inexpensive, and on a nice day the open-air waterside setting is unbeatable (£10-16 main courses, £10 large portion fish-and-chips, £25 seafood platter, June-Sept daily 12:00-21:00, closed Oct-May, reservations smart, tel. 07840/650-669, www.obanseafoodrestaurant.co.uk). A free-for-customers eight-minute ferry to the marina leaves from Oban's North Pier—look for the sign near the recommended Piazza restaurant (departs hourly at :10 past each hour).

Fish-and-Chip Joints: Oban Fish and Chip Shop, run by husband-and-wife team George and Lillian (with Lewis and Sammy working the fryer), serves praiseworthy haddock and mussels among other tasty options in a cheery blue cabana-like dining room. Consider venturing away from basic fish-and-chips into a world of more creative seafood dishes, all at a great price (£8 haddock-and-chips, £7-11 main courses, 116 George Street, tel. 01631/567-000 or 01631/569-828).

At **The Oban Bay Fish & Chips,** which is also family-run, Renato serves all things from the sea (plus an assortment of Scottish classics) battered and fried. Choose between the casual restaurant or take-away counter, where you can give fried haggis a try (£7-10 meals, slightly cheaper for take-away, "Fish Tea" for £8, daily 12:00-23:00, on the harborfront at 34 George Street, below Skipinnish, tel. 01631/565-855).

Lunch

The green **shellfish shack** at the ferry dock is the best spot to pick up a seafood sandwich or a snack. Get freshly caught and boiled seafood in Styrofoam cups to go; request a paper plate and bread to make a light meal (often free salmon samples, meal-size £3 salmon sandwiches, inexpensive coffee, picnic tables nearby, open daily from 10:00 until the boat unloads from Mull around 17:45).

The Kitchen Garden is fine for soup, salad, or sandwiches. It's a deli and gourmet-foods store with a charming café upstairs (£4 sandwiches to go, £5-8 dishes upstairs, Mon-Sat 9:00-17:30, Sun 10:00-16:30, closed Sun Jan-mid-Feb, 14 George Street, tel. 01631/566-332).

Oban Connections

By Train from Oban: Trains link Oban to the nearest transportation hub in **Glasgow** (3-4/day, just 1/day Sun in winter, 3 hours); to get to **Edinburgh,** you'll have to transfer in Glasgow (2/day, 4.25 hours). To reach **Fort William** (a transit hub for the Highlands), you'll take the same Glasgow-bound train, but transfer in Crianlarich—the direct bus is easier (see next). Oban's small train station has limited hours (ticket window open Mon-Sat 7:15-18:00, Sun 10:45-18:00, same hours apply to lockers, train info tel. 08457-484-950, www.nationalrail.co.uk).

By Bus: Bus #918 passes through Ballachulish—a half-mile from **Glencoe**—on its way to **Fort William** (3/day in summer, 2/day off-season, never on Sun; 1 hour to Ballachulish, 1.5 hours total to Fort William). Take this bus to Fort William, then transfer to bus #919 to reach **Inverness** (3.75 hours total, with a 20-minute layover in Fort William) or bus #915 or #916 to **Portree** on the Isle of Skye (2/day, 4.5-5 hours total). A different bus (#976 or #977) connects Oban with **Glasgow** (3-6/day, 2.75-3 hours, some with transfer in Tyndrum), from where you can easily connect by bus or train to **Edinburgh** (figure 4.5 hours total). Buses arrive and depart from a roundabout, marked by a stubby clock tower, just before the entrance to the train station (tel. 08712/663-333, www .citylink.co.uk).

By Boat: Ferries fan out from Oban to the **southern Hebrides** (see information on the islands of Iona and Mull, later). Caledonian MacBrayne Ferry info: Tel. 01631/566-688, free booking tel. 0800-066-5000, www.calmac.co.uk.

Between Glasgow and Oban

The drive from Glasgow (or Edinburgh) to Oban provides dreamy vistas and your first look at the dramatic landscapes of the Highlands. Drivers coming from the south can consider these stopovers, which are listed in order from Glasgow to Oban.

Loch Lomond

Within about an hour's drive of half the population of Scotland is the centerpiece of the country's leading national park, the scenic lake called Loch Lomond. It's a favorite retreat for Scots as well as foreign tourists. Leaving Glasgow on the A-82, you'll soon be driving along Loch Lomond. The first picnic turnout has the best lake views, benches, a park, and a playground. Twenty-four miles long and speckled with islands, Loch Lomond is second in size only to Loch Ness.

Loch Lomond is well-known mostly because of its easy proximity to Glasgow (about 15 miles away)—and also because its bonnie, bonnie banks inspired a beloved folk song: "Ye'll take the high road, and I'll take the low road, and I'll be in Scotland afore ye... For me and my true love will never meet again, on the bonnie, bonnie banks of Loch Lomond." As you'll be humming that all day, here's one interpretation of the song's poignant meaning: After the disastrous Scottish loss at the Battle of Culloden, the English brought the Jacobite ringleaders to London for a series of show trials. The Scottish were all executed, and their bodies transported back to Scotland by coaches along the "high road," while the wives, girlfriends, and families—who had walked to London for the trials—had to return along the commoners' "low road"— both ending up, at least in spirit, back in Scotland.

• *Halfway up the loch, at Tarbet, take the "tourist route" left onto the A-83, driving along Loch Long toward Inveraray.*

Rest-and-Be-Thankful Pass

As you climb into more rugged territory, be mindful that the roads connecting the Lowlands with the Highlands (like this one) were originally a military project designed to facilitate the English

OBAN

quelling of the Highland clans. A low-profile pullout on the A-83 just west of the A-82 offers a pleasant opportunity to stretch your legs and get your first taste of that rugged Scottish countryside. The colorful name comes from the 1880s, when second- and third-class coach passengers got out and pushed the coach and first-class passengers up the hill.

Inveraray

Nearly everybody stops at this lovely, seemingly made-for-tourists castle town on Loch Fyne. Park near the pier and browse the wide selection of restaurants and tourist shops.

Inveraray's **TI** sells bus and ferry tickets, has Internet access, and offers a free mini-guide and an exhibit about the Argyll region (daily June-Aug 9:00-17:30, Sept-Oct and April-May 10:00-17:00, Nov-March 10:00-16:00, Front Street, tel. 01499/302-063). Public WCs are at the end of the nearby pier.

The town's main "sight" is the **Inveraray Jail,** an overpriced, corny, but mildly educational former jail converted into a museum. This "living 19th-century prison" includes a courtroom where mannequins argue the fate of the accused. You'll have the opportunity to be locked up for a photo op by a playful guard (£9, daily April-Oct 9:30-18:00, Nov-March 10:00-17:00, last entry one hour before closing, Church Square, tel. 01499/302-381, www.inverary jail.co.uk).

You'll spot the dramatic **Inveraray Castle** (which you may recognize as Duneagle Castle from the PBS series *Downton Abbey*) on the right as you cross the bridge coming from Glasgow. This impressive-looking stronghold of one of the more notorious branches of the Campbell clan is striking from afar but dull inside; save your time for better castles elsewhere in the Highlands.

• *To continue on to Oban, leave Inveraray through a gate (at the Woolen Mill) to the A-819, and go through Glen Aray and along Loch Awe. The A-85 takes you into Oban.*

Islands of Mull and Iona

For the easiest one-day look at two of the dramatic and historic Hebrides (HEB-rid-eez) islands, take the Iona/Mull tour from Oban. (For a more in-depth look, head north to Skye—see next chapter.)

Here's the game plan: You'll take a ferry from Oban to Mull (45 minutes), ride a West Coast Motors tour bus across Mull (1.25 hours), then board a quick ferry from Mull to Iona. The total round-trip travel time is 5.5 hours (all of it incredibly scenic), plus about two hours of free time on Iona. Buy your strip of six tickets—one for each leg—at the West Coast Motors office in Oban (£38, for Iona/Mull tour, no tours Nov-March, book one day ahead in July-Sept if possible, bus tickets can sell out during busy summer weekends, office open daily 8:30-17:30, 1

Queens Park Place, a block from train station, tel. 01631/566-809 or 01631/563-221). For directions on how to buy individual tickets for various legs of this journey (for example, if you plan to sleep in Iona or spend a longer day there), see page 898.

You'll leave in the morning from the Oban pier on the huge Oban-Mull ferry run by Caledonian MacBrayne (boats depart Sun-Fri at 9:50, Sat at 9:30, board at least 20 minutes before departure; boats return daily around 17:45). As the schedule can change slightly from year to year, confirm your departure time carefully in Oban. The best inside seats on the ferry—with the biggest windows—are in the sofa lounge on the uppermost deck (level 4) at the back end of the boat. (Follow signs for the toilets, and look for the big staircase to the top floor; this floor also has its own small snack bar with hot drinks and £3 sandwiches.) On board, if it's a clear day, ask a local or a crew member to point out Ben Nevis, the tallest mountain in Great Britain. The ferry has a fine cafeteria with select-your-own lunch bags (£4, includes sandwich, chips, drink, and fruit) and a bookshop (though guidebooks are cheaper in Oban). Five minutes before landing on Mull, you'll see the striking 13th-century Duart Castle on the left (www .duartcastle.com).

Walk-on passengers disembark from deck 3, across from the bookshop (port side). Upon arrival in Mull, find your tour company's bus for the entertaining and informative ride across the Isle of Mull (bus may not have name on it; ask the drivers). The right (driver's) side offers better sea views during the second half of the journey to Fionnphort, while the left side has fine views of Mull's rolling wilderness. The bus drivers spend the entire ride chattering away about life on Mull, slowing to point out wildlife, and sharing adages like, "If there's no flowers on the gorse, snogging's gone out of fashion." They are hardworking local boys who make historical trivia fascinating—or at least fun. Your destination is Mull's westernmost ferry terminal (Fionnphort), where you'll board a small, rocking ferry for the brief ride to Iona. Unless you stay overnight, you'll have only about two hours to roam freely around the island before taking the ferry-bus-ferry ride in reverse back to Oban.

Oban & the Southern Highlands

SKYE

ARMADALE

MALLAIG

RUM

ARISAIG

A-

	CASTLE
•••	FERRY ROUTES (NOT ALL SHOWN)

20 MILES

20 KM

COLL

TOBERMORY

DUART
CASTLE

MULL

TRESHNISH

STAFFA

CRAIG-
MURE

IONA

A-849

SEIL

FIONNPHORT

COLONSAY

JURA

SOUTHERN HIGHLANDS

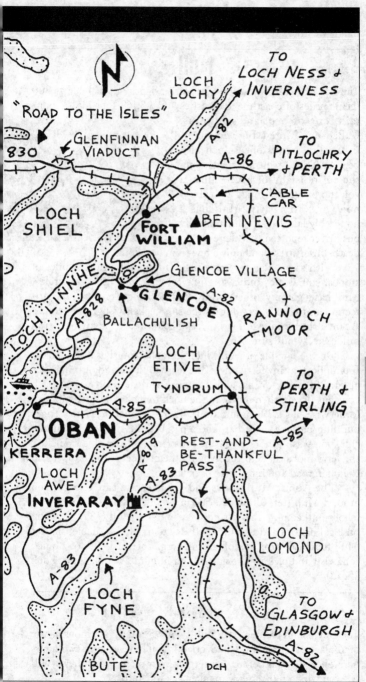

Though this trip is spectacular when it's sunny, it's worthwhile in any weather.

Mull

The Isle of Mull, the second-largest in Scotland, has nearly 300 scenic miles of coastline and castles and a 3,169-foot-high mountain, one of Scotland's Munros.

Called Ben More ("Big Mountain" in Gaelic), it was once much bigger. At 10,000 feet tall, it made up the entire island of Mull—until a volcano erupted. Things are calmer now, and, similarly, Mull has a noticeably laid-back population. My bus driver reported that there are no deaths from stress, and only a few from boredom.

With steep, fog-covered hillsides topped by cairns (piles of stones, sometimes indicating graves) and ancient stone circles, Mull has a gloomy, otherworldly charm. Bring plenty of rain protection and wear layers in case the sun peeks through the clouds. As my driver said, Mull is a place of cold, wet, windy winters and mild, wet, windy summers.

On the far side of Mull, the caravan of tour buses unloads at Fionnphort, a tiny ferry town. The ferry to the island of Iona takes about 200 walk-on passengers. Confirm the return time with your bus driver, then hustle to the dock to make the first trip over (otherwise, it's a 30-minute wait). There's a small ferry-passenger building/meager snack bar (and a pay WC). After the 10-minute ride, you wash ashore on sleepy Iona (free WC on this side), and the ferry mobs that crowded you on the boat seem to disappear up the main road and into Iona's back lanes.

The **About Mull Tours and Taxi** service can also get you around Mull (tel. 01681/700-507 or mobile 0788-777-4550, www .aboutmull.co.uk). They also do day tours of Mull (£35), focusing on local history and wildlife (half-day tours also available, shorter Mull tours can drop you off at Iona ferry dock at 15:00 for a quick Iona visit and pick you up at 18:00, minimum 2 people, must book ahead).

Iona

The tiny island of Iona, just 3 miles by 1.5 miles, is famous as the birthplace of Christianity in Scotland. You'll have about two hours here on your own before you retrace your steps (your driver will tell you which return ferry to take back to Mull).

History of Iona

St. Columba, an Irish scholar, soldier, priest, and founder of monasteries, got into a small war over the possession of an

illegally copied psalm book. Victorious but sickened by the bloodshed, Columba left Ireland, vowing never to return. According to legend, the first bit of land out of sight of his homeland was Iona. He stopped here in 563 and established an abbey.

Columba's monastic community flourished, and Iona became the center of Celtic Christianity. Missionaries from Iona spread the gospel throughout Scotland and northern England, while scholarly monks established Iona as a center of art and learning. The *Book of Kells*—perhaps the finest piece of art from "Dark Ages" Europe—was probably made on Iona in the eighth century. The island was so important that it was the legendary burial place for ancient Scottish and even Scandinavian kings (including Shakespeare's Macbeth).

Slowly, the importance of Iona ebbed. Vikings massacred 68 monks in 806. Fearing more raids, the monks evacuated most of Iona's treasures to Ireland (including the *Book of Kells*, which is now in Dublin). Much later, with the Reformation, the abbey was abandoned, and most of its finely carved crosses were destroyed. In the 17th century, locals used the abbey only as a handy quarry for other building projects.

Iona's population peaked at about 500 in the 1830s. In the 1840s, a potato famine hit, and in the 1850s, a third of the islanders emigrated to Canada or Australia. By 1900, the population was down to 210, and today it's only around 100.

But in our generation, a new religious community has given the abbey fresh life. The Iona Community is an ecumenical gathering of men and women who seek new ways of living the Gospel in today's world, with a focus on worship, peace and justice issues, and reconciliation.

SOUTHERN HIGHLANDS

A pristine quality of the light and a thoughtful peace pervades the stark, (nearly) car-free island and its tiny community. With buoyant clouds bouncing playfully off distant bluffs, sparkling-white crescents of sand, and lone tourists camped thoughtfully atop huge rocks just looking out to sea, Iona is a place that's perfect for meditation. To experience Iona, it's important to get out and take a little hike; you can follow the "Welcome to Iona" walk outlined below. And you can easily climb a peak—nothing's higher than 300 feet above the sea.

Staying Longer on Iona: For a chance to really experience peaceful, idyllic Iona, consider spending a night or two. Scots bring their kids and stay on this tiny island for a week. If you want to overnight in Iona, don't buy your tickets at the bus-tour office in Oban—they require a same-day return. Instead, buy each leg of the ferry-bus-ferry (and return) trip separately. Get your Oban-Mull ferry ticket in the Oban ferry office (one-way for walk-on passengers-£5.40, round-trip-£9, ticket good for 5 days). Once you arrive in Mull (Craignure), follow the crowds to the tour buses and buy a ticket directly from the driver (£14 round-trip). When you arrive at the ferry terminal (Fionnphort), walk into the small trailer ferry office to buy a ticket to Iona (£2.50 each way). If it's closed, just buy your ticket from the ferry worker at the dock (cash or credit/debit cards accepted; leaving Iona, do the same as there's no ferry office).

If you want to spend more time on Iona (about four hours) and return to Oban the same day, you have another option. Take the first boat of the day, usually around 7:45, then connect at Mull to bus #496, which takes you to Fionnphort and the Iona ferry (no tour narration, buy each leg separately as described earlier). The benefit of taking the tour—besides the helpful commentary—is the guarantee of a seat each way. Ask at the bus tour office for details.

Orientation to Iona

The village, Baile Mòr, has shops, a restaurant/pub, enough beds, and no bank (get cash back with a purchase at the grocery store). The only taxi on Iona is **Iona Taxi** (tel. 07810-325-990, www.ionataxi.co.uk). Up the road from the ferry dock is a little **Spar** grocery (Mon-Sat 9:00-17:15, Sun 12:00-16:00, shorter hours and closed Sun Oct-April, free island maps). Iona's official website (www.isle-of-iona.net) has good information about the island.

Self-Guided Walk

Welcome to Iona

With a couple of hours, I recommend this basic route, which includes the nunnery ruins, abbey/chapel, a hilltop overview, and a pretty beach.

From the ferry dock, head directly up the single paved road that passes through the village and up a small hill to visit the **Nunnery Ruins**, one of Britain's best-preserved medieval nunneries (free). Turn right on North Road to reach the chapel and abbey.

St. Oran's Chapel, in the graveyard of the **Iona Abbey**, is the oldest church building on the island. Inside the chapel you'll find several grave slabs carved in the distinctive Iona School style, which was developed by local stone-carvers in the 14th century. Look for the depictions of medieval warrior aristocrats. Many more of these carved graves have been moved to the abbey, where you can see them in its cloisters and old infirmary. It's free to see the graveyard and chapel; the abbey itself has an admission fee, but it's worth the cost just to sit in the stillness of its lovely, peaceful interior courtyard (£7.10, not covered by bus tour ticket, includes audioguide and 30-minute guided tour, £5 guidebook, daily April-Sept 9:30-17:30, Oct-March 9:30-16:30, tel. 01681/700-512, www.historic-scotland.gov.uk). While the present abbey, nunnery, and graveyard go back to the 13th century, much of what you'll see was rebuilt in the 20th century.

Across from the abbey is the **Iona Community's welcome center** (free WCs), which runs the abbey with Historic Scotland and hosts modern-day pilgrims who come here to experience the birthplace of Scottish Christianity. (If you're staying longer, you could attend a worship service at the abbey—check the schedule here; tel. 01681/700-404, www.iona.org.uk.) Its gift shop is packed with books on the island's important role in Christian history.

After you leave the abbey, turn right and continue on North Road. A 10-minute walk brings you to the footpath for **Dun I**, a steep but short climb with good views of the abbey looking back toward Mull.

From Dun I, walk another 20-25 minutes to the end of the paved road, where you'll arrive at a gate leading through a sheep- and cow-strewn pasture to Iona's pristine white-sand **North Beach**. Dip your toes in the Atlantic and ponder what this Caribbean-like alcove is doing in Scotland. Be sure to allow at least 40 minutes to return to the ferry dock.

With Extra Time: The **Heritage Centre**, on your left past the nunnery ruins, is small but well done, with displays on local and natural history and a tiny tearoom (£2.50, Mon-Sat 10:30-16:15, closed Sun and Nov-mid-April).

Sleeping and Eating on Iona

(area code: 01681)
In addition to the options listed below, there are many B&Bs, apartments, and a hostel on the island (see www.isle-of-iona.net/accommodation).

$$$ Argyll Hotel, built in 1867, proudly overlooks the waterfront, with 16 cottage-like rooms and pleasingly creaky hallways lined with bookshelves (Sb-£63-68, D-£72-79, Db-£93-99, larger Db-£136-144, cheaper off-season, extra bed for kids-£15, reserve far in advance for July-Aug, free Wi-Fi, comfortable lounge and sunroom, tel. 01681/700-334, www.argyllhoteliona.co.uk, reception @argyllhoteliona.co.uk). Its white-linen dining room is open to the public for lunch (12:30-14:00, tea served until 16:00) and dinner (£12-20 main courses, 18:30-20:00). Both the hotel and restaurant are closed from November through mid-March.

$$$ St. Columba Hotel, situated in the middle of a peaceful garden with picnic tables, has 27 institutional rooms and spacious lodge-like common spaces (Sb-£70-83, Db-£120-140, huge view Db-£180, front rooms have sea views but windows are small, discounts for stays of 4 or more nights, extra bed for kids-£15, free guest computer, closed Nov-March, next door to abbey on road up from dock, tel. 01681/700-304, www.stcolumba-hotel.co.uk, info@stcolumba-hotel.co.uk). Their fine 21-table restaurant, overlooking the water, is open to the public for lunch (£5-10, daily 12:00-14:30), tea (14:00-17:00), and dinner (£10-13, 18:30-20:00). Even if you're not staying here, you can stop by to use the Internet (£0.50/15 minutes).

$$ Calva B&B, near the abbey, has three spacious rooms (Db-£65, second house on left past the abbey, look for sign in window and gnomes on porch, tel. 01681/700-340; friendly Janetta, Ken, and Jack the bearded collie).

Glencoe

This valley is the essence of the wild, powerful, and stark beauty of the Highlands. Along with its scenery, Glencoe offers a good dose of bloody clan history: In 1692, British Redcoats (led by a local Campbell commander) came to the valley, and were sheltered and fed for 12 days by the MacDonalds—whose leader had been late in swearing an oath to the British monarch. Then, the morning of February 13, the soldiers were ordered to rise up early and kill their sleeping hosts, violating the rules of Highland hospitality and earning the valley the name "The Weeping Glen." It's fitting that such an epic, dramatic incident should be set in this equally epic, dramatic valley, where the cliffsides seem to weep (with running streams) when it rains.

Orientation to Glencoe

The valley of Glencoe is just off the main A-828/A-82 road between Oban and points north (such as Fort William and Inverness). If you're coming from the north, the signage can be tricky—at the roundabout south of Fort William, follow signs to *Crianlarich* and *A-82*. The most appealing town here is the one-street Glencoe village, while the slightly larger and more modern town of Ballachulish (a half-mile away) has more services. Though not quite quaint, the very sleepy village of Glencoe is worth a stop for its folk museum and its status as the gateway to the valley. The town's hub of activity is its grocery store (ATM, daily June-Aug 7:30-21:00, Sept-May 8:00-20:00).

Tourist Information

Your best source of information (especially for walks and hikes) is the **Glencoe Visitors Centre,** described later. The nearest **TI** is well-signed in Ballachulish (daily Easter-Sept 9:00-17:00, Oct-Easter 10:00-16:00, bus timetables, free phone to call area B&Bs, café, shop, tel. 01855/811-866, www.glencoetourism.co.uk). For more information on the area, see www.discoverglencoe.com.

Sights in Glencoe

Glencoe Village

Glencoe village is just a line of houses sitting beneath the brooding mountains.

Glencoe and North Lorn Folk Museum

Two tiny, thatched-roof, early-18th-century croft houses are jammed with local history, creating a huggable museum filled with humble exhibits gleaned from the town's old closets and attics. When one house was being re-thatched, its owner found a cache of 200-year-old swords and pistols hidden there from the British Redcoats after the disastrous battle of Culloden. Be sure to look for the museum's little door that leads out back, where you'll find exhibits on the Glencoe Massacre, native slate, farm tools, and more.

Cost and Hours: £3, call ahead for hours—generally Easter-Oct Mon-Sat 10:00-16:30, last admission at 16:00, closed Sun and off-season, tel. 01855/811-664, www.glencoemuseum.com.

In Glencoe Valley

▲▲Driving Through Glencoe Valley

If you have a car, spend an hour or so following the A-82 through
the valley, past the Glencoe Visitors Centre
(see next listing), into the desolate moor
beyond, and back again. You'll enjoy grand
views, dramatic craggy hills, and, if you're
lucky, a chance to hear a bagpiper in the
wind—roadside Highland buskers (most often
seen on good-weather summer weekends). If
you play the recorder (and no other tourists
are there), ask to finger a tune while the piper
does the hard work. At the end of the valley
you hit the vast Rannoch Moor—500 bleak
square miles with barely enough decent land
to graze a sheep.

Glencoe Visitors Centre

This modern facility, a mile up the A-82 past Glencoe village (off
to the right) into the dramatic valley, is designed to resemble a
clachan, or traditional Highlands settlement. The information desk
inside the shop at the ranger desk is your single best resource for
advice (and maps or guidebooks) about local walks and hikes, some
of which are described next. At the back of the complex you'll
find a viewpoint with a handy 3-D model of the hills for orientation. There's also a pricey £6.50 exhibition about the surrounding
landscape, the region's history, mountaineering, and conservation. It's worth the time to watch the more-interesting-than-it-
sounds video on geology and the 14-minute film on the Glencoe
Massacre, which thoughtfully traces the events leading up to the
tragedy rather than simply recycling romanticized legends.

Cost and Hours: Free; April-Oct daily 9:30-17:30; Nov-
March Thu-Sun 10:00-16:00, closed Mon-Wed; last entry 45 minutes before closing, free parking, WCs, café, tel. 01855/811-307,
www.glencoe-nts.org.uk.

Walks

For a steep one-mile hike, climb the Devil's Staircase (trailhead
just off the A-82, 8 miles east of Glencoe). For a three-hour hike,
ask at the visitors center about the Lost Valley of the MacDonalds
(trailhead just off the A-82, 3 miles east of Glencoe). For an easy
40-minute walk above Glencoe, head to the mansion on the hill
(over the bridge, turn left, fine loch views, well-signed). This
mansion was built in 1894 by Canadian Pacific Railway magnate
Lord Strathcona for his Canadian wife. She was homesick for the
Rockies, so he had the grounds landscaped to represent the lakes,
trees, and mountains of her home country. It didn't work, and they
eventually returned to Canada. The house originally had 365 win-

dows, to allow a different view each day.

Glencoe's Burial Island and Island of Discussion

In the loch just outside Glencoe (near Ballachulish), notice the burial island—where the souls of those who "take the high road" are piped home. (Ask a local about "Ye'll take the high road, and I'll take the low road.") The next island was the Island of Discussion—where those in dispute went until they found agreement.

Sleeping in Glencoe

(area code: 01855)

Glencoe is an extremely low-key place to spend the night between Oban or Glasgow and the northern destinations. These places are accustomed to one-nighters just passing through, but some people stay here for several days to enjoy a variety of hikes. The following B&Bs are along the main road through the middle of the village, and all are cash-only.

$$ Inchconnal B&B is a cute, renovated house with a bonnie wee potted garden out front, renting two bright rooms with views—one cottage-style, the other woodsy (Db-£50-54, tel. 01855/811-958, www.inchconnal.com, enquiries@inchconnal.com, warm Caroline MacDonald).

$$ Tulachgorm B&B has one comfortable room with a private bathroom in a modern house with fine mountain views (D-£50, tel. 01855/811-391, mellow Ann Blake and friendly border collie Jo).

$$ Grianan B&B, across from the grocery store, comes with a homey feeling and two large rooms sharing a bath (D-£46-48, great for families, also rents self-catering cottages, tel. 01855/811-322, donaldyoung@hotmail.co.uk, Jane).

$$ Morven Cottage offers two rooms with free Wi-Fi, a breakfast room overlooking the gardens, owners with plenty of character, and a son who was an extra in a Harry Potter movie (Db-£50, can accommodate double/twin/family, dogs welcome, tel. 01855/811-544, www.morvenbnb.com, Freddie and Bob).

$$ Ghlasdrum B&B, next to the police station and set back from A-82, has four large rooms, a cozy dining room with a fireplace, and the nicest bathrooms (Sb-£35, Db-£55, tel. 01855/811-593, Maureen@ken110.orangehome.co.uk, Maureen, Ken, and shih tzu Daisy).

Outside of Town: **$$$ Clachaig Inn,** which runs three popular pubs on site, also rents 23 rooms, all with private bath (Db-£100-104, tel. 01855/811-252, 3 miles from Glencoe, www.clachaig.com). It works well for hikers who want a comfy mountain inn, or Harry Potter fans who want a glimpse of where part of the movie was filmed. Nothing remains from the movie, but that doesn't seem to matter to die-hard fans. For directions to the inn, see "Eating in Glencoe," next.

Eating in Glencoe

The choices around Glencoe are slim—this isn't the place for fine dining. But four options offer decent food a short walk or drive away. For evening fun, take a walk or ask your B&B host where to find music and dancing.

In Glencoe: The only real restaurant is **The Glencoe Gathering & Inn,** with lovely dining areas and a large outdoor deck. Choose between the quirky, fun pub, specializing in seafood with a Scottish twist, or the fancier restaurant (£8-15 main courses, food served daily 12:00-22:00, at junction of A-82 and Glencoe village, tel. 01855/811-245).

The **Glencoe Café,** also in the village, is just right for soups and sandwiches, and Justine's homemade baked goods—especially the carrot loaf—are irresistible (£4 soups, £8.50 soup and *panini* lunch combo, daily 9:30-17:00, last order at 16:15, free Wi-Fi).

Near Glencoe: **Clachaig Inn,** set in a stunning valley, serves food all day long in three pubs to a clientele that's half locals and half tourists. This unpretentious and very popular social hub features billiards, live music, pub grub, and over 300 whiskies and 15 hand-pulled ales (£5-13 main courses, open daily for lunch and dinner, music Sat from 21:00, tel. 01855/811-252). Drive to the end of Glencoe village, cross the bridge, and follow the little single-track road for three miles, past campgrounds and hostels, until you reach the inn on the right.

In Ballachulish: **Laroch Bar & Bistro,** in the next village over from Glencoe (toward Oban), has a nice patio and is family-friendly (£6-9 pub grub, food served daily 18:00-21:00, Sat-Sun also open for lunch 12:00-14:30, tel. 01855/811-274). Drive into Ballachulish village, and you'll see it on the left.

Glencoe Connections

Unfortunately, buses don't actually drive down the main road through Glencoe village. Some buses (most notably those going between Glasgow and Fort William) stop near Glencoe village at a place called **"Glencoe Crossroads"**—a short walk into the village center. Other buses (such as those between Oban and Fort William) stop at the nearby town of **Ballachulish,** which is just a half-mile away (or a £3 taxi ride). Tell the bus driver where you're going ("Glencoe village") and ask to be let off as close to there as possible.

From **Glencoe Crossroads,** you can catch bus #914, #915, or

#916 (8/day) to **Fort William** (30 minutes) or **Glasgow** (2.5 hours).

From **Ballachulish,** you can take bus #918 (3/day in summer, 2/day off-season, never on Sun) to **Fort William** (30 minutes) or **Oban** (1 hour). Bus info: Tel. 08712/663-333, www.citylink.co.uk.

To reach **Inverness** or **Portree** on the Isle of Skye, transfer in Fort William. To reach **Edinburgh,** transfer in Glasgow.

Fort William

Laying claim to the title of "outdoor capital of the UK," Fort William is well-positioned between Oban, Inverness, and the Isle of Skye. This crossroads town is a transportation hub and has a pleasant-enough, shop-studded, pedestrianized main drag, but few charms of its own. Most visitors just pass through...and should. But while you're here, consider buying lunch and stopping by the TI to get your questions answered.

Tourist Information: The TI is on the car-free main drag (July-Sept Mon-Sat 9:30-18:30, Sun 9:30-17:00; Easter-June Mon-Sat 9:00-17:00, Sun 10:00-17:00; shorter hours off-season; Internet access £1/20 minutes, free public WCs up the street next to parking lot; follow signs to short-term parking, £1/2 hours, 15 High Street, tel. 01397/701-801).

Sights in Fort William

West Highland Museum

This humble-but-well-presented museum is Fort William's only real sight. It features exhibits on local history, wildlife, dress, Jacobite memorabilia, and more.

Cost and Hours: Free, guidebook-£1, Mon-Sat 10:00-17:00, Nov-Dec and March until 16:00, closed Sun and Jan-Feb, on Cameron Square, tel. 01397/702-169, www.westhighlandmuseum.org.uk.

Near Fort William

The appealing options described below lie just outside of town.

Ben Nevis

From Fort William, take a peek at Britain's highest peak, Ben Nevis (4,406 feet). Thousands walk to its summit each year. On a clear day, you can admire it from a distance. Scotland's only mountain cable cars—at the **Nevis Range Mountain Experience**—can take you to a not-very-lofty 2,150-foot perch on the slopes of Aonach Mor for a closer look (£11.50, daily July-Aug 9:30-18:00,

Sept-June 10:00-17:00, 15-minute ride, shuts down in high winds and mid-Nov–mid-Dec—call ahead, signposted on the A-82 north of Fort William, tel. 01397/705-825, www.nevisrange.co.uk). They also have high-wire obstacle courses (£24.50, under age 17–£16.75, sessions run throughout the day, call for more information).

Toward the Isle of Skye:
The Road to the Isles and the Jacobite Steam Train

The magical steam train that scenically transports Harry Potter to the wizarding school of Hogwarts runs along a real-life train line. The West Highland Railway Line chugs 42 miles from Fort William west to the ferry port at Mallaig. Along the way, it passes the iconic **Glenfinnan Viaduct,** with 416 yards of raised track over 21 supporting arches. This route is also graced with plenty of loch-and-mountain views and, near the end, passes along a beautiful stretch of coast with some fine sandy beaches. While many people take the Jacobite Steam Train to enjoy this stretch of Scotland, it can be more rewarding to drive the same route—especially if you're headed for the Isle of Skye.

By Train: The **Jacobite Steam Train** (they don't actually call it the "Hogwarts Express") offers a small taste of the Harry Potter experience...but many who take this trip for that reason alone are disappointed. (For more Harry Potter sights in Britain, see page 1028.) Although one of the steam engines and some of the coaches were used in the films, don't expect a Harry Potter theme ride. However, you can expect beautiful scenery. Along the way, the train stops for 20 minutes at Glenfinnan Station (just after the Glenfinnan Viaduct), and then gives you way too much time (1.75 hours) to poke around the dull port town of Mallaig before heading back to Fort William (one-way—£28 adults, £17 kids; round-trip—£33 adults, £19 kids; £3.25 booking fee, more for first class, tickets must be purchased in advance—see details next, 1/day Mon-Fri mid-May-Oct, 2/day Mon-Fri early June-Aug, also 1/day Sat-Sun late-June-late-Sept, departs Fort William at 10:15 and returns at 16:00, afternoon service in summer departs Fort William at 14:30 and returns at 20:24, about a 2-hour ride each way, WCs on board, tel. 0844/850-4680 or 0844/850-4682, www .westcoastrailways.co.uk).

Note: Trains leave Fort William from the main train station, but you must book ahead online or by phone—you cannot buy tickets for this train at the Fort William or Mallaig train-station ticket offices. There may be a limited amount of seats available each day on a first-come, first-served basis (cash only, buy from conductor), but in summer, trips are often sold out.

The 84-mile round-trip from Fort William takes the better part of a day to show you the same scenery twice. Modern

"Sprinter" trains follow the same line—consider taking the steam train one-way to Mallaig, then speeding back on a regular train to avoid the long Mallaig layover and slow return (£11.40 one-way between Fort William and Mallaig, 1.5 hours, 2-4/day, book at least two days ahead July-Aug, tel. 08457-550-033, www.scotrail .co.uk). Note that you can use this train to reach the Isle of Skye: Take the train to Mallaig, walk onto the ferry to Armadale (on Skye), then catch a bus in Armadale to your destination on Skye (tel. 08712/663-333, www.citylink.co.uk).

There are lockers for storing luggage at the Fort William train station (£4-5/24 hours, station open Mon-Sat 7:20-22:10, Sun 11:30-22:10).

By Car: While the train is time-consuming and expensive, driving the same **"Road to the Isles"** route (A-830)—ideally on your way to Skye—can be a fun way to see the same famous scenery more affordably and efficiently. The key here is to be sure you leave enough time to make it to Mallaig before the Skye ferry departs—get timing advice from the Fort William TI. I'd allow at least 1 hour and 20 minutes to get from Fort William to the ferry landing in Mallaig (if you keep moving, with no stops en route)—and note that vehicles are required to arrive 30 minutes before the boat departs. As you leave Fort William on the A-830, a sign on the left tells you what time the next ferry will depart Mallaig. For more tips on the Mallaig-Armadale ferry, see "Getting to the Isle of Skye" on page 911.

Sleeping in Fort William

(area code: 01397)

These two B&Bs are on Union Road, a five-minute walk up the hill above the main pedestrian street that runs through the heart of town. Each place has three rooms, one of which has a private bathroom in the hall.

$$ Glenmorven Guest House is a friendly, flower-bedecked, family-run place at the end of the road. The hospitality, special extras, and views of Loch Linnhe are worth the walk (Db-£65-70, free pick-up from train or bus station with advance notice, laundry service, welcome whisky, Fort William, tel. 01397/703-236, www .glenmorven.co.uk, glenmorven@yahoo.com, Anne and Colin Jamieson).

$$ Gowan Brae B&B ("Hill of the Big Daisy") has three antique-filled rooms with loch or garden views in a hobbit-cute house (Db-£70 in high season, £60 off-season, free Wi-Fi, tel. 01397/704-399, www.gowanbrae.co.uk, gowan_brae@btinternet .com, Jim and Ann Clark).

FORT WILLIAM

Eating in Fort William

All three places listed below are on the main walking street, near the start of town; the first two serve only lunch.

Hot Roast Company sells beef, turkey, ham, or pork sandwiches, topped with some tasty extras, along with soup, salad, and coleslaw (£3 take-away, a bit more for sit-down service, Mon-Sat 9:30-15:30, sandwiches from 11:00, closed Sun, free Wi-Fi, 127 High Street, tel. 01397/700-606).

Café 115 features good food and modern bistro decor (£4-8 meals, £6 fish-and-chips, daily 10:00-17:00, mid-July-Aug until 21:30, 115 High Street, tel. 01397/702-500).

The Grog & Gruel serves real ales, good pub grub, and Tex-Mex and Cajun dishes, with unusual meals such as vegetarian haggis with Drambuie sauce, boar burgers, and venison chili (£5-12 meals, food served daily 12:00-23:30, Sun in winter 17:00-23:30, free Wi-Fi, 66 High Street, tel. 01397/705-078, www.grogand gruel.co.uk). Their upstairs restaurant features the same menu (daily 17:00-23:30).

Fort William Connections

Fort William is a major transit hub for the Highlands, so you'll likely change buses here at some point during your trip.

From Fort William by Bus to: Glencoe (all Glasgow-bound buses—#914, #915, and #916; 8/day, 30 minutes), **Ballachulish** near Glencoe (Oban-bound bus #918, 3/day in summer, 2/day off-season, never on Sun, 30 minutes), **Oban** (bus #918, 3/day in summer, 2/day off-season, never on Sun, 1.5 hours), **Portree** on the Isle of Skye (buses #915 and #916, 3/day, 3.5 hours), **Inverness** (Citylink bus #919 or Stagecoach bus #19, 10/day, 2 hours), **Glasgow** (buses #914, #915, and #916; 8/day, 3 hours), **Edinburgh** (bus #913, 1/day direct, 4 hours; more with transfer in Glasgow on buses #900 and #914/915, 5 hours). Bus info: Tel. 0871-266-3333, www.citylink.co.uk or www.stagecoachbus.com.

Route Tips for Drivers

From Oban to Glencoe and Fort William: From Oban, follow the coastal A-828 toward Fort William. After about 20 miles, you'll see the photogenic Castle Stalker marooned on a lonely island. At North Ballachulish, you'll reach a bridge spanning Loch Leven; rather than crossing the bridge, turn off and follow the A-82 into the Glencoe Valley for about 15 minutes. After exploring the valley, make a U-turn and return through Glencoe. To continue on to Fort William, backtrack to the bridge at North Ballachulish (great view from bridge) and cross it, following the A-82 north. (For a scenic shortcut directly back to Glasgow or Edinburgh, head north only as far as Glencoe, and then cut to Glasgow or Edinburgh on the A-82 via Rannoch Moor and Tyndrum.)

From Fort William to Loch Ness and Inverness: Follow the Caledonian Canal north along the A-82, which goes through Fort Augustus (and its worthwhile Caledonian Canal Heritage Centre) and then follows the north side of Loch Ness on its way to Inverness. Along the way, the A-82 passes Urquhart Castle and two Loch Ness Monster exhibits in Drumnadrochit. These attractions are described in the Inverness and the Northern Highlands chapter.

From Fort William to the Isle of Skye: You have two options for this journey: Head west on the A-830 (the Road to the Isles), then catch the ferry from Mallaig to Armadale on the Isle of Skye (described on page 911); or head north on the A-82 to Invergarry, and turn left (west) on the A-87, which you'll follow (past Eilean Donan Castle) to Kyle of Lochalsh and the Skye Bridge to the island. Consider using one route one way, and the other on the return trip—for example, follow the "Road to the Isles" from Fort William to Mallaig, and take the ferry to Skye; later, leaving Skye, take the A-87 east from the Skye Bridge past Eilean Donan Castle to Loch Ness and Inverness.

ISLE OF SKYE

*The Trotternish Peninsula • More Sights
on the Isle of Skye • Portree • Kyleakin*

The rugged, remote-feeling Isle of Skye has a reputation for unpredictable weather ("Skye" means "cloudy" in Old Norse, and locals call it "The Misty Isle"). But it also offers some of Scotland's best scenery, and it rarely fails to charm its many visitors. Narrow, twisty roads wind around Skye in the shadows of craggy, black, bald mountains.

Skye seems to have more sheep than people; 200 years ago, many human residents were forced to move off the island to make room for more livestock during the Highland Clearances. The people who remain are some of the most ardently Gaelic Scots in Scotland. The island's Sleat Peninsula is home to a rustic but important Gaelic college. Half of all native island residents speak Gaelic (which they pronounce "gallic") as their first language. A generation ago, it was illegal to teach Gaelic in schools; today, Skye offers its residents the opportunity to enroll in Gaelic-only education, from primary school to college.

Set up camp in one of the island's home-base towns, Portree or Kyleakin. Then dive into Skye's attractions. Drive around the appealing Trotternish Peninsula, enjoying stark vistas of jagged rock formations with the mysterious Outer Hebrides looming on the horizon. Explore a gaggle of old-fashioned stone homes, learn about Skye's ancient farming lifestyles, and pay homage at the grave of a brave woman who rescued a bonnie prince. Climb the dramatic Cuillin Hills, and drive to a lighthouse at the end of the world. Visit a pair of castles—the familial thought-provoking Dunvegan, and nearby but not on Skye, the photo-perfect Eilean Donan.

Planning Your Time

With a week in Scotland, Skye merits two nights, with a full day to hit its highlights (Trotternish Peninsula, Dunvegan Castle, Cuillin Hills, Talisker Distillery). Mountaineers need extra time for hiking and hillwalking. Because it takes time to reach, Skye (the northernmost destination in this book) is skippable if you only have a few days in Scotland—instead, focus on Edinburgh and the more accessible Highlands sights near Oban.

Skye fits neatly into a Highlands itinerary between Oban/Glencoe and Loch Ness/Inverness. To avoid seeing the same scenery twice, it works well to drive the "Road to the Isles" from Fort William to Mallaig, then take the ferry to Skye; later, leave Skye via the Skye Bridge and follow the A-87 east toward Loch Ness and Inverness, stopping at Eilean Donan Castle en route.

Getting to the Isle of Skye

By Car: Your easiest bet is the slick, free **Skye Bridge** that crosses from Kyle of Lochalsh on the mainland to Kyleakin on Skye (for more on the bridge, see page 924).

The island can also be reached from the mainland via a pair of **car ferry** crossings. The major ferry line connects the mainland town of Mallaig (west of Fort William along the "Road to the Isles" and the Harry Potter steam-train line—see page 906) to Armadale on Skye (£23.50/car, £4.50/passenger, late March-late Oct 8/day each way, 4-6/day on Sun, late Oct-late March very limited Sat-Sun connections, check-in closes 30 minutes before sailing, can be canceled in rough weather, 30-minute trip, operated by Caledonian MacBrayne, www.calmac.co.uk). A tiny, six-car, proudly local "turntable" ferry crosses the short gap between the mainland Glenelg and Skye's Kylerhea (£14/car with up to 4 passengers, £20 round-trip, roughly Easter-Oct daily every 20 minutes 10:00-18:00, June-Aug until 19:00, no need to book ahead, no boats off-season, Skye Ferry, www.skyeferry.com).

By Public Transportation: Skye is connected to the outside world by a series of Scottish Citylink **buses** (www.citylink.co.uk), which use Portree as their Skye hub. Rates listed are rough estimates for one-way travel. From Portree, buses connect to **Inverness** (£30, bus #917, 3-4/day, 3.25 hours), **Glasgow** (£40, buses #915 and #916, 3/day, 6.5-7.5 hours, also stops at **Fort William** and **Glencoe**), and **Edinburgh** (£50, 4/day, 7.5-8 hours, transfer in Inverness or Glasgow).

There are also some more complicated connections possible for the determined: Take the train from Edinburgh, Glasgow, or Inverness to Fort William; transfer to the steam train to Mallaig; take the ferry across to Armadale; and catch a bus to Portree.

Isle of Skye

ISLE OF SKYE

1. Sligachan Hotel & Rest.
2. MacKinnon Country House Hotel, White Heather Hotel, Cliffe House B&B; Taste of India Restaurant
3. Three Chimneys Restaurant
4. Waverly Restaurant
5. Broadford Hotel & Rest.

CASTLE

FERRY ROUTES (NOT ALL SHOWN)

SELF-GUIDED DRIVING ROUTE

KYLE OF LOCHALSH

TO INVERNESS

A-890

KYLE AKIN

A-87

DORNIE

EILEAN DONAN CASTLE

10 MILES

10 KM

KYLERHEA

A-87

GLENELG

TO FORT WILLIAM & LOCH NESS

"ROAD TO THE ISLES"

A-830

TO FORT WILLIAM

DCH

Alternatively, you can take the train from Edinburgh or Glasgow to Inverness, take the train to Kyle of Lochalsh, then take the bus to Portree.

Orientation to the Isle of Skye

The Isle of Skye is big (over 600 square miles), with lots of ins and outs—but you're never more than five miles from the sea. The island is punctuated by peninsulas and inlets (called "sea lochs"). Skye is covered with hills, but the most striking are the mountain-like Cuillin Hills in the south-central part of the island.

There are only about 11,000 people on the entire island; roughly a quarter live in the main village, Portree. Other population centers include Kyleakin (near the bridge connecting Skye with the mainland) and Broadford (a tidy string of houses on the road between Portree and the bridge, with the biggest and handiest grocery store and gas station on the island, open daily 9:00-22:00). A few of the villages—including Broadford and Dunvegan—have **TIs**, but the most useful one is in Portree.

Getting Around the Isle of Skye

By Car: Once on Skye, you'll need a car to enjoy the island. (Even if you're doing the rest of your trip by public transportation, a car rental is worthwhile here to bypass the frustrating public-transportation options; I've listed some car-rental options in Portree on page 927.) If you're driving, a good map is a must (look for a 1:130,000 map that covers the entire island with enough detail to point out side roads and attractions; Philip's and Ordnance Survey are good). You'll be surprised how long it takes to traverse this "small" island. Here are driving-time estimates for some likely trips: Kyleakin and Skye Bridge to Portree—45 minutes; Portree to Dunvegan—30 minutes; Portree to the tip of Trotternish Peninsula and back again—1.5-2 hours; Portree to Armadale—1 hour; Uig (on Trotternish Peninsula) to Dunvegan—45 minutes.

By Bus: Skye is frustrating by bus, especially on Sundays, when virtually no local buses run (except for a few long-distance buses to the ferry dock and mainland destinations). Portree is the hub for bus traffic. Most Skye buses are operated by Stagecoach. The company is experimenting by adding a new hop-on, hop-off bus service (#60); this open-top motor coach, which operates only in summer, stops in Sligachan, Dunvegan Castle, and the Trotternish Peninsula (www.stagecoachbus.com/highlands, time-table info from Traveline, tel. 0871-200-2233, www.traveline.org .uk). If you'll be using buses a lot, consider a Skye Dayrider ticket (£8/day, includes Kyle of Lochalsh) or the Skye North Island Megarider (£31/7 days, covers the northern half of Skye, including

Portree, Dunvegan, and the Trotternish Peninsula; no Megarider for southern half of the island). You can buy either of these tickets from any driver.

From Portree, you can go around the **Trotternish Peninsula** (#57, Mon-Sat 4-5/day in each direction—clockwise and counterclockwise; none on Sun), and to **Dunvegan** (#56, 5/day Mon-Fri, 3/day Sat, none on Sun, 40 minutes, goes right to the castle, catch a bus that leaves no later than 12:45 to have enough time at the castle). To bus it from Portree to **Kyleakin**, you'll need to travel on Scottish Citylink (#917, 4/day, 55 minutes).

By Tour: If you're without a car, consider taking a tour. Several operations on the island take visitors to hard-to-reach spots on a half-day or full-day tour. Some are more educational, while others are loose and informal. Look for brochures around the island, or ask locals for tips. **Kathleen MacAskil** with Skye Tours gives small-group tours by car or minibus (£22.50/person, 4 hours, minimum 4 people, tel. 01470/582-306, www.skyetours .co.uk, kathleenmacaskil@aol.com).

The Trotternish Peninsula

This inviting peninsula north of Portree is packed with windswept castaway scenery, unique geological formations, and some offbeat sights. In good weather, a spin around Trotternish is the single best Skye activity (and you'll still have time to visit Dunvegan Castle or the Cuillin Hills later on).

Self-Guided Driving Tour

Peninsula Loop
The following loop tour starts and ends in Portree, circling the peninsula counterclockwise. If you did it without stopping, you'd make it back to Portree within two hours—but it deserves the better part of a day. Note that from Portree to Uig, you'll be driving on a paved single-track road; use the occasional "passing places" to pull over and allow faster cars to go by.

The Drive Begins
Begin in the island's main town, Portree. (If you're heading up from Kyleakin, you'll enjoy some grand views of the Cuillin Hills on your way up—especially around the crossroads of Sligachan, described on page 920.) For sightseeing information on Portree—and the nearby Aros visitors center—see page 927.

• *Head north of Portree on the A-855, following signs for* Staffin. *About*

ISLE OF SKYE

three miles out of town, you'll begin to enjoy some impressive views of the Trotternish Ridge. As you pass the small loch on your right, straight ahead is the distinctive feature called the...

Old Man of Storr: This 160-foot-tall tapered slab of basalt stands proudly apart from the rest of the Storr. The unusual landscape of the Trotternish Peninsula is due to massive landslides (the largest in Britain). This block slid down the cliff about 6,500 years ago and landed on its end, where it was slowly whittled by weather into a pinnacle. The lochs on your right have been linked together to spin the turbines at a nearby hydroelectric plant that once provided all of Skye's electricity.

• *After passing the Old Man, enjoy the scenery on your right, overlooking...*

Nearby Islands and the Mainland: Some of Skye's most appealing scenery isn't the island itself, but the surrounding terrain. In the distance, craggy mountains recede into the horizon. The long island in the foreground, a bit to the north, is called Rona. This military-owned island, and the channel behind it, were used to develop and test one of Margaret Thatcher's pet projects, the Sting Ray remote-control torpedo.

• *After about five miles, keep an eye out on the right for a large parking lot near a wee loch. Park and walk to the viewpoint to see...*

Kilt Rock: So named because of its resemblance to a Scotsman's tartan kilt, this 200-foot-tall sea cliff has a layer of volcanic rock with vertical lava columns that look like pleats (known as columnar jointing), sitting atop a layer of horizontal sedimentary rock.

• *After continuing through the village of Staffin (whose name means "the pinnacle place"), you'll begin to see interesting rock formations high on the hill to your left. When you get to the crossroads, head left toward the Quiraing (a rock formation). This crossroads is a handy pit stop—there's a public WC in the Staffin Community Hall (in the same building as the licensed grocer, on your left as you pass through).*

Now twist your way up the road to the...

Quiraing: As you drive up, notice (on your left) a couple of modern cemeteries high in the hills, far above the village. It seems like a strange spot to bury the dead, in the middle of nowhere. But it's logical since the earth here is less valuable for development, and since it's not clay, like down by the water, it also provides better drainage.

You'll enjoy fine views on the right of the jagged, dramatic northern end of the Trotternish Ridge, called the Quiraing—rated ▲▲. More landslides caused the dramatic scenery in this

area, and each rock formation has a name, such as "The Needle" or "The Prison." As you approach the summit of this road, you'll reach a parking area on the left. This marks a popular trailhead for hiking out to get a closer look at the formations. If you've got the time, energy, and weather for a

sturdy 30-minute uphill hike, here's your chance. You can either follow the trail along the base of the rock formations, or hike up to the top of the plateau and follow it to the end (both paths are faintly visible from the parking area). Once up top, your reward is a view of the secluded green plateau called "The Table," another landslide block, which isn't visible from the road.

• *You could continue on this road all the way to Uig, at the other end of the peninsula, but it's worth backtracking, then turning left onto the main road (A-855), to see the...*

Tip of Trotternish: A few miles north, you'll pass a hotel called **Flodigarry,** with a cottage on the premises that was once home to Bonnie Prince Charlie's rescuer, Flora MacDonald (her story is explained later; the cottage is now part of the hotel and not open to the public).

Soon after, at the top of the ridge at the tip of the peninsula, you'll see the remains of an old **fort**—not from the Middle Ages or the days of Bonnie Prince Charlie, but from World War II, when the Atlantic was monitored for U-boats from this position.

Farther down the road, you'll pass (on the right) the crumbling remains of another fort, this one much older: **Duntulm Castle,** which was the first stronghold on Skye of the influential MacDonald clan. The castle was abandoned around 1730 for Armadale Castle on the southern end of Skye; according to legend, the family left after a nursemaid accidentally dropped the infant heir out a window onto the rocks below. In the distance beyond, you can see the **Outer Hebrides**—the most rugged, remote, and Gaelic part of Scotland. (Skye, a bit closer to the mainland, belongs to the Inner Hebrides.)

• *A mile after the castle, you'll come to a place called Kilmuir. Watch for the turn-off on the left to the excellent...*

Skye Museum of Island Life: This fine little stand of seven thatched stone huts, organized into a family-run museum and worth ▲▲, explains how a typical Skye family lived a century and a half ago (£2.50, Easter-Oct Mon-Sat 9:30-17:00, closed Sun and Nov-Easter, tel. 01470/552-206, www.skyemuseum.co.uk). Though there are ample posted explanations, the £1.25 guidebook is worthwhile.

The three huts closest to the sea are original (more than 200 years old). Most interesting is the one called The Old Croft House, which was the residence of the Graham family until 1957. Inside you'll find three rooms: kitchen (with peat-burning fire) on the right, parents' bedroom in the middle, and a bedroom for the 12 kids on the left. Nearby, The Old Barn displays farm implements, and the Ceilidh House contains some dense but very informative displays about crofting (the traditional tenant-farmer lifestyle on Skye—explained later), Gaelic, and other topics.

The four other huts were reconstructed here from elsewhere on the island, and now house exhibits about weaving and the village smithy (which was actually a gathering place). As you explore, admire the smart architecture of these humble but deceptively well-planned structures. Rocks hanging from the roof keep the thatch from blowing away, and the streamlined shape of the structure embedded in the ground encourages strong winds to deflect around the hut rather than hit it head-on.

• *After touring the museum, drive out to the very end of the small road that leads past the parking lot, to a lonesome cemetery. The tallest Celtic cross at the far end of the cemetery (you can enter the gate to reach it) is the...*

Monument to Flora MacDonald: This local heroine sup-

posedly rescued beloved Scottish hero Bonnie Prince Charlie at his darkest hour. After his loss at Culloden, and with a hefty price on his head, Charlie retreated to the Outer Hebrides. But the Hanover dynasty, which controlled the islands, was closing in. Flora MacDonald rescued the prince, disguised him as her Irish maid, Betty Burke, and sailed him to safety on Skye. (Charlie pulled off the ruse thanks to his soft, feminine features—hence the nickname "Bonnie," which means "beautiful.") The flight inspired a popular Scottish folk song: "Speed bonnie boat like a bird on the wing, / Onward, the sailors cry. / Carry the lad that's born to be king / Over the sea to Skye." For more on Bonnie Prince Charlie and the Battle of Culloden, see page 956.

• *Return to the main road and proceed about six miles around the peninsula. On the right, notice the big depression.*

The Missing Loch: This was once a large loch, but it was drained in the mid-20th century to create more grazing land for sheep. If you look closely, you may see a scattering of stones in the middle of the field. Once a little island, this is the site of a former monastery...now left as high, dry, and forgotten as the loch. Beyond the missing loch is Prince Charlie's Point, where the bonnie prince supposedly came ashore on Skye with Flora MacDonald.

• *Soon after the loch, you'll drop down over the town of...*

Uig: Pronounced "OO-eeg," this village is the departure point for ferries to the Outer Hebrides (North Uist and Harris islands, 2-3/day). It's otherwise unremarkable, but does have a café with good sandwiches (follow *Uig Pier* signs into town—look for a white building with blue *Café* sign, next to ferry terminal at entrance to town).

• *Continue past Uig, climbing the hill across the bay. Near the top is a large parking strip on the right. Pull over here and look back to Uig for a lesson about Skye's traditional farming system.*

Crofting: You'll hear a lot about crofts during your time on Skye. Traditionally, arable land on the island was divided into

plots. If you look across to the hills above Uig, you can see strips of demarcated land running up from the water—these are crofts. Crofts were generally owned by landlords (mostly English aristocrats or Scottish clan chiefs, and later the Scottish government) and rented to tenant farmers. The crofters lived and worked under very difficult conditions, and were lucky if they could produce enough potatoes, corn, and livestock to feed their families. Rights to farm the croft were passed down from father to son over generations, but always under the auspices of a wealthy landlord.

Finally, in 1976, new legislation kicked off a process of privatization called "decrofting." Suddenly crofters could have their land decrofted, then buy it for an affordable price (£130 per quarter-hectare, or about £8,000 for one of the crofts you see here). Many decroftees would quickly turn around and sell their old family home for a huge profit, but hang on to most of their land and build

ISLE OF SKYE

a new house at the other end. In the crofts you see here, notice that some have a house at the top of a strip of land and another house at the bottom. Many crofts (like most of these) are no longer cultivated, but that should change, as crofters are now legally required to farm their land...or lose it. In many cases, families who have other jobs still hang on to their traditional croft, which they use to grow produce for themselves or to supplement their income.

• *Our tour is finished. From here, you can continue along the main road south toward Portree (and possibly continue from there on to the Cuillin Hills). Or take the shortcut road just after Kensaleyre (B-8036), and head west on the A-850 to Dunvegan and its castle. Both options are described later.*

More Sights on the Isle of Skye

▲▲Cuillin Hills

These dramatic, rocky "hills" (which look more like mountains to me) stretch along the southern coast of the island, dominating Skye's landscape. More craggy and alpine than anything else you'll see in Scotland, the Cuillin seem to rise directly from the deep. You'll see them from just about anywhere on the southern two-thirds of the island, but no roads actually take you through the heart of the Cuillin—that's reserved for hikers and climbers, who love this area. To get the best views with a car, consider these options:

Near Sligachan: The road from the Skye Bridge to Portree is the easiest way to appreciate the Cuillin (you'll almost certainly drive along here at some point during your visit). These mountains are all that's left of a long-vanished volcano. As you approach, you'll clearly see that there are three separate ranges (from right to left): red, gray, and black. The steep and challenging Black Cuillin is the most popular for serious climbers; the granite Red Cuillin ridge is more rounded.

The crossroads of Sligachan, with an old triple-arched bridge and a landmark hotel (see page 929), is nestled at the foothills of the Cuillin, and is a popular launch pad for mountain fun. The 2,500-foot-tall cone-shaped hill looming over Sligachan, named Glamaig ("Greedy Lady"), is the site of an annual 4.5-mile race in July: Speed hikers begin at the door of the Sligachan Hotel, race to the summit, run around a bagpiper, and scramble back down to the hotel. The record: 44 minutes (30 minutes up, 13 minutes down, 1 minute dancing a jig up top).

Elgol: For the best view of the Cuillin, locals swear by the drive from Broadford (on the Portree-Kyleakin road) to Elgol, at the tip of a small peninsula that faces the Black Cuillin head-on. While it's just 12 miles as the crow flies from Sligachan, give it a half-hour each way to drive (mostly on single-track roads) into Elgol from Broadford. To get an even better Cuillin experience, take a boat excursion from Elgol into Loch Coruisk, a "sea loch" (fjord) surrounded by the Cuillin (April-Oct, various companies do the trip several times a day, fewer on Sun and off-season, generally 3 hours round-trip including 1.5 hours free time on the shore of the loch, figure £15-22 round-trip).

▲Dunvegan Castle

Perched on a rock overlooking a sea loch, this ancestral castle is a strange and intriguing artifact of Scotland's antiquated, nearly

extinct clan system. Dunvegan Castle is the residence of the MacLeod (pronounced "McCloud") clan—along with the MacDonalds, one of Skye's preeminent clans. Worth ▲▲▲ to people named MacLeod, the castle offers an interesting look at aristocratic life and is a good way to pass the time on a rainy day. The owners claim it's the oldest continuously inhabited castle in Scotland.

Cost and Hours: £9.50, April-mid-Oct daily 10:00-17:30, last entry 30 minutes before closing, mid-Oct-March Mon-Fri open by appointment only, no interior photos, café, tel. 01470/521-206, www.dunvegancastle.com.

Getting There: It's near the small town of Dunvegan in the northwestern part of the island, well-signposted from the A-850. As you approach Dunvegan on the A-850, the two flat-topped plateaus you'll see are nicknamed "MacLeod's Tables."

You can also get to the castle by bus from Portree (#56, 5/day Mon-Fri, 3/day Sat, none on Sun; leave Portree no later than 12:45 to have time to tour the castle).

Background: In Gaelic, *clann* means "children," and the clan system was the traditional Scottish way of passing along power—similar to England's dukes, barons, and counts. Each clan traces its roots to an ancestral castle, like Dunvegan. The MacLeods (or, as they prefer, "MacLeod of MacLeod") eventually fell on hard times. Having run out of male heirs in 1935, Dame Flora MacLeod of MacLeod became the 28th clan chief. Her grandson, John MacLeod of MacLeod, became the 29th chief after her death in 1976. With their castle looking rough around the edges and their leaky roof in need of fixing, John MacL of MacL threatened to sell the Black Cuillin ridge of hills (which technically belonged to him)

ISLE OF SKYE

for £10 million to pay for a new roof. The deal outraged locals, but it wasn't concluded prior to the chief's passing in early 2007. The current clan chief, Hugh Magnus MacLeod of MacLeod, is a film producer who divides his time between London and the castle, where his noble efforts are aimed at preserving Dunvegan (roof included) for future generations.

❍ Self-Guided Tour: Unlike medieval castles, the interior feels lived in; you'll notice the MacLeods proudly display their heritage—old photographs and portraits of former chiefs—like any family decorating the walls of their home. You'll wander through halls, the dining room, and the library, and peer down into the dungeon's deep pit. Pick up the laminated flier in each room to discover some of the history. In the **Drawing Room,** look for the tattered silk remains of the Fairy Flag, a mysterious swatch with about a dozen different legends attached to it (most say that it was a gift from a fairy, and somehow it's related to the Crusades). It's said that the clan chief can invoke the power of the flag three times, in the clan's darkest moments. It's worked twice before on the battlefield—which means there's just one use left.

The most interesting historical tidbits are in the **North Room,** which was built in 1360 as the original Great Hall. The family's coat of arms in the middle of the carpet has a confused-looking bull and the clan motto, "Hold Fast"—recalling an incident where a MacLeod saved a man from being gored by a bull when he grabbed its horns and forced it to stop. (Notice the book in the display case along the wall. It's opened to a different coat of arms claiming MacLeod heritage—this one with lions instead of a bull.) Also in the room, find the Dunvegan Cup and the Horn of Rory Mor. Traditionally, this horn would be filled with nearly a half-gallon of claret (Bordeaux wine), which a potential heir had to drink without stopping (or falling) to prove himself fit for the role. (The late chief, John MacLeod of MacLeod, bragged that he did it in less than two minutes...but you have to wonder if Dame Flora chug-a-lugged.) Other artifacts in the North Room include bagpipes and several relics related to Bonnie Prince Charlie (including a lock of his hair and his vest). Look for a portrait of Flora MacDonald and some items that belonged to her.

At the end of the tour, you can wander out onto the **terrace** (overlooking a sea loch) and, in the cellar, watch a **video** about the clan. Between the castle and the parking lot are five acres of enjoyable **gardens** to stroll through while pondering the fading clan system. You can also take a **boat ride** on Loch Dunvegan to visit a seal colony on a nearby island (£6, boats run mid-April-Sept only, 10:00-17:00, last trip around 16:30, 25 minutes, tel. 01470/521-500).

The flaunting of inherited wealth and influence in some English castles rubs me the wrong way. But here, seeing the rough edges of a Scottish clan chief's castle, I had the opposite feeling: sympathy and compassion for a proud way of life that's slipping into the sunset of history. You have to admire the way they "hold fast" to this antiquated system (in the same way the Gaelic tongue is kept on life support). Paying admission here feels more like donating to charity than padding the pockets of a wealthy family. In fact, watered-down McClouds and McDonalds from America, eager to reconnect with their Scottish roots, help keep the Scottish clan system alive.

▲Neist Point and Lighthouse

To get a truly edge-of-the-world feeling, consider an adventure on the back lanes of the Duirinish Peninsula, west of Dunvegan.

This trip is best for hardy drivers looking to explore the most remote corner of Skye and undertake a strenuous hike to a lighthouse. (The lighthouse itself is a letdown, so do this only if you believe a journey is its own reward.) Although it looks close on the map, give this trip 30 minutes each way from Dunvegan, plus 30 minutes or more for the lighthouse hike.

The owner of this private property has signs on his padlocked gate stating that you enter at your own risk—which many walkers happily do. (It's laughably easy to walk around the unintimidating "wall.") From here you can enjoy sheep and cliff views, but you can't see the lighthouse itself unless you do the sturdy 30-minute hike (with a steep uphill return). After hiking around the cliff, the lighthouse springs into view, with the Outer Hebrides beyond.

Getting There: Head west from Dunvegan, following signs for *Glendale.* You'll cross a moor, then twist around the Dunvegan sea loch, before heading overland and passing through rugged, desolate hamlets that seem like the setting for a BBC sitcom about backwater Britain. After passing through Glendale, carefully track *Neist Point* signs until you reach an end-of-the-road parking lot.

Eating: It's efficient and fun to combine this trek with lunch or dinner at the pricey, recommended **Three Chimneys Restaurant,** on the road to Neist Point at Colbost (reservations essential; see page 931).

▲Talisker Distillery

Opened in 1830, Talisker is a Skye institution (and the only distillery on the island). If you've tried only mainland whisky, island whisky is worth a dram to appreciate the differences. Island whisky is known for having a strong smoky flavor, due to the amount of peat smoke used during the malting of the barley. The Isle of Islay has the smokiest, and Talisker workers describe theirs as "medium smoky," which may be easier for non-connoisseurs to take. Talisker produces single-malt whisky only, so it's a favorite with whisky purists: On summer days, this tiny distillery swarms with visitors from all over the world.

Cost and Hours: £7 for a 45-minute tour, a wee dram, and a £3 voucher toward a bottle, £25 tasting tour offered on selected weekdays—call ahead; April-Oct Mon-Sat 9:30-17:00, closed Sun except in June-Aug when it's open 11:00-17:00, last tour one hour before closing; Nov-March Mon-Fri 10:00-16:30, tours at 10:30, 12:00, 14:00, and 15:30, closed Sat-Sun, call ahead; no photos or mobile phones, down a tiny road in Carbost village, tel. 01478/614-308, www.discovering-distilleries.com.

Skye Bridge

Connecting Kyleakin on Skye with Kyle of Lochalsh on the mainland, the Skye Bridge severely damaged B&B business in the towns it connects. Environmentalists worry about the bridge disrupting the habitat for otters—keep an eye out for these furry native residents. But it's been a boon for Skye tourism—making a quick visit to the island possible without having to wait for a ferry.

The bridge, which was Europe's most expensive toll bridge per foot when it opened in 1995, has stirred up a remarkable amount of controversy among island-dwellers. Here's the Skye natives' take on things: A generation ago, Lowlanders (city folk) began selling their urban homes and buying cheap property on Skye. Natives had grown to enjoy the slow-paced lifestyle that came with living life according to the whim of the ferry, but these new transplants found their commute into civilization too frustrating by boat. They demanded a new bridge be built. Finally a deal was struck to privately fund the bridge, but the toll wasn't established before construction began. So when the bridge opened—and the ferry line it replaced closed—locals were shocked to be charged upward of £5 per car each way to go to the mainland. A few years ago, the bridge was bought by the Scottish Executive, the fare was abolished, and the Skye natives were appeased...for now.

▲▲Near the Isle of Skye: Eilean Donan Castle

This postcard castle, watching over a sea loch from its island perch, is conveniently and scenically situated on the road between the Isle of Skye and Loch Ness. Famous from such films as Sean Connery's *Highlander* (1986) and the James Bond movie *The World Is Not Enough* (1999), Eilean Donan (EYE-lan DOHN-an) might be Scotland's most photogenic countryside castle (chances are good it's on that Scotland calendar you bought during your trip).

Though it looks ancient, the castle is actually less than a century old. The original castle on this site (dating from 800 years ago) was destroyed in battle in 1719, then rebuilt between 1912 and 1932 by the MacRae family as their residence.

Even if you're not going inside, the castle warrants a five-minute photo stop. But the interior—with cozy rooms—is worth a peek if you have time. Walk across the bridge and into the castle complex, and make your way into the big, blocky keep. First you'll see the claustrophobic, vaulted Billeting Room (where soldiers had their barracks), then head upstairs to the inviting Banqueting Room. Docents posted in these rooms can tell you more. Another flight of stairs takes you to the circa-1930 bedrooms. Downstairs is the cute kitchen exhibit, with mannequins preparing a meal (read the recipes posted throughout). Finally, you'll head through a few more assorted exhibits to the exit.

Cost and Hours: £6.50, good £3.50 guidebook; daily July-Aug 9:00-18:00, March-June & Sept-Oct 10:00-18:00; generally closed Nov-Feb but may be open a few times a week—call ahead, last entry one hour before closing; café, tel. 01599/555-202, www.eileandonancastle.com.

Getting There: It's not actually on the Isle of Skye, but it's quite close, in the mainland town of Dornie. Follow the A-87 about 15 minutes east of Skye Bridge, through Kyle of Lochalsh and toward Loch Ness and Inverness. The castle is on the right side of this road, just after a long bridge.

Portree

Skye's main attraction is its natural beauty, not its villages. But of the villages, the best home base is Portree (say poor-TREE fast, comes from Port Righ, literally, "Royal Port"). This village (with less than 3,000 people, too small to be con-

sidered a "town") is Skye's largest settlement and the hub of activity and transportation.

ISLE OF SKYE

Portree

P PARKING   B BUS STOP

100 YARDS
100 METERS

🔭 VIEW

A-87 TO UIG & DUNVEGAN

PLAY FIELDS

A-855 TO STAFFIN & TROTTERNISH PENINSULA

SCHOOL

SOMERLED SQUARE

HARBOR

FERRY TERMINAL

A-87 TO ❶, AROS CENTRE, SLIGACHAN & KYLE OF LOCHALSH

SOUND OF RAASAY

ISLE OF SKYE

❶ To Almondbank Guest House
❷ Marine House
❸ Pink Guest House; Lower Deck & Sea Breezes Restaurants
❹ Braeside B&B
❺ Bayview House
❻ Bayfield Backpackers Hostel
❼ Rosedale Restaurant & Café Arriba
❽ The Café
❾ The Bosville Hotel Bistro
❿ Co-op Grocery
⓫ School Library (Internet)
⓬ Hostel (Launderette) & Bike Rental

Orientation to Portree

This functional village has a small harbor and, on the hill above it, a tidy main square (from which buses fan out across the island and to the mainland). Surrounding the central square are just a few streets. Homes, shops, and B&Bs line the roads to other settlements on the island.

Tourist Information

Portree's helpful TI is a block off the main square. They can help you sort through bus schedules, give you maps, and book you a room for a £4 fee (Mon-Sat 9:00-18:00, closes at 17:00 off-season; Sun 10:00-16:00; Bayfield Road, just south of Bridge Road, tel. 01478/612-992 or 0845-225-5121). Public WCs are across the street and down a block, across from the hostel.

Helpful Hints

Internet Access: The **TI** has two terminals in the back (£1/20 minutes), and the big **Aros Centre** outside of town has several computers as well (£2/hour, see listing under "Sights in Portree," later). You can get online at the **library** in Portree High School (free, picture ID required, Mon-Fri 9:15-17:00, Tue and Thu until 20:00, Sat 10:00-16:00, closed Sun, Viewfield Road, tel. 01478/614-823).

Laundry: The **Independent Hostel,** just off the main square, has a self-service launderette down below (about £4 self-service, £8 full-service, usually 11:00-21:00, last load starts at 20:00, The Green/A-855, tel. 01478/613-737).

Supermarket: A **Co-op** is on Bank Street (daily 7:00-23:00).

Bike Rental: Island Cycles rents bikes in the middle of town, also just off the main square (£8.50/half-day, £15/24 hours, Mon-Sat 9:00-17:00, closed Sun, The Green/A-855, tel. 01478/613-121).

Car Rental: M2 Motors will pick you up at your B&B or the bus station (£45-55/day, half-day available, Dunvegan Road, tel. 01478/613-344). Other places to rent a car are outside of town, on the road toward Dunvegan. The **MacRae Dealership** is a 10-minute walk from downtown Portree (£46-52/day, Mon-Fri 9:00-17:00, Sat 9:00-12:00, no pick-up Sun, call at least a week in advance in summer, tel. 01478/612-554); farther along the same road are **Jansvans** (£57/day, Mon-Sat 8:00-17:30, closed Sun, tel. 01478/612-087) and **Portree Coachworks** (£48/day, Mon-Fri 8:30-17:30, Sat 9:00-13:00, no pick-up Sun, book in advance, tel. 01478/612-688).

Parking: As you enter town, a free parking lot is off to the right—

ISLE OF SKYE

look for the sign. You can also pay to park in the main town square or in front of the TI.

Sights in Portree

Harbor

Portree has some shops to peruse, but the best activity is to simply wander along the colorful harbor, where boat captains offer £18 1.5-hour excursions out to the sea-eagle nests and around the bay (ask at TI).

Aros Centre

This visitors center and cinema, a mile outside of town on the road to Kyleakin and Skye Bridge, overlooks the sea loch. It offers a humble but earnest exhibit run by the Royal Society for the Protection of Birds (RSPB) about the island's wildlife (mainly its birds; ask if there's still a heron nest in the trees at the far end of the parking lot). Enjoy the 20-minute movie with spectacular aerial photos of otherwise-hard-to-reach parts of Skye, and chat with the ranger. The exhibit also describes the local sea eagles. These raptors were hunted to extinction on Skye but have been reintroduced to the ecosystem from Scandinavia. A live webcam shows their nests nearby—or, if there are no active nests, a "greatest hits" video of past fledglings.

Cost and Hours: £4.75, Easter-Oct daily 9:00-17:00, last entry 30 minutes before closing, closed Nov-Easter, café, gift shop, a mile south of town center on Viewfield Road, tel. 01478/613-649, www.aros.co.uk.

Sleeping in Portree

(area code: 01478)

$$$ **Almondbank Guest House,** on the road into town from Kyleakin, works well for drivers and has great views of the loch from the public areas. It has four tidy, homey rooms (two with sea views for no extra charge) and is run by friendly Effie Nicolson (Sb-£68, Db-£85, free Wi-Fi, Viewfield Road, tel. 01478/612-696, j.n.almondbank@btconnect.com).

$$ **Marine House,** run by sweet Skye native Fiona Stephenson, has three simple, homey rooms (two with a private bathroom down the hall) and fabulous views of the harbor (S-£25-30, D-£66-70, Db-£70-72, cash only, 2 Beaumont Crescent, tel. 01478/611-557, stephensonfiona@yahoo.com).

$$ At **Pink Guest House,** energetic Robbie and Fiona rent 11 bright, spacious rooms (8 with sea views) on the harbor. The rates include a full Scottish breakfast and the hosts' youthful enthusiasm (Db-£70, sea-view Db-£80, large family rooms, free Wi-Fi,

---

Sleep Code

(£1 = about $1.60, country code: 44)
S = Single, **D** = Double/Twin, **T** = Triple, **Q** = Quad, **b** = bathroom, **s** = shower only. Unless otherwise noted, credit cards are accepted at hotels and hostels—but not B&Bs—and breakfast is included.

To help you sort easily through these listings, I've divided the accommodations into three categories based on the price for a standard double room with bath (during high season):

$$$ Higher Priced—Most rooms £75 or more.
  $$ Moderately Priced—Most rooms between £50-75.
    $ Lower Priced—Most rooms £50 or less.

Prices can change without notice; verify the hotel's current rates online or by email.

Quay Street, tel. 01478/612-263, www.pinkguesthouse.co.uk, info@pinkguesthouse.co.uk).

$$ Braeside B&B has three comfortable rooms at the top of town, up from the Bosville Hotel (Db-£70, Tb-£90, £5 cheaper without breakfast, cash only, steep stairs, Stormyhill, tel. 01478/612-613, www.braesideportree.co.uk, mail@braesideportree .co.uk, Ruth).

$$ Bayview House has seven small and basic rooms, well-located on the main road just below the square (Db-£50-60, no breakfast, free Wi-Fi, Bridge Road, tel. 01478/613-340, www.bay viewhouse.co.uk, info@bayviewhouse.co.uk, Murdo and Alison). If there's no answer, walk down the stairs to Bayfield Backpackers, described next.

Hostel: **$ Bayfield Backpackers**—run by Murdo and Alison from the Bayview House (see listing above)—is a modern-feeling, institutional, cinderblock-and-metal hostel with 24 beds in 4- to 8-bed rooms (£16-17/bunk, pay Wi-Fi, kitchen, tel. 01478/612-231, www.skyehostel.co.uk, info@skyehostel.co.uk).

Sleeping near Portree, in Sligachan

$$$ Sligachan Hotel, a compound of related sleeping and eating options, is a local institution and a haven for hikers. It's been in the Campbell family since 1913. The hotel's 21 renovated rooms are comfortable, if a bit simple for the price, while the nearby campground and bunkhouse offer a budget alternative. The setting—surrounded by the mighty Cuillin Hills—is remarkably scenic (May-Sept: Db-£135, superior Db-£155; April and Oct: Db-£110, superior Db-£135; March: Db-£95, superior Db-£115;

ISLE OF SKYE

closed Nov-Feb, campground-£6/person, bunkhouse-£20/person in 4- to 6-bed rooms, pay guest computer in pub, free Wi-Fi for hotel guests, on the A-87 between Kyleakin and Portree in Sligachan, hotel and campground tel. 01478/650-204, bunkhouse tel. 01478/650-458, www.sligachan.co.uk, reservations@sligachan.co.uk).

Eating in Portree

Note that Portree's few eateries tend to close early (21:00 or 22:00), and during busy times, lines begin to form soon after 19:00. Eating early works best here.

On the Waterfront: A pair of good eateries vie for your attention along Portree's little harbor. **Lower Deck** feels like a salty sailor's restaurant, decorated with the names of local ships (£6-10 lunches, £10-14 dinners, daily 12:00-14:30 & 18:00-21:30, closed Nov-March, tel. 01478/613-611). **Sea Breezes,** with a more contemporary flair, serves tasty cuisine with an emphasis on seafood (£8-12 lunches, £12-20 dinners, £18 two-course early-bird specials 17:00-18:00, open daily June-Aug 12:30-14:00 & 17:00-21:30, shorter hours generally in April-May and Sept-Oct, closed Nov-March, reserve ahead for dinner, tel. 01478/612-016, www.seabreezes-skye.co.uk).

Rosedale Restaurant, with just a dozen tables and stunning views of the harbor, is the place for fresh, local seafood. Willie and Fiona work the front of the house while son-in-law Robert creates delicious, local dishes featuring all things shellfish (£7-13 lunches, £12-20 dinners, £60 seafood platter for two, daily 12:00-14:00 & 17:30-21:00, reservations smart, tel. 01478/613-214, www.portreerestaurant.co.uk).

Elsewhere in Portree: **Café Arriba** tries hard to offer eclectic flavors in this small Scottish town. With an ambitious menu that includes local specialties, Mexican, Italian, and more, this youthful, colorful, easygoing eatery's hit-or-miss cuisine is worth trying. Drop in to see what's on the blackboard menu today (£4-9 meals, lots of vegetarian options, daily 8:00-18:00, Quay Brae, tel. 01478/611-830).

The Café, a few steps off the main square, is a busy, popular hometown diner serving good crank-'em-out food to an appreciative local crowd. The homemade ice-cream stand in the front is a nice way to finish your meal (£9-10 lunches and burgers, £10-15 dinners, also does take-away, daily 8:30-15:30 & 17:30-21:00, Wentworth Street, tel. 01478/612-553).

The Bosville Hotel Bistro offers a popular selection of inexpensive, casual dishes (£7-9 lunch sandwiches, £10-16 lunches, £11-22 dinners, daily 12:00-14:00 & 17:30-21:00, until 21:30 in

ISLE OF SKYE

June-Aug). Their 19 rooms are expensive, but worth considering (Db-£128-165, tel. 01478/612-846, www.bosvillehotel.co.uk).

Eating Elsewhere on the Isle of Skye

In Sligachan

Sligachan Hotel (described earlier) has a lovely dining room and a microbrew pub serving up mountaineer-pleasing grub. Its setting is extremely scenic, nestled in the Cuillin Hills (traditional dinners in restaurant, served nightly 18:30-21:00; pub grub—£7-11, served until 21:30; pub closed Oct-Feb, on the A-87 between Kyleakin and Portree in Sligachan, tel. 01478/650-204).

In Colbost, near Dunvegan

Three Chimneys Restaurant is your big-splurge-on-a-small-island meal. The high-quality Scottish cuisine, using local ingredients, earns rave reviews. Its 16 tables fill an old three-chimney croft house, with a stone-and-timbers decor that artfully melds old and new. It's cozy, classy, and candlelit, but not stuffy. Because of its remote location—and the fact that it's almost always booked up—reservations are absolutely essential, ideally several weeks if not months ahead, although it's worth calling in case of last-minute cancellations (lunch: £28.50 for two courses, £37 for three courses; dinner: £60 for three courses, £90 for seven-course "showcase menu"; dinner served nightly from 18:15, last booking at 21:45, lunch mid-March-Oct Mon-Sat 12:15-13:45, no lunch Sun or Nov-mid-March, closed for 3 weeks in Jan, tel. 01470/511-258, www.threechimneys.co.uk, Eddie and Shirley Spear). They also rent six swanky, pricey suites next door (Db-£295-415, less off-season).

Getting There: It's in the village of Colbost, about a 10- to 15-minute drive west of Dunvegan on the Duirinish Peninsula (that's about 45 minutes each way from Portree). To get there, first head for Dunvegan, then follow signs toward Glendale. This single-track road twists you through the countryside, over a moor, and past several dozen sheep before passing through Colbost. You can combine this with a visit to the Neist Point Lighthouse (described earlier), which is at the end of the same road.

Kyleakin

Kyleakin (kih-LAH-kin), the last town in Skye before the bridge, used to be a big tourist hub...until the bridge connecting it to the

mainland made it much easier for people to get to Portree and other areas deeper in the island. Today this unassuming little village, with a ruined castle (Castle Moil), a cluster of lonesome fishing boats, and a forgotten ferry slip, still works well as a home base.

If you want to pick up information on the island before you drive all the way to Portree, stop by the tiny **TI** in Broadford, about 15 minutes farther up the road from Kyleakin, where the friendly "one 'ell of a Callum" helps travelers sort out options (April-Oct Mon-Sat 9:30-17:00—until 18:00 July-Aug, Sun 10:00-16:00, closed Nov-March, maps and hiking books, in Co-op parking lot, WCs across street next to church; no phone or email in Kyleakin office, but questions answered by Visit Scotland at tel. 0845-225-5121, info@visit scotland.com).

Helpful Hints

Internet Access: If you're desperate, **Saucy Mary's** store/bar has a laptop and printer available for visitors to use (Main Street, tel. 01599/534-845).

Laundry: Saucy Mary's offers laundry service (£12 wash/dry); there is also a launderette in Broadford, next to the Co-op supermarket (daily 6:00-20:00, shorter hours in winter).

Supermarkets: A **Co-op** is across the bridge in Kyle of Lochalsh (daily 7:00-23:00, Bridge Road, tel. 01599/530-190), and another is up the road in Broadford (daily 9:00-22:00, Main Street, tel. 01471/820-420).

Car Rental: You can rent a car for the day from **Skye Car Hire** (about £45/day, daily 9:00-17:00, in Kyle of Lochalsh, free delivery within 5 miles, tel. 01599/534-323, www.skyecarhire .co.uk).

Taxi: For taxi services or local tours, contact **Kyle Taxi** (also in Kyle of Lochalsh, same phone number as Skye Car Hire, www.lochalsh.net/taxi).

ISLE OF SKYE

Sleeping in Kyleakin

(area code: 01599)

$$$ MacKinnon Country House Hotel is my favorite country-side home base on Skye. It sits quietly in the middle of five acres of gardens just off the bustling Skye Bridge and boasts of famous visitors such as Queen Elizabeth II and Winston Churchill. Ian and Carol Smith Tongs have lovingly restored this old 1912 country home with Edwardian antiques and 18 clan-themed rooms, an inviting overstuffed-sofa lounge, and a restaurant with garden views in nearly every direction (Sb-£50-55, Db-£110-150 depending on room size and amenities, 10 percent discount when you mention this book in 2014, about 20 percent cheaper Oct-Easter, room fridges, free Wi-Fi; 10-minute walk from Kyleakin, at the turnoff for the bridge; tel. 01599/534-180, www.mackinnonhotel .co.uk, info@mackinnonhotel.co.uk). Ian also serves a delicious dinner to guests and non-guests alike (see "Eating in Kyleakin," later). Moss, the border collie, will try to take you for a walk.

$$$ White Heather Hotel, run by friendly and helpful Gillian and Craig Glenwright, has nine small but nicely decorated rooms with woody pine bathrooms, across from the waterfront and the castle ruins (Sb-£52, Db-£76, family rooms, cheaper for stays longer than 2 nights, free guest computer and Wi-Fi, lounges, washer and dryer available, closed late Oct-Feb, The Harbour, tel. 01599/534-577, www.whiteheatherhotel.co.uk, info@white heatherhotel.co.uk).

$$$ Cliffe House B&B rents three rooms in a white house perched at the very edge of the water. All of the rooms, including the breakfast room, enjoy wonderful views over the strait and the bridge (Db-£70-80, cash only, closed Dec-Jan, tel. 01599/534-019, www.cliffehousebedandbreakfast.co.uk, info@cliffehousebed andbreakfast.co.uk, Ian and Mary Sikorski).

Eating in and near Kyleakin

Locals like the **Taste of India,** just past the roundabout outside Kyleakin on the A-87 toward Broadford (£8-13 main courses, also does take-away, daily 17:00-23:00, tel. 01599/534-134). For a nice dinner, head up to the recommended **MacKinnon Country House Hotel** (£15-20 main courses, nightly 19:00-20:30, just outside Kyleakin at roundabout, tel. 01599/534-180). Little Kyleakin also has a few pubs; ask your B&B host for advice.

In Kyle of Lochalsh: If you can get reservations, eat fresh Scottish cuisine at the **Waverly Restaurant,** a tiny six-table place with locally sourced food, across the bridge from Kyleakin in Kyle

ISLE OF SKYE

of Lochalsh (£13-20 main courses, £12.75 two-course dinner special 17:30-19:00, open Fri-Tue 17:30-21:30, closed Wed-Thu, reservations essential, Main Street, across from Kyle Hotel and up the stairs, tel. 01599/534-337, www.waverleykyle.co.uk, Dutch chef/owner Ank).

In Broadford: Up the road in Broadford are more eateries, including the renovated **Broadford Hotel,** overlooking the bay (£9-17 main courses, Torrin Road at junction with Elgol, tel. 01471/822-204). It was here that a secret elixir—supposedly once concocted for Bonnie Prince Charlie—was re-created by hotelier James Ross after finding the recipe in his father's belongings. Now known as Drambuie, the popular liqueur, which caught on in the 19th century, is made with Scottish whisky, honey, and spices. With its wide variety of Drambuie drinks, the Broadford is the place to try it.

INVERNESS AND THE NORTHERN HIGHLANDS

Inverness • Loch Ness • Culloden Battlefield • Clava Cairns

Filled with more natural and historical mystique than people, the northern Highlands are where Scottish dreams are set. Legends of Bonnie Prince Charlie linger around crumbling castles as tunes played by pipers in kilts swirl around tourists. Explore the locks and lochs of the Caledonian Canal while the Loch Ness monster plays hide-and-seek. Hear the music of the Highlands in Inverness and the echo of muskets at Culloden, where the English drove Bonnie Prince Charlie into exile and conquered his Jacobite supporters.

I've focused my coverage on the handy hub of Inverness, with several day-trip options into the surrounding countryside. For Highlands sights to the south and west, see the Oban and the Southern Highlands chapter; for the Isle of Skye off Scotland's west coast, see the previous chapter.

Planning Your Time

Though it has little in the way of sights, Inverness does have a workaday charm and is a handy spot to spend a night or two en route to other Highland destinations. One night here gives you time to take a quick tour of nearby attractions. With two nights, you can find a full day's worth of sightseeing nearby.

Note that Loch Ness is on the way toward Oban or the Isle of Skye. If you're heading to one of those places, it makes sense to see Loch Ness en route, rather than as a side trip from Inverness.

For a speedy itinerary through the Highlands that includes Inverness and Loch Ness, see page 876.

Getting Around the Highlands

With a car, the day trips around Inverness are easy. Without a car, you can get to Inverness by train (better from Edinburgh or Pitlochry) or by bus (better from Skye, Oban, and Glencoe), then side-trip to Loch Ness, Culloden, and other nearby attractions by public bus or with a package tour.

Inverness

The only city in the north of Scotland, Inverness is pleasantly situated on the River Ness at the base of a castle (now a courthouse, not

a tourist attraction). Inverness' charm is its normalcy—it's a nice, midsize Scottish city that gives you a palatable taste of the "urban" Highlands, and is well-located for enjoying the surrounding countryside sights. Check out the bustling, pedestrian downtown or meander the picnic-friendly riverside paths—best

at sunset, when the light hits the castle and couples hold hands while strolling along the water and over the many footbridges.

Orientation to Inverness

Inverness, with about 60,000 people, is the fastest-growing city in Scotland. Marked by its castle, Inverness clusters along the River Ness. Where the main road crosses the river at Ness Bridge, you'll find the TI; within a few blocks (away from the river) are the train and bus stations and an appealing pedestrian shopping zone. The best B&Bs huddle atop a gentle hill

behind the castle (a 10-minute uphill walk, or a £5 taxi ride, from the city center).

Tourist Information

At the centrally located TI, you can pick up activity and day-trip brochures, the self-guided *Historic Trail* walking-tour leaflet, a map of the trail from Culloden to Clava Cairns, and the *What's On* weekly events sheet for the latest theater, music, and film showings (all free). The office also has a bulletin board with timely local event information, books rooms for a £4 fee, and offers tours (open July–mid-Sept Mon-Sat 9:00-18:30, Sun 9:30-18:00; mid-Sept–June Mon-Sat 9:00-18:00, Sun 9:30-18:00; Internet access, free WCs up behind TI, Castle Wynd, tel. 01463/252-401).

Helpful Hints

Festivals and Events: In mid-June, the city fills up for the **RockNess Music Festival** (www.rockness.co.uk), and there's a **marathon** the last week of September or first week of October (www.lochnessmarathon.com); book ahead for these times. For a real Highland treat, catch a **shinty match** (a combination of field hockey, hurling, and American football—but without pads). Inverness Shinty Club plays at Bought Park, along Ness Walk (the TI or your B&B can tell you if there are any matches on, or check www.spanglefish .com/invernessshintyclub).

Internet Access: You can get online at the **TI** (£1/20 minutes), or for free at the Neoclassical **library** behind the bus station (30-minute limit, Mon-Tue and Fri 9:00-18:30, Wed 10:00-18:30, Thu 9:00-20:00, Sat 9:00-17:00, closed Sun, computers shut down 15 minutes before closing, photo ID required, tel. 01463/236-463). **New City Launderette,** listed below, also has Internet access (£1/20 minutes).

Baggage Storage: The train station has lockers (£3-5/24 hours, open Mon-Sat 6:45-19:45, Sun 10:45-18:15), and the bus station offers daily baggage storage (£4/bag, daily 8:45-17:30).

Laundry: New City Launderette is just across the Ness Bridge from the TI (£5-6 for self-service, about £10 for same-day full-service, price calculated by weight, Internet access, Mon-Sat 8:00-18:00, until 20:00 Mon-Fri June-Oct, Sun 10:00-16:00 year-round, last load one hour before closing, 17 Young Street, tel. 01463/242-507). **Thirty Degrees Laundry** on Church Street is another option (£8 full-service only, drop off first thing in the morning for same-day service, Mon-Sat 8:30-17:30, closed Sun, 84 Church Street, tel. 01463/710-380).

Supermarkets: The **Co-operative** (Mon-Sat 7:00-22:00, Sun 7:00-20:00, 59 Church Street) and **Marks & Spencer** (described in "Eating in Inverness," later) are handy for picnics.

Charity Shops: Inverness is home to several pop-up charity shops. Occupying vacant rental spaces, these are staffed by volunteers who are happy to talk about their philanthropy. You can pick up a memorable knickknack, adjust your wardrobe for the weather, and learn about local causes.

Inverness

1 Craigside Lodge B&B
2 Eildon Guesthouse
3 Dionard Guest House
4 Ardconnel House & Crown Hotel Guest House
5 Ryeford Guest House
6 Heathmount Hotel & Restaurant
7 Inverness Palace Hotel & Spa
8 Premier Inn Inverness Centre River Ness
9 Mercure Inverness & The Joy of Taste Restaurant
10 Waterside Inverness
11 Inverness Student Hotel & Bazpackers Hostel
12 Café 1; Pockets Snooker & Pool Bar
13 Number 27 Restaurant
14 La Tortilla Asesina Rest.
15 Hootananny Café/Bar
16 Rocpool Restaurant
17 The Mustard Seed
18 The Kitchen
19 Rajah Indian Restaurant
20 Leakey's Bookshop & Café
21 The Gellions Pub
22 Marks & Spencer (Groceries)
23 Co-op Supermarket
24 Library (Internet)
25 Launderettes (2)

FRIARS
BR.
OLD HIGH CHURCH
RIVER
TO A-862
CELT
HUNTLY
KENNETH
"BOUNCY" BRIDGE
FOOT BR.
GREIG ST.
8
18
N
TOMNAHURICH
GLENURQUHART
ARDROSS ST.
NESS WALK
TO A-82
CALEDONIAN CANAL,
FORT WILLIAM,
LOCH NESS (WEST) & OBAN
TO BOUGHT PARK

INVERNESS

Tours in Inverness

Walking Tours

Happy Tours

Cameron—a.k.a. "the man in the kilt"—at Happy Tours offers history walks by day, and "Crime and Punishment" tours by night. These one-hour walks are cheeky, and peppered with his political opinions—a fun mix of history, local gossip, Scottish culture, and comedy. Cameron also offers other tours, guides bike tours to

Loch Ness, and rents bikes for £15 per day (tours-£6/person; history tour daily April-Sept at 11:00, 13:00, and 15:00; Crime and Punishment at 19:00 and 20:30; tours leave from steps of TI, just show up, tel. 07828/154-683, www.happy-tours.biz).

Excursions from Inverness

While thin on sights of its own, Inverness is a great home base for day trips. The biggest attraction is Loch Ness, a 20-minute drive southwest. Tickets are available at the TI, and tours depart from somewhere nearby. It's smart to book ahead, especially in peak season.

Jacobite Tours

This outfit runs a variety of tours, from a one-hour basic boat ride to a 6.5-hour extravaganza. Most tours run daily (£13-40, tours fill up in summer—book in advance). Their 3.5-hour "Sensation" tour includes a guided bus tour with live narration, a half-hour cruise of Loch Ness with recorded commentary, and an hour apiece at Urquhart Castle and the better of the two Loch Ness exhibits (£30, includes admissions to both sights, departs at 10:30 from Bank Street, near the TI; ticket/info counter in bus station open daily 9:00-16:00, tel. 01463/233-999, www.jacobite.co.uk).

Highland Experience Tours

Choose from several daylong tours, including one that focuses on the Isle of Skye, with stops along Loch Ness and at scenic Eilean Donan Castle. You'll get a few hours on Skye; unfortunately, it only takes you as far as the Sleat Peninsula at the island's southern end, rather than to the more scenic Trotternish Peninsula (£45, departs from Bridge Street outside the TI at 9:30, returns at 19:30; mid-May-Sept runs daily, mid-April-mid-May and most of Oct runs several days a week, no tours late-Oct-mid-April, reservations recommended, tel. 01463/719-222, www.highlandexperience.com). For more on the Isle of Skye, see the previous chapter.

More Options

Several companies host daily excursions to whisky distilleries, the Orkney Islands, and the nearby bay for dolphin-watching (ask at TI). Skip the City Sightseeing hop-on, hop-off bus tour (whose main objective is connecting you with Jacobite—their sister company—cruise docks).

Self-Guided Walk

Humble Inverness has meager conventional sights, but its fun history and quirky charm become clear as you take this short self-guided walk.

• *Start at the clock tower and TI.*

Clock Tower and TI: Notice the Scottish language on signs all around you. While nobody speaks Gaelic as a first language and few Scottish people speak it at all, the old Celtic Scottish language symbolizes the strength of the local culture. The recommended Gellions Bar (across from the TI and described later, in "Nightlife in Inverness") flies two Scottish flags.

The steeple towering 130 feet above you is all that remains of a tollbooth building erected in 1791. This is the highest spire in town, and for generations was a collection point for local taxes. Here, four streets—Church, Castle, Bridge, and High—come together, integrating God, defense, and trade—everything necessary for a fine city. This is naturally the center of Inverness.

About 800 years ago, a castle was built on the bluff overhead and the town of Inverness coalesced right about here. In 1854 the train arrived, injecting energy from Edinburgh and Glasgow, and the Victorian boom hit. Before the Industrial Age the economy was based on cottage industries. Artisans who made things also sold them. With the Industrial Age came wholesalers, distributors, mass production, and affluence. The cityscape is neo-Gothic—over-the-top and fanciful, like the City Hall, built in 1882. With the Victorian Age also came tourism.

Look across the street at the Bible quotes chiseled into the wall. A city leader, tired of his council members being drunkards, edited these Bible verses for maximum impact, especially the bottom two.

Inverness Castle is just up the hill—with some of the best views of Inverness looking west and south. Today the building holds a courthouse without a lot of action. In the last 30 years, there have been only two murders to prosecute. Locals like to say "no guns, no problems." While hunters can own a gun, gun ownership in Scotland is complicated and tightly regulated.

By the way, every day and night in peak season, from this spot, Cameron ("the man in the kilt" who gave me the material for this walk) gives entertaining hour-long guided walks (see "Tours in Inverness," earlier).

• *Walk a few steps uphill to the Scottish hamburger restaurant that caught on big-time in the USA.*

Mercat Cross and Old Town Center: Standing in front of the City Hall is a well-worn mercat cross, which designated the market in centuries past. This is where the townspeople gathered to hear important proclamations, share news, watch hangings, gossip, and so on. The scant remains of a prehistoric stone at the base of the cross are what's left of Inverness' "Stone of Destiny." According to tradition, whenever someone moved away from Inverness, they'd take a tiny bit of home with them in the form of a chip of this stone—so it's been chipped and pecked almost to oblivion.

A yellow Caledonian building faces McDonald's at the base of High Street. (Caledonia was the ancient name of Scotland.) It was built in 1847, complete with Corinthian columns and a Greek-style pediment, as the leading bank in town, back when banks were designed to hold the money of the rich and powerful...and intimidate working blokes. A few doors up High Street from here is the Victorian Gothic Royal Tartan Warehouse, with Queen Victoria's august coat of arms, indicating that the royal family shopped here. Notice how nicely pedestrianized High Street welcomes people and seagulls...but not cars.

Church Street to the Church: The street art at the start of Church Street is *Earthquake*, a reminder of the quake that hit Inverness in 1816. According to the statues, the town's motto is "Open Heartedness, Insight, and Perseverance."

Stroll down Church Street. Look up above the modern storefronts to see Old World facades. Union Street (first corner on the right)—stately, symmetrical, and neo-Classical—was the best street in the Highlands when it was built in the 19th century. Its buildings had indoor toilets. That was big news.

Midway down the next block of Church Street (on the right), an alley marked by an ugly white canopy leads to the Victorian Market. Explore this gallery of shops under an iron-and-glass domed roof dating from 1876. (If this entrance is closed, there are other entrances around the block.)

Continuing down Church Street, on the next corner you come to Hootananny, famous locally for its live music (pop in to see what's on tonight). Next door is Abertarff, the oldest house in Inverness. It was the talk of the town in 1593 for its "turnpike" (spiral staircase) connecting the floors.

The lane on the left leads to the "Bouncy Bridge" (where we'll finish this walk). Opposite that lane (on the right) is the Dunbar Hospital, with four-foot-thick walls. In 1668, Alexander Dunbar was a wealthy landowner who built this as a poor folks' home. You can almost read the auld script in his coat of arms above the door.

Walk through the iron gate and churchyard (ignoring the church on left and focusing on the one on the right). Looking at the WWI and WWII memorials on the church's wall, it's clear which war hit Britain harder. While no one famous is buried here, many tombstones go back to the 1700s. Being careful not to step on a rabbit, head for the bluff overlooking the river.

Old High Church: There are a lot of churches in Inverness (46 Protestant, two Catholic, and two Gaelic-language) but, these days, most are used for other purposes. This one, dating from the 11th century, is the most historic (but is generally closed). It was built on what was likely the site of a pagan holy ground. Early Christians called upon St. Michael to take the fire out of pagan spirits, so it only made sense that the first Christians would build their church here and dedicate the spot as St. Michael's Mount.

In the sixth century the Irish evangelist monk St. Columba brought Christianity to northern England, the Scottish Lowlands (at Iona), and the Scottish Highlands (in Inverness). He stood here amongst the pagans and preached to King Brude and the Picts.

Study the bell tower from the 1600s. The small door to nowhere (about one floor up) indicates that back before the castle offered protection, this tower was the place of last refuge for townsfolk under attack. They'd gather inside and pull up the ladder. The church became a prison for Jacobites after the Battle of Culloden, and executions were carried out in the churchyard.

Every night at 20:00, the bell in the tower rings 100 times. It has rung like this since 1730 to remind townsfolk that it's dangerous to be out after dinner.

• *From here you can circle back to the lane leading to the "Bouncy Bridge" and then hike out onto the bridge, or you can just survey the countryside from this bluff.*

River Ness: "Inverness" means the area around the river. "Ness" means river. So River Ness means "River River." Emptying out of Loch Ness and flowing seven miles to the sea (a mile from here), this is the shortest river in the country. While it's shallow (you can almost walk across it), there are plenty of fish in it. A 64-pound salmon was recently pulled out of the river right here. In the 19th century, Inverness was smaller, and across the river stretched nothing but open fields. Then, with the Victorian boom, the suspension footbridge (a.k.a. "Bouncy Bridge") was built in 1881 to connect new construction across the river with the town.

• *Your tour is over and you are now free to enjoy the bridge.*

Sights in Inverness

Inverness Museum and Art Gallery

This free, likable town museum is worth poking around on a rainy day to get a taste of Inverness and the Highlands. The ground-floor exhibits on geology and archaeology peel back the layers of Highland history: Bronze and Iron ages, Picts (including some carved stones), Scots, Vikings, and Normans. Upstairs you'll find the "social history" exhibit (everything from Scottish nationalism to hunting and fishing) and temporary art exhibits.

Cost and Hours: Free; April-Oct Tue-Sat 10:00-17:00, closed Sun-Mon; Nov-March Thu-Sat 10:00-17:00, closed Sun-Wed; cheap café, in the modern building behind the TI on the way up to the castle, tel. 01463/237-114, http://inverness.highland.museum.

Inverness Castle

Inverness' biggest nonsight has nice views from its front lawn, but the building itself isn't worth visiting. A wooden fortress that stood on this spot was replaced by a stone structure in the 15th century. In 1715, that castle was made Fort George to assert English control over the area. In 1745, it was destroyed by Bonnie Prince Charlie's Jacobite army and remained a ruin until the 1830s, when the present castle was built. The statue (from 1899) outside depicts Flora MacDonald, who helped Bonnie Prince Charlie escape from the English (see page 956). Today the castle is used as a courthouse, and when trials are in session, loutish-looking men hang out here, waiting for their bewigged barristers to arrive.

River Walks

As with most European cities, where there's a river, there's a walk. Inverness, with both the River Ness and the Caledonian Canal, does not disappoint. Consider an early-morning stroll along the Ness Bank to capture the castle at sunrise, or a post-dinner jaunt to Bought Park for a local shinty match (see "Helpful Hints—Festivals and Events," earlier). From the Ness Bridge, the Caledonian Canal is also less than a 15-minute walk (follow Tomnahurich Street, which turns into Glenurquhart Road; it's a straight shot to the canal—when you see the gates for the Commonwealth War Graves you're two minutes away). Where Tomnahurich Bridge crosses the canal you'll find paths on either bank, allowing you to walk along the Great Glen Way until you're ready to turn around. On your way back to town, instead of retracing the route, turn right on Bought Drive (or Bought Road—your choice) and circle around Queens Park to connect with the Ness Bank back into the city.

Nightlife in Inverness

Scottish Folk Music

While you're likely to find traditional folk music sessions in pubs and hotel bars anywhere in town, two places are well established as the music pubs. **The Gellions** has live folk and Scottish music nightly. Just across the street from the TI, it has local ales on tap and brags it's the oldest bar in town (14 Bridge Street, tel. 01463/233-648, www.gellions.co.uk). **Hootananny** is an energetic place with several floors of live rock, blues, or folk music, and drinking fun nightly. Upstairs is the Mad Hatter's nightclub (Thu-Sun only), complete with a "chill-out room" (bar open 18:00-24:00, music begins at 21:30, 67 Church Street, tel. 01463/233-651, www.hootananny.co.uk). They also serve dinner; see their listing in "Eating in Inverness," later.

Pockets Snooker & Pool Bar

If you'd rather just shoot some pool, try this modern sports bar, a local hangout with free darts, pool, and snooker (snooker and pool-£4/hour, nightly until 24:00, across from the Castle at #67 Castle Street).

Sleeping in Inverness

B&Bs on and near Ardconnel Street and Old Edinburgh Road

These B&Bs are popular; book ahead for June through August (and during the marathon in late September or early October), and be aware that some require a two-night minimum during busy

---

Sleep Code

(£1 = about $1.60, country code: 44, area code: 01463)
S = Single, **D** = Double/Twin, **T** = Triple, **Q** = Quad, **b** = bathroom,
s = shower only. Unless otherwise noted, you can assume credit cards are accepted at hotels and hostels—but not B&Bs—and breakfast is included.

To help you sort easily through these listings, I've divided the accommodations into three categories based on the price for a standard double room with bath (during high season):

$$$ Higher Priced—Most rooms £75 or more.
  $$ Moderately Priced—Most rooms between £45-75.
    $ Lower Priced—Most rooms £45 or less.

Prices can change without notice; verify the hotel's current rates online or by email. For the best prices, always book direct.

---

times. The rooms are all a 10-minute walk from the train station and town center. To get to the B&Bs, either catch a taxi (£5) or walk: From the train and bus stations, go left on Academy Street. At the first stoplight (the second if you're coming from the bus station), veer right onto Inglis Street in the pedestrian zone. Go up the Market Brae steps. At the top, turn right onto Ardconnel Street toward the B&Bs and hostels.

$$ Craigside Lodge B&B has five large, comfortable, cheery rooms with a tasteful modern flair mirroring the energy of the hosts. Guests share an inviting sunroom and a cozy lounge with a great city view (Sb-£40-45, Db-£70-75, prices depend on season, free Wi-Fi, just above Castle Street at 4 Gordon Terrace, tel. 01463/231-576, www.craigsideguesthouse.co.uk, enquiries@craigsideguesthouse.co.uk, Ewan and Amy).

$$ Eildon Guesthouse, set on a quiet corner, offers six tranquil rooms with spacious baths at an excellent value. The cute-as-a-button 1890s countryside brick home exudes warmth and serenity from the moment you open the gate (Sb-£30-35, Db-£60-70, Tb-£90-105, family rooms available, in-room fridges, free Wi-Fi, parking, 29 Old Edinburgh Road, tel. 01463/231-969, eildonguesthouse@yahoo.co.uk, www.eildonguesthouse.co.uk, Jacqueline).

$$ Dionard Guest House, just up Old Edinburgh Road from Ardconnel Street, has cheerful common spaces and six pleasant rooms, including two on the ground floor (Sb-£50, Db-£67-85 depending on size, no single-occupancy rate during high season, in-room fridges, free Wi-Fi, 39 Old Edinburgh Road, tel.

01463/233-557, www.dionardguesthouse.co.uk, enquiries@dionard guesthouse.co.uk, Brian and Doris).

$$ Ardconnel House offers a nice, large guest lounge and a warm welcome, along with six spacious and comfortable rooms (Sb-£45, Db-£75, family room-£95, family deals but no children under 10, slightly cheaper off-season or for 2 or more nights, free Wi-Fi, 21 Ardconnel Street, tel. 01463/240-455, www.ardconnel -inverness.co.uk, ardconnel@gmail.com, John and Elizabeth).

$$ Crown Hotel Guest House has six clean, bright rooms and an enjoyable breakfast room (Sb-£35, Db-£60, family room-£80-100, lounge, 19 Ardconnel Street, tel. 01463/231-135, www .crownhotel-inverness.co.uk, reservations@crownhotel-inverness .co.uk, friendly Catriona—pronounced "Katrina"—Barbour).

$$ Ryeford Guest House is a decent value, with six flow-ery rooms and plenty of teddy bears (Sb-£45, Db-£70, Tb-£105, family deals, vegetarian breakfast available, small twin room #1 in back has fine garden view, free Wi-Fi in front lounge, above Market Brae steps, go left on Ardconnel Terrace to #21, tel. 01463/242-871, www.scotland-inverness.co.uk/ryeford, joananderson @uwclub.net, Joan and George Anderson).

Hotels

The following hotels may have rooms when my recommended B&Bs are full.

$$$ Heathmount Hotel's understated facade hides a chic retreat for comfort-seeking travelers. Its eight uniquely decorated elegant rooms come with free Wi-Fi, parking, and fancy extras (Sb-£79-95, Db-£95-140, Kingsmill Road, tel. 01463/235-877, info@heathounthotel.com, www.heathmounthotel.com). Their restaurant is also recommended; see "Eating in Inverness."

$$$ Inverness Palace Hotel & Spa, a Best Western, is a fancy splurge with a pool, a gym, and 88 overpriced rooms. It's located right on the River Ness, across from the castle (Db-£209-229, but you can almost always get a much better rate—even half-price—if you book a package deal on their website, £89 last-minute rooms, prices especially soft on weekends, river/castle view rooms about £40 more than rest, breakfast extra, elevator, free Wi-Fi, free parking, 8 Ness Walk, tel. 01463/223-243, www.inverness palacehotel.co.uk, palace@miltonhotels.com).

$$$ Premier Inn Inverness Centre River Ness, along the River Ness, offers 99 predictable rooms, all with private bath. What the hotel lacks in charm and glitz it makes up for in afford-able rates and location (Db-£60-120, £29 rooms not uncommon if booked online well in advance; Wi-Fi free for 30 minutes, then £3/day; 19-21 Huntly Street, tel. 01463/246-490, www.premierinn .com).

$$$ Mercure Inverness, across the river from the Premier Inn, has 106 rooms, a gym, pool, and spa, and feels less commercial than other chain hotels (Db-£125-175, much cheaper rates if booked in advance online, free Wi-Fi, parking-£2/night; entrance is at Church Street, tel. 0844/815-9006, sales.mercureinverness @jupiterhotels.co.uk, www.mercureinverness.co.uk).

$$$ Waterside Inverness, in a nice location along the River Ness, has 35 crisp, recently updated rooms and a riverview restaurant (Sb-£75, Db-£140, superior Db-£170, Qb-£190, call or check website for deals as low as Db-£79, 19 Ness Bank, tel. 01463/233-065, www.thewatersideinverness.co.uk, info@thewaterside inverness.co.uk).

Hostels on Culduthel Road

For inexpensive dorm beds near the center and the recommended Castle Street restaurants, consider these friendly side-by-side hostels, geared toward younger travelers. They're about a 12-minute walk from the train station.

$ Inverness Student Hotel has 57 beds in nine rooms and a cozy, inviting, laid-back lounge with a bay window overlooking the River Ness. The knowledgeable, friendly staff welcomes any traveler over 18. Dorms come in some interesting shapes, and each bunk has its own playful name (£17-18 beds in 6- to 10-bed rooms, price depends on season, breakfast-£2, free tea and coffee, cheap guest computer, free Wi-Fi, full-service laundry for £3.50, kitchen, 8 Culduthel Road, tel. 01463/236-556, www.inverness studenthotel.com, info@invernessstudenthotel.com).

$ Bazpackers Hostel, a stone's throw from the castle, has a quieter, more private feel and 20 beds in basic 4- to 6-bed dorms (beds-£17, D-£44, cheaper Oct-May, linens provided, reception open 7:30-23:00 but available 24 hours, no curfew, pay guest computer, free Wi-Fi, £4 laundry service, 4 Culduthel Road, tel. 01463/717-663, www.bazpackershostel.co.uk). They also rent a small apartment nearby (£70-80, sleeps up to 4).

Eating in Inverness

You'll find a lot of traditional Highland fare—game, fish, lamb, and beef. Reservations are smart at most of these places, especially on summer weekends.

Near the B&Bs, on or near Castle Street

The first three eateries line Castle Street, facing the back of the castle.

Café 1 serves up high-quality modern Scottish and international cuisine with trendy, chic bistro flair. This popular place fills up on weekends, so it's smart to call ahead (£12-20 main courses, lunch and early-bird dinner specials 17:30-18:45, open Mon-Fri 12:00-14:00 & 17:30-21:30, Sat 12:00-15:30 & 18:00-21:30, closed Sun, 75 Castle Street, tel. 01463/226-200).

Number 27 has a straightforward, crowd-pleasing menu that offers something for everyone—burgers, pastas, and more. The food is surprisingly elegant for this price range (£9-13 main courses, £8 two-course lunch Mon-Fri; open daily 12:00-21:00, generous portions, local ales on tap, noisy bar up front not separated from restaurant in back, 27 Castle Street, tel. 01463/241-999).

La Tortilla Asesina has Spanish tapas, including spicy king prawns (the house specialty). It's an appealing and vivacious dining option that feels like Spain (£3-7 cold and hot tapas—three make a meal, cheap tapas combo-specials; April-Sept daily 12:00-22:00; Oct-March daily 12:00-21:00; 99 Castle Street, tel. 01463/709-809).

The recommended **Heathmount Hotel** serves good food in their quiet dining room (£6-9 lunches, £11-19 dinners, Mon-Fri 12:00-14:30 & 17:00-22:00, Sat-Sun 12:30-21:30, 5-minute walk down Argyle Street to Kingsmills Road, tel. 01463/235-877).

In the Town Center

Hootananny mixes an energetic pub and live music with Scottish staples like lamb stovies (stew) and cullen skink (fish chowder). It's got a great join-in-the-fun vibe at night (£4-8 dishes, food served Mon-Sat 12:00-15:00 & 17:00-21:30, no food on Sun; see "Nightlife in Inverness," earlier).

Rocpool Restaurant is a hit with locals and good for a splurge. Owner/chef Steven Devlin serves creative modern European food in a sleek—and often crowded—chocolate/pistachio dining room. Reserve ahead or be sorry (£15 lunch specials, £17 early-bird special before 18:45 Mon-Fri, £13-21 dinners; open Mon-Sat 12:00-14:30 & 17:45-22:00, closed Sun; across Ness Bridge from TI at 1 Ness Walk, tel. 01463/717-274, www.rocpoolrestaurant.com).

The Mustard Seed serves Scottish food with a modern twist in an old church with a river view. It's pricey, but worth considering for a nice lively-at-lunch, mellow-at-dinner meal. Ask for a seat on the balcony if the weather is cooperating. Reservations are essential on weekends (£7 lunch specials, £12 early-bird specials 17:30-19:00, £15-20 meals, daily 12:00-15:00 & 17:30-22:00, on the corner of Bank and Fraser Streets, 16 Fraser Street, tel. 01463/220-220, www.mustardseedrestaurant.co.uk).

The Kitchen is the sister restaurant of The Mustard Seed. Equally good and popular, they serve fantastic homemade comfort food—pizza, pasta, and burgers—in an ultra-modern townhouse (daily 12:00-22:00, similar specials, directly across the river at 15

Huntly Street, tel. 01463/259-119, www.kitchenrestaurant.co.uk).

Rajah Indian Restaurant provides a tasty break from meat and potatoes, with vegetarian options served in a classy red-velvet, white-linen atmosphere (£8-14 meals, 10 percent less for takeout, Mon-Sat 12:00-23:00, Sun 15:00-23:00, last dine-in order 30 minutes before closing, just off Church Street at 2 Post Office Avenue, tel. 01463/237-190).

The Joy of Taste serves up European cuisine along with altruism—a portion of their profits goes to charity, and volunteers (including local teachers and newspaper reporters) donate their time to fill shifts. The menu changes with the fancy of the chef, but usually includes staples such as steak, seafood, and slow-cooked shoulder of lamb (£5-7 lunch salads and sandwiches, £13/£16 early evening specials 17:30-18:45, £13-18 main dishes; open Mon-Sat 12:00-15:00 & 17:30-21:30, also open Sun late July-Sept; 25 Church Street, tel. 01463/241-459, www.thejoyoftaste.co.uk).

Leakey's Bookshop and Café, located in a converted church built in 1649, has the best lunch deal in town. Browse through stacks of musty old books and vintage maps, warm up by the wood-burning stove, and climb the spiral staircase to the loft for hearty homemade soups, sandwiches, and sweets (£3-4 light lunches, limited menu, Mon-Sat 10:00-16:30, bookstore stays open until 17:30, closed Sun, in Greyfriar's Hall on Church Street, tel. 01463/239-947, Charles Leakey).

Picnic: The **Marks & Spencer** food hall is best (you can't miss it—on the main pedestrian mall, near the Market Brae steps at the corner of the big Eastgate Shopping Centre; plastic utensils at the registers, Mon-Sat 8:00-18:00, Thu until 20:00, Sun 11:00-17:00, tel. 01463/224-844).

Inverness Connections

From Inverness by Train to: Pitlochry (every 1-2 hours, 1.5 hours), **Stirling** (every 1-2 hours, 2.75-3 hours, some transfer in Perth), **Kyle of Lochalsh** near Isle of Skye (4/day, 2.5 hours), **Edinburgh** (every 1-2 hours, 3.5-4 hours, some with change in Perth), **Glasgow** (11/day, 3 hours, 4 direct, the rest change in Perth). ScotRail does a great sleeper service to **London** (generally £140-190 for first class/single private compartment or £100-150 for standard class/twin shared compartment with breakfast, not available Sat night, www.firstscotrail.com). Consider dropping your car in Inverness and riding to London by train. Train info: tel. 0845-748-4950, www.nationalrail.co.uk.

By Bus: To reach most destinations in western Scotland, you'll first head for **Fort William** (10/day, 2 hours). For connections onward to **Oban** (figure 4 hours total) or **Glencoe** (3 hours total), see "Fort William Connections" on page 908. To reach **Portree** on the Isle of Skye, you can either take the direct bus (3-4/day, 3.25 hours), or transfer in Fort William. These buses are run by Scottish Citylink; for schedules, see www.citylink.co.uk. You can buy tickets in advance by calling Citylink at tel. 0871-266-3333 or stopping by the Inverness bus station (daily 8:45-17:30, £0.50 extra for credit cards, daily baggage storage-£4/bag, 2 blocks from train station on Margaret Street, tel. 01463/233-371). For bus travel to England, check National Express (www.nationalexpress.com) or Megabus (http://uk.megabus.com).

Route Tips for Drivers

Inverness to Edinburgh (150 miles, 3 hours minimum): Leaving Inverness, follow signs to the A-9 (south, toward Perth). If you haven't seen the Culloden Battlefield yet (described later), it's an easy detour: Just as you leave Inverness, head four miles east off the A-9 on the B-9006. Back on the A-9, it's a wonderfully speedy, scenic highway (A-9, M-90, A-90) all the way to Edinburgh. If you have time, consider stopping en route in Pitlochry (just off the A-9; see the Between Inverness and Edinburgh chapter).

    To Oban, Glencoe, or Isle of Skye: See the "Route Tips for Drivers" at the end of the Oban and the Southern Highlands chapter.

Sights near Inverness

Inverness puts you in the heart of the Highlands, within easy striking distance of a gaggle of famous and worthwhile sights: Squint across Loch Ness looking for Nessie—or, if you're a skeptic, just appreciate the majesty of Britain's largest body of water (by volume). (I'm thankful the loch is in Scotland, where property laws make it extremely difficult to buy or build along its banks, and not in California.) Commune with the Scottish soul at the historic Culloden Battlefield, where Scottish, English, and world history reached a turning point. Ponder three mysterious Neolithic cairns, which remind visitors that Scotland's history goes back even before Braveheart. And enjoy a homey country castle at Cawdor.

Loch Ness

I'll admit it: I had my zoom lens out and my eyes on the water. The local tourist industry thrives on the legend of the Loch Ness Monster. It's a thrilling thought, and there have been several

Inverness & the Northern Highlands

TO ULLAPOOL

TO THURSO & JOHN O'GROATS

A-835

A-832

MORAY FIRTH

NAIRN

TO ABERDEEN

A-96

CAWDOR CASTLE

Cawdor

INVERNESS

TO KYLE OF LOCHALSH & ISLE OF SKYE

Loch Ness Monster Exhibits

A-831

DAVIOT

CULLODEN

CLAVA CAIRNS

A-939

TO ABERDEEN

URQUHART CASTLE

INVERMORISTON

Dores

LOCH NESS

A-9

A-938

A-95

TO KYLE OF LOCHALSH & ISLE OF SKYE

A-87

A-887

B-862

B-852

AVIEMORE

FORT AUGUSTUS

INVERGARRY

LOCH OICH

CAIRNGORM

TO MALLAIG VIA "ROAD TO THE ISLES"

A-830

LOCH LOCHY

A-82

A-86

DALWHINNIE

MOUNTAINS

BEN NEVIS

A-9

BLAIR CASTLE

BLAIR ATHOLL

FORT WILLIAM

GLENCOE

PITLOCHRY

TO OBAN

GLENCOE VILLAGE

BALLA-CHULISH

RANNOCH MOOR

TO STIRLING & EDINBURGH

TO LOCH LOMOND & GLASGOW

20 MILES

20 KM

■ CASTLE

✈ AIRPORT

DCH

NORTHERN HIGHLANDS

seemingly reliable "sightings" (by monks, police officers, and sonar images). But even if you ignore the monster stories, the loch is impressive: 23 miles long, less than a mile wide, the third-deepest in Europe (754 feet), and containing more water than in all the freshwater bodies of England and Wales combined.

Getting There: The Loch Ness sights are a quick drive southwest of Inverness. Various buses go from Inverness to Urquhart Castle and Drumnadrochit in about 35-40 minutes (buses #19, #19a, and #919, 8/day, fewer on Sun, figure £14 round-trip to Urquhart, confirm routes at Inverness bus station or TI).

Sights on Loch Ness

Loch Ness Monster Exhibits

In July of 1933, a couple swore that they saw a giant sea monster shimmy across the road in front of their car by Loch Ness. Within

days, ancient legends about giant monsters in the lake (dating as far back as the sixth century) were revived—and suddenly everyone was spotting "Nessie" poke its head above the waters of Loch Ness. Further sightings and photographic "evidence" have bolstered the claim that there's something mysterious living in this unthinkably deep and murky lake. (Most sightings take place in the deepest part of the loch, near Urquhart Castle.) Most witnesses describe a waterbound dinosaur (resembling the real, but extinct, plesiosaur). Others cling to the slightly more plausible theory of a gigantic eel. And skeptics figure the sightings can be explained by a combination of reflections, boat wakes, and mass hysteria. The most famous photo of the beast (dubbed the "Surgeon's Photo") was later discredited—the "monster's" head was actually attached to a toy submarine. But that hasn't stopped various cryptozoologists from seeking photographic, sonar, and other proof.

And that suits the thriving local tourist industry just fine. The Nessie commercialization is so tacky that there are two different monster exhibits within 100 yards of each other, both in the town of Drumnadrochit. Each has a tour-bus parking lot and more square footage devoted to their kitschy shops than to the exhibits. The overpriced exhibitions are actually quite interesting—even though they're tourist traps, they'll appease that small part of you that knows the *real* reason you wanted to see Loch Ness.

▲Loch Ness Centre & Exhibition

This exhibit—the better option of the two—is headed by a naturalist who has spent many years researching lake ecology and scientific phenomena. With a 30-minute series of video bits and special effects, this exhibit explains the geological and historical environment that bred the monster story, as well as the various searches that have been conducted. Refreshingly, it retains an air of healthy skepticism instead of breathless monster-chasing. It also has some artifacts related to the search, such as a hippo-foot ashtray used to fake monster footprints and the *Viperfish*—a harpoon-equipped submarine used in a 1969 Nessie search.

Cost and Hours: £7, daily Easter-June and Sept-Oct 9:30-17:00, July-Aug 9:30-18:00, Nov-Easter 10:00-15:30, in the big

The Caledonian Canal

Two hundred million years ago two tectonic plates collided, creating the landmass we know as Scotland and leaving a crevice of thin lakes slashing right across the country. Called the Great Glen Fault, this diagonal slash across Scotland from Inverness to Oban is easily visible on any map.

Two hundred years ago, British engineer Thomas Telford connected the lakes with a series of canals so ships could avoid the long trip around the north of the country. The Caledonian Canal runs 62 miles from Scotland's east to west coasts, and 22 miles of it is man-made. Telford's great feat of engineering took 19 years to complete, opening in 1822 at a cost of one million pounds. But the timing was bad, and the canal was a disaster commercially. Napoleon's defeat in 1815 meant that ships could sail the seas more freely. And by the time the canal opened, commercial ships were generally too big for its 15-foot depths. Just a couple decades after the Caledonian Canal opened, the arrival of the train made the canal almost useless...except for Romantic Age tourism. From the time of Queen Victoria (who cruised the canal in 1873), the canal has been a popular tourist attraction. To this day the canal is a hit with vacationers, recreational boaters, and lock-keepers who compete for the best-kept lock.

The scenic drive from Inverness along the canal is entertaining, with Urquhart Castle (Nessie centers), Fort Augustus (five locks), and Fort William (under Ben Nevis, Neptune's

Staircase). You'll follow Telford's work—20 miles of canals and locks between three lakes, raising ships from sea level to 51 feet (Ness), 93 feet (Lochy), and 106 feet (Oich).

While "Neptune's Staircase," a series of eight locks near Fort William, has been cleverly named to sound intriguing, the best lock stop is midway, at Fort Augustus, where the canal hits the south end of Loch Ness. In Fort Augustus, the **Caledonian Canal Visitor Centre,** three locks above the main road, gives a good rundown on Telford's work (see page 955). Stroll past several shops and eateries to the top of the locks for a fine view.

Seven miles north in the town of Invermoriston is another Telford structure worthy of a quick detour—a stone bridge, dating from 1805, which spans the Morriston Falls as part of the original road. Look for a small parking lot just before the junction at A-82 and A-887, on your right as you drive from Fort Augustus. Carefully cross the A-82 and walk three minutes back the way you came. The bridge, which took eight years to build and is still in use today, is on your right.

stone mansion right on the main road to Inverness, tel. 01456/450-573, www.lochness.com.

Nessieland Castle Monster Centre

The other exhibit (up a side road closer to the town center, affiliated with a hotel) is less serious. It's basically a tacky high-school-quality photo report and a 30-minute *We Believe in the Loch Ness Monster* movie, which features credible-sounding locals explaining what they saw and a review of modern Nessie searches. (The most convincing reason for locals to believe: Look at the hordes of tourists around you.) It also has small exhibits on the area's history and on other "monsters" and hoaxes around the world.

Cost and Hours: £6, daily May-Sept 9:00-19:00, Oct-April 9:00-17:00, tel. 01456/450-342, www.loch-ness-monster-nessieland.com.

▲Urquhart Castle

The ruins at Urquhart (UR-kurt), just up the loch from the Nessie exhibits, are gloriously situated with a view of virtually the entire lake.

Cost and Hours: £8, guidebook-£4, daily April-Sept 9:30-18:00, Oct 9:30-17:00, Nov-March 9:30-16:30, last entry 45 minutes before closing, café, tel. 01456/450-551, www.historic-scotland.gov.uk.

Visiting the Castle: Its visitors center has a tiny exhibit with interesting castle artifacts and a good eight-minute film taking

you on a sweep through a thousand years of tumultuous history—from St. Columba's visit to the castle's final destruction in 1692. The castle itself, while dramatically situated and fun to climb through, is a relatively empty shell. After its English owners blew it up to keep the Jacobites from taking it, the largest medieval castle in Scotland (and the most important in the Highlands) wasn't considered worth rebuilding or defending, and was abandoned. Well-placed, descriptive signs help you piece together this once mighty fortress. As you walk toward the ruins, take a close look at the trebuchet (a working replica of one of the most destructive weapons of English King Edward I), and ponder how this giant slingshot helped Edward grab almost every castle in the country away from the native Scots.

Fort Augustus

Perhaps the most idyllic stop along the Caledonian Canal is the little lochside town of Fort Augustus. It was founded in the 1700s—before there was a canal here—as part of a series of garrisons and military roads built by the English to quell the Highland clansmen, even as the Stuarts kept trying to take the throne in London. Before then, there were no developed roads in the Highlands—and without roads, it's hard to keep indigenous people down.

From 1725 to 1733 the English built 250 miles of hard roads and 40 bridges to open up the region; Fort Augustus was a central Highlands garrison at the southern tip of Loch Ness, designed to awe clansmen. It was named for William Augustus, Duke of Cumberland—notorious for his role in destroying the clan way of life in the Highlands. (When there's no media and no photographs to get in the way, ethnic cleansing has little effect on one's reputation.)

Fort Augustus makes for a delightful stop if you're driving through the area. Parking is easy. There are plenty of B&Bs, charming eateries, and an inviting park along the town's four lochs. You can still see the capstans, surviving from the days when the locks were cranked open by hand.

The fine little **Caledonian Canal Visitor Centre** nicely tells the story of the canal's construction (free, daily Easter-Oct 10:00-17:30, closed Nov-Easter, tel. 01320/366-493).

You can eat reasonably at eateries along the canal. If picnicking, pick up good sandwiches at the MacVean Supermarket. Their restaurant out back has peaceful tables overlooking the river (not the canal), where you can eat your grocery store purchases for just a few pence more than the grocery price.

Culloden Battlefield

Jacobite troops under Bonnie Prince Charlie were defeated at Culloden (kuh-LAW-dehn) by supporters of the Hanover dynasty (King George II's family) in 1746. This last major land battle fought on British soil spelled the end of Jacobite resistance and the beginning of the clan chiefs' fall from power. Wandering the desolate, solemn battlefield, you sense that something terrible occurred here. Locals still bring white roses and speak of "the '45" (as Bonnie Prince Charlie's entire campaign is called) as if it just happened. The battlefield at Culloden and its high-tech visitors center together are worth ▲▲▲.

Orientation to Culloden

Cost and Hours: £10.50, daily April-May and Sept-Oct 9:00-17:30, June-Aug 9:00-18:00, Nov-Dec and Feb-March 10:00-16:00, closed Jan, last entry 30 minutes before closing.

Information: £5 guidebook, café, tel. 0844-493-2159, www.nts .org.uk/culloden.

Tours: Tours with live **guides** are included with your admission. Check for a schedule—there are generally 3-4/day, focusing on various aspects of the battle. **Audioguides** are free, with good information tied by GPS to important sites on the battlefield (pick up before 17:00 at the end of the indoor exhibit and return by 17:15; earlier off-season).

Getting There: It's a 15-minute **drive** east of Inverness. Follow signs to *Aberdeen*, then *Culloden Moor*, and the B-9006 takes you right there (well-signed on the right-hand side). Parking is £2. Public **buses** leave from Inverness' Queensgate Street and drop you off in front of the entrance (£3.60 round-trip ticket, bus #2B, roughly hourly, 40 minutes, ask at the TI for route/schedule updates and confirm that bus is going all the way to the battlefield).

Length of This Tour: Allow 2-2.5 hours.

Background

The Battle of Culloden (April 16, 1746) marks the end of the power of the Scottish Highland clans and the start of years of repression of Scottish culture by the English. It was the culmination of a year's worth of battles, known collectively as "the '45." At the center of it all was the charismatic, enigmatic Bonnie Prince Charlie (1720-1788).

Charles Edward Stuart, from his first breath, was raised with a single purpose—to restore his family to the British throne. His grandfather was King James II, deposed in 1688 by Parliament for his tyranny and pro-Catholic bias. In 1745, young Charlie crossed the Channel from exile in France to retake the throne for the Stuarts. He landed on the west coast of Scotland and rallied support for the "Jacobite" cause (from the Latin for "James"). Though Charles was not Scottish-born, he was the rightful heir directly down the line from Mary, Queen of Scots—and so many Scots joined the Stuart family's rebellion out of resentment at being ruled by a foreign king (English royalty of German descent).

Bagpipes droned, and "Bonnie" (beautiful) Charlie led an army of 2,000 tartan-wearing, Gaelic-speaking Highlanders across Scotland, seizing Edinburgh. They picked up other supporters of the Stuarts from the Lowlands and from England. Now 6,000 strong, they marched south toward London, and King George II made plans to flee the country. But anticipated support for the Jacobites failed to materialize in the numbers they were hoping for (both in England and from France). The Jacobites had so far been victorious in their battles against the Hanoverian government forces, but the odds now turned against them. Charles retreated to the Scottish Highlands, where many of his men knew the terrain and might gain an advantage when outnumbered. The English government troops followed closely on his heels.

Against the advice of his best military strategist, Charles' army faced the Hanoverian forces at Culloden Moor on flat, barren terrain that was unsuited to the Highlanders' guerrilla tactics. The Scots—many of them brandishing only broadswords and spears—were mowed down by English cannons and horsemen. In less than an hour, the government forces routed the Jacobite army, but that was just the start. They spent the next weeks methodically hunting down ringleaders and sympathizers (and many others in the Highlands who had nothing to do with the battle), ruthlessly killing, imprisoning, and banishing thousands.

Charles fled with a £30,000 price on his head. He escaped to the Isle of Skye, hidden by a woman named Flora MacDonald (her grave is on the Isle of Skye, and her statue is outside Inverness Castle). Flora dressed Charles in women's clothes and passed him off as her maid. Later, Flora was arrested and thrown in the Tower of London before being released and treated like a celebrity.

Charles escaped to France. He spent the rest of his life wandering Europe trying to drum up support to retake the throne. He drifted through short-lived romantic affairs and alcohol, and died in obscurity, without an heir, in Rome.

Though usually depicted as a battle of the Scottish versus the English, in truth Culloden was a civil war between two opposing dynasties: Stuart (Charlie) and Hanover (George). In fact, about one-fifth of the government's troops were Scottish, and several redcoat deserters fought along with the Jacobites. However, as the history has faded into lore, the battle has come to be remembered as a Scottish-versus-English standoff—or, in the parlance of the Scots, the Highlanders versus the Strangers.

The Battle of Culloden was the end of 60 years of Jacobite rebellions, the last major battle fought on British soil, and the final stand of the Highlanders. From then on, clan chiefs were deposed; kilts, tartans, and bagpipes became illegal paraphernalia; and farmers were cleared off their ancestral land, replaced by more-profitable sheep. Scottish culture would never recover from the events of the campaign called "the '45."

NORTHERN HIGHLANDS

Self-Guided Tour

Culloden's visitors center, opened in 2008, is a state-of-the-art £10 million facility. The ribbon was cut by two young local men, each descended from soldiers who fought in the battle (one from either side). On the way up to the door, look under your feet at the memorial stones for fallen soldiers and clans, mostly purchased by their American and Canadian descendants. Your tour takes you through two sections: the exhibit and the actual battlefield.

The Exhibit

The initial part of the exhibit provides you with some background. As you pass the ticket desk, note the **family tree** of Bonnie Prince Charlie ("Prince Charles Edward") and George II, who were essentially distant cousins. Next you'll come across the first of the exhibit's shadowy-figure **touchscreens,** which connect you with historical figures who give you details from both the Hanoverian and Jacobite perspectives. A **map** here shows the other power struggles happening in and around Europe, putting this fight for political control of Britain in a wider context. This battle was no small regional skirmish, but rather a key part of a larger struggle between Britain and its neighbors, primarily France, for control over trade and colonial power. In the display case are **medals** from the early 1700s, made by both sides as propaganda.

Your path through this building is cleverly designed to echo the course of the Jacobite army. Your short march gets under way as Charlie sails from France to Scotland, then finagles the support of Highland clan chiefs. As he heads south with his army to take London, you, too, are walking south. Along the way, maps show the movement of troops, and wall panels cover the build-up to the attack, as seen from both sides. Note the clever division of information: To the left and in red is the story of the "government" (a.k.a. Hanoverians/Whigs/English, led by the Duke of Cumberland); to the right, in blue, is the Jacobites' perspective (Prince Charlie and his Highlander/French supporters).

But you, like Charlie, don't make it to London—in the dark room at the end, you can hear Jacobite commanders arguing over whether to retreat back to Scotland. Pessimistic about their chances of receiving more French support, they decide to U-turn, and so do you. Heading back up north, you'll get some insight into some of the strategizing that went on behind the scenes.

By the time you reach the end of the hall, it's the night before the battle. Round another bend into a dark passage, and listen to the voices of the anxious troops. While the English slept soundly in their tents (recovering from celebrating the Duke's 25th birthday), the scrappy and exhausted Jacobite Highlanders struggled through the night to reach the battlefield (abandoning their plan of a surprise attack at Nairn and instead retreating back toward Inverness).

At last the two sides meet. As you wait outside the theater for the next showing, study the chart depicting how the forces were arranged on the battlefield. Once inside the theater, you'll soon be surrounded by the views and sounds of a windswept moor. An impressive four-minute **360° movie** projects the re-enacted battle with you right in the center of the action (the violence is realistic; young kids should probably sit this one out). If it hasn't hit you already, the movie drives home how truly outmatched the Jacobites were, and what a hopeless and tragic day it was for them.

Leave the movie, then enter the last room. Here you'll find **period weapons,** including ammunition and artifacts found on the battlefield, as well as **historical depictions** of the battle. You'll also find a section describing the detective work required to piece together the story from historical evidence. On the far end is a huge map, with narration explaining the combat you've just experienced while giving you a bird's-eye view of the field through which you're about to roam.

The Battlefield

Collect your free **audioguide** and go outside. From the back wall of the visitors center, survey the battlefield. In the foreground is a cottage used as a makeshift hospital during the conflict (it's decorated as it would have been then). To the east (south of the River Nairn) is the site that Lord George Murray originally chose for the action. In the end, he failed to convince Prince Charlie of its superiority, and the battle was held here—with disastrous consequences. Although not far from Culloden, the River Nairn site was miles away tactically, and things might have turned out differently for the Jacobites had the battle taken place there instead.

Head left, down to the battlefield. Your GPS guide knows where you are, and the attendant will give you directions on where to start. As you walk along the path, stop each time you hear the "ping" sound (if you keep going, you'll confuse the satellite). The basic audioguide has 10 stops—including the Jacobite front line, the Hanoverian front line, and more—and takes a minimum of 30 minutes, which is enough for most people. At the third stop, you have the option of detouring along a larger loop (6 extra stops—figure another 30 minutes minimum) before rejoining the basic route. Each stop has additional information on everything from the Brown Bess musket to who was standing on what front line—how long this part of the tour takes depends on how much you want to hear. Notice how uneven and boggy the ground is in parts, and imagine trying to run across this hummocky terrain with all your gear, toward almost-certain death.

As you pass by the **mass graves,** marked by small headstones, realize that entire clans fought, died, and were buried together. (The fallen were identified by the clan badge on their caps.) The Mackintosh grave alone was 77 yards long.

When you've finished your walking tour, re-enter the hall, return your audioguide, then catch the last part of the exhibit, which covers the aftermath of the battle. As you leave the building, hang a left to see the wall of **protruding bricks,** each representing a soldier who died. The handful of Hanoverian casualties are on the left (about 50); the rest of the long wall's raised bricks represent the multitude of dead Jacobites (about 1,500).

If you're having trouble grasping the significance of this battle, play a game of "What if?" If Bonnie Prince Charlie had persevered on this campaign and taken the throne, he likely wouldn't have plunged Britain into the Seven Years' War with France (his ally). And increased taxes on either side of that war led directly to the French and American revolutions. So if the Jacobites had won...the American colonies might still be part of the British Empire today.

Clava Cairns

Scotland is littered with reminders of prehistoric peoples—especially along the coast of the Moray Firth—but the Clava Cairns are

among the best-preserved, most interesting, and easiest to reach. You'll find them nestled in the spooky countryside just beyond Culloden Battlefield. These "Balnauran of Clava" are Neolithic burial chambers dating from 3,000 to 4,000 years ago. Although they appear to be just some giant piles of rocks in a sparsely forested clearing, they warrant a closer look to appreciate the prehistoric logic behind them. (The site is well-explained by informative plaques.) There are three structures: a central "ring cairn" with an open space in the center but no access to it, flanked by two "passage cairns," which were once covered. The entrance shaft in each passage cairn lines up with the setting sun at the winter solstice. Each cairn is surrounded by a stone circle, injecting this site with even more mystery.

Cost and Hours: Free, always open.

Getting There: Just after passing Culloden Battlefield on the B-9006 (coming from Inverness), signs on the right point to *Clava Cairns.* Follow this twisty road to the free parking lot by the stones. You can also walk from Culloden Battlefield (the Inverness

TI has maps as well as information on the Cairns; about 3 miles round-trip). Skip the cairns if you don't have a car or if the weather is bad.

Cawdor Castle

Homey and intimate, this castle is still the residence of the Dowager (read: widow) Countess of Cawdor, a local aristocratic

branch of the Campbell family. The castle's claim to fame is its connection to Shakespeare's *Macbeth*, in which the three witches correctly predict that the protagonist will be granted the title "Thane of Cawdor." The castle is not used as a setting in the play—which takes place in

Inverness, 300 years before this castle was built—but Shakespeare's dozen or so references to "Cawdor" are enough for the marketing machine to kick in. Today, virtually nothing tangibly ties Cawdor to the Bard or to the real-life Macbeth. But even if you ignore the Shakespeare lore, the castle is worth a visit.

Cost and Hours: £9.75, good £5 guidebook explains the family and the rooms, May-Sept daily 10:00-17:30, last entry at 17:00, gardens open until 18:00, closed Oct-April, tel. 01667/404-401, www.cawdorcastle.com.

Getting There: It's on the B-9090, just off the A-96, about 15 miles east of Inverness (6 miles beyond Culloden and the Clava Cairns). Public transportation no longer goes to Cawdor Church, making it difficult to visit without a car.

Visiting the Castle: The chatty, friendly docents (including Jean at the front desk, who can say "welcome" and "mind your head" in 60 different languages) give the castle an air of intimacy—most are residents of the neighboring village of Cawdor and act as though they're old friends with the Dowager Countess (many probably are). Entertaining posted explanations—written by the countess' late husband, the sixth Earl of Cawdor—bring the castle to life and make you wish you'd known the old chap. While many of today's castles are still residences for the aristocracy, Cawdor feels even more lived-in than the norm—you can imagine the Dowager Countess stretching out in front of the fireplace with a good book. Notice her geraniums in every room.

Stops on the tour include a tapestry-laden bedroom and a "tartan passage" speckled with modern paintings. In another bedroom (just before the stairs back down) is a tiny pencil sketch by Salvador Dalí. Inside the base of the tower, near the end of the tour, is the castle's proud symbol: a holly tree dating from 1372. According to the beloved legend, a donkey leaned against this tree to mark the spot where the castle was to be built—which it was, around the tree. (The tree is no longer alive, but its withered trunk is still propped up in the same position. No word on the donkey.)

The **gardens,** included with the ticket, are also worth exploring, with some 18th-century linden trees, a hedge maze (not open to the public), and several surprising species (including sequoia and redwood). In May and June, the laburnum arbors drip with yellow blossoms.

The nine-hole **golf course** on the castle grounds is bigger than pitch-and-putt and plenty of fun even for non-golfers (£12.50/person; golf shack staff generally include clubs and balls without an extra rental fee).

Nearby: The close but remote-feeling **village of Cawdor**—with a few houses, a village shop, and a tavern—is also worth a look if you've got time to kill.

BETWEEN INVERNESS AND EDINBURGH

Pitlochry • Stirling

To break up the trip between Inverness and Edinburgh (3 hours by car, 3.5 hours by train), consider stopping over at one of these two worthwhile destinations. The town of Pitlochry, right on the train route, mixes whisky and hillwalking with a dash of countryside charm. Farther south, the historic city of Stirling boasts an impressive castle, a monument to a Scottish hero (William "Braveheart" Wallace), and one of the country's most important battle sites (Bannockburn).

Planning Your Time

Visiting both Pitlochry and Stirling on a one-day drive from Inverness to Edinburgh is doable but busy (especially since part of Pitlochry's allure is slowing down to taste the whisky).

Pleasant Pitlochry is well-located, a quick detour off the main A-9 highway from Inverness to Edinburgh (via Perth) or an easy stop for train travelers. The town deserves an overnight for whisky-lovers, or for those who really want to relax in small-town Scotland. Though many find the town of Pitlochry appealing, it lacks the rugged Highlands scenery and easy access to other major sights found in Oban and Glencoe.

Stirling, off the busy A-9/M-9 motorway between Perth and Edinburgh, is well worth a sightseeing stop, especially for historians and romantics interested in Scottish history. (If skipping Stirling, notice that you can take the M-90 due south over the Firth of Forth to connect Perth and Edinburgh.) Stirling also works well as a stop-off between Edinburgh and points west (such as Glasgow or Oban)—just take the northern M-9/A-80 route instead of the more direct M-8.

Between Inverness & Edinburgh

TO THURSO & JOHN O'GROATS

MORAY FIRTH

NORTH SEA

NAIRN

A-96

A-98

INVERNESS

CAWDOR CASTLE

CLAVA CAIRNS

CULLODEN

TO ABERDEEN

A-82

TO ISLE OF SKYE

FORT AUG.

LOCH NESS

A-9

A-939

A-87

A-82

AVIEMORE

DAL-WHINNIE

BALMORAL CASTLE

A-93

GRAMPIAN

BALLATER

TO ABERDEEN

TO OBAN

MTNS.

A-93

BLAIR CASTLE

BLAIR ATHOLL

PITLOCHRY

A-90

A-82

A-923

A-85

DUNDEE

NORTH SEA

TO OBAN

PERTH

LEUCHARS

LOCH LOMOND

A-9

A-92

ST. ANDREWS

M-90

A-955

ANSTRUTHER

STIRLING

FIRTH OF FORTH

A-82

FALKIRK

M-8

EDINBURGH

GLASGOW

M-74

A-702

TO BERWICK-UPON-TWEED

A-68

TO AYR

A-80

TO CARLISLE & LAKE DISTRICT

TO JEDBURGH

🏰 CASTLE

✈ AIRPORT

DCH

Pitlochry

This likable tourist town, famous for its whisky and its hillwalking (both beloved by Scots), makes an enjoyable overnight stop

on the way between Inverness and Edinburgh. Just outside the craggy Highlands, Pitlochry is set amid pastoral rolling hills that offer plenty of forest hikes (brochures at TI). A salmon ladder climbs alongside the lazy river (free viewing area—salmon can run April-Oct, best in May and June, 10-minute walk from town).

Orientation to Pitlochry

Plucky little Pitlochry (pop. 2,500) lines up along its tidy, tourist-minded main road, where you'll find the train station, bus stops, TI, and bike rental. The town exists thanks to the arrival of the train, which conveniently brought Romantic Age tourists from the big cities to the south with this lovely bit of Scotland. Queen Victoria herself visited three times in the 1860s, putting Pitlochry on the tourist map. The Victorian architecture on the main street makes it clear that this was a delightful escape for city folks back in the 19th century. The River Tummel runs parallel to the main road, a few steps away. Most distilleries are a short drive out of town, but you can walk to the two best (see my self-guided hillwalk). Navigate easily by following the black directional signs to Pitlochry's handful of sights.

Tourist Information

The helpful TI provides bus and train schedules, has Internet access, and books rooms for a £4 fee. It sells maps for local hillwalks and scenic drives, including the £1 *Pitlochry Path Network* brochure, which has a handy map and is a good guide (July-early Sept Mon-Sat 9:00-18:30, Sun 9:30-17:30; April-June and early-Sept-Oct Mon-Sat 9:30-17:30, Sun 10:00-16:00; Nov-March Mon-Sat 9:30-16:30, closed Sun; exit from station and follow small road to the right with trains behind you, turn right on Atholl Road, and walk 5 minutes to TI on left, at #22; tel. 01796/472-215, www.perthshire.co.uk, pitlochry@visitscotland.com).

Helpful Hint

Bike Rental: Escape Route Bikes, located across the street and a block from the TI (away from town), rents a variety of bikes for adults and kids (£16-35/5 hours, £25-40/24 hours, price varies by type of bike and includes helmet and lock if you ask, Mon-Sat 9:00-17:30, Sun 10:00-17:00, shorter hours and sometimes closed Thu in winter, 3 Atholl Road, tel. 01796/473-859, www.escape-route.co.uk).

Self-Guided Hillwalk

Pitlochry Whisky Walk

You can spend an enjoyable afternoon hillwalking from downtown Pitlochry to a pair of top distilleries. The entire loop trip takes two to three hours, depending on how long you linger in the distilleries (at least 45 minutes to an hour of walking each way). It's a good way to see some green rolling hills, especially if you've only experienced urban Scotland. The walk is largely uphill on the way to the Edradour Distillery; wear good shoes, bring a rain jacket just in case, and be happy that you'll stroll easily downhill *after* you've had your whisky samples.

At the TI, pick up the *Pitlochry Path Network* brochure. You'll be taking the **Edradour Walk** (marked on directional signs with the yellow hiker icons; on the map it's a series of yellow dots). Leave the TI and head left along the busy A-924. The walk can be done by going either direction, but I'll describe it counterclockwise.

Within 10 minutes, you'll come to **Bell's Blair Athol Distillery.** If you're a whisky buff, stop in here (described later, under "Sights in Pitlochry"). Otherwise, hold out for the much more atmospheric Edradour. After passing a few B&Bs and suburban homes, you'll see a sign (marked *Edradour Walk*) on the left side of the road, leading you up and off the highway. You'll come to a clearing, and as the road gets steeper, you'll see signs directing you 50 yards off the main path to see the "Black Spout"—a wonderful waterfall well worth a few extra steps.

At the top of the hill, you'll arrive in another clearing, where a narrow path leads along a field. Low rolling hills surround you in all directions. It seems like there's not another person around for miles, with just the thistles to keep you company. It's an easy 20 minutes to the distillery from here.

Stop into the **Edradour Distillery** (also described later). After the tour, leave the distillery, heading right, following the paved road (Old North Road). In about five minutes, there's a sign that seems to point right into the field. Take the small footpath that runs along the left side of the road. (If you see the driveway with stone lions on both sides, you've gone a few steps too far.)

You'll walk parallel to the route you took getting to the distillery, and then you'll head back into the forest. Cross the footbridge and make a left (as the map indicates), staying on the wide road. You'll pass a B&B and hear traffic noises as you emerge out of the forest. The trail leads back to the highway, with the TI a few blocks ahead on the right.

Sights in Pitlochry

Distillery Tours
The cute **Edradour Distillery** (ED-rah-dower), the smallest in Scotland, takes pride in making its whisky with a minimum of

machinery. Small white-and-red buildings are nestled in an impossibly green Scottish hillside. Wander through the buildings and take the £7.50 guided tour (2-3/hour in summer, 1/hour in winter, 60 minutes). They offer a 10-minute video and, of course, a free sample dram. Unlike the bigger distilleries, they allow you to take photos of the equipment. If you like the whisky, buy some here and support the Pitlochry economy—this is one of the few independently owned distilleries left in Scotland (May-Oct Mon-Sat 10:00-17:00, Sun 12:00-17:00; Nov-April Mon-Sat 10:00-16:00, Sun 12:00-16:00 except Nov-Feb, when it's closed on Sun; last tour departs one hour before closing, tel. 01796/472-095, www.edradour.com). Most come to the distillery by car (follow signs from the main road, 2.5 miles into the countryside), but you can also get there on a peaceful hiking trail that you'll have all to yourself (follow my "Pitlochry Whisky Walk," earlier).

The big, ivy-covered **Bell's Blair Athol Distillery** is more conveniently located (about a half-mile from the town center) and more corporate-feeling, offering 45-minute tours with a wee taste at the end (£6.50, Easter-Oct tours depart 2/hour daily 10:00-17:00, July-Aug until 17:30, possibly closed Sun in spring, last tour departs one hour before closing; shorter hours, fewer tours, and closed Sat-Sun off-season; tel. 01796/482-003, www.discovering -distilleries.com/blairathol).

Pitlochry Power Station
The station's visitors center, adjacent to the salmon ladder, offers a mildly entertaining exhibit about hydroelectric power in the region.

Cost and Hours: Free, salmon viewing and exhibit open April-Oct Mon-Fri 10:00-17:00, closed Sat-Sun except Bank

Holidays and in July-Aug, closed Nov-March, tel. 01796/473-152.

Getting There: Walkers can reach this easily in about 15 minutes by crossing the footbridge from the town center. Drivers will head east out of town (toward Bell's Blair Athol Distillery), then turn right on Bridge Road, cross the river, and backtrack to the power station.

Pitlochry Festival Theatre

From about May through October, this theater presents a different play every night and concerts on some Sundays (tickets cost £15-28 for Mon-Thu shows and Sat matinee, £18-33 for Fri-Sat shows; purchase tickets online, by phone, or in person; visit Just the Ticket, in town at 89 Atholl Road, or the theater—same price, box office open daily 10:00-20:00, restaurant, tel. 01796/484-626, www.pitlochryfestivaltheatre.com).

Explorers Garden

Adjacent to the theater, this six-acre woodland garden features plants and wildflowers from around the world.

Cost and Hours: £4, April-Oct daily 10:00-17:00, last entry at 16:15, tel. 01796/484-626, www.explorersgarden.com.

John Muir Exhibit

On the main street in the center of town is **The Wild Space**, established to raise awareness of the John Muir Trust and the man who inspired it. Muir (1838-1914) was born in Scotland, moved to the US when he was 10, and later helped establish the world's first national park system in the US. There's a tiny exhibit with a feel-good nature video and a small art gallery.

Cost and Hours: Free, Mon and Wed-Sat 10:00-16:00, closed Tue, off the A-9 at corner of Station and Atholl roads, www.jmt.org.

Northeast of Pitlochry

Balmoral Castle

The Queen stays at her 50,000-acre private estate, located within Cairngorms National Park, from August through early October. The grounds and the castle's ballroom are open to visitors part of the year, but they're overpriced.

Cost and Hours: £10, includes audioguide, April-July daily 10:00-17:00, closed Aug-March, last entry 30 minutes before closing, tel. 013397/42534, www.balmoralcastle.com.

Getting There: Balmoral is on the A-93, midway between Ballater and Braemar, about 50 miles northeast of Pitlochry and about 75 miles southeast of Inverness.

Nearby: For a free peek at another royal landmark, stop at **Crathie Kirk,** the small but charming parish church where the royal family worships when they are at Balmoral, and where Queen

Victoria's beloved servant John Brown is buried. The church is just across the highway from the Balmoral parking lot.

Sleeping in Pitlochry

$$ Craigroyston House is a quaint, large Victorian country house with eight Laura Ashley-style bedrooms, run by charming Gretta and Douglas Maxwell (Db-£94 July-Sept, less off-season, family room, cash only, Wi-Fi, above and behind the TI—small gate at back of parking lot—and next to the church at 2 Lower Oakfield, tel. 01796/472-053, www.craigroyston.co.uk, reservations@craig royston.co.uk).

$ Pitlochry's fine **hostel** has 53 beds in 12 rooms, including some private and family rooms. It's on Knockard Road, well-signed from the town center, about a five-minute walk above the main drag and offering nice views (£18 bunks in 3- to 6-bed rooms, Db-£60; £2 more for non-members, breakfast-£5-6, packed lunch-£5.50, closed Nov-Feb, pay guest computer, pay Wi-Fi, self-service laundry, kitchen, office open 7:00-10:00 & 16:30-23:00, tel. 01796/472-308, www.syha.org.uk, pitlochry@syha.org.uk).

Eating in Pitlochry

Plenty of options line the main drag, including several bakeries selling picnic supplies. For a heartier meal, try **Victoria's** restaurant and coffee shop, located midway between the train station and the TI (£6-10 sandwiches, £10-11 pizzas, £10-16 lunches, £13-25 dinners, daily 10:00-20:30, patio seating, free Wi-Fi, at corner of memorial garden, 45 Atholl Road, tel. 01796/472-670), or **Fern Cottage,** just behind Victoria's (pre-theater £18-22 dinner specials 17:30-18:45, Ferry Road, tel. 01796/473-840). **Port-na-Craig Inn** is a fancy option on the river, just downhill from the theater (tel. 01796/472-777).

Pitlochry Connections

The train station is open Monday to Saturday 8:00-18:30 and Sunday 10:30-18:00 (may have shorter hours in winter).

From Pitlochry by Train to: Inverness (every 1.5-2 hours, 1.5 hours), **Stirling** (every 1.5-2 hours, 1.25 hours, some transfer in Perth), **Edinburgh** (8/day direct, 2 hours), **Glasgow** (9/day, 1.75-2 hours, some transfer in Perth). Train info: tel. 08457-484-950, www.nationalrail.co.uk.

Stirling

Once the Scottish capital, the quaint city of Stirling (pop. 41,000) is a mini-Edinburgh with lots of character and a dramatic castle dripping with history and boasting sweeping views. Just outside of town are the William Wallace Monument, honoring the real-life Braveheart, and the Bannockburn Heritage Centre, marking the site of Robert the Bruce's victorious battle.

Orientation to Stirling

Stirling's old town is situated along a long, narrow, steep hill, with the castle at its apex. The old town feels like Edinburgh's Royal Mile—only steeper, shorter, and less touristy. From the castle it's a long, steep 10-block descent before you hit the thriving commercial district.

Tourist Information: The TI is near the base of the old town, just inside the gates of the touristy Old Town Jail attraction (daily 10:00-17:00, Internet access—£1/20 minutes, St. Johns Street, tel. 01786/475-019, stirling@visitscotland.com).

Getting Around: The city's three main sights (Stirling Castle, the Wallace Monument, and the Bannockburn Heritage Centre) are difficult to reach by foot from the center of town, but are easily accessible by frequent public bus (the bus station is a short walk from the train station) or by taxi (about £5 to each one).

Sights in Stirling

▲Stirling Castle

"He who holds Stirling, holds Scotland." These fateful words have proven, more often than not, to be true. Stirling Castle's strategic position—perched on a volcanic crag overlooking a bridge over the River Forth, the primary passage between the Lowlands and the Highlands—has long been the key to Scotland. This castle of the Stuart kings is one of Scotland's most historic and popular. Offering spectacular views over a gentle countryside, and an interesting exhibit inside, Stirling is worth a look.

Cost and Hours: £14, daily April-Sept 9:30-18:00, Oct-March 9:30-17:00, last entry 45 minutes before closing, Regimental Museum closes 45 minutes before castle, café.

Information: Tel. 01786/450-000, www.stirlingcastle.gov.uk.

Tours: Posted information is skimpy, so consider a tour or audioguide to help bring the site to life. You can take the included 45-minute **guided tour** (generally hourly 10:00-16:00, less off-season, depart from the well outside the Fort Major's House), or rent the £3 **audioguide**. Docents posted throughout can tell you more.

Getting There: Similar to Edinburgh's castle, Stirling Castle sits at the very tip of a steep old town. If you enter Stirling by car, follow the *Stirling Castle* signs uphill through town to the esplanade, and park at the £4 lot just outside the castle gate. In summer, there's a park-and-ride option: Leave your car at the Castleview Park-and-Ride off the A-84 and hop on the shuttle bus (£1 round-trip, runs June-Sept 7:30-18:00, 15-minute ride). Without a car, you can hike the 20-minute uphill route from the train or bus station to the castle, or take a taxi (about £5).

Background: Stirling marks the site of two epic medieval battles where famous Scotsmen defeated huge English armies despite terrible odds: In 1297, William Wallace (a.k.a. "Braveheart") fended off an invading English army at the Battle of Stirling Bridge. And in 1314, Robert the Bruce won the battle of nearby Bannockburn. Soon after, the castle became the primary residence of the Stuart monarchs, who turned it into a showpiece of Scotland (and a symbol of one-upmanship against England). But when the Crown moved to London, Stirling's prominence waned. The military, which took over the castle during the Jacobite Wars of the 18th century, bulked it up and converted it into a garrison—destroying its delicate beauty. While restored now, it feels new, with almost no historic artifacts.

❍ Self-Guided Tour: My tour covers the castle's top spots. Begin on the esplanade, just outside the castle entrance, with its grand views.

The Esplanade: Spectacularly set on a volcanic crag to oversee the place where the Lowlands meet the Highlands, Stirling Castle was the preferred home of Scottish kings and queens in the Middle Ages.

But because of its strategic setting, the castle had to weather lots of sieges. Two of the most important battles in Scottish history were fought within sight of its ramparts: Stirling Bridge (1297) and Bannockburn (1314). A statue of the hero of Bannockburn, King Robert the Bruce, stands strong on the esplanade, as if still rallying his people. The fortified grand entry showed all who approached that James IV (r. 1488-1513) was a great ruler with a powerful castle.

Stirling Castle's glory days were in the 16th century, when it provided a splendid showcase for the Stuart court. It last saw action when besieged by Jacobite forces in 1746. After the end of the Scottish threat, it became a British garrison, home base of the Argyll and Sutherland regiments. It still flies the Union Jack of Great Britain. Its esplanade, a military parade ground in the 19th century, is a tour-bus parking lot in the 21st century.

Entry and Castle Exhibition: Just inside the gate, buy your ticket (ask about tour times, and consider renting the audioguide). Pass through the inner gate, then follow the passage to the left into a delightful grassy courtyard called the Queen Anne Garden. This was the royal family's playground in the 1600s. Imagine doing a little lawn bowling with the queen here.

In the casemates (from 1710) lining the garden is the Castle Exhibition. Its "Come Face to Face with 1000 Years of History" exhibit provides an entertaining and worthwhile introduction to the castle. The video leaves you thinking that re-enactors of Jacobite struggles are even more spirited than our Civil War re-enactors.

• *Return to the Outer Close (where you'll notice the Grand Battery, with its cannons and rampart views and, underneath that, the Great Kitchens). We'll see both of those at the end of this walk. Now, turn left and hike up through the main gateway and into the center of the castle, the Inner Close.*

Inner Close: Standing at the center of Stirling Castle, you're surrounded by Scottish history. This courtyard was the core of the 12th-century castle and continued to be its center as new buildings were added.

Notice the Renaissance statues looking down on the castle courtyard from royal apartments. In 1540 King James V, inspired by French Renaissance châteaus he'd seen, had the castle covered with about 200 statues and busts to "proclaim the peace, prosperity and justice of his reign" and to validate his rule. Imagine the impression all these classical gods and goddesses had on visitors. The message: James' rule was a Golden Age for Scotland.

Each of the very different buildings in this complex was constructed by a different monarch. While all are historic, they are entirely rebuilt and none have the patina of age. Facing downhill, you'll see the Great Hall. The Chapel Royal, where Mary, Queen of Scots was crowned in 1543, is to your left. The Royal Palace with the Royal Apartments is to your right. The Stirling Heads Gallery is above that. And behind you is the Regimental Museum.

The Great Hall: Step inside the largest secular space in medieval Scotland. Dating from around 1500, this was a grand setting for the great banquets of Scotland's Renaissance kings. The impressive hammerbeam roof is a modern reconstruction, modeled on the early 16th-century roof at Edinburgh Castle.

The Chapel Royal: One of the first Protestant churches built in Scotland, the Chapel Royal was constructed in 1594 by James VI for the baptism of his first son, Prince Henry. The faint painted frieze high up survives from Charles I's coronation visit to Scotland in 1633. Clearly the holiness of the chapel ended in the 1800s when the army moved in.

The Royal Palace and Royal Apartments: Within the palace you can visit six ground-floor apartments, colorfully done up as they might have looked in the mid-16th century when James V and his queen, Mary of Guise, lived here. Costumed performers play the role of palace attendants, happy to chat with you about medieval life. Notice the 60 carved and colorfully painted oak medallions on the ceiling in the king's presence chamber. The medallions are carved with the faces of Scottish and European royalty. These are copies, painstakingly reconstructed after expert research—you'll soon see the originals up close in the Stirling Heads Gallery.

• *Outside the apartments, a staircase leads up to...*

The Stirling Heads Gallery: This is, for me, the castle's highlight—a chance to see the originals of the elaborately carved and painted portrait medallions that decorated the ceiling of the king's presence chamber.

Regimental Museum: At the top of the Inner Close, in the King's Old Building, is the excellent **Argyll and Sutherland Highlanders Museum.** Another highlight of the castle, it's barely mentioned in castle promotional material because it's run by a different organization. With lots of tartans, tassels, and swords, it shows how the spirit of Scotland was absorbed by Britain. The "In the Trenches" exhibit is a powerful look at World War I, with accounts from the battlefield. The two regiments, established in the 1790s to defend Britain in the Napoleonic age and combined in the 1880s, have served with distinction in over two centuries of British military campaigns. Their pride shows here in the building that's their headquarters, where they've been stationed since 1881.

Rampart Walk to the Kitchen: The skinny lane between church and museum leads to the secluded Douglas Gardens at the rock's highest point. From here you can walk the ramparts downhill to the Grand Battery, with its cannon rampart at the Outer Close. As you stroll the ramparts, look across the valley at the dramatic lone tower—the National Wallace Monument. The Outer Close was the service zone, with a well and the kitchen (below the cannon rampart). The great banquets of James VI didn't happen all by themselves, as you'll appreciate when you explore the fine medieval kitchen exhibit (where mannequin cooks oversee medieval recipes).

• *Your castle visit ends here, but your castle ticket includes Argyll's Lodging, a fortified noble mansion (described next).*

Argyll's Lodging

Just below the castle esplanade and across the street is a 17th-century nobleman's fortified mansion. European noblemen wanted to live near power—such as this spot below the king's palace, where the Earl of Argyll's family resided for about a century. Its hours are erratic—and you must book a tour at the castle beforehand (most likely open in peak season, June-Aug). While Stirling Castle is pretty sterile, Argyll's Landing is less so and worth a few minutes.

▲William Wallace Monument

Commemorating the Scottish hero better known to Americans as "Braveheart," this sandstone tower—built during a wave of

Scottish nationalism in the mid-19th century—marks the Abbey Craig hill on the outskirts of Stirling. This is where Wallace gathered forces for his largest-scale victory against England's King Edward I, in 1297: the Battle of Stirling Bridge. The victory was a huge boost to the Scottish cause, but England came back to beat the Scots the next year. (To learn more about William Wallace, see page 766.)

Cost and Hours: £8.50, audioguide-£1, daily July-Aug 10:00-18:00, April-June and Sept-Oct 10:00-17:00, Nov-March 10:30-16:00, last entry 45 minutes before closing, café and gift shop, tel. 01786/472-140, www.nationalwallacemonument.com.

Getting There: It's two miles northeast of Stirling on the A-8, signposted from the city center. You can catch a public bus from the Stirling bus station (a short walk south of the train station) to the monument's parking lot (several buses run on this route, 10/hour, 9-15 minutes). Taxis cost about £5-7. From the parking lot's Visitors Pavilion, you'll need to hike (a very steep 10 minutes) or take a shuttle bus up the hill to the monument itself.

Visiting the Monument: From the base of the monument, you can see Stirling Bridge—a stone version that replaced the original wooden one. Looking out from the same vantage point as Wallace, imagine how the famous battle played out, and consider why the location was so important in the battle (explained in more detail inside the monument).

After entering the monument, pick up the worthwhile audioguide. You'll first encounter a passionate talking Wallace replica, explaining his defiant stand against Edward I. As you listen, ogle Wallace's five-and-a-half-foot-long broadsword (and try to imagine drawing it from a scabbard on your back at a dead run). Then take a spin through a hall of other Scottish heroes. Finally, climb the 246 narrow steps inside the tower for grand views. The stairways are extremely tight and require some maneuvering—claustrophobes be warned.

STIRLING

▲Bannockburn Heritage Centre

Just to the south of Stirling proper is the newly rebuilt Bannockburn Heritage Centre, commemorating what many Scots view as their nation's most significant military victory over the invading English: the Battle of Bannockburn, won by a Scottish army led by Robert the Bruce against England's King Edward II in 1314. The new and improved center is closed through March of 2014, when it reopens for the battle's 700th anniversary. Later in 2014, on September 18, Scotland will vote on a referendum for complete independence from England.

Cost and Hours: Likely £10, check online or call ahead; closed until March 2014, after that open March-Oct daily 10:00-17:30, Nov-Feb daily 10:00-17:00; café, tel. 0844/493-2139, www.nts.org.uk.

Anniversary Events: Major celebrations marking the battle's 700th anniversary will be held June 28-30, 2014. A re-enactment of the Battle of Bannockburn is planned, with 15,000 people expected to attend each of the three days (£22, requires advance purchase, heritage center not open during re-enactment except for those with special £83 King's Ticket, see www.battleofbannockburn.com for more information).

Getting There: It's two miles south of Stirling on the A-872, off the M-80/M-9. For non-drivers, it's an easy bus ride from the Stirling bus station (a short walk south from the train station; several buses run on this route, 8/hour, 9-15 minutes).

Visiting Bannockburn Heritage Centre: The rebuilt center will feature an interactive 3-D battle simulation and a short 360-degree film, along with audio narrations from fictional combatants and bystanders.

In simple terms, Robert—who was first and foremost a politician—found himself out of political options after years of failed diplomatic attempts to make peace with the strong-arming English. William Wallace's execution left a vacuum in military leadership, and eventually Robert stepped in, waging a successful guerrilla campaign that came to a head as young Edward's army marched to Stirling. Although the Scots were greatly outnumbered, their strategy and use of terrain at Bannockburn allowed them to soundly beat the English and drive Edward out of Scotland for the time being. (For more about Robert the Bruce, see page 769.)

This victory is so legendary among the Scots that the country's unofficial national anthem, "Flower of Scotland"—written 600 years after the battle—focuses on this one event. (CDs with a version of this song performed by The Corries can be purchased at the heritage center. Buy one and learn the song, and you might soon find yourself singing along at a pub.)

Stirling Connections

From Stirling by Train to: Edinburgh (roughly 2/hour, 1 hour), **Glasgow** (3/hour, 30-45 minutes), **Pitlochry** (every 1.5-2 hours, 1.25 hours, some transfer in Perth), **Inverness** (every 1.5-2 hours, 2.75-3 hours, some transfer in Perth). Train info: tel. 08457-484-950, www.nationalrail.co.uk.

BRITAIN: PAST AND PRESENT

Britain was created by force and held together by force. It's a nation shaped by the 19th century, when its rich Victorian-era empire reached a financial peak. Its traditional industry, buildings, and the pervasive notion of "Great" Britain are the products of its past wealth.

To best understand the many fascinating tour guides you'll encounter in your travels, have a basic handle on the sweeping story of this land and its capital, London. (Generally speaking, the nice and bad stories guides tell are not true...and the boring ones are.)

Basic British History for the Traveler

When Julius Caesar landed on the misty and mysterious isle of Britain in 55 B.C., England entered the history books. The primitive Celtic tribes Caesar fought were themselves invaders (who had earlier conquered the even more mysterious people who built Stonehenge). About 90 years later, the Romans came back, building towns and roads and establishing their capital at Londinium. The Celtic natives in Scotland and Wales—consisting of Gaels, Picts, and Scots—were not easily subdued. The Romans built Hadrian's Wall near the Scottish border as protection against their troublesome northern neighbors. Even today, the Celtic language and influence are strongest in these far reaches of Britain.

As Rome fell, so fell Roman Britain—a victim of invaders and internal troubles. Barbarian tribes from Germany and Denmark, called Angles and Saxons, swept through the southern part of the island, establishing Angle-land. These were the days of the real King Arthur, possibly a Christianized Roman general who fought valiantly—but in vain—against invading barbarians. In 793,

Get It Right

Americans tend to use "England," "Britain," and the "United Kingdom" (or "UK") interchangeably, but they're not quite the same.

- **England** is the country occupying the center and southeast part of the island.
- **Britain** is the name of the island.
- **Great Britain** is the political union of the island's three countries: England, Scotland, and Wales.
- The **United Kingdom (UK)** adds a fourth country, Northern Ireland.
- The **British Isles** (not a political entity) also includes the independent Republic of Ireland.
- The **British Commonwealth** is a loose association of possessions and former colonies (including Canada, Australia, and India) that profess at least symbolic loyalty to the Crown.

You can call the modern nation either the United Kingdom ("the UK"), "Great Britain," or simply "Britain."

England was hit with the first of two centuries of savage invasions by barbarians from Norway, called the Vikings or Norsemen. The island was plunged into 500 years of Dark Ages—wars, plagues, and poverty—lit only by the dim candle of a few learned Christian monks and missionaries trying to convert the barbarians. The sightseer sees little from this Anglo-Saxon period.

Modern England began with yet another invasion. William the Conqueror and his Norman troops crossed the English Channel from France in 1066. William crowned himself king in Westminster Abbey (where all subsequent coronations would take place) and began building the Tower of London. French-speaking Norman kings ruled the country for two centuries. Then followed two centuries of civil wars, with various noble families vying for the crown. In the bitterest feud, the York and Lancaster families fought the Wars of the Roses, so-called because of the white and red flowers the combatants chose as their symbols. Rife with battles, intrigues, and kings, nobles, and ladies imprisoned and executed in the Tower, it's a wonder the country survived its rulers.

England was finally united by the "third-party" Tudor family. Henry VIII, a Tudor, was England's Renaissance king. He was handsome, athletic, highly sexed, a poet, a scholar, and a musician. He was also arrogant, cruel, gluttonous, and paranoid. He went through six wives in 40 years, divorcing, imprisoning, or executing them when they no longer suited his needs. (To keep track of each one's fate, British kids learn this rhyme: "Beheaded, divorced, died; beheaded, divorced, survived.")

Henry "divorced" England from the Catholic Church, establishing the Protestant Church of England (the Anglican Church) and setting in motion years of religious squabbles. He also "dissolved" the monasteries (c. 1540), left just the shells of many formerly glorious abbeys dotting the countryside, and pocketed their land and wealth for the crown (for more on Henry, see the sidebar on page 132).

Henry's daughter, Queen Elizabeth I, who reigned for 45 years, made England a great trading and naval power (defeating the Spanish Armada) and presided over the Elizabethan era of great writers (such as William Shakespeare) and scientists (such as Sir Francis Bacon). But Elizabeth never married, so the English Parliament asked the Protestant ruler to the north, Scotland's King James (Elizabeth's first cousin twice removed), if he'd like to inherit the English throne. The two nations have been tied together, however fitfully, ever since (though recent stirrings toward Scottish independence may indeed shake up this longstanding union).

The enduring quarrel between England's divine-right kings and Parliament's nobles finally erupted into a civil war (1643). Parliament forces under the Protestant Puritan farmer Oliver Cromwell defeated—and beheaded—King Charles I. This civil war left its mark on much of what you'll see in Britain. Eventually, Parliament invited Charles' son to take the throne. This "restoration of the monarchy" was accompanied by a great colonial expansion and the rebuilding of London (including Christopher Wren's St. Paul's Cathedral), which had been devastated by the Great Fire of 1666. Parliament gained ultimate authority over the throne when it deposed Catholic James II and imported the Dutch monarchs William and Mary in 1688, guaranteeing a Protestant succession.

Queen Victoria
(1819-1901)

Plump, pleasant, and barely five feet tall, Queen Victoria, with her regal demeanor and 64-year reign, came to symbolize the global dominance of the British Empire during its greatest era.

Born in Kensington Palace, Victoria was the granddaughter of "Mad" King George III, the tyrant who sparked the American Revolution. Her domineering mother raised her in sheltered seclusion, drilling into her the strict morality that would come to be known as "Victorian." At 18, she was crowned queen. Victoria soon fell madly, deeply in love with Prince Albert, a handsome German nobleman with mutton-chop sideburns. They married and set up house in Buckingham Palace (the first monarchs to do so) and at Windsor Castle. Over the next 17 years, she and Albert had nine children, whom they eventually married off to Europe's crowned heads. Victoria's royal descendants include Kaiser Wilhelm II of Germany (who started World War I); the current monarchs of Spain, Norway, Sweden, and Denmark; and England's Queen Elizabeth II, who is Victoria's great-granddaughter.

Victoria and Albert promoted the arts and sciences, organizing a world's fair in Hyde Park (1851) that showed off London as *the* global capital. Just as important, they were role models for an entire nation; this loving couple influenced several generations with their wholesome middle-class values and devoted parenting. Though Victoria is often depicted as dour and stuffy—she supposedly coined the phrase "We are not amused"—in private she was warm, easy to laugh, plainspoken, thrifty, and modest, with a talent for sketching and journal writing.

In 1861, Victoria's happy domestic life ended. Her mother's death was soon followed by the sudden loss of her beloved Albert to typhoid fever. A devastated Victoria dressed in black for the funeral—and for her remaining 40 years never again wore any other color. She hunkered down at Windsor with her family. Critics complained she was an absentee monarch. Rumors swirled that her kilt-wearing servant, John Brown, was not only her close friend but also her lover. For two decades, she rarely appeared in public.

Over time, Victoria emerged from mourning to assume her

Britain grew as a naval superpower, colonizing and trading with all parts of the globe (although it lost its most important colony to those ungrateful Americans in 1776). Admiral Horatio Nelson's victory over Napoleon's fleet at the Battle of Trafalgar secured her naval superiority ("Britannia rules the waves"), and 10 years later, the Duke of Wellington stomped Napoleon on land at Waterloo. Nelson and Wellington—both buried in London's St. Paul's Cathedral—are memorialized by many arches, columns, role as one of history's first constitutional monarchs. She had inherited a crown with little real power. But beyond her ribbon-cutting ceremonial duties, Victoria influenced events behind the scenes. She studiously learned politics from powerful mentors (especially Prince Albert and two influential prime ministers) and kept well-informed on what Parliament was doing. Thanks to Victoria's personal modesty and honesty, the British public never came to disdain the monarchy, as happened in other countries.

Victoria gracefully oversaw the peaceful transfer of power from the nobles to the people. The secret ballot was introduced during her reign, and ordinary workers acquired voting rights (though this applied only to men—Victoria opposed women's suffrage). The traditional Whigs and Tories morphed into today's Liberal and Conservative parties. Victoria personally promoted progressive charities, and even paid for her own crown.

Most of all, Victoria became the symbol of the British Empire, which she saw as a way to protect and civilize poorer peoples. Britain enjoyed peace at home, while its colonial possessions doubled to include India, Australia, Canada, and much of Africa. Because it was always daytime someplace under Victoria's rule, it was often said that "the sun never sets on the British Empire."

The Victorian era saw great changes. The Industrial Revolution was in full swing. When Victoria was born, there were no trains. By 1842, when she took her first train trip (with much fanfare), railroads crisscrossed Europe. The telegraph, telephone, and newspapers further laced the world together. The popular arts flourished—it was the era of Dickens novels, Tennyson poems, Sherlock Holmes stories, Gilbert and Sullivan operettas, and Pre-Raphaelite paintings. Economically, Britain saw the rise of the middle class. Middle-class morality dominated—family, hard work, honor, duty, and sexual modesty.

By the end of her reign, Victoria was wildly popular, both for her personality and as a focus for British patriotism. At her Golden Jubilee (1887), she paraded past adoring throngs to Westminster Abbey. For her Diamond Jubilee (1897), she did the same at St. Paul's Cathedral. Cities, lakes, and military medals were named for her. When she passed away in 1901, it was literally the end of an era.

and squares throughout England.

Economically, Britain led the world into the Industrial Age with her mills, factories, coal mines, and trains. By the time of Queen Victoria's reign (1837-1901), Britain was at its zenith of power, with a colonial empire that covered one-fifth of the world (for more on Victoria, see sidebar).

The 20th century was not kind to Britain. After decades of rebellion, Ireland finally gained its independence—except for the more Protestant north. Two world wars devastated Britain's population. The Nazi Blitz of World War II reduced much of London to rubble, although the freedom-loving world was inspired by Britain's determination to stand up to Hitler. Britain was rallied through difficult times by two leaders: Prime Minister Winston Churchill, a remarkable orator, and King George VI, who overcame a persistent stutter. After the war, the colonial empire dwindled to almost nothing, and Britain lost its superpower economic status.

One post-Empire hot spot—Northern Ireland, plagued by the "Troubles" between Catholics and Protestants—heated up, and then finally started cooling off. In the spring of 2007, the unthinkable happened when leaders of the ultra-nationalist party sat down with those of the ultra-unionist party. London returned control of Northern Ireland to the popularly elected Northern Ireland Assembly. Perhaps most important of all, after almost 40 years, the British Army withdrew from Northern Ireland that summer.

The tradition (if not the substance) of greatness continues, presided over by Queen Elizabeth II, her husband, Prince Philip, and their son Prince Charles. It seems you can't pick up a British newspaper without some mention of the latest event, scandal, or oddity involving the royal family.

The sons of Prince Charles and the late Princess Diana generate the biggest tabloid buzz. The older son, Prince William (b. 1982), is a graduate of Scotland's St. Andrews University and served as a search-and-rescue helicopter pilot with the Royal Air Force. In 2011, William married Catherine "Kate" Middleton, who is now the Duchess of Cambridge and will eventually become Britain's queen. Their son, Prince George Alexander Louis, born in 2013, will ultimately succeed William as sovereign. (A conveniently timed change in the law ensured that William and Kate's firstborn would inherit the throne, regardless of gender.)

William's brother, redheaded Prince Harry (b. 1984), has mostly shaken his reputation as a bad boy: He's proved his mettle as a career soldier, completing a tour in Afghanistan, doing charity work in Africa, and serving as an Apache aircraft commander pilot with the Army Air Corps. Nonetheless, Harry's romances and high-wire party antics are popular tabloid topics.

For years, their parents' love life was also fodder for the British press: Charles' marriage to Princess Di, their bitter divorce, Diana's dramatic death, and the ongoing drama with Charles' longtime girlfriend—and now wife—Camilla Parker Bowles. Camilla, trying to gain the respect of the Queen and the public, doesn't call herself a princess—she uses the title Duchess of Cornwall. (And even when Charles becomes king, she will not be Queen Camilla—instead she plans to call herself the "Princess Consort.")

Britain's Royal Families

Royal Lineage

802-1066	Saxon and Danish kings
1066-1154	Norman invasion (William the Conqueror), Norman kings
1154-1399	Plantagenet (kings with French roots)
1399-1461	Lancaster
1462-1485	York
1485-1603	Tudor (Henry VIII, Elizabeth I)
1603-1649	Stuart (civil war and beheading of Charles I)
1649-1653	Commonwealth, no royal head of state
1653-1659	Protectorate, with Cromwell as Lord Protector
1660-1714	Restoration of Stuart dynasty
1714-1901	Hanover (four Georges, William IV, Victoria)
1901-1910	Saxe-Coburg (Edward VII)
1910-present	Windsor (George V, Edward VIII, George VI, Elizabeth II)

Royal Sightseeing

You can see the trappings of royalty at Buckingham Palace (the Queen's London residence) with its Changing of the Guard; Kensington Palace—with a wing that's home to Will, Kate, and baby George, and a cottage that serves as Harry's bachelor pad—plus good exhibits on Victoria, William and Mary, and the Hanovers; Clarence House, the London home of Prince Charles and Camilla; Althorp Estate (80 miles from London), the childhood home and burial place of Princess Diana; Windsor Castle, a royal country home near London; and the crown jewels in the Tower of London.

Your best chances to actually see the Queen are on three public occasions: State Opening of Parliament (mid-May, next in 2015), Remembrance Sunday (early November, at the Cenotaph), or Trooping the Colour (one Saturday in mid-June, parading down Whitehall and at Buckingham Palace).

Otherwise, check the "Latest news and diary" section of www.royal.gov.uk, where you can search for future royal events.

Charles' siblings are occasionally in the news: Princess Anne, Prince Andrew (who married and divorced Sarah "Fergie" Ferguson), and Prince Edward (who married Di look-alike Sophie Rhys-Jones).

Through it all, Queen Elizabeth has stayed above the fray, and most British people still jump at an opportunity to see royalty. With the worldwide hubbub surrounding Prince William's marriage to Kate (more than two billion people tuned in to watch) and the birth of their son, it is clear that the concept of royalty is still alive and well in the third millennium. (And, according to pollsters, just one-fifth of the Queen's subjects are in favor of abolishing the monarchy.)

In 2012, Queen Elizabeth marked her 60th year on the throne—her Diamond Jubilee. Only her great-great-grandmother, Queen Victoria (see sidebar on page 980), had a longer reign—but Elizabeth is on pace to overtake her in September of 2015. While many wonder who will succeed her—and when—the situation is straightforward: The Queen sees her job as a lifelong position, and legally, Charles (who wants to be king) cannot be skipped over for his son William. Given the longevity in the family (the Queen's mum, born in August of 1900, made it to the ripe old age of 101), Charles may be in for a long wait.

For more on the monarchy, see www.royal.gov.uk.

Architecture in Britain

From Stonehenge to Big Ben, travelers are storming castle walls, climbing spiral staircases, and snapping the pictures of 5,000 years of architecture. Let's sort it out.

The oldest ruins—mysterious and prehistoric—date from before Roman times back to 3000 B.C. The earliest sites, such as Stonehenge and Avebury, were built during the Stone and Bronze ages. The remains from these periods are made of huge stones or mounds of earth, even man-made hills, and were created as celestial calendars and for worship or burial. Britain is crisscrossed with imaginary lines said to connect these mysterious sights (ley lines). Iron Age people (600 B.C.-A.D. 50) left desolate stone forts. The Romans thrived in Britain from A.D. 50 to 400, building cities, walls, and roads. Evidence of Roman greatness can be seen in lavish villas with ornate mosaic floors, temples uncovered beneath great English churches, and Roman stones in medieval city walls. Roman roads sliced across the island in straight lines. Today, unusually straight rural roads are very likely laid directly on these ancient roads.

As Rome crumbled in the fifth century, so did Roman Britain. Little architecture survives from Dark Ages England,

Mysterious Ruins

Inverness •
♆ CLAVA CAIRNS

SCOTLAND   ♆ = Major
            Prehistoric
            Sites

Keswick • ♆ CASTLERIGG

W
A
L
E
S   ENGLAND

         AVEBURY
         ↓   London •
Bath •
CERNE ♆ ♆ STONEHENGE
ABBAS ♆ ↑
GIANT   GLASTONBURY

♆ SCORHILL

the Saxon period from 500 to 1000. Architecturally, the light was switched on with the Norman Conquest in 1066. As William earned his title "the Conqueror," his French architects built churches and castles in the European Romanesque style.

English Romanesque is called Norman (1066-1200). Norman churches had round arches, thick walls, and small windows; Durham Cathedral and the Chapel of St. John in the Tower of London are prime examples. The Tower of London, with its square keep, small windows, and spiral stone stairways, is a typical Norman castle. You can see plenty of Norman castles around England—all built to secure the conquest of these invaders from Normandy.

Gothic architecture (1200-1600) replaced the heavy Norman style with light, vertical buildings, pointed arches, soaring spires, and bigger windows. English Gothic is divided into three stages. Early English Gothic (1200-1300) features tall, simple spires; beautifully carved capitals; and elaborate chapter houses (such as the Wells Cathedral). Decorated Gothic (1300-1400) gets fancier, with more elaborate tracery, bigger windows, and ornately carved pinnacles, as you see at Westminster Abbey. Finally, the Perpendicular Gothic style (1400-1600, also called "rectilinear") returns to square towers and emphasizes straight, uninterrupted vertical lines from ceiling to floor, with vast windows and exuberant decoration, including fan-vaulted ceilings (King's College Chapel at Cambridge). Through this evolution, the structural ribs (arches meeting at the top of the ceilings) became more and more decorative and fanciful (the most fancy being the star vaulting and fan vaulting of the Perpendicular style).

As you tour the great medieval churches of Britain, remember that almost everything is symbolic. For instance, on the tombs of knights, if the figure has crossed legs, he was a Crusader. If his feet rest on a dog, he died at home; but if his legs rest on a lion, he died

Typical Church Architecture

History comes to life when you visit a centuries-old church. Even if you wouldn't know your apse from a hole in the ground, learning a few simple terms will enrich your experience. Note that not every church has every feature, and that a "cathedral" isn't a type of church architecture, but rather a designation for a church that's a governing center for a local bishop.

Aisles: The long, generally low-ceilinged arcades that flank the nave.

Altar: The raised area with a ceremonial table (often adorned with candles or a crucifix), where the priest prepares and serves the bread and wine for Communion.

Apse: The space beyond the altar, often bordered with small chapels.

Barrel Vault: A continuous round-arched ceiling that resembles an extended upside-down U.

Choir ("quire" in British English): A cozy area, often screened off, located within the church nave and near the high altar where services are sung in a more intimate setting.

Cloister: Covered hallways bordering a (usually square shaped) open-air courtyard, traditionally where monks and nuns got fresh air.

Facade: The exterior surface of the church's main (west) entrance, viewable from outside and usually highly decorated.

Groin Vault: An arched ceiling formed where two equal barrel vaults meet at right angles. Less common usage: term for a medieval jock strap.

Narthex: The area (portico or foyer) between the main entry and the nave.

Nave: The long, central section of the church (running west to east, from the entrance to the altar) where the congregation sits or stands through the service.

Transept: In a traditional cross-shaped floor plan, the transept is one of the two parts forming the "arms" of the cross. The transepts run north-south, perpendicularly crossing the west-east nave.

West Portal: The main entry to the church (on the west end, opposite the main altar).

in battle. Local guides and books help us modern pilgrims understand at least a little of what we see.

Wales is particularly rich in English castles, which were needed to subdue the stubborn Welsh. Edward I built a ring of powerful castles in North Wales, including Conwy and Caernarfon.

Gothic houses were a simple mix of woven strips of thin wood, rubble, and plaster called wattle and daub. The famous black-and-white Tudor (or "half-timbered") look came simply from filling in heavy oak frames with wattle and daub.

The Tudor period (1485-1560) was a time of relative peace (the Wars of the Roses were finally over), prosperity, and renaissance. But when Henry VIII broke with the Catholic Church and disbanded its monasteries, scores of Britain's greatest churches were left as gutted shells. These hauntingly beautiful abbey ruins (Glastonbury, Tintern, Whitby, Rievaulx, Battle, St. Augustine's in Canterbury, St. Mary's in York, and lots more), surrounded by lush lawns, are now pleasant city parks.

Although few churches were built during the Tudor period, this was a time of house and mansion construction. Heating a home was becoming popular and affordable, and Tudor buildings featured small square windows and many chimneys. In towns, where land was scarce, many Tudor houses grew up and out, getting wider with each overhanging floor.

The Elizabethan and Jacobean periods (1560-1620) were followed by the English Renaissance style (1620-1720). English architects mixed Gothic and classical styles, then Baroque and classical styles. Although the ornate Baroque never really grabbed Britain, the classical style of the Italian architect Andrea Palladio did. Inigo Jones (1573-1652), Christopher Wren (1632-1723), and those they inspired plastered Britain with enough columns, domes, and symmetry to please a Caesar. The Great Fire of London (1666) cleared the way for an ambitious young Wren to put his mark on London forever with a grand rebuilding scheme, including the great St. Paul's Cathedral and more than 50 other churches.

The celebrants of the Boston Tea Party remember Britain's Georgian period (1720-1840) for its lousy German kings. But in architectural terms, "Georgian" is English for "Neoclassical." Its architecture was rich and showed off by being very classical. Grand ornamental doorways, fine cast-ironwork on balconies and railings, Chippendale furniture, and white-on-blue Wedgwood ceramics graced rich homes everywhere. John Wood Sr. and Jr. led the way, giving the trendsetting city of Bath its crescents and circles of aristocratic Georgian row houses.

The Industrial Revolution shaped the Victorian period (1840-1890) with glass, steel, and iron. Britain had a huge new erector

Typical Castle Architecture

Castles were fortified residences for medieval nobles. Castles come in all shapes and sizes, but knowing a few general terms will help you understand them.

The Keep (or Donjon): A high, strong stone tower in the center of the castle complex that was the lord's home and refuge of last resort.

Great Hall: The largest room in the castle, serving as throne room, conference center, and dining hall.

The Yard (or Bailey or Ward): An open courtyard inside the castle walls.

Loopholes: Narrow slits in the walls (also called embrasures, arrow slits, or arrow loops) through which soldiers could shoot arrows at the enemy.

Towers: Tall structures serving as lookouts, chapels, living quarters, or the dungeon. Towers could be square or round, with either crenellated tops or conical roofs.

Turret: A small lookout tower projecting up from the top of the wall.

Moat: A ditch encircling the wall, often filled with water.

Motte-and-Bailey: A traditional form for early English castles, with a small fort on top of a hill (motte) next to an enclosed and fortified yard (bailey).

Wall Walk (or Allure): A pathway atop the wall where guards could patrol and where soldiers stood to fire at the enemy.

Parapet: Outer railing of the wall walk.

Crenellation: A gap-toothed pattern of stones atop the parapet.

Hoardings (or Gallery or Brattice): Wooden huts built onto the upper parts of the stone walls. They served as watch towers, living quarters, and fighting platforms.

---

set (so did France's Mr. Eiffel). This was also a Romantic period, reviving the "more Christian" Gothic style. London's Houses of Parliament are Neo-Gothic—they're just 140 years old but look 700, except for the telltale modern precision and craftsmanship. Whereas Gothic was stone or concrete, Neo-Gothic was often red brick. These were Britain's glory days, and there was more building in this period than in all previous ages combined.

The architecture of the mid-20th century obeyed the formula "form follows function"—it worried more about your needs than your eyes. But more recently, the dull "international style" has been nudged aside by a more playful style, thanks to cutting-edge architects such as Lord Norman Foster and Renzo Piano. In the last several years, London has added several creative buildings to its skyline: the City Hall (nicknamed "the Armadillo"), the Swiss Re Tower ("the Gherkin"), and the tallest building in the

Machicolation: A stone ledge jutting out from the wall, fitted with holes in the bottom. If the enemy was scaling the walls, soldiers could drop rocks or boiling oil down through the holes and onto the enemy below.

Barbican: A fortified gatehouse, sometimes a stand-alone building located outside the main walls.

Drawbridge: A bridge that could be raised or lowered, using counterweights or a chain-and-winch.

Portcullis: A heavy iron grille that could be lowered across the entrance.

Postern Gate: A small, unfortified side or rear entrance used during peacetime. In wartime, it could become a "sally-port" used to launch surprise attacks, or as an escape route.

European Union, the pointy Shard London Bridge (called...um, "the Shard").

Even as it sets trends for the 21st century, Britain treasures its heritage and takes great pains to build tastefully in historic districts and to preserve its many "listed" (government-protected) buildings. With a booming tourist trade, these quaint reminders of its past—and ours—are becoming a valuable part of the British economy.

Britain Today

Regardless of the revolution we had 230-some years ago, many American travelers feel that they "go home" to Britain. This most popular tourist destination has a strange influence and power over us. The more you know of Britain's roots, the better you'll get in touch with your own.

What's So Great About Britain?

Geographically, the Isle of Britain is small (about the size of Uganda or Idaho)—600 miles long and 300 miles at its widest point (and just 75 miles at its narrowest). Similar in size to Louisiana, England occupies the southeastern part of Britain (with about 60 percent of its land and 80 percent of its population). England's highest mountain (Scafell Pike in the Lake District) is 3,206 feet, a foothill by our standards. The population is a fifth that of the United States'. At its peak in the mid-1800s, Britain owned one-fifth of the world and accounted for more than half the planet's industrial output. Today, the Empire is down to the Isle of Britain itself and a few token, troublesome scraps, such as the Falklands, Gibraltar, and Northern Ireland (though many larger nations—including Canada and Australia—still consider themselves part of the "British Commonwealth").

Economically, Great Britain's industrial production is about 5 percent of the world's total. After emerging from a recession in 1992, Britain's economy enjoyed its longest period of expansion on record. But in 2008, the global economic slowdown, tight credit, and falling home prices pushed Britain back into a recession.

Culturally, Britain is still a world leader. Her heritage, culture, and people cannot be measured in traditional units of power. London is a major exporter of actors, movies, and theater; of rock and classical music; and of writers, painters, and sculptors.

Ethnically, the British Isles are a mix of the descendants of the early Celtic natives (in Scotland, Ireland, Wales, and Cornwall), the invading Anglo-Saxon "barbarians" who took southeast England in the Dark Ages, and the conquering Normans of the 11th century...not to mention more recent immigrants from around the world. Cynics call the United Kingdom an English Empire ruled by London, whose dominant Anglo-Saxon English (50 million) far outnumber their Celtic brothers and sisters (10 million).

Politically, Britain is ruled by the House of Commons, with some guidance from the mostly figurehead Queen and House of Lords. Just as the United States Congress is dominated by Democrats and Republicans, Britain's Parliament has traditionally been dominated by two parties: left-leaning Labour and right-leaning Conservative ("Tories"). But recently the center-left Liberal Democrats ("Lib Dems") have made inroads, and the current administration is a coalition between the Lib Dems and Tories.

Strangely, Britain's "constitution" is not one single document; the government's structures and policies are based on centuries of tradition, statutes, and doctrine, and much of it is not actually in writing. While this might seem potentially troublesome—if not dangerous—the British body politic takes pride in its ethos of civility and mutual respect, which has long made this arrangement work.

The prime minister is the chief executive. He or she is not elected directly by voters; rather, he or she assumes power as the head of the party that wins a majority in Parliamentary elections. In the interest of protocol, the Queen symbolically invites the winner to form a "government" (administration). Instead of imposing term limits, the Brits allow their prime ministers to choose when to leave office. The ruling party also gets to choose when to hold elections, as long as it's within five years of the previous one—so prime ministers carefully schedule elections for times that (they hope) their party will win. (Breaking with tradition, David Cameron's government announced their election date as soon as they took office: May 7, 2015.) When an election is announced, the Queen dissolves the Parliament so the parties can focus on a short-and-sweet, one-month campaign.

In the 1980s, Conservatives were in charge under Prime Minister Margaret Thatcher and Prime Minister John Major. As proponents of traditional, Victorian values—community, family, hard work, thrift, and trickle-down economics—they took a Reaganesque approach to Britain's serious social and economic problems. In ending costly government subsidies to old-fashioned heavy industries, they caused many dated factories to close (earning working-class ire), but also nudged Britain toward a more 21st-century economy.

In 1997, a huge Labour victory brought Tony Blair to the prime ministership. Labour began shoring up a social-service system (health care, education, minimum wage) undercut by years of Conservative rule. Blair started out as a respected and well-liked PM, but his legacy became tarnished after he followed US President George W. Bush into war with Iraq. In 2007, Blair's Chancellor of the Exchequer and longtime colleague, Gordon Brown, succeeded him as prime minister. Elections in May of 2010 pitted a floundering Brown (who never achieved Blair's level of popularity) against a Conservative opponent, David Cameron, and a third-party Liberal Democrat challenger, Nick Clegg. No party won the number of seats needed for a majority, but the Conservatives and the Lib Dems formed a coalition government (the first since World War II)—vaulting David Cameron into the prime ministership. While Cameron's push for "austerity" (government-spending cutbacks) was initially met with approval, the promised results have not materialized; the election scheduled for May of 2015 will be a referendum on his approach.

In 2012, the Brits hosted two huge events: the Olympics and the Queen's Diamond Jubilee. The flurry of investment that swept Britain in the lead-up to that summer have left this already

Prime Minister David Cameron

David Cameron succeeded Gordon Brown as prime minister in May of 2010, and lives at #10 Downing Street with his wife, Samantha, and their young children. Elected at age 43, Cameron was the youngest PM in two centuries. He heads the Conservative Party (the "Tories"), but has never quite fit the stodgy Conservative image. Rumors still swirl of wild parties and illicit drugs in his student days at Oxford. He's known as "Dave" to his friends, and he developed a habit of riding his bike to work. Cameron rose quickly through the political ranks: He worked to re-elect Conservative PM John Major (1992), assisted the finance minister at #11 Downing Street (1992-1994), and was himself elected to Parliament in 2001, becoming head of the Conservative Party in 2005. By 2008, he was on the cover of *Time* magazine, which hailed him as the future of conservatism.

In 2010, Cameron's Conservative Party came to power, but it was hardly a sweeping Conservative mandate: Three parties split the vote, forcing Cameron's Conservatives to form a coalition with the (more left-leaning) Liberal Democrat Party. The Labour Party, which had held power in Britain for 13 years under Gordon Brown and Tony Blair, is the coalition's chief opposition.

Politically, Cameron is a moderate Conservative who is more pragmatic than ideological. Socially, he's "liberal" in the classical sense, advocating for personal freedoms—gay rights, decriminalization of drugs, allowing hunting and smoking, and ensuring

spruced-up country looking better than ever. This is the icing on top of a decades-long effort to rejuvenate some of Britain's former urban wastelands; cities like Liverpool and Cardiff have reclaimed their deserted, industrial waterfronts and converted them into hip, thriving people zones.

Current Challenges

From early 2008 to late 2009, the British economy shrank more than 6 percent—the largest decline since the Great Depression. Facing a huge—and growing—budget deficit, soon after his election Prime Minister Cameron announced an austerity program that dramatically cut back spending and increased the VAT (Value-Added Tax—the national sales tax) to 20 percent. The prime minister's budget eliminated more than 500,000 public-sector jobs, shortened long-term unemployment benefits to 12 months, imposed higher rents on public housing, slashed funding for the arts and the BBC, cut police services, and raised the retirement age to 66 by 2020. (Visitors might notice reduced bus schedules and unexpected closures of TIs or minor sights.) The initial result of these efforts was a double-dip recession (in 2012).

citizens' privacy against government intrusion. Fiscally, he rails against big-government waste. His fiscal policies have emphasized austerity and belt-tightening in order to get the budget under control. The immediate result was a double-dip recession. His most right-of-center stance is his support for distancing Britain from the euro and the European Union; his veto of EU treaty amendments during the euro crisis led some to predict "the beginning of the end" of Britain's EU membership.

Despite his personal appeal, Cameron can't quite shake the Conservatives' image as the party of the upper class. Cameron was born rich, married rich, and has worked within the corporate culture. His colleagues form an old boys' network from his days at Eton, England's most exclusive prep school. The mayor of London, Boris Johnson, is not only an old Oxford frat buddy but also a distant cousin. Cameron's reputation has been tarnished by his links to discredited media mogul Rupert Murdoch, and some have questioned his handling of riots in London and other urban centers in the summer of 2011.

As the Conservatives try to unite the country to solve Britain's severe economic and cultural problems, it remains to be seen whether David Cameron has brought a fresh enough approach to #10. The people of Britain will get a chance to weigh in on May 7, 2015, when Cameron's party is up for re-election.

The economy showed some signs of recovery in early 2013—but skeptics remain concerned that the growth isn't sustainable.

Other hot-button topics in Britain include terrorism, immigration, and binge-drinking.

Like the US, Britain has been coping with its own string of terrorist threats and attacks. On the morning of July 7, 2005, London's commuters were rocked by four different bombs that killed dozens across the city. In the summer of 2006, authorities foiled a plot to carry liquid bombs onto a plane (resulting in the liquid ban air travelers are still experiencing today). On June 29, 2007, two car bombs were discovered (and defused) near London's Piccadilly Circus, and the next day, a flaming car drove into the baggage-claim level at Glasgow Airport. Most Brits have accepted that they now live with the possibility of terrorism at home—and that life must go on.

Britain has taken aggressive measures to prevent future attacks, such as installing CCTV (closed-circuit television) surveillance cameras everywhere, in both public and private places. (You'll frequently see signs warning you that you're being recorded.) As Brits trade their privacy for security, many wonder if they've given up too much.

The terrorist threats have also highlighted issues relating to Britain's large immigrant population (nearly 4 million). Three of the four suicide bombers responsible for the July 2005 attacks were second-generation Muslims, born in Britain. Some Brits reacted to the event known as "7/7" as if all the country's Muslims were to blame. At the same time, a handful of radical Islamic clerics attempted to justify the bombers' violent actions.

The large Muslim population is just one thread in the tapestry of today's Britain. While nine out of ten Brits are white, the country has large minority groups, mainly from Britain's former colonies: India, Pakistan, Bangladesh, Africa, the Caribbean, and many other places. Despite the tensions between some groups, for the most part Britain is relatively integrated, with minorities represented in most (if not all) walks of life.

But unemployment, the economic downturn, and cuts to programs for the working class have strained relations between communities within Britain. In August of 2011, London police shot and killed a young black man named Mark Duggan, inflaming tensions between the police and the black community. A peaceful protest against the police was followed by violent riots and looting. British society as a whole was left to grapple with its causes and social implications: Were the riots a sign of rising racial and economic tensions, or simply a chance for poor young people to grab a shiny new smartphone?

Throughout the British Isles, you'll also see many Eastern Europeans (mostly Poles, Slovaks, and Lithuanians) working in restaurants, cafés, and B&Bs. These transplants—who started arriving after their home countries joined the EU in 2004—can make a lot more money working here than back home. British small-business owners have found these new arrivals to be polite, responsible, and affordable. While a few Brits complain that the new arrivals are taking jobs away from the natives, and others are frustrated that their English can be far from perfect, for the most part Britain has absorbed this new set of immigrants gracefully.

In 2003, Tony Blair's Licensing Act deregulated alcohol sales and did away with the government-mandated 23:00 closing time for pubs. The goal was to encourage a lively, late-night café culture in Britain, but an unintended consequence has been an epidemic of binge-drinking among young people. A 2007 study revealed that one out of every three British men, and one out of every five British women, routinely drinks to excess. It's become commonplace for young adults (typically from their mid-teens to mid-20s) to spend weekend nights drinking at pubs and carousing in the streets. (And they ratchet up the debauchery even more when celebrating a "stag night" or "hen night"—bachelor and bachelorette parties.) While sociologists and politicians scratch their heads about this phenomenon, tourists are complaining about weekend noise and obnoxious (though generally harmless) young drunks on the streets.

British TV

Although it has its share of lowbrow reality programming, much British television is still so good—and so British—that it deserves a mention as a sightseeing treat. After a hard day of castle climbing, watch the telly over tea in the living room of your village B&B.

For many years there were only five free channels, but now nearly every British television can receive a couple dozen. BBC television is government-regulated and commercial-free. Broadcasting of its eight channels (and of the five BBC radio stations) is funded by a mandatory £145.50-per-year-per-household television and radio license (hmmm, 60 cents per day to escape commercials and public-broadcasting pledge drives...not bad). Channels 3, 4, and 5 are privately owned, are a little more lowbrow, and have commercials—but those "adverts" are often clever and sophisticated, providing a fun look at British life. About 60 percent of households pay for cable or satellite television.

Whereas California "accents" fill our airwaves 24 hours a day, homogenizing the way our country speaks, Britain protects and promotes its regional accents by its choice of TV and radio announcers. See if you can tell where each is from (or ask a local for help).

Commercial-free British TV, while looser than it used to be, is still careful about what it airs and when. But after the 21:00 "watershed" hour, when children are expected to be in bed, some nudity and profanity are allowed, and may cause you to spill your tea.

American programs (such as *Game of Thrones, CSI, Friends, Frasier, How I Met Your Mother, The Simpsons, Family Guy,* and trash-talk shows) are very popular. But the visiting viewer should be sure to tune the TV to more typically British shows, including a dose of British situation- and political-comedy fun, and the top-notch BBC evening news. British comedies have tickled the American funny bone for years, from sketch comedy *(Monty Python's Flying Circus)* to sitcoms *(Are You Being Served?, Fawlty Towers, Absolutely Fabulous,* and *The Office).* Quiz shows and reality shows are taken very seriously here *(American Idol, America's Got Talent, Dancing with the Stars, Who Wants to Be a Millionaire?,* and *The X Factor* are all based on British shows). Jonathan Ross is the David Letterman of Britain for sometimes edgy late-night talk. Other popular late-night "chat show" hosts include Graham Norton and Alan Carr. For a tear-filled, slice-of-life taste of

British soaps dealing in all the controversial issues, see the popular and remarkably long-running *Emmerdale, Coronation Street*, or *EastEnders*. The costume drama *Downton Abbey*, the long-running sci-fi serial *Doctor Who*, and the small-town dramedy *Doc Martin* have all become hits on both sides of the Atlantic.

Notable Brits of Today and Tomorrow

Only history can judge which British names will stand the test of time, but these days big names in the UK include politicians (David Cameron, Nick Clegg, Ed Miliband), actors (Helen Mirren, Emma Thompson, Helena Bonham Carter, Jude Law, Stephen Fry, Ricky Gervais, Robert Pattinson, Daniel Radcliffe, Kate Winslet), musicians (Adele, Chris Martin of Coldplay, James Arthur, Emeli Sandé), writers (J. K. Rowling, Hilary Mantel, Tom Stoppard, Nick Hornby, Ian McEwan, Zadie Smith), artists (Damien Hirst, Rachel Whiteread, Tracey Emin, Anish Kapoor), athletes (David Beckham, Bradley Wiggins), entrepreneurs (Sir Richard Branson, Lord Alan Sugar)...and, of course, William and Kate.

APPENDIX

Contents

Tourist Information

Tourist Information Offices

The Visit Britain website contains a wealth of knowledge on destinations, activities, accommodations, and transport in Great Britain. Families will especially appreciate the "Britain for Kids" travel suggestions. Maps, airport transfers, sightseeing tours, and theater tickets can be purchased online (www.visitbritain.com, www.visitbritainshop.com/usa for purchases). Also try these official tourism board websites: www.visitengland.com, www.visitwales.com, and www.visitscotland.com.

In Britain, your best first stop in every town is generally the tourist information office—abbreviated **TI** in this book (and abbreviated locally as "TIC," for "tourist information centre"). In London, the City of London Information Centre is helpful; see page 54.

TIs are good places to get a city map, information on public transit (including bus and train schedules), walking tours, special events, and nightlife. Due to funding constraints, some of Britain's

TIs are struggling; village TIs may be staffed by volunteers who need to charge you for maps and informational brochures that more fully funded TIs give out for free.

Many TIs have information on the entire country or at least the region, so try to pick up maps for destinations you'll be visiting later in your trip. If you're arriving in town after the TI closes, call ahead to get your questions answered and try to pick up a map in a neighboring town.

For all the help TIs offer, steer clear of their room-finding services (bloated prices, booking fees, and commissions that come from the pocket of your B&B host).

Communicating

Telephones

Smart travelers use the telephone to book or reconfirm rooms, get tourist information, reserve restaurants, confirm tour times, or phone home. Generally, it's cheapest to use an international phone card in Britain. This section covers dialing instructions, phone cards, and types of phones (for more in-depth information, see www.ricksteves.com/phoning).

How to Dial

Calling from the US to Britain, or vice versa, is simple—once you break the code. The European calling chart in this chapter will walk you through it.

Dialing Domestically Within Britain

The following instructions apply whether you're dialing from a landline (such as a pay phone or your hotel-room phone) or a British mobile phone.

Britain, like the US, uses an area-code dialing system. To make domestic calls within Britain, punch in just the phone number if you're dialing locally, and add the area code (which starts with 0) if calling long distance.

Area codes are listed (with phone numbers) in this book, displayed by city on phone-booth walls, and available from directory assistance (dial 118-500, £0.64/minute). Certain phone numbers, however, are considered "nongeographical" and don't have area codes. These include mobile phone, toll-free, and toll numbers.

Mobile phone numbers begin with 074, 075, 076, 077, 078, and 079 (and are more expensive to call than a landline). Numbers starting with 080 are toll-free, but those beginning with 084, 087, or 03 are inexpensive toll numbers (£0.10/minute maximum from a landline, £0.20-40/minute from a mobile). Numbers beginning with 09 are pricey toll lines. If you have questions about a prefix,

The British Accent

In the olden days, a British person's accent indicated his or her social standing. Eliza Doolittle had the right idea—elocution could make or break you. Wealthier families would send their kids to fancy private schools to learn proper pronunciation. But these days, in a sort of reverse snobbery that has gripped the nation, accents are back. Politicians, newscasters, and movie stars have been favoring deep accents over the Queen's English. While it's hard for American ears to pick out all of the variations, most Brits can determine where a person is from based on his or her accent...not just the region, but often the village, and even the part of town.

call 100 for free help.

If you're dialing within Britain using your US mobile phone, you may need to dial as if it's a domestic call, or you may need to dial as if you're calling from the US (see "Dialing Internationally," next). Try it one way, and if it doesn't work, try it the other way.

Dialing Internationally to or from Britain

If you want to make an international call, follow these steps:

• Dial the international access code (00 if you're calling from Britain, 011 from the US or Canada). If you're dialing from a mobile phone, you can replace the international access code with +, which works regardless of where you're calling from. (On most mobile phones, you can insert a + by pressing and holding the 0 key.)

• Dial the country code of the country you're calling (44 for Britain, or 1 for the US or Canada).

• Dial the area code (without the initial zero) and the local number. (The European calling chart on page 1004 lists specifics per country.)

Calling from the US to Britain: To call a London hotel from the US, dial 011 (US access code), 44 (Britain's country code), 20 (London's area code without its initial 0), then 7730-8191 (the hotel's number).

Calling from any European Country to the US: To call my office in Edmonds, Washington, from anywhere in Europe, I dial 00 (Europe's access code), 1 (US country code), 425 (Edmonds' area code), and 771-8303.

Mobile Phones

Traveling with a mobile phone is handy and practical. There are two basic options: roaming with your own phone (expensive but easy) or buying and using SIM cards with an unlocked phone (a bit

Smartphones and Data Roaming

I take my smartphone to Europe, using it to make phone calls (sparingly) and send texts, but also to check email, listen to audio tours, and browse the Internet. You may have heard horror stories about people running up outrageous data roaming bills on their smartphones. But if you understand the options, it's easy to avoid these fees and still stay connected. Here's how.

For voice calls and text messaging, smartphones work like any mobile phone (as described under "Roaming with Your US Mobile Phone," below). To avoid roaming charges, connect to free Wi-Fi, and use Skype, FaceTime, or other apps to make cheap or free calls (see "Calling over the Internet," later).

To get online with your phone, you have two options: Wi-Fi and mobile data. Because free Wi-Fi hotspots are generally easy to find in Europe (at most hotels, many cafés, and even some public spaces), the cheap solution is to use Wi-Fi wherever possible.

But what if you just can't get to a hotspot? Fortunately, most providers offer an affordable, basic data-roaming package for Europe: $25 or $30 buys you about 100 megabytes—enough to view 100 websites or send/receive 1,000 text emails. If you don't buy a data-roaming plan in advance, but use data in Europe anyway, you'll pay staggeringly high rates—about $20 per megabyte, or about 80 times what you'd pay with a plan.

While a data-roaming package is handy, your allotted megabytes can go quickly—especially if you stream videos or music.

more hassle, but potentially much cheaper).

Roaming with Your US Mobile Phone: This pricier option can be worthwhile if you won't be making or receiving many calls, don't want to bother with SIM cards, or want to stay reachable at your US number. Start by calling your mobile-phone service provider to ask whether your phone works in Europe and what the rates are (likely $1.29-1.99 per minute to make or receive calls, and 20–50 cents to send or receive text messages). Tell them to enable international calling on your account, and if you know you'll be making multiple calls, ask your carrier about any global calling deals to lower the per-minute costs. When you land in Europe, turn on your phone and—bingo!—you have service. Because you'll pay for receiving calls and texts, be sure your family knows to call only in an emergency. Note that Verizon and Sprint use a different technology than European providers, so their phones are less likely to work abroad; if yours doesn't, your provider may be able to send you a loaner phone (arrange in advance).

Buying and Using SIM Cards in Europe: If you're comfortable with mobile-phone technology, will be making lots of calls,

To keep a cap on usage and avoid incurring overage charges, I manually turn off data roaming on my phone whenever I'm not actively using it. (To turn off data and voice roaming, look in your phone's menu—try checking under "Cellular" or "Network," or ask your mobile-phone provider how to do it.) As I travel through Europe, I jump from hotspot to hotspot. But if I need to get online at a time when I can't easily access Wi-Fi—for example, to download driving directions when I'm on the road to my next hotel—I turn on data roaming just long enough for that task, then turn it off again. You can also limit how much data your phone uses by switching your email settings from "push" to "fetch" (you choose when to download messages rather than having them automatically "pushed" to your device). By carefully budgeting my data this way, my 100 megabytes last a long time.

If you want to use your smartphone exclusively on Wi-Fi—and not worry about either voice or data charges—simply turn off both voice and data roaming (or put your phone in "Airplane Mode" and then turn your Wi-Fi back on). If you're on a long trip, are positive you won't be using your phone for voice or data roaming, and want to save some money, ask your provider about suspending those services altogether while you're gone.

By sticking with Wi-Fi wherever possible and budgeting your use of data, you can easily and affordably stay connected while you travel.

and want to save some serious money, consider this very affordable alternative: Carry an unlocked mobile phone, and use it with a European SIM card to get much cheaper rates.

Getting an **unlocked phone** may be easier than you think. You may already have an old, unused mobile phone in a drawer somewhere. When you got the phone, it was probably "locked" to work only with one company—but if your contract is now up, your provider may be willing to send you a code to unlock it. Just call and ask. Otherwise, you can simply buy an unlocked phone: Search your favorite online shopping site for an "unlocked quad-band phone" before you go, or wait until you get to Europe and buy one at a mobile-phone shop there. Either way, a basic model costs less than $50.

Once in Europe, buy a **SIM card**—the little chip that inserts into your phone (either under the battery, or in a slot on the side)—to equip the phone with a European number. (Note that smaller "micro-SIM" or "nano-SIM" cards—used in some iPhones—are less widely available.) SIM cards are sold at mobile-phone shops, department-store electronics counters, and some newsstand kiosks for $5–10, and usually include about that much prepaid calling credit (making the card itself virtually free). In most places, buying a SIM card is as easy as buying a pack of gum—and almost as cheap. (In some countries—including Italy, Germany, and Hungary—it can take a bit longer, because you have to show your passport and be registered.) Because SIM cards are prepaid, there's no contract and no commitment (in fact, they expire after just a few months of disuse); I buy one even if I'm in a country for only a few days.

When using a SIM card in its home country, it's free to receive calls and texts, and it's cheap to make calls—domestic calls average 20-30 cents per minute (though toll lines can be substantially more). Rates are higher if you're roaming in another country, but as long as you stay within the European Union, these fees are capped (about 30 cents per minute for making calls or 10 cents per minute for receiving calls). Texting is cheap even if roaming in another country. Particularly inexpensive SIM card brands (such as Lebara) let you call either within Europe or to the US for less than 10 cents per minute.

When purchasing a SIM card, always ask about fees for domestic and international calls, roaming charges, and how to check your credit balance and buy more time. If text or voice prompts are in another language, ask the clerk whether they can be switched to English.

It's also possible to buy an **inexpensive mobile phone in Europe** that already comes with a SIM card. While these phones are generally locked to work with just one provider (and therefore can't be reused on future trips), they may be less hassle than buying an unlocked phone and a SIM card separately.

Mobile-Phone Calling Apps: If you have a smartphone, you can use it to make free or cheap calls in Europe by using a calling app such as Skype or FaceTime when you're on Wi-Fi; for details, see the next section.

Calling over the Internet

Some things that seem too good to be true...actually are true. If you're traveling with a smartphone, tablet, or laptop, you can make free calls over the Internet to another wireless device, anywhere in the world, for free. (Or you can pay a few cents to call from your computer or smartphone to a telephone.) The major providers are Skype, Google Talk, and (on Apple devices) FaceTime. You can get online at a Wi-Fi hotspot and use these apps to make calls without ringing up expensive roaming charges (though call quality can be spotty on slow connections). You can make Internet calls even if you're traveling without your own mobile device: Many European Internet cafés have Skype, as well as microphones and webcams, on their terminals—just log on and chat away.

Landline Telephones

Just like Americans, these days most Europeans make the majority of their calls on mobile phones. But you'll still encounter landlines in hotel rooms and at pay phones.

Hotel-Room Phones: Calling from your hotel room can be great for local calls, and for international calls if you have an international phone card (described later). Otherwise, hotel-room phones can be an almost criminal rip-off for long-distance or international calls. Many hotels charge a fee for local and sometimes even "toll-free" numbers—always ask for the rates before you dial.

Phones are rare in **B&Bs**, but if your room has one, the advice above applies. If there's no phone in your B&B room, and you have an important, brief call to make, politely ask your hosts if you can use their personal phone. Ideally use a cheap international phone card with a toll-free access number, or offer to pay your host for the call.

Public Pay Phones: These are relatively easy to find in Britain, but they're expensive. Unlike phones in most of Europe, British pay phones don't use dedicated, insertable phone cards; instead, you'll pay with a major credit card (which you insert into the phone—minimum charge for a credit-card call is £1.20) or coins (have a bunch handy; minimum fee is £0.60). The phone clearly shows how your money supply's doing. Only unused coins will be returned, so put in biggies with caution. Avoid using an international phone card at a pay phone (see below).

Telephone Cards

International phone cards can be used with any type of phone (and will generally save you plenty of money, especially on overseas calls). With these cards, phone calls from Great Britain to the US can cost less than 10 cents a minute, as long as you don't call from a phone booth. British Telecom levies a hefty surcharge for using international phone cards from a pay phone (so instead of 100 minutes for a £5 card, you'll get less than 10 minutes—a miserable deal). But they're still a good value if you use them when calling from your hotel-room phone or mobile phone with a European SIM card.

To use the card, dial a toll-free access number, then enter your scratch-to-reveal PIN code. (If you have several access numbers listed on your card, you'll save money overall if you choose the toll-free one starting with 0800.) To call the US or Britain, see "How to Dial," earlier. To make calls within Britain using an international calling card, you must dial the area code even if you're just

APPENDIX

European Calling Chart

Just smile and dial, using this key:
AC = Area Code, LN = Local Number.

European Country	Calling long distance within ...	Calling from the US or Canada to ...	Calling from a European country to ...
Austria	AC + LN	011 + 43 + AC (without initial zero) + LN	00 + 43 + AC (without initial zero) + LN
Belgium	LN	011 + 32 + LN (without initial zero)	00 + 32 + LN (without initial zero)
Bosnia-Herzegovina	AC + LN	011 + 387 + AC (without initial zero) + LN	00 + 387 + AC (without initial zero) + LN
Croatia	AC + LN	011 + 385 + AC (without initial zero) + LN	00 + 385 + AC (without initial zero) + LN
Czech Republic	LN	011 + 420 + LN	00 + 420 + LN
Denmark	LN	011 + 45 + LN	00 + 45 + LN
Estonia	LN	011 + 372 + LN	00 + 372 + LN
Finland	AC + LN	011 + 358 + AC (without initial zero) + LN	999 (or other 900 number) + 358 + AC (without initial zero) + LN
France	LN	011 + 33 + LN (without initial zero)	00 + 33 + LN (without initial zero)
Germany	AC + LN	011 + 49 + AC (without initial zero) + LN	00 + 49 + AC (without initial zero) + LN
Gibraltar	LN	011 + 350 + LN	00 + 350 + LN
Great Britain & N. Ireland	AC + LN	011 + 44 + AC (without initial zero) + LN	00 + 44 + AC (without initial zero) + LN
Greece	LN	011 + 30 + LN	00 + 30 + LN
Hungary	06 + AC + LN	011 + 36 + AC + LN	00 + 36 + AC + LN
Ireland	AC + LN	011 + 353 + AC (without initial zero) + LN	00 + 353 + AC (without initial zero) + LN
Italy	LN	011 + 39 + LN	00 + 39 + LN

APPENDIX

European Country	Calling long distance within ...	Calling from the US or Canada to ...	Calling from a European country to ...
Latvia	LN	011 + 371 + LN	00 + 371 + LN
Montenegro	AC + LN	011 + 382 + AC (without initial zero) + LN	00 + 382 + AC (without initial zero) + LN
Morocco	LN	011 + 212 + LN (without initial zero)	00 + 212 + LN (without initial zero)
Netherlands	AC + LN	011 + 31 + AC (without initial zero) + LN	00 + 31 + AC (without initial zero) + LN
Norway	LN	011 + 47 + LN	00 + 47 + LN
Poland	LN	011 + 48 + LN	00 + 48 + LN
Portugal	LN	011 + 351 + LN	00 + 351 + LN
Russia	8 + AC + LN	011 + 7 + AC + LN	00 + 7 + AC + LN
Slovakia	AC + LN	011 + 421 + AC (without initial zero) + LN	00 + 421 + AC (without initial zero) + LN
Slovenia	AC + LN	011 + 386 + AC (without initial zero) + LN	00 + 386 + AC (without initial zero) + LN
Spain	LN	011 + 34 + LN	00 + 34 + LN
Sweden	AC + LN	011 + 46 + AC (without initial zero) + LN	00 + 46 + AC (without initial zero) + LN
Switzerland	LN	011 + 41 + LN (without initial zero)	00 + 41 + LN (without initial zero)
Turkey	AC (if there's no initial zero, add one) + LN	011 + 90 + AC (without initial zero) + LN	00 + 90 + AC (without initial zero) + LN

- The instructions above apply whether you're calling to or from a European landline or mobile phone.

- If calling from any mobile phone, you can replace the international access code with "+" (press and hold 0 to insert it).

- The international access code is 011 if you're calling from the US or Canada.

- To call the US or Canada from Europe, dial 00, then 1 (country code for US and Canada), then the area code and number. In short, 00 + 1 + AC + LN = Hi, Mom!

calling across the street. These cards, which are sold at newsstands, work only within the country of purchase (e.g., one bought in Britain won't work in France). Buy a lower denomination in case the card is a dud.

US calling cards, such as the ones offered by AT&T, Verizon, or Sprint, are a rotten value and are being phased out. Try any of the options outlined earlier.

Useful Phone Numbers and Websites

Emergencies
Police and Ambulance: Tel. 999

Embassies and Consulates in London
US Consulate and Embassy: Tel. 020/7499-9000 (all services), no walk-in passport services; for emergency 36-hour passport service, email LondonEmergencyPPT@state.gov or call all-services number, 24 Grosvenor Square, Tube: Bond Street, www.usembassy.org.uk
Canadian High Commission: Tel. 020/7258-6600, passport services available Mon-Fri 9:30-13:00, 38 Grosvenor Street, Tube: Bond Street, www.unitedkingdom.gc.ca

Travel Advisories
US Department of State: Tel. 888-407-4747, from outside US tel. 1-202-501-4444, www.travel.state.gov
Canadian Department of Foreign Affairs: Canadian tel. 800-387-3124, from outside Canada tel. 1-613-996-8885, www.travel.gc.ca
US Centers for Disease Control and Prevention: US tel. 800-CDC-INFO (800-232-4636), www.cdc.gov/travel

Directory Assistance
Operator Assistance: Tel. 100 (free)
Directory Assistance: Toll tel. 118-500 (£0.64/minute, plus £0.23/minute connection charge from fixed lines)
International Directory Assistance: Toll tel. 118-505 (£1.99/minute, plus £0.69 connection charge)

Trains and Buses
Train information for Trips within Britain: Tel. 0845-748-4950, overseas tel. 011-44-20-7278-5240, www.nationalrail.co.uk
Eurostar (Chunnel Info): Tel. 0843-218-6186, overseas tel. 011-44-12-3361-7575, www.eurostar.com
National Express Buses: Tel. 0871-781-8178, www.nationalexpress.com

Citylink Buses: Tel. 0871-266-3333, www.citylink.co.uk

Airports
Heathrow (LHR): Tel. 0870-000-0123, www.heathrowairport
.com
Gatwick (LGW): Tel. 0844-892-0322, www.gatwickairport.com
Stansted (STN): Tel. 0844-335-1803, www.stanstedairport.com
Luton (LTN): Tel. 01582/405-100, www.london-luton.com
London City Airport (LCY): Tel. 020/7646-0088, www.london
cityairport.com
Southend Airport (SEN): Tel. 01702/608-100,www.southendair
port.com
Edinburgh Airport (EDI): Tel. 0844-448-8833, www.edinburgh
airport.com

Airlines
Aer Lingus: Tel. 0871-718-2020, www.aerlingus.com
Air Canada: Tel. 0871-220-1111, www.aircanada.com
Alitalia: Tel. 0871-424-1424, www.alitalia.com
American: Tel. 0844-499-7300, www.aa.com
British Airways: Tel. 0844-493-0787, www.ba.com
Brussels Airlines: Toll tel. 0905-609-5609 (40p/minute), www
.brusselsairlines.com
easyJet: Tel. 0870-600-0000, www.easyjet.com
KLM Royal Dutch: Tel. 0871-231-0000, www.klm.com
Lufthansa: Tel. 0871-945-9747, www.lufthansa.com
Ryanair: Tel. 0871-246-0000, www.ryanair.com
Scandinavian Airlines (SAS): Tel. 0871-226-7760, www.flysas
.com
United Airlines: Tel. 0845-607-6760, www.united.com
US Airways: Tel. 0845-600-3300, www.usairways.com

Heathrow Airport Car-Rental Agencies
Avis: Tel. 0844-581-0147, www.avis.co.uk
Budget: Tel. 0844-544-3439, www.budget.co.uk
Enterprise: Tel. 0800-800-227, www.enterprise.co.uk
Europcar: Tel. 0871-384-1087, www.europcar.co.uk
Hertz: Tel. 0870-844-8844, www.hertz.co.uk

Internet Access
It's useful to get online periodically as you travel—to confirm trip
plans, check train or bus schedules, get weather forecasts, catch
up on email, blog or post photos from your trip, or call folks back
home (explained earlier, in "Calling over the Internet").

   Your Mobile Device: The majority of accommodations in
Britain offer Wi-Fi, as do many cafés, making it easy for you to

get online with your laptop, tablet, or smartphone. Access is often free, but sometimes there's a fee. At hotels that charge for a certain number of hours, save money by logging in and out of your account on an as-needed basis. You should be able to stretch a two-hour Wi-Fi pass over a stay of a day or two.

Some hotel rooms and Internet cafés have high-speed Internet jacks that you can plug into with an Ethernet cable.

Public Internet Terminals: Many accommodations offer a guest computer in the lobby with Internet access. If you ask politely, smaller places may let you sit at their desk for a few minutes just to check your email. If your hotelier doesn't have access, ask to be directed to the nearest place to get online.

Security: Whether you're accessing the Internet with your own device or at a public terminal, using a shared network or computer comes with the potential for increased security risks. If you're not convinced a connection is secure, avoid accessing any sites (such as your bank's) that could be vulnerable to fraud.

Mail

You can mail one package per day to yourself worth up to $200 duty-free from Europe to the US (mark it "personal purchases"). If you're sending a gift to someone, mark it "unsolicited gift." For details, visit www.cbp.gov and search for "Know Before You Go."

The British postal service works fine, but for quick transatlantic delivery (in either direction), consider services such as DHL (www.dhl.com).

Transportation

By Car or Public Transportation?

If you're debating between public transportation and car rental, consider these factors: Cars are best for three or more traveling together (especially families with small kids), those packing heavy, and those scouring the countryside. Trains and buses are best for solo travelers, blitz tourists, city-to-city travelers, and those who don't want to drive in Europe. While a car gives you more freedom, trains and buses zip you effortlessly and scenically from city to city, usually dropping you in the center, often near a TI. Cars are an expensive headache in places like London.

In Britain, my choice is to connect big cities by train (e.g., London, Bath, York, Edinburgh, and Glasgow) and to explore

Public Transportation Routes in Britain

Legend:
- Rail
- Eurostar
- Bus
- Ferry with crossing time (8H)

Ferry Note:
Dover - Calais–1.5H
Dover - Boul–1.5 H

N

50 Kilometers
50 Miles

Orkney Islands
Burwick
Thurso
John o' Groats
Lewis
Skye
Portree
Elgin
Inverness
Culloden
Kyle
Loch Ness
Aviemore
Aberdeen
Mallaig
SCOTLAND
Fort William
Pitlochry
Mull
Iona
Oban
Perth
Dundee
Leuchars
St. Andrews
Stirling
Edinburgh
Glasgow
Berwick
Holy Island
Cairnryan
Hexham
Newcastle
To Amsterdam (15H)
Larne
Stranraer
Carlisle
Durham
North Sea
Belfast
NORTHERN IRELAND
Keswick
Penrith
Danby
Whitby
Scarborough
Windermere
Noth York Moors
Isle of Man
ENGLAND
Irish Sea
Blackpool
York
Leeds
Hull
To Zeebrugge (10H)
Dublin
Preston
Liverpool
Grimsby
Dun Laoghaire
Holyhead
Conwy
Manchester
Lincoln
Bangor
Chester
REPUBLIC OF IRELAND
Caernarfon
Betws-y-Coed
Stoke
Derby
Peterborough
King's Lynn
Norwich
Pwllheli
Blaenau Ffest.
Telford
Wolv.
Harlech
Ely
To Esbjerg (18 H)
Aberystwyth
Ironbridge Gorge
Birmingham
Coventry
Cambridge
Harwich
Stratford
Warwick
WALES
Cheltenham
Moreton
Stow
Oxford
To Hoek van Holland (6H)
Fishguard
Carmarthen
Newport
Ebbsfleet
Rosslare
Swansea
Cardiff
Bath
Reading
London
Canterbury
Dover
Bristol
STONEHENGE
Woking
Ashford
Calais
Wells
West-bury
Salisbury
Glastonbury
Brighton
Atlantic Ocean
Exeter
Newhaven
EUROSTAR (2.5H)
Dartmoor
Southampton
Portsmouth
To Dieppe (4H)
Truro
St. Ives
Plymouth
English Channel
To Paris & Brussels
Penzance
Falmouth
To Roscoff (6H)
To Cherbourg (3H)
To Ouistreham (6H)
FRANCE
(2H)
(2.3H)
(8H)
(7H)
(2-3H)
(3.5H)

rural areas (such as the Cotswolds, North Wales, the Lake District, and the Scottish Highlands) footloose and fancy-free by rental car. You might consider a BritRail & Drive Pass, which gives you various combinations of rail days and car days to use within two months' time.

Public Transportation

Trains

Regular tickets on Britain's great train system (15,000 departures from 2,400 stations daily) are the most expensive per mile in all of Europe. For the greatest savings, either book in advance or leave after rush hour (after 9:30).

Now that Britain has privatized its railways, it can be tricky to track down all your options; a single train route can be operated by several companies. However, one British website covers all train lines (www.nationalrail.co.uk), and another covers all bus and train routes (www.traveline.org.uk—for information, not ticket sales). Another good resource, which also has schedules for trains throughout Europe, is German Rail's timetable (www.bahn.com).

As with airline tickets, British train tickets can come at many different prices for the same journey. A clerk at any station can figure out the cheapest fare for your trip (or call the helpful National Rail folks at tel. 0845-748-4950, 24 hours daily). Savings can be significant. For a London-Edinburgh round-trip (standard class), if you book the day of departure for travel after 9:30, it may be around £130; and the cheapest fare, booked a couple of months in advance as two one-way tickets, can cost as little as £75.

While not required on British trains, reservations are free and can normally be made well in advance. They are an especially good idea for long journeys or for travel on Sundays or holidays. Make reservations at any train station or over the phone or Internet when you buy your ticket. With a point-to-point ticket, you can reserve up to two hours before train time, but railpass holders should book seats at least 24 hours in advance.

For information on the high-speed Eurostar train through the "Chunnel" to Paris or Brussels, see page 223.

Buying Train Tickets in Advance: The best fares go to those who book their trips well in advance of their journey. (While only a 7-day minimum advance booking is officially required for the cheapest fares, these sell out fast—especially in summer—so booking 6-8 weeks in advance is often necessary.) Keep in mind that when booking in advance, "return" (round-trip) fares are not always cheaper than buying two "single" (one-way) tickets. Cheap advance tickets often come with the toughest refund restrictions, so be sure to nail down your travel plans before you reserve. To book ahead, go in person to any station, book online at www

APPENDIX

Sample Train Journey

Here is a typical example of a personalized train schedule printed out at Britain's train stations. At the Llandudno Junction station in North Wales, I told the clerk I wanted to leave after 15:00 for Moreton-in-Marsh in the Cotswolds.

Stations	Arrive	Depart	Class
Llandudno Junction	—	15:27	Standard
Hereford	18:12	18:48	Standard
Great Malvern	19:14	19:44	Standard
Moreton-in-Marsh	20:39	—	—

Even though the trip involved two transfers, this schedule allowed me to easily navigate the rails.

In many stations, train departures are listed on overhead boards by their final destination; intermediate stops typically are not listed. Ask at the info desk—or any conductor—for the final destination of your next train so you can quickly figure out which platform it's departing from. For example, after checking with the conductor, I know that I'll need to look for *Oxford* to catch the train for Moreton-in-Marsh.

Often the conductor on your previous train can even tell you which platform your next train will depart from, but it's wise to confirm. The platforms often display scrolling screens that list the next train that's arriving and all its intermediate stops.

Any train system can experience delays, so don't schedule your connections too tightly if you need to reach your destination at a specific time.

.nationalrail.co.uk, or call 0845-748-4950 (from the US, dial 011-44-20-7278-5240, phone answered 24 hours) to find out the schedule and best fare for your journey; you'll then be referred to the appropriate vendor—depending on the particular rail company—to book your ticket. If you order online, be sure you know what you want; it's tough to reach a person who can change your online reservation. You'll pick up your ticket at the station, or you may be able to print it at home. (BritRail passholders, however, cannot use the Web to make reservations.)

A company called **Megabus** (through their subsidiary Megatrain) sells some discounted train tickets well in advance on a few specific routes, though their focus is mainly on selling bus tickets (info tel. 0871-266-3333, www.megatrain.com).

Buying Train Tickets as You Travel: If you'd rather have the flexibility of booking tickets as you go, you can save a few pounds by buying a round-trip ticket, called a "return ticket" (a same-day

Railpasses

Prices listed are for 2013 and are subject to change. For the latest prices, details, and train schedules (and easy online ordering), see my comprehensive *Guide to Eurail Passes* at www.ricksteves.com/rail.

"Standard" is the polite British term for "second" class. "Senior" refers to those age 60 and up. No senior discounts for standard class. "Youth" means under age 26. For each adult or senior BritRail or BritRail England pass you buy, one child (5–15) can travel free with you (ask for the **"Family Pass,"** not available with all passes). Additional kids pay the normal half-adult rate. Kids under 5 travel free.

Note: Overnight journeys begun on the final night of your pass can be completed the day after your pass expires—only BritRail allows this trick. A bunk in a twin sleeper costs $75.

BRITRAIL CONSECUTIVE PASS

	Adult 1st Class	Adult Standard	Senior 1st Class	Youth 1st Class	Youth Standard
3 consec. days	$319	$215	$269	$255	$169
4 consec. days	395	265	339	319	215
8 consec. days	565	375	479	455	305
15 consec. days	839	565	715	675	455
22 consec. days	1065	709	909	855	569
1 month	1259	839	1075	1009	675

BRITRAIL FLEXIPASS

	Adult 1st Class	Adult Standard	Senior 1st Class	Youth 1st Class	Youth Standard
3 days in 2 months	$395	$269	$339	$319	$215
4 days in 2 months	495	335	419	395	269
8 days in 2 months	719	479	615	575	385
15 days in 2 months	1079	725	919	865	585

BRITRAIL & DRIVE PASS

Any 4 rail days and 2 car days in 2 months.

	1st Class	2nd Class	Extra Car Day
Mini	$610	$430	$48
Economy	619	439	57
Compact	627	447	65
Compact Auto	658	478	96
Intermed. Auto	672	492	110
Minivan Auto	755	560	193

Prices are per person, two traveling together. Third and fourth persons sharing car buy a regular BritRail pass. To order a Rail & Drive pass, call Rail Europe at 800-438-7245. *Not sold by Europe Through the Back Door.*

Map key:

Approximate point-to-point one-way standard-class fares in US dollars by rail (solid line) and bus (dashed line). First class costs 50 percent more. Add up fares for your itinerary to see whether a railpass will save you money.

BRITRAIL ENGLAND CONSECUTIVE PASS

	Adult 1st Class	Adult Standard	Senior 1st Class	Youth 1st Class	Youth Standard
3 consec. days	$255	$169	$219	$205	$139
4 consec. days	319	215	269	255	169
8 consec. days	449	305	385	365	245
15 consec. days	675	449	575	539	365
22 consec. days	855	569	729	685	459
1 month	1009	675	859	809	539

Covers travel only in England, not Scotland, Wales, or Ireland.

BRITRAIL ENGLAND FLEXIPASS

Type of Pass	Adult 1st Class	Adult Standard	Senior 1st Class	Youth 1st Class	Youth Standard
3 days in 2 months	$319	$215	$269	$255	$175
4 days in 2 months	395	269	339	319	215
8 days in 2 months	575	385	489	465	309
15 days in 2 months	865	585	735	695	469

Covers travel only in England, not Scotland, Wales, or Ireland.

BRITRAIL LONDON PLUS PASS

	Adult 1st Class	Adult Standard
2 out of 8 days	$225	$149
4 out of 8 days	309	239
7 out of 15 days	385	285

Covers much of SE England (see London Plus Coverage Map, online). Includes vouchers to cover two trips on the Heathrow, Stansted, or Gatwick Express, separate from your counted travel days, which can be used up to 6 months from the date you validate the pass in Britain (but not before pass is validated for the 8- or 15-day travel window). Many trains are standard class only. The 7 p.m. rule for night trains does not apply. Kids 5–15 half price; under 5 free.

BRITRAIL SOUTH WEST CONSECUTIVE PASS

	Adult 1st Class	Adult Standard	Senior 1st Class	Youth 1st Class	Youth Standard
3 consec. days	$225	$149	$189	$179	$125
4 consec. days	279	189	239	225	149
8 consec. days	395	265	339	319	215
15 consec. days	589	395	505	475	319
22 consec. days	749	499	639	599	399
1 month	885	589	755	709	475

BRITRAIL SOUTH WEST FLEXI PASS

	Adult 1st Class	Adult Standard	Senior 1st Class	Youth 1st Class	Youth Standard
3 days in 2 months	$279	$189	$239	$225	$155
4 days in 2 months	349	235	295	279	189
8 days in 2 months	505	339	429	405	275
15 days in 2 months	759	509	645	609	409

Covers most trains in SW England operated by First Great Western (but not east of Portsmouth), South West Trains, and Heathrow Express (see coverage map online); not other operators. Includes Newport-Cardiff-Swansea main line trains in Wales. Many trains offer Standard class only.

round-trip, called a "day return," is particularly cheap); buying before 18:00 the day before you depart; traveling after the morning rush hour (this usually means after 9:30 Mon-Fri); and going standard class instead of first class. Preview your options at www.nationalrail.co.uk.

Senior, Youth, and Family Deals: To get a third off the price of most point-to-point rail tickets, seniors can buy a Senior Railcard (for ages 60 and above), and younger travelers can buy a 16-25 Railcard (for ages 16-25, or for full-time students 26 and above with a valid ISIC card). A Family and Friends Railcard allows adults to travel about 33 percent cheaper while their kids ages 5 to 15 receive a 60 percent discount for most trips (maximum of 4 adults and 4 kids). Each Railcard costs £30; see www.railcard.co.uk. Any of these cards are valid for a year on almost all trains except special runs, such as the Heathrow Express or the Eurostar to Paris or Brussels (fill out application at station, brochures on racks in info center, need to show passport; passport-type photo needed for 16-25 Railcard).

Railpasses: Consider getting a railpass, which offers hop-on flexibility and no need to lock in reservations, except for overnight sleeper cars. The BritRail pass comes in "consecutive day" and "flexi" versions, with price breaks for youths, seniors, off-season travelers, and groups of three of more. Most allow one child under 16 to travel free with a paying adult. If you're exploring Britain's backcountry with a BritRail pass, standard class is a good choice since many of the smaller train lines don't even offer first-class cars. BritRail passes cover England as well as Scotland and Wales.

More BritRail options include England-only passes, Scotland-only passes, Britain/Ireland passes, "London Plus" passes (good for travel in most of southeast England but not in London itself), South West passes (good for the Cotswolds, Bath, Dorset, Devon, Cornwall, plus part of South Wales), and BritRail & Drive passes (which offer you some rail days and some car-rental days). These BritRail passes, as well as Eurail passes, get you a discount on the Eurostar train that zips you to continental Europe under the English Channel. These passes are sold outside of Europe only. For specifics, see www.ricksteves.com/rail.

Buses

Although buses are about a third slower than trains, they're also a lot cheaper. Most buses are operated by **National Express** (tel. 0871-781-8178, www.nationalexpress.com). Note that Brits distinguish between "buses" (for in-city travel with lots of stops) and "coaches" (long-distance cross-country runs)—though for simplicity in this book, I call both "buses."

Round-trip bus tickets usually cost less than two one-way

fares. And buses go many places that trains don't. Budget travelers can save a wad with a bus pass. National Express sells **Brit Xplorer bus passes** for unlimited travel on consecutive days (£79/7 days, £139/14 days, £219/28 days, sold over the counter, non-UK passport required, tel. 0871-781-8178, www.nationalexpress.com). Check their website to learn about online deals; senior/youth/family cards and fares; and discounts for advance booking.

If you want to take a bus from your last destination to the nearest airport, you'll find that National Express often offers **airport buses.** Bus stations are normally at or near train stations (in London, the main bus station is a block southwest of Victoria Station).

Megabus sells very cheap promotional fares on certain routes, often beating National Express in price. But you have to book far ahead for the best rates, and journey times tend to be longer than those on National Express (info tel. 0871-266-3333, www.mega bus.com). Megabus also sells discounted train tickets on selected routes.

If you're focusing on Scotland, consider Citylink's **Explore Scotland pass,** which allows flexibility within specific time spans (£41/3 days in 5-day period, £62/5 days in 10-day period, £93/8 days in 16-day period, tel. 0871-266-3333, www.citylink.co.uk).

Renting a Car

If you're renting a car in Britain, bring your driver's license. It's recommended, but not required, that you also have an International Driving Permit (sold at your local AAA office for $15 plus the cost of two passport-type photos; see www.aaa.com); however, I've frequently rented cars in Britain and traveled problem-free with just my US license.

Rental companies in Britain require you to be at least 23 years old. Drivers under the age of 25 or over the age of 70 may incur a young- or older-driver surcharge (some rental companies do not rent to anyone 75 or older). If you're considered too young or old, look into leasing (covered later), which has less-stringent age restrictions.

Research car rentals before you go. It's cheaper to arrange most car rentals from the US. Call several companies and look online to compare rates, or arrange a rental through your hometown travel agent.

Most of the major US rental agencies (including Avis, Budget, Enterprise, Hertz, and Thrifty) have offices throughout Europe. It can be cheaper to use a consolidator, such as Auto Europe (www .autoeurope.com) or Europe by Car (www.europebycar.com), which compares rates at several companies to get you the best deal. However, my readers have reported problems with consolidators,

APPENDIX

British Radio

Local radio broadcasts can be a treat for drivers sightseeing in Britain. While most rental cars have CD players, very few have adapter ports for portable media players—so you may wind up listening to a lot of British radio, whether you want to or not.

Many British radio stations broadcast nationwide; your car radio automatically detects the local frequency a station plays on and displays its name (not its frequency) on your radio's digital readout.

The BBC has five nationwide stations, which you can pick up in most of the country. These government-subsidized stations have no ads.

BBC **Radio 1** plays today's pop music, with youthful DJs spinning top 40 hits and interviewing big-name bands. Many of the same songs and artists air stateside, but Radio 1 will acquaint you with British acts that aren't yet known "across the pond." And many hit singles (even those by American groups) get a lot of play here months before they turn up on US radios. You'll be ahead of the curve when you get home, hear a hot "new" song on the radio, and wink knowingly to your friends, "This was a huge hit in the UK last summer."

BBC **Radio 2**—the highest-rated station nationwide—aims at a slightly more mature audience, with adult contemporary, retro pop, and other "middle of the road" music with broad popular appeal.

ranging from misinformation to unexpected fees; because you're going through a middleman, it can be more challenging to resolve disputes that arise with the rental agency.

Regardless of the car-rental company you choose, always read the fine print carefully for add-on charges—such as one-way drop-off fees, airport surcharges, or mandatory insurance policies—that aren't included in the "total price." You may need to query rental agents pointedly to find out your actual cost.

For the best deal, rent by the week with unlimited mileage. To save money on fuel, ask for a diesel car. I normally rent the smallest, least-expensive model with a stick-shift (generally much cheaper than automatic). Almost all rentals are manual by default, so if you need an automatic, request one in advance; be aware that these cars are usually larger models (not as maneuverable on narrow, winding roads). But weigh this against the fact that in Britain you'll be sitting on the right side of the car, and shifting with your left hand...while driving on the left side of the road. The floor pedals are in the same locations as in the US, and the gears are found in the same basic "H" pattern as at home.

For a one-week rental, allow roughly $150 per person (based

BBC **Radio 3** features mostly classical music (including live broadcasts of all the concerts in the annual BBC-sponsored Proms music festival), with some jazz and world music.

BBC **Radio 4** is all talk. It's reminiscent of public radio back home—current events, entertaining chat shows, special-interest topics such as cooking and gardening, and lots of radio plays.

BBC **Radio 5 Live**—less widely broadcast than the "big four"—features sporting events, as well as news and sports talk programs.

You'll encounter regional variations of BBC stations, such as BBC London, Radio York, or BBC Scotland. At the top of the hour, many BBC stations broadcast the famous "pips" (indicating Greenwich Mean Time) and a short roundup of the day's news.

Beyond the BBC offerings, several private stations broadcast music and other content with "adverts" (commercials). While many of these are unique to a specific city or region, others are nationwide, including **XFM** (alternative rock), **Classic FM** (classical), **Absolute Radio** (pop), and **Capital FM** (pop).

Traffic Alerts: If you want to stay up-to-date on traffic conditions, ask your rental-car company about turning on automatic traffic alerts that play on the car radio. Once these are enabled (look for the letters *TA* or *TP* on the radio readout), traffic reports for the area you are driving in will periodically interrupt programming.

on two people sharing) for a small economy car with unlimited mileage. Allow extra for insurance, fuel, tolls, and parking. For trips of three weeks or more, look into leasing; you'll save money on insurance and taxes.

You can usually get a GPS unit with your rental car or leased vehicle for an additional fee (around $15/day; be sure it has all the maps you need before you drive off). Or, if you have a portable GPS device at home, consider taking it with you to Europe (buy and upload European maps before your trip). GPS apps are also available for smartphones, but downloading maps in Europe could lead to an exorbitant data-roaming bill (for more details, see the sidebar on page 1000).

Big companies have offices in most cities; ask whether they can pick you up at your hotel. Small local rental companies can be cheaper but aren't as flexible. If you pick up the car in a smaller city, such as Bath, you'll more likely survive your first day on the British roads.

Compare pickup costs (downtown can be less expensive than the airport) and explore drop-off options. For a trip covering both Britain and Ireland, you're better off with two separate car rentals.

Always check the hours of the location you choose: Many rental offices close from midday Saturday until Monday morning and, in smaller towns, at lunchtime.

When selecting a location, don't trust the agency's description of "downtown" or "city center." In some cases, a "downtown" branch can be on the outskirts of the city—a long, costly taxi ride from the center. Before choosing, plug the addresses into a mapping website. You may find that the "train station" location is handier. But returning a car at a big-city train station or downtown agency can be tricky; get precise details on the car drop-off location and hours, and allow ample time to find it.

When you pick up the rental car, check it thoroughly and make sure any damage is noted on your rental agreement. Find out how your car's lights, turn signals, wipers, and fuel cap function. Ask what type of fuel your car takes before you fill up. When you return the car, make sure the agent verifies its condition with you.

Car Insurance Options

When you rent a car, you are liable for a very high deductible, sometimes equal to the entire value of the car. Limit your financial risk with one of these three options: Buy Collision Damage Waiver (CDW) coverage from the car-rental company, get coverage through your credit card (free, if your card automatically includes zero-deductible coverage), or buy coverage through Travel Guard.

CDW includes a very high deductible (typically $1,000-1,500). Though each rental company has its own variation, basic CDW costs $15-35 a day (figure roughly 25 percent extra) and reduces your liability, but does not eliminate it. When you pick up the car, you'll be offered the chance to "buy down" the basic deductible to zero (for an additional $10-30/day; this is sometimes called "super CDW").

If you opt for **credit-card coverage,** there's a catch. You'll technically have to decline all coverage offered by the car-rental company, which means they can place a hold on your card (which can be up to the full value of the car). In case of damage, it can be time-consuming to resolve the charges with your credit-card company. Before you decide on this option, quiz your credit-card company about how it works.

Finally, you can buy collision insurance from **Travel Guard** ($9/day plus a one-time $3 service fee covers you for up to $35,000, $250 deductible, tel. 800-826-4919, www.travelguard.com). It's valid everywhere in Europe except the Republic of Ireland, and some Italian car-rental companies refuse to honor it. Note that various states differ on which products and policies are available to their residents—check with Travel Guard *before* you rent your car.

For more on car-rental insurance, see www.ricksteves.com/cdw.

APPENDIX

Leasing

For trips of three weeks or more, consider leasing (which automatically includes zero-deductible collision and theft insurance). By technically buying and then selling back the car, you save lots of money on tax and insurance. Leasing provides you a brand-new car with unlimited mileage and a 24-hour emergency assistance program. You can lease for as little as 21 days to as long as six months. Car leases must be arranged from the US. One of many reliable companies offering affordable lease packages is Europe by Car (US tel. 800-223-1516, www.ebctravel.com).

Driving in Britain

Driving in Britain is basically wonderful—once you remember to stay on the left and after you've mastered the roundabouts. Every year, however, I get a few notes from traveling readers advising me that, for them, trying to drive in Britain was a nerve-racking and regrettable mistake. If you want to get a little slack on the roads, drop by a gas station or auto shop and buy a green *P* (probationary driver with license) sign to put in your car window (don't get the red *L* sign, which means you're a learner driver without a license and thus prohibited from driving on motorways).

Many Yankee drivers find the hardest part isn't driving on the left, but steering from the right. Your instinct is to put yourself on the left side of your lane, which means you may spend your first day or two constantly drifting into the left shoulder. It can help to remember that the driver always stays close to the center line.

Road Rules: Be aware of Britain's rules of the road. Seat belts are mandatory for all, and kids under age 12 (or less than about 4.5 feet tall) must ride in an appropriate child-safety seat. It's illegal to use a mobile phone while driving—pull over or use a hands-free device. In Britain, you're not allowed to turn

STOP AND LEARN THESE ROAD SIGNS

Speed Limit (mph) — Yield — No Passing — End of No Passing Zone

One Way — Intersection — Main Road — Freeway

Danger — No Entry — No Entry for cars — All Vehicles Prohibited

Parking — No Parking — Customs — Peace

left on a red light unless a sign or signal specifically authorizes it. For more information about driving in Britain, ask your car-rental company, read the Department for Transport's *Highway Code* (www.direct.gov.uk—click on "Motoring" and look for "The Highway Code" link), or check the US State Department website (www.travel.state.gov, click on "International Travel," then specify your country of choice and click "Traffic Safety and Road Conditions").

Speed Limits: Speed limits are 30 mph in town, 70 mph on the motorways, and 50 or 60 mph elsewhere (though, as back home, many British drivers consider these limits advisory). The national sign for 60 mph is a white circle with a black slash. Motorways have electronic speed limit signs; posted speeds can change depending on traffic or the weather. Follow them accordingly.

Note that road-surveillance cameras strictly enforce speed limits. Any driver (including foreigners renting cars) photographed speeding will get a nasty bill in the mail. (Cameras—in foreboding gray boxes—flash on rear license plates to respect the privacy of anyone sharing the front seat with someone he or she shouldn't.) Signs (an image of an old-fashioned camera) alert you when you're entering a zone that may be monitored by these "camera cops." Heed them.

Roundabouts: Don't let a roundabout spook you. After all, you routinely merge into much faster traffic on American highways back home. Traffic flows clockwise, and cars already in the roundabout have the right-of-way; entering traffic yields (look to your right as you merge). You'll probably encounter "double-roundabouts"—figure-eights where you'll slingshot from one roundabout directly into another. Just go with the flow and track signs carefully. When approaching an especially complex roundabout, you'll first pass a diagram showing the layout and the various exits. And in many cases, the pavement is painted to indicate the lane you should be in for a particular road or town.

Freeways (Motorways): The shortest distance between any two points is usually the motorway (what we'd call a "freeway"). In Britain, the smaller the number, the bigger the road. For example, the M-4 is a freeway, while the B-4494 is a country road.

Motorway road signs can be confusing, too few, and too late. Miss a motorway exit and you can lose 30 minutes. Study your map before taking off. Know the cities you'll be lacing together, since road numbers are inconsistent. British road signs are never

How to Navigate a Roundabout

NOTE:

- TRAFFIC IN ROUNDABOUTS FLOWS IN A CLOCKWISE DIRECTION.
- WHITE CARS ARE ENTERING THE ROUNDABOUT, GRAY CARS ARE EXITING.
- VEHICLES ENTERING A ROUNDABOUT MUST YIELD TO VEHICLES IN THE ROUNDABOUT.
- LOOK TO YOUR RIGHT AS YOU MERGE! ☺

marked with compass directions (e.g., *A-30 West*); instead, you need to know what major town or city you're heading for *(A-30 Penzance)*. The driving directions in this book are intended to be used with a good map. Get a road atlas, easily purchased at gas stations in Britain, or download digital maps before your trip.

Unless you're passing, always drive in the "slow" lane on motorways (the lane farthest to the left). The British are very disciplined about this; ignoring this rule could get you a ticket (or into a road-rage incident). Remember to pass on the right, not the left.

Rest areas are called "services" and often have a number

APPENDIX

Britain by Car: Mileage & Time

m = miles
h = hours

Note: Your times may vary based on traffic, sheep, construction & road conditions.

To John o'Groats

Portree
35m • 1h
Kyle of Lochalsh
85m • 2h
120m • 2.5h
105m • 2.75h
Inverness
20m • .5h
65m • 1.5h
Loch Ness (Urquhart Castle)
90m • 1.75h
Aberdeen
90m • 2.5h
SCOTLAND
Glencoe
90m • 2.75h
Pitlochry
80m • 1.75h
70m • 1.5h
60m • 1.5h
80m • 2h
Oban
35m • 1h
Fionn-port
Craig-nure
85m • 1.75h
100m • 2.5h
25m • .5h
Stirling
40m • 1h
St. Andrews
50m • 1.5h
Glasgow
50m • 1h
Edinburgh
135m • 2.5h
130m • 3h
100m • 2.5h
75m • 2h
Holy Island
80m • 1.75h
125m • 2.75h
90m • 2.25h
145m • 3h
Hadrian's Wall (Housesteads Fort)
Cairnryan
65m • 1.5h
50m • 1h
Durham
Keswick (N. Lake Dist.)
20m • .5h
120m • 3h
75m • 1.5h
65m • 2h
Whitby
Windermere (S. Lake Dist.)
50m • 1h
35m • 1h
20m • .5h
100m • 2h
York
Blackpool
Preston
40m • 1h
160m • 3h
220m • 4h
145m • 2.75h
130m • 3.5h
75m • 2h
Holyhead
60m • 1.25h
Conwy
30m • 1h
Liverpool
25m • .5h
15m • .5h
Caernarfon
30m • 1h
Ruthin
25m • .75h
60m • 1.5h
Snowdonia (Betws-y-Coed)
170m • 4h
150m • 3.5h
Ironbridge Gorge
ENGLAND
70m • 1.75h
10m • .5h
Warwick
10m • .25h
Stratford
110m • 2h
Cambridge
WALES
Cotswolds (Chipping Campden)
90m • 2h
100m • 2h
65m • 1.75h
60m • 1.5h
60m • 1.25h
Cardiff
55m • 1.25h
20m • 75m
Bath
Avebury
85m • 1.75h
London
Wells
50m • 1.25h
30m • 1h
100m • 2h
75m • 1.5h
Glastonbury
10m • .25h
Salisbury (Stonehenge)
Dover
180m • 4h
To Land's End

of useful amenities, such as restaurants, cafeterias, gas stations, shops, and motels.

Fuel: Gas (petrol) costs about $10 per gallon and is self-serve. Pump first and then pay. Diesel rental cars are common; make sure you know what kind of fuel your car takes before you fill up. Unleaded pumps are usually green. Note that self-service gas pumps and automated toll booths and parking garages often accept only a chip-and-PIN credit card or cash. It might help if you know the PIN for your US credit and debit cards, but just in case a machine rejects them, be sure to carry sufficient cash. For more on chip and PIN, see page 16.

Driving in Cities: Whenever possible, avoid driving in cities. Be warned that London assesses a congestion charge (see page 71). Most cities have modern ring roads to skirt the congestion. Follow signs to the parking lots outside the city core—most are a 5- to 10-minute walk to the center—and avoid what can be an unpleasant grid of one-way streets (as in Bath) or roads that are only available to public transportation during the day (as in Oxford).

Driving in Rural Areas: Outside the big cities and except for the motorways, British roads tend to be narrow. In towns, you may have to cross over the center line just to get past parked cars. Adjust your perceptions of personal space: It's not "my side of the road" or "your side of the road," it's just "the road"—and it's shared as a cooperative adventure. If the road's wide enough, traffic in both directions can pass parked cars simultaneously, but frequently you'll have to take turns—follow the locals' lead and drive defensively. Some narrow country lanes are barely wide enough for one car. Go slowly, and if you encounter an oncoming car, look for the nearest pullout (or "passing place")—the driver who's closest to one is expected to use it, even if it means backing up to reach it. If another car pulls over and blinks its headlights, that means, "Go ahead; I'll wait to let you pass." British drivers—arguably the most courteous on the planet—are quick to offer a friendly wave to thank you for letting them pass (and they appreciate it if you reciprocate). Pull over frequently—to let faster locals pass and to check the map.

Parking: Parking can be confusing. One yellow line marked on the pavement means no parking Monday through Saturday during work hours. Double yellow lines mean no parking at any time. Broken yellow lines mean short stops are OK, but you should always look for explicit signs or ask a passerby. White lines mean you're free to park.

In towns, rather than look for street parking, I generally just pull into the most central and handy pay-and-display parking lot I can find. To pay and display, feed change into a machine, receive a timed ticket, and display it on the dashboard or stick it to the driver's-side window. Rates are reasonable by US standards, and locals love to share stickers that have time remaining. If you stand by the machine, someone on their way out with time left on their sticker will probably give it to you. Keep a bag of coins in the console or glove box for these machines and for parking meters.

In some municipalities, drivers will see signs for "disc zone" parking. This is free, time-limited parking. But to use it, you must obtain a clock parking disc from a shop and display it on the dashboard (set the clock to show your time of arrival). Return within the signed time limit to avoid being ticketed.

The AA: The services of Britain's Automobile Association are included with most rentals (www.theaa.com), but check for this when booking to be sure you understand its towing and emergency road-service benefits.

Cheap Flights

London is the hub for many cheap, no-frills airlines, which affordably connect the city with other destinations in the British Isles and throughout Europe. If you're considering a train ride that's more than five hours long, a flight may save you both time and money. When comparing your options, factor in the time it takes to get to the airport and how early you'll need to arrive to check in.

The best comparison search engine for both international and intra-European flights is www.kayak.com. For inexpensive flights within Europe, try www.skyscanner.com or www.hipmunk.com. If you're not sure who flies to your destination, check its airport's website for a list of carriers.

The low-cost airline **easyJet** flies from London (Gatwick, Luton, Southend, and Stansted airports) as well as Liverpool. Prices are based on demand, so the least popular routes make for the cheapest fares, especially if you book early (tel. 0870-600-0000, www.easyjet.com).

Irish-owned **Ryanair** flies from London (mostly Stansted Airport, though also Gatwick and Luton), Liverpool, and Glasgow to often obscure airports near Dublin, Frankfurt, Stockholm, Oslo, Venice, Turin, and many others (Irish toll tel. 0818-303-030, British tel. 0871-246-0000, www.ryanair.com). However, be warned that Ryanair charges additional fees for nearly everything. Online check-in is mandatory (£7 charge), from 15 days to four hours before your flight (no airport check-in). You must also print a boarding pass before going to the airport; if you show up without it, there's an additional £70 charge. You can carry on only a small day bag; you'll pay a fee for each checked bag (price depends on the season; up to two bags allowed per passenger).

Brussels Airlines (formerly Virgin Express) is a Brussels-based company with good rates and hubs in Bristol, Birmingham,

Heathrow, and Manchester (US tel. 516/296-9500, British toll tel. 0905-609-5609—£0.40/minute, www.brusselsairlines.com).

Be aware of the potential drawbacks of flying on the cheap: nonrefundable and nonchangeable tickets, minimal or nonexistent customer service, treks to airports far outside town, and stingy baggage allowances with steep overage fees. If you're traveling with lots of luggage, a cheap flight can quickly become a bad deal. To avoid unpleasant surprises, read the small print before you book.

Resources

Resources from Rick Steves

Rick Steves' Great Britain is one of many books in my series on European travel, which includes country guidebooks, city guide-

books (London, Paris, Rome, Florence, etc.), Snapshot Guides (excerpted chapters from my country guides), Pocket Guides (full-color little books on big cities, including London), and my budget-travel skills handbook, *Rick Steves' Europe Through the Back Door*. Most of my titles are available as ebooks. My phrase books—for Italian, French, German, Spanish, and Portuguese—are practical and budget-oriented. My other books include *Europe 101* (a crash course on art and history designed for travelers); *Mediterranean Cruise Ports* and *Northern European Cruise Ports* (how to make the most of your time in port), and *Travel as a Political Act* (a travelogue sprinkled with tips for bringing home a global perspective). A more complete list of my titles appears near the end of this book.

Video: My public television series, *Rick Steves' Europe,* covers European destinations in 100 shows, including 10 episodes on Great Britain. To watch episodes online, visit www.hulu.com; for scripts and local airtimes, see www.ricksteves.com/tv.

Audio: My weekly public radio show, *Travel with Rick Steves,* features interviews with travel experts from around the world. I've also produced free self-guided audio tours of the top sights and neighborhoods in London (and other great cities). All of this audio content is available for free at Rick Steves Audio Europe, an extensive online library organized by destination. Choose whatever interests you, and

Begin Your Trip at www.ricksteves.com

At our travel website, you'll discover a wealth of free information on European destinations, including fresh monthly news and helpful tips from thousands of fellow travelers. You'll find my latest guidebook updates (www.ricksteves.com/update), a monthly travel enewsletter, my personal travel blog, and my free Rick Steves Audio Europe smartphone app (if you don't have a smartphone, you can access the same content via podcasts). You can also follow me on Facebook and Twitter.

Our **online Travel Store** offers travel bags and accessories that I've designed specifically to help you travel smarter and lighter. These include my popular bags (rolling carry-on and backpack versions), money belts, totes, toiletries kits, adapters, other accessories, and a wide selection of guidebooks, planning maps, and DVDs.

Choosing the right **railpass** for your trip—amid hundreds of options—can drive you nutty. Our website will help you find the perfect fit for your itinerary and your budget.

Want to travel with greater efficiency and less stress? We organize **tours** with more than three dozen itineraries and 600 departures reaching the best destinations in this book...and beyond. We offer a 14-day England tour, a 10-day Scotland tour, and a 7-day in-depth London city tour. You'll enjoy great guides, a fun bunch of travel partners (with small groups of 24 to 28 travelers), and plenty of room to spread out in a big, comfy bus when touring between towns. You'll find European adventures to fit every vacation length. For all the details, and to get our Tour Catalog and a free Rick Steves Tour Experience DVD (filmed on location during an actual tour), visit www.ricksteves.com or call us at 425/608-4217.

download it for free via the Rick Steves Audio Europe smartphone app, www.ricksteves.com/audioeurope, iTunes, or Google Play.

Maps

The black-and-white maps in this book are concise and simple, designed to help you locate recommended places and get to local TIs, where you can pick up more in-depth maps of towns or regions (usually free). Better maps are sold at newsstands and bookstores. Before you buy a map, make sure it has the level of detail you want.

If you'll be lingering in London, buy a city map at a London newsstand; the red *Benson's Handy London Map & Guide* is excellent. Even the vending-machine maps sold in Tube stations are good. The *Rough Guide* map to London is well designed (sold at London and US bookstores). The *Rick Steves' Britain, Ireland & London City Map* has a good map of London (www.ricksteves .com). Many Londoners, along with obsessive-compulsive tourists, rely on the highly detailed *London A-Z* map book (called "A to Zed" by locals, available at newsstands and www.a-zmaps.co.uk).

If you're driving, get a road atlas covering all of Britain. Ordnance Survey, AA, and Bartholomew editions are all available at tourist information offices, gas stations, and bookstores. Drivers, hikers, and cyclists may want more in-depth maps for the Cotswolds, the Lake District, and Snowdonia (North Wales).

Other Guidebooks

If you're like most travelers, this book is all you need. But if you're heading beyond my recommended destinations, $40 for extra maps and books can be money well-spent. If you'll be focusing on London or England, consider *Rick Steves' London 2014* or *Rick Steves' England.*

The following books are worthwhile, though most are not updated annually; check the publication date before you buy. The *Lonely Planet* and *Let's Go* guidebooks on London and on Britain are fine budget-travel guides. *Lonely Planet*'s guidebooks are more thorough and informative; *Let's Go* books are youth-oriented, with good coverage of nightlife, hostels, and cheap transportation deals. For cultural and sightseeing background, look into *Michelin* and *Cadogan* guides to London, England, and Britain. *Secret London* by Andrew Duncan leads the reader on unique walks through a less touristy London. If you're a literature fan, consider picking up *The Edinburgh Literary Companion* (Lownie).

Recommended Books and Movies

To learn more about Britain past and present, check out a few of these books or films.

Nonfiction

For a serious historical overview, wade into *A History of Britain,* a three-volume collection by Simon Schama. *Literary Trails* (Hardyment) reunites famous authors with the environments that inspired them. *A Traveller's History of England* (Daniell), *A Traveller's History of Scotland* (Fisher), and *A History of Wales* (Davies) all provide good, succinct summaries of British history.

Other options include the humorous *Notes from a Small Island,* (Bryson), *The Matter of Wales* (Morris), or any of the books by Susan Allen Toth on her British travels. If you'll be spending time in the Cotswolds, try *Cider with Rosie,* Laurie Lee's boyhood memoir set just after World War I. If you'll be visiting Scotland, consider reading *Crowded with Genius* (Buchan) or *How the Scots Invented the Modern World* (Herman), which explains the influence the Scottish Enlightenment had on the rest of Europe. *The Guynd* (Rathbone) is a memoir of a woman who married into a historic

Harry Potter Sights

Harry Potter's story is set in a magical Britain, and all the places mentioned in the books, except London, are fictional, but you can visit many real film locations. Many of the locations are closed to visitors, though, or are an unmagical disappointment in person, unless you're a huge fan. For those diehards, here's a sampling.

Spoiler Alert: The information below will ruin surprises for the three of you who haven't yet read or seen the Harry Potter series.

London

In the first film, *The Sorcerer's Stone* (2001), Harry first realizes his wizard powers when talking with a boa constrictor, filmed at the **London Zoo's Reptile House** in Regent's Park (Tube: Great Portland Street). Hagrid takes Harry shopping for school supplies in the glass-roofed **Leadenhall Market** (Tube: Bank). The goblin-run Gringotts Wizarding Bank was filmed in the marble-floored Exhibition Hall of **Australia House** (Tube: Temple), home of the Australian Embassy.

Harry catches the train to Hogwarts, the wizarding prep school, at **King's Cross Station.** The fanciful exterior in *The Chamber of Secrets* (2002) was actually shot at nearby **St. Pancras International Station.** Inside, Harry heads to platform 9¾. (For a fun photo-op, head to the station's western departures concourse to find the *Platform 9¾* sign and the luggage cart that looks like it's disappearing into the wall, between tracks 8 and 9.)

In *The Prisoner of Azkaban* (2004), Harry careens through London on a three-decker bus that dumps him at the Leaky Cauldron pub. The exterior was shot on rough-looking Stoney Street at the southeast edge of **Borough Street Market,** by The Market Porter pub (Tube: London Bridge).

In *The Order of the Phoenix* (2007), the Order takes to the night sky on broomsticks over London, passing over plenty of identifiable landmarks, including the **London Eye, Big Ben,** and **Buckingham Palace.** The **Millennium Bridge** is attacked and collapses into the Thames in the dramatic finale to *The Half-Blood Prince* (2009). For *Order of the Phoenix* and the first *Deathly Hallows* (2010), the real government offices of **Whitehall** serve as exteriors for the Ministry of Magic. Other London settings, like Diagon Alley, only exist at **Leavesden Film Studios** (20 miles north of London), where most of the films' interiors were shot. Leavesden has opened its doors to Harry Potter pilgrims (see page 155).

Elsewhere in England

Many scenes showing Hogwarts were filmed in the **Gloucester Cathedral cloisters,** north of Bath. In *The Sorcerer's Stone,* when Harry and Ron set out to save Hermione, they look down a long, dark Gloucester hallway to see a 20-foot troll at the far end.

In this film, Harry walks with his white owl, Hedwig, through a snowy cloister courtyard located in **Durham's Cathedral** (see listing on page 639).

Scotland

Many of the movies' exterior shots—especially scenes of the Hogwarts grounds—were filmed in craggy, cloudy, mysterious Scotland (much of it in the Fort William and Glencoe areas).

The **Hogwarts Express train** that carries Harry, Ron, and Hermione to school each year was filmed along an actual steam-train line that runs between Fort William and Mallaig (tourists can ride this Jacobite Steam Train—see page 906).

In *The Prisoner of Azkaban*, Hogwarts Lake was filmed using Loch Shiel, Loch Eilt, and Loch Morar near Fort William, and Hagrid skips stones across the water at **Loch Eilt. Steal Falls,** a waterfall at the base of Ben Nevis, is the locale for Harry's battle with a dragon for the Triwizard Tournament in *The Goblet of Fire*.

Other scenes filmed in the Highlands include a desolate hillside with Hagrid's stone hut in **Glencoe,** which was the main location for outdoor filming in *The Prisoner of Azkaban*. Exterior scenes for *The Half-Blood Prince* were filmed in Glencoe as well as in the small village of **Glenfinnan.**

Highlands estate. And the obsessive world of British soccer is illuminated in Nick Hornby's memoir, *Fever Pitch*.

Fiction

For the classics of British fiction, read anything—and everything—by Charles Dickens, Jane Austen, and the Brontës.

Kidnapped, by Robert Louis Stevenson, is a fantastic adventure story set in Scotland. Sharon Kay Penman brings 13th-century Wales to life in *Here Be Dragons*. In the romantic, swashbuckling *Outlander* series (Gabaldon), the heroine time-travels between the Scotland of 1945 and 1743.

Pillars of the Earth (Follett) traces the building of a fictional 12th-century cathedral in southern England. For a big book on the era of King Richard III, try *The Sunne in Splendour*, one in a series by Sharon Kay Penman. *Wolf Hall* and *Bring Up the Bodies* (Mantel) transport readers to the court of Henry VIII through the eyes of Thomas Cromwell, while *Restoration* (Tremain) returns readers to the time of King Charles II.

Set in the 19th-century Anglican church, *The Warden* (Trollope) dwells on moral dilemmas. *Brideshead Revisited* (Waugh) satirizes the British obsession with class and takes place between the World Wars. A rural village in the 1930s is the social battlefield for E. F. Benson's *Mapp and Lucia*. A family saga spanning the interwar years and beyond, *Atonement* (McEwan) takes an intense look at England's upper-middle class. For evocative Cornish settings, try Daphne du Maurier's *Rebecca* or *The House on the Strand*.

Mystery novels have a long tradition in Britain. *A Morbid Taste for Bones* (Peters) features a Benedictine monk-detective in 12th-century Shropshire. Agatha Christie's Miss Marple was introduced in 1930 in *The Murder at the Vicarage*. And Ian Rankin's troubled Inspector Rebus first gets his man in *Knots and Crosses*, set in present-day Edinburgh. For other modern mysteries, try any of the books in the Inspector Lynley series by Elizabeth George.

For a more contemporary read, check out *Bridget Jones's Diary* (Fielding), *Behind the Scenes at the Museum* (Atkinson), *White Teeth* (Smith), *Saturday* (McEwan), or anything by Nick Hornby *(High Fidelity, About a Boy)*.

Film and Television

In terms of world influence, Britain's filmmaking rivals its substantial literary contributions. Here are some films that will flesh out your understanding of this small island, past and present.

For a taste of Tudor-era London, try *Shakespeare in Love* (1999), which is set in the original Globe Theatre. In *A Man for All Seasons* (1966), Sir Thomas More faces down Henry VIII.

Showtime's racy, lavish series *The Tudors* (2007-2010) is an enter-taining, loosely accurate chronicle of the marriages of Henry VIII. For equally good portraits of Elizabeth I, try *Elizabeth* (1998) and its sequel *Elizabeth: The Golden Age* (2007), or the BBC/HBO miniseries *Elizabeth I* (2005).

Written and set in the early 19th century, the works of Jane Austen have fared well in film. Among the many versions of *Pride and Prejudice,* the 1995 BBC miniseries starring Colin Firth is the winner. *Persuasion* (1995) was partially filmed in Bath. Other Austen adaptations include *Sense and Sensibility* (1995, with Emma Thompson, Hugh Grant, and Kate Winslet) and *Emma* (1996, with Gwyneth Paltrow). The 1995 SoCal teen comedy *Clueless* also (freely) reinterprets *Emma.* Charlotte Brontë's *Jane Eyre* has been made into a movie at least nine times, most recently in 2011 (with Mia Wasikowska and Michael Fassbender).

In *The Elephant Man* (1980), the cruelty of Victorian London is starkly portrayed in black and white. *Sweeney Todd* (2007) cap-tures the gritty Victorian milieu, as do two highly stylized *Sherlock Holmes* films (2009 and 2011). Sherlock shows up again in an excel-lent British TV update of the detective's story, set in present-day London (2010-present).

How Green Was My Valley (1941), which won the Academy Award for Best Picture, was set in a 19th-century Welsh mining village.

In 1995, Scottish history had a mini-renaissance, with *Braveheart,* another winner of the Best Picture Oscar, and *Rob Roy,* which some historians consider the more accurate of the two films. The UK television series *Monarch of the Glen* (2000), set on Loch Laggan, features stunning Highland scenery and the eccen-tric family of a modern-day Laird.

The upstairs-downstairs Edwardian era of the early 20th century has inspired many films. Producer Ismail Merchant and director James Ivory teamed up to create many well-regarded films about this era, including *Howard's End* (1992, which captures the stifling societal pressure underneath the gracious manners), *A Room with a View* (1985), and *The Remains of the Day* (1993).

The all-star *Gosford Park* (2001) is part comedy, part mur-der mystery, and part critique of England's stratified class system in the 1930s. Its screenwriter, Julian Fellowes, went on to create the wildly popular *Downton Abbey* (2011-present), a spot-on por-trayal of aristocratic life before and after World War I (filmed at Highclere Castle, about 70 miles west of London). *Chariots of Fire* (1981), about British track stars competing in the 1924 Paris Olympics, ran away with the Academy Award for Best Picture.

Wartime London has been captured in many fine movies. *The King's Speech* (2010) won the Best Picture Oscar, with Colin Firth named Best Actor for his portrayal of King George VI on the eve of World War II. *Hope and Glory* (1987) is a semi-autobiographical story of a boy growing up during WWII's Blitz. In *Foyle's War*, a BBC series (2002-2013), detective Christopher Foyle solves crime amid wartime in southern England.

British acts became all the rage in the States in the 1960s, thanks to a little band called the Beatles, whose *A Hard Day's Night* (1964) is filled with wit and charm. During this time, "swinging London" also exploded o   International scene, with films such as *Alfie* (1966), *Blowup* (1   d *Georgy Girl* (1966). For a swinging spoof of this time, t.   ustin Powers comedies.

England goes main   n in a series of 1990s hits: Hugh Grant charms the ladies in *Four Weddings and a Funeral* (1994) and *Notting Hill* (1999); Gwyneth Paltrow lives two lives in *Sliding Doors* (1998); and John Cleese, Jamie Lee Curtis, and Kevin Kline hilariously double-cross one another in *A Fish Called Wanda* (1988).

For a departure from the typical Hollywood fare, see *My Beautiful Laundrette* (1986), a gritty story of two gay men (with Daniel Day-Lewis). For another portrayal of urban London—and the racial tensions found in its multiethnic center—look for *Sammy and Rosie Get Laid* (1987). *Lock, Stock and Two Smoking Barrels* (1998) is a violent crime caper set in the city.

Billy Elliot (2000), about a young boy ballet dancer, and *Bend It Like Beckham* (2003), about a young girl of Punjabi descent who plays soccer, were both huge crowd-pleasers. *An Education* (2009), about a bright schoolgirl who falls for an older man, takes place in 1960s London. *V for Vendetta* (2006), based on a British graphic novel, shows a sci-fi future of a London ruled with an iron fist. Alfonso Cuarón's *Children of Men* (2006) takes place in a dystopian future London.

In *The Queen* (2006), Helen Mirren expertly channels Elizabeth II during the days after Princess Diana's death. If you enjoy *The Queen*, don't miss two other reality-based films by the same screenwriter and with many of the same cast members (most notably Michael Sheen as Tony Blair): *The Special Relationship* (2010, about the friendship between Tony Blair and Bill Clinton) and *The Deal* (2003, about Tony Blair's early relationship with Gordon Brown).

Britain has offered up plenty of comedy choices over the years. If you're in the mood for something completely different, try *Monty Python and the Holy Grail* (1975), a surreal take on the Arthurian legend. The BBC's deeply irreverent "mockumentary" series *The Office* (by Ricky Gervais and Stephen Merchant) inspired the gentler US television show. In *The Full Monty* (1997), some working-class Yorkshire lads take it all off to pay the bills.

For Kids: If you're traveling to London or Great Britain with children, consider watching *Mary Poppins* (1964), *My Fair Lady* (1964), *A Little Princess* (1995), the Wallace & Gromit movies, Rowan Atkinson's *Mr. Bean* television series and movies, and the Harry Potter films (adults can watch them, too).

Holidays and Festivals

This list includes national holidays observed throughout Great Britain plus selected festivals. Many sights and banks close on national holidays—keep this in mind when planning your itinerary. Throughout Britain, hotels get booked up during Easter week; over the Early May, Spring, and Summer Bank Holidays; and during Christmas, Boxing Day, and New Year's Day. On Christmas, virtually everything shuts down, even the Tube in London. Museums also generally close December 24 and 26.

Many British towns have holiday festivals in late November and early December, with markets, music, and entertainment in the Christmas spirit (for instance, Keswick's Victorian Fayre).

Before planning a trip around a festival, make sure to verify its dates by checking the festival website or the Visit Britain website (www.visitbritain.com).

Here are some major holidays:

Jan 1	New Year's Day
Jan 2	New Year's Holiday, Scotland
Jan 25	Burns Night, Scotland (poetry readings, haggis)
Mid-Feb	London Fashion Week (www.londonfashionweek.co.uk)
Mid-Feb	Jorvik Viking Festival, York (costumed warriors, battles; www.jorvik-viking-centre.co.uk)
March 1	St. David's Day, Wales (parades)
Early March	Bath Literature Festival (www.bathlitfest.org.uk)
Easter Sunday	April 20, 2014; April 5, 2015
Easter Monday	April 21, 2014; April 6, 2015
Early May Bank Holiday	May 5, 2014; May 4, 2015
Early May	Keswick Jazz Festival (www.keswickjazzfestival.co.uk)
Late May	Chelsea Flower Show, London (www.rhs.org.uk/chelsea)

Spring Bank Holiday	May 26, 2014; May 25, 2015
Late May-early June	Bath International Music Festival (www.bathmusicfest.org.uk)
Late May-early June	Bath Fringe Festival (alternative music, dance, and theater; www.bathfringe.co.uk)
Early June	Keswick Beer Festival (music, shows; www.keswickbeerfestival.co.uk)
Mid-June	Royal Highland Show, Edinburgh (Scottish-flavored county fair, www.royalhighlandshow.org)
Early-mid-June	Trooping the Colour, London (military bands and pageantry, Queen's birthday parade; www.trooping-the-colour.co.uk)
Late June	Royal Ascot horse races (near Windsor; www.ascot.co.uk)
Mid-late June	Golowan Festival, Penzance (midsummer celebrations, www.golowan.org)
Late June-early July	Wimbledon Tennis Championship, London (www.wimbledon.org)
Early July	International Eisteddfod, Llangollen (near Ruthin, Wales; folk songs, dances; www.international-eisteddfod.co.uk)
Mid-July	Early Music Festival, York (www.ncem.co.uk)
Late July-early Aug	Cambridge Folk Festival (www.cambridgefolkfestival.co.uk)
Aug	Edinburgh Military Tattoo (massing of military bands, www.edinburgh-tattoo.co.uk)
Aug	Edinburgh Fringe Festival (offbeat theater and comedy, www.edfringe.com)
Aug	Edinburgh International Festival (music, dance, shows; www.eif.co.uk)
Aug 5	Summer Bank Holiday, Scotland (not England or Wales)
Late Aug	Notting Hill Carnival, London (costumes, Caribbean music, www.thenottinghillcarnival.com)
Summer Bank Holiday	Aug 25, 2014; Aug 31, 2015; England and Wales only (not Scotland)
Late Aug-late Oct	Blackpool Illuminations (waterfront light festival, www.visitblackpool.com/illuminations)

Mid-Sept	London Fashion Week (www.londonfashionweek.co.uk)
Mid-Sept	Jane Austen Festival, Bath (www.janeausten.co.uk)
Late Sept	York Food and Drink Festival (www.yorkfoodfestival.com)
Nov 5	Guy Fawkes Night (fireworks, bonfires, effigy-burning of 1605 traitor Guy Fawkes)
Nov 30	St. Andrew's Day, Scotland (dancing and other cultural events)
Dec 1	St. Andrew's Day Bank Holiday
Dec 24-26	Christmas holidays
Dec 31–Jan 2	Hogmanay, Scotland (music, street theater, carnival, www.hogmanay.net)

APPENDIX

Conversions and Climate

Numbers and Stumblers

- In Europe, dates appear as day/month/year, so Christmas 2015 is 25/12/15.
- What Americans call the second floor of a building is the first floor in Britain.
- On escalators and moving sidewalks, Brits keep the left "lane" open for passing. Keep to the right.
- To avoid the British version of giving someone "the finger," don't hold up the first two fingers of your hand with your palm facing you. (It looks like a reversed victory sign.)
- And please...don't call your waist pack a "fanny pack" (see the British-Yankee Vocabulary list on page 1039).

Metric Conversions

Britain uses the metric system for nearly everything. Weight and volume are typically calculated in metric: A kilogram is 2.2 pounds, and one liter is about a quart (almost four to a gallon). Temperatures are generally given in Celsius, although some newspapers also list them in Fahrenheit.

1 foot = 0.3 meter	1 square yard = 0.8 square meter
1 yard = 0.9 meter	1 square mile = 2.6 square kilometers
1 mile = 1.6 kilometers	1 ounce = 28 grams
1 centimeter = 0.4 inch	1 quart = 0.95 liter
1 meter = 39.4 inches	1 kilogram = 2.2 pounds
1 kilometer = 0.62 mile	32°F = 0°C

Imperial Weights and Measures

Britain hasn't completely gone metric. Driving distances and speed limits are measured in miles. Beer is sold as pints (though milk can be measured in pints or liters), and a person's weight is measured in stone (a 168-pound person weighs 12 stone).

1 stone = 14 pounds
1 British pint = 1.2 US pints
1 imperial gallon = 1.2 US gallons or about 4.5 liters

Clothing Sizes

When shopping for clothing, use these US-to-Britain comparisons as general guidelines (but note that no conversion is perfect).
- Women's dresses and blouses: Add 4
  (US women's size 10 = UK size 14)
- Men's suits, jackets, and shirts: US and UK sizes are the same
- Women's shoes: Subtract 2½ (US size 8 = UK size 5½)
- Men's shoes: Subtract about ½ (US size 9 = UK size 8½)

Britain's Climate

First line, average daily high; second line, average daily low; third line, average days without rain. For more detailed weather statistics for destinations in this book (as well as the rest of the world), check www.wunderground.com.

	J	F	M	A	M	J	J	A	S	O	N	D
LONDON												
	43°	44°	50°	56°	62°	69°	71°	71°	65°	58°	50°	45°
	36°	36°	38°	42°	47°	53°	56°	56°	52°	46°	42°	38°
	16	15	20	18	19	19	19	20	17	18	15	16
CARDIFF (SOUTH WALES)												
	45°	45°	50°	56°	61°	68°	69°	69°	64°	58°	51°	46°
	35°	35°	38°	41°	46°	51°	54°	55°	51°	46°	41°	37°
	13	14	18	17	18	17	17	16	14	15	13	13
YORK												
	43°	44°	49°	55°	61°	67°	70°	69°	64°	57°	49°	45°
	33°	34°	36°	40°	44°	50°	54°	53°	50°	44°	39°	36°
	14	13	18	17	18	16	16	17	16	16	13	14
EDINBURGH												
	42°	43°	46°	51°	56°	62°	65°	64°	60°	54°	48°	44°
	34°	34°	36°	39°	43°	49°	52°	52°	49°	44°	39°	36°
	14	13	16	16	17	15	14	15	14	14	13	13

Fahrenheit and Celsius Conversion

Britain uses both Celsius and Fahrenheit to take its temperature. For a rough conversion from Celsius to Fahrenheit, double the number and add 30. For weather, remember that 28°C is 82°F—perfect. For health, 37°C is just right.

APPENDIX

Packing Checklist

Whether you're traveling for five days or five weeks, here's what you'll need to bring. Pack light to enjoy the sweet freedom of true mobility. Happy travels!

- ❏ 5 shirts: long- & short-sleeve
- ❏ 1 sweater or lightweight fleece
- ❏ 2 pairs of pants
- ❏ 1 pair of shorts
- ❏ 5 pairs of underwear & socks
- ❏ 1 pair of shoes
- ❏ 1 rainproof jacket with hood
- ❏ Tie or scarf
- ❏ Swimsuit
- ❏ Sleepwear
- ❏ Money belt
- ❏ Money—your mix of:
  - ❏ Debit card
  - ❏ Credit card(s)
  - ❏ Hard cash ($20 bills)
- ❏ Documents plus photo-copies:
  - ❏ Passport
  - ❏ Printout of airline eticket
  - ❏ Driver's license
  - ❏ Student ID, hostel card, etc.
  - ❏ Railpass/train reservations/ car-rental voucher
  - ❏ Insurance details
- ❏ Guidebooks & maps
- ❏ Address list (for sending emails & postcards)
- ❏ Notepad & pen
- ❏ Journal
- ❏ Daypack
- ❏ Toiletries kit:
  - ❏ Toiletries
  - ❏ Medicines & vitamins
  - ❏ First-aid kit
  - ❏ Glasses/contacts/ sunglasses (with prescriptions)
- ❏ Small towel/washcloth
- ❏ Laundry supplies:
  - ❏ Laundry soap
  - ❏ Clothesline
- ❏ Sewing kit

- ❏ Electronics—your choice of:
  - ❏ Camera (& related gear)
  - ❏ Mobile phone
  - ❏ Portable media player (iPod or other)
  - ❏ Laptop/netbook/ tablet
  - ❏ Ebook reader
  - ❏ Headphones or earbuds
  - ❏ Chargers for each of the above
  - ❏ Plug adapter(s)
- ❏ Alarm clock
- ❏ Earplugs
- ❏ Sealable plastic baggies
- ❏ Empty water bottle
- ❏ Postcards & photos from home

If you plan to carry on your luggage, note that all liquids must be in 3.4-ounce or smaller containers and fit within a single quart-size sealable baggie. For details, see www.tsa.gov/travelers.

British-Yankee Vocabulary

For a longer list, plus a dry-witted primer on British culture, see *The Septic's Companion* (Chris Rae). Note that instead of asking, "Can I help you?" many Brits offer a more casual, "You alright?" or "You OK there?"

advert: advertisement

afters: dessert

anticlockwise: counterclockwise

Antipodean: an Australian or New Zealander

aubergine: eggplant

banger: sausage

bangers and mash: sausage and mashed potatoes

Bank Holiday: legal holiday

bap: small roll

bespoke: custom-made

billion: a thousand of our billions (a million million)

biro: ballpoint pen

biscuit: cookie

black pudding: sausage made from dried blood

bloody: damn

blow off: fart

bobby: policeman ("the Bill" is more common)

Bob's your uncle: there you go (with a shrug), naturally

boffin: nerd, geek

bollocks: all-purpose expletive (a figurative use of testicles)

bolshy: argumentative

bomb: success or failure

bonnet: car hood

boot: car trunk

braces: suspenders

bridle way: path for walkers, bikers, and horse riders

brilliant: cool

brolly: umbrella

bubble and squeak: cabbage and potatoes fried together

candy floss: cotton candy

caravan: trailer

car-boot sale: temporary flea market, often for charity

car park: parking lot

cashpoint: ATM

casualty: emergency room

cat's eyes: road reflectors

ceilidh (KAY-lee): informal evening of song and folk fun (Scottish and Irish)

cheap and cheerful: budget but adequate

cheap and nasty: cheap and bad quality

cheers: good-bye or thanks; also a toast

chemist: pharmacist

chicory: endive

Chinese whispers: playing "telephone"

chippy: fish-and-chips shop

chips: French fries

chock-a-block: jam-packed

chuffed: pleased

chunter: mutter

cider: alcoholic apple cider

clearway: road where you can't stop

coach: long-distance bus

concession: discounted admission

concs (pronounced "conks"): short for "concession"

coronation chicken: curried chicken salad

cos: romaine lettuce

cot: baby crib

cotton buds: Q-tips

courgette: zucchini

craic (pronounced "crack"): fun, good conversation

(Irish/Scottish and spreading to England)

crisps: potato chips

cuppa: cup of tea

dear: expensive

dicey: iffy, risky

digestives: round graham cookies

dinner: lunch or dinner

diversion: detour

dogsbody: menial worker

donkey's years: ages, long time

draughts: checkers

draw: marijuana

dual carriageway: divided highway (four lanes)

dummy: pacifier

elevenses: coffee-and-biscuits break before lunch

elvers: baby eels

face flannel: washcloth

fag: cigarette

fagged: exhausted

faggot: sausage

fancy: to like, to be attracted to (a person)

fanny: vagina

fell: hill or high plain (Lake District)

first floor: second floor

fiver: £5 bill

fizzy drink: pop or soda

flutter: a bet

football: soccer

force: waterfall (Lake District)

fortnight: two weeks (shortened from "fourteen nights")

fringe: hair bangs

Frogs: French people

fruit machine: slot machine

full Monty: whole shebang, everything

gallery: balcony

gammon: ham

gangway: aisle

gaol: jail (same pronunciation)

gateau (or gateaux): cake

gear lever: stick shift

geezer: "dude"

give way: yield

glen: narrow valley (Scotland)

goods wagon: freight truck

gormless: stupid

goujons: breaded and fried fish or chicken sticks

green fingers: green thumbs

half eight: 8:30 (not 7:30)

hard cheese: bad luck

heath: open treeless land

hen night: bachelorette party

holiday: vacation

homely: homey or cozy

hoover: vacuum cleaner

ice lolly: Popsicle

interval: intermission

ironmonger: hardware store

ish: more or less

jacket potato: baked potato

jelly: Jell-O

jiggery-pokery: nonsense

Joe Bloggs: John Q. Public

jumble (sale): rummage sale

jumper: sweater

just a tick: just a second

kipper: smoked herring

knackered: exhausted (Cockney: cream crackered)

knickers: ladies' panties

knocking shop: brothel

knock up: wake up or visit (old-fashioned)

ladybird: ladybug

lady fingers: flat, spongy cookie

lady's finger: okra

lager: light, fizzy beer

left luggage: baggage check

lemonade: lemon-lime pop like 7-Up, fizzy

lemon squash: lemonade, not fizzy

let: rent

licenced: restaurant authorized to sell alcohol

lift: elevator

listed: protected historic building

loo: toilet or bathroom

lorry: truck

mack: mackintosh raincoat

mangetout: snow peas

marrow: summer squash

mate: buddy (boy or girl)

mean: stingy

mental: wild, memorable

mews: former stables converted to two-story rowhouses

moggie: cat

motorway: freeway

naff: tacky or trashy

nappy: diaper

natter: talk on and on

neep: Scottish for turnip

newsagent: corner store

nought: zero

noughts & crosses: tic-tac-toe

off-licence: liquor store

on offer: for sale

OTT: over the top, excessive

panto, pantomime: fairy-tale play performed at Christmas (silly but fun)

pants: (noun) underwear, briefs; (adj.) terrible, ridiculous

pasty (PASS-tee): crusted savory (usually meat) pie from Cornwall

pavement: sidewalk

pear-shaped: messed up, gone wrong

petrol: gas

piccalilli: mustard-pickle relish

pillar box: mailbox

pissed (rude), **paralytic, bevvied, wellied, popped up, merry, trollied, ratted, rat-arsed, pissed as a newt**: drunk

pitch: playing field

plaster: Band-Aid

plonk: cheap, bad wine

plonker: one who drinks bad wine (a mild insult)

prat: idiot

publican: pub owner

public school: private "prep" school (e.g., Eton)

pudding: dessert in general

pukka: first-class

pull, to be on the: on the prowl

punter: customer, especially in gambling

put a sock in it: shut up

queue: line

queue up: line up

quid: pound (£1)

randy: horny

rasher: slice of bacon

redundant, made: laid off

Remembrance Day: Veterans' Day

return ticket: round trip

revising; doing revisions: studying for exams

ring up: call (telephone)

roundabout: traffic circle

rubber: eraser

rubbish: bad

sausage roll: sausage wrapped in a flaky pastry

Scotch egg: hard-boiled egg wrapped in sausage meat

Scouser: a person from Liverpool

self-catering: accommodation with kitchen

Sellotape: Scotch tape

services: freeway rest area
serviette: napkin
setee: couch
shag: intercourse (cruder than in the US)
shambolic: chaotic
shandy: lager and 7-Up
silencer: car muffler
single ticket: one-way ticket
skip: Dumpster
sleeping policeman: speed bumps
smalls: underwear
snap: photo (snapshot)
snogging: kissing, making out
sod: mildly offensive insult
sod it, sod off: screw it, screw off
sod's law: Murphy's law
soda: soda water (not pop)
soldiers (food): toast sticks for dipping
solicitor: lawyer
spanner: wrench
spend a penny: urinate
stag night: bachelor party
starkers: buck naked
starters: appetizers
state school: public school
sticking plaster: Band-Aid
sticky tape: Scotch tape
stone: 14 pounds (weight)
stroppy: bad-tempered
subway: underground walkway
suet: fat from animal rendering (sometimes used in cooking)
sultanas: golden raisins
surgical spirit: rubbing alcohol
suspenders: garters
suss out: figure out
swede: rutabaga
ta: thank you

take the mickey/take the piss: tease
tatty: worn out or tacky
tattie scone: potato pancake
taxi rank: taxi stand
telly: TV
tenement: stone apartment house (not necessarily a slum)
tenner: £10 bill
theatre: live stage
tick: a check mark
tight as a fish's bum: cheapskate (watertight)
tights: panty hose
tin: can
tip: public dump
tipper lorry: dump truck
top hole: first rate
top up: refill (a drink, mobile-phone credit, petrol tank, etc.)
torch: flashlight
towel, press-on: panty liner
towpath: path along a river
trainers: sneakers
Tube: subway
twee: quaint, cutesy
twitcher: bird-watcher
Underground: subway
verge: grassy edge of road
verger: church official
way out: exit
wee (adj.): small (Scottish)
wee (verb): urinate
Wellingtons, wellies: rubber boots
whacked: exhausted
whinge (rhymes with hinge): whine
wind up: tease, irritate
witter on: gab and gab
wonky: weird, askew
yob: hooligan
zebra crossing: crosswalk
zed: the letter Z

INDEX

INDEX

INDEX

INDEX

INDEX

MAP INDEX

MAP INDEX

Audio Europe

Rick's Free Travel App

Get your FREE **Rick Steves Audio Europe**™ app to enjoy…

- Dozens of self-guided tours of Europe's top museums, sights and historic walks

- Hundreds of tracks filled with cultural insights and sightseeing tips from Rick's radio interviews

- All organized into handy geographic playlists

- For iPhone, iPad, iPod Touch, Android

With Rick whispering in your ear, Europe gets even better.

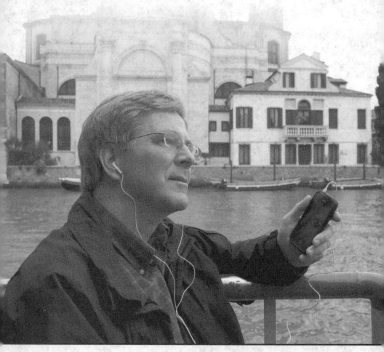

Find out more at ricksteves.com

Join a Rick Steves tour

Enjoy Europe's warmest welcome... with the flexibility and friendship of a small group getting to know Rick's favorite places and people. It all starts with our free tour catalog and DVD.

Great guides, small groups, no grumps.

Free information and great gear to

▶ Plan Your Trip

Browse thousands of articles and a wealth of money-saving tips for planning your dream trip. You'll find up-to-date information on Europe's best destinations, packing smart, getting around, finding rooms, staying healthy, avoiding scams and more.

▶ Eurail Passes

Find out, step-by-step, if a railpass makes sense for your trip—and how to avoid buying more than you need. Get free shipping on online orders

▶ Graffiti Wall & Travelers Helpline

Learn, ask, share—our online community of savvy travelers is a great resource for first-time travelers to Europe, as well as seasoned pros.

Rick Steves®

www.ricksteves.com

Rick Steves guidebooks are published by Avalon Travel,
a member of the Perseus Books Group.

Cameron Hewitt

Cameron writes and edits guidebooks for Rick Steves, specializing in Eastern Europe. For this book, he scoured the moors of Dartmoor, ventured to Land's End in Cornwall, took in some Shakespeare in Stratford, and pondered Tintern Abbey. When he's not traveling, Cameron lives in Seattle with his wife, Shawna.

Mark Seymour

Mark, specializing in England and Wales, leads tours and researches guidebooks for Rick Steves. He loves to explore the prehistoric sites of Britain and to toast the sunset from within stone circles. Mark lives in western France with his tour-guide wife, Toni.

Lynne McAlister

Lynne, from a small town in Tennessee, popped out of the Westminster Tube on a drizzly London evening to spy the glow of Big Ben and the Houses of Parliament. It was love at first sight. The history, art, architecture, parks, and people kept her coming back. Now she writes about travel from her flat in Notting Hill, where she lives with husband, Tony, and dog, Coco.

Contributor
Gene Openshaw

Gene is the co-author of 10 Rick Steves books. For this book, he wrote material on Europe's art, history, and contemporary culture. When not traveling, Gene enjoys composing music, recovering from his 1973 trip to Europe with Rick, and living everyday life with his daughter.

Acknowledgments

Thanks to Cameron Hewitt for his original work on several of the Scotland chapters (particularly St. Andrews and the Isle of Skye), to Jennifer Hauseman for the original version of the Glasgow chapter, and to friends listed in this book who put the "Great" in Great Britain.

Chapter Images

The following list identifies the chapter-opening images and credits their photographers.

Introduction: Keswick — Rick Steves
England: Salisbury Cathedral — Cameron Hewitt
London: Houses of Parliament — Rick Steves
Greenwich, Windsor & Cambridge:
    Windsor's Changing of the Guard — Lauren Mills
Bath: Pulteney Bridge — Cameron Hewitt
Near Bath: Avebury Stone Circle — David C. Hoerlein
The Cotswolds: Typical Cotswold Scene — Dominic Bonuccelli
Stratford-Upon-Avon:
    Anne Hathaway's Cottage — Rick Steves
Warwick and Coventry: Warwick Castle — Cameron Hewitt
Ironbridge Gorge: The Iron Bridge — Lauren Mills
Liverpool: Albert Dock — Cameron Hewitt
Lake District: Derwentwater — Rick Steves
York: York Minster — Rick Steves
Durham and Northeast England:
    Durham Cathedral — David C. Hoerlein
Wales: Snowdonia — Cameron Hewitt
North Wales: Snowdonia — David C. Hoerlein
Scotland: Niest Point — Cameron Hewitt
Edinburgh: Edinburgh Castle — Rick Steves
St. Andrews: The Old Course — Cameron Hewitt
Glasgow: Cityscape from The Lighthouse — David C. Hoerlein
Oban and the Southern Highlands:
    Oban — Jennifer Hauseman
Isle of Skye: Kyleakin Harbor — Cameron Hewitt
Inverness and the Northern Highlands:
Inverness — Jennifer Hauseman
Between Inverness and Edinburgh:
    View from Stirling Castle — Cameron Hewitt
Britain: Past and Present:
    Castlerigg Stone Circle — Rick Steves